The West in the World

A Mid-Length Narrative History

Second Edition

Updated

DENNIS SHERMAN

John Jay College
City University of New York

JOYCE SALISBURY

University of Wisconsin–Green Bay

McGraw Hill

Boston   Burr Ridge, IL   Dubuque, IA   Madison, WI   New York   San Francisco   St. Louis
Bangkok   Bogotá   Caracas   Kuala Lumpur   Lisbon   London   Madrid   Mexico City
Milan   Montreal   New Delhi   Santiago   Seoul   Singapore   Sydney   Taipei   Toronto

The McGraw-Hill Companies

McGraw Hill | **Higher Education**

THE WEST IN THE WORLD : A MID-LENGTH NARRATIVE HISTORY, SECOND EDITION, UPDATED EDITION
Published by McGraw-Hill, a business unit of The McGraw-Hill Companies, Inc., 1221 Avenue of the Americas, New York, NY, 10020.
Copyright © 2006, 2004, 2001 by The McGraw-Hill Companies, Inc. All rights reserved. No part of this publication may be reproduced or distributed in any form or by any means, or stored in a database or retrieval system, without the prior written consent of The McGraw-Hill Companies, Inc., including, but not limited to, in any network or other electronic storage or transmission, or broadcast for distance learning.

Some ancillaries, including electronic and print components, may not be available to customers outside the United States.

This book is printed on acid-free paper.

1 2 3 4 5 6 7 8 9 0 DOW/DOW 0 9 8 7 6 5 4

ISBN 0-07-297317-X

Publisher: *Lyn Uhl*
Sponsoring editor: *Monica Eckman*
Developmental editor: *Angela W. Kao*
Marketing manager: *Katherine Bates*
Senior media producer: *Sean Crowley*
Project manager: *Jill Moline-Eccher*
Production supervisor: *Carol A. Bielski*
Design manager: *Laurie J. Entringer*
Lead supplement producer: *Marc Mattson*
Photo research coordinator: *Alexandra Ambrose*
Freelance photo researcher: *Christine Pullo*
Art manager: *Robin Mouat*
Art director: *Jeanne Schreiber*
Permissions editor: *Marty Granahan*
Cover design: *Jenny El-Shamy*
Interior design: *Jenny El-Shamy*
Typeface: *10.5/12 Goudy*
Compositor: *Cenveo*
Printer: *R. R. Donnelley and Sons*

Cover Photos (left to right, top to bottom)
© Valley of The Kings, Thebes / Giraudon Paris / SuperStock; © National Portrait Gallery, London / SuperStock; © Superstock; © Rijksmuseum, Amsterdam / SuperStock

Page 745
"Dulce et Decorum Est" by Wilfred Owen from *The Collected Poems of Wilfred Owen*. Copyright © 1963 by Chatto & Windus, Ltd. Reprinted by permission of New Directions Publishing Corporation.

Library of Congress Cataloging-in-Publication Data

Sherman, Dennis.
    The West in the world : a mid-length narrative history / Dennis Sherman, Joyce Salisbury.
        p. cm.
    Includes index.
    Contents: v. 1. To 1715—v. 2. From 1600—v.3. Renaissance to present.
    ISBN 0-07-297318-8 (v. 1 : softcover : alk. paper) — ISBN 0-07-297319-6 (v. 2 : softcover : alk. paper) — ISBN 0-07-297320-X (v. 3 : softcover : alk. paper)
        1. Civilization, Western—History—Textbooks. I. Salisbury, Joyce E. II. Title.
CB245.S465 2006
909'.09821—dc22

2004056179

www.mhhe.com

IMPORTANT:

HERE IS YOUR REGISTRATION CODE TO ACCESS

YOUR PREMIUM McGRAW-HILL ONLINE RESOURCES.

For key premium online resources you need THIS CODE to gain access. Once the code is entered, you will be able to use the Web resources for the length of your course.

If your course is using **WebCT** or **Blackboard**, you'll be able to use this code to access the McGraw-Hill content within your instructor's online course.

Access is provided if you have purchased a new book. If the registration code is missing from this book, the registration screen on our Website, and within your WebCT or Blackboard course, will tell you how to obtain your new code.

Registering for McGraw-Hill Online Resources

TO gain access to your McGraw-Hill web resources simply follow the steps below:

1. USE YOUR WEB BROWSER TO GO TO: **www.mhhe.com/sherman2updated**
2. CLICK ON **FIRST TIME USER**.
3. ENTER THE REGISTRATION CODE* PRINTED ON THE TEAR-OFF BOOKMARK ON THE RIGHT.
4. AFTER YOU HAVE ENTERED YOUR REGISTRATION CODE, CLICK **REGISTER**.
5. FOLLOW THE INSTRUCTIONS TO SET-UP YOUR PERSONAL UserID AND PASSWORD.
6. WRITE YOUR UserID AND PASSWORD DOWN FOR FUTURE REFERENCE. KEEP IT IN A SAFE PLACE.

TO GAIN ACCESS to the McGraw-Hill content in your instructor's **WebCT** or **Blackboard** course simply log in to the course with the UserID and Password provided by your instructor. Enter the registration code exactly as it appears in the box to the right when prompted by the system. You will only need to use the code the first time you click on McGraw-Hill content.

Thank you, and welcome to your McGraw-Hill online Resources!

 **Higher Education**

* YOUR REGISTRATION CODE CAN BE USED ONLY ONCE TO ESTABLISH ACCESS. IT IS NOT TRANSFERABLE.

0-07-311176-7 T/A SHERMAN: WEST IN THE WORLD, 2/E UPDATED

REGISTRATION CODE

7250-R6OJ-0E2J-IMGG-3LP4

 **Higher Education**

About the Authors

DENNIS SHERMAN

Dennis Sherman is Professor of History at John Jay College, the City University of New York. He received his B.A. (1962) and J.D. (1965) degrees from the University of California at Berkley, and his Ph.D. (1970) from the University of Michigan. He was visiting Professor at the University of Paris (1978–79, 1985). He received the Ford Foundation Prize Fellowship (1968–69, 1969–70), a fellowship from the Council for Research on Economic History (1971–72), and fellowships from the National Endowment for the Humanities (1973–1976). His publications include *A Short History of Western Civilization*, Eighth Edition (coauthor), *Western Civilization: Sources, Images, and Interpretations*, Sixth Edition, *World History: Sources, Images, and Interpretations*, Third Edition, a series of introductions in the Garland Library of War and Peace, several articles and reviews on nineteenth-century French economic and social history in American and European journals, and several short stories in literary reviews.

JOYCE SALISBURY

Joyce Salisbury is Frankenthal Professor of History at the University of Wisconsin–Green Bay where she has taught undergraduates for almost twenty years. She received a PhD in medieval history from Rutgers University in New Jersey. She is a respected historian who has published many articles and has written or edited ten books, including the critically acclaimed *Perpetua's Passion: Death and Memory of a Young Roman Woman; The Beast Within: Animals in the Middle Ages, Encyclopedia of Women in the Ancient World* and *The Blood of Martyrs*. Salisbury is also an award-winning teacher, who was named *"Professor of the Year for Wisconsin in 1991"* by CASE (Council for Advancement and Support of Education), a prestigious national organization.

Brief Contents

Primary Source Documents   xxi

List of Maps   xxiii

Preface   xxv

CHAPTER 1
The Roots of Western Civilization: The Ancient Middle East to 500 B.C.   3

CHAPTER 2
The Contest for Excellence: Greece, 2000–338 B.C.   45

CHAPTER 3
The Poleis Become Cosmopolitan: The Hellenistic World, 323–150 B.C.   83

CHAPTER 4
Pride in Family and City: Rome from Its Origins through the Republic, 753–44 B.C.   117

CHAPTER 5
Territorial and Christian Empires: The Roman Empire, 31 B.C. to A.D. 410   149

CHAPTER 6
A World Divided: Western Kingdoms, Byzantium, and the Islamic World, ca. 376–1000   189

CHAPTER 7
The Struggle to Restore Order: The Middle Ages, ca. 750–1000   227

CHAPTER 8
Order Perfected: The High Middle Ages, 1000–1300   261

CHAPTER 9
Despair in the West, Empires in the East: The Late Middle Ages, ca. 1300–1500   301

CHAPTER 10
A New Spirit in the West: The Renaissance, ca. 1300–1640   331

CHAPTER 11
"Alone Before God": Religious Reform and Warfare 1500–1648   369

CHAPTER 12
Faith, Fortune, and Fame: European Expansion, 1450–1700   407

CHAPTER 13
The Struggle for Survival and Sovereignty: Europe's Social and Political Order, 1600–1715   443

CHAPTER 14
A New World of Reason and Motion: The Scientific Revolution and the Enlightenment, 1600–1800   483

CHAPTER 15
Competing for Power and Wealth: The Old Regime, 1715–1789   515

CHAPTER 16
Overturning the Political and Social Order: The French Revolution and Napoleon, 1789–1815   553

CHAPTER 17
Factories, Cities, and Families in the Industrial Age: The Industrial Revolution, 1780–1850   587

CHAPTER 18
Coping with Change: Ideology, Politics, and Revolution, 1815–1850   619

CHAPTER 19
Nationalism and State Building: Unifying Nations, 1850–1870   653

CHAPTER 20
Mass Politics and Imperial Domination: Democracy and the New Imperialism, 1870–1914   675

CHAPTER 21
Modern Life and the Culture of Progress: Western Society, 1850–1914   705

CHAPTER 22
Descending into the Twentieth Century: World War and Revolution, 1914–1920   737

Brief Contents

CHAPTER 23
Darkening Decades: Dictators, Depression, and World War II, 1920–1945 769

CHAPTER 24
Superpower Struggles and Global Transformations: The Cold War, 1945–1980s 811

CHAPTER 25
Into the Twenty-First Century: The Present in Perspective 851

Glossary G-1

Credits C-1

Index I-1

Contents

Primary Source Documents xxi
List of Maps xxiii
Preface xxv

CHAPTER 1

The Roots of Western Civilization: The Ancient Middle East to 500 B.C. 3

Timeline: The Big Picture 4

Before Western Civilization 4
  Out of Africa: The Paleolithic Period, 600,000–10,000 B.C. 4
  The Neolithic Period: The First Stirrings of Agriculture, 10,000–3000 B.C. 6
  Map 1.1: Mesopotamia and Egypt, ca. 2000 B.C. 7

Struggling with the Forces of Nature: Mesopotamia, 3000–ca. 1000 B.C. 8
  The Origins of Western Civilization 9
  Life in a Sumerian City 10
  Gods and Goddesses of the River Valley 11
  The Development of Writing 12
  Laws and Justice 14
  Indo-Europeans: New Contributions in the Story of the West 15

Rule of the God-King: Ancient Egypt, ca. 3100–1000 B.C. 17
  Prosperity and Order: The Old Kingdom, ca. 2700–2181 B.C. 17
  Global Connections: Nubia: The Passage from the Mediterranean to the Heart of Africa 19
  Hieroglyphs: Sacred Writing 20
  Pyramids and the Afterlife 20
  Changing Political Fortunes, ca. 2200–1570 B.C. 22
  Political Expansion: The New Kingdom, 1570–1085 B.C. 23
  Map 1.2: The Ancient Near East, ca. 1450 B.C. 24
  The Religious Experiment of Akhenaten, ca. 1377–1360 B.C. 25
  The Twilight of the Egyptian Empire, 1360–ca.1000 B.C. 25

Biography Hatshepsut (R. 1473–1458 B.C.) and Thutmose (1482?–1450 B.C.) 26

Merchants and Monotheists: Peoples of the Mediterranean Coast, ca. 1300–500 B.C. 26
  The Phoenicians: Traders on the Sea 27
  The People of the One God: Early Hebrew History, 1500–900 B.C. 29
  Map 1.3: Mediterranean Coast in the First Millennium B.C. 31
  A Jealous God, 1300–587 B.C. 31
  Judaism in Exile 32

Terror and Benevolence: The Growth of Empires, 1200–500 B.C. 33
  The Age of Iron 33
  Rule by Terror: The Assyrians, 911–612 B.C. 34
  Map 1.4: The Assyrian Empire, ca. 662 B.C. 34
  Babylonian Rule, 612–539 B.C. 36
  Rule by Tolerance: The Persian Empire, ca. 550–330 B.C. 37
  Map 1.5: The Persian Empire, ca. 500 B.C. 37

Timeline: A Closer Look 38

Summary 40

Review, Analyze, and Anticipate 40

Beyond the Classroom 41

Document 1.1 An Egyptian Nobleman Writes His Obituary

Document 1.2 King Solomon Secures His Realm's Fortune

Document 1.3 The Assyrians Wage War and Develop Scholarship

CHAPTER 2

The Contest for Excellence: Greece, 2000–338 B.C. 45

Timeline: The Big Picture 46

The Rise and Fall of Ancient Heroes, 2000–800 B.C. 46
  The Greek Peninsula 46
  Map 2.1: The World of the Greeks 47
  The Minoans, 2000–1450 B.C. 48
  Mycenaean Civilization: The First Greeks, 2000–1100 B.C. 49

From "Dark Ages" to Colonies   50
Map 2.2 The Greek Colonies in About
   500 B.C.   51

Emerging from the Dark: Heroic Beliefs
and Values   52
Heroic Values Preserved   52
The Family of the Gods   53
Studying the Material World   54

Life in the Greek Poleis, 700–489 B.C.   55
The Invention of Politics   56
The Heart of the Polis   56
Fears and Attachments in Greek Emotional Life   58
Athens: City of Democracy   59
Sparta: Model Military State   61
The Love of the Contest: Olympic Games   63

Imperial Athens, 489–431 B.C.   64
The Persian Wars, 490–479 B.C.   64
Map 2.3: The Persian Wars, 490–480 B.C.   65
Herodotus: The Father of History   66
Athens Builds an Empire, 477–431 B.C.   66
Artistic Athens   67
Greek Theater: Exploring Complex Moral Problems   68

Destruction, Disillusion, and a Search for
Meaning   70
The Peloponnesian War, 431–404 B.C.   70
Philosophical Musings: Athens Contemplates Defeat   71
Map 2.4: The Peloponnesian War, 431 B.C.   72

Biography   Alcibiades (450?—404 B.C.)   73
Tragedy and Comedy: Innovations in Greek Theater   75
Hippocrates and Medicine   76
The Aftermath of War, 404–338 B.C.   76

Summary   77

Timeline: A Closer Look   78

Review, Analyze, and Anticipate   78

Beyond the Classroom   80

Document 2.1   Theseus Founds the City of Athens

Document 2.2   Xerxes Invades Greece

Document 2.3   Ten Thousand Greek Mercenaries
Return Home

CHAPTER 3

The Poleis Become Cosmopolitan: The Hellenistic World, 323–150 B.C.   83

Timeline: The Big Picture   84
The Conquest of the Poleis   84

Tribal Macedonia   84
Philip II: Military Genius   85
Death of the King   86
Alexander's Conquests   86
Map 3.1: Alexander's Empire   88
A Young Ruler's Legacy   89

The Successor Kingdoms, 323–ca. 100 B.C.   90
Egypt under the Ptolemies   90
Map 3.2: The Successor States after the Death of Alexander,
   ca. 240 B.C.   91

Biography   Arsinoë II (315–270? B.C.)   92
The Seleucids Rule Asia   94
Antigonids in Greece   95
Global Connections: The Mauryan Dynasty Unifies India   96

East Meets West in the Successor Kingdoms   97
Money in the New Cosmopolitan Economies   97
Armies of the Hellenistic World   99
A True Cultural Blending?   100
Struggles and Successes: Life in the Cosmopolitan
   Cities   101
Patronage, Planning, and Passion: Hellenistic Art   102
Resistance to Hellenism: Judaism, 323–76 B.C.   104

The Search for Truth: Hellenistic Thought,
Religion, and Science   106
A Life of Learning   106
Theater and Literature   106
Cynics, Epicureans, and Stoics: Cosmopolitan
   Philosophy   107
New Religions of Hope   109
Hellenistic Science   110

Summary   111

Review, Analyze, and Anticipate   111

Timeline: A Closer Look   112

Beyond the Classroom   114

Document 3.1   Philip of Macedon Conquers Greek
Cities

Document 3.2   Antiochus and Stratonice Marry: A
Hellenistic Love Story

Document 3.3   Judas Maccabaeus Prevails in
Jerusalem

CHAPTER 4

Pride in Family and City: Rome from Its Origins Through the Republic, 753–44 B.C.   117

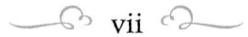

Timeline: The Big Picture   118

The Rise of Rome, 753–265 B.C.   118
   A Great City Is Founded   118
   The Etruscan Influence   119
   The Roman Monarchy, ca. 753–509 B.C.   119
   Governing an Emerging Republic   120
   Informal Governance: Patrons and Clients   123
   Dominating the Italian Peninsula   123
   Map 4.1: Rome During the Republic   124

Family Life and City Life   124
   A Pious, Practical People   125
   Map 4.2: Italy, 265 B.C.   125
   Loyalty to the Family   126
   The Challenges of Childhood   127
   Life in the City   128

Expansion and Transformation, 265–133 B.C.   129
   The Romans' Victorious Army   130
   Wars of the Mediterranean   130
   Map 4.3: Expansion of the Roman Empire,
      264–44 B.C.   133
   An Influx of Slaves   134

Biography Publius Terentius Afer (190?–159 B.C.)—
      Terence   135
   Economic Disparity and Social Unrest   136

The Hellenizing of the Republic   136
   Roman Engineering: Fusing Utility and Beauty   137
   Concrete: A New Building Material   137
   Latin Comedy and the Great Prose Writers,
      240–44 B.C.   139

The Twilight of the Republic, 133–44 B.C.   139
   The Reforms of the Gracchi, 133–123 B.C.   140
   Populares vs. Optimates: The Eruption of Civil Wars,
      123–46 B.C.   141
   Julius Caesar 100–44 B.C.   142

Summary   144

Review, Analyze, and Anticipate   144

Beyond the Classroom   145

Timeline: A Closer Look   146

Document 4.1 Hannibal Triumphs at the Battle of
      Cannae

Document 4.2 Conspirators Assassinate Julius Caesar

CHAPTER 5

Territorial and Christian Empires:
The Roman Empire, 31 B.C. to A.D. 410   149

Timeline: The Big Picture   150

The Pax Romana—27 B.C. to A.D. 192   150
   Augustus Takes Power   150
   A New Form of Governing   151
   Challenges to the Principate, A.D. 69–193   153
   Map 5.1: City of Rome During the Empire   155
   Global Connections: China's Han Dynasty and the
      Silk Road   156
   Map 5.2: Silk Road ca. A.D. 200   157
   A Vibrant Far-Flung Empire   158
   Map 5.3: The Roman Empire, 44 B.C.–A.D. 284   159

Life During the Peace of Rome   161
   A New Decadence   161
   The Problem with Population   161
   Sexual and Medical Misunderstandings   162
   The Games   163

Crisis and Transformation, A.D. 192–ca. 400   164
   The Military Monarchy   164
   The Reforms of Diocletian, A.D. 284–305   166
   Map 5.4: Diocletiaris Division of the Empire, A.D. 304   167
   The Capital Moves East   168

The Longing for Religious Fulfillment   169
   Stoicism and Platonism   170
   Mystery Cults   170
   The Four Faces of Judaism   171
   Map 5.5: Israel at the Time of Jesus   172
   The Jesus Movement   173
   Map 5.6: The Spread of Christianity to A.D. 311   175
   Early Christian Communities   176

From Christian Persecution to the City of God,
A.D. 64–410   177
   Looking for Christian Scapegoats   177
   Constantine: The Tolerant Emperor   177
   The Empire Adopts Christianity   178
   The New Roman   181

The Holy Life   181

Biography Melanie the Younger (385—439?)   182
   The Influence of Holy People   183

Summary   184

Review, Analyze, and Anticipate   184

Beyond the Classroom   185

Timeline: A Closer Look   186

Document 5.1 Augustus Tallies His
      Accomplishments

Document 5.2 A Great Fire Consumes Rome

Document 5.3 Diocletian Becomes "Lord"

Document 5.4 Titus Destroys Jerusalem

CHAPTER 6

A World Divided: Western Kingdoms, Byzantium, and the Islamic World, ca. 376–1000 189

Timeline: The Big Picture 190

The Making of the Western Kingdoms, ca. 376–750 190
 Life in a German Clan and Family 190
 Germanic Clothing and Food 191
 Heroic Society 192
 Infiltrating the Roman Empire, 376–476 193
 Map 6.1: Germanic Invasions, Fifth Century 194
 Did Rome "Fall"? 195
 The Growing Power of the Popes 197
 Monasteries: Peaceful Havens 198
 Rise and Fall of a Frankish Dynasty, ca. 485–750 199
 Accomplishments and Destruction in Italy, ca. 490–750 200
 The Visigoths in Spain, 418–711 201

The Byzantine Empire, ca. 400–1000 202
 Justinian and Theodora, r. 527–565 203
 Map 6.2: Map of Justinian's Conquests, 554 205
 Constantinople: The Vibrant City 205
 Military Might and Diplomatic Dealings 206
 Breaking Away from the West 208
 Converting the Slavs, 560–ca. 1000 209
 Map 6.3: Map of the Byzantine Empire, Eighth Century 210

Islam, 600–1000 210
 The Prophet 211
 The Religion 211
 The Spread of Islam 212
 Map 6.4: The Expansion of Islam to 750 213
 Creating an Islamic Unity 214
 The Gracious Life 215
 Forces of Disunity 215
 Global Connections: Yemen: Monotheism Spreads to Southern Arabia 216
 Heirs to Hellenistic Learning 218
 Map 6.5: Map of Islam, ca. 1000 219

Biography Avicenna (Ibn Sina) (980–1037) 220
 Islam and the West 222

Timeline: A Closer Look 222

Summary 223

Review, Analyze, and Anticipate 224

Beyond the Classroom 224

Document 6.1 The Huns Menace Rome

Document 6.2 The Silk Industry Comes to Byantium

Document 6.3 Shahrazad Mollifies a Murderous King

CHAPTER 7

The Struggle to Restore Order: The Middle Ages, ca. 750–1000 227

Timeline: The Big Picture 228

Bringing Order with Laws and Leadership 228
 The Rule of Law 228

Anglo-Saxon England: Forwarding Learning and Law 230
 The Venerable Bede: Recording Science and History 230
 Map 7.1: Anglo-Saxon Kingdoms, ca. 700 230
 Governing the Kingdom 231
 Alfred the Great: King and Scholar 232
 Map 7.2: England in 886 233

Charlemagne and the Carolingians: A New European Empire 234
 Charlemagne's Kingdom 234
 Linking Politics and Religion 235
 Map 7.3: The Empire of Charlemagne, ca. 800 236
 Negotiating with Byzantium and Islam 238
 An Intellectual Rebirth 238
 Global Connections: The 'Abbasid Caliphate and Charlemagne 239

Struggle for Order in the Church 240
 Monasteries Contribute to an Ordered World 241

Order Interrupted: Vikings and Other Invaders 242
 Competing for the Realm: Charlemagne's Descendants 242
 Map 7.4: Partition of the Carolingian Empire, 843–Treaty of Verdun 243
 "The Wrath of the Northmen": Scandinavian Life and Values 243

Biography Dhuoda, Bernard, and William, ca. 840 244
 Map 7.5: Invasions of Europe, Ninth and Tenth Centuries 245
 Viking Travels and Conquests 247
 An Age of Invasions: Assessing the Legacy 248

Manors and Feudal Ties: Order Emerging from Chaos 249
 Peasants and Lords: Mutual Obligations on the Medieval Manor 249
 Life in the Manorial Village 251
 Noble Warriors: Feudal Obligations Among the Elite 251
 Merriment, Marriage, and Medicine: A Noble's Life 253

Summary   255

Review, Analyze, and Anticipate   255

Timeline: A Closer Look   256

Beyond the Classroom   257

Document 7.1   The Visigoths Lay Down the Laws

Document 7.2   Charlemagne Promotes Educational Reforms

Document 7.3   A Comet Predicts Disaster

Document 7.4   Feudal Relationship Grows Complex

CHAPTER 8

Order Perfected: The High Middle Ages, 1000–1300   261

Timeline: The Big Picture   262

Those Who Work: Agricultural Labor   262
- *Harnessing the Power of Water and Wind*   262
- *New Agricultural Techniques*   263
- *The Population Doubles*   263
- *Map 8.1: German Migration Eastward*   264

Those Outside the Order: Town Life   264
- *Communes and Guilds: Life in a Medieval Town*   265
- *Map 8.2: Trade Routes, Twelfth and Thirteenth Centuries*   266
- *The Widening Web of Trade*   267
- *The Glory of God: Church Architecture*   268
- *The Rise of Universities*   268
- *Scholasticism: The Height of Medieval Philosophy*   270
- *Map 8.3: Medieval Universities*   271

Biography   Ramon Lull (1232?–1316)   273
- *Discovering the Physical World*   274

Those Who Fight: Nobles and Knights   275
- *Castles: Medieval Homes and Havens*   276
- *The Ideals of Chivalry*   276
- *The Literature of Chivalry*   277
- *In Praise of Romantic Love*   278

The Rise of Centralized Monarchies   279
- *England: From Conquest to Parliament*   279
- *Map 8.4: Medieval France, England, and Germany, Tenth Through Fourteenth Centuries*   280
- *The Spanish Reconquer Their Lands*   282
- *Map 8.5: Christian Expansion in Iberia*   282
- *France and Its Patient Kings*   283

The Myth of Universal Rule: The Holy Roman Empire   284

Those Who Pray: Imperial Popes and Expanding Christendom   285
- *A Call for Church Reform*   285
- *The Investiture Controversy*   286
- *Christians on the March: Crusades, 1096–1291*   287
- *Map 8.6: The Early Crusades, 1096–1192*   290
- *Map 8.7: The Late Crusades, 1201–1270*   291
- *Criticism of the Church*   292
- *The Church Accommodates: Franciscans and Dominicans*   292
- *The Church Suppresses: The Albigensian Crusade and the Inquisition*   293

Summary   294

Review, Analyze, and Anticipate   295

Beyond the Classroom   295

Timeline: A Closer Look   296

Document 8.1   Guibert of Nogent Describes His Education

Document 8.2   Pope Innocent III Prohibits Trade with Muslims

Document 8.3   Papal Reformers Impose Clerical Celibacy

Document 8.4   Walter of Henley Writes an Agricultural Instruction Manual

CHAPTER 9

Despair in the West, Empires in the East: The Late Middle Ages, ca. 1300–1500   301

Timeline: The Big Picture   302

Economic and Social Misery   302
- *Famine*   302
- *The Black Death: Bubonic Plague*   303
- *Map 9.1: The Spread of the Black Death*   304
- *The Peasants and Townspeople Revolt*   305

Imperial Papacy Besieged   306
- *Popes Move to Avignon*   307
- *Things Get Worse: The Great Schism*   307
- *The Conciliar Movement*   307
- *New Critics of the Church*   308
- *Map 9.2: The Great Schism, 1378–1417*   309

More Destruction: The Hundred Years' War, 1337–1453   310
  England vs. France   310
  Map 9.3: The Hundred Years' War, 1337–1453   311
  Joan of Arc   312

Biography Edward: The Black Prince, 1330–1376   313
  Results of the War   315

Responses to Disaster and Despair   315
  William of Ockham Reconsiders Scholasticism   315
  New Literary Giants   316
  A New View: Jan van Eyck   318

Empires in the East   319
  Eastern Universalism: The Mongols   319
  Map 9.4: The Mongol Empire, ca. 1300   319
  The Ottoman Empire, ca. 1300–1566   320
  *Global Connections: The Mongols Establish the Yuan
    Dynasty in China*   321
  Map 9.5: The Ottoman Empire, 1300–1566   322
  Russia: The Third Rome   323
  Map 9.6: The Rise of Moscow, 1325–1533   324

Summary   325

Review, Analyze, and Anticipate   325

Timeline: A Closer Look   326

Beyond the Classroom   328

Document 9.1 Edward III of England Seeks Allies

Document 9.2 Pope Boniface VIII Wrests Control of
    the Church from Kings

Document 9.3 Joan of Arc Is Defiant

CHAPTER 10

A New Spirit in the West: The Renaissance,
ca. 1300–1640   331

Timeline: The Big Picture   332

A New Spirit Emerges: Individualism, Realism, and
Activism   332
  The Renaissance: A Controversial Idea   332
  Why Italy?   333
  A Multifaceted Movement   333
  Humanism: The Path to Self-Improvement   335

Biography Isabella d'Este (1474–1539)   336
  The Generosity of Patrons: Supporting New Ideas   338

*The Invention of the Printing Press: Spreading
    New Ideas*   339
  Map 10.1: The Spread of Printing Before 1500   340

The Politics of Individual Effort   341
  The Italian City-States   341
  Florence: Birthplace of the Renaissance   341
  Map 10.2: Italy in 1454   342
  Venice: The Serene Republic?   343
  *Map 10.3: The Venetian Empire in the
    Fifteenth Century*   344
  Milan and Naples: Two Principalities   345
  The Papal States   345
  The Art of Diplomacy   346

Individualism as Self-Interest: Life During the
Renaissance   347
  Growing Intolerance   347
  Economic Boom Times   348
  Slavery Revived   349
  Finding Comfort in Family   350
  Children's Lives   351

An Age of Talent and Beauty: Renaissance Culture
and Science   352
  Artists and Artisans   352
  Architecture: Echoing the Human Form   353
  Sculpture Comes into Its Own   355
  Painting from a New Perspective   355
  Science or Pseudoscience?   357
  Leonardo da Vinci: The "Renaissance Man"   358

Renaissance of the "New Monarchies" of the North:
1453–1640   359
  France Under the Italian Influence   360
  *Map 10.4: France in the Fifteenth and Sixteenth
    Centuries*   361
  English Humanism   362
  Renaissance London: A Booming City   362
  England's Pride: William Shakespeare   363

Timeline: A Closer Look   364

Summary   364

Review, Analyze, and Anticipate   366

Beyond the Classroom   366

Document 10.1 The Friar Savonarola Ignites a
    "Bonfire of the Vanities"

Document 10.2 Isabella d'Este's Implores Leonardo
    da Vinci to Paint for Her

Document 10.3 Leonardo Seeks a Patron

CHAPTER 11

"Alone Before God": Religious Reform and Warfare 1500–1648   369

Timeline: The Big Picture   370

The Clash of Dynasties, 1515–1555   370
Land-Hungry Monarchs   370
Map 11.1: Europe in 1526–Habsburg-Valois Wars   371
Map 11.2: The Ottoman Empire, 1520–1566   372
The Changing Rules of Warfare   372
Winners and Losers   373

Biography Martin Guerre (1524–1594)   374
The Habsburg-Valois Wars, 1521–1544   375

A Tide of Religious Reform   376
The Best Path to Salvation?   376
Desiderius Erasmus: "Prince of Humanists"   376
Luther's Revolution   377
Protestant Religious Ideas   378
The Reformed Church Takes Root in Germany   379
Bringing Reform to the States in Switzerland   381
Anabaptists: The Radical Reformers   382
Calvinism and the Growing Middle Class   382
Henry VIII and the English Church   383

The Catholic Reformation   386
The Stirring of Reform in Spain   386
Map 11.3: Religions in Europe, ca. 1600   387
The Society of Jesus   388
The Council of Trent, 1545–1563   388
Catholics on the Offense   390

Europe Erupts Again: A Century of Religious Warfare, 1559–1648   391
French Wars of Religion, 1562–1598   391
A "Council of Blood" in the Netherlands, 1566–1609   393
The Thirty Years' War, 1618–1648   394
Peace at Westphalia   395
Map 11.4: The Thirty Years' War, 1618–1648   396
Map 11.5: Europe in 1648   397

Life After the Reformation   398
New Definitions of Courtship and Marriage   398
Forging a Link Between Education and Work   399
Anxiety and Spiritual Insecurity   400
Searching for Scapegoats: The Hunt for Witches   400

Timeline: A Closer Look   402

Summary   404

Review, Analyze, and Anticipate   404

Beyond the Classroom   405

Document 11.1 Germans Rage Against Papal Exploitation

Document 11.2 An English Historian Chronicles the Execution of Anne Boleyn

Document 11.3 A Ducal Order Mandates Persecution of Anabaptist Women

CHAPTER 12

Faith, Fortune, and Fame: European Expansion, 1450–1700   407

Timeline: The Big Picture   408

The World Imagined   408
The Lure of the "East"   408
Imagined Peoples   409
Ptolemy's Map   409

The World Discovered   410
Fame, Fortune, and Faith: The Drive to Explore   410
New Technologies and Travel   411
Map 12.1: Exploration and Conquest: Fifteenth and Sixteenth Centuries   412
The Portuguese Race for the East, 1450–1600   412
Spain's Westward Discoveries, 1492–1522   413
The Northern Europeans Join the Race, 1600–1650   414

Confrontation of Cultures   415
The Original Americans   415
Map 12.2: European Expansion, ca. 1700   416
Early Contacts   418
Map 12.3: Indigenous Empires in the Americas, ca. 1500   418
Conquest of the Great Empires, 1520–1550   419
Global Connections: The Inca Empire Falls   421
Life and Death Under European Rule, 1550–1700   422
The African Slave Trade   423
Gathering Souls in the New Lands   425

The World Market and Commercial Revolution   427
High Prices and Profits: Trading on the World Stage   427
The Rise of Commercial Capitalism   428
Mercantilism: Controlling the Balance of Trade   429
The Growth of Banking   430
The Danger of Overspending: Spain Learns a Lesson   430
Redefining Work Roles   430
Piracy: Banditry on a World Scale, 1550–1700   431

The World Transformed   432
European Culture Spreads   432
European Culture Transformed   433

Biography Maria Sibylla Merian (1647–1717)   434
  A New Worldview   435

Summary   437

Timeline: A Closer Look   438

Review, Analyze, and Anticipate   438

Beyond the Classroom   439

Document 12.1   Explorers Describe Prester John, a Mythical Christian King in Africa

Document 12.2   Amerigo Vespucci Describes the New World

Document 12.3   Thomas Mun Praises Trade

 CHAPTER 13

The Struggle for Survival and Sovereignty: Europe's Social and Political Order,
1600–1715   443

Timeline: The Big Picture   444

Stresses in Traditional Society   444
  Mounting Demands on Rural Life   444
  Pressures on the Upper Orders   446

Royal Absolutism in France   447
  Henry IV Secures the Monarchy   447
  Richelieu Elevates Royal Authority   448
  Mazarin Overcomes the Opposition   448
  The Sun King Rises   449
  Map 13.1: France under Louis XIV, 1661—1715   454

The Struggle for Sovereignty in
Eastern Europe   455
  Centralizing the State in Brandenburg-Prussia   455
  Austria Confronts the Ottomans and Expands its Control   455
  Map 13.2: Central and Eastern Europe, 1648   456
  Russia and Its Tsars Gain Prominence   457
  Global Connections: The Rise and Fall of the Mughal Empire in India   459
  The Victory of the Nobility in Poland   460

The Triumph of Constitutionalism   460
  Map 13.3: Central and Eastern Europe, 1640—1725   461
  The Nobility Loses Respect   462
  Protestantism Revitalized   463
  James I Invokes the Divine Right of Kings   464
  Charles I Alienates Parliament   464

"God Made Men and the Devil Made Kings": Civil War, 1642–1649   465
  Map 13.4: The English Civil War, 1642—1649   465
  The King Laid Low   466
  A Puritan Republic Is Born: The Commonwealth, 1649–1660   468
  Who Has the Power to Rule?   468
  The Monarchy Restored, 1660–1688   469
  The Glorious Revolution   471
  Royalism Reconsidered: John Locke   471

Biography Samuel Pepys (1633—1703)   472
  The Netherlands: The Sovereignty of Local Authority   473
  Map 13.5: The United Provinces and the Spanish Netherlands, 1609   474

Summary   477

Review, Analyze, and Anticipate   477

Timeline: A Closer Look   478

Beyond the Classroom   478

Document 13.1   Bishop Bossuet Justifies Monarchical Absolutism

Document 13.2   Louis XIV Describes Monarchical Rights and Duties

Document 13.3   Charles II Arrives in England

Document 13.4   England's Parliament Presents A Bill of Rights

Document 13.5   An Ambassador Describes the Dutch Government

CHAPTER 14

A New World of Reason and Reform: The Scientific Revolution and the Enlightenment,
1600–1800   483

Timeline: The Big Picture   484

Questioning Truth and Authority   484
  The Old View   484
  Undermining the Old View   485

Developing a Modern Scientific View   486
  Astronomy and Physics: From Copernicus to Newton   486
  The Revolution Spreads: Medicine, Anatomy, and Chemistry   489
  The Methodology of Science Emerges   491

Supporting and Spreading Science   492
  Courts and Salons   492

Contents

The Rise of Royal Societies   493
Religion and the New Science   494
The New Worldview   494

Laying the Foundations for the Enlightenment   495
Science Popularized   495
Skepticism and Religion   497
Broadening Criticism of Authority and Tradition   498

The Enlightenment in Full Stride   498
The Philosophes   499
The Encyclopedia   500
Battling the Church   500
Reforming Society   501

Biography Jean-Jacques Rousseau (1712–1778)   502
The Culture and Spread of the Enlightenment   506

Timeline: A Closer Look   508

Summary   510

Review, Analyze, and Anticipate   510

Beyond the Classroom   511

Document 14.1 Kepler and Galileo Exchange Letters about Science

Document 14.2 Isaac Newton: God in a Scientific Universe

Document 14.3 Frances Bacon Promotes a New Method of Inquiry

Document 14.4 Concorcet Lauds the Power of Reason

Document 14.5 Cesare Beccaria on Crimes and Punishment

CHAPTER 15

Competing for Power and Wealth: The Old Regime, 1715–1789   515

Timeline: The Big Picture   516

Statebuilding and War   516
Rising Ambitions in Eastern Europe   516
Map 15.1: Europe, 1721   517
Map 15.2: The Expansion of Russia and the Partition of Poland, 1721–1795   519
Map 15.3: Prussia and the Austrian Empire, 1721–1772   522
Warfare in the Eighteenth Century   522
Western Europe and the Great Colonial Rivalry   524
Map 15.4: Overseas Colonies and Trade, 1740   525
Global Connections: Western Africa, Brazil, and the Atlantic Slave Trade   530

Map 15.5: India 1756–1805   531

The Twilight of Monarchies? The Question of Enlightened Absolutism   531
Maps 15.6 and 15.7: North America, 1755 and 1763   532

Changes in Country and City Life   533
The Agricultural Revolution   534
Manufacturing Spreads in the Countryside: Cottage Industry   535
More People, Longer Lives   536
Deepening Misery for the Poor   537
Prosperity and the Bourgeoisie   539

The Culture of the Elite: Combining the Old and the New   539
The Advent of the Modern Novel   539
Pride and Sentiment in Art and Architecture   540
Reaching New Heights in Music   541

Biography Wolfgang Amadeus Mozart (1756–1791)   542
The Grand Tour   543

Culture for the Lower Classes   544
Festivals and Popular Literature   544
Gin and Beer   544
Religious Revivals   545

Foreshadowing Upheaval: The American Revolution   545
Insults, Interests, and Principles: The Seeds of Revolt   545
A War for Independence   546
Creating the New Nation   547

Summary   547

Timeline: A Closer Look   548

Review, Analyze, and Anticipate   548

Beyond the Classroom   550

Document 15.1 Landlords and Serfs in Russia

Document 15.2 Austria's Empress Explains the Diplomatic Revolution

Document 15.3 Olaudah Equiano Describes the Middle Passage

CHAPTER 16

Overturning the Political and Social Order: The French Revolution and Napoleon, 1789–1815   553

Timeline: The Big Picture   554

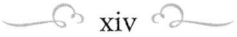

"A Great Ferment": Trouble Brewing in France   554
  The Financial Crisis Weakens the Monarchy   554
  The Underlying Causes of the Revolution   555
  The "Tennis Court Oath"   557
  Storming the Bastille   559
  The End of the Old Order   559

The Constitutional Monarchy: Establishing a
New Order   560
  Maps 16.1 and 16.2: Reorganizing France in 1789   561
  The King Discredited   562
  Reactions Outside France   562

To the Radical Republic and Back   563
  War and the Breakdown of Order   563
  Radical Republicans Struggle for Power   564
  The Terror   565

Biography Manon Roland (1754–1793)   566
  The Republic of Virtue   568
  The Revolution Spreads Outside of France   569
  Resistance to the Republic Rises   570
  Reaction: The "White" Terror and the Directory   571

Napoleon Bonaparte   571
  Napoleon's Rise to Power   572
  Map 16.3: France and Its Sister Republics   573
  Napoleon Consolidates Control   574
  Reforming France   574
  Creating the Empire   575
  War and Conquest   576
  Map 16.4: Europe, 1810   577
  The Impact Overseas   578
  Map 16.5: Latin America After Independence   579
  Decline and Fall   579

Timeline: A Closer Look   582

Summary   582

Review, Analyze, and Anticipate   584

Beyond the Classroom   584

Document 16.1 New Laws End the Feudal System in
  France

Document 16.2 The Jacobins' Revolutionary Politics

Document 16.3 Napoleon Issues an Imperial Decree
  at Madrid

CHAPTER 17

Factories, Cities, and Families in the Industrial Age: The Industrial Revolution, 1780–1850   587

Timeline: The Big Picture   588

The Industrial Revolution Begins   588
  A Booming Commercial Economy in the West   589
  *Global Connections: Cross-Cultural Misunderstandings:
    China and Great Britain*   590
  Britain's Unique Set of Advantages   591
  Map 17.1: Eighteenth-Century England   591
  A Revolution in Agriculture   592

New Markets, Machines, and Power   592
  The Rising Demand for Goods   592
  Cotton Leads the Way   593
  Iron: New Processes Transform Production   593
  The Steam Engine and the Factory System   594
  Coal: Fueling the Revolution   595
  Railroads: Carrying Industrialization Across the Land   595
  Britain's Triumph: The Crystal Palace Exhibition   597

Industrialization Spreads to the Continent   598

Balancing the Benefits and Burdens of
Industrialization   599
  The Middle Class   600
  Map 17.2: The Industrial Revolution in Europe, 1850   600
  The Working Classes   601
  Developing Working-Class Consciousness   602

Life in the Growing Cities   603
  The Promise and Pitfalls of Work in the Cities   604
  Living with Urban Growth   604
  Worrying about Urban Society: Rising Crime   605

Public Health and Medicine in the
Industrial Age   606
  The Danger of Disease   606
  Map 17.3: The Spread of A Cholera Epidemic   607
  Seeking Medical Care   607
  Promising Developments for Public Health   608

Family Ideals and Realities   609
  Middle-Class Ideals: Affection, Children, and Privacy   609
  *Separate Spheres: Changing Roles for Middle-Class Women
    and Men*   610
  Working-Class Realities   611

Biography The Cadburys   612
  Prostitution   614
  Stress and Survival in the Working Classes   614

Timeline: A Closer Look   614

Summary   615

Review, Analyze, and Anticipate   616

Beyond the Classroom   616

Document 17.1 Andrew Ure Defends Industrial
  Capitalism

Document 17.2 Factory Owners Establish Discipline
  for Workers

Document 17.3 A Middle-Class Reformer Describes Workers' Housing

CHAPTER 18

Coping with Change: Ideology, Politics, and Revolution, 1815–1850 619

Timeline: The Big Picture 620

The Congress of Vienna: A Gathering of Victors 620
   Map 18.1: Europe, 1815 622
   The Concert of Europe: Securing the Vienna Settlement 623

Ideologies: How the World Should Be 623
   Conservatism: Restoring the Traditional Order 623
   Liberalism: Individual Freedom and Political Reform 624
   Nationalism: A Common Identity and National Liberation 625

   Biography John Stuart Mill (1806–1873) and Harriet Taylor (1807–1858) 626
   Romanticism: Freedom, Instinct, and Spontaneity 628
   Early Socialism: Ending Competition and Inequalities 632
   "Scientific Socialism": Karl Marx and the Communist Manifesto 634

Restoration and Repression 635
   The Return of the Bourbons in France 635
   Reaction and Repression in the German States 635
   Restoration in Italy 636
   Conservatism in Russia 636
   Holding the Line in Great Britain 636

A Wave of Revolution and Reform 637
   The Greek War for Independence 638
   Liberal Triumphs in Western Europe 638
   Testing Authority in Eastern and Southern Europe 640
   Liberal Demands in Great Britain 640
   Map 18.2: European Revolts, 1820–1831 641

The Dam Burst: 1848 642
   The "Glory Days" 643
   Map 18.3: European Revolts, 1848–1849 645
   The Return to Order 645
   What Happened? 647

Timeline: A Closer Look 648

Summary 648

Review, Analyze, and Anticipate 649

Beyond the Classroom 650

Document 18.1 A Conservative Theorist Attacks Political Reform

Document 18.2 France's Provisional Government Issues Decrees

Document 18.3 German Liberals and Nationalists Rally for Reform

CHAPTER 19

Nationalism and Statebuilding: Unifying Nations, 1850–1870 653

Timeline: The Big Picture 654

Building Unified Nation-States 654

The Drive for Italian Unification 654
   Map 19.1: The Unification of Italy 656

Germany "By Blood and Iron" 657
   Map 19.2: The Unification of Germany 659

The Fight for National Unity in North America 660
   Global Connections: Japan Opens to the West 661

Divided Authority in the Austrian and Ottoman Empires 662
   Map 19.3: Language Groups of Austria-Hungary 663

Using Nationalism in France and Russia 664
   Napoleon III and the Second Empire 664
   Map 19.4: The Decline of the Ottoman Empire, 1683–1914 665
   Alexander II and Russia 666

Biography Florence Nightingale (1820–1910) 668

Timeline: A Closer Look 670

Summary 671

Review, Analyze, and Anticipate 672

Beyond the Classroom 672

Document 19.1 Garibaldi Appeals to Italians for Support

Document 19.2 Bismarck Masters Politics in Prussia

Document 19.3 A Serf Reacts to the Russian Emancipation Proclamation

CHAPTER 20

Mass Politics and Imperial Domination: Democracy and the New Imperialism, 1870–1914 675

Timeline: The Big Picture 676

Demands for Democracy   676
  Liberal Democracy in Western Europe   677
  For and Against Democracy in Central and Eastern Europe   679

Insiders and Outsiders: Politics of the Extremes   680
  The Spread of Unions   681

Biography Jean Jaurès (1859–1914)   682
  Socialism Gains Strength   682
  Anarchism: Freedom from All Authority   684
  Anti-Semitism and Ultranationalism   684
  Still Outsiders: Women, Feminism, and the Right to Vote   686
  Map 20.1: Jewish Migration, 1870–1914   687

Emigration: Overseas and Across Continents   688
  Leaving Europe   688

The New Imperialism: The Race for Africa and Asia   690
  Money and Glory   690
  The Tools of Conquest   691
  The Scramble for Africa   692
  Map 20.2: Imperialism in Africa, ca. 1885   693
  Map 20.3: Imperialism in Africa, 1914   694
  Establishing Control in Asia   695
  Map 20.4: Imperialism in Asia, 1840–1914   698
  The Legacy of Imperialism   700

Timeline: A Closer Look   700

Summary   702

Review, Analyze, and Anticipate   702

Beyond the Classroom   702

Document 20.1 Kaiser Wilhelm II Links Nationalism and Imperialism

Document 20.2 Economics and Imperialism in Africa

CHAPTER 21

Modern Life and the Culture of Progress: Western Society, 1850–1914   705

Timeline: The Big Picture   706

The Second Industrial Revolution   706
  Steel Leads the Way   706
  New Transportation and Communication Networks   707
  The Birth of Big Business   708
  The Lure of Shopping   708
  Winners and Losers in the Race for Wealth   709

The New Urban Landscape   709
  Rebuilding Cities   709
  Global Connections: Economic Transformation in Latin America   710
  Sewers and Subways   711

City People   712
  On Top of It All: The Urban Elite   712
  Pride and Success: The "Solid" Middle Class   712
  Hardworking and Hopeful: The Lower Middle Class   713
  The "Other Half": The Working Classes   714
  What to Do About "Them"   715

Sports and Leisure in the Cities   716
  Building Character Through Athletics   716
  The New Tourist   716

Private Life: Together and Alone at Home   716
  Family: The Promise of Happiness   716
  A Home of One's Own   717
  Poor Housing   718
  Intimacy and Morality   718
  Sexual Realities   719
  Psychic Stress and Alcoholism   719

Science in an Age of Optimism   720
  Science, Evolution, and Religion   720
  Mysteries of the Material and Human World   722
  Germs, Cures, and Healthcare   723

Culture: Accepting the Modern World   724
  Realism and Naturalism: The Details of Social Life   725
  Impressionism: Celebrating Modern Life   726

Biography Claude Monet (1840–1926)   727

From Optimism to Uncertainty   728
  Everything Is Relative   728
  Sex, Conflict, and the Unconscious   729
  Fear of Social Disintegration   730
  Disenchantment Sets In   730
  Art Turns Inward   731

Summary   732

Review, Analyze, and Anticipate   733

Beyond the Classroom   733

Timeline: A Closer Look   734

Document 21.1 John Stuart Mill Argues for Women's Rights

Document 21.2 Walter Bagehot on "Natural Selection" and Human History

Document 21.3 Beeton's Guide for Women

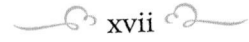

CHAPTER 22

Descending Into the Twentieth Century: World War and Revolution, 1914–1920 737

Timeline: The Big Picture 738

On the Path to Total War 738
Rivalries and Alliances 738
Crises in the Balkans 739
Map 22.1: The Balkans, 1878 740
Map 22.2: The Balkans, 1914 740

The Front Lines 741
Off to Battle 741
The Schlieffen Plan 742
Slaughter and Stalemate on the Western Front 742
Map 22.3: World War I 743
Map 22.4: The Western Front 744
Victory and Defeat on the Eastern and Southern Fronts 746
The War Spreads Across the Globe 747

War on the Home Front 747
Mobilizing Resources 747
New Gender Roles 748
Maintaining the Effort 748

To the Bitter End 749

Biography Käthe Kollwitz (1867–1945) 750

Assessing the Costs of the War 752

The Peace Settlement 753
Gathering at Versailles 753
A Victors' Peace 754
Redrawing the Map of Europe 754
Map 22.5: Europe, 1923 755
Legacy of the Peace Treaty 756

Revolutions in Russia 756
The First Warnings: 1905 756
The Fall of the Tsar 757
The Provisional Government 759
The Rise of the Bolsheviks 759
Communism and Civil War 761
Map 22.6: Civil War in Russia, 1919 762

Summary 763

Review, Analyze, and Anticipate 763

Timeline: A Closer Look 764

Beyond the Classroom 764

Document 22.1 A Russian Socialist Supports the War Effort

Document 22.2 In the Trenches and Beyond

Document 22.3 Keynes Warns of the Economic Consequences of the Peace

CHAPTER 23

Darkening Decades: Dictators, Depression, and World War II, 1920–1945 769

Timeline: The Big Picture 770

Trying to Recover from the Great War, 1919–1929 770
The Victors Just Hold On 771
Continuing Crises in Germany 772
Conciliation and a Glimpse of Prosperity 772
The Roaring Twenties? 773
The Anxious Twenties 776

Turning Away From Democracy: Dictatorships and Fascism, 1919–1929 777
Authoritarianism in East-Central Europe 777
The Rise of Fascism in Italy 777

Transforming the Soviet Union: 1920–1939 779
Lenin's Compromise: The NEP 780
The Struggle to Succeed Lenin 780
Stalin's Five-Year Plans 781
Blood and Terror: The Great Purges 783

The Great Depression: 1929–1939 784
Crash! 784
In the Teeth of the Depression 784
Searching for Solutions 785

Nazism in Germany 785
The Young Adolf Hitler 785
The Birth of Nazism in Germany's Postwar Years 786
The Growth of the Nazi Party 786
The Appeal of Nazism 787
Hitler Takes Power 787
Life in Nazi Germany 787
Rebuilding and Rearming the New Germany 790

The Road to War: 1931–1939 790
International Affairs Break Down 790
Civil War in Spain 791
Map 23.1: The Spanish Civil War, 1936–1939 792
Map 23.2: German Expansion, 1936–1939 793
Trying to Cope with Germany 793

World War II, 1939–1945 794
Triumph of the German Blitzkrieg 794
War in North Africa and the Balkans 795
Operation Barbarossa: Germany Invades the Soviet Union 796

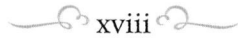

Japan Attacks   796
Global Connections: The Rise of Japanese
   Ultranationalism   797
Map 23.3: World War II in Europe   798
Behind the Lines: The Struggle and the Horror   799
Map 23.4: World War II in the Pacific   799

Biography *Josip Broz (Tito) (1892–1980)*   802
   Turning the Tide of War   803

Summary   804

Review, Analyze, and Anticipate   805

Timeline: A Closer Look   806

Beyond the Classroom   807

Document 23.1   Postwar Strains in Germany

Document 23.2   Nazi Propaganda Pamphlet

Document 23.3   The Nazi Extermination Camps

CHAPTER 24

Superpower Struggles and Global Transformations: The Cold War, 1945–1980s   811

Timeline: The Big Picture   812

From Peace to Cold War   812
   The Settlement   812
   Origins of the Cold War   813
   Map 24.1: Europe After World War II   814
   The Heart of the Cold War   815
   Map 24.2: Europe During the Cold War   816
   The Global Impact of the Cold War   817
   Map 24.3: Cold War Alliances and Conflicts   818
   Map 24.4: Vietnam and Southeast Asia   820
   Détente   822

East and West: Two Paths to Recovery in Europe   823
   Tight Control in the Soviet Union and Eastern Europe   823
   Parliamentary Politics and Prosperity in the
      Western Democracies   825
   Assessing the Paths Taken   827

The Twilight of Colonialism   828
   Revolts in Southern Asia   828
   Conflict in the Middle East   829
   Map 24.5: The Arab-Israeli Conflict, 1947–1982   830
   Liberating Africa   830

A Sense of Relativity in Thought and Culture   831
   Global Connections: Apartheid in South Africa   832

Map 24.6: Decolonization   833
Existentialism: Responsibility and Despair   833
A Culture of Contrasts and Criticism   834

Protests, Problems, and New Politics: The 1960s to the 1980s   835
   A Flurry of Social Protests and Movements   836

Biography *Simone de Beauvoir (1908–1986)*   838
   Stagnant Growth and Rising Inflation   839
   The New Political Landscape   840

Postindustrial Society   841
   Changing Fortunes in the Postindustrial Society   841
   The Baby Boom and the Booming Cities   842
   The Shifting Foundations of Family and Private Life   842
   The "Sexual Revolution" and the Youth Culture   843

Breakthroughs in Science   843
   From the Universe Above to the Universe Within   844
   The Information Revolution   844
   Transforming Medicine   844

Summary   845

Timeline: A Closer Look   846

Review, Analyze, and Anticipate   847

Beyond the Classroom   848

Document 24.1 The Cold War and Nuclear Weapons

Document 24.2 A Warning about the United States

Document 24.3 An Oxford Student Explains
   Revolutionary Attitudes

CHAPTER 25

Into the Twenty-First Century: The Present in Perspective   851

Timeline: The Big Picture   852

The Collapse of Communism   852
   Undermining Communism in the Soviet Union   852
   Gorbachev Launches Reforms   853
   Revolutions in Eastern Europe   854

Biography *Václav Havel (1936–   )*   856
   The Soviet Union Disintegrates   858
   Map 25.1: Eastern Europe, 1989   858
   Life After the Collapse of Communism   859
   Map 25.2: The Dissolution of the Soviet Union, 1991   860
   Nationalism Unleashed   861
   Maps 25.3 and 25.4: Disintegration of Czechoslovakia and
      Yugoslavia in the 1990s   862

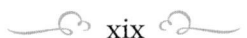

Contents

Repercussion and Realignments in the West   863
  The United States Unchallenged and Germany
    Rising   863
  Politics Shift to the Right   864
  Toward European Integration   864
  Map 25.5: The European Union, 1999   865

The World and the West from a Global
Perspective   866
  East Asia and the Rise of the Pacific Rim   867
  The Challenge of Islam   867
  International Terrorism and War   868
  Map 25.6: Israel and the Occupied Territories, 2003   869
  Map 25.7: The Middle East and Iraq, 2003   870
  Across Borders: Cultural Conflict and Convergence   871
  Map 25.8: Afghanistan, Kashmia, and South Central Asia,
    2002   872
  Beyond Borders: Uncertainty and Opportunity in a
    Shrinking World   874
  Map 25.9: The Growth of Cities   875

  Map 25.10: Global Environmental Problems   876

Summary   878

Review, Analyze, and Anticipate   879

Beyond the Classroom   879

Timeline: A Closer Look   880

Document 25.1   The Perils of the New Nationalism

Document 25.2   The Information Revolution Inspires
    Vision of New Potential

Document 25.3   Ecological Problems Threaten Nature

Glossary   G-1

Credits   C-1

Index   I-1

Primary Source Documents

Document Number		Page Number
D1.1	An Egyptian Nobleman Writes His Obituary	D1.1
D1.2	King Solomon Secures His Realm's Fortune	D1.1
D1.3	The Assyrians Wage War and Develop Scholarship	D1.2
D2.1	Theseus Founds the City of Athens	D2.1
D2.2	Xerxes Invades Greece	D2.2
D2.3	Ten Thousand Greek Mercenaries Return Home	D2.2
D3.1	Philip of Macedon Conquers Greek Cities	D3.1
D3.2	Antiochus and Stratonice Marry: A Hellenistic Love Story	D3.2
D3.3	Judas Maccabaeus Prevails in Jerusalem	D3.3
D4.1	Hannibal Triumphs at the Battle of Cannae	D4.1
D4.2	Conspirators Assassinate Julius Caesar	D4.1
D5.1	Augustus Tallies His Accomplishments	D5.1
D5.2	A Great Fire Consumes Rome	D5.2
D5.3	Diocletian Becomes "Lord"	D5.3
D5.4	Titus Destroys Jerusalem	D5.3
D6.1	The Huns Menace Rome	D6.1
D6.2	The Silk Industry Comes to Byzantium	D6.1
D6.3	Shahrazad Mollifies a Murderous King	D6.2
D7.1	The Visigoths Lay Down the Laws	D7.1
D7.2	Charlemagne Promotes Educational Reforms	D7.2
D7.3	A Comet Predicts Disaster	D7.2
D7.4	Feudal Relationship Grows Complex	D7.3
D8.1	Guibert of Nogent Describes His Education	D8.1
D8.2	Pope Innocent III Prohibits Trade with Muslims	D8.1
D8.3	Papal Reformers Impose Clerical Celibacy	D8.2
D8.4	Walter of Henley Writes an Agricultural Instruction Manual	D8.3
D9.1	Edward III of England Seeks Allies	D9.1
D9.2	Pope Boniface VIII Wrests Control of the Church from Kings	D9.1
D9.3	Joan of Arc is Defiant	D9.2
D10.1	The Friar Savonarola Ignites a "Bonfire of the Vanities"	D10.1
D10.2	Isabella d'Este's Implores Leonardo da Vinci to Paint for Her	D10.1
D10.3	Leonardo Seeks a Patron	D10.2
D11.1	Germans Rage Against Papal Exploitation	D11.1
D11.2	An English Historian Chronicles the Execution of Anne Boleyn	D11.1
D11.3	A Ducal Order Mandates Persecution of Anabaptist Women	D11.2
D12.1	Explorers Describe Prester John, a Mythical Christian King in Africa	D12.1
D12.2	Amerigo Vespucci Describes the New World	D12.2
D12.3	Thomas Mun Praises Trade	D12.3
D13.1	Bishop Bossuet Justifies Monarchical Absolutism	D13.1
D13.2	Louis XIV Describes Monarchical Rights and Duties	D13.2

Contents

D13.3	Charles II Arrives in England	D13.2
D13.4	England's Parliament Presents a Bill of Rights	D13.4
D13.5	An Ambassador Describes the Dutch Government	D13.4
D14.1	Kepler and Galileo Exchange Letters About Science	D14.1
D14.2	Isaac Newton: God in a Scientific Universe	D14.1
D14.3	Francis Bacon Promotes a New Method of Inquiry	D14.2
D14.4	Concorcet Lauds the Power of Reason	D14.2
D14.5	Cesare Beccaria on Crimes and Punishment	D14.3
D15.1	Landlords and Serfs in Russia	D15.1
D15.2	Austria's Empress Explains the Diplomatic Revolution	D15.1
D15.3	Olaudah Equiano Describes the Middle Passage	D15.2
D16.1	New Laws End the Feudal System in France	D16.1
D16.2	The Jacobins' Revolutionary Politics	D16.1
D16.3	Napoleon Issues an Imperial Decree at Madrid	D16.2
D17.1	Andrew Ure Defends Industrial Capitalism	D17.1
D17.2	Factory Owners Establish Discipline for Workers	D17.1
D17.3	A Middle-Class Reformer Describes Workers' Housing	D17.2
D18.1	A Conservative Theorist Attacks Political Reform	D18.1
D18.2	France's Provisional Government Issues Decrees	D18.1
D18.3	German Liberals and Nationalists Rally for Reform	D18.2
D19.1	Garibaldi Appeals to Italians for Support	D19.1
D19.2	Bismarck Masters Politics in Prussia	D19.1
D19.3	A Serf Reacts to the Russian Emancipation Proclamation	D19.2
D20.1	Kaiser Wilhelm II Links Nationalism and Imperialism	D20.1
D20.2	Economics and Imperialism in Africa	D20.1
D21.1	John Stuart Mill Argues for Women's Rights	D21.1
D21.2	Walter Bagehot on "Natural Selection" and Human History	D21.1
D21.3	Beeton's Guide for Women	D21.2
D22.1	A Russian Socialist Supports the War Effort	D22.1
D22.2	In the Trenches and Beyond	D22.1
D22.3	Keynes Warns of the Economic Consequences of the Peace	D22.2
D23.1	Postwar Strains in Germany	D23.1
D23.2	Nazi Propaganda Pamphlet	D23.1
D23.3	The Nazi Extermination Camps	D23.2
D24.1	The Cold War and Nuclear Weapons	D24.1
D24.2	A Warning about the United States	D24.1
D24.3	An Oxford Student Explains Revolutionary Attitudes	D24.2
D25.1	The Perils of the New Nationalism	D25.1
D25.2	The Information Revolution Inspires Vision of New Potential	D25.1
D25.3	Ecological Problems Threaten Nature	D25.2

List of Maps

1.1 Mesopotamia and Egypt, ca. 2000 B.C. 7
1.2 The Ancient Near East, ca. 1450 B.C. 24
1.3 Mediterranean Coast in the First Millennium B.C. 31
1.4 The Assyrian Empire, ca. 662 B.C. 34
1.5 The Persian Empire, ca. 500 B.C. 37
2.1 The World of the Greeks 47
2.2 The Greek Colonies in About 500 B.C. 51
2.3 The Persian Wars, 490–480 B.C. 65
2.4 The Peloponnesian War, 431 B.C. 72
3.1 Alexander's Empire 88
3.2 The Successor States after the Death of Alexander, ca. 240 B.C. 91
4.1 Rome During the Republic 124
4.2 Italy, 265 B.C. 125
4.3 Expansion of the Roman Republic, 264–44 B.C. 133
5.1 City of Rome During the Empire 155
5.2 The Silk Road, ca. A.D. 200 157
5.3 The Roman Empire, 44 B.C.–A.D. 284 159
5.4 Diocletian's Division of the Empire, A.D. 304 167
5.5 Israel at the Time of Jesus 172
5.6 The Spread of Christianity to A.D. 311 175
6.1 Germanic Invasions, Fifth Century 194
6.2 Map of Justinian's Conquests, 554 205
6.3 Map of the Byzantine Empire, Eighth Century 210
6.4 The Expansion of Islam to 750 213
6.5 Map of Islam, ca. 1000 217
7.1 Anglo-Saxon Kingdoms, ca. 700 230
7.2 England in 886 233
7.3 The Empire of Charlemagne, ca. 800 236
7.4 Partition of the Carolingian Empire, 843–Treaty of Verdun 243
7.5 Invasions of Europe, Ninth and Tenth Centuries 245
8.1 German Migration Eastward 264
8.2 Trade Routes, Twelfth and Thirteenth Centuries 266
8.3 Medieval Universities 271
8.4 Medieval France, England, and Germany, Tenth Through Fourteenth Centuries 280

8.5 Christian Expansion in Iberia 282
8.6 The Early Crusades, 1096–1192 290
8.7 The Late Crusades, 1201–1270 291
9.1 The Spread of the Black Death 304
9.2 The Great Schism, 1378–1417 309
9.3 The Hundred Years' War, 1337–1453 311
9.4 The Mongol Empire, ca. 1300 319
9.5 The Ottoman Empire, 1300–1566 322
9.6 The Rise of Moscow, 1325–1533 324
10.1 The Spread of Printing Before 1500 340
10.2 Italy in 1454 342
10.3 The Venetian Empire in the Fifteenth Century 344
10.4 France in the Fifteenth and Sixteenth Centuries 361
11.1 Europe in 1526–Habsburg-Valois Wars 371
11.2 The Ottoman Empire, 1520–1566 372
11.3 Religions in Europe, ca. 1600 387
11.4 The Thirty Years' War, 1618–1648 396
11.5 Europe in 1648 397
12.1 Exploration and Conquest: Fifteenth and Sixteenth Centuries 412
12.2 European Expansion, ca. 1700 416
12.3 Indigenous Empires in the Americas, ca. 1500 418
13.1 France under Louis XIV, 1661–1715 454
13.2 Central and Eastern Europe, 1648 456
13.3 Central and Eastern Europe, 1640–1725 461
13.4 The English Civil War, 1642–1649 465
13.5 The United Provinces and the Spanish Netherlands, 1609 474
15.1 Europe, 1721 517
15.2 The Expansion of Russia and the Partition of Poland, 1721–1795 519
15.3 Prussia and the Austrian Empire, 1721–1772 522
15.4 Overseas Colonies and Trade, 1740 525
15.5 India, 1756–1805 531
15.6 and 15.7 North America, 1755 and 1763 532
16.1 and 16.2 Reorganizing France in 1789 561
16.3 France and its Sister Republics 573
16.4 Europe, 1810 577
16.5 Latin America After Independence 579
17.1 Eighteenth-Century England 591

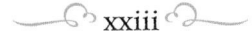

17.2   The Industrial Revolution in Europe, 1850   600
17.3   The Spread of A Cholera Epidemic   607
18.1   Europe, 1815   622
18.2   European Revolts, 1820–1831   641
18.3   European Revolts, 1848–1849   645
19.1   The Unification of Italy   696
19.2   The Unification of Germany   659
19.3   Language Groups of Austria-Hungary   663
19.4   The Decline of the Ottoman Empire, 1683–1914   665
20.1   Jewish Migration, 1870–1914   687
20.2   Imperialism in Africa, ca. 1885   693
20.3   Imperialism in Africa, 1914   694
20.4   Imperialism in Asia, 1840–1914   698
22.1   The Balkans, 1878   740
22.2   The Balkans, 1914   740
22.3   World War I   743
22.4   The Western Front   744
22.5   Europe, 1923   755
22.6   Civil War in Russia, 1919   762
23.1   The Spanish Civil War, 1936–1939   792

23.2   German Expansion, 1936–1939   793
23.3   World War II in Europe   798
23.4   World War II in the Pacific   799
24.1   Europe After World War II   814
24.2   Europe During the Cold War   816
24.3   Cold War Alliances and Conflicts   818
24.4   Vietnam and Southeast Asia   820
24.5   The Arab-Israeli Conflict, 1947–1982   830
24.6   Decolonization   833
25.1   Eastern Europe, 1989   858
25.2   The Dissolution of the Soviet Union, 1991   860
25.3 and 25.4   Disintegration of Czechoslovakia and Yugoslavia in the 1990s   862
25.5   The European Union, 1999   865
25.6   Israel and the Occupied Territories, 2003   869
25.7   The Middle East and Iraq, 2003   870
25.8   Afghanistan, Kashmir, and South-Central Asia, 2002   872
25.9   The Growth of Cities   875

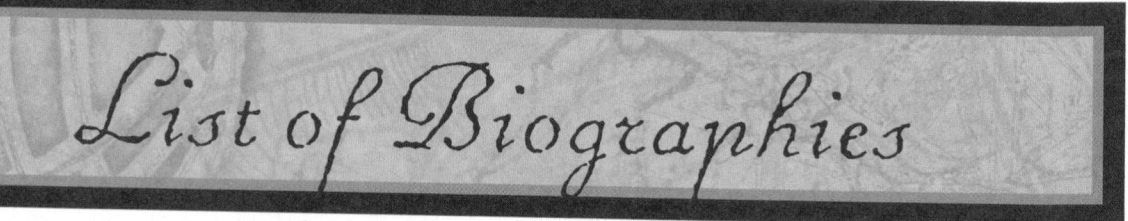

List of Biographies

Hatshepsut and Thutmose   26
Alcibiades   73
Arsinoë II   92
Publius Terentius Afer–Terence   135
Melania the Younger   182
Avicenna (Ibn Sina)   218
Dhuoda, Bernard, and William   244
Ramón Lull   273
Edward: The Black Prince   313
Isabella D'Este   336
Martin Guerre   374
Maria Sibylla Merian   434
Samuel Pepys   472

Jean-Jacques Rousseau   502
Wolfgang Amadeus Mozart   542
Manon Roland   566
The Cadburys   612
John Stuart Mill and Harriet Taylor   626
Florence Nightingale   668
Jean Jaurès   682
Claude Monet   726
Kathe Kollwitz   750
Josip Broz (Tito)   802
Simone de Beauvoir   838
Václev Havel   856

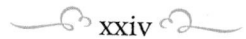

Preface

WHAT'S DIFFERENT AND WHY

Western civilization influences—and is influenced by—peoples all over the world today; it remains a fascinating (and at times controversial) subject. While many have studied the strong contributions of the West to the world, too often the reverse influences have not been stressed. In fact, one of the hallmarks of Western civilization has been its power to be transformed through contact with people outside its center. This quality has contributed to the West's capacity to keep changing as it embraces new ideas, new people, and new challenges. We chose the title of this book—*The West in the World*—to emphasize this characteristic, and we have written the story of the West in a way that reveals its complex interactions with the surrounding world.

When we first prepared to write this book, we set five goals for ourselves:

- To demonstrate the complex relationship between Western and world history
- To weave a strong social-history "thread" into the political/cultural framework
- To write a book that would hold readers' attention and that would convey the drama and interest inherent in the story of the past
- To integrate some unique features that would enhance the narrative and support learning on the part of readers
- To make the book an attractive, manageable length

With each chapter and each round of revision, we reminded ourselves of these five goals and asked our reviewers to hold us accountable for achieving them.

To address the first goal, we dealt with the thorny issue of the relationship between Western and world history. In doing so, we chose to present the concept of Western civilization as an ever-changing pattern of culture that first emerged in the ancient Middle East and that then moved west through the Mediter-ranean lands, north to Europe, and, in the sixteenth century, across the Atlantic. Throughout the narrative we have tried to emphasize the importance of the interactions—economic, social, and cultural as well as political—that have created our modern civilization that in the twenty-first century is in many ways a world civilization.

Civilizations grow and are shaped through the decisions and actions of people, and we have kept this idea in mind as we wove the story of the West. To meet our second goal, we integrated social history, including women's history, throughout this text, acknowledging that people of all ages and walks of life have affected the course of history. Social historians have sometimes written about "the masses" while losing touch with the individual men and women whose lives have shaped the past. We frequently "stop the music" for a moment to let the words and experiences of individuals illustrate broad developments, and in addition we have presented biographical portraits of people who experienced some of the developments discussed in each chapter.

To meet our third goal, we sought to capture both the art and science of history. We strove for an engaging narrative of Western civilization (the "art") that would also analyze the events, individuals, ideas, and developments (the "science"). We designed the book to draw students in as they follow the unfolding of Western culture from its earliest roots to the present.

As scholars who care as much about teaching as we do about history, and to fulfill our fourth goal, we have designed a number of unique pedagogical features to complement and support the narrative. For example, we treat art works and maps in an unusual way. Each illustration is discussed in the text itself rather than presented as a separate, optional feature or mere ornamentation. This approach not only brings the past alive for today's highly visual audience, it also helps teach students how to interpret art works and other illustrations. Maps are also treated as more than a visual aid. Each map comes with an analytical guide that encourages readers to consider connections between geography, politics, and other developments. A picture by itself is not worth a thousand words, but in this text the illustrations and maps serve as a central feature for learning.

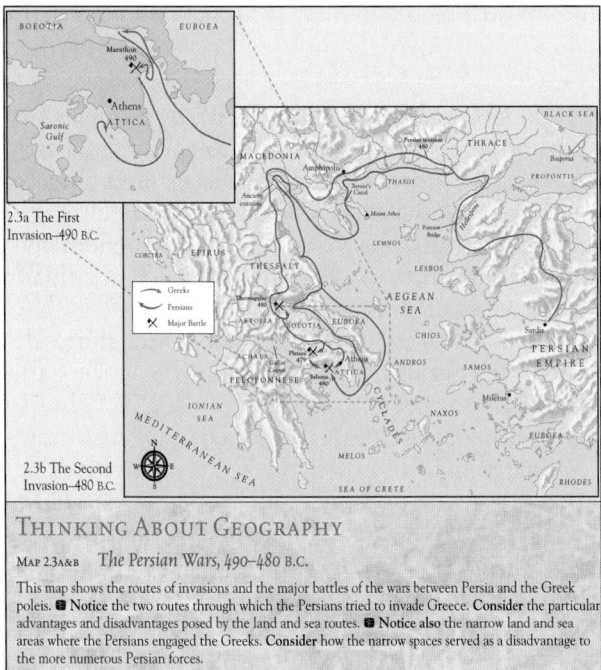

2.3a The First
Invasion–490 B.C.

2.3b The Second
Invasion–480 B.C.

THINKING ABOUT GEOGRAPHY

MAP 2.3A&B   *The Persian Wars, 490–480 B.C.*

This map shows the routes of invasions and the major battles of the wars between Persia and the Greek poleis. ■ **Notice** the two routes through which the Persians tried to invade Greece. **Consider** the particular advantages and disadvantages posed by the land and sea routes. ■ **Notice also** the narrow land and sea areas where the Persians engaged the Greeks. **Consider** how the narrow spaces served as a disadvantage to the more numerous Persian forces.

To achieve our final goal of making this book an attractive size, we selected a length that is unusual for a Western civilization textbook. Long texts, while of great value, can be intimidating to students in their level of detail and can make the assigning of supplementary readings difficult, if not impossible—we've all had this experience. Brief texts, while leaving plenty of time for additional readings, are typically lacking in necessary coverage and detail, thus making it a remarkable challenge for the authors to achieve the kind of braided, nuanced narrative that history deserves. Medium in length, **The West in the World** is long enough to present a strong, rich narrative while allowing instructors the flexibility to use other sources and books as supplements.

NEW TO THIS SECOND UPDATED EDITION

We have made the following substantial changes—both in content and in pedagogical features—in this second edition of *The West in the World.*

- Many instructors have asked for more primary sources to complement the text. In this Updated Edition, we have answered their request with two new important features:

  1) Primary source document readings at the end of each chapters, and
  2) *A Primary Source Investigator* (PSI) CD that contains more than 200 additional primary source readings, images, interactive maps, glossary, and quiz questions.

While links to additional primary sources on the internet have always been available on our website (www.mhhe.com/sherman2updated), in this edition, we have integrated more primary sources into the narrative and provide many more at your fingertips on the PSI CD.

- To further highlight the book's well-received emphasis on the West within a world context, we have added the new "Global Connections" feature. These boxed essays, which appear in half of the chapters, build on the chapter's content and showcase the West's interaction with the wider world. In this updated edition, we have added two more Global Connection essays in chapters 6 and 21: "Yemen: Monotheism Spreads to Southern Asia" and "Economic Transformation in Latin America".

- Several important developments in the West and the world—such as the rise of international terrorism—have taken center stage in recent years. We have extensively revised Chapter 25 to reflect those developments, and have updated earlier chapters to lay the foundation for understanding the new material. For example, Chapter 6 now includes a new section on "Islam and the West."

- The pedagogical tools in the first edition have been very well received, and we have built on them in the new edition. For example, we have added critical-thinking questions as "Chapter Opening Points" to focus students' reading, and we have revised the questions attached to the "Biography" feature. The "Global Connections" boxes also begin with points to stimulate students' critical thinking and help them link the material to the chapter's content.

- We have appreciated the positive comments on the analytical and integrated treatment of maps

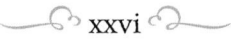

and visuals in the first edition. Therefore, we have strengthened these features in the new edition, revising many maps for increased clarity. In this updated edition, we have also created a new map to support expanded historical coverage on the Middle East and Iraq.

- We have listened closed to students', professors', and reviewers' comments, and we have considered how recent scholarship has modified our understanding of the past. Accordingly, we have revised aspects of every chapter.

Despite these improvements, we have taken care to hold true to the subtitle of this book: *A Mid-Length Narrative History*. The book retains the manageable length and the emphasis on a flowing narration that marked it in the first edition.

ORGANIZATION AND COVERAGE

The West in the World is organized in a way that reflects the typical Western civilization course. The twenty-five chapters follow the history of Western civilization chronologically, and the subheadings allow professors to select portions of chapters to suit their syllabi. Three volume splits are also available to provide flexibility for two-semester courses. While this organization makes it easy for instructors to use this text, it also allows us to cover traditional topics in fresh ways.

Narrative

Students and instructors often complain that history texts are dry. We agree. The strong narrative approach of this book reflects our belief that the various dimensions of an historical era—political, intellectual, social, and cultural—are best presented as part of an integrated whole rather than separate chapters or occasionally referenced in a discussion. The story of the West is a compelling one, and we have worked hard to tell it in a lively way that includes analysis (the "why" of history) as well as events and ideas (the "what"). For example, in Chapter 7, the discussion of Charlemagne's wars and his relation with the papacy are framed in a larger theoretical discussion of the

benefits of linking politics with religion. Similarly, in Chapter 11, a chronology of warfare is informed by an analysis of technological and social change.

Integration of Political and Social History

History is about people, and we keep that point "front and center" in our narrative, which integrates political and social history. Women, families, peasants, and workers are not treated as an afterthought, but as essential players in the evolving story. Our "Biography" feature as well as illustrative anecdotes throughout, regularly reminds readers that the human past emerged through the interaction of all members of society and that human agency is an essential component of the past. For example, Chapter 17 begins by comparing the differing experiences of industrialization for a middle-class couple with that of a railroad worker. That comparison is then used to reflect broader developments and leads to an analysis of the causes of the Industrial Revolution. The same theme is echoed in the chapter's *Biography* section, *The Cadburys*.

Art and Culture

In addition to written evidence, paintings, sculpture, ceramics, photographs, and buildings all provide valuable historical information. In this book, the examples of material culture and art do far more than just beautify the presentation. Each visual source is discussed and interpreted within the narrative. For example, we analyze a painting of a nineteenth-century middle-class family to show gender roles, attitudes toward children, the place of servants, and relationships to the outside world. Similarly, we use a beautiful Rubens painting of the miracles of Saint Ignatius Loyola to comment on the theology and sensibilities of sixteenth-century Catholicism. All this is discussed within the narrative of the text. Visuals serve as sources of history and encourage students to arrive at richer insights than they would have gained solely through reading the text.

Science and Medicine

An enthusiasm for science and technology has been a hallmark of Western civilization. Like many developments in the story of the West, this enthusiasm has ebbed and flowed over time. To meet the growing interest among today's students and scholars, we emphasize these topics throughout the narrative. For example, a discussion of medieval technology reveals the significant inventions that brought mechanical power to a central point in society, and students will also see how other cultures—like early Muslim societies—performed surgery, dispensed drugs, and established hospitals. Even in the modern period, we discuss the experience of going to a doctor in addition to reporting on new developments in medicine, such as antiseptics, anesthetics, and antibiotics. Consistent with our use of art as history, illustrations such as Caroline Naudet's "Journey of a Dying Man to the Other World" are used to reveal both typical medical practices and common attitudes toward physicians.

PEDAGOGICAL FEATURES

We believe that telling a good story is only part of the task facing those who teach the history of the West. Instructors also have to engage students in the enterprise of learning, and the more actively engaged they are, the more they learn. Therefore, we have designed

Wall painting of a woman playing a cithara
The Romans believed that their greatness derived first from the family, in which aristocratic fathers and mothers were educated and devoted to instilling traditional values in their children. This illustration shows one such cultured mother playing a cithara for her child.

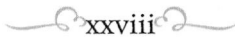

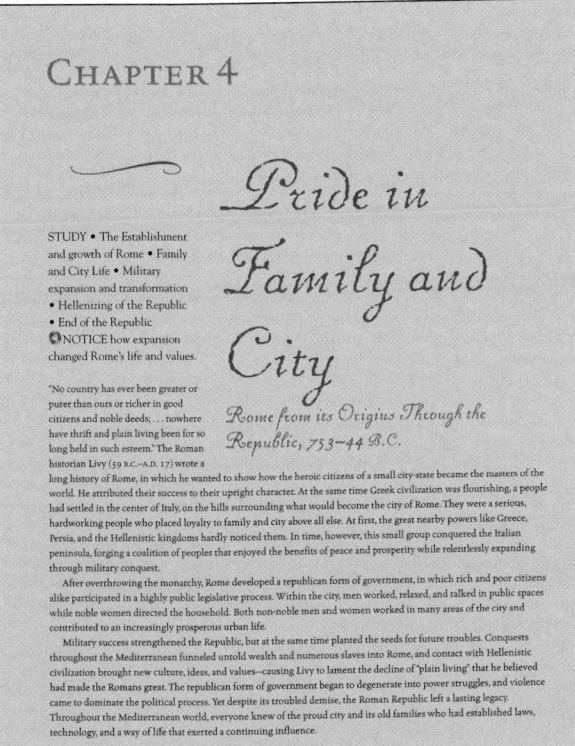

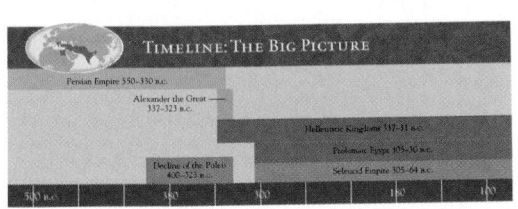

and included a number of pedagogical features to help students participate actively in the learning process. These can be used by students alone or become part of classroom activity.

Chapter Previews and Summaries

Each chapter opens with a short preview and telling anecdote that, together, set the stage for understanding the material. Chapters then end with a summary of key themes. Rather than dry outlines, these features instead preserve the engaging narrative style while satisfying the pedagogical dictum: "tell them what they'll learn; teach them, then tell them what they have learned." The chapter previews and reviews help students stay focused on the main themes in the narrative.

Time Lines and Reminder Dates

Many instructors and reviewers have told us that students lack a sense of chronology. We believe that this problem stems in part from the way history texts are written—as the narrative progresses in a linear way,

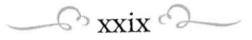

TIMELINE: A CLOSER LOOK

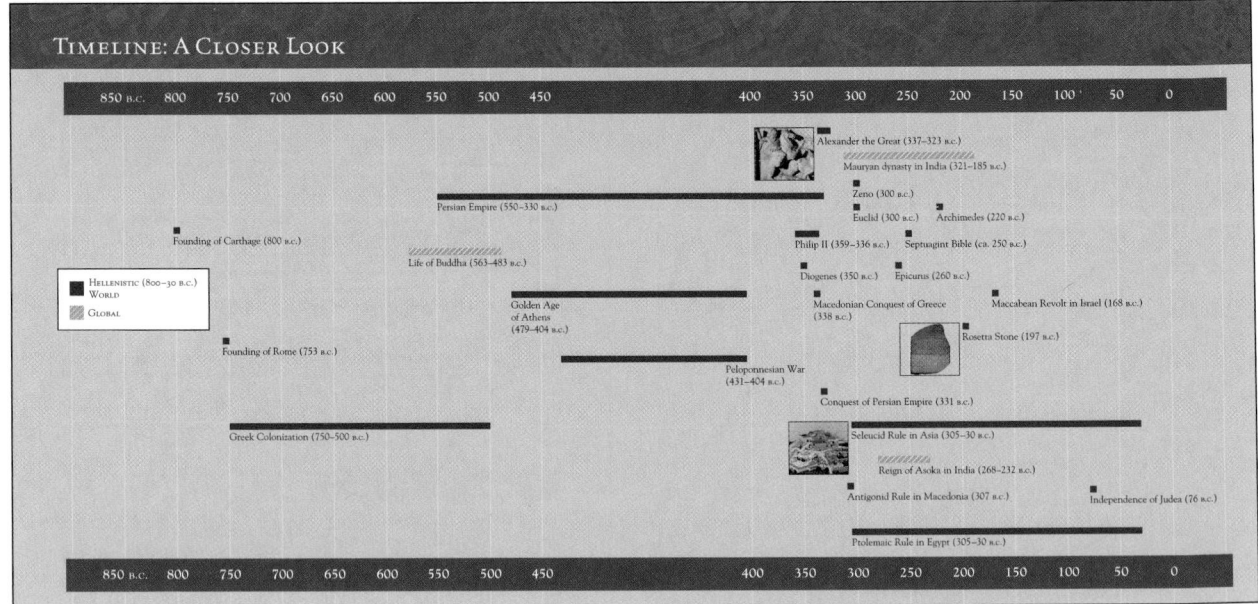

students lose track of simultaneous developments, and indeed of the dates themselves. We have added several features to strengthen readers' sense of chronology. For example, we include dates in the chapter titles and many of the chapter subheadings. We have also sprinkled important dates throughout the narrative and whenever key individuals are named.

As a significant feature to address the understanding of chronology, we have included time lines at the beginning and end of each chapter. The beginning lines that we have called "The Big Picture" show blocks that indicate the large events, periods, or dynasties that will be covered within the chapter.

The ending lines, called "A Closer Look," detail events and people that were covered within the text. Both these lines depict simultaneous developments in a memorable, visual way and provide a sense of broad chronological context. Finally, we have made sure that the time lines draw from the material in the previous and forthcoming chapters. Again, this technique emphasizes connectedness and continuity in the story of Western civilization.

Map Exercises

Because a sense of geography is essential to the study of history, we have included a wealth of full-color maps, and we treat them uniquely. As instructors know very well, too often students just glance at

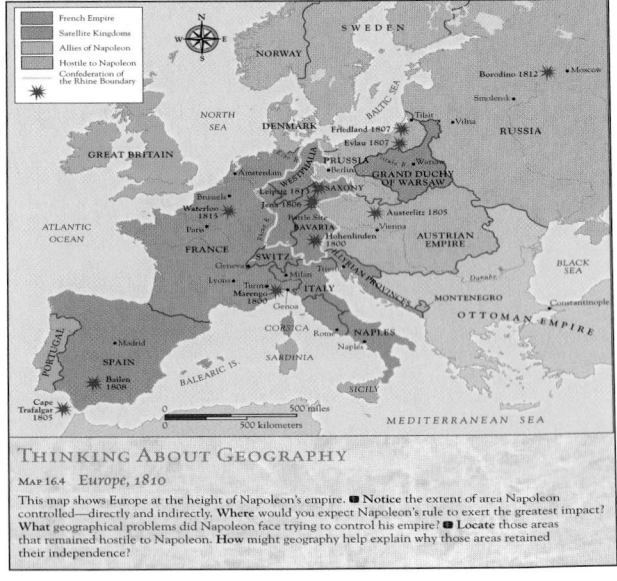

THINKING ABOUT GEOGRAPHY

MAP 16.4 *Europe, 1810*
This map shows Europe at the height of Napoleon's empire. ■ **Notice** the extent of area Napoleon controlled—directly and indirectly. **Where** would you expect Napoleon's rule to exert the greatest impact? **What** geographical problems did Napoleon face trying to control his empire? ■ **Locate** those areas that remained hostile to Napoleon. **How** might geography help explain why those areas retained their independence?

maps without understanding them or engaging them critically. To address this, we have included a feature called "Thinking about Geography," which provides analytical exercises that invite students to delve into the meaning of each map. We hope this approach will not only help students remember particular maps, but will also get them into the habit of actively seeking to understand how geographic features shape human events.

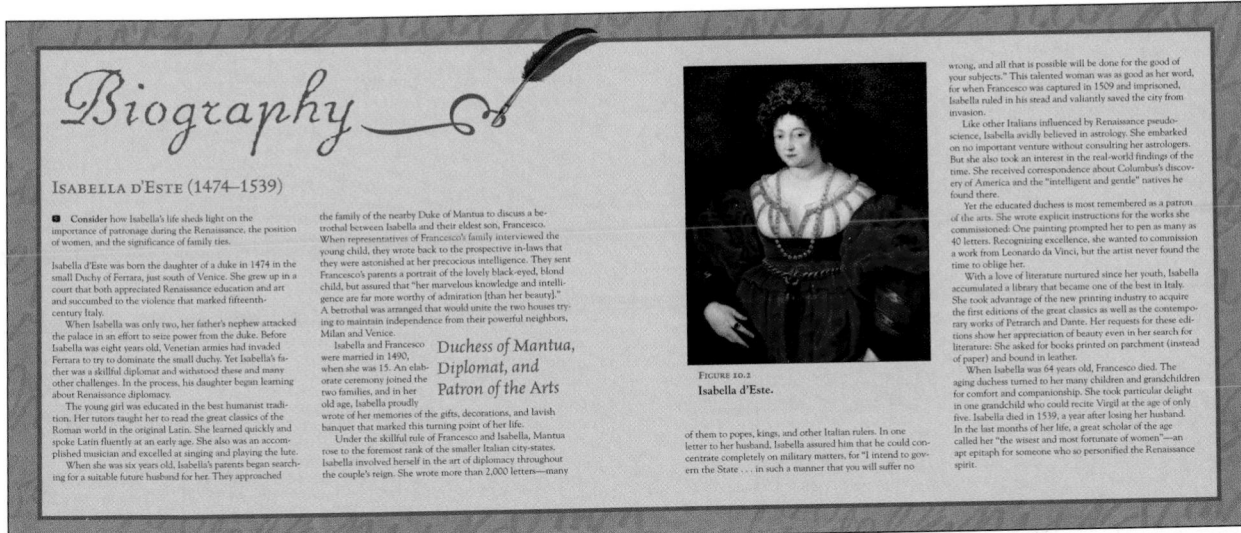

Biographies

Each chapter features a biographical essay of a man or woman who embodies major themes from the chapter. The individuals selected are not necessarily the most celebrated nor the most typical, but instead are powerful illustrative examples. Each biography serves as a reminder of the major themes—another kind of review—and provides a concrete way to discuss some of the more abstract concepts covered, and each biography includes questions that guide students to think critically about the individual's life and connect it with the chapter's themes. We designed the biographies to bring the past to life, as well as to encourage students to think about how large developments affect individuals. For example, the biography of Isabelle D'Este, found in Chapter 10, illustrates the Renaissance by her patronage of the arts, her political struggles, and her strong family ties. Similarly, the biography of Jean-Jacques Rousseau in Chapter 14 analyzes his life as well as how it reflects the broad themes of the Enlightenment.

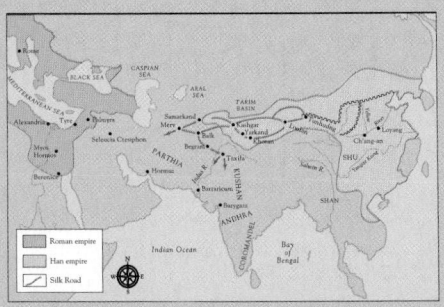

Global Connections

CHINA'S HAN DYNASTY AND THE SILK ROAD

■ **Consider** the importance of centralized authority and trade to the growth of cultures in the West and the East. **NOTICE** how long-term economic ties with eastern Asia influenced the Roman Empire.

In 206 B.C., while the Roman Republic was expanding, a strong Chinese military commander, Liu Bang, brought order to warring factions in China. Liu established the Han dynasty (named after his native land), which would endure for more than 400 years. The Han emperors developed a centralized authority supported by a large bureaucracy, and they built an extensive network of roads and canals to facilitate communication throughout the realm. The emperors also knew the value of educated royal servants. Thus, in 124 B.C., Emperor Han Wudi established an imperial university. This university incorporated Confucianism as the basis for its curriculum, so the Confucian tradition took root in China. Like the Romans in the West, the Han emperors developed an influential body of law, written first on bamboo and silk. Their legal system became the most comprehensive and best organized in the world.

The centralized, ordered rule of the Hans facilitated trade. It also led to the development of the "silk road," which linked China and the West in significant ways. Luxury items moved from China and India to Mesopotamia and the Mediterranean basin. Incoming goods arrived through a complex series of trades. Roman sailors used the prevailing monsoon winds to sail their ships from Red Sea ports to the mouth of the Indus River in India at Barygaza. There, they traded their goods—mostly gold and silver—for Indian spices and silks. The Indian merchants took their share of the merchandise and proceeded to trade with the Han merchants.

Chinese traders shipped spices—ginger, cinnamon, cloves, and others—that Westerners craved both as flavorings and medicines. However, the most prized commodity was Chinese silk, which gave its name to the trade route. By the first century A.D., Romans were willing to pay premium prices for the prized fiber. The Chinese knew how to feed silkworms on mulberry leaves and harvest the cocoons before the moths chewed through the precious silk strands. The silk traveled in bales—either as woven cloth or raw yarn—and went to processing centers, most of them in Syria. There workers ungummed the rolls and unwound the fiber before weaving the fabric that sold for top prices throughout the Roman Empire. For hundreds of years, the trade flourished bringing West and East into close contact. This contact sparked the exchange of ideas as well as goods. Unfortunately, it also spread diseases that dramatically reduced populations in China as well as in the Roman Empire.

Despite the thriving trade, the later Han emperors proved unable to maintain the centralization and prosperity that had marked the early centuries of their reign. In the face of social and economic tensions, as well as epidemic diseases, disloyal generals grabbed more and more power. By A.D. 200, the Han dynasty had collapsed and the empire lay in pieces. The trade along the silk road suffered too, but stories of the prosperous East continued to capture the imaginations of Westerners.

MAP 5.2 *The Silk Road ca.* A.D. 200.

FIGURE 16.9
Antoine-Jean Gros, *Battle of Nazareth*, 1801. Musée des Beaux-Arts, Nantes.

NAPOLEON CONSOLIDATES CONTROL

Napoleon quickly outmaneuvered his partners. He had a new "short and obscure" constitution drawn up and accepted by members of the old legislature. *First consul* In a national plebiscite where people could vote to accept or reject the new constitution, the French overwhelmingly approved it (though the government falsified the results to give it a more lopsided victory). As one observer explained, people "believed quite sincerely that Bonaparte . . . would save us from the perils of anarchy." Napoleon named himself "first consul" and assumed the powers necessary to rule—all with the ready support of the Senate. The remaining two consuls, as well as voters and the handpicked legislative bodies they thought they were electing, had only minimal powers. Next, Napoleon placed each of France's 83 departments under the control of a powerful agent of the central government—the *prefect*. Thus at both the local and the national levels, Napoleon ended meaningful democracy in France.

With the touch of a skilled authoritarian politician, Napoleon proceeded to gather support. He welcomed former Old Regime officials as well as moderate Jacobins into his service. By approving the end of serfdom and feudal privileges as well as all transfers of property that had occurred during the Revolution, he won favor with the peasantry. He gained the backing of the middle class by affirming the property rights and formal equality before the law that adult males had secured during the Revolution. He welcomed back to France all but the most reactionary émigrés, most of whom had come from France's old aristocracy. The educated elite admired Napoleon for patronizing science and inviting leading scientists to join him in his government. To deter opposition, he created a secret police force, suppressed independent political organizations, and censored newspapers and artistic works. Finally, for those who displayed the highest loyalty and the most spectacular achievements (particularly in the military), he created the prestigious Legion of Honor.

Keenly aware of the political and social importance of religion—once calling religion "excellent stuff for keeping the common people *The Concordat* quiet"—Napoleon made peace with the pope and ended the 10-year struggle between the French revolutionary governments and the Roman Catholic church. Their Concordat (formal agreement) of 1801 declared the Catholic religion the religion of the majority of the French people, but ensured freedom for Protestants. Later, Napoleon granted new rights to Jews, as well. Under his rule, the clergy was paid by the state and required to take an oath of allegiance to the state. Confiscated Catholic Church property was not returned.

REFORMING FRANCE

Napoleon followed up this pattern of blending compromise and authoritarian control with a remaking of France's legal, financial, and educational systems. The Civil Code of *Napoleonic Code* 1804 (the Napoleonic Code), for example, generally affirmed the Enlightenment-inspired legal reforms that the early French revolutionaries had sought. Progressives throughout Europe and even overseas would embrace this law code. For men, the code

574

GLOBAL CONNECTIONS

These essays, which focus on important connections between the West and the non-Western world, appear in half of the book's chapters. They illustrate varying degrees of interaction between the West and the world. In some cases the connection was strong and continuous—like the Silk Road (Chapter 5) linking Rome with China. In other cases, connections were brief but left a lingering impact on non-Western regions—as with the growth of the Indian Empires after the withdrawal of Alexander the Great (Chapter 3). However, in each essay, we have reinforced the notion that the West has always developed within a world context. We have also used Global Connections to consider history from the perspective of non-Westerners.

Clear Headings and Marginal Notes

Each chapter has clear thematic titles and precise headings that guide students through the narrative. Throughout, brief marginal notes help students focus on the key concepts, terms, and events and provide a tool for reviewing the chapter.

Review, Analyze, and Anticipate

At the end of each chapter are questions that not only ask students to think about the material discussed within the chapter, but also encourage them to place the material within the context of what has come before and what is coming next. The summary paragraphs included within these sections offer continuous reviews and previews of material, once again helping students to retain the larger picture while learning new details.

Beyond the Classroom

These sections, found at the end of each chapter, list resources that students can use to gain additional ideas and information. These include suggestions of primary sources (many of which are available free on the book's online learning center), Internet links to a variety of materials, and books briefly reviewed and organized according to the chapter's main headings.

Glossary and Pronunciation Guide

Important terms are briefly defined in the Glossary at the end of the book (that is conveniently marked by a color border to make it easy to locate). All the words, except the most simple, come with a pronunciation guide. This feature allows students to readily review terms, while giving them the confidence in pronunciation to help make the terms part of their vocabulary.

New End of Chapter Document Excerpts

New to this edition, we have added two to four primary source excerpts at the end of each chapter. Each excerpt begins with an introduction and "Investigate the Document" questions to prompt critical analyses of each primary source.

New Marginal Icons

Throughout the text, you'll notice the following icons:

The CD icon indicates that a primary source reading is available on PSI.

The video icon indicates that a video is available on PSI

The following is a reproduction of a textbook page showing the "Review, Analyze, and Anticipate" and "Beyond the Classroom" features:

REVIEW, ANALYZE, AND ANTICIPATE

REVIEW THE PREVIOUS CHAPTER

Chapter 7—"The Struggle to Restore Order"—described manorialism and the feudal contract as the organizing structures of medieval life. It also described the invasions of the ninth and tenth centuries that undermined the developing order in the West.

1. Review the obligations of peasants and the nature of village life described in Chapter 7 and consider the strengths of these structures that allowed for the agricultural boom in the eleventh century.

2. Review the invasions by Vikings and others that caused a decentralization of power and the weakening of kings. How did this decentralization influence the growth of England and France from the eleventh through the thirteenth centuries?

ANALYZE THIS CHAPTER

Chapter 8—"Order Perfected"—traces the High Middle Ages and follows the fortunes of the social groups and political entities that made up the West.

1. Consider the growth of towns and the related developments of trade. How did towns govern themselves? How was the prevalence of Gothic cathedrals and pilgrimages related to the growing prosperity of towns?

2. One of the themes of this chapter is the struggle between popes and emperors or kings to decide who should lead a Christian Europe. Review these struggles and consider the advantages and disadvantages of each party's position.

3. Review the Crusades. Why did the crusaders go to the Holy Land, and what did they accomplish?

ANTICIPATE THE NEXT CHAPTER

Chapter 9—"Despair in the West, Empires in the East"—shows how the disasters of the fourteenth century undermined the structures that had ordered western Europe for centuries, and also shows the growth of empires in eastern Europe.

1. What structures—manorialism, feudal contracts, centralized monarchies, or a central church organization—do you think would be most vulnerable to social, economic, and military disasters? Why?

BEYOND THE CLASSROOM

THOSE WHO WORK: AGRICULTURAL LABOR

Hanawalt, B. *The Ties That Bind: Peasant Families in Medieval England.* New York: Oxford University Press, 1986. An eminent historian provides a vivid and engaging picture of peasant life.

Sweeny, Del, ed. *Agriculture in the Middle Ages: Technology, Practice and Representation.* Philadelphia, PA: University of Pennsylvania Press, 1995. Presents a collection of essays on various aspects of medieval agriculture that also shows the sources for such information.

THOSE OUTSIDE THE ORDER: TOWN LIFE

Bennet, Judith M. *Ale, Beer, and Brewsters in England: Women's Work in a Changing World.* Oxford: Oxford University Press, 1999. An excellent discussion of the changing economic roles of women as the medieval economy grew.

Evans, G.R. *Philosophy and Theology in the Middle Ages.* New York: Routledge, 1993. A sound, comprehensive survey of intellectual thought, showing the ties between philosophy and theology.

Gies, Frances, and Joseph Gies. *Cathedral, Forge, and Waterwheel: Technology and Invention in the Middle Ages.* New York: HarperCollins, 1994. An engaging discussion of the many inventions of the Middle Ages that shows the influence of the East in spreading innovations.

Herlihy, David. *Opera Muliebria: Women and Work in Medieval Europe.* New York: McGraw-Hill, 1990. A short, yet scholarly, summary of the varied jobs of women in the Middle Ages that considers the way their work changed over time.

295

Documents

DOCUMENT 6.1
The Huns Menace Rome

Many of the Germanic tribes who invaded the Roman Empire during the fourth century were fleeing the Huns, nomadic peoples from central Asia. This account by the Roman historian Ammianus Marcellinus describes the Huns' frightening qualities.

■ Investigate the Document

Notice how the historian pointedly shows the Huns as strikingly different from the "civilized" Romans. Which characteristics of the Huns might the Romans have found most frightening? How might this description have shaped Roman policy toward the Huns?

At the very moment of their birth the cheeks of their infant children are deeply marked by an iron, in order that the usual vigor of their hair, instead of growing at the proper season, may be withered by the wrinkled scars; and accordingly they grow up without beards, and consequently without any beauty, like eunuchs, though they all have closely knit and strong limbs and plump necks; they are of great size, and bow-legged, so that you might fancy them two-legged beasts, or the stout figures which are hewn out in a rude manner with an axe on the posts at the end of bridges.

They are certainly in the shape of men, however uncouth, but are so hardy that they neither require fire nor well-flavored food, but live on the roots of such herbs as they get in the fields, or on the half-raw flesh of any animal, which they merely warm rapidly by placing it between their own thighs and the back of their horses.

They wear linen clothes, or else garments made of the skins of field-mice; nor do they wear a different dress out of doors from that which they wear at home; but after a tunic is once put round their necks, however much it becomes worn, it is never taken off or changed till, from long decay, it becomes actually so ragged as to fall to pieces.

Source: *The Great Events by Famous Historians.* Edited by Rossiter Johnson. The National Alumni. 1905. Volume III. pp. 353-354.

DOCUMENT 6.2
The Silk Industry Comes to Byzantium

The Byzantine Empire thrived in part on the wealth derived from its silk industry, which had previously belonged exclusively to China. In the sixth century, the emperor Justinian learned the secret of producing the valued fabric. Through the excerpt below, the ancient historian Procopius describes this pivotal moment.

■ Investigate the Document

Why did the traveling monks say that Justinian should no longer buy silk from the Persians? What challenges did the Byzantines face in starting the new industry?

About the same time there came from India certain monks; and when they had satisfied Justinian Augustus that the Romans no longer should buy silk from the Persians, they promised the emperor in an interview that they would provide the materials for making silk so that never should the Romans seek business of this kind from their enemy the Persians, or from any other people whatsoever. They said that they were formerly in Serinda, which they call the region frequented by the people of the Indies, and there they learned perfectly the art of making silk. Moreover, to the emperor who plied them with many questions as to whether he might have the secret, the monks replied that certain worms were manufacturers of silk, nature itself forcing them to keep always at work; the worms could certainly not be brought here alive, but they could be grown easily and without difficulty; the eggs of single hatchings are innumerable; as soon as they are laid men cover them with dung and keep them warm for as long as it is necessary so that they produce insects. When they had announced these tidings, led on by liberal promises of the emperor to prove the fact, they returned to India. When they had brought the eggs to Byzantium, the method having been learned, as I have said, they

Source: Halsall Medieval Sourcebook, online at www.mhhe.com_shennanl.

D6.1

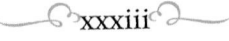

The Online Learning Center icon indicates that a primary source reading is available on the book's website at *www.mhhe.com/sherman2 updated*.

And at the end of each chapter a quiz icon reminds students that pertinent quiz questions are available on PSI to test your reading skills.

These multimedia assets are fully integrated throughout the book and represent a mere sampling of the resources available on the Primary Source Investigator CD. You'll also find images, maps, chapter summaries, and a variety of quizzing materials on the PSI CD and Online Learning Center.

TO YOU, THE STUDENT: HOW TO USE THIS BOOK

Welcome to the study of Western civilization! The word "West" does not refer to one geographic location, but rather a series of cultures that first emerged in the ancient Middle East, spread to the Mediterranean world and Europe, and eventually crossed the seas to the Americas and elsewhere. Today, there is scarcely any culture in the world not touched by the West. Yet from the beginning, the West has also been powerfully influenced by its interactions with cultures outside its moving center. The *West in the World* emphasizes this global, interactive quality rather than analyzing the West's story in isolation. To get the most out of this book, we suggest you use the process described below as you read each chapter. (Try these same techniques with textbooks in your other courses, too—you'll likely find them just as valuable there.)

1. *Preview the chapter.* Find out what the chapter is about before you start reading it. Look at the "chapter points" at the beginning, and read the preview that appears next to the opening illustration. These two features set the stage for what you are about to read. You might also take a peek at the "Analyze This Chapter" questions at the end of the chapter; they can give you an idea of what to expect. Finally, a chapter outline from our on-line study guide is also available at *www.mhhe.com/sherman2updated*.

2. *Read the chapter as you would a good story.* Try to get engaged in the narrative. That is, don't read the chapter too slowly. However, *do* notice each sub-heading in the chapter—these signal what's coming next. Also, resist the urge to highlight *everything!* We've provided marginal notes to help you review. We've also included descriptions and analyses of the illustrations. So, when you come to an illustration, pause and look carefully at it. This process will help you get used to interpreting visual sources. The illustrations will also trigger your memory of the chapter's content when you study the chapter later.

3. *Examine and think about the maps.* Geography plays a huge role in history, so it's vital that you know how to read and interpret maps. We've provided questions with each amp to help you understand how it fits in with the chapter as a whole. Try to answer the questions (even if you're note sure how)—they'll help you review the material in the chapter. Also, sharpen your map skills by practicing the interactive map exercises for each chapter in the on-line study guide.

4. *Examine and think about the "Biography" and "Global Connections" features.* These boxes provide more information about the time period covered in the chapter. Information in the chapter connects directly to these features, so watch carefully for these relationships. These two features can serve as an additional review of the chapter while helping you understand one topic more deeply. By answering the "consider" questions at the head of each box, you build your critical-thinking skills while you review.

5. *Review the timelines.* Some people may lose track of chronology—that is, the sequence in which major developments and events occurred—while they're reading narrative histories. The chapter's two timelines will help you keep track of chronology. The first timeline (at the beginning of the chapter) gives you the large developments; the "Closer Look" timeline (at the end of the chapter) features detailed events as well as key individuals. As you examine these, make sure everything in them is familiar. If you see something you don't understand in a timeline, go back into the chapter to

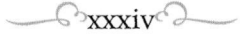

fill in the gaps. These timelines make excellent review tools.

6. *Review the chapter.* Answer the "Review, Analyze, and Anticipate" questions at the end of the chapter, even if you just compose your responses in your mind. Better yet, talk over your responses with other students in your class. The "Review the Previous Chapters" questions will help you connect the material you just read with preceding chapters; the "Analyze This Chapter" questions focus on the material in the current chapter; and the "Anticipate the Next Chapter" questions point you to future chapters. Don't worry if you don't know what's coming next. Making educated guesses helps you build your thinking skills. Even more important, you'll soon realize that history is a seamless web that is only artificially divided into chapters.

7. *Use the primary source documents at the end of each chapter.* Within each chapter's narrative are references to relevant primary sources. These sources appear at the end of each chapter. Each source begins with a short introduction and "Investigate the Document" questions. This feature is new to the updated edition and one that we hope will prove useful. For instance, in chapter 11, after you have learned the chief reason behind Henry VIII's break with the Roman Catholic Church, read an account of Anne Boleyn's execution. When was this eyewitness account written? Who was the author? Is his account reliable? Consider each document as a window on to another aspect of the political, cultural, and social environment of the times. If you are particularly interested in one document, you may want to conduct further research.

8. *Conduct further research.* Do you have to write a paper, or (better yet!) are you simply curious and want to learn more? Are you looking for more primary or secondary sources on a specific topic? The readings listed at the end of each chapter will get you started with a list of texts at your school library. Icons placed in the margins of the chapter also signal that multi-media assets are available on either the Primary Source Investigator CD or the Online Learning Center. The former contains over 200 additional readings, images, interactive maps, and quiz questions, while the latter contains links to recommended online primary sources.

The steps described above should help you better understand the story of *The West in the World.* We hope you enjoy the unfolding history of the West as much as we have enjoyed bringing it to you.

Dating System

The various civilizations across the world do not all use the same dating system. For example, Muslims use the date 622 (when the Prophet fled from Mecca to Medina) as year 1 in their history. The Hebrew calendar counts the Western year 3760 B.C. as year 1—which some consider to be when the world was created.

The western world generally uses a dating system that counts backward and forward from the birth of Christ—which Westerners consider year 1. Events that took place "Before Christ" ("B.C.") are counted backward from year 1. Thus, something that happened 300 years before Christ's birth is dated 300 B.C. The events described in the first four chapters of *The West in the World* all took place B.C. Events that took place after the birth of Christ are also dated from the hypothetical year 1 and are labeled A.D.— which stands for the Latin *anno Domini,* meaning "in the year of the lord." In Chapter 5, we've marked all dates with A.D., but because everything after that time is A.D., we then drop the designation. Some people—especially world historians—prefer to keep the same numerical system, but use the designation "B.C.E."—"Before the common Era"— and "C.E."— "Common Era." We have kept B.C. and A.D., because this system is customarily used in the teaching of Western civilization.

SUPPLEMENTS

For the Instructor

Instructor's Manual, by Carol Bresnahan, The University of Toledo. The Instructor's Manual includes chapter summaries, main themes, points for discussion, map exercises, essay questions, terms for identification, and a pronunciation guide. In addition, the Instructor's Manual draws on some of the unique features of the text, including a guide to visual analysis, discussion questions derived from the book's

integrated coverage of visual material and boxed biographies, World Wide Web-related exercises accompanied by a listing of relevant websites for each chapter, and video suggestions. The Instructor's Manual is available online at www.mhhe.com/sherman2updated and on the Instructor's Resource CD-ROM.

Test Bank, by David Hudson, California State University at Fresno. The Test Bank includes short answer and essay questions, identification questions, multiple choice, fill-in-the-blank questions, mapping exercises, true/false questions and chronology exercises. Like the Instructor's Manual, it offers a range of questions that highlight the distinctive features of the text. The Test Bank is available on the Instructor's Resource CD-ROM, and in the computerized format described below.

Computerized Test Bank McGraw-Hill's EZ Test is a flexible and easy-to-use electronic testing program. The program allows instructors to create tests from book specific items. It accommodates a wide range of question types and instructors may add their own questions. Multiple versions of the test can be created and any test can be exported for use with course management systems such as WebCT, BlackBoard or PageOut. The program is available for Windows, Macintosh and Linux environments.

Overhead Transparencies This comprehensive packet of approximately 140 transparencies is designed to support the text's unique integrated art program. Fine art, photos, and maps—many pulled directly from the text— allow instructors to easily illustrate classroom lectures.

Slide Set Available through your McGraw-Hill sales representative, instructors can choose from a list of hundreds of fine art slides to create a customized slide set to complement the text and enhance classroom lectures.

Instructor's Resource CD-ROM The McGraw-Hill presentation manager organizes a diverse range of instructor's tools on one CD. Instructors can illustrate classroom lectures and discussions with text-specific PowerPoint presentations including outlines, maps, and photos for each chapter. The Instructor's Manual and Test Bank are also included on this CD, as well as links to web-based research assignments.

Instructor's Online Learning Center
www.mhhe.com/sherman2updated
At the homepage to the text-specific website, instructors will find a series of online tools to meet a range of classroom needs. The Instructor's Manual and most PowerPoint shows can be downloaded by instructors, but are password-protected to prevent tampering. Instructors can also create web-based homework assignments or classroom activities by linking to the Student Online Learning Center, and can create an interactive course syllabus using McGraw-Hill's **PageOut** (*www.mhhe.com/pageout*).

PageOut
www.mhhe.com/pageout
On the PageOut website, instructors can create their own course websites. PageOut requires no prior knowledge of HTML, no long hours of coding, and no design skills on the instructor's part. Simply plug the course information into a template and click on one of 16 designs. The process takes no time at all and leaves instructors with a professionally designed website. Powerful features include an interactive course syllabus that lets instructors post content and links, an online gradebook, lecture notes, bookmarks, and even a discussion board where instructors and students can discuss course-related topics.

Videos Created and narrated by Joyce Salisbury, this three-video collection illuminates the author's lectures on the Middle Ages with the sculpture and fine art of the times. Available to adopters through your local McGraw-Hill representative, this unique series contains a video on each of the following topics: medieval women, medieval Judaism, and medieval life.

A wide range of videos on classic and contemporary topics in history is available through the Films for the Humanities and Sciences collection. Instructors can illustrate classroom discussion and enhance lectures by selecting from a series of videos that are correlated to complement **The West in the World.** Contact your local McGraw-Hill sales representative for further information.

For the Student

After the Fact Interactive is a multimedia tool that enables students to work as historians, developing their own understanding of historiography while examining a variety of multimedia primary source materials. Each CD-ROM prompts students to ask questions, research, and formulate arguments, supporting their own thesis with evidence and a conclusion. Both the "Tracing the Silk Roads" and "Envisioning the Atlantic World" CD-ROMS are available with the

combined volume, while "Tracing the Silk Roads" is offered with Volume I and "Envisioning the Atlantic World" is offered with Volumes II and III.

Tracing the Silk Roads: In this interactive exercise, students explore the sources of the Silk Roads, the most important zone of cross-cultural encounter during the classical period. Far from isolated pockets of civilization, the rise of complex and unified classical societies made possible an extensive network of trade routes between the Mediterranean and East Asia, and were in turn transformed (some even destroyed) by the forces unleashed through those exchanges.

Envisioning the Atlantic World: Students here delve into the discovery of the Atlantic Basin during the age of exploration. Once a nearly impassable barrier, Columbus and subsequent explorers ripped the veil of ignorance and uncertainty cloaking the Atlantic. In doing so, they opened a new, dramatic chapter of cross-cultural encounters whose cultural, political, economic, and biological exchanges transformed the modern world.

Student Study Guide, by Bruce Venarde, University of Pittsburgh, Megan McLean, University of Pittsburgh, and Melissa McGary, University of Pittsburgh; second edition revised by Megan McLean.

Available in two volumes, this guide helps students to process and master important concepts covered in the text. For each chapter of the text, the study guide offers valuable pedagogical tools such as chapter summaries and reviews, chapter outlines that include the main theme of each chapter, objective questions, short answer and essay questions, and mapping exercises. Visual learning exercises, chronology exercises based on the text's timeline, and questions that make use of the text's many biography sections highlight some of most distinctive features found in **The West in the World.** A unique guide to history on the Internet can be found at the front of the study guide.

Map Workbooks Students need all the work they can get on geography, and this supplement offers the opportunity for extra mapping practice. The workbooks are available in two volumes, and each builds upon the many unique map exercises found throughout the text.

Student Online Learning Center
www.mhhe.com/sherman2updated

At the homepage to the text-specific website, students can link to an interactive study guide, including online essay questions, timelines, mapping exercises, and a variety of objective questions to guide students through the text material. Links to related websites make the student Online Learning Center a great place to begin web-based research.

Qualifications As a full service publisher of quality education products, McGraw-Hill does much more than just sell textbooks to your students. We create and publish an extensive array of print, video, and digital supplements to support instruction on your campus. Orders of new (versus used) textbooks help us to defray the cost of developing such supplements, which is substantial. Please consult your local McGraw-Hill sales representative to learn about the availability of the supplements that accompany *The West in the World.*

ACKNOWLEDGMENTS

We have nurtured this book through many drafts, and every page has benefited from the advice of numerous reviewers, some of whom we have gone back to several times. For their thoughtful comments and generous contribution of time and expertise, we would like to thank the following reviewers:

For the Second Edition

Joseph Appiah
Virginia Community College

Douglas C. Baxter
Ohio University

Jonathan Bone
William Patterson University

Suzanne Bowles
William Patterson University

April Brooks
South Dakota State University

Katherine Clark
University of Kansas

Sandi Cooper
City University of New York

Florin Curta
University of Florida

Norman C. Delany
Del Mar College

David D. Flaten
Plymouth State College

Marsha L. Frey
Kansas State University

Bruce Garver
University of Nebraska at Omaha

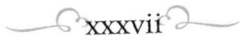

Carla Hay
Marquette University

Holly Hurlburt
Southern Illinois University

Andrew Keitt
University of Alabama at Birmingham

Dave Kelly
Colorado State University

Jason Knirck
Humboldt State University

Mark W. McLeod
University of Delaware

Carol Menning
University of Toledo

Jeffrey Lee Meriwether
Roger Williams University

Zachary Morgan
William Patterson University

Michael Myers
University of Illinois

Max Okenfuss
Washington University

Jack Pesda
Camden County College

Dolores Davison Peterson
Foothill College

Paul Rempe
Carroll College

Harry Rosenberg
Colorado State University

Shawn Ross
William Patterson University

Glenn Sanders
Oklahoma Baptist University

Marc Schwarz
University of New Hampshire

David Stefanic
Saint Mary's College

Aliza Wong
Texas Technical University

Michael A. Zaccaria
Cumberland County College

For the First Edition

Edward Anson
University of Arkansas

William S. Arnett
West Virginia University

Richard Berthold
University of New Mexico

Robert Blackey
California State University–San Bernardino

Hugh Boyer
Michigan Technical University

Carol Bresnahan-Menning
University of Toledo

April Brooks
South Dakota State University

Nathan Brooks
New Mexico State University

Blaine T. Browne
Broward Community College

Donald Butts
Gordon College

Frederick Corney
University of Florida

Jeffrey Cox
University of Iowa

Florin Curta
University of Florida

Norman Delaney
Del Mar College

Robert Dise
University of Northern Iowa

Chris Drake
Houston Community College–Northwest

Lawrence G. Duggan
University of Delaware

Laird Easton
California State University–Chico

Gregory Elder
Riverside Community College

Nancy Erickson
Erskine College

Chiarella Esposito
University of Mississippi

Gary Ferngren
Oregon State University

Nancy Fitch
California State University–Fullerton

Elizabeth Lane Furdell
University of North Florida

Frank Garosi
California State University–Sacramento

Don Gawronski
Mesa Community College

Paul Goodwin
University of Connecticut

Anita Guerrini
University of California –Santa Barbara

Louis Haas
Duquesne University

Alice Henderson
University of South Carolina–Spartanburg

Jennifer Hevelone-Harper
Gordon College

Steven Hill
Wake Technical Community College

Laura J. Hilton
Ohio State University

Karen Holland
Providence College

David Hudson
California State University–Fresno

Gary Johnson
University of Southern Maine

Jonathan G. Katz
Oregon State University

Andrew Keitt
University of Alabama–Birmingham

Charles Killinger
Valencia Community College

Lisa Lane
Mira Costa College

John Livingston
University of Denver

David Longfellow
Baylor University

Donna Maier
University of Northern Iowa

James I. Martin, Sr.
Campbell University

Carol Miller
Tallahassee Community College

Eileen Moore
University of Alabama–Birmingham

Frederick I. Murphy
Western Kentucky University

Max J. Okenfuss
Washington University

Michael Osborne
University of California–Santa Barbara

John P. Pesda
Camden County College

Russell Quinlan
Northern Arizona University

Patricia Ranft
Central Michigan University

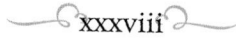

Roger Reese
Texas A&M University

Harry Rosenberg
Colorado State University

Constance M. Rousseau
Providence College

Jay Rubenstein
University of New Mexico

Claire Sanders
Texas Christian College

Alan Schaffer
Clemson University

Daryl Schuster
University of Central Florida

Marc Schwarz
University of New Hampshire

David Shearer
University of Delaware

Arlene Sindelar
University of Central Arkansas

James Sisson
Central Texas College

Ronald D. Smith
Arizona State University

Saulius Suziedelis
Millersville University of Pennsylvania

Hunt Tooley
Austin College

Kevin Uhalde
Northern Illinois University

David Ulbrich
Kansas State University

Bruce Venarde
University of Pittsburgh

Charlotte Wells
University of Northern Iowa

Michael Wilson
University of Texas–Dallas

Robert Wise
University of Northern Iowa

Bill Wrightson
American River College

We would also like to offer a special thank-you to the reviewer focus group participants. We appreciate your generous contribution of time and attention to this book, from its inception to the final design touches.

In addition, we would like to thank Lauren Johnson, who served as the developmental editor, for her detailed line-by-line editing, and Peter Seelig, Karen Lewis, and William Whiting for their research assistance.

Last, but certainly not least, we would like to thank the many professors who choose to use this text in their classrooms. It is they who will fulfill our hope for this text—that it will bring the past to life for many undergraduates and will perhaps awaken in them a love for history and an awareness that understanding the past is the key to our future.

A Note from the Authors

What's the best way to write an interesting, accessible, and accurate account of the West's complex history? This question confronts everyone who approaches this huge and important task. On the one hand, we believed strongly that different authors' perspectives would give readers a sense of the richness of the past. On the other hand, we wanted a seamless narrative that read like a good story. We decided that a careful two-author collaboration would best enable us to achieve both goals.

We brought our different backgrounds, research interests, and teaching experiences to the table. We talked over our ideas and read and struggled with one another's words. Throughout, we never lost sight of our goal: to bring the compelling history of the West in the world to students of the twenty-first century.

Dennis Sherman

I was in the twelfth grade in west Los Angeles when I first realized I had a flair for history. Our teacher wisely gave us much latitude in selecting topics for two lengthy papers. I chose ancient Egypt (I liked the National Geographic visuals) as my first topic, and Tasmania as the second. (I was the only one who seemed to know that Tasmania was an island below Australia). Assembling the material and writing the papers just came easily to me, as did any questions our history teacher posed in class (though I was an otherwise fading-into-the-background student). I more or less blundered into different majors in college and then slid through law school (which taught me how to be succinct) before returning to history. At the beginning of my first semester of graduate school, I met my advisor who asked me what courses I wanted to take. I ticked off four selections: History of South Asia; Nineteenth Century Europe; Twentieth Century America; European Intellectual History. "You're a generalist," he said. Indeed I was. He wisely counseled me to narrow my focus. However, throughout my studies and professional career I have found the

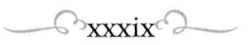

big picture—the forest rather than the trees—the most interesting aspect of history.

A few years later I moved to the front of the classroom and, never forgetting what it was like to be a student, found my heart in teaching. Teaching and writing about the sweep of Western civilization within the broadest possible context has remained my greatest interest over the years. That is why I have written this book with Joyce.

Joyce Salisbury

I grew up in Latin America (10 years in Brazil and 5 in Mexico). Through those years, I attended American schools filled with expatriates. There I studied a curriculum of Western culture, which in those days was equated with European history. But even as a young girl, I knew I wasn't getting the whole story. After all, we celebrated Mardi Gras (a Christian holiday) to an African drumbeat, and the national museum of Mexico was bursting with Napoleonic artifacts. I knew that the history and culture of the West was intimately tied to that of the rest of the world.

In the more than 20 years that I've been teaching Western civilization, I've brought this global perspective to the classroom, and now Dennis and I have brought it to this book. It is very satisfying to me to work with my students as we trace the unfolding history of the West and to see that all my students—with their own rich and varied cultural backgrounds—recognize their stories within the larger narrative.

We live in the present with
what remains of the past,
scarcely knowing all that we
take for granted.

Egyptian Scribe, ca. 2400 B.C.

Historians study the written word, and much of the West's heritage comes from texts that were carefully and laboriously written by people of the past. This scribe, with a roll of papyrus in his lap and a now-lost pen in his right hand, represents the tens of thousands of anonymous scribes who diligently recorded the events and developments of their day.

CHAPTER 1

The Roots of Western Civilization

The Ancient Middle East to 500 B.C.

STUDY • Prehistory through the Neolithic • Mesopotamia • Ancient Egypt • Phoenicians and Hebrews • Growth of Empires ⊕NOTICE how these civilizations developed through interactions with regions far from their centers.

"Since time immemorial, since the seedcorn first sprouted forth . . . [powerful men] have been in charge for their own benefit. The workingman was forced to beg for his bread; the youth was forced to work for others." In 2400 B.C. the Sumerian ruler Uruinimgina wrote these words as he took power in a Mesopotamian city. He claimed that his reforms freed citizens from usury, burdensome controls, hunger, theft, and murder—troubles that, in varying forms, have periodically plagued civilization since it first arose in cities. With his thoughtful policies and passionate sense of justice, Uruinimgina embodied another important characteristic of Western civilization: the occasional rise to power of people who strive to correct social injustice.

In the growing cities of Mesopotamia, Egypt, and the coast of the eastern Mediterranean Sea, other ideas developed that would also form the basis of civilization in the West. Societies practicing social stratification, sophisticated religious ideas, and concepts of law emerged in the same environment that spawned the social ills Uruinimgina briefly corrected. Perhaps most important, these early peoples invented writing, which preserved their cultures in the tablets and scrolls that reveal their world to us as we explore ancient cultures. The culture of the West was born in the Fertile Crescent of what we now know as the Middle East.

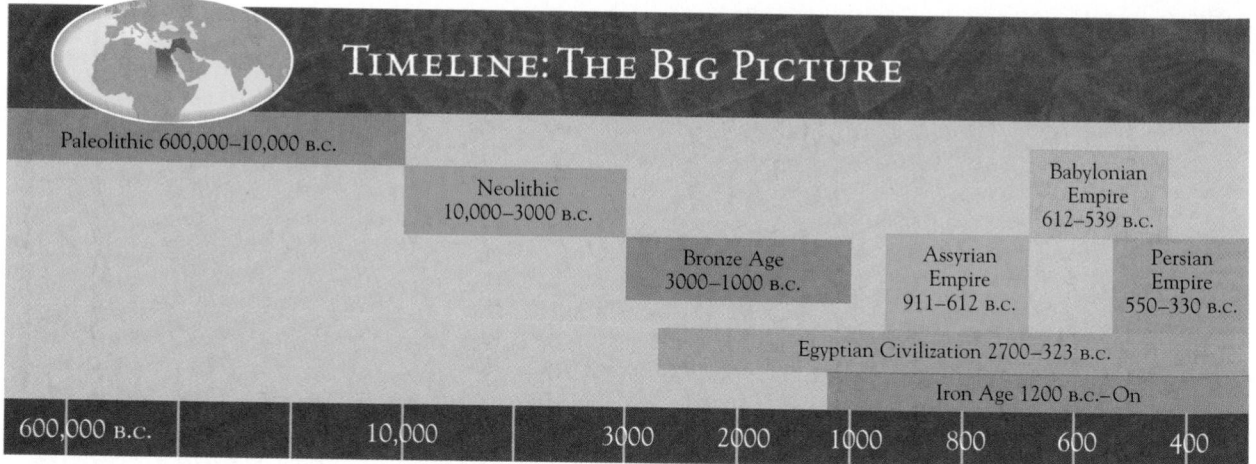

TIMELINE: THE BIG PICTURE

Paleolithic 600,000–10,000 B.C.

Neolithic 10,000–3000 B.C.

Babylonian Empire 612–539 B.C.

Bronze Age 3000–1000 B.C.

Assyrian Empire 911–612 B.C.

Persian Empire 550–330 B.C.

Egyptian Civilization 2700–323 B.C.

Iron Age 1200 B.C.–On

600,000 B.C. 10,000 3000 2000 1000 800 600 400

Before Western Civilization

In 2500 B.C., a Sumerian schoolboy wrote an essay about his struggles to learn reading and writing. He claimed in his essay that he practiced these skills in school all day. He took his writing tablet home to his father, who praised the boy's progress. That night, the boy ate his dinner, washed his feet, and went to bed. The next day, however, he had a difficult time in school. He arrived late and was beaten for his tardiness and several other offenses, including poor handwriting. In despair, the boy invited the schoolmaster home to dinner. The father gave the teacher gifts, and the boy began having fewer problems in school.

This narrative, dating from 4,500 years ago, is perhaps most remarkable for its timeless themes. Tardy students, schools, and concerned parents are all a part of life for most of us today. Here, in the village of this young boy, we can find the roots of what we have come to call Western civilization (or "the West"). This term does not define one location, but instead refers to a series of cultures that slowly evolved and spread to impact societies all over the world. This book traces the development and expansion of the West. Here, however, at the very beginning, we can identify certain characteristics that define Western civilization, and which gave it an advantage—for better or worse—over other competing cultures. Western civilization began in the Middle East, which enjoyed the striking advantage of having plants for agriculture and animals for domestication native to the region. Then large cities arose with attendant division of labor and social stratification based on relationships other than family. Another dramatic advantage was the development of writing, which gave schoolboys so much difficulty, but allowed the preservation and transmission of advantageous developments.

Finally, one of the hallmarks of Western civilization was that it never developed in isolation. Throughout its recorded history, the peoples of the Mediterranean basin traded with other societies, and the resulting cultural diffusion strengthened all the cultures involved. For example, crops from the ancient Middle East spread westward as far as Britain as early as about 4000 B.C., and by the second millennium B.C. wheat, barley, and horses from the Middle East reached as far east as China. In fact, the trade routes from the Middle East to India and China, and west and south to Africa and Europe have a permanence that dwarfs the accomplishments of conquerors and empire builders. These constant and fruitful interactions with other cultures perhaps gave Western civilization its greatest advantage.

Trade

Yet, recorded history represents less than one percent of the time that humans have lived on the earth. Hundreds of thousands of years before this day in the life of a young, urban Sumerian, life for human beings was completely different. Before we begin the story of the development of Western civilization, we must explore the life of the first humans in the lush lands of sub-Saharan Africa.

OUT OF AFRICA: THE PALEOLITHIC PERIOD, 600,000–10,000 B.C.

Human beings first evolved in sub-Saharan Africa hundreds of thousands of years ago. Archaeologists have classified the remains of these early humans into various species and subspecies, most of which were evolutionary dead ends. Modern humans belong to *Homo sapiens sapiens* ("thinking, thinking man"), a subspecies that migrated north and northeast from Africa. These earliest ancestors first appeared some 40,000 years ago and ultimately colonized the world. The first humans used tools made from materials at hand, including wood and bone, but the most useful tools were those made of stone. Initial stone tools were sharpened only roughly, but later humans crafted stones into finely finished flakes ideal for spearheads, arrowheads, and other blades. These tools have led archaeologists to name this long period of human pre-history the Old Stone Age, or the Paleolithic.

Our ancient ancestors were nomadic peoples who lived in small kin groups of about twenty to thirty people and who ate animals that they hunted and plants that they gathered. Fossil teeth indicate that *Trade networks* their diet consisted mostly of plants, and clans had to roam long distances to avoid exhausting the resources of one particular area. Evidence from the late Paleolithic Age tells us that groups of humans returned seasonally to the same regions instead of wandering endlessly to new areas. As they traveled, kin groups encountered other clans and traded goods as well as stories. Archaeological evidence indicates that shells and especially stone tools were often traded in places far from their original sites. For example, late Stone Age people living in what is now Scotland rowed small boats to an off-shore island to bring back precious bloodstone that flaked accurately into strong tools. This bloodstone spread widely across northern Europe through trade with the original sailors. Commerce thus became established as an early human enterprise.

Art joined commerce as a defining quality of early human society. Beginning in about 15,000 B.C., people in southern France and northern Spain painted *Cave art* extraordinary pictures on walls deep inside caves. Figure 1.1 shows one of these paintings. This reproduction cannot convey the power of the original work, which is about six feet long and utilizes the contours of the cave wall to delineate parts of the figure. People returned seasonally to the same caves and painted new figures near earlier ones, and sometimes over them. Some caves show evidence of repeated painting over an astonishing span of 10,000 years, revealing the preservation of traditions over lengths of time that are almost unimaginable today. Scholars believe that the paint-

ings served some ritual purpose—perhaps to ensure the continued abundance of the great game animals they represented. The repeated visits to the deep, nearly inaccessible caves also may have coincided with groups gathering periodically for trade and other interactions, and perhaps the paintings preserved tribal memories. However, we are so removed from those Stone Age times that we can hardly do more than admire these magnificent, mysterious creations.

By the end of the Paleolithic Age (about 10,000 B.C.), the human population of Europe stood at about 20,000. These numbers may seem *Stone monuments* sparse by today's standards, but they suggest that *Homo sapiens sapiens* had gained a sturdy foothold on the European continent. By the late Stone Age, these early Europeans practiced agriculture and copper metallurgy, but their most enduring remains are huge stone monuments (called *megaliths*), of which Stonehenge in western England (shown in Figure 1.2) is probably the most famous. Stonehenge was built in stages over millennia beginning in about 7000 B.C., although most of the stones were erected about 3,000 B.C. In its present form, it consists of about 160 massive rocks, some weighing up to 50 tons, which are arranged in concentric circles and semicircles. People moved the heavy stones

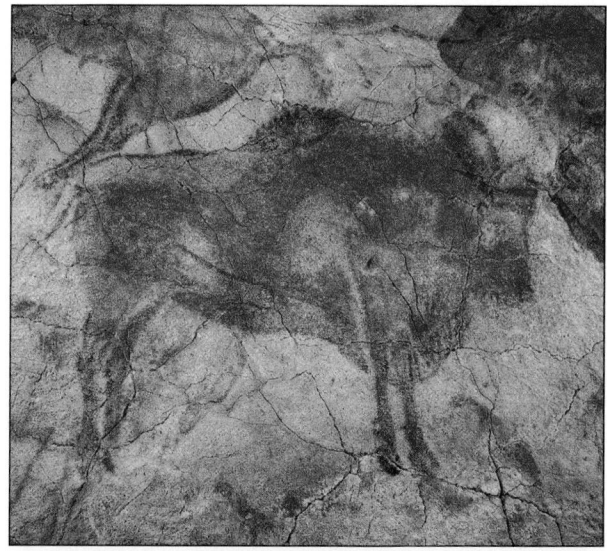

FIGURE 1.1
Bison cave painting.

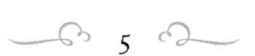

long distances without using wheels, which were unknown in Europe at this time, and shaped many of them with only stone tools. Most scholars believe that the stones were carefully aligned to show the movements of the sun and moon. If this is so, the astonishing structure shows both a long tradition of studying the heavens and humans' impressive curiosity. Whatever the purpose of these stone structures that dot Europe, they all suggest highly organized societies that were able to marshal the labor needed for such complex building projects. (Map 1.1 shows the range of the megaliths.)

However, although these early Europeans displayed some characteristics that would mark Western civilization—agriculture, a curiosity about nature, and a highly developed political structure—these great builders in stone lacked a critical component: writing. Although wisdom transmitted solely through memory can be impressive, it is also fragile, and thus engineering skills and astronomical knowledge of the earliest Europeans were lost. The real origins of Western civilization lay in the Middle East, where an agricultural revolution occurred that changed the course of human history, and where writing preserved the story of the developing West.

THE NEOLITHIC PERIOD: THE FIRST STIRRINGS OF AGRICULTURE, 10,000–3000 B.C.

Sometime around 10,000 B.C., people living in what we call the Middle East learned how to plant and cultivate the grains that they and their ancestors had gathered for millennia. With this skill, humankind entered the Neolithic era, or the New Stone Age. Agriculture did not bring complete improvement in people's lives compared to hunting and gathering. Diets were often worse (with a reliance on fewer foods), sewage and animal wastes brought more health problems, and farming was a lot of work. As we will see on page 9, people adopted this way of life because the environment changed, but once people learned how to plant crops instead of simply gathering what grew naturally, human society changed dramatically.

FIGURE 1.2
Stonehenge, southern England, ca. 7000-1500 B.C.

Just as people discovered how to control crops, they also began to domesticate animals instead of hunting them. Dogs had been domesticated as hunting partners during the Paleolithic, but around 8500 B.C., people first domesticated sheep as a source of food. Throughout the Middle East, some people lived off their herds as they traveled about looking for pasturage. Others lived as agriculturalists, keeping their herds near stationary villages.

Domestic animals

These two related developments—agriculture and animal domestication—fostered larger populations than hunting and gathering cultures, and gradually agricultural societies prevailed. In large part, the success of the Western civilization in eventually spreading throughout the world lay in its agricultural beginnings in the Middle East. Why were people in this region able to embrace agriculture so successfully? The main answer is luck—the Middle East was equipped with the necessary resources.

Of the wealth of plant species in the world—over 200,000 different varieties—humans eat only a few thousand. Of these, only a few hundred have been more or less domesticated, but almost 80 percent of the world's human diet is made up of about a dozen species (primarily cereals). The Middle East was home to the highest number of the world's prized grains, such as wheat and barley, which are easy to grow and contain the highest levels of protein. By contrast, people

Middle East plants and animals

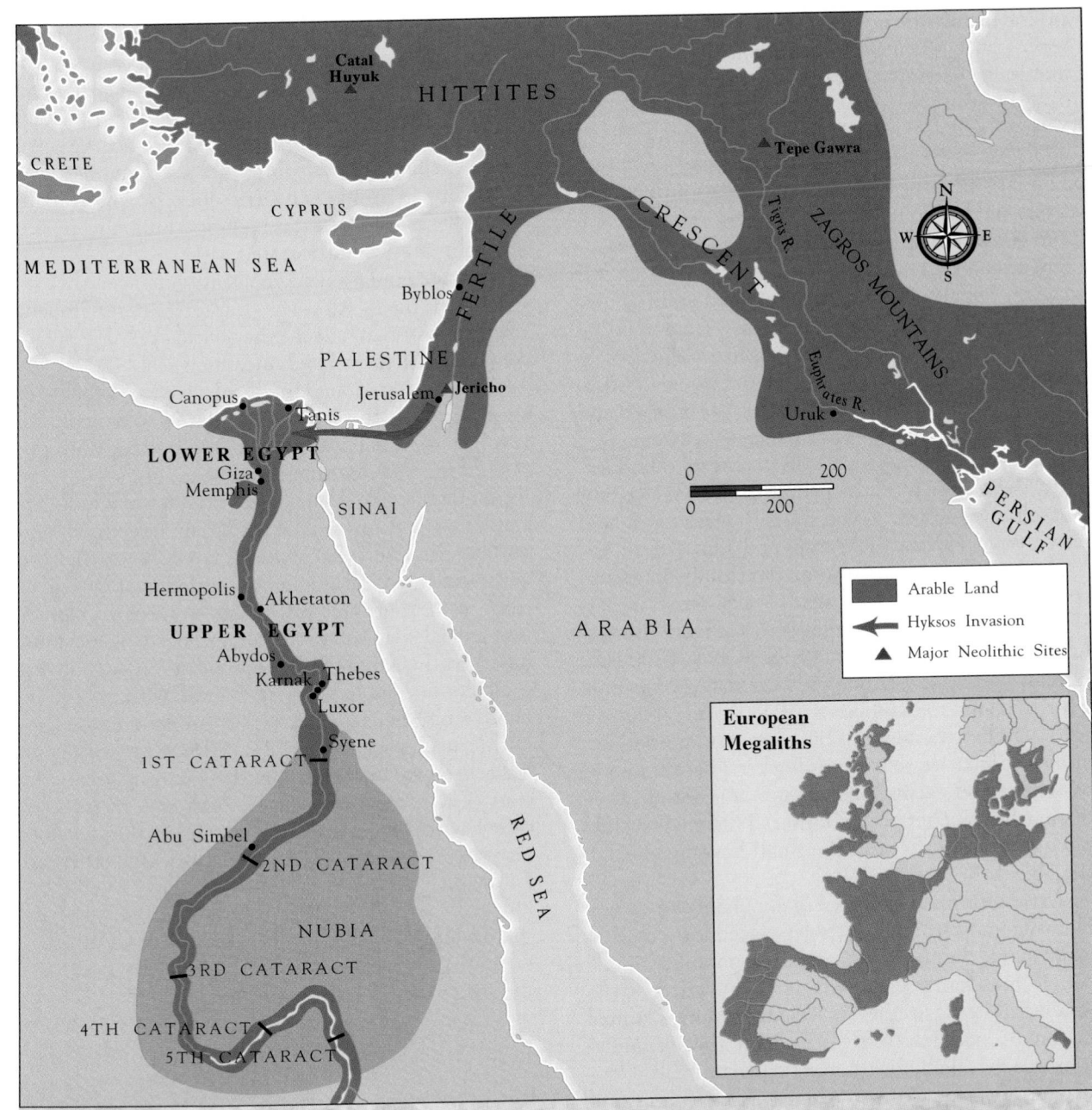

THINKING ABOUT GEOGRAPHY

MAP 1.1 *Mesopotamia and Egypt, ca.* 2000 B.C.

This map shows the cradles of Western civilization in Mesopotamia, the coast of the Mediterranean Sea, and Egypt. ✒ **Notice** the major Neolithic sites marked on the map, and the European stone monuments in western Europe. ✒ **Notice** how far those sites are from the cradle of Western civilization. **Consider** how these distances affected the relative development of all these cultures. ✒ **Notice also** how convenient the communication routes were between Mesopotamia and Egypt. **What** advantages did the locations of the rivers offer the growing cultures?

who independently domesticated local crops in other regions did not enjoy the same abundance. In New Guinea, for example, early agriculturalists in about 7000 B.C. were able to domesticate only sugarcane and bananas—crops that could not offer a complete diet.

The Middle East maintained the same advantage when it came to animals for domestication. Very few species yield to domestication; beyond the most common—dogs, sheep, goats, cows, pigs, and horses—there are only a few others—from camels to reindeer to water buffalo. Because domesticated animals provide so many benefits to humans—from food to labor—the distribution of animals fit for domestication helped determine which societies would flourish. Most of these animals were confined to Europe and Asia, and seven—including goats, sheep, and cattle—were native specifically to the Middle East. With these resources, the people of the Middle East created civilization, which quickly spread east and west (along with valuable crops and animals).

With the rise of agriculture, some small kin groups stopped wandering and instead slowly settled in permanent villages to cultivate the surrounding land. As early as 8000 B.C., Jericho (see Map 1.1) boasted about 2,000 people who lived in round huts scattered over about 12 acres. Human social forms broadened from small kin groups to include relative strangers. The schoolboy, whom we met earlier, had to make a point of introducing his teacher to his father. This effort would have been unheard of in the small hunting clans of the Paleolithic.

Population growth

Agriculture also sparked a major change in values. Hunting and gathering societies placed low value on possessions because they impeded mobility. Such people had to carry everything they owned—even small children—as they traveled. Farming, animal husbandry, and fixed settlement led to the accumulation of goods, including domesticated animals. Consequently, a new social differentiation arose in agricultural villages as some people acquired more belongings than others.

The social stratification that arose in the earliest cities included slavery as part of what people thought of as the natural order of things. There were various ways to become a slave in ancient Middle Eastern society. Sometimes economic catastrophe caused parents to sell their children or even themselves into slavery to repay their debts, and children born to slaves were automatically enslaved.

Slavery

Although slavery was part of ancient societies, it was a slavery that could be fairly fluid—unlike the slavery of the early modern world, it was not a racial issue. Slaves could save money to purchase their freedom, and children born of a freewoman and a slave were free. Ancient slavery, while taken for granted, was based on an individual's bad luck or unfortunate birth, so a servile status did not hold the severe stigma it later would acquire.

The accumulation of goods also changed the nature of warfare. Although hunter-gatherers fought over territory at times, the skirmishes tended to be short lived and small scale because the individuals involved were too valuable to waste through this sort of conflict. The agricultural revolution pushed warfare to a larger scale. With the population increase that the revolution fueled, there were more people to engage in conflict and more rewards for the winners, who could gain more goods and enslave the losers. Excavations have shown that the early settlement of Jericho was surrounded by a great stone wall about three yards thick—one of the earliest humanmade defensive structures. Indeed, people must have greatly feared their neighbors in order to invest the labor needed to build such a wall with only stone hand tools. Settlements arose throughout the Neolithic in Europe and in Asia Minor (as well as in many regions in Asia), but the mainstream in the story of the West arose further east in a river valley where writing preserved the details of the development of even larger and more sophisticated cities.

New warfare

Struggling with the Forces of Nature: Mesopotamia, 3000–ca. 1000 B.C.

Between 3000 and 1000 B.C., people began to cultivate a broad curve of land that stretched from the Persian Gulf to the shores of the Mediterranean (Map 1.1). This arc, the Fertile Crescent, has been called the cradle or birthplace of Western civilization. It earned this appellation in part because of its lucky possession of essential plants and animals and its central location that placed it at a crossroad for mingling of ideas and peoples. The ancient Greeks called this region "Mesopotamia," or "land between the rivers," emphasizing the importance of the great Tigris

Bronze Age

and Euphrates rivers to the life of the area. The earliest cities in which civilization took root were located in the southern part of Mesopotamia. During the late Neolithic period, people living in this region used agriculture; sometime after 3000 B.C., they learned to smelt metals to make tools and weapons. By smelting, they developed a process to combine copper and tin to make a much stronger metal, bronze. At last, there was a substance that improved on stone, and archaeologists note this innovation by calling this period the Bronze Age.

Life in southern Mesopotamia was harsh but manageable. Summer temperatures reached a sweltering 120 degrees Fahrenheit, and the region received a meager average rainfall of less than ten inches a year. Yet the slow-running Euphrates created vast marshlands that stayed muddy and wet even during the dry season. Villagers living along the slightly higher ground near the marshes poled their boats through the shallow waters as they netted abundant river fish and shot waterfowl with their bows and arrows. Domesticated cattle and sheep grazed on the rich marsh grass while agriculturalists farmed the fertile high ground, which was actually made up of islands in the marshland. The villagers used the marsh reeds as fuel and as material to make sturdy baskets, and they fashioned the swamp mud into bricks and pottery.

THE ORIGINS OF WESTERN CIVILIZATION

In about 3000 B.C., a climate change occurred that forced the southern Mesopotamians to alter their way of life. As they did so, they created a more complex society that we call Sumerian—the earliest civilization. Starting around 3200 B.C., the region became drier. The rivers no longer flooded as much of the land as before, and more and more of the marshes evaporated. When the rivers flooded, they still deposited fertile soil in the former marshlands, but the floods came at the wrong times of the year for easy agriculture. Fed by the melting snows in the Zagros Mountains (see Map 1.1), the Tigris flooded between April and June—a time highly inconvenient for agriculture in a region where the growing season runs from autumn to early summer. Furthermore, the floods were unpredictable; they could wash away crops still ripening in the fields or come too early to leave residual moisture in the soil for planting. Men and women had to learn how to use the

river water efficiently to maintain the population that had established itself during centuries of simpler marsh life. Now people began to dig channels to irrigate the dry land and save the water for when they needed it, but these efforts were never certain because the floods were unpredictable. Mesopotamians developed an intense pessimism that was shaped by the difficult natural environment of the land between the rivers that could bring seemingly random abundance or disaster.

To manage the complex irrigation projects and planning required to survive in this unpredictable environment, the Sumerians developed a *Administration* highly organized society—they worked hard to bring order to the chaos that seemed to surround them. Their resourcefulness paid off; by 3000 B.C., the valley had become a rich food-producing area. The population of Uruk, shown on Map 1.1, expanded to nearly 10,000 by about 2900 B.C. Neighbors no longer knew each other, and everyone looked to a centralized administration to organize daily life.

Priests and priestesses provided the needed organization. In exchange, these religious leaders claimed a percentage of the land's produce. With their new wealth, they built imposing temples that dominated the skylines of cities like Uruk. Figure 1.3 is a modern-day photograph of one of those temples,

FIGURE 1.3
Ziggurat at Ur, ca. 2100 B.C.

which was built about 2100 B.C. The temple shown here consists of levels of steps that were designed to lead the faithful up toward heaven. Known as a "ziggurat," the structure was intended to bridge the gap between gods and humans. These huge structures were located in a temple complex that spanned several acres. A statue of a god or goddess was placed in a sacred room at the top, and after priests and priestesses conducted a ritual dedication of the statue, people believed the deity dwelled symbolically within the temple, bringing blessings to the whole community. The scale and wealth committed to the ziggurat revealed the dominant role that religion played in the Sumerians' lives.

Ziggurats also served as administrative and economic centers of cities, with storehouses and administrative rooms housed in the lower levels. They were **Economic functions** bustling places as people came to bring goods and socialize with neighbors. Just as religion was at the center of the Sumerian world, these buildings, rising like mountains out of the mud plains, served as the center of city life.

The labor and goods of the local men and women belonged to the deity who lived in the inner room at the top of the temple. In one temple dedicated to a goddess, attendants washed, clothed, and perfumed the statue every day, and servants burned incense and played music for the statue's pleasure. Meanwhile, temple administrators organized irrigation projects and tax collection in the cities to foster the abundance that allowed the great cities to flourish and serve their patron deities. Through these centralized religious organizations, ancient loyalties to family and clan were slowly replaced by political and religious ties that linked devoted followers to the city guarded by their favored deity. This was a crucial step in creating the large political units that were to become a hallmark of Western civilization.

LIFE IN A SUMERIAN CITY

In the shadow of the ziggurats, people lived in mud-brick houses with thick walls that insulated them from heat, cold, and noise. Women and slaves prepared the family meals, which consisted mostly of barley (in the south) or wheat (in the north). Vegetables, cheese, fish, figs, and dates supplemented the Sumerian diet. A large portion of the calories people consumed came from ale. Forty percent of all the grain grown in the region was brewed for ale by women in their homes, not only for their family's consumption but also for sale.

Although Mesopotamia offered early settlements the significant advantage of indigenous plants and animals, the area had some severe shortages. **Trade** The river valleys lacked metal or stone, which were essential for tools and weapons. The earliest settlements depended on long-distance trade for these essential items, and soon the wheel was invented to move cartloads of goods more easily. Materials came from Syria, the Arabian Peninsula, and even India, and Mesopotamian traders produced goods for trade. The most lucrative products were textiles. Traders transported woven wool great distances in their quest for stone, metal, and, later, luxury goods. Mesopotamian goods, animals, and even plants moved slowly as far as China as the ancient cultures of the Eurasian land embarked on mass trade. The essential trade routes that marked the whole history of Western civilization appeared at the dawn of its inception.

In the bustling urban centers, families remained the central social tie. Parents arranged marriages for their sons and daughters and bound the contract with an exchange of goods that women brought to the marriage as their dowry. The earliest written **Families** laws regulated married life in an attempt to preserve public peace through private ties. Adultery was a serious crime punished by death, but divorce was permitted. If a woman who was above reproach as a wife wished a divorce, she could keep her dowry. If, however, a wife neglected her home and acted foolishly in public, she would lose her dowry. Her husband could then insist that she remain as a servant in his house even when he remarried. The laws also recognized that men kept concubines in addition to their legal wives and provided ways for children of such informal unions to be considered legitimate. All these laws attempted to preserve the family as an economic unit and as the central social unit in a complex, changing society.

Sumerian women worked in many shops in the cities—as wine sellers, tavern keepers, and merchants. Some women were prostitutes, **Women's work** although in time Sumerians came to view this profession as a threat to more traditional ties. Late in Mesopotamian history, laws arose that insisted on special clothing to distinguish "respectable" women from prostitutes. Ordinary women were expected to veil their heads in public, whereas prostitutes and slaves were forced to go about their day with bare heads. At the end of Mesopotamian ascendancy, these laws were made extremely strict—any slave woman who dared to wear a veil was punished by having her ears cut off. In this society, in which people did not know each other, city residents strove mightily to distinguish social ranks. City life came with increasing emphasis on social stratification as the cornerstone of urban order.

GODS AND GODDESSES OF THE RIVER VALLEY

The men and women of the Tigris-Euphrates river valley believed that all parts of the natural world were invested with will. For example, if a river flooded, the event was interpreted as an act of the gods. People also viewed intercity warfare as a battle between each city's gods. On a broader level, the Sumerians saw themselves and their deities as combatants locked in a struggle against a mysterious chaos that could destroy the world at any moment—just as sometimes the unpredictable rivers flooded and brought destruction. People viewed themselves as slaves of the gods and provided the deities with everything they needed—from sacrifices to incense to music—to try to keep order in their uncertain world. In spite of their appeasements, however, when disorder appeared in the form of natural disasters or disease, the pessimistic Sumerians were not surprised.

In addition to venerating their city's patron, Sumerians in time invested their universe with a bewildering number of demons who needed placating. Demons caused illness, and magicians or priests—rather than physicians—were called on for cures. To understand the world, priests tried to read the future in the entrails of animals (a practice known as augury). Magic, omens, and amulets rounded out the Mesopotamian religious world, as people struggled to try to control what seemed to be a world in which people owed everything to capricious deities.

An anonymous Sumerian poem of despair expresses the anxiety that came with this view of religious responsibility. In this poem, a once-prosperous

Sumerian pessimism man suffers a reversal of fortune. He laments:

My ill luck has increased, and I do not find the right.
I called to my god, but he did not show his face,
I prayed to my goddess, but she did not raise her head.

The man seeks out diviners and dream priests, but no one can tell him the omission that brought about his downfall. In his despair, he can only hope that continued devotion to the gods will restore his prosperity—but his tone is not optimistic.

Neither the Sumerians nor their eventual conquerors envisioned an attractive afterlife. They believed that the spirits of the dead went to a shadowy, disagreeable place from where they might occasionally affect the living, usually for ill. Sumerians' only hope for happiness lay in the present life, and that happiness hinged on capricious deities who cared little for humans.

These beliefs prevailed in the Fertile Crescent from the fourth millennium B.C. up to the middle of the first millennium B.C., even as conquests **Sargon** changed the prevailing rulers. During that time, conquerors made a conscious effort to appease the local deities, and this accommodation serves as a model for the continuing interchange of ideas that was one of the strengths of Western culture. For example, when the Akkadian ruler Sargon invaded Sumer in about 2350 B.C., he had to facilitate peace among the Akkadian northerners and the Sumerian southerners. The bronze head probably depicting Sargon shown in Figure 1.4 was designed to show the power of this great king. His long beard, carefully curled, was a symbol of masculine strength, and he wears a band around his head showing his royal office.

Sargon chose religion as the key to uniting the people and appointed his daughter Enheduanna as high priestess of both the Akkadian and Sumerian goddesses. In the inset in Figure 1.4, the priestess (the second figure from the left) is shown wearing the elaborate clothing appropriate to her rank, surrounded by her attendants as she moves to the altar to worship. Enheduanna wrote beautiful hymns (which have survived to the present) in which she identified the Sumerian goddess Inanna with her Akkadian counterpart, Ishtar. She proved so successful in reconciling goddesses in this way that Sargon's successors continued the practice of making their daughters high priestesses, thus forging a link between the cultures of the region. As kings began to handle earthly administration, sky gods became more crucial in the heavenly hierarchy. Fearsome war gods like Marduk sometimes demanded human sacrifices in exchange for victory over invading tribes. The heavenly hierarchy grew more elaborate and demanding.

FIGURE 1.4

Akkadian king Sargon, ca. 2350 B.C. Inset: Limestone disk depicting Sargon's Daughter, Enheduanna (second from left)

some men and women looked to a more personal alliance, just as the despairing poet we met earlier cried out for a divine explanation of his plight. This longing led individuals to ponder the concept of immortality, wondering whether death was avoidable. In the celebrated poem *The Epic of Gilgamesh*, the poet articulates this search for meaning in death while telling an engaging story of a Sumerian hero and his fortunes. This is an early example of an important literary genre called the "epic of quest." Gilgamesh (shown in Figure 1.5) was a king who ruled Uruk (see Map 1.1) in about 2700 B.C. Sometime after 2000 B.C., stories about the by-then semi-mythical king were collected and written down in the epic. In one of Gilgamesh's adventures, his best friend, Enkidu, is killed and the reality of death strikes home. Gilgamesh refuses to bury Enkidu; in his grief he is unwilling to give up his friend. When the reality of decomposition confronts the king, he travels to find the secret of immortality. At the bottom of the sea he finds a plant that will give eternal life, only to see the magic herb stolen by a snake before he can bring it back to Enkidu. Gilgamesh is left facing the reality of death and the equally important reality of the value of finding joy in the present. This pessimistic epic once again reveals the Sumerian assumption that humans are doomed to struggle endlessly in a difficult universe.

Individual longings

The carving of Gilgamesh shown in Figure 1.5 was made in the eighth century B.C. and shows the enduring popularity of the Sumerian legend. Here Gilgamesh is shown with the long curled beard of a king—which looks remarkably like Sargon's in Figure 1.4. The captured lion illustrates his hunting prowess. These characteristics of kings—power and strength—persist through the ancient world.

THE DEVELOPMENT OF WRITING

Although religion dominated Mesopotamian thought, the Sumerians' real impact on the future of Western civilization derived from their more practical inventions. As Mesopotamian cities expanded and grew wealthy, the need arose for a system of keeping records that would prove more enduring and accurate than the spoken word. In response, the Sumerians developed a system of writing. Some scholars believe that writing first emerged from a system of trade tokens. For example, if a merchant

By the third millennium B.C., earthly society in the ancient Middle East mirrored the hierarchical heavenly one. Kingship was universally accepted as the correct political order, and castes of nobles and priests were also deemed natural. Inequality among people was seen as normal and theologically justified, and people accepted their place in this highly ordered world with kings on top and slaves on the bottom. Individuals' longings for social justice and hopes for improving their situations all took place within a frame of reality that was very different from ours—one that assumed inequality was natural.

Sometime during the second millennium B.C., the Sumerians began to reflect on individuals' relationships with the gods. Instead of being content with a corporate association between a city and its guardian, wanted to verify the amount of sheep someone else was supposed to deliver, he would count out tokens to represent the sheep and seal them in a clay envelope that would be broken open upon delivery. The tokens left an imprint in the clay, and in time people realized that they could omit the tokens entirely and simply mark the clay.

At first, Sumerian writing consisted of stylized pictures of the objects represented—birds, sheep, or bowls to signify food. Soon the characters became more abstract and indicated sounds as well as objects. By 2800 B.C., the Sumerians had developed a sophisticated writing system called cuneiform (named from the Latin word that means "wedge"). Scribes imprinted wedge-shaped characters into wet clay tablets, which became highly durable when dried. Figure 1.6 shows a tablet of cuneiform script made in about 2600 B.C., which lists quantities of various commodities.

Cuneiform

Scribes labored for many years to memorize the thousands of characters of cuneiform script. By 2500 B.C., scribal schools were established to train the numerous clerks needed to serve the palaces and temples. Some surviving cuneiform tablets reveal that these students also studied mathematics and geometry. At first, girls attended these scribal schools, and records testify to a number of successful female scribes. Later, however, the occupation became exclusively male, but the reasons for this change have been lost. The schoolboy described at the beginning of this chapter was one of the lucky few who were trained to read and write. Anyone possessing these skills was assured a prosperous future.

Most of the Sumerian tablets that have been excavated refer to inventories, wills, contracts, payrolls, property transfers, and correspondence between monarchs. Such content reflects both the complexity of this civilization and the everyday necessity of tracking economic transactions. However, writing also let people record more abstract subject matter. *The Epic of Gilgamesh* and other myths preserved the dreams and hopes of these early civilizations, and the hymns of the priestess-poet Enheduanna attest to their spiritual longings and aesthetic sensibilities. However, beyond providing us a glimpse of this long-lost civilization, the invention of writing gave Western culture a distinct advantage over other societies that depended only on human memory to recall their achievements. Writing

Written records

FIGURE 1.5
Gilgamesh holding a conquered lion.

enabled the transfer and dissemination of knowledge, which allowed people to build on previously acquired advancements instead of continually rediscovering and relearning the same material.

LAWS AND JUSTICE

Writing also fostered the emergence of another element that would remain an essential component of Western civilization: a written law code. Recording laws in writing was an attempt to establish order in the land between the rivers that seemed so susceptible to chaos. But these laws also tried to express principles of justice that outlasted the ruler who issued them. As early as 2500 B.C., Uruinimgina tried to reform his society by passing laws that protected the powerless while preserving the socially stratified society that all took for granted. This tradition continued throughout Mesopotamian history and formed a powerful precedent for subsequent civilizations. In about 2100 B.C., Ur-Nammu, king of Ur, wrote laws to preserve "the principles of truth and equity."

The most famous and complete of the ancient law codes was that of the Babylonian king Hammurabi (1792?–1750 B.C.), who ruled the southern Mesopotamian valley. In the prologue to his law code, which is preserved in cuneiform script on a stone column, the king expressed the highest principles of justice: "I established *Code of Hammurabi* law and justice in the language of the land and promoted the welfare of the people." Studying Hammurabi's code, which was a compilation of existing laws, opens a window into the lives of these ancient urban dwellers. It regulated everything from family life to physicians' fees to building requirements. The king seemed determined to order his society, for he introduced harsh penalties that had been absent from earlier laws. His code literally demanded an "eye for an eye"—one law stipulated that "should a man destroy another's eye, he shall lose his own." Another stated that a son who strikes his father shall have his hand cut off.

Hammurabi's code clearly expressed the strict social hierarchy that Mesopotamian society counted as natural. The laws specified different penalties for the three social orders: elites, freemen, and slaves. The elites included everyone from officials to priests and

FIGURE 1.6
Clay tablet with cuneiform script, ca. 2600 B.C.

warriors. Beneath them were freemen, including artisans, merchants, professionals, and some farmers. Slaves occupied the bottom stratum, but they, too, had some rights under Hammurabi's laws—for example, they might own land and marry free persons. Many of the laws sought to protect the powerless so, as the prologue says, "that the strong may not oppress the weak."

Many laws tried to protect women and children from unfair treatment and limited the authority of husbands over their households. *Women and children* For example, women could practice various trades and hold public positions. Husbands could not accuse their wives of adultery without proof, for the penalty for proven adultery was harsh—the adulterous wife and her lover would be drowned. However, a woman could obtain a divorce from her husband. In spite of these protections, women still remained largely the property of their husbands. For example, if a man could not pay his debts, his wife could be sold into slavery to repay the obligation.

Perhaps one of the most significant things about Hammurabi's code was that he intended his laws to outlast his own rule. On the tablet, he inscribed: "For all future time, may the king who is in the land observe the words of justice which I have written upon my monument!" Writing, and written law in particular, gave kings and reformers like Hammurabi hope for the establishment of timeless justice and a chance for a kind of personal immortality for the king.

INDO-EUROPEANS: NEW CONTRIBUTIONS IN THE STORY OF THE WEST

While the people in the Fertile Crescent developed many of the elements that contributed to the formation of Western civilization—agriculture, writing, and law—the emerging culture remained subject to transformation. As we have seen, one of the advantages of the ancient Middle East was its location, which permitted it to benefit from influences from the far reaches of Asia. Of course, this geographic openness also contributed to instability—ideas often came with invaders and destruction. The region north of the Black Sea and the Caucasus Mountains (see Map 1.4 on page 34) produced peoples living on the steppes who waged war on the peoples of the Fertile Crescent and developed a culture that eventually had a profound influence on the West.

Linguists, who analyze similarities in languages, have labeled these people Indo-European because their language served as the basis for virtually all subsequent European languages (except Finnish, Hungarian, and Basque). Figure 1.7 shows the relationship of the Indo-European languages to each other as well as *Indo-European languages* to the other world languages. This language family separates the Indo-Europeans from most of the original inhabitants of the Fertile Crescent, who spoke "Semitic" languages. The steady influx of Indo-European invaders (later called Celts, Latins, Greeks, or Germans) formed the dominant population of Europe. Other Indo-Europeans moved east and settled in India or traveled south into modern-day Turkey and Iran. Some Indo-Europeans periodically attacked the kingdoms of Mesopotamia and other regions in the western Mediterranean.

The Indo-Europeans were led by a warrior elite, who were buried in elaborate graves. Excavations of these graves have allowed scholars to analyze the prized possessions and weapons that were buried with these rulers, yielding many insights into this society. Some archaeologists refer to the Indo-Europeans as "battle-axe people" because of the many axes found in their burial sites. *Mounted warriors* They also rode horses, which they first domesticated for riding in about 2000 B.C. Riding on horseback gave Indo-European warriors the deadly advantages of speed, mobility, and reach over the Stone and Bronze Age archers they encountered in their travels.

The warrior elite of the Indo-Europeans excelled in battle and moved their families with them as they journeyed and fought. They carried their belongings in heavy carts outfitted with four solid, wooden wheels. With these carts, they were able *Contributions* to wander into the most northern reaches of Europe. The carts were a significant departure from the Sumerian two-wheeled chariots, which proved too unstable over long distances. The heavy carts traveled best over flat surfaces, and evidence indicates that as early as 2000 B.C., wooden roadways were built across boglands in northern Europe to accommodate the movement of people and their goods.

When the Indo-Europeans moved into the Fertile Crescent, they were not literate, but they preserved their values in oral traditions. Later, influenced by the literary traditions of those they conquered, Indo-Europeans developed their own written languages, and many of these tales were written down and preserved. Ideals of a warrior elite and worship of gods who lived in the sky instead of on the earth continued, as did the Indo-European language. These elements were among the Indo-European contributions to Western civilization. In turn, early in the history of the Indo-Europeans (long before they acquired a written language), they adopted some things from the Mesopotamian cradle of civilization. They acquired many of the grains and other foods that were native to Mesopotamia and spread them widely. The successful culture of the Fertile Crescent was making its impact known far outside the river valleys that spawned it.

In about 1650 B.C., an Indo-European group called the Hittites established a kingdom in Asia Minor (modern Turkey) with their capital at Hattusas (see Map 1.2, p. 24). The location of the Hittite kingdom offered many opportunities for interaction *Hittites* with the other ancient civilizations of the region, and as we shall see, the Hittite kingdom influenced the fortunes of Egypt and the other lands of

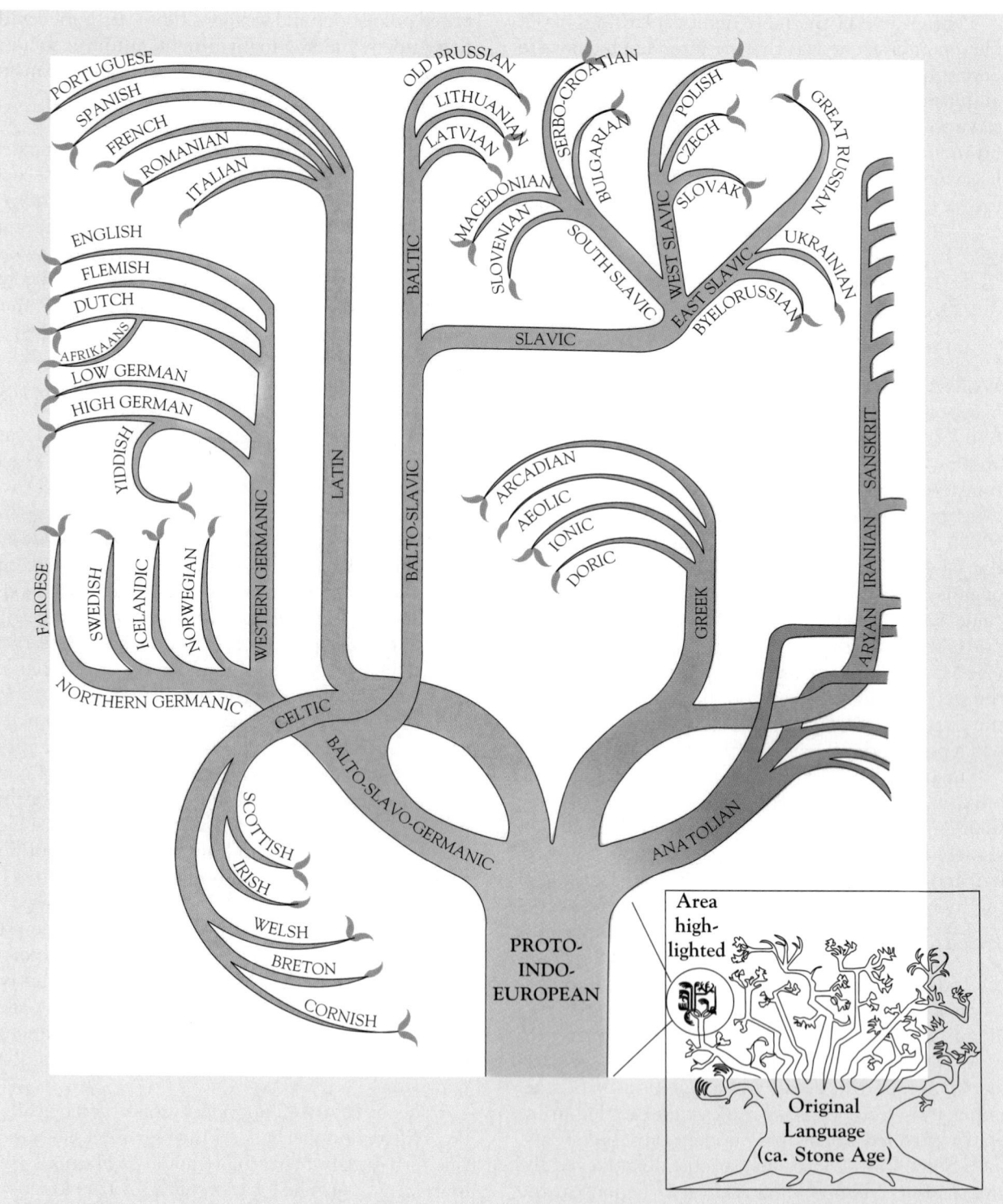

FIGURE 1.7

Tree of Indo-European Languages. Inset: The small branch of Indo-European languages relative to the other languages of the world.

the ancient Middle East. Fortunately for historians, the Hittites learned the art of writing from the Mesopotamians. At Hattusas, archaeologists have excavated about 10,000 cuneiform tablets, which enable us to follow the fortunes of this early Indo-European kingdom. While the peoples of Mesopotamia and the surrounding regions built their civilizations and struggled with nature and their neighbors, another civilization arose to the south and west in another river valley—one that was kinder to its inhabitants.

Rule of the God-King: Ancient Egypt, ca. 3100–1000 B.C.

The food crops that proved so successful in Mesopotamia spread to Egypt, stimulating another ancient civilization that arose on the banks of a great river—the roots of Western civilization moved farther west. The Nile River in Egypt flows more than 4,000 miles, from central Africa north to the Mediterranean Sea. Just as in Mesopotamia, a climate change forced dependence on the great river. In about 6000 B.C. the prevailing Atlantic rains shifted, changing great grassy plains into desert and forcing people to move closer to the Nile to use its waters.

Nile Valley

Unlike the Tigris and Euphrates, the Nile reliably overflowed its banks every year at a time convenient for planting—flooding in June and receding by October. During this flood, the river deposited a layer of fertile black earth in time for a winter planting of cereal crops. In ancient times, the Nile also provided the Egyptians with an excellent communication and transportation system. The river flowed north, encouraging traffic in that direction, but the prevailing winds blew from north to south, helping ships to sail against the current.

Egypt was more isolated than the other ancient civilizations to the northeast. The deserts to the Nile's east and west stymied most would-be invaders, and in the southern Sudan a vast marsh protected the area from encroachers. Potential invaders from the Mediterranean Sea confronted shallows that prevented ships from easily approaching the Egyptian coast. As a result, Egyptian civilization developed without the fear of conquest or the resultant blending and conflict among cultures that marked the

Mesopotamian cities. By about 3100 B.C., a king from Upper Egypt (in the south) who according to tradition was named Menes, consolidated his rule over the entire Egyptian land.

PROSPERITY AND ORDER: THE OLD KINGDOM, CA. 2700–2181 B.C.

Ancient Egyptians believed that the power of the gods was visible in the natural world—in the Nile and in the people and animals that benefited from its bounty. Consequently, they worshiped the divine spirit that was expressed through heavenly bodies, animals, and even insects. Over time, some gods were exalted over others, and deities were combined and blurred. However, through most of Egypt's history the most important deities were the sun god Re (or Amon) and the Nile spirits Isis, her husband-consort Osiris, and their son, the falcon-god Horus. Unlike the Mesopotamians, the Egyptians were optimistic about their fortunes. They believed they were blessed by the gods, who brought such a regular and fertile flooding of the Nile, not cursed by their chaotic whims. The Mesopotamians issued law codes to try to create order, but the Egyptians simply assumed order and worked to preserve it. This optimism infused Egyptian culture with extraordinary persistence—why change something that brought such blessings?

At the heart of their prosperity was the king, whom Egyptians considered the living embodiment of the deity, and this linking of political power with religion reinforced the stability of the Old Kingdom. While Mesopotamians believed their kings served as priests to their gods, Egyptians believed their rulers *were* gods, who had come to earth to bring truth, justice, and order—all summarized in the word *ma'at*. In return, the populace was obligated to observe a code of correct behavior that was included in the concept of *ma'at*. In about 2450 B.C., a high palace official named Ptahhotep left a series of instructions for his son, in which he urged the boy to follow the precepts of *ma'at:* "He who departs from its laws is punished. . . . Evil may win riches, but it is the strength of *ma'at* that endures long." For millennia, kings and advisors like Ptahhotep believed strongly that the importance of proper behavior brought prosperity to the land, and such beliefs contributed to a stable society. (The funeral inscription in Document 1.1 on page D1.1 shows

Perserving order

these enduring values.) This ordered society was ruled by a god-king later called *pharaoh* ("great house"), a term that referred to the general institution of the monarchy as well as the ruler.

The Old Kingdom period (ca. 2700–2181 B.C.) saw astonishing prosperity and peace, as farming and irrigation methods provided an abundance of crops *Trade* and wealth to many. Unlike the Mesopotamian valley, Egypt had ready access to mineral resources, most importantly copper, which was in great demand for tools. Egyptians refined copper ore at the site of the surface mines, and ingots of copper were transported by caravans of donkeys overland to the Nile. From there, the precious ores were manufactured or used to trade abroad. Egypt was also happily situated to capitalize on trade with Nubia which gave access to the resources of sub-Saharan Africa. (See "Global Connections" on page 19). From Nubia, Egyptians gained gold, ivory, ebony, gems and aromatics in exchange for Egyptian cloth and manufactured goods. With the surpluses of metals and grains, Egyptians could import goods from the Middle East and beyond. In addition to textiles, Egyptians desperately needed wood to make large seagoing vessels for their trade and navy. All this industry generated prosperity for many people, and in the Old Kingdom, people used these resources to support close families.

Ptah-hotep advised his son to start a family as soon as he could afford to: "If you are prosperous you should es- *Family life* tablish a household and love your wife as is fitting. . . . Make her heart glad as long as you live." The artwork of the time suggests that many Egyptians took Ptah-hotep's advice and established loving families during this prosperous era. Figure 1.8 shows a limestone carving of one such family. Seneb, the man depicted in the portrait, was a dwarf who had made a successful career in the court. He headed the court's weaving

mill and then became the priest of the dead for two kings. His success was acknowledged when he married a member of the royal house. Husband and wife are shown side by side, suggesting that women had an equal place in the household during the time of the Old Kingdom. In this sculpture, the couple embrace affectionately and smile with seeming self-satisfaction while they tower protectively over the children below. The two figures at the lower left are each placing a finger over their lips, the Egyptian sign for "child." Stylized portraits like these suggest the success,

FIGURE 1.8
Egyptian family: Seneb with his wife and children, ca. 2320–2250 B.C.

Global Connections

NUBIA: THE PASSAGE FROM THE MEDITERRANEAN TO THE HEART OF AFRICA

Consider how geography made Nubia so important throughout the ancient world. **NOTICE** how Egypt provided a link between Africa and the Mediterranean.

From the dawn of civilization, the history of the West and the history of Africa developed together through cultural interactions that unfolded along the Nubian corridor. And throughout history, diverse groups—who spoke languages different from Egyptian—mingled in ancient Nubia, which was populated with black Africans. At times these groups even managed to unite into large kingdoms—one of which would conquer Egypt itself. Late in ancient Egyptian history, Nubian kings even became Egyptian pharaohs.

Lush and flat, the northern Nile valley stimulated the ancient Egyptians' agriculture and settlement. But near Aswan, in the south, the land changed. Here sandstone cliffs dropped directly from the desert plateau to the riverbank, and the river churned as it descended through a succession of swift rapids. These rapids are the first of six cataracts that impeded navigation south along the great river. Early rulers of Egypt marked the First Cataract as a natural southern border of their kingdom. However, later Egyptians pushed south beyond the First Cataract into Nubia. Egyptians had strong motivation to do so: Nubia provided the only reliable route around the Sahara desert to the riches that lay deep within the interior of the African continent.

In Nubia, goods moved north to the Mediterranean and south from Egypt and Mesopotamia. From the beginning, both Nubians and northerners recognized the benefits of this trade. As early as 3000 B.C., domestic goats and sheep that had originated in Mesopotamia showed up in Nubia. Sometime after that, Nubians began to cultivate the domestic grains from Mesopotamia along the valley of the southern Nile beyond the First Cataract.

As early as the Old Kingdom in Egypt, kings valued the goods that came through Nubia, and even the sparse records from this ancient time reveal the importance of the trade with the south. For example, the Egyptian princes who governed Aswam bore the title "Keeper of the Door of the South," and sometime around 2250 B.C., the pharaohs sent a prince of Aswam named Herkhuf (or Harkhuf) on three journeys into Nubia to trade and to recruit mercenary troops to fight in Egypt's armies. Herkhuf headed south on the Nile, his ships propelled against the current by the prevailing north winds. The skilled navigators he employed negotiated the roiling rapids. The proud records carved on Herkhuf's tomb do not indicate how far beyond the Second Cataract he traveled, for we cannot identify the names of the various tribes he encountered. Yet most scholars think he made it to the Third Cataract. Seven months later, Herkhuf returned from one journey with 300 donkeys laden with incense, ebony, oil, leopard skins, elephant tusks, boomerangs, and other goods. His bounty revealed that Nubia served as a trading hub for luxuries and staples far beyond the Nile. The lure of Nubia was only increased when rich gold mines were discovered there in about 1980 B.C.

During the Middle Kingdom under the reign of Senwosret I (ca. 1980 B.C.), Egyptians began to mine for gold in Nubia, and the rich mines brought Nubia into the politics as well as the trade of the north. (Indeed, "Nubia" means "gold" in Egyptian.) Egyptians began to fortify the Nile, and Nubia engaged in the wars of the north. The fall of the ancient Egyptian kingdom did not end the importance of Nubia, which remained the major passage to the heart of Africa.

contentment, and prosperity of many Old Kingdom families—at least those with enough wealth to commission portraits.

HIEROGLYPHS: SACRED WRITING

Sometime around 3000 B.C., Egyptians—probably influenced by Sumerians—developed a system of writing. However, Egyptian writing was not cuneiform, nor was it used primarily for accounting purposes. While Egyptian administrators surely had as much need for clear records as the Sumerians, they primarily used writing to forward religious and magical power. Every sign in their writing system represented a real or mythical object and was designed to express that object's power. The ancient Greeks saw these images on temples and named Egyptian script "hieroglyph," meaning "sacred writing."

Hieroglyphs were more than a series of simple pictures. Each symbol could express one of three things: the object it portrayed, an abstract idea associated with the object, or one or more sounds of speech from the spoken Egyptian word for the object. (The technical terms for these three uses are "pictogram," "ideogram," and "phonogram.") Because this writing had ceremonial religious use, it changed little over the centuries as scribes carved it into stone monuments. An example of hieroglyphic writing can be seen in the background of Figure 1.10 (p. 22).

However, hieroglyphs were too cumbersome for everyday use, so scribes learned two other simplified scripts—called Hieratic and Demotic—to keep records or write literature. Whereas many of the hieroglyphs were carved into stone, everyday records were more often written on papyrus, a kind of paper made from the Nile's abundant papyrus reeds. This versatile, sturdy reed could be reused—much like recycled paper today—and in the dry desert air was very durable. Often in Egypt's history, the lucrative export of papyrus increased the royal treasury.

Scribes studied for many years to master the complicated, varied Egyptian scripts. As in Mesopotamia, there are early records of women scribes, but the occupation later became restricted to men. The scribe shown at the beginning of this chapter is writing on a papyrus scroll and is portrayed with the dignity and honor accorded to the profession. On one surviving papyrus fragment, a scribe praised his occupation:

"Writing for him who knows it is better than all other professions. It pleases more than bread and beer, more than clothing and ointment. It is worth more than an inheritance in Egypt, than a tomb in the west."

PYRAMIDS AND THE AFTERLIFE

Scribes furthered the prosperity of the god-kings by carefully tracking the rulers' finances as they grew rich from state monopolies and taxes on all the products created in the fertile land. Whenever they had excess income, the kings proved their greatness *Scribes* by building pyramids, monuments to their glory that in some cases survive today. Imhotep, the chief advisor to the Egyptian king Djoser in about 2650 B.C., designed and built the first pyramid at Sakkara (near Memphis, shown on Map 1.2 on page 24). This early pyramid, depicted in Figure 1.9a, is called a "step pyramid," and its design shows the influence of the Mesopotamian ziggurats. Like those earlier monuments, Egyptian pyramids were intended to join heaven and earth. An inscription on one pyramid explains: "A staircase to heaven is laid for [the king] so that he may mount up to heaven thereby." Unlike the ziggurats, which were made of dried clay bricks, these pyramids were built of cut stone—a remarkable building innovation.

The Old Kingdom rulers made the pyramids the great symbol of Egyptian power and longevity. An anonymous architect refined the early pyramid design and built the Great Pyramid as a burial tomb for the Fourth Dynasty ruler, Khufu (also known as Kheops), in about 2590 B.C. This pyramid became the model for the later Old Kingdom tombs that were built in Giza, which continue to dominate the skyline there. Figure 1.9b shows the pyramids at Giza with the Great Pyramid of Khufu on the left. The pyramid of Khufu's son is in the back; it appears taller because it is on higher ground. Khufu's pyramid covers about 13 acres and is made of more than 2 million stone blocks. Peasants labored on these pyramids before planting season during the months when the Nile was in flood. Ancient Greek historians later claimed that the Great Pyramid of Giza took twenty years to build and required the labor of 100,000 workers. Modern estimates tend to agree with these calculations. The pyramids—so visible in the ancient skyline—proclaimed the god-king's immortality and the permanence of the order he brought to the land along the Nile.

Pyramids—and later mortuary temples—were built as tombs for the god-kings or, more precisely, as houses for their departed spirits. The departed's soul was sustained in the tomb by the same food and goods that had sustained the living body. The Egyptian notion of immortality marked an important contribution to the world of ideas, for the afterlife Egyptians conceived of was dramatically different from the dark world of the Mesopotamian dead. We do not have an exact idea of how the Egyptians visualized the afterlife, but it seems to have been an improved version of this world—a heavenly Nile valley. Some poets even wrote of death as a pleasant release:

Afterlife

Death is before me today
Like a man's longing to see his home
When he has spent many years in
captivity.

Upon the death of a king, or in later years a nobleman who could afford a burial, the body was embalmed. Embalmers removed the internal organs through an incision in the abdomen and placed them in a vessel filled with a salty preserving solution. The body cavity was then probably dried in a pile of natron crystals. Later in Egypt's history, embalmers used resin-soaked linen to pack the body cavity. Finally the embalmers wrapped the body in more linen with resin. The wrapped, embalmed body—the mummy—along with a box containing the internal organs, were then placed in a chamber deep within the pyramid. Stocking the tomb with an array of food, household goods, and precious jewels for the pharaoh to enjoy in the afterlife completed the burial process.

Burial rituals

Pyramids from the Old Kingdom contained no images, but later artists painted the interior walls of tombs with scenes of activities that the deceased could expect to enjoy in the afterlife, and these scenes offer us a glimpse of how Egyptians viewed the next world. Figure 1.10 shows a happy scene that was painted on the walls of a New Kingdom tomb. In this picture, the noble family frolics on a bird-hunting trip that yields far more abundance than any real-life trip ever could. Under their boat swims a fish so fat it belongs in a fisherman's paradise. A child grips her father's leg while he catches birds with the help of his hunting falcon. His well-dressed wife stands in the background. Even the family cat enjoys an abundant afterlife, catching three birds at once.

FIGURE 1.9

(a) Step pyramid of King Djoser, ca 2680 B.C. (b) Pyramids at Giza, with the Great Pyramid of Khufu (Kheops) on the left, ca. 2590 B.C.

FIGURE 1.10
Egyptian family on a hunting trip in the afterlife, 1400 B.C.

This illustration reveals how much the Egyptian "heaven" had changed from the Mesopotamian dark netherworld.

CHANGING POLITICAL FORTUNES, CA. 2200–1570 B.C.

The order and prosperity promised by the pyramids proved less enduring than the Egyptians expected. At the end of the Old Kingdom period, the climate turned against the god-kings. As drought in southern Nubia led to a series of low floods in Egypt, crops failed, and people pillaged the countryside in a desperate search for food. There was even one account of cannibalism. Under such pressure, Egypt needed a strong ruler to preserve *ma'at*, but one was not forthcoming. Near the end of the Old Kingdom, one king—Pepi II (ca. 2270–2180 B.C.)—reputedly ruled for over 90 years, which was an extraordinary feat in an age when a decade or two was considered a substantial rule and when 40 years of age was the normal life expectancy. However, the old

Famine

king was unable to keep a strong rule; during his reign, authority broke down, and he outlived his heirs. After his death a succession of little-known kings with very short reigns followed—a clear indication that all was not well within Egypt. Sources indicate that one of these ephemeral rulers was a woman —Nitocris—who ruled for about two years. During these times of weak central authority, local nobles exerted power, and Egypt suffered a period of social and political instability called the First Intermediate Period (2181–2140 B.C.).

A contemporary witness wrote poignantly of the widespread misery experienced during these hard years: "Everything is filthy: there is no such thing as clean linen these days. The dead are thrown into the river. . . . The ladies of the nobility exclaim: 'If only we had something to eat!' They are forced to prostitute their daughters. They are reduced to sleeping with men who were once too badly off to take a woman."

During these difficult times, people began to hope for a more pleasant afterlife, which many began to believe was possible for more than just the royal family. In the First Intermediate Period, anyone who could afford the appropriate burial rituals and magic spells could expect to achieve immortality. Still, prosperity continued to elude the Nile valley.

In about 2060 B.C., Amenemhat I of Thebes finally restored peace to the crippled valley and introduced what has come to be called the "Middle Kingdom" period (2060?–1785 B.C.). Egypt prospered once again, and one pharaoh wrote:
Middle Kingdom "None was hungry in my years, none thirsted then; men dwelled in peace." During these years, the kings conquered Nubia and grew rich on the gold of that kingdom. This conquest also brought black sub-Saharan Africa into closer contact with the Mediterranean world, and continued trade with Nubia integrated African goods and elements of their culture into Egypt and into the developing western culture in general. The funeral inscription in Document 1.1 (page D1.1) testifies to the increased trade. Egypt's rulers also introduced impressive engineering projects that expanded Egypt's amount of irrigated land by more than 17,000 acres. The Egyptians also began engaging in lucrative trade with the peoples of the Fertile Crescent. This practice had a price, however: It drew Egypt into the volatile politics of the ancient Middle East.

In the eighteenth century B.C., trouble struck again. The Nubians in the south revolted and broke away from Egyptian control, taking their gold with them. The kings' authority lessened again, and in 1650 B.C., the Hyksos who had settled *Egypt conquered* in the lowland where the Nile poured into the Mediterranean (the Delta) rose to power (see Map 1.1). The Hyksos brought with them a new technology of warfare. They fought with bronze weapons, chariots, and body armor against the nearly nude Egyptians, who used only javelins and light copper weapons. The Hyksos established a kingdom in the Delta and this uneasy time, the Second Intermediate Period, extended from about 1785 to 1575 B.C.

POLITICAL EXPANSION: THE NEW KINGDOM, 1570–1085 B.C.

In about 1560 B.C., the Egyptians adopted the new technology of warfare. With bronze weapons and chariots of their own, they liberated themselves from the hated Hyksos and established a new dynasty that introduced what historians call the New Kingdom (1570–1085 B.C.). While these kings—now officially called pharaohs—intended to restore the conservative glory of the Old Kingdom, they nevertheless remembered the lesson of the invasion from the north and no longer relied on Egypt's geographical isolation to protect their way of life. Instead, the newly militant god-kings embarked on a series of foreign wars to build an empire that would erect a territorial barrier between Egypt and any potential invaders. Map 1.2 shows the extent of the Egyptian Empire by 1450 B.C.

As the Egyptian Empire expanded, it was in turn shaped by Fertile Crescent politics and culture. For example, the riches that poured into the Nile valley from foreign conquests often ended up in the hands of temple priests, who began rivaling the pharaohs in power. Slaves, captured abroad and brought to Egypt, introduced new languages, views, and *Egyptian Empire* religions to the valley. Not surprisingly, the lives of Egyptian soldiers, battling in foreign wars, changed for the worse. The scribe we met earlier, who praised his own occupation above all others, wrote about the grim life of a soldier of the New Kingdom: "He is called up for Syria. He may not rest. There are no clothes, no sandals. He drinks water every third day; it is smelly and tastes of salt. His body is ravaged by illness. He does not know what he is about. His body is weak, his legs fail him." As Map 1.2 shows, the imperial expansion of

Egypt encroached on the borders of the strong Hittite Empire, which soon threatened the restored New Kingdom.

The imperial pharaohs successfully built their empire and made Egypt prosperous again, but critics periodically worried about the new direction of Egyptian policy that was changing the old homogeneous society. Hatshepsut (1504?–1482 B.C.) was one

Hatshepsut

such critic (see "Biography," p. 26) who apparently tried to revive Egypt's isolationist ways. She led one military exhibition to Nubia but focused mostly on peaceful pursuits of trade and rebuilding. Her inscriptions claim that she repaired the damage done by the Hyksos, an achievement that made her popular among her people.

Hatshepsut had to reconcile her traditional views with her unusual status as a woman in the position of pharaoh. Women in a pharaoh's family had always held the important position of consort to their brother-husbands. They joined them in being descended from gods, but the king had always been the incarnation of the principal deity. Hatshepsut used artistic representations to overcome this problem, ordering that all statues of her portray her as a man. In Figure 1.11 on page 27, a formal portrait, she is dressed in the traditional male royal style—bare-chested and wearing a short, stiff skirt. She even wears an artificial, ceremonial beard.

Hatshepsut's successors reversed her traditional politics and revived Egypt's imperial ambitions. The New

Empire building

Kingdom reached its apogee in expansion and prosperity under the reign of Amenhotep III (r. 1412?–1375? B.C.). This confident pharaoh built huge statues of himself and a spacious new temple. His luxurious lifestyle,

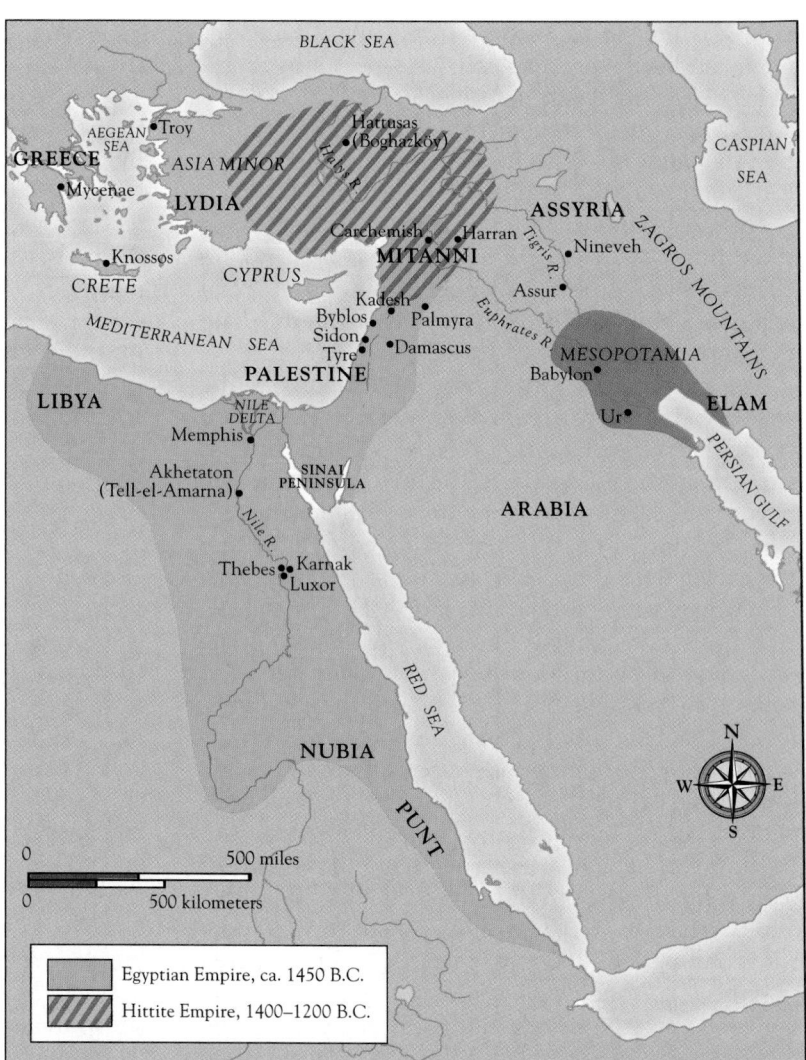

THINKING ABOUT GEOGRAPHY

MAP 1.2 *The Ancient Near East, ca. 1450 B.C.*

This map shows the growth of the Egyptian Empire, the large Hittite Kingdom, and their relationship to the Mesopotamian kingdoms. ❧ **Notice** the extent of the Egyptian Empire. **Compare** it to Egypt in Map 1.1. **What** new areas were conquered during Egypt's imperial period? ❧ **Consider** the impact of such expansion on the old civilization of the Nile valley. ❧ **Notice** the location of Nubia. **Consider** what the conquest of this region might mean for the interaction between sub-Saharan Africa and the rest of the Mediterranean world and the Fertile Crescent.

however, took its toll on him. He died at age 38, and his mummified remains reveal a balding, overweight man with rotted teeth.

THE RELIGIOUS EXPERIMENT OF AKHENATEN, 1377?–1360 B.C.

During the New Kingdom period, the traditional relationship between the god-king and his priests began to change. Priests of Amon became almost as powerful as the pharaohs in administering the kingdom. The priests of Osiris grew popular with wealthy people, to whom they offered the possibility of immortal life in return for money. Within this increasingly tense environment arose a reformer who tried to create a religious revolution.

Amenhotep IV (r. 1377?–1360 B.C.), the son of Amenhotep III, tried to renounce the many divine principles worshiped in all the temples of Egypt and institute worship of a single god whom he called Aten, the sun-disk. The god-king changed his name *Akhenaten's religion* from Amenhotep ("Amon is satisfied") to Akhenaten ("useful to Aten, the sun-disk"). Then he withdrew his support from the old temples and tried to dissolve the powerful priesthoods. Akhenaten also departed from tradition by introducing a new naturalism in art, in which he allowed himself to be portrayed realistically, protruding belly and all (see Figure 1.12 on page 28). However, the artwork in Aten's new temples often featured portraits of Akhenaten's beautiful wife, Nefertiti, without the pharaoh, suggesting that the queen may have played a large role in planning the new cult.

Figure 1.12 shows a casual family portrait of Akhenaten, Nefertiti, and three of their daughters. Husband and wife are shown the same size. Both wear regal headdresses that suggest an unusual equality, and Akhenaten affectionately kisses one of his daughters in a remarkably informal portrayal. The sun-disk is above and shines down on both, indicating that the family not only is blessed by the sun deity, but also that they can serve to bring the blessings of the sun to their people.

A beautiful hymn to Aten has survived, perhaps written by Akhenaten himself. In the hymn, the pharaoh praises Aten as the only god: "O sole god, like whom there is no other! Thou didst create the world according to thy desire." In a development remarkable for the ancient world, Akhenaten declares

this god to be universal, belonging to all peoples: "Their tongues are separate in speech, and their natures as well; Their skins are distinguished, As thou distinguishest the foreign peoples. . . . The lord of all of them, . . . The lord of every land." In the ancient world, gods were associated with individual peoples and cities, so Akhenaten's praise of a universal god is extraordinary.

Many scholars have speculated about the motives behind this dramatic religious innovation. Had Akhenaten been influenced by Israelites living in Egypt? Was his declaration of a single god a political move to reduce the power of the priests of Amon? Or was the king a sickly dreamer, who merely had a strange spiritual vision? We will never know Akhenaten's motives, but his reign caused turmoil in Egypt. He neglected the imperial administration in his religious quest, and the powerful Hittites were able to take many of the northern imperial lands. The disruptions gave support to the offended priests and people alike who did not trust this new deity.

THE TWILIGHT OF THE EGYPTIAN EMPIRE, 1360–CA. 1000 B.C.

Akhenaten was succeeded by Tutankhaton (r. 1347–1338 B.C.), who lacked the commitment and strength to carry on the religious reforms of his father-in-law. The priests of the old cults had grown increasingly resentful of Akhenaten—whom they called "the criminal"—and the young king changed his name to Tutankhamen as he renounced the old pharaoh's religious convictions. Tutankhamen died at just 18 years of age, and the general who succeeded him as pharaoh—Harmhab—destroyed Akhenaten's temples and restored the worship of the old gods.

Egypt showed a hint of its former greatness during the reign of Ramses II (1279–1213 B.C.), who reestablished the imperial frontiers in Syria and restored peace under Egypt's traditional gods. Ramses negotiated a treaty with the Hittites that is believed to be the first recorded nonaggression pact. Ramses' success in bringing peace allowed him to free resources for huge building projects, most notably a great temple carved out of the rocky cliffs along the Nile. But the prosperity proclaimed by the colossal buildings was not enduring. Subsequent pharaohs, through the end of the New Kingdom in 1085 B.C., tried to shore up the fragile empire. However, major

Biography

HATSHEPSUT (R. 1473–1458 B.C.) AND THUTMOSE (1482?–1450 B.C.)

Consider how Hatshepsut's career showed both the political realities of the New Kingdom's involvement with other regions, as well as the Egyptian desire to maintain isolation.

The Egyptian pharaoh Thutmose I had three children by his favorite wife—two sons who died in their youths, and a daughter, Hatshepsut. In the complex households of the pharaohs, the succession to the throne was never clear, for Thutmose I also had a son by a lesser wife. This son, Thutmose II, married his half-sister Hatshepsut and succeeded his father as pharaoh. Thutmose II apparently was sickly and died in 1504 B.C. after he and Hatshepsut had a daughter, Neferure. The succession again went to a son by a concubine. However, this next son, Thutmose III, was less than 10 years old when his father died. The logical regent was his aunt/stepmother, Hatshepsut. Although it was customary for a man to rule, Hatshepsut wanted to be pharaoh, not regent. To this end, she cultivated the support of the powerful priests of Amon, and of the army, and had herself declared pharaoh. Thutmose III had to accept a position of titular co-ruler with no actual authority. Hatshepsut seems to have treated her young charge well. Contemporaries praised his extraordinary skills in reading and writing and his study of military arts. He was also healthy and a strong athlete.

His remains show that he escaped even the severe dental decay that appears in many royal mummies. Thutmose III was probably married to his aunt's daughter, Neferure, to guarantee his succession.

Hatshepsut grappled with two major challenges during her reign: how to forward her political vision for Egypt and how to ensure her credibility. She approached both tasks shrewdly, ever aware of the importance of appearances as well as policy. In her political vision, she focused attention on trade and peaceful pursuits, apparently trying to restore Egypt's former position of glorious isolation. To prove her rule, she turned to art and building in the traditional royal Egyptian way. She commissioned portraits that showed her dressed as a male king, and she built a magnificent funerary temple intended to stand forever and proclaim her passage into the land of the gods.

Powerful Queen and Vengeful Son-in-Law

While Hatshepsut focused on internal building projects, she kept the army strong, because Egypt's neighbors did not feel powerful enough to threaten the borders. The accomplishments she seemed proudest of, however, were in

challengers arose to confront the god-kings. Libyans to the west and Nubians from the south invaded the Nile valley and took power for a while. Eventually, greater empires to the east and north would conquer Egypt permanently, and the center of Western civilization would move to other lands. However, the advanced culture, ordered life, and intense spirituality of the rich land of the Nile would again exert a profound impact on the early peoples of the West, as we will see in Chapter 3.

Merchants and Monotheists: Peoples of the Mediterranean Coast, ca. 1300–500 B.C.

Along the eastern coast of the Mediterranean Sea, various civilizations arose and became part of the power struggles plaguing the Middle East. Most of

FIGURE I.II

Hatshepsut, ca. 1460 B.C.

any case, this wealthy sub-Saharan kingdom had been the destination of several trade missions during the Middle Kingdom, and all knew of the wealth that was available. The carving depicts the pharaoh meeting with the Queen of Punt—an obese and powerful woman—and bringing back many luxury items of trade. Hatshepsut's ships were filled with incense, ebony, gold, ivory, animal skins, and even live baboons, sacred to Egyptian gods. The pharaoh brought these great luxuries back to Egypt and used much of the wealth in her monumental building projects.

When Thutmose III grew to manhood, he gained control of the army and seemed ready to rule without Hatshepsut's guidance. The early death of this wife Neferure weakened his ties to Hatshepsut, and sources hint that the woman pharaoh was murdered (or simply deposed) in 1458 B.C. Late in his reign, the pharaoh Thutmose III tried to eradicate all memory of Hatshepsut. He had her temples and most of her statues destroyed and her name scraped off stone monuments. Was he angry about his long regency? Did he object to Hatshepsut's gender? Or did he disapprove of her popular political agenda of isolationism? We can never know the answers to these questions. Fortunately for students of history, Thutmose was unable to erase all the evidence that tells of his remarkable predecessor.

Thutmose III was a great leader, although his political vision for Egypt differed markedly from that of his aunt. Specifically, he believed that Egypt should be an imperial power. During his 54-year reign, he led military expeditions and established the empire that defined Egypt during the New Kingdom. In the story of Hatshepsut and Thutmose, we see two accomplished pharaohs with conflicting visions of Egypt—one looking backward to its Old Kingdom greatness, the other looking forward to the empire building of the future. Both rules embodied major, dramatic themes in Egyptian history.

trade. She commissioned a great carving that recounted her successful trade mission to "Punt," an African kingdom that we can no longer exactly identify, although some historians suggest it may be near modern-day Somalia (see Map 1.2). In

these Mediterranean cultures eventually were absorbed by their neighbors and disappeared. However, two of them—the Phoenicians and the Hebrews—made a lasting impact as they vigorously expanded their fortunes and furthered the worship of their gods.

THE PHOENICIANS: TRADERS ON THE SEA

The Phoenicians were successful traders whose culture was based in the coastal cities of Sidon, Tyre, and Byblos (see Map 1.2 on page 24). These seagoing merchants made the most of their location by engaging in prosperous trade with Egypt and the lands in the Fertile Crescent. The Phoenicians controlled forests of cedar trees that were highly prized in both Mesopotamia and Egypt. They also had an even more lucrative monopoly on purple dye made from coastal shellfish. Phoenician weavers dyed cloth purple and sold it throughout the Middle East and western Mediterranean for huge profits to wealthy people for whom nobility was demonstrated by wearing purple clothing.

FIGURE 1.12
Akhenaten, Nefertiti, and three of their daughters enjoying the blessings of the sun-disk.

Explorers from the Phoenician cities traveled widely throughout the Mediterranean Sea. By 950 B.C., these remarkable sailors traded as far west as Spain, and even into the Atlantic down the west coast of Africa. Like all ancient sailors, *Trading colonies* they hugged the coast as they traveled so they could stop each night to beach the ships and sleep. To guarantee safe harbors, Phoenician traders established merchant colonies all along the north coast of Africa; by some estimates there was a colony about every thirty miles. The most important colony was Carthage, which was founded about 800 B.C. and would become a significant power in the Mediterranean (see Chapter 4). Through these colonies, the Phoenicians spread the culture of the ancient Middle East—from their trading expertise to their gods and goddesses—around the Mediterranean. Among the Phoenician remains, archaeologists have discovered the solid-gold belt shown in Figure 1.13. The designs on the belt portray men fighting lions—a typical theme in the Middle East. This belt was found in Spain, testifying to the spread of eastern culture to the western edges of the Mediterranean. The gold also confirms the amazing wealth the Phoenicians accumulated through their trade.

The Phoenicians' most important contribution to Western culture was their remarkable alphabet. *Phoenician alphabet* In developing a writing system, the Phoenicians improved on the Sumerian script by creating a purely phonetic alphabet of only twenty-two letters. This system was simpler than the unwieldy cuneiform and hieroglyph that dominated the rest of the Middle East. The Phoenician alphabet spread rapidly and allowed other later cultures to write without the long apprenticeships that characterized the proud scribes like the one shown at the beginning of this chapter. Through adopting a Phoenician-style alphabet, cultures of the West achieved a significant advantage over cultures whose written languages remained the exclusive province of the elite.

FIGURE 1.13
Phoenician gold belt found in Spain, fifth century B.C.

THE PEOPLE OF THE ONE GOD: EARLY HEBREW HISTORY, 1500–900 B.C.

Phoenician society in the Near East ultimately disappeared as an independent state, but not before it had performed an immense service as a transmitter of culture throughout the Mediterranean. The Phoenicians' neighbors, the Hebrews, followed an entirely different course. The Hebrews resiliently withstood both time and conquest, and emerged from a difficult journey with their culture intact.

While the Sumerians and their successors in Mesopotamia developed complex civilizations based on irrigation and built ziggurats to their many deities, the seminomadic Hebrews moved their flocks from Mesopotamia into the land of Canaan, comprising much of the modern states of Israel, Lebanon, and western Syria. As they traveled, they shared many of the ancient stories of Mesopotamia, such as the tale of a great flood that destroyed the land (present in

The Epic of Gilgamesh described earlier) and a lost Garden of Eden. The Hebrews, perhaps seeing the Mesopotamian ziggurats from a distance, also viewed their neighbors as overly proud. The Hebrew story of the ill-fated Tower of Babel captures this theme of overweening pride.

Sometime before 1500 B.C., the early leaders of the Hebrews, the patriarchs—Abraham, Isaac, and Jacob—led these seminomadic tribes that roamed the eastern Mediterranean and beyond. Jacob *Patriarchs* changed his name to "Israel" ("he who prevails with God"), and this name marked Jacob's followers as having a special relationship with one God. Consequently, historians refer to these tribes as the Israelites. Several clans traveled to Egypt, where Israelite texts claim they were enslaved by the Egyptians, although their status is not clear. They might simply have been employed in the labor-intensive Egyptian work projects, and their position may have changed over time to a more restrictive relationship. Some historians identify the Israelites with a group who helped build the huge projects of the Egyptian pharaoh

Ramses II (r. 1279–1213 B.C.). According to the Bible, Moses led this same group from Egypt. This "Exodus" (which means "journey out" in Greek) transformed them into a nation with a specific religious calling.

The details of the history of the Israelites are found in the Hebrew Scriptures (called the Old Testament by subsequent Christians). Made up of writings from oral and written traditions and dating from about 1250 to 150 B.C., these Scriptures record laws, wisdom, legends, literature, and the history of the ancient Israelites. The first five books (known as the Pentateuch), constitute the Torah, or law code, which governed the people's lives. The Bible contains some information that is historically accurate and can be generally confirmed by archaeological evidence. For example, as early as 1208 B.C., the pharaoh Marneptah, the son of Ramses II, erected a victory stone recording his triumphs, including the conquest of Israel: "Israel is laid waste, his seed is no more. . . ." The Egyptian god-king would not have bothered to *Hebrew Scriptures* brag about the conquest of the Israelites if this accomplishment had not been fairly substantial, so we know that the Bible's descriptions of a strong Israelite kingdom in Palestine during the second millennium B.C. are well founded.

Historians must be cautious when using the Bible as a source, because it is basically a religious book that reveals faith, not science. Archaeology and history can illuminate the events of the ancient Israelites, but these sciences can shed no light on the faith that underlies the text. Used carefully, though, the Bible is an important source of information on these early Israelites, for they made a point to record and remember their own history—they wove teachings and morality into a historical narrative. Thus, Hebrew religion was rooted in history rather than myth, and from this text we can begin to re-create the early history of this profoundly influential people.

According to the Bible, the Hebrews from Egypt eventually returned to ancient Palestine and slowly reconquered the land, uniting the other nearby Hebrew tribes in the process. During this period of settlement, between about 1200 and 1050 B.C., Israelites experienced a change in leadership. Instead of relying solely on tribal leaders, people turned to "judges"—charismatic leaders who helped unite the people against the threats of their neighbors. In time, the elders of the tribes felt they needed a king to lead the people, declaring, "then we shall be like other nations, with a king to govern us, *Establishing a kingdom* to lead us out to war and fight our battles" (1 Sam. 8:20). The people insisted that Samuel, the last of the judges, anoint their first king Saul (r. 1024?–1000? B.C.).

Saul's successor, David (r. 1000?–961? B.C.), began encouraging the tribes to settle in a fixed location, with their capital at Jerusalem. David's successor, Solomon (r. 961?–922? B.C.), brought Phoenician craftsmen to Jerusalem to build a great temple there. The artist's rendition in Figure 1.14 shows what archaeologists imagine the temple looked like, with its large interior and great sacrificial altar in front. Now a territorial power like others in the Fertile Crescent, the Hebrews worshiped their God, Yahweh, in the temple overlooking a majestic city. But the costs of the temple were exorbitant, causing increased taxes and the growth of an administrative structure to collect them.

Solomon was a king in the Mesopotamian style. If the biblical account is to be believed, he used marriage to forge political alliances, accumulating 300 wives and many

FIGURE 1.14
Artist's rendition of Solomon's Temple in Jerusalem.

hundreds more concubines, including the daughter of an Egyptian pharaoh. The Biblical excerpts in Document 1.2 on page D1.1 show Solomon's fame, long-distance trade, and the difficulties accompanying his many marriages. However, the

Dividing a kingdom unified kingdom of tribes barely outlasted Solomon's reign. After his death, the northern tribes—particularly angry about Solomon's taxation and adzto form the separate kingdom of Israel (Map 1.3). The southern state was called Judah, with its capital at Jerusalem, and at this time the southern Israelites began to be called Jews. Israel was the more prosperous of the two kingdoms and was tied more closely to Phoenicia by trade and other contacts. Judah adhered more rigorously to the old Hebrew laws. The two kingdoms often fought one another as they participated in the shifting alliances of their neighbors. Dominating all politics, however, was their commitment to their one God, Yahweh.

The authors of the Scriptures developed an overriding theme in Jewish history: the intimate relationship between obedience to God's laws and the unfolding of the history of the Jewish people. As these authors recorded their recollection of events, they told of periodical violations of the uncompromising covenant with God and the resulting punishments that God imposed.

A JEALOUS GOD, 1300–587 B.C.

When Moses led his people out of Egypt, they reportedly wandered for 40 years in the wilderness of the Sinai Peninsula before returning to the land of Canaan (see Map 1.3). During that time,

The Covenant Moses bound his people to Yahweh in a special covenant, or agreement, through

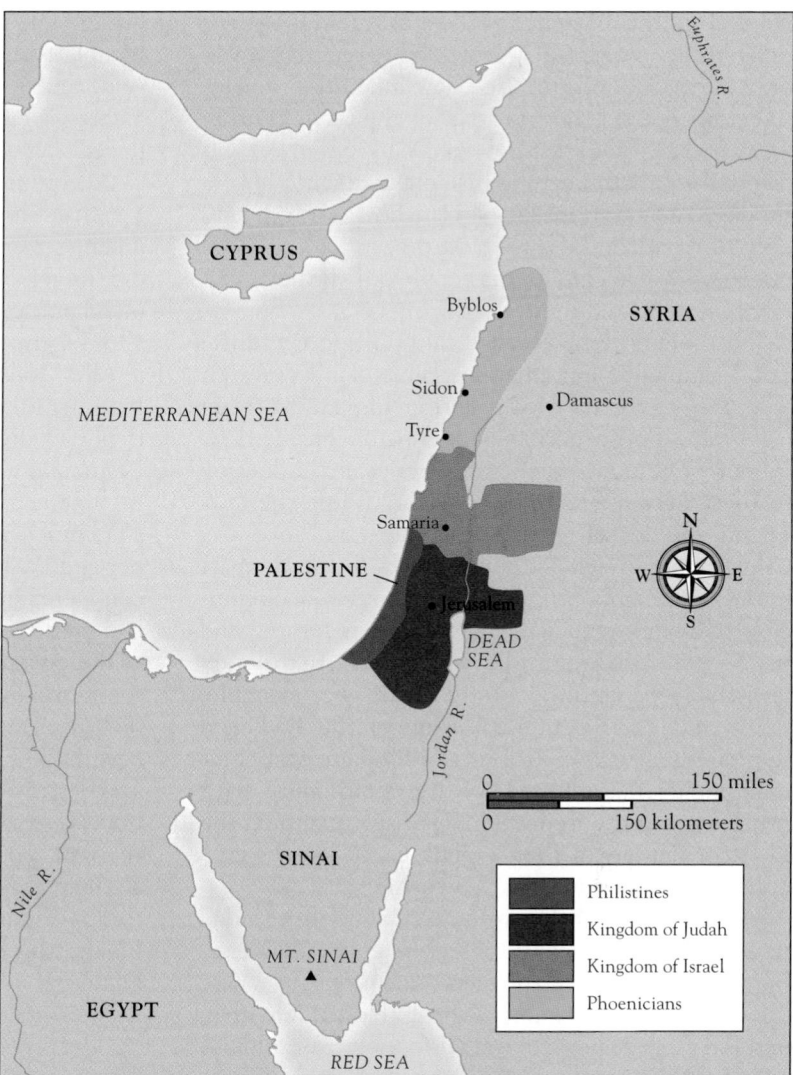

THINKING ABOUT GEOGRAPHY

MAP 1.3 *Mediterranean Coast in the First Millennium* B.C.

This map shows the major kingdoms of the Mediterranean coast, including the Philistines, Hebrews, and Phoenicians.
◾ **Notice** the scale of the map and **consider** how their proximity contributed to the many ties between them.
◾ **Locate** the Philistines. **Consider** why there were so many battles between the Philistines and the Hebrews.

which the Jews would be God's "chosen people" in return for their undivided worship. The ancient Hebrews were not strictly monotheistic, for they believed in the existence of the many deities of their neighbors. For Moses' people, however, there was only one God, and this God demanded their exclusive worship. As the historian of the sixth century B.C. wrote in the Bible's Book of Deuteronomy, "He is the faithful God, keeping his covenant of love to a thousand generations of those who love him and keep his commands." This promise was a conditional one: God would care for his people only if they practiced his laws, and there were many laws.

The core of the Hebrew legal tradition lay in the Ten Commandments that the Bible claims Yahweh gave to Moses during his exodus from Egypt, and these were supplemented by other requirements listed in the Scriptures. Adhering to these laws defined one as a Jew. While the laws bound the Jewish people together—to "love thy neighbor as thyself"—they also set the Jews apart from their neighbors. For example, boys were circumcised as a mark of the covenant between Yahweh and his people. In addition, Jews observed strict dietary laws that separated them from others—for example, they could eat no pork nor any animal that had been improperly slaughtered. But the fundamental commandment that allowed for no compromise with non-Jews was the injunction against worshiping the idols, or deities, of their neighbors. A jealous god, Yahweh demanded exclusive worship.

Around the eighth century B.C., Jews were called to even higher ethical standards by a remarkable series of charismatic men—the prophets. These men, such as Amos, Micah, Hosea, Jeremiah, and Isaiah, were neither kings nor priests nor soldiers. Instead, they were common people—shepherds or tradesmen—who cared nothing for power or glory. They were brave men who urged their people to return to the covenant and traditional Hebrew law. In times of social distress, they became the conscience of Israel, and in turn they helped shape the social conscience that was to become part of Western civilization. The prophets reminded the Jews to care for the poor: "Seek justice, relieve the oppressed, Judge the fatherless, plead for the widow" (Isa. 1:17). In doing so, they emphasized the direct ethical responsibility of every individual. Unlike the other religions of the ancient Middle East, Judaism called to individuals to follow their consciences to create a more ethical world. Religion was no longer a matter of rituals of the temple, but a matter of people's hearts and

Hebrew laws

Prophets

minds. The prophets preached a religion that would be able to withstand turmoil and political destruction, and it is fortunate that they did so, for the Hebrews would suffer much adversity which they believed was a form of testing by their God.

According to the Bible, King Solomon had a weakness that stemmed from his polygamy. (See Document 1.2 on page D1.1.) Not only did he violate the biblical command not to take foreign wives, but to please them he allowed the worship of other deities (especially the fertility goddess Astarte), even in the holy city of Jerusalem. Prophets claimed that it was his impiety that had divided the kingdom against itself. Later events showed a similar theme. Ahab (r. 869–850 B.C.), king of the northern kingdom of Israel, married a Phoenician princess, Jezebel, and erected an altar to her god Baal in order to please her. When Israel was conquered in 721 B.C. by the Assyrians, prophets who had predicted its downfall pointed to Ahab's breach of the covenant as the cause of the misfortune. The southern kingdom of Judah fared little better than Israel in trying to escape the aggressions of its neighbors. In 587 B.C., the Babylonians captured Jerusalem and destroyed Solomon's magnificent temple. Many Jews were exiled and enslaved in Babylon, and the "chosen people" were once more without a country or a religious center. From then on, there would be substantial numbers of Jews who lived outside Israel or Judah, who later would be collectively known as the Diaspora. Instead of renouncing their God, however, the Jews reaffirmed their covenant in a different way.

"God's punishments"

JUDAISM IN EXILE

Hebrew priests in exile worried that Diaspora Jews living among non-Jews would forget the old traditions and be assimilated into the cultures of their neighbors. Therefore, they carefully compiled and edited the Scriptures to preserve their unique view of religion and history. These written accounts helped Judaism survive without a geographic center. The authors of the Scriptures arranged the history of the Jews to show that, despite hardships, God had always cared for his people. The priests felt convinced that the destruction of the two Hebrew kingdoms had come because people either did not know the laws or had failed to obey them. As a result, Hebrew teachers emphasized the study of and strict adherence to the purity laws to keep the followers of Yahweh separate from others even when they lived in close proximity as neighbors.

Without the temple in Jerusalem to serve as the center of worship, Jewish worship began to convene in more local establishments—synagogues and the home itself. This movement had an important impact on the status of women in Jewish culture. The emphasis on details of purity law to keep the chosen people separate reduced women's roles in formal prayer because the law stressed that anyone worshipping Yahweh had to be "clean." Women, seen as sometimes unclean because of menstrual blood or childbirth, were excluded from participating in the formal worship rituals. On the other hand, the experience of exile strengthened the family as a social and religious unit, a change that improved women's lives in other ways. For example, concubinage disappeared and women presided over the household, upholding the dietary laws and household rituals that preserved the Jewish culture wherever they lived.

In time, however, the Hebrews were able to reestablish their religious center in Jerusalem. After *"Second Temple" period* ruling Judah for 48 years, the Babylonians were, in turn, conquered by new peoples, the Persians. The Persians proved much more tolerant than the Babylonians of the varied beliefs of their subject people. In 538 B.C. the Persian king, Cyrus, let the Jewish exiles return to Jerusalem. The Jews built a new temple in 515 B.C., an event that introduced the "Second Temple" period. Again, the Jews had a temple and center of worship like other Mesopotamian peoples. However, all Jews did not return to Israel, and the question of the relationship between Diaspora Jews and the cultures in which they lived would reemerge periodically throughout history as followers of this old covenant interacted with their neighbors.

The ancient Hebrews made a tremendous impact on the future of Western civilization. They believed *Hebrew contributions* that God created the world at a specific point in time, and this notion set them apart dramatically from their neighbors, such as the Egyptians, who believed in the eternity of the world. Their view of history as a series of purposeful, morally significant events was unprecedented in the ancient world. Their concept of ethical monotheism, in which a single God of justice interacted with humans in a personal and spiritual way,

offered a vision of religion that eventually dominated in the West. The many deities and demons that ruled the Mesopotamian and Egyptian worlds would in time be rendered insignificant by the God of the Hebrews, who transcended nature. The Hebrews believed that there was a profound distance between people and God, and thus individuals took more responsibility for the events of this world even as they worshiped and held in awe the deity who had made a deep and abiding covenant with the Jewish people.

Terror and Benevolence: The Growth of Empires, 1200–500 B.C.

By the second millennium B.C., many people could see the value of centralized control over larger territories. The Egyptians were establishing an empire, and the Hebrews had united into a kingdom. Size not only offered the potential for larger armies, but expansion westward also secured access to valuable seaborne trade (that was making the Phoenicians wealthy) and would secure the strategically important region of Syria and Palestine. Perhaps most importantly, people wanted to expand their territories to acquire the metals so necessary for military and economic success. These impulses led to the growth of a new political form in the West—huge empires based on a new technology, iron.

THE AGE OF IRON

Before the eleventh century B.C., ancient civilizations depended on bronze, an alloy of copper and tin. All across Europe and the Middle East, people used bronze plows to cultivate the land and employed bronze-tipped weapons to make war. While agriculture remained the most important enterprise, the economies of these civilizations were fueled by trade in copper and tin. Initially, these essential metals came largely from Asia Minor (see Map 1.2 on page 24), Arabia, and India. Later, sources of these metals were also found in the western Mediterranean.

In about 1200 B.C., warfare disrupted the usual trade routes, making tin scarce. Pure copper is a soft metal, and without the tin needed to make bronze, smiths could not produce effective tools and weapons. To overcome the tin shortage, Hittite metal-workers in Asia Minor first began to employ iron, an abundant mineral in that region. Unforged iron is not much stronger than copper. However, when it is repeatedly heated in a hot charcoal furnace, carbon molecules combine with iron molecules to form a very reliable metal known as carbon steel. Even low-carbon steel is stronger than bronze, and when it is cold hammered, the strength more than doubles. People—and particularly soldiers—gained a huge advantage by using the new metal.

Iron Age

The technology used to create the superior forged iron spread rapidly throughout the Mediterranean world, and from about 1000 B.C. on it was used in tools, cookware, and weapons. The use of iron spread to sub-Saharan Africa through Nubia, and iron working became prominent throughout much of that continent that was rich in iron ore. Soldiers wielding iron weapons easily vanquished those armed with bronze. The Age of Iron had dawned, and it dominated the world until the late nineteenth century when metalsmiths developed new ways to make iron into steel without the carbon method (Bessemer steel). Iron Age kings in Mesopotamia forged enough weapons and fielded armies so large that their extensive conquests introduced a new political entity into the history of Western civilization: multiethnic empires.

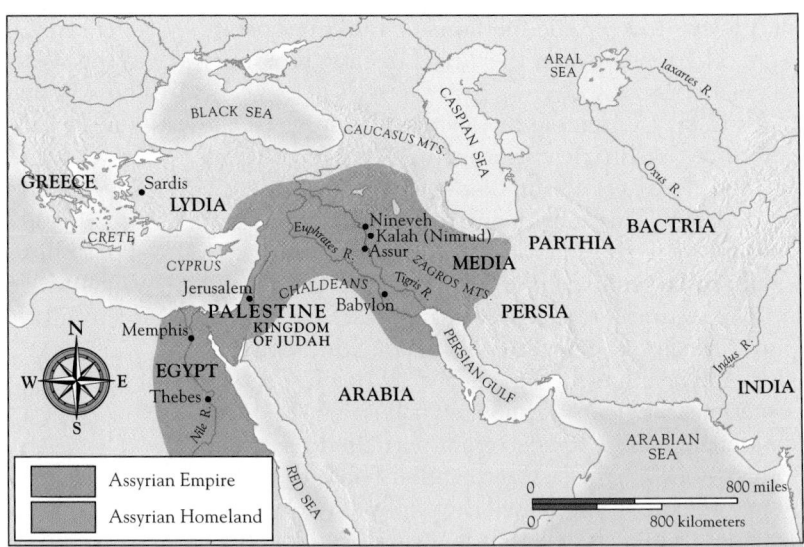

THINKING ABOUT GEOGRAPHY

MAP 1.4   *The Assyrian Empire, ca. 662 B.C.*

This map shows the expansion of the Assyrian Empire in the seventh century B.C. as it conquered the older centers of Western civilization. ◙ **Compare** this map with Maps 1.1, 1.2, and 1.3. **Notice** how many cultures were included in this large empire. ◙ **What** problems might you expect to arise when governing such a diverse empire? ◙ **Notice** the location of the Assyrian homeland. **Consider why** that location might have facilitated Assyrian conquests.

RULE BY TERROR: THE ASSYRIANS, 911–612 B.C.

The Assyrians, a people living originally in the northern Tigris-Euphrates valley, had traded profitably with their neighbors for centuries. In the early tenth century B.C., they began arming themselves with iron weapons and following the one command of their god Assur: expand the frontiers of Assyria so that Assur finally rules over all. Map 1.4 shows the striking success of the Assyrians as they cut a swath through the civilizations of the ancient Near East.

The Assyrians' success stemmed from the skill of their armies and their willingness to engage in almost constant warfare to follow the command of Assur. Assyrian histories recounting their military campaigns were written as propaganda pieces to instill fear in their enemies. (See Document 1.3 on page D1.2.) The historians accomplished their goal, and the cold-blooded details cemented the Assyrians' reputation for ruthlessness. King Sargon II's (r. 722–706 B.C.) description of his conquest of Babylon is one chilling example of these accounts: "I blew like the onrush of a hurricane and enveloped the city like a fog. . . . I did not spare his mighty warriors, young or old, but filled the city square with their corpses."

Beyond sheer brutality, the Assyrians relied on some of the most advanced military techniques that

FIGURE 1.15
Fugitives swimming underwater, ca. 883 B.C.

the ancient world had seen. They employed a corps of military engineers to build bridges, tunnels, and efficient siege weapons capable of penetrating strongly fortified cities. Furthermore, they had a highly trained and well-rewarded officer corps who became the elite in Assyrian society.

The Assyrians portrayed their military achievements in their art as well as in their writings. But along with interminable portrayals of destruction and carnage, Assyrian art occasionally reveals unusual details of experience during the ninth century B.C. The carving shown in Figure 1.15 depicts three men fleeing Assyrian archers as they swim the river toward the fortified town on the right. Two of the swimmers hold pigskins filled with air to breathe underwater, offering a surprising glimpse of an underwater swimming technique. This carving captures an incident that may have been particularly memorable due to the fugitives' creative escape. However, although the fugitives eluded the archers, the Assyrians later conquered the town.

The Assyrians were first both to acquire such a large territory and to try to govern it cohesively. In many ways, they proved to be skilled administrators. For example, they built roads to unify their holdings, and kings appointed governors and tax collectors to serve as their representatives in the more distant territories. One of the elements that facilitated governing and trade over large area was the Assyrians' use of Aramaic as a common language. This was a Semitic language originally spoken by the Aramaeans, successful merchants who lived in Mesopotamia in about 1100 B.C. Aramaic remained the official language of subsequent empires—it *Governing an empire* was even spoken by Jesus. In spite of the Assyrians' reputation for violence, the Greek historian Herodotus (484?–424? B.C.) recalled the peaceful accomplishments of Queen Semiramis, who built "magnificent embankments to retain the river [Euphrates], which till then used to overflow and flood the whole country around Babylon."

Many Assyrian rulers also appreciated the wealth of knowledge and culture that had accumulated in these lands for centuries. The great Assyrian king Ashurbanipal (669–627 B.C.) collected a huge library from which 20,000 clay tablets have survived. Within this collection, the king *Preserving learning* preserved the best of Mesopotamian literature, including *The Epic of Gilgamesh*. The highly educated Ashurbanipal took pride in his accomplishments: "I acquired the hidden treasure of all scribal knowledge, the signs of the heaven and the earth. . . . I have solved the laborious problems of division and multiplication . . . I have read the artistic script of Sumer and the obscure Akkadian." This quotation offers an excellent example of how a written language served to preserve and disseminate the culture developing in the ancient Middle East. The proverbs in Document 1.3 (page D1.2) show a sophisticated ethical development.

Although the Assyrians were skilled in making both war and peace, they still faced the problem that *Fall of Assyrians* confronted all empire builders: how to keep the empire together when subject peoples resisted. The Assyrians used terror to control their far-flung territories. When individuals dissented, they were publicly tortured; when cities revolted, they were razed to serve as examples to others. To break up local loyalties, Assyrian commanders uprooted and moved entire populations. These methods worked for a while; eventually, however, they catalyzed effective opposition.

Ashurbanipal ruled from his capital in Nineveh—reputedly so well fortified that three chariots could ride abreast along the top of the walls surrounding the city. However, even those great walls could not save the king's successors. A coalition including Babylonians from southern Mesopotamia; Medes, an Indo-European tribe from western Iran; and Egyptians gathered against the Assyrian domination. Because the empire was so large it overextended the Assyrians' resources, and the provinces gave way quickly. Nineveh itself finally collapsed in 612 B.C. after a brutal two-year siege. In an ironic turn of events, the great city was defeated by the very river that had sustained it for so long—the Tigris flooded higher than normal and eroded Nineveh's defensive wall. Assyrian rule came to an ignominious end. However, the Assyrians left an enduring legacy for Western civilization: centralized empires that ruled over extended lands and different peoples.

BABYLONIAN RULE, 612–539 B.C.

After vanquishing the Assyrians, the Medes left Mesopotamia and returned to their homeland near the Zagros Mountains (see Map 1.4). The Babylonians (also called Chaldeans, or Neo-Babylonians, to distinguish them from the earlier kingdom of Hammurabi) remained and ruled the lands of the former Assyrian Empire. The new rulers emulated the Assyrian use of terror to enforce their will on subject peoples. King Nebuchadrezzar (r. 605–561 B.C.) kept penalties similar to the Code of Hammurabi for civil crimes, but introduced extreme punishments for enemy rulers and their followers. When captured, these people were often flayed or burned alive. It was this severity that led Nebuchadrezzar to destroy Jerusalem in 587 B.C. and lead the Jews into captivity. This in-

cident was the formative "Babylonian Captivity" discussed earlier that shaped much of subsequent Jewish history.

The Babylonians also continued the Assyrian passion for art and education. The king rebuilt his capital city of Babylon in such splendor that it was admired *Culture and commerce* throughout the ancient world. His architects constructed huge ziggurats in praise of the Babylonian god Marduk and fortified the structures with walls more impressive than even Nineveh's had been. Under Nebuchadrezzar, Babylon blossomed into an impressive city graced by gardens, palaces, and temples.

The magnificent architecture that marked Babylon cost a fortune, and the Babylonian kings obtained these funds largely through fostering the commerce that often guided their military policies. One king, for example, besieged Tyre for thirteen years, hoping to win control over the Phoenicians' far-reaching trade. Another king established himself in Arabia in an attempt to control a new trade—in incense—that came from southern Arabia to the Mediterranean Sea.

Kings used their new wealth not only to decorate their cities, but also to foster learning. Within the cosmopolitan city, Babylonian priests excelled in astronomy and mathematics. They observed the heavens in an effort to understand the will of the gods, and in the process they charted the skies with impressive accuracy; they could predict solstices, equinoxes, and other heavenly phenomena. Their *Astronomy and mathematics* passion for predictions led them to develop another innovation with which they sought to foretell the future for individuals: astrology. By the fifth century B.C., Babylonian astrologers had divided the heavens into twelve signs—including the familiar Gemini, Scorpio, Virgo, and others—and began to cast horoscopes to predict people's futures based on their birth dates. The earliest surviving example of a horoscope was for a child born in 410 B.C. and marks the beginning of a long-standing practice.

As part of their astronomical calculations, Babylonians developed advanced mathematics. Their tablets show that they regularly used multiplication, division, calculations of square and cube roots, algebra, and other operations. In addition, they based their numerical system on the number 60, working out an elaborate method of keeping time that led to the division of hours and minutes that we use today. The benefits of the Babylonians' impressive intellectual achievements were not spread widely through society. More subjects resented Babylonian rule than benefited from its accomplishments.

RULE BY TOLERANCE: THE PERSIAN EMPIRE, CA. 550–330 B.C.

OLC

In 553 B.C., the fortunes of the Babylonian Empire changed. The Persians, a people from east of the Zagros Mountains, overran the land of their Indo-European relatives, the Medes. Under their wise king, Cyrus the Great (r. 559–530 B.C.), the Persians expanded westward to establish an empire even larger than that of the Assyrians (Map 1.5). They quickly conquered the kingdom of Lydia in Asia Minor and then turned southeast to the Babylonian Empire. The Babylonian rulers found few supporters against the invaders even among their own people, and in 539 B.C. Babylon fell to the Persians virtually without a struggle.

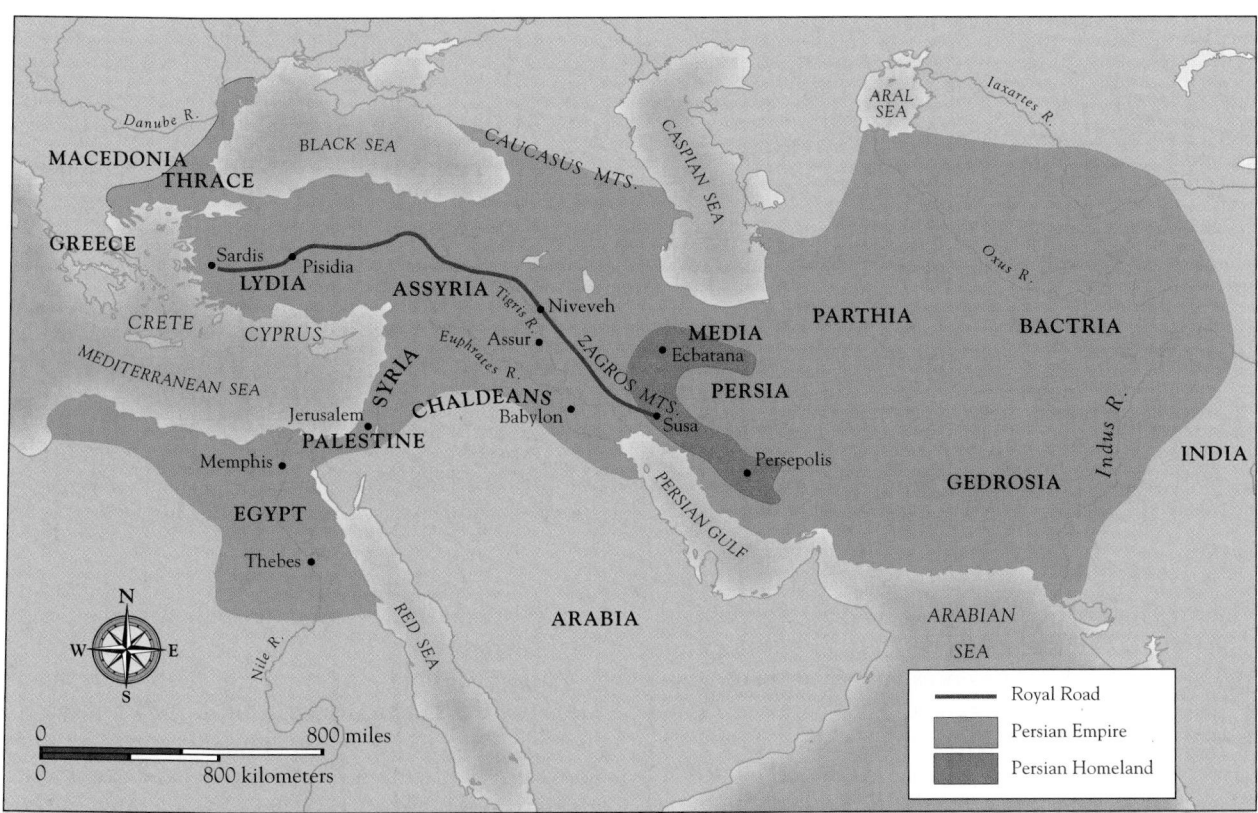

THINKING ABOUT GEOGRAPHY

MAP 1.5 *The Persian Empire, ca. 500 B.C.*

This map shows the Persian Empire that replaced and greatly expanded the previous Assyrian domain.
❧ **Compare** the extent of this empire with that of the Assyrians shown in Map 1.4. **What** additional problems might the Persians have encountered due to these increased distances and diverse cultures?
❧ **Notice** the long Royal Road. **How** might that road help to meet some of the challenges in administering such a large empire? ❧ **Notice** the location of the Persian capital Persepolis.
Consider what additional influences Mesopotamian culture might have faced by having an imperial capital so far to the east.

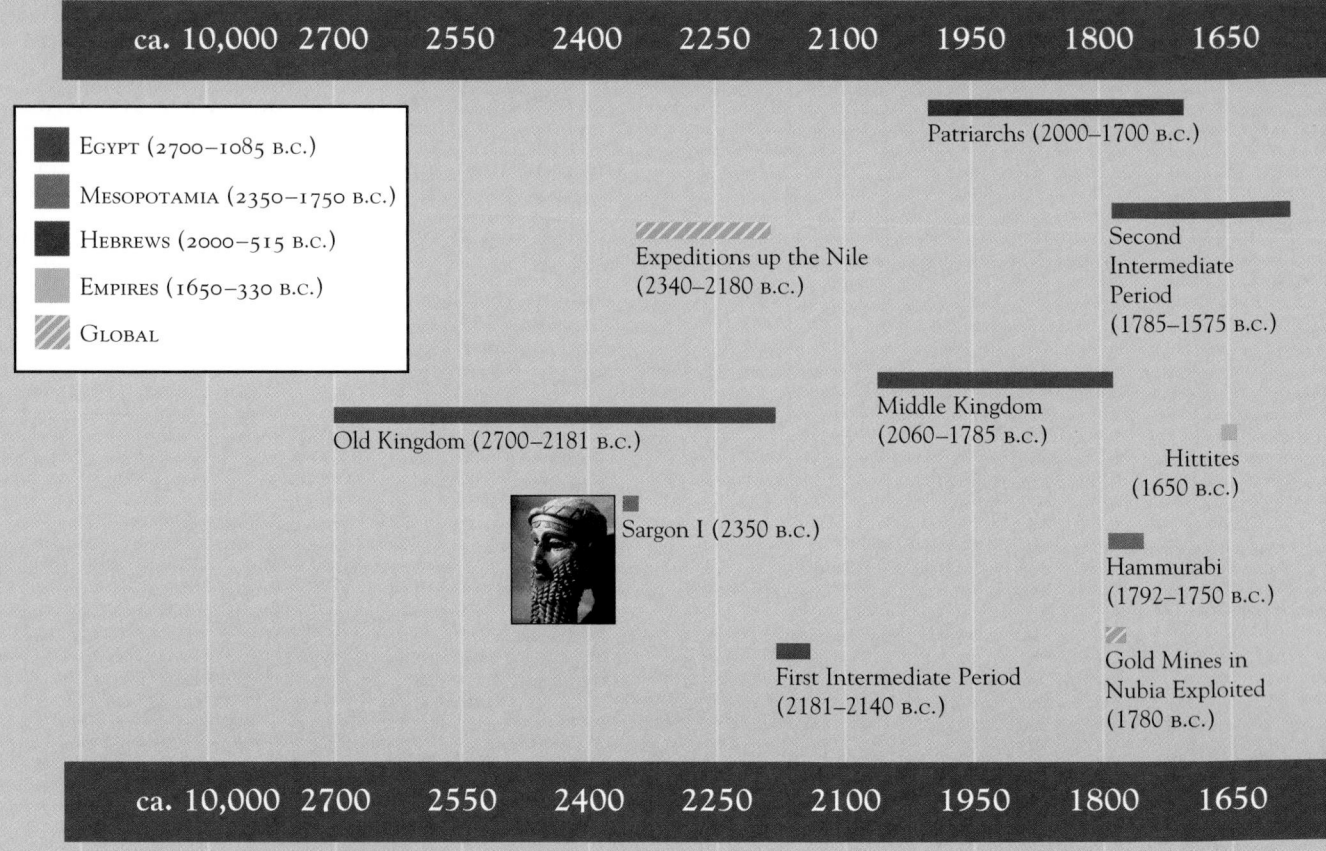

ca. 10,000	2700	2550	2400	2250	2100	1950	1800	1650

■ EGYPT (2700–1085 B.C.)
■ MESOPOTAMIA (2350–1750 B.C.)
■ HEBREWS (2000–515 B.C.)
■ EMPIRES (1650–330 B.C.)
▨ GLOBAL

Patriarchs (2000–1700 B.C.)

Expeditions up the Nile
(2340–2180 B.C.)

Second
Intermediate
Period
(1785–1575 B.C.)

Old Kingdom (2700–2181 B.C.)

Middle Kingdom
(2060–1785 B.C.)

Hittites
(1650 B.C.)

Sargon I (2350 B.C.)

Hammurabi
(1792–1750 B.C.)

First Intermediate Period
(2181–2140 B.C.)

Gold Mines in
Nubia Exploited
(1780 B.C.)

ca. 10,000	2700	2550	2400	2250	2100	1950	1800	1650

Cyrus rejected the Assyrian policies of terror and sought to hold his vast empire together by tolerating differences among his many subject peoples. As mentioned earlier, in 538 B.C. he allowed the Jewish captives in Babylon to return to Jerusalem and rebuild their temple. At the same time, he appeased Babylonians by claiming he was "friend and companion" to their god Marduk. In the conquered provinces—or "satrapies"—Cyrus retained local officials, but installed Persian governors called "satraps." He controlled the satraps' power by appointing additional officials who were directly responsible to the king. The Persians required subject peoples to pay reasonable taxes and serve in their armies, but Cyrus's system prevented local officials from abusing their power excessively. Conquered peoples could worship their own gods and follow their own customs, and under Cyrus's reign, the ancient civilizations enjoyed a long period of peace. The great king (as his subjects called him) was

Persian administration

seen as a semidivine figure, who ruled benignly from his golden throne.

A unified empire allowed the Persians to adopt ideas that had proven successful in the civilizations that preceded them. For example, Persians retained Aramaic as the common language of commerce, making communication easier across many cultures, and they fostered the trade routes that had brought so much wealth to the Babylonians. Persian astrologers learned from their Babylonian predecessors as well. These wise men, or "magi," became celebrated for their knowledge of the heavens.

Of all the conventions the Persians borrowed from the inhabitants of their diverse empire, the adoption of coinage had the greatest long-term impact. The Lydians seem to have invented the use of coins in the seventh century B.C. Before this time, traders either bartered or used cumbersome bars of precious metals to purchase goods. For example, in Egypt in 1170 B.C., a burial vault that was priced at five pounds

Coins

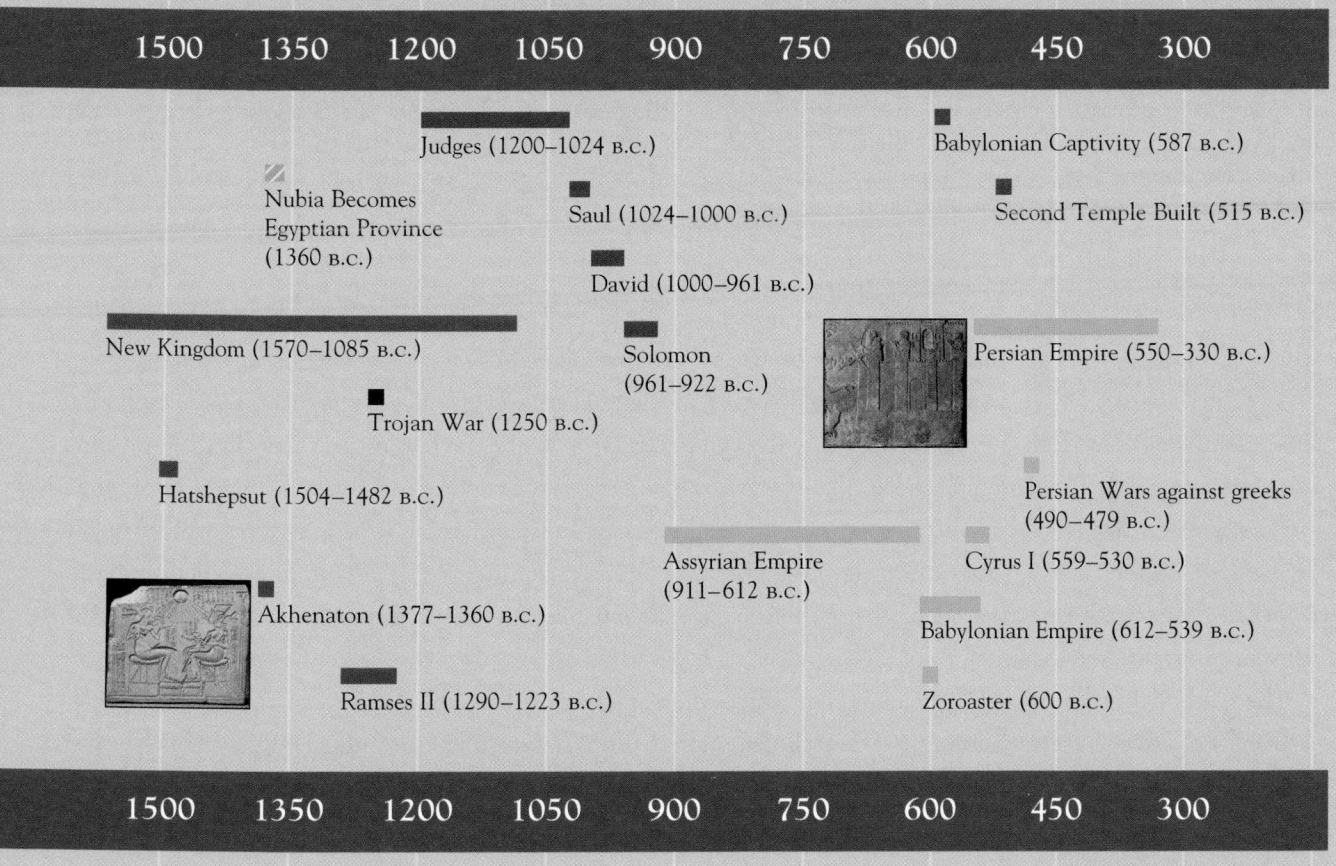

Judges (1200–1024 B.C.)

Babylonian Captivity (587 B.C.)

Nubia Becomes
Egyptian Province
(1360 B.C.)

Saul (1024–1000 B.C.)

Second Temple Built (515 B.C.)

David (1000–961 B.C.)

New Kingdom (1570–1085 B.C.)

Solomon
(961–922 B.C.)

Persian Empire (550–330 B.C.)

Trojan War (1250 B.C.)

Hatshepsut (1504–1482 B.C.)

Persian Wars against greeks
(490–479 B.C.)

Assyrian Empire
(911–612 B.C.)

Cyrus I (559–530 B.C.)

Akhenaton (1377–1360 B.C.)

Babylonian Empire (612–539 B.C.)

Ramses II (1290–1223 B.C.)

Zoroaster (600 B.C.)

1500　1350　1200　1050　900　750　600　450　300

of copper might have been bought with two and one-half pounds of copper, one hog, two goats, and two trees. By minting coins with precise, identifiable values, kingdoms greatly facilitated trade. The kings of Lydia were said to have grown fabulously rich after their invention, and the Persians rapidly spread the use of coins throughout their far-flung lands. From this time on, coins became a valuable primary source of information about the societies that produced them.

While the Persians adopted many novelties of their predecessors, they also made a unique contribution of their own: a new movement in religious **Zoroastrianism** thought initiated by the talented prophet Zoroaster (628?–551 B.C.). One of the most important religious reformers of the ancient world, Zoroaster founded a new religion (later called Zoroastrianism) that contained the seeds of many modern belief systems. Zoroaster experienced a revelation given to him by the one god, Ahura Mazda, the Lord of Light. In this revelation, recorded in a holy book called the Avesta, Zoroaster was called to reform Persian religion by eliminating polytheism and animal sacrifice. In the tradition of Uruinimgina, Hebrew prophets, and others throughout the early history of Western civilization who called for social justice, Zoroaster also urged people to live ethical lives and to show care for others. Finally, the prophet believed that the history of the world was one of ongoing conflict between Ahura Mazda and the forces of the evil god Ahriman. Zoroaster also felt confident that Ahura Mazda would ultimately prevail over evil, and eventually the dead would be resurrected. Believers would go to paradise, while evildoers would fall into a hell of perpetual torture.

The Persian kings claimed to rule the earth as Ahura Mazda's viceroys, but slowly the old nature worship returned and became incorporated into Zoroastrian beliefs. For example, people began to venerate Mithra, the ancient sun god, as an assistant to Ahura Mazda. Zoroaster's ideas had an influence that far outlasted the Persian rulers. During the Roman Empire, the worship of Mithra would be an important cult (see Chapter 5). Furthermore, followers of Zoroastrianism still exist today, and even in the ancient world many of the prophet's ideas influenced other religions as well. Over time, some believers transformed Zoroaster's monotheism into a dualistic belief in two gods, one good and one evil. Judaism—and, later, Christianity—seem to have been influenced by his vision, for Jewish texts began to write of the power of a devil and of a final struggle between good and evil. Zoroaster was the first prophet whose ideas would spread throughout a large political empire, but he would not be the last.

Summary

In the 3,000 years that make up the history of the ancient Middle East, many elements that characterize Western civilization emerged. Great cities sprang up, introducing commerce, excitement, diversity, and extremes of wealth and poverty that the West both values and struggles with even today. Tyranny and oppression arose, as did the laws and principles designed to hold them in check. Sophisticated religions provided vehicles for metaphysical reflection, and artists expressed those hopes and dreams in beautiful forms. Perhaps most important, writing systems evolved to let people preserve their accumulated knowledge for future generations, including ours. Finally, these early centuries established a pattern of interaction and cross-fertilization of goods and ideas that would mark Western civilization from its beginnings through today.

The great civilizations of the Tigris-Euphrates valley—the Sumerians, Akkadians, Babylonians, and others— were ultimately absorbed by larger empires. Yet their contributions endured as a result of the mutual influence that always occurs when cultures mingle. The same was true for the complex civilization of Egypt. The Hebrews, too, contributed much to the growing body of Western ideas and values. By 500 B.C., the Persian kings had united the region, creating an empire rich with the diversity of many peoples and thousands of years of history. The Persian Empire marks a culmination of the first stirrings of Western civilization in the ancient Middle East. The next developments in the story of the West would come from different peoples: the Greeks.

REVIEW, ANALYZE, AND ANTICIPATE

REVIEW AND ANALYZE THIS CHAPTER

Chapter 1 traces the development of Western civilization from its earliest beginnings in the cities of the ancient Middle East through the establishment of great empires. One of the significant themes throughout this chapter is the interaction among the various cultures that allowed each to assimilate and build on the innovations of the others.

1. *What environmental advantages did the ancient Middle East have that permitted the growth of agriculture and cities? What disadvantages did the Middle East have? How did environmental conditions affect the various cultures?*

2. *Review the long-standing contributions of the Sumerians, Egyptians, Nubians, Phoenicians, and Hebrews.*

3. *How were the Jews able to maintain their integrity while being part of the Diaspora?*

4. *Review the empires—Assyrian, Babylonian, Persian—that arose in the ancient Middle East, and note the strengths and weaknesses of each.*

ANTICIPATE THE NEXT CHAPTERS

In Chapters 3 and 4—"The Poleis Become Cosmopolitan" and "Pride in Family and City"—we will see new empires established in the Western world that, like the replaced Persians, will face problems of governing multiethnic lands.

1. *What lessons do you think future empires will learn from the different governance styles of the Assyrians and Persians?*

2. *Consider the Jews' history of preserving their identity while living outside Israel, and consider what kinds of relationships they might have with future empires. What problems might they face?*

3. *Review the map of the Persian Empire (Map 1.5). In Chapter 2, we will see the Persian Empire going to war once again. What peoples do you believe will next come into conflict with that empire?*

BEYOND THE CLASSROOM

BEFORE WESTERN CIVILIZATION

Diamond, Jared. *Guns, Germs, and Steel*. NY: W.W. Norton & Co., 1997. A brilliant Pulitzer-Prize winning global analysis of the natural advantages that gave Western civilization its head start.

STRUGGLING WITH THE FORCES OF NATURE: MESOPOTAMIA, 3000–CA. 1000 B.C.

Binford, Lewis R. *In Pursuit of the Past*. NY: Thames and Hudson, 1988. An archaeological study of the transformation of human society.

Crawford, Harriet. *Sumer and the Sumerians*. NY: Cambridge University Press, 1991. A summary of the historical and archaeological evidence that offers a solid survey of the field.

Frankfort, Henri. *Before Philosophy*. Harmondsworth, England: Penguin, 1951. An attempt to understand the view ancient peoples took of the world.

Hawkes, Jacquetta. *The Atlas of Early Man*. NY: St. Martin's Press, 1993. An accessible study of human thought.

Hooker, Jeremy T. *Reading the Past: Ancient Writing from Cuneiform to the Alphabet*. Berkeley: University of California Press, 1991. An exploration of the stages of the ancient scripts of past civilizations.

Kramer, Samuel N. *The Sumerians: Their History, Culture, and Character*. Chicago: University of Chicago Press, 1963. A historical outline of Sumerian civilization describing topics like literature, education, and psychology.

Postgate, Nicholas. *Early Mesopotamia: Society and Economy at the Dawn of History*. NY: Routledge, Chapman and Hall, 1992. A narrative depiction of the life of the peoples of early Mesopotamia.

Redman, Charles L. *The Rise of Civilization: From Early Farmers to Urban Society in the Ancient Near East*. NY: Freeman, 1978. A look at cultural change as a cumulative phenomenon.

Ruhlen, Merritt. The *Origin of Language: Tracing the Evolution of the Mother Tongue*. NY: John Wiley and Sons, Inc., 1996. A lucid explanation of the processes of phonetic and semantic change and the reconstruction of protolanguages.

Saggs, H.W. *Civilization before Greece and Rome*. New Haven: Yale University Press, 1991. A fine account of various cultures, including Babylonian, Assyrian, Sumerian, Medean, and Hittite civilizations.

RULE OF THE GOD-KING: ANCIENT EGYPT, CA. 3100–1000 B.C.

Capel, A.X. and G.E. Markoe. *Mistress of the House, Mistress of Heaven: Women in Ancient Egypt*. NY: Hudson Hills Press, 1996. A beautifully illustrated study of the roles of women in ancient Egypt.

Grimal, N. A *History of Ancient Egypt*. Oxford: Oxford University Press, 1994. Insights into the essence of Egyptian culture and its relations with outsiders throughout its history.

Trigger, B.C. *Ancient Egypt: A Social History*. Cambridge: Cambridge University Press, 1983. A study of early dynastic periods through the late period, ending with Egypt's conquest by Alexander; offers a nice look at social life.

Tyldesley, Joyce. *Daughters of Isis: Women of Ancient Egypt*. NY: Penguin, 1995. A highly readable, illustrated account of women in Egypt.

Wilson, John A. *The Culture of Ancient Egypt*. Chicago: University of Chicago Press, 1956. This remains the best single-volume account of Ancient Egypt that is both comprehensive and accessible.

MERCHANTS AND MONOTHEISTS: PEOPLES OF THE MEDITERRANEAN COAST, CA. 1300–500 B.C.

Grant, Michael. *Ancient Israel*. NY: Macmillan Publishing Company, Inc., 1984. A close analysis of the Hebrew Bible with findings of modern archaeology.

Smith, Mark K. *Early History of God: Yahweh* and *the Other Deities in Ancient Israel*. San Francisco: Harper, 1990. A controversial look at the convergence and differentiation of deities toward monotheism in Israel.

TERROR AND BENEVOLENCE: THE GROWTH OF EMPIRES, 1200–500 B.C.

Boardmen, John. *Assyrian and Babylonian Empires and Other States of the Near East from the Eighth to the Sixth Centuries*

B.C. NY: Cambridge University Press, 1991. A comprehensive look at the subject.

Cook, J.M. *The Persian Empire*. NY: Schocken Books, 1983. A discussion of the origins of the Medes and Persians surveying the sources for Persian history from 550 to 330 B.C.

🌐 GLOBAL CONNECTIONS

Adams, William Y. *Nubia: Corridor to Africa*. Princeton: Princeton University Press. 1977. Comprehensive history of Nubia from prehistory through the nineteenth century.

Keating, Rex. *Nubian Rescue*. NY: Hawthorn Books, Inc., 1975. Engaging account of the history of Nubia from prehistory through the Christian sixth century. The narrative is framed and shaped by the United Nations successful efforts to save many of the Nubian archaeological treasures that would be flooded by the building of the Aswan Dam in 1970.

Trigger. Bruce G. *Nubia under the Pharaohs*. Boulder, CO: Westview Press, 1976. Detailed archaeological account of the ancient Nubians from prehistory through the fall of the Egyptian New Kingdom.

Unfamiliar words? See our Glossary at the back for pronunciation and definitions.

See our Web Page at www.mhhe.com/sherman2updated for additional readings, map exercises, practice quizzes, and more activities.

For quiz questions that tie the book to the videos and additional primary sources, please go to the Primary Source Investigator CD.

QUIZ

Documents

DOCUMENT 1.1

An Egyptian Nobleman Writes His Obituary

Egyptian nobles proudly served their pharaohs as merchants, military men, and administrators. They also ordered records of their accomplishments inscribed in their tombs. This excerpted obituary reveals what one nobleman, Ameni (Amenemhet), counted as his greatest deeds in his years of service during Egypt's early Middle Kingdom (ca. 1950 B.C.).

■ **Investigate the Document**

Where did this nobleman travel in the course of his service? What kinds of accomplishments did he most want readers of this inscription to remember about him? What does this inscription reveal about the values of ancient Egypt?

First Expedition

I followed my lord when he sailed southward to overthrow his enemies among the four barbarians. I sailed southward, as the son of a count, wearer of the royal seal, and commander in chief of the troops of the Oryx nome, as a man represents his old father, according to [his] favor in the palace and his love in the court. I passed Kush, sailing southward, I advanced the boundary of the land, I brought all gifts; my praise, it reached heaven. Then his majesty returned in safety, having overthrown his enemies in Kush the vile. I returned, following him, with ready face. There was no loss among my soldiers.

Second Expedition

I sailed southward, to bring gold ore for the majesty of the King of Upper and Lower Egypt, Kheperkere (Sesostris I), living forever and ever. I sailed southward together with the hereditary prince, count, oldest son of the king, of his body, Ameni. I sailed southward, with a number, 400 of all the choicest of my troops, who returned in safety, having suffered no loss. I brought the gold exacted of me; I was praised for it in the palace, the king's-son praised god for me.

Source: James Henry Breasted, Ancient Records of Egypt, vol 1. (Chicago: University of Chicago Press, 1906), pp. 251–253.

Ameni's Able Administration

I was amiable, and greatly loved, a ruler beloved of his city. Now, I passed years as ruler in the Oryx nome. All the imposts of the king's house passed through my hand. The gang-overseers of the crown possessions of the shepherds of the Oryx nome gave to me 3,000 bulls in their yokes. I was praised on account of it in the palace each year of the loan-herds. I carried all their dues to the king's house; there were no arrears against me in any office of his. The entire Oryx nome labored for me.

Ameni's Impartiality and Benevolence

There was no citizen's daughter whom I misused, there was no widow whom I oppressed, there was no [peasant] whom I repulsed, there was no shepherd whom I repelled, there was no overseer of serf-laborers whose people I took for (unpaid) imposts, there was none wretched in my community, there was none hungry in my time. When years of famine came I plowed all the fields of the Oryx nome, as far as its southern and northern boundary, preserving its people alive and furnishing its food so that there was none hungry therein. I gave to the widow as (to) her who had a husband; I did not exalt the great above the small in all that I gave. Then came great Niles, possessors of grain and all things, (but) I did not collect the arrears of the field.

DOCUMENT 1.2

King Solomon Secures His Realm's Fortune

In the ancient world, leaders secured the fortunes of their kingdoms through marriages with neighboring peoples. This posed a problem for the new Hebrew kingdom, which was founded on the idea of a special relationship with one God. These two passages from the Book of Kings in the Bible tell of King Solomon's fame and relationship with women. The first passage describes the wealthy Queen of Sheba (modern Yemen) who brought great wealth to Solomon. (See the Global Connections essay in chapter 6.) The second passage describes Solomon's many marriages.

■ **Investigate the Document**

How does the story of the Queen of Sheba show the importance of long-distance trade to the new Hebrew state? What caused King Solomon's downfall? How does this account reflect the particular challenge most ancient Jews faced?

Now when the queen of Sheba heard of the fame of Solomon concerning the name of the Lord, she came to test him with hard questions. She came to Jerusalem with a very great retinue, with camels bearing spices, and very much gold, and precious stones; and when she came to Solomon, she told him all that was on her mind. And Solomon answered all her questions; there was nothing hidden from the king which he could not explain to her. And when the queen of Sheba had seen all the wisdom of Solomon, the house that he had built, the food of his table, the seating of his officials, and the attendance of his servants, their clothing, his cupbearers, and his burnt offerings which he offered at the house of the Lord, there was no more spirit in her.

And she said to the king, "The report was true which I heard in my own land of your affairs and of your wisdom, but I did not believe the reports until I came and my own eyes had seen it; and behold, the half was not told me; your wisdom and prosperity surpass the report which I heard . . . then she gave the king a hundred and twenty talents of gold, and a very great quantity of spices, and precious stones; never again came such an abundance of spices as these which the queen of Sheba gave to King Solomon (1 Kings 10:1–7, 10).

Now King Solomon loved many foreign women: the daughter of Pharaoh, and Moabite, Ammomite, Edomite, Sidonian, and Hittite women, from the nations concerning which the Lord had said to the people of Israel, "You shall not enter into marriage with them, neither shall they with you, for surely they will turn away your heart after their gods"; Solomon clung to these in love. He had seven hundred wives, princesses, and three hundred concubines; and his wives turned away his heart. For when Solomon was old his wives turned away his heart after other gods; and his heart was not wholly true to the Lord his God, as was the heart of David his father. For Solomon went after Ashtoreth the goddess of the

Source: Bible. 1 Kings 10:1–13, 1 Kings 11:1–13 (*New Oxford Annotated Bible with the Apocrypha* NY: Oxford Univ. Press, 1973).

Sidonians and after Milcom the abomination of the Ammonites. So Solomon did what was evil in the sight of the Lord, and did not wholly follow the Lord as David his father had done. Then Solomon built a high place for Chemosh the abomination of Moab, and for Molech the abomination of the Ammonites, on the mountain east of Jerusalem. And so he did for all his foreign wives, who burned incense and sacrificed to their gods. And the Lord was angry with Solomon . . . (1 Kings 11:1–9).

DOCUMENT 1.3
The Assyrians Wage War and Develop Scholarship

Assyrian kings carefully cultivated their reputation for ruthless warfare as the first reading below reveals through details about the Assyrians' conquest of Judah in 701 B.C. At the same time, Assyrian scholars preserved old texts and developed their own scholarship. The second reading lists some selected proverbs of Ahikar the Wise. Ahikar reputedly wrote those proverbs for his nephew, Nadan, to prepare him to take his place at court. Together these two sources show the complex range of Assyrian culture.

■ **Investigate the Document**

What techniques did the Assyrians use for siege warfare? What did they take as tribute for their victories? Do you approve of the advice in the proverbs? Why or why not?

From The Sennacherib Prism

In my third campaign I marched against Hatti, Luli, king of Sidon, whom the terror-inspiring glamor of my lordship had overwhelmed, fled far overseas and perished. . . . As to Hezekiah, the Jew, he did not submit to my yoke. I laid siege to his strong cities, walled forts, and countless small villages, and conquered them by means of well-stamped earth-ramps and battering-rams brought near the walls with an attack by foot soldiers, using mines, breeches as well as trenches. I drove out 200,150 people, young and old, male and female, horses, mules, donkeys, camels, big and small cattle beyond counting, and considered them slaves. Himself I made a prisoner in Jerusalem, his royal residence, like a bird in a cage. I surrounded him with earthwork in order to molest those who were his city's gate. Thus I reduced his country, but I still increased the tribute and the presents to me as overlord which I imposed upon him beyond the former tribute, to be delivered annually. Hezekiah himself, did send me, later, to Nineveh, my lordly city, together with 30 talents of fold, 800 talents of silver, precious stones, antimony, large cuts of red stone, couches inlaid with ivory, nimeduchairs inlaid with ivory, elephant-hides, ebony-wood, boxwood and all kinds of valuable treasures, his own daughters and concubines.

Selected Proverbs of Ahikar The Wise

1. Hear, O my son Nadan, and come to the understanding of me, and be mindful of my words, as the words of God.

5. My son, commit not adultery with the wife of thy neighbor; lest others should commit adultery with thy wife.

6. My son, be not in a hurry, like the almond tree whose blossom is the first to appear, but whose fruit is the last to be eaten; but be equal and sensible, like the mulberry tree whose blossom is the last to appear, but whose fruit is the first to be eaten.

Source: "The Sennachrib Prism: in Ancient History Sourcebook, Halsall@murray.fordham.edu; "Selected Proverbs of Ahikar the Wise," http:pwl.netcom.com~aldewood_ahikar.htm.

7. My son, it is better to remove stones with a wise man than to drink wine with a fool.

8. My son, with a wise man thou wilt not be depraved, and with a depraved man thou wilt not become wise.

9. My son, the rich man eats a snake, and they say, he ate it for medicine. And the poor man eats it, and they say, for his hunger he ate it.

10. My son, if thine enemy meet thee with evil, meet thou him with wisdom.

11. My son, walk not in the way unarmed; because thou knowest not when thy enemy shall come upon thee.

12. My son, let thy words be true, in order that thy lord may say to thee, 'Draw near me,' and thou shalt live.

14. My son, smite with stones the dog that has left his own master and followed after thee.

18. My son, I have carried salt and removed lead; and I have not seen anything heavier than that a man should pay back a debt which he did not borrow.

19. My son, better is he that is blind of eye than he that is blind of heart; for the blind of eye straightway learneth the road and walketh in it: but the blind of heart leaveth the right way and goeth into the desert.

Bronze Warrior, ca. 450 B.C.

This bronze statue of a Greek warrior illustrates the qualities of heroic strength, beauty, and physical perfection that the ancient Greeks so valued. Artists strove to portray ideal types of humans, and their surviving works reveal the qualities they treasured. This figure's confident stance and strength symbolize Greek civilization at its height.

CHAPTER 2

The Contest for Excellence

Greece, 2000–338 B.C.

STUDY • Minoans and Myceneans • Greek values and religion • Life in the city-states • Imperial Athens • Peloponnesian War and the rise of philosophy. NOTICE how the value of individualism shaped ancient Greek history.

"It is the greatest good every day to discuss virtue . . . for life without enquiry is not worth living for a man. . . ." The Greek philosopher Socrates reputedly spoke these words and they have become a famous articulation of the value of the spirit of inquiry. But the society that produced Socrates was also one that spawned an often-violent competition among men and among cities. Violence even swept up Socrates' voice of rationalism, for his memorable words were spoken at his trial as his neighbors accused him of undermining their way of life. Yet the philosopher/stonemason claimed he would rather die than give up challenging his neighbors to think about everything from truth and beauty to life and death. Because he refused to be silent, he was condemned to die. Fortunately his call for rational inquiry did not die with him, but flourished in the contentious city-states of Greece, ultimately to become a fundamental characteristic of Western civilization.

The Greeks grappled with other challenges in addition to new philosophical approaches. Two brilliant Aegean civilizations, the Minoans and the Mycenaeans, rose and fell. In city-states such as Athens and Sparta, Greek citizens battled powerful neighbors such as the Persians, fought over spheres of influence, and invented unprecedented forms of participatory government. The individualistic Greeks also created magnificent works of art that set the standard of beauty for millennia and literature that inspires readers even in modern times. Ancient Greeks believed that in a heroic search for excellence, a man could accomplish anything. In some cases, they were almost right. However, in their quest for excellence—whether in war or peace—they also planted the seeds of their own downfall by valuing competition over cooperation.

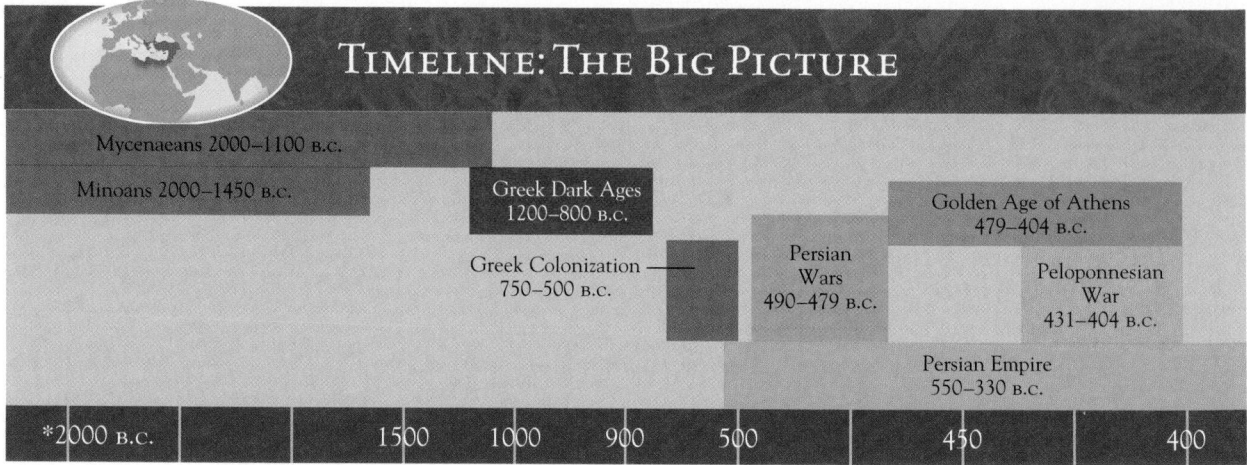

Mycenaeans 2000–1100 B.C.

Minoans 2000–1450 B.C.

Greek Dark Ages
1200–800 B.C.

Greek Colonization
750–500 B.C.

Golden Age of Athens
479–404 B.C.

Persian
Wars
490–479 B.C.

Peloponnesian
War
431–404 B.C.

Persian Empire
550–330 B.C.

*2000 B.C.   1500   1000   900   500   450   400

*For clarity, the dates in this line are not drawn to scale.

The Rise and Fall of Ancient Heroes, 2000–800 B.C.

Ancient Greek men and boys gathered in the household hall in the evenings to enjoy songs of heroic deeds recited by skilled performers. (Literary texts also show that women and girls listened from the seclusion of their own rooms.) For centuries, poets recited accounts that later were gathered together to form the epic poem the *Iliad*. This work, by the eighth-century poet Homer, told of 50 days in the 10-year war between the Greeks and the Trojans, a people living on the coast of Asia Minor. The *Iliad* was also a story of the Greek mythic hero Achilles, whose prowess in battle overcame great odds. Despite his successes, Achilles was subject to outbursts of monumental anger—a trait that, as Homer wrote, "brought the Greeks so much suffering." The leader of the Greeks, King Agamemnon, provoked a quarrel with Achilles. When exerting his right to take the booty seized in war, he took Briseis, a woman who first had been allotted to Achilles. In protest, the wrathful warrior sat in his tent and refused to fight while many of his compatriots died under the Trojan onslaught. As one Greek leader in the story said, "Now look at Achilles. He is a brave man, yet who but he will profit by that bravery?"

Modern historians understandably have questioned the accuracy of certain details in Homer's epics, but the ancient Greeks saw these poems differently. For centuries, people believed that the epics portrayed Achilles' actions accurately. Indeed, many aspiring heroes strove to emulate the mythical soldier whose mere presence or absence on the battlefield could change the course of the war. By reading or listening to these accounts of a lost age, young men learned about heroism and about the destructiveness of human weakness. The tension between heroic aspirations and dangerous individual pride became a prominent theme throughout the history of the ancient Greeks as they built their civilization on a rocky peninsula in the Aegean Sea.

THE GREEK PENINSULA

The Greek peninsula is dominated by striking mountain ranges. Lacking the plains and large rivers that would have provided natural communication links, the ancient Greek civilization consisted of separate communities scattered throughout the peninsula and the numerous Aegean islands. The mountain ranges protected the Greeks from large-scale invasions, but the rocky soil made agriculture difficult. The Greeks had to grow their wheat and barley on the scarce lowland, and in time they came to depend on imports for the grain they needed. The Greek historian Herodotus summed up the difficulties of agriculture when he wrote "Greece has always poverty as her companion." As Map 2.1 indicates, most places in Greece enjoyed a close proximity to the sea, which allowed overseas trade to become an essential part of ancient Greek society. This orientation toward the

THINKING ABOUT GEOGRAPHY

MAP 2.1 *The World of the Greeks*

This map shows the Greek peninsula with the surrounding seas. ■ **Consider** how this landscape would influence localism and the importance of sea trade. ■ **Notice** the location of Asia Minor. **How** would travelers best proceed from Asia Minor to the Greek mainland? ■ **Notice** the location of the Cyclades, the narrow Hellespont, and the strategic location of Troy, all of which shaped the future of Greek history. ■ **Locate** Athens and Sparta. **Notice** how their locations influenced their domination of sea and land, respectively.

sea stimulated the many cultural contacts that marked the development of Western civilization (as discussed in Chapter 1). In fact, the earliest advanced civilization that arose in this region originated on an island that lay at the heart of the eastern Mediterranean.

THE MINOANS, 2000–1450 B.C.

By 2000 B.C. the islanders living on Crete boasted the wealthiest, most advanced civilization in the Mediterranean. They were not Greek—nor Indo-European—but were probably a Semitic people related to those living in the eastern and southern Mediterranean. At the height of its economic and political power, Crete consisted of a number of principalities, each dominated by a great palace. But the king of Knossos (see Map 2.1) ruled over them all. Early Greek historians identify the ruler of Crete as King Minos, and thus modern excavators named "Minoan" society after this legendary king. Minoan prosperity permitted the growth of a relatively large, peaceful population. During the golden age of this culture, the population of Crete reached an impressive 250,000, with 40,000 living in Knossos alone.

By trading with the peoples of the Fertile Crescent, the Minoans learned much of the best of early *Economic power* Western civilization. They learned to make bronze from the Sumerians, and their foundries produced a steady stream of valuable bronze tools and weapons. Minoan ships were the best-made in the region. With their heavy construction and high front prows, these vessels cut effortlessly through rough seas and proved reliable in conditions that the islanders' shore-hugging contemporaries deemed impossible.

Centers of economic as well as political power, Minoan palaces comprised vast mazes of storerooms, workrooms, and living quarters. These structures were markedly different from the huge buildings in Sumeria and Egypt, where architects of pyramids and ziggurats valued symmetry. Minoan architects preferred to build palace rooms of different sizes that wandered without any apparent design. The Greeks later called these palaces labyrinths. Kings controlling the trade through which wealth poured into Crete stashed goods away in the huge palace storerooms. One room in the palace at Knossos contained clay jars for olive oil that totaled a remarkable capacity of 60,000 gallons.

Like many maritime civilizations, the Minoans learned much from their encounters with other peoples. For example, their artwork reveals the influence of Egyptian colors and styles. The Minoans also learned writing from the Sumerians, and their script (called "Linear A") was also a pictographic script written on clay tablets. As in Sumer, archaeologists have excavated clay tablets in Crete that seem to have been used for accounting and for tracking the movement of merchandise. So far, the symbols of Linear A have not been translated, so to learn about Minoan society, we must rely on archaeological remains, including their riveting artwork.

The Minoans decorated their palaces with magnificent frescoes, created by mixing paint with plaster and crafting the image as part of the *Religious ritual* wall. These paintings portrayed many of the everyday objects and activities that Minoans held dear, including religious rituals. Many statuettes from Crete showing goddesses holding snakes suggest that the predominant Minoan deity was a fertility goddess. The fresco in Figure 2.1 shows a ritual in which men and women performed gymnastic activities with a wild bull. In this painting, one woman grabs the bull's horns to prepare to vault over it, while a man is already at the apex of his leap. Another woman waits to guide the jumper's descent. Some scholars suggest that this dangerous event may have been a religious ritual that culminated with the sacrifice of the bull and an opulent banquet at which men and women feasted on the meat and celebrated the goddess's generosity in bringing abundance to the society.

In the centuries after the Minoans, the ancient Greeks often told their history in the form of myths that recounted heroic acts from the *Minoan destruction* Greek past. Some of these myths recalled the eventual destruction of Minoan society. The Greeks remembered a time when Greece owed tribute to Crete, including young people to be sacrificed to the Minotaur—a creature that was half human and half bull. The king of Knossos may have worn the head of a bull on ceremonial occasions, and perhaps it was this tradition that gave rise to the legend of the Minotaur. One mythical Greek hero, Theseus, joined the sacrificial group, killed the Minotaur, and escaped the palace labyrinth by following a thread he had unraveled as he entered. This myth may hold a core of truth, for archaeological evidence

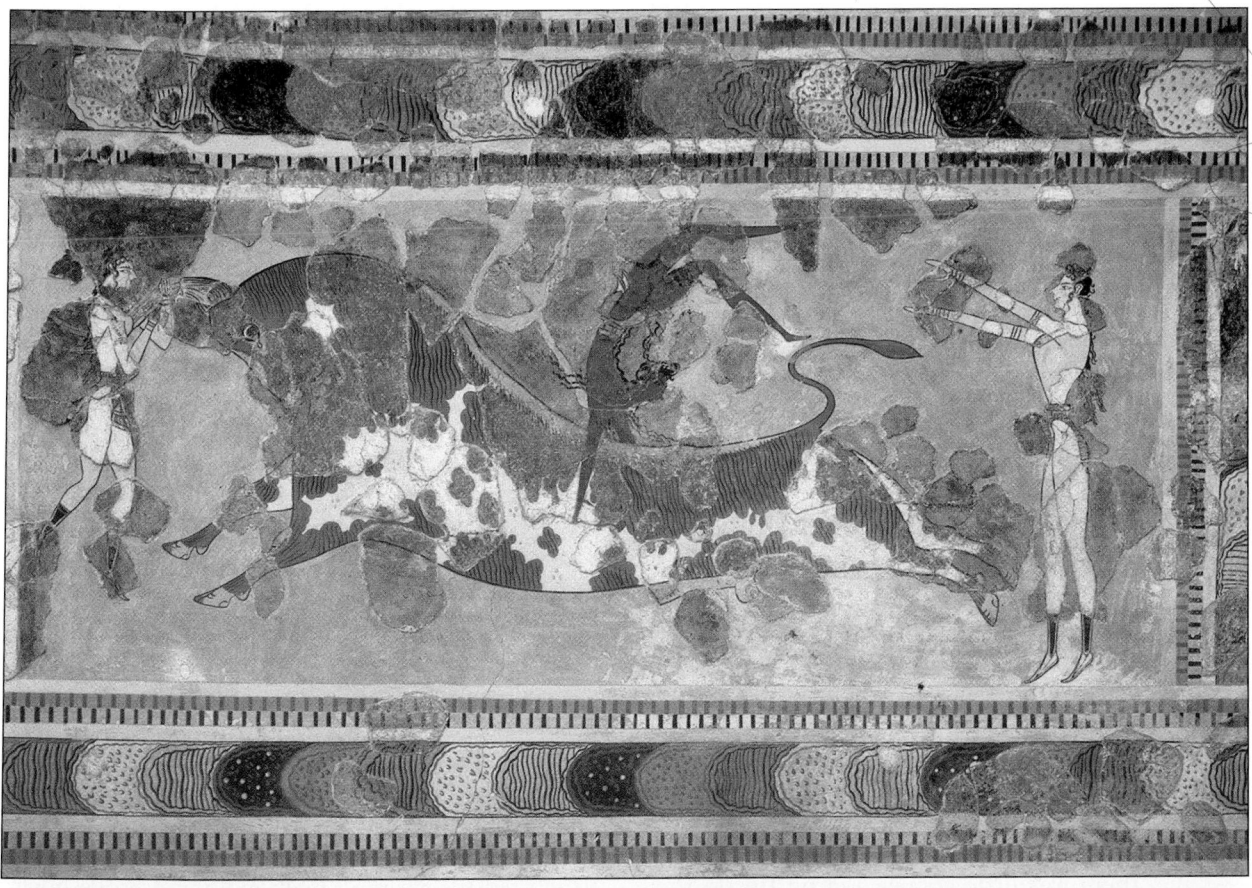

FIGURE 2.1
Minoan man and women leaping over a bull, ca. 1500 b.c.

shows that Minoan society was toppled by invaders from across the sea. The great Minoan palaces apparently were burned by invaders who destroyed the unfortified cities. A man named Theseus may not have killed a minotaur, but it seems that Greeks killed the king of Crete.

Historians have looked further for the cause of the Minoans' downfall. Some suggest that a natural disaster contributed to their decline. In about 1450 B.C., a volcanic explosion on the nearby island of Thera caused a tidal wave that may have destroyed the Minoans' protective fleet. However, this explanation is uncertain because other scholars question the date of the eruption, placing it two centuries earlier than the burning of Crete. Whatever the cause, Minoan society was overwhelmed and transformed by invaders from the Greek mainland, and the center of Aegean civilization passed to the earliest Greeks, whom we call the Mycenaeans.

MYCENAEAN CIVILIZATION: THE FIRST GREEKS, 2000–1100 B.C.

Sometime after 2000 B.C., Indo-European Greek-speaking people settled on the mountainous Greek peninsula. By 1600 B.C. they were increasingly influenced by the Minoans, and developed a wealthy, hierarchic society centered in the city of Mycenae (see Map 2.1). Excavations of their shaft graves have yielded golden crowns and masks and, like other Indo-European burials, many weapons, perhaps confirming ancient writers' characterizations of these people as the "war-mad Greeks." Yet, these early Greeks were also traders, and much of their wealth came from the growing commerce in the Aegean. As the Mycenaeans traded with wealthy Minoans, they learned much from them, evidenced by the strong Minoan influences in Mycenaean artwork. Mycenaean Greeks even learned to write from the Minoans, and their script is called "Linear B" for its similarity to Minoan characters. Because Linear B recorded an early form of the spoken Greek language, linguists have been able to translate Mycenaean tablets.

After Minoan society was destroyed in about 1450 B.C., the Mycenaeans took over as the commercial masters of the Mediterranean. As their wealth increased, so did the complexity of their governing system, which had a hierarchy of kings, nobles, and slaves. Powerful kings built palaces of stones so large that later Greeks thought they must have been constructed by giants. Unlike Minoan palaces, these structures were walled, indicating to archaeologists that there was a great deal of warfare to necessitate defensive fortifications. This conclusion is reinforced by written sources claiming that the kings surrounded themselves with soldiers.

Mycenaean states were not self-sufficient. Like the civilizations of the ancient Middle East, they de-

Trade pended on trade for many essentials. For example, there was little copper and no tin on the peninsula, so they had to trade for ore to make bronze weapons and tools. The vast expanse of Mycenaean trade is clear. Mycenaean pottery has been found on the coast of Italy, and after the destruction of Crete, Mycenaean pottery replaced Minoan pottery in Egypt, Syria, Palestine, and Cyprus. These pottery remnants testify to the beginnings of the trade that linked the fortunes of the ancient Greeks intimately with those of their neighbors.

In about 1200 B.C., violence and a wide-ranging movement of peoples disrupted the eastern Mediter-

Violence and disruption ranean. A scarcity of sources does not allow historians to detail the exact causes of the upheaval, but we can see the effects on kingdoms and individuals. The Egyptian Empire was besieged and lost territory as Syria and cities all along the coast confronted invaders. A letter from the king of the island of Cyprus urged the king of a city in Syria to hold firm against invaders: "You have written to me: enemy ships have been seen at sea. . . . Where are your troops and chariots? . . . Await the enemy steadfastly." Archaeological evidence shows

towns sacked and burned throughout the region during these times of trouble. The important trade in copper from Cyprus was interrupted, and as we saw in Chapter 1, this violent era stimulated the dawning of the Iron Age.

The Mycenaeans were surely involved in these invasions that disrupted the ancient civilizations. According to later Greek myths, part of this violence included the Mycenaean invasion of Troy (see Map 2.1) in about 1250 B.C. The Trojan War became the basis of Homer's influential epics. Greek mythology attributes the conflict to a rivalry over a beautiful Greek woman, Helen, who was seduced by the Trojan prince, Paris. Less-romantic historians believe the war stemmed primarily from the intensifying economic competition and growing violence in the eastern Mediterranean. Either way, the fighting was relentless and devastating—Homer claimed that the Greeks besieged Troy for 10 years. At the end of this ordeal, Troy was destroyed (demonstrated by evidence from archaeological excavations).

Sometime after 1200 B.C., Mycenaean civilization itself dissolved. Later Greeks attributed this downfall to the Trojan War, which supposedly kept the Mycenaean leaders and soldiers away from home for so long. Archaeological evidence, however, shows that during and shortly after the Trojan War, the highly structured life on the Greek mainland broke down. Amid crop failures due to drought and internal instability, more Greek invaders from the north (later called Dorian Greeks) moved into the peninsula, especially the southern part, the Peloponnese. Population dropped dramatically. Excavations in one region reveal 13 villages during the Mycenaean period; by 1100 B.C. only three remained. We do not know exactly what happened, but the flourishing Bronze Age Mycenaean society came to such a complete end that even the valuable art of writing was lost. All the great Mycenaean centers, except Athens, were destroyed. Life on the Greek mainland now consisted of a smattering of small villages, where people survived largely through subsistence farming.

From "Dark Ages" to Colonies

The period after the fall of Mycenae is called the "Dark Ages" (which extend from about 1100 B.C. to about 800 B.C.), because with the loss of writing, we have no texts that illuminate life during this time. For three centuries, life went on in the small villages,

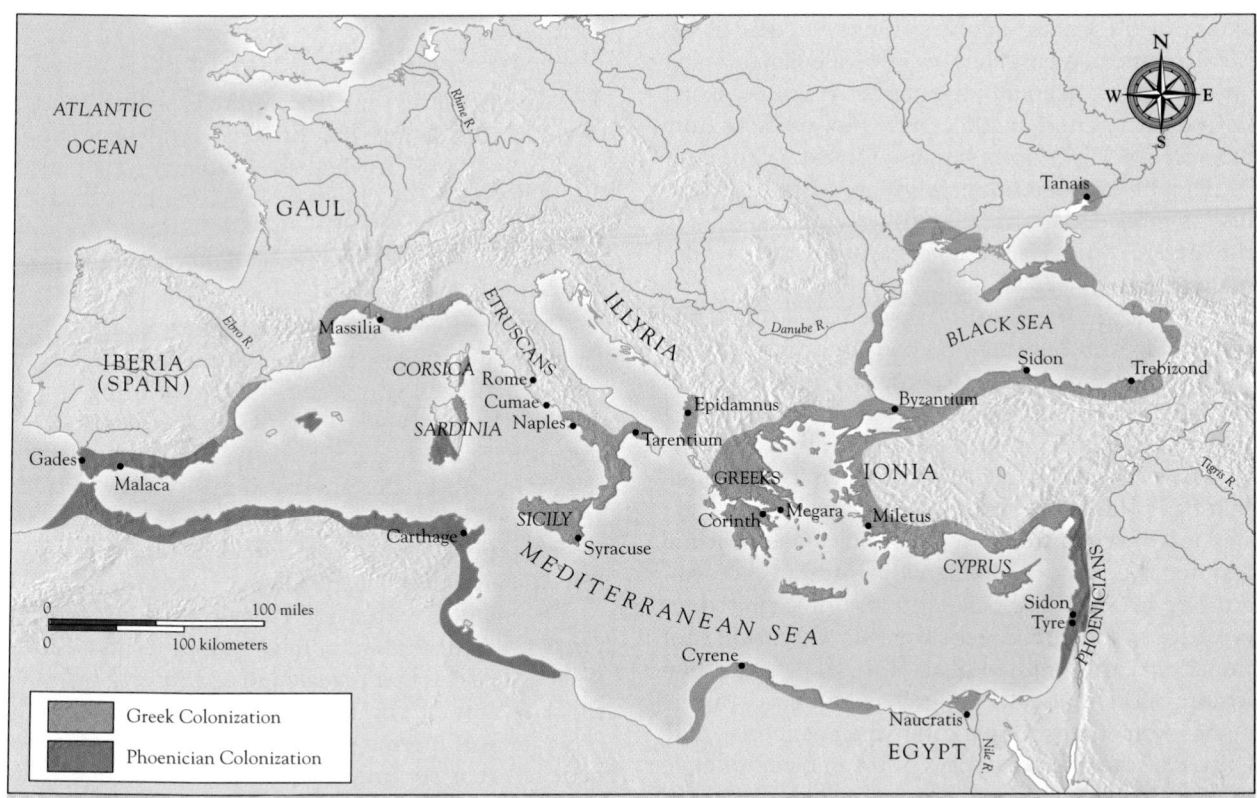

THINKING ABOUT GEOGRAPHY

MAP 2.2   *The Greek Colonies in About 500 B.C.*

This map shows the locations of the Greek and Phoenician colonies. ❧ **Notice** the extent of Greek and Phoenician colonies. **Consider** how the locations would facilitate the growth of maritime trade in the Mediterranean. **What** spheres of influence are implied by the locations of their respective colonies? ❧ **Consider** in what regions Greeks would most likely come in conflict with other powers.

and people told tales that preserved their values. At the end of the Dark Ages, in about 800 B.C., Homer recorded some of these oral tales. The details he included offer glimpses into life during the previous three centuries. For example, Homer's descriptions of the cremation of the dead, which had not been practiced in Mycenaean civilization, suggest that cremation was developed after the fall of the early Greeks. As tantalizing as these bits of literary evidence are, most of our information for this period nevertheless must come from archaeology.

Excavations show that during these years, bronze gave way to iron as the primary metal used in weapons and tools. Archaeological findings also reveal that near the end of the Dark Ages trade of

wine, olive oil, and other goods began to flourish again all over the Mediterranean. By tracing the movement of Greek goods through the remnants of pottery and other artifacts excavated around the Mediterranean, archaeologists have discovered that Greek culture spread through the many colonies Greeks established in the region. At first, Greeks fled the disasters on the peninsula by settling on the numerous islands of the Aegean and the coast of Asia Minor (called Ionia). Later, colonists may have left the peninsula to escape overpopulation and seek new land and prosperity. Some aristocrats in Greek cities used the founding of new colonies as a way to diffuse social unrest by sending the dissatisfied elsewhere. Map 2.2 shows the

Founding colonies

extent of the Greek colonies along the coast of the Mediterranean Sea. They were rivaled in number only by the Phoenicians, the master colonists we met in Chapter 1. Greek colonies were very different from modern colonial efforts because Greeks in the new settlements arranged themselves in cities that were just as independent as the mother city. The ties to the original cities were ones of emotion, not of colonial control.

For a time, Greeks in the new colonies remained independent from the other civilizations around them—the neighboring Phoenicians and the Babylonian and Persian Empires. However, while trading with their neighbors, the Greeks participated in the growth of Western civilization by adopting much that had gone before. For example, they derived their systems of weight from Babylonia and Phoenicia and adopted the practice of making coins from the Lydians (see Chapter 1). Societies transform acquired innovations, and the Greeks were no exception. For their coins, they minted silver (instead of the Lydian white gold) and usually placed secular images on the coins—sometimes illustrating their exports, like grapes or fish, and sometimes using emblems of civic pride. However, when describing Greek use of others' inventions, the Greek philosopher Plato (428–348 B.C.) characteristically gave the Greeks undue praise, boasting, "Whatever the Greeks have acquired from foreigners, they have in the end turned into something finer."

Emerging from the Dark: Heroic Beliefs and Values

Through their trade with the Phoenicians, the Greeks acquired and adapted the Phoenician alphabet, and writing reemerged among the Greeks around 800 B.C. Once more Greek society was illuminated for historians. The Greeks used writing not only for trade and contractual agreements—the Phoenician alphabet was simpler than other scripts, so it lent itself to a wider use. Talented Greeks used writing to record and transmit powerful and inspiring poetry that had been preserved for centuries only through human memory, and the ideas of the ancient Greeks once more came to light; the "Dark Ages" were over.

HEROIC VALUES PRESERVED

The earliest of this Greek literature preserved a series of values that define what historians call a heroic society, in which individuals seek fame through great deeds and advocate values such as honor, reputation, and prowess.

As we saw in the opening account of Achilles, the most influential Greek poet was Homer, who historians believe lived in the early eighth century B.C. Homer's two greatest epics were the *Iliad*, the tale of Achilles' heroic wrath, and the *Odyssey*, the story of the Greek warrior Odysseus's 10-year travels to return home from Troy. The *Iliad* became a seminal text for later ancient Greeks—schoolchildren and adults never tired of this tale of heroic deeds that captured details from Homer's times and preserved many Mycenaean values.

Homer

The highest virtue for Homer (and subsequent Greeks) was *arete*—manliness, courage, and excellence. *Arete* was best revealed in a "contest," whether sporting, warfare, or activities extending into many other areas of life and recreation. The ancient Greeks believed that striving for individual supremacy enhanced one's family honor, and the hero's name would live in poetic memory. Such beliefs and values helped fuel the greatness of ancient Greece. However, this striving for excellence—for heroism—was not always beneficial. At times it created a self-centered competitiveness that caused much suffering—just as Achilles' heroic-scale rage was said to have caused his companions' deaths. Harboring such intense competitive spirit, Greeks also held a deep disregard for all cultures other than their own (and they even had disdain for neighboring Greeks from different cities). Greeks distinguished themselves from "barbarians" who "spoke other languages" and felt it demeaned them to work alongside such foreigners. Individuals adhering to "heroic" values brought a combination of good and bad results, and the best of the Greeks from Homer on recognized this ambiguity.

Hesiod, an early Greek poet who wrote around 750 B.C., left almost as important a mark as Homer. His *Works and Days* describes farm life, wisdom, and values near the end of the Greek Dark Ages. Like social critics who had come before him, Hesiod complained of the powerful who cheat and exploit the poor and strive only for riches. Deploring the selfish "age of iron" in which he lived, Hesiod lamented the

Hesiod

loss of what he believed were more virtuous heroic ages of "gold" and "bronze." He was no doubt wrong in assuming that the leaders of the Mycenaean age were less corrupt than those in his time, but his vision reveals the desire to imagine better times.

Hesiod lived in poverty—cheated out of his inheritance by a greedy brother and corrupt officials—yet he still articulated the ideals of heroic individualism. However, he clearly saw that the pursuit of excellence was a two-sided coin. At the end of *Works and Days,* he wrote of two kinds of "strife." One was good—a healthy spirit of competitiveness that Hesiod believed made people work and achieve their best. The other kind of strife, however, was bad, and led to some people exploiting others, as happened in Hesiod's own life. This tension within heroic values marked Greek life, values, and even their gods and goddesses.

THE FAMILY OF THE GODS

The ancient Greek historian Herodotus (482–425 B.C.) claimed that Homer and Hesiod powerfully shaped subsequent Greek religious beliefs. As Herodotus observed, these early poets "gave the gods their epithets, divided out offices and functions among them and described their appearance." The poems of Homer's and Hesiod's day were indeed populated by an extended family of gods and goddesses, loosely ruled by Zeus and his wife, Hera. This family included 10 other main deities, among them Aphrodite, goddess of love; Athena, goddess of wisdom and war; Poseidon, god of the sea; Apollo, god of music, divination, and healing; and Demeter, goddess of fertility. These gods lived on Mount Olympus and periodically interfered in human affairs.

The Greek gods and goddesses resembled humans so much that one Greek critic from the sixth century B.C. observed that "Homer and Hesiod ascribed to the gods everything that among men is a shame and disgrace: theft, adultery, and deceiving one another." It is true that the gods shared human flaws, but they also shared admirable human qualities. Like the Greeks themselves, they loved beauty, banquets, processions, athletic competitions, music, and theater. The Greeks therefore infused all these activities with a feeling of worship. Religious rituals, for example, had an intensely festive air, and ancient Greek writings characterize religious activities as "sacrificing and having a good time."

As with the ancient religions of the Middle East, proper worship for the Greeks involved sacrificing a portion of human production to the gods. In contrast to the Mesopotamians, Greeks sacrificed things of relatively little value—the fat-wrapped thigh bones or internal organs of sacrificial animals—while keeping the best parts for themselves. Families, magistrates, and citizen assemblies were primarily responsible for observing proper respect for the gods. As a result, unlike in Egypt and Mesopotamia, powerful religious institutions never developed in ancient Greek society. Each temple had a priest or priestess, but these were usually part-time activities requiring little training.

The real religious professionals were oracles—people who interpreted divine will. Among these, the Delphic oracle, a woman who reputedly could *Oracles* enter into a trance and receive cryptic messages from Apollo, was the most famous. Oracle messages were received in the form of ambiguous riddles and had to be interpreted by humans, so a central role for human agency remained in Greek religion. Perhaps the most famous inquiry at Delphi was made by King Croesus of Lydia in about 546 B.C. Croesus was worried about the Persian king Cyrus, who was threatening his kingdom (see Chapter 1), and asked the oracle whether he should wage war against Persia. The priests of Delphi returned with the answer: If Croesus were to make war on the Persians, he would destroy a mighty empire. Croesus was elated, but he had misinterpreted the oracle: The mighty empire that fell was that of Croesus as Cyrus defeated the Lydians. Messages from oracles needed to be interpreted very carefully, indeed.

Just as they envisioned their gods with all the qualities and foibles of humans, the Greeks embraced all facets of human behavior, even the irrational. To Homer's list of *Worship of Dionysus* Olympians, subsequent Greeks added the worship of Dionysus, the god of wine and fertility. Men worshiped this god during lavish banquets, but the cult had special appeal to women. During worship of Dionysus, women temporarily escaped their domestic confinement and engaged in drinking, ecstatic dancing, and sometimes sexual license as part of the ritual. On the painted plate shown in Figure 2.2, women dance around the statue of the god. The woman to the left of Dionysus plays a flute, while the one to his right dances with wild abandon. At the far right, another woman carries a staff covered with ivy, the distinctive symbol for this particular ritual. In some cities, women's worship of Dionysus proved even more frenzied than this scene shows. Women followed the "handsome god" to the mountains, where they danced, drank, and became so swept up by the moment that they ripped apart small animals and ate the raw flesh.

Greek religious thought marked a significant departure from the forms of worship of the ancient Middle East. In Greece, the gods *Impact of religious ideas* were so much like humans that worshiping them encouraged people to aspire to the greatest in human accomplishments and to acknowledge the worst in human frailties. It was this view, for instance, that caused them to count Achilles as a flawed, yet powerful, hero. The Greeks did add a cautionary warning in their praise of humanity. If people exhibited overweening pride or arrogance (called "hubris"), the gods would punish them. Yet, they still had a great deal of room to celebrate human accomplishments. As Greek thinkers placed humans rather than gods at the center of their understanding of the world, and as they studied reality from a human perspective, they began to transform the Mesopotamian view that had contributed so much to Western civilization. Humans were no longer impotent before a chaotic world ruled by arbitrary deities; instead, they were encouraged to understand and master their world.

FIGURE 2.2
Women dancing in worship of Dionysus, ca. 490 b.c.

STUDYING THE MATERIAL WORLD

The Greeks had great confidence in their ability to learn everything about the world. They rejected many earlier explanations and began an objective, almost scientific, approach to comprehending nature. This special search for knowledge was termed philosophy ("love of wisdom") and would become the Greeks' most important intellectual invention. The earliest known scholar of this kind was Thales of Miletus (624?–548? B.C.). The location of Miletus on the Ionian coast (see Map 2.2 on page 51) shows how Greek culture and its tremendous influence had moved beyond the Greek mainland itself.

Thales reputedly studied astronomy and geometry in Egypt and brought this knowledge to practical use by measuring pyramids, based on *Thales and Democritus* the length of their shadows, and predicting a solar eclipse. Departing from most of his Egyptian and Mesopotamian predecessors, Thales believed in an orderly cosmos that was accessible to human reason. This formed the heart of much subsequent Greek (and Western) inquiry. He sought a single primal element that would explain a cosmic unity, and Thales believed that element was water. Although Thales' conclusion was wrong, his assumption of an orderly universe accessible to human inquiry was pivotal to the future of Western thought.

Thales was followed by others who continued the rational approach to the natural world. Democritus (460?–370? B.C.), for example, posited an infinite universe of tiny atoms with spaces between them. Although his ideas were not widely supported in ancient Greece, they were proven by early-twentieth-century physicists.

Pythagoras (582?–507 B.C.) made even greater discoveries in the fields of mathematics and astronomy. He believed that order in the universe was based on *Pythagoras* numbers (not water), and that mathematics was the key to understanding reality. Pythagoras is credited with being the first to suggest that the number 13 is unlucky, but his mathematics extended far beyond such attempts to quantify fortune. He developed the Pythagorean Theorem, the geometrical statement that the square of the hypotenuse of a right triangle is equal to the sum of the squares of the

FIGURE 2.3
Tunnel of Eupalinus. 6th century B.C.

3,000-foot-long tunnel through a mountain in order to bring water from a spring into a city. To accomplish this feat, he used only hand tools, and he had to work in the *Practical applications* dark because he lacked a light source. Most extraordinary, he dug from both sides of the mountain—and the two parts of the tunnel met in the middle with only a slight adjustment needed. Figure 2.3 shows a modern photograph of this tunnel that gives an idea of how impressive this engineering feat was. Pythagoras was on Eupalinus's island of Samos at about the time the tunnel was dug, so some scholars speculate that the mathematician helped in the process. Others have suggested that Eupalinus used a system of mirrors to line up the tunnel and illuminate the interior as he excavated. However he managed this feat, he counts among the most accomplished Greeks who applied reason to practical matters.

While modern scholars admire these early Greek thinkers, many contemporaries looked with suspicion on those who studied the world while *Fears of "impiety"* seemingly ignoring the gods. Even though the Greeks worshiped humanlike gods and goddesses, they still revered them, and accusations of impiety always hovered on the borders of scientific inquiry. In 432 B.C. the democratic assembly of Athens made it a crime to "deny the gods, or disseminate teachings about the things that take place in the heavens." This law was precipitated by the teachings of Anaxagoras (500?–428? B.C.), who claimed that the sun was a white-hot stone instead of a god. Even in the field of rational inquiry, in which the Greeks made such impressive strides, the ambiguities that marked this dynamic society are evident. The same culture that produced impressive thinkers like Anaxagoras and Socrates (whom we met at the beginning of this chapter) sometimes recoiled from the results of their studies. Nevertheless, Greek intellectual accomplishments formed one of their central contributions to Western civilization.

other two sides. He went on to explore additional theories of proportion that have contributed to much modern mathematics. Pythagoras was also among the first to claim that the earth and other heavenly bodies were spherical and that they rotated on their axes. The mathematician was so respected that his followers later developed a religious cult in his name.

These philosophers, in a dramatic way, changed the direction of thinking about the world. They rejected the mythopoeic approach to understanding the world and made the first attempts to understand and explain the world in a scientific and philosophical way. Because they had little experimental equipment and no prior knowledge to draw upon, their ideas were not necessarily accurate by our standards, but we would not be who we are without them.

Men like Thales, Democritus, and Pythagoras operated on an abstract level of almost pure science. Yet the Greeks also practiced an applied technology, with results that continue to astound us. The sixth-century B.C. engineer Eupalinus, for example, constructed a

Life in the Greek Poleis, 700–489 B.C.

As we saw in Chapter 1, ancient societies had taken for granted a natural order of society that placed kings and priests in charge, and the Mycenaean Greeks had shared this view. With the brisk trade that comes so naturally to sea peoples, however, a new prosperity based on commercial expansion emerged, creating an urban middle class of merchants and artisans who owed no loyalty to aristocratic landowners.

By 700 B.C. changes in warfare brought about in part by the growth of Greek trade also made aristo-

Hoplite armies cratic warriors less important. First, the growing commercial classes became wealthier, and at the same time the increased trade brought down the price of metals. Now more men could afford to arm themselves and go to war. New armies of infantrymen (called *hoplites*) dominated the art of making war. Common citizens armed with swords, shields, and long thrusting spears formed a "phalanx"—a tight formation about eight men deep and as wide as the number of troops available. As long as these soldiers stayed tightly pressed together, they were virtually impenetrable. Elite warriors once could rely on their own heroism and on their monopoly of horses and cavalry to ensure victory on the battlefield. Now that a hoplite phalanx could withstand cavalry charges, the aristocracy no longer maintained a privileged position; they needed the support of citizen armies. This dependence further weakened aristocratic rule.

THE INVENTION OF POLITICS

Between 650 and 550 B.C., civil war broke out in many cities as the lower classes rose to overthrow the

Tyrants aristocracy. This violence led to the rule of men who became rulers by physical force. Although kingship had a long-standing tradition in the West, this was a new form of authority—based on power, not hereditary right. The Greeks called such rulers *tyrants* to distinguish them from more traditional kings. At first the term had no pejorative connotation—one could easily be a kind tyrant, and indeed some were sincere reformers seeking to end aristocratic exploitation. For example, some tyrants gained popular support by such reforms as freeing slaves, eliminating debts, redistributing land. Later, however, as these rulers relied on force to hold power, the term *tyrant* acquired the negative meaning it holds today. Tyrants often favored the commercial classes to try to hold onto power, but such alliances proved insubstantial. In some city-states, tyrants were replaced by various forms of participatory governments.

Greek citizens—especially those who controlled the lucrative trade and fought in the successful

phalanxes—thus began to take charge of the political life of their cities. A Greek city-state was called a *polis* (plural *poleis*). It was a small but au-

City-states tonomous political unit that generated intense loyalty from its citizens, who conducted their political, social, and religious activities in its heart. The poleis frequently included a fortified high ground—called an *acropolis*, and the most famous is in Athens. They also had a central place of assembly and market, called the *agora* (pl. *agorae*). Surrounding villages began to consolidate and share a political identity, and the word *polis* came to mean the city-state itself and its surrounding countryside. Each city-state was an independent governing entity, but in the view of its residents, a polis was also a state of mind. Unlike in Mesopotamia, Egypt, and Mycenae, poleis inhabitants did not think of themselves as subjects of a king or as owing obedience to a priesthood. Instead, they were "citizens" who were actively responsible for guiding their poleis.

Each city-state created its own form of government, and most retained some form of oligarchy (rule by a few). Athens, however, developed an early form of democracy that was strikingly new in the West, and which generated ideas that continue to influence our views. Aristotle (384–322 B.C.) even characterized humans by their participation in politics (the word *politics* is derived from the word *polis*), arguing that "man is a political animal" (although a more accurate translation is "man is an animal of the polis"). Even in city-states with less participatory democracy than Athens, in the central agorae Greek men who fought together in the hoplite armies gathered, traded, and discussed matters of governance.

THE HEART OF THE POLIS

The heart of the polis was the household, which consisted of a male citizen, his wife and children, and their slaves. This configuration formed the basis for both the rural and urban economies. In the villages outside the walls of the city itself, household members herded sheep and goats, worked in the vineyards and olive groves, and struggled to plant crops in the rocky ground. Olive trees yielded abundant fruit, but harvesting required a good deal of labor. As the vase in Figure 2.4 shows, one man climbed the tree to pick the olives within reach while two others knocked olives down from the far branches and a fourth picked up the ones that had fallen.

FIGURE 2.4
Cultivating olives, late sixth century B.C.

Olive harvesting was well worth the effort, however, for the olives and their precious oil brought much wealth into some of the city-states. Athens's economy in particular depended upon its olive oil exports. A well-known story about the philosopher Thales illustrates the economic importance of olives to the Greeks. His neighbors mocked him, saying, "If you are smart, why aren't you rich?" In response, he purchased the use of all the local olive presses cheaply during the off season. Then, when everyone was trying to press their olives after the harvest, they had to buy the use of the presses from Thales. He made a fortune and silenced his neighbors. As his final retort, Thales pointed out that philosophers could easily become rich, but they loved the life of the mind more than money.

In addition to olive harvesting, craftsmanship and trade completed the polis economy. Artisans in the polis labored at their crafts or sold their merchandise in the open market during the mornings. After a large afternoon meal, they napped, and then either returned to their shops or (more likely) went to the gymnasium to *Men's and women's role* exercise and talk with other citizens. The gymnasium grew up as part of the Greek belief in cultivating perfection in all things; thus a skilled artisan or philosopher also needed to cultivate his physical prowess as part of his pursuit of excellence. The gymnasium proved an enduring feature of life in the Mediterranean city-states. This was a highly public life for male citizens; work, exercise, and talk were all central activities of the masculine life.

Within the household, responsibilities were strictly divided by gender. A text from the early fourth century B.C. describes how a husband educated his 15-year-old wife on domestic responsibilities. He told her that men belonged outdoors: "For a man to remain indoors . . . is a thing discreditable." Women, on the other hand, should stay inside, teaching female slaves necessary skills, managing the goods brought into the household, and presiding over the spinning and weaving. When men entertained their peers at dinner parties or visited, "respectable" women stayed home and out of sight along with their female slaves and children. (As we will see, life for women in Sparta marked an exception to this pattern.)

In addition to strictly defined gender roles, Greek society depended heavily on slave labor; virtually every household had a few slaves. In the *Slave labor* earliest years of the poleis, just as elsewhere in the ancient Middle East, slaves were either captives of war or debtors. By the sixth century B.C., debt slavery had been virtually banned throughout the Greek world, but slavery itself remained a central institution. However, in many ways slaves' lives resembled those of their owners. Numerous slaves worked alongside free men and women in almost every occupation. (There were even slave policemen in Athens.) Slaves frequently lived in their own residences, worked in a trade, and earned their own money. Sometimes called "pay-bringers," they owed their owners a portion of their income but could retain some of the money they earned. With this revenue, some slaves in turn bought slaves for themselves or purchased their own freedom. Many Greek cities even had benefit clubs that lent slaves enough money to buy their freedom and repay the loan later. Numerous bright, ambitious slaves gained their freedom and became quite prosperous.

FIGURE 2.5

Assassination of Hipparchus in a lover's dispute, ca. 470 B.C.

All slaves did not enjoy this relatively easy life. Some slaves had brutal masters and suffered all forms of abuse; in Athens, some slaves who tried to flee their condition bore a brand of a runaway on their foreheads. Slaves who lived under the worst conditions were those who had the misfortune to work in the silver mines, an essential source of income for Athens. In these mines, they were fed just enough to stay strong and were beaten regularly to keep them working in the mines that produced immense wealth for free Greeks. For the most part, however, slavery was treated as a simple fact of life—an essential tool for getting necessary work done.

FEARS AND ATTACHMENTS IN GREEK EMOTIONAL LIFE

The extreme separation of men and women seems to have contributed to a wide range of insecurities and emotional attachments in Greek society. Many Greek writers expressed a great suspicion of women. As one poet, Semonides of Amorgos, wrote: "God made the mind of women a thing apart." The strict segregation of men and women through their lives may have contributed to misunderstandings. Men with little experience with women believed that virtuous women were scarce. Many husbands feared that their wives would escape their seclusion and take lovers, and thereby raise questions about the paternity of their children. These fears permeate many writings by Greek men.

Perhaps as part of their overall praise of masculinity, many ancient Greeks accepted bisexuality, at least among wealthy urban dwellers. The ideal of such a relationship took the form of *Bisexual relations* a mentoring arrangement between a well-connected older man and a "beardless youth" (although school-aged, free-born boys were protected from such liaisons). As the pair matured, the elder man would marry and take up his family responsibilities, and the younger would serve as a mentor to a new youth. Such relationships were seen as a natural part of a world in which men feared female sexuality, spent all their time together, exercised nude in the gymnasia, and praised the male body as the ideal of beauty. Indeed, many Greeks believed that the male-male relationship offered the highest possibility for love and that such ties usually brought out the best in each partner, making both braver and nobler.

The examples of homosexual relationships mentioned in Greek historical narratives, poetry, and even legal cases reveal how accepted and prevalent they were. Some relationships were even said to have shaped public policies. The vase painting in Figure 2.5 portrays a widely told story of two Athenian lovers—Aristogiton and Harmodius—who assassinated Hipparchus, a man who had tried to win the younger man from his elder companion. This scene shows the traditionally expected relationship by depicting the two elder men as bearded. Although the pair of lovers murdered the rival primarily for emotional reasons, Athenians appended a political motivation to the crime because Hipparchus was the brother of Athens's tyrant, Hippias. When the tyrant heard about the assassination, he believed that it was part of a conspiracy to overthrow him, and he became more suspicious and oppressive in his rule, only to be ousted four years later in 510 B.C. After Hippias's overthrow, Athenians recast the assassination of Hipparchus, glorifying it as a political act that helped bring down tyranny and introduce democracy to the polis. In ancient Greece, the personal was almost always framed in political terms, and Harmodius and Aristogiton became national heroes.

We have fewer examples of women engaging in homosexual be-

Sappho of Lesbos havior, probably because their lives were conducted in privacy and were not recorded in as many historical documents. However, one sixth-century B.C. poet, Sappho from the island of Lesbos, expressed passionate love for the young women in her social circle. Her poetry has since been both highly respected for its beauty and severely criticized for its content. The philosopher Plato admired Sappho so much that he referred to her as a goddess of poetry, but some Greek playwrights dismissed and ridiculed her as an ugly woman who could not attract a man. Nevertheless, Sappho's poetry was so influential that the word "Lesbian," meaning a resident of Sappho's island of Lesbos, has become synonymous with female homosexuality.

Not all women were confined to the home. While respectable women stayed carefully indoors, some women—slaves or foreigners—who had no economic resources or family ties became prostitutes and courtesans who shared men's public lives at dinners and

Courtesans drinking parties. Prostitutes were even registered and taxed in many Greek city-states, and thereby became a legitimate part of social and economic life. Men and prostitutes drank freely together from the wine bowls abundantly filled at banquets. These bowls were decorated inside and out with appropriate themes. Figure 2.6 shows a prostitute dressed in loose, seductive clothing who holds a wine bowl in each hand as she plays a Greek drinking game in which the participant twirls the drinking vessel until the dregs go flying. Such exuberant images not only portrayed scenes from the parties but also were intended to spur people on to greater abandon. Women in ancient Greece, particularly Athens, were thus placed in the peculiar situation of being invisible if they were "respectable," and mingling with and influencing powerful men only if they were not.

All the city-states shared many of these elements of urban life, from work to pleasure. However, each

FIGURE 2.6
Courtesan at a drinking party, fifth century B.C.

polis had its own distinctive character, as citizens structured their political lives to suit themselves. Two well-known Greek cities, Athens and Sparta, offer examples of the broad range of governing styles in the ancient Greek poleis.

ATHENS: CITY OF DEMOCRACY

Document 2.1 (on page D2.1) relates the founding myth of Athens, and suggests that participatory democracy was at the heart of the origins of the city. The reality of a growing democratic form of

Oligarchy government was more complicated. By 700 B.C., Athenian aristocrats established a form of government that allowed them to run and control the growing city. Three (and later nine) administrators—called *archons*—were elected by an assembly of male citizens (the *Ecclesia*) and ran the business of the city. They served for only one year, and after their tenure they permanently entered a council called the

Areopagus (eventually numbering 300 men), which held the real power because it was composed of senior men who could not be removed from office. This government in which the wealthy effectively controlled power proved unable to respond to changing economic fortunes, which had profound political consequences.

By about 600 B.C., the weaknesses in the Athenian economy became apparent. Small farmers could not produce enough to feed the growing population, and many fell into debt and even slavery by offering themselves as security in exchange for food. At about the same time, the hoplite armies caused the aristocracy to lose its monopoly over the military. A social crisis was in the making, but it was resolved by a far-sighted Athenian aristocrat, Solon, who was elected as sole archon in 594 B.C. Like so many men in the West who periodically tried to alleviate social ills, Solon introduced reforms intended to appease these lower classes while keeping aristocrats in power.

Solon's reforms

Solon first addressed the alarming debt crisis by introducing reforms called "the Shaking off of Burdens"—that canceled (or limited) existing debts and banned debt slavery altogether. Solon also introduced some agricultural reforms, striking at the economic heart of the problem. He ordered that no agricultural product could be exported except olive oil, thus stimulating the cultivation of the valuable olives that would become the basis of Athens's prosperity. He also standardized the weights used by the Athenians, making it easier for them to trade with other poleis. With the economic reforms in place, Solon turned to the political structures that had proved inadequate to prevent civil strife.

Solon did not try to eliminate the old families from power; instead, he paved the way for the newly wealthy to participate in government. He first divided up all citizens into four groups based on wealth (instead of birth), and only members of the top two groups were eligible to become archons (and subsequently members of the Areopagus). While this preserved some privilege of rank, it nevertheless appeased the newly wealthy, who were now permitted to aspire to the highest offices. Solon then revitalized the assembly of citizens, and to further weaken the power of the Areopagus, he created a Council of 400 to set the agenda for the Ecclesia. To round out the reforms, Solon tried to ensure justice for everyone by

Increased democracy

establishing a special people's court of appeal intended to offer protection against the abuse of power by archons.

Solon's reforms were balanced and attempted to provide a compromise among the contentious social groups in Athens. However, his attempts to placate the various factions were unsuccessful because each party tried to gain more privileges. During the resulting civil strife, Athens turned to tyranny, bringing Peisistratus to power in 560 B.C. He ruled (between periods of exile) until 527 B.C., when his son Hippias tried to continue the rule. He was to be the last of Athens's tyrants. He fell to a coalition of aristocrats and Greeks from other city-states hoping to gain some political advantage for themselves. (The lovers' quarrel depicted in Figure 2.5 received the credit for Hippias's fall). The period of tyranny broke the power of the aristocrats and paved the way for full democracy.

Tyranny

The people rallied to Cleisthenes, a nobleman who stood for popular interests. In 508 B.C., Athens adopted the Constitution of Cleisthenes, which refined Solon's reforms and brought a remarkable degree of direct democracy to the city. The chart in Figure 2.7 outlines Athens' democratic system. As you can see from Figure 2.7, Cleisthenes kept Solon's basic structure, but his major innovation (which has earned him the credit for establishing democracy in Athens) was to redistrict the city in a way that old alliances of geography and clan were broken and could no longer control the city offices. Everyone was divided up into ten tribal units, and this was how they were represented in the Assembly. Furthermore, Solon's old Council of 400 was increased to 500—each tribal unit could select 50 members by lot. By breaking the old alliance system, Cleisthenes secured a remarkable form of direct democracy for Athens with provisions to curb the power of any group that might become too strong.

Although the Ecclesia offered a new level of participation to the men of the ancient world and a model of representation that has been praised since, it was not a perfect democracy. It still represented only about 20 percent of the population of Athens, for it excluded women and slaves. Also excluded were the *metics*, resident foreigners who lived and worked in Athens in manufacturing and commerce and who represented nearly one-third of the free population of Athens. Furthermore, recent scholarship shows that

Assessing democracy

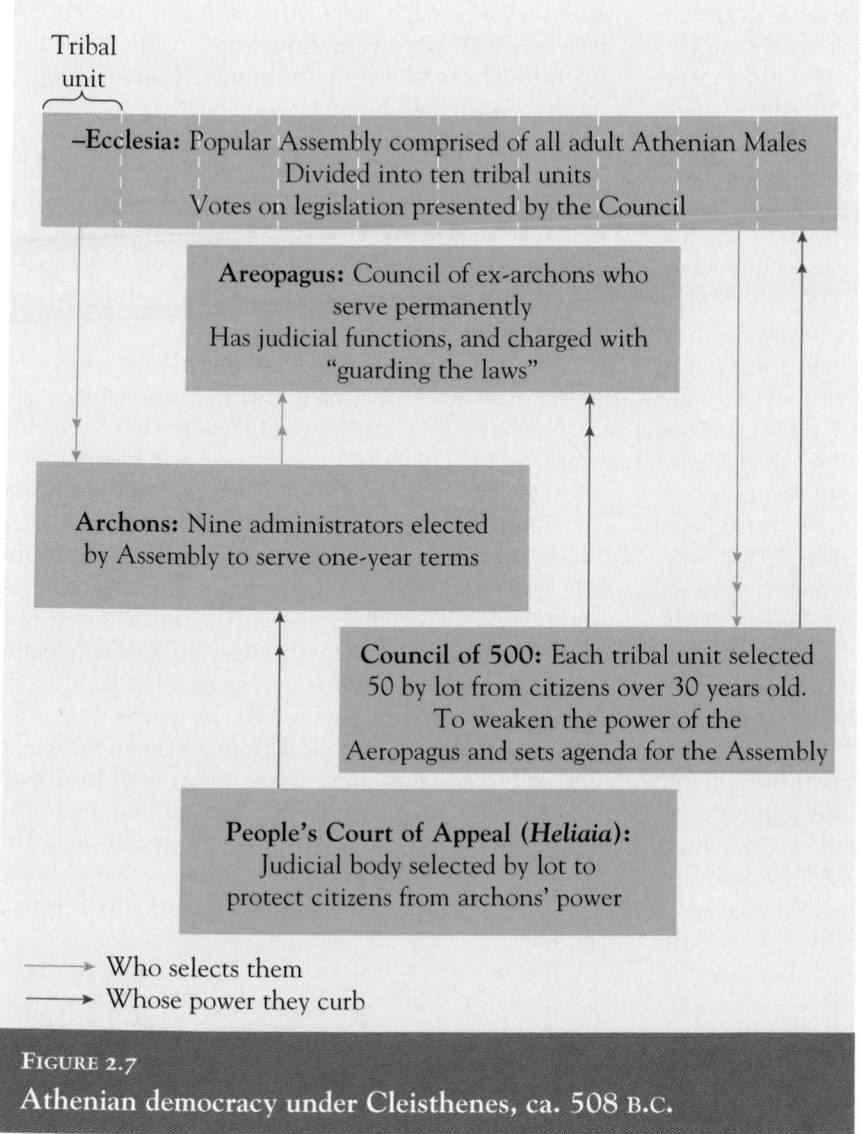

Tribal unit

Ecclesia: Popular Assembly comprised of all adult Athenian Males
Divided into ten tribal units
Votes on legislation presented by the Council

Areopagus: Council of ex-archons who serve permanently
Has judicial functions, and charged with "guarding the laws"

Archons: Nine administrators elected by Assembly to serve one-year terms

Council of 500: Each tribal unit selected 50 by lot from citizens over 30 years old.
To weaken the power of the Aeropagus and sets agenda for the Assembly

People's Court of Appeal (*Heliaia*):
Judicial body selected by lot to protect citizens from archons' power

→ Who selects them
→ Whose power they curb

FIGURE 2.7
Athenian democracy under Cleisthenes, ca. 508 B.C.

(instead of by election or other device) removed much of the influence of wealth and personal power from the political process. The Council set the agenda for the Ecclesia, preparing forms of legislation for the assembly's action. Its influence was enormous, but the full governing power remained in the direct democracy of the Ecclesia. These practices assumed that all citizens could fulfill the duties of government, and this egalitarian assumption is astonishing for the ancient world (and perhaps for the modern one as well). The great leader of Athens, Pericles, in a famous funeral oration preserved (or paraphrased) by the historian Thucydides, rightly observed: "Our constitution is called a democracy because it is in the hands not of the few but of the many."

The people did recognize that sometimes individuals could threaten the rule of the many, and to protect *Ostracism* the democracy, Cleisthenes instituted an unusual procedure early in the sixth century B.C.: ostracism. Once a year, Athenians could vote for the man they considered most dangerous to the state by inscribing his name on a scrap of pottery (called an *ostracon*). If a man received 6,000 votes, he was sent into exile for 10 years. Although Athenian democracy was not perfect, it was an extraordinary new chapter in the history of the West, and one that has held long-standing appeal.

only a minority of the qualified citizens could attend the assembly at any given time—only about 6,000 can fit into the meeting place, a small sloping hillside. It seems that when the meeting place was full, no one else could enter and a quorum was declared. Thus, probably many of the same people (those living nearby) attended the Ecclesia regularly.

However, other parts of the Athenian government made sure the principle of egalitarian democracy prevailed. The Council of 500 was chosen annually by lot from male citizens over age 30, and citizens could not repeat tenure. Choosing representatives by lot

☙ SPARTA: MODEL MILITARY STATE

Sparta's development led to the emergence of a state thoroughly different from Athens, with a markedly different set of values. Whereas Athenians were creative, artistic, and eloquent, Spartans were militaristic, strict, and sparing of words (our word *laconic* comes from the Greek word for "Spartans" or the region they inhabited). The nature of their state was shaped by an early solution to their land hunger. Instead of sending out colonists or negotiating partnerships with the peoples in their vicinity (like the Athenians had done), the Spartans conquered their neighboring districts and enslaved the local populations. The slaves, called *helots*, were treated harshly. As one Spartan poet observed, they were like "donkeys worn down by intolerable labor." Sparta's helots greatly outnumbered free citizens and always seemed to threaten rebellion. To keep the helots in slavery, the Spartans virtually enslaved themselves in a military state of perpetual watchfulness. They consoled themselves by observing that at least they had chosen their harsh life, whereas their helots had not.

The Spartan constitution—reputedly introduced by the semilegendary Lycurgus in about 600 B.C.—reflected their deep conservatism and made a minimal concession to democracy. Figure 2.8 illustrates the governmental structure erected by Sparta's constitution. Authority was carefully kept in the hands of the elders. In this oligarchy, citizen representation was firmly guided by age and experience, and many outsiders admired Sparta's "mixed constitution" that seemed to balance democracy with oligarchy.

Life in Sparta was harsh, although it was much admired by many Greeks who appreciated the Spartans' powers of self-denial. At birth, each child was examined by elders, and if deemed physically deficient, the child would be exposed—left outdoors to die. At the age of seven, boys were turned over to the state and spent the next 13 years in training to learn military skills, endurance, and loyalty to the polis. At 20, young men entered the army and lived the next 10 years in barracks. They could marry, but could visit their wives only by eluding the barracks guards. At 30, men became full citizens and could live at home. Nevertheless, they were expected to take all meals in the military dining hall, where food was sparse and plain.

Spartan life

While their men lived isolated in the barracks, Spartan women had far more freedom than Greek women of other city-states. Because men concentrated on their military activities, women handled most of the household arrangements and had wide economic powers. They attended contests to cheer the brave and mock the losers, but they were not simply spectators. Women, too, trained in athletic endurance, and the fierceness of Spartan women was said to match that of their men. The Greek biographer Plutarch (A.D. 46?–120?) recorded a series of quotations that were supposedly the words of Spartan women. The most famous is from a woman who tells her son to come back from war either with his shield (victorious) or on it (dead). Such resolve made the armies of Sparta the best in Greece, and though the Spartans created no works of art, they probably would have said that their own lives were masterpiece enough.

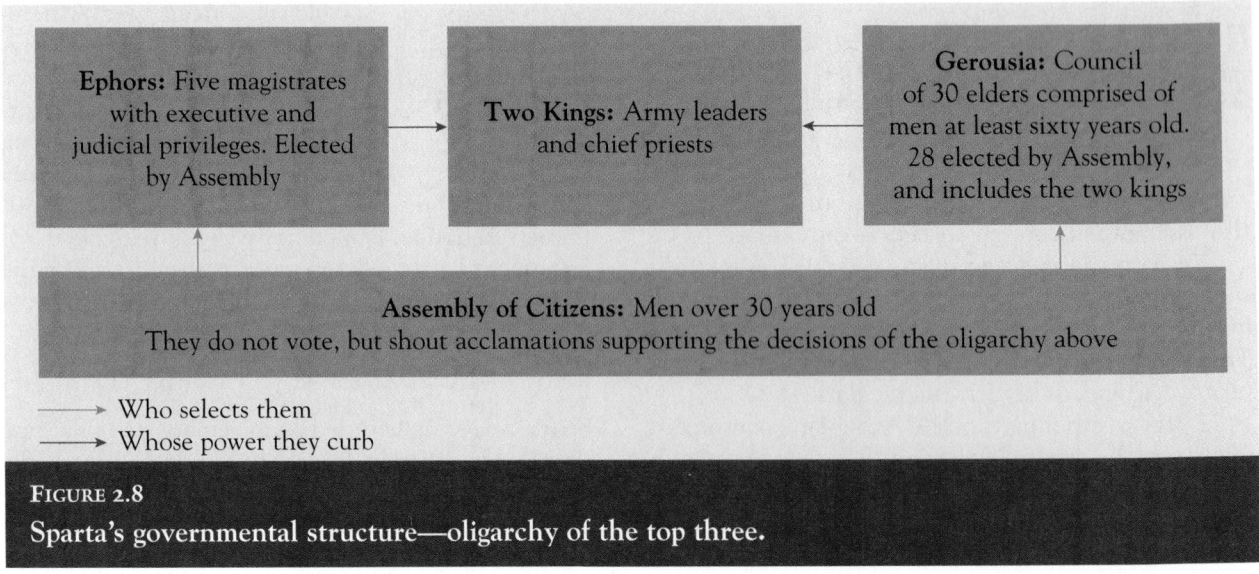

Ephors: Five magistrates with executive and judicial privileges. Elected by Assembly

Two Kings: Army leaders and chief priests

Gerousia: Council of 30 elders comprised of men at least sixty years old. 28 elected by Assembly, and includes the two kings

Assembly of Citizens: Men over 30 years old
They do not vote, but shout acclamations supporting the decisions of the oligarchy above

→ Who selects them
→ Whose power they curb

FIGURE 2.8
Sparta's governmental structure—oligarchy of the top three.

FIGURE 2.9
Athletes preparing for the Olympic Games, late sixth century B.C.

THE LOVE OF THE CONTEST: OLYMPIC GAMES

Athens and Sparta were only two examples of the many varieties of city-states that developed with fierce independence on the Greek mainland and in the colonies throughout the Mediterranean. But, although there was much rivalry among the poleis, they still shared a certain sense of identity. They spoke the same language, worshiped the same gods, cherished Homer's poetry, and had a passionate love for individual competition. They recognized these affinities, calling themselves *Hellenes* (the Romans later called them "Greek" after a Greek colony), and they considered all Hellenes to be better than other peoples. The Hellenes gathered periodically at a religious festival dedicated to Zeus, and they even stopped their almost interminable warfare to come together and celebrate their love of the contest.

The first pan-Hellenic Olympic Games were held in 776 B.C. At first, the event consisted only of a *Olympic Games* footrace, but soon the games expanded to include boxing, wrestling, chariot racing, and the grueling pentathlon, which consisted of long jumping, discus and javelin throwing, wrestling, and the 200-meter sprint. Olympic victors brought glory to their home cities and were richly rewarded there with honor and free meals.

The Olympics were so popular that they served as an inspiration to many artists. The athletes shown in Figure 2.9 demonstrate the perfection that people expected from their athletic heroes. The scene portrays several of the contests: the footrace, the javelin throw, and, in the center of the relief, the most difficult event, wrestling. The athletes tense all their muscles as they begin the contest that virtually defined Greek life. Critics, such as the playwright Euripides (485–406 B.C.), chided Greeks for their adulation of athletes. "We ought rather to crown the good man and the wise man," he scolded. Nevertheless, spectators flocked to the games.

Olympic planners prohibited women from attending the contest, although they could purchase a chariot and horses with which men *Women at Olympics* would compete in their names. One woman defied the convention and dressed as a trainer so she could watch her son compete. After he won, she jumped over a fence in her excitement and accidentally revealed her gender. Olympic officials promptly passed a law requiring all future trainers to attend the games in the nude to prevent further disguises.

Some women conducted games of their own separately from the men's. These games, dedicated to Zeus's wife Hera, involved footraces run by unmarried women of various ages. Women judged and sponsored the games and awarded the fastest competitors crowns of olive branches. However, these winners did not receive the high level of acclaim or wealth accorded to male victors, who brought prestige to their cities and fame for themselves through their athletic prowess. Although the Olympic Games offered a safe outlet for the Greeks' love of competition, Greek history was shaped by more devastating strife in which city-states tried to outdo each other on the battlefields.

Imperial Athens, 489–431 B.C.

Greek colonists who settled in Asia Minor built their city-states in lands that the Persian Empire claimed by 500 B.C. As we saw in Chapter 1, the Persians were tolerant of the various subject peoples within their territories, so they did not object to the growing spirit of independence that accompanied the prosperity of these successful commercial cities. However, open revolt was another matter.

In 499 B.C. the Greek tyrant ruling in the city of Miletus (Map 2.3) offended the Persian rulers. Hoping to avoid retribution, he staged a revolt against Persian rule and asked for help from his compatriots on the Greek mainland. Sparta refused, but Athens sent twenty ships—only enough to anger the Persians but not to save Miletus. The Greek city was sacked, and the Persians turned their attention to the Greek peninsula. They planned an invasion in part to punish Athens for its involvement in the Miletus uprising.

THE PERSIAN WARS, 490–479 B.C.

Any forces seeking to invade the Greek mainland had to negotiate the mountainous terrain and the narrow passes that afforded the only access to the interior. Furthermore, an invading land army had to be supplied by a shore-hugging fleet that backed up the infantry while navigating the narrow straits of the Aegean shoreline. In 490 B.C. the Persian king Darius I (r. 522–486 B.C.), therefore, sailed across the Aegean, attacked Eretria, and landed near Athens. Map 2.3a depicts the route of the invading Persian army and the battle site located on the plain of Marathon.

At the Battle of Marathon, the Athenians and their allies were far outmatched by the numerous Persians. The worried Greeks asked their Spartan compatriots for reinforcements, but the Spartans replied that they had to complete their religious festival first—then it would be too late to repel the Persians. Athens and its allies had to stand alone. In spite of being outnumbered, the Athenians decided to march from Athens to meet the Persians near their landing site on the plain of Marathon. Confident of an easy victory, the Persians launched their attack. Things did not go as expected for the Persians, however. The Athenian general, Miltiades, developed a clever strategy that helped them outwit the lightly armed Persians. Weakening the center of their line and strengthening the two wings, the Athenians outflanked the advancing Persian force and inflicted severe damage. The Greeks also made a running advance, a novelty that surprised and confused their enemy. Athenian innovation and energy won the day, bringing a decisive and stunning victory to the Greeks. According to the texts, 6,400 Persians perished in the battle, compared with only 192 Athenians. This unexpected victory of the polis over the huge empire of Persia earned Athens great prestige. The strong, confident soldier shown in the illustration at the beginning of the chapter embodies the triumphant spirit of this proud city-state, and the Athenian victory also inspired confidence in the newly emerging democracy itself.

Battle of Marathon

One of the heroes of Marathon was a fast runner, Philippides, who ran approximately 150 miles in two days to request the help of the Spartans. However, he is more remembered for a probably untrue story that claims he ran to Athens to deliver the news of victory to the polis and then died on the spot from his exertions. Modern-day races are called *marathons* in commemoration of Philippides' legendary 26-mile run from the plain of Marathon to Athens.

Athens had fended off the invaders, but the humiliated Persians were determined to try again. Ten years after the disaster at Marathon, Darius's successor, Xerxes (r. 486–465 B.C.), plotted a full-scale invasion of the Greek mainland. (Document 2.2 on page D2.2 describes the logistical problems.) Xerxes brought the best of ancient engineering to the invasion to try to avoid the disaster of the first war. To move a large infantry force, he built a pontoon bridge across the Hellespont and marched 180,000 soldiers to Greece. Even more impressive, he ordered his men to build a canal a mile and a quarter long through a peninsula in northern Greece so his fleet could supply the ground force. Historians have debated for decades about whether the canal existed,

A second invasion

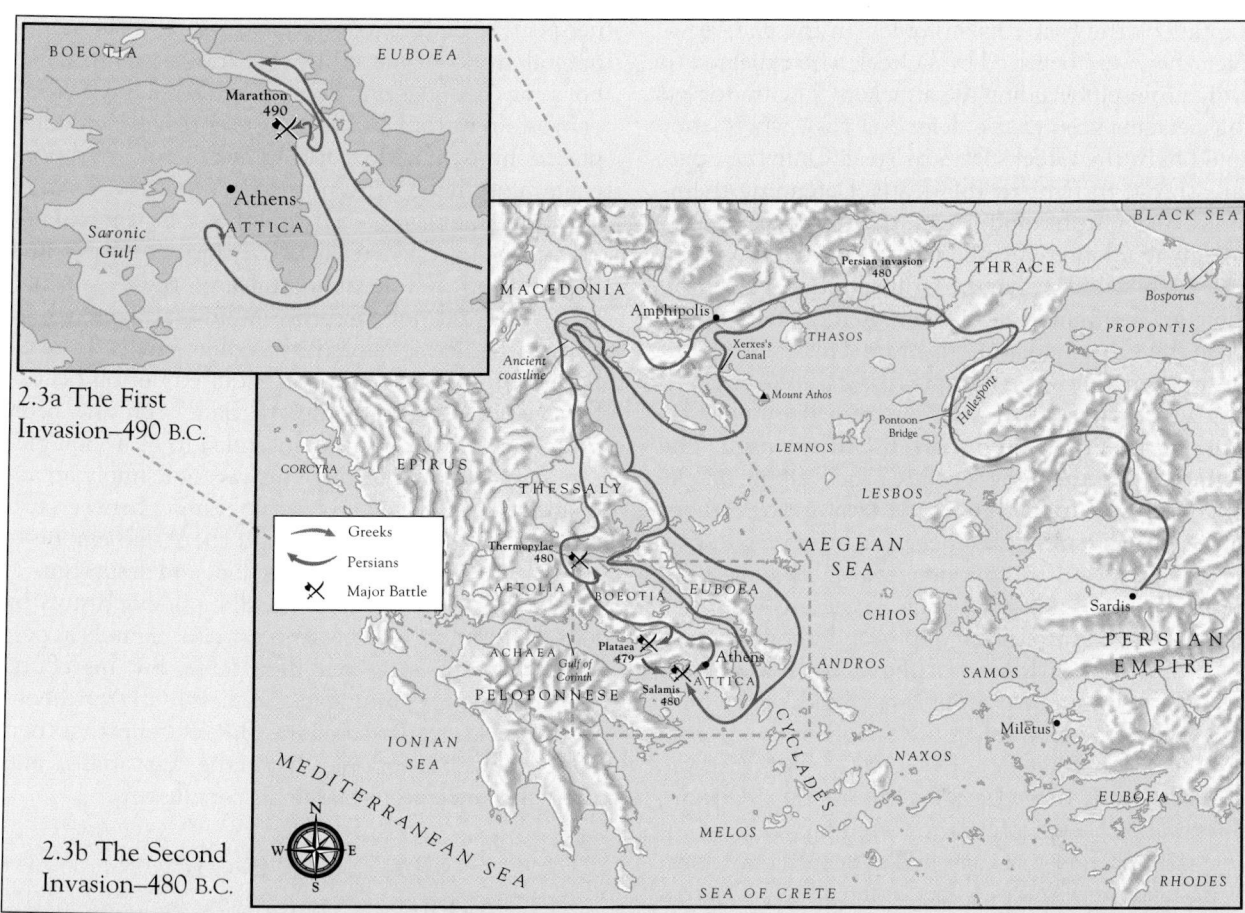

2.3a The First Invasion–490 B.C.

2.3b The Second Invasion–480 B.C.

Legend:
- Greeks
- Persians
- ✕ Major Battle

THINKING ABOUT GEOGRAPHY

MAP 2.3A&B   *The Persian Wars, 490–480 B.C.*

This map shows the routes of invasions and the major battles of the wars between Persia and the Greek poleis. ✎ **Notice** the two routes through which the Persians tried to invade Greece. **Consider** the particular advantages and disadvantages posed by the land and sea routes. ✎ **Notice also** the narrow land and sea areas where the Persians engaged the Greeks. **Consider** how the narrow spaces served as a disadvantage to the more numerous Persian forces.

but recently, scientists from Britain and Greece proved conclusively that the canal was built. It spanned about 100 feet at the surface, just wide enough for two war galleys to pass. It was an astonishing engineering feat and showed Xerxes's determination. (Both the bridge and canal are shown on Map 2.3b).

As the Persians invaded, several Greek city-states in the north surrendered quickly to the Persian Great King. Meanwhile, Athens had readied its own fleet, assuming that the best way to withstand the Persians was to control the Aegean and therefore the supply routes to troops on the march. Athens also secured the participation of Sparta and its allies to aid in the battle.

For the Persian army, the gateway to the south lay through the pass at Thermopylae (see Map 2.3b). Yet, the narrow pass, held by a small coalition of Greeks led by Spartans, *Thermopylae* turned the Persians' greater numbers into a liability. The Greeks held the pass for days against repeated assaults by the best Persian forces. In the end, however, they were betrayed by a Greek who expected to enrich himself by aiding the attackers. The traitor led the Persians around the defended pass, where they could fight the Greeks from the rear. Only the Spartans stayed to fight to the death. Defending themselves from front and back, the Spartans fought fiercely in a long-remembered feat of bravery, and all died with sword in hand. An inscription placed on their graves immortalized their heroic stand: "Tell them the news in Sparta, passer by. That here, obedient to their words, we lie."

The Persians' success at Thermopylae opened a route for them to march south to Athens itself. The outmatched Athenians consulted the Delphic oracle, who told them to trust in wooden walls. The Athenian leader, Themistocles, persuaded the people that the oracle meant the wooden "walls" of their ships, not the walls of Athens, so the Athenians scattered, taking refuge in their fleet and abandoning the polis for nearby islands. Many horrified Greeks were close enough to watch as the Persians plundered Athens and burned the temples on the Acropolis as an act of revenge for their previous losses. Yet, as in Marathon, the tide again turned against the mighty Persians, this time in the bay of Salamis (see Map 2.3b).

Artemisia, queen of Caria in Persia and commander of a squadron of Xerxes' fleet, immediately saw that the Persians would lose their advantage in numbers fighting in a narrow bay and strongly advised the Persian king against it. *Greek naval victory* Her military wisdom proved well founded; the swift Greek vessels rallied and crushed almost the entire Persian fleet. Artemisia managed to escape through her remarkable strategy and bravery. Xerxes withdrew from the melee after sending his children home to safety on Artemisia's ship. The despondent emperor, watching Artemesia's success and the destruction of the rest of his fleet, lamented: "My men have become women, and my women men." The next year, the Spartans led a coalition that defeated the remnants of the Persian army at Plataea (see Map 2.3b). The individualistic, disbursed Greeks had triumphed once more over the vast, unified Persian Empire.

HERODOTUS: THE FATHER OF HISTORY

In a famous work called simply *The History*, the Greek historian Herodotus recorded the great deeds of the Persian Wars with a combination of a broad perspective and an attention to detail. This monumental work—some 600 pages long—was so pathbreaking that he is universally considered the "father" of Western history. With his first sentence, Herodotus placed himself within the Greek heroic tradition, claiming to have written in order "that the deeds of men may not be forgotten, and that the great and noble actions of the Greeks and Asiatics may not lose their fame." While immortalizing these warriors, Herodotus did not take the traditional approach of converting heroic deeds into godlike myths. Instead, he drew from oral traditions acquired during his extensive travels—the things he had "seen and been told"—and wrote what he intended to be a total picture of the known world. This was not simply an account of a war, but a heroic-scale conflict between two types of societies, the poleis and the Asian empire—or, for Herodotus, between freedom and despotism.

Herodotus did much for the discipline of history by striving to record historical events as accurately as possible and separating fact from fable, but his efforts marked only a beginning in the quest for historical objectivity. He clearly shared the Greeks' belief that their culture was far superior to that of the "barbarians," and these preconceptions biased his conclusions.

ATHENS BUILDS AN EMPIRE, 477–431 B.C.

Although Herodotus wrote a lively, fascinating history, as we will see, he was wrong in identifying the Persians as the Greeks' worst enemies. Just as a Greek had betrayed the Spartans at Thermopylae, the Greeks themselves would one day bring about their own downfall. But for the time being, they gloried in their astounding victory over Persia, the great power of Asia. The Greeks' defeat of the Persians, though sweet, presented the fiercely independent poleis with a new dilemma. The Persian Empire was still powerful. How would the Greek city-states work together to remain vigilant in the face of this threat, and who would lead them? The most effective defense of Greece lay in controlling the Aegean, and the Athenians possessed the strongest fleet.

In 477 B.C. most maritime poleis on the coasts and the islands of the Aegean finally decided to form a defensive league. Each member of the *Delian League* league contributed money to maintain a large fleet for the defense of them all. The treasury for the alliance was held on the island of Delos (see

Map 2.1 on page 47), so the coalition was called the Delian League. Theoretically, all league members were entitled to an equal voice in decision making, but Athens was the strongest member and began to dominate league policy.

As early as the 470s B.C., some members took offense at Athens's prominent role and sought to withdraw from the arrangement. But the Athenians swiftly made the situation clear: This was not a league of independent states after all, but an Athenian empire with subject cities. In 454 B.C. the Athenians dropped any pretense of the member states' autonomy and moved the league's treasury from Delos to Athens. They then proceeded to use the wealth to create an Athenian Golden Age. One critic of Athenian policy complained that, because the smaller Aegean states depended on seaborne imports and exports for their survival, they did not dare to defy the Athenian "rulers of the sea." Nevertheless, the Athenian Empire did succeed in protecting the mainland from further Persian assaults and conferred other benefits: The poleis of the Aegean and Asia Minor were free to trade safely under the protection of the Greek ships. They received peace in exchange for autonomy.

During the Persian Wars, the Athenian military commanders had understandably acquired a good deal of power. Officials called *strategoi* (sing. *strategos*) were elected as commanders of the tribal army units, and during Athens's imperial age, a particularly strong strategos came to be the chief officer of the state. The political architect of Athens's Golden Age was the statesman Pericles (495–429 B.C.), who was elected strategos every year from 443 B.C. to his death in 429 B.C. He so dominated Athenian affairs that many compared him to a tyrant, yet this powerful aristocrat eloquently championed democracy in the assembly of Athens and encouraged democratic principles within the states of the league. However, he did not permit independent action by subject states. Thus, Pericles supported Athens's removal of the league treasury. As he pointed out, it was only right that Athenians should enjoy the money, given that they had led the victory over Persia in the first place and their city had been burned in the process. Pericles followed up this argument by playing an instrumental role in plans for spending the money.

Pericles' closest companion and most influential advisor was the talented courtesan Aspasia, who headed an establishment that boasted the most cultured young

Pericles

courtesans in Athens and in the mid-440s B.C., she became Pericles' mistress. Despite her status with Pericles, Aspasia drew intense criticism for her "undue" influence over Athens's great leader. For example, the Athenians suspected her of persuading Pericles to involve Athens in military alliances advantageous to her native city of Miletus. Rumors also circulated that she helped write the orator's speeches. The ever-loyal Pericles ignored all these complaints, however, and maintained his close relationship with Aspasia until his death.

Pericles forwarded democracy within Athens by trying to ensure that even poor citizens could participate fully in Athenian politics and culture. Figure 2.10 shows the changes Pericles made to Cleisthenes' constitution, including the advent of paying the people who served as jurors or on the Council of 500. Now all male citizens—not just the rich—could participate in the democracy. Equally important, he used much of the treasury to employ citizens on a project designed to beautify the public spaces of Athens. He organized armies of talented artists and artisans and paid thousands of workers to participate in the project. Finally, he put about 20,000 Athenians on the municipal payroll, a move that stimulated widespread involvement in the democratic proceedings of the city.

Pericles' democracy

ARTISTIC ATHENS

Pericles' leadership made Athens the political and cultural jewel of Greece. At the heart of the reconstruction program lay a plan to rebuild the Acropolis that the Persians had destroyed. The restored Acropolis consisted of several temples and related buildings. The largest temple in the Acropolis was the Parthenon, located on the highest point and dedicated to Athena, the patron goddess of the city. The temple had a magnificent statue of the goddess (now lost) created by Phidias, the greatest sculptor of the day, whose reputation for excellence continues today. The Parthenon (shown in Figure 2.11) followed the form of classical Greek temples, although it was the grandest such structure on the Greek peninsula. Designed with extraordinary care, it was built according to principles of mathematical proportion, which the Greeks (following in the footsteps of Pythagoras) believed underlay the beauty of the universe. At the same time, the builders knew that human beings cannot visually perceive absolute, mathematical perfection.

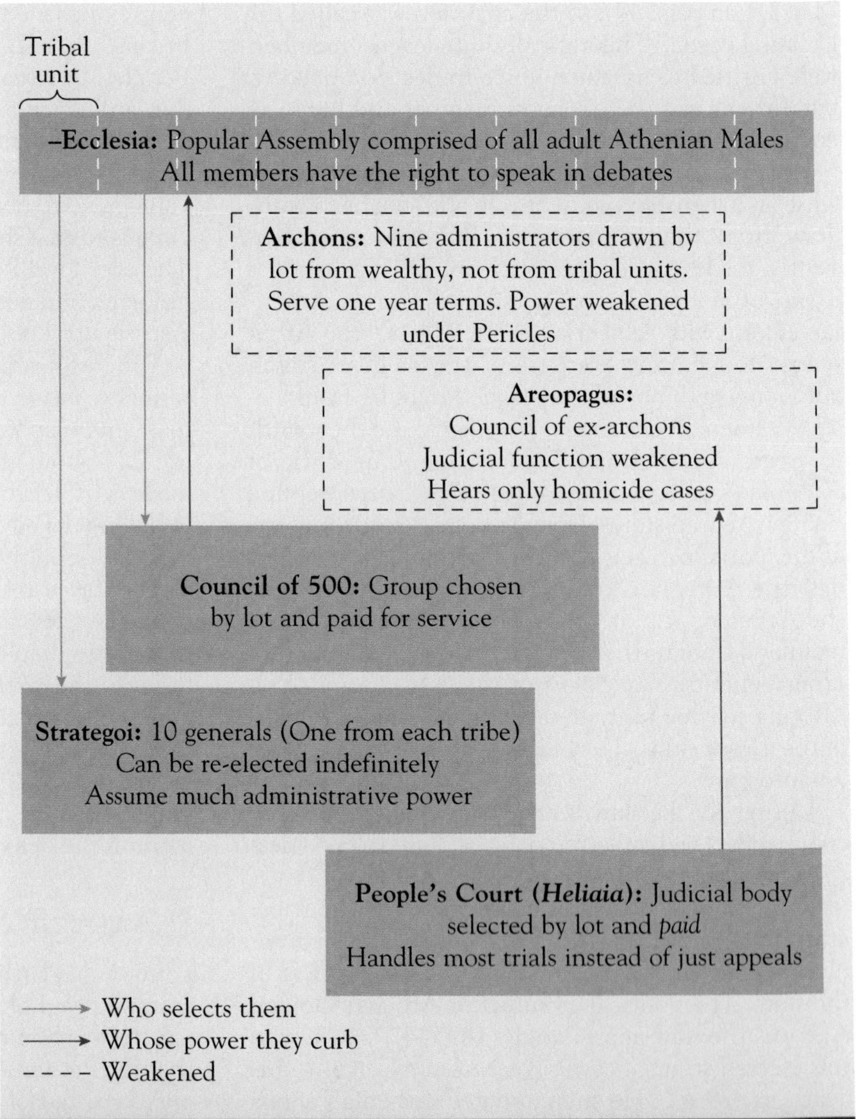

The architects, therefore, compensated for the limits of human vision by creating an optical illusion: curving some of the Parthenon's lines so they would appear straight to the human eye. This building represents the highest accomplishment of Greek architects who used practical means to strive for abstract perfection.

The Athenians adorned the Parthenon with many sculptures and statues of both gods and humans. (Today, few statues remain in Athens—most are in museums elsewhere.) Most of these figures were done in bronze (like the soldier at the beginning of the chapter) or marble. These statues, which all bear a strong resemblance to one another, echo the Greek belief that gods and humans had much in common.

Figures 2.12 and 2.13, photos of sculptures from the Parthenon, depict both gods and ordinary Athenians. The gods and goddess in Figure 2.12 are seated, waiting for the procession of the Athenians to begin. They are shown posed and dressed as Athenian citizens. At the same time, the Athenian youths in Figure 2.13 who ride in the procession are as beautifully formed and as serenely confident as gods. By blurring humanity and divinity in their visual arts in this way, the Greeks explored the highest potential of humanity in their artwork. Their sculpture represented an idealized humanity, not real people.

GREEK THEATER: EXPLORING COMPLEX MORAL PROBLEMS

In addition to their architecture and sculpture, the Athenians' theatrical achievements set new standards for Greek culture. Greek theater grew as part of the religious celebration of Dionysus, held in the late spring. Every year, Athens's leaders chose eight playwrights to present serious and comic plays at the festival in a competition as fierce as the Olympics. The plays were performed in open-air theaters with simple staging (Figure 2.14). Men played both male and female parts, and all actors wore stylized masks. The themes of these plays centered on weighty matters such as religion, politics, and the deep dilemmas that arose as people grappled with their fates.

Tribal unit

–Ecclesia: Popular Assembly comprised of all adult Athenian Males
All members have the right to speak in debates

Archons: Nine administrators drawn by lot from wealthy, not from tribal units. Serve one year terms. Power weakened under Pericles

Areopagus:
Council of ex-archons
Judicial function weakened
Hears only homicide cases

Council of 500: Group chosen by lot and paid for service

Strategoi: 10 generals (One from each tribe)
Can be re-elected indefinitely
Assume much administrative power

People's Court (*Heliaia*): Judicial body selected by lot and *paid*
Handles most trials instead of just appeals

⟶ Who selects them
━━▶ Whose power they curb
---- Weakened

FIGURE 2.10
Athenian democracy under Pericles, ca. 420 B.C.

FIGURE 2.11
Acropolis of Athens with the Parthenon, ca. 430 B.C.

During Athens's Golden Age, playwrights reminded the Athenians that, even at the height of their power, they faced complex moral problems.

One of Athens's most accomplished playwrights was Aeschylus (ca. 525–456 B.C.), who had fought at the Battle of Marathon. His earliest play, *The Persians*, added thoughtful nuance to the celebrations that the Athenians had enjoyed after their victory. Instead of simply praising Athenian success, Aeschylus studied Persian *Aeschylus and Sophocles* loss, attributing it to Xerxes' hubris at trying to upset the established international order. This also subtly warned the Athenians not to let their own arrogant pride bring about their own destruction.

The most revered playwright of this period, however, was Sophocles (496?–406 B.C.), who is best known for *The Theban Plays*, a great series about the mythological figure Oedipus and his family. All Athenians would have known the story of Oedipus, an ill-fated man whose family was told by a soothsayer at his birth that he was doomed to kill his father and marry his mother. The family exposed the baby to die, but he was rescued by a shepherd and raised as a prince in a faraway land. When he was grown, a soothsayer in his new land repeated the prediction, and when Oedipus fled to avoid killing the man he believed was his father, he returned to his original home, where unintentionally fulfilled the prophecy. In Sophocles' hands, the play became a study in the range of human emotions measured

FIGURE 2.12
Gods on the Parthenon, ca. 430 B.C.

by how man responds to tragic fates. Oedipus moves from pride in his own position as king to deep agony and humility as he discovers the horrifying truth of his life. The play concludes with a reminder to all spectators who might feel complacent in their own lives: "Behold, what a full tide of misfortune swept over his head. Then learn that mortal man must always look to his ending, and none can be called happy until that day when he carries his happiness down to the grave in peace." Sophocles' plays, written at the height of Athenian glory, repeatedly warned the Greeks that happiness can be achieved by wisdom and fear of the gods, without which pride brings destruction.

FIGURE 2.13
Parthenon relief of Athenian horsemen riding in procession to the Acropolis, ca. 430 B.C.

Destruction, Disillusion, and a Search for Meaning

Sadly for the Athenians, they failed to heed Sophocles' warnings about pride and impiety. Their era of prosperity came to a violent end with the onset of the Peloponnesian War, a long, destructive conflict between Athens and Sparta and their respective allies. Like the Persian Wars, this new contest generated its own historian. Thucydides (460–400 B.C.), an even more objective historian than Herodotus, wrote: "I began my history at the very outbreak of the war, in the belief that it was going to be a great war. . . . My belief was based on the fact that the two sides were at the very height of their power and preparedness. . . ." Historians today share his desire for intellectual analysis of the facts, but might come to different conclusions about the results. In any case, as a result of Thucydides' *History of the Peloponnesian War,* we now have the earliest, most carefully detailed record of a war—and of the destruction of a way of life.

Thucydides

THE PELOPONNESIAN WAR, 431–404 B.C.

To counter growing Athenian power, Sparta gathered together allies—the Peloponnesian League—to challenge the power of the Athenian Empire. While the flash point of the conflict was a dispute between two poleis, Thucydides recorded the Spartan viewpoint: "What made war inevitable was the growth of Athenian power and the fear which this caused in Sparta." At its core, this was a war to preserve the independence of each city-state and the unique brand of competitiveness among all the poleis. Athens had grown too strong, and the contest too uneven. Sparta felt compelled to take action when Athens increased its imperial ambitions.

The actual fighting proved awkward and difficult, for Athens and Sparta each had differing strengths and military styles. Athens was surrounded by long walls that extended to the shore (see inset in Map 2.4). Therefore, as long as the Athenian navy controlled the sea, Athens could not be successfully besieged. Thus Athens preferred to conduct battle with its navy and harried Spartan and allied territories from the sea. Sparta, on the other hand, put its trust in its formidable infantry. Bolstering their individual strengths, Athens's allies surrounded the Aegean Sea, while Sparta's allies were largely land based, as Map 2.4 shows. As the Spartans marched across the isthmus near Megara to burn Athens's crops and fields, Athenians watched safely from behind their walls and supplied their needs with their massive fleet. However, there were bloody clashes as young Athenians tried to stop the Spartans, who were ravaging the countryside, and Athenians

FIGURE 2.14
Theater at Delphi.

suffered inside the city that was overcrowded with refugees. Under these conditions, plague struck the city in 430–429 B.C. Even Pericles succumbed, along with about one-quarter of the population. Athenian leadership fell to lesser men, whom contemporaries denounced as selfish and impulsive (such as Alcibiades, featured in the Biography on page 73).

Athens's long-held principles deteriorated further with the city-state's shameful treatment of Melos, an island that sought neutrality in 416 B.C. in the conflict between Athens and Sparta. Athens argued that its *Melos destroyed* superior strength gave it the right to force Melos into serving as its ally. Maintaining that they had the right to make their own choices, the Melians held their ground. The furious Athenians struck back, killing every last man on Melos and enslaving the women and children. Dismayed by this atrocity, Thucydides observed that the ravages of war had reduced "men's characters to a level with their fortunes." By this he meant that, under the relentless pressure of war, the Athenians had sacrificed their ideals of justice in favor of expediency.

The turning point of the war came when Alcibiades, one of the new leaders of Athens, persuaded residents of the polis to meddle in a dispute between two Greek city-states in Sicily. Alcibiades saw this involvement as a way to gain glory for himself, and perhaps as a ploy by which Athens could extend its

control outside the Aegean Sea. It may have worked, for if Athens could control the sea trade between Greece and Italy *Athens loses* (the Ionian Sea), Sparta's commercial allies would have been ruined. However, the venture ended in disaster: Athens lost as many as 200 ships and 40,000 men. Its fleet severely weakened, Athens could no longer rule the Aegean, and its reluctant "allies" began to fall away. Although eight years would elapse between the Sicilian disaster and Athens's final defeat, the city-state could not recover enough to prevail. The Peloponnesian League's fleet, partially financed by a Persia eager to help weaken Athens, destroyed the remnants of the Athenian fleet. Cut off from the trade that would have let them survive a siege, the Athenians were forced to surrender in 404 B.C. Their defeat would have profound political and philosophic ramifications.

PHILOSOPHICAL MUSINGS: ATHENS CONTEMPLATES DEFEAT

During the devastating war, some Athenians started asking themselves sobering questions about justice and the meaning of life. The answers they came up with led them down new pathways of thought—pathways that would permanently alter the direction of Western philosophy. Athenian politicians like Alcibiades and the architects of the Melos atrocity had promulgated the principle of moral relativism—whatever was good for them was right. At the time, some philosophers in Athens shared this belief. These *Sophists* (or "wise ones") doubted the existence of universal truths and instead, taught their followers how to influence public opinion and how to forward their own fortunes. Rather than seeking truth, the Sophists argued that "man is the measure of all things," and that people should therefore act in accordance with their own needs and desires—exactly what Alcibiades had done during the Peloponnesian conflict.

Socrates (470?–399 B.C.), the first great philosopher of the West, developed his ideas as a reaction against the Sophists' moral relativism. Supposedly, the

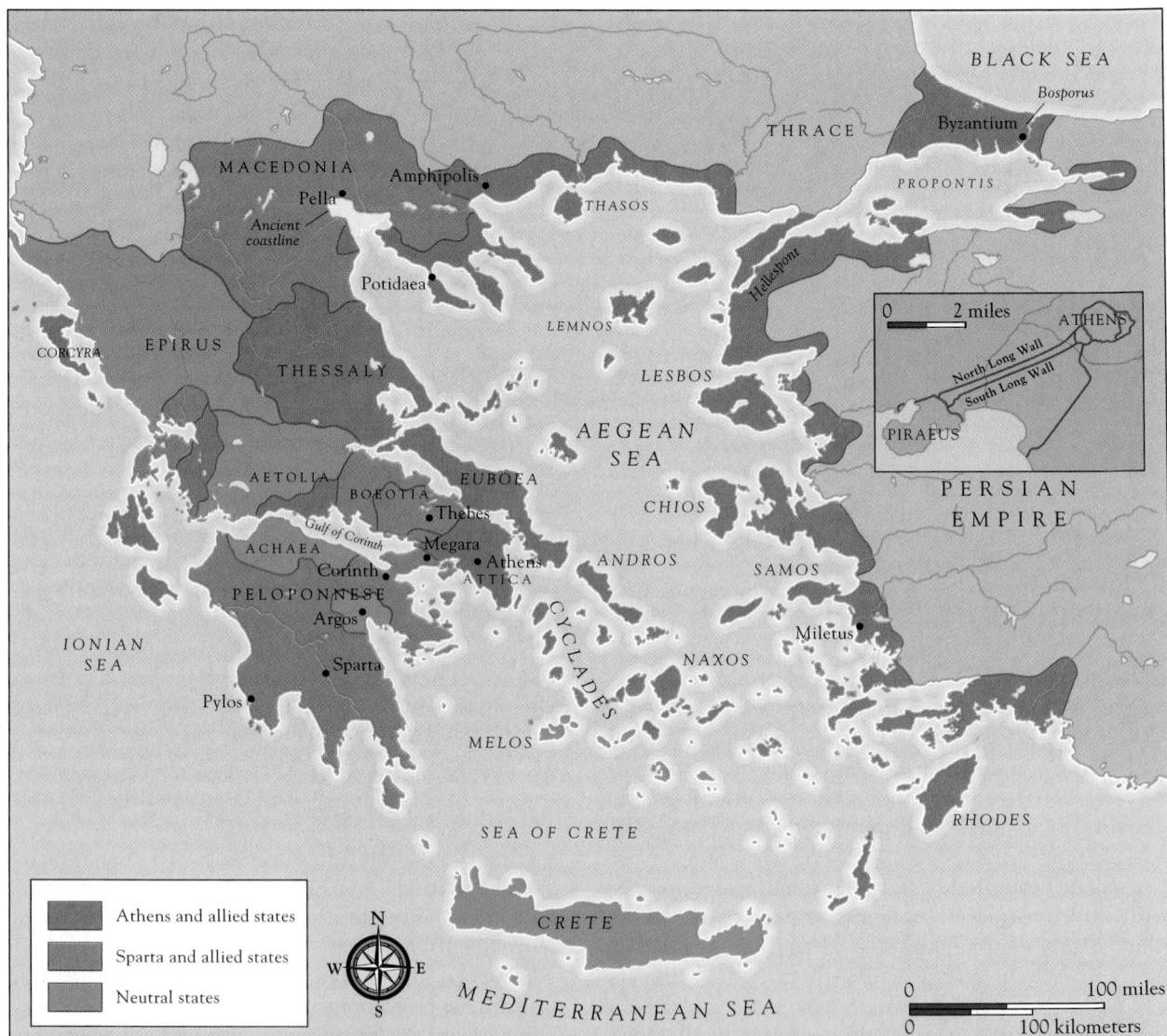

THINKING ABOUT GEOGRAPHY

MAP 2.4   *The Peloponnesian War, 431 B.C.*

This map shows Athens and Sparta and their allies during the Peloponnesian war. ✉ **Notice** how Athens is surrounded on land and thus had to rely on its fleet and its allies in the Aegean. ✉ **Notice** how Athens' long walls (shown in the inset) extend to protect its harbor. **What** does this indicate about the importance of Athens' fleet? ✉ **Notice** how many of Athens' allies bordered the Persian Empire. **Consider,** given this location, whether Persia will be drawn into this war.

Biography

ALCIBIADES (450?–404 B.C.)

⬧ **Consider** how Alcibiades' life illustrates the concept of the contest for excellence and the drive for personal greatness at any expense.

⬧ **Consider** also how Alcibiades' relationship to Socrates might have contributed to the philosopher's condemnation.

Alcibiades was born to a well-placed family in Athens, but his father died when the boy was only about three. The child was then raised in the house of Pericles, the talented leader of Athens, who was his mother's cousin. Tall, handsome, wealthy, charming, and a skilled orator (in spite of a lisp), Alcibiades had all the advantages of a privileged Athenian youth. The philosopher Socrates took a personal interest in the promising young man and spent a great deal of time teaching him. Alcibiades was perfectly positioned to succeed Pericles as a leader in Athens. However, he lacked his foster father's integrity and his teacher's sense of virtue. Instead, he seems to have been overly proud and impulsive and placed his own interests above those of his polis.

The outbreak of the Peloponnesian War in 431 B.C. gave the young man the opportunity to win the admiration of his countrymen. At one point in the war, Alcibiades shared a tent with Socrates, who saved his life during a skirmish but allowed the youth to take credit for heroism. Alcibiades' political career was launched on the battlefield, where Athenian men traditionally proved their manhood.

Alcibiades married a well-born woman, Hipparete, with whom he had a son. Hipparete quickly learned of Alcibiades' character flaws and licentiousness and tried to divorce him. Family ties and political expedience were against her, however, and she was forced to remain a dutiful wife. She chose to ignore her husband's philandering, while he built his reputation in public life.

When the war against Sparta subsided temporarily after 421 B.C., Alcibiades turned to other means to buttress his fame. In 416 B.C., he entered seven four-horse teams in the chariot races of the Olympics and won the top prizes. Except for one Greek king, no one had ever before spent so much money on the races, and no one had won so much. Yet Alcibiades saw war as the real path to glory. He maneuvered to revive the conflict with Sparta and urged Athens to request a deputation from Sicily, which wanted Athens's assistance against Syracuse. Alcibiades saw in this alliance an opportunity to win riches and land, and he persuaded the Athenians to send a large expedition to Sicily.

Before the expedition could depart, however, the Athenians were shocked by a display of impiety that seemed to bring a bad omen. The statues of Hermes that adorned the city had been smashed and mutilated. During an investigation into this desecration, which struck at the very heart of Athenian pride, the citizens heard testimony that implicated Alcibiades himself. In addition, one of his own slaves accused Alcibiades of ridiculing the sacred "mysteries" of Demeter by drunkenly mocking the goddess's religious rituals at a dinner party. The charge seems to have been true and shows the tension between those Athenians who had little fear of the gods and those who found impiety terrifying.

Hero, Military Genius, and Traitor

As the proceedings against Alcibiades dragged on, the summer sailing season began to wane. The Athenian expedition left for Sicily with Alcibiades in the lead. However, the fleet had not even reached Sicily when Alcibiades was recalled to answer the mounting charges against him. The Sicilian expedition ended in disaster, but Alcibiades was not there to see it.

Instead of returning to Athens, Alcibiades fled to Sparta, offering advice and leadership to his traditional enemy. He impressed the Spartans with his obvious talents and with his seeming ability to live with no luxuries. He stayed in Sparta for two years, helping his newfound allies plot against Athens.

Alcibiades' luck evaporated when he reputedly seduced the Spartan king's wife. To escape the king's ire, he fled to Persia, the enemy of both Sparta and Athens. The Persians, too, were impressed with Alcibiades' talents. He negotiated an alliance with the Persians that would prove damaging to Sparta and then returned triumphant to Athens. When war broke out again between Sparta and Athens, Alcibiades was given command of the Athenian fleet and the opportunity to assume the kind of power that Pericles had held. However, the Spartan commander, Lysander, won a spectacular victory. The loss was not Alcibiades' fault, but the Athenians blamed him and he was again forced to flee. In 404 B.C. the Spartans and Persians arranged the assassination of Alcibiades. In an ironic twist, the heroic opportunist who chose personal glory over allegiance to his polis died at the hands of his former partners in treachery.

Delphic oracle had reported that there was "no man wiser than Socrates." After this revelation, the philosopher spent the rest of his life roaming the streets of Athens, questioning his fellow citizens in an effort to find someone wiser than he. His questions took the form of dialogues that forced people to examine their beliefs critically and confront the logical consequences of their ideas. Socrates came to the conclusion that, indeed, he was the wisest man because he alone understood that he knew nothing, and that wisdom lies in the endless search for knowledge. Athenians came to know the rather homely man, whose father worked as a stonemason and whose mother was a midwife. Socrates, who saw himself as giving birth to ideas, claimed to have followed his mother's occupation more closely than his father's.

Socrates left no writings, so we know of his ideas only from the words of one of his students, Plato. According to these texts, Socrates expressed the idea that there were absolutes of truth and justice and excellence, and that a dormant knowledge of these absolutes rested within all people. In these enquiries, Socrates not only departed from the Sophists, but from the early philosophers like Thales who wanted to know the nature of the world—Socrates wanted to explore the nature of right action. The method he employed was that of questioning and refuting students' answers, and with this method—now called the "Socratic" method—he brought students to see the truth.

Socrates called himself a "gadfly" for his efforts to goad other Athenians into examining their opinions —but gadflies that sting painfully are seldom appreciated. Socrates began his enquiries in the dynamic period before the Peloponnesian War, but in the times of disillusionment after the war, Athenian jurors were suspicious of anyone who seemed to oppose the democracy—even by pointing out humankind's inadequacies. Socrates was brought to trial and accused of impiety and corruption of the young. The latter charge was no doubt forwarded by the reprehensible behavior of Alcibiades, who had been Socrates' student, but the former charge had no basis. Socrates was found guilty, even though he shrewdly discounted the charges during his trial. His friends urged him to stop questioning others and to simply flee, to which he replied with the famous words that began this chapter: "Life without enquiry is not worth living." He received the death penalty and drank a cup of the deadly poison hemlock.

Socrates' ideas, however, did not die with him, but lived on in his students. Plato, his best-known follower, wrote many dialogues in which he seems to have preserved his teacher's ideas, although historians are uncertain where Socrates' teachings end and Plato's begin. Plato believed that truth and justice existed only as ideal models, or "forms," but that humans could apprehend those realities only to a limited degree. Real people, he argued, lived in the imperfect world of the senses, a world that revealed only shadows of reality. This was his answer to the relativist Sophists, who saw the imperfect world as the true measure of right and wrong. For Plato, the goal of philosophical inquiry was to find the abstract and perfect "right" that was so elusive in this world. He established a school in Athens called the Academy to educate young Greek men in the tenets of virtue, for he believed that only through long training in philosophy could one learn to understand the ideal forms that exist outside the human world.

Plato was disillusioned with the democracy that had killed his teacher, Socrates, and admired Sparta's rigorous way of life. This political affinity shaped what is perhaps Plato's best-known work, *The Republic,* in which he outlined the ideal form of government. Instead of encouraging democracy, he explained, states should be ruled autocratically by philosopher-kings. In this way, the world might exhibit almost perfect justice. In some respects, this work expresses an articulate disillusionment with the failure of Athenian democracy to conduct a long war with honor or to tolerate a decent man pointing out citizens' shortcomings.

Plato's perfect state was never founded, but nevertheless, his ideas had an enduring impact on Western civilization. Subsequent philosophers would confront his theory of ideal forms as they created other philosophic systems. His call for introspection and an awareness of self as the way to true knowledge would also have profound intellectual and religious implications.

Plato's ideas were not accepted universally in the Greek world. The career of his student Aristotle is one example. The son of a physician, Aristotle studied at Plato's Academy and then spent another twenty years refining his thinking, debating his ideas, and writing. As much as Aristotle valued his teacher, he departed from Plato's theory of "perfect forms" and declared that ideas cannot exist

Socrates

Plato

Aristotle

outside their physical manifestations. Therefore, he concluded, to study anything—from plants to poetics to politics—one had to observe and study actual entities. Through his practical observations, Aristotle divided knowledge into categories, which remained the organizing principle of learning for over a thousand years. He said there were three categories of knowledge: ethics, or the principles of social life; natural history, the study of nature; and metaphysics, the study of the primary laws of the universe. He approached these studies through logic, which, in his hands, became a primary tool of philosophy and science. Aristotle's approach represented a major departure from the perspective of Plato, who argued that one should think about ideals instead of studying the imperfect nature of this world.

Aristotle also departed from his teacher on the subject of politics. As was his custom, the philosopher studied the different kinds of governments—monarchies, aristocracies, and republics—and discussed how each style could degenerate into corruption. He thought the ideal state was a small polis with a mixed constitution and a powerful middle class to prevent extremes. Aristotle recoiled from extremes in all aspects of life and argued for a balance—in his famous phrase, a "golden mean"—that would bring happiness. The philosopher extended his idea of moderation to the realm of ethics, arguing that the lack of excess would yield virtue.

TRAGEDY AND COMEDY: INNOVATIONS IN GREEK THEATER

Athens's disillusioning war with Sparta had prompted philosophers to explore challenging questions of justice and virtue. Athenian theater, too, underwent change during the conflict. The playwright Euripides (485–406 B.C.) wrote tragedies in which people grappled with anguish on a heroic scale. In these plays he expressed an intense pessimism and the lack of a divine moral order that marked Athens after the Peloponnesian War. In *Women of Troy*, written in the year of Alcibiades' expedition against Sicily, Euripides explored the pain of a small group of captured Trojan women. Though set in the era of the war immortalized by Homer, *Women of Troy* also had a strong contemporary message. In part, it represented a criticism of Athens's treatment of Melos and of the enslavement of Greek women

Euripedes

and children. When a character in *Women of Troy* mused, "Strange how intolerable the indignity of slavery is to those born free," Euripedes was really asking the Athenians to reflect on their own actions. In foretelling destruction to the Greeks who abused the women of Troy, Euripides predicted the eventual downfall of Athens.

Tragedy was not the only way to challenge contemporary society; talented playwrights also used comedy. As Greeks laughed at the crudest of sexual jokes and bathroom humor, they criticized public figures and conquered their own anxieties. These plays appeal less to modern audiences than do the Greek tragedies for, in their intense fascination with human nature, Greeks embraced even our basest inclinations. The comedies of this era also reveal much about Greek perceptions of the human body and their lack of modesty. Just as their character flaws became the subject of tragedies, their bodies were often the focus of comedies.

The vase in Figure 2.15 portrays a typical scene from Greek comedy. In this rendering, each actor sports a long, artificial phallus hanging well below his tunic, and padded buttocks to increase the comic effect. The actors also wear highly stylized masks. In the window is a man wearing a woman's mask. The scene portrays Zeus trying to seduce the woman in the window and the extreme costuming highlights the bawdy and disrespectful subject matter. Although we often find such graphic portrayals tasteless at best, Greek society was surrounded with them, and we cannot fully understand the Greeks without recognizing the way they accepted their humanity in its fullest sense.

Aristophanes

While people laughed at these comic portrayals, the greatest of the comic playwrights also used humor for serious purposes. Aristophanes (455–385 B.C.), for example, used costumes and crude humor to deliver biting political satire. This esteemed Athenian playwright was a conservative Athenian trying to preserve traditional values, and he delivered a ruthless criticism of contemporary Athens. Like many citizens, Aristophanes longed for peace. In 411 B.C.—at the height of the Peloponnesian War—he wrote *Lysistrata*, a hilarious antiwar play in which the women of Athens force their men to make peace by refusing to have sexual intercourse with them until they comply. With *Lysistrata*, Aristophanes reminded people that life and sex were more important than death and war.

FIGURE 2.15
Vase with a scene from a Greek comedy, fourth century B.C.

HIPPOCRATES AND MEDICINE

While philosophers and playwrights mulled over abstract notions of life and human nature, Greek physicians turned to a practical study of the human body, influencing subsequent opinions of medicine. Previous ancient societies had made a number of strides in medical knowledge—the Babylonians and Assyrians kept catalogs of healing herbs, and the Egyptians were famed for medical treatments such as setting fractures, amputating limbs, and even opening skulls to relieve pressure on head injuries. However, most of the medical knowledge that influenced the West for centuries came from the Greeks, whose systematic treatises really began to separate medicine from the supernatural. Hippocrates (460?–377? B.C.), considered the father of modern Western medicine, supposedly claimed that "every disease has a natural cause, and without natural causes nothing ever happens." With this statement Hippocrates rejected the ancient belief that spirits were responsible for human ailments.

Hippocrates was a highly respected physician and gave his name to a body of medical writing known as the *Hippocratic Collection*, compiled between the fifth and third centuries B.C. The *Collection* established medicine on a rational basis devoid of supernatural explanations of disease—a major innovation in Western culture. Consistent with other Greek thinkers from Thucydides to Aristotle, it also emphasized careful observation. This body of writings contains more than 400 short observations about health and disease—for example, "People who are excessively overweight are far more apt to die suddenly than those of average weight," or "Extremes in diet must be avoided." Overall, this new approach to medicine put human beings, rather than the gods, at the center of study. The human-centered outlook of Greek medicine culminated in a long-standing idea expressed in the Hippocratic Oath. Modern physicians still take this oath, in which they vow first to do no harm to their patients.

Though Athens suffered some dark days of war and disillusionment, this difficult era also witnessed the rise of geniuses who used the hard times as a backdrop for exploring the complex nature of humanity. Greek philosophers, playwrights, and physicians created brilliant works and conceived of ideas that transcended their time despite the turmoil of the age.

THE AFTERMATH OF WAR, 404–338 B.C.

As a condition of its surrender at the end of the Peloponnesian War, Athens agreed to break down its defensive walls and reduce its fleet to only 12 ships. These harsh measures not only ended the Athenian Empire but also erased any possibility for a politically united Greece. The Spartans left a garrison in Athens and sent the rest of its troops home to their barrack state to guard their slaves. Sparta's subsequent attempts to assemble a political coalition foundered on its high-handed and inept foreign policy. Sparta's major allies, especially Corinth, opposed the Peloponnesian peace treaty, accusing Sparta of grabbing all the tribute and objecting to what they saw as lenience toward Athens. The generous treaty also stipulated that the Greek states in Asia Minor be given to Persia as the price for Persia's aid to Sparta, further eroding Greek unity.

All these postwar developments heightened competition among the poleis in the years after Athens's loss. For example, Corinth and Thebes *Power struggles* fought wars to earn control of other Greek city-states while Sparta ineptly struggled to preserve some leadership. Persia remained involved in Greek affairs, shrewdly offering money to one side and then another so that the Greeks would continue to fight each other. In this way, Persia kept the poleis from marshaling their strength against their longtime imperial enemy.

These wars among the poleis only aggravated serious weaknesses within each city. Democracy in Athens as a political form, for example, had been deeply threatened by the long, devastating war. Antidemocratic feelings expressed in the works of Plato erupted as Athens fell. As Thucydides had noted, democracy was not safe during turbulent times. As the war came to an end in 404 B.C., a brutal tyranny of 30 men took over and tried to stamp out the vestiges of democracy. Fifteen hundred democratic leaders were killed in the coup, and 5,000 more were exiled. This oligarchy lasted only eight months before democracy was restored, but the revived government had only a shadow of its former vigor. Fed by an involved citizenry, democracy had flourished in Athens. Now, without its empire and large fleet, fewer citizens became wealthy, and political involvement waned.

Traditional participatory government in all the poleis unraveled further with innovations in military tactics. Under skillful generals, lightly armed javelin throwers, slingers, and archers began to defeat the heavily armed citizen hoplite armies that had once been the glory of Greece. Moreover, in the century following the Peloponnesian War, more and more Greeks served as mercenaries. See Document 2.3 on page D2.2 for a famous account of Greek mercenaries fighting in Persia. These paid soldiers, owing allegiance to no city, added further disruption to an already unstable time. In this period of growing anarchy, every major Greek polis endured at least one war or revolution every 10 years.

The nascent collective power of the Greek city-states also deteriorated during the postwar era. None of the poleis had succeeded in forging a lasting Hellenic coalition. The sovereignty of each city remained the defining idea in Greek politics. With this principle as a backdrop, individualism and loyalty to one's own city overrode any notions of a larger civic discipline. This competitive attitude had fueled the greatest of the Greeks' accomplishments in the arts, athletics, and politics, but it also gave rise to men like Alcibiades, who could not see beyond their own self-interests. In the midst of the troubled fourth century B.C., many Greeks feared that Persia would return to conquer a weakened Greece. As we will see in the next chapter, they should have worried about the "backward" people to the north instead.

Summary

Small city-states nestled in the mountains of the Greek peninsula rerouted the course of Western civilization. These fiercely independent cities developed participatory forms of government that encouraged men to take active roles in all aspects of their cities. Through their vigorous involvement in the life of their poleis, the men of ancient Greece created magnificent works of art, theater, and architecture that came to define Western aesthetics. These men also developed a rational approach to inquiry that has enriched Westerners' understanding of life, history, philosophy, and medicine even in modern times.

But the pride in individual accomplishment that catalyzed such extraordinary accomplishments also contained the seeds of Greece's own political destruction. The future leadership of the eastern Mediterranean would come from a people who could set aside their heroic individualism to support a larger unity. However, this influx of new ideas did not erase the legacy of Greek achievement. The newcomers would ultimately spread the accomplishments of this complex culture as far east as India as they forged a new empire.

TIMELINE: A CLOSER LOOK

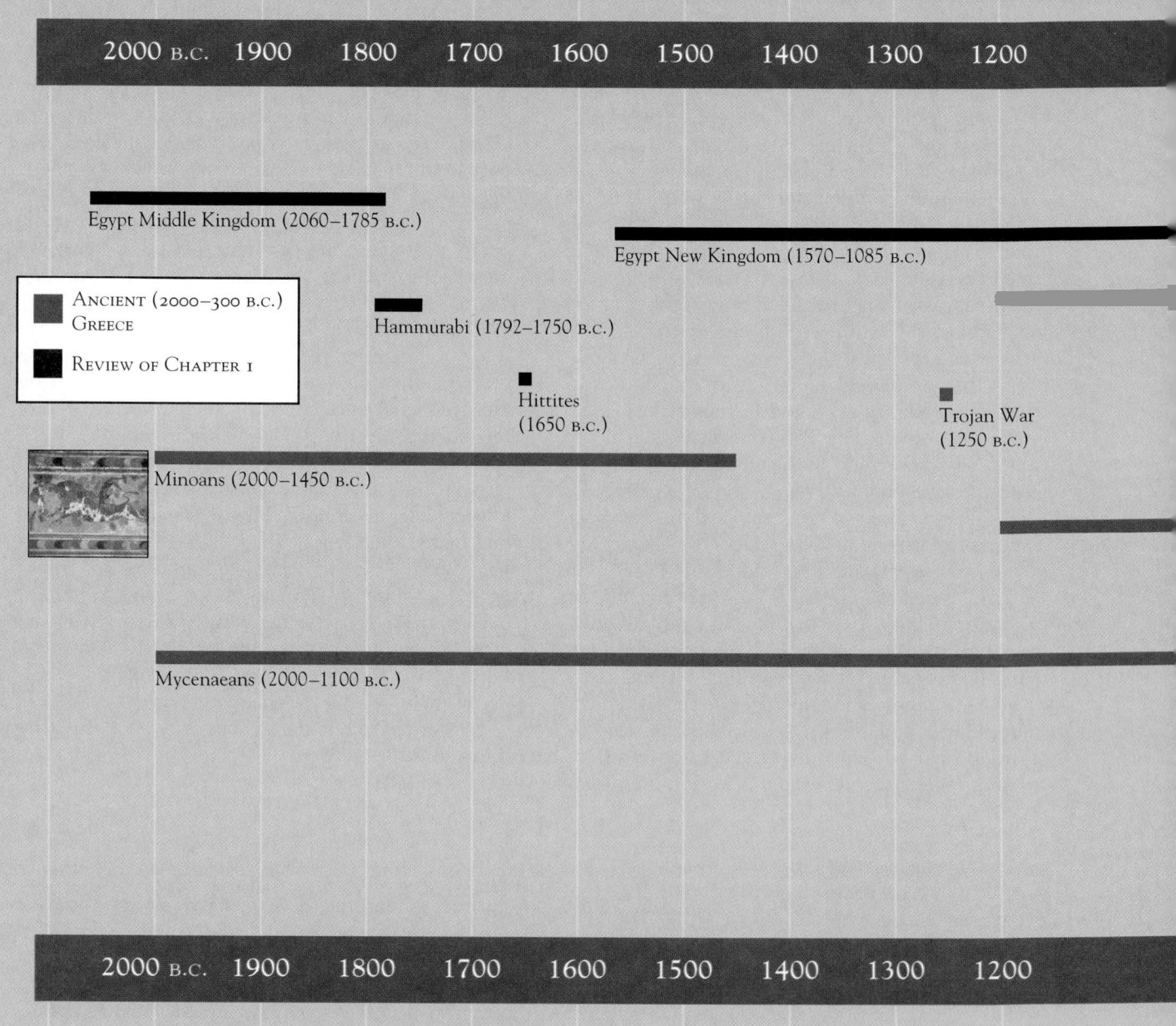

| 2000 B.C. | 1900 | 1800 | 1700 | 1600 | 1500 | 1400 | 1300 | 1200 |

Egypt Middle Kingdom (2060–1785 B.C.)

Egypt New Kingdom (1570–1085 B.C.)

ANCIENT (2000–300 B.C.) GREECE

REVIEW OF CHAPTER 1

Hammurabi (1792–1750 B.C.)

Hittites (1650 B.C.)

Trojan War (1250 B.C.)

Minoans (2000–1450 B.C.)

Mycenaeans (2000–1100 B.C.)

| 2000 B.C. | 1900 | 1800 | 1700 | 1600 | 1500 | 1400 | 1300 | 1200 |

REVIEW, ANALYZE, AND ANTICIPATE

REVIEW THE PREVIOUS CHAPTER

Chapter 1—"The Roots of Western Civilization"—described the growth and development of the civiliza-tions of Mesopotamia, Egypt, and the eastern Mediter-ranean coast, highlighting their contributions to the future of Western civilization. It also described the growth of empires in that region.

1. *Review the growth of empires in the ancient Middle East and contrast that process with the political development of Greece.*

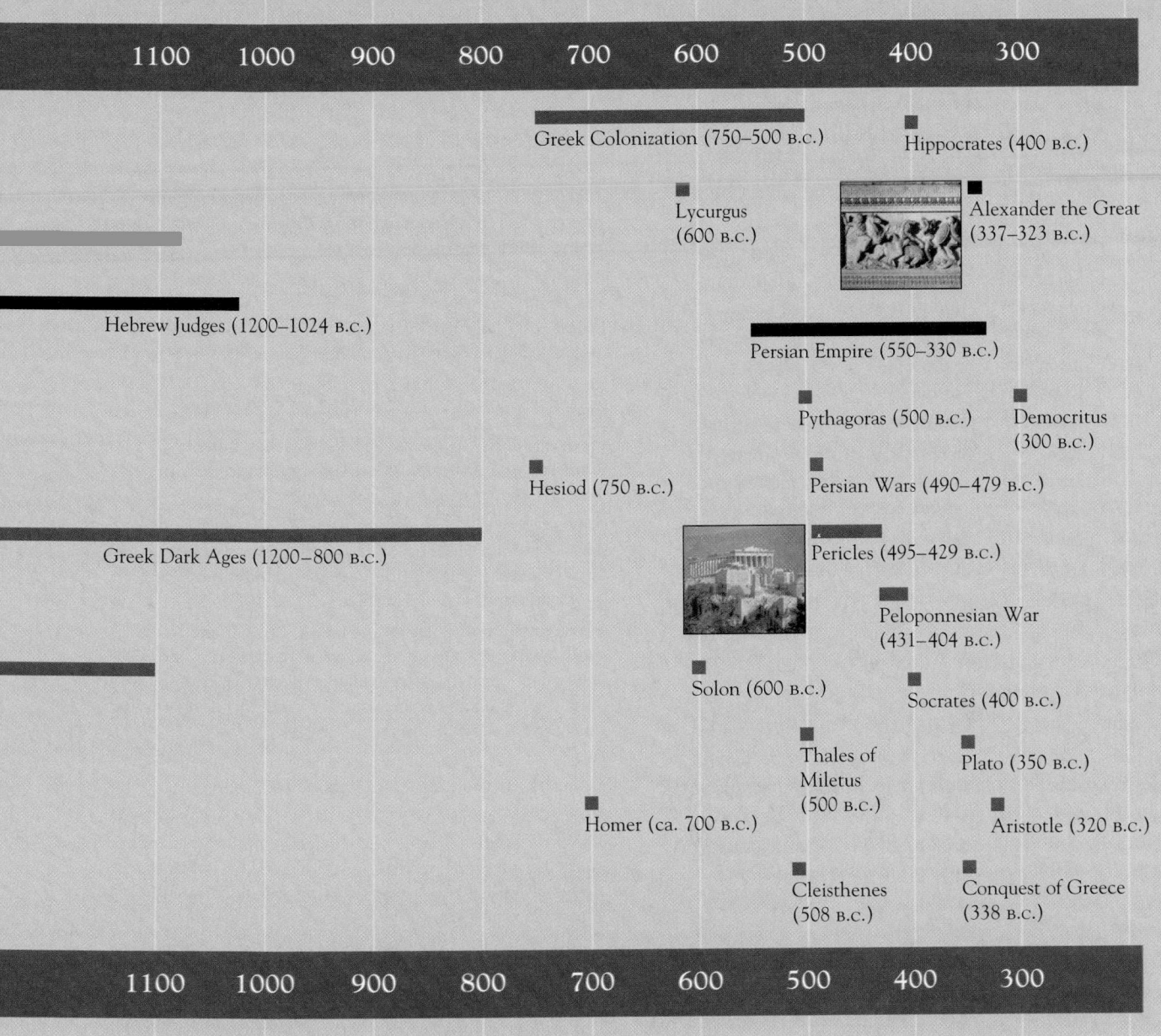

1100 1000 900 800 700 600 500 400 300

Greek Colonization (750–500 B.C.)

Hippocrates (400 B.C.)

Lycurgus (600 B.C.)

Alexander the Great (337–323 B.C.)

Hebrew Judges (1200–1024 B.C.)

Persian Empire (550–330 B.C.)

Pythagoras (500 B.C.)

Democritus (300 B.C.)

Hesiod (750 B.C.)

Persian Wars (490–479 B.C.)

Greek Dark Ages (1200–800 B.C.)

Pericles (495–429 B.C.)

Peloponnesian War (431–404 B.C.)

Solon (600 B.C.)

Socrates (400 B.C.)

Thales of Miletus (500 B.C.)

Plato (350 B.C.)

Homer (ca. 700 B.C.)

Aristotle (320 B.C.)

Cleisthenes (508 B.C.)

Conquest of Greece (338 B.C.)

1100 1000 900 800 700 600 500 400 300

2. *Review the characteristics of Phoenician society discussed in Chapter 1. Consider what qualities the Phoenicians had in common with the early Greeks that might have led both peoples to be such successful colonizers.*

ANALYZE THIS CHAPTER

Chapter 2—"The Contest for Excellence"—looks at the rise and fall of the civilizations in the Aegean region culminating in the growth of classic Greek civilization. It describes life in ancient Greece, the political fortunes of the city-states, and the dramatic accomplishments in culture and science that influenced the future.

1. *Review the causes of the decline of the Minoans, the Mycenaeans, and the Athenian Empire.*

2. *Review the economic life of the Greek city-states, and consider the impact of geography on their economic choices. Also consider how the Greek economy influenced political decisions.*

3. *Compare and contrast Athens and Sparta and their political and social systems. Why did Spartan women play a more meaningful role in society than did Athenian women?*

4. *Consider the Greeks' views on religion and review how these views influenced their approach to other aspects of their lives, like science and medicine.*

5. *Review Greek accomplishments in the arts, sciences, and political life, and consider why they would be so influential on future societies.*

ANTICIPATE THE NEXT CHAPTER

In Chapter 3—"The Poleis Become Cosmopolitan" —we will see Greek influences spread as far east as India and explore Hellenism's confrontation with many other cultures.

1. *Which of the accomplishments you reviewed in Question 5 above might most readily be adopted by political entities larger than poleis? Which might be most transformed in the process?*

2. *Do you think Greek traditions of participatory government will survive in large, multiethnic empires?*

BEYOND THE CLASSROOM

THE RISE AND FALL OF ANCIENT HEROES, 2000–800 B.C.

Burkert, Walter. *Greek Religion.* Cambridge, MA: Harvard University Press, 1985. A masterful reconstruction of Greek festival activities that addresses the problem of rituals of animal sacrifice.

Fitton, J. Lesley. *The Discovery of the Greek Bronze Age.* Cambridge, MA: Harvard University Press, 1996. An informed and elegantly written account of the history of archaeological investigations.

Graves, Robert. *The Greek Myths: Complete Edition.* NY: Viking Penguin, 1993. An in-depth study of the major Greek myths.

Larson, Jennifer. *Greek Heroine Cults.* Madison: University of Wisconsin Press, 1995. A solid study of an unusual and little explored phenomenon: women venerated as heroes.

Lloyd, Geoffrey E.R. *Early Greek Science: Thales to Aristotle.* NY: Norton, 1970. A study of branches, theories, methods, and problems of Greek science from the beginning of Thales to the death of Aristotle.

Martin, Thomas R. *Ancient Greece: From Prehistoric to Hellenistic Times.* New Haven, CT: Yale University Press, 1996. A skillful blend of social, cultural, political, and military data to create a panoramic view of the Greek world.

LIFE IN THE GREEK POLEIS, 700–489 B.C.

Dodds, Eric R. *The Greeks and the Irrational.* Berkeley: University of California Press, 1968. A classic study of human experience through the Greek mind.

Dover Kenneth, J. *Greek Homosexuality.* Cambridge, MA: Harvard University Press, 1978. A description of homosexual behavior and sentiment in Greek art and literature between the eighth and second centuries B.C.

Fantham, E., H.P. Foley, N.B. Hampen, S.B. Pomeroy, and H.A. Shapiro. *Women in the Classical World.* NY: Oxford University Press, 1995. A readable, illustrated, chronological survey of Greek and Roman women's lives, focusing on vivid cultural and social history.

Hooker, J. *The Ancient Spartans.* London: J.M. Dent, 1980. Comprehensive in scope, with good illustrations.

Hornblower, Simon. *The Greek World.* NY: Routledge, 2002. Uses up-to-date archaeological and epigraphical evidence to study the full Greek world—Egypt, Cyrene, Asia Minor, Etaly—as well as the city-states of the Greek mainland. Informative and accessible.

Kennell, Nigel M. *The Gymnasium of Culture: Education and Culture in Ancient Sparta.* Chapel Hill, NC: University of North Carolina, 1995.

Pedley, John Griffiths. *Greek Art and Archaeology.* NY: H.N. Abrams, 1993. A study of the architecture, sculpture, pottery, and wall paintings of ancient Greece.

Sealey, R. *Athenian Democracy.* University Park, PA: Pennsylvania State University Press, 1987. An interpretation of Athenian constitutional history.

IMPERIAL ATHENS, 489–431 B.C.

Herodotus. *The History of Herodotus,* trans. D. Grene. Chicago: University of Chicago Press, 1987. The primary source for the Persian Wars by the acknowledged "Father of History."

McGregor, Malcolm F. *The Athenians and Their Empire*. Vancouver: University of British Columbia Press, 1987. The standard brief history of the Athenian Empire.

Powell, Anton. *Constructing Greek Political Power and Social History from 478 B.C.* NY: Routledge, 1991. An introduction to Greek history from 478 to 411 B.C.; includes a chapter on women in Athens.

Wood, Ellen M. *Peasant-Citizen and Slave: The Foundations of Athenian Democracy*. NY: Routledge, Chapman and Hall, 1988. Controversial piece disputing two modern myths—that of the idle mob and that of slavery—as the basis of Athenian democracy.

DESTRUCTION, DISILLUSION, AND A SEARCH FOR MEANING

Lloyd, Geoffrey E.R. *Greek Science After Aristotle*. NY: Norton, 1973. Deals with the social background of Hellenistic science, the Lyceum after Aristotle, Epicureans and Stoics, Hellenistic mathematics, astronomy, biology, and medicine.

Reale, Giovanni. *A History of Ancient Philosophy, Vol. II—Plato and Aristotle*. NY: State University of New York Press, 1990. A look at the remarkable heights of thought achieved by Plato and Aristotle.

Snell, Bruno. *The Discovery of the Mind: The Greek Origins of European Thought*. NY: Harper & Row, 1960. A study of how Western thought was based on the Greeks.

Sutton, D. *Self and Society in Aristophanes*. Washington, DC: University Press of America, 1980. A sophisticated analysis of the portrayal of Greek society in the plays of Aristophanes.

Thucydides, *The Peloponnesian War*, trans. J.H. Finley. NY: The Modern Library, 1951. The great primary source on the Peloponnesian War, which forms the starting point for any study.

For quiz questions that tie the book to the videos and additional primary sources, please go to the Primary Source Investigator CD.

QUIZ

Old Market Woman, third or second century B.C.

In the great cosmopolitan cities of the Hellenistic world, many people lived in poverty and struggled all their lives just to survive. Artists began to portray these people in realistic images that were much less heroic than those favored by earlier Greek artists. Change was afoot in the Greek world.

CHAPTER 3

The Poleis Become Cosmopolitan

The Hellenistic World, 323–150 B.C.

STUDY • Alexander's conquests • Establishment of successor kingdoms • Hellenistic economy and culture • Hellenistic philosophy, religion, and science. ⊕NOTICE how Greek culture was transformed by its spread eastward into Asia.

Alexander "conducted himself as he did out of a desire to subject all the races in the world to one rule and one form of government making all mankind a single people." The Greek biographer Plutarch (A.D. 46–119) wrote these words 400 years after the death of the Macedonian king Alexander the Great (356–323 B.C.). In his description of Alexander, Plutarch attributed high ideals to the young conqueror that Alexander himself may not have held. However, the biographer's glowing portrayal captured the reality of Alexander's conquests, whereby he joined the great civilizations of the ancient Middle East and classical Greece in a way that transformed them both.

In this new world, described as "Hellenistic" (meaning "Greek-like") by nineteenth-century historians, the ideal Greek poleis changed from scattered, independent city-states into large, multiethnic urban centers—what the Greeks called "world cities," or cosmopolitan sites—firmly anchored within substantial kingdoms. Greek colonists achieved high status in the new cities springing up far from the Greek mainland, making the Greek language and culture the ruling ideal from Egypt to India. In this Hellenistic world, classical Greek culture was in turn altered through the influences of the subject peoples, and the new world left the old world of the Greek mainland behind. Society, economy, and politics all played out on a larger scale, and kings, rather than citizens, now ruled. Royal patronage stimulated intellectual and cultural achievement among the privileged classes, while ordinary people struggled to find their place in a new world.

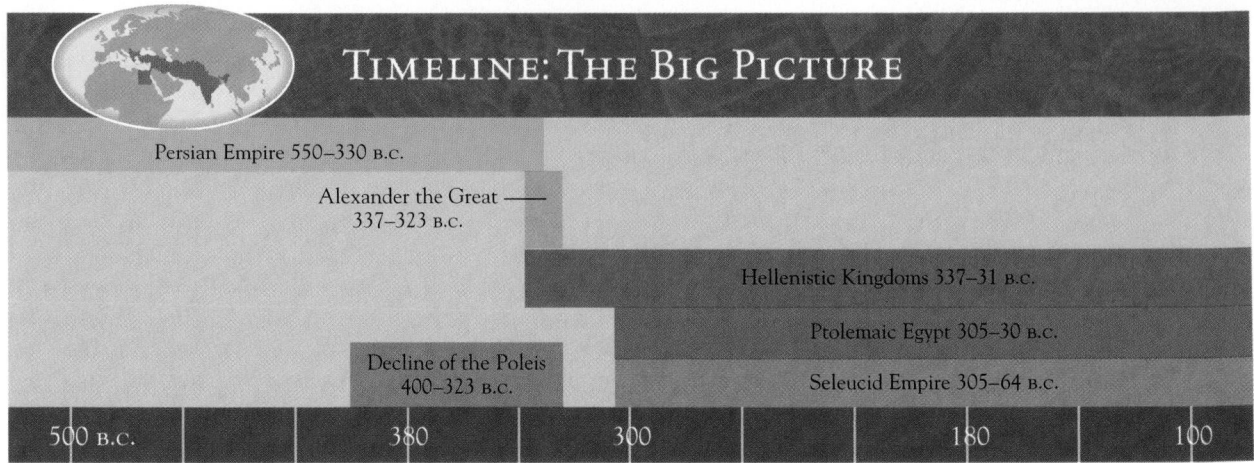

TIMELINE: THE BIG PICTURE

Persian Empire 550–330 B.C.

Alexander the Great ——
337–323 B.C.

Hellenistic Kingdoms 337–31 B.C.

Ptolemaic Egypt 305–30 B.C.

Decline of the Poleis
400–323 B.C.

Seleucid Empire 305–64 B.C.

500 B.C.   380   300   180   100

The Conquest of the Poleis

In 220 B.C., an Egyptian father appealed to the Greek king to help him resolve a domestic dispute. He claimed that his daughter, Nice, had abandoned him in his old age. According to the father, Nice had promised to get a job and pay him a pension out of her wages every month. To his dismay, she instead became involved with a comic actor and neglected her filial duties. The father implored the king, Ptolemy IV, to force Nice to care for him, pleading, "I beg you O king, not to suffer me to be wronged by my daughter and Dionysus the comedian who has corrupted her."

This request—one of many sent to the king during this period—reveals several interesting points about Mediterranean life in the Hellenistic era. For example, it suggests that women worked and earned money instead of staying carefully guarded within the home. It also shows a loosening of the tight family ties that had marked the Greek poleis and the ancient Middle East civilizations—a father could no longer exert authority over his rebellious daughter and could no longer count on his children to care for him in his old age. Finally, it indicates people's view of their king as the highest authority in redressing personal problems. These were dramatic changes, and to trace their origins, we must look to Macedonia, a province on the northeast border of Greece. There, in a land traditionally ruled by strong monarchs, a king arose who would redefine life in the ancient world.

TRIBAL MACEDONIA

Although Macedonia was inhabited by Greek-speaking people, it had not developed the poleis that marked Greek civilization on the peninsula. Instead, it had retained a tribal structure in which aristocrats selected a king and served in his army bound by ties of loyalty and kinship. The southern Greek poleis—populated by self-described "civilized" Greeks—had disdain for the Macedonians, whom they saw as backward because they did not embrace the political life of the city-states.

The Macedonian territory consisted of two distinct parts: the coastal plain to the south and east, and the mountainous interior. The plain offered fertile land for farming and lush pastures in which fine warhorses grazed along with sheep and oxen. The level land of the coastline bordered two bays that afforded access to the Aegean Sea. The Macedonian interior, by contrast, was mountainous and remote, and posed the same problems for rulers that the Greek landscape presented. Kings struggled to exert even a little authority over the fierce tribes in the hills. Yet, concealed within the mountains were precious reserves of timber and metals, including abundant veins of gold and silver in the more remote locations.

Geography

For centuries, the Macedonian kings failed to take full advantage of such treasures in large part because they could not control the remote tribes. Repeated invasions of Macedonia by its neighbors to the north only added to the problem. Throughout this turbulent period, the mainland Greeks thought of Macedonia only as an area to exploit for its natural resources. The Greeks neither helped nor feared their beleaguered relatives to the north and instead focused on keeping their old enemy, Persia, at bay. Nevertheless, eventually a Macedonian king arose who not only succeeded in marshaling the resources of his land, but also rerouted the direction of Greek history.

Uniting the tribes

This great king, Philip II (r. 359–336 B.C.) had participated in some of the many wars that disrupted Greece during the fourth century B.C. (see Chapter 2), and as a result had been held hostage as a young man in the Greek city-state of Thebes for three years. During his captivity, he learned much about the strengths and weaknesses of Greek politics and warfare. Document 3.1 on page D3.1 describes the formative development of this great king. When he returned to Macedonia, he used his new knowledge to educate his people. As his son, Alexander, later reminded the Macedonians: "Philip took you over when you were helpless vagabonds mostly clothed in skins, feeding a few animals on the mountains. . . . He gave you cloaks to wear instead of skins, he brought you down from the mountains to the plains. . . . He made you city dwellers and established the order that comes from good laws and customs."

PHILIP II: MILITARY GENIUS

OLC

The pride of the Macedonian army was the cavalry, led by the king himself and made up of his nobles, known as "companions." Yet Philip showed his military genius in the way he reorganized the supporting forces. The shrewd monarch changed the traditional Greek phalanx, already threatened by a new fighting style that favored lightly armed—and therefore more mobile—foot soldiers. Philip strengthened the phalanx by arming his soldiers with 13-foot pikes instead of the standard 9-foot weapons. Then he instructed the infantry to arrange themselves in a more open formation, which let them take full advantage of the longer pikes. Philip also hired lightly armed, mobile mercenaries who could augment the Macedonian phalanx with arrows, javelins, and slings.

In battle, the long Macedonian pikes kept opponents at a distance, while the cavalry made the deci-*Military innovations* sive difference in almost every battle. The mounted warriors surrounded the enemy and struck at their flank, leaving the lightly armed mercenaries to move in to deliver the final blow. This strategy, which combined traditional heavily armed foot soldiers with the mobility of cavalry and light troops, would prove virtually invincible.

Philip also developed weapons for besieging walled cities. During the Peloponnesian War, even mighty Sparta's only strategy against the sturdy walls of Athens had been to starve the inhabitants to death—a slow and uncertain method. Philip is credited with using a torsion catapult that twisted launching ropes to gain more force than the older models that used counterweights. With this new device, his forces could fire rocks at city walls with deadly force. Although Philip is credited with developing these siege weapons, his son would be the one to successfully use them against many fortified cities.

With his forces reorganized and equipped with the latest weapons, Philip readied himself to expand his kingdom. First, he consolidated his own highlands and the lands to the north and east. These conquests allowed him to exploit the gold and silver mines in the hills, which yielded the riches he needed to finance his campaigns. With his northern flank secure and his treasury full, the conqueror then turned his attention to the warring Greek cities to the south.

Philip dreamed of uniting the Greek city-states under his leadership. Some southern Greeks shared this dream, looking to the Macedonian king to save them from their own inter-*Greek responses* city violence. Isocrates (436–338 B.C.), an Athenian orator and educator, made eloquent speeches in which he supported Philip's expansionist aims. Expressing a prevalent disillusionment with democracy, Isocrates argued that the Greeks were incapable of forming a cohesive union without a leader like Philip. In his view, this form of participatory governance had become so corrupt that "violence is regarded as democracy, lawlessness as liberty, impudence of speech as equality. . . ." Isocrates believed that only Philip could unify the Greeks and empower them to face Asia as one people finally to vanquish their ancient enemy, Persia.

Isocrates' words were compelling. But Athens had another great orator who opposed Philip and who proved more convincing than Isocrates. Demosthenes (384–322 B.C.) argued brilliantly for a position that rejected union under a tyrant like Philip in order to preserve Athens's traditional freedom and the self-government of the polis. As we saw in Chapter 2, the classic polis had eroded in the aftermath of the Peloponnesian War, but the orator was looking backward to a more golden age of democracy. Historians have characterized Demosthenes as everything from a stubborn, old-fashioned orator to the last champion of the lost cause of Athenian freedom. Ultimately, however, the spirited debate about Philip became moot. The question of freedom was answered not in the marketplace of Athens, but on the battlefield.

In 338 B.C., Philip and his armies marched south toward the peninsula, where they confronted a Greek coalition led by Athens and Thebes, long-time rivals who at last joined in cooperation. The belated cooperation among the Greeks came too late. At the Battle of Chaeronea near Thebes, the powerful left wing of Philip's phalanx enveloped the approaching Greeks. The Macedonian cavalry, led by Philip's talented son, Alexander, slaughtered the surrounded Greeks. The victory paved the way for Philip to take control of the Greek city-states (except Sparta).

Greece conquered

Philip proved a lenient conqueror; he charged the Greeks no tribute, but instead united them in a league under his command, so they were technically allies with Macedonia. No longer allowed to wage war against each other, the poleis joined the combined army of Greeks and Macedonians. Isocrates' hope was fulfilled, and the Greeks reluctantly renounced internal warfare. Now they prepared to follow Philip to attack the Persian Empire that extended far beyond the borders of the Persian homeland into Asia.

DEATH OF THE KING

Philip's brilliance on the battlefield exceeded his judgment in domestic matters. In the tradition of Macedonian kings, Philip had taken at least six wives. The most important was Olympias, daughter of the king of Epirus (which was southwest of Macedonia and bordered the Greek city-states) and mother of Alexander. According to Plutarch, who drew from earlier sources, Olympias and Alexander were highly insulted when Philip, in his forties, took a young bride, Cleopatra. At the wedding, Cleopatra's uncle made a toast implying that he hoped Philip would disinherit Alexander. Jealousy in the royal circle intensified even further when Philip, who followed the Greek practice of mentoring and loving young men, seemed to prefer a new youth over his previous favorite, Pausanias.

These political and personal resentments came to a head in 336 B.C. at the wedding of Alexander's sister, also named Cleopatra. On the morning of the festivities, members of the court attended the theater. Philip was escorted by his son, the bridegroom, and his bodyguards. As the little group separated to enter the theater, Pausanias,

Philip murdered

Philip's jilted companion, saw his opportunity. He stepped in and mortally stabbed the king. Pursued by the guards, Pausanias ran outside but tripped and fell. A guard drew his sword and killed him on the spot.

Alexander, suspecting a conspiracy behind the assassination, vigorously investigated the murder. He tried and executed the diviner who had predicted good omens for the day, and he put to death anyone whom he thought had even a remote claim to the Macedonian throne. Later, even Philip's wife Cleopatra and their infant child were killed, an act that finally eliminated Alexander's rivals. Because of insufficient evidence, historians have never ascertained the full reasons for Philip's assassination. Some ancient sources accused Olympias of organizing the murder; others blame a conspiracy of nobles; still others consider the killing the solitary act of a jealous courtier. Whatever the cause, Alexander was now king.

The young monarch buried his father in a massive tomb with all the traditional honors. Excavated in 1977, Philip's tomb is the only unplundered burial site from this era. The excavations confirm that Philip and one of his wives (probably the murdered Cleopatra) had been buried with high ceremony and mounds of treasure. Archaeologists found two solid-gold caskets containing cremated remains wrapped in valuable purple and gold cloth. Figure 3.1 shows the beautifully preserved gold casket of the king. The sunburst design on the top is the symbol of Macedonia, and the fine craftsmanship of the item attests to the patronage of the arts that Philip had cultivated and that his son continued. The king's casket held a solid-gold wreath of oak leaves. The tomb also contained solid-gold diadems (narrow ornamental headbands)—the mark of Macedonian royalty, which as we will see, subsequent kings also adopted.

Philip's tomb

ALEXANDER'S CONQUESTS

The brilliant king was dead, but Philip's son Alexander would make an even greater mark on the world than his father had. Alexander (r. 337–323 B.C.) was born in 356 B.C. and raised by his parents expressly to rule. Philip diligently taught the young boy the arts of Macedonian warfare, including horsemanship, an essential skill for service in the cavalry. Philip and Olympias also encouraged Alexander's intellectual

FIGURE 3.1
Burial casket of Philip II of Macedon, third century B.C.

development. They appreciated the accomplishments of the classical Greeks and hired the revered philosopher Aristotle (384–322 B.C.) to tutor their promising heir. We cannot know the exact influence of the philosopher on his young student, but Aristotle certainly imparted a love of Greek culture and literature to Alexander. Moreover, he may well have cultivated Alexander's curiosity about the world, which would fuel the young man's later urge to explore. However, Alexander seems to have rejected Aristotle's prejudice against non-Greek "barbarians." Philip's son imagined a world much wider than that of Aristotle's ideal, small city-state.

As soon as Alexander ascended the Macedonian throne, he consolidated his rule in the region, showing a decisive ruthlessness that marked all his subsequent campaigns. For example, when the Greeks revolted after hearing false rumors of Alexander's death, the king promptly marched south, sacked the *Military exploits* city of Thebes, and slaughtered or enslaved the inhabitants. With the Greeks subdued, he then turned to implementing Philip's planned war against the Persian Empire. In 334 B.C., Alexander advanced into Asia Minor with an army of 30,000 hoplites and 5,000 cavalry. He was joined by Callisthenes, Aristotle's nephew, who later wrote the history of Alexander's campaigns. Although this text has been lost, it served as a pro-Macedonian, but carefully detailed source for

Alexander's early campaigns, and subsequent chroniclers who had access to the work have passed elements of it on to us.

After several decisive victories in Asia Minor, Alexander engaged the full power of Persia at the Battle of Issus (Map 3.1), where he matched with Persian forces and Greek mercenaries led by the Persian Great King Darius III. Through skillful deployment and swift action, Alexander's armies defeated a force more than twice as large as their own. Darius fled the battle, leaving his mother, wife, and children. The young king captured Darius's family, but treated them with respect and courtesy. In this way, he showed his belief that savagery should be reserved for the battlefield.

Before driving deeper into Asia, Alexander turned south along the Phoenician coast, shrewdly recognizing the problem of the superior Persian fleet that was reinforced by Phoenician vessels. He captured the great coastal cities of Sidon, Tyre, and finally Gaza, thus rendering the fleet useless without ever engaging it. The brilliant young strategist also perfected the art of siege warfare, improving on Philip's catapults and adding siege towers erected next to the defensive walls that allowed attackers to penetrate the fortresses. As the proud cities fell one by one, Alexander gained a reputation for brutal warfare but generosity to subject peoples. Subsequent cities surrendered quickly and joined the rapidly growing Macedonian Empire.

After conquering Gaza, Alexander swept into Egypt virtually unopposed in 332 B.C. The Egyptian priests declared Alexander the incarnation of their god, Amon and crowned him pharaoh. Now the god-king of Egypt, the young Macedonian founded a new city, Alexandria, on the Delta. This development brought Egypt more fully into Mediterranean economy and culture than it had ever been before, as the new northern, coastal capital encouraged trade and attracted colonists from elsewhere—a cosmopolitan center was founded in Egypt. With his western flank thus secured, Alexander once again headed for Asia to revive his pursuit of the Persian "Great King," Darius.

After crossing the Euphrates and Tigris rivers, Alexander encountered Darius at Gaugamela in 331 B.C. The Persian ruler had fitted chariots with sharp scythes to cut down the Macedonian infantry, and his forces far outnumbered Alexander's army—by about 250,000 to 47,000 (although these figures are certainly exaggerated). Despite the Persian strength,

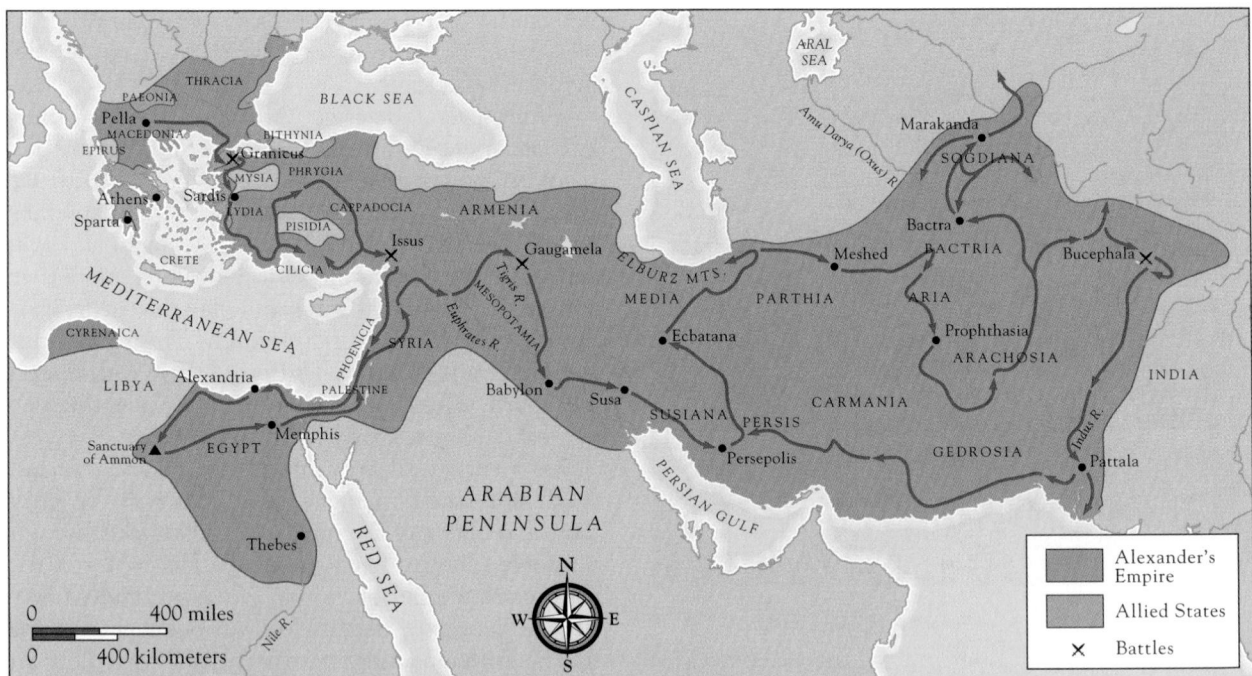

THINKING ABOUT GEOGRAPHY

MAP 3.1   *Alexander's Empire*

This map shows the vast territory Alexander conquered, the route he took, and the major battle sites.
◼ **Notice** the scale on the map and calculate the distance Alexander traveled during his conquests.
Consider the difficulties of supplying an army over these distances and of holding such an extensive empire.

Alexander's superior strategy vanquished the Persian warriors yet again. He forced the Persians to turn to confront his wheeling formation and thus opened fatal gaps in the long Persian line. His cavalry set upon the trapped Persian infantry. In the ensuing slaughter, about 50,000 Persians died before Darius again escaped and the Persian force collapsed. Alexander never again succeeded in meeting Darius face to face in battle, for the Persian king was assassinated the following year by one of his own guards. By that time, Alexander had taken Babylon and other cities in the heart of the Persian Empire and was crowned Great King.

Remembering Aristotle's lessons in Greek literature, Alexander thought of himself as a powerful, semidivine Greek hero in the tradition of Achilles and Heracles (whom we remember by the Roman name Hercules). The shrewd conqueror was also a skilled propagandist, and his identification with ancient heroes helped consolidate his authority in the minds of Greeks raised on the stories of Homer. Figure 3.2 shows a portion of a beautifully carved sarcophagus from the city of Sidon, on the Phoenician coast of the Mediterranean. The local royalty buried here had commissioned a scene of Alexander's victory over Darius to grace the side of the coffin, recognizing the moment that the Sidonian king changed his allegiance from Persia to Macedonia. Alexander sits astride a rearing horse at the left, while the defeated Persians fall before him. The conqueror wears a lion skin on his head, in a typical portrayal of Heracles. It is highly unlikely that Alexander fought in anything other than the traditional Macedonian armor, but the artistic license reveals the popular view of Alexander as a true Greek hero.

The Greek hero

Alexander himself identified most strongly with the hero Achilles, from whom he claimed descent. According to Plutarch, Alexander slept with a copy of Homer's *Iliad*, edited by Aristotle, under his pillow, and "esteemed it a perfect portable treasure of all military virtue and knowledge." Through Alexander, then, the heroic values of the Greek world endured and spread, and as Plutarch maintained, "thanks to Alexander, Homer was read in Asia. . . . "

The war against Persia had finally ended, but the young conqueror was still not satisfied. Having studied world geography as documented by the ancient *India* Greeks, Alexander yearned to push his conquests to the edge of the known world. He mistakenly believed that this enticing frontier lay just beyond the Indus River in India. A last major battle against an Indian king eliminated opposition in northern India, and Alexander made plans to press farther into the subcontinent. However, his Macedonian troops had had enough and refused to go on. Alexander wept in his tent for days at the mutiny of his beloved troops, but he finally conceded and turned back. However, instead of returning along the northern route, he led his troops south to explore the barren lands at the edge of the Arabian Sea (see Map 3.1). His exhausted, parched army finally reached the prosperous lands of Mesopotamia. Yet their relief was marred by an ironic tragedy: Alexander, seriously weakened by ever-growing alcohol abuse, caught a fever and died in Babylon in 323 B.C. He was just 32 years old. Others would have to rule the lands conquered by Alexander the Great.

A Young Ruler's Legacy

Was Plutarch right in thinking that Alexander wanted to make "all mankind a single people"? This ideal, which marked a radical departure from traditional Greek attitudes, has provoked intense historical debate virtually from the time of Alexander's life to the present. The Macedonian conqueror implemented several policies that some have interpreted as his desire to rule over a unified rather than a conquered people. One such policy, and certainly the most influential, was his founding of cities. In all his conquered territories, Alexander established an array of new cities. He intended these urban centers in part to re-create the Greek city life that he and his father had so admired. To this end, the conqueror helped settle numerous Greek and Macedonian colonists in the new cities. Hundreds of thousands of Greeks emigrated to the newly claimed lands in Asia, taking privileged positions. We will see that as they introduced their culture into Asia, these colonists inevitably influenced and were changed by the subject peoples. These culturally rich cities rank among Alexander's most enduring legacies.

Alexander also strongly supported the intermarriage of Greeks and Macedonians with Asians. He himself married the daughter of Darius and later wedded Roxane, the daughter of an Asian tribal king who ruled near modern-day Afghanistan. Alexander also presided over the weddings *Intercultural marriages* of 100 of his generals to highborn Persian women. As Plutarch said, he "joined together the greatest and most powerful peoples into one community by wedlock." Ten thousand more of Alexander's soldiers also married Asian women. Alexander might well have imagined that the offspring of these marriages would help seal the union of the two populations.

Finally, Alexander had a constant need for additional soldiers to support his campaigns, and he obtained these men from the conquered peoples. He

FIGURE 3.2

Alexander mounted in battle defeating the Persians, 315? B.C.

accepted both Persian soldiers and commanders into his companies. Preparing for the future, he also chose about 30,000 Asian boys whom he slated to learn the Greek language and the Macedonian fighting style. These boys would become the next generation of soldiers to fight for the king in a combined army.

Alexander's cultural blending disturbed those upper-crust Greeks and Macedonians who saw themselves as conquerors rather than as equals among the subject peoples. Indeed, while in Persia, Alexander adopted Persian robes and courtly ceremonies, including having his subjects prostrate themselves on the ground in his presence. Without a doubt, this ritual helped Persians accept their new king—but it also offended the proud Macedonians. Alexander's inclusion of Asians in the military elite only intensified Macedonian resentment. At one point, an outcry arose among Alexander's soldiers when the king apparently sought to replace some of them with Asians. Alexander squelched these objections decisively, executing 13 leaders and suggesting that the rest of them go home so that he could lead the Asian troops to victory. The Macedonians backed down, pleading for their king's forgiveness. Alexander resolved the incident with a lavish banquet of reconciliation, at which Asians and Macedonians drank together and Alexander prayed for harmony (sometimes mistranslated as "brotherhood") between them.

Resentments

Alexander died too soon for historians to be certain of his exact plans for ruling his vast, multiethnic empire. For all we know, he might well have intended that Greeks and Macedonians would remain a ruling elite. The cities and colonies guaranteed a continued Greek presence, as did the invaders' weddings to local women. The conqueror's inclusive army might have been simply a practical means of ensuring a large enough force to fulfill his ambitions. Whatever his intentions, Alexander created a fertile combination by joining the cultures of the ancient Middle East and classical Greece.

Alexander's legacy included more than his political conquests—which in some regions hardly outlasted the young king himself. The memory of his accomplishments have endured in an embellished way far beyond even his most impressive victories. For example, Plutarch's interpretation of Alexander's desire for a blending of peoples made this notion a foundational characteristic of Western culture, regardless of whether the king

Alexander's memory

truly held this ideal. Moreover, a highly imaginative version of Alexander's accomplishments, titled *The Alexander Romance,* was translated into 24 languages and found its way from Iran to China to Malaysia. The idea of a great empire ruled by one king may have exerted an influence as far as the Han dynasty in China (see, "Global Connections" in Chapter 5). It certainly shaped Mediterranean thinking, where would-be conquerors reverently visited Alexander's tomb in the spectacular Egyptian city of Alexandria that he founded.

The Successor Kingdoms, 323–ca. 100 B.C.

Admirers across the world may have romanticized Alexander's supposed dream of a unified kingdom. In reality, however, brutal politics sullied the picture soon after the great king's death. Legends preserve the probably false tale that as Alexander lay dying, he told his comrades that the kingdom should go "to the strongest." Even if Alexander never said this, the story reflects the reality of the violent fighting that broke out among the Macedonian generals shortly after the king died. Alexander's wife Roxane was pregnant when he succumbed, and presumably the empire should have gone to his infant son, Alexander IV. But within 13 years of Alexander's death, both Roxane and her young son had been murdered. Moreover, the Macedonian generals had carved up the great empire into new, smaller kingdoms that became the successors to Alexander's conquests. Map 3.2 shows the successor kingdoms.

EGYPT UNDER THE PTOLEMIES

Upon Alexander's death, one of his cavalry "companions," Ptolemy, moved toward Egypt with his own loyal troops to take control of that wealthy region. Ptolemy diverted the king's corpse, which was being returned to Macedon for burial, and took it to Alexandria, where he erected an imposing tomb for Alexander. It seems that Ptolemy believed the presence of the conqueror's remains would help legitimize his own rule. Fending off attempts by Alexander's other generals to snatch the rich land of the Nile, Ptolemy and his successors ruled as the god-kings of Egypt for the next 300 years.

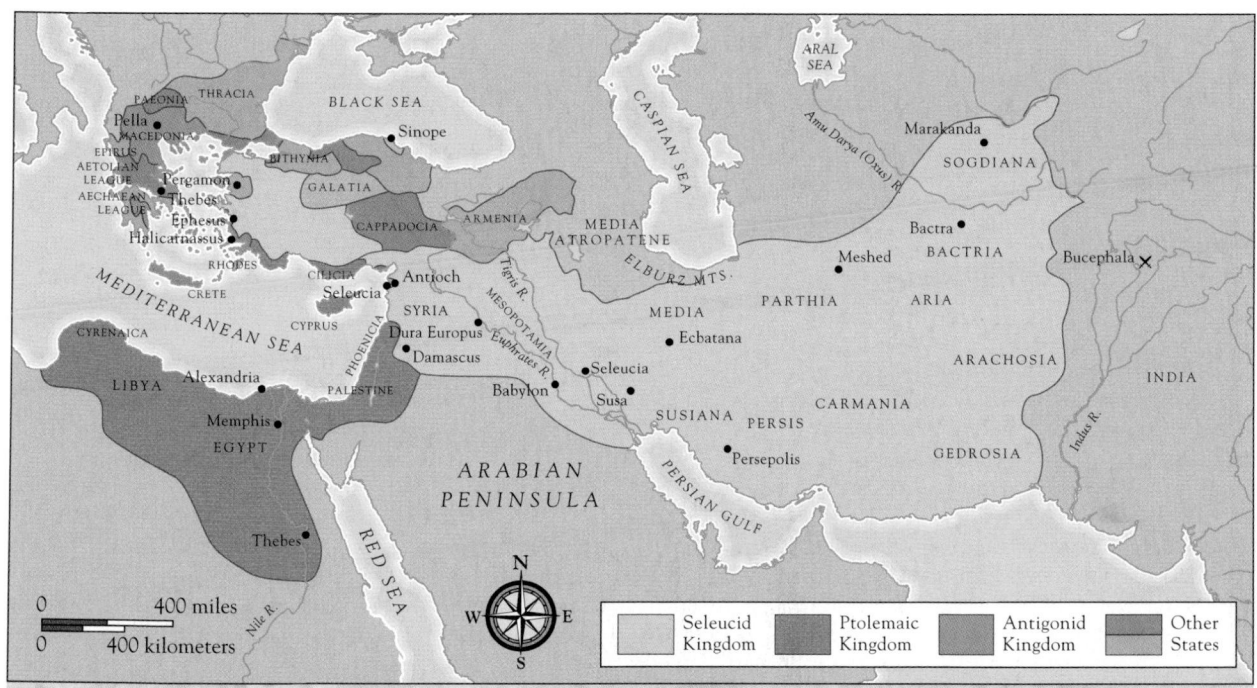

THINKING ABOUT GEOGRAPHY

MAP 3.2 *The Successor States After the Death of Alexander, ca. 240 B.C.*

This map shows how Alexander's empire broke apart into three successor states. ■ **Notice** the relative sizes of the successor kingdoms. **Consider** the historical and geographic reasons why they were so different. ■ **Notice** the locations of the two capitals of Egypt—the old one at Thebes and the new one at Alexandria. **Consider** how Alexandria offered more of a focus on the Mediterranean and the old Greek heartland.

The Ptolemies inherited a land with a long tradition of obedience to authority. Accordingly, the new kings wisely struck a bargain with the Egyptian priests, promising to fulfill the traditional duty of the pharaohs to care for the temples (and the priests) in *Continuity of life* exchange for protection of their legitimacy. Through most of their history, the Ptolemies lived in luxury in Alexandria, conducting official business in Greek while Egyptian peasants continued to obey the age-old dictates of the Nile, the priests, and the tax collectors. Life away from the court under the new order changed very little, which made it easier for the new dynasty to rule. The parallel practicing of both Egyptian and Greek ways continued throughout most of the Ptolemaic rule. In fact, the majority of these Greek kings rarely

carried out traditional ritual functions, and some were probably not even formally crowned. For their part the priests honored the Ptolemies while still governing in the traditional way.

However, in one significant way the Hellenistic rulers departed from their Egyptian predecessors—their queens took a more prominent role. (See Document 3.2 on page D3.2.) Many of the Ptolemaic rulers engaged in brother-sister marriages as *Hellenistic queens* the ancient Egyptians had done, but many women ruled completely on their own, without the problems faced by Egyptian women like Hatshepsut (see the Biography in Chapter 1). Hellenistic queens derived much of their power from controlling substantial wealth and spending it on public works (and on hiring large armies). The height of the

Biography

ARSINOË II (315–270? B.C.)

❧ **Consider** in what ways the reign of Arsinoë II contributed to the blending of Greek and Egyptian culture that marked the Ptolemaic dynasty.

The Hellenistic dynasties created by the successor states to Alexander's empire set new precedents for the ancient world by bringing strong women to power. These queens of all three dynasties (Seleucid, Antigonid, and Ptolemaic) derived their power from two main things: their descent from the original founders of the dynasties and their great wealth. Many of these women strongly influenced the great events of the day. The story of Arsinoë II, queen of Egypt, reveals the violent world of Hellenistic politics and shows the fierce will to power that women leaders often needed to rule effectively.

Arsinoë was the daughter of the first Ptolemy, Alexander's successor who took over Egypt. Like most Hellenistic princesses, she was well educated and raised to rule. She was married at age 15 to the king of Thrace, Lysimachus, an old companion-in-arms of

Brilliant and Ruthless Queen of Egypt

Ptolemy. (See Map 3.1.) Lysimachus renounced his first wife in favor of the young, and very beautiful, Arsinoë. By the time Arsinoë was 30, she had borne three sons and had begun to plan for their (and her) future. To position her sons to inherit the throne, she accused Lysimachus's son by his first wife of treason and had him poisoned.

Yet despite Arsinoë's plans, her family became ensnared in one of the seemingly endless Hellenistic wars of power. First, Seleucus marched from Asia to Thrace to conquer Lysimachus. Amid the combat, Arsinoë's husband (now nearing 80 years old) died. Then as Arsinoë fled with her children to Greece, her half-brother Ceraunus seized control of her old realm. Ceraunus well understood the benefits of legitimacy that Arsinoë's bloodline could provide, her lust for power, and the advantages of her great wealth. He offered to marry her and make her children his heirs. She agreed, but he betrayed her, killing her two youngest children in order to secure the kingdom for his own progeny. She and her eldest son managed to escape to Egypt to seek the protection of her brother, Ptolemy.

Safe in Egypt, Arsinoë moved to rebuild her power. Not content to be simply sister to the king, she had Ptolemy's wife exiled and married him herself to assure herself the title of queen. She was the elder of the two, and sources credit her with the idea for the marriage. From then on, she and her brother were known as "sibling-lovers" (*philadelphus*). If we are to believe the poets of the period, the couple genuinely loved each other. One poet wrote, "No more splendid wife than she ever clasped in bridal chamber her bridegroom, loving him from her heart, her brother and her lord." Satisfied with her newly secured position as the head of Egypt's ruling family, Arsinoë ignored her husband's many mistresses, although she quickly killed any political rivals who tried to reduce her authority.

Hellenistic queens of Egypt came with the last one—Cleopatra VII—who challenged the growing power of Rome (discussed in Chapter 4).

Under the Ptolemies, the port city of Alexandria became the premier city of the Hellenistic world. It *Alexandria* was a dynamic cosmopolitan city that by the end of the first century B.C. boasted almost one million inhabitants. Alexandria was a bustling port city where the main enterprise was the pursuit of wealth. The harbors were busy and the markets thronging, and international banks grew up to serve the people. To make sure ships could enter the port safely, Hellenistic scientists built a huge lighthouse on an island (Pharos) outside the harbor.

FIGURE 3.3A

Arsinoë

The sibling marriage not only gave Arsinoë the power she craved, it also helped consolidate the power of the dynasty by bringing the Ptolemies closer to traditional Egyptian practices. Sometimes Egyptian pharaohs had married their sisters. However, the Greek Macedonians decried the practice as incest and forbade it. In marrying one another, Arsinoë and Ptolemy reclaimed an older form of legitimacy that had shaped the Egyptian ruling families. Artistic portrayals of Queen Arsinoë depict this movement toward traditional Egyptian practices. Figure 3.3a shows her in the traditional Greek fashion, crowned only by the slim band that marked Macedonian rulers. Figure 3.3b, on the other hand, shows Arsinoë wearing the traditional headdress of the Egyptian rulers. The Greek queen had become an Egyptian one. During the next centuries, the Ptolemies in Egypt followed the precedent set by Arsinoë and Ptolemy. They preserved much of their Macedonian ways while adopting enough Egyptian traditions to let them rule the ancient country effectively. Historians have argued over how much political influence Arsinoë wielded. However, we should perhaps believe the ancient historian, Memnon, when he wrote, "Arsinoë was one to get her own way."

In addition, in a decree after her death, Ptolemy wrote that he followed the "policy of his ancestors and of his sister in his zeal for the freedom of the Greeks." Arsinoë's zeal for free-

FIGURE 3.3B

Arsinoë

dom" stemmed more from her hostility to the Antigonid rulers of Macedonia (who had driven her from her lands in Thrace) than from any abstract ideals of independence. The queen wanted to be sure her Egyptian dynasty would be free from intrusion from the successors of Alexander coming from the north, so she even traveled to the front to survey the defenses. Furthermore, she and Ptolemy knew that their safety in Egypt would hinge on sea power, so they expanded the Egyptian fleet significantly.

Even while securing the independence of Egypt, the Ptolemies did not forget the Greek love of learning that marked all the successor kingdoms. As their greatest accomplishment, they constructed an immense library in Alexandria, which served as the center of learning in the Mediterranean world for almost the next thousand years.

Even before Arsinoë's death, Egyptian priests followed Ptolemy's lead in worshiping her as a goddess, making her the first Macedonian queen to receive that honor. Following her death in about 270 B.C., Ptolemy issued edicts and built shrines to stimulate her cult. Poets described Arsinoë as a special patron of sailors, claiming, "She will give fair voyages and will smooth the sea even in midwinter in answer to prayer." The veneration of Queen Arsinoë by Egyptians and Greeks alike ensured that the cultural blending that emerged during her lifetime continued long after her death.

The structure was 440 feet high, and the light from the lantern at the top was intensified by a system of reflectors. Ships approaching the harbor were guided by the beam of the lighthouse that was looked on as one of the seven wonders of the ancient world.

For all its commercial value, Alexandria under the Ptolemies also became an intellectual and cultural center. The rulers established a world-famous museum (the word museum means "temple to the muses," the Greek goddesses who served as inspiration to creativity). At the museum, scholars from around the Mediterranean and Asia gathered to study texts and discuss ideas. The Greek rulers founded a great library as part of this museum and ambitiously designed it to stand as the West's first complete collection of published works. Well established by 280 B.C., the library boasted more than 700,000 volumes just one century later, making it the largest collection the ancient world had seen.

Eventually, however, the Ptolemies encountered both internal and external pressure to change. Under the reign of Ptolemy V (r. 205?–183? B.C.), a boy not yet in his teens, priests began demanding that the young king be more involved in religious rituals. The boy-king's problems only worsened when sub-Saharan Nubians (see "Global Connections," Chapter 1), detecting his weakness, clamored for their own pharaoh. In addition, the armies of Alexander's successor in Asia were threatening Egypt's borders. Pressured on all sides, Ptolemy offered concessions to the powerful priests in return for their support in rallying the Egyptians to his cause. The young ruler reduced taxes on the peasants and increased payments to the priests. In return for his cooperation, the priests brought Ptolemy to Memphis, the traditional capital of the pharaohs, where they placed the great double crown of Egypt—the sign of royalty—on his head. Finally, they ordered that Ptolemy V be worshiped in every Egyptian shrine. To make good on this policy, they demanded that scribes write all the accomplishments of Ptolemy V "on a slab of hard stone, in the writing of the words of god, the writing of documents and the letters of the Northerners, and set it up in all the temples. . . . "

Figure 3.4 shows the Rosetta Stone, the tablet that resulted from this decree, which was unearthed in 1799. Demonstrating the presence of both Greeks and Egyptians in the kingdom of the Ptolemies, the stone records Ptolemy's deeds in three written versions: the sacred hieroglyphics at the top, Egyptian cursive administrative script at the center, and Greek ("the letters of the Northerners") at the bottom. In the hieroglyphic section the king's name is enclosed in circles, which supposedly protected his name and because the names of pharaohs had always been so encircled, it also signaled to all who saw it that Ptolemy was indeed the rightful god-king. Equally significant, the Rosetta Stone provided the key that finally let nineteenth-century scholars decipher hieroglyphic writing. Without the stone, the meaning embedded in the great carvings of the ancient Egyptians might still remain a mystery.

Rosetta Stone

FIGURE 3.4
The Rosetta Stone, 197? B.C.

THE SELEUCIDS RULE ASIA

In the violent political jockeying that broke out after the death of Alexander, one of Ptolemy's lieutenants, Seleucus, entered Babylon in 311 B.C. and captured the imperial treasure there. With this money, Seleucus laid claim to the old heartland of the Persian Empire. Yet the extensive eastern lands that Alexander had conquered eluded his grasp. As early as 310 B.C., Seleucus gave northwest India back to its native rulers in return for 500 war elephants, and by the third century B.C., eastern Asia Minor fell away. (See "Global Connections" box.) Nevertheless, Seleucus founded a long-standing kingdom that continued the Hellenizing process begun by Alexander.

Like Alexander, the Seleucids founded cities and populated them with imported Greek and Macedonian bureaucrats and colonists. Seleucia, about 50

Commercial cities miles north of Babylon, was established as the new capital of the kingdom, and Dura Europus, near the midpoint of the Euphrates River, was another important center. Their locations reveal that the Seleucid kings recognized the crucial role of eastern trade in the prosperity of their kingdom. These cities controlled the trade routes through the Tigris-Euphrates valley and the caravan trails that crossed the desert from Damascus and, along with Antioch, became vital political and economic centers within the former Persian lands (see Map 3.2).

While the Ptolemies could depend on an established Egyptian priesthood to facilitate their control of *Seleucid colonists* their kingdom, the Seleucids had no such ready-made institution. Instead, they relied in part on Macedonian and Greek colonists to secure their hold on their Asian lands. After Alexander's death, the Seleucids settled at least 20,000 Macedonian colonists in Syria and Asia Minor. This number was supplemented by others from Macedonia who came looking for riches and privileges.

The Macedonian settlers viewed themselves as world conquerors and expected to maintain their high-status positions in the new lands. The Seleucid kings, who saw the colonists as the backbone of their armies, granted them considerable farmlands. Some charters from this time show that certain colonists were exempt from paying taxes and even received free food until their first crops could be harvested. These colonists did not expect to work the land themselves; instead, resident dependent laborers farmed the land for their foreign conquerors. Again, as in Egypt, the resident peasantry served their Greek-speaking masters. Not surprisingly, the Seleucid kings gained a loyal following among the elite with these allocations of land.

Although Greek sovereignty faded quickly in the easternmost edges of the Seleucid lands, evidence remains of the impact of the Greek presence there. To illustrate, consider the great king of northern India, Aśoka (r. 268?–233? B.C.) described in "Global Connections" page 96. Aśoka is perhaps most remembered for spreading the ideals of Buddhism through inscriptions on stones. Like the Rosetta Stone, these Rock Edicts testify to the Hellenic presence in India, because Aśoka's sayings were preserved in both the Indian language of Prakrit and in Greek. In wise phrases such as, "Let them neither praise themselves nor disparage their neighbors, for that is vain," the ideas of Buddhism met the language of Hellenism in the farthest lands of Alexander.

ANTIGONIDS IN GREECE

The Seleucid kings concentrated on ruling the western portions of their Asian provinces, ever watchful for opportunities to gain advantage over the Ptolemies or the Macedonian leaders who now ruled in Macedonia and Greece. These kings, known as the Antigonids, were descended from Antigonus the One-Eyed (382–301? B.C.), a general who had joined in the struggle for succession after Alexander's death. Antigonus failed to score a decisive military victory, however, and died on the battlefield at the venerable age of 80, still trying to win control of the entire Macedonian Empire. Nevertheless, his descendants eventually took power in Macedonia and Greece and introduced the Antigonid dynasty.

The Antigonids ruled a land that had changed little with the growth of Alexander's empire. The great king's conquests had exerted scanty *Life in Macedonia* long-term impact on Macedonia itself. At first, wealth poured from the east into the young king's homeland. Indeed, near the end of his life, Alexander sent home one shipment of booty that proved so large that 110 warships were needed to escort the merchant vessels on their return journey. Numismatic evidence also confirms the volume of wealth that initially flowed into Macedonia, for its mint churned out about 13,000,000 silver coins immediately after Alexander's reign. Much of this coinage came into wide circulation, for officials used it to pay troops and provide stipends for veterans' widows and orphans. Yet the money did not profoundly alter Macedonian society. By the reign of Antigonus's great-grandson, Demetrius II (r. 239–229 B.C.), life in Macedonia had changed little from even as far back as Philip II's time. The army still consisted mainly of Macedonian nobles, who fought as companions to their king. Invaders from the north still threatened; indeed, in the 280s B.C., the Gauls, a tribe on the Macedonians' northern border, launched an attack that cost Macedonia dearly. To make matters worse, the Greeks to the south, who had never really accepted Macedonian rule, kept revolting.

The Greek city-states experienced more change than Macedonia did, for the traditional democracy of

Global Connections

THE MAURYAN DYNASTY UNIFIES INDIA

Consider how one Indian ruler took advantage of Alexander's conquest and the subsequent break up of his empire. **NOTICE** how Buddhism began to grow into a world religion.

Sometimes great historical events (like Alexander's conquest) indirectly generate unforeseen consequences. This happened in the Indian subcontinent. In the late 320s B.C. as Alexander the Great was conquering the small kingdoms that dotted the prosperous western side of the Indian subcontinent, an ambitious Indian warrior named Chandragupta calculated how to take advantage of Alexander's incursion. Chandragupta lived in the eastern kingdom of Magadha (on the Ganges River along the wealthy trade route near the Bay of Bengal). Perhaps eager to emulate the Macedonian general, he began to consolidate his power by conquest. By 321 B.C., he had overthrown the ruling dynasty and established the Mauryan Dynasty. After Alexander withdrew from the Punjab region of the west, Chandragupta annexed the region. For the first time, an Indian monarch ruled from the Arabian Sea on the west to the Bay of Bengal on the East.

Meanwhile, Alexander's successors began carving out kingdoms in the west, while the Seleucids held the eastern lands. (See Map 3.2.) In 305 B.C., King Seleucus Nicator (r. 305-280) crossed the Indus in the hope of reclaiming Alexander's Indian lands. But Chandragupta fended him off. Seleucus not only withdrew, but also ceded enough land to extend the Mauryan frontier west to the Hindu Kush mountains, in modern Afghanistan. In return, Seleucus received the modest prize of 500 war elephants—hardly enough to save face. The Mauryan Empire was now impressive indeed.

Chandragupta's accomplishments were memorable, but those of his famous grandson, Emperor Aśoka, proved more

---

Athens and the other poleis had evaporated. The poleis relaxed their notions of citizenship, so many immigrants and freed slaves became citizens, but at *Changes in Greece* the same time people had less attachment to their cities. Many jobs—from soldier to athlete—became the province of specialists, not citizens, and thus international professionals replaced the native competitors who brought glory and wealth to their cities. Furthermore, the new economy of the Hellenistic world widened the gulf between rich and poor, and the disparity undermined participatory government: Rich Greeks took over governance and frequently forgot that they had any responsibility to the poor.

Despite these tensions, outright revolution never materialized. The relentless warfare plaguing the poleis simply proved too distracting. In addition, Greeks from all walks of life continued emigrating to the other Hellenistic kingdoms in search of a better life, and this exodus helped ease population pressures at home. Bureaucrats and scientists headed for the Greek colonies to take advantage of the tempting opportunities there—for example, a talented mathematician, Apollonius, worked first in Alexandria, Egypt, and then was lured to the Seleucid kingdom in the east. The polis, which in the old days had claimed people's loyalty, had given way to cosmopolitan cities. Now individuals sought to enhance their own fortunes in a wider world.

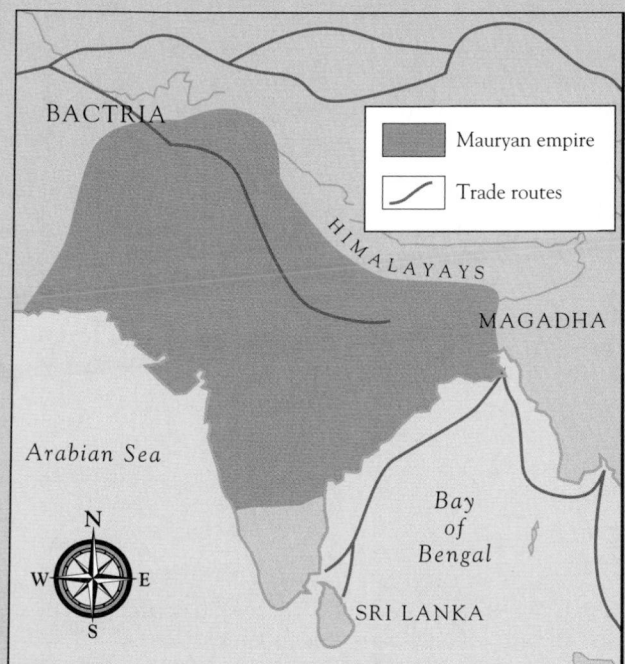

MAP 3.3 *The Mauryan Empire.*

so. Aśoka ruled from about 274 until his death in 232. According to legend, he ascended the throne after murdering many of his brothers. The young emperor expanded Mauryan territory even further by fighting a brutal war against the Kalinga people in the southeast of India. Purportedly, the violence of the war, in which 100,000 people perished, shocked even Aśoka, who responded to the carnage by converting to Buddhism. He spent the rest of his life promoting the religion. He sent missionaries as far north as Afghanistan and south to the island of Ceylon.

Aśoka's rule is most remarkable because he combined the roles of talented monarch and pious monk. His rock edicts (described in the text) record both his deeds and his ideas for bringing about a better world. For example, he abolished war within his empire after his victory over the Kalingas and never fought again. In this way, he lived the philosophy expressed on Rock Edict 13: "the chiefest conquest is the conquest of Right and not of Might." Most scholars credit Aśoka for helping Buddhism ascend from a regional sect of Hinduism to a world religion. Yet, the emperor did not neglect his secular duties. Under his leadership, India prospered with improved irrigation for agriculture and a boom in trade owing to roads that he commissioned.

Aśoka died in about 232 B.C. He was succeeded by his grandson, who lacked his forebear's talent. Staggering under economic difficulties, the empire fragmented into various provinces. The Mauryan Empire grew in part thanks to Alexander's conquests, and it established a fertile ground for the growth and spread of Buddhism that would influence west and east alike.

East Meets West in the Successor Kingdoms

OLC The vast breadth of the Hellenistic kingdoms stimulated the West's economy to new heights. Trade rhythms quickened, and merchants raked in unprecedented wealth. Under Alexander and his successors in the various kingdoms, Greek became the universal language of business. Now traders could exchange goods across large distances without confronting confusing language barriers. The Greeks also advanced credit, a business practice that let merchants ply their trade without having to transport unwieldy quantities of hard currency.

MONEY IN THE NEW COSMOPOLITAN ECONOMIES

The Hellenistic kings standardized currency as well, another boon for trade. There were two weights of coins in the Hellenistic world: One was based on Alexander's standard, in which one drachma contained 4.3 grams of silver. The Ptolemies in Egypt abided by a different standard, using only 3.5 grams of silver in the drachma. Despite the dual standards, the consistency of both

Coinage and trade

helped merchants buy and sell with ease throughout the extensive region. Figure 3.5 shows two coins from this era. Coin 3.5a is a gold coin from Egypt worth eight drachmas. It shows Ptolemy II with his wife Arsinoë (featured in the "Biography") on the front and Ptolemy's parents, Ptolemy I and Berenice, on the obverse. By showing two generations of royalty, the coin is proclaiming a dynastic succession that was traditionally important in Egypt. Coin 3.5b shows a silver coin, a "tetradrachma," from Pergamum in Asia worth four drachmas. It shows king Perseus of Macedon with an eagle—a symbol of royalty—on the obverse. These coins show that the Hellenistic kingdoms had much in common. Both coins show the monarchs in the style of Macedonian rulers, wearing the simple diadem that since Philip II's time had marked Macedonian kingship, and both are based on the drachma. They also graphically represent both the wealth that the Macedonian conquests generated and the spread of Greek cultural influence throughout the region as trade intensified.

Goods moved briskly through the Hellenistic kingdoms, reshaping old patterns of trade and consumption. Athens initially benefited from the widespread demand for Greek goods like pottery and weapons, but a century after the death of Alexander, Alexandria had replaced Athens as the commercial capital of the eastern Mediterranean. The small islands of Rhodes and Delos also rose to prominence because of their advantageous locations along the routes that connected the north and southeast areas of the Mediterranean with Greece and Italy.

Heightened trade led to new approaches to agriculture as people rushed to develop and sell novel delicacies. As one example, Greek farmers began planting their precious olive trees and grapevines in the eastern kingdoms, permanently altering the ecosystems in those regions. In turn, eastern spices transformed cooking on the Greek mainland and in Egypt. Agricultural crossbreeding also became common, though it failed in some cases—even seeds imported from Rhodes to cross with Egypt's bitter cabbage could not sweeten that pungent vegetable of the Nile valley.

While commerce made countless merchants rich, the individual kingdoms also benefited—mainly by **Command economies** taking control of economic activity. In Egypt, where pharaohs traditionally controlled much trade and industry—a system called a command economy—the Ptolemies

FIGURE 3.5
Coins of the Hellenistic period. (a) Eight drachma coin of Ptolemy II, 284–247 B.C. (b) Tetradrachma of Perseus of Macedonia, 178–168 B.C.

increased their controls to funnel the riches of the Nile valley into the royal treasury. They converted the most successful industries into royal monopolies, controlling such essentials as sesame oil, salt, perfumes, and incense. Their most successful venture, however, was the beer industry, which had been a royal monopoly since the Old Kingdom. The Ptolemies insisted that the millions of gallons of beer consumed each year in Egypt be manufactured in the royal breweries, though many women doubtless continued to brew the beverage for household consumption as they had always done.

Kings also levied taxes on imports and exports, such as grain, papyrus, cosmetics, timber, metals, and horses. These policies required a complex administrative system, which in turn led to the proliferation of Greek-speaking bureaucrats. Equally important, the kings used their new riches not only to live lavishly, but also to fund the expensive wars that ravaged the Hellenistic world.

ARMIES OF THE HELLENISTIC WORLD

One of the most famous statues of the Hellenistic world, shown in Figure 3.6, is the Nike of Samothrace—called "Winged Victory" because Nike was the Greek goddess of victory—and it is a perfect symbol of the war-dominated Hellenistic age. Originally part of a sculptural group that included a war galley, Nike strides confidently into the wind, certain of victory. However, the battles of the Hellenistic world seemed to bring endless suffering more often than clear victory.

The Macedonian kings thought of themselves as conquerors and derived their legitimacy in large part from their military successes. Like Alexander, whom they strove to emulate, these monarchs fully expected to participate in the hardships of battle and the dangers of combat. Consequently, they regularly made war on each other in hopes of gaining land or power. The ideal of conquest thus persisted after Alexander's death. However, the scale of warfare had broadened.

This broadening occurred partly because of the larger territories in dispute. Some boundaries now far *Mercenary armies* surpassed the dimensions of the earlier Greek poleis. To cover these daunting distances, monarchs accumulated vast armies. Philip had conquered Greece with a force of about 30,000 men, and Alexander had increased the numbers significantly as he moved east. Alexander's force in India may have exceeded 100,000—exceptional for ancient armies. The Hellenistic kings, however, regularly fielded armies of between 60,000 and 80,000 troops. These large armies no longer consisted primarily of citizen-soldiers, but mercenaries—who were loyal only to their paymaster and who switched sides with impunity. Tellingly, Hellenistic theater often featured mercenary soldiers who returned home with lots of money to spend and a newly cynical outlook.

The Macedonian armies were also influenced by their contact with the far eastern provinces. For example, in these distant lands they encountered war *War elephants* elephants for the first time. Just as horses had offered mounted warriors advantages of mobility and reach over foot soldiers, soldiers mounted on elephants had an even greater military advantage. Furthermore, elephants participated in the fray, trampling men and using their trunks as weapons. As mentioned previously, the earliest Seleucids had exchanged territory in India for the prized elephants, and these formidable animals eventually became part of the Hellenistic armory. The Seleucids tried to breed elephants in Syria, but had to keep trading with India for more elephants when their efforts failed. To retain their advantage, the Seleucid kings cut off the Ptolemies' trade in Asian elephants, forcing the Egyptians to rely on the smaller, less effective African breed. The Greek historian Polybius (200?–118? B.C.) described a confrontation between the two classes of pachyderms: The African elephants, "unable to stand the smell and trumpeting of the Indian elephants and terrified, I suppose, also by their great size and strength, . . . at once turn tail and take to flight." As impressive as the Asian elephants were, foot soldiers learned to dodge the beasts and stab or hamstring them. However, the massive animals remained a

FIGURE 3.6
Nike of Samothrace, sometimes known as "Winged Victory."

valuable tool for moving heavy siege engines to walled cities and attacking fortified positions.

On every level, war became more brutal than ever during the Hellenistic era. Large, wealthy, and well-equipped armies now routinely toppled defensive walls, and kings followed Alexander's ruthless model of wiping out any city that showed even a hint of defiance. Mercenaries, too, cared little for civilians, and historical sources describe soldiers drunkenly looting private homes after a conquest. The countryside also suffered from the warfare, and peasants repeatedly petitioned kings to ease their burdens. Peasants faced increased taxes levied to fund expensive wars, and then frequently confronted violence from marauding mercenaries. To an unprecedented level, civilians became casualties in wars waged between kings.

The incessant warfare also changed the nature of slavery in the Greek world. As we have seen, during the classical Greek period—as throughout the ancient world—slavery was taken for granted. *Slavery* Every household had one or two domestic slaves, and most manufacturing and other labor was done by slaves. Alexander's immediate successors generally avoided mass enslavement of prisoners, but traditionally it was customary to enslave losers in battle. Therefore, by the late third century B.C., prisoners began to be enslaved in huge numbers. This changed the scale of the institution of slavery and, ultimately, the treatment of the slaves themselves. By 167 B.C. the island of Delos in the Aegean Sea housed a huge slave market. Claiming that 10,000 slaves could arrive and be sold in a day on Delos, the Greek historian Strabo quoted a contemporary saying about the slave markets that suggested how quickly the slave-traders sold their human cargo: "Merchant, put in, unload—all's sold." Although these large numbers are surely an exaggeration, they testify to the huge increase in numbers of slaves that began to be moved around the eastern Mediterranean. Wealthy households now could have hundreds of slaves, and others worked in gangs in agriculture and mining. This new scale of slavery further dehumanized those who had been taken, and slaves joined civilians as a new population suffering under the new kingdoms.

A True Cultural Blending?

Whether or not Alexander had envisioned a complete uniting of east and west, in reality a full blending of peoples never occurred in the lands he conquered. The Hellenistic kingdoms in Egypt and Asia consisted of local native populations ruled by a Greek/Macedonian elite who made up less than 10 percent of the population. However, this elite was not limited to people of direct Macedonian descent; it also included those who acquired Greek language and culture through formal or informal education. Alexander's conquests opened opportunities for people from many ethnic backgrounds to join the elite—a development that inevitably transfigured Greek culture itself.

The intermingling of East and West intensified with the movement of travelers, which the common use of the Greek language and the size of the kingdoms facilitated. Travelers included merchants and mercenaries and diplomats seeking political and economic advantages or opportunities to spy. Perhaps most instrumental in blending cultures were the artists and artisans who journeyed widely in search of patrons and prizes. *Travelers*

In this new, cosmopolitan world, even women traveled with a freedom unheard of in the classical Greek poleis. Female musicians, writers, and artists embarked on quests for honors and literary awards. One inscription on a commemorative stone recalls "Aristodama, daughter of Amyntas of Smyrna, an epic poetess, who came to the city and gave several readings of her own poems." The citizens were so pleased with this poet's work that they granted her citizenship. During such readings, authors shared experiences from one part of the world with the people of another, enhancing the diversity that marked this vibrant time.

Such diversity showed up vividly in the art of the period. For example, classical Greek artists had sometimes depicted black Africans in their works. In the Hellenistic age such portrayals grew more frequent. Figure 3.7 exemplifies the cultural blending that occurred in the visual arts of this period. This bronze figure was cast in the Greek style, yet it shows a youth from sub-Saharan Africa, possibly Nubia, which partook in continued close interaction with Egypt. (Discussed in "Global Connections" in Chapter 1.) The subject's pose suggests that he may have once held a lyre, a traditional Greek (not African) musical instrument. The young man might well have been a slave, given that the Hellenistic kingdoms traded heavily in slaves of all ethnic backgrounds. Or he might have been one of the many traveling performers who earned a living by entertaining newly wealthy, cosmopolitan audiences. *Diverse art*

All travelers left some evidence of their visits in the farthest reaches of the Hellenistic world. In the third century B.C., for example, the Greek philosopher Clearchus discovered a Greek-style city, complete with a gymnasium at the center, on the northern frontier of modern Afghanistan. In the gymnasium, Clearchus erected a column inscribed with 140 moral maxims taken from a similar pillar near the shrine of Apollo at Delphi. Like the Rock Edicts of Aśoka, the pillar of Clearchus preserves in stone the mingling of ideas at the fringes of the Hellenistic world.

STRUGGLES AND SUCCESSES: LIFE IN THE COSMOPOLITAN CITIES

The new cities founded by Alexander and his successors were in many ways artificial structures—they did not grow up in response to local manufacturing or commercial needs. Instead, they were simply created by rulers as showcases of their wealth and power. Expensive to maintain, these cities burdened local peasants with extra taxes and produced little wealth of their own. However, they played a crucial role as cultural and administrative centers, and they became a distinctive feature of Hellenistic life. Modeled on the Greek city-states, these cities still differed markedly from the poleis in several important ways, including the opportunities for women.

The travelers and the diversity of the cities helped break down the tight family life and female seclusion that had marked traditional Greek cities. *Women* Women were more free to move about in public. Furthermore, many texts indicate that Hellenistic women had more independence of action than their Greek counterparts. For example, a marriage contract explicitly insists that a couple will make joint decisions: "We shall live together in whatever place seems best to Leptines and Heraclides, deciding together." These new opportunities for independence made possible the situation at the opening of this chapter, when the young working woman ran off with her lover.

The Hellenistic cities also differed from their Greek counterparts in that they owed allegiance to larger political entities, the kingdoms. *Cities and kings* Now Greek monarchies had replaced Greek city-states as the influential political form in the developing history of the West. The relationship between the Hellenistic kings and the new cities derived from both Macedonian and Greek traditions. For example, during and after Alexander's reign, monarchs advocated democracy within the cities they founded. Cities were governed by magistrates and councils, and popular assemblies handled internal affairs. In return, the kings demanded tribute and special taxes during times of war. However, these taxes were not onerous, and a king might even exempt a city from taxation. In response, many cities introduced a civic religious cult honoring their kings. As one example, to show this dual allegiance to both their king and city, citizens of the city of Cos had to swear the following oath: "I will abide by the established democracy . . . and the ancestral laws of Cos, . . . and I will also abide by the friendship and alliance with King Ptolemy."

These cities flourished under the patronage of their kings, but they also struggled with all the problems endemic in any urban area. To feed the townspeople,

FIGURE 3.7
African boy playing an instrument, second century B.C.

city officials often had to import supplies from distant sources. Following Hellenistic ideas of a command economy, these urban leaders set grain prices and sometimes subsidized food to keep the costs manageable. They also regulated millers and bakers to prevent them from making large profits from cheap grain. Finally, the cities suffered the unavoidable problems of what to do about sewerage and water drainage; the largest urban centers had drainpipes under the streets for these purposes. Gangs of slaves owned by the city maintained the drainage system and cleared the streets.

Urban problems

City leaders gave little attention to public safety. They hired a few night watchmen to guard some public spaces, but for the most part, they considered safety a personal matter. Consequently, people mingling in the crowded markets or venturing out at night were often victims of robberies, or worse. Danger lurked everywhere, but especially in the many fires that broke out from residents' use of open flames to cook and heat their wooden homes. Despite the perils of fire, crime, and lack of sanitation, however, cities still offered the best hope of success for enterprising people.

The greatest of the new cities—Alexandria, Antioch, Seleucia—drew people from around the world. No longer connected to the original Greek city-states, such newcomers felt little obligation to participate in democratic politics or to profess loyalty to a clan or polis. Greeks, Phoenicians, Jews, Babylonians, Arabs, and others gathered in the cosmopolitan centers to make their fortunes. As the most ambitious among them took Greek names, the old divisions between Greek and "barbarian" blurred. Traditional family ties dissolved, too, as we saw in the story that opened this chapter.

City dwellers improved their lot in several ways, some of them advancing through successful military activities. The Greek Scopas, for example, unable to find work in his home city, "turned his hopes toward Alexandria," where he got a job in the army. Within three years, Scopas had risen to command the armies of Ptolemy V. Women, too, had opportunities to participate in the public sphere. One stone inscription from the first century B.C. honors Phile as the first woman to hold the public office of magistrate. The inscription also tells us that Phile "constructed at her own expense the reservoir for water and the city aqueduct." With her unusual wealth, Phile seems to have transcended gender and succeeded in holding public office.

New opportunities

Though cities opened up new opportunities, they also spawned miseries. Many poor people were forced to continue working well into their old age; indeed, the elderly market woman shown at the beginning of the chapter would have been a common sight in the Hellenistic period. The father in the chapter's opening story looked to his king to spare him an impoverished old age. His pleas probably went unheard, however; cities and their royal patrons tended to ignore the mounting problems of poverty. Slums cropped up, becoming just as characteristic of Hellenistic cities as the palaces of the wealthy and the libraries of the wise.

In some cities, destitute people designed institutions to help themselves. Artisans' guilds, for example, offered a sense of social connection to people bewildered by the large, anonymous cosmopolitan cities. Some people organized burial clubs, in which members contributed money to ensure themselves a decent interment at the end of lives that had little material security. Historical evidence suggests that some rich city dwellers worried about the possibility of social revolution. As one illustration of this fear, the citizens of a city in Crete were required to include the following statement in their oath of citizenship: "I will not initiate a redistribution of land or of houses or a cancellation of debts."

PATRONAGE, PLANNING, AND PASSION: HELLENISTIC ART

The monarchs who were becoming fabulously wealthy did not spend much money on the urban poor. What did they do with the mounds of coins that filled their coffers? In part, they spent fortunes as patrons of the arts, commissioning magnificent pieces that continue to be treasured today. However, not all critics have admired the products of the Hellenistic artists. For example, early in the first century A.D., the prolific Roman commentator Pliny the Elder (A.D. 23–79) energetically discussed Greek art. A passionate admirer of classical Athenian art, Pliny claimed that after the accomplishments of Lysippus (380?–318? B.C.), "art stopped." His dismissal of the Hellenistic world's artistic contributions has since been shared by many observers who admire the idealized poses of classical Greek works. But art did not stop with Lysippus; it merely changed as its center migrated from Athens to the great cosmopolitan centers of the East.

Classical Greek artists had been supported by public funding by democratic poleis. By contrast, Hellenistic artists received their funding *Royal patrons* from wealthy kings seeking to build and decorate their new cities. Royal patronage began with monarchs who wanted their newly established cities to reflect the highest ideals of Greek aesthetics. At the same time, this policy served the political agenda of promoting Greek culture. These rulers hired architects to design cities conducive to traditional Greek life, with its outdoor markets and meeting places, and employed artists to decorate the public spaces. Pergamum (see Map 3.2) posed a special challenge to architects: Its center was perched on a high hill, so city planners had to take the steep slopes into account in designing the city. In the end, they arranged the royal palaces at the top of the hill—visibly proclaiming the king's ascendancy—and the markets at the bottom. The layout of this magnificent city is typical of many Hellenistic urban centers.

Citizens in Pergamum shopped in the colonnaded building shown at the lower left corner of Figure 3.8. Higher up the hill was an altar to Zeus and higher still, a temple to Athena that served as the entrance to the library. The heights were dominated by the

royal palaces and barracks. (The temple shown at the center of the hilltop was built later by Roman conquerors.) On the left side of the model, we can see theater seats built into the hillside, where some 10,000 spectators could gather to watch the latest dramatic productions. The city preserved the gracious outdoor life of the classical Greek cities, yet was dominated by the majesty and power of the new kings.

After cities were designed, kings commissioned sculptors to decorate the great public buildings, especially temples. Throughout the Hellenistic *Sculpture* period, sculptors also found a market in the newly wealthy, who hired these artists to create works of beauty to decorate their homes. Hellenistic sculpture built on classical models in the skill with which artists depicted the human form and in the themes that harked back to the age of Greek heroes and the Trojan War. Still, Hellenistic artists departed from the classical style in significant ways. Classical Greek sculptors sought to portray the ideal—that is, they depicted scenes and subjects that were above the tumult and passion of this world. By contrast, Hellenistic artists faced passion and emotion head-on. Their works exhibit a striking expressiveness, violence, and

FIGURE 3.8
Restored model of Pergamum.

sense of movement, along with contorted poses that demonstrate these artists' talents for capturing human emotion in marble.

The great altar to Zeus in Pergamum is graced by several figures that reveal this startling range of human emotion. One of these sculptures, shown in Figure 3.9, depicts a soldier from Gaul who had been defeated in war. The piece exudes noble despair. The soldier has killed his wife and prepares to stab himself so that neither will be taken captive by their Macedonian conquerors. The figure gives us a glimpse at the horrors of war from the perspective of the loser rather than the winner. Contrast this piece with the classical, idealized Greek warrior shown at the beginning of Chapter 2, who barely seems affected by the grim realities of war.

FIGURE 3.9
Gaul and his wife, late third century B.C.

Hellenistic artists also portrayed themes that the classical artists in Athens would have considered undignified or even demeaning. These themes included realistic portrayals of everyday life. For example, classical artists, in their search for ideal beauty instead of imperfect reality, would have ignored subjects such as the market woman shown at the beginning of the chapter. The boxer in Figure 3.10 also exemplifies the contrast to the Olympic heroism that we saw in Chapter 2. Here the artist shows his knowledge of Greek idealism in the perfectly crafted hair and musculature of the bronze figure. Yet this boxer is tired, not heroic. He rests his taped hands on his knees and his shoulders sag in exhaustion, or perhaps defeat. The marks of his contest show clearly on his face—his cheek bleeds, his nose is broken, and his ear is deformed from too many blows. Many art critics, like Pliny who mourned the "death of art," have condemned Hellenistic artists for not striving to portray perfection. Nonetheless, they had remarkable courage in showing the flawed reality of cosmopolitan life.

RESISTANCE TO HELLENISM: JUDAISM, 323–76 B.C.

Much of Hellenistic art and life in the cosmopolitan cities reflected a deep, and in many ways, successful blending of classical Greek culture with that of the ancient Middle East and Egypt. Yet, Alexander's desire to make "all mankind a single people" did not appeal to everyone in the Hellenistic world. Throughout their history, Jews had worked to preserve their distinctive identity, and this desire came directly into conflict with spreading Hellenism (ancient Greek culture). Although Judea remained an independent political unit under Alexander and the Ptolemies, the successor kingdoms offered opportunities for Jews from Palestine to trade and settle throughout the Hellenistic world. In the new multiethnic areas, urban Jews struggled to clarify and sustain their sense of identity. The most pious among them lived together in Jewish quarters where they could observe the old laws and maintain a sense of separate community. Alexandria and Antioch had substantial Jewish quarters, and most large cities had a strong Jewish presence.

Some Jews compromised with Hellenism, learning Greek and taking advantage of the opportunities available to those who at least had the appearance of

In Palestine, too, Jews and Gentiles, or non-Jews, met and mingled. Palestine had many Greek settlements, and even in Jerusalem Jews faced the question of what it meant for them to compromise with Hellenism. Jesus Ben Sirach, a Jewish scribe and teacher in Jerusalem, wrote a text called *Ecclesiasticus* (ca. 180 B.C.) in which he scolded believers who had turned away from the traditional Jewish Law of Moses and warned them that God would exact vengeance for their impiety. In an ironic twist, his text was translated into Greek by his grandson.

These uncertainties within the Jewish community came to a head when the Seleucid kings wrested Palestine from the Ptolemies in 200 B.C. The pace of Hellenization quickened after this pivotal event. Both Jewish and pagan historical sources claim that the Seleucid king Antiochus IV (r. 175–163 B.C.) intended to change Jewish observance in order to "combine the peoples"—that is, to Hellenize the Jews. According to an early Jewish text, even the high priest of Jerusalem supported the king and "exercised his influence in order to bring over his fellow-countrymen to the Greek ways of life." Antiochus established Greek schools in Jerusalem and went so far as to enter Jewish contestants in the Greek-style athletic games celebrated at Tyre. In 168 B.C., he ordered an altar to Zeus to be erected in the Temple of Jerusalem and sacrifices to be offered to the Greek god. The Roman historian Josephus (A.D. 75?) later described the sacrilege: "He sacrificed swine upon the altars and bespattered the temple with their grease, thus perverting the rites of the Jews and the piety of their fathers."

Antiochus's policies proved too much for pious Jews, and in 166 B.C., Judas Maccabeus (Judas the Hammer) led an armed revolt against the Seleucids. (See Document 3.3 on page D3.3.) *Maccabean Revolt* The account of the Maccabean Revolt is preserved in a text titled *The First Book of the Maccabees,* probably written in 140 B.C. by a Jew in Judea. The author articulated the goal of Antiochus clearly: "Then the king wrote to his whole kingdom that all should be one people, and that each should give up his customs." This decree of Antiochus is reminiscent of Plutarch's praise of Alexander quoted at the beginning of this chapter, and it confirms the differing, intensely felt opinions that people often have about cultural blending.

In the end, the Maccabeans prevailed. In 164 B.C. the Jewish priests rededicated the Temple, and the Jews celebrated the restoration of their separate

Hellenism. As they learned to speak and write in Greek and studied the classical texts, some of their *Hellenized Jews* traditional beliefs changed, especially where they sought to reconcile Judaism with Hellenism. Sometime in the third century B.C., the Hebrew Scriptures were translated into Greek, in the influential document known as the *Septuagint.* (The name derives from the Latin word for "seventy," recalling the legendary group of 72 translators who were credited with the accomplishment.) In great cities like Alexandria, Jews gathered in synagogues to pray in a traditional fashion, but in many of these centers of worship, the Scriptures were read in Greek.

identity. The historian of *First Maccabees* wrote that "Judas and his brothers and all the assembly of Israel determined that every year at that season the days of the dedication of the altar should be observed with gladness and joy for eight days." This declaration instituted the feast of Hanukkah, which Jews continue to celebrate today.

The Maccabean revolutionaries established a new theocratic state of Judea, which the Seleucids were

Independent Judea

too busy with war on their eastern borders to challenge. The reinvigorated Jewish state continued its conquests of neighboring states, including Greek cities in Galilee, and by 76 B.C. the Jews had established a kingdom almost as extensive as that of Solomon (r. 970–931 B.C.) (see Chapter 1). Though they had revolted to preserve their cultural and religious purity, the new rulers proved intolerant of their Gentile subjects, forcing many to convert and insisting that non-Jewish infant boys be circumcised. These practices worsened the instability already plaguing the region.

The Search for Truth: Hellenistic Thought, Religion, and Science

Hellenistic rulers from Alexander on consciously spread Greek ideas and learning. To do this, they vigorously supported education, which they saw as key to the preservation of Greek ideals and the training ground for new Hellenized civil servants. Within these educated circles occurred most of the intellectual and cultural blending that had created the brilliance of Hellenistic art as well as the struggles of cultural identity. However, these communities of the educated also proved a fertile ground for intellectual inquiry in which great minds eagerly sought truth about the world, religion, and the meaning of life.

A Life of Learning

Great speculations, however, began first in the schoolrooms. Families who wanted their boys to succeed invested heavily in education. At the age of seven, boys attended privately funded schools and practiced Greek and writing. The parchment samples of their assignments reveal a strong anti-"barbarian" prejudice in which the culture of all non-Greeks was

dismissed. Thus, even early schooling aimed to inculcate Greek values among non-Greek peoples. This indoctrination was reinforced by an emphasis on Homer's works as the primary literary texts.

At fourteen, boys expanded their education to include literary exercises, geography, and advanced studies of Homer. Successful students then continued their studies in the gymnasium, the heart of Hellenistic education and culture. Most cities boasted splendid gymnasia as their central educational institutions. Often the most beautiful building in the city, the gymnasium sported a running track, an area for discus and javelin throwing, a wrestling pit, and baths, lecture halls, and libraries. Here Greek-speaking boys of all ethnic backgrounds gathered, exercised naked, and finished an education that allowed them to enter the Greek ruling class.

Hellenistic kings cultivated education just as they served as patrons of the arts. They competed fiercely to hire sought-after tutors for their families and schools and to purchase texts for their libraries. The best texts were copied by hand on Egyptian papyrus or carefully prepared animal hide called parchment. (The word *parchment* derives from *Pergamena charta*, or "Pergamum paper," which refers to where the best quality parchment was made.) Texts were prepared in scrolls rather than bound in books and were designed to be unrolled and read aloud.

This advocacy of education yielded diverse results. Many scholars produced nothing more than rather shallow literary criticism; others created literature that captured the superficial values of much of Hellenistic life; and some created highly sophisticated philosophy and science. The range of these works, however, contributed important threads to the tapestry of Western civilization.

THEATER AND LITERATURE

The tragedies and comedies of classical Greek theater had illuminated profound public and heroic themes ranging from fate and responsibility to politics and ethics. Theater proved extremely popular in the Hellenistic cities as well. Though some cosmopolitan playwrights wrote tragedies, few of these works have survived. We do have many comedies from this era, which contrast so starkly with the classic Greek examples of this genre that this body of work is called "New Comedy." Hellenistic plays were almost devoid of political satire and focused instead on the plights of individuals.

The best-known playwright of New Comedy is Menander (342?–292? B.C.), whose works often centered on young men who fell in love with women who were unattainable for some reason. Most of these *New comedies* plots ended happily with the couples overcoming all obstacles. In general, New Comedy characters were preoccupied with making money or indulging themselves in other ways. This focus on individual concerns reflected the realities of cosmopolitan life—ruled by powerful and distant kings, individuals had limited personal power. Menander and the other playwrights of the age shed light on this impotence by focusing on the personal rather than on larger questions of good and evil.

A new genre of escapist literature—the Hellenistic novel—also emerged in this environment. The themes in these novels echo those of the plays: Very young men and women fall in love (usually at first *Hellenistic novels* sight), but circumstances separate them. (The historical account in Document 3.2 bears a striking resemblance to this genre raising doubts about its veracity!) They must endure hardships and surmount obstacles before they can be reunited. Surprisingly, most of these novels portray young women as resourceful and outspoken individuals. For example, a remarkable heroine in the novel *Ninos* dresses in gender-ambiguous clothing and leads a band of Assyrians to capture a fortified city. Although wounded, she makes a brave escape while elephants trample her soldiers.

Both the New Comedy and the Hellenistic novel sought to provide an escape from the realities of cosmopolitan life. Yet they also reflected new ideals in this society that often looked to the personal rather than to the polis for meaning. For example, unlike the writings of classical Greece, Hellenistic texts expressed an ideal of affection within marriage. The philosopher Antipater of Tarsus wrote, "The man who has had no experience of a married woman and children has not tasted true and noble happiness." The literature of the day also revealed an increased freedom of Hellenistic women to choose their partners. While families still arranged most marriages, some women (and men) began to follow their hearts in choosing a spouse. The woman we read about at the beginning of this chapter, who abandoned her father for the comic actor, was one example. Women also gained more freedom in divorce laws. Like men, they could seek divorce if their husbands committed adultery. One marriage contract from as early as 311 B.C. included clauses forbidding the husband to "insult" his wife with another woman. Taken together, all these themes expressed a new emphasis on love within the family.

CYNICS, EPICUREANS, AND STOICS: COSMOPOLITAN PHILOSOPHY

Like their literary counterparts, Hellenistic philosophers also narrowed the focus of their inquiry. Most of them no longer tackled the lofty questions of truth and justice that had preoccupied Socrates and Plato. Instead, they considered how an individual could achieve happiness in an age in which vast, impersonal kingdoms produced the kind of pain and weariness embodied by the market woman pictured at the beginning of the chapter.

The sensibilities of the Hellenistic age had been first foreshadowed by Diogenes (400?–325? B.C.), an early proponent of the philosophic school called "Cynicism." Diogenes was disgusted with the hypocrisy and materialism emerging around him in the transformed life of Athens as traditional polis life deteriorated. Diogenes and his followers believed that the only way for people to live happily in a fundamentally evil world was to involve themselves as little as possible in that world. The Cynics therefore claimed that the more people rejected the goods and connections of this world—property, marriage, religion, luxury—the more they would achieve spiritual happiness.

To demonstrate his rejection of all material things, Diogenes reputedly lived in a large tub. The carving in Figure 3.11 shows him in the tub, oblivious *Cynics* to the lavish villa behind him. He is talking to Alexander the Great, enacting a likely apocryphal story in which Alexander offers the famous philosopher anything in the world. Diogenes simply asks Alexander to "stand out of my light and let me see the sun." The dog perched on top of the tub symbolizes Cynicism. (The word *cynic* derives from the Greek word *kunos*, which means "of a dog," or dog-like, because Cynics supposedly lived as simply and as filthily as dogs.)

Although Plato had dismissed Diogenes as "Socrates gone mad," Cynicism became popular during the Hellenistic period as people searched for meaning in their personal lives, rather than justice for their polis. Some men and women chose to live an ascetic life of the mind instead of involving themselves in the day-to-day activities of the Hellenistic cities. However, most found it difficult to reject material goods completely.

FIGURE 3.11
Diogenes and Alexander.

teaching of the wise, and to gaze down from that elevation on others wandering aimlessly in a vain search for the way of life." Of course, this "greatest joy" required money with which to purchase the pain-free pleasures that Epicurus advocated. His was not a philosophy that everyone could afford.

While Epicurus honed his philosophy in his private garden, the public marketplace of Athens gave rise to a third great Hellenistic philosophy: Stoicism. Named after *stoa*, the covered walkways surrounding the marketplace, the school of Stoicism was founded by Zeno (335?–261? B.C.). Zeno exemplified the cosmopolitan citizen of the Hellenistic world, for he was born in Cyprus of non-Greek ancestry and spent most of his life in Athens.

Stoics

At age 22 Zeno was a follower of Crates the Cynic, but later abandoned his early connection to Cynicism, arguing that people could possess material goods as long as they were not emotionally attached to them. Indeed, the Stoic philosophers advocated indifference to external things. While this attitude paralleled Epicurus's desire to avoid pain, Zeno and the Stoics did not frame their philosophy in terms of the materialism of an atomic universe. Instead, they argued for the existence of a Universal Reason or God that governed the universe. As they explained, seeds of the Universal Reason lay within each individual, so everyone was linked in a universal brotherhood. In quasi-religious terms, this belief validated Alexander's supposed goal of unifying diverse peoples.

The Stoics' belief in a Universal Reason led them to explain the apparent turbulence of the world differently than the Epicureans. Stoics did not believe in random events, but instead posited a rational world with laws and structures—an idea that would have a long history in the West. While individuals could not control this universe, they could control their own responses to the apparent vagaries of the world. Followers were implored to pursue virtue in a way that kept them in harmony with rational nature,

Other Hellenistic philosophies offered more practical solutions to the question of where to find personal happiness in an impersonal world. Epicurus (342?–270? B.C.), for example, founded a school of philosophy that built on Democritus's (460–370 B.C.) theory of a universe made of atoms (described in Chapter 2). Envisioning a purposeless world of randomly colliding atoms, Epicurus proclaimed that happiness came from seeking pleasure while being free from pain in both body and mind. From a practical standpoint, this search for happiness involved pursuing pleasures that did not bring pain. Activities such as overeating or overdrinking, which ended in pain, should thus be avoided. In Epicurus's view, the ideal life was one of moderation, which consisted of being surrounded by friends and free of the burdens of the public sphere. His circle of followers included women and slaves. The Roman Epicurean Lucretius Carus (99?–55? B.C.) articulated Epicurus's ideal: "This is the greatest joy of all: to stand aloof in a quiet citadel, stoutly fortified by the

Epicurus

not fighting it. The ideal Stoic renounced passions (including anger) even while enduring the pain and suffering that inevitably accompany life. Through self-control, Stoics might achieve the tranquility that Epicureans and Cynics desired.

Cynicism, Epicureanism, and Stoicism had many things in common. Arising in settings where individuals felt unable to influence their world, they all emphasized control of the self and personal tranquility. Whereas the classical Greeks had found meaning through participation in the public life of their poleis, Hellenistic philosophers claimed that individuals could find contentment through some form of withdrawal from the turbulent life of the impersonal cosmopolitan cities. Moreover, all three philosophies appealed primarily to people with some measure of wealth. The indifferent, pain-free life of both the Epicureans and the Stoics required money, and the self-denial of the Cynics seldom appealed to really destitute people.

New Religions of Hope

For most ordinary people, the philosophies of the Hellenistic age had little relevance. These people looked instead to new religious ideas for a sense of meaning and hope. During this period, the gods and goddesses of the poleis gave way to deities that had international appeal and that were accessible to ordinary individuals—two features that marked a dramatic departure from previous religions of the West. Furthermore, the new religions offered hope in an afterlife that provided an escape from the alienation of the Hellenistic world. The international component paved the way for a blending of religious ideas—syncretism—and individuals felt a deeply passionate spiritual connection to their deities. The most popular new cults were known as "mystery religions" because initiates swore not to reveal the insights they received during the highest ceremonies. The historical roots of these cults stretched back to early Greece, Egypt, and Syria, but they acquired a new relevance throughout the Hellenistic era.

Mystery cults included worship of fertility goddesses like Demeter and Cybele, and a revitalized *"Mystery religion"* cult of Dionysus. However, the most popular was that of the Egyptian goddess Isis, who achieved a remarkable universality. Inscription stones offering her prayers claim that Isis ruled the world and credited her with inventing writing and cultivation of grain, ruling the heavenly bodies, and even transcending fate itself—the overarching destiny that even the old Homeric gods could not escape. Isis reputedly declared: "I am she who is called Lawgiver. . . . I conquer Fate. Fate heeds me." In other inscriptions, worshipers claimed that Isis was the same goddess that other peoples called by different names: "In your person alone you are all the other goddesses named by the peoples."

Figure 3.12, a marble relief from Athens, demonstrates religious syncretism in action. The piece was carved in the classical technique showing an apparently traditional Greek family worshiping at an altar. At the right of the altar, standing before the veil of mystery, is the Egyptian goddess Isis, depicted in traditional Greek style. The god seated at the right resembles Zeus, but he is Isis' brother/husband Osiris, the traditional Egyptian consort of the goddess-queen. This figure shows the syncretic nature of the new Hellenistic religions, in which patron deities of particular cities acquired international appeal. In their worship of these mysteries, the people of the Hellenistic kingdoms may have almost achieved Alexander's rumored ideal of universalism.

Men and women who wanted to experience the mysteries of these new religions believed that they had been summoned by a dream or other supernatural

FIGURE 3.12
Worship of Isis and Osiris, later second century B.C.

call. They took part in a purification ritual and an elaborate public celebration, including a procession filled with music and, sometimes, ecstatic dance in which people acted as if possessed by the goddess or god. Finally, the procession left the public spaces and entered the sacred space of the deity, where the initiate experienced a profound connection with the god or goddess. Many mysteries involved sacred meals through which people became godlike by eating the flesh of the deity. Such believers emerged from this experience expecting to participate in an afterlife. Here lay the heart of the new religious impulses: the hope for another, better world after death. The mystery religions would continue to draw converts for centuries, and perhaps paved the way for Christianity—the most successful mystery religion of all.

HELLENISTIC SCIENCE

The philosophic and religious longings of the Hellenistic world bred long-standing consequences for the future. People living in later large, impersonal cities turned to the philosophies of indifference and religions of hope. Equally impressive were the improvements on classical Greek science and technology that emerged in the Hellenistic learning centers. This flourish of intellectual activity was fostered in part by the generous royal patronage that made Alexandria and Pergamum scholastic centers, and in part by the creative blending of ideas from old centers of learning.

One scholar who benefited from the new Hellenistic world of learning was Herophilus (335?–280? B.C.), who traveled to Alexandria from the Seleucid lands near the Black Sea to study medicine. The first physician to break the strong Greek taboo against cutting open a corpse, Herophilus performed dissections that led him to spectacular discoveries about human anatomy. (His curiosity even reputedly led him to perform vivisections on convicted criminals to learn about the motion of living organs.) His careful studies *Medical advances* yielded pathbreaking knowledge: He was the first to recognize the brain as the seat of intelligence and to describe accurately the female anatomy, including the ovaries and fallopian tubes. However, all physicians were not as willing as Herophilus to treat the human body as an object of scientific study. Even in intellectually advanced Alexandria, dissection became unpopular, and subsequent physicians focused on techniques of clinical treatment rather than on anatomy. However, they made major strides in pharmacology, carefully studying the influence of drugs and toxins on the body.

In spite of these noteworthy advances, the most important achievements of the Hellenistic scientists occurred in the field of mathematics. Euclid (335–270 B.C.), who studied in Alexandria, is considered one of the most accomplished mathematicians of all time. In his most famous work, *Elements* (300? B.C.), Euclid presented a geometry based on increasingly complex *Mathematics and astronomy* axioms and postulates. When Euclid's patron, King Ptolemy, asked the mathematician whether there was an easier way to learn geometry than by struggling through these proofs, Euclid replied that there was no "royal road" (or shortcut) to understanding geometry. Euclid's work became the standard text on the subject, and, even today, students find his intricate proofs both challenging and vexing.

Euclid's mathematical work laid the foundation for Hellenistic astronomy. Eratosthenes of Cyrene (275?– 195 B.C.), for example, used Euclid's theorems to calculate the circumference of the earth with remarkable accuracy—he erred only by about 200 miles. Aristarchus of Samos (310?–230? B.C.) posited a heliocentric, or sun-centered, universe (against prevailing Greek tradition) and attempted to use Euclidian geometry to calculate the size and distance of the moon and sun. Although Aristarchus's contemporaries rejected his work, he and other astronomers introduced a striking change into the study of the heavens: They eliminated superstition and instead approached their work with mathematics.

Another beneficiary of Euclid's mathematics was Archimedes (287?–212 B.C.), often considered the greatest inventor of antiquity. Like so *Archimedes* many cosmopolitan scholars, Archimedes, who was born in Syracuse, traveled to Alexandria to study. He later returned to Syracuse, where he worked on both abstract and practical problems. He built further on Euclid's geometry, applying the theorems to cones and spheres. In the process, he became the first to determine the value of pi—essential in calculating the area of a circle. He also applied geometry to the study of levers, proving that no weight was too heavy to move. He reportedly coined the optimistic declaration: "Give me a place to stand, a long enough lever, and I will move the earth."

Archimedes did more than advance theoretical mathematics: He also had a creative, practical streak. For example, he invented the compound pulley, a

valuable device for moving heavy weights. His real challenge, however, came at the end of his life. As we will see in Chapter 4, Syracuse, the city of Archimedes' birth, was besieged by Rome, a rising power in the Mediterranean. Throughout the siege, Syracuse used both offensive and defensive weapons that Archimedes had invented. Yet the great man's inventions could not save the Sicilian city. The Romans ultimately prevailed, and in 212 B.C. Archimedes was struck down by a Roman soldier as he was drawing a figure in the sand.

Archimedes serves as an apt symbol for the Hellenistic world that produced him. He was educated with the best of Greek learning, and combined it with the rich diversity of Asia and the Mediterranean lands—a blending that gave Western civilization dramatic impetus. The Hellenistic scientist died at the hands of a new peoples—the Romans—who embraced the practical applications of men like Archimedes and who next took up the torch of Western culture.

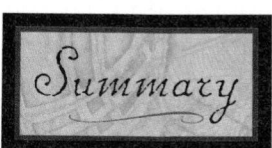

The Macedonian kings Philip and Alexander permanently transformed the life of the polis that had marked the glory of Greece. Their conquests of Greece, and then Egypt and the Persian Empire in Asia, created a unique blend of these ancient civilizations. By establishing a ruling elite of Greeks and Macedonians in cities from the Mediterranean to India, Alexander and his successors spread key elements of Greek civilization. Yet they also reshaped the culture of the polis. Political and cultural centers moved from the Greek city-states to bustling cosmopolitan areas, where people from all over the Hellenistic world mingled. Some benefited greatly from the new opportunities for personal enrichment that cosmopolitan life offered; many more sank to unprecedented levels of poverty. Some peoples embraced the cultural blending; others rejected it.

Though the armies of the Hellenistic kings competed endlessly for land and power, kings still had the resources to support culture and learning. Scientists, artisans, and scholars of this complex age made impressive advances. However, a new force was gathering momentum in the West, one that would profoundly impact the fate of Hellenistic civilizations.

REVIEW, ANALYZE, AND ANTICIPATE

REVIEW THE PREVIOUS CHAPTER

In Chapter 1—"The Roots of Western Civilization"—we explored the beginnings of city life in Mesopotamia. Chapter 2—"The Contest for Excellence"—looked at the life, culture, and political fortunes of the classical Greek city-states.

1. *Contrast the culture of classical Athens with artistic and philosophic ideas of the Hellenistic world, and consider what contributed to the transformation in ideas.*

2. *Review the urban experiences of Mesopotamia and Greece, and compare and contrast them with those of people in the cosmopolitan cities of the Hellenistic world. What do you think are the most significant differences, and what elements of urban life remained constant?*

3. *Chapter 1 summarized the early history of the Jews. Consider how their past contributed to the Maccabean Revolt under the Seleucids.*

ANALYZE THIS CHAPTER

Chapter 3—"The Poleis Become Cosmopolitan"—describes the conquest of Greece by Macedonia, and traces the spread of Greek culture as far east as India, as vibrant new monarchies combined Greek culture with the diversity of many other peoples to create the Hellenistic world.

1. *What contributed to the conquest of the Greek city-states by Macedonia? Consider both the weaknesses of the poleis and the strengths of Macedonia.*

2. *What elements of Hellenic culture were most transformed, and in what ways were the cultures of*

TIMELINE: A CLOSER LOOK

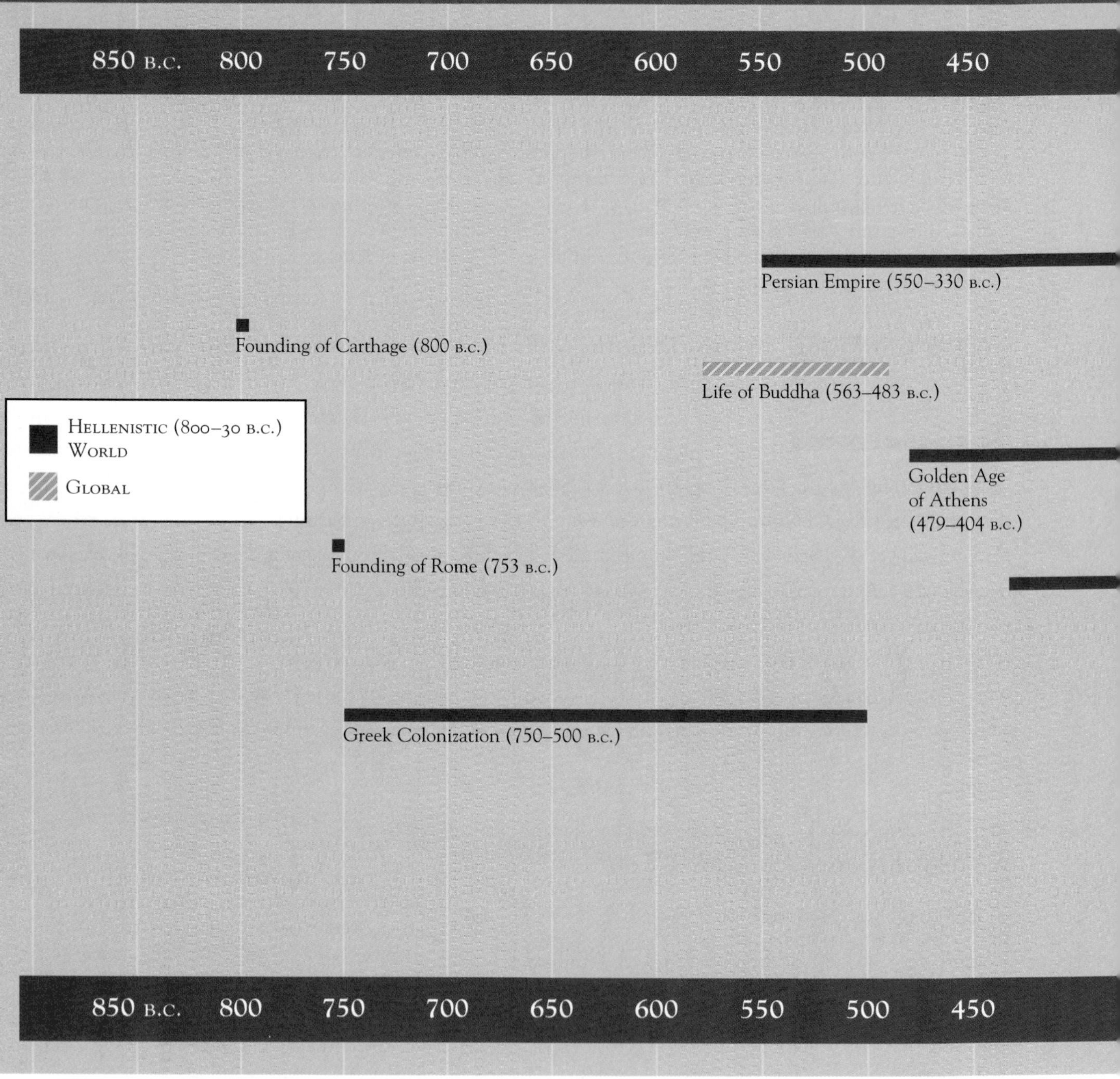

850 B.C.	800	750	700	650	600	550	500	450

Persian Empire (550–330 B.C.)

Founding of Carthage (800 B.C.)

■ HELLENISTIC (800–30 B.C.)
WORLD

⧄ GLOBAL

Life of Buddha (563–483 B.C.)

Golden Age
of Athens
(479–404 B.C.)

Founding of Rome (753 B.C.)

Greek Colonization (750–500 B.C.)

850 B.C.	800	750	700	650	600	550	500	450

the Persian Empire changed by contact with
Greek culture?

3. Describe the changes in economics and warfare that
were introduced in the Hellenistic world.

4. How did the opportunities for women change under
the Hellenistic monarchies?

5. How did the Hellenistic world affect places as far
away as India?

112

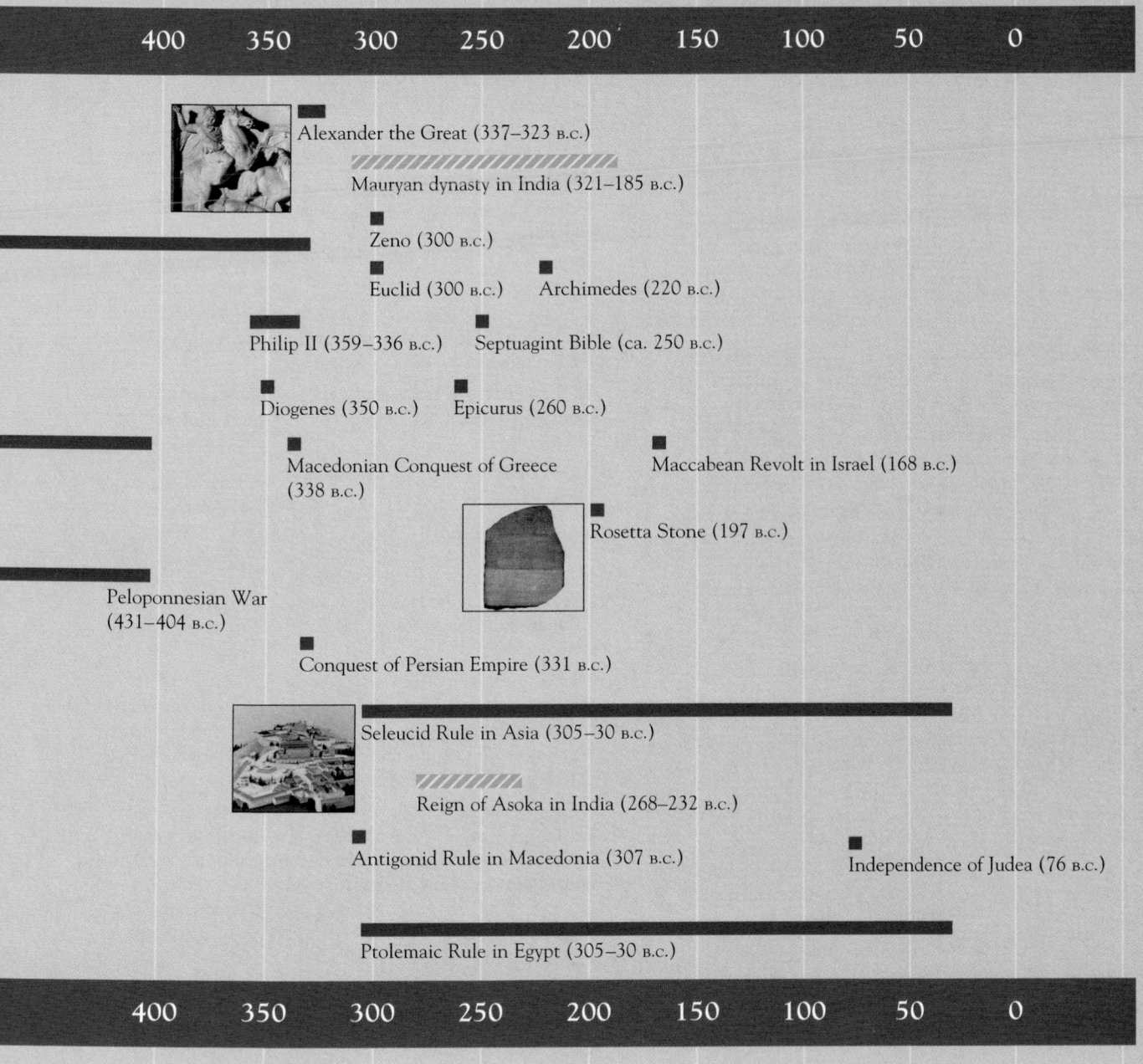

| 400 | 350 | 300 | 250 | 200 | 150 | 100 | 50 | 0 |

Alexander the Great (337–323 B.C.)

Mauryan dynasty in India (321–185 B.C.)

Zeno (300 B.C.)

Euclid (300 B.C.)   Archimedes (220 B.C.)

Philip II (359–336 B.C.)   Septuagint Bible (ca. 250 B.C.)

Diogenes (350 B.C.)   Epicurus (260 B.C.)

Macedonian Conquest of Greece (338 B.C.)   Maccabean Revolt in Israel (168 B.C.)

Rosetta Stone (197 B.C.)

Peloponnesian War (431–404 B.C.)

Conquest of Persian Empire (331 B.C.)

Seleucid Rule in Asia (305–30 B.C.)

Reign of Asoka in India (268–232 B.C.)

Antigonid Rule in Macedonia (307 B.C.)   Independence of Judea (76 B.C.)

Ptolemaic Rule in Egypt (305–30 B.C.)

| 400 | 350 | 300 | 250 | 200 | 150 | 100 | 50 | 0 |

ANTICIPATE THE NEXT CHAPTER

In Chapter 4—"Pride in Family and City"—we will see the Hellenistic monarchies conquered by a new empire growing in the West.

1. *Which elements of the Hellenistic world do you think might endure and which might change? Why? Include in your consideration political organization, military strategy, and cultural elements.*

BEYOND THE CLASSROOM

THE CONQUEST OF THE POLEIS

Borza, Eugene N. *In the Shadow of Olympus: The Emergence of Macedon*. Princeton, NJ: Princeton University Press, 1992. Chronological survey seeking to trace the emergence of Macedon as a major force in the political affairs of the fourth-century B.C. Balkans.

Bosworth, A.B. *Conquest and Empire: The Reign of Alexander the Great*. Cambridge, England: Cambridge University Press, 1988. Considers Alexander's impact on Macedon, the Greek world, and the former Persian Empire.

Cawkwell, G. *Philip of Macedon*. London: Faber & Faber, 1978. A standard history tracing the rise of Philip and the development of Macedon into a world power.

Green, Peter. *Alexander of Macedon, 356–323 B.C.: A Historical Biography*. Hammondworth, England: Penguin, 1974. A fresh interpretation of the life of Alexander.

Harding, Philip. *From the End of the Peloponnesian Wars to the Battle of Ipsus*. NY: Cambridge University Press, 1985. A sophisticated analysis of the late Greek world before its conversion into the Hellenistic world by Alexander's conquest.

THE SUCCESSOR KINGDOMS, 323–100 B.C.

Engels, Donald. *Alexander the Great and the Logistics of the Macedonian Army*. Berkeley, CA: University of California Press, 1978. Tries to answer two questions: How did Alexander secure provisions for his army in Asia, and how did these logistical problems affect his progress?

Grant, M. *From Alexander to Cleopatra: The Hellenistic World*. NY: Scribner, 1982. A general survey of the Hellenistic world.

Green, P. *From Alexander to Actium*. Berkeley, CA: University of California Press, 1990. A complex analysis of the Hellenistic world's politics, literature, art, philosophy, and science.

EAST MEETS WEST IN THE SUCCESSOR KINGDOMS

Billows, Richard A. *Kings and Colonists: Aspects of Macedonian Imperialism*. NY: E.J. Brill, 1995. An in-depth study of the problems of Macedonian imperial rule.

Cohen, Getzel M. *The Hellenistic Settlements in Europe, the Islands and Asia Minor*. Berkeley, CA: University of California Press, 1995. A good general history of Hellenistic settlement—its founders, early history, and organization.

Laks, Andre, and Malcolm Schofield. *Justice and Generosity: Studies in Hellenistic Social and Political Philosophy*. NY: Cambridge University Press, 1995. A comprehensive guide to the social and political philosophies in a period of increasing interest to classicists, philosophers, and cultural and intellectual historians.

Stewart, Andrew. *Faces of Power: Alexander's Image and Hellenistic Politics*. Berkeley, CA: University of California Press, 1993. A remarkable look at art as a legitimate source of historical evidence.

Tcherikover, V. *Hellenistic Civilization and the Jews*. NY: Macmillan Publishing Company, Inc., 1970. A study of the Jewish influence on Greek civilization.

Walbank, F.W. *The Hellenistic World*. Cambridge, MA: Harvard University Press, 1993. A thorough, comprehensive survey.

THE SEARCH FOR TRUTH: HELLENISTIC THOUGHT, RELIGION, AND SCIENCE

Hicks, R.D. (trans.). *Diogenes Laertius: Lives of the Eminent Philosophers*. Cambridge: Loeb Classical Library, 1922. An excellent primary source on the giants of speculative thought in Greece.

Martin, Luther H. *Hellenistic Religions: An Introduction*. NY: Oxford University Press, 1987. A well-written survey of Hellenistic religions, their characteristic forms and expressions, differences and relationships, and their place in the Hellenistic system of thought.

Pollitt, J.J. *Art in the Hellenistic Age*. NY: Cambridge University Press, 1986. An accessible and well-illustrated look at Hellenistic art as an expression of cultural experience and aspirations of the Hellenistic age.

Sharples, R.W. *Stoics, Epicureans and Sceptics*. NY: Routledge, 1996. A readable account of the principal doctrines of these Hellenistic philosophies.

GLOBAL CONNECTIONS

Sedlar, Jean W. *India and the Greek World: A Study in the Transmission of Culture*. Totowa, NJ: Rowman & Littlefield. 1980. Well-researched study of the interaction between India and Greece that yields important insights into the mingling of cultures.

Smith Vincent Arthur. *Asoka, the Buddhist Emperor of India*. Delhi: S. Chand, 1964. A short accessible biography made more valuable by its detailed discussion of his important rock edicts.

Documents

Philip of Macedon Conquers Greek Cities

The seeds of Alexander the Great's accomplishments were planted by the experiences of his father, Philip. In this account by the Roman historian Justin, we see the origins of Philip's appreciation of Greek culture. We also see how Philip combined military vigor with leniency toward conquered peoples. Finally, the account sheds light on the dynastic violence and the strength of queens that marked future Hellenistic kingdoms.

■ **Investigate the Document**

*Why was Philip in Greece? **What** role did Philip's mother play in his ascent to power? **How** did Philip treat defeated Greek cities? **What** similarities do you see between Philip's actions and those of his son Alexander?*

Alexander II [King of Macedon] at the very beginning of his reign purchased peace from the Illyrians [the peoples north and west of Macedon] with a sum of money, giving his brother Philip as a hostage. Some time later, also, he made peace with the Thebans by giving the same hostage, a circumstance which afforded Philip fine opportunities for improving his extraordinary abilities; for being kept as a hostage at Thebes for three years, he received the first rudiments of a boy's education at a city famous for its strict discipline, and in the house of Epaminondas, who was eminent as a philosopher as well as a great general. Not long afterward Alexander perished by a plot of his mother Eurydice, whom Amyntas [her husband]—when she was once convicted of a conspiracy against him—had spared for the sake of their children, little imagining that one day she would be their destroyer. Perdiccas, too—Alexander II's brother—was taken off by like treachery. Horrible, indeed, it was that children should

Source: Justin, "The Beginning of Philip of Macedon's Reign," in *Ancient History Sourcebook*, www.Hallsall@morray.fordham.edu (on the OLC).

have been deprived of life to gratify the passion of a mother—whom a regard for those very children had saved from the reward for her crimes. The murder of Perdiccas seemed all the viler in that not even the prayers of his little son could win him pity from this mother. Philip, for a long time, acted not as king, but as guardian to this child; but when dangerous wars threatened, and it was too long to wait for the cooperation of a prince who was yet so young, he was forced by the people to take the government upon himself.

When he took possession of the throne, great hopes were formed of him by all, both on account of his abilities, which promised that he would prove a great man, and on account of certain old oracles touching Macedonia, which foretold that "when one of the sons of Amyntas should be king, the country should be extremely flourishing," to fulfill which expectations the iniquity of his mother had left only him.

At the beginning of his reign, when both the treacherous murder of his brother, and the multitude of his enemies, and the poverty of the kingdom exhausted by successive wars, bore hard upon the immature young king, he gained respite from attack by his many foes, some being put off by offers of peace, and others being bought off. However, he attacked such of his enemies as seemed easiest to be subdue, in order that by a victory over them he might confirm the wavering courage of his soldiers, and alter any feelings of contempt which his foes might feel for him. His first conflict was with the Athenians [who sent a fleet to sustain one Manteias, a pretender to Philip's throne] whom he surprised by a strategem, but—though he might have put them all to the sword—he yet, from dread of a more formidable war, allowed them to depart—uninjured, and without [even] a ransom. Later, leading his army against the Illyrians he slew several thousand of his enemies and took the famous city of Larissa. He then fell suddenly upon Thessaly (when it was fearful of anything but a war)—not from a desire of spoil but because he wished to add the strength of the Thessalian cavalry to his own troops; and he thus incorporated a force of horse and foot in one invincible army.

DOCUMENT 3.2

Antiochus and Stratonice Marry: A Hellenistic Love Story

For members of Hellenistic dynasties, marriage provided a doorway to power. Indeed, the descendants of Alexander's followers attributed their right to rule to their bloodlines. Thus, marriages frequently provoked bloodshed as families jockeyed for power. In the excerpt below, Plutarch tells of one marriage that was the exception: this union was based on love—but a forbidden love of a stepson for his stepmother. In the tradition of Hellenistic novels, this story ended happily.

Here's a bit of background to the story: One of Alexander's successors, Seleucus, had married a Persian woman, Apame, and had a son with her named Antiochus. Seleucus then married Stratonice, the daughter of his Macedonian rival, Demetrius. Stratonice also bore Seleucus a son. The historian Plutarch tells what happened next:

■ **Investigate the Document**

> **What** *caused Antiochus' illness?* **What** *does the diagnosis tell you about the beliefs of Hellenistic physicians?* **Why** *did Seleucus allow the marriage between Antiochus and Stratonice?* **What** *does this incident tell you about the importance of dynastic marriages during the Hellenistic world?*

For Antiochus, it appears, had fallen passionately in love with Stratonice, the young queen, who had already made Seleucus the father of a son. He struggled very hard with the beginning of this passion, and at last, resolving with himself that his desires were wholly unlawful, his malady past all cure, and his powers of reason too feeble to act, he determined on death, and thought to bring his life slowly to extinction by neglecting his person and refusing nourishment, under the pretence of being ill. Erasistratus, the physician who attended him, quickly perceived that love was his distemper, but the difficulty was to discover the object. He therefore waited continually in his chamber, and when any of the beauties of the court made their visit to the sick prince, he observed the emotions and alterations in the countenance of Antiochus, and watched for the changes which he knew to be indicative of the inward passions and inclinations of the soul. He took notice that the presence of other women produced no effect upon him; but when Stratonice came, as she often did, alone, or in company with Seleucus, to see him, he observed in him all Sappho's famous symptoms,—his voice faltered, his face flushed up, his eyes glanced steathily, a sudden sweat broke out on his skin, the beatings of his heart were irregular and violent, and, unable to support the excess of his passion, he would sink into a state of faintness, prostration, and pallor.

Erasistratus, reasoning upon these symptoms, and, upon the probabilities of things, considering that the king's son would hardly, if the object of his passion had been any other, have persisted to death rather than reveal it, felt, however, the difficulty of making a discovery of this nature to Seleucus. But, trusting to the tenderness of Seleucus for the young man, he put on all the assurances he could, and at last, on some opportunity, spoke out and told him the malady was love, a love impossible to gratify or relieve. The king was extremely surprised, and asked, "Why impossible to relieve?" "The fact is," replied Erasistratus, "he is in love with my wife." "How!" said Seleucus, "and will our friend Erasistratus refuse to bestow his wife upon my son and only successor, when there is no other way to save his life?" "You," replied Erasistratus, "who are his father, would not do so, if he were in love with Stratonice." "Ah, my friend," answered Seleucus, "would to heaven any means, human or divine, could but convert his present passion to that; it would be well for me to part not only with Stratonice, but with my empire, to save Antiochus." This he said with the greatest passion, shedding tears as he spoke; upon which Erasistratus, taking him by the hand replied, "In that case, you have no need of Erasistratus; for you, who are the husband, the father, and the king, are the proper physician for your own family." Seleucus, accordingly, summoning a general assembly of his people, declared to them, that he had resolved to make Antiochus king, and Stratonice queen, of all the provinces of Upper Asia, uniting them in marriage; telling them, that he thought he had sufficient power over the prince's will that he should find in him no repugnance to obey his commands; and for Stratonice, he hoped all his friends would endeavour to make her sensible, if she should manifest any reluctance to such a marriage, that she ought to esteem those things just and honourable which had been determined upon by the king as nec-

Source: Plutarch. "Demetrius" in *The Lives of the Noble Grecians and Romans*, trans. John Dryden (NY: The Modern Library, n.d.) pp. 1095–1096.

essary to the general good. In this manner, we are told, was brought about the marriage of Antiochus and Stratonice.

DOCUMENT 3.3

Judas Maccabaeus Prevails in Jerusalem

Hellenistic empires brought together diverse populations with different religious beliefs. This blending posed a particularly acute problem for the Jews, whose spiritual tenets forbade compromise with polytheism. The following document describes an incident that occurred during a war waged by the Jewish leader Judas Maccabaeus against the Hellenistic king Antiochus in 165 B.C.

■ **Investigate the Document**

What *religious motivations undergirded this war?* **How** *did the Maccabees compromise their own religious beliefs to fight the war?* **How** *did this conflict resemble modern controversies regarding fighting during Ramadan or Christmas?*

[Judas Maccabaeus] overthrew the idol altar and cried out, "If," said he, "anyone be zealous for the laws of his country and for the worship of God, let him follow me"; and when he had said this he made haste into the desert with his sons, and left all his substance in the village. Many others did the same also, and fled with their children and wives into the desert and dwelt in caves; but when the King's generals heard this, they took all the forces they then had in the citadel at Jerusalem, and pursued the Jews into

the desert; and when they had overtaken them, they in the first place endeavored to persuade them to repent, and to choose what was most for their advantage and not put them to the necessity of using them according to the law of war; but when they would not comply with their persuasions, but continued to be of a different mind, they fought against them on the Sabbath day, and they burned them as they were in the caves, without resistance, and without so much as stopping up the entrances of the caves. And they avoided to defend themselves on that day because they were not willing to break in upon the honor they owed the Sabbath, even in such distresses; for our law requires that we rest upon that day.

There were about a thousand, with their wives and children, who were smothered and died in these caves; but many of those that escaped joined themselves to Mattathias and appointed him to be their ruler, who taught them to fight even on the Sabbath day, and told them that unless they would do so they would become their own enemies by observing the law [so rigorously] while their adversaries would still assault them on this day, and they would not then defend themselves; and that nothing could then hinder but they must all perish without fighting. This speech persuaded them, and this rule continues among us to this day, that if there be a necessity we may fight on Sabbath days.

Source: *The Great Events by Famous Historians.* Edited by Rossiter Johnson. (No city) The National Alumni. 1905. Volume II. p. 247.

For quiz questions that tie the book to the videos and additional primary sources, please go to the Primary Source Investigator CD.

Wall painting of a woman playing a cithara

The Romans believed that their greatness derived first from the family, in which aristocratic fathers and mothers were educated and devoted to instilling traditional values in their children. This illustration shows one such cultured mother playing a cithara for her child.

CHAPTER 4

Pride in Family and City

Rome from its Origins Through the Republic, 753–44 B.C.

STUDY • The Establishment and growth of Rome • Family and City Life • Military expansion and transformation • Hellenizing of the Republic • End of the Republic ⊕NOTICE how expansion changed Rome's life and values.

"No country has ever been greater or purer than ours or richer in good citizens and noble deeds; . . . nowhere have thrift and plain living been for so long held in such esteem." The Roman historian Livy (59 B.C.–A.D. 17) wrote a long history of Rome, in which he wanted to show how the heroic citizens of a small city-state became the masters of the world. He attributed their success to their upright character. At the same time Greek civilization was flourishing, a people had settled in the center of Italy, on the hills surrounding what would become the city of Rome. They were a serious, hardworking people who placed loyalty to family and city above all else. In time, this small group conquered the Italian peninsula, forging a coalition of peoples that enjoyed the benefits of peace and prosperity while relentlessly expanding through military conquest.

After overthrowing the monarchy, Rome developed a republican form of government, in which rich and poor citizens alike participated in a highly public legislative process. Within the city, men worked, relaxed, and talked in public spaces while noble women directed the household. Both non-noble men and women worked in many areas of the city and contributed to an increasingly prosperous urban life.

Military success strengthened the Republic, but at the same time planted the seeds for future troubles. Conquests throughout the Mediterranean funneled untold wealth and numerous slaves into Rome, and contact with Hellenistic civilization brought new culture, ideas, and values—causing Livy to lament the decline of "plain living" that he believed had made the Romans great. Yet despite its troubled demise, the Roman Republic left a lasting legacy. Throughout the Mediterranean world, everyone knew of the proud city and its old families who had established laws, technology, and a way of life that exerted a continuing influence.

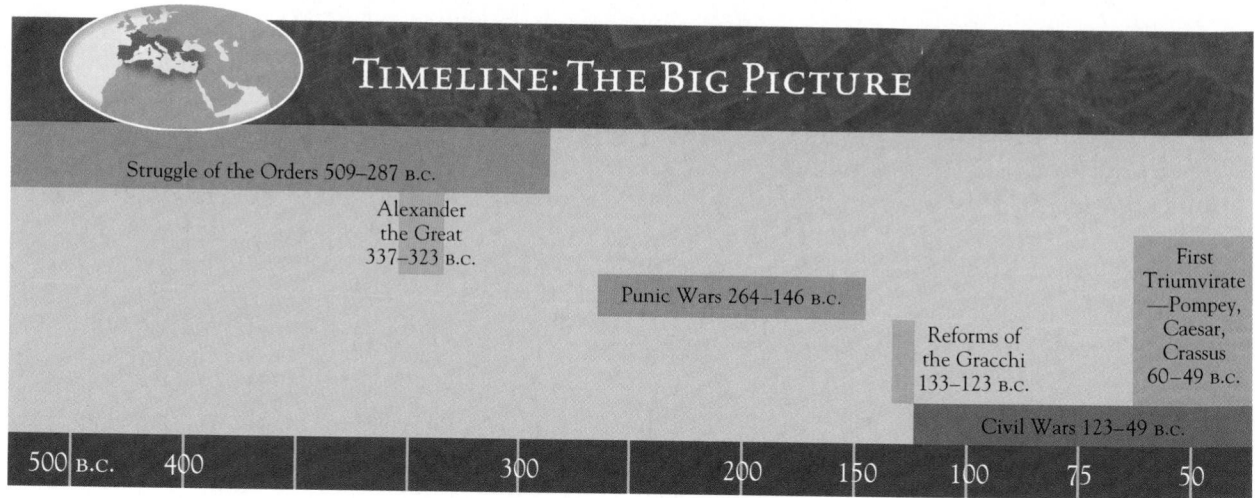

TIMELINE: THE BIG PICTURE

Struggle of the Orders 509–287 B.C.

Alexander the Great 337–323 B.C.

Punic Wars 264–146 B.C.

Reforms of the Gracchi 133–123 B.C.

First Triumvirate —Pompey, Caesar, Crassus 60–49 B.C.

Civil Wars 123–49 B.C.

500 B.C.   400   300   200   150   100   75   50

The Rise of Rome, 753–265 B.C.

On a warm spring day in 458 B.C., a Roman farmer was plowing the land adjacent to his small, round hut when the Senate recognized an imminent threat from a nearby tribe. In the face of such emergencies, the Roman Senate could offer one man supreme power for the duration of the crisis, giving him the title "dictator." The Senate offered the dictatorship to the farmer, Cincinnatus. He accepted the task and successfully led his armies to defeat the invaders. His grateful fellow villagers asked him to continue his leadership after the crisis, but he refused, preferring to return to his plow. Throughout the next centuries, this story of the strong, unassuming farmer Cincinnatus was told and retold by conservative Romans who looked back to the "ways of the fathers" *mos maiorum* for models of virtue. (The American city Cincinnati was so named to honor George Washington—another savior farmer-general.) Romans preserved stories like this to remember their heroes and transmit their values to their families. Though they exist on the border between history and legend, these stories offer a glimpse of the origins of the greatness that would become Rome.

A GREAT CITY IS FOUNDED

The historian Livy did not mind mixing history with myth, for he said: "There is no reason to object when antiquity draws no hard line between the human and the supernatural; it adds dignity to the past." Romans regularly remembered their history in terms of legends. Perhaps the most beloved of these stories told Romans how their city was founded. Like the story of Cincinnatus, the tale of the birth of Rome is filled with drama, conflict, heroes, and values. The tale begins with Aeneas, a Trojan hero who escaped from the destruction of his city after the Trojan War (described in Chapter 2). A royal female descendant of Aeneas decided to dedicate her life to serving the gods. She became pregnant by the god Mars and bore twin boys, Romulus and Remus. The princess's uncle did not believe in the miraculous conception, nor did he want her sons to threaten his rule, so he threw the infant boys in the Tiber River. Soon, a shepherd found them being suckled by a wolf and raised them as his own sons. Many years later, after the boys had grown up, Romulus killed his brother during a quarrel and became the first king of the newly founded city of Rome. The traditional date of the founding of the city is 753 B.C., and archaeological evidence confirms the existence of a settlement there by this time.

Figure 4.1 shows a well-known statue from the fifth century B.C. that depicts the two brothers, Romulus and Remus, being suckled by the wolf that saved them. The age of the original statue—which was only of the nursing wolf—reveals how much the Romans treasured this myth of their city's founding. The twins were added about 2,000 years later, during the Renaissance, showing the continued attraction of the myth. Images like this helped Romans remember and carry on their valued traditions from generation to generation. Reflecting this sense of destiny and heroic action, Livy concluded that "with reason did gods and men choose this site for our city—all its advantages make it of all places in the world the best for a city destined to grow great."

Rome was located on hills overlooking a fertile, low-lying plain and the Tiber River, which afforded access to the Mediterranean Sea and to the inland regions. The geography of the surrounding Italian

FIGURE 4.1
"Wolf of Rome," fifth century B.C.

peninsula offered a number of advantages that would ultimately favor the growth of the young city. In contrast to Greece, whose mountainous terrain discouraged political unification, the large plains along Italy's western and eastern shores fostered trade, communication, and agriculture. The Apennine mountain range that marches down through the peninsula also creates abundant rainfall on the western plain. Therefore, Rome's fields were better situated for large-scale agriculture than had been possible for the Greek city-states. In addition, calm, accessible harbors along the western coast opened avenues for trade throughout the Mediterranean, which was further enhanced by Italy's central location in that important sea.

Geography

The initial settlers of Rome, like many of the other tribes in the region, were Indo-Europeans, those ubiquitous migrants from near the Black Sea whom we first saw in Chapter 1. They farmed, living in round huts and plowing their land. Cato the Elder (234–149 B.C.), a Roman political leader known for expressing traditional Roman values, summarized the Romans' pride in this way of life: "From farmers come the bravest men and sturdiest soldiers." Yet Rome also grew stronger through absorbing some of the culture and ways of its particularly talented neighbors. Greek colonies were well established in southern Italy and Sicily; Phoenician colonies prospered along the coast of North Africa. Most influential, however, were the Romans' immediate neighbors to the north, the Etruscans.

THE ETRUSCAN INFLUENCE

Historians are uncertain about the origins of the Etruscans; they were not an Indo-European people, and scholars have not yet deciphered all their writings. We do know that they were a prosperous people who traded all over the Mediterranean, importing luxury items from Greece and elsewhere. One of the best sources of information about this culture is the surviving artwork. From these works, a picture emerges of a people who apparently enjoyed a gracious way of life.

Figure 4.2 shows an Etruscan sarcophagus, or stone coffin, adorned by a carving of a married couple. The couple recline together as they would have at dinner, and their poses suggest much affection between them. Indeed, women's active participation in this society surprised many of the Etruscans' contemporaries. The famous Greek philosopher Aristotle (384–322 B.C.), writing centuries later, described with some shock how even respectable Etruscan women joined in banquets with men.

Etruscan kings ruled Rome for a time, and the Romans absorbed much from their civilization. Romans adopted Etruscan engineering skills and used them to drain the lowland marsh, which formed the center of their growing city. Romans also learned to use divination—interpreting the will of the gods in the entrails of sacrificial animals—which became a central feature of Roman religion. Finally, the Romans acquired the Etruscan alphabet and began using it to write in their own Latin language. The Italian region of Tuscany is named after this early people who exerted such an influence on the growing culture of Rome.

THE ROMAN MONARCHY, 753?–509 B.C.

Like other ancient civilizations, the early Romans were ruled by kings, but to work out the details of the monarchy, historians have to struggle with combinations of history and legend. Romulus (753?–715? B.C.) was the first king, and more unverifiable legends claim he was followed by four more monarchs. By the seventh century B.C., Rome seems to have been ruled by an Etruscan dynasty that governed for almost a century from about 616 to about 509 B.C.

By the end of the sixth century B.C., the Roman aristocracy had come to chafe against the Etruscan kings' authority. Roman tradition holds that rebellion against the Etruscans erupted in response to the

FIGURE 4.2
Etruscan sarcophagus, late sixth century B.C.

violation of Lucretia, a virtuous Roman matron. According to Livy, Sextus, son of the Etruscan king Tarquin the Proud, raped Lucretia at knifepoint. Her husband, Collatinus, told her not to blame herself, but after extracting her husband's promise to exact vengeance, she committed suicide. She was remembered as a chaste, heroic woman who chose death over dishonor. After her death, Romans rallied around the leadership of an Etruscan nobleman—Brutus—who joined Collatinus in a revolt that toppled the monarchy. The story of Lucretia illuminates the values of bravery and chastity held by early Roman men and women, but it also became a symbol of Romans' revulsion against kings, which would be a continuing theme throughout their history.

Overthrow of Etruscans

The legend accurately concluded that the Etruscan monarchy was overthrown, but the historical reality was more complex. All Romans did not support the overthrow of the monarchy—many in the lower classes relied on the monarchy to control the power of the noble families (the patricians), and some patricians who were related to kings also supported the monarchy. With these competing social forces, simply overthrowing a monarchy would not resolve social issues. However, just as the Greek poleis had overthrown their own kings and replaced them with oligarchies of nobles during their early history, the situation was repeated in Rome. The erection of a stable governmental form would require time and struggle.

GOVERNING AN EMERGING REPUBLIC

Although the Romans introduced a government ruled by old aristocratic families after the fall of the monarchy just as the Greek poleis had done, the Romans put their own stamp on the oligarchy. As the conservative Romans established a new form of government, they tried to preserve many of the institutions that had helped kings govern, and in doing so they created a complex form of government that was very different from the governments of the classical Greek poleis. In this government, wealth and family connections emerged as the most important factors, but a structure was established that tried to prevent the growth of centralized power. The Greek historian Polybius (203?–123 B.C.) offers the most detailed description of the Roman constitution, but his summary also illustrates the complexity of the structure: "No one could say for certain, not even a native, whether the constitution as a whole were an aristocracy or democracy or despotism." Power was shared by the influential in the Senate, the people in the city and in the army, and elected leaders (consuls and tribunes) who exerted executive powers. As complicated as the structure was, Polybius joined many others in seeing Roman political organization as the source of Roman greatness.

The Romans called this form of government a republic, a Latin word that meant "public matter" (often rendered "public realm" or "commonwealth" in English), which they distinguished from the "private realm" of the Etruscan kings. For Romans, this meant that power rested with the people assembled together and that magistrates served the state. This influential vision of government was in striking contrast to that of the Hellenistic kings, who generally viewed their kingdoms as their own property, their spoils of war, their private realm.

However, this impressive political theory did not deter individual nobles from enriching themselves and their families. Many abused their power and oppressed the commoners in their charge, even enslaving many because of debts they incurred. By the fifth century B.C., social relations between patrician and commoner (plebeian) had deteriorated enough that a social revolution occurred, which historians have called the "Struggle of the Orders." Two main issues fueled this controversy: First, the poor wanted guarantees against the abuses of the powerful, and second, the wealthy plebeians wanted a role in government. This struggle was not a civil war, but instead a series of political reforms forced on the aristocracy from about 509 to 287 B.C.

Plebeians began their revolution by establishing themselves as a political alternative to the patricians. They withdrew from the city, held their own assemblies, established their own temple to counter the patrician cults, and even elected their own leaders, called "tribunes," who were to represent plebeian interests. Tribunes could veto unfavorable laws and represent plebeians in law courts for example. Patricians also had a practical reason to listen to the voice of the people through their tribunes, because they needed the plebeians to fight in the infantry. Just as Greek citizens forced concessions from aristocrats who needed armies, Roman citizen-soldiers threatened to refuse military service unless some of their demands were met. This was an effective threat; slowly, plebeians gained in political skill and, through the pressure of their tribunes, extracted meaningful concessions.

Plebeians won a number of important rights: First they gained a written law code that could be consistently enforced. Between 451 and 449 B.C., the laws were written down and displayed in a form called the Twelve Tables. Subsequent Romans looked back proudly to this accomplishment, which established a Roman commitment to law that became one of Rome's most enduring contributions to Western culture. To mark the importance of the establishment of written law, Roman children continued to memorize the Twelve Tables for up to four centuries later. Plebeians also won the right to hold sacred and political offices. While in practice, offices more readily went to the wealthy, upward mobility was possible. Perhaps the greatest concession the plebeians eventually won was the right to marry patricians. This removed birth as the most serious impediment to the rise of talented and wealthy plebeians.

The plebeian struggle for representation culminated in 287 B.C., when the Tribal Assembly became the principal legislative body. Figure 4.3 shows this new republican structure. This group was named because the assembly was organized in "tribes" or regions, urban and rural, where plebeians lived. Laws passed by the Tribal Assembly did not need Senate approval, but bound everyone—rich or poor. The resulting society in Rome contained three main social classes: patricians, wealthy plebeians—later called equestrians (or knights) because they could afford to be in the cavalry—and the *Governing the Republic* poorer plebeians. Money and connections dominated Roman politics as patricians and equestrians fought to increase their power. But Polybius recognized the important influence the people held: "For the people is the sole fountain of honor and of punishment; and it is by these two things and these alone that dynasties and constitutions and, in a word, human society are held together."

Struggle of Orders

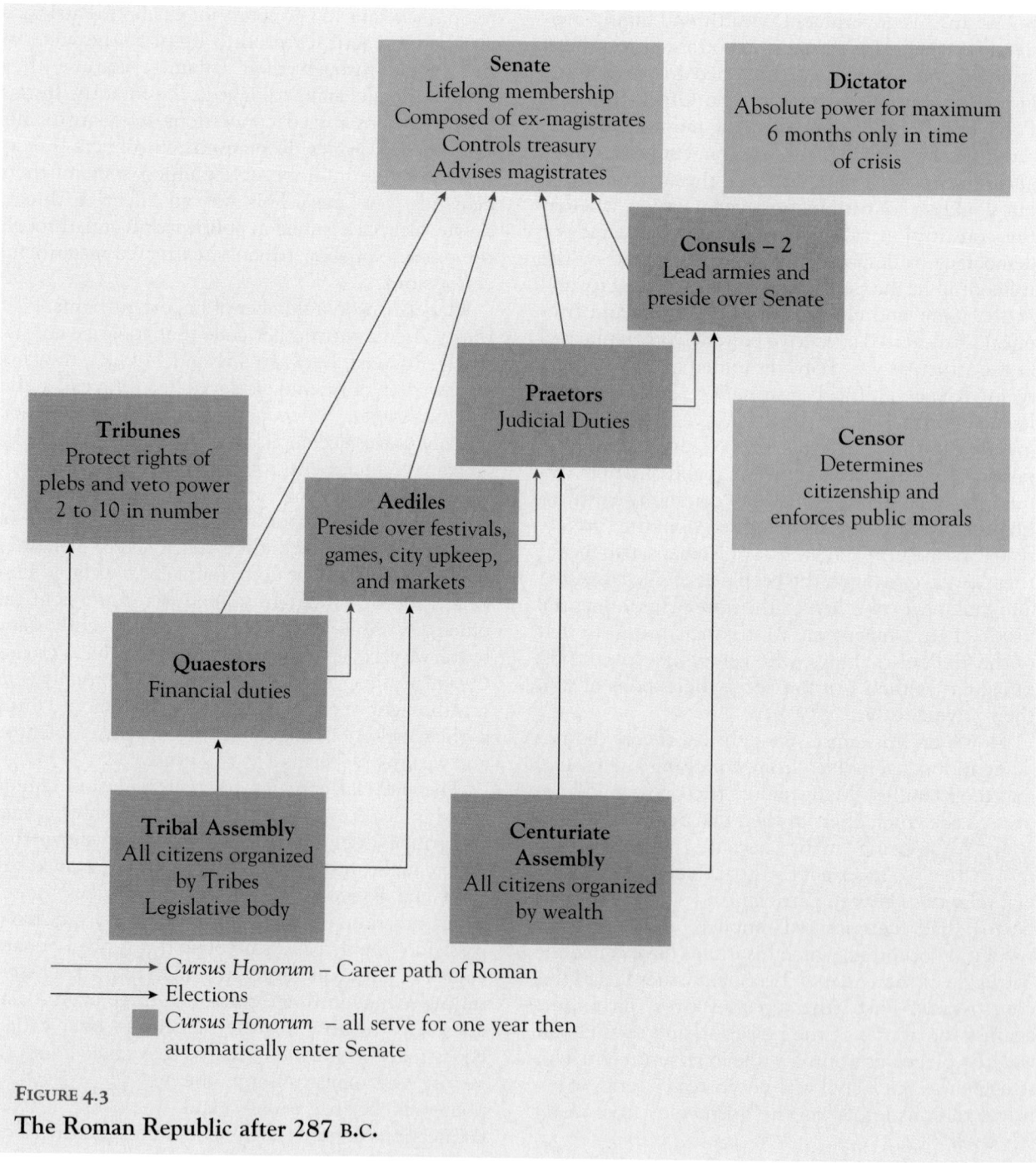

Senate
Lifelong membership
Composed of ex-magistrates
Controls treasury
Advises magistrates

Dictator
Absolute power for maximum
6 months only in time
of crisis

Consuls – 2
Lead armies and
preside over Senate

Tribunes
Protect rights of
plebs and veto power
2 to 10 in number

Praetors
Judicial Duties

Censor
Determines
citizenship and
enforces public morals

Aediles
Preside over festivals,
games, city upkeep,
and markets

Quaestors
Financial duties

Tribal Assembly
All citizens organized
by Tribes
Legislative body

**Centuriate
Assembly**
All citizens organized
by wealth

Cursus Honorum – Career path of Roman

Elections

Cursus Honorum – all serve for one year then
automatically enter Senate

FIGURE 4.3
The Roman Republic after 287 B.C.

As Figure 4.3 shows, the Roman constitution was complex, but logical. All citizens participated in the two Assemblies that elected the magistrates who served the state. Roman men with money and influence could move through the *Cursus Honorum*, the career path of a successful public official. A man would be elected to each office for one year, and then (through the late Republic) automatically become a member of the Senate—that venerable institution which by now had no actual constitutional power but a great deal of influence. The Roman system probably worked in part because most of the political life took place within a more informal system.

INFORMAL GOVERNANCE: PATRONS AND CLIENTS

From the earliest years of the Republic, Romans relied on semiformal ties to smooth social and even political intercourse. Powerful members of society, called patrons, surrounded themselves with less powerful people—clients—in a relationship based on informal yet profoundly important ties. Patrons provided clients with what they called "kindnesses," such as food, occasional financial support, and help in legal disputes. Clients consisted of people from all walks of life: aristocratic youths who looked to powerful patrons for help in their careers (or hoped to be remembered in a rich patron's will), businessmen who wanted to use a patron's political influence to profit in their enterprises, poets who needed money, or freed slaves who remained attached to their former owners. Because Rome remained overwhelmingly an agricultural society, the largest group of clients were small farmers, who depended on their patrons to help them survive in a land that was becoming dominated by powerful aristocratic landowners. Clients owed their patrons duties, such as financial and political support.

Many clients gathered at their patrons' doors every morning as the cock crowed—failure to appear would jeopardize one's tie of clientage. This mixed crowd *Clients' role* numbering in the tens to hundreds received ritual gifts, assuring that the poorest would eat and the richest were remembered, and everyone was invited into the patron's home to greet him. The patron was supposed to exert a moral authority over his clients, helping them to be good citizens. As the Roman poet Horace (65–8 B.C.) wrote, "A wealthy patron governs you as a good mother might do and requires of you more wisdom and virtue than he possesses himself."

In the public world of Mediterranean society, clients provided patrons visible proof of their authority. After the morning greeting, clients accompanied their patron to the center of the city, where the day's business took place. A patrician surrounded by hundreds of clients was a man to be reckoned with. Political life of the Republic was conducted in the Forum, a large gathering area surrounded by temples and other public buildings. The Forum included the Senate chamber, the people's assembly, and a speaker's platform—called the *Rostra*—where politicians addressed the Roman people. Map 4.1 shows the City of Rome with its important public spaces, including the Rostra and the Senate chamber. Clients would cheer their patron, shout down his opponents, and offer their votes to his agenda. An aristocrat who abandoned this public life that gave him stature and dignity was described sadly: "He will have no more entourage, no escort for his sedan chair, no visitors in his antechamber."

The Struggle of the Orders created a republic in which rich and poor both had a voice. In fact, it was a system dominated by wealth and an aristocracy who used its influence in the Senate and the Forum to preserve traditional privileges. However, the wealthy never forgot they needed the support of the Roman clients who gathered at their doors in the morning, shouted their support in the Forum, and manned Rome's armies.

DOMINATING THE ITALIAN PENINSULA

As the Republic gathered strength, territorial wars between Rome and its neighbors broke out almost annually. What led Rome into these repeated struggles? Romans themselves claimed that they responded only to acts of aggression, so their expansion was self-defensive. The reality, however, was more complicated. Rome felt a continual land hunger and was ever eager to acquire land to establish colonies of its plebeians. Roman leaders also had a hunger for glory and plunder that would let them acquire and reward clients—victorious generals were well placed to dominate Rome's political life. Thus, farmers often had to drop their plows, as Cincinnatus did, to fight.

By the beginning of the fourth century B.C., Rome was increasingly involved in wars in the Italian peninsula. From an early period, Romans were united by fellow Latin tribes in religious and military ties; by the early Republic, this alliance was *Italian Wars* known as the Latin League. Under Rome's leadership, the Latin League successfully defended its borders during the fifth and fourth centuries B.C. However, Rome's allies became increasingly resentful of Rome's leadership and revolted in 340 B.C. Two years later, Rome decisively defeated the rebellious allies and dissolved the League. Here, however, Rome showed its genius for administration. Instead of crushing the rebellious

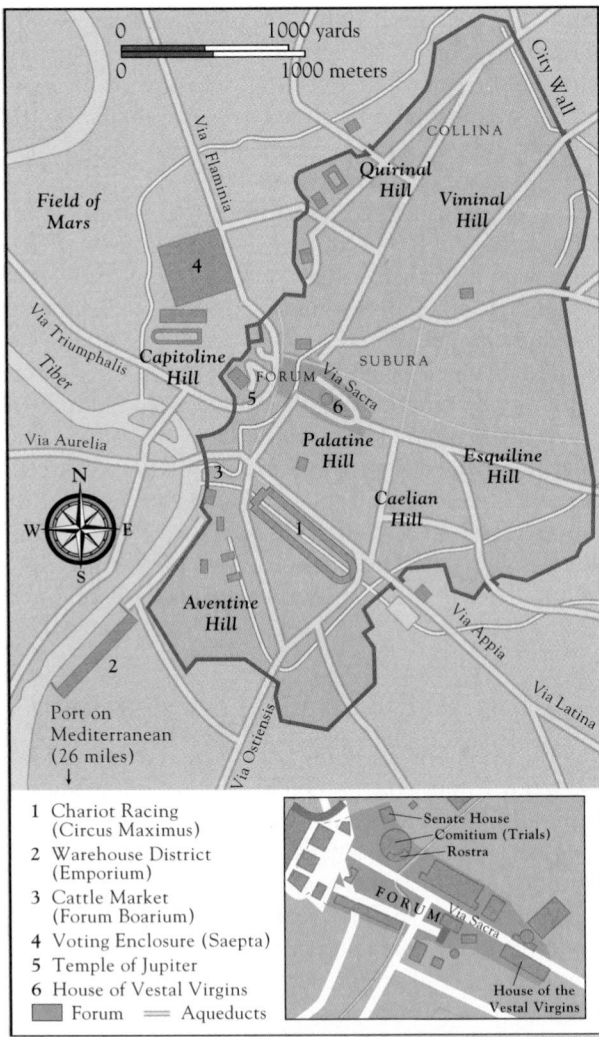

1 Chariot Racing
   (Circus Maximus)
2 Warehouse District
   (Emporium)
3 Cattle Market
   (Forum Boarium)
4 Voting Enclosure (Saepta)
5 Temple of Jupiter
6 House of Vestal Virgins
   ▨ Forum ═ Aqueducts

THINKING ABOUT GEOGRAPHY

MAP 4.1 *Rome During the Republic*

This map shows the city of Rome during the late Republic. ▨ **Which** elements in the Forum and in the center of the city show how political life and religious institutions dominated the life in Rome? ▨ **Notice** the *Subura*, the most famous slum district dominated by lower-class apartment buildings. **Consider** the political implications of its location so near the Forum and the Palantine Hill, where the wealthiest Romans lived.

states, Rome extended varying degrees of citizenship to the Latins. Some received the rights of full Roman citizenship, while others became partial citizens who could earn full citizenship by moving to Rome. This benign policy allowed Rome with its allies to confront and conquer other peoples of the peninsula.

As Map 4.2 shows, Rome acquired territories to the south and north. This was not a time of endless victories, however. In 390 B.C., the Gauls of northern Italy (a Celtic tribe) sacked much of the city before being bribed to leave with a large tribute payment, but it would be another 800 years before a foreign army once more set foot in the city. However, their invasion had weakened the Etruscan cities of the north, so by 295 B.C., Roman armies controlled the north of the peninsula. By the middle of the third century B.C., Rome dominated most of the Italian peninsula.

The Romans' successful expansion in part stemmed from their renowned courage and tenacity in battle. Most of their success, however, came from their generosity in victory. Although Map 4.2 looks as if Rome had "united" Italy, in fact, the peninsula remained a patchwork of diverse states allied to Rome by separate treaties. These treaties were varied, but all were generous to conquered peoples. Romans allowed all the tribes to retain full autonomy in their own territories and to elect their own officials, keep their own laws, and collect their own taxes. These peoples were required to supply troops for Rome's armies and to avoid pursuing independent foreign policy. Many of the conquered peoples did have to give up some territory for Rome to use as colonies to feed their land hunger, but the colonies served to help Rome watch over and control its ever-widening borders of influence. As a result of Rome's leadership, the conquered territories at times enjoyed more peace and freedom than they ever had. Rome's sensible policy toward the territories bought the loyalty of many states and created a relatively cohesive unit that would fuel further imperial expansion.

Foreign policy

Family Life and City Life

The great Roman orator Cicero (106–43 B.C.) wrote that the Romans were like other peoples except in their religious fervor: "In reverence for the gods, we are far superior." Perhaps more than other ancient civilizations, the Romans saw the world as infused with spirits; in their view, almost every space was governed by some divinity. Rome itself was guarded by three deities that protected the state—Jupiter, Juno, and Minerva—but there were gods for even smaller spaces. There were goddesses for the countryside, for the hills, and for the valleys. There were three gods to guard entrances—one for the door, another for the hinges, and a third for the lintel, the door's upper supporting beam. The remaining spaces within the home were equally inhabited by spirits that demanded worship and sacrifice.

A PIOUS, PRACTICAL PEOPLE

Formal worship of the many gods and goddesses took place at the temples, where priests presided over sacrifices and divination officials looked for favorable omens in the entrails of sacrificial animals. The Vestal Virgins, six priestesses who presided over the temple of Vesta, goddess of the hearth, kept the sacred fire of the state hearth burning. (See the major Temple of Jupiter and the House of the Vestal Virgins in Map 4.1.)

According to the Roman people, their success hinged on proper worship, which meant offering sacrifices. Sacrifices could be as small as a drop of wine or a honeycake, or as large as an ox, but the Romans believed their destiny was deeply tied to their proper observation of religious rituals. When Rome was sacked by the Gauls in 390 B.C., Livy reported that one Roman general supposedly said, "All things went well when we obeyed the Gods, but badly when we disobeyed them."

In addition to piety, Romans valued moral seriousness. These hardworking men and women prized duty

THINKING ABOUT GEOGRAPHY

MAP 4.2 *Italy, 265 B.C.*

This map shows the peoples of the Italian Peninsula conquered by the Romans, the dates of the conquests, and the nearby Carthaginian territories. ◼ **Notice** the location of the Tiber River. **Consider** how its location would yield advantages for Rome's developing trade. ◼ **Notice** how much territory was controlled by Rome, and how much was controlled by Carthage. **Consider** how Rome's expansion in the western Mediterranean would be impeded by Carthage's possessions. ◼ **Locate** Messana (where Rome and Carthage would first clash). **Consider** how its location might be strategically important.

to family, clients, patrons, and the Republic itself. They rejected the individualism of the Greeks and would have found the idea of Achilles sulking in his tent while his compatriots died incomprehensible. These serious men and women, who stressed collective responsibility and obedience both to secular and religious authority, would one day rule the entire Mediterranean world.

LOYALTY TO THE FAMILY

Roman religion, duty, and loyalty began in the family. A father, in theory, had complete authority over everyone in his household, including his wife, children, slaves, and even ex-slaves. The father served as guardian of the family's well-being and shared with his wife the responsibility for venerating the household gods. In addition to recognizing all the spirits who guarded the home, families worshipped their ancestors, whom they considered the original source of their prosperity. The best families displayed busts of their important ancestors in niches in the home. Figure 4.4 shows a Roman man holding the busts of his forefathers revealing the piety and ancestor worship so vital to Romans at that time.

Marriages in early Rome were arranged, to make politically advantageous alliances between families and ensure the continuation of the family through children. A woman could be given in

Marriage patterns

marriage in two ways. Her family of origin might transfer her to her husband's control, in which case she became part of his family and participated in the worship of his ancestors. Or she might remain under her father's "hand," never becoming a full part of her husband's family. In this case, the woman's family of origin kept more political and financial control of her resources. Figure 4.5 shows a modest, serious Roman couple with their child. They do not touch, and they stand together looking into the distance. This gravestone contrasts strikingly with the affectionate Etruscan couple shown in Figure 4.2 and suggests that Romans considered marriage a serious duty.

Despite the authority of husbands, women still played an important role in the family. They instilled the values of Rome in their children and raised them to be responsible and obedient citizens. Historical evidence such as letters indicate that mothers exerted as much stern authority as fathers and therefore wielded

FIGURE 4.4
Patrician with the busts of his ancestors, first century A.D.

some political power through their sons. Livy recounted the popularly told story of one such influential mother—Veturia, who in the fifth century B.C. saved the city from her son Coriolanus, an exiled patrician, who was leading an army of Latins against Rome. She traveled to his camp and reprimanded him for being an enemy of the Republic. Chastened, he suspended the invasion. In another case, when the

FIGURE 4.8
Roman warship

conquer the dispu
gan the first of t
Rome and Cartha
meant "Phoenicia
the origins of the (

But to broaden
the Romans neede
some money and b
ing admirals who
The Romans neve
tenacity and desi

New Roman navy   cl
                    Be
at sea was rammir
ing the second. S
opposing ship to
ten. The Roman
new vessel that f
lowed many infar
proached an opp
then board the er
a style that was
Carthaginian na
brought them s
ships. Before the
however, a platf
swept across, taki
ship. The Roma
own destroyed sl
Figure 4.8 show
with infantryme
tiveness of the i

FIGURE 4.5
Gravestone of Lucius Vibius and his wife and child. First century B.C.

Gauls attacked Rome in 390 B.C., citizens had to raise tribute to persuade the invaders to leave. The senators failed to collect enough, so the women of Rome came forward and contributed their own wealth and jewels.

THE CHALLENGES OF CHILDHOOD

Birth in a Roman home always involved great risk to the newborn. When a child was born, the midwife inspected it, even before the umbilical cord was cut, to judge whether it was physically perfect. If it was not, she would likely cut the cord too closely, thus killing the child. A healthy newborn was placed at the father's feet. If he accepted the infant, picking up a boy or acknowledging a girl, then the child was raised. If he did not, the baby would be "exposed"— placed outside to die or to be taken in and raised as a slave. Roman law required the father to raise one daughter, but he could choose to raise all his daughters, as many families did. However, it is impossible to know how many children were exposed and how many died as a result. In one chilling letter, a soldier matter-of-factly instructs his pregnant wife to keep the child if it is a boy and to expose it if it is a girl.

We can only conclude that the practice of exposure was not considered extraordinary.

When the child was accepted, however, he or she received endless attention. Influential physicians like Soranus and Galen (second century A.D.) detailed explicit instructions on how to raise an infant, and all the child-rearing ad- *Child-rearing practices*
vice focused on
molding the baby to be shapely, disciplined, and obedient. Newborns were tightly bound in strips of cloth for two months to ensure that their limbs would grow straight. Once a day they were unwrapped to be bathed in a tepid bath. Parents would then stretch, massage, and shape the screaming babies before tightly wrapping them again. Noble children were usually breast-fed by a wet nurse (a slave woman who had recently had a child), and many physicians recommended that children begin to drink sweet wine at six months. Infant mortality was high despite the recommendations of physicians and the attentions of loving parents— fewer than half of the newborns raised reached puberty. As we will see in Chapter 5, Rome would have trouble maintaining its population throughout its history, and some historians have suggested that childcare practices may have contributed to the problem.

At the age of six or seven, children were put in the care of tutors, and their formal education began. Patrician children of both genders were expected to receive an education so as to transmit Roman culture to the next generations. Girls also learned to spin and weave wool, activities that consumed much of their time in their adult years.

By age twelve, boys graduated to higher schooling, learning literature, arithmetic, geometry, music, astronomy, and logic. This general education prepared boys for public life—the honorable and expected course for a wealthy boy. If a boy was talented, at age sixteen he began an advanced study of rhetoric. This skill would help him later to speak persuasively to the crowds that had so much influence on the political life of the Republic.

As we saw in the exampl
of the Republic was mad
set aside their work to
Rome's leaders believed t
eign invaders, the cons
Forum. Then free houseb
tory—that is, tax-payin;
seventeen and forty-six–
within thirty days. From
and military tribunes ch

THE ROMANS' VI

By the early Republic, t
gions of about 4,000 m
100 men each, althoug
constituted a legion or
These were mostly foot
Weapons and discipline in t
an c
army until death or the
able strength of this citi
discipline. For example,
mation" in which one sc
disobeyed an order or fa
fare in the Mediterrane
rules that allowed surr
fered extensive losses.
hated to return home
would prevent him fror
where everyone met fa

The Roman army
fighting machine under
ers. Roman soldiers ate
only water while at wa
some vinegar. Sometim
the wheat ran out, the
they feared the meat w
their invincibility. Th
who slept heavily on w
probably gave them co

The victorious repu
season of fighting wit
hand and the pride of
relentless series of suc
had unified virtually tl
Map 4.2). However,
and power clashed wi
sula. These contests
the Republic itself.

Hannibal expected Rome's subject peoples to rise up in his support, and while some did, the inner core of central Italy stayed loyal. The strong alliance system that Rome had built gave it a huge advantage. Nevertheless, the astonishing general handed Rome its worst defeat ever at the Battle of Cannae in 216 B.C., in which some 30,000 Romans died (see Map 4.3). Document 4.1 on page D4.1 describes this significant battle. Romans were shocked and frightened—for years Roman mothers would scare naughty children with the threat "Hannibal will get you"—and yet the Romans would not surrender. They adopted a defensive attitude of delay and refusal to fight while the Carthaginian forces marched up and down Italy for almost 17 years—wreaking havoc along the way.

FIGURE 4.9
War elephant plate.

Finally, Rome produced a general who could match Hannibal's skill. Publius Cornelius Scipio (236–183 B.C.) had studied Carthaginian battlefield tactics and had the skill to improve on them. Scipio took Carthage's Spanish lands, and then sailed to North Africa, bringing the war to Carthage. Hannibal had to leave Italy to defend his homeland, and he had to face the Romans virtually unaided. The Roman control of the sea prevented the Carthaginian ally, Philip V of Macedonia (of the Hellenistic Macedonian kingdom discussed in Chapter 3), from helping, and Carthaginian support in North Africa was weak. Scipio decisively defeated Hannibal at the Battle of Zama in 202 B.C. (see Map 4.3) and won the surname "Africanus" to commemorate his great victory that saved Rome. Carthage again sued for peace—giving up Spain and promising not to wage war without Rome's permission. But peace would prove temporary.

Carthage was placed in a difficult position, for Numidia, one of Rome's allies in North Africa, was encroaching on its territory. Yet Carthage could not wage war against Numidia without *Third Punic War* Rome's permission, and Rome withheld it. The Senate was led by Cato the Elder (234–149 B.C.), who was virulently anti-Carthaginian. Plutarch recorded his famous rousing speech in 150 B.C. as he tried to spur his countrymen to resume the fighting against Carthage. He reminded the Senate that Carthage was "only three days' sail from Rome," and he ended all his speeches with the phrase "Carthage must be destroyed." Cato spoke for many Romans who wanted to take on their old enemy again. The inflammatory language worked, and the Third Punic War began. After a long siege of the citadel at the top of the hill overlooking the town, Rome crushed the city of Carthage in 146 B.C. The Carthaginian general surrendered, and his wife, accusing him of cowardice, committed suicide by leaping with her two children into the flames of the burning city. The Roman general—another Scipio called Aemilianus—reputedly shed tears at the sight of the ruin of the great city. The once-shining city of Carthage would lie in ruins for a century until Rome itself recolonized it.

Map 4.3 shows the lands in North Africa and Spain that Rome acquired as a result of the defeat of Carthage. Although the government *Eastern conquests* of Rome remained a republic, it now controlled an empire. As you can see from the map, Rome's expansion continued after the Punic

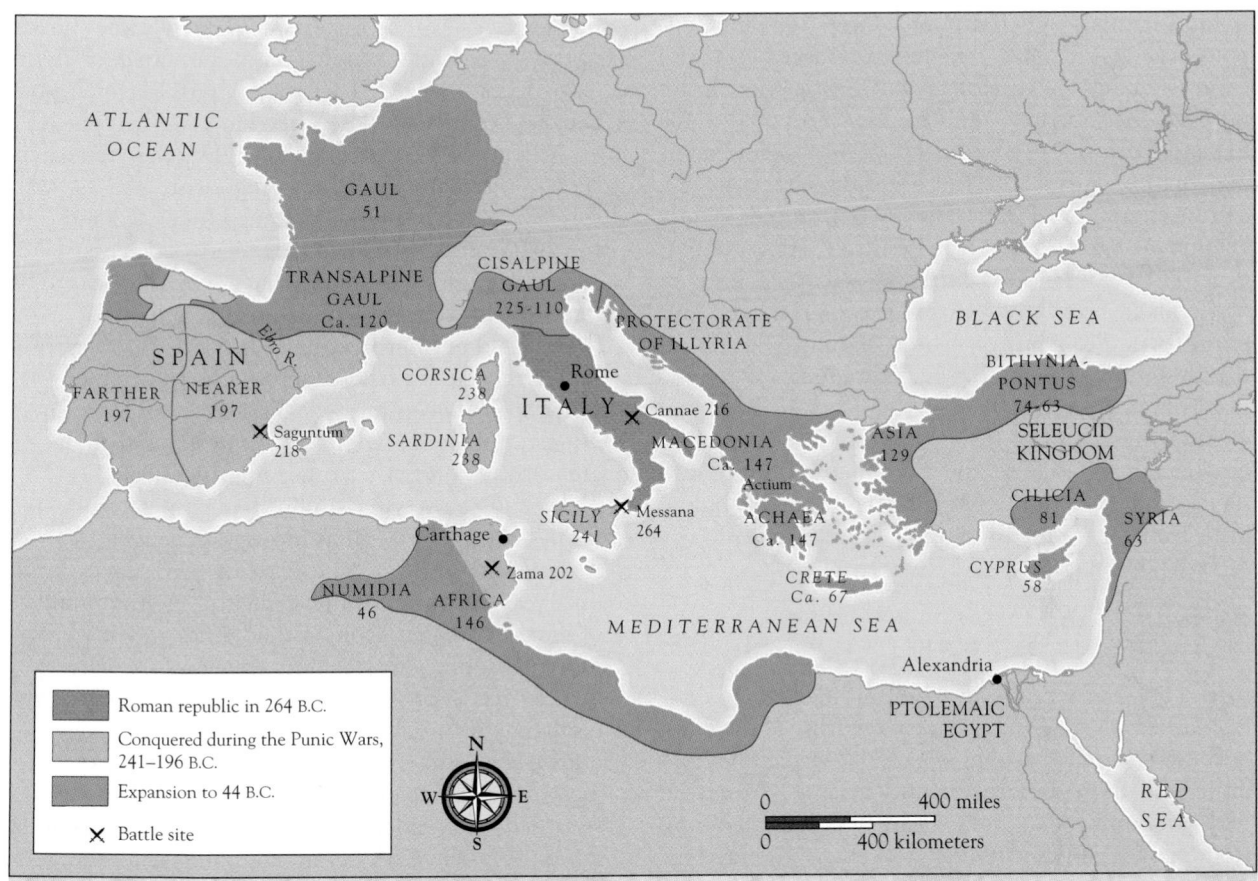

Map legend:
- Roman republic in 264 B.C.
- Conquered during the Punic Wars, 241–196 B.C.
- Expansion to 44 B.C.
- ✗ Battle site

THINKING ABOUT GEOGRAPHY

MAP 4.3 *Expansion of the Roman Empire, 264–44 B.C.*

This map shows the expansion of the Roman Empire as it fought victorious wars against Carthage and the Macedonian and Seleucid kingdoms in the East. **Notice** how far away Spain is from Italy, using the scale to estimate the distances. **Consider** the difficulties Hannibal had transporting his army and his elephants. **Locate** the Hellenistic kingdoms of the Seleucids and the Ptolemies. **Consider** how likely they were to come into conflict with an expanding Rome. **Consider** how Rome became influenced by the Hellenistic world as it expanded east.

Wars. Historians still disagree about Rome's motives for continuing the warfare. Rome often marched to protect its allies—waging what they called "just wars." At the same time, some Romans were becoming rich in these enterprises, and Roman generals saw war as the road to upward mobility. Now the path to success for an ambitious Roman lay not in impressing his fellow citizens in the Forum, but in leading victorious armies.

Rome did not always annex territories outright. Sometimes it operated through client states, leaving local rulers in place. Sometimes victorious Romans established the conquered territories as provinces— one in Africa, one in Asia, and later across the Alps in Gaul (southern France) in an area that is still called "Provence." Within the provinces, people lived as they had in the past, but Rome's leaders expected these states to conform to their wishes (which at times caused friction). Governors were appointed by the Roman Senate to preserve peace and administer justice to Roman citizens. Other duties were given to private individuals, who could make fortunes performing administrative duties. For example, tax collectors received a contract to collect a certain amount of taxes, and they could legally keep some profits they squeezed from local populations. The governors were supposed to make sure tax collectors did not abuse their privilege, but, not surprisingly, many of them took full advantage of this system and extracted huge amounts of money from helpless residents. The conquests in Italy had yielded most profits from land. In the provinces, on the other hand, people made money from land, slaves, and graft. In the process, the Roman Republic itself was transformed in various ways by its military success abroad.

An Influx of Slaves

In the ancient world, successful military campaigning earned a victor not just new territory and riches, but also slaves. As Rome expanded, it accumulated more and more bondsmen and women. After the Second Punic War, more than 200,000 men and women were captured as prisoners of war and brought to Italy as slaves. Numbers like these changed the nature of Roman society. Now, instead of each small householder having one to three slaves (as we saw was the pattern in ancient Greece), rich households might have hundreds of domestic slaves. By the end of the Republic, there were between two and three million slaves in Italy, an astounding 35 to 40 percent of the population.

Thousands of slaves labored in agriculture or mining, working in large anonymous gangs. However, in the cities, slaves and citizens often worked in the same occupations, and all could earn money through their labor. The most undesirable jobs—

Slave occupations

garbage collection, mining, acting, or prostitution—were generally reserved for slaves, although freed men and women, while technically citizens, were willing to do the most lucrative of these jobs. Often slaves dominated some of the higher-status jobs. After Rome's conquest of Greece (ca. 148 B.C.), most of the tutors and teachers to Roman children were Greek slaves. The biography on page 135 describes the successful career of a playwright who

had been a slave. Most physicians were either Greek or trained in Greece, and it was not unusual for physicians to be succeeded by their Greek slaves, whom they had trained and then freed to take their place.

All but the poorest Roman infants were nursed by slaves, and many free children grew up playing with the household's slave children. Under Roman law, the head of a household was to consider his slaves part of his family, and many slaves could expect to be freed in the course of their lifetimes. In these cases they would ordinarily remain attached to the household as clients instead of slaves. Such intimate relationships between masters and slaves could not help but be ambiguous at times—sometimes stimulating great loyalty and other times intense anger.

Perhaps not surprisingly, Romans often feared their slaves. The Stoic philosopher Seneca (4 B.C.–A.D. 65) wrote that "the least of your slaves holds over you the power of life or death." As the numbers of slaves increased, Romans had more and more reason to worry, and they passed laws to try to protect themselves. For example, the punishment for murdering one's master was severe—all the slaves in the household were to be executed. The Roman historian Tacitus (A.D. 56?–120?) recorded an incident when an ex-consul was murdered by a slave. A senator arguing that the state should enforce the harsh law and kill the whole household said: "Whom will a large number of slaves keep safe, when four hundred could not protect Pedanius Secundus? . . . In every wholesale punishment there is some injustice to individuals, which is compensated by the advantage to the state." Not only did individual instances of slave treachery crop up, but large-scale slave rebellions broke out as well.

Slave revolts

Three great slave uprisings disrupted Italy and Sicily between 135 and 71 B.C. The most famous was led by the gladiator Spartacus between 73 and 71 B.C. Spartacus escaped his master with 70 of his fellow gladiators. Many others joined them as his army of almost 70,000 slaves ravaged portions of Italy. They succeeded in defeating many of the soldiers sent after them. Some sources suggest that Spartacus even tried to take his army to Sicily to rally the slaves there, but could not gather enough ships to cross the sea. Spartacus was finally killed and the rebellion crushed. Six thousand of Spartacus' followers were crucified—the brutal form of execution reserved for slaves. This revolt was suppressed, but Rome did not forget the

OLC

Biography

PUBLIUS TERENTIUS AFER (190?–159 B.C.) — TERENCE

Consider how Rome's control of North Africa led to an increasingly diverse, cosmopolitan life in Rome and how it led to the Hellenization of the empire.

During the peaceful interlude between the First and Second Punic Wars, a slave trader in Carthage purchased a young man named Terence. We have no idea how Terence came into the hands of a slave dealer; we do know he was not a prisoner of war. However, many North Africans were enslaved by the Carthaginians; Terence may have come from one such slave family. His surname, "Afer," meaning "the African," suggests that he was not originally from Carthage. He was described as being "of medium stature, graceful in person, and of dark complexion," and some scholars have suggested that he was from a black sub-Saharan family. The ambiguity of Terence's background points to the cosmopolitan, highly diverse nature of the city of Carthage. It was one of the jewels of the Mediterranean—a bustling city where people mingled from all over and shared in a dynamic cultural life. Terence's early experience in the cosmopolitan city no doubt prepared him to contribute to Rome's growing interest in Hellenistic literature.

The young slave was brought to Rome and sold to a senator, M. Terentius Lucanus, who must have recognized the youth's promise. The senator had him educated as a freeman and then granted him his freedom. This is but one example of many talented slaves who were freed by their owners during the optimistic years of the Republic. Terence then pursued a literary career.

The intellectual gifts that had won Terence his freedom earned him the acceptance of an aristocratic circle of young men who were interested in literature. These educated youths were actively involved in fostering Greek literature, and such literary circles had much influence in Hellenizing Roman society.

At first, Terence was outside the guild of poets and the working playwrights. He made his artistic breakthrough when he got a chance to submit one of his plays for production to the aging but well-established poet Caecilius. Terence found out where the poet was dining and approached him as he reclined on his couch eating with friends. Because Terence was a stranger and plainly dressed, Caecilius invited him only to sit on a stool and recite from his work. After a few verses, however, the old poet was so impressed with Terence's talent that he invited him to join him on the couch and share the festive dinner. The budding playwright's career was launched.

Terence wrote six plays based on traditional Greek models, even specifying that they be performed in Greek dress. These plays show Terence's talent and understanding of both human nature and the social realities in Rome. Yet he received mixed reactions from the Romans. During his short lifetime, Terence was much criticized by other playwrights, and like so much else in Rome, these critiques were conducted publicly. Terence addressed his critics (and attacked other playwrights) in the prologues to the plays. These public debates tell us much about the openly competitive nature of the artistic world during the Republic.

Terence was accused first of plagiarism, meaning that someone else claimed to have been the first to translate Greek plays into Latin. In a prologue, Terence flatly denies "any knowledge of the play's previous Latinization." Terence was also charged with being "untraditional"—a serious insult to Romans. According to his accusers, he did not remain true to the Greek originals. Terence admitted that he combined plots ### A Talented Slave and created interesting works of art rather than translations. As he put it, precise translations often turned "the best Greek plays . . . into Latin flops." These criticisms reveal a people struggling to discover a new art form and to determine the rules with which to judge it.

Terence challenged his audiences to judge his works on their own merits. Not surprisingly, many of his contemporaries appreciated his talent, for he did more than reproduce classic plays—he gave them his own stamp. For example, instead of simply relying on slapstick humor (like Plautus did), Terence developed a clever use of language to provide humor. He also used suspense as a dynamic device that would have a long history in the theater. His fame long outlasted him. Long after Terence's death, Cicero and Caesar, both known for their eloquence, praised his work as a model of elegant language. Audiences ever since have found his plays brilliant.

Unfortunately, Terence died while still in his prime. In 159 B.C., the 31-year-old undertook a journey to Greece, possibly to study theater or to escape the jealous rumors of his rivals. He died on the way, either from illness or shipwreck. He left a revered body of work that people still enjoy and appreciate today. Perhaps equally important, Terence exemplified the kind of upward mobility available to educated slaves during an age when Rome fell in love with Greek intellectual life.

potential for violence that simmered within the many men and women they had enslaved in their imperial expansion.

ECONOMIC DISPARITY AND SOCIAL UNREST

Just as the expansion of Rome altered the nature of slavery, it transformed many other aspects of life in the Republic. These changes were noted sadly by many conservative Romans who watched their traditional way of life fade. One Roman (Silius Italicus) lamented the aftermath of Rome's victory in the Punic Wars: "[I]f it was fated that the Roman character should change when Carthage fell, would that Carthage was still standing." But, such qualms were too late; the Republic was transmuting into something else entirely, even as some Romans mourned it.

One of the most noticeable changes came in the form of increasing disparity between rich and poor. Many of the upper classes had grown very rich indeed. Governors of provinces had the opportunity to make fortunes undreamed of in the Republic's earlier years. Other enterprising Romans made fortunes in shipbuilding contracts, banking, slave trading, and many other high-profit occupations. Rome had become a Hellenistic state like the successor states of Alexander the Great (see Chapter 3), with a growing distance between the rich and the poor.

While some Romans amassed great fortunes, others suffered a worsening of their economic situations. The example of Cincinnatus, who fought for only one season and then returned to his plow, was impossible to repeat when foes were far away and wars long. During the Punic Wars, military time was extended. As a result, more than 50 percent of adult males spent over 7 years in the army, and some spent as long as 20 years. Throughout most of the Republic, the army was not formally paid, and this caused both some hardship and a particularly strong relationship between soldiers and their generals. By right, generals controlled all booty taken in war, and they distributed some of it to their troops. Thus generals acted as patrons to their client soldiers, who increasingly owed loyalty to their general rather than to Rome itself. Meanwhile, as soldiers stayed longer in the army, their family fields remained unplowed. Numerous farmers went bankrupt, and soldiers returned to their homes to find them sold and their wives and children turned out of the family farm.

Newly rich men and women eagerly purchased these neglected lands, and small landholders were replaced by large plantations worked by gangs of new slaves. Fields that had cultivated wheat were slowly transformed to produce olives and wine grapes, much more lucrative crops. Other great landowners in Italy grew rich on ranches that raised animals for meat, milk, or wool. Now Romans had to import their wheat from abroad, particularly North Africa.

Spurred by economic hardship, the displaced citizens flocked to the city. The population swelled with a new class of people—propertyless day laborers who were unconnected to the *New poverty* structures of patronage and land that had defined the early Republic. These mobs created more and more problems for the nobility because they always represented a potentially revolutionary force in the Forum. Aristocrats tried to keep them happy and harmless by subsidizing food. But this short-term solution could not solve the deeper problem of lost jobs taken by newly captured slaves and land seized by the newly rich. The situation had become volatile indeed.

The Hellenizing of the Republic

As if these social tensions were not disruptive enough, new intellectual influences further modified Rome's traditional value system. As the Republican armies conquered some of the great centers of Hellenistic culture from Greece to North Africa, Romans became deeply attracted to many of the Hellenistic ways. As the Roman poet Horace (65–8 B.C.) observed: "Captive Greece took her Captor Captive." With the capture of slaves from Greece, Greek art, literature, and learning came to Rome, and many in the Roman aristocracy became bilingual, adding Greek to their native Latin. Rome became a Hellenized city, with extremes of wealth and poverty and a growing emphasis on individualism over obedience to the family.

Cato the Elder (234–149 B.C.)—the antiCarthaginian orator—was one Roman who feared the changes that came with the increasing wealth and love of things Greek, and when he held the office of censor (see Figure 4.3), he tried to stem the tide of Hellenization. The office of censor had come to be an influential one. During the early Republic, censors had made lists of citizens and their property qualifications, but in time the censors became so powerful that they revised the lists of senators, deleting those whose behavior they deemed objectionable. To preserve the old values, Cato tried taxing luxury goods and charging fines to those who neglected their farms, but his efforts were in vain. Romans had added an appreciation of Greek beauty to their own practical skills, and they adopted a new love of luxury and power that seemed to erode the moral strength of old Rome. To men like Cato, the Republic was becoming unrecognizable.

Resising change

ROMAN ENGINEERING: FUSING UTILITY AND BEAUTY

Most of the great building projects that so characterize Rome arose in the building boom during the early years of the empire, as we will see in the next chapter. However, the techniques that led to those projects were developed during the Republic and were refined by the influx of Greek ideas and artists during the wars of expansion in the third and second centuries B.C. During these years Rome developed a new aesthetic sense that combined its traditional love of utility with the Hellenistic ideals of beauty.

As we have seen, the Romans had learned much about engineering from the Etruscans, especially techniques for draining swamps and building conduits to move water. The early Romans had a strong practical side themselves and greatly admired feats of science and engineering. The Roman orator Cicero revealed this admiration when he traveled to Syracuse in 75 B.C. to visit the grave of Archimedes, the esteemed engineer we met in Chapter 3. When Cicero discovered that Archimedes' countrymen had forgotten him, he found the old engineer's grave and restored it.

Engineering

Rome's military success stemmed in part from the engineering achievements that supported the legions. For example, armies had to forge many rivers, and the Roman engineers invented ingenious devices to help them. General Julius Caesar (100–44 B.C.), in his account of one military campaign, described how he had to sink heavy timbers into the fast-moving Rhine River to build a bridge. The task was completed in 10 days, and the army crossed. Engineers could build pontoon bridges even faster by floating flat-bottomed boats down the river and anchoring them at the intended crossing.

Perhaps Rome's greatest military engineering lay in the area of siege engines. Caesar described how the Romans patiently built a tall, fortified mound and tower next to a city they were besieging. As some soldiers fought from the top of the tower, they protected others who were beneath sturdy beams below. These hidden soldiers were then able to dismantle the bottom of the wall, causing it to collapse so the army could enter and take the city. Some Roman siege engines were so impressive that even Chinese sources documented them.

Engineering skills also brought many benefits to civilian life. The arch is a key example. The Greeks used post and lintel construction, which limited the variety of structures they could build. By using arches, Romans enhanced the size, range, and flexibility of their constructions. The use of the arch can most readily be seen in the aqueducts—perhaps the greatest examples of Roman civil engineering. Aqueducts brought water from rivers or springs into cities. Figure 4.10 shows the aqueduct of Segovia, Spain, built in about A.D. 10. This aqueduct is constructed of a double row of arches, which strengthen the structure without adding much mass. Furthermore, the arches allowed the engineers to adjust the height of the aqueduct to regulate the rate of the water flowing through the channel at the top. The water finally entered the city at a height of about 92 feet, which created sufficient pressure to regulate water flow within the city. Rome itself had a huge appetite for water and by the end of the first century A.D., nine aqueducts each directed an astonishing 22,237,000 gallons of water into the city each day. (Map 4.1 shows the locations of Rome's aqueducts.) These structures were marvels of engineering and represented the best of Roman engineering—solid design, practical application, and visual appeal.

Aqueducts

CONCRETE: A NEW BUILDING MATERIAL

In the late third century B.C., Roman architects discovered a new building material that opened even more architectural possibilities than the perfection of the arch. Masons found that mixing volcanic

FIGURE 4.10
Aqueduct in Segovia, Spain, ca. A.D. 10.

theon, a temple dedicated to all the gods, shown in Figure 4.11. It was built in A.D. 125 on the site of a previous temple that had been constructed during the late Republic. The structure is a perfect *Pantheon* combination of Roman and Hellenistic styles, and thus embodies the transformation of republican Rome imposed by Hellenistic influences. The front of the temple has a classical rectangular porch with columns and a pediment, the triangular structure on top of the columns. From the front, the Pantheon resembles the Greek temples we saw in Chapter 2. Inside the temple, however, any resemblance to Hellenistic architecture disappears.

The interior of the Pantheon consists of a massive round space (visible in Figure 4.11) covered by a high dome, revealing the Romans' engineering skills. A heavy concrete base supports the weight of the whole, while the upper walls are constructed of a lighter mix of concrete. The center of the dome has an opening that lets in natural light—and rain, though drainpipes beneath the ground (which still function today) took care of flooding problems.

brick-earth with lime and water resulted in a strong, waterproof building material—concrete. With this new substance, architects could design large, heavy buildings in a variety of shapes.

Combining concrete construction with the knowledge of the arch allowed for even more flexibility than before. After they had mastered the arch, Romans built with barrel vaults, a row of arches spanning a large space. As early as 193 B.C., builders constructed a gigantic warehouse in Rome using this technique. Concrete and barrel vaults also made possible the design of large bathhouses, for the concrete was strong enough to withstand the heat of steam rooms. Finally, the new technology permitted the design of the oval amphitheaters that so characterized Rome.

Of course, people as religious as the Romans applied their architectural skills to their temples as well. Although most structures in Rome were made of brick or concrete covered with stucco, the growing Hellenization began to influence architectural tastes. Marble columns would soon grace the traditional buildings. In this new architecture, we can see the degree of the Greek slaves' influence on the Romans and Rome's own growing appreciation of Hellenistic art.

The fullest development of this temple construction took place early in the empire. The outstanding example of Roman religious architecture is the Pan-

FIGURE 4.11
The Pantheon, A.D. 125.

LATIN COMEDY AND THE GREAT PROSE WRITERS, 240–44 B.C.

In the third century B.C., Roman literature emerged. Written in Latin, it reflected the elements we have discussed throughout this chapter: Roman values, society, and influence of Hellenistic culture. The earliest surviving examples of Roman literature are comic plays. Latin comedy flowered with the works of Plautus (205–185 B.C.) and Terence (190–159 B.C.), who wrote plays based on Hellenistic models but modified them for their Italian audience. Plautus and Terence wrote in verse, but unlike their Greek predecessors, they added a good deal of music. The masked street musicians portrayed in Figure 4.8, playing the flutes and cymbals that traditionally accompanied such productions, may be performing a scene from one of these comic plays.

Like the Hellenistic plays, most comedies involved the triumph of love over obstacles. In Plautus' works particularly, the humor centered on jokes and elaborate puns within the stories and were marked by slapstick, bawdy humor. For example, in one play Plautus described a confrontation in which a man threatened to beat a slave. The man said: "Whoever comes here eats my fists." The slave responded: "I do not eat at night, and I have dined; Pray give your supper to those who starve." The audience would have laughed at the play on words associating a punch with food, as well as the suggestion that the nobles were not really charitable to the starving. The plays included all types of Romans, from smart, scheming slaves to boastful soldiers and clever prostitutes, to many clients and patrons. Thus, Romans who watched these plays recognized and laughed at all the types of people that populated their world.

The Latin prose literature of the Republic emphasized the serious side of Roman character. The best of the prose writers were men who combined literary talent with public service—for example, Cicero and Julius Caesar.

Cicero Latin literature was shaped—indeed defined—by the writings of Cicero, whose career coincided with the decline of the Republic. His skillful oratory and strong opinions about Roman values placed him in the center of public life, but his long-standing influence derived from his prose, not his political involvement. His writings cover an extraordinary range of topics, from poetry to formal orations to deeply personal letters. From his more than 900 letters, we get a revealing picture of the personality of this influential man. He was deeply concerned about public affairs and political morality, writing "our leaders ought to protect civil peace with honor and defend it even at the risk of life itself." At the same time, his letters reveal him to be vindictive, mercurial of mood, and utterly self-centered. Although scholars are ambivalent about the character of this complex man, there is no doubt about his influence. Cicero's writings defined the best use of Latin language, and his works were used as textbooks of how to construct elegant prose.

Caesar's writings Julius Caesar's literary legacy also grew out of his active political life. As Caesar rose to power, he used literature to enhance his reputation in Rome. His accounts of his dazzling military campaigns in Gaul (across the Alps in modern France), vividly told in his *Commentaries*, intensified his popularity and have fascinated generations ever since. His Latin is clear and accessible, and his narrative vivid and exciting.

By the middle of the second century B.C., the Roman Republic had reached a crucial threshold. Vibrant, wealthy, and victorious in war, the Republic had established political and social structures that steadily fueled its success. But in crafting their society, the Romans had unwittingly planted the seeds of their own undoing. Their much-loved precepts, established in a simpler age, would prove unsustainable in a future where Rome boldly sought to extend its reach farther than ever before.

The Twilight of the Republic, 133–44 B.C.

In the mid-second century B.C., Rome suffered a sudden economic downturn. The wars of expansion had brought vast riches into Rome, and this wealth drove prices up. When the wars ended, the influx of slaves and wealth subsided. Furthermore, an unfortunate grain shortage made grain prices skyrocket. This shortage worsened in 135 B.C. with the revolt of the slaves in Sicily. Half of Rome's grain supply came from Sicily, so the interruption of grain flow threatened to starve the masses of people who had fled to Rome when their own small farms had been taken over. To stave off disaster, two tribunes of the plebeians, Tiberius and Gaius Gracchus, proposed reforms. (The brothers were known as the Gracchi, which is the plural form of their name in Latin.)

THE REFORMS OF THE GRACCHI, 133–123 B.C.

The Gracchi brothers came from a noble family, yet they devoted their lives to helping the Roman poor. They credited their mother, Cornelia, with giving them the education and motivation they needed to use their privilege for the good of the Roman people. The Gracchi seemed to many Romans to represent the best of republican men—devoted to a public life. Of course, many modern historians have observed that helping the poor would increase their own clients and prestige. Regardless of the motivations of the brothers, they set themselves apart from many aristocrats who no longer obeyed the rigorous demands of public service, preferring private pleasures instead. There were too few nobles willing to sacrifice their own interests for those of Rome when Tiberius became tribune of the plebeians in 133 B.C.

In Tiberius's view, Rome's problems came from the decline of the small farmer, which in turn prompted migrations into the city and a shift to large-scale and cash-crop agriculture. *Tiberius's reforms* Tiberius compassionately expressed the plight of the displaced soldier-farmers: "They are styled masters of the world, and have not a clod of earth they can call their own." Tiberius recognized an additional problem with the growing landlessness—Rome did not have a pool of soldiers, for men had to meet a property qualification to enter the army. Thus, the newly poor could neither farm nor serve in the army—Rome had moved a long way from the days of the farmer-soldier Cincinnatus.

Tiberius proposed an agrarian law that would redistribute public land to landless Romans. The idea may have made a difference, but it alarmed greedy landlords. The law passed, but the Senate appropriated only a tiny sum to help Tiberius administer the law. Many senators were particularly worried when Tiberius announced he was running for reelection. Although in the distant past, tribunes had run for a second term, that had not been done for a long time, and Tiberius's opponents argued that it was illegal. In the ensuing turmoil, a riot occurred at an assembly meeting, and some senators with their followers beat Tiberius and 300 of his followers to death. With one stroke, a new element emerged in Roman political life: political murder.

Tiberius's land law continued to operate for a time, but not very effectively. In 123 B.C., Tiberius's brother Gaius became tribune in an effort to continue his brother's work, and he wisely appealed *Gaius's reforms* to a broad sector of the Roman people. He built granaries, roads, and bridges to improve the distribution of grain into the city, and these projects created jobs for many Romans. Gaius also tried to fix the price of grain to keep it affordable, and he appealed to the equestrian order by giving them more influence in the wealthy provinces. Gaius opened the new Asian provinces to equestrian tax collectors and placed equestrians in the courts that tried provincial governors accused of abusing their powers. Many senators believed these reforms were politically motivated to destroy the Senate (which had destroyed Tiberius), and it was true that cheap grain might weaken the patron-client relationship that represented the backbone of senatorial power. The Senate moved to undo his reforms as soon as Gaius was out of office, and he and some 250 supporters were murdered in 122 B.C.—their deaths were arranged by one of the consuls supporting the Senate.

Noble Romans may not have liked the reforms of the Gracchi, but they remembered and praised the way Cornelia comported herself after their deaths. After the murders, she continued her life in a noble fashion, praising the accomplishments of her sons and bearing her grief without tears. She was remembered as the embodiment of Roman virtue not only because she had raised her sons for public service, but also because she willingly gave them up to the city they served. Her admirers erected a statue of Cornelia seated graciously—the first public statue of a Roman woman who was not a priestess. Figure 4.12 shows a replica of this statue of Cornelia, which became a model for respected public women who followed her.

Nevertheless, the Gracchi's sacrifices did not solve the Republic's problems. Their careers focused Rome's attention on its worries, but the brothers had also established a new style of republican government. From their time on, a struggle unfolded in Rome between men like the Gracchi who enjoyed popular support (*populares*), and *optimates* who intended to save the Republic by keeping power in the Senate. The old image of a nobility surrounded by and caring for its clients became supplanted by a

FIGURE 4.12
Fourth century statue of a women that replicates the seated statue of Cornelia.

populares. To address the problem of the African wars and the shortage of soldiers noted by Tiberius, Marius initiated a way of enlisting new soldiers that would redefine the Roman military. He created a professional army, eliminating the previous requirement that soldiers own property. In addition, he formally put the soldiers on the payroll, making official the previous informal patron-client relationship between generals and their troops. Marius also promised them land after their term of service. In this way, he cultivated an army with many rootless and desperate men who were loyal only to him. Although Marius could not forsee the results, his policies established a dangerous pattern that continued through the rest of Roman history. With his new army at his back, the victorious general decisively defeated first the Numidians in Africa, and then the Celts to the north. In the process he won great popular power.

Marius

New crises paved the way for the *optimates* to restore their own power under another general, the aristocrat Lucius Cornelius Sulla (138?–78 B.C.). The first threat to Rome's safety came from within Italy itself—the Italian allies who had first been conquered wanted a greater share in the prosperity that Rome's conquests were bringing. The violent fighting that took place between 90 and 88 B.C., finally forced Rome eventually to give full citizenship to the Italian allies. But the violence that devastated much of the countryside further weakened the Republic. As one of the consuls for 88 B.C., Sulla commanded six legions in the final stages of the Italian wars, and his successes earned him a governorship in Asia, where he was given the command to lead the armies against a second threat to Rome—Mithridates (120–63 B.C.), a king in Asia Minor who was threatening Rome's borders. However, fearing Sulla's growing strength, the assembly called Marius out of retirement and tried to give him control of Sulla's army. Perhaps Sulla's most dramatic moment came when he marched his army directly into Rome to confront Marius. The hostilities between the two generals made a permanent mark on the city, changing the peaceful Forum into a war zone. After defeating Mithridates, Sulla returned to Rome in 83 B.C. to take up the cause of the *optimates.*

Sulla

Sulla assumed the long-dormant office of dictator (see Figure 4.3), but violated tradition by making the term unlimited. He also repealed laws that favored equestrians and he killed off his political opponents. He buttressed the power of the Senate by passing

much more confrontational model. The Gracchi were only the first to die in this struggle, and perhaps the greatest legacy of the Gracchi was the subsequent violence that descended upon the political arena. Roman public life would not be the same again.

POPULARES VS. OPTIMATES: THE ERUPTION OF CIVIL WARS, 123–46 B.C.

Even as Rome experienced violence in its political life, life in the provinces, too, seemed threatened. In North Africa, Rome's old ally Numidia caused trouble, and the Gauls threatened Italy from the north. Just as the military emerged as a primary instrument of political power, the generals, especially, had new opportunities to play a role in internal politics. The political struggle between the *populares* and the *optimates* catalyzed by the Gracchi was continued by popular generals.

The first general to come to power based on the support of the army was Gaius Marius (157?–86 B.C.). an equestrian tribune, Marius took up the cause of the laws to guarantee it, instead of allowing the tradition of Senate leadership to suffice. The venerable Roman constitutional system was becoming changed, and power politics began to fill the vacuum.

With the wars of Marius and Sulla, a new question confronted Roman politicians: how to protect the citizens from people seeking power and personal gain. Clearly, the old system of checks and balances no longer worked. The next group of popular leaders bypassed most of the formal structures and made a private alliance to share power. Modern historians have called this agreement the First Triumvirate, or the rule by three men. A contemporary called it a "three-headed monster."

The First Triumvirate (60?–49 B.C.) was made up of three men who appealed to various sectors of Roman society. Pompey, beloved of the *optimates*, was a brilliant general who had won striking battles in the

First Triumvirate

east against Sulla's old enemy, Mithridates, and Mediterranean pirates. Julius Caesar was probably an even more talented general and brilliant orator, who won wars in Gaul and Britain, and had the support of the *populares*. The third man was Crassus, a fabulously rich leader of the business community who had also led armies (including defeating the rebel slave Spartacus). In keeping with tradition in Roman society, the political alliance was sealed by marriage between Pompey and Caesar's daughter, Julia. Instead of bringing peace, however, the triumvirate simply became an arena in which the three powerful figures jockeyed for control.

Events soon came to a head. Crassus perished leading armies to confront a new threat in Rome's eastern frontier. Julia died in childbirth, along with her infant. With her death, little remained to hold Caesar and Pompey together. *Optimates* in the Senate co-opted Pompey in their desire to weaken the popular Caesar, and they declared Pompey sole consul in Rome. The Senate further ordered Caesar to give up command of his armies. Caesar defied the Senate, who had forbidden him to bring his army into Italy, and in 49 B.C. marched across the Rubicon River into Italy. There was no retreating from this defiant act—a new civil war had erupted.

JULIUS CAESAR 100–44 B.C.

Julius Caesar came from one of the oldest noble families of Rome. As with the Gracchi, his family associated itself with the *populares*. In the civil wars to come, Caesar enjoyed a high degree of support from the plebeians, but before he could take power, he needed the backing of an army. This he achieved in his wars of conquest in Gaul. Both his military successes and his captivating literary accounts of them won him broad popularity. According to the ancient writers, this accomplished general was tall with a fair complexion and piercing black eyes. The bust of Caesar shown in Figure 4.13 reveals his memorable strength of character. Clearly a brilliant man in all fields, he enthralls historians today much as he fascinated his contemporaries.

The civil war between Caesar and Pompey that began in 49 B.C. was not limited to Italy; battles broke out throughout the Roman world. Caesar's and Pompey's armies clashed in Greece, North Africa,

FIGURE 4.13
Julius Caesar.

and Spain. After losing a decisive battle in Greece in 48 B.C., Pompey fled to Egypt where he was assassinated. When Caesar followed Pompey to Egypt, he *Civil war* became involved with Queen Cleopatra VII (r. 51–30 B.C.) (also discussed in Chapter 5), who was engaged in a dynastic struggle with her brother. Caesar supported her claims with his army, spent the winter with her, and fathered her child; then he left in the spring to continue the wars that consolidated his victory over Pompey's supporters. In 46 B.C. Caesar returned to Rome.

Cleopatra joined Caesar in Rome as he took up a task harder than winning the civil war: governing the Republic. The new leader faced two major challenges. First, he had to untangle the economic problems that had plagued the Republic since before the Gracchi attempted reform. Second, Rome needed a form of government that would restore stability to the factions that had burdened the city with so much violence.

Caesar applied his genius for organization to these practical tasks. He reformed the grain dole and established an ambitious program of public works to create jobs for the unemployed. To help displaced peasants, he launched a program of colonization all around the Mediterranean. Caesar's policies extended widely. With the help of an Egyptian astronomer who had accompanied Cleopatra to Rome, Caesar even reformed the calendar. The new "Julian calendar" introduced the solar year of 365 days and added an extra day every four years (the prototype of the "leap year"). With modifications made in 1582, the Julian calendar has remained in use throughout the West.

Despite his organizational skill, Caesar could not solve the problem of how to govern the Republic. In 48 B.C., he accepted the title of "dictator," the venerable title Romans reserved for those who stepped in *Political titles* during a crisis. Unlike Cincinnatus (the Roman with whom we began this chapter), Caesar did not renounce the title when the emergency was over, but ultimately proclaimed himself "dictator for life," a shocking departure from the traditional six-month tenure. He reportedly refused the title of "king" to avoid offending the republicans, yet he took on many of the trappings of a monarch. He wore royal regalia and established a priesthood to offer sacrifice to his "genius"—what the Romans called each person's spirit. In 44 B.C., Caesar had his image placed on coins—perhaps the first time a living Roman was so honored. (Some historians believe

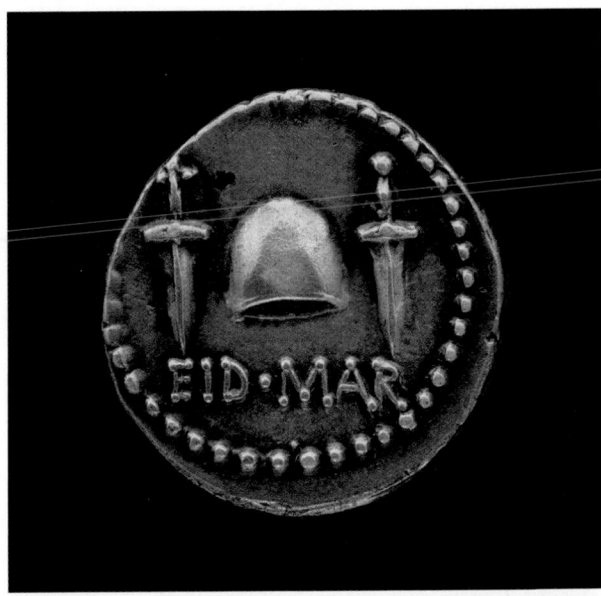

FIGURE 4.14
Coin commemorating the murder of Caesar, 43 B.C.

Pompey may have beat Caesar to that distinction.) Some people began to question whether the Republic of Rome was changing too radically.

The peace and order that Caesar brought to Rome pleased many, particularly the *populares* whose support had lifted Caesar to power. However, many Romans, even among his supporters, were *Conspiracy* outraged by the honors Caesar took for himself. He had shrunken the role of the *optimates*, and peace seemed to come at the price of the traditional Republic, and at the expense of the old power structure. Some conspirators were simply self-serving, hoping to increase their own power. Sixty senators with various motives entered into a conspiracy to murder their leader. Even Brutus, a friend and protégé of Caesar, joined in the plot. He would be like the Brutus of early Rome who had avenged Lucretia and freed Rome from the Etruscan kings. This Brutus would save Rome from a new king—Caesar.

Caesar was planning a military campaign for March 18, 44 B.C., so the assassins had to move quickly. On March 15, the date the *Caesar's murder* Romans called the "ides," or middle of the month, they surrounded the unwary dictator as he approached the Senate meeting place. Suddenly they drew knives from the folds of their togas and plunged them into his body. He died at the foot of the statue of Pompey, his old enemy. Most of the killers seem to have genuinely believed they had done what was best for Rome. They saw themselves as "liberators" who had freed Rome from a dictator and who would restore the Republic. In 43 B.C. they issued the coin shown in Figure 4.14. The coin depicts the assassins' daggers and reads "Ides of March." On the other side of the coin is a portrait of Brutus.

This attempt to celebrate a great victory on the coin was mere propaganda. The conspirators had no real plan beyond the murder. They apparently had made no provision for control of the army, nor for ensuring peace in the city. In the end, their claim to "save the Republic" rang hollow. Document 4.2 on page D4.1 reveals the chaos of the assassination. After Caesar's death, one of his friends supposedly lamented, "If Caesar for all his genius, could not find a way out, who is going to find one now?"

The Republic of Rome, with its emphasis on family and city, rose to great power from 509 B.C. to the death of Caesar in 44 B.C. By that year, Rome controlled much of the Mediterranean world, and a system of wealthy slave owners and a large standing army had replaced the citizen farmer-soldier who had laid the foundation for the Republic's success. Whereas the early Romans had emphasized the ties between citizens, now violent power struggles tore at the social fabric. A people who had preserved stories of serious Roman heroes began to treasure Greek models of beauty and individualism.

Julius Caesar became a central figure in Rome's transformation from republic to empire. Since Caesar's death, historians have argued about his qualities. Was he a great man who detected the inability of the republican form of government—designed to govern a city-state—to adapt to the changed circumstances of empire and social unrest? Or was he a power-hungry politician who craved control and blocked his fellow citizens from having any political involvement in the Republic? The truth no doubt falls somewhere between these extremes. One thing is certain: Despite the assassins' confident claims, Caesar's murder did not solve anything. More violence would ensue until a leader arose who could establish a new form of government that would endure even longer than the Republic.

REVIEW, ANALYZE, AND ANTICIPATE

REVIEW THE PREVIOUS CHAPTER

Chapter 1—"The Roots of Western Civilization"—discussed the rise of the first empires of the West—the Assyrian and the Persian. In Chapter 3—"The Poleis Become Cosmopolitan"—we saw the rise of large Hellenistic monarchies throughout the old empires of the ancient world. Rome inherited much from these empires.

1. *Review the Persians' and the Assyrians' treatment of conquered peoples and consider which most closely resembled the Romans' approach. To what degree did the Romans' treatment of their subjects contribute to their success as an imperial power?*

2. *Compare and contrast Roman and Greek governments.*

3. *In what ways do you think Rome came to resemble the great Hellenistic cities, and what problems did they share?*

ANALYZE THIS CHAPTER

This chapter—"Pride in Family and City"—traces the rise of the small city of Rome to a Hellenistic power whose territory extended throughout the Mediterranean world. In the course of this expansion, the old values of Rome were transformed and new constructs were slowly and violently implemented.

1. *Review these changes in early Roman life and values as the armies successfully expanded Roman influence.*

2. *Review the political structure of the Roman Republic. What were its strengths and weaknesses? How did the patron-client system contribute to the strengths and weaknesses of the political system?*

3. *What were the strengths of the Roman army? Consider how and why Rome expanded its territories so extensively.*

4. *Review Rome's contributions to the fields of art and technology.*

ANTICIPATE THE NEXT CHAPTER

Chapter 5—"Territorial and Christian Empires"—will continue the story of the development of Rome as it becomes an empire that endures for centuries.

1. *The Hellenistic cities we studied in Chapter 3 produced the important philosophies of Epicureanism and Stoicism, which the Romans learned about in the course of their expansion. Given their traditions of duty and respect for law, which philosophy do you think the Romans would be drawn to in Chapter 5?*

2. *After the death of Caesar, one of the major challenges facing Rome was establishing an effective form of government. Given what you have learned about Roman traditions in this chapter, what form of government do you think might be formed? What do you think would be the strengths and weaknesses of any new government?*

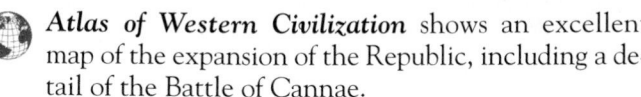

BEYOND THE CLASSROOM

Atlas of Western Civilization shows an excellent map of the expansion of the Republic, including a detail of the Battle of Cannae.

THE RISE OF ROME, 753–265 B.C.

Cornell, Tim. *Beginnings of Rome: Italy from the Bronze Age to the Punic Wars*. NY: Routledge, Chapman and Hall, Inc., 1995. A clear chronological survey of the period, focusing on the development of the Roman state and society.

Meyer, J.C. *Pre-Republican Rome*. Odense, Denmark: Odense University Press, 1983. A highly illustrated archaeological look at pre-republican Rome.

Mitchell, Richard E. *Patricians and Plebeians: The Origin of the Roman State*. NY: Cornell University Press, 1990. A description of the separate patrician and plebeian systems.

Pallottino, Massimo. *The Etruscans*. Bloomington, IN: Indiana University Press, 1975. An informed and interesting interpretation of Etruscan history.

FAMILY LIFE AND CITY LIFE

Aldrete, Gregory S. *Gestures and Acclamations in Ancient Rome*. Baltimore: Johns Hopkins University Press, 1999. An accessible, fascinating discussion on the verbal and non-verbal communications between Roman crowds and their leaders, nicely illustrated.

Bradley, Keith R. *Discovering the Roman Family: Studies in Roman Social History*. NY: Oxford University Press, 1991. Essays that study the composition of the Roman family and household-central features of the Roman state.

Gardner, J.F. *Women in Roman Law and Society*. Bloomington, IN: Indiana University Press, 1986. An interesting look at the ways in which the practice of law affected women in various aspects of their lives.

Orlin, Eric M. *Temples, Religion and Politics in the Roman Republic*. NY: E.J. Brill U.S.A., Inc., 1996. An exploration into the relationship between the individual and the community.

Robinson, O.F. *Ancient Rome: City Planning and Administration*. NY: Routledge, 1994. A remarkable study of the level of organization, laws, and local governmental arrangements made to allow a large population to live together in the ancient world.

Stambaugh, John E. *The Ancient Roman City*. Baltimore: Johns Hopkins University Press, 1988. A user-friendly guide that explains facets of everyday life in Roman cities.

EXPANSION AND TRANSFORMATION, 265–133 B.C.

Bagnall, Nigel. *The Punic Wars*. London: Hutchinson, 1990. A detailed, chronological study of the different campaigns, studying them strategically, operationally, and tactically.

Harris, William V. *War and Imperialism in Republican Rome*. NY: Oxford University Press, 1985. A solid account of the expansion of the Republic.

Rich, J. and G. Shipley. *War and Society in the Roman World*. NY: Routledge, 1993. A study of the impact of expansion and the army on Rome.

THE HELLENIZING OF THE REPUBLIC

Ogilvie, R.M. *Roman Literature and Society*. Harmondsworth, England: Penguin, 1980. A brief introduction to and fresh opinion of major Latin writers.

Rawson, Elizabeth. *Intellectual Life in the Late Roman Republic*. Baltimore: John Hopkins University Press, 1985. A summary intending to capture the full range of intellectual activity in the Republic.

Wheeler, Mortimer. *Roman Art and Architecture*. NY: Praeger, 1964. A fully illustrated and thought-provoking interpretation of Roman art and architecture.

Timeline: A Closer Look

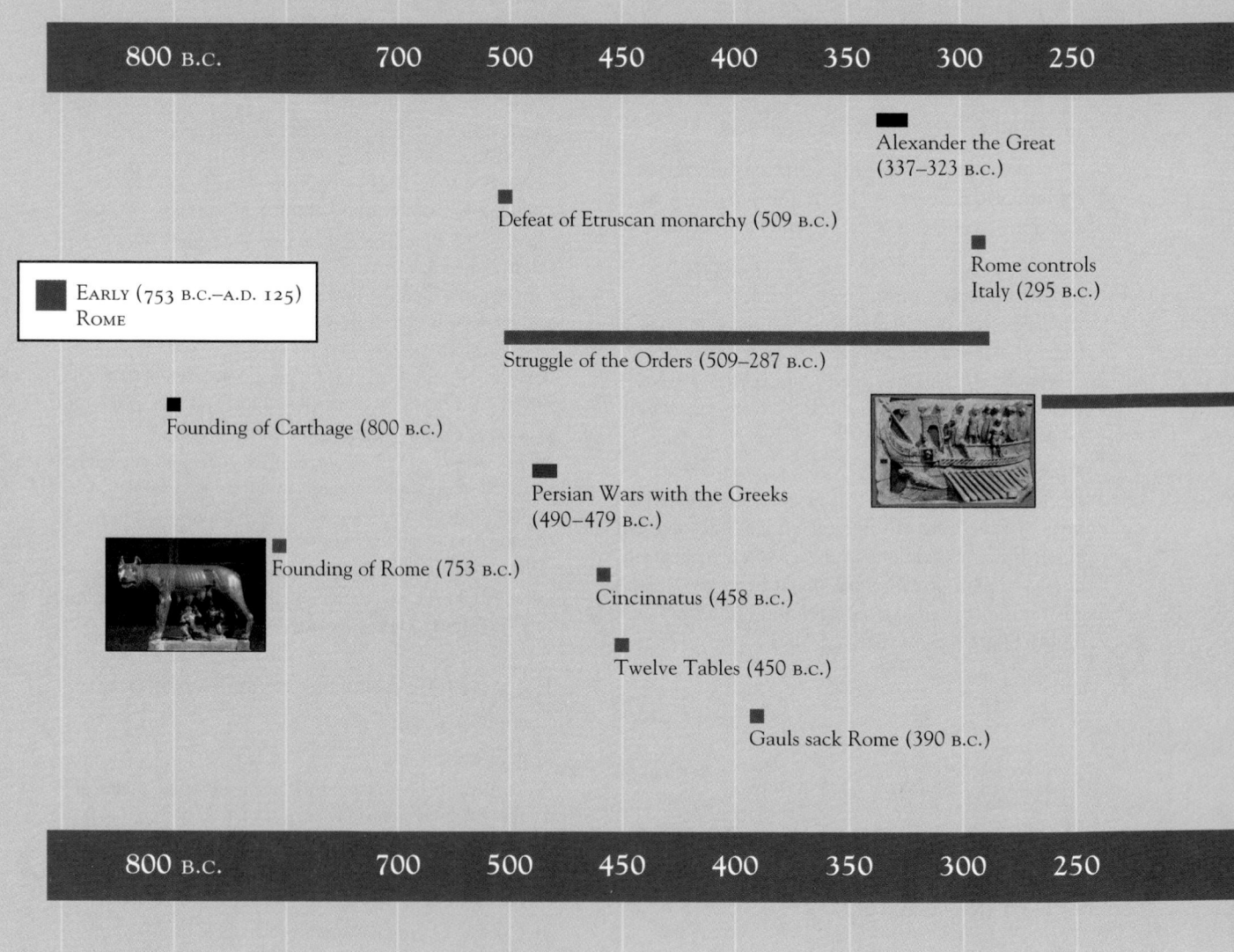

800 B.C.		700	500	450	400	350	300	250

Alexander the Great (337–323 B.C.)

Defeat of Etruscan monarchy (509 B.C.)

Rome controls Italy (295 B.C.)

EARLY (753 B.C.–A.D. 125) ROME

Struggle of the Orders (509–287 B.C.)

Founding of Carthage (800 B.C.)

Persian Wars with the Greeks (490–479 B.C.)

Founding of Rome (753 B.C.)

Cincinnatus (458 B.C.)

Twelve Tables (450 B.C.)

Gauls sack Rome (390 B.C.)

800 B.C.		700	500	450	400	350	300	250

THE TWILIGHT OF THE REPUBLIC, 133–44 B.C.

Lacey, W.K. *Cicero and the Fall of the Republic*. NY: Barnes and Noble, 1978. An in-depth study of all aspects of the man—speaker, author, philosopher—that shows how elements of Cicero's character developed over time in reaction to the social conditions of his age.

Langguth, A.J. *A Noise of War: Caesar, Octavian and the Struggle for Rome*. NY: Simon and Schuster, 1994. A chronologically organized focus on the personalities of these influential men.

Shotter, David. *The Fall of the Roman Republic*. NY: Routledge, 1994. A brief survey of the elements surrounding the fall of the Roman Republic—a good introductory survey.

Taylor, L.R. *Party Politics in the Age of Caesar*. Berkeley, CA: University of California Press, 1949. A study of the bitter partisan strife during the last years of the Republic.

200	150	100	50	0	50	100	150	A.D. 200

Destruction of Carthage (146 B.C.)

Reforms of the Gracchi (133–123 B.C.)

Pantheon Built (A.D. 125)

Civil Wars—Marius and Sulla (123–49 B.C.)

Revolt of Spartacus (72 B.C.)

Punic Wars (264–146 B.C.)

Cleopatra VII of Egypt (69–30 B.C.)

First Triumvirate—Pompey, Caesar, Crassus (60–49 B.C.)

Siege of Syracuse (212 B.C.)

Death of Julius Caesar (44 B.C.)

Rule of Caesar Augustus (12 B.C.–A.D. 14)

Cicero (50 B.C.)

Caesar and Pompey at war (49–45 B.C.)

200	150	100	50	0	50	100	150	A.D. 200

For quiz questions that tie the book to the videos and additional primary sources, please go to the Primary Source Investigator CD.

QUIZ

Altar of Augustan Peace (Ara Pacis Augustae)

This altar was built in 9 B.C. to praise the peace and prosperity that Caesar Augustus brought to the Roman people. Carvings of goddesses join flowers and fruits to promise abundance; processions carved on the sides show the imperial family and the Roman senators. The whole altar perfectly captures the spirit of the "Roman Peace" in which gods and civil servants alike contributed to the well-being of the new empire.

CHAPTER 5

Territorial and Christian Empires

The Roman Empire, 31 B.C.—A.D. 410

STUDY • The political and economic life of the Roman Empire • Daily life • Crisis and transformation of the empire • Religious developments • Creation of a Christian empire • Holy men and women. ⊕NOTICE how the far-flung empire was multiethnic with extensive trade networks.

"...[T]he newborn babe shall end that age of iron, [and] bid a golden dawn upon the broad world...." With these words, the Roman poet Virgil foretold the birth of a child who would save the world from the civil wars plaguing the late Roman Republic. For many Romans, that child arrived in the person of Caesar Augustus, a talented leader whose political and economic policies introduced almost 200 years of internal peace. But this *Pax Romana* was no cure-all. The Romans still faced the challenges of unifying a multiethnic empire while ensuring a succession of capable emperors. They also struggled to preserve their concept of private morality, and they grappled with the complexity of people's political involvement under an imperial system. In the third century A.D., economic and political hardship nearly wiped out the empire, but the reforms of two great rulers—Diocletian and Constantine—temporarily held Rome's extensive dominions together.

Meanwhile, another child born in the time of Caesar Augustus inspired a new creed that seemed to offer salvation. Followers of Jesus grew steadily in numbers through the first centuries A.D. At first the empire ignored them and occasionally persecuted them, but it later adopted Christianity as its own. This fusion of Roman and Christian ideas created a new Christian empire that many ancient Romans believed fulfilled the promise of the child Virgil praised. Both empires—Roman and Christian—contributed a great deal to the continuing development of the West.

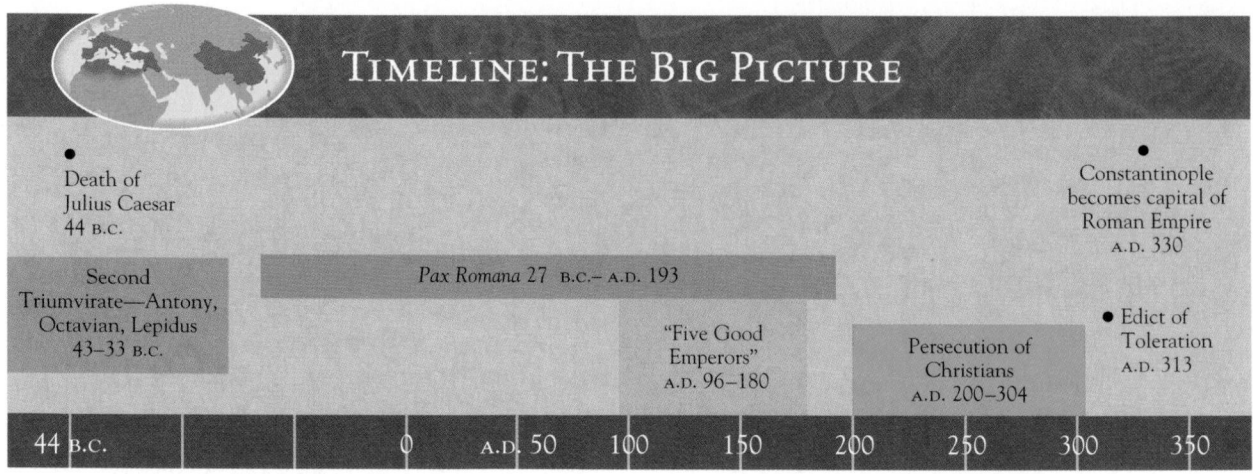

Death of
Julius Caesar
44 B.C.

Constantinople
becomes capital of
Roman Empire
A.D. 330

Second
Triumvirate—Antony,
Octavian, Lepidus
43–33 B.C.

Pax Romana 27 B.C.– A.D. 193

"Five Good
Emperors"
A.D. 96–180

Persecution of
Christians
A.D. 200–304

Edict of
Toleration
A.D. 313

44 B.C.   0   A.D. 50   100   150   200   250   300   350

The *Pax Romana*,
27 B.C.– A.D. 192

On the eve of their wedding, a young Roman couple, couple, Vespillo and Turia, paused during the celebration to reflect on a sad memory. Turia's parents had perished in the civil war that had elevated Julius Caesar to power, but the troubled times were not over for the young couple. During new civil wars, Turia had to sell her jewelry to help her husband escape the political strife in the city, and even had to beg for a pardon for Vespillo. Finally, the wars were over, and the couple "enjoyed quiet and happy days" through 41 years of their marriage, although sadly they produced no children. They were representative of many Romans who struggled through the violence after Julius Caesar's death finally to enjoy a long "Roman Peace" that was introduced by his successor.

AUGUSTUS TAKES POWER

In 43 B.C. three powerful men emerged who established a new triumvirate to rule the Republic. Unlike the first, the Senate legitimized this "Second Triumvirate," which ruled from 43 to 33 B.C. and which seemed to offer a way to bring peace to the turbulent land. Marc Antony, who managed Caesar's vast fortune, was a strong general who seemed to challenge senatorial power. To balance his power, the Senate turned to Julius Caesar's grandnephew and adopted son, Octavian—a remarkably talented 19-year-old who played on popular sympathy for the murdered dictator by calling himself Caesar. The young Octa-

vian offered respect to the Senate as he jockeyed for position against Mark Antony. The two brought into their partnership one of Julius Caesar's loyal governors and generals, Lepidus. At first, the three men controlled various parts of the empire: Octavian based his power in Italy and the provinces to the west; Lepidus held North Africa, and Mark Antony governed Egypt, Greece, and the provinces to the east. However, like the First Triumvirate, the second soon deteriorated into a power struggle among the three rulers. Octavian forced Lepidus into retirement in 36 B.C., and he and Antony vied for sole control of the empire.

As was traditional in Rome, politics was intimately bound up with family and with the women who, through childbearing, held the key to future family alliances. Not surprisingly, the political struggles between Octavian and Antony were to some degree played out in the bedroom. Having lost Julius Caesar, Cleopatra sought to continue her ruling dynasty through a new alliance with a new ruler of Rome. Figure 5.1 is a portrait bust of Queen Cleopatra showing her regal bearing and her fairly ordinary looks. She seduced Antony with the wit and charm that had so impressed the ancient biographers and bore him twins. Antony, however, was not yet committed to an alliance with Egypt's ruling house. Octavian's popularity in Rome was too high for Antony to risk offending the Roman people. Rumors already circulated in Rome's Forum that Antony wanted to move the Roman capital to Alexandria, so Antony had to negotiate a marriage that would be more acceptable to the public.

Antony and Octavian finally negotiated a peace that was to be secured by Antony's marriage to Octavian's sister, the young, beautiful Octavia. Octavia soon became pregnant, so the two families had the opportunity to seal their agreement permanently. But Antony left Octavia and traveled to Egypt. It *Civil war* is uncertain whether he decided that a strong political ally like Cleopatra afforded better security against Octavian than marriage to his rival's sister, or whether he was driven by the Egyptian queen's allure. In either case, the alliance bound through marriage dissolved. Octavian and Antony resumed their battle over who would rule all of Rome.

The war between the two leaders finally came to a head in 31 B.C., when Antony and Cleopatra, surrounded by Octavian's forces, risked all on a sea battle near the city of Actium, off the western coast of Greece. During this famous battle, Cleopatra and Antony proved less determined than Octavian, for Cleopatra's squadron left for Egypt in the course of the battle, and Antony followed her. They abandoned their navy and about twenty legions of their troops. Octavian's navy destroyed the Egyptian fleet and his land forces quickly occupied Egypt.

Antony committed suicide, and Octavian personally inspected his corpse to be sure his rival was dead. Cleopatra refused to be taken prisoner and ordered her servant to bring her a poisonous snake. She committed suicide by its bite. Although robbed of an imprisoned Egyptian Queen, Octavian stood as sole ruler of Rome. With Cleopatra's death in 31 B.C., the last Macedonian kingdom fell, ending the Hellenistic age that had begun with the empire of Alexander the Great. Now the new empire of Rome dominated the Mediterranean world.

FIGURE 5.1
Bust of Cleopatra VII, ca. 30 B.C.

A New Form of Governing

Unlike his uncle, Julius Caesar, Octavian successfully established a form of government that let him rule without offending the traditions of conservative Romans. This delicate balance between his leadership *The principate* style and the old ways earned him widespread popularity. On January 1, 27 B.C., the young general appeared before the Senate and claimed that he had brought peace and was thus returning the rule of the state to the Senate and the people of Rome. Octavian acted in the spirit of Cincinnatus (see Chapter 4), the general who gave up rule to return to his plow, and the tradition-loving Romans appreciated his gesture. The Senate showed its gratitude by giving him the title "Augustus," a name that implied majesty and holiness. It is by this informal title that his people addressed him and historians remember him. Augustus, however, modestly referred to himself as the *princeps*—that is, the "first citizen." The government he established was in turn called the *principate*, after the first citizen upon whom everyone depended.

The principate transformed the republican form of government, and historians roughly date the beginning of the Roman Empire *Governmental structure* from 27 B.C.—the date of Augustus' famous renunciation and acceptance of power. Under this new imperial form, the traditional representatives of government—the Senate and the Roman people—continued to exist and appoint the traditional magistrates to carry out their public business. The Senate continued to make disbursements from the traditional treasury and, in fact, slowly increased its power as it began to take over elections from the popular assemblies. The Senate also maintained control over some of the provinces—the older ones that did not require so many soldiers to guard the borders. In these ways, Augustus avoided offending the senators as Julius Caesar had done.

However, the vast extent of the empire and the increased complication of public affairs required a special magistrate—the princeps—to coordinate the whole, and more importantly to control the army. By A.D. 70, the princeps was more often called "emperor," a title with which troops had customarily hailed their generals. Augustus exerted his control in part by assuming the powers of the traditional Roman offices (of consul and tribune) while others held the actual offices. Perhaps more important, he used his enormous personal wealth to balance the national treasury, to rebuild Rome, and to fund gladiator shows and other popular spectacles. Indeed, his "Altar of Peace," shown at the beginning of this chapter, shamelessly praised his public piety and largesse (the location of the altar is shown in Map 5.1 on page 155). In 2 B.C. the Senate awarded Augustus the title "Father of the Fatherland." In a culture that depended on the father to guard his family's prosperity and honor, perhaps no other title could convey greater respect.

Of course, all these titles and honors, though significant, had little to do with the day-to-day practical problems of managing a large empire. Like any good father, Augustus ran the empire as one would run a household. He kept authority for himself, but the everyday business was handled by freedmen and slaves in his household. Although Rome itself remained governed largely by the traditional forms, Augustus made dramatic changes in governing the provinces.

Administering an empire

Augustus kept about half of the provinces—including wealthy Egypt—under his direct control, sending out representatives to govern there in his name. He began to create a foreign service drawn from the equestrian class (wealthy, upwardly mobile non-nobles), whose advancement depended upon their performance. This reform eliminated some of the worst provincial abuses that had gone on during the late Republic—for example, Augustus began eliminating private tax collectors. To keep the peace on the borders, Augustus stationed troops permanently in the provinces; the empire began to maintain fixed borders with military camps along the frontiers. Document 5.1 on page D5.1 includes Augustus' own assessment of his accomplishments.

For all these reforms, even by ancient standards, the empire was astonishingly undermanaged—a few thousand individuals controlled some 50 million people. The genius of the system lay in a combination of limited goals on top—maintain peace, collect taxes, and prevent power from accumulating—with actual power exerted at the local level. Through its relative simplicity, the principate established by Augustus continued to function efficiently even during years of remarkably decadent rulers. The Roman people recognized Augustus's accomplishments by according him a level of respect almost suiting a god, and this veneration would dramatically shape the future of the principate.

Figure 5.2 reveals the Romans' love of this strong, wise leader. This famous statue—named for the villa of Augustus's wife, Livia, where the sculpture stood—captures the people's hopes for Augustus. The statue portrays him as a strong, young soldier in his prime. His bare feet indicate that he is a hero, perhaps even semidivine. The cupid astride the dolphin refers to the claim that Augustus's family was descended from the goddess Venus, mother of Cupid. The symbols on Augustus' breastplate—a victorious general and a generous Mother Earth—promise divine aid and prosperity. Although Augustus refused to let himself be portrayed explicitly as a god, these associations left no doubt about his near-divine status. Although Augustus allowed altars in his name to be erected in the provinces, he refused to allow Romans to worship their "first citizen." His formal deification would come after his death.

This image of Augustus as a divine being was reinforced in the great literature produced under his patronage. Virgil's famous epic, the *Aeneid* (ca. 29–19 B.C.), is a mythological tale of the wandering of the Trojan hero Aeneas, who founded the city of Rome. However, in spite of its *Virgil's Aeneid* echoes of Homer, Aeneas was a kind of hero different from Achilles, and in this portrayal, Virgil was able to show that the virtues of the past could work in the new age of the principate. Aeneas refuses to yield to his weaknesses or his passions and is rewarded with a vision of the future in which his descendants would extend Rome's rule "to the ends of the earth." In his epic, Virgil promises:

OLC

. . . yours will be the rulership of nations.
Remember Roman, these will be your arts:
to teach the ways of peace to those you conquer,
to spare defeated peoples, tame the proud.

The *Aeneid* did for Rome what Homer had done for classical Greece: It defined the Roman Empire and its values for subsequent generations, and in the process it contributed to the deification of Augustus. It was also a fine example of Augustus's talent for propaganda.

What Virgil did for Roman literature, Livy (59 B.C.–A.D. 17) did for the empire's recorded history. In his long, detailed work, *The History of Rome* (26? B.C.–A.D. 15), Livy recounted the development of his city from the earliest times to the principate, and he included many speeches that brought the past to life. Like Virgil, Livy emphasized Roman religion and morality, looking nostalgically back to republican values. And again like Virgil, the historian recognized that the future lay with the new imperial form of government. His history strongly influenced subsequent ancient historians and has remained a central source of information today.

Livy's Historia

The system established by Augustus was not perfect, but Augustus lived for so long that the principate became tradition. The Roman historian Tacitus (A.D. 56–120) wrote that by Augustus' death in A.D. 14, no one left alive could remember any other way to govern. For the next two centuries his successors ruled with the benefits of the imperial system that Augustus had established. But they also inherited major problems he left unresolved—Who should succeed the "first citizen"? How should one best govern such a large empire, and how would rulers handle such power?

CHALLENGES TO THE PRINCIPATE, A.D. 69–193

Augustus's long tenure as emperor postponed the problem of imperial succession, but this weakness in the principate showed up soon after his death. The next four emperors all ascended the throne based on their ties to Augustus's family, and this succession showed how flimsy the concept of "first citizen" really was. An imperial dynasty had been established, and it did not matter that the rulers lacked the moral stature of Augustus or traditional republican virtues. During the Republic, leaders regularly confronted the Roman

Augustus's successors

FIGURE 5.2
Augustus of Prima Porta, ca. 20 B.C.

people in the Forum and yielded to the pressure of scorn or applause. However, the new rulers of the empire experienced no such corrective public scrutiny, and the successors of Augustus immediately proved that power corrupted. The careful (if scandalous)

FIGURE 5.3
Cameo of Emperor Claudius and his wife Agrippina the Younger. In background are Germanicus and his wife Agrippina the Elder.

historian Suetonius (A.D. 69–130) explained the decline of Augustus's successor, his stepson Tiberius (r. 14–37): "No longer feeling himself under public scrutiny, he rapidly succumbed to all the vicious passions which he had for a long time tried, not very successfully, to disguise." Tiberius "made himself a private sporting house where sexual extravagances were practiced for his secret pleasure," and in his isolation his paranoia grew. He even executed people for insulting his stepfather's memory if they carried a coin bearing Augustus's image into a lavatory or brothel. Such excesses continued throughout the dynasty of Augustus's heirs.

One of the heirs in this dynasty was Caligula (r. 37-41), an irrational—if not insane—ruler who wanted to be worshiped as a god. Upon Caligula's assassination, the guard who was present at the murder found a retiring, neglected relative—Claudius—in the palace and promptly declared him emperor. Claudius (r. 41–54) was regarded by many Romans as an imbecile subject to the whims of his wives, but the power of the connection to the family of Augustus prevailed to solidify his rule. The cameo in Figure 5.3 is a beautiful piece of propaganda as well as art. It shows Claudius and his wife Agrippina the Younger

in the foreground superimposed on Germanicus—Caligula's father—and his wife Agrippina the Elder (the younger's mother). The superimposition on the cameo emphasizes the family connections that gave Claudius the right to rule as "first citizen," and the horns of plenty on the front allude to the prosperity this dynasty promised to bring to the Romans. However, in contrast to the calm portrayal on the cameo, the dynasty only brought more family feuds.

Suetonius's history of those years tells of a series of murders within the family as they vied for the power of the princeps. Nero (r. 54–68) marked the most excessive of the murderers, for he killed many of his family members, mostly using his favorite means, poison. He even killed his mother, although it was not easy. He poisoned her three times, but she had taken a preventive antidote. Nero then tried to arrange for the ceiling of her room to collapse on her and for her boat to sink. When all these techniques failed, he simply sent an assassin to kill her and make it appear that she had committed suicide.

Nero was so despised that even his personal guard deserted him, and to avoid being captured and publicly executed, Nero commanded his slave to slit his throat, saying, "How ugly and vulgar my life has become!" It is not surprising that there were no more members of Augustus's *A new dynasty* family left to claim the succession, and the armies fought a bloody civil war to see which family would succeed to the imperial throne. Fortunately for Rome, Vespasian took power in A.D. 69 and restored some order to the empire, but even so fine an emperor could not ensure that his son would be equally competent. Each subsequent dynasty would eventually end through the weakness or corruption of one of the rulers and the flaws in the succession policy were repeatedly highlighted. The assassination of Vespasian's murderous son Domitian (r. 81–96) introduced a new period, that of the "Five Good Emperors" (96–180). These rulers increasingly centralized their power at the expense of the Senate, but they ruled with a long-remembered integrity. From Nerva (r. 96–98) to Marcus Aurelius (r. 161–180), these emperors established a tone of modest simplicity and adherence to republican values.

Marcus Aurelius represented the highest expression of a ruler whose political life was shaped by moral philosophy. He was highly educated in law, poetry, and philosophy, but the latter was his greatest love. When he was only 11, he adopted the coarse dress

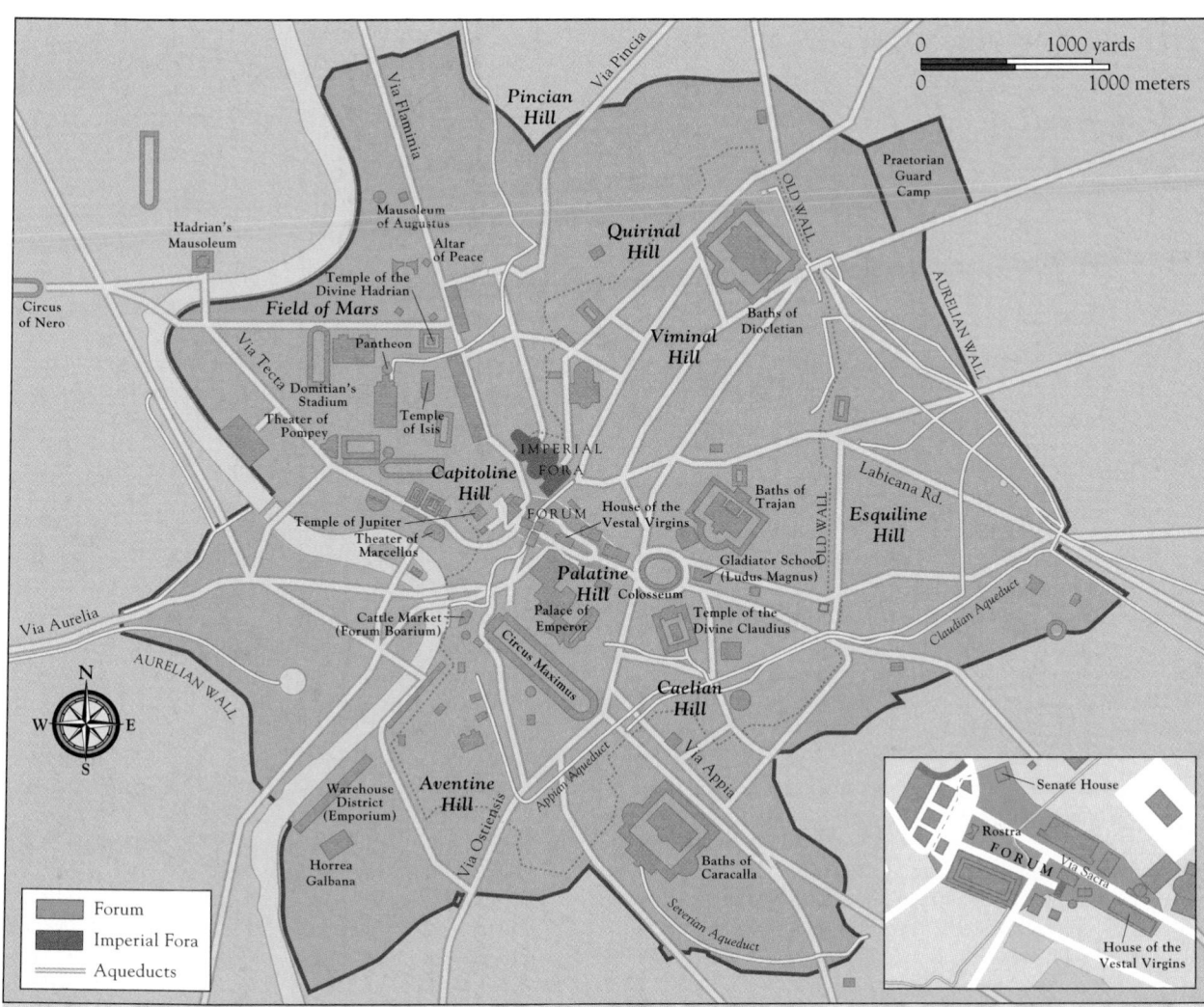

THINKING ABOUT GEOGRAPHY

MAP 5.1 *City of Rome During the Empire*

This map shows the City of Rome during the empire, indicating the new buildings constructed by the emperors. ❧ **Compare** the old city walls with the new to see how Rome has expanded in size under the empire. ❧ **Notice** the large new buildings that dominated the city. **What** were their functions? ❧ **Notice** the new Fora (pl. of Forum) built by the emperors next to the old Forum, and how the emperor's palace completely took over the Palatine Hill. **Consider** how these urban features indicate how emperors displaced old republican centers of power. ❧ **Compare** this map with Map 4.1, Rome under the Republic, and see how the city was now dominated by imperial power and locations for entertainment.

and sparse life of Stoic philosophers (discussed in Chapter 3), and when he became emperor, he continued to act based on the self-containment embodied in Stoic principles. His ideas have been preserved in a collection of his contemplative notes, called his *Meditations* (171–180?). Within these notes he wrote a caution that should have been followed by all who rose to great power: When one is seduced by fame

Global Connections

CHINA'S HAN DYNASTY AND THE SILK ROAD

🔳 **Consider** the importance of centralized authority and trade to the growth of cultures in the West and the East. **NOTICE** how long-term economic ties with eastern Asia influenced the Roman Empire.

In 206 B.C., while the Roman Republic was expanding, a strong Chinese military commander, Liu Bang, brought order to warring factions in China. Liu established the Han dynasty (named after his native land), which would endure for more than 400 years. The Han emperors developed a centralized authority supported by a large bureaucracy, and they built an extensive network of roads and canals to facilitate communication throughout the realm. The emperors also knew the value of educated royal servants. Thus, in 124 B.C., Emperor Han Wudi established an imperial university. This university incorporated Confucianism as the basis for its curriculum, so the Confucian tradition took root in China. Like the Romans in the West, the Han emperors developed an influential body of law, written first on bamboo and silk. Their legal system became the most comprehensive and best organized in the world.

The centralized, ordered rule of the Hans facilitated trade. It also led to the development of the "silk road," which linked China and the West in significant ways. Luxury items moved from China and India to Mesopotamia and the Mediterranean basin. Incoming goods arrived through a complex series of trades. Roman sailors used the prevailing monsoon winds to sail their ships from Red Sea ports to the mouth of the Indus River in India at Barygaza. There, they traded their goods—mostly gold and silver—for Indian spices and silks. The Indian merchants took their share of the merchandise and proceeded to trade with the Han merchants.

Chinese traders shipped spices—ginger, cinnamon, cloves, and others—that Westerners craved both as flavorings and medicines. However, the most prized commodity was Chinese silk, which gave its name to the trade route. By the first century A.D., Romans were willing to pay premium prices for the prized fiber. The Chinese knew how to feed silkworms on mulberry leaves and harvest the cocoons before the moths chewed through the precious silk strands. The silk traveled west in bales—either as woven cloth or raw yarn—and went to processing centers, most of them in Syria. There workers ungummed the rolls and unwound the fiber before weaving the fabric that sold for top prices throughout the Roman Empire. For hundreds of years, the trade flourished bringing West and East into close contact. This contact sparked the

and flattery, one should remember how flatterers are frequently wrong on other occasions, so one should remain humble. Unfortunately, too many emperors did not share Marcus' wise self-containment.

Through these years, the City of Rome was transferred from a center of republican power to a glorification of imperial power. As Map 5.1 shows, the entertainment centers—baths, games—offered by the emperors began to dominate the city, and temples to divine emperors sprang up.

Throughout the reigns of emperors good and bad, the borders had to be guarded. Armies fought in the east and as far away as Britain. Centuries of Roman military presences *Provincial defense* along the frontiers had brought Roman-style cities and agriculture—indeed, Roman civilization—to the edges of the empire. This long-term presence of Rome in lands far from Italy served to add Roman culture to the growing Western civilization in the north of Europe as well as the Mediterranean.

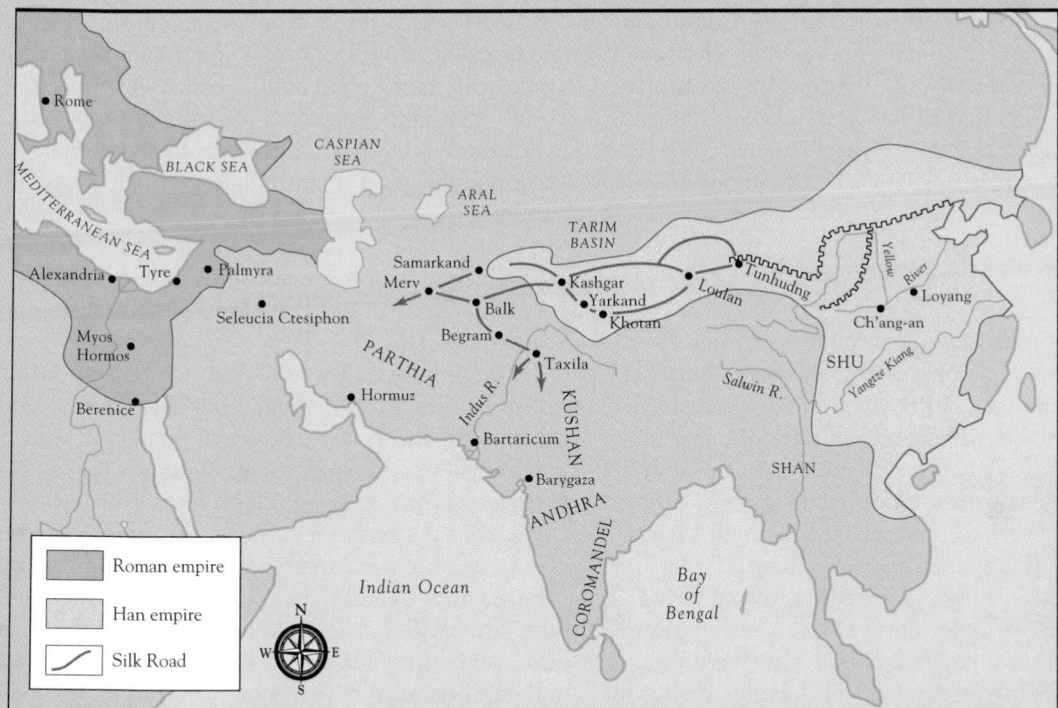

MAP 5.2 *The Silk Road ca.* A.D. 200.

exchange of ideas as well as goods. Unfortunately, it also spread diseases that dramatically reduced populations in China as well as in the Roman Empire.

Despite the thriving trade, the later Han emperors proved unable to maintain the centralization and prosperity that had marked the early centuries of their reign. In the face of social and economic tensions, as well as epidemic diseases, disloyal generals grabbed more and more power. By A.D. 200, the Han dynasty had collapsed and the empire lay in pieces. The trade along the silk road suffered too, but stories of the prosperous East continued to capture the imaginations of Westerners.

However, holding such extensive lands caused many of these soldier-emperors to be away from Rome for extended periods. Hadrian (r. 117–138) spent 12 of his 21 ruling years traveling around the provinces, establishing fortifications, and checking on provincial administration. However, it was one thing to establish definite borders and quite another to hold them. The Stoic emperor Marcus Aurelius spent the better part of 13 years in fierce campaigns to keep the border tribes out of the empire and he died while on campaign. His death brought an end to the era of the "good emperors," caused once again by a decadent son.

The long rule by good emperors may have been more the result of biological accident than anything else: Four of the emperors had no sons, so each of them adopted as his successor a man he thought best able to rule. However, Marcus Aurelius fathered a son, Commodus (r. 180–192), who unfortunately brought the age of the Five Good Emperors to an ignoble end through his cruel reign. Commodus seems to have been a simpleminded man who loved the games. He even shocked Rome by fighting in the arena as a gladiator. With Commodus's murder (he was strangled by his wrestling partner), the Roman Peace came crashing down in a fresh outbreak of civil war.

A VIBRANT, FAR-FLUNG EMPIRE

One must credit the genius of Augustus's political system and the steadfastness of the Roman administrators for the empire's ability to flourish even during years of imperial decadence. In our age of rapid communication and many levels of administrators and financial managers, it is difficult to imagine how hard it must have been to govern, with a small bureaucracy, an area as large as the Roman Empire. Map 5.3 shows the extent of the empire through A.D. 284. Although this map looks impressive, it still requires some imagination to understand the meaning of these distances in the third century. For example, in good sailing weather, it took three weeks to sail from one end of the Mediterranean Sea to the other, and travel overland was even harder. Hauling goods by wagon train with escorts armed against bandits took so much time and manpower that it was cheaper to send a load of grain all the way across the Mediterranean than to send it 75 miles overland. Information moved almost as slowly as goods. What could hold the empire together against the centrifugal force of these distances?

The empire found a partial answer in Romanization. From the time of the Republic, Romans had established colonies for military veterans in the *Colonies* provinces, and such colonial expansion continued under the empire. Furthermore, to boost the strength of his army, Augustus recruited auxiliary troops from the noncitizen population all over the empire. After serving 24 years, these veterans were awarded with citizenship and land in the colonies. These auxiliary troops also served to spread Roman culture. Colonies became the cities that grew up in Britain, North Africa, Germany, and the East, bringing Roman culture to the most distant corners of the empire. The cities boasted all the amenities that Romans had come to expect: theaters, baths, a colosseum, roads, and townhouses. These urban communities had so much in common that they seemed to erase the huge distances that separated them.

In these scattered, Romanized centers, local officials ruled. Town councils, for example, collected taxes and maintained public works, such as water systems and food markets. To collect taxes, officials maintained census figures on both the human population and agricultural produce *Provincial administration* and reported all to their superiors in Rome. This combination of local rule, Romanization, and some accountability to the central authority helped hold the fabric of the huge empire together.

The provinces not only depended on the administrative skills of local officials, but also on their philanthropy. In the best tradition of ancient Rome, men and women used their private resources for the public good. Inscriptions recalling private contributions survive in towns and cities all over the empire and reveal how essential such charity was to the maintenance of the Roman Peace. One woman in central Italy bequeathed 1,000,000 coins in her will for the town to use to provide monthly child-assistance payments for all children until boys reached 16 years of age and girls 14. In another instance, the governor of the Asian city of Troy observed that the city was "ill-supplied with baths and that the inhabitants drew muddy water from their wells." The governor persuaded Emperor Hadrian to contribute 3,000,000 coins to build an aqueduct, but when costs rose to 7,000,000 the governor paid for the difference from his own pocket. Philanthropists assured that Roman life prospered all over the empire by contributing funds for baths, libraries, poor relief, and even public banquets.

The empire also remained unified through the marvels of Roman engineering. Fifty thousand miles of roads supplemented the great rivers as primary means of transportation. As today, the upkeep of these roads posed a constant challenge, and the empire collected tolls on goods in transit to fund this maintenance. Roman authorities also established a transportation system that provided travelers with horses and carriages and that monitored the move- *Roads and transportation* ment of heavy goods. Regulations established maximum loads but were frequently ignored by inspectors who often took bribes. With these elaborate networks of roads, lightly burdened travelers could cover an astonishing 90 miles a day— an extraordinary feat in ancient times.

During the early centuries of the empire, goods moved over great distances not only along the road network, for there was also a great deal of shipping.

THINKING ABOUT GEOGRAPHY

MAP 5.3 *The Roman Empire,* 44 B.C.–A.D. 284

This map shows the greatest extent of the Roman Empire. ■ **Notice** how much of this territory was acquired during the Republic (before Augustus' rule). **Notice also** the subsequent expansion to A.D. 284, and consider the logic of this expansion. ■ **What** geographical features did Rome take advantage of as natural defenses as the legions established their frontiers? ■ **Notice** the location of Hadrian's Wall. ■ **Notice** the scale of this map. Consider the difficulties in transportation. For example, allowing for a rapid travel of ninety miles a day, how long would it take a message to go from Rome to Hadrian's Wall?

For the first time in the ancient world, the Roman navy kept the Mediterranean Sea relatively free of pirates, so shipping flourished. The sea had become a virtual Roman lake, and the Romans confidently called it *Mare Nostrum* ("our sea") to show the degree to which the Mediterranean world was united under Rome.

The peace and unity of the empire allowed merchants to increase trade with the furthest reaches of Asia. The fabulous "silk road" brought spices and

silks from as far away as China and only whetted the appetite of wealthy Romans for exotic goods from the East. The "Global Connections" feature on page 156–157 discusses the Chinese empire that also profited from trade between the West and East.

Finally, the movement of people and armies also held the empire together. The Roman Empire boasted a remarkably multiethnic and multicultural population. Many educated provincials, for example, spoke at least three languages: Greek, Latin, and a local dialect. The imperial lands included a bewildering array of climates and geological features as well. Figure 5.4 shows the 80-mile-long wall of Hadrian, the northern outpost of the empire in Britain built in the early second century. Here, Roman forts dotted the wall at one-mile intervals. Roman soldiers peered into the damp fog, on alert against the fierce northern tribes who threatened to swarm across the imperial boundary. By contrast, Figure 5.5 shows the forum of the ruins of Dougga, a Roman city in North Africa. You can see the desert in the background that marked the southern border of the empire. Beyond the great groves of olive trees that, together with abundant fields of grain, produced much of the agricultural wealth of North Africa, Roman legions stood watch against the Bedouin tribesmen who came galloping out of the desert to menace the edge of the empire.

Imperial diversity

With this remarkable diversity came the constant movement of people. Merchants traveled with their goods, and just as in the Hellenistic world, enterprising people moved about to seek their fortunes. Furthermore, to defend the empire's 6,000 miles of border, Roman authorities moved approximately 300,000 soldiers to wherever they were needed. The armies usually did not patrol their own regions. A garrison of black sub-Saharan Africans, for example, was stationed in the foggy north along Hadrian's Wall, and Germans from the north patrolled the desert. At the height of the *Pax Romana*, this flexible system seemed to ensure peace within Rome's borders.

As we will see, in time the centrifugal forces began to work against the ability of such a far-flung empire to hold together. The expense and difficulties of long-distance trade caused more and more provinces to produce their goods locally. Outside the empire itself, as more tribes wanted to enter and share

FIGURE 5.4
Hadrian's Wall, Northern England.

FIGURE 5.5
Roman ruins at Dougga, Tunisia.

Rome's prosperity, the borders would become all too permeable. But for the first 200 years of the empire, it seemed as if the promise of a glorious new age had been fulfilled.

Life During the Peace of Rome

Just as Augustus wanted to return politics to the traditional morality of the Roman Republic, he also tried to revive the old morality in the private lives of Rome's citizens. As Roman legions conquered new territories during the early empire, booty and new taxes made wealth pour from the provinces into Rome. Throughout the Roman Peace, increased commerce brought even more wealth to some Romans well placed to profit.

A NEW DECADENCE

Although the growing separation between rich and poor that began under the Republic continued through the empire, those getting more wealthy began to flaunt their riches. Silks and embroidery replaced the rough wool of republican virtue, and satirists wrote scathingly of women sporting makeup, high heels, elaborate hair styles, and lots of jewelry. Men, too, indulged in similar excesses to ensure their appearance reflected their wealth and status. Augustus and subsequent moralists would fight a losing battle against such decadent displays.

Figure 5.6 captures this sense of excess. In this wall painting an elegantly dressed and bejeweled lady leisurely pours perfume. The painting not only reveals the opulent lifestyle of people who could afford expensive luxuries like jewels and perfume, but it was also a status symbol in itself. Only the wealthiest of homes boasted such exquisite artwork. Romans fortunate enough to display such possessions were naturally reluctant to return to the days of classic simplicity.

THE PROBLEM WITH POPULATION

During the Republic, marriage and family ties were central values of the Roman people. Augustus brought those same values to the new empire, using his power to support families. The princeps promoted legislation that assessed penalties on people who remained unmarried and instituted strong laws against adultery. These laws, though intended to strengthen the family, fell far short of their mark. Morality is singularly hard to legislate, and the Roman historian Tacitus observed that many people simply ignored the laws. Augustus himself experienced this phenomenon firsthand: unable to control his own daughter's behavior (that he perceived as inappropriate), he ended up exiling her.

At heart, however, the laws were probably as much about children as about morality. The future of Rome, like the succession of the emperor, depended on offspring to carry on the family and other cultural traditions. Yet throughout the empire, Romans had a particularly hard time reproducing. Augustus even promoted a law that exempted women from male guardianship if they bore three children (four children for a freed slave). These numbers are a far cry from Cornelia, mother of the Gracchi, who earned praise for bearing 12 children! Fecundity in the empire certainly had plummeted to alarmingly low levels.

Birthrates

This phenomenon had cultural as well as physical causes. Wealthy Roman men and women often wanted few children, so as to preserve their inheritance intact. Yet Augustus's law specifically tried to influence women. This law is particularly interesting in its assumptions: It recognized women's desire for freedom, and it assumed that women controlled their own fecundity. The former assumption may have been accurate, but the latter was only partially so. Sometimes women used birth-control methods based on herbs, spermicidal drugs, or douches. The texts also refer to abortion, although drugs strong enough to abort a fetus often endangered the life of the mother. The causes of Roman infertility lay in a full complex of medical misunderstandings combined with cultural practices.

SEXUAL AND MEDICAL MISUNDERSTANDINGS

Despite the scandalized commentary lamenting the sexual excess of "loose" women and decadent emperors, Romans in fact were very circumspect about sex. Medical wisdom warned men against the fatiguing effects of sexual activity, which they thought deprived the body of vital spirit. Roman physicians believed semen was made of brain fluid, and urged men to conserve it carefully. Physicians recommended sexual intercourse in the evening after a light meal, followed by a therapeutic massage. Women were to be modest in the marriage bed, always wearing an article of clothing during intercourse.

By contrast, physicians did not believe that sexual intercourse weakened females. Indeed, medical advice for women focused on helping them to

FIGURE 5.6
Woman pouring perfume, ca. 20 B.C.

bear as many children as possible. Yet, medical misinformation actually contributed to Rome's falling birthrate. Physicians concluded, incorrectly, that women were most fertile soon after their menstrual periods, so they recommended reserving intercourse for that time. Furthermore, some doctors thought that women had to have intercourse before puberty in order to mature correctly. Medical misunderstanding about women's bodies and child healthcare contributed to a low birthrate. These factors combined with other cultural issues—the desire to restrict children to keep from reducing inheritances, for example—help explain why Rome had so much trouble maintaining its population.

Despite the confusion regarding human reproduction, Roman medicine proved highly influential for the next 1,500 years. In particular, the physician Galen (131–201) popularized views that have prevailed even into modern times. Galen used some modern scientific techniques—for example, he performed vivisections on pigs to see the process of digestion—but his conclusions were strongly rooted in the classical world. He embraced the notion of moderation that was so central to ancient thought (recall Aristotle's "golden mean," discussed in Chapter 2), and therefore saw disease as the result of an imbalance, or excess. Galen believed that good health resulted from a balance among the four "humors," or bodily fluids—blood, bile, urine, and phlegm. He argued that each of these humors had its own properties—warm, cold, dry, and moist—and when a person was out of balance—that is, when one humor dominated—the cure was to restore an appropriate equilibrium. For example, if a person were feverish and flushed, he or she was considered to have an excess of blood. An application of bloodsucking leeches or the initiation of bleeding would reduce the blood and restore the balance. These ideas may not have improved people's health, but they formed the subsequent basis for medical treatment.

Galen

THE GAMES

Families may have formed the basis of Roman society, but as we saw in Chapter 4, during the Republic, men forged critical ties in the world of civic affairs centered in the Roman Forum. Under the empire this focus changed; real power moved from the Forum to the emperor's household. Yet the Roman people still needed a public place to gather and express their collective will. Over time, they began satisfying this need at the great games and spectacles held in the amphitheaters across the empire. During the late Republic, wealthy men who craved the admiration of the people, and politicians who sought the loyalty of the crowd, spent fortunes producing chariot races in the *Circus Maximus* and hunts and gladiator games. After the time of Augustus, the emperors had a virtual monopoly on providing entertainment in Rome, although in the provinces others could produce spectacles. These games always had a religious significance to the Roman people, ritualizing Roman power and authority.

Figure 5.7 shows the Roman Colosseum, built by Emperor Vespasian (r. 69–79) as a gift to his subjects. Map 5.1 shows its location within the city. This structure was the largest of its kind in the Roman world and held about *From Forum to arena* 50,000 people. The photograph on the right (see Figure 5.7) shows what remains of the interior, showing the subterranean passages that held animals and prisoners. The photograph on the left shows the exterior that dominated the skyline of Rome. All major Roman cities throughout the provinces featured an amphitheater where local officials presented games and where Roman power was expressed. Men and women would flock to the arena in the mornings to watch men hunt exotic animals that had been transported to Rome from the farthest reaches of the empire. Augustus proudly claimed to have provided a total of 3,500 animals in these hunts; other emperors were equally lavish in their displays.

The crowds then witnessed the public executions of criminals who were either set aflame or put in the path of deadly wild animals. Through such rituals, Rome displayed its power over its enemies. Figure 5.8 shows a criminal being attacked by a leopard in the arena. This horrifying scene suggests that it was not easy to make animals attack humans; the victims had to be immobilized and the animals goaded into aggression. The very existence of the mosaic, however, which was displayed in a private home, reveals the Romans' pride in the empire's dominance over its perceived enemies. As we will see, these enemies would eventually include Christians.

Afternoons at the Colosseum were reserved for the main event, the gladiator contests. Gladiators were condemned criminals who were trained in the gladiator school near the Colosseum (see Map 5.1 on page 155). They then received the right to live a while

FIGURE 5.7
The Colosseum.

longer by training to fight against each other in the arena. In time, the gladiatorial ranks were increased by slaves who were specifically bought and *Gladiators* trained for this purpose. Gladiators armed with weapons were paired to fight until one was killed, and the winner won the right to live until his next fight. At first, gladiator contests were part of funeral rites, and the death blood of the losers was seen as an offering to the recently departed. Later, however, emperors sponsored contests featuring hundreds of gladiators. At the end of a gladiator contest, the man who had been overpowered was supposed to bare his throat unflinchingly to the killing blade of the victor. Not all defeated gladiators were killed; those who had fought with extreme bravery and showed a willingness to die could be freed by the emperor's clemency.

It is easy to judge these activities as wanton displays of brutality. Yet, from the Roman perspective, these rituals actually exemplified and perpetuated Roman virtue. In the arenas, private honor and public good intersected: The private generosity that funded the games served the community's need for ritual, and the emperor's sponsorship strengthened the community's loyalty to its leaders. Finally, individuals learned to face death bravely by watching people die; as the historian Livy (59 B.C.–A.D. 17) wrote: "There was no better schooling against pain and death." Nevertheless, all these demonstrations of Roman largesse, prowess, and courage could not stave off the threats to the empire that came at the end of the *Pax Romana*.

Crisis and Transformation, A.D. 192–ca. 400

The assassination of Marcus Aurelius's decadent son Commodus in 192 marks the traditional end of the Roman Peace. From the subsequent struggles, the principate established by Augustus was transformed to withstand the new challenges facing the empire. The armies had grown strong under the military policy of the Five Good Emperors, so armies became the king makers. Septimius Severus (r. 193–211) was a new kind of emperor—a North African general who came to power because of his army's support. A military man to the core, he also embodied the multicultural elements of the empire. He spoke Latin with a North African accent and seemed to feel more at home among provincials than among the old, wealthy families of Rome.

THE MILITARY MONARCHY

Under Septimius's rule, the principate was transformed into a military dictatorship. The new emperor increased the size of the army and raised soldiers' pay. He also militarized the government, placing able generals in key positions of power. The efficiency of Septimius's leadership kept Rome's fundamental problems at bay, but only temporarily. This soldier-emperor's successors would bear the full brunt of the threats to the empire that Septimius left unresolved.

As the army gathered strength during Septimius's reign, the chaos that so threatened in the mid-third century worsened. The powerful army became more expensive to maintain because of the increased salary and attention the soldier-emperors gave to their troops. But these expenditures did not guarantee the army's loyalty to the state. Instead, the army's power *Threats to empire* contributed to some instability. From 235 to 285, the number of claimants to the throne exploded. In one nine-year period, the emperor Gallienus fought off as many as 18 challengers. As soldiers became central to the imperial rule, the traditional rivalry that had existed between army units became expressed in rival claimants to the throne. A unit whose general became emperor increased its own status—this was worth fighting for.

At the same time, Rome's borders were threatened. The Persian Empire to the east had grown stronger in the third century and was able to encroach on Rome's eastern provinces. A Persian rock inscription celebrates the Persian victory: "We attacked the Roman Empire and annihilated . . . a Roman force of 60,000." Rome could not respond with its customary vigor because, at the same time, Germanic tribes on the northern borders made substantial incursions. As if these internal and external pressures were not enough, a severe economic downturn loomed.

At the height of the empire, certain families accumulated astonishing wealth. Even though they gave some of it back to the public in the form of monuments or games, they still lived lavishly. Not only did they buy jewels and fine silks, *Economic recession* but they gave banquets featuring exotic (and expensive) imported foods. One menu from a Roman cookbook recommends rare dishes from the far reaches of the empire: sow's udders stuffed with salted sea urchins, Jericho dates, boiled ostrich, roast parrot, boiled flamingo, and African sweet cakes.

This kind of luxury spending seriously damaged an already weakening economy for two reasons: It drained hard currency from the West and transferred it to the Far East, which supplied many of the luxuries; and it kept money from circulating, thus limiting the avenues for the growth of a prosperous middle class. As the poor in Rome received more and more food subsidies, the city had to spend more money on imported grain, further reducing the treasury. With the increase in imports from the East, the western centers of the empire began to suffer a shortage of hard currency, as money flowed to the great eastern centers that supplied most of the imports. As we will see, this shifting of wealth to the East had profound ramifications for the governing of the empire.

There was a further inherent weakness in the imperial economy: When territorial expansion stopped, there was little to bring new wealth into the empire. Instead, a growing bureaucracy, increased military expenses, and costly military rivalries served to drain money. The economy stagnated while expenses increased. As usual, the burden fell mostly on the poor, whose plight worsened. The rich grew richer, and the poor lived off the generosity of those in power.

Emperors throughout the centuries tried to address the problem of a shortage of hard currency by debas- *Inflation* ing the coinage, which meant that plenty of money still circulated, but it was not worth as much as it had been before. Gold coins virtually disappeared from circulation, and by the mid-third century the silver content of coins dropped to a negligible 1 percent.

FIGURE 5.8
Men condemned to the beasts, ca. second century A.D.

Not surprisingly, inflation struck. The price of grain climbed so much that a measure that cost two coins in A.D. 200 cost 330 coins just a century later. Inflation always hits the poor hardest, and many people turned to banditry out of desperation. The resulting fear and unrest further rocked life in the empire.

To worsen matters, plague spread through the empire from China along with the luxury goods that came along the silk road. (See "Global Connections, page 156). Just as in China, the disease caused intense suffering and depleted the already low Roman population. Labor became as scarce as hard currency. The Roman government turned to the tribes outside its borders to replenish its armies. Mercenaries crossed the borders to fight for Rome, and the legions of Rome

increasingly came to resemble the "barbarians" from the outside. Structures like Hadrian's Wall no longer clearly separated the "civilized" from the "uncivilized."

All the problems of the late second and third centuries clearly demonstrated that the Roman Peace was over. The borders between Roman and non-Roman had dissolved, and hungry, restless residents agitated within the empire. Medical knowledge was helpless in the face of pandemics like the mid-third century plague, and Roman families could no longer populate the empire. The empire seemed to teeter on the brink of collapse.

THE REFORMS OF DIOCLETIAN, A.D. 284–305

Considering the many disasters facing the empire in the mid-third century, it is a wonder that Rome did not fall then. In fact, it was the dramatic measures of Diocletian, an autocratic new emperor, that helped Rome avert ultimate disaster—at least for the time being. Diocletian (r. 285–305) was a general who rose from the ranks to wear the imperial purple. Not content to be called emperor, he assumed the title "lord" and demanded that his subjects worship him as a living god. (See Document 5.3 on page D5.3) The change in title marked the formal end of the principate founded by Augustus—from then on, emperors were no longer "first citizens." Diocletian had a shrewd, practical side and used his considerable administrative talents to address the problems plaguing the empire. The new Roman lord was up to the task and stopped the decline.

Turning to the problems of communication, administration, and succession, Diocletian organized the government into a "tetrarchy," or rule by four men. Diocletian ruled in the wealthier *Tetrarchy* eastern region of the empire while assigning his partner, Maximian, to rule in the west. To address the issue of succession, each of these "augusti" adopted a "caesar" who would succeed him. In the Roman tradition dating back to Octavian, each caesar married his augustus's daughter, sealing the alliance through family bonds. Figure 5.9 depicts the ideals behind the tetrarchy. The four emperors—all military men—rest their hands on their swords. They also embrace one another. The overall arrangement of their figures conveys the concept of a unified rule by four men. Map 5.4 shows the territorial division of the tetrarchy.

FIGURE 5.9
Tetrarchs, ca. A.D. 305.

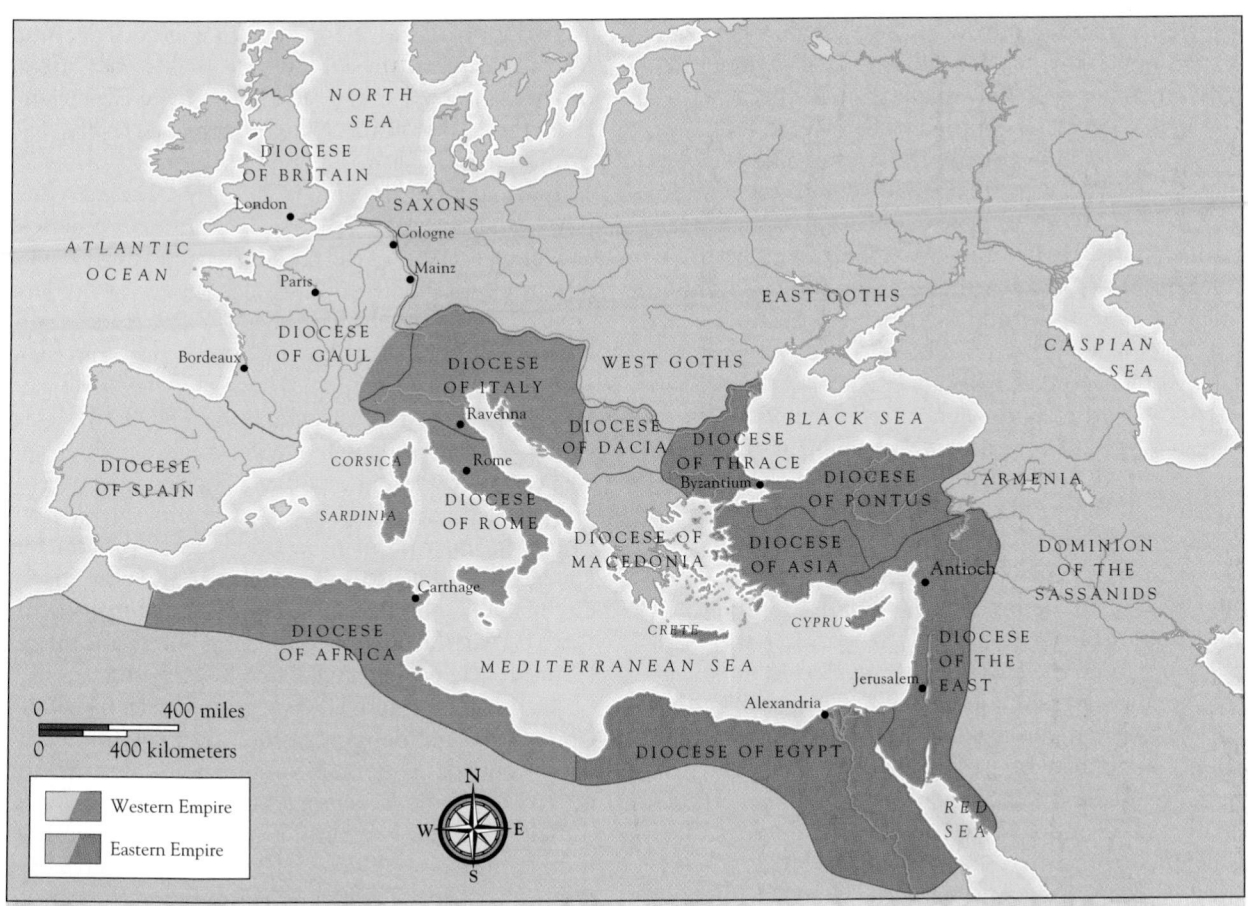

NORTH SEA

DIOCESE OF BRITAIN

London

SAXONS

ATLANTIC OCEAN

Cologne

Mainz

Paris

DIOCESE OF GAUL

Bordeaux

EAST GOTHS

CASPIAN SEA

DIOCESE OF ITALY

WEST GOTHS

Ravenna

DIOCESE OF DACIA

BLACK SEA

DIOCESE OF SPAIN

CORSICA

Rome

DIOCESE OF ROME

SARDINIA

DIOCESE OF THRACE

Byzantium

DIOCESE OF PONTUS

ARMENIA

DIOCESE OF MACEDONIA

DIOCESE OF ASIA

Antioch

DOMINION OF THE SASSANIDS

Carthage

CRETE

CYPRUS

DIOCESE OF AFRICA

MEDITERRANEAN SEA

Jerusalem

DIOCESE OF THE EAST

DIOCESE OF EGYPT

Alexandria

RED SEA

0   400 miles
0   400 kilometers

Western Empire

Eastern Empire

N W E S

THINKING ABOUT GEOGRAPHY

MAP 5.4 *Diocletian's Division of the Empire,* A.D. 304

This map shows Diocletian's administrative reform of the empire and its division into four units to be guided by the tetrarchy. ❂ **Notice** the primary division into east and west, each guided by an Augustus. ❂ **Consider** why Diocletian himself took the eastern portion. ❂ **Notice** the locations of Ravenna in Italy and Byzantium on the Black Sea—both would become the capitals of the two halves of the empire. **What** advantages did each city's location offer for trade and defense?

Diocletian then turned his administrative talents to problems other than succession. He recognized *Military reforms* that the military that had created so many emperors from the time of Septimius Severus onward was a threat to political stability. He brought the army under control in part by reversing Septimius's policy of uniting civil and military offices. He separated the two, so that provincial governors could not command armies. He thus made it harder for generals to aspire to the purple. To address the problem of incursions along the imperial frontiers, Diocletian rearranged the armies. Instead of placing his greatest martial strength along the borders, he stationed mobile legions deep inside the empire. That way, they could move quickly to meet a threat rather than just react as outsiders encroached. The Germanic tribes on the northern borders were particularly eager to enter the empire, looking for wealth.

Diocletian recruited many of these Germans to serve in this new army, further diluting its traditional Roman character even as he made it more effective.

Finally, Diocletian turned to the severe economic problems troubling the empire. In the same way Augustus had tried to improve morality by decree, Diocletian issued economic edicts. He addressed the rampant inflation by freezing prices and wages, but these policies simply led merchants to withdraw goods from the open market to participate in informal black market exchanges. The emperor also raised taxes to pay for an expanding army, but he reformed the tax system so that it was partially based on payment in goods instead of in the inflated, scarce coins. This kind of authoritarian approach could not solve the empire's most deep-seated economic troubles, but it kept the economy from collapsing altogether.

Economic reforms

The last problem that Diocletian addressed was the simple shortage of people to perform the tasks needed to keep the empire running. Again, he sought solutions in decrees. He identified "essential" occupations—ranging from soldier, farmer, baker, and tax collector—and froze people in these jobs. Furthermore, he made these occupations hereditary. His decrees had a serious unintended consequence: They weakened the willingness of well-off locals to contribute to the public works and the games that had so defined imperial life. Instead, great estates became more self-contained, pulling away from the central authority and maintaining their own mercenary armies. People increasingly complained about the tax collectors and the central government that seemed to ask more and more of its citizens while providing less and less.

THE CAPITAL MOVES EAST

Diocletian's attempts to stabilize the succession barely outlasted him. He and his co-augustus stepped down in 305 as planned, leaving the empire to be ruled by their two caesars, but Diocletian's hopes for a smooth transition proved overly optimistic. There were years of intrigue and civil war as several rulers fought for the throne. Finally, one of the caesars was succeeded by an ambitious son, Constantine (r. 306–337), who defeated his rivals to assume sole control of the empire. He kept Diocletian's economic and military reforms, but put his own unique stamp on the empire.

In 330, Constantine made a momentous decision for the future of the empire: He built a new urban center on the site of the old Greek city of Byzantium. Later the city would be called Constantinople, after its founder, and become a second capital to the empire, eclipsing Rome itself in power and grandeur. Rome was no longer a practical site for the capital of the empire because it was too far from the center of the military actions on the borders, and the conservative old Roman nobility made it very difficult for emperors to implement vigorous new ideas. Constantine could not have chosen a better site for a new capital city, which he called his "new Rome." It was easily defended and located along the rich eastern trade routes. Since Diocletian, when emperors ruled autocratically based in cities away from Rome, the great Roman Senate that had governed in concert with Augustus had shrunk to no more than a city council. The Roman Empire seemed to have little to do with "Rome" anymore and bore scant resemblance to the principate created by Augustus.

Constantinople

As the capital moved east, the western provinces came under increasing pressure from the Germanic tribes outside the empire. Great estates in the provinces—called *latifundia*—became more self-sufficient, needing nothing from the central authority. The mosaic in Figure 5.10 shows one such estate in North Africa. The figures surrounding the central house show the abundance and prosperity produced by the great manor, but the thick-walled manor house that looks more like a fort than a traditional villa testifies to the new role of the provincial landowners—defense.

After the death of Constantine in 337, emperors reacted to Germanic invaders by inviting some tribes into the empire to settle and become allies. The borders had already proved permeable, and with the continued population decline within the empire, there seemed to be enough space for everyone. This influx, however, carried the seeds of the empire's eventual disintegration. The Visigoths (more fully described in Chapter 6) were one of the tribes the Romans invited across the border to settle. However, the Romans treated them abysmally, giving them land they could not farm, raping their women, and forcing them to sell their children into slavery in return for food. The warlike tribe went on a rampage.

In 378 at the Battle of Adrianople, the emperor Valens (r. 364–378) suffered a resounding military defeat at the hands of one of the Germanic tribes and was killed on the field. This battle dispelled the aura of invincibility that had surrounded the Roman legions for centuries—it seemed that military might now was possessed by the "barbarians" rapidly pouring through the borders. The Visigoths not only were able to raid Italy, but in 410 actually plundered the "eternal city" of Rome itself. Masses of panicked Romans (like Melania in the Biography on page 182) fled to Africa and the East.

It seemed that an era had passed and that the empire had finally fallen—but the end had not come *Twilight of the empire* quite yet. The Visigoths left Rome and settled in Spain as allies of the empire, just as many other tribes had done in other provinces. An emperor remained in the west, ruling from Italy, and a co-ruler continued to govern in the east, from Constantinople. But by 410 the western region had disintegrated so much that soon there seemed to be no point in referring to a "Roman Empire" in the west at all.

For the last few centuries, historians have spent a great deal of thought (and paper) exploring what has come to be known as the "fall" of the Roman Empire that began in the turmoil of the third century. Historians point to dwindling population, economic problems, civil warfare, and moral decay as the causes of the decline. All of these factors con-*Rome's "Fall"* tributed to the transformation of the old Roman world, but perhaps more important than anything else was the great influx of peoples from the north who invaded the empire. These invasions (which we will explore in more detail in Chapter 6) caused the breakup of the huge empire that had dominated the Mediterranean world since the time of Augustus. The territorial empire was ending, but throughout these years of power and turmoil a religion arose that would give a new source of unity to the Mediterranean world.

The Longing for Religious Fulfillment

As we saw in Chapter 4, the Romans were a deeply religious people who carefully linked their deities to cherished spaces. As the empire controlled more and more land, its subjects seemed increasingly distanced from their traditional gods. In part, worship of the emperor served as a unifying religious cult. By the middle of the third century, some 20 festival days honored deified emperors or their families each year. However, for all the reverence given to the emperors, a spiritual dissatisfaction still gnawed at the Roman people. Many Romans seemed to long for a closer relationship to a truly transcendent divinity, and Romans expressed this longing through a rise in various philosophic and religious movements.

We can see this attempt to bring the gods a little closer to earth in the increasing numbers of spells and charms that Roman men and women purchased. People tried everything from healing and love charms to curses placed on chariot racers. Prophets, magicians, and charlatans also proliferated. One late-second-century writer described a man who made a fortune by pretending to

FIGURE 5.10
Mosaic of a North African *latifundium.*

prophesy through a giant serpent that he wrapped around himself. However, all the religious movements of the Roman world were not as superficial as magical curses and false prophets.

STOICISM AND PLATONISM

The Hellenistic philosophies (Chapter 3) all continued to offer religious satisfaction to some educated Romans. The great Roman Stoic Seneca (4? B.C.–A.D. 65) wrote that by focusing on their own ethical behavior, people could locate the divinity that dwells within each person. As mentioned earlier, the Stoic emperor Marcus Aurelius used this philosophy to bring meaning to the challenges of his life. Like the reflective emperor, many people found in Stoicism ethical principles to help guide their lives, and Stoicism exerted an important influence on both Christianity and Western ideas in general.

The most influential philosophical system, however, came with a new form of Platonism that *Neo-Platonism* emerged during the late empire. In the third century, these neo-Platonists created a complex system that offered an explanation for the link between the divine and the human. Like Stoics, Platonists believed that each person contained a spark of divinity that longed to join the divinity that had created it. Through study, contemplation, and proper living, people could cultivate that bit of divinity within themselves and thereby reduce the distance between the human and the divine.

These philosophies, though intriguing, had limited appeal. Just as in the earlier Hellenistic kingdoms, they attracted people with leisure, education, and a respectable income. Most people instead tried to satisfy their spiritual desires through one or more of the mystery cults that gained popularity in the second century.

MYSTERY CULTS

The mystery cults that had become popular during the Hellenistic world (Chapter 3) had an even stronger appeal in the difficult times of the late empire. These cults had always offered hope to individuals seeking meaning in their lives and ecstatic celebrations that seemed to transport individuals outside themselves into the world of the gods. Some cults claimed to offer a universality lacking in many of the Roman deities, and many offered hopes of a better afterlife to people disenchanted with their current existence.

The ancient Greek cult of Dionysus is one example of a cult that promised all these things. In this popular worship, men and women cel- *Cult of Dionysus* ebrated the mysteries of the god of wine and rebirth by drinking, engaging in sex acts, and ritually eating the raw flesh of beasts. Figure 5.11 shows a painting discovered in Pompeii that probably depicts the worship of Dionysus. The young woman on the left is being whipped, probably to bring about an ecstatic state. The woman on the right dances in naked ecstasy with a cymbal while the woman before her prepares to hand her the staff marking her entrance into the mysteries. Such ceremonies appealed to people's need to feel personally connected with the divine.

The cult of Isis, the Egyptian goddess of fertility, enjoyed remarkable popularity throughout the empire. Septimius Severus and his wife por- *Cult of Isis* trayed themselves as Isis and her consort Serapis. As we saw in Chapter 1, the ancient Egyptians called Isis' husband "Osiris," but in the Hellenistic period, when many of the Egyptian deities were assimilated into the Greek pantheon, Osiris began to be called "Serapis." As the noted Greek biographer Plutarch (A.D. 46?–120?) explained, "Serapis received this name at the time when he changed his nature. For this reason Serapis is a god of all peoples in common." In his new form as Serapis, the old god Osiris left his traditional home of the Nile and brought protection to wide areas of the empire. Thus, Serapis was an appropriate incarnation for Septimius, a North African emperor who wanted to combine imperial worship with that of a popular mystery religion to try to overcome Rome's lack of a single, unifying religion.

While some cults, like that of Serapis, strove for universal appeal, the worship of other deities was not intended to be for everyone. Instead, initiates prided themselves on participating in an exclusive and difficult worship. For example, some men and women celebrated the mystery of the Great Mother, the female goddess who brought fertility and comfort. In these frenzied rituals, celebrants flogged themselves until their blood flowed, and some men castrated themselves as an ultimate sacrifice to the goddess. In another example, imperial soldiers felt particularly

FIGURE 5.11
Introduction into the mysteries, ca. mid-first century B.C.

drawn to the mysteries of Mithraism, whose followers were exclusively men, and the religion's emphasis on self-discipline and courage made it very popular with the armies of Rome. These soldiers gathered in special buildings, ritualistically ate bread and water, and awaited salvation.

These different mysteries practiced throughout the Roman world reflected the multicultural nature of the empire. People were willing to partake in mysteries of any origin, whether Egyptian, Syrian, or Persian. All these practices emphasized the irrational at the expense of the rational, in contrast to the Stoic or Platonist approaches. But in the ancient world,

people did not feel compelled to choose only one path to spiritual fulfillment. The famous second-century author Apuleius, for example, was a magician, a Platonist, and an initiate into the mysteries of Isis.

THE FOUR FACES OF JUDAISM

Although Palestine had struggled for religious purity while under the Hellenistic kings, the Jews under Roman rule were not exempt from the religious angst that swept the empire. At the time of Julius Caesar, the kingdom of Judah had been ruled by descendants of Judas Maccabees (see Chapter 3), but the kingdom was swept into the turmoil of Rome's civil wars following the death of Julius Caesar. Finally, Herod, a member of a prominent family in Hebron, south of Jerusalem, rose to power, and with the support of Octavian, the Senate of Rome made him king of Judea and subject to Rome. Map 5.5 shows the kingdom of Herod and illustrates its central location in the trade of the Middle East. Herod was unpopular with the Jews, and during this kingdom, controversies grew. The struggles of four main Jewish groups shaped the religious and political future of this region and beyond.

The Sadducees largely comprised members of priestly families. They emphasized Jewish worship at the Temple in Jerusalem, which they saw as the cult center of the Israelites. (In Chapter 3 we saw that the Temple had been rebuilt in the sixth century B.C., and this structure—which had been further rebuilt in 19 B.C.—is known as the "Second Temple.") The Sadducees were religious conservatives who rejected any "new" ideas

Sadducees and Pharisees that they did not find in the Torah—the first five books of the Bible. These innovations included the ideas of angels and resurrection of the dead, both of which began to win more adherents. The Sadducees were also willing to compromise with the Hellenized world and the Roman rulers as long as the Temple cult remained secure. However, the Sadducees would not continue as a viable force after Titus destroyed the Temple in A.D. 70.

The Pharisees, on the other hand, emphasized Jewish purity laws. They refused all compromise with the Hellenized world and adhered strictly to dietary rules and rituals to reinforce their separateness from all non-Jews.

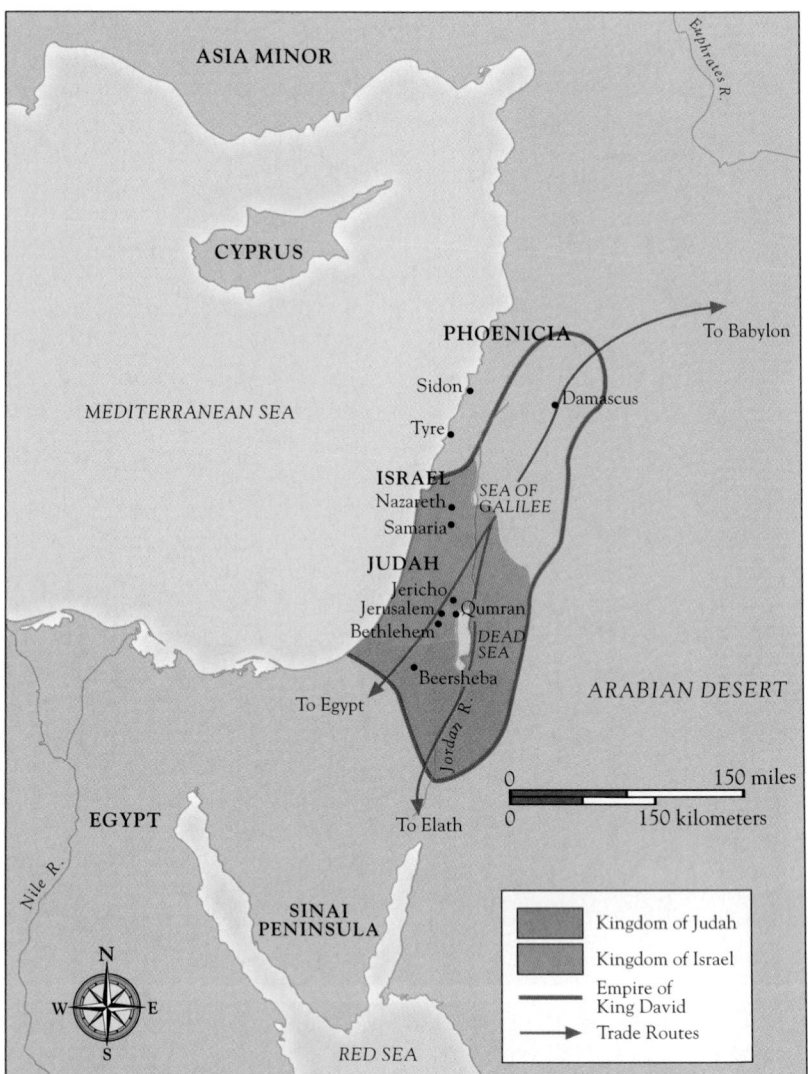

THINKING ABOUT GEOGRAPHY

MAP 5.5 *Israel at the Time of Jesus*

This map shows the kingdom of Herod under the rule of Rome. It also shows how this kingdom reunited Judah and Israel, which previously had been separated. ❧ **Notice** the arrows that denote the trade routes to the major regions in the eastern Mediterranean. **Consider** the diverse influences Judaism might have been exposed to by the many travelers that passed through the small kingdom. ❧ **Locate** the major sites of Jesus' ministry. **Notice** the distances involved. **Compare** this scale with the large distances shown in Map 5.6.

However, the Pharisees did accept new ideas of the resurrection of the just and the existence of angels. For Pharisees, Judaism did not center on public worship in the Temple, but on the private observances of Jews all over the Roman world. The Pharisees also supported sayings and interpretations of Jewish scholars, such as the influential Hillel the Elder (30? B.C.–A.D. 10?), that later became part of the Jewish tradition. It was the work of the Pharisees that would ultimately lead to the expanded writings that updated the practice of the Torah.

Although the Pharisees believed strongly in separating themselves from the surrounding non-Jewish world, they avoided political revolution. Another group in Palestine, the Zealots, took a different approach. This group looked back to the successful revolt of the Maccabees against Seleucid rule and urged political revolt against Roman rule as a way to restore Israel to an independent state. Not surprisingly, clashes between the Zealots and Roman troops broke out throughout the early first century A.D.

Despite their differences, all these groups were struggling in some way with the same question that *Essenes* had plagued Jews since the first Hellenistic conquest: how to maintain a separate identity within the Roman world. The fourth group, the Essenes, tried to avoid the problem altogether by withdrawing from the social world. The Essenes moved to separate communities and attempted to live pure lives, seemingly alienating themselves from the Temple cult. The Essenes have drawn much scholarly attention because they probably authored one of the most exciting archaeological finds in biblical history, the Dead Sea Scrolls.

In 1947, a shepherd boy discovered a deep cave containing ancient pottery jars holding hundreds of scrolls of texts dating from as early as 250 B.C. The scrolls include such valuable works as the oldest version of portions of the Hebrew Bible and other documents revealing the historical context of the biblical texts. Most of the works are severely damaged and have been reconstructed from hundreds of tiny fragments, which leaves lots of room for differing interpretations. Although many of the texts have been studied since the 1950s, there is still no scholarly consensus surrounding these precious scrolls.

Most scholars believe these texts were produced by the Essenes in their mountain retreat in Qumran (see Map 5.5)—a desert community fifteen miles from Jerusalem, near the Dead Sea—and hidden in the cave during the turbulent times when Rome was exerting its dominance in the region. All the writings were completed before A.D. 68, when the Romans destroyed the settlement at Qumran. Some scholars believe the writings came from a large library of various Hebrew documents, and thus they may reveal the origins of the many strains of Judaism, perhaps even the early Jesus movement. It is certain that continued analysis of these texts will shed a good deal of light on these early centuries that were so fertile to spiritual impulses.

In this time of spiritual longing, many Jews believed that a savior—a Messiah—would come to liberate them. Some believed that he would *The Messiah* be a political figure who would liberate the Jews from foreign domination, and people like the Zealots were poised to fight for this political leader. Others, however, expected a spiritual savior—a Chosen One who would bring a kingdom of righteousness to earth. The Essenes may have withdrawn to the desert community to wait for the spiritual Messiah—their "Teacher of Righteousness." It was into this volatile religious time that Jesus of Nazareth was born.

THE JESUS MOVEMENT

During the reign of Augustus (r. 27 B.C.–A.D. 14) at the beginning of the empire, a child named Jesus was born in about 4 B.C., possibly in Bethlehem (about 10 miles southeast of Jerusalem, shown on the Map 5.5). This event dramatically influenced the empire by the fourth century. Thus, we must return to the time of Augustus to trace the fortunes of a small religious sect in Judea that would ultimately conquer Rome itself.

The information we have on Jesus' life and teachings is drawn largely from the Gospels of the New Testament of the Bible, which were written some time after his death by people who never knew him. (Estimates on the time of the composition of the Gospels range from 30 to 90 years after Jesus' death.) The Gospels offer little information about the first 30 years of Jesus' life. They do tell us that he was the son of a woman named Mary and a carpenter named Joseph and that he excelled in his religious studies, for he confounded the priests of the Temple with his knowledge of matters of faith.

According to the limited historical information available, Jesus drew from the rich religious environment in the Jewish lands. Like the Pharisees, he appealed to the poor, and many of his sayings resembled those of Hillel the Elder. His teachings also had some qualities in common with the Essenes, who had written of a coming "Teacher of Righteousness." Unlike the Zealots, Jesus spoke of a heavenly kingdom rather than a violent revolution and attracted a large following of those who longed for a better life. Jesus began his ministry after being baptized by John the Baptist, and the Gospels tell the story of his activities after this defining event in some detail. For many, Jesus was the awaited Messiah who would save and transform the world. Many called him "Christ"—the Lord's Anointed, the Messiah.

Jesus' ideas

While Jesus' ideas resembled those of some of his contemporaries, the totality of his message was strikingly new and changed the course of Western civilization. For about three years, Jesus preached in Judea and Galilee, drawing huge crowds to listen to his message of peace, love, and care for the poor and suffering. He was accompanied by a small group of devoted followers—the apostles—who carried on his message after his death. Many people also believed that he performed miracles and cures. His growing popularity alarmed both Jewish leaders and Roman authorities, who constantly watched for uprisings in Judea. In about A.D. 29, the Roman governor, Pontius Pilate, sentenced Jesus to crucifixion, the cruel death reserved for many of Rome's enemies. The Romans nailed a sign on Jesus' cross identifying him as the "king of the Jews," perhaps mistranslating the powerful notion of Messiah as "king," and certainly underestimating the nature and appeal of Jesus and his message.

Jesus' brief, three-year ministry had come to an end. However, three days later, Jesus' followers believed they saw him risen from the dead and subsequently taken into heaven. They believed this proof of Jesus' divinity promised a resurrection for his followers, and the apostles wanted to spread this good news to other Jews.

A small group of Jesus' followers led by the apostles Peter and James formed another Jewish sect that modern historians call the "Jesus movement" to identify the period when followers of Jesus continued to identify themselves as Jews. The apostles appealed to other Jews by preaching and praying at the Temple and at small gatherings of the Jewish faithful. The earliest history of this Jesus movement is

Apostles

recorded in Acts in what Christians call the New Testament of the Bible. Like others throughout the Roman world, these Jews believed that prophecy and miracles marked the presence of the divine. Thus, the apostles, the followers who had known Jesus personally, began traveling to bring his message to others. They spoke in prophetic tongues and appeared to work miracles. They also began preaching in Jewish communities around the Mediterranean world.

The early Jesus movement could have taken various different directions. Would Jesus' followers withdraw from society like the Essenes and John the Baptist had done? The apostle James moved to Jerusalem and centered his leadership of the church there, thus choosing not to lead a sect in the wilderness. A more thorny issue was the question of accepting Gentiles—non-Jews—into the new religion. James took a position of conservative Judaism, insisting that Christianity required its adherents to follow the circumcision and strict dietary laws that had marked the people of Yahweh. The apostle Peter seems to have been more willing to preach to Gentiles, particularly "God-fearing" Greeks who were interested in the ethical monotheism of the Jews. Peter believed they would not have to be circumcised nor keep all the Jewish festivals, but they would have to follow the dietary restrictions.

However, the man who would be remembered as the "Apostle to the Gentiles" had not known Jesus before his crucifixion. Saul of Tarsus A.D. 5?–64?), whom we remember by the name of Paul, was a Hellenized Jew and a Roman citizen who had at first harassed Christians. After he experienced a vision of the risen Jesus, he converted and took up the mission of bringing the Christian message beyond the particularity of the Jewish communities to the wider world of the Roman Empire and beyond. He moved beyond Peter by eliminating all dietary restrictions on Christians, and he traveled widely through the eastern portion of the empire establishing new Christian communities. Map 5.6 shows where Paul journeyed and how the Christian message slowly spread throughout the Roman world. Paul's influence on the young church was immense, and his letters became part of the Christian Scriptures.

Paul of Tarsus

Religious tensions between Jews and Roman authorities in Palestine culminated shortly after the deaths of Peter and Paul. Rome finally decided to take strong action against those in Judea, including Zealots, who were rebelling against Roman rule. In the course

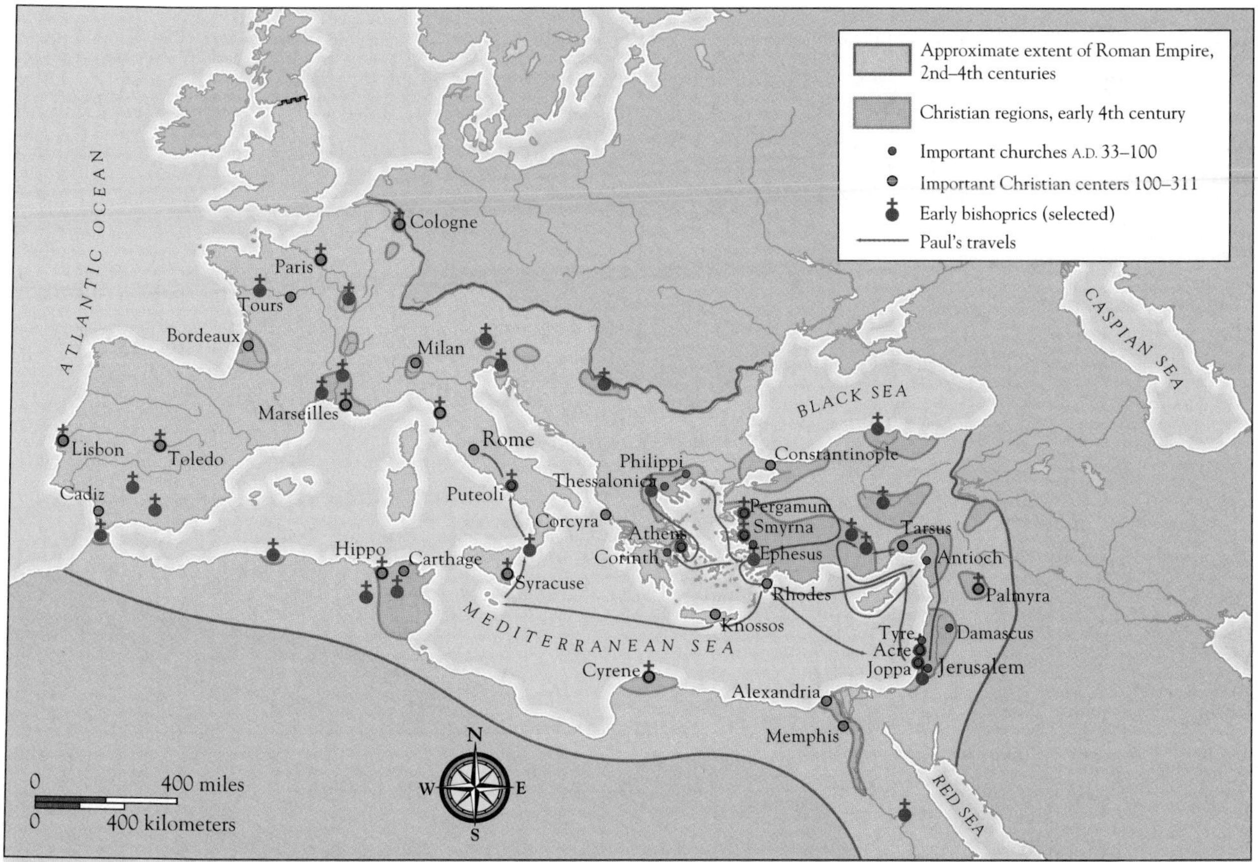
Approximate extent of Roman Empire, 2nd–4th centuries
Christian regions, early 4th century
Important churches A.D. 33–100
Important Christian centers 100–311
Early bishoprics (selected)
Paul's travels
ATLANTIC OCEAN
CASPIAN SEA
BLACK SEA
MEDITERRANEAN SEA
RED SEA
Cologne
Paris
Tours
Bordeaux
Milan
Marseilles
Lisbon
Toledo
Cadiz
Rome
Puteoli
Philippi
Thessalonica
Constantinople
Pergamum
Smyrna
Ephesus
Tarsus
Antioch
Palmyra
Corcyra
Athens
Corinth
Hippo
Carthage
Syracuse
Rhodes
Knossos
Tyre
Acre
Damascus
Joppa
Jerusalem
Cyrene
Alexandria
Memphis
400 miles
400 kilometers
N
W
E
S

THINKING ABOUT GEOGRAPHY

MAP 5.6 *The Spread of Christianity to A.D. 311*

This map shows the areas of Christian strength by the fourth century, and also traces Paul's journeys as he conducted his missionary work. **Notice** the areas of greatest Christian concentration. **How** influential will Greek and eastern thought be for the future development of the church? **Notice also** how important North Africa was for the development of Christian ideas. **Notice** that many of the Christian spaces coincide with regions of commerce. **Why** would that be so? **Notice also** that Christianity spread mostly within the borders of the empire. **Why** was that so?

Destruction of the Temple

of the suppression, the Essene community at Qumran was destroyed (but not before they had buried their precious scrolls, which we call the Dead Sea Scrolls), and then the armies proceeded against Jerusalem. In A.D. 70, the son of Emperor Vespasian, Titus (who later became emperor in his own right), led Roman legions into Jerusalem, burned the city, and destroyed the Second Temple. (See Document 5.4 on page D5.3)

Titus returned to Rome in a triumphal procession and built a great arch celebrating his accomplishment. Figure 5.12 shows a marble relief from that arch. In the relief, Titus's troops return victorious from Jerusalem clutching spoils from the Temple. This figure shows soldiers carrying an important symbol of Judaism, the great menorah—a candelabra that held seven candles—that had been sacked from the holy place. The Temple was never rebuilt. Many Jews

FIGURE 5.12
Menorah procession on the Arch of Titus, ca. A.D. 81.

were scattered from Judea all over the Mediterranean after this devastation, and with them traveled numerous followers of the Jesus movement.

The destruction of the Temple inadvertently resolved the tensions within Judaism. The Sadducees, Essenes, and Zealots were all destroyed, and the Phar-

Dispersion of Jews
isees made peace with the Romans and recentered Judaism on synagogue worship. An emphasis on prayer and the law replaced sacrifices at the Temple. After A.D. 70, the Hebrew canon of Scriptures came to be closed and the Hebrew Bible—what the Christians would call the Old Testament—was completed. Followers of the great teacher Hillel reached a compromise with the authority of Rome that let Jews maintain an identity within the empire, and future rabbis would study scripture and interpret the ways Jews should act while living among Gentiles.

The conquest of Jerusalem also settled any question about whether Christianity was to be centered in Jerusalem. Early Christianity, like Diaspora Judaism, was to be a religion that was not bound to one city,

and it began to claim universality. The Jesus movement within Judaism was transformed and was now more accurately called the early Christian church.

EARLY CHRISTIAN COMMUNITIES

The spread of Christianity was slow. Small groups of converts in the major cities of the empire gathered in each other's houses because there were no designated churches for the new movement. When members of the small communities met together at least once a week, people took turns reading Scripture, praying, and offering other forms of worship. As Paul wrote: "When you come together, each one has a hymn, a lesson, a revelation, a tongue, or an interpretation" (1 Cor. 14:26). "Tongues and interpretations" refers to speaking prophetically, which people in the communities believed proved the presence of God in their midst. The culmination of the service was the Eucharist—the commemoration of Jesus' last supper—in which the faithful shared cups of wine and pieces of bread. Members then offered prayers of thanksgiving for Christ's sacrifice and death, which the faithful believed offered them salvation and eternal life.

The relatively small numbers of Christians grew consistently throughout the first few centuries after the death of Jesus. Some estimates suggest that the total number of Christians at the beginning of the third century A.D. was about 200,000, or less than 0.5 percent of the total population. Although this is a small percentage, the actual number is significant—Christians were slowly becoming more visible. The church father Tertullian (A.D. 160?–217?) wrote that there were "thousands" of Christians in Carthage in about A.D. 200, and he was probably accurate—a few thousand Christians in a population of about 500,000. This small but growing number would periodically come in conflict with the power of Rome.

From Christian Persecution to the City of God, A.D. 64–410

Conservative Romans looked askance at any innovations, particularly religious novelties. It was one thing for Christians to worship someone who had died within living memory as a divinity, but it was quite another for them to reject the traditional Roman assortment of gods. Furthermore, outrageous rumors circulated about Christian rituals. One third-century Roman described the accusations against Christians: They gathered together with "the lowest dregs of society and credulous women," and engaged in incest, cannibalism, and orgies after indulging in shocking "love feasts." Such rumors came from misunderstandings of communion meals in which Christians commemorated Jesus' sacrifice and sealed their fellowship with "kisses of peace." Early Christians seemed to violate the traditional Roman social order by including the poor, slaves, and women as equals in their congregations, but the more shocking charges against them were never demonstrated.

LOOKING FOR CHRISTIAN SCAPEGOATS

To quell accusations that he was responsible for a devastating fire in Rome (described in Document 5.2 on page D5.2), Emperor Nero looked for scapegoats and implemented the first large-scale persecution of Christians in Rome in A.D. 64. He executed hundreds of Roman Christians, possibly including the apostles Peter and Paul, and set a precedent that would be repeated periodically over the next two centuries. During the contentious years, provincial officials played a leading role in the persecutions. Some of these authorities chose to harass Christians; others ignored the new religion. Whatever their policy, however, the texts make it clear that when Christian men and women were brought to the arena, many died so bravely that some Roman spectators promptly converted.

During the third century when the empire confronted many internal and external problems, its policy toward Christians grew harsher. Under Emperor Decius (r. 249–251) and then again under Emperor Diocletian (r. 285–305), all imperial residents were to sacrifice to the emperor and receive a document recording their compliance. Diocletian, the autocratic emperor who legislated wages, prices, and military matters, thought he could decree religious beliefs as well. But this wide-scale demand for conformity only provoked many more Christians to die for their beliefs. Map 5.6 reflects the extent of Christian strength after the persecutions of Diocletian had ended.

CONSTANTINE: THE TOLERANT EMPEROR

In the long tradition of Roman emperors, Constantine looked for supernatural help in his wars with his rivals. According to the Greek historian Eusebius (260?–340?), as Constantine prepared for a crucial battle he saw in the sky a vision of a cross with Greek writing reading, "In this sign, conquer." That night he had a prophetic dream explaining that soldiers would triumph only if they fought under Christian symbols. He obeyed the dream and won a decisive victory. To the Romans, dreams and omens carried crucial religious messages, and Constantine's nighttime message convinced him of the power of the Christian God. In 313 he issued a decree of toleration (the Edict of Milan) for all the religions of the empire, including Christianity, and the martyrdoms ended.

Constantine did more than simply tolerate Christians. He actively supported the church. He returned property to Christians who had been persecuted, gave *Constantine supports church* tax advantages to Christian priests, and let Christian advisors play a role in his court's inner circle. Constantine's support of Christians probably derived in part from his military victory under the sign of the cross. The women in his family exerted a strong influence on him as well. His half-sister Constantia and his mother Helena were both Christians.

Under Constantine's patronage, the Christian movement grew rich and powerful, and the emperor built beautiful churches in support of the religion. Romans had always believed religious cults were linked to geographic spaces, and Constantine was no different. As part of his respect for Christianity, he decided to restore the Holy Places at Jerusalem and Palestine to Christian worship. Helena toured the region to identify the sacred spaces, but this was quite a feat, for since the destruction of the Temple, Jerusalem had become a Roman city that had lost all identification with its Jewish past. Nevertheless, Helena located what she believed were key sites in the life of Jesus, building great churches where he was born and where he died. Christians before Constantine's rule had focused on the afterlife instead of historical places associated with Jesus. With the backing of Constantine and his family, however, Jerusalem was revived as a holy place, and Christians began to make pilgrimages there. These journeys began a tradition of Christian claim on that land that would continue throughout the Middle Ages.

Constantine was finally baptized on his deathbed, but throughout his life he practiced a toleration toward all religions as most Romans from the time of the Republic had done, but he established a relationship between church and state that moved Christianity in a new direction: It would continue to flourish and grow in the shadow of the imperial throne. Subsequent emperors moved from toleration toward sole Christian worship.

THE EMPIRE ADOPTS CHRISTIANITY

Theodosius I (r. 379–395) put the final cap on the movement toward Christianity by forbidding the public worship of the old Roman cults. With this mandate, Christianity became the official religion of the Roman Empire. Of course, everyone did not immediately convert to Christianity; Judaism remained strong, and those who clung to traditional Roman religious beliefs came to be called "pagans." This word came from *pagani,* a derogatory term for backward peasants, and its etymology shows how Christianity spread first from urban centers.

This merging of a political and Christian empire irrevocably changed both Rome and Christianity.

After the fourth century, Christian communities looked very different from those of two centuries earlier. Instead of gathering secretly in each other's homes, Christians met *Christianity changes* publicly in churches that boasted the trappings of astounding wealth. Indeed, where once people converted to Christianity in spite of the danger of persecution, the influential church father Augustine

FIGURE 5.13
Christ as the Good Shepherd, second century.

FIGURE 5.14
Mosaic depicting Christ as the Good Shepherd, ca. A.D. 450.

(354–430) complained that some people now converted only to impress the rich and powerful.

Figures 5.13 and 5.14 illustrate this shift in the status of Christianity. In Figure 5.13 a second-century statue of Christ depicts him as the Good Shepherd. He appears as an unpretentious peasant, wearing the typical shepherd costume of the day. The Good Shepherd was the most popular portrayal of Christ in the early, simple centuries of Christianity. Figure 5.14 shows a very different Good Shepherd. In this fifth-century mosaic, Christ wears the royal purple cloth of emperors. Now the Lord, he watches over his flock rather than working to convert nonbelievers. The gold in the mosaic demonstrates the new wealth of the church, as the image of Christ is transformed from that of a simple man to Lord of the universe.

As the empire embraced Christianity, the organization of the church began to duplicate the civil order of Rome. The emperor Diocletian had clustered provinces into larger units, called dioceses, for ease of administration. The church retained these divisions and placed bishops in charge of the major communi-

Christian organization

ties. Bishops were in charge of all aspects of church life, from finances to spiritual guidance, and as early as the third century in most regions they were paid by a church depending increasingly on their administrative skills. For example, by A.D. 245, the province of North Africa had 90 bishops, and each was served by a well-developed hierarchy of priests and deacons. The ecclesiastical structure of the dioceses was divided into parishes, presided over by priests who reported to the bishops.

With Constantine's support, the church had become powerful. In the political world, power meant the ability to impose a uniformity of practice and even belief. Emperor Constantine tried to guide the church toward this kind of unity, and the church fathers began looking to authority figures to help them resolve differences. Prophecy—so important to the early church—became suspect, replaced by obedience to authority. As leaders began to look to a hierarchical organization for guidance in religious matters, it was perhaps inevitable that questions would arise over who should lead—religious or secular leaders. Ambrose (r. 374–397), the Bishop of Milan in Italy, was one of the earliest bishops to challenge the power of the emperors and set a precedent for later bishops. In 390, Ambrose reprimanded Emperor Theodosius for massacring some rebellious citizens: The bishop excommunicated the emperor, forbidding him to participate in church services until he repented. Theodosius acceded to the bishop's demands, and later bishops of Rome (who came to be called popes) looked to this example of the church leading the state.

In the eastern part of the empire, the relationship between bishops and emperor took a different turn. Beginning with Constantine, emperors in the East had involved themselves directly in religious disputes. Since the early third century, for example, Christians had quarreled over the nature of Christ.

Religious disagreements "Had he always existed," they asked themselves, "or did God bring him forth at a particular time?" In about 320, Arius, bishop of Alexandria, raised a furor when he argued that Jesus had been created by God. Arius's teachings polarized believers all over the empire, and Constantine did not want such a dispute raging in his lands. Therefore, he called a meeting that was the first "ecumenical" council—purportedly with representatives of the whole inhabited world. In 325, Constantine vigorously presided over the bishops he had summoned to the Council of Nicaea to resolve Arius's dispute over the nature of Christ. With the formulation of the Nicene Creed, which stated that Christ had always existed, Constantine and his bishops hoped to put that controversy to rest. However, as we shall see in Chapter 6, Arius's beliefs had already spread, and the church would have to face the problem of Arianism again. The council also set the precedent that orthodox Christians could exert their authority over those who believed otherwise.

Similarly in North Africa, Christians split over what to do about bishops and others who had "lapsed" during the years of persecution. This controversy was called the "Donatist" heresy, named after one of the protesting bishops. Church leaders believed it was essential to protect the notion that sacraments—like baptism and the Eucharist—were valid regardless of the behavior of the presiding priest, so they declared that bishops who had proven weak when threatened by torture could continue to hold their offices. The Donatists disagreed saying that lapsed priests could *not* conduct the sacraments. Yet, passions had run so high over this issue that Donatists separated and tried to start a new church. The dispute catalyzed much violence in North Africa for centuries until the barbarian invasions created enough turmoil to move this issue to the background.

These and many other religious quarrels that spilled into secular politics raised the question of the relationship between church and state. In the early church, the relationship had been simple— *City of God* Christianity focused on the next world while enduring an antagonistic earthly relationship with an unsympathetic state. Now, with church and state combined, the situation had become exceedingly complex. Many Christians felt ill at ease with all the resulting uncertainty. In his influential work *City of God* (413–427), Augustine tried to address these very complexities. Writing after the Visigoths had sacked Rome and terrified Romans had fled the city in waves, he explained that Christians should not look at the current disasters with despair, nor see in them divine punishment. Instead, the church father drew from his strong background in neo-Platonism to explain worldly pain much as Plato had (described in Chapter 2), but with a Christian understanding. Augustine claimed that the world—and worldly cities—were made up of individuals who were constantly in struggle between their spiritual and earthly selves. Those people in whom the spiritual dominated belonged to a "City of God," and those in whom the earthly dominated belonged to an earthly city. The perfect community of the faithful—the "City of God"—could exist only outside this world and would dominate at the end of time. In the meantime, all communities were mixed with members of both cities. Therefore, people ought to obey the political order and focus on the worthiness of their own souls rather than the purity of the reigning political institutions. They need not worry even when the city of Rome was sacked.

For Augustine and other religious thinkers, church and state were not incompatible. In fact, these men believed that the state should play an active role in ensuring the health of the church. In the early centuries of Christianity, heresy (expressing opinions that differed from official church doctrine) could be considered treason punishable by civil sanctions. Augustine, for example, suggested confiscating the property of the Donatists to persuade them to conform. However, in the late fourth century, a Christian heretic (Priscillian) was sentenced to death. As the ultimate power of the empire was brought to issues of conscience in these ways, church members learned that the path to salvation lay in obedience. Inevitably, there were Christians who objected to this direction, but the majority saw in this Christian order a fulfillment of God's plan—a victory for the earthly church.

THE NEW ROMAN

Like political institutions and the church itself, everyday Roman life was also transformed with the burgeoning strength of Christianity. As church fathers in many regions of the empire wrote on matters of religion, they also addressed the larger question of how the new Christian Roman was to behave. In some areas of life it was easy simply to prohibit certain behaviors. For example, the church fathers wrote that Christians should not attend gladiator shows nor arena games. Over time, the great amphitheaters fell out of use. Instead, Christian Romans satisfied their appetite for spectacle with chariot races, which remained hugely popular for centuries. In other areas, religious leaders and the populace reached a compromise—Christians could read the beloved traditional literature, such as Virgil or Homer (even though it praised pagan gods and suspect morality), but they were to try to extract a Christian message from it. (This is a major reason why such literature has survived.)

Christians also reshaped the social fabric of Roman life. For example, they did not believe in exposing unwanted children. Indeed, through the early centuries, they actively rescued foundling infants and raised them as Christian. Furthermore, they placed enormous priority on caring for the poor and needy. By the middle of the third century, church records show that in Rome alone the bishop provided charity for more than 1,500 widows and others in need.

Views on sexuality also shifted with the influence of the church fathers. As we have seen, although the Romans showed a certain cautiousness in their sexual *Christian sexuality* lives, they also passionately believed that people had a duty to marry and procreate. Some Christian leaders, on the contrary, strongly advocated celibacy as the ideal life. Numerous Roman men complied with this recommendation, and many women used Christian celibacy as a way to free themselves from the expectations that they would marry and bear children. The influential church father Jerome (348?–420) surrounded himself with chaste women who studied and traveled with him and founded monasteries. The Biography featuring Melania the Younger tells of one such fourth-century woman who was famous and admired during her lifetime and who spent her vast wealth establishing enduring religious institutions.

The most influential writer on sexuality was Augustine. In his widely read work *The Confessions*, he described his inability to give up his mistress and his "habit" of lust. As he explained, only with God's help was he able to summon the resolve to renounce these vices. This experience convinced Augustine that human beings were born with original sin and that this sin was passed to subsequent generations through semen during sexual intercourse. Because of original sin, Augustine concluded, people had to keep constant vigil against the force of lust—even marital intercourse was somewhat suspect. The church father urged people to avoid things that might inspire too much lust—for example, birth-control methods and some sexual positions. Through this kind of thinking, religious leaders involved themselves in people's private lives, and this watchfulness continued for centuries through a growing body of church law. Hardly any aspect of Roman life was left untouched by the Christianization of the empire.

The Holy Life

For early Christians, the path to God came through community; congregations of the faithful gathered together to help each other withstand the pressure of a hostile society. By the fourth century, some Christians chose another path to spiritual perfection. Men and women by the thousands left society to

Biography

MELANIA THE YOUNGER (385–439?)

Consider how Melania's life reveals both the old Roman values of family and wealth and the new Christian respect for chastity and poverty.

Melania was born in A.D. 385, the daughter of a rich Roman patrician. By the time of her birth, Christianity was the official religion of the empire, and as a young girl she experienced the conflict of values that confronted so many Christian Roman families. Starting in her youth, Melania longed to follow a life of ascetic chastity like that of earlier holy women. As a daughter of Rome, however, she was expected to marry and bear children. As was the custom in a society in which women married young, when Melania was 14 years old her family arranged for her to marry Pinian.

The young bride begged her new husband to live chastely with her so they could better worship God. Pinian wanted first to ensure the worldly succession of his family, so he told Melania she must bear two children before he would consider her request. A daughter was born to the young couple. Melania became pregnant again, but during this pregnancy she practiced many austerities in her search for a holy life. For example, she repeatedly prayed on her knees all night against the advice of her physician and the pleas of her mother. Furthermore, as a symbol of her commitment, she began to wear rough wool under the smooth silk clothing of the upper class. It is ironic that this return to republican simplicity was seen as rebellion by her family.

Melania's father tried to exert his paternal authority and make her care for herself and her unborn child in the traditional ways, but Christian beliefs and introduced competing loyalties into family life. The young woman disobeyed her father, and her son was born prematurely. The infant boy died shortly after being baptized. Melania's and Pinian's daughter died soon after that. Like so many Roman families, this young couple was unable to produce heirs. They saw the will of God in their children's deaths, however, and at age 20, Melania persuaded Pinian to join her in a vow of chastity.

As her first demonstration of religious commitment, she sought to liquidate her property. Her biographer's description of the problems involved in this task suggest the scale of wealth that many imperial Roman families had accumulated. For example, Melania owned thousands of slaves that she could not free without contributing adversely to Rome's unemployment problem. Furthermore, her house was so expensive even the emperor could not afford to buy it. However, the turmoil of the times helped resolve the difficulties of disposing of her property. The Visigoths who sacked Rome burned Melania's home, and she was able to sell the ruined property easily. As she and Pinian fled to Africa in the wake of the invasion, Melania used her money to ransom captives and buy islands for fellow ascetics to use as holy retreats.

After liquidating most of her wealth, Melania escalated her personal renunciations. She began to fast regularly, eating only some moldy bread twice a week. Beyond that, she spent her days reading and writing. She knew both Latin and Greek and studied the

A Model of Holiness

scriptures and the writings of church leaders. As her reputation for holiness grew, people began to come to her to listen to her teach.

Melania and Pinian then traveled from North Africa to Jerusalem to tour the holy places that Constantine had identified. From there, they visited the holy men and women living in the deserts of Egypt. Finally, Melania decided to found monasteries in Jerusalem, where she and Pinian could embark on a communal life dedicated to spirituality. Joined by 90 virgins and some reformed prostitutes, Melania spent the rest of her life studying, teaching and traveling to holy sites. Shortly after her death, the faithful began to venerate her burial place where miracles reputedly took place.

Melania's life exemplifies the Roman world transformed. She began as a well-off young girl, wearing silk and expecting to carry on the traditions of an upper-class Roman. After the disastrous barbarian invasions, she settled in the holy land, wearing rough wool and embodying the new values of the Christian world.

live alone in the deserts of Egypt and Syria, and their experiences profoundly influenced Christian life and thought.

Some Christians fled into the desert to escape the persecutions and chaos of the mid-third century. *Flight to the desert* Others left during the fourth and fifth centuries because they objected to the union of church and state that developed after Constantine's rule. Still others fled the tax collectors. Whatever the reasons, the popularity of this movement reached enormous proportions. Historians estimate that by 325, as many as 5,000 men and women lived as hermits along the banks of the Nile, each in his or her own small cell. The fame of these holy people spread. Jerome advocated an ascetic life even for urban people and persuaded numerous wealthy Roman women to join him. Romans were scandalized when one of Jerome's young charges starved herself to death in her zeal for asceticism, but such was the passion for what many perceived was a holy life.

Many of these holy men and women survived extraordinary feats of self-denial—enduring lack of food, sleep, and other basic necessities. Some people insisted on living for decades on platforms perched high on poles. Women in particular sealed themselves into tombs that had only a tiny opening through which they could receive a small loaf of bread, and they eked out their lives in cramped, filthy solitude. These people's contemporaries found their behaviors so unusual that they concluded that to endure such hardships, the holy men and women must be recipients of God's power.

Of course, the extreme deprivation of heroic abstinence was not for everyone. Some people wanted simply to withdraw from the distractions of the world so as to worship God without enduring the rigors of *Monastic communities* the desert hermits. Communal monasticism developed as a parallel movement to the hermits and offered an appealing alternative to life in the thick of Roman society. Discipline was strict in these pious oases, but participants had contact with other people, and conditions were not as harsh as those in the desert. Not everyone who seeks God is suited to a harsh life alone in a cell, and communal monasticism provided a palatable alternative. In time, communal monasteries were brought into the overall structure of the church. Monks and nuns took vows of obedience to the monastery head (the abbot or abbess), and the monastic leader answered to the local bishop.

THE INFLUENCE OF HOLY PEOPLE

The earliest holy people had been the Christian martyrs. Faithful observers witnessing their brave deaths concluded that God had invested their bodies with the power to withstand torture. People believed that martyrs' remains contained sacred power and saved and venerated their bones, or relics. One woman in North Africa was reprimanded by her bishop for bringing a sacred bone to church and kissing it repeatedly. This kind of veneration strengthened the notion of resurrection of the flesh, in which the tortured flesh itself would receive its reward. Christianity thus became a religion that accepted the body. Believers wanted the holy dead to be buried near them, and by the fourth century, most altars included relics. In a very short time, the faithful and the enterprising began to engage in a brisk trade in relics that would be lucrative and influential throughout the Middle Ages. Historians have uncovered letters in which people solicit relics to help increase the power of their churches, and some of the correspondence is quite poignant. Bishop Braulio in seventh-century Spain responded to one such request, writing that he had many valuable relics, but all the labels had been lost. He could no longer identify the bones, but asked if the correspondent wanted them anyway.

Relics were preserved, treasured, and displayed in reliquaries—containers often covered in precious metals and jewels that displayed the precious bones that lay within. These reli- *Saints' cults* quaries spread all over Europe and became a visible feature of the growing religion. Exquisite jeweled containers were supposed to express both the power of the relic and the incorruptibility of heaven, where people believed the saint dwelled.

The desert fathers and mothers eventually supplanted the martyrs. They, too, seemed to embody holiness physically, and their *Sayings* reinforced the idea that people could not find spirituality without somehow sanctifying the flesh itself. Ironically, these holy people had traveled to the desert to find God and instead discovered their own humanity. They learned about the hunger that could drive one mad and about sexual urges that could relentlessly haunt their dreams. They even discussed nocturnal emissions and reflected on how to overcome boredom. The thinking of these spiritual people gave Christianity a profoundly human touch.

Like the martyrs, many of these holy people became venerated upon their deaths. The cult of saints became *Ascetic influence* a strong part of Christian faith. Just as people believed that martyrs could intercede for them with God, so they felt convinced that prayer to a holy man or woman might also help them attain their desires. Holy men and women who had learned so much about their humanity by transcending it seemed accessible even to the most ordinary of people. Saints gained reputations for doing everything from raising the dead and healing the sick to extending a too-short wooden beam so an overworked carpenter would not have to cut another. The conversion of the northern European countryside was inspired largely by living and dead holy people who had brought God's power down to the community.

The ascetic practices of the monasteries also shaped the lives of everyday Christians. Even for people who did not adhere to the strict rules of the monasteries, the luxuries of the Roman world seemed shameful when compared with the purity of the monasteries. Over time, people concluded that the ideal Christian life should be simple, and some Christians looked with disdain at those who surrounded themselves with comfort and pleasure. This tendency of monastic rigor to influence Christian life continued throughout the Middle Ages.

Monasteries always served as both havens during stormy political times and as outlets for those who sought a highly spiritual life. For centuries, these communities rejuvenated the Christian world and helped the church meet people's changing spiritual needs. Men and women in search of personal spiritual perfection would ultimately become powerful social forces for the medieval world.

The conservative Romans who mourned the death of Julius Caesar and celebrated the victory of his young nephew Octavian (Augustus) would hardly have recognized the world of Augustine or of the late-fourth-century emperor Theodosius. The great territorial empire governed 400 years earlier by Augustus and his successors in the name of the Senate and the people of Rome was still impressive. However, it was now a Christian empire ruled from Constantinople by an emperor who governed in the name of God and was advised by bishops.

The huge borders of the "civilized" world were still guarded by Roman legions, but by the fourth century these borders had become porous. The guarding legions more often than not wore the trousers of the Germanic peoples and rode horses instead of marching in the disciplined ranks of the tunic-clad Romans.

Sadly for Rome, the centrifugal forces pulling this radically transformed empire apart would prevail. As we will see in Chapter 6, the Roman Empire eventually split into three parts: Byzantium in the east, the Muslim world in the south, and the Germanic kingdoms in the west. However, the glory and accomplishments of Rome would remain in the West's memory for centuries more and periodically inspire people to try reviving its greatness.

REVIEW, ANALYZE, AND ANTICIPATE

REVIEW THE PREVIOUS CHAPTER

Chapter 4—"Pride in Family and City"—described the rise and fall of the Roman Republic and the way expansion changed Roman life and values.

1. *Review the "twilight of the Republic" that led to the civil wars and the murder of Julius Caesar. How did Augustus avoid the fate of Julius Caesar? What reforms did Augustus make to help the new empire endure?*

2. *Review the strengths and virtues that made the early Roman Republic so successful. Which of those were lost through the fourth-century reforms of Diocletian and Constantine? To what degree did these reforms contribute both to the decline of the empire and to its preservation?*

ANALYZE THIS CHAPTER

Chapter 5—"Territorial and Christian Empires"—continues the story of the Roman Empire as it dominated the Mediterranean region for hundreds of years. The empire survived many crises and in turn was dramatically transformed by Christianity.

1. Consider the economic advantages of the great territorial empire of the Romans. Who benefited most from the Mediterranean trade? Who benefited least? What central weakness did the economy have during the empire?

2. What was the "silk road?" What goods traveled along it and why was it so important to both the Roman and Han empires?

3. Describe the social, cultural, and medical ideas that contributed to Rome's declining population.

4. Review the situation in Judea and the various ideas within Judaism during the time of Jesus. How did the political and cultural environment in Judea affect the growth of Christianity?

5. Review the relationship between the early Christians and the Roman authorities. How did Christianity move from a persecuted sect to the religion of the Roman Empire?

6. The adoption of Christianity by the Roman Empire created profound transformations in both the early Christian church and the empire itself. Review these changes and consider which might have the longest standing impact on the future of Western culture.

ANTICIPATE THE NEXT CHAPTER

Chapter 6—"A World Divided"—looks at the fortunes of various parts of the Roman Empire as it began to disintegrate. Three new cultures will be created as the eastern, western, and southern portions of the Mediterranean basin go their separate ways.

1. Given what you know about the economy and geography of the region, which of the empire's parts—the eastern or western portions—do you think might be the most prosperous and secure in the next centuries? Which do you think will be the most vulnerable? Why?

2. Historians have always looked to the rise and fall of the Roman Empire for lessons that could benefit modern societies. What do you think we can learn from the fate of the empire?

BEYOND THE CLASSROOM

THE Pax Romana, 27 B.C.–A.D. 192

Duncan-Jones, Richard. Money and Government in the Roman Empire. New York, NY: Cambridge University Press, 1994. A detailed essay in economic history that begins to explain the relationship between economics and politics.

LeBohec, Yann. The Imperial Roman Army. New York, NY: Hippocrene Books, 1994. A good description of the all-important Roman military.

LIFE DURING THE PEACE OF ROME

August, Roland. Cruelty and Civilization: The Roman Games. New York: Routledge, 1994. An exciting history of gladiators, chariot racing, and other games that offers an explanation of their appeal and function within society.

Dupont, Florence. Daily Life in Ancient Rome. Oxford: Basil Blackwell, 1993. Offers an informative interpretation that describes and analyzes the everyday experiences of the Romans.

Garnsey, Peter. The Roman Empire: Economy, Society and Culture. Berkeley, CA: University of California Press, 1987. Essays devoted to imperial bureaucracy, economic relations, social classes, and family life.

Jackson, Ralph. Doctors and Diseases in the Roman Empire. Norman, OK: University of Oklahoma Press, 1988. A broad and concise account of classical medicine as it culminated in the Roman Empire.

Weidmann, Thomas. Adults and Children in the Roman Empire. New Haven, CT: Yale University Press, 1989. An interpretative analysis that traces changes in adult attitudes toward childhood.

CRISIS AND TRANSFORMATION, A.D. 192–CA. 400

Barnes, T.D. The New Empire of Diocletian and Constantine. Cambridge, MA: Harvard University Press, 1982. A basic factual framework for a notoriously obscure period of history.

Gamsey, Peter D. Famine and Food Supply in the Graeco-Roman World: Response to Risk and Crisis. New York: Cambridge University Press, 1988. Concerns and responses of both urban and rural dwellers to food crises, actual or anticipated.

Jones, A.H.M. The Later Roman Empire, 284-602, 2 volumes. London: Basil Blackwell, 1964. The most comprehensive classic study on the subject by a master historian.

THE LONGING FOR RELIGIOUS FULFILLMENT

Riches, John. The World of Jesus: First-Century Judaism in Crisis. New York: Cambridge University Press, 1990. An examination of the ways in which Jewish figures and groups of the first century—including Jesus—reacted to the basic social, economic, and political realities of the time.

Turcan, Robert. The Cults of the Roman Empire. Cambridge, MA: Blackwell Publishers, 1996. A sound study of the cults during the Roman period.

Timeline: A Closer Look

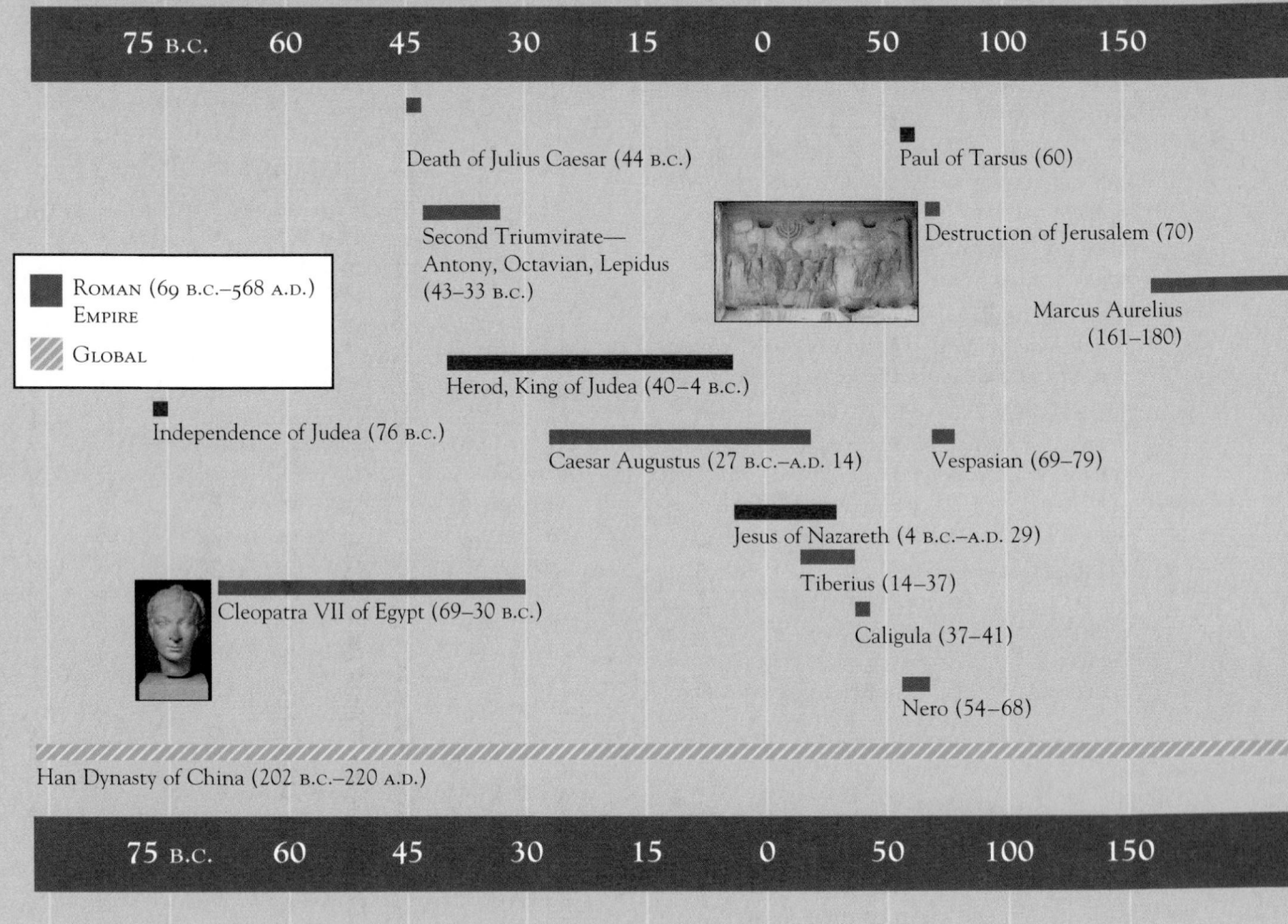

| 75 B.C. | 60 | 45 | 30 | 15 | 0 | 50 | 100 | 150 |

Death of Julius Caesar (44 B.C.)

Paul of Tarsus (60)

Second Triumvirate—
Antony, Octavian, Lepidus
(43–33 B.C.)

Destruction of Jerusalem (70)

ROMAN (69 B.C.–568 A.D.)
EMPIRE
GLOBAL

Marcus Aurelius
(161–180)

Herod, King of Judea (40–4 B.C.)

Independence of Judea (76 B.C.)

Caesar Augustus (27 B.C.–A.D. 14)

Vespasian (69–79)

Jesus of Nazareth (4 B.C.–A.D. 29)

Tiberius (14–37)

Cleopatra VII of Egypt (69–30 B.C.)

Caligula (37–41)

Nero (54–68)

Han Dynasty of China (202 B.C.–220 A.D.)

| 75 B.C. | 60 | 45 | 30 | 15 | 0 | 50 | 100 | 150 |

From Christian Persecution to the City of God, A.D. 64–410

Brown, Peter. *Power and Persuasion in Late Antiquity: Toward a Christian Empire*. Madison: University of Wisconsin Press, 1992. Reopens the question of how the empire's transformation from paganism to Christianity affected its civic culture.

Frend, W.H.C. *The Rise of Christianity*. Philadelphia: Fortress Press, 1984. A comprehensive summary of the growth of Christianity, which includes the major figures and controversies of the movement.

Salisbury, J.E. *The Blood of Martyrs: Unintended Consequences of Ancient Violence*. New York: Routledge, 2004. The ancient Christian martyrdoms transformed many modern western ideas, including images of the body, sacrifice, anti-Semitism,

motherhood, suicide, and others, and this book explores these relationships.

Salisbury, J.E. *Perpetua's Passion: The Death and Memory of a Young Roman Woman*. New York: Routledge, 1997. Describes the cultural, social, and religious environment of early-third-century Carthage as it tells the story of a young martyr.

Stark, Rodney. *The Rise of Christianity: A Sociologist Reconsiders History*. Princeton, NJ: Princeton University Press, 1996. A controversial but influential analysis of how Christianity spread.

The Holy Life

Brown, Peter R.L. *The Body and Society: Men, Women, and Sexual Renunciation in Early Christianity*. New York: Columbia University Press, 1988. A classic study of the

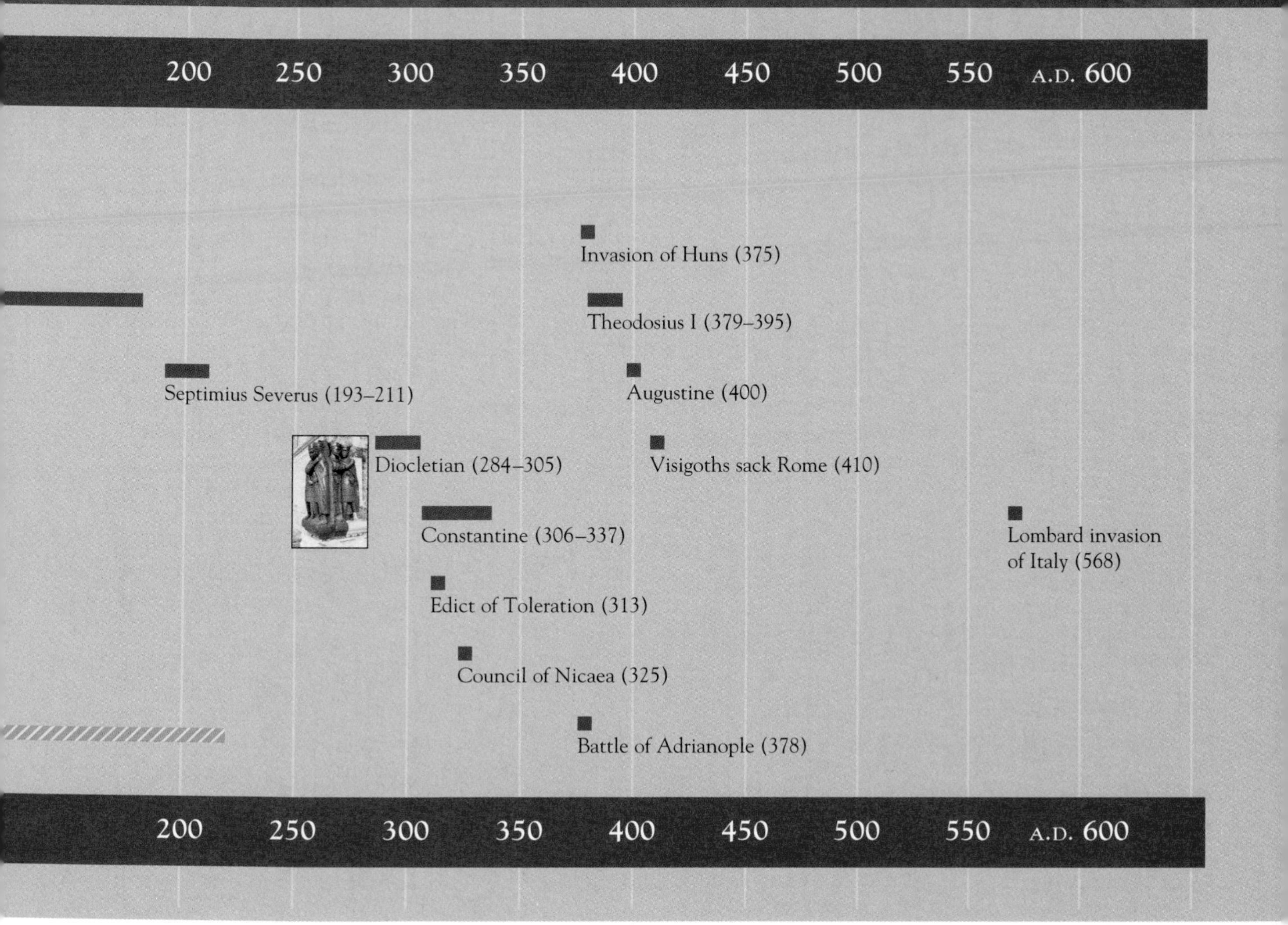

| 200 | 250 | 300 | 350 | 400 | 450 | 500 | 550 | A.D. 600 |

Invasion of Huns (375)

Theodosius I (379–395)

Septimius Severus (193–211)

Augustine (400)

Diocletian (284–305)

Visigoths sack Rome (410)

Constantine (306–337)

Lombard invasion
of Italy (568)

Edict of Toleration (313)

Council of Nicaea (325)

Battle of Adrianople (378)

| 200 | 250 | 300 | 350 | 400 | 450 | 500 | 550 | A.D. 600 |

ascetic movements and their impact by the major scholar of late antiquity.

Bynum, Caroline Walker. *The Resurrection of the Body in Western Christianity, 200-1336*. New York: Columbia University Press, 1995. A fascinating look at the impact of martyrs and saints on ideas of the body and the afterlife.

 GLOBAL CONNECTIONS

Boulnois, Luce. *The Silk Road*. Translated by D. Chamerlain. New York, Dutton, 1966. Easy-to-read and highly accurate account of trade and travel on the important silk route.

Miller, J. Innes. *The Spice Trade of the Roman Empire. 29 B.C. to A.D. 641*. Oxford, Clarendon Press, 1969. Studies the long-distance trade of the empire with great attention to detail and scholarly analysis.

Pratt, Keith L. *Visitors to China: Eyewitness Accounts of Chinese History*. NY: Praeger Publishers, 1970. An older book that remains one of the most engaging and informative short works detailing contacts between westerners and China.

For quiz questions that tie the book to the videos and additional primary sources, please go to the Primary Source Investigator CD.

Documents

DOCUMENT 5.1
Augustus Tallies His Accomplishments

Shortly before he died, Emperor Augustus left a number of state papers with the Vestal Virgins. These documents included an account of his accomplishments, which he wanted inscribed on bronze pillars to be installed in front of Augustus' mausoleum. The document below gives us a glimpse into this early period of the principate, which set the stage for subsequent imperial success. The short excerpts included here reveal the source of Augustus' political power.

■ **Investigate the Document**

Why *was Augustus so popular with the Roman people?* **Which** *offices did he accept and which did he refuse?* **Notice** *the blurring of private and public funds.* **How** *would that blending contribute to Rome's stability and Augustus's office?*

3. I waged many wars throughout the whole world by land and by sea, both civil and foreign, and when victorious I spared all citizens who sought pardon. Foreign peoples who could safely be pardoned I preferred to spare rather than to extirpate. About 500,000 Roman citizens were under military oath to me. Of these, when their terms of service were ended, I settled in colonies or sent back to their own municipalities a little more than 300,000, and to all of these I allotted lands or granted money as rewards for military service. I captured 600 ships, exclusive of those which were of smaller class than triremes.

4. Twice I celebrated ovations, three times curule triumphs, and I was acclaimed *imperator* twenty-nine times. When the senate decreed addition triumphs to me, I declined them on four occasions. . . .

5. The dictatorship offered to me in the consulship of Marcus Marcellus and Lucius Arruntius by the people and by the senate, both in my absence and in my presence, I refused to accept. In the midst of a critical scarcity of grain I did not decline the supervision of the grain supply, which I so administered that within a few days I freed the whole people from imminent panic and danger by my expenditures and efforts. The consulship, too, which was offered to me at that time as an annual office for life, I refused to accept.

6. In the consulship of Marcus Vinicius and Quintus Lucretius, and again in that of Publius Lentulus and Gnaeus Lentulus, and a third time in that of Paullus Fabius Maximus and Quintus Tubero, though the Roman senate and people unitedly agreed that I should be elected sole guardian of the laws and morals with supreme authority, I refused to accept any office offered me which was contrary to the traditions of our ancestors. The measures which the senate desired at that time to be taken by me I carried out by virtue of the tribunician power. In this power I five times voluntarily requested and was given a colleague by the senate. . . .

15. To the Roman plebs I paid 300 sesterces apiece in accordance with the will of my father; and in my fifth consulship I gave each 400 sesterces in my own name out of the spoils of war; and a second time in my tenth consulship I paid out of my own patrimony a largess of 400 sesterces to every individual; in my eleventh consulship I made twelve distributions of food out of grain purchased at my own expense; and in the twelfth year of my tribunician power for the third time I gave 400 sesterces to every individual. These largesses of mine reached never less than 250,000 persons. In the eighteenth year of my tribunician power and my twelfth consulship I gave sixty *denarii* to each of 320,000 persons of the urban plebs. And in my fifth consulship I gave out of the spoils of war 1,000 sesterces apiece to my soldiers settled in colonies. This largess on the occasion of my triumph was received by about 120,000 persons in the colonies. In my thirteenth consulship I gave sixty *denarii* apiece to those of the plebs who at that time were receiving public grain; the number involved was a little more than 200,000 persons. . . .

17. Four times I came to the assistance of the treasury with my own money, transferring to those in charge of the treasury 150,000,000 sesterces. And in the consulship of Marcus Lepidus and Lucius Arruntius I transferred out of my own patrimony 170,000,000 sesterces to the soldiers' bonus fund,

Source: Naphtali Lewis and Meyer Reinhold, *Roman Civilization: Sourcebook II: The Empire*, (NY: Harper Torchbooks, 1966), pp. 10, 11, 14, 16, 19.

which was established on my advice for the purpose of providing bonuses for soldiers who had completed twenty or more years of service. . . .

22. I gave a gladiatorial show three times in my own name, and five times in the names of my sons or grandsons; at these shows about 10,000 fought. Twice I presented to the people in my own name an exhibition of athletes invited from all parts of the world, and a third time in the name of my grandson. I presented games in my own name four times, and in addition twenty-three times in the place of other magistrates. On behalf of the college of fifteen, as master of that college, with Marcus Agrippa as my colleague, I celebrated the Secular Games in the consulship of Gaius Furnius and Gaius Silanus. In my thirteenth consulship I was the first to celebrate the Games of Mars, which subsequently the consuls, in accordance with a decree of the senate and a law, have regularly celebrated in the succeeding years. Twenty-six times I provided for the people, in my own name or in the names of my sons or grandsons, hunting spectacles of African wild beasts in the circus or in the Forum or in the amphitheaters; in these exhibitions about 3,500 animals were killed.

23. I presented to the people an exhibition of a naval battle across the Tiber where the grove of the Caesars now is, having had the site excavated 1,800 feet in length and 1,200 feet in width. In this exhibition thirty beaked ships, triremes or biremes, and in addition a great number of smaller vessels engaged in combat. On board these fleets, exclusive of rowers there were about 3,000 combatants. . . .

34. In my sixth and seventh consulships, after I had put an end to the civil wars, having attained supreme power by universal consent, I transferred the state from my own power to the control of the Roman senate and people. For this service of mine I received the title of Augustus by decree of the senate, and the doorposts of my house were publicly decked with laurels, the civic crown was affixed over my doorway, and a golden shield was set up in the Julian senate house, which, as the inscription on this shield testifies, the Roman senate and people gave me in recognition of my valor, clemency, justice, and devotion. After that time I excelled all in authority, but I possessed no more power than the others who were my colleagues in each magistracy.

35. When I held my thirteenth consulship, the senate, the equestrian order, and the entire Roman people gave me the title of "father of the country" and decreed that this title should be inscribed in the vestibule of my house, in the Julian senate house, and in the Augustan Forum on the pedestal of the chariot which was set up in my honor by decree of the senate. At the time I write this document I was in my seventy-sixth year.

DOCUMENT 5.2

A Great Fire Consumes Rome

In A.D. 64, a raging fire consumed most of the city of Rome. Residents perished or lost their homes, and rumors spread that the emperor Nero had either started the blaze or played music callously while Rome burned. In this account, the Roman historian Tacitus described how Nero persecuted Christians in his search for someone to blame for the disaster.

■ **Investigate the Document**

> **How** did Nero try to appease the Roman people? **Why** did these measures fail? **What** characteristics of Hellenistic cities contributed to their vulnerability to fire?

There followed a dreadful disaster, whether fortuitously or by the wicked contrivance of the prince is not determined, for both are asserted by historians; but of all the calamities which ever befell this city from the rage of fire, this was the most terrible and severe. It broke out in that part of the Circus which is contiguous to mounts Palatine and Cælius, where, by reason of shops in which were kept such goods as minister aliment to fire, the moment it commenced it acquired strength, and being accelerated by the wind, it spread at once through the whole extent of the Circus; for neither were the houses secured by enclosures nor the temples environed with walls, nor was there any other obstacle to intercept its progress; but the flame, spreading every way impetuously, invaded first the lower regions of the city, then mounted to the higher; then again ravaging the lower, it baffled every effort to extinguish it, by the rapidity of its destructive course, and from the liability of the city to conflagration, in consequence of the narrow and intricate alleys, and the irregularity of the streets in ancient Rome.

Source: *The Great Events by Famous Historians*. Edited by Rossiter Johnson. The National Alumni. 1905. Volume III. pp. 128–129.

Add to this the wailings of terrified women, the infirm condition of the aged, and the helplessness of childhood; such as strove to provide for themselves and those who labored to assist others; these dragging the feeble, those waiting for them; some hurrying, others lingering; altogether created a scene of universal confusion and embarrassment; and while they looked back upon the danger in their rear, they often found themselves beset before and on their sides; or, if they had escaped into the quarters adjoining, these, too, were already seized by the devouring flames; even the parts which they believed remote and exempt were found to be in the same distress. At last, not knowing what to shun or where to seek sanctuary, they crowded the streets and lay along in the open fields. Some, from the loss of their whole substance, even the means of their daily sustenance, others, from affection for their relations whom they had not been able to snatch from the flames, suffered themselves to perish in them, though they had opportunity to escape. Neither dared any man offer to check the fire, so repeated were the menaces of many who forbade to extinguish it; and because others openly threw firebrands, with loud declarations "that they had one who authorized them"; whether they did it that they might plunder with the less restraint or in consequence of orders given.

Nero, who was at that juncture sojourning at Antium, did not return to the city till the fire approached that quarter of his house which connected the palace with the gardens of Mæcenas; nor could it, however, be prevented from devouring the house and palace and everything around. But for the relief of the people, thus destitute and driven from their dwellings, he opened the field of Mars and the monumental edifices erected by Agrippa, and even his own gardens. He likewise reared temporary houses for the reception of the forlorn multitude, and from Ostia and the neighboring cities were brought, up the river, household necessaries, and the price of grain was reduced to three sesterces the measure. All which proceedings, though of a popular character, were thrown away, because a rumor had become universally current "that at the very time when the city was in flames, Nero, going on the stage of his private theatre, sang *The Destruction of Troy*, assimilating the present disaster to that catastrophe of ancient times."

DOCUMENT 5.3
Diocletian Becomes "Lord"

By the early fourth century A.D., the public demeanor of emperors had changed dramatically in Rome. Whereas Augustus had cultivated a reputation as the "first citizen," emperors now took pains to present themselves as aloof and godlike. This description by the Roman historian Aurelius Victor traces this transformation.

■ **Investigate the Document**

> **How** did Diocletian present himself to the Roman public? **What** innovations does Aurelius Victor describe? **Did** this historian approve of Diocletian's actions? **Why** do you think the Romans accepted such a kinglike demeanor in Diocletian when they so clearly resented it in Julius Caesar?

By decision of the generals and [military] tribunes, Valerius Diocletian, commander of the palace guards, was chosen emperor because of his wisdom. A mighty man he was, and the following were characteristics of his: he was the first to wear a cloak embroidered in gold and to covet shoes of silk and purple decorated with a great number of gems. Though this went beyond what befitted a citizen and was characteristic of an arrogant and lavish spirit, it was nevertheless of small consequence in comparison with the rest. Indeed, he was the first after Caligula and Domitian to allow himself to be publicly called "lord," and to be named "god," and to be rendered homage as such. . . . But Diocletian's faults were counterbalanced by good qualities; for even if he took the title of "lord," he did act [toward the Romans] as a father.

DOCUMENT 5.4
Titus Destroys Jerusalem

In A.D. 70, the Roman legions led by Titus besieged Jerusalem in their war to control Judea. Josephus was a Jew who first opposed the Romans in the war and then joined Rome. He later wrote all the events of the war in a history that is a vital source for this period. In this excerpt, Josephus describes first the internal dissensions

Source: Naphtali Lewis and Meyer Reinhold, *Roman Civilization: Sourcebook II: The Empire.* (NY: Harper Torchbooks, 1966) p. 456.

*among the Jews themselves (whom he calls the "seditious")
then relates the fearful destruction that burnt the Second
Temple.*

■ **Investigate the Source**

> **How** *did the Jewish internal problems contribute to their defense of
> Jerusalem?* **Notice** *how thoroughly Titus destroyed the city?* **Why**
> *did he do so?* **How** *would the dissension among the Jews affect
> them after their dispersion?*

The legions had orders to encamp at the distance
of six furlongs from Jerusalem, at the mount called
the Mount of Olives, which lies over against the city
on the east side, and is parted from it by a deep valley,
interposed between them, which is named Cedron.

Now, when hitherto the several parties in the city
had been dashing one against another perpetually,
this foreign war, now suddenly come upon them after
a violent manner, put the first stop to their con-
tentions one against another; and as the seditious
now saw with astonishment the Romans pitching
three several camps, they began to think of an awkward sort of concord, and said one to another: "What
do we here, and what do we mean, when we suffer
three fortified walls to be built to coop us in, that we
shall not be able to breathe freely? While the enemy
is securely building a kind of city in opposition to us,
and while we sit still within our own walls and become spectators only of what they are doing, with our
hands idle, and our armor laid by, as if they were
about somewhat that was for our good and advantage.
We are, it seems (so did they cry out), only courageous against ourselves [in mutual argument], while
the Romans are likely to gain the city without blood-

shed by our sedition." Thus did they encourage one
another when they were gotten together and took
their armor immediately and ran out upon the Tenth
legion and fell upon the Romans with great eager-
ness, and with a prodigious shout, as they were forti-
fying their camp. . . . [After a long and bloody siege,
the Romans finally entered the city.]

Now the number of those that were carried captive during this whole war was collected to be ninety-
seven thousand; as was the number of those that
perished during the whole siege eleven hundred
thousand, the greater part of whom was indeed of the
same nation [with the citizens of Jerusalem], but not
belonging to the city itself. . . . Now this vast multitude is indeed collected out of remote places, but the
entire nation was now shut up by fate as in prison,
and the Roman army encompassed the city when it
was crowded with inhabitants. Accordingly the multitude of those that therein perished exceeded all the
destructions that either men or God ever brought
upon the world; for, to speak only of what was publicly known, the Romans slew some of them, some
they carried captives, and others they made a search
for underground, and when they found where they
were they broke up the ground and slew all they met
with. There were also found slain there above two
thousand persons, partly by their own hands and
partly by one another, but chiefly destroyed by the
famine. . . . An now the romans set fire to the extreme parts of the city, and burned them down, and
entirely demolished its walls.

Source: *The Great Events by Famous Historians*, edited by Rossiter
Johnson. The National Alumni, 1905, Volume III, 151, 205-06.

The Dome of the Rock, Jerusalem, ca. 691

This Muslim pilgrimage site is located on the holiest place in Jerusalem. Jews revere the site as the place where they believe Abraham was told to sacrifice his son, Isaac. Muslims believe that the prophet Muhammad ascended to heaven from this spot. Christians respect it as the location of the Temple where Jesus walked. This building symbolizes the dramatic cultural transformations that unfolded as the Roman Empire dissolved, and it stands on one of the most contested pieces of land in history.

CHAPTER 6

A World Divided

Western Kingdoms, Byzantium, and the Islamic World, ca. 376–1000

STUDY • Germanic life, values, and the establishment of their kingdoms in western Europe • The Byzantine Empire, its characteristics and relationship with its neighbors • Islamic religion, life, and expansion. ◉NOTICE that as the Roman Empire breaks up, the Islamic world confronts the West.

"The harsh nature of war! The malevolent fate of all things! How proud kingdoms fall, suddenly in ruins! Blissful housetops that held up for long ages now lie torched, consumed beneath a huge devastation." These lines, written by Radegund, a nun living in sixth-century Gaul, poignantly express the turbulent world in which she lived. The Roman Empire was no longer a political unit that people could rely on for peace within its borders. The once mighty empire had fragmented into three culturally distinct parts separated by religion, language, and loyalties. In the west, Germanic invaders established new kingdoms and converted to Christianity. In the east, the political form of the Roman Empire continued at least nominally for another thousand years. However, centered in the great city founded by Constantine, and separated from Rome, Byzantium began developing its own distinct character. The language of government changed to Greek, and people began to mingle more with the Slavic tribes to the north than with the Latins in the west. Finally, the desert of Arabia produced a prophet, Muhammad, who profoundly influenced the religious beliefs of millions. Followers of the new religion of Islam swept out of the desert and conquered the eastern and southern shores of the Mediterranean, as well as most of Spain. These three civilizations—the heirs of Rome—existed in uneasy, sometimes violent, proximity. Their differences and conflicts would remake the map of Europe and shatter the Roman unity that had graced the land for so long.

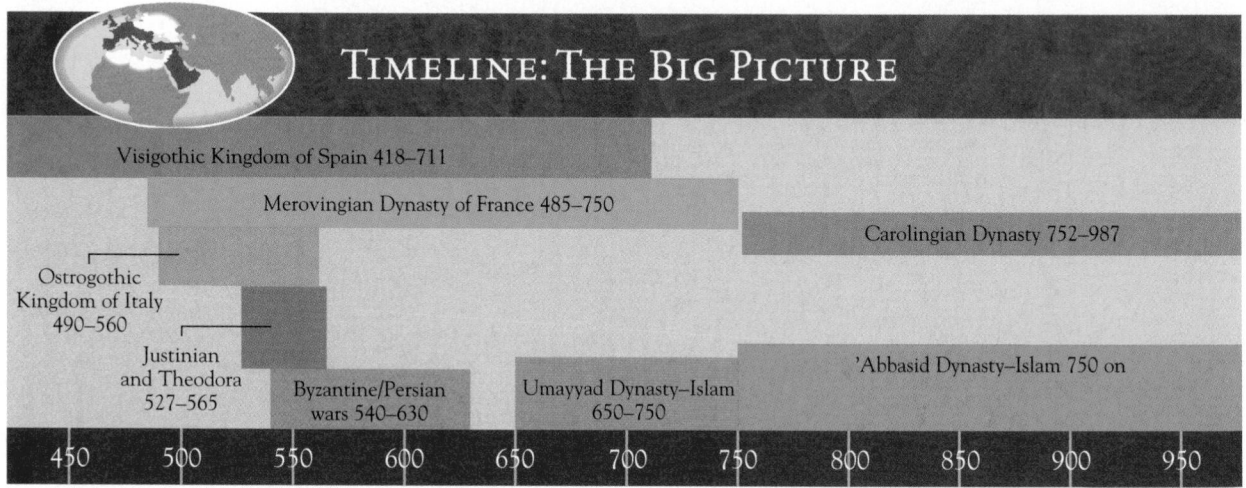

TIMELINE: THE BIG PICTURE

Visigothic Kingdom of Spain 418–711

Merovingian Dynasty of France 485–750

Carolingian Dynasty 752–987

Ostrogothic Kingdom of Italy 490–560

Justinian and Theodora 527–565

Byzantine/Persian wars 540–630

Umayyad Dynasty–Islam 650–750

'Abbasid Dynasty–Islam 750 on

450   500   550   600   650   700   750   800   850   900   950

The Making of the Western Kingdoms, ca. 376–750

Sidonius Apollinaris (431?–480?) was a Roman nobleman living in Gaul. He received a classical Roman education and wrote letters to his friends that brimmed with stories of the gracious life of a provincial Roman. In his missives, he described a lifestyle blessed by culture, ease, and luxury. Yet Sidonius also witnessed much turmoil in his lifetime. In one letter he wrote, "Our town lives in terror of a sea of tribes which find in it an obstacle to their expansion and surge in arms all round it." He defended the walls of his town against the invading Visigoths and was imprisoned by the attackers. Later his captors released him, and he lived out the rest of his days tranquilly, serving as bishop in a town now governed by Visigoths. His Roman world had been reshaped, but not obliterated. To understand the changes that Sidonius experienced, we must first meet the Germans, who played such a major role in the remaking of the Roman Empire.

LIFE IN A GERMAN CLAN AND FAMILY

Who were these "Germani" that the Romans called "barbarians?" In about 500 B.C., when the earliest Romans were settling on the seven hills of their city and beginning their republic, groups of Indo-European Scandinavian people began to migrate south into the Baltic states and Germany and east into Ukraine. As they fanned out across the land, their tribes took on a bewildering array of separate names: East Goths (Ostrogoths), West Goths (Visigoths), Burgundians, Franks, Saxons, and so forth. These tribes traded with Rome and sometimes threatened its northern borders throughout the history of the empire. Whereas Chapter 5 focused on life within the empire, here we will move back in time to describe the culture of the early Germans and follow the fortunes of the tribes as they entered the empire.

Because the Germanic tribes had originally come from a small region in Scandinavia, they shared many cultural similarities. Their settlements were based on clans—families joined in kinship groups. A whole tribe made up of many clans might number no more than 100,000 people, including only about 20,000 warriors. Historians studying their early history are hampered by the fact that they did not write and thus left no written records. Instead, we must piece together their history from archaeology, Roman descriptions of the tribes, and texts based on imperfect memories written centuries later.

The earliest descriptions by Romans are not objective. Some Roman accounts depict the Germans as "barbarians" ("outsiders") whose language sounded like babbling and whose personal hygiene was objectionable. One Roman wrote, "Happy [is] the nose that cannot smell a barbarian." However, the earliest and most famous text, Tacitus's *Germania*, written at the end of the first century, praises the Germans in order to criticize Roman society by contrast. Therefore, Tacitus portrays the Germans as strong and brave people who cared for their families and raised sturdy children. He writes: "With them good customs are of more avail than good laws elsewhere." However, readers must be cautious not to accept his descriptions uncritically—he

Roman sources

OLC

was no objective reporter, and he was interested in urging Romans to adopt more virtuous customs. Nevertheless, by carefully using these imperfect sources in conjunction with archaeological finds, we can piece together a picture of the lives of the early Germanic peoples.

FIGURE 6.1
Germanic girl's corpse discovered in a bog, first century A.D.

Tacitus praised the Germans' devotion to marriage—"This they consider their strongest bond"— and the children it produced. Although Tacitus somewhat romanticized the marriage bonds, without a doubt they forged the essential ties that bound society together. Within marriages, men and women had clearly defined and equally essential roles. Men cared for the cattle (a clan's greatest measure of wealth) and took primary responsibility for crop tending, iron working, and war making. Women owned property and received a share of their husbands' wealth upon marriage. Women also performed agricultural labor, but they were mainly responsible for pottery and textile production and household care. In addition, they brewed the all-important alcoholic beverages—honey-sweetened ale and mead, a fermented concoction of honey and water—that provided much of the caloric intake needed for survival. Preserving knowledge of herb lore, women also cared for the sick and injured members of the clan. Perhaps in part because of their knowledge of brewing and healing, women were reputed to have a gift for prophecy, so men often consulted their wise female elders regarding important forthcoming enterprises.

Marriage patterns

Women were considered "peace-weavers," for through their arranged marriages they were supposed to bring peace between two families. However, family feuds often transcended family ties. Because the purpose of marriage was to join families, men were not limited to one wife. On the contrary, the more wives a man had, the larger his kin network became. The meager sources suggest that many pre-Christian Germans were polygynous; men had as many wives and concubines as they could support. Under these polygynous marriages, husbands and wives did not necessarily live in the same household, so women had a good deal of independence and maintained close ties with their birth families. Although Tacitus claimed adultery was rare, anthropological studies indicate that polygyny may encourage infidelity among women, and there is no reason to doubt that adultery occurred among these tribes. Adultery, however, deeply threatened the strong kinship ties that marriage forged and was severely punished.

Figure 6.1 shows the corpse of a 14-year-old girl who was executed in the first century A.D. by drowning, probably for committing adultery. Such bodies— well preserved by the northern European bogs—offer a wealth of information about the lives of these early Germanic peoples. This young girl's head was shaved, and she was blindfolded before her death. Her right hand is frozen in an obscene gesture—perhaps her last act of defiance toward her executioners. This find offers eloquent, though silent, testimony to the importance of the marriage ties holding Germanic communities together, and the gruesome penalty for violation.

GERMANIC CLOTHING AND FOOD

Germanic peoples differed from the more southerly Romans in more ways than family traditions. Their clothing styles and diets also set them dramatically apart. Germanic men wore trousers, a long-sleeved jacket, and a flowing wool or fur cape secured by a large brooch or pin (or even a thorn if the wearer was impoverished). With their elaborate, luxurious detail, some of these brooches signified wealth and prestige. Figure 6.2 shows six examples of Germanic jewelry from the sixth century A.D. There are clasps (also called *fibulae*) to secure the capes and clothing and a silver belt buckle. The valuable gold pieces are inlaid with precious stones; the fibula on the upper left is

FIGURE 6.2
Early Germanic jewelry, ca. sixth century A.D.

of the south that merely scratched the surface of the sandier land there, this plow could turn over the heavy clay soils of the north. Furthermore, it encouraged co-operation—for to use a plow of this size, members of the community had to work together. But even this technology did not yield enough grain for a healthy diet, for the northern growing season was short. In addition, the disruptions of wars—even raids—upset agriculture and led to frequent hunger.

Archaeologists have learned about the Germanic diet through studying the stomach contents of people (like the woman in Figure 6.1) whose remains have been preserved in bogs. The last meals of many of the dead consisted of mostly weeds—flax, grass, nettle, hemp, and so forth. These people also ate small amounts of bread, which they ground with a hand-held stone. The grinding process left small stone particles in the flour that wore people's teeth down to stumps. While it is hard to tell whether the stomach contents of the surviving corpses were typical, experts agree that the diet of the ancient Germans was not adequate. Due to malnutrition, the average Germanic woman stood just under five feet; the average man, five feet six inches.

HEROIC SOCIETY

Like the ancient Greeks, the Germanic tribes of the north cherished the heroic ideals. Warfare played a central role in this society. The Roman historian Tacitus remarked on the German preference for war over work when he wrote: "They think it tame and stupid to acquire by their sweat what they can purchase by their blood." Although Tacitus understated the agricultural productivity of the tribes, these warriors did prefer raiding and plundering. Through such adventures, they acquired both wealth and fame. In the evening gatherings after a day of war making, a poet might praise a particularly heroic deed, and the warrior's name would be permanently preserved in the "word-hoard" or poetry of his people.

Just as Homer had recorded the dramatic deeds of Achilles and Odysseus, anonymous Germanic poets composed works remembering the heroes of the north. The Anglo-Saxon poem *Beowulf* is a written version of one such heroic account. *Beowulf* not only tells of the accomplishments of the monster-killing hero, but also gives us a glimpse into traditional Germanic society: The warriors gather in the hall to

less valuable because it is partially made of silver. As the pieces show, most of the design work of the ancient tribes utilized patterns rather than representations, a preference believed to demonstrate the Germans' awareness of the complex patterns symbolizing how fate wove together people's destinies.

Germanic women wore ankle-length dresses of linen or woven wool, which they colored with vegetable dyes. Like the men, they wore capes for warmth. They also dressed their hair with elaborate combs and hairpins and wore patterned jewelry as marks of wealth and prestige.

The Germans' diets were not as elaborate as their fashion accessories. The German peoples raised cattle *Agriculture and diet* but seldom ate the meat—the animals were too valuable for the milk and labor they provided. Instead, most of the clans were primarily agricultural. They apparently invented a large, wheeled plow that only a team of six to eight oxen had the strength to pull. Unlike the small plows boast, drink, and prepare for their military feats; the women serve in the hall but also speak their minds; and the king takes responsibility for guarding his people and doling out gifts to ensure their loyalty.

Each clan within the larger tribe was led by its own chieftain, who served as priest, main judge, and war leader. However, this was no absolute ruler, for the warrior elite (comitatus) was continually consulted in the decisions made for the whole clan. At times, small groups of warrior bands *Warrior bands* (usually less than 35 strong) set out to raid neighboring villages and bring back booty and tales of bravery. Sometimes when chiefs decided to conduct longer campaigns, they sent out a call to summon young, adventurous warriors who fought for their chief in return for arms, food, and with luck, treasure. Sometimes the whole tribe decided to move, bringing along all the related clans and escorting their women and children. According to Tacitus, women traveling with these fighting tribes stayed behind the battle lines, probably within a protective circle of ox carts. If their men seemed to be losing, the women goaded the warriors to victory by baring their breasts behind the battle lines to remind them of their responsibility to protect their dependents.

INFILTRATING THE ROMAN EMPIRE, 376–476

While there was periodic, fierce fighting on the borders of the empire between the German tribes and the Romans, there was also a growing relationship based on mutual advantage. After the third century, Rome relied more and more on mercenaries to guard the empire's borders (described in Chapter 5). By the late fourth century, then, many tribes had a great deal of contact with the empire. Numerous young Germanic warriors no longer farmed but instead used Roman pay to support their families. Nearby tribes had learned to value Roman coins as much as cattle and jewelry (their traditional forms of wealth), and Rome had come to depend on the Germans' impressive skill in war.

This mutually satisfying relationship changed in the late fourth century when a Mongolian tribe originating in northern China came sweeping out of the steppes of Asia. These Huns (known as Hsiung-hu in their homeland) struck terror in the hearts of the Germanic tribes in their path. Map 6.1 shows the route of the Huns as they galloped out of the east beginning in about 375. The Huns were a fierce people (even by Germanic standards) who charged across the continent on small ponies that *The Huns* seemingly needed no rest. Contemporary descriptions of the Huns reveal the dread and disgust generated by this wild and remarkably successful people. For example, the Roman historian Ammianus Marcellinus (354?) wrote: They "are so prodigiously ugly and bent that they might be two-legged animals. Their shape, however disagreeable, is human." With their tattooed arms and cheeks purposefully scarred, the Huns made a terrifying picture. (See Document 6.1 on page D6.1 for an excerpt of this influential source.) Some Germanic tribes fled across the boundaries of the empire in search of safer territory. One such tribe, the Visigoths, crossed into the empire looking for land and ended up sacking Rome itself in 410 (discussed in Chapter 5). As the map reveals, the Visigoths were only one of many Germanic peoples who crossed into the empire in the early fifth century.

As we saw in Chapter 5, by the late third century, the Romans faced severe economic problems that kept them from successfully defending *Federate treaties* their borders against these new encroachments. They could not even afford to pay for the minimum defense, for the empire spent about 30 gold pieces a year for each soldier. An army of only 30,000 would have cost the entire annual budget of the western empire, so the Romans had to develop a new, less expensive way to defend its borders. To address this need, the Romans offered some encroaching tribes a treaty that made them "federates," or allies, of Rome. Through this treaty, the warrior tribes received permission to live within the borders of the empire, and in exchange, they agreed to fight the enemies of Rome. The Visigoths became federates for enough grain to feed their warriors and families; in return they agreed to fight their traditional enemies, the Germanic Vandals. The Visigoths were later called north to protect the Italian borders. As more tribes were awarded federate status, the western empire began to be transformed by the blending of peoples.

The federate treaties allowed the Germanic tribes to live within the empire and govern themselves by their own laws and customs, using their own leaders. This model of separate, coexisting cultures almost immediately proved to be utopian. In most of the territories, such as Spain or North Africa, the Germans

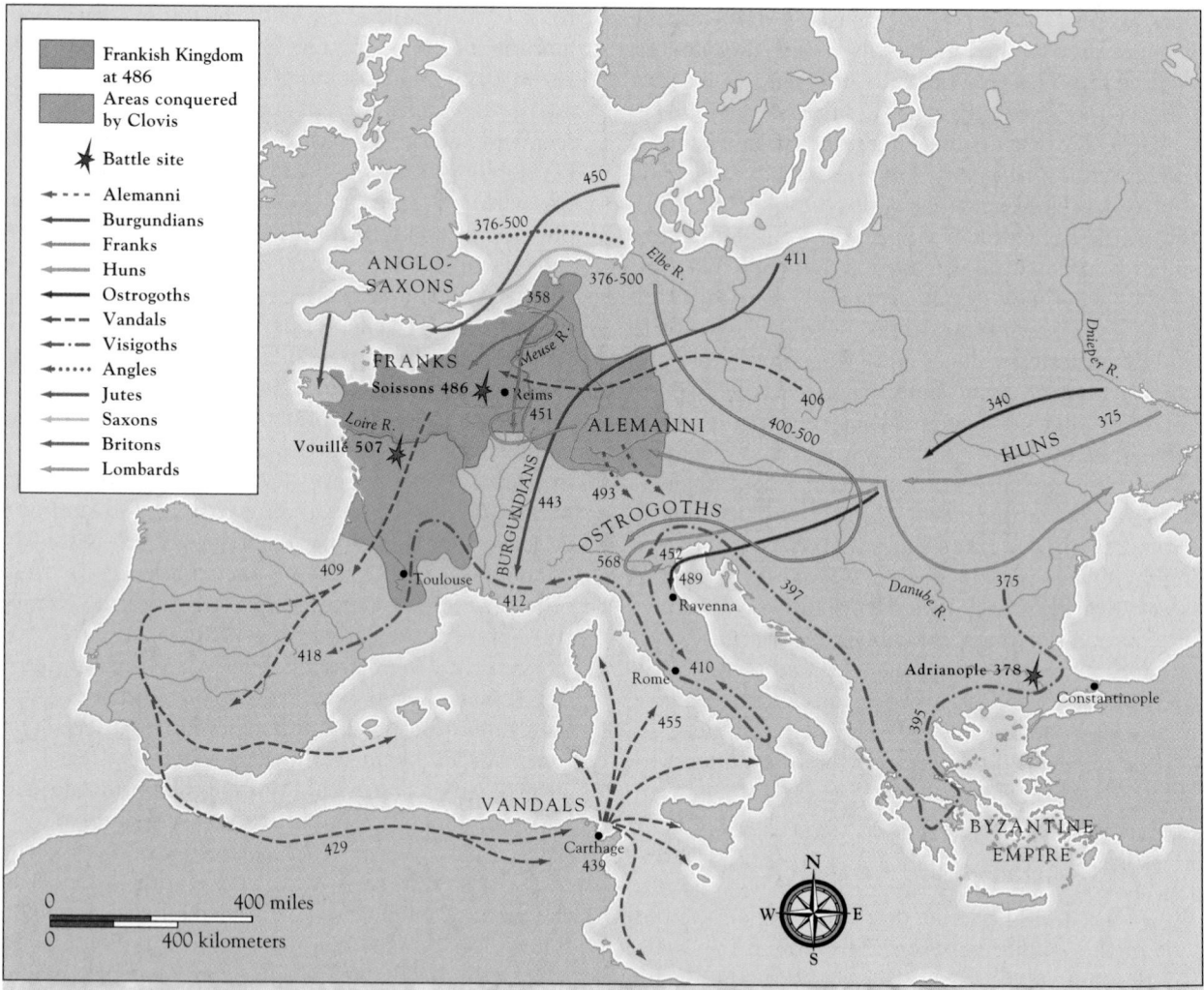

THINKING ABOUT GEOGRAPHY

MAP 6.1 *Germanic Invasions, Fifth Century*

This map shows the routes of the various Germanic tribes as they invaded the Roman Empire, and gives the dates of their invasions of various lands. ✒ **Notice** the various tribes entering the empire. **Review** where they moved and where they eventually settled. **Consider** what regions might be centers of continued contention. ✒ **Notice** the strategic location of Constantinople and why it would control the important trade with the Far East.

were very much in the minority, so their culture was transformed by contact with neighboring Romans. For example, tribal leaders began to be called and treated as kings, although competing German noblemen consistently resorted to assassination to maintain their traditional voice in tribal affairs.

In many cases, two religions also existed side by side. Some pagan tribes (Anglo-Saxons, for example) restored paganism to parts of the nominally Christian empire. Other tribes (Visigoths and Ostrogoths) were Christian but had been converted by a missionary named Ulfila (310?–381?), whose

Christian ideas had been shaped before Arius's teachings had been condemned at the Council of Nicaea in 325 (see Chapter 5). Ulfila's parents had been captured by Goths, and he grew up speaking the early Germanic language, so he was the natural candidate to convert the Germans. Thus, many of the Goths were converted to Arian Christianity, and they used a Gothic-language Bible that Ulfila had translated for them. However, this translation reflected Ulfila's Arian beliefs. By the fifth-century settlements, the Arian tribes associated their religious beliefs with their ethnic identity, and this impeded their relationship with the orthodox Catholics living in the disintegrating empire.

Arian Christianity

A fifth-century North African Catholic (Victor of Vita) chronicled the invasion of the Vandals, and he particularly lamented the religious strife that erupted. He wrote that the Vandals "gave vent to their wicked ferocity . . . against the churches, . . . cemeteries and monasteries, so that they burned houses of prayer with fires greater than those used against cities." Although Victor probably exaggerated the villainy of the Vandals, his description pointed to the disintegration of the empire. When the emperor could not protect his Catholic subjects from his Arian ones, the religious differences further splintered an already weakened central authority.

In addition to its disputes with the federate tribes, the empire lost some provinces altogether. In about 407, Rome recalled legions from Britain to help defend Italy against invaders. This left the Celtic Britons, who were Christian and lived in the Roman manner, alone to defend themselves against invaders from Scotland and from the Scandinavian countries. As Map 6.1 shows, tribes of Angles, Saxons, and Jutes entered and settled the eastern portions of Britain, pushing most of the Celtic Britons to Wales and Ireland, the western edges of the British Isles. In the midst of these invasions, one British war chief won a great victory at the Battle of Badon (about the late fifth century) over the Anglo-Saxons. This victory stemmed the tide of the invasions, but only for a while. The deeds of this war chief, Arthur of Britain, were nevertheless remembered in the western Celtic lands and formed the basis for the famous Arthurian romances composed in the twelfth century (see Chapter 8). Britain was lost to Rome and became a mosaic of small Germanic kingdoms.

Loss of provinces

North Africa also fell away from the empire. At first the Vandals were settled as federates in the northern lands of Africa, but they soon broke off their allegiance to Rome and created a separate kingdom with their capital in Carthage. By the middle of the fifth century, Rome lost the rich tax shipments of grain and oil that had come in a steady stream from North Africa. Struggling with this and other territorial losses, the empire in the west was slowly disintegrating.

DID ROME "FALL"?

By the fifth century, the provincial armies in the west were dominated by Germans, so it is not surprising that many rose to military power in Rome itself. When the Visigoths invaded Italy, the Roman defense was led by a Vandal general, which shows how ineffective the Roman emperors in the west had become. During the invasion, the Visigoths' leader even captured Emperor Honorius's (r. 395–423) sister, Galla Placidia, and took her with him as he sacked Rome itself. When Rome finally signed a treaty with the Visigoth Athaulf, the Goth married Galla Placidia to seal the bargain.

Such efforts merely delayed the seemingly inevitable replacement of Roman emperors with Germanic kings. Finally, in 476, the military leader Odovacar deposed the last western emperor (who, ironically, was named Romulus Augustulus after Romulus, the founder of the city of Rome and Augustulus, "little Augustus," after Augustus, the first Roman emperor). Odovacar disdained the practice of dual emperorship that the Romans had established and shipped the imperial regalia off to the east. He then appointed himself regent in Italy.

The western empire did not "fall" with a cataclysmic crash. People like Sidonius in Gaul probably did not even use words such as "fall" to describe the times. After all, the eastern regions still had an emperor to whom people could give their allegiance if they wished, and in fact, many in the east celebrated the fact that there was once again one emperor who ruled the Mediterranean world. However, Sidonius and his contemporaries knew that the Roman Empire overall had undergone a major shift. Historians frequently use the term "late antique" to describe this period during which there was so much continuity with the Roman world. But this world was changed.

Transformation not "Fall"

The empire's declining population played a key part in this transformation. The shrinking populace left plenty of room for the Germanic tribes to settle without severely dislocating residents. Even after the Germanic settlements, as much as 20 percent of the arable land was abandoned in some areas of the empire. As we saw in Chapter 5, economic and social problems had also eaten away at the empire for centuries. Finally, plagues and warfare had decimated the already fragile population. The empire, therefore, did not "fall"; instead, it was transformed as new people moved into the territory that the Romans failed to populate.

The urban life that had so characterized Roman culture was the first thing to go. The violence of the times crippled the towns, and the Germanic preference for rural living shifted attention to the countryside. The urban tax base shriveled as powerful Romans began to refuse to pay taxes to Rome. The Germans, for their part, were not often vigilant in collecting them. The roads and bridges that connected the empire fell into disrepair, and people's focus narrowed to the local level.

There were always Romans like Sidonius who continued their correspondence with Romans elsewhere, but they became fewer and fewer. Even Roman clothing changed; the toga that had symbolized the civilized life of the city was abandoned in favor of trousers more suited to country life. (Churchmen continued to wear more traditional Roman robes. Indeed, to this day, Catholic vestments resemble the clothing of the ancient Roman upper class.)

Of course, change happens in both directions when different peoples intermingle. The Germans were as much influenced by the Romans as the Romans were by Germanic culture. *Germans transformed* Slowly, the Germanic pagans and Arians converted to orthodox Christianity and began to intermarry with resident Romans. In southern Europe, Germans began to speak the local Latin-derived dialects instead of their native Gothic. This is why the southern European languages (French, Spanish, Portuguese, Italian, Romanian) are called "Romance" languages—they are based on the language of the Romans. The Germans also became literate and began to produce written texts.

Figure 6.3 shows a page depicting the beginning of the Gospel of Matthew, from a manuscript made probably in Ireland in about the seventh century. Whereas the theme of the image is Christian, the

FIGURE 6.3

Manuscript illustration of a man from the Gospel of Matthew, ca. 660.

aesthetics resemble those of the Germanic tribes, which were shared by the Celtic inhabitants of Ireland. The beautiful patterning in the border and in the man's cloak resembles the gold work on the jewelry in Figure 6.2. The Germans and the Romans, through their mutual influence, were creating a whole new culture—that of the medieval west—and this illustration reveals the blending of the two ways of life. After invading, the Germanic tribes settled down and created new political entities—kingdoms, instead of tribal units. These new entities formed the basis for the medieval kingdoms that defined the West in the centuries to come.

THE GROWING POWER OF THE POPES

As central authority fell away in western Europe, some people—especially in the cities—looked to their local bishops to handle things previously left to secular authorities. Bishops sometimes organized aqueduct repair or food relief, and perhaps not surprisingly, the bishop of the most prestigious city—Rome—began slowly to come to the fore. In these tumultuous centuries, the bishops of Rome began to claim earthly as well as spiritual authority, and in doing so, established precedents that would reach well into the future.

All Christian bishops were believed to be the successors of the original apostles and as such held the authority to guide the faithful. However, as early as the fourth century, the bishops of Rome began to assert their supremacy over all the other bishops. Many bishops during the early church period were called *popes*, based on the Latin word for "father," but the bishops of Rome slowly began to claim exclusive use of that title to set themselves apart from other bishops. On what did the popes base their claims of leadership? In part, the early-fourth-century popes claimed primacy because Rome had been the capital of the empire. However, as the imperial city faded in importance, the popes began pointing to biblical writings to justify their leadership of the church. They based their claim mainly on a passage from the Book of Matthew (Matt. 16:18–19) in which Christ said: "And I tell you, you are Peter, and on this rock I will build my church. . . . I will give you the keys of the kingdom of heaven. . . ." The early popes had claimed that Peter had been the first bishop of Rome, so each subsequent pope claimed to be the spiritual descendant of Peter—thus also controlling heaven's keys.

Figure 6.4, an illustration from an early-eleventh-century manuscript, portrays Christ giving Peter the keys to heaven. A crowd of people stand behind Peter, suggesting their dependency on *Petrine Doctrine* him. This image appealed strongly to medieval Europeans because it visually expressed the idea that the pope (Peter's successor) should head the church. The claim that the supremacy of the pope is based on Christ's words to Peter is called the

FIGURE 6.4
Christ giving the keys of heaven to Peter, ca. 1007.

"Petrine" doctrine of papal supremacy. Not surprisingly, some people—especially the emperors in the east and some other bishops—disagreed with this interpretation of the Bible.

Since the fourth century, some popes had involved themselves in politics. As we saw in Chapter 5, Bishop Ambrose had forced Emperor Theodosius to bend to his will, and in the following century, Pope Leo I (r. 440–461) successfully negotiated with invading Huns and Vandals to spare Rome. At the end of the fifth century, Pope Gelasius (r. 492–496) tried to resolve this issue of who had power by describing authority on earth as two swords: one wielded by kings and the other by the church. In Gelasius's view, the church's sword was the greater because it was spiritual—popes were responsible for the souls of kings. In a metaphorical sense, then, Gelasius converted St. Peter's keys to heaven into an earthly blade.

However, these early popes could exert only sporadic authority, and they had little real power. It was Pope Gregory the Great (r. 590–604) who dramatically forwarded the case for papal supremacy, as much through his actions as his words. A talented, energetic administrator, he defined the role of the pope in broad terms. For example, he took over the day-to-day administration of Rome, reorganizing estates and managing them in such a way as to generate extra revenue to feed the poor. When the Lombards invaded the peninsula, Gregory directed the defense of the city and negotiated the truce. Acting the part of a territorial ruler, he even exerted his authority outside Italy, writing letters to settle disputes and offering financial assistance to distant churches. Gregory's influence extended far beyond sixth-century Italy: In the ninth century, when the Anglo-Saxon king Alfred (see Chapter 7) selected seminal works to translate from Latin to Anglo-Saxon, Gregory's writings were prominently featured. With Gregory's precedent, popes of the eighth century and beyond were prepared to claim influence throughout western Christendom, although it would take until the thirteenth century for them to fully wield such authority over a Christian world. In these early centuries, there was still too much chaos for any institution to come decisively to the fore. Many people preferred to withdraw from the turbulence of the times and seek a spiritual life behind monastery walls.

Gregory the Great

MONASTERIES: PEACEFUL HAVENS

As the Germanic tribes were sweeping into the western empire, many men and women sought refuge from the chaotic times in monasteries, where they could concentrate on their spiritual growth. As we saw in Chapter 5, communal monasticism began to appeal to many Christians throughout the empire. In the west, the most influential founder of communal monasticism was the Italian, Benedict of Nursia (480?–543). His twin sister Scholastica shared his calling and founded monasteries for women. Like many other churchmen, Benedict disapproved of people who lived independently like the holy ascetics we met in Chapter 5. He feared that without guidance, such individuals might go astray, and he complained of wandering holy men, saying: "Whatever they think of or choose to do, that

Benedict of Nursia

they call holy; what they do not like, that they regard as illicit." Instead, Benedict wrote a book of instruction—a *Rule*—to guide monks and nuns in their communal lives.

Benedict eschewed the extreme fasts and bodily mortifications that had marked the eastern holy men and women, writing: "We hope to ordain nothing that is harsh or heavy to bear." Benedict's *Rule* required that people spend a balanced day divided into work and prayer, with moderate and regular meals. The requirement to work encouraged monks and nuns to study and copy the precious manuscripts that preserved classical learning. Benedict himself called his monastery a "schoolhouse for the Lord," which was an apt description for an institution that served a central role in education throughout the Middle Ages.

Although Benedict did not require heroic asceticism, the monk insisted that individuals ignore their own desires—whether for extra food, different work, or even extra hardships—and live in strict obedience to the head monk or nun. These monastic leaders, called "abbots" or "abbesses," eventually became powerful figures in medieval life, extending their influence far outside monastery walls. By requiring a vow of obedience from monks and nuns, Benedict created an effective mechanism for bringing otherwise independent religious people into the Christian hierarchy.

Monasteries formed an effective avenue through which Christianity spread to the pagan outposts. In the early fifth century, a Romano-British Christian named Patrick (390?–461) was kidnapped by Irish raiders and enslaved in Ireland. He later escaped to Britain, where he became a bishop. However, he decided his calling was to return to Ireland to convert the pagan Irish. He established monasteries in Ireland, and the Irish consider him the founder of Irish Christianity. Ireland had never been part of the Roman Empire, so it lacked the ecclesiastical structure that characterized the rest of the Christian West. Without the established Roman administrative structures, bishops in Ireland exercised less authority than the heads of monasteries. The strong Irish monastic tradition in Ireland created monks who made great strides in preserving learning and stimulating ideals of asceticism in the West. Furthermore, some Irish monks became missionaries to the pagan Anglo-Saxons in Britain.

Irish Christianity

In fact, scholars give the Irish monks a great deal of credit for preserving the classical wisdom and transmitting it on to subsequent civilizations of the West.

Pope Gregory the Great—a monk himself—was also interested in converting the Anglo-Saxons and bringing them into the orbit of Roman Christianity. The pope sent monks to Britain in 597 to convert the natives—a task they slowly, but successfully, achieved. However, the monks sent from Rome came in contact with those sent from *Conversion of Britain* Ireland, and it became clear that the two strands of Christianity had developed differing opinions on certain points (the most important was the date of Easter). In 664, the Anglo-Saxon king called a council in Whitby to resolve the discrepancy. After ascertaining that all the monks agreed on the primacy of the apostle Peter, the king decreed that Peter's heir in Rome should prevail. Thus, the practices of Roman—instead of Irish—Christianity prevailed throughout Europe.

Beyond their missionary roles, monasteries served as quiet havens from a tempestuous world. In these retreats, men and women worked, prayed, and studied—keeping ancient texts alive for a time when learning could again emerge from behind monastery walls. Through the sixth and seventh centuries, however, the focus of Europe was on the violent kingdoms being established in the rubble of the Roman Empire.

RISE AND FALL OF A FRANKISH DYNASTY, CA. 485–750

In the sixth century, the Germanic Franks established a powerful kingdom in the old Roman province of Gaul (see Map 6.1 on page 194). The Franks were ruled by the Merovingian family (named after a legendary ancestor, Merovech). The most famous Merovingian was Clovis (r. 485–511), a brutal man who murdered many of his own relatives to consolidate his rule. Clovis's descendants were no less brutal, and the accounts of subsequent reigns tell of feuds and assassinations involving Merovingian princesses as well as princes.

Gregory, the bishop of Tours (538–594), wrote a history of the Franks that offers a detailed account of the reigns of Clovis and his successors. Within this vivid narrative, the bishop reveals the brutality of day-to-day life in this Germanic kingdom. He describes in a matter-of-fact account how one queen

sent an assassin to kill one of her relatives, and when "he returns without success, she has his feet and hands cut off." Such incidents multiplied throughout the reign of the Merovingians.

Clovis is significant not only because he unified large portions of the Frankish kingdom, but also because he converted to Roman Christianity. According to Gregory, Clovis's wife, Clotilda, was a Christian and was influential in persuading the king to convert. In the tradition of Constantine before him, Clovis reputedly vowed to *Christian Merovingians* convert if he won a significant battle. He won and fulfilled his vow around the year 500 (although the date is controversial). Unlike the Visigoths and other Germans, Clovis converted to orthodox, not Arian, Christianity, and this began a long relationship between the popes and the Frankish kings. As was traditional with the German tribes, the conversion of the king meant the conversion of his people, which paved the way for the slow transformation of Germanic culture through the influence of the Roman church.

Figure 6.5 shows the baptism of Clovis—the defining moment during which the Frankish people (on the right) joined with the church hierarchy (on the left). In the center, an uncharacteristically innocent looking Clovis is blessed by the dove of the Holy Spirit hovering above him. This illustration captures the king's central role in uniting the various groups in

FIGURE 6.5
Baptism of Clovis.

his society. The dove symbolized the Franks' belief that God had guided Clovis in his consolidation and conversion. This conversion also brought papal support to the Frankish kingdom. Like the manuscript illustration in Figure 6.3, this image testifies to the blending of Roman, Christian, and Germanic cultures that would characterize the early Middle Ages.

In the Merovingian territory, Christianity made significant strides through the efforts of a number of royal women who founded monasteries and supported education. Radegund, whose poetry opened this chapter, is one example. This Merovingian queen, one of the several wives of King Clothar (d. 562), left her husband to found a convent. With her royal family ties, her financial independence, and the force of her personality, she overcame the anger of both her husband and the local bishop and established a house for women who wanted to dedicate themselves to God. She and her ladies spent their days praying, reading, copying manuscripts, and helping the sick and poor in the neighborhood. The king may have declared his people Christian, but leaders like Radegund did much more to win individual hearts to the new religion.

Although Clovis had been highly skilled in forging a Christian kingdom from the ashes of the Roman Empire in Gaul, the subsequent Merovingians were not as competent. By the seventh century the authority of these kings had deteriorated—frequently, children inherited the throne and in turn died young, leaving the throne to another child. Real power began to be exerted by the "mayors of the palace," an office controlled by another noble family, the Carolingians. This enterprising family included a number of skilled leaders, and as we will see, the Carolingian Charles Martel won a great victory in 733 to save the land. His son, Pepin the Short (r. 747–768) forwarded the fortunes of the family. Pepin wanted more than just to rule; in fact, he craved the royal title as well. Just as Clovis had enhanced his authority through Christian ritual, Pepin looked to the spiritual leader of Christendom for help. The shrewd Carolingian wrote to Pope Zachary (r. 741–752), asking him who should hold the title of king: he who actually exercised the power or he who had the name of king but no actual authority. The pope favored Pepin, and the mayor of the palace then gathered all the Frankish bishops and nobles, who promptly proclaimed him their king. The last of the ineffectual Merovingian kings was

Fall of Merovingians

forced to cut his long hair (a symbol of his power) and lived out his days in a monastery. Armed with the support of the church, the vigorous new dynasty was now in a position to bring centralized order to western Europe. We will follow the fortunes of the Carolingians in Chapter 7.

ACCOMPLISHMENTS AND DESTRUCTION IN ITALY, CA. 490–750

As the Franks established their kingdom in the sixth century, another Germanic kingdom took shape on the Italian peninsula. The story began when Theodoric (r. 493–526), an Ostrogothic leader, ousted Odovacar (who had deposed the last Roman emperor) and declared himself ruler of Italy. Theodoric had received a Roman education and proved a talented and balanced ruler—at first. The Ostrogoths were Arian Christians, so Theodoric had difficulty uniting Goths and Romans in Italy. Nevertheless, he seems to have exhibited a surprising religious toleration in an age that had little.

Theodoric fostered learning at his court and supported a number of scholars who had a profound influence on Western culture. Boethius, for example—a high official in Theodoric's court—was a man of great education. He translated works of Aristotle from Greek to Latin, and these translations became the basis for the study of logic for centuries. He also had an inventive streak and built a water clock for his patron. But *Fostering learning* Theodoric's court was plagued with intrigue, and Boethius was unjustly accused of treason and jailed. He wrote his most influential work, *The Consolation of Philosophy*, while in prison. In *The Consolation*, Boethius thought about the injustices of life and found comfort in philosophy. This profound and sensitive work was extremely popular among educated Europeans throughout the Middle Ages as Christians interpreted Boethius's work in a religious context, and it remains much studied today. However, it did not save Boethius, for Theodoric had him executed.

Dionysius Exiguus, a Greek-speaking monk, was one of the most respected scholars in Theodoric's Italy. A skilled mathematician, the monk calculated the date of Easter (which changes each year), and Dionysius apparently was the first to suggest that calendars be dated from his estimation of when the Incarnation of Christ occurred (our B.C./A.D. system). Although modern scholarship shows that his dates were slightly wrong—Christ was probably born about 4 B.C.—Dionysius' dating system is still used. His student, Cassiodorus (490–585), succeeded Boethius in the king's court, and his name is remembered much more than his master Dionysius.

Thoroughly trained in Roman writings like the *Aeneid* and Livy's *History* (both discussed in Chapter 5), Cassiodorus seems to have recognized the power of historical writing to create and preserve a people's identity. Consequently, he wrote a historical chronicle, the *Origin of the Goths*, that was designed to show that the Goths had as impressive and ancient a history as the Romans. By showing that the history of the Goths resembled the epic scope of the Roman past, Cassiodorus helped assimilate the histories of both peoples. Although the original of this seminal work is lost, excerpts survive in the quotations of later historical writings. Through this work and its subsequent emulators, the history of the Germans was incorporated into the history of the Roman Empire—the Germanic tribes were slowly but surely merging with the peoples of the old empire they had inhabited.

Theodoric was succeeded by his daughter, Amalasuintha, who ruled at first as regent for her young son and then as queen after the boy's death. She was well *Fall of Ostrogoths* educated and well suited to rule, but the unruly Germans were unused to being governed by a woman. Amalasuintha corresponded with the Byzantine emperor Justinian to gain support for her rule, writing: "We hope that the peaceful relations that you maintain toward us—and that you continue to uphold for my sake especially—may be extended." However, all her diplomatic skills could not save her from internal intrigue. In 535, she was murdered—according to Gregory of Tours, locked in an overheated steam bath where she was scalded to death.

Justinian used her death as an excuse to begin his reconquest of Italy as part of his ambitious plan to retake the western portions of the empire. The emperor's forces crushed the Ostrogothic kingdom. The scholar Boethius's widow seems to have received some satisfaction after the reconquest, for the emperor gave her permission to destroy statues of Theodoric as revenge for her husband's death. But few others celebrated the conquest that brought down the religiously tolerant and impressive rule of the Ostrogoths.

Justinian had overextended his resources, and the reconquest of Italy did not last long. A Germanic tribe that had fought as allies of the Byzantine army learned about the riches of Italy during the campaign against the Ostrogoths. In 568, these Lombards ("longbeards") moved south and took over most of the peninsula (see Map 6.1 on page 194). Italy would be now ruled by a tribe much less Romanized than the Ostrogoths and the slow struggle to achieve a synthesis between Germans and Romans began again. The fierce Lombards ruled the northern part of the peninsula until they confronted the growing power of the Franks in the north. Pepin conquered the Lombards in the mid-eighth century, and northern Italy came under the rule of the Frankish Carolingians.

Pepin did not forget his debt to the papacy that had supported his coronation, and when the Byzantines demanded that he return the Italian conquests to them, Pepin angrily refused. He said he fought his war for St. Peter, and it was to Peter (that is the papacy) that he would hand over his conquests. From this time onward, the pope ruled in central Italy as an independent monarch, and the "Donation of Pepin" marked the beginning of the Papal States that endured until the nineteenth century.

THE VISIGOTHS IN SPAIN, 418–711

The history of the Visigoths in Spain resembles that of the other growing kingdoms. Like the Ostrogoths, Visigoths were Arian Christians when they became federates of Rome, and the two cultures, Roman and Goth, lived separate though parallel lives in Spain. However, in the 580s the Visigothic kings converted to Roman Christianity and paved the way for a close church and state rule. Like the Ostrogoths, Visigothic kings fostered learning in their land. The most famous Visigothic writer was Isidore of Seville (560?–636), who compiled collections of Roman works that preserved classical knowledge for subsequent generations.

Two flaws marred Visigothic civilization, however. The first was a delight in political assassination, which even the violent Franks called the "Visigothic curse." Church and state repeat- *Visigothic weaknesses* edly condemned people who "turned their hand against the king," but the assassinations continued, weakening the kingdom. The second problem was Visigothic anti-Semitism. Kings passed strict laws against the many Jews living in Spain, undermining their communities and dampening their loyalty.

The Visigothic kingdom was ultimately destroyed by invasions of Muslims from North Africa. As we will see later, followers of the new religion of Islam swept across North Africa, crossed the narrow straits known as the Pillars of Hercules (now the Straits of Gibraltar), and in 711 conquered most of the Iberian Peninsula.

Figure 6.6 shows Iberian Christians taken into slavery by the victorious Muslims. The conquerors include the mounted leaders in the background towering over their bound captives and the African foot soldiers in the foreground guarding the new slaves. The mules, cattle, and long-haired sheep on the right represent the great wealth of the Visigothic kingdom that now came into the hands of the Muslims. The only remaining Christian territory on the peninsula lay in the northwest hills. From there the Iberians would spend the next 700 years reconquering their land. The invasion, the interaction between Christians and Muslims, and the long era of reconquest left the Visigothic kingdom in ruins and shaped the subsequent history and culture of Spain.

FIGURE 6.6
Christians led into slavery by conquering Muslims.

The Byzantine Empire,
ca. 400–1000

As early as the beginning of the fourth century, Roman emperors had recognized the unique strategic and economic advantages of the eastern portion of the empire. In 330, when Constantine moved his capital to the old city of Byzantium and renamed it Constantinople, he imagined he was creating a new Rome. During the turbulent fifth and sixth centuries, the eastern Roman Empire held firm as the western provinces fell away to the Germanic tribes. However, the eastern empire did not remain unchanged; instead, Constantine planted seeds that would later flower into a dramatically different empire. By the eighth century, the eastern Roman Empire had changed so much that historians call it the Byzantine Empire, or Byzantium, to distinguish it from the Latin Roman Empire that it succeeded. As with the emergence of the western Germanic kingdoms, the rise of the Byzantine Empire did not represent a sudden break from the past, but simply another aspect of the Roman Empire's transformation.

When the Visigoths sacked Rome in 410, the eastern emperor, Theodosius II, began to build a great wall to protect Constantinople from a similar fate. This structure stood firm even during the violent fifth and sixth centuries—inhabitants of Constantinople watched from the safety of the top of the wall as smoke rose from villages set aflame by the Germanic tribes and the Huns surging westward. The wall continued to protect the new capital for almost a thousand years. Only western crusaders conquered the city in 1204 and held it briefly before the Byzantine emperors restored their rule. Beyond that, the capital of eastern Christendom stood firm behind the great walls until the Turks successfully besieged the city with cannons in 1453.

The wave of invasions separated the eastern and western portions of the old Roman Empire. While the *A separate empire* western portion adopted some aspects of Germanic culture, the easterners consciously rejected such changes. For example, at the end of the fourth century, residents of Constantinople were forbidden to wear Germanic clothing, such as pants and any clothing made from furs. Between A.D. 400 and 1000, the Byzantine Empire distanced itself more and more from the concerns of the west and turned its focus north and east instead. One eastern emperor stood out as an exception to this tendency and turned his attention again to the west.

JUSTINIAN AND THEODORA, R. 527–565

Justinian was born in 483 to peasant parents living in a province near Macedonia. A promising youth, he was adopted by an uncle in the royal court. His uncle became emperor, which paved the way for Justinian to take the crown at his uncle's death in 527. The most influential person in Justinian's court was his wife, Theodora. She, too, had come from a humble background. She had been an actress, and according to the Byzantine historian Procopius (d. 562) (whose *Secret History* is biased against Justinian, so it may not be fully accurate), Theodora won the emperor's heart with her skill as an erotic dancer.

Early in Justinian's reign, Theodora established her role in the emperor's court when a violent riot (remembered as the *Nika* riot for the rioters' rallying cry *Nika*, which means "victory") broke out in Constantinople between two rival political factions who supported different chariot racing teams. In an uncommon alliance, *Nika riot* they joined forces to try to oust Justinian. When the rest of his advisors urged Justinian to flee the city, Theodora insisted that Justinian confront the rioters, saying, "For one who has been an emperor it is intolerable to be a fugitive." Justinian's forces brutally squelched the riot—probably 30,000 were killed—and this victory broke any political opposition.

During the *Nika* riot, much of Constantinople was burned, so Justinian and Theodora embarked on an ambitious reconstruction plan. The most impressive outcome of this effort was the design and construction of a massive church, the Hagia Sophia (Holy Wisdom). Figure 6.7, a modern photograph of the interior of the Hagia *Rebuilding the city* Sophia, shows the great church in its full glory and captures the piety and engineering skill of the Byzantines. The central dome, with its diameter of 101 feet, is the largest such structure in the world. Two half-domes double the interior length of the church to 200 feet. After the Muslims captured the city in 1453, the church became a mosque, and the spheres with the Arabic calligraphy date from the Muslim years. Today the magnificent structure is a museum, but it still showcases the impressive Byzantine engineering along with the blend of cultures that marks this region.

Besides the Hagia Sophia, Justinian left another enduring contribution: the codification of Roman law. From the earliest codification—the Twelve Tables (Chapter 4)—Roman law continued growing and changing. Emperors and senators had passed decrees, judges had made precedent-setting decisions, and

FIGURE 6.7
Hagia Sophia in Constantinople, mid-sixth century.

FIGURE 6.8
Mosaic of Justinian and attendants, mid-sixth century.

However, he succeeded only in taking North Africa from the Vandals and Italy from the Ostrogoths.

Under the newly established control of Justinian, a great church was built in Ravenna, in the north of Italy. Figures 6.8 and 6.9 are sixth-century mosaics of Justinian and Theodora that adorned this Church of San Vitale, and they reveal much about how people perceived the royal couple. As befitting highest royalty, the two rulers wear royal purple and costly jewels and are surrounded by their retinue. The halos over their heads reflect their claim to rule as God's representatives. These mosaics signify the power, authority, and veneration that Justinian and Theodora acquired. It was a worthy celebration of the victorious conquest of Italy, but the accomplishment proved more ephemeral than the magnificent mosaics.

Map 6.2 shows the extent of Justinian's reconquest. As impressive as it looked, it was destructive and costly. While the North Africans welcomed the

jurists had written complicated legal interpretations. By Justinian's time, the collections were full of obscurities and internal contradictions, and the emperor wanted them organized and clarified. The enterprise was immense, as Justinian himself noted: "We turned our attention to the great mass of venerable jurisprudence and, as if crossing the open sea, we completed a nearly hopeless task." The results of this formidable project were published in 50 books called the *Corpus Iuris Civilis* (the *Body of Civil Law*) (533?). In this form, Roman law survived and was revived in western Europe in about the thirteenth century. From there it has influenced Western legal codes through today.

Legal codification

Finally, as we have seen, after the murder of the Ostrogothic queen Amalasuintha, Justinian tried to reconquer the western territories that had fallen to Germanic tribes. In part, he wanted to recapture lost tax revenues, but probably the ambitious emperor also hoped to resurrect the Roman Empire to its past glory.

Reconquering the west

FIGURE 6.9
Mosaic of Theodora and attendants, mid-sixth century.

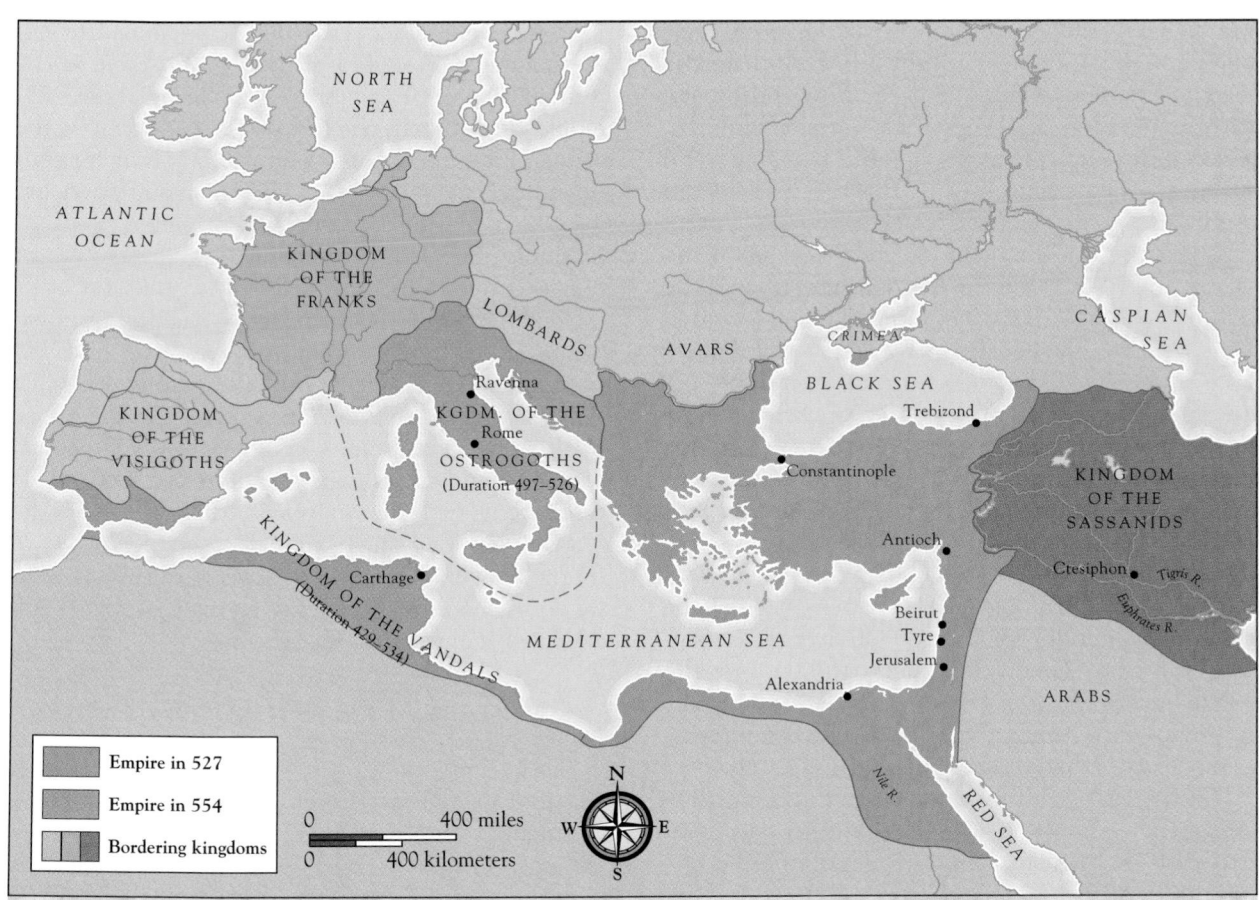

THINKING ABOUT GEOGRAPHY

MAP 6.2 *Map of Justinian's Conquests, 554*

This map shows the extent of the Roman Empire at A.D. 527 after the western provinces had fallen away, and it also shows the extent of Justinian's reconquest. ❧ **Notice** which regions Justinian conquered and the limits to the conquest. **Consider** what facilitated his conquest. ❧ **What** might contribute to the loss of these lands? **Compare** this map with Map 6.3 to see how fragile this reconquest proved to be.

rule of the orthodox emperor over the Arian Vandals, the Italians, who were governed by the tolerant Ostrogoths, were less thrilled. The new regime brought more violence and taxation. Worse, Justinian had to rely on German mercenaries to win these battles. As we saw on page 201, this strategy paved the way for the Lombards to conquer Italy in 568. Although Justinian temporarily accomplished some of his goals, the reconquest led only to failure in the long run. He could not maintain a firm grip on the western provinces, and the constant battling drained the eastern empire of needed resources. Justinian's dream of reuniting and reconnecting with the empire's old homeland in Rome would vanish forever.

CONSTANTINOPLE: THE VIBRANT CITY

Constantinople not only was the administrative and cultural center of the east, it also served as the economic hub. The great city's wealth stemmed in part from commerce: Trade routes to the Far East all passed through Constantinople, so spices, silks, rare woods, and perfumes poured into the Byzantine capital. These luxury items brought a fine profit to the men and women who resold them. Streets thronged with shopkeepers displaying their wares: goldsmiths, silversmiths, furniture makers, textile merchants, and so on. Shoppers bargained at the booths, and the sounds of commerce rang through the streets.

The Byzantine Empire also grew rich producing luxury items. Artisans in Constantinople and the *Lucrative industries* other major cities of the east crafted expensive fabrics, fine jewelry, glassware, and ivory works as Document 6.2 on page D6.1 describes. The empire imported silkworms from China in the sixth century, which opened a new, lucrative industry. The royal court held a monopoly on silk production, and the finest silk was made in the emperor's palace itself. The court also controlled the profitable industry of purple dye, which was produced from mounds of shellfish left to rot on the shores of the eastern Mediterranean. Everyone, from east to west, who wanted to demonstrate their nobility or royalty had to have purple dye. The long purple robes worn by Justinian and Theodora in Figures 6.8 and 6.9 testify to more riches than the couple's gold and jewels.

While great wealth was available in the bustling city, it came to only a few. The Byzantines had abandoned the ancient Roman tradition of offering free food to the urban poor, but officials offered food to those who worked in imperial bakeries or on aqueduct repair. The palace also established a number of charitable institutions for the needy, including poorhouses, hospitals, and the first orphanages recorded in Western tradition. Even while the court made provision for the poor, it believed more of a social threat came from those in a position to gain great wealth.

Prosperity brought temptation, and emperors and other highly placed officials began to favor eunuchs as a way to control corruption. Easterners from the time of the ancient Persian Empire believed that eunuchs were less prone to corruption than other men. Because eunuchs had no children, they were expected to have little motivation to acquire wealth to pass along to subsequent generations. As eunuchs gained favor in high places, some poor families even had a son castrated to prepare him for a prosperous career. In addition to the emperor's closest aides, highly placed bureaucrats, some army and navy commanders, and some high church officials were eunuchs. Doctors who were eunuchs were allowed to treat women, though some women's hospitals insisted on letting only female doctors attend to their patients.

A society and economy that so prominently featured eunuchs would have been unthinkable in the Roman Empire of Augustus. Yet, the Byzantines did retain some Roman characteristics. For example, the Roman tradition of public political involvement continued in Constantinople, as Justinian and Theodora discovered during the riots. In this vibrant city, people argued about the great *Chariot races* religious questions, political issues, and the ever-intriguing chariot races. In Rome, men and women had gathered in the Forum or the Colosseum to express their collective opinion; in Constantinople they flocked to see the chariot races. The great race track—the hippodrome—could seat 40,000 people, and the emperor frequently addressed his people there. The two chariot teams, the Blues and the Greens, signified much more than simply a love of sports. People aligned themselves with the teams as we do with political parties—by wealth, religion, social class, and political inclination.

MILITARY MIGHT AND DIPLOMATIC DEALINGS

Constantinople's walls kept the empire safe from the Germanic tribes heading west, but external enemies still posed a threat. The Byzantines clashed regularly with the powerful Persians and kept a vigilant eye on the tribes to the north. As we will see, the Muslim people to the south also represented a constant danger. To withstand these challenges, the Byzantines carefully considered both military and diplomatic science.

While the emperors kept the administration of Constantinople in civilian hands, they entrusted the care of the provinces to military men. Rulers divided up their empire into about 25 provinces, called *themes*, governed by military commanders. (See Map 6.3 on page 210 for the *theme* divisions.) Assemblies composed of "heads of house- *Provincial organization* holds" empowered to make judicial and financial decisions administered the villages within each *theme*. Governors designated most village families as "military households," which meant they owed one fully equipped man to the empire's army. In this way, the provinces were guarded by armies made up of local residents who had a strong stake in the protection of their homes.

In addition, the Byzantine army was disciplined, well paid, and thoroughly armed. Its backbone, the heavy cavalry, provided the army with extraordinary

FIGURE 6.10
Greek fire.

flexibility. Protected by mail armor and outfitted with lances and swords as well as bows and arrows, these fighters could shoot from a distance as archers or do battle at close range while heavily armed. The cavalry in turn was supported by an efficient infantry. Though only about 120,000 men at its height, this standing army was supplemented by a large number of camp followers. Slaves and engineers accompanied the infantry everywhere. Unlike the Roman legions, who constructed their own camps every night, the Byzantines depended on camp slaves to carry out such tasks. The army also developed a finely tuned medical corps, complete with ambulance carts that moved the wounded to safety.

The army

In addition to its land army, the empire continued the Roman tradition of maintaining a strong navy. It was particularly essential that the Byzantines sustain naval superiority after Muslims threatened shipping in the Mediterranean, so they continued to invest considerable resources in their warships. In the seventh century, Byzantine scientists invented "Greek fire," a deadly new weapon that gave the navy a crucial competitive edge. Figure 6.10 shows a manuscript illustration of the use of Greek fire in a naval battle. The substance was made of combustible oil that was pumped through tubes or placed in containers to be launched from a catapult. The liquid then burst into flames on contact with the target. This weapon proved particularly effective at sea; because the oil floated, it kept burning on the water. Not surprisingly, the Byzantines closely guarded the secrets of Greek fire.

The Byzantines' military success stemmed from more than strategic and technical innovations. Unlike their western counterparts, the easterners continued and improved the ancient Romans' highly developed diplomatic techniques to protect their empire. Many Byzantine emperors considered diplomacy as important as war, and therefore worthy of just as much investment. As a matter of policy, these rulers used spies, lies, and money to weaken their enemies, and sometimes even turned their enemies against each other. Indeed, today the term "Byzantine diplomacy" still connotes expedient and tricky negotiations. However, such complex diplomacy needed money to succeed. As long as the empire was wealthy enough to keep funding bribes, spies, and counterintelligence efforts, it stood firm. Later in the Middle Ages, the empire's diplomatic powers faded after an economic downturn.

Diplomacy

Nevertheless, the world learned much from the Byzantines about using diplomacy instead of war as a way to resolve conflict.

BREAKING AWAY FROM THE WEST

As early as the rule of Diocletian (r. 284–305) (discussed in Chapter 5), the emperors in the east claimed to be sacred people appointed by God and worthy of veneration. As one sign of their devotion, subjects dropped full length to the floor in the presence of royalty. Such ceremonies began to steer the eastern empire away from the traditions of the west. After Justinian's reconquest attempt ended in the loss of the western provinces, the Byzantines turned their focus eastward. The two sections of the former Roman Empire grew increasingly dissimilar in every way, especially in their language and religious attitudes.

Justinian was the last eastern emperor to use Latin as the official language. After the seventh century, the language of the Byzantine bureaucracy changed to Greek. This made sense given that the native language of most educated people in the east was Greek rather than Latin, but it accelerated the east's drift away from the west. The split became even more pronounced after people living in the Germanic kingdoms gradually forgot how to speak and read Greek. Men and women living in the two sections of the old Roman Empire could no longer converse except through interpreters.

During the late Roman Empire, Christianity had linked the faithful of many regions and backgrounds together in one worship. However, *Religious controversy* even this unifying force began to weaken between the seventh and eleventh centuries. In part, the religious separation had its roots in the language difference. As the official language in the east became Greek, church services and writings were conducted in Greek, while the west continued to preserve Latin as the ecclesiastical language.

The question of who should lead the church posed another problem. As we have seen, the power vacuum caused by the invasions allowed the popes to emerge as independent political leaders. In the east, however, the self-styled sacred emperors were "Caesaropapist," that is they led both church and state. Note, for example how the images of Justinian and Theodora in Figures 6.8 and 6.9 include religious symbols in addition to emblems of their secular offices. Emperors led the church, appointed the patri-

archs (the eastern equivalents of the highest ranking archbishops), led church councils, and involved themselves in theological controversies.

Just as Constantine had called the Council of Nicaea in 325 to discuss the origin of Christ (see Chapter 5), the Byzantine emperor Marcian called the Council of Chalcedon in 451 to resolve questions about the human and divine natures of Christ. The council decided that Jesus was both fully human and fully divine. This position seemed eminently logical to the pope in the west. Yet some men and women in portions of the east were shocked by this conclusion. In their view, this statement seemed to reduce the power of God by acknowledging that Jesus remained human. The anger catalyzed by this resolution further separated portions of the eastern empire from the west.

In the eighth century, another religious controversy convulsed the east and brought the growing differences between the Latin and Greek churches to the forefront. From the fifth through the sixth centuries, the worship of the faithful in the eastern church had focused on icons—images of Jesus, Mary, and the saints. People viewed these depic- *Iconoclasm* tions as more than simple portrayals; they believed that the images contained spirituality that had become material and thus could bring divine help. Byzantine monasteries in particular had amassed huge wealth by painting and selling icons. In the west, men and women also venerated images of saints, but not to the same degree.

The Byzantine emperor Leo III (r. 717–741) ordered all icons destroyed, and in an autocratic style, he intended for his decree to apply to all of Christendom, east and west. In part this dictate represented a belief common in the Asiatic provinces, that veneration of icons amounted to worshipping idols. Leo's policy also had a political side. The eastern emperors wanted to challenge the growing power of the monasteries that were producing most of the icons. This controversy raged for a century in the east, during which many mosaics in Constantinople and Asia Minor were destroyed, leaving Ravenna as the most important repository of the old mosaics. Finally, less controversial emperors withdrew their support from the *iconoclasts* ("icon destroyers"). In the meantime, however, the western popes did not acknowledge the emperor's authority, and Pope Gregory II (r. 715–731) defied Leo's edict. The tensions resulting from this struggle strained relations between the eastern and western churches even further.

Over the centuries, two branches of Christianity grew more and more apart until they became two separate churches—the Catholic west and the Orthodox east. The Orthodox church rejected the concept of Papal supremacy that was growing in the west and preserved the idea that the church should be led by five bishops (called patriarchs) who presided in the five major cities. Rome, Constantinople, Jerusalem, Alexandria, and Antioch. Each of the five patriarchs—called the Pentarchs—exerted jurisdiction in his own area and met with the other patriarchs in council to regulate matters of dogma and church discipline. Over time, they rejected decisions made outside these councils by the Popes alone. Questions of language, theology, hierarchy, the wording of the creeds, and even the date of Easter finally severed ties between east and west.

Orthodox Church

In 1054, the two churches broke apart. The pope and the patriarch of Constantinople excommunicated each other, and the unified Christian church became two. (The mutual excommunications were finally withdrawn, but not until 1965.) Both the Roman Catholic and Greek Orthodox churches would grow and find adherents all over the world into the twenty-first century.

CONVERTING THE SLAVS, 560–CA. 1000

Starting in the sixth century, the several Slavic groups settling along the Danube River that had once formed the northeastern boundary of the Roman Empire represented yet another challenge to Byzantine unity. These pagan tribes included Serbs, Croats, and Avars. In 679, the Bulgars, a Turko-Mongolian people came out of the steppes of Russia and built a powerful kingdom just north of the Danube. Map 6.3 shows generally where these peoples settled. In the ninth century, Scandinavian traders (and raiders) established a kingdom in Kiev (modern Ukraine) made up of Slavic people ruled by Scandinavian princes. (This principality, called Kievan Rus, became the origin of the name "Russia.") All these peoples alternately raided and traded with the eastern empire and personally experienced the famed Byzantine diplomacy. Some tribes were bribed into peace, other kings were offered Byzantine brides, and occasionally tribes were tricked into fighting each other.

The Byzantines sought a way to bring these peoples within the eastern empire's influence by converting them to Christianity. In 863, the Byzantine emperor Michael III (r. 842–867) sent two missionaries, Cyril and Methodius, to the Slavs. The missionaries realized that conversion depended in part on literacy. The Slavs, who had no written language, could not read the church services. Therefore, Cyril and Methodius developed a Slavonic written language based on the Greek alphabet.

Cyril and Methodius

Their mission was successful. Serbs and Russians embraced Greek Christianity and the alphabet that Cyril and Methodius developed to transmit the religion became known as the "Cyrillic alphabet" (named after St. Cyril). It is still used in Russia and in portions of the Balkan peninsula today. The Bulgar leader also converted to Othodox Christianity in the 890s and adopted the Cyrillic alphabet.

The state of Kievian Rus was brought to Christianity by a bargain struck between the reputedly ruthless prince of Kiev, Vladimir (r. 978–1015), and the Byzantine emperor Basil II (r. 976–1025). Basil wanted to secure Vladimir's military assistance and bring the growing eastern Slavic state into Byzantium's sphere of influence. Vladimir agreed to convert to Greek Orthodox Christianity and help Basil if the emperor would give his own sister, Anna—a princess "born to the purple"—as Vladimir's bride. The Kievan prince already had several wives, but Basil had little choice. Anna went north and Vladimir established churches along the Byzantine model. Vladimir's "conversion" in 989 marks the traditional date for the beginning of Christianity in Russia.

Conversion of Russia

Like its Byzantine counterparts, the Catholic church also sent missionaries who successfully converted tribes in portions of the east. The Poles, Bohemians, Hungarians, and Croats adopted Catholic Christianity and the Latin alphabet that came with it. These divisions in religion, loyalty, and alphabet divided eastern Europe, and, indeed, cultural divisions established during this period have continued to color the politics of the region into the twenty-first century.

By the tenth century, the Byzantine Empire had entered a sort of "golden age." It had occupied and assimilated the strong Bulgarian kingdom and the eastern emperor exerted his authority from the Adriatic to the Black Sea. The empire was prosperous and secure. The Byzantine culture and the western kingdoms would interact for centuries, during which the West gained a great deal

"Golden age"

THINKING ABOUT GEOGRAPHY

MAP 6.3 *Map of the Byzantine Empire, Eighth Century*

This map shows the extent and the organization of the Byzantine Empire in the eighth century and the peoples who surrounded the empire. ✒ **Notice** the internal structure of the empire—its division into *themes*. **Consider** how this might be an effective way to manage decentralized provinces. ✒ **Notice** the names and locations of the Bulgars, Slavs, Croats, Serbs, and the other peoples in the Balkan region. **Consider** how difficult it was for the Byzantines to withstand pressure from all these peoples.

from Byzantium. The western legal system owed much to Justinian's codification, western scholars would gain from the Greek texts preserved in the east, and western kingdoms owed their survival to Byzantium serving as a buffer state against incursions from the east. The eastern empire and the Orthodox church left an enduring cultural influence in eastern Europe that continues to affect political life today. In the seventh century, the Mediterranean world grew even more complex: A third great power was rising in the south and this new civilization would come to challenge both the West and Byzantium.

Islam, 600–1000

In the early seventh century, the Arabian peninsula was part of neither the Byzantine nor the Persian Empires. The region contained both oases with settled populations and great reaches of desert. In the desert, nomadic Bedouin tribes roamed, living on milk, meat, and cheese from camels and goats; dates; and some grain from the oases. These tribes emphasized family and clan loyalty and fought, raided, and feuded with each other to protect their honor and their possessions. The Arabs were pagan, worshipping natural objects such as stones, springs, and a large ancient meteor that had fallen into the Arabian desert long before human memory.

The success of Bedouin life stemmed in large part from the use of domesticated camels. These magnificent desert animals could carry heavy loads for many miles without water, and proved a speedy form of transportation in the raids of desert warfare. The Bedouins sold camels to the Arabs of the oases, who in turn used them for the long-distance trade that brought prosperity to the small cities of the oases.

During the wars between Byzantium and Persia (540–630?), the land route to the Far East through Mesopotamia became dangerous. For safety's sake, some traders from Constantinople and Egypt decided to travel through Mecca in Arabia to reach a water route through the Red Sea. Others crossed the Arabian peninsula to leave by sea from the Persian Gulf. This trade brought even more wealth to the thriving oasis cities, the most important of which was Mecca. Mecca housed an important pagan shrine, the Ka'bah, containing an ancient meteorite, which drew Bedouins and other Arabs to gather in peace for trade. But trading had another consequence beyond stimulating commerce: It brought Arabs in contact with Christians and Jews, and as a result, new ideas filtered into the Arabian peninsula.

The Prophet

The new ideas generated by Arab, Christian, and Jewish interaction came to be embodied in the person of a man named Muhammad. Muhammad (570–632) was an orphan who grew up in Mecca in the care of his uncle. He became a merchant and made an excellent marriage to a wealthy widow and businesswoman, Khadijah. The couple had seven children and lived a prosperous life. As a merchant, Muhammad earned a reputation for being a good and honest man. His nickname was "al-Amin"—"the trustworthy."

In his fortieth year, Muhammad began to have visions. First an angel appeared to him while he was sleeping and said: "Read! Thy Lord . . . taught by the pen, taught that which they knew not unto men." When Muhammad awoke from this vision, he saw a huge man with his feet astride the horizon. This man claimed to be the angel Gabriel

The Qur'an

and told Muhammad to be the apostle to his people. According to Islamic tradition, Muhammad received an additional 114 revelations over the next 20 years. These revelations were recorded as the word of Allah (God) given in the Arabic language. Accounts of the revelations were collected after Muhammad's death and became the book of inspired scripture of the new religion. This scripture is called the Qur'an (sometimes written in English as "Koran").

Muhammad believed the God who spoke through him was the same God worshiped by Jews and Christians. Muhammad said that five major prophets had come before him: Adam, Noah, Abraham, Moses, and Jesus. Muhammad said each had brought truth, but Christians and Jews had departed from the prophets' messages—the Jews had ignored Jesus, and Christians had embellished the simple message of the Gospels by adding theological complexities. Therefore, Allah had decided to speak through Muhammad, who is known simply as the Prophet. The religion he founded is called Islam, and its followers are known as Muslims.

The Religion

The nature of Islam is as clear and stark as the Arabian desert itself. "Islam" means "surrender to God," and this idea lies at the heart of the religion, for a follower of the religion is called a Muslim—"one who submits." Christians had to study for years before converting and had to understand the subtlety of various creeds. For a man or woman to convert to Islam, he or she merely needed to testify, "There is no God but Allah and Muhammad is his prophet." Whenever children were born in Muslim lands, midwives and parents whispered this creed into their ears so that they would grow immediately into faith. After this simple creed, Muslims were to follow the Five Pillars of Faith.

The first pillar of faith is the "Profession of Faith" itself. Believers adhere to a strict monotheism. (For example, Muslims believe that the Christian belief in the Trinity of the Father, Son, and Holy Spirit signaled a departure from the command to have only one God.) Further, Muslims believe that the Qur'an represents the word of God. The power of the written word had come to light in Muhammad's first vision, which emphasized the importance of reading and of a God who brought the truth through

Faith

a written text. Many of the faithful memorize the entire Qur'an (which is about as long as the Christian New Testament).

Figure 6.11 shows a page from the Qur'an. The beautiful calligraphy of the Arabic letters, and the gold leaf make precious manuscripts like this one as much works of art as religious objects. Muslims believe that the Qur'an must not be translated from the original language, so all the manuscripts are copied in Arabic. This figure shows how strikingly different the Arabic alphabet is from the Greek and Latin scripts that dominated in the West. This visual signal points to the language barrier that would separate Muslim from Christian lands.

The first pillar concerned private behavior, indicating the faith within, but the next four reinforced the first through public actions of all believers. The second pillar of faith is prayer, an activity that the faithful perform five times a day. In addition, every Friday, Muslims gather to pray together at the local mosque, called there by a human voice beckoning from the mosque towers, or minarets. (Christians are called by bells, and Jews by horns. Muslims believe the angel Gabriel told Muhammad to use the human voice to call his followers to prayer.)

Public rituals

Unlike Christian churches, mosques display no images of God. Muslims take the biblical prohibition against the idolatry of graven images literally. It may be that the Byzantine iconoclast movement was influenced by the example of the strict interpretation of the Muslims. Instead of images of God, mosques are decorated with beautiful geometric patterns. These designs are intended to help the faithful in their prayers by focusing their attention on the divine pattern of the universe. An example of mosaic patterning appears on the photograph of the Dome of the Rock shown at the opening of this chapter.

The third pillar of faith is almsgiving. Muslims are to donate a portion of what they earn to the needy, and this giving purifies the rest of their earnings. The fourth pillar of faith is fasting. All Muslims fast during the month of Ramadan, a time based on the lunar calendar that comes at a different point every year, which commemorates the month Allah revealed the Qur'an to Muhammad. During this month, the faithful ingest no food nor drink nor engage in sexual relations during the day, but eat and celebrate every night after sundown. This month is much loved by Muslims because it lets them attend to spiritual matters and family in a concentrated way.

The last pillar of faith is pilgrimage. All Muslims try to make a journey to Muhammad's holy city of Mecca once in their lifetime. This trip—called the *Haj*—is made during a designated pilgrimage month, so the city throngs with Muslims from all over the world during this special time. Muslims today continue to follow all the pillars of faith, including the Haj.

THE SPREAD OF ISLAM

When Muhammad began to speak of his visions, his wife Khadijah became his first convert. However, aside from her and some close friends, few people living in the market city of Mecca paid any attention to his message. This city had grown prosperous in part because of pilgrims coming to worship at the pagan shrine of the Ka'bah, so the city leaders had little interest in the words of a new prophet.

In 622, Muhammad and his small group of followers fled Mecca to another city 250 miles to the north. This city was later named Medina, which simply means "the city." Muslims consider this flight, called the *Hijra* (or *Hegira*), the turning point in the acceptance of the new religion. Just as Christians mark the birth of Christ as a turning point by dating the calendar from that year, Muslims remember the Hijra by using the year 622 as the year "1" in their calendar. The dating system uses A.H. (*Anno Hijrah*) instead of A.D. (*Anno Domini*).

Hijra

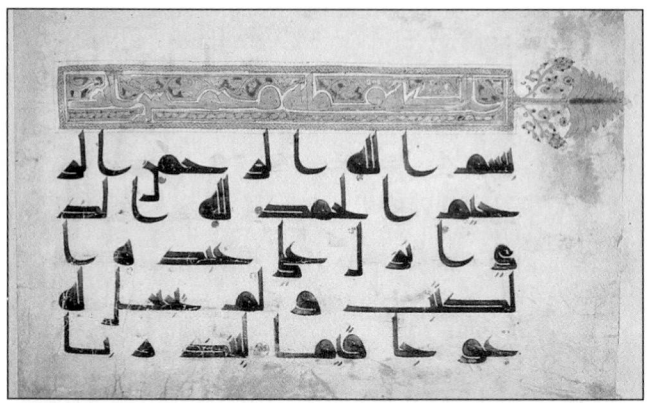

FIGURE 6.11
Page from the Qur'an.

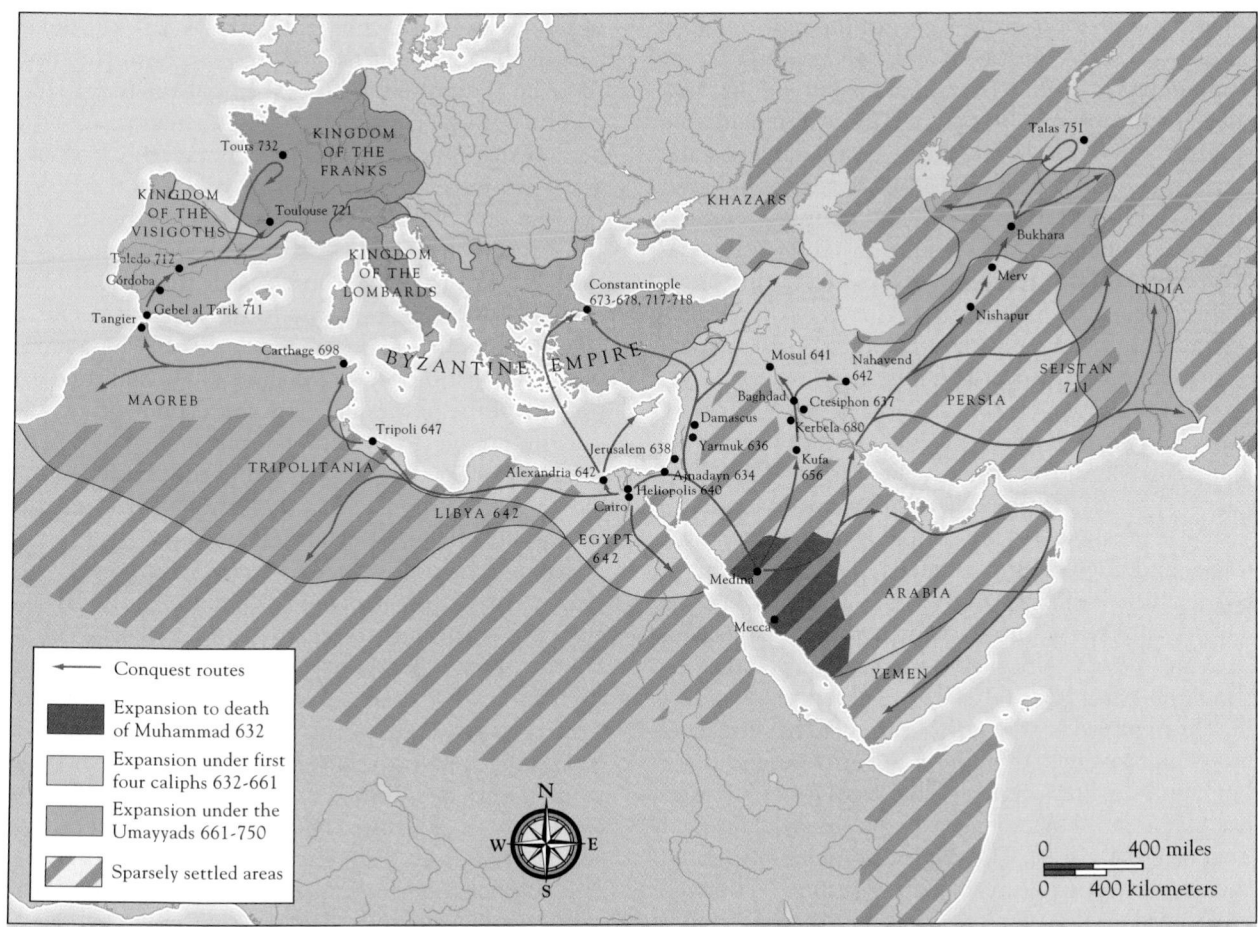

Map showing the expansion of Islam with locations and dates including: Tours 732, KINGDOM OF THE FRANKS, KINGDOM OF THE VISIGOTHS, Toulouse 721, Toledo 712, Córdoba, Tangier, Gebel al Tarik 711, Carthage 698, KINGDOM OF THE LOMBARDS, MAGREB, Tripoli 647, TRIPOLITANIA, LIBYA 642, Alexandria 642, Heliopolis 640, Cairo, EGYPT 642, Jerusalem 638, Yarmuk 636, Amadayn 634, Medina, Mecca, ARABIA, YEMEN, BYZANTINE EMPIRE, Constantinople 673-678, 717-718, KHAZARS, Damascus, Baghdad, Ctesiphon 637, Kerbela 680, Kufa 656, Mosul 641, Nahavend 642, PERSIA, SEISTAN 711, Nishapur, Merv, Bukhara, Talas 751, INDIA

Legend:
→ Conquest routes
Expansion to death of Muhammad 632
Expansion under first four caliphs 632-661
Expansion under the Umayyads 661-750
Sparsely settled areas

0 400 miles
0 400 kilometers

THINKING ABOUT GEOGRAPHY

Map 6.4 *The Expansion of Islam to 750*

This map shows the expansion of Islam from the Arabian peninsula to dominate the southern and eastern Mediterranean. It also gives the dates of the expansion. ❧ Which sections of the Byzantine Empire were lost to the Muslims? ❧ **Notice** the scale on the map. **Consider** the difficulties in governing such a large area. ❧ **Locate** Mecca, Damascus, and Baghdad—each in turn would become the capital of the Muslim world. **Which** regions might be most influenced by the change in capitals? **Where** might the Islamic rulers be most likely to focus their efforts while based in each city?

From his new base in Medina, Muhammad spread his ideas to the desert Bedouins. Tribe by tribe, the Arabians converted and began to focus their warfare on "unbelievers" instead of on each other, eventually coalescing into a unified group. In 628, Muhammad returned victorious to Mecca, where the large numbers of his followers persuaded the urban dwellers that his message was true. He kept the great shrine at

the Ka'bah, convinced that the large meteor within it was sacred to Allah. Pilgrims still journey to this holy place and it is the focal point of the prayer of Muslims worldwide.

Map 6.4 shows the extent of Islam at the death of the Prophet in 632. At first, Muhammad's closest followers proclaimed themselves *caliphs*, ("deputies" or "successors") of the Prophet. The map shows how rapidly the first four caliphs spread the new religion. These successes continued, and only a century after Muhammad's death, Islam held sway in an area stretching from India to Spain. After this remarkable spread, many people who were not Arabs became Muslims, and although all learned to speak Arabic so they could read the Qur'an, sometimes tensions emerged between Arab and non-Arab believers. Nevertheless, the spectacular growth of this compelling new creed obliterated the Persian Empire, shrank the Byzantine Empire, and conquered the Vandal and Visigothic kingdoms.

In the summer of 732, the forces of Islam drove through the passes of the Pyrenees into the Merovingian kingdom of the Franks. The army was made up *Battle of Tours* of a large body of light cavalry and was about 80,000 strong. It was a formidable force, and the Muslim generals were confident of their ability to conquer the less-organized Franks. They easily swept through the southern lands, destroying the opposition and taking great plunder. As the Arab chronicler relates, "All the nations of the Franks trembled at that terrible army." The retreating forces approached the Merovingian household for help, and the great general Charles Martel ("Charles the Hammer") led a force to a large grassy plain near Tours (see Map 6.4). The Arab chronicler recognized the momentous nature of this meeting: "The two great hosts of the two languages and the two creeds were set in array against each other." The battle was fierce and tens of thousands died, but Charles won a decisive victory. The remaining Muslim force retreated across the Pyrenees, and the storm of Islamic conquests in the west was halted.

In spite of Charles's victory, the Islamic conquests were impressive. Why did Islam spread so quickly? There are a number of reasons. In part, its success came from the military strength of the recently unified Bedouin and oasis Arabs. Form-
Reasons for success ing a new "tribe" based on religion, these formerly separate groups now made an effective fighting unit. Islamic armies also benefited from a new attitude toward religious warfare; Muslims believed that Allah had called for a holy war—a *jihad*—to defend the faith. Warriors fought with extra zeal in this cause because they believed that to die in a *jihad* brought salvation and entry into paradise. During the *jihad*, Muslim armies may have forced pagans to convert or be killed, for the Qur'an said "Fight in the path

of God with those who fight with you . . . kill them; such is the reward of the infidels. . . . Fight them till there be no dissent, and the worship be only to God."

The expansion of Islam also drew strength from the benign attitude of the Muslim conquerors. Christians and Jews, whom Muslims called "people of the Book" because they all shared the same sacred scripture and worshipped the same God that Muslims venerated, were allowed to believe and pray as they liked. They had only to pay taxes to the Muslim rulers. In one of the earliest political documents of Islam, Muhammad wrote a "constitution" for Medina in 622 outlining the policies of the new religion. In this document, he laid out the principle of toleration and mutual aid: "The Jews must bear their expenses and the Muslims their expenses. Each must help the other against anyone who attacks the people of this document."

Many Christians, especially in Syria, Egypt, and North Africa, had rejected the policies of the Byzantine emperors and willingly tolerated Islam. For example, some Christians believed in Christ's total divinity (rather than his combined divinity and humanity as required by the Council of Chalcedon in 451), and the North African Donatists believed that priests who had sinned should no longer give the sacraments. Within Byzantium, such men and women had been forbidden to continue in their beliefs. Under the Muslims, who cared little about the subtleties of Christian theology, they could believe as they liked. Jews, too, were free to practice their religion without the pressure they had experienced before, particularly under the Visigoths. For all these people, the "conquerors" seemed far preferable to Christian rulers, and in time, many Christians converted to Islam. The rise of Islam had created a wholly new culture in the Mediterranean world.

CREATING AN ISLAMIC UNITY

The Muslim armies not only conquered large expanses of land, they also quickly transformed the society and culture of these territories. Anyone traveling in the Mediterranean world today can see immediately that life in Algeria is strikingly different from life in Italy. This was not so during Roman times.

What was it about Muslim rule that made Islamic culture take root so powerfully in these formerly Christian regions? Language played a large role. Because the Qur'an was not to be translated, believers

of Islam had to learn Arabic. Therefore, Arabic became the language of business, government, and literature in Islamic strongholds. Prayer
Unifying elements and pilgrimage also served to solidify the Muslim world. As the faithful all looked to Mecca five times a day during prayer and made pilgrimages to the holy places, men and women broadened their attention and loyalties beyond their local kingdoms. Over time, they began to think of themselves as part of a larger group.

Law was another important unifying force. The Islamic governments were ruled by Muslim law based on the Qur'an and the Sunna, which is a collection of cultural traditions based on the life of the Prophet. These laws, administered by Muslim judges, governed most aspects of Islamic life. Uniform enforcement of the laws contributed to a growing cultural homogeneity.

Finally, the great Muslim trade network that extended from India to the Mediterranean powerfully united the Islamic world. The freedom that Muslim rulers allowed merchants and artisans fueled economic development. Arabic coins, *dinars*, began to replace Byzantine or Persian coins as the main trade medium, and the Muslims developed advanced banking techniques to facilitate trade. For example, they initiated the use of bank checks, which would not be employed in the West for another 800 years.

THE GRACIOUS LIFE

With large-scale trade came dramatic changes in Muslim society. The conquerors adopted the best of both the Persian and Hellenistic worlds and created a
Women way of life that was comfortable and pleasant, at least for the wealthy. Muslim households built on traditions drawn from the Bedouin tribes combined with practices from the Persian Empire. Previously, men had been allowed to have an unlimited number of wives, as in the Persian harems. However, the Qur'an limited a man to four wives, and this only if he could demonstrate that he had enough money to provide each wife with her own quarters and her own slaves. If husbands and wives did not get along, they could appeal to a judge who acted as an arbiter. If arbitration failed to resolve a conflict, either the man or the woman could obtain a divorce. Women's status under Islam improved in other ways as well: They were no longer treated strictly as prop-

erty as they had been in pagan Arabic tribal society, and under Islamic law, Muslim women could inherit and keep their property even after marriage.

Within the household, women were separated from the company of men, and this seclusion continued when they went outdoors. Muslims adopted Syrian Christian women's practice of wearing heavy veils to cover themselves, and this practice continues in many Muslim countries today. Within the households, women presided over the many slaves generated from the conquests and subsequent trade, and created a lifestyle that was the envy of many in the Mediterranean world.

Persians taught the Arabian Muslims to play chess and backgammon; from Syria, Muslims learned to wear wide trousers instead of the traditional
Daily life Arab robes. They also began to eat at tables instead of sitting cross-legged on the floor. These seemingly small matters, when taken together, reflected a prosperous, relatively homogeneous society.

Figure 6.12 reveals several unique aspects of Islamic society. In this illustration, two wealthy Muslim men are served wine by a Christian slave probably captured in Spain. (Islamic society depended heavily on slavery just as the Persian and Roman cultures had.) This picture also captures Muslim attitudes toward alcohol. The Qur'an forbids drinking of wine, but many Muslims routinely violated this prohibition. Indeed, some beautiful Arabic poetry even extols the pleasures of good wine. As this illustration indicates, Muslim culture was developing into something very different from life in western Europe and Byzantium.

FORCES OF DISUNITY

For all its cultural commonalties, the Muslim world was not without strife. Two related problems led to conflict within the Muslim territories. One problem centered on ethnicity—specifically, relations between Arabs and other Muslim peoples. The other involved a pressing political question: Who would rule after the death of the Prophet?

Some Muslims believed that the caliphs should be spiritual leaders who based their authority on the Prophet's family. In the mid-seventh-
Shi'ite Muslims century, amid much controversy over the succession, the Prophet's son-in-law and cousin, 'Ali, became the caliph. 'Ali promoted the idea of

Global Connections

YEMEN: MONOTHEISM SPREADS TO SOUTHERN ARABIA

■ **CONSIDER** the relationship between long-distance trade and the spread of religious ideas. **Notice** the similarities and differences in how religious controversies were expressed in Yemen and the Mediterranean basin.

Trade is the greatest stimulant to human interaction. Throughout history, men and women have willingly journeyed vast distances to sell or acquire luxury items like jewelry, fine clothing, and spices, as well as to trade everyday, useful objects like pots, knives, and basic ingredients for meals. But as merchants and entrepreneurs talked business and conducted deals along the major trade routes, they transported ideas in addition to merchandise. The ancient trade between the Mediterranean world and the southernmost tip of Arabia brought together peoples separated by immense deserts and exposed them to one another's religious ideas and controversies. As notions of religion spread, the lives of peoples from these two markedly different worlds began to be inextricably connected. Of course, the shifting sands of southern Arabia's deserts and the monsoon winds that whipped across the Red Sea posed daunting obstacles to people seeking to travel from southern Arabia, or Yemen, to the Mediterranean. Yet, these enterprising individuals found ways to interact with their counterparts in the eastern Mediterranean.

Some scholars suggest that after Africa, Yemen was the earliest area of human migration out of the African continent. Bold Africans crossed the Arabian Sea at the narrow straits separating the Red Sea from the Gulf of Adan, and the human expansion out of Africa had begun. The fertile plateaus of Yemen's highlands and the abundant sea coasts allowed early villages to flourish. As far back as 1,000 B.C. several wealthy kingdoms cropped up in this promising new land. Historians of technology are particularly impressed by the ruins of the ancient Marib Dam that settlers built in about 500 B.C. This astonishing structure allowed the ancient residents of the City of Saba (the Sabeans) to irrigate about 25,000 acres of land—and secure their food supply for the next thousand years.

But Yemen's real wealth came from trade. The region grows rare, brush-like trees that produce strong-smelling resins from which ancient peoples produced frankincense and myrrh. These resins—used in perfumes, medicines, and religious cere-

equality for all believers, rather than privileged status for Arabs who had initially spread the Prophet's message. Although he hoped to serve less as a governor and tax collector than a spiritual leader, 'Ali had to devote much of his reign to fighting political rivals.

In 661, as 'Ali was entering a mosque to pray, an assassin supporting another political faction plunged a dagger into the caliph, but 'Ali's notion of the caliphate remained alive. Men and women who followed his ideal were called Shi'ites. They continue to believe that the Islamic world should be ruled by *imams,* men descended from 'Ali who act as true spiritual heads of the community. The Shi'ite faithful proclaimed 'Ali's two sons, Hasan and Husayn, the second and third Imams. Husayn is particularly revered by Shi'ites today because followers of the caliph killed him and his infant son. Although Shi'ites look upon the usurpation of 'Ali's rights to rule as the beginning of their movement, Husayn's death—which they saw as a martyrdom—served as the emotional rallying point for the Shi'ites. To this day, the death of Husayn is the most fervently celebrated event in the Shi'ite monies—were prized throughout the ancient Mediterranean world. By 1,000 B.C., domestication of the camel enabled merchants to trade extensively across the Arabian desert. As one result, demand for frankincense and myrrh spread widely in the northern parts of Arabia and throughout the Mediterranean basin. One ancient writer described a caravan of three thousand camels which would have extended over 25 miles as it arrived at Mediterranean ports laden with the precious incenses. Certainly the best-known caravan of cherished goods from Saba was brought by the Queen of Sheba (Saba) to the court of the Jewish King Solomon. This trade mission is described in both the Bible (1 Kings 10:1-13) and the Qur'an (27-16-44). For centuries, people throughout the ancient world continued to value frankincense and myrrh: The Roman scholar, Pliny the Elder, noted that the Emperor Nero burned an entire year's harvest of frankincense to mark his mother's funeral. Indeed, southern Arabia prospered so much during this earliest era that the Romans called it "Arabia Felix" which translates to "Happy Arabia."

But even Happy Arabia was swept into the religious turmoil that raged through the Mediterranean world in the centuries after the birth of Christ. During the fourth and fifth centuries AD, missionaries traveling the caravan routes began converting the southern Arabian tribes to monotheism. Their efforts spawned tensions. For example, In the early six century A.D., the Sabean king ordered all Christians in his realm to convert to Judaism. When twenty thousand of them refused, he ordered them executed. The Christian king of Ethiopia retaliated by seizing Yemen in A.D. 525. However, the Christian reign he initiated lasted just 50 years, crumbling when the Persians conquered the Yemeni kingdoms in 575. In 628, the Persian governor of Yemen embraced Islam, and the new religion spread quickly through the tribes of southern Arabia. As

early as 630 (before the death of the Prophet) the first mosques rose in Yemen's cities. Still, the conversion of the Yemenis to Islam could not heal the religious divisions that had long plagued the region.

When the Muslim faithful split into factions (Sunni and Shi'ite) over the question of who should rule after the death of Muhammad, the faithful in Yemen also eventually took sides in the dispute. In the early eighth century, Shi'ites argued that the succession went to the grandsons of Husayn. (See page 216 for more information on Husayn.) Most of the Shi'ites recognized Husayn's elder son, Muhammad al-Baqir as the fifth Imam. But some dissidents recognized the younger son, Zayd, as the legitimate successor. Both Zayd and his son were killed in subsequent battles and so could not fulfill their supposed destiny. However, many Shi'ites contended that while the next Imam must be a descendent of Husayn or his brother Husan, he need not be the eldest of the siblings. This became one of several points of difference among the Shi'ite communities. Holding firm to their positions, a number of Zaydi sects emerged and formed a separate branch of the Shi'ite movement. In the late eighth century, some Zaydis fled to the mountainous region of Yemen. There, in 901, they established a Zaydi state. This long-standing branch of Shi'ism remains a significant minority in Yemen today.

As the centuries have unfolded, Yemen has continued to take part in the political and religious struggles marking interactions between the Western and Islamic worlds—from its conquest by the Ottoman Empire in the sixteenth century, to its engagement in Cold War politics during the mid-twentieth century, to the near-sinking of the U.S. battleship Cole in one of its harbors in 2000. In ancient times, the trade in precious resins brought this land into contact with the West and its fortunes have remained intertwined with those of the West ever since.

calendar. From these early centuries, Shi'ites believe that *imams* are endowed with the Divine Light Wisdom that enables them to interpret complicated passages in the Qur'an. Shi'ites today are a significant minority in the Muslim world and continue to disagree with the Sunnis, who advocate a political, rather than purely spiritual, caliphate. The "Global Connection" on page 216 shows how this struggle influenced events in southern Arabia (modern Yemen).

After the murder of 'Ali, the caliphate was taken over by the Umayyad family, who established a dynasty that lasted almost a century. The Umayyads located their capital in Damascus and created a government that favored Arabs. This dynasty represented the traditional military and economic leaders of the Arabs. Nevertheless, dissent stirred even within the Umayyad caliphate. The Dome of the Rock (shown at the beginning of this chapter) was built by one Umayyad caliph in 691 who wanted to de-emphasize Mecca. He encouraged the faithful to visit the rock in Jerusalem from where Muslims believed Muhammad

Umayyad caliphate

had ascended to heaven. He was successful; the Dome of the Rock today is a much-loved shrine. Unfortunately, it stands on land that Jews and Christians also venerate, and the site continues to generate controversy.

In 750, the 'Abbasids overthrew the Umayyad caliphate. They intended to restore more spiritual authority to the caliphate and to broaden authority from the Arabs to other believers, but most important, they moved the capital from Damascus to Baghdad. This newly built city, located on the banks of the Tigris River, was perfectly suited to take advantage of the rich trade from the Far East. Its land was rich, and the caliph was particularly impressed with its cool nights and freedom from mosquitoes. The founder claimed, "It will surely be the most flourishing city in the world," and he was not wrong. The great city, fortified by three concentric round walls, was the administrative center of Islam and by the tenth century had a population of about 1.5 million people. This extraordinary city helped the Muslim world focus toward the old Persian provinces, with their rich trade routes to the east. Seen from this magnificent cosmopolitan city, rivaled only by Constantinople, western Europe seemed very primitive indeed. (See "Global Connections" in Chapter 7 on page 239.) However, the move to the east did not help the 'Abbasids eliminate political dissension. The Umayyads continued to hold power in Spain, and the Shi'ites refused to support the 'Abbasids.

'Abbasid caliphate

Beyond the disunity percolating within the ruling dynasties, there was the ever-present tendency toward local control. Caliphs in Baghdad growing rich on eastern trade had little authority over commanders as far away as Spain, and by the tenth century A.D. (fourth century of the Islamic calendar), military commanders, called *emirs*, took power in their local areas. Although they theoretically followed the rule of the caliphs, they frequently acted with a good deal of autonomy. As Map 6.5 shows, the huge Muslim

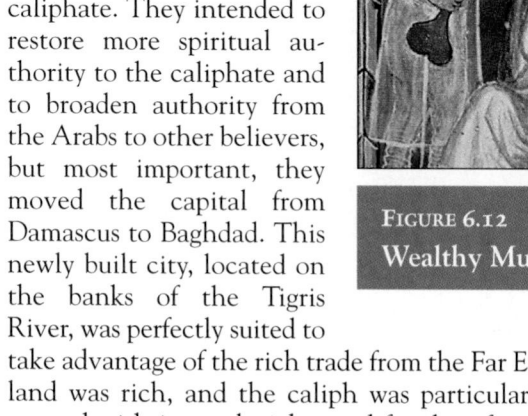

FIGURE 6.12
Wealthy Muslim household in Spain, ca. 1283.

world, which formed a strong cultural unity, suffered from the centrifugal forces that separated all the ancient empires.

HEIRS TO HELLENISTIC LEARNING

Despite all the political tensions, the Muslim world still managed to make astonishing gains in the arts and sciences, and in fact remained the intellectual center of the Mediterranean world for centuries. By the eighth century, the caliphs had collected Persian, Greek, and Syriac scientific and philosophical works and had them translated into Arabic. In the ninth century, the 'Abbasids ruling in Baghdad maintained this support of science. They built the House of Wisdom in Baghdad, which included a library, a translation center, and a school. This careful cultivation of learning and the blending of so many traditions led to remarkable accomplishments. Muslim scientists and physicians were by far the best in the Western world.

Muslim doctors did not slavishly follow the great classical physicians, Hippocrates and Galen, even though the works of these men circulated widely. Instead they combined this ancient *Medicine* wisdom with practical and empirical observation. Islamic rulers required doctors to be licensed, so the practice of medicine was well regulated. Some Islamic physicians wrote extensively and exerted a

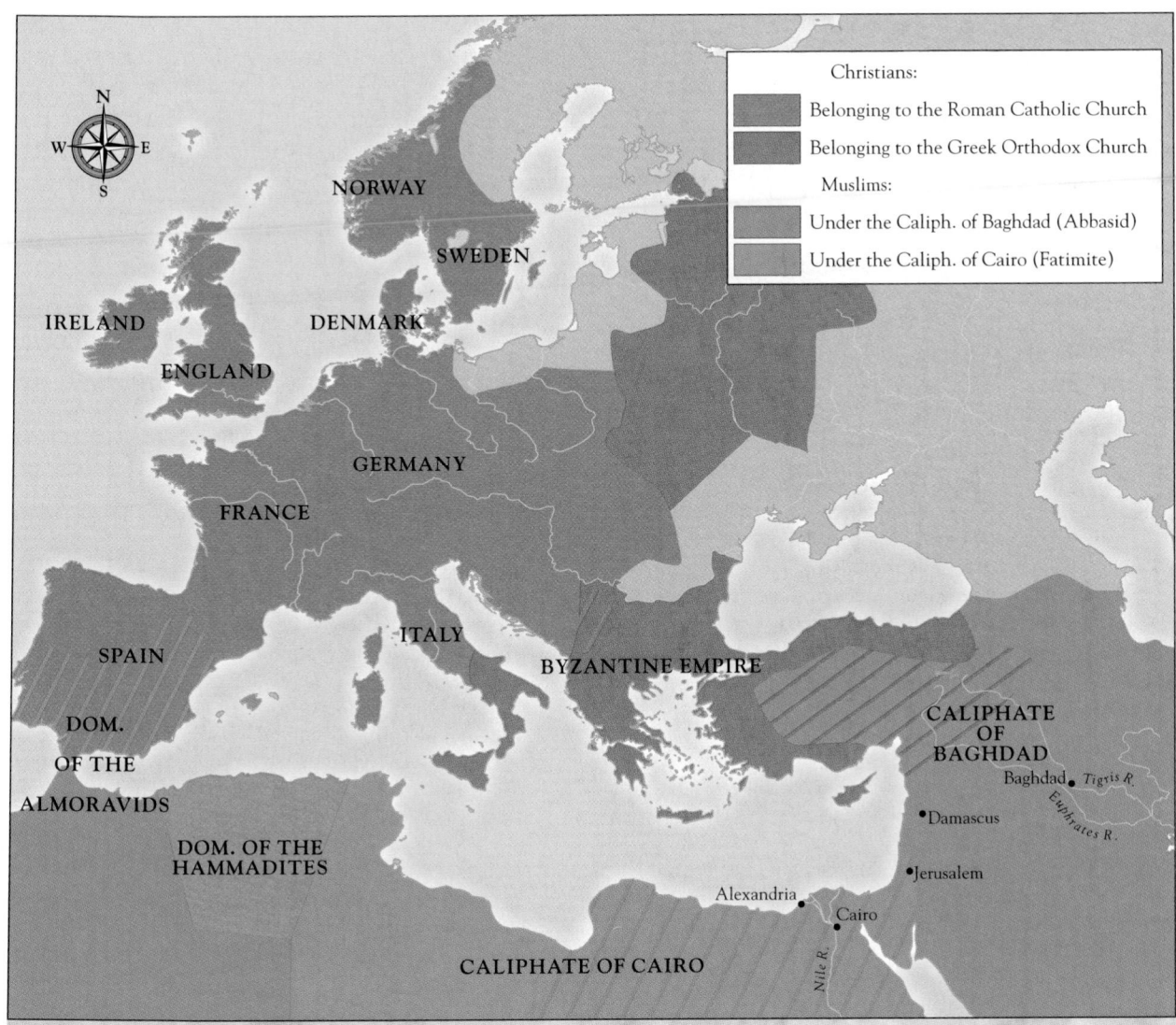

Christians:

- Belonging to the Roman Catholic Church
- Belonging to the Greek Orthodox Church

Muslims:

- Under the Caliph. of Baghdad (Abbasid)
- Under the Caliph. of Cairo (Fatimite)

NORWAY

SWEDEN

IRELAND

DENMARK

ENGLAND

GERMANY

FRANCE

ITALY

SPAIN

BYZANTINE EMPIRE

DOM.
OF THE
ALMORAVIDS

CALIPHATE
OF
BAGHDAD

Baghdad • Tigris R.

•Damascus

Euphrates R.

DOM. OF THE
HAMMADITES

•Jerusalem

Alexandria •

• Cairo

CALIPHATE OF CAIRO

Nile R.

THINKING ABOUT GEOGRAPHY

MAP 6.5 *Map of Islam, ca. 1000*

This map shows how the world of Islam divided to be ruled by various leaders. ❧ **Notice** how the 'Abbasid caliphate focuses toward the east with its capital at Baghdad. ❧ **Notice** the scale of the map and the distances between the Dominion of the Almoravids in Spain and North Africa. **Consider** how such distances would serve as a hindrance to a strongly centralized authority.

profound influence on western medicine. Razi (865–925) (called Rhazes in the West) authored more than 100 books on medicine. He was the first to diagnose smallpox and prescribe an effective treatment for it. Ibn Sina (980–1037) (known as Avicenna in the West) wrote *Canon of Medicine*, an encyclopedia of medicine that laid the foundation for experimental science.

Biography

AVICENNA (IBN SINA) (980–1037)

◼ **Notice** how Avicenna's life shows the high respect for learning found among the ancient Muslims.

◼ **Notice** also how the forces of disunity within the Muslim world affected Avicenna's life.

Avicenna was born in 980, the son of a wealthy governor of an outlying province in modern-day Afghanistan. His father was Turkish and his mother Iranian. Because education played an important role in Muslim families, Avicenna and his younger brother Mahmud had tutors from a young age. The young man showed great intellectual curiosity and talent, and by the age of 10, he had memorized the entire Qur'an. Within his home, he also explored philosophy, theology, and mathematics. For a while, the avid scholar studied with an Indian surveyor, from whom he learned Indian mathematics.

A turning point came in Avicenna's life when his father hired a well-known philosopher to live with the family and tutor him. Avicenna learned so quickly that the tutor was stunned. The young man found medicine and natural science so easy that, by the age of 16, he was practicing medicine and teaching other physicians. However, it was logic and geometry that captured the young man's imagination. After much struggle, Avicenna mastered Aristotle's logic and was so grateful for this new knowledge that he gave extra alms to the poor as a way to thank Allah. The young man so voraciously consumed all the works of the great thinkers that by the age of 18, he claimed that he had mastered all knowledge. He accomplished this prodigious feat of learning without renouncing the pastimes that engaged other young men: He was well known for satisfying his passions for wine and women as well as for knowledge.

A Muslim Scientist

The young scholar became a court physician to a sultan when he was only 18, and he began his prolific writing career during these years. He wrote on subjects ranging from ethics to the law to the Qur'an. However, this happy time in his life came to a tragic end at age 22, when Avicenna's father died. Forced to earn a more substantial living, he entered government service, moving among the courts of various emirs.

Muslim surgeons performed remarkably complex operations. They practiced vascular and cancer surgery and developed a sophisticated technique for operating on cataracts of the eyes that involved using a tube to drain the fluid from the cataract. This technique was employed even in modern times, until physicians developed procedures for removing the cataracts completely. A wide range of anesthetics, from opium mixed in wine to more sophisticated drugs, made surgery tolerable for Muslim patients. Hospitals, too, sprang up throughout the Muslim world and included outpatient treatment centers and dispensaries for the many medicines being developed. Thanks to the careful sharing of knowledge and the development of advanced procedures and study, Muslim physicians provided outstanding medical care between the seventh and twelfth centuries.

Scientists made dramatic progress in other areas as well. Mathematicians brought the use of "Arabic" numerals from India, and these replaced the Roman numerals that had been used **Mathematics** throughout the former empire. The major advantage of Arabic numerals was that they included the zero, which makes complex calculations manageable. By

Occupied with public affairs during the day, Avicenna at night continued his studies and writings. He composed treatises on arithmetic, music, and language and invented a unique form of rhythmic poetry that was emulated by subsequent poets. However, his most significant contributions came in the fields of medicine and philosophy. When the Western universities recovered the works of Aristotle in the twelfth century, the texts included Avicenna's commentaries. In this way, the Muslim scholar's interpretations of Aristotle's ideas influenced the West's intellectual revival. Furthermore, Avicenna's *Canon of Medicine* served as the main medical text for more than six centuries and was copied throughout the Mediterranean world. In the West, the *Canon* was probably second only to the Christian Bible in the number of times it was reproduced. Some scholars suggest that his techniques of experimentation and observation gave birth to the modern scientific method.

In 1037 Avicenna fell ill. In hopes of stealing his money, one of his slaves tried to kill him by contaminating his food with opium. The scholar survived this attempt by treating himself. However, his illness killed him shortly thereafter. Nevertheless, Avicenna represented the best of the Muslim world that valued education and applied science. His theories on the sources of infectious diseases, his explanation of sight, his invention of longitude, and his use of the astrolabe have all caused modern scientists to praise his genius. The scholar accomplished all this while negotiating the hazards of a world dependent on uncertain politics and disloyal slaves. To this day, the outstanding body of work that he left behind continues to earn wide admiration and respect.

While he was still in his early twenties, Avicenna began to teach Abu 'Ubaid al-Juzjani, who stayed with him throughout much of the remainder of his life and who wrote Avicenna's biography. Al-Juzjani moved with the philosopher as he went from court to court negotiating the complex Islamic political scene. He had resisted his father's attraction to Shi'ism and was imprisoned only once, for corresponding with an emir who was seen as a rival to the man he served.

the tenth century, Muslim mathematicians had perfected the use of decimals and fractions and had invented algebra. The word *algebra* comes from Arabic and means "the art of bringing together unknowns to match a known quantity." Today students all over the world continue to learn this art.

The accomplishments of Muslim society ranged far beyond science. The Qur'an is written in beautiful **Literature** Arabic rhymed prose, and its study contributed to a lively appreciation for literature. Muslim writers throughout the Middle Ages would pen magnificent poetry that celebrated beauty, love, and the sensual life. Perhaps the most famous literary work was the tales of the *Arabian Nights*. This widely admired collection of stories was set in Baghdad in the court of the most famous 'Abbasid caliph, Harun al-Rashid (r. 786–809) and has delighted readers in the east and west for centuries. Read Document 6.3 on page D6.2 for an excerpt of this engaging work.

Even the religious architecture developed by the Muslims put a unique imprint on the appearance of the southern Mediterranean cities. Whereas Christians emphasized religious images based on the human form, Muslims developed exquisite patterning

TIMELINE: A CLOSER LOOK

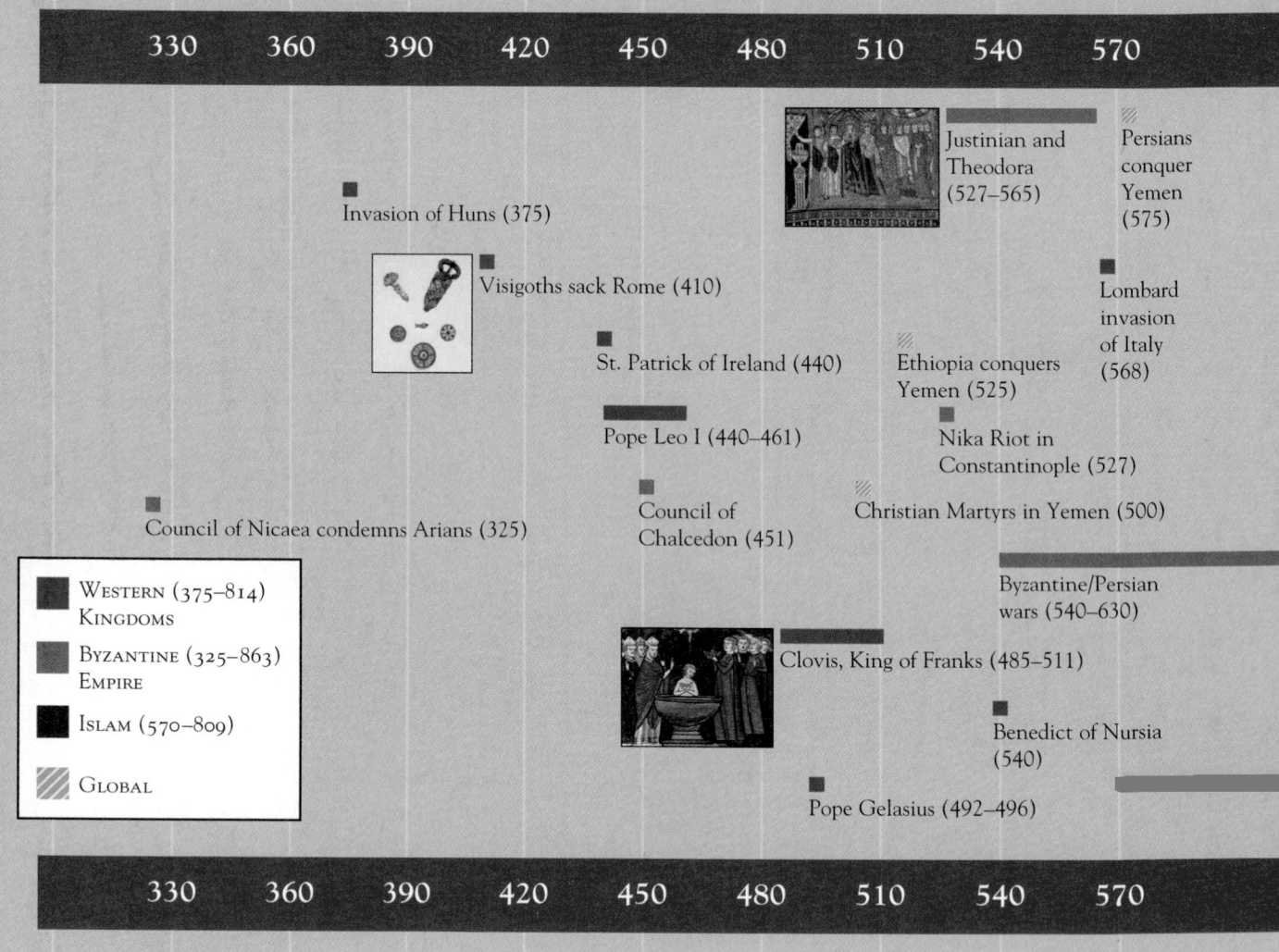

330	360	390	420	450	480	510	540	570

Justinian and Theodora (527–565)

Persians conquer Yemen (575)

Invasion of Huns (375)

Visigoths sack Rome (410)

Lombard invasion of Italy (568)

St. Patrick of Ireland (440)

Ethiopia conquers Yemen (525)

Pope Leo I (440–461)

Nika Riot in Constantinople (527)

Council of Nicaea condemns Arians (325)

Council of Chalcedon (451)

Christian Martyrs in Yemen (500)

WESTERN (375–814) KINGDOMS

BYZANTINE (325–863) EMPIRE

ISLAM (570–809)

GLOBAL

Byzantine/Persian wars (540–630)

Clovis, King of Franks (485–511)

Benedict of Nursia (540)

Pope Gelasius (492–496)

330	360	390	420	450	480	510	540	570

designs. Domes and minarets gracing impressive mosques gave the skylines of eastern and southern cities their own distinct character.

ISLAM AND THE WEST

Before the seventh century, the story of the West unfolded rather organically from the Fertile Crescent around the Mediterranean basin and into northern Europe. Throughout these millennia, western culture developed with contact from as far away as east Asia, until during the Roman Empire, people identified themselves as participating in one empire—albeit a diverse, multicultural one. After Muhammad's visions and the spread of Islam, that experience changed. The Mediterranean world was split into two separate cultures. Historians have argued over the degree to which trade or travel was interrupted by the division, but none questions the cultural divide. From the seventh century on, Islam and the West would take two different paths, always interacting at some level, but always conscious of the difference between them.

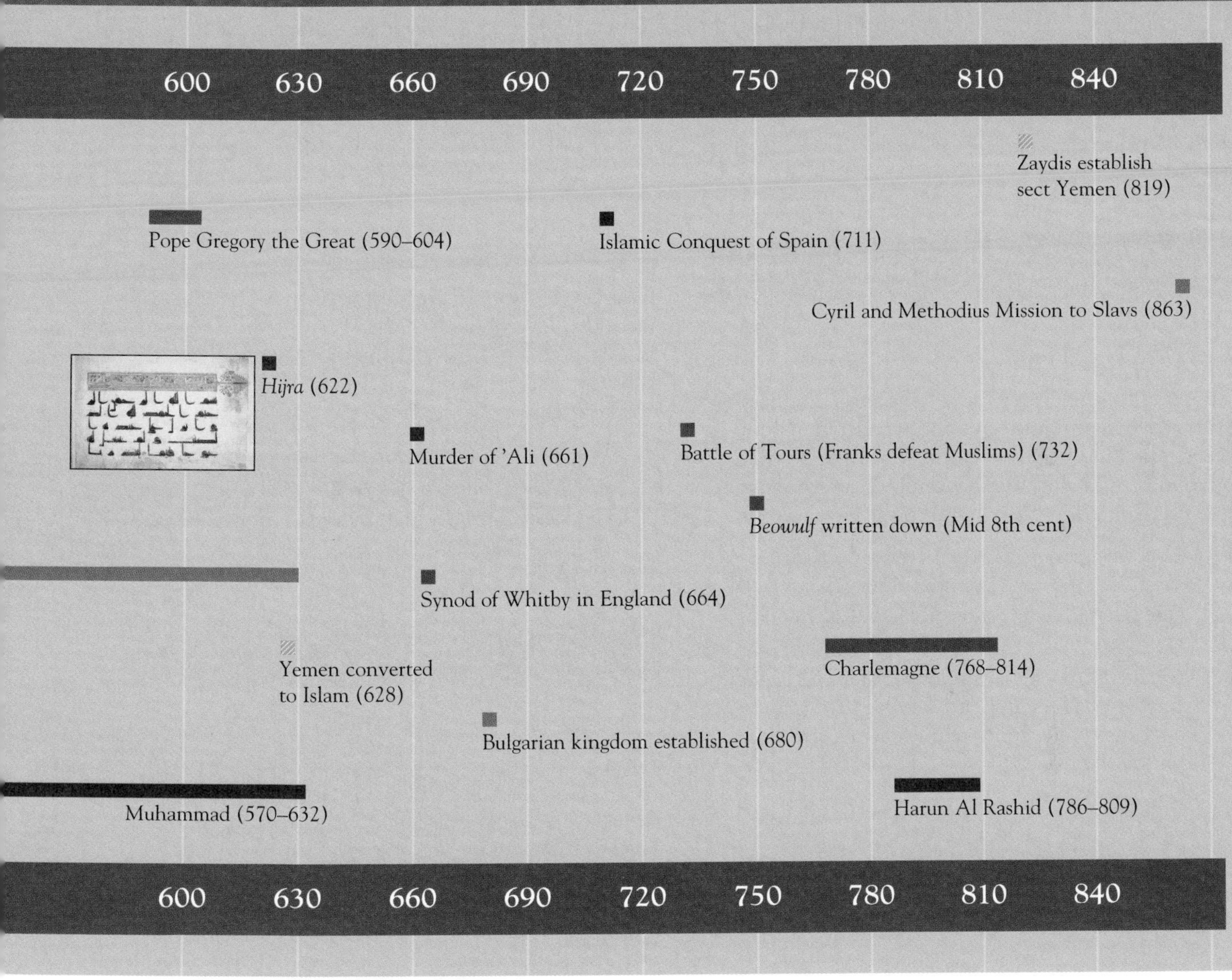

| 600 | 630 | 660 | 690 | 720 | 750 | 780 | 810 | 840 |

Zaydis establish
sect Yemen (819)

Pope Gregory the Great (590–604) Islamic Conquest of Spain (711)

Cyril and Methodius Mission to Slavs (863)

Hijra (622)

Murder of 'Ali (661) Battle of Tours (Franks defeat Muslims) (732)

Beowulf written down (Mid 8th cent)

Synod of Whitby in England (664)

Yemen converted
to Islam (628) Charlemagne (768–814)

Bulgarian kingdom established (680)

Harun Al Rashid (786–809)

Muhammad (570–632)

| 600 | 630 | 660 | 690 | 720 | 750 | 780 | 810 | 840 |

Summary

After the sixth century, the Mediterranean world of the old Roman Empire underwent a dramatic transformation. The Roman Empire in the west dissolved in the face of the rising Germanic kingdoms. The empire persisted in the east, but in a drastically changed form known as the Byzantine Empire. In the south, armies of the new religion of Islam conquered vast territories to create a new society and culture. Islam arose in part as a reaction to the Byzantine Empire and Christianity. Although they worshipped the same God as Christians and Jews, Muslims worshiped in a different way. Consequently, they developed a new way of life that led to a vigorous synthesis of the cultures of the many lands they conquered.

The emergence of this third culture in the lands of the old Roman Empire brought warfare, suffering, and religious tensions, but also a rejuvenated intellectual life. The West and Byzantium did not adopt Islamic religion, but they learned much from Muslim philosophers, scientists, and poets. From this time forward, the interactions among these three great cultures—western European, Byzantine, and Muslim—would profoundly shape the history of the West.

REVIEW, ANALYZE, AND ANTICIPATE

REVIEW THE PREVIOUS CHAPTER

Chapter 5—"Territorial and Christian Empires"—followed the difficulties of the late Roman Empire and studied Diocletian's reforms in which he tried to reorganize and preserve the empire, and Constantine's movement of the capital to the east.

1. *What elements of Diocletian's reforms did the Byzantine emperors continue? Why did many of these reforms endure more in the East than in the West?*

2. *Review the reasons Constantine moved his capital. In what ways did his decision prove to be sound in the face of the events of the fifth and sixth centuries?*

ANALYZE THIS CHAPTER

Chapter 6—"A World Divided"—shows how three distinct cultures emerged in the old territory of the Roman Empire.

1. *Review the various characteristics of the societies of the Byzantine Empire, the Muslim lands, and the western kingdoms. What are the strengths and weaknesses of each?*

2. *Compare and contrast the beliefs of Christianity, Judaism, and Islam.*

3. *What accounted for the rapid expansion of Islam?*

4. *As the Slavs converted to Christianity, they established cultural patterns that would affect Europe for millennia. Review the Slavic settlements and their conversion to Christianity.*

5. *Review the main elements of Muslim culture, including the forces of unity and disunity that helped shape the lands of Islam.*

ANTICIPATE THE NEXT CHAPTER

Chapter 7—"The Struggle to Restore Order"—will trace the development of the Western kingdoms, and in Chapter 8—"Order Perfected"—we will see the three powers—Byzantium, Islam, and the West—confront each other again on the battlefield.

1. *Which of the Western kingdoms do you expect to emerge first as the most powerful? Why?*

2. *Over what territory and what issues do you expect the three great powers to clash? Why?*

BEYOND THE CLASSROOM

THE MAKING OF THE WESTERN KINGDOMS

Ferrill, Arthur. *The Fall of the Roman Empire: The Military Explanation.* New York: Thames and Hudson, 1990. Explains the fall of the empire by focusing on the generals and their armies as a critical component of the decline.

Glob, P.V. *The Bog People; Iron Age Man Preserved.* Translated by R. Bruce-Mitford. Ithaca, NY: Cornell University Press, 1969. One of the most fascinating archaeological studies of Iron Age People and their culture, based on the excavations of corpses from the bogs.

Grant, Michael. *The Fall of the Roman Empire.* New York: Macmillan Publishing Company, 1990. A highly illustrated text illuminating why the fall of the western Roman Empire has been regarded as one of the most significant transformations in history.

Noble, T.F.X. *The Republic of St. Peter: The Birth of the Papal State, 680–825.* Philadelphia: University of Pennsylvania Press, 1984. A clear study of the growth of the papacy in these early, little-studied centuries.

Owen, Francis. *The Germanic People: Their Origin, Expansion and Culture.* New York: Dorset Press, 1990. Looks at the question of the origin and expansion of the Germanic people through the fields of linguistics, archaeology, anthropology, and history.

Richards, Jeffrey. *The Popes and the Papacy in the Early Middle Ages*. New York: Routledge, 1979. Develops the theory that the papal development was shaped by the religious and political events of each pope's reign, not by a larger ideology.

Russell, James C. *The Germanization of Early Medieval Christianity: A Sociohistorical Approach to Religious Transformation*. New York: Oxford University Press, 1994. An inquiry into Christianization efforts among the German peoples that considers the influence of the Germans on Christianity.

Todd, Malcolm. *The Early Germans*. Cambridge, MA: Blackwell Publishers, 1992. Looks at the European tribes and peoples from their origins in prehistory to the present day.

Wallace-Hadrill, J.M. *The Barbarian West, 400–1600*. New York: Oxford University Press, 1985. The classic work on the subject that summarizes the major events in the early Middle Ages.

THE BYZANTINE EMPIRE

Cavallo, Guglielmo. *The Byzantines*. Chicago: University of Chicago Press, 1996. A brief survey of the life and citizens of Byzantine civilization.

Conte, Francis. *The Slavs*. New York: Columbia University Press, 1995. Summarizes the ancient Slavic world—its characteristics, internal and external contacts, and the influences that shaped its development.

Gojda, Martin. *The Ancient Slavs: Settlement and Society*. New York: Columbia University Press, 1991. Offers a good summary of the subject.

Hussey, Joan M. *The Orthodox Church in the Byzantine Empire*. New York: Oxford University Press, 1990. Explores the development of the church in the Byzantine Empire from the reshaping of the policies in the post-Justinian period of the seventh century to the fall of Byzantium in the fifteenth century.

Rodley, Lyn. *Byzantine Art and Architecture*. New York: Cambridge University Press, 1996. A well-illustrated introduction to the material culture of the Byzantine Empire.

ISLAM

Bidwell, Robin. *The Two Yemens*. Boulder, CO: Westview Press, 1983. An engaging history of Yemen from ancient to present times.

Lewis, B. *The Muslim Discovery of Europe*. New York: W.W. Norton, 1982. Examines historical sources to describe the attitudes of the Muslims toward Europe and European civilization.

Momen, Moojan. *An Introduction to Shi'i Islam*. Oxford: George Ronald, 1985. A clear explanation of this branch of Islam written by a practicing Shi'ite.

Roberts, Robert. *The Social Laws of the Qur'an*. Atlantic Highlands, NJ: Humanities Press, 1990. A fine analysis of the laws in the Qur'an and how they impact society.

Rubin, Uri. *The Eye of the Beholder: The Life of Muhammad as Viewed by the Early Muslims*. Princeton, NJ: Darwin Press, Inc., 1995. Explores differing versions of Muhammad's life in order to understand the changing image of the Prophet as perceived by believers.

Savage, Elizabeth. *A Gateway to Hell, A Gateway to Heaven: The North African Response to the Arab Conquest*. Princeton, NJ: Darwin Press, Inc., 1996. Studies the response of one community in North Africa to see the actual effect of the conquest.

Stowasser, Barbarra. *Women in the Qur'an: Traditions and Commentaries*. New York: Oxford University Press, 1994. A scripture-based examination of differing women's status in family and society.

For quiz questions that tie the book to the videos and additional primary sources, please go to the Primary Source Investigator CD.

Documents

DOCUMENT 6.1
The Huns Menace Rome

Many of the Germanic tribes who invaded the Roman Empire during the fourth century were fleeing the Huns, nomadic peoples from central Asia. This account by the Roman historian Ammianus Marcellinus describes the Huns' frightening qualities.

■ **Investigate the Document**

> **Notice** *how the historian pointedly shows the Huns as strikingly different from the "civilized" Romans.* **Which** *characteristics of the Huns might the Romans have found most frightening?* **How** *might this description have shaped Roman policy toward the Huns?*

At the very moment of their birth the cheeks of their infant children are deeply marked by an iron, in order that the usual vigor of their hair, instead of growing at the proper season, may be withered by the wrinkled scars; and accordingly they grow up without beards, and consequently without any beauty, like eunuchs, though they all have closely knit and strong limbs and plump necks; they are of great size, and bow-legged, so that you might fancy them two-legged beasts, or the stout figures which are hewn out in a rude manner with an axe on the posts at the end of bridges.

They are certainly in the shape of men, however uncouth, but are so hardy that they neither require fire nor well-flavored food, but live on the roots of such herbs as they get in the fields, or on the half-raw flesh of any animal, which they merely warm rapidly by placing it between their own thighs and the back of their horses.

They wear linen clothes, or else garments made of the skins of field-mice; nor do they wear a different dress out of doors from that which they wear at home; but after a tunic is once put round their necks, however much it becomes worn, it is never taken off or changed till, from long decay, it becomes actually so ragged as to fall to pieces.

Source: *The Great Events by Famous Historians.* Edited by Rossiter Johnson. The National Alumni. 1905. Volume III. pp. 353–354.

DOCUMENT 6.2
The Silk Industry Comes to Byzantium

The Byzantine Empire thrived in part on the wealth derived from its silk industry, which had previously belonged exclusively to China. In the sixth century, the emperor Justinian learned the secret of producing the valued fabric. Through the excerpt below, the ancient historian Procopius describes this pivotal moment.

■ **Investigate the Document**

> **Why** *did the traveling monks say that Justinian should no longer buy silk from the Persians?* **What** *challenges did the Byzantines face in starting the new industry?*

About the same time there came from India certain monks; and when they had satisfied Justinian Augustus that the Romans no longer should buy silk from the Persians, they promised the emperor in an interview that they would provide the materials for making silk so that never should the Romans seek business of this kind from their enemy the Persians, or from any other people whatsoever. They said that they were formerly in Serinda, which they call the region frequented by the people of the Indies, and there they learned perfectly the art of making silk. Moreover, to the emperor who plied them with many questions as to whether he might have the secret, the monks replied that certain worms were manufacturers of silk, nature itself forcing them to keep always at work; the worms could certainly not be brought here alive, but they could be grown easily and without difficulty; the eggs of single hatchings are innumerable; as soon as they are laid men cover them with dung and keep them warm for as long as it is necessary so that they produce insects. When they had announced these tidings, led on by liberal promises of the emperor to prove the fact, they returned to India. When they had brought the eggs to Byzantium, the method having been learned, as I have said, they

Source: Halsall Medieval Sourcebook, online at www.mhhe.com_sherman2.

changed them by metamorphosis into worms which feed on the leaves of mulberry. Thus began the art of making silk from that time on in the Roman Empire.

DOCUMENT 6.3
Shahrazad Mollifies a Murderous King

The best literary works not only entertain but also reveal the values of the society that produced them. This is true of the well-known Muslim work The Arabian Nights, *also called* The Thousand and One Nights. *The story tells of a jealous king who marries a virgin each night and kills her in the morning so that his wives can never be unfaithful. The lovely Shahrazad escapes this fate by weaving a compelling story for the king every evening for a thousand and one nights. This excerpt explains what happened to Shahrazad after her years of storytelling.*

■ **Investigate the Document**

> **What** *does this text say about the Muslim view of women?* **What** *light does the story shed on the household of the caliph?*

SHARAZÁD, during this period, had borne the King three male children; and when she had ended these tales, she rose upon her feet, and kissed the ground before the King, and said to him, O King of the time, and incomparable one of the age and period, verily I am thy slave, and during a thousand and one nights I have related to thee the history of the preceding generations, and the admonitions of the people of former times: then have I any claim upon

Source: Edward William Lane, trans. *The Arabian Nights' Entertainments—or The Thousand and One Nights*, (NY: Tudor Publishing Co., 1927), pp. 962–963.

thy majesty so that I may request of thee to grant me a wish? And the King answered her, Request: thou shalt receive, O Shahrazád. So thereupon she called out to the nurses and the eunuchs, and said to them, Bring ye my children. According they brought them to her quickly; and they were three male children: one of them walked, and one crawled, and one was at the breast.

And when they brought them, she took them and placed them before the King, and, having kissed the ground, said, O King of the age, these are thy children, and I request of thee that thou exempt me from slaughter, as a favour to these infants; for if thou slay me, these infants will become without a mother, and will not find among women one who will rear them well. And thereupon the King wept, and pressed his children to his bosom, and said, O Shahrazád, by Allah, I pardoned thee before the coming of these children, because I saw thee to be chaste, pure, ingenuous, pious. May God bless thee, and thy father and thy mother, and thy root and thy branch! I call God to witness against me that I have exempted thee from every thing that might injure thee.—So she kissed his hands and his feet, and rejoiced with exceeding joy; and she said to him, May God prolong thy life, and increase thy dignity and majesty! . . .

So they decorated the city in a magnificent manner, the like of which had not been seen before, and the drums were beaten and the pipes were sounded, and all the performers of sports exhibited their arts, and the King rewarded them munificently with gifts and presents. He bestowed alms also upon the poor and needy, and extended his generosity to all his subjects, and all the people of his dominions. And he and the people of his empire continued in prosperity and joy and delight and happiness until they were visited by the terminator of delights and the separator of companions.

Saint Matthew, ca. 700

This illustration of Saint Matthew, from a gospel book made in Anglo-Saxon England, shows the importance of writing and learning. The illustration also provides a glimpse of the new synthesis between Germanic, Roman, and Christian elements that was forged in this era: In Matthew's chair and in the corners of the border, we can see the Germanic love of patterns; in the drapery and the realistic portrayals of the men, we can see the influence of classical Roman drawing; and the theme of Saint Matthew at work is profoundly Christian.

CHAPTER 7

The Struggle to Restore Order

STUDY • Early Germanic laws • Growth of Anglo-Saxon England • Charlemagne and the Carolingian Empire • Cluniac monastic Reform • Vikings and other invaders • Manorial and Feudal structures. NOTICE how order was brought to Western Europe.

The Early Middle Ages, ca. 750–1000

"Since I had not wherewith to feed and clothe myself, I wish to commend myself to you and to put myself under your protection. I have done so, . . . and as long as I live I shall never have the right to withdraw from your power and protection." With these words, drawn from a legal document, eighth-century noblemen placed themselves in a mutually-binding contract with their superior. After the disruptions of the fifth, sixth, and seventh centuries, western Europeans struggled to restore order to their society, and they did it by trying to join all members of society in ties of law and loyalty. From the eighth to the tenth centuries, rulers worked to organize their kingdoms, and in doing so, they created a new culture that combined elements of the old Germanic tribes, the Roman Empire they inherited, and the Christian beliefs they embraced.

As kings worked to establish frameworks for their fragile new kingdoms, they discovered that written law codes and highly organized social structures gave their lands a relative peace that brought a growing prosperity. As law codes regulated people's behavior, nobles and peasants alike defined their relationships in terms of personal and contractual ties that stabilized day-to-day life for everyone. Kings also encouraged intellectual and cultural growth, which had stalled during the previous volatile centuries. Western civilization seemed poised to flourish again in a new form.

Anglo-Saxon England developed traditions of local government and law that planted the early seeds of constitutional government. However, the most successful combination of Germanic and Roman culture took place on the continent, where Frankish rulers slowly consolidated an empire. With the peace brought by these new strong kings, the church, too, began to reassert its authority and its role in maintaining the Christian order. Although a new series of invasions in the tenth century undermined all these efforts, we can still find in them the roots of ideas and institutions that would shape the lives of men and women in the West for centuries.

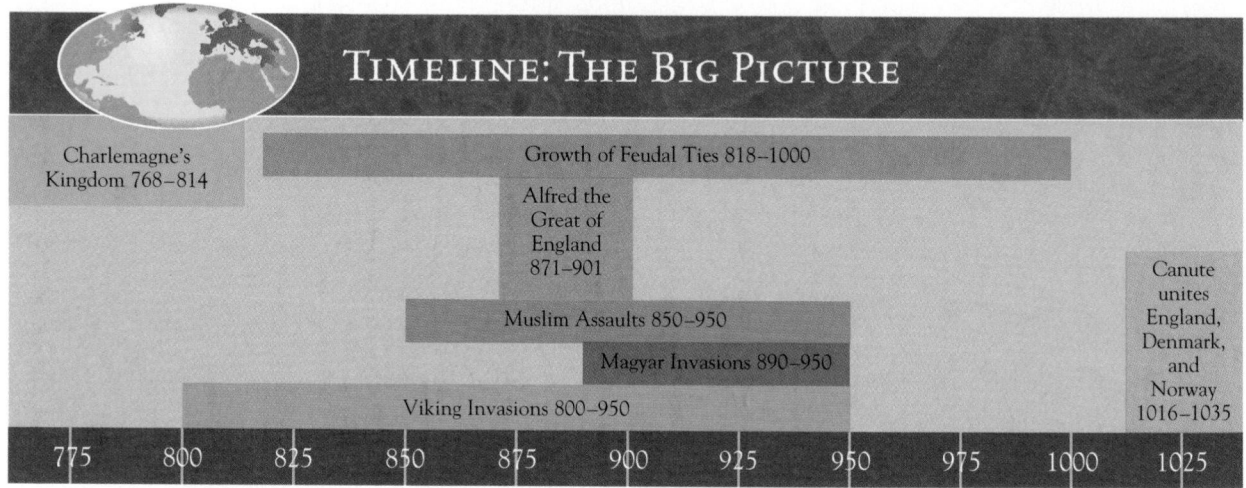

Charlemagne's Kingdom 768–814

Growth of Feudal Ties 818–1000

Alfred the Great of England 871–901

Muslim Assaults 850–950

Magyar Invasions 890–950

Viking Invasions 800–950

Canute unites England, Denmark, and Norway 1016–1035

775 800 825 850 875 900 925 950 975 1000 1025

Bringing Order with Laws and Leadership

Early in the eighth century, in the northern England town of York, a small child was sent to the newly founded school at the church. As the young boy grew, he became an accomplished scholar who corresponded with Latin-speaking scholars all over western Europe. In time, his Anglo-Saxon name, probably Alhwini, changed to the Latin form of Alcuin, and it is by this name that he is remembered today. In 766, when Alcuin was about 30 years old, he became headmaster of the church school, and he never lost his commitment to education. The illustration that opens this chapter portrays a scholar similar to Alcuin, writing with a quill pen on a parchment book.

As we will see, Alcuin's career did not end in York—he went on to travel and profoundly influence the most celebrated courts of the time, even encouraging the emperor Charlemagne to pass laws establishing schools for all freeborn children. In preserving and teaching Latin literature and working to strengthen the Christian church, Alcuin was instrumental in furthering the synthesis of Germanic, Roman, and Christian culture that shaped the early Middle Ages. Alcuin's career and dedication to learning was made possible in large part because the violence that had characterized the centuries after the fall of the Roman Empire was slowly being brought under control by talented kings.

THE RULE OF LAW

Long before their penetration into the Roman Empire (see Chapter 6), the Germanic tribes had valued the force of law. Laws were not written down, however, nor legislated by king or council. Instead, laws constituted the customs of the past enforced by individuals and families. Traditionally, kings could arbitrate between conflicting parties, but people believed the law transcended any individual ruler, and law was administered by assemblies of the people. The German assemblies had developed some unusual means to help determine the truth in disputed cases. For example, they might consider the character (or value to the community) of the accused, and in a practice called *compurgation,* 12 honorable men testified to the character of the accused (without any necessary knowledge of the facts of the incidents under discussion). Or, the assembly might appeal to the supernatural, in a process called *ordeal* (the word originally meant "judgment"). In an ordeal, the accused might pick up a red-hot iron or immerse his hand in boiling water. If the hand was not severely burned, the accused was judged innocent. Later in the Middle Ages, ordeals by battle would also be used to determine guilt, and in late witchcraft trials, women were thrown into the water to see if they sank. Floating—an indication that the water rejected the woman—was seen as a sign of guilt.

In the late fifth century, the kings from the western Germanic kingdoms—who inherited the Roman traditions of the lands they held—began to codify their people's laws, and they were helped by their Roman subjects trained in classical law. The ancient laws of the Germanic peoples began to be | Legal codes | written down in Latin and began to incorporate some of the principles of Roman law. The laws of the land became yet another example of the slow blending of cultures that shaped the medieval world. The codes of the Franks, Lombards, Visigoths, and Anglo-Saxons offer historians important insights into these early

OLC

kingdoms. The prologues of these codes continued to insist that the kings were not making laws, but simply recording the people's will—the old Germanic tradition of law was preserved.

In villages (which might have as few as a dozen families), the most respected people in the community assembled periodically to administer their local affairs. They debated questions such as how land should be used or what should be done about a dangerous dog in the village, and they discussed issues such as where wolf traps in the vicinity were located so children could be warned away. In many ways, these day-to-day decisions, made by people gathering together at a crossroad in the village, were more important to these people's lives than the larger policies set by kings. These villagers were participating in an ancient custom of self-governance at the most local level. Document 7.1 on page D7.1 gives examples of rural legislation in the Visigothic code.

Like the villagers, the nobles of the Germanic tribes also had traditions for resolving disputes; they depended upon private vengeance for justice. According to the recorded laws, the principal preoccupation was to find ways to stop the bitter feuds that broke out between extended families who cherished their ability to protect their people and their honor above all else. The written law codes became a first step toward regularizing and perhaps controlling the violence to bring order to the growing kingdoms.

Feuding was slowly regulated by placing limits on the occasions where vengeance was allowed. For example, a family was not permitted to seek revenge if **Wergeld** one of their number was killed while committing a crime. Nor could a family strike back before an offender from another family was proven guilty. However, the most important mechanism for regulating violence was persuading family groups to accept compensation (in money or goods) instead of vengeance. If a member of one's kin was killed or injured, for example, the guilty party had to restore the victim's monetary worth to his or her family. This amount of money was called *wergeld,* or "man gold"—in other words, the worth of a man. A free peasant was worth about 200 shillings; a nobleman six times that. The Germanic laws used the techniques of ordeal and compurgation to determine who should pay wergeld.

The written Germanic law codes reveal rulers' hopes that wergeld would compensate peacefully for the various injustices that inevitably cropped up as

people—especially heavily armed men who spent a lot of time drinking—lived together. Wergeld covered quarrels—offenders had to pay 30 shillings for cutting off an ear, 60 shillings for removing a nose, and 8 shillings for knocking out a front tooth—as well as damaged reputations. For slandering an earl, the penalty was 60 shillings; for cutting his hair to insult him, 10 shillings; for damaging his beard—his symbol of masculinity—20 shillings.

This intricate system of fines included outrages committed against all members of the tribe, from women and children to livestock. Wergeld was assessed for the rape of young women or nuns, for adultery committed with a married woman, and even for crimes as specific as watching a woman who was modestly hiding behind a bush to urinate. The early laws of the Franks penalized anyone who hit a pregnant woman, and the penalty was increased if the woman died, thus killing the unborn child. The laws recognized that part of a woman's value included her potential for bearing children; if someone killed a post-menopausal woman, he had to pay one-third of the fine for killing a woman during her childbearing years. The lists of penalties extended protection to the livestock of the village from chickens to oxen, and even to the bells that the animals wore so their owners would not lose them.

These law codes that so precisely reveal the details of life in the early Germanic kingdoms may appear strange to us because they put a price on everything from an insult to a toe injury. However, they represented an important step in the emerging synthesis between Germanic and Roman societies, as kings began to record the customs of the people. These records were intended to bring peace and order to the kingdoms, but in this they were only partially successful: The early medieval kings never succeeded in weaning their subjects completely from their need for vengeance. In spite of the efforts of kings, the eighth and ninth centuries remained an era of rampant lawlessness, largely because these laws were too difficult to enforce. However, important seeds were planted in the legal traditions that we have come to identify with Western civilization.

The eighth-century monarchs slowly insinuated themselves and their royal officers between feuding families, and written law codes became an instrument by which royal power could be slowly increased. Wergeld, compurgation, and trial by ordeal became major legal pillars of the early Middle Ages, adding to the judicial tradition left by the Romans. The Germanic custom of trial by assemblies became an important base for the growth of representative institutions that would emerge in the Middle Ages. The concept of the rule of law—in which law superseded individual inclination and played a central role in keeping order—proved highly resilient and helped consolidate these early monarchies.

Anglo-Saxon England: Forwarding Learning and Law

As the eighth century opened, Anglo-Saxon England consisted of several kingdoms (shown in Map 7.1). The most powerful were Northumbria, Mercia, and Wessex. At this time, these kingdoms were separate and struggling to integrate their new Christianity and the new learning they inherited from the Roman texts that Christian leaders brought to the island.

The Anglo-Saxons had been converted to Christianity in the seventh century, and after the Synod of Whitby in 664 (discussed in Chapter 6), the English church began to be organized along the Roman model—with a clearer hierarchy of bishops and priests—instead of a monastic, missionary organization. In 669, Pope Vitalian sent Theodore of Tarsus to be the archbishop of Canterbury, and this erudite man from the eastern Roman Empire significantly forwarded learning in Britain. He established a school at Canterbury and brought other scholars with him who founded Benedictine monasteries in the north of England—at Wearmouth and Jarrow—that also became centers of learning. By the end of the seventh century, England was poised to be a center of intellectual activity.

The illustration on page 226 was produced at Jarrow and shows the intellectual skill that had grown in this island outpost of Christianity. *Beowulf*, the most famous Old English poem that has immortalized the heroic values of the Germanic tribes (described in Chapter 6), was probably written down during this period of monastic scholarship. Although the English monastic schools created valuable manuscripts, their proudest creation was probably the greatest scholar since the decline of the Roman world: the Venerable Bede (672?–735).

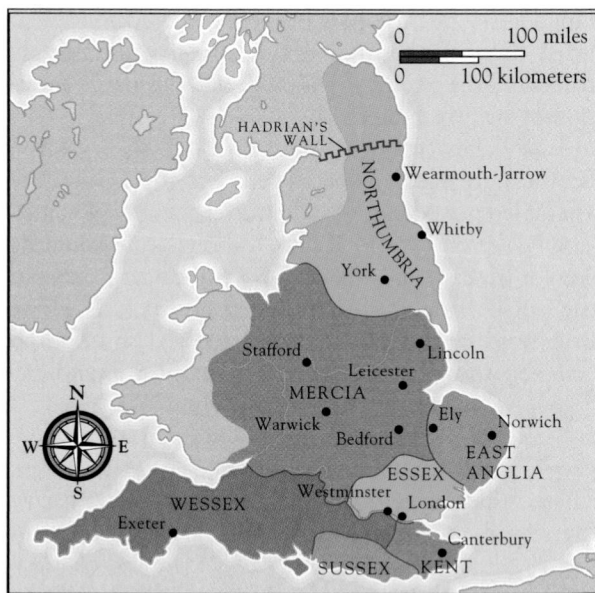

Thinking About Geography

Map 7.1 *Anglo-Saxon Kingdoms, ca. 700*

This map shows the seven Anglo-Saxon kingdoms that had emerged by the eighth century. ⬛ **Notice** the locations of the three major kingdoms—Wessex, Mercia, and Northumbria. **Consider** which will be most vulnerable to invasion from the northerners. ⬛ **Notice** the locations of the major intellectual centers—Canterbury, and the monasteries at Wearmouth and Jarrow, and consider the advantage of their placement at the northern and southern ends of the kingdoms.

The Venerable Bede: Recording Science and History

In the early eighth century, Bede studied in Jarrow, and the young scholar mastered all the texts available to him. His writings interpreted the ancient works and made them accessible to his contemporaries. As a product of the monasteries, he wrote in Latin—the language of the church and of the educated—and his writings became essential to generations of subsequent Latin scholars. Bede was primarily a teacher who wrote a number of works intended as educational tracts. In these works he drew from previous scholars, thus preserving and expanding upon knowledge from previous centuries. For example, in an influential text—*The Nature of Things*—Bede incorporated much from the Roman encyclopedist Pliny (23–79) and the Visigothic scholar Isidore of Seville (560?–636), but he added his own interpretations. For example, *The Nature of Things* attempted to explain the orbits of the earth, heavens, stars, and planets. In this widely copied and read work, Bede described the earth as a globe and discussed its geography, and this tract was counted among the most important scientific texts of the early Middle Ages.

Bede's most famous work, however, is the *Ecclesiastical History of the English People*, in which he tells

Bede's History the history of early Anglo-Saxon England to 731. This enterprise was pathbreaking in that he took as his canvas an entire nation—not just a local region, as was customary. This was all the more remarkable from a man who probably never went farther than seven miles from the place he was born. But his vision helped shape the English into a cohesive entity. Bede drew from sources that are now lost, so his work is invaluable to our understanding of this early period of the Middle Ages. Further, Bede was careful to distinguish between knowledge and rumor, so he established principles of historical writing that had been virtually forgotten since the Roman historians. Perhaps the most influential aspect of Bede's history was that he adopted Dionysius Exiguus's B.C./A.D. dating system (described in Chapter 6). Not many people had read Dionysius's tract, but Bede's was read and translated for centuries, and our adoption of Dionysius's historical dating system can be largely attributed to Bede.

Centuries of readers were not captivated by these technical details. Instead, they were drawn to his powerful prose that brought to life the centuries in which the Germanic tribes seemed very foreign to Roman Christian missionaries. He wrote of how the first missionaries ordered to go to England in 596 by Pope Gregory recoiled at the prospect: "For they were appalled at the idea of going to a barbarous, fierce, and pagan nation, of whose very language they were ignorant." Readers followed these timid missionaries as they slowly converted the Anglo-Saxon kings and

established monasteries that by the late seventh century could spawn a scholar of Bede's stature. The missionaries had done their work so well that when royal courts were ready, learning could leave the monasteries and enter secular life.

GOVERNING THE KINGDOM

Like the other Germanic kingdoms, the Anglo-Saxon kings developed detailed law codes that combined wergeld with some principles of Roman jurisprudence. Indeed, the small island developed an enduring legal tradition that has become known as common law, which differs from the "statutory law" that is based on mandates passed by a legislative body. The common-law tradition preserves a vestige of the Germanic tradition in which the customs of the people are law.

The Christian kings claimed to rule by the grace of God, but they did so with the approval and advice of the powerful men in their court. A king **Witan** could succeed to the throne only with the approval of the *Witan*, or circle of "wise men" of the realm. (The full assembly was called the Witenagemot.) In addition, the king periodically called the Witenagemot to meet with him and discuss matters important to the governing of the realm. Like the laws themselves, the assembly had arisen through custom and tradition rather than any constitutional authority. Moreover, its power ebbed and flowed in accordance with the king's power. For example, if a monarch were weak (or young), the witan exerted a great deal of influence. A strong monarch, on the other hand, might call his lords together merely to confirm his decision. Over time, however, all kings governed with the assistance of this body of powerful men.

In an age of slow communication, kings depended on other officials as well to govern their realms. Monarchs divided their kingdoms into shires **Royal offices** (roughly the size of modern counties) and appointed royal representatives to govern in their name. These aristocratic earls had many responsibilities, including mustering the local men into armies if the king needed them, and leading warriors into battle. Earls also served as the principal judges, presiding over shire courts and executing royal commands.

Some earls amassed so much power that they governed several shires. This tendency might have weakened royal authority and essentially created new kingdoms had not the Anglo-Saxon monarchs moved to name additional royal officials. For example, kings appointed shire reeves (who later were called sheriffs) to help the earls fulfill their duties, but the sheriffs answered only to the kings, not to the earls. In this way, rulers kept a firm grip on power, even down to the shire level.

Yet in this preindustrial world, in which people had no mail system or telephone network to connect them, kings had to do more than just appoint earls and sheriffs to keep order. For instance, collecting taxes and resolving legal disputes were matters for face-to-face contact. These emerging kingdoms struggled to provide the means for such contact and the ways by which to control it. The Anglo-Saxons accomplished this feat not only by assigning royal representatives to govern at the shire level, but also by recognizing that some tasks were best handled at the local village level. Village laws enforced by community elders formed the basic level of administrative order, and parish priests and local tax collectors joined sheriffs and earls in structuring a network that could govern the new kingdoms.

ALFRED THE GREAT: KING AND SCHOLAR

The administrative organization and the patronage of the arts flourished in England under the reign of king Alfred the Great (r. 871–901) of Wessex. Alfred is the only English king who has been called "the Great" in memory of his military victories and his support of learning and culture in his realm.

Alfred's contemporary biographer, Asser, offered an engaging picture of the young prince and emphasized his early love of learning: "As he passed through his childhood and boyhood he appeared fairer in form than all his brothers, and more pleasing in his looks, his words and his ways. . . . From his cradle, Alfred had been drawn to wisdom." Despite his intelligence, Alfred did not learn to read until he was 12 years old. In adulthood, he would make up for lost time. He studied Latin, collected books, and invited scholars to his court. His interests extended to the arts, for he encouraged singers to fill his court with sacred music and traditional folk songs.

By the time Alfred became king, the political divisions shown in Map 7.1 had been shaken by a wave of outside invaders—the Danes from across the North Sea. As early as the late eighth century, raiders from the Scandinavian countries had begun raiding northern England. The great monastery of Jarrow had been looted and destroyed, and the intellectual flowering in the north that had produced Bede came to an end. A Danish raid with some 350 ships plundered London, and it looked as if the Anglo-Saxon kingdoms would all fall to the northmen.

However, King Alfred had reorganized the military to confront the invaders, and he built the first English navy to patrol the coast against the raiders. After some English victories, the *Danelaw* Danes and the English signed a treaty in 886. Under its terms, Alfred and the Danish king Guthrum agreed to divide England between them. Map 7.2 shows the division the two leaders agreed upon. The northern lands later became known as the "Danelaw" to recognize that they were governed by laws different from those in the southern parts of the land. As part of this settlement, Guthrum agreed to convert to Christianity (which would ultimately make it easier for the peoples to share the land). The treaty also paved the way for Alfred to forge a unified kingdom in the south and to focus on the laws and learning that were his passions.

Alfred worked to bring southern England into the intellectual world of wider Europe through literature. From his own educational experience, Alfred knew that Latin texts *Alfred's translations* were not accessible to many inquiring minds. In a letter to one of his bishops, Alfred expressed the opinion (highly unusual in his time) that intellectual ideas should be available to everyone. He wrote, "It seems better to me for us also to translate some of the books which are most needful for all men to know into the language which we can all understand." The wise king followed his own advice and translated, or helped to translate, some of the great books of literature into Old English so his own people could read them. Among other works, he translated Boethius's *Consolation of Philosophy* (discussed in Chapter 6). Although Alfred valued the classical texts, he never lost his central interest in his own people, so his literary patronage extended to recording the history of their deeds. He translated Bede's *Ecclesiastical History of the English People* and initiated the writing of the *Anglo-Saxon Chronicle*, a history of England that continued Bede's effort to narrate the story of the English.

The precious jewel shown in Figure 7.1 beautifully illustrates the cultural flowering that took place under Alfred's reign. The Alfred Jewel (as it is now called) depicts a man who personifies sight, and who embodies the concept of "seeing" truth by learning. Yet the jewel also symbolizes the blending of Roman and Germanic cultures that Alfred advocated. The figure of sight was drawn from the Roman tradition that Alfred brought to England through his translations. The filigree goldwork reflects the style of the ancient Germanic heroes (notice the similarities with Figure 6.2 in the previous chapter) and echoes Alfred's efforts to preserve the Germanic history of the English people. The back plate of the jewel comes from France, representing England's connection with the continent through trade and the exchange of ideas. Finally, around the jewel are the words "Alfred had me made" written in Old English. This declaration again expresses the idea that the order brought to this Anglo-Saxon world came from the skilled governance of kings. (The jewel is now in the Ashmolean Museum in Oxford, England.)

The rule of Alfred the Great marked the high point of the accomplishments of Anglo-Saxon England. Much of the southern portion of the island was ruled by this skilled king who brought the benefits of law and learning to his land. However, a century before Alfred's reign, across the English Channel, comparable developments had taken place on the continent, where an even more powerful king had unified the lands of western Europe and established an empire that shone even more brightly than that of Alfred.

THINKING ABOUT GEOGRAPHY

MAP 7.2   *England in 886*

This map shows the division of England between Alfred the Great and Guthrum the Dane in the treaty of 886. **Compare** this map with Map 7.1. **Notice** how many of the old Anglo-Saxon kingdoms were united by Alfred and which were taken by the Danes. **Consider** the advantages of Alfred's southern kingdoms, which shared a closer connection to the continent and encompassed the areas that had been more influenced by Roman occupation.

and who restored the centralized order that had disappeared with the fall of Rome. Charlemagne represented the high point in the process of the combining of classical, Germanic, and Christian cultural elements that we saw beginning in Chapter 6. Figure 7.2 shows a ninth-century bronze statue that reputedly portrays this powerful ruler. In a conscious link with the classical past, the statue depicts him in the pose of the Roman emperor Marcus Aurelius—riding with no stirrups, as the Romans did, even though by Charlemagne's time the Germans did use stirrups. However, the rider also wears a Germanic cloak, a style that Einhard insists Charlemagne refused to abandon. In addition, he carries an orb representing his empire and wears a crown adorned with the symbol of office bestowed on him by the pope. In all these ways, this statue symbolizes the synthesis of cultures that restored a new kind of order to western Europe.

CHARLEMAGNE'S KINGDOM

This impressive warrior undertook 53 campaigns throughout his reign—and won most of them. A pious man as well, Charlemagne established himself as a leader and reformer of the church. Finally, he had a deeply curious intellect. He knew the importance of education, recognized the worth of scholars like Alcuin, and energetically sponsored learning by establishing schools and hiring scholars. The political, ecclesiastical, and intellectual order that Charlemagne brought to the continent has been called the Carolingian Renaissance, to emphasize the rebirth of learning that he initiated. Just as in England, publicly fostered intellectual life depended upon a relatively ordered society, and in the early Middle Ages, this stability was purchased by military victories.

The map of Charlemagne's realm (Map 7.3 on page 236) shows the vast span of territory—from northern Spain to the North Sea, from the English Channel well into Germany, and across the Alps into northern Italy—that this accomplished leader brought under his control. If we contrast this area with the smaller Anglo-Saxon kingdoms shown on Maps 7.1 and 7.2, we can imagine the challenges Charlemagne faced in administering this territory.

Administering the realm

Like his English counterparts, Charlemagne put noblemen in charge of the various provinces he controlled and tried to use laws to bring order to his lands. However, his approach differed from that of

FIGURE 7.1
King Alfred's Jewel, tenth century.

Charlemagne and the Carolingians: A New European Empire

The Carolingian king Charles (later known as Charles the Great, or Charlemagne) earned that accolade by the force of his personality and the breadth of his talents. About six feet tall and physically powerful, Charlemagne boasted a full head of red hair and a prominent belly. Charlemagne the man has generated a lively debate among historians. His contemporary biographer, Einhard, left us with tantalizing bits of information about this man, who dominated the late eighth and early ninth centuries in western Europe, the Anglo-Saxons in that, instead of having fixed sheriffs at his command, Charlemagne sent traveling agents (called *missi dominici*) throughout his territory to examine conditions in his name and to redress certain abuses. These royal representatives traveled in pairs—a bishop and a nobleman—representing both the secular and religious arms of Charlemagne's realm. An edict issued by Charlemagne in 802 describes the high expectations he had for his officials, who were sent "throughout his whole kingdom, and through them he would have all the various classes of persons . . . live in accordance with the correct law . . . and let no one, through his cleverness or craft, dare to oppose or thwart the written law, as many are wont to do." The king knew that his rule depended upon his subjects obeying his laws.

Charlemagne enhanced his authority further by requiring his nobles to attend two assemblies a year. As the men gathered in the outdoor meeting fields, they listened to the emperor's latest decrees and offered some opinions—but then went home and obeyed their ruler. In this way, Charlemagne moved from the original Germanic legal practice of the king simply recording the customs of the people; the Frankish king actually issued legal commands, and these carefully recorded capitularies serve as rich historical sources of his times.

In all these ways, Charlemagne departed from the Anglo-Saxon model and, in a strikingly new departure from traditional Germanic practice, sought to maintain a personal, centralized control over his unwieldy kingdom without appointing local administrators. Of course, personal rule hinges on the ruler's physical presence. Charlemagne met this requirement by traveling frequently throughout his lands, enjoying the hospitality of his noblemen. It is to Charlemagne's credit that this system worked as well as it did during his lifetime. As we will see, his administrative structure would not survive the loss of his personal attention.

Linking Politics and Religion

Charlemagne's political order had close links to his religious policies. He followed his father's lead in ensuring that his success as emperor was firmly tied to the fortunes of the church. This religious policy manifested itself in his treatment of the Saxons, a fierce people living on the northern borders of the empire. The Saxons had raided Frankish territory for gen-

Figure 7.2
Bronze statue of Charlemagne, ninth century.

erations. Charlemagne marched north in 772 and again in 775 and won decisive victories against the ferocious Saxons, but each time he left, they rose in revolt again. The emperor surmised that only by forcibly Christianizing the Saxons could he make them permanent members of his kingdom. In 785, after a particularly punitive campaign in which Charlemagne crushed the Saxon armies, the emperor forced the Saxon leader to convert to Christianity. Then Charlemagne established priests and monks in the conquered lands and punished relapses into paganism or other religious disobedience as treason. After some thirty years of religious coercion (that the scholar Alcuin opposed), Charlemagne's program worked—Christian Saxony no longer rebelled, again demonstrating how the church could serve his political ends.

northern kingdom had begun. In his political activities and his personal life, the Frankish emperor personified the artful integration of God and politics.

NEGOTIATING WITH BYZANTIUM AND ISLAM

As Charlemagne forged a new empire out of the fragmented kingdoms in the west, he naturally attracted the notice of the neighboring Byzantine and Islamic leaders. Not surprisingly, his taking the title of emperor irked the Byzantine court, but Irene ran out of time to object strenuously. She was overthrown in 802 by Nicephorus, a Byzantine aristocrat, who continued the diplomatic negotiations over the status of the Frankish ruler's title. Finally, in 813, both parties agreed that Charlemagne could be emperor of the Franks and the Byzantine emperor would be emperor of the Romans. This decision solved the immediate dispute, but the political split between east and west continued to widen. Einhard, friend and biographer of Charlemagne, summarized the uneasy relations between east and west by repeating a proverb he said was used in the east: "It is better that a Frank be your friend than your neighbor."

Charlemagne had more promising relations with the Islamic caliph in Baghdad, Harun Al Raschid (r. 786–809). Einhard said, "Charlemagne was on such friendly terms that Harun valued his goodwill more than the approval of all the other kings in the entire world." There were many diplomatic exchanges between the two courts, as it was in both their interests to forge a friendly bond against their mutual enemy, the Byzantine Empire. The Frankish sources say Harun even gave Charlemagne jurisdiction over the Christian holy places in Palestine, certainly a gracious, though empty, diplomatic gesture—Harun reportedly said, the holy land is "so far away that [Charlemagne] cannot defend it from the barbarians. . . . [Therefore] I myself will rule over it as his representative." Nevertheless, the two rulers exchanged many more tangible gifts to seal their friendship— among them an elephant that Harun gave Charlemagne in 802. The elephant lived eight more years and traveled with Charlemagne as he patrolled his kingdom, causing quite a stir among his subjects who had never seen such a beast. The "Global Connections" feature describes this relationship from the Muslim point of view.

Charlemagne's negotiations and the relative peace that came within his lands (in spite of almost incessant warfare on the borders) served to stimulate trade that had declined during the previous tumultuous centuries. Through the ninth century, Venice, in Italy, had assumed a leading role in the southern Mediterranean trade. Venetian merchants sent grain, wine, and timber to Constantinople in exchange for silk cloth and other luxury goods. Other Italian cities also joined in the growing trade, and the Mediterranean trade that had been one of the hallmarks of the west continued to link the region and its varied peoples. More trade brought increased prosperity into Charlemagne's lands, and the great emperor used a portion of it to forward intellectual endeavors.

AN INTELLECTUAL REBIRTH

As memorable as Charlemagne's political and diplomatic victories were, his most enduring impact came in the area of intellectual achievement. Although Charlemagne himself had never learned to write, he had always shown a wide-ranging intellectual curiosity that as a powerful ruler he was able to indulge. Like the Anglo-Saxon cultural revival, the Carolingian rebirth built upon learning that had been preserved in monasteries. Furthermore, the cultural revivals in England and on the continent were directly linked in the person of the scholar Alcuin.

In the late eighth century, Alcuin, the head of the library at York and a product of the same training that had encouraged the genius of Bede, sailed across the English Channel to visit the pope in Rome. On his way home, he met the young Frankish king, Charlemagne, who was so impressed by the English scholar that he asked Alcuin to visit his court and help him reform the education there. The 50-year-old Alcuin readily agreed to come, and he guided the revival of learning on the continent under Charlemagne's patronage.

Charlemagne's motivation for fostering learning stemmed primarily from his concern for the religious health of his kingdom. (Charlemagne's letter, included as Document 7.2 on page D7.2 tells of his motives in his own *Establishing schools* words.) The emperor had observed that even many of the priests serving in his parishes could not read well enough to recite the proper form of the liturgy. Nor were they sufficiently educated to guide their

Global Connections

The 'Abbasid Caliphate and Charlemagne

⬛ **NOTICE** the differences in sophistication between the Muslim capital and Charlemagne's court. **Consider** how these differences affected the two leaders' diplomatic exchanges.

Chroniclers during Charlemagne's reign proudly wrote about diplomatic contacts between the Carolingian king and the Muslim caliph Harun al-Raschid that took place between 797 and 802. This diplomacy was stimulated by the exchange of kind words and gifts, including the famous elephant named Abulabbas, that the caliph presented to Charlemagne. Chroniclers of the 'Abbasid caliphate, on the other hand, never mentioned these interactions. To the sophisticated Muslims, Charlemagne must have ranked among the minor rulers who exchanged goods with Harun al-Raschid, whose name means "the well guided."

When the 'Abbasids conquered the previous caliphate, the Umayyads, they moved their capital from Damascus (in modern-day Syria) to a new city, Baghdad (in modern-day Iraq). (See Map 6.5.) Thus the heart of Islam moved east, away from the Mediterranean basin. The capital blossomed into a cosmopolitan city. One Muslim poet did not exaggerate when he described the magnificent city: "Baghdad, in the heart of Islam is the city of well-being; in it are elegance and courtesy. Its winds are balmy and its science penetrating. In it are to be found the best of everything and all that is beautiful." Harun al-Raschid (r. 786–809) guided the 'Abbasid caliphate at the height of its success. Another Muslim poet praised the leader, writing, "Did you not see how the sun came out of hiding on Harun's accession and flooded the world with light?" Indeed, the revered caliph fostered prosperity, science, and poetry throughout his lands.

By the late ninth century, the Persian Gulf had become the main trade route to the Indian Ocean and the East. Muslim traders grew immensely wealthy. Their ships sailed to Ceylon and other southeast Asian ports and brought jewels, spices, and even elephants back to Baghdad. So many spices became available through the trade that Islamic cookbooks recommended using liberal quantities of pepper, nutmeg, cinnamon, musk, ginger, and cloves for the sophisticated palates of Baghdad. According to the famous fictional account *Thousand and One Nights*, even Harun was a skilled cook. Considering the delicacies that graced Eastern tables and households, it is perhaps not surprising that Charlemagne's gifts of hunting dogs caused little stir among Muslim chroniclers.

Why did Harun al-Raschid bother to engage in diplomatic relations with Charlemagne at all? The answer probably lay in the Byzantine Empire that bordered the 'Abbasid lands. As a teenager leading his father's armies, Harun had won some glorious victories over the Byzantine forces, and as ruler, he planned to continue his encroachments on the weakening Byzantine territory. Charlemagne, too, had provoked tensions among the Byzantines, particularly after he took the title of Emperor. (The Byzantine Emperor felt that he alone could claim that title.) Despite deep differences in religion and culture, Harun al-Raschid discovered that he had something in common with the Carolingian emperor: a shared enemy. Politics can create unlikely allies.

parishioners to what the emperor considered the correct understanding of a Christian life. To address these matters, Charlemagne issued an edict ordering that "In the villages and townships the priests shall open schools," and that the clergy must accept all interested children without charging them fees—although he did allow teachers to accept "the small gifts offered by the parents." From this pool of literate children, Charlemagne expected to produce a clergy educated, as one of his edicts said, "in the psalms, musical notation, chant, the computation of years and season, and in grammar."

Providing schools was not enough; Charlemagne noted that this education depended upon the proper books, ordering "all books used shall be carefully corrected." To accomplish this, the emperor gathered scholars from all over Europe to assemble a canon of corrected readings. When he invited Alcuin to his court, he was not disappointed, for Alcuin drew scholars from throughout the continent to visit the emperor and to share their wisdom. The scholars took up residence in the emperor's court and were very well paid for their labors—Alcuin, for example, ended his life an extremely wealthy man.

These scholars revived a curriculum (originally proposed by fifth-century scholars) that would dominate medieval universities and profoundly influence modern liberal-arts education. To create this course of study, they divided knowledge into seven liberal arts. The most basic of these was the trivium, in which students learned grammar, rhetoric, and logic. With these tools, students could read texts, explain them, and understand the way to think about them. Next came the more advanced curriculum, the quadrivium: arithmetic, music, geometry, and astronomy. Whereas to us these four subjects may not seem obviously related, to medieval thinkers they all shared one characteristic: They involved the patterns by which God organized the world. Because scholars of the Middle Ages saw this organization as consistent, they believed they could study music, for example, to understand mathematics or the movement of the heavens.

The scholars also contributed much to text reform. Before the invention of the printing press, scribes copied books laboriously by hand onto animal skins (called parchment or vellum) with quill pens and ink. (The illustration on page 226 portrays such scribal activity.) Copyists sometimes needed a full day to copy just 6 to 10 manuscript pages. Moreover, there was a shortage of these scribes. Today, we learn to read and write at the same time. During the Middle Ages, however, these two skills were considered separate. Although many people could read, not so many could write.

The problems associated with handwriting only compounded these difficulties. Handwriting was not standardized, and copyists ran words together and employed contractions in an effort to use as little of the precious parchment as possible. Copyists not fluent in Latin (as few were) also made many mistakes. By the eighth century, these errors had been

Correcting texts

multiplying for several hundred years. The sample of Anglo-Saxon manuscript presented in Figure 7.4a shows how difficult this script was to read—words are connected and each small mark above the words means that one or more letters was deleted.

The scholars who gathered at Charlemagne's court school attacked these problems in two ways. First, they compared many versions of the same text to prepare a correct rendition. Second, they developed a standardized handwriting so that future copyists could accurately preserve the corrected text. Figure 7.4b shows a sample of Carolingian handwriting—called Carolingian minuscule. Notice that the letters are well formed and the words more clearly spaced than in the Anglo-Saxon sample. This reformed handwriting style reduced errors, thus saving much wisdom for future generations. Moreover, the Carolingian handwriting style formed the basis for our own lowercase letters and the printing-press letters invented 600 years later. The scholars carefully working on texts played a crucial role in preserving the intellectual contributions of the classical world.

Struggle for Order in the Church

Established long before the Roman Empire disintegrated, the church had adopted the Roman administrative system in which bishops presided in dioceses (see Chapter 5). At the local level, priests in parishes cared for their flocks in manorial villages. Parish priests were accountable to their bishops, who in turn were accountable to archbishops, ruling in the largest urban center of the region. Archbishops called their subordinates together periodically to discuss church issues. During these meetings, bishops also learned about new church rules or ideas, which they then took back to their dioceses and communicated to their priests. This whole structure was designed to weave the Christian world and its administrators into a tight fabric of personal ties.

However, this structure sounds better on paper than it worked in practice during these tumultuous early medieval centuries. Communication among churchmen was always disrupted during warfare, and there was no certainty that competent priests and bishops would be appointed when a church office became vacant. Nor did the theoretical structure mean

FIGURE 7.4

Ancient handwritings: Anglo-Saxon and Carolingian minuscule. (a) Anglo-Saxon page from *Bede's Ecclesiastical History*, eighth century. (b) Carolingian minuscule from the first Bible of Charles the Bald, ninth century.

that the church operated independently of local warlords. Even during the years of relative peace under strong Carolingian kings such as Charlemagne, the church was dominated by monarchs, who felt responsible for bringing order to their churches. Nevertheless, during the eight and ninth centuries, the church planted seeds of order that would fully flower in the High Middle Ages (see Chapter 8).

MONASTERIES CONTRIBUTE TO AN ORDERED WORLD

Bringing structure to the ecclesiastical order was not limited to priests, bishops, popes, and kings. As we saw in Chapter 6, Benedict of Nursia (480?–543) had established a monastic rule that brought men and women into obedience to their monastic leader, who in turn obeyed the local bishop. This kind of monastic structure had proved immensely popular. By the late seventh century, monasteries had sprung up throughout the northern regions of Europe, including Anglo-Saxon England. Monasteries for men and women provided one of the few avenues for social mobility for promising individuals, and for women, the monastic life offered the possibility of a voice in church affairs.

Monasteries performed an essential service in copying and preserving texts and learning. Bede and Alcuin were only two of numerous men and women who excelled in scholarship in an age that valued warfare more. The manuscript painting in Figure 7.5 emphasizes the importance of this monastic learning. The illustration, taken from a Bible copied in a monastery, depicts the Abbess (identified as "Hitda" in the image) offering a manuscript to the woman who commissioned its creation (identified as "Saint Walburga"). Walburga was an eighth-century Anglo-Saxon nun who traveled to Germany to establish a monastery to carry out missionary work among the Germans, and this image emphasizes the importance of both monastic missions and the careful transmission of texts from one house to another.

Monasteries also became involved in the growing political issues of the day. As we have seen, nobles and kings exerted control over priests and bishops in

Cluniac reform

their lands, and they believed they could exert the same authority over monasteries. To many spiritual reformers this seemed to subordinate spiritual values to secular politics, and in the early tenth century, reformers took a step to correct this imbalance.

In 910, a group of monks persuaded a duke in southern France to found a new monastery at Cluny. The Cluniac founding charter refined the Benedictine Rule by insisting that the monastery was exempt from local control—owing only prayers for the donor and as Duke William wrote in the founding charter, "subject neither to our yoke, nor to that of our relatives, nor to the sway of royal might, nor to that of any earthly power." To do this, Cluny was established to be directly subordinate to the pope, and all subsequent Cluniac foundations were to be accountable to the abbot at Cluny, and through him, the pope. This tenth-century movement established a strong, reinvigorated monasticism that helped increase papal authority (as we will see in Chapter 8). However, all these developments establishing order and hierarchy in the church would be shaken—and almost destroyed—by a new cycle of violence that engulfed western Europe.

FIGURE 7.5
Abbess Hitda gives a manuscript to Saint Walburga.

Order Interrupted: Vikings and Other Invaders

Although Charlemagne valued much of classical culture, such as education and even the title of Emperor, his imperial rule was different from that of an early Roman emperor. His sense of empire remained highly personal. Like the innumerable German kings before him, he saw his kingdom as consisting of subjects loyal to him and to his family, not to an abstract political entity. He viewed his realm as his to divide up among his sons, not as an entity separate from

himself and his family. This perception put him firmly in the Germanic tradition. However, in the end it undermined the order that he had built, as the emperor's descendants vied for control of the lands he bequeathed them.

COMPETING FOR THE REALM: CHARLEMAGNE'S DESCENDANTS

Charlemagne's only son, Louis the Pious (r. 814–840), inherited the empire, but during the course of his reign problems began to appear. Document 7.3 on page D7.2 shows a contemporary witness's perception of the growing difficulties. However, the final disintegration of Charlemagne's empire took place after Louis' death, when his kingdom was divided among his surviving three sons: Charles the Bald (r. 843–877), Lothair I (r. 840–855), and Louis the German (r. 843–876). The

Treaty of Verdun three brothers succumbed to the Germanic tendency toward civil war, each seeking to increase his power at the expense of the others. Their violent clashes struck at the foundation of what Charlemagne had constructed, and they brought untold hardship to the subjects of the once unified kingdom (see Biography). Map 7.4 shows the division of the lands established at the Treaty of Verdun in 843, which effectively destroyed Charlemagne's creation of a united western Europe.

The Treaty of Verdun anticipated some important nationalistic developments in western Europe, because for the first time, linguistic differences that would divide the lands seemed to be solidifying. When Charles the Bald and Louis the German took oaths (called the Strasbourg Oaths) to support each other in this division, the oaths were recorded in two languages so the subjects of each would understand them—Charles pledged in a Romance (Latin-derived) language, and Louis spoke in an early Germanic tongue. This showed how the two sections of Charlemagne's empire were already separating culturally and linguistically.

Map 7.4 further suggests how vulnerable the central lands were, because by 870, Charles the Bald and Louis the German divided up the middle kingdom between them. These central lands—the modern regions of Alsace and Lorraine—remained in dispute off and on into the twentieth century.

Battered by the disruptions of war, the already local economy became even more isolated. The long-distance trade that began to enrich the Italian cities as well as the Carolingian kings virtually evaporated, and money went out of circulation. If it had even a brief respite from this dynastic turmoil, the Carolingian Empire might have recovered from mismanagement by Charlemagne's grandsons—but this was not to be. Instead, the weakened empire would succumb to new invaders from the north, south, and east.

Map 7.5 shows the impact of these invasions on Europe. Part of the pressure came from the south, as Muslim maritime raiders sailed across the Mediter-

New invaders ranean Sea and penetrated most of the southern coasts of Europe. Sicily fell to the forces of Islam, as did the islands in the western Mediterranean. In spite of Charlemagne's foresight in establishing protective tributary peoples on his eastern flank, eastern Europe reeled from a serious blow with the invasion of the Magyars (now known

as Hungarians, a name derived from one group of Magyars). Magyar warlords led their people in raids across Germany, France, and Italy before they settled down and established the kingdom of Hungary. The influx of Muslims and Magyars left an indelible imprint on Europe. However, the invaders who wreaked the most violence, and ultimately settled the most widely, came from the north—bands of Scandinavian warriors known as Vikings.

"THE WRATH OF THE NORTHMEN": SCANDINAVIAN LIFE AND VALUES

Back when Charlemagne had forcefully converted the Saxons to Christianity, the people living farther north, in what we know as Denmark, Norway, Sweden, and

OLC

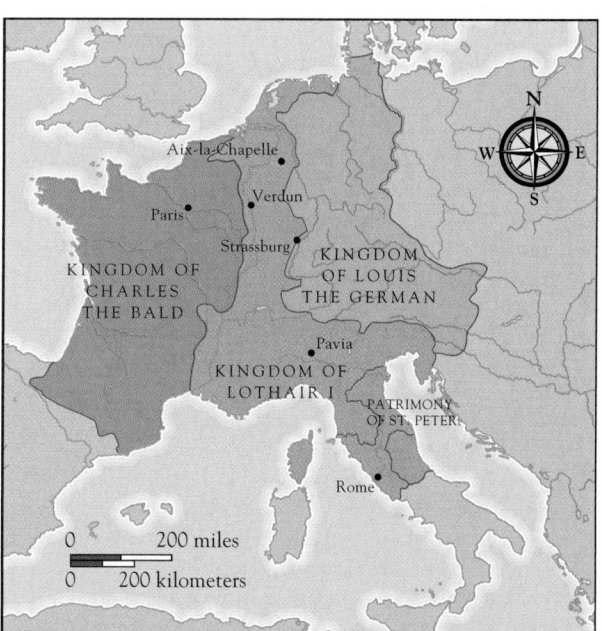

THINKING ABOUT GEOGRAPHY

MAP 7.4 *Partition of the Carolingian Empire, 843—Treaty of Verdun*

This map shows the division of Charlemagne's lands under his grandsons. ✍ **Notice** the extent and location of the three kingdoms. **Which** lands might be most vulnerable to external attack? **Which** brother's lands might be most susceptible to encroachment from the other kings?

Biography

CD DHUODA, BERNARD, AND WILLIAM, CA. 840

■ **Consider** how Dhuoda's life was affected by the turmoil of the breakdown of Charlemagne's central authority.

■ **Consider also** how important marriage and other ties of family and loyalty were to medieval people.

The political turmoil that marked the breakup of the empire assembled by Charlemagne destroyed the family of an educated, pious, remarkable woman named Dhuoda. This young woman was married at the palace of Emperor Louis the Pious in 824 to Bernard of Septimania, a relative of the emperor who served as a knight in Louis's court. Although marriage to such a high-born man seemed a good match, it was not to be a happy companionship. At first, Dhuoda joined her husband in his travels, but then Bernard sent her away to live in a small town in the south of France. The sources do not explain his reasoning—it could have been anything from personal to political. Nevertheless, he visited her periodically. In the meantime, Dhuoda spent her days quietly, immersed in books and prayer. She also followed the fortunes of her husband avidly, writing, "I rejoice in his campaigns." Dhuoda and Bernard had two sons: William, born in 826, and Bernard Jr., born in 841.

In spite of Louis the Pious's advocacy of marriage and his opposition to concubinage, his kinsman Bernard was one of many nobles who took it as their right to have many lovers. Bernard was not a loyal husband to Dhuoda during his absences, and he was particularly indiscreet in his choice of a companion. Accused of committing adultery with Louis's wife and of other treasonous conspiracy against his king, he lost the position of governor of Septimania. His relatives, too, paid dearly for his transgressions. Bernard's sister, a nun, was accused of sorcery, sealed in a wine cask, and thrown into the river to drown. His brother was blinded and imprisoned after being accused of participating in Bernard's treason. In the Middle Ages, families were considered linked together in innocence and guilt, and even the life of a nun could be jeopardized by the misbehavior of her brother.

Bernard's fall from grace foretold his inability to negotiate the civil wars that erupted among Charlemagne's grandsons after Louis's death in 840. Just as Bernard's sister had paid the highest price for his infidelity, so Dhuoda and her sons would suffer because of Bernard's actions. In 841, Bernard returned to Dhuoda to attend the birth of their second son, Bernard Jr. He then took both boys from her and left. To curry favor with his new overlord, Charles the Bald, Bernard gave his 14-year-old son, William, to Charles as a hostage.

Dhuoda missed her boys acutely, especially William. In 841 she began writing a book of instructions for him that she completed in 843. The book not only reveals her love for William, it also reflects the central values of the ninth century. Dhuoda's writings urged her son to have faith in God and in the feudal

A Carolingian Family Tragedy

ties that bound men together. She warned him, "Never let the idea of disloyalty against your lord be born or thrive in your heart." She also encouraged him to read, to give it the "same attention and zeal that others give to . . . a game of backgammon."

Yet all of Dhuoda's care and advice could not save this family caught in the crossfire of feudal conflict. Bernard shifted his allegiance from his own lord Charles to Pepin and was captured as he tried to leave for Pepin's army. Charles accused Bernard of treason and had him publicly beheaded. Fulfilling Germanic ideas of vengeance, young William tried to avenge his father's death, but Charles executed the 24-year-old youth. Like so many noble Carolingian families, Bernard, William, and Dhuoda were damaged by the jockeying for power wrought by the fall of Charlemagne's empire. In medieval families, political developments profoundly influenced personal matters. Even by devoting oneself to God, like Bernard's sister, or studying and writing in solitude, like Dhuoda, women could not escape political storms when their lives were joined to men who allied themselves with the wrong lord. Dhuoda's tender care and eloquent missives tell us of both the hopes and tragedies of a typical Carolingian family. It is only through her love and thoroughness in writing to William that we have such a poignant glimpse of medieval life.

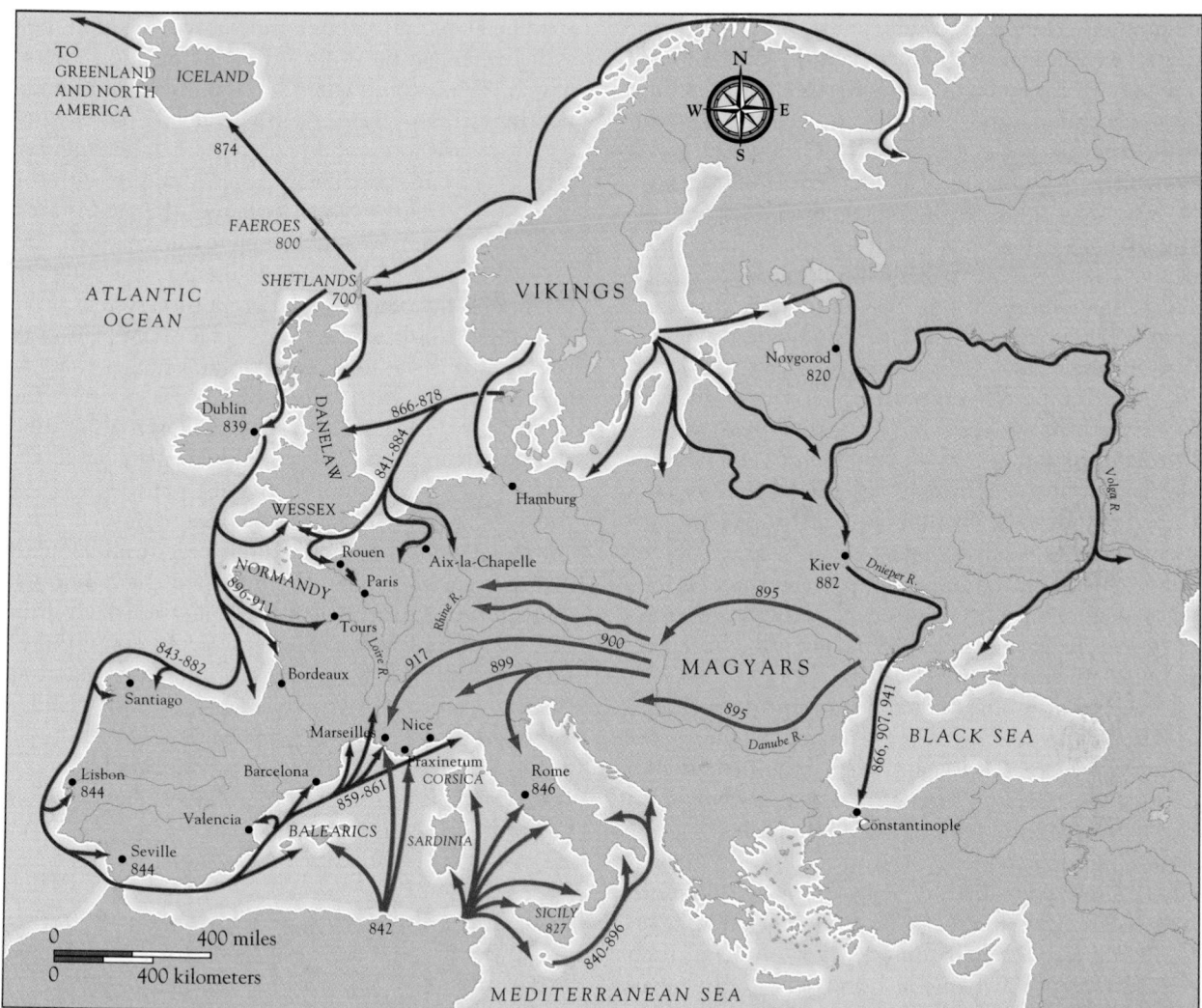

THINKING ABOUT GEOGRAPHY

MAP 7.5   *Invasions of Europe, Ninth and Tenth Centuries*

The arrows on this map show the invasion routes of the major peoples who threatened Europe during the ninth and tenth centuries. The map also shows the dates of the invasions. ◪ **Notice** the pressure that invaders put on the Carolingian Empire from the south, east, and north. ◪ **Compare** this map with Map 7.4. **Which** of the kingdoms might be most affected by which invaders? ◪ **Notice** the various routes the Vikings took. **Which** rivers did they take advantage of the most? **How** important would it be for the Vikings to have ships that could easily navigate rivers?

Finland, remained pagan. For the most part, these Scandinavians lived on farms rather than in communal villages; they grew crops and kept cows and sheep. The short growing seasons of the north made agricul-

ture especially challenging, and the people supplemented their produce by fishing in the cold, stormy waters of the North Sea. Over time they became skilled seamen and even engaged in long-distance commerce. They traded furs, amber, and honey for finely wrought jewelry, glass, cloth, or weapons. These rugged seamen from the north drew a fine line between trading and pirating, and crossed it often. Still, their activities prompted the spread of goods from all over Europe to Scandinavian farms.

Who were these northern peoples? The Scandinavians were Germanic, so their way of life resembled that of the Germanic tribes who had earlier invaded the Roman Empire. The Scandinavians cherished heroic values and sought fame in notable deeds and through the works of poets who recorded those deeds. In their literature—both the poetry and the old Norse prose narratives called sagas that preserve their history—we can detect a people who valued words and wit as much as strength and courage. They worshiped gods similar in function to those of the ancient Greeks and Romans, but with different names—Wodin, Thor, and Freya are three deities whose names have been preserved in the English days of the week: Wodin's Day (Wednesday), Thor's Day (Thursday), and Freya's Day (Friday).

The powerful and violent Scandinavians shared another trait with the early Germanic people: a passion for revenge. Although these northerners tried to control their feuding through a system of compensation involving wergeld, they had much less success stemming their tendency toward violence than even the Anglo-Saxons had. A saying from Viking literature succinctly expresses how violent Scandinavian life could be: "A man should never move an inch from his weapons when out in the fields for he never knows when he will need his spear." The sagas, too, recount many a bloody feud. Indeed, it may have been this very violence that prompted numerous Vikings to leave Scandinavia in search of new, more peaceful lands overseas. Some may have left to avoid feuds, and the sagas suggest that others emigrated to escape the growing power of kings who tried to impose peace on many violent men who did not want to submit to authority.

All Northmen did not emigrate to avoid or seek violence. Many were drawn by the wealth that had accumulated in Europe during the prosperous years of the Carolingians and Anglo-Saxons. All *Viking ships* these movements during the ninth and tenth centuries—raids, trading, and settlements—left a deep impact on European life. Map 7.5 shows the Northmen's movements to the western and eastern edges of Europe. Their success in these campaigns stemmed largely from their innovative ships and their skill in navigating them. The Viking ships, one of which is shown in Figure 7.6, were marvels of engineering. They were highly valued possessions, guarded with honor and praised in Scandinavian poetry. Often built of oak and designed to flex with the rough waters of the North Atlantic, the vessels each carried between 50 and 100 men who manned oars on either side. A large sail, usually decorated in bright colors, completed the propulsion system.

Figure 7.6 also shows another unique feature of these ships: a shallow keel, the long timber that extended the length of the ship and supported the frame. This feature allowed the Vikings to pilot their ships up rivers during raids. It also let them beach the crafts easily and launch them back out to sea before their surprised victims could mount an effective counterattack. The ships and the ferocity and bravery of the men who sailed them earned the Scandinavians a widespread, fearsome reputation. A ninth-century chronicler wrote how Northmen "inflicted much harm," and he sharply captures the suffering: "The steel of the heathen glistened; excessive heat; a famine followed," as too many were dead to bring in a good crop. Many a European repeated the oft-quoted Anglo-Saxon prayer for God to "save us from the wrath of the Northmen."

FIGURE 7.6
The Gokstad Ship, Norway.

VIKING TRAVELS AND CONQUESTS

As Map 7.5 suggests, the unmatched navigational skills of the Vikings gave them access to many parts of Europe. Some Northmen traveled east down the Dnieper River to the Black Sea and the rich city of Constantinople, at times settling along this rich trade route. The oldest Russian chronicle contains the story of an invitation to the Northmen to come and rule, for there was no order in their land. As we saw in Chapter 6, the Scandinavians established a strong state centered in Kiev. Other Vikings traveled to Constantinople and served as soldiers of fortune in the Byzantine emperor's service. Throughout the tenth century, the emperor's personal guard—the Varangians—was composed entirely of Scandinavians. The most famous of these—Harald Sigurdson of Norway (r. 1046–1066)—grew so wealthy while serving in Constantinople that when he returned to Norway he became a great king. Archaeologists have discovered early-eleventh-century Byzantine coins in Norway that may have come from the hoard that Harald shipped home.

Harald's hoard of coins was not unique. Archaeologists have found some 1,700 treasure hoards, each containing on average about 300 coins. These (primarily silver) coins were mostly eastern—Byzantine or Islamic. Great piles of treasure like these continue to draw our imagination, but the fact that so many were simply buried tells us that the Scandinavian eastern trade in the eighth and ninth centuries did not contribute much to the overall European economy. Most gold was not circulated; it was either hidden during the violence that dominated the age or used as jewelry to show status. For example, the coins shown in Figure 7.7 were joined to hooks so the coins could be worn as jewelry instead of circulated as currency. This hoard of solid gold also indicates the volume of wealth that was plundered by the Vikings in their raids. However, great wealth like this may have contributed to the status of kings like Harald, but it did not improve the plight of hardworking Scandinavian farmers. Trade needs peace to benefit more people, and peace would have to wait.

Still other Scandinavians sailed west across the North Atlantic, seeking other lands and wealth. Although some Europeans may have imagined the *Western explorations* world as flat, people who sailed westward out of sight of land and who watched ships return from the eastern horizon knew better. Like many ancients, Scandinavian

FIGURE 7.7
Viking jewelry of gold and silver coins.

sailors perceived the world as round. With these views, Scandinavians sailed confidently into the open seas in their sturdy, versatile ships. They established permanent settlements in Iceland and a settlement in Greenland that lasted for centuries. In the late tenth century, an expedition led by the Norwegian Leif Erikson (970–1035) traveled all the way to North America, which Erikson dubbed Vinland. Although the Vikings did not establish a permanent settlement there, their arrival on this distant coast counts as one of history's most extraordinary feats of sailing, and the difficult passage earned the captain the name "Leif the Lucky."

As the Vikings explored Greenland and North America, they naturally encountered peoples who already lived there. Because they considered these natives inferior, they called them by the contemptuous term "Skraelings," which defies exact translation. They used this term to refer to Eskimos in northern Greenland and tribes they encountered in North America. The Scandinavians who settled in southern Greenland mostly ignored their neighbors to the north. In North America, the encounter proved more dramatic. At first, these tribes and the Scandinavians engaged in some trading. Amerindians especially valued the Vikings' red cloth and milk. They also coveted the Scandinavians' weapons, but the newcomers refused to give them up.

Relations between the two peoples soon soured. Several confrontations occurred in which parties on both sides were killed. The sagas described one incident in which Amerindians in skin-covered boats and armed with arrows and catapults attacked. In another case, only the courage of a pregnant Scandinavian woman saved the day for the Vikings. According to the story, the woman picked up a sword and slapped it on her bare breast as the natives charged her. Unnerved by this odd sight, the attackers fled, and the woman won praise for her bravery. After this confrontation, the Vikings concluded that, although the North American land was bountiful, they could not live there safely because of the ferocity of its inhabitants. They abandoned North America and returned to Greenland, Iceland, and other areas where they could settle more easily.

Within western Europe, Vikings (or their descendants) made permanent conquests in northern France (Normandy), Sicily, and England. As previously mentioned, one group of Vikings, the Danes,

European settlements conquered most of northeast England by the middle of the ninth century, until they were stopped by Alfred the Great in 886. However, the British Isles remained a tempting target for the Northmen. In the summer of 1016, a great fleet led by King Swein of Denmark and his son Canute sailed for England. The Anglo-Saxon king Edmund Ironside (r. 1016) was beaten, and Canute became king of a united England. He was an able ruler, and was one of many who demonstrated that the Northmen were effective administrators as well as skilled warriors. In 1066, the Norwegian king Harald Sigurdson—the enterprising Varangian who brought a fortune back from Constantinople—set himself a final goal of conquering all of England. He died in the attempt, and the sources say that the only English land he claimed was the "seven feet of soil" required to bury this tall warrior.

AN AGE OF INVASIONS: ASSESSING THE LEGACY

The invasions from the north, south, and east brought sporadic violence to western Europe for about 200 years. With this kind of pressure, Viking,

Magyar, and Muslim conquests all disrupted the newly established order that had reigned in Europe for more than a century. In Charlemagne's Frankish Empire, the onslaughts from many foreign fronts accelerated the disintegration initiated by the emperor's feuding descendants, and the central authority envisioned by Charlemagne could not hold.

Learning also suffered as people devoted more and more attention and resources to war. Charlemagne's great palace school in Aachen that had drawn scholars from all over Europe ceased functioning. Again, learning took place primarily behind monastery walls. However, this time monks and nuns had the benefit of texts that had been corrected during Charlemagne's rule. In time, these carefully preserved sources of knowledge would once more play a role in centers of learning, but not until peace returned to western Europe.

Finally, the order in the church crumbled under the tenth-century turmoil. In Ireland and on the western coasts of Britain, the magnificent Celtic monasteries were almost completely destroyed by Vikings looking for plunder. The invaders damaged monasteries in France as well. This violence took a massive personal toll on men and women seeking God. As just one example, texts tell of houses of women who feared that the Vikings would rape them and thus violate their vows of virginity. To avert this disaster, the women cut off their noses and lips as the Vikings approached their gates, and greeted the invaders with mutilated faces.

The church structure of parishes and bishops under the control of the pope also deteriorated. Bishops and priests placed themselves under the protection of local lords instead of looking to Rome for help. Sometimes lords simply took over church lands, as a Frankish law declared: "because of threats of war and the invasions of some of the border tribes, we shall . . . take possession of a part of the land belonging to the church . . . for the support of our army." The church itself became fragmented in the service of war. In the end, the notion of a Christian Europe with both a pope and an emperor at its head disappeared into the wreckage of lives and property as the invasions dragged on.

In the eleventh century, the violence at last spent itself. The traditional Scandinavian farming and trading life was easier to conduct in peace rather than in war. And as the invaders settled in newly conquered territories, they absorbed some of the structures already in place there. The Scandinavians also eventually converted to Christianity and thus became fully integrated into Christian Europe. Harald Sigurdson's brother, Olaf (r. 1016–1030), for example, converted the Norwegians by force of arms and his own charisma in the early eleventh century. Leif Erikson "the Lucky" introduced Christianity to Iceland and Greenland around the same time. Canute, who ruled England, Denmark, and Norway, converted to Christianity and brought priests from England to complete the conversion of the Northmen.

Vikings convert

The Vikings may have settled down, but the centralization that had unraveled through the centuries of chaos would not be restored easily. However, throughout this time people had created another kind of order—one that was not imposed by royal officials, like Charlemagne's *missi dominici*, traveling through the land. Instead, people bound themselves to each other in solemn contracts like the one quoted at the beginning of this chapter. These local ties formed a new order from which the medieval world would build again.

Manors and Feudal Ties: Order Emerging from Chaos

As early as the eighth century, Carolingian nobles began to develop mutual contracts that bound people together in personal relationships. In a modified version of the ties that bound the Germanic tribes, these structures were personal, tying each person to a superior. In the modern West, we often judge a society in terms of the freedom of its citizens, but in the Middle Ages, social order was defined by connections rather than degree of freedom. All men and women—from the peasantry all the way up to the king—were connected to someone above or below them in a contractual system of mutual obligations. The obligations did not fall equally on everyone, but each person had explicitly defined commitments to someone else. Everyone in society expected to live within a hierarchy that ordered nature, the church, and society. This social order was not a product of rational planning, but instead developed slowly over centuries—and the chaos of the tenth century escalated the development.

PEASANTS AND LORDS: MUTUAL OBLIGATIONS ON THE MEDIEVAL MANOR

Manors developed from the agricultural estates of the old Roman Empire (described in Chapter 5) and the new divisions of the land made by early medieval kings. In various forms, manors existed throughout the Mediterranean world, including the Byzantine and Islamic Empires. In western Europe during the Carolingian Empire, manors developed a characteristic pattern of serfs and lords that marked the medieval west for almost the next millennium. Virtually all manors consisted of the lord's home and outbuildings (barn, mill, etc.) and at least one village in which the peasants resided and worked.

Figure 7.8 shows the layout of a typical manor. Notice that unlike today's farm communities, where farmers live on their cropland and travel into the village, medieval peasants lived close together in the village and traveled out to their fields. The fields were organized in strips, with each peasant family using some and the lord owning a large number himself. The church, too, owned some strips for the priest's support. However, the pasture, woodlands, and water were as important as the cultivated land, because they supported the village's animals.

Manor layout

The survival of the peasants depended not only on the crops they grew on their plowed strips, but also on their wise use of the other spaces identified in Figure 7.8. Serfs grazed their oxen and working horses, as well as their sheep and goats, on the common pastureland. They relied on the large draft animals to help with the hard labor of plowing, especially in the heavy, clay soils of northern Europe. The animals also provided essential leather and wool for clothing and other uses. In our age of cotton and synthetic fabrics, it is easy to forget how important medieval animals were for clothing. Farm animals supplemented a grain diet as well, with milk and cheese (especially from goats) and some meat. Peasants ate very little meat because their animals were too valuable to be disposed of in this way. However, sometimes the lord gave the peasants his unwanted portions of meat (tails, hoofs, or entrails) to make soup.

The forests of the manor also played a key role in village life. Although the trees and the game animals belonged to the lord, peasants were allowed to gather fallen branches as firewood. Pigs could browse in

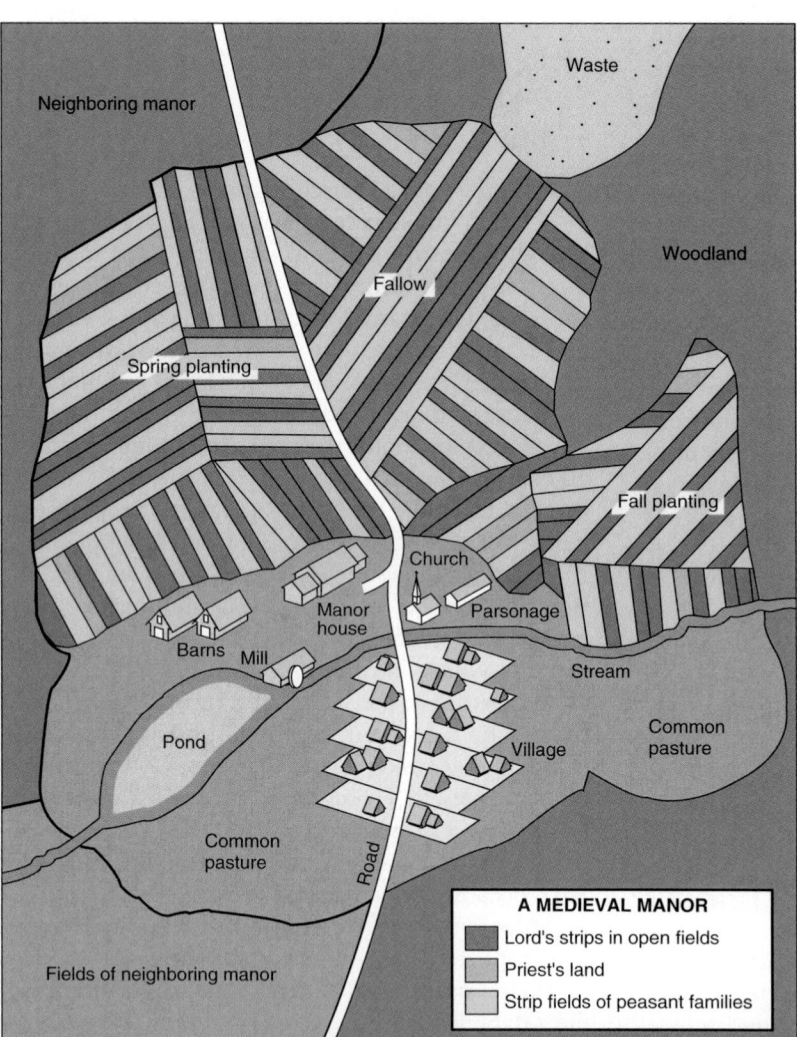

FIGURE 7.8
Hypothetical medieval manor.

semi-free in this way—that is, personally free yet not free to move from their village—were called serfs.

Beyond their obligation to remain on the land, serfs owed their lords many other things— *Serfs' obligations* roughly divided into goods and labor. For example, they had to give the lord a percentage of their crops or whatever livestock they raised—perhaps a tenth of their grain, a piglet, a number of eggs from their hens, or some of the cheese made from the milk of their goats. They also owed him their labor. On some manors, serfs had to work as many as three days a week on the lord's demesne lands, those set aside for his own consumption and use. Serfs had to plant his crops, build roads, erect walls or buildings, dig ditches, and do anything else the lord ordered. Serfs did not owe military service—fighting was the privilege of the nobility.

Peasant women worked as hard as the men. They did all the domestic chores, toiled in the fields, tended vegetable gardens, and fed the animals. In addition, they performed the time-consuming task of producing cloth. Women sheared the sheep, cleaned and prepared the wool, spun it into thread, and wove it into cloth. As serfs, women also shared the labor obligations of their husbands. They, too, owed the lord a portion of what they produced (from cloth to garden vegetables) and owed the lord and lady of the manor a certain amount of their labor for domestic chores, spinning, and weaving. Peasant children bore obligations as well. Children as young as six were responsible for the care of their younger siblings, and older children worked in the fields alongside their parents.

In exchange for peasant services, lords provided things that required a large investment of capital: mills, barns, ovens, large draft animals, and the like. However, the lords primarily offered justice and protection to their serfs. In times of war, for example, the presence of a well-armed warrior and his followers

the forest as long as the lord got a share of the pork. Finally, in times of hunger, villagers gathered acorns in the oak forests and ground them into flour to make bread.

Medieval European peasants were at the bottom of the social order in that they had obligations to people "above" them, but no one below them owed them any commitments. Most medieval peasants were personally free (that is they were not slaves), but they were bound to the land. When a lord received a land grant from the king, he also gained the service of the peasants who worked the land. Peasants who were could make the difference between a village's survival and its destruction. When an attacking army neared the vicinity, peasants with their flocks rushed inside the armed fortress of the lord to stay until the battle ended. However, they often had to watch as their crops and villages were raided and burned, and when the war ended they were left to begin again.

All serfs did not enter voluntarily into this contract in which they exchanged their labor for safety (especially since safety was never absolutely assured). Sometimes armed lords who needed their lands cultivated forced peasants into servitude on their estates. Late in the Middle Ages, as we will see in Chapter 9, many serfs decided the benefits of protection were not worth the price. However, the newly restored order that established the medieval structure was built on the labor of peasants bound to work the land, which was divided up into manors—agricultural estates under the control of a lord.

Life in the Manorial Village

The village itself formed the center of the peasant community, functioning much as it had long before the medieval system of obligations between serfs and lords. The adult male heads of the household met there to resolve property disputes and other local issues that had formed the core of customary Germanic law. Serfs also gathered in the village square to celebrate festivals, marriages, and saints' days. They sang, danced, and drank together, and so strengthened the bonds that made the village a cohesive, productive agricultural and social unit.

Village life

As another way to forge social connections, families arranged marriages among young villagers. Only those peasants who had enough resources—strips of cultivated land and some livestock—to support a family could marry; indeed, many never accumulated sufficient income to do so, and had to work as hired hands throughout their lives. The lord of the manor also had a stake in the marriages of his serfs. He wanted the serfs to produce children to replenish his labor force; however, he did not want to lose the labor of serfs who might marry into another manor. Lords thus had to approve all marriages among serfs and sometimes charged a fee for the privilege of matrimony.

Most lords did even more to encourage the growth of serf families. In many manors, pregnancy warranted special privileges. For example, the lord granted an expectant mother the right to pick fruit whenever she wished and to keep any fish she caught in the manorial streams or rivers. In spite of such benefits, childbirth was difficult and dangerous. Many women died, and as a result, a man might have a series of wives in the course of his life. Child mortality was also very high, owing to disease, poor nutrition, and accidents as older children cared for infants while their parents worked. The manorial lord's support of marriage and pregnancy went only so far in overcoming these problems.

Noble Warriors: Feudal Obligations Among the Elite

The medieval manors were structured and organized to provide food for everyone. However, in the medieval mind these manors served an additional function: They were the economic and agricultural base which supported the fighting forces that allowed rulers like Charlemagne and Alfred to conduct their campaigns. Armies were expensive. It took about 10 peasant families to support one mounted soldier, so an efficient manorial organization was essential to produce an army. However, the Carolingians developed a way to organize the fighting men as well. Like the serfs, noble warriors were also bound to their lord in a system of mutual obligation. The legal formula that opened this chapter bound a noble fighting man. This system was a fluid one—each contract could be different, and some men might be bound to more than one lord. Nevertheless, a general system slowly developed that was based on the exchange of land for military service. In its most general sense, this system—that historians in the sixteenth century called "feudalism"—formed the political structure of the elites in medieval society. Many historians today prefer to avoid the term feudalism because it seems to suggest a clearly organized structure instead of the loose system that varied from place to place. Regardless of modern disagreements, it is clear that medieval people saw themselves linked in a chain of mutual obligation, only the forms of those obligations were varied.

As we saw in Chapter 6, men in the Germanic tribes saw themselves as linked in loyalty to their chief. This was a personal tie that bound fighting men together. Charlemagne's grandfather, Charles Martel (r. 714–741) (who defeated the Muslims at the Battle of Tours as we described in Chapter 6), seems to have at times joined these personal ties to the land that people occupied. Charles had seen the virtues of having an army made up of heavily armed men on horseback to replace the more lightly armed citizen foot soldiers that made up the Anglo-Saxon armies, for example. But armed, mounted knights were expensive. Instead of trying to raise money to support an army of this kind, Charles drew from what he had in abundance: land. He granted huge tracts of land, including the serfs who lived on them, to his followers in exchange for their military service. This process laid the foundation for a complex system that later brought order to the fighting men of the land.

The feudal system that grew out of Charles Martel's innovation bound men together in a series of *Lords and vassals* mutual obligations, but what set it apart from other bonds of loyalty was the linking of loyal service with land. When a nobleman bound himself in service to a lord, he swore a solemn oath of fealty (that is, to be faithful to his vows and his lord) by placing his hands between those of his lord. The nobleman now became the lord's "vassal"—bound to him for life. In return, the vassal would receive his *fief*—usually land, but it might be something else that would generate enough income to support the vassal. The illustration in Figure 7.9 cleverly portrays the solemn bonds. The standing vassal, shown with four arms, simultaneously places his hands between those of his lord and points to the stalks of wheat that stand for his fief.

The lord (who could be a king or any other man with land to bestow) gave away enough land to support the lifestyle of his noble vassals. These nobles' main function was warfare; they did not work the land as serfs did. Later, vassals took on other titles, like baron or duke, that showed their position relative to other greater or lesser vassals, but the word "vassal" remained a general term that applied to all noblemen bound in contract and loyalty to a lord. Theoretically, a vassal only held his fief as long as he was able to fight for his lord, but in fact, by the ninth century, vassals expected to be able to pass their fiefs on to their sons. A son was expected to place his hands between those of his lord and renew his father's vows before he took full possession of the fief, but as fiefs became hereditary possessions, the lord's control over his fiefs was reduced.

Each party owed something to the other. Lords owed their vassals "maintenance" (usually land) and military protection. In recalling the old Germanic legal principle of compurgation, the lord was also to act as his vassal's advocate in public court. Vassals owed lords "aid and counsel." The primary "aid" took the form of military service. Just as serfs owed their own lords labor, nobles owed their superiors specified periods of fighting time, which varied, but an average length of service might be 40 days a year. Vassals also owed monetary "aid." When a lord incurred certain expenses, such as for his daughter's wedding or his son's knighting, the vassals paid extra taxes to fund the event. In addition, vassals owed their lord "counsel," or advice at the lord's command. This obligation, along with the witenagemot discussed earlier, paved the way for the parliamentary system that developed later in the Middle Ages (see Chapter 8). Both parties owed the other fealty—that is, good faith to do the other no harm—and this was granted by a solemn kiss that sealed the pact.

Because this was a system of mutual obligation, if either party breached the contract, the arrangement could be rendered null. For instance, if a vassal failed to fight or give counsel, the lord could declare his land forfeit and give it to someone else. Of course, enforcement became complicated when armies

FIGURE 7.9
Vassal pledging fealty and receiving a fief from his lord.

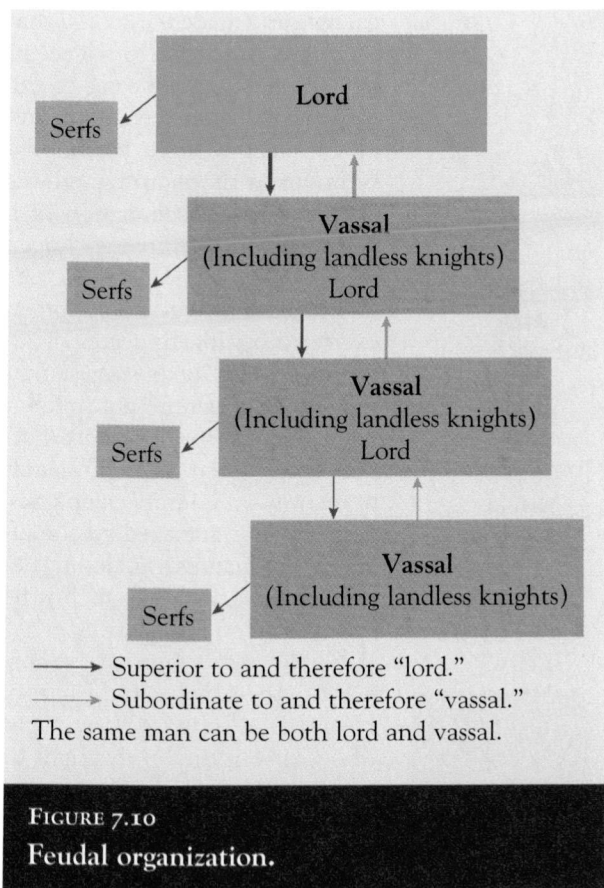

Serfs

Lord

Vassal
(Including landless knights)
Lord

Serfs

Vassal
(Including landless knights)
Lord

Serfs

Vassal
(Including landless knights)

Serfs

⟶ Superior to and therefore "lord."
⟶ Subordinate to and therefore "vassal."
The same man can be both lord and vassal.

FIGURE 7.10
Feudal organization.

one person's relationship with another. The chart in Figure 7.10 outlines the complexities of this relationship of superior and subordinate.

These feudal bonds were remarkably flexible because they were adapted to each place, time, and individual. Furthermore, the feudal ties kept society from disintegrating altogether in the face of the invasions and decentralization of the ninth century. In spite of these benefits, feudal ties also had features that further decentralized society, and even contributed to increased violence. In most cases, the vow of fealty was not necessarily exclusive, and in time the notion of personal loyalty became secondary to the idea of acquiring more property. Many vassals would serve different lords in exchange for different fiefs. Several sources showing the obligations and growing ambiguities of the feudal ties are in Document 7.4 on page D7.3.

The chart in Figure 7.11 adds the complexities of vassals who served several masters. Of course, one can readily see the potential for divided loyalties built into this structure. What if both lords of one vassal were at war? Sometimes—very practically—vassals followed the lord who gave him the largest fief. At other times, the vassal's first vow was the one that bound. Other vassals probably just tried to back the lord most likely to win the engagement. Beginning in the eleventh century in France and spreading from there over the next centuries, kings tried to establish the concept of liege lord—that is, the lord who could claim unreserved loyalty. Kings were able to enforce this with mixed success—the kings in England were successful, but in Germany they were less so (as we will see in Chapter 8). These systems of divided loyalty strained attempts to exert central authority in western Europe, so while feudal ties reduced the chaos, they still preserved some measure of violence. No doubt most people did not reflect upon these abstract considerations as they lived their lives. Feudal ties became simply one more reality of life in the Middle Ages.

MERRIMENT, MARRIAGE, AND MEDICINE: A NOBLE'S LIFE

The daily life of the nobility revealed the sense of community engendered by the feudal system. The feudal lords with their wives and children lived together with crowds of their own vassals and their servants. All ate together on long tables in the common hall of the manor house. The nobles amused themselves with

of men were involved, but the system did establish the idea of the primacy of contract law that bound people together in a more ordered society. However, because the feudal system varied from place to place and across time, historians disagree on exactly how formal or influential these contractual bonds were. Nevertheless, in the most general sense, feudal ties joined older kinship bonds in linking medieval warriors and their families together.

In this system, a nobleman could be both a vassal to someone over him and a lord to someone under him. A powerful vassal who had received large tracts *Feudal complexities* of land from his overlord might offer portions of it to other nobles who, in turn, would become his vassals. The lowest vassal in this structure was still a lord to the serfs who worked the land (who were lords to no one). Medieval people did not find ambiguity in these flexible terms, because the words "lord" and "vassal" were not absolute—they expressed a legal condition that defined

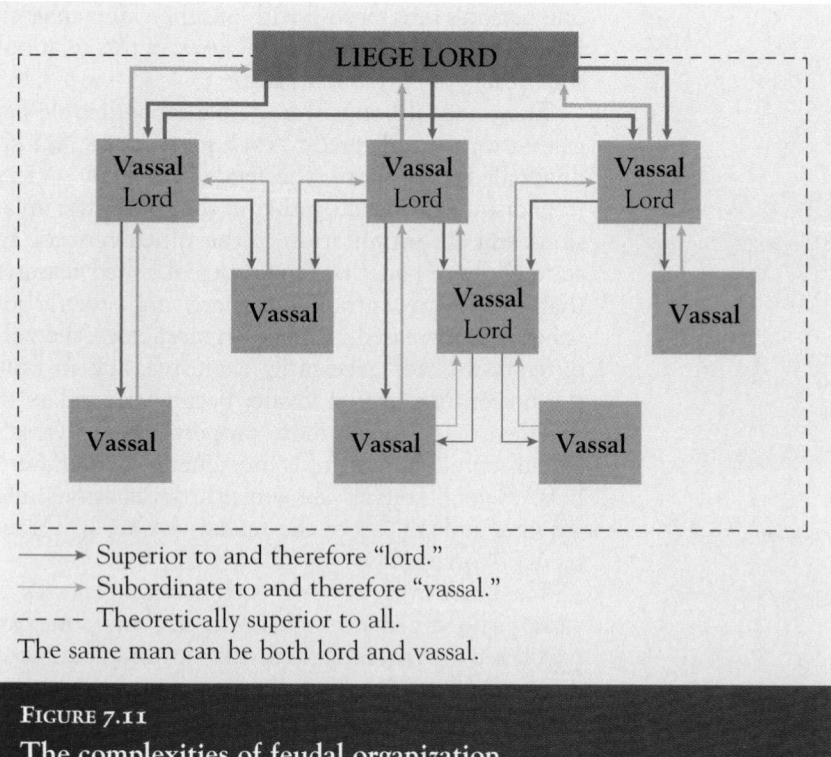

> → Superior to and therefore "lord."
> → Subordinate to and therefore "vassal."
> ---- Theoretically superior to all.
> The same man can be both lord and vassal.

FIGURE 7.11
The complexities of feudal organization.

music, dance, and games like backgammon, chess, and dice. Archaeologists have even found loaded dice in an Anglo-Saxon excavation, so cheating at such games is not a modern invention. In times of peace, both noble men and women indulged their passion for hunting with hawks, horses, and hounds. Hunting was intended to keep their skills sharp for their real purpose: warfare.

Just as in the Germanic tribes, noble families in the feudal system were bound to each other by the *Marriage ties* important ties of marriage. Yet, the institution of marriage changed during the Carolingian years. In the tradition of the Germanic tribes, Charlemagne had taken a number of wives—renouncing the marriage ties with one in order to marry another—and he even kept a number of concubines at the same time. However, under his religious son Louis the Pious, churchmen began to regulate the marriage bond, emphasizing monogamy and urging married men to give up their concubines. Although the church intruded more and more into the marriage relationship, it never persuaded all noblemen to make this sacrifice. Nonetheless, the church's interventions enhanced the status of the le-

gal wife and made it essential that she, and only she, produce an heir. As a new bride came to the wedding with great ceremony, and as she emerged from the nuptial bedroom in the morning, crowds cheered the consummation of a marriage that everyone hoped would produce offspring. As highly placed wives, noblewomen exerted a significant degree of autonomy. Many texts suggest that such women were responsible for managing the royal treasury. Furthermore, when their husbands were away on military campaigns, noblewomen managed all the affairs of the manors—including defending the castles from hostile invaders when necessary.

Noble girls married young, many of them between the ages of 12 and 14, if not younger. A girl who was betrothed early might be raised in the household of her fiance's family until she was deemed old enough for the marriage to be consummated. As they awaited their wedding day, girls learned household management, cloth making, and often reading and writing. Women could also inherit and hold land, but they still owed the feudal obligations that structured this society. If an unmarried girl's father died, she was placed under the wardship of the lord her father had served, because her future husband would become that lord's vassal. Widows, too, became wards until their lord arranged another marriage for them, but lords at times relinquished their rights of wardship in exchange for money, so wealthy widows might well control their own lives. Orphans were under the lord's control until they grew old enough to take their place in the lord's army or marry someone who could do so.

Germanic women had traditionally been responsible for medical care, and this continued through the early medieval period. Medicines consisted *Medicine* primarily of herbs, as suggested by the manuscripts from this era that preserve what are probably long-treasured medical recipes. Nasturtium, for example, was recommended for indigestion, wormwood for sleep disorders, and frankincense and oil for sore hands and fingers.

Even food was considered medicinal if prepared properly; therefore, women were also in charge of designing a healthful diet. Just as our notion of a "balanced" diet changes with the latest research, early medieval ideas about nutritious eating relied on contemporary understanding of health. For example, people during this period continued the classical idea that health depended on a balance between the body's "humors": wet, dry, cold, and hot. A proper diet must be "tempered"—that is, feature a balance of foods in each category of humor. For example, beans were considered "cold," so they were supplemented by "hot" spices to balance them. Likewise, illness was treated by correcting an imbalance of the humors. For example, if a person was considered too hot, the patient was given predominantly "cold" foods to bring his or her humors back into balance. This system also applied to the preparation of food. Charlemagne's biographer tells about the emperor's growing "dislike" of his physician after Charlemagne was forced to forgo his beloved roast meat in favor of boiled fare. Food and medicine were considered interchangeable in this era, and knowledgeable men and women alike prescribed medicinal diets.

Summary

At the beginning of the eighth century, the Germanic tribes that had precipitated the collapse of the Roman Empire in the west established kingdoms and converted to Christianity. Monasteries revealed the intellectual treasures from the classical world that they had painstakingly preserved in their libraries. Kings began to forge an effective synthesis between Germanic, Roman, and Christian cultures and create vigorous new societies governed by the rule of law. The culmination of these developments was Charlemagne's assumption of the imperial crown; it seemed as if a unified empire would exist again in western Europe.

However, the ninth- and tenth-century invasions by Scandinavians, Muslims, and Magyars broke down this progress, introducing another dark period of violence and retreat to local authority. Yet, the settlement of the Northmen and their conversion to Christianity paved the way for a new restoration of European order. This time rulers did not have to reinvent the political and economic structures of Europe; they simply had to restore them. They built on a decentralized order that had flourished in the dark days after the fall of the Carolingian Empire. This included a manorial system that secured effective agricultural production and a feudal system that supplied a political organization uniting people in law and loyalty. In the late eleventh century, it remained for kings, emperors, and popes to take charge and bring about the high point of medieval culture in western Europe.

REVIEW, ANALYZE, AND ANTICIPATE

REVIEW THE PREVIOUS CHAPTER

Chapter 6—"A World Divided"—described the breakup of the Roman Empire into western kingdoms, the Byzantine Empire, and the Muslim world. It also described the three cultures as the old Mediterranean world split.

1. *Review Germanic culture and values. Which elements did Charlemagne, Alfred the Great, and the Vikings retain?*

2. *Compare the illustration on page 226 with that in Figure 6.3. Both portray Saint Matthew, but in very different ways. Explain how the differences reflect Germanic and Roman culture.*

ANALYZE THIS CHAPTER

Chapter 7—"The Struggle to Restore Order"—traces the slow establishment of order in Europe as kings instituted laws for their kingdoms and as Charlemagne forged a new empire in western Europe. It also describes new destruction as migrating tribes again wreaked havoc on the continent.

1. *How did Alfred the Great and Charlemagne structure the administration of their respective kingdoms? How did the large size of Charlemagne's empire pose particular challenges for the ruler?*

TIMELINE: A CLOSER LOOK

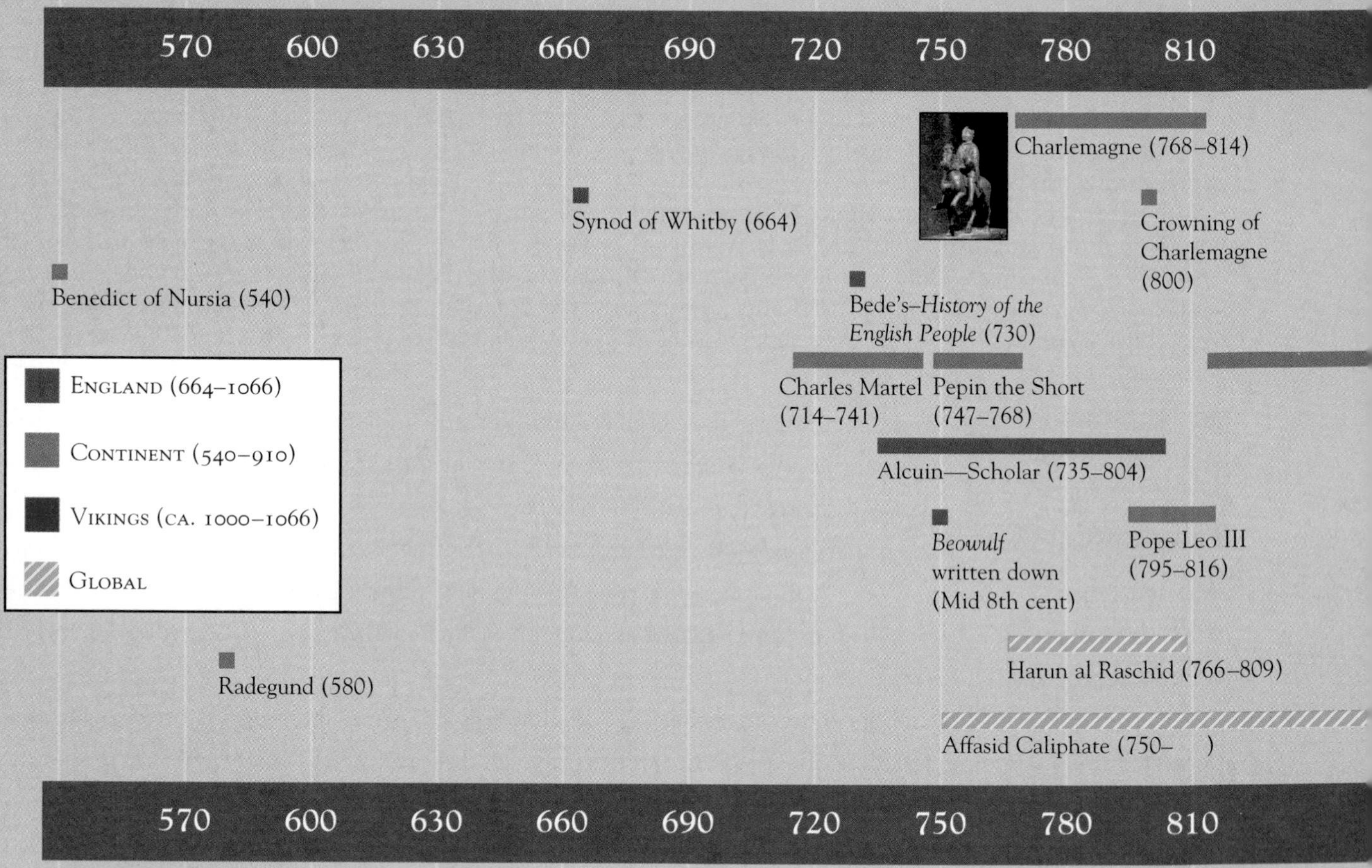

570	600	630	660	690	720	750	780	810

Charlemagne (768–814)

Synod of Whitby (664)

Crowning of
Charlemagne
(800)

Benedict of Nursia (540)

Bede's–*History of the
English People* (730)

ENGLAND (664–1066)

CONTINENT (540–910)

VIKINGS (CA. 1000–1066)

GLOBAL

Charles Martel Pepin the Short
(714–741)   (747–768)

Alcuin—Scholar (735–804)

Beowulf
written down
(Mid 8th cent)

Pope Leo III
(795–816)

Harun al Raschid (766–809)

Radegund (580)

Affasid Caliphate (750–   )

570	600	630	660	690	720	750	780	810

2. *Review Charlemagne's diplomatic negotiations with the Byzantine Empire and the 'Abbasid Caliphate. Why did each ruler act the way he/she did?*

3. *What was the basis for papal claims of supremacy over the church? What helped the church exert an order over its organization, and what forces prevented it from doing so?*

4. *Review the intellectual accomplishments of the Anglo-Saxon and Carolingian kingdoms.*

5. *Review the invasions of the ninth and tenth centuries. Who invaded? Where did they go, and what impact did they have on European society?*

ANTICIPATE THE NEXT CHAPTER

In Chapter 8—"Order Perfected"—we will follow the fortunes of the medieval kingdoms and the church as they grow in wealth and power, and we will see the fulfillment of medieval civilization.

1. *As England and France develop their own governmental forms, they create different kinds of parliaments. Given the differences between the administrative structures of Alfred and Charlemagne, can you imagine which is more likely to depend on a centralized bureaucracy and which would more likely build on representative institutions?*

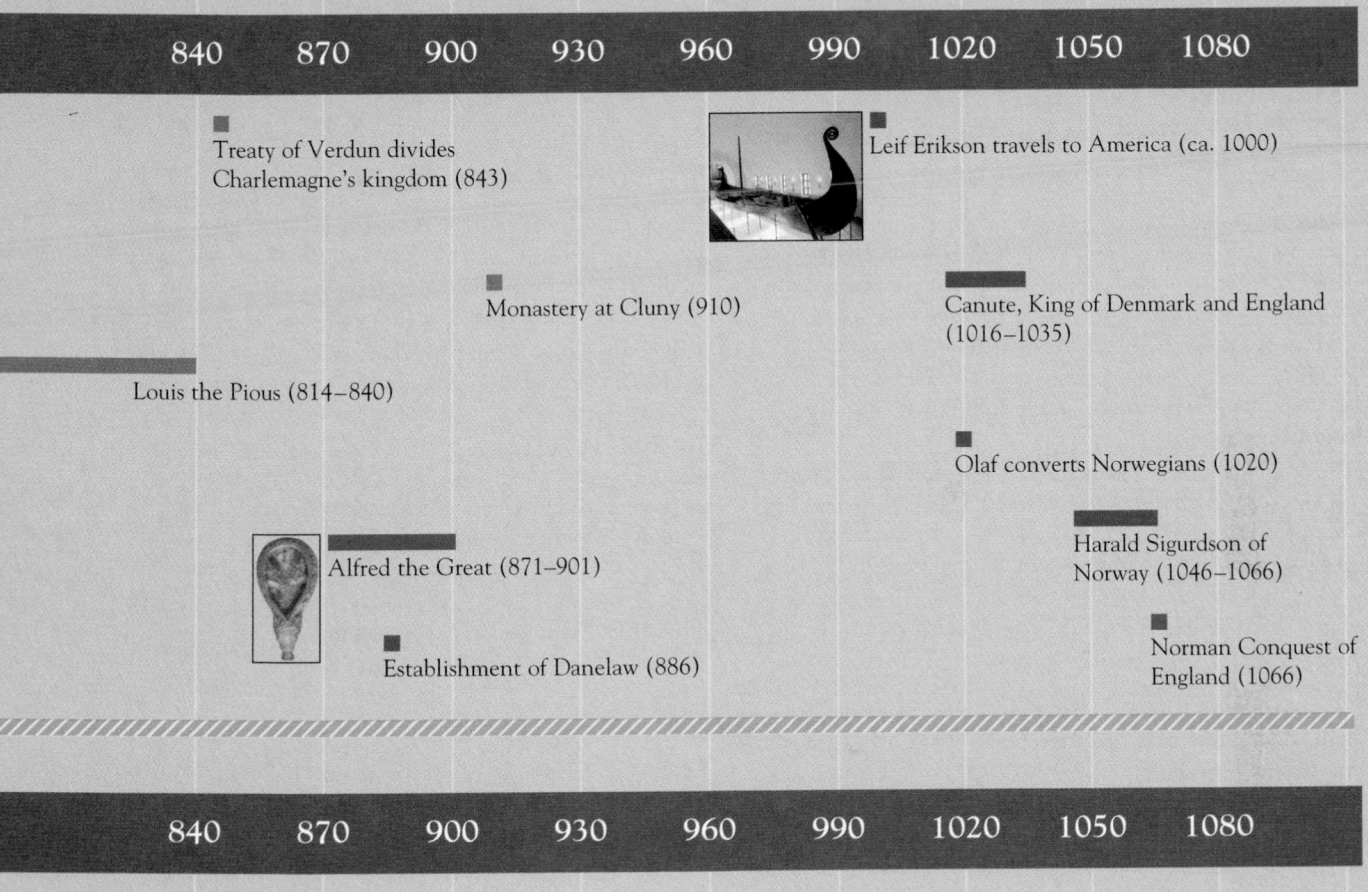

840	870	900	930	960	990	1020	1050	1080

Treaty of Verdun divides
Charlemagne's kingdom (843)

Leif Erikson travels to America (ca. 1000)

Monastery at Cluny (910)

Canute, King of Denmark and England
(1016–1035)

Louis the Pious (814–840)

Olaf converts Norwegians (1020)

Alfred the Great (871–901)

Harald Sigurdson of
Norway (1046–1066)

Establishment of Danelaw (886)

Norman Conquest of
England (1066)

840	870	900	930	960	990	1020	1050	1080

2. *Charlemagne and Leo introduced the question of who should rule a Christian society—pope or emperor. What form do you expect that controversy might take as it is revisited in Chapter 8?*

BEYOND THE CLASSROOM

BRINGING ORDER WITH LAWS AND LEADERSHIP

Meyers, Henry A., and H. Wolfram. *Medieval Kingship.* Chicago: University of Chicago Press, 1982. A solid study of the institution of kingship as it changed over time in western Europe.

Wallace-Hadrill, J.M. *Early Germanic Kingship in England and on the Continent.* Oxford: Clarendon Press, 1971. A clear, classic study by one of the acknowledged masters of the field.

ANGLO-SAXON ENGLAND: FORWARDING LAW AND LEARNING

Bassett, Steven. *The Anglo-Saxon Kingdoms.* New York: St. Martin's Press, 1989. A clear and fascinating study of the origins of the Anglo-Saxon kingdoms and kingship.

Mayr-Harting, Henry. *The Coming of Christianity to Anglo-Saxon England.* University Park, PA: Pennsylvania State University Press, 1991. Attempts to show how Christianity itself was changed in Anglo-Saxon society.

Smyth, Alfred P. *King Alfred the Great*. Oxford: Oxford University Press, 1995. A controversial look at the life and times of Alfred the Great that argues against the historical value of Asser's life of the king.

CHARLEMAGNE AND THE CAROLINGIANS: A NEW EUROPEAN EMPIRE

Bullough, David. *Carolingian Renewal: Sources and Heritage*. New York: St. Martin's Press, 1992. A clear and interesting study of the spirit of the age with a solid analysis of the sources.

Butzer, Paul L. *Science in Western and Eastern Civilization in Carolingian Times*. Boston, MA: Birkhäuser Verlag, 1993. Skillfully juxtaposes the heritage of classical science in western Europe with the Byzantine and Arab traditions of astronomy and mathematics.

Dhuoda. *Handbook for William: A Carolingian Woman's Counsel for Her Son*. Translated by Carol Neel. Lincoln: University of Nebraska Press, 1991. A good translation with commentary of the letter by Dhuoda featured in the Biography.

THE STRUGGLE FOR ORDER IN THE CHURCH

Knowles, David. *Christian Monasticism*. New York: McGraw-Hill, 1969. Offers a short and clear look at monastic life and its literature—a classic.

Lawrence, C.H. *Medieval Monasticism: Forms of Religious Life in Western Europe in the Middle Ages*, 2nd edition. New York: Longman, 1988. A comprehensive study of the growth of the western monastic condition, placing it solidly within the social context.

ORDER INTERRUPTED: VIKINGS AND OTHER INVADERS

Clark, Helen. *Towns in the Viking Age*. New York: St. Martin's Press, 1994. An insightful archaeological investigation of early medieval towns in northern Europe.

Logan, Donald F. *Vikings in History*. New York: Routledge, Chapman, and Hall, Inc., 1992. Focuses on Viking expeditions—across the seas, through river systems, and even overland.

MANORS AND FEUDAL TIES: ORDER EMERGING FROM CHAOS

Bloch, Marc. *Feudal Society*. Translated by L.A. Manyon. Chicago: University of Chicago Press, 1961. A classic study of the growth and nature of feudalism in its broad social context, but see Reynolds for a revised view.

Collins, Roger. *Early Medieval Europe, 300–1000*. New York: St. Martin's Press, 1991. A study of the people, politics, and religion of early medieval Europe.

Reynolds, Susan. *Fiefs and Vassals: The Medieval Evidence Reinterpreted*. Oxford: Oxford University Press, 1994. An important work that revises traditional approaches and considers whether the terms *fiefs* and *vassals* were used in the early Middle Ages as they are by modern scholars.

Strayer, J.R. *Feudalism*. Princeton, NJ: Princeton University Press, 1985. This work revises and refines the classic study of Bloch.

GLOBAL CONNECTIONS

Clot, André. *Harun al-Rashid*. Translated by John Howe. NY: New Amsterdam, 1989. An easy-to-read biography based on the Muslim sources. It ranges more widely than just the caliph's life to discuss the political, economic, social, and cultural times of the caliphate centered in Baghdad.

Von Grundebaum, G. E. *Classical Islam: A History, 600–1258*. NY: Barnes and Noble, 1970. A classic, scholarly work that examines the relationship between the Islamic world and the Mediterranean countries and India.

For quiz questions that tie the book to the videos and additional primary sources, please go to the Primary Source Investigator CD.

QUIZ

Documents

DOCUMENT 7.1
The Visigoths Lay Down the Laws

When the Germanic tribes began to record their customary laws, they wrote down many dictates that shed light on everyday rural life. Thus, these laws are valuable sources of information about facets of life that most historical sources ignore. Here are some examples of Visigothic laws documented in about the seventh century. These mandates aimed to regulate problems in the remote villages. Notice that the laws use the principle of wergeld *to resolve conflicts between neighbors.*

■ **Investigate the Document**

> **What** *kinds of animals did the villagers have?* **What** *kinds of problems arose among neighbors?* **How** *were these problems resolved?*

I. Where a Horse, or any other Animal, which has been Tied Up, is Removed, or Injured, in any way, Without the Consent of the Owner.

If any person should free a horse, or any other animal belonging to another, from its halter, or from its hobbles, without the knowledge of the owner, he shall pay him a *solidus*. If said horse, or other animal, should die, in consequence, said person shall give its owner another of equal value. If he should use said animal to travel, or to work with elsewhere, without the knowledge of the owner, he shall be compelled to give him another of equal value; provided the owner should find him on that day, or on the following one. If said animal should not be found by the third day, the person who took it shall be deemed guilty of theft.

III. Where the Mane or Tail of a Horse, or of any Other Animal, is cut off by Anyone.

Anyone who disfigures the mane of a horse belonging to another, or cuts off its tail, must at once give to the owner of the same another animal of equal value. Should any other animal be mutilated in this manner, the third part of a *solidus* must be paid for every one so mutilated.

Source: S. P. Scott, Trans. *The Visigothic Code (Forum Judicum)*, (Boston: The Boston Book Co., 1910), pp. 284, 285, 286, 291.

IV. Where Anyone Castrates an Animal Belonging to Another.

Whoever castrates any quadruped used for racing purposes, without the knowledge or consent of the owner; or castrates any animal which ought not to be castrated; shall be compelled to pay double the value of said animal to the owner of the same, who has been damaged on account of his malice.

V. Where Anyone Produces an Abortion upon a Beast of Burden Belonging to Another.

Whoever produces an abortion upon a mare, shall give to the owner of the same a foal, one year old, by way of compensation.

VI. Where Anyone Produces an Abortion upon any kind of Animal Belonging to Another.

If anyone should produce an abortion upon a cow, he shall be compelled to give another, along with her calf, to the owner; and he himself shall be entitled to the animal injured. This Law shall also apply to the cases of all other quadrupeds.

VII. Where Animals of any kind Injure One Another.

Where beasts of burden, or any kind of cattle, injure others belonging to another person, the owner of those that caused the damage shall give to the owner of the former, others of equal value, and the injured ones shall become his own property.

XIX. Where a Dog that has been Irritated, whether the Provocation was Wanton or not, is Proved to have Injured, or Killed Anyone.

Where a dog bites another person not his owner, and said person is known to have been crippled or killed, in consequence thereof, no responsibility shall attach to the owner of the dog, unless it shall be proved that he caused said dog to make the attack. If, however, he should encourage his dog to seize a thief, or any other criminal, and the latter should be bitten while in flight, and should be crippled, or die from the effects of the bite, the owner of said dog shall incur no liability therefor. But if he should cause said dog to injure an innocent person, he must render satisfaction according to law, in the same manner as if he himself had inflicted the wound.

King Oswald with his bishop Aiden, ca. 1200

This illustration shows the hierarchy of medieval society: The king and his bishop talk at the table while the poor laborers sit at the great men's feet, soliciting charity. A fortified castle frames the whole picture, and represents the structure of the medieval order in which some fight (kings), others pray (bishops), and the rest work (laborers).

CHAPTER 8

Order Perfected

The High Middle Ages, 1000–1300

STUDY • Medieval Agriculture • Town Life, Universities, and Philosophy • Ideals of Chivalry • Growth of Centralized Kingdoms • Church Reform and Crusades NOTICE both the peaceful and violent interactions between the West and Islam.

"From the beginning, mankind has been divided into three parts—men of prayer, farmers, and men of war. . . . " These words written by Bishop Gerard of Cambrai in the eleventh century capture the social order as the people of the High Middle Ages understood it. In this highly organized world, everyone was expected to keep his or her place, or "order." And these orders were arranged by their function—prayer, warfare, and labor on the land. This understanding of the world ignored the important role of commerce in the growing cities.

After the year 1000, medieval society began to expand in all respects. Agricultural advances spurred population growth; commerce quickened in thriving cities; fortified houses for the nobility sprang up across Europe. After the devastation of the tenth century, kings again tried to consolidate their rule, and nobles resisted their incursion. Intellectual life also flourished with the new prosperity of the age, and philosophers, poets, and artists created works that still inspire us today.

The church, too, grew stronger, and popes began to exert their authority over secular matters. Church leaders called for crusades against Islam, luring western Europeans far from their homelands. Finally, the church's growing role in secular life ignited criticism from some people, who felt that it had forgotten its true purpose. In the face of such criticism, religious leaders responded by both reforming some church policies and repressing those who complained. It was indeed a dynamic age.

Carolingian Dynasty
752–987
France

Saxon (or Ottonian)
Dynasty 919–1024
Germany

Norman Dynasty
1066–1154
England

Salian Dynasty
1024–1125
Germany

Angevin
Dynasty
1154–1216
England

Hohenstaufen Dynasty
1138–1268 Germany

Habsburg Dynasty 1250 Germany

Plantagenet Dynasty 1216–1399 England

Capetian Dynasty 987–1328 France

Spanish Reconquest of Iberian Peninsula 900–1492

900   1000   1100   1200   1300   1400

Those Who Work: Agricultural Labor

In the late twelfth century, a noble knight, William Marshall, rested in the woods while on a journey accompanied only by his squire. He was awakened from his sleep by the sound of a woman's voice saying "Ah, God, how weary I am." Opening his eyes, William saw a well-dressed couple riding along. William quickly mounted and rode to introduce himself and offer help, but the man was not pleased to see the knight. As the stranger drew his sword, his hood fell off and William saw by his tonsured hair that he was a monk—the handsomest one that he had ever seen. Filled with shame, the monk confessed he had run from his monastery with his lady love: "I have carried her off from her own country." William reprimanded the young woman and offered to escort her back to her brother so she would avoid the shame of the path she had chosen. She refused, and William did not persist. However, the knight did show continued concern, asking them how they would live. The monk showed a belt bulging with coins and said that they would lend money and live off the interest. The good knight William was horrified, "Upon usury? By God's sword, you shall not." He told his squire to take the money to save the couple from falling into the additional shame of moneylending. He sent the couple on their way (penniless) and took the money to the local inn, where William generously treated his friends to abundant food and drink with the purloined coins.

In this story of a noble knight—preserved in a long poem written by his son—we can see the Middle Ages coming into full flower. Knights acted with courtesy to help women who may have been in distress, and they were generous with money (that may not even have been their own). Wealth and love were to be had, and some people—even monks and women—began to explore new ways to live their lives. All this was stimulated by a technological and agricultural boom.

HARNESSING THE POWER OF WATER AND WIND

After 1000, Europeans used more mechanical power than any previous society had; and this power helped fuel the expansion of population, commerce, and political power in western Europe. Water mills provided the major source of mechanical power. In England in 1086, there were often as many as three mills for every mile of river. Water mills ground grain with extraordinary efficiency, and their technology spread rapidly across Europe. Figure 8.1 shows two women bringing sacks of grain to a mill. The women must cross a bridge over the river that powers the great waterwheel. The nearby buildings reveal the prosperity of the mill owner—prosperity he has acquired by charging a fee for the use of the mill. In the picture, the man at the left stands ready to collect the women's fees.

How did the mills actually work? A cam, projecting from the axle of the waterwheel, converted rotary motion to vertical motion, which let mill workers accomplish tasks from forging iron to softening wool cloth to making beer and paper. By the twelfth century, creative builders developed ways to bring mechanical power to regions without rivers to drive water mills. Windmills (first developed in Persia) used wind to generate power in many parts of Europe, and tide mills sprang up around the North Sea. Harnessing all this power accomplished what technology in the ancient world had never achieved: it released human power for other uses.

New Agricultural Techniques

Peasants supplemented water power with effective use of animal muscle. In the early Middle Ages, as in the ancient world, people harnessed horses with the same kind of yoke they used on oxen. This device was highly inefficient on horses, however, because the yoke rested on their necks and impeded their breathing when they lowered their heads to pull. By the eleventh century, a new padded horse collar that had been developed in China appeared in western Europe. This harness rested on the animal's shoulders, making it possible for people to use horses for heavy plowing and pulling. Because horses can work 50 percent faster and two hours a day longer than oxen, the advantages were huge. Of course, now the peasant walking behind the team of horses also had to work longer and harder. Not surprisingly, the improvement was not as popular with workers as it was with their lords. The Agricultural Instruction manual in Document 8.4 on page D8.3 gives a contemporary view of agricultural innovations. Nevertheless, the amount of land under cultivation expanded dramatically with increased use of the horse.

The increased use of animal power required peasants to cultivate more land for fodder and hay. Traditionally—since Roman times—most peasants used what is called a two-field system, in which half the land was left fallow (unplanted) while half was planted. The fertility of the fallow land was restored to yield more crops the following year. However, to accommodate the need to cultivate more land, manors slowly adopted a three-field system that further increased agricultural yields. In this system, plots of land were divided into thirds: One-third was planted in the spring, another in the fall, and the remaining third was left fallow. The three-field system also stimulated the growth of new crops that boosted production. Villagers began to plant legumes, such as peas and beans, which add nitrogen to the soil, thus fertilizing the subsequent grain crop. Legumes also provided an excellent source of protein, which vastly improved the villagers' diets.

Three-field cultivation

FIGURE 8.1
Women carrying grain to be ground at a water mill, 1470.

The Population Doubles

These agricultural improvements (and the declining violence after the ninth- and tenth-century invasions ended) led to unprecedented population growth. Although it is impossible to get exact figures, estimates of population growth indicate that from the eleventh through the thirteenth centuries, the population of Europe approximately doubled—from about 37 million to 74 million. Women in particular benefited from the addition of legumes to their diet because the iron in these foods helped replenish blood lost through menstruation and childbirth, and it enabled healthy women to have fewer miscarriages and nurse stronger babies. With such improvements, women began outnumbering men during these centuries, and even some medieval commentators noted this disparity, considering it a "problem."

Throughout this period, infant and child deaths remained high due to diseases and accidents, and the overall mortality rates were much higher than in modern times. But anyone surviving past the years normally devoted to warfare or childbearing could expect to live as long as people do today. Indeed, the Biography on page 273 features a man who was vigorous well into his 80s. And in

Life span

1204, one 97-year-old representative of the pope participated in the Crusades. There were plenty of gray heads and seasoned minds in the villages, castles, and churches of the Middle Ages.

To accommodate the ballooning population, western Europeans expanded their settlements. Hardworking villagers on the northwest coast (later the Low Countries) built dikes to hold back the ocean itself to expand their agricultural lands. Sometimes groups of villagers left an overcrowded area and cultivated new land, a process called "assarting." The resulting "assart" was great open fields that the peasants divided into strips as they established new villages and manors. Primarily they moved eastward. Probably as many as 3,000 new villages were established in lands east of the Elbe River in modern-day northern Germany. As they migrated east, settlers spread western European culture into the lands of the Slavs. Map 8.1 shows some of the eastern settlements that were founded as western Europeans relentlessly sought new lands.

Why would peasants leave their established villages to go east and do the hard work needed to clear new agricultural lands? The texts show that people *New freedoms* had two motivations: the possibility of better lands and more freedom. The twelfth-century chronicler Helmod of Bosau described how Count Adolf II of Holstein (1128–1164) attracted settlers to his new lands: He insisted that "whoever might be in difficult straits because of a shortage of fields should come with their families to accept land which was excellent, spacious, fertile with fruits, abounding in fish and meat, and favorable to pastures." Still, the peasants drove a hard bargain—many surviving charters show that the new settlers gained many freedoms from the feudal obligations of serfdom. For example, the Charter of the twelfth-century village of Lorris read: "No man shall pay a tax upon his food. Nor for measuring the grain which he obtains from his own labor or that of his animals. Nor shall he pay any tax on the wine which he obtains from his own vineyards." With such incentives, the spread to new lands blossomed, and western European culture flourished.

Few expansions offer unmixed blessings, and the population growth had dire environmental consequences. To build their new settlements, people *Environmental consequences* clear-cut huge swaths of forest, often using slash-and-burn techniques that left clouds of smoke and ash hanging in the air. The settlers also dumped human waste and the remains of slaughtered animals in the

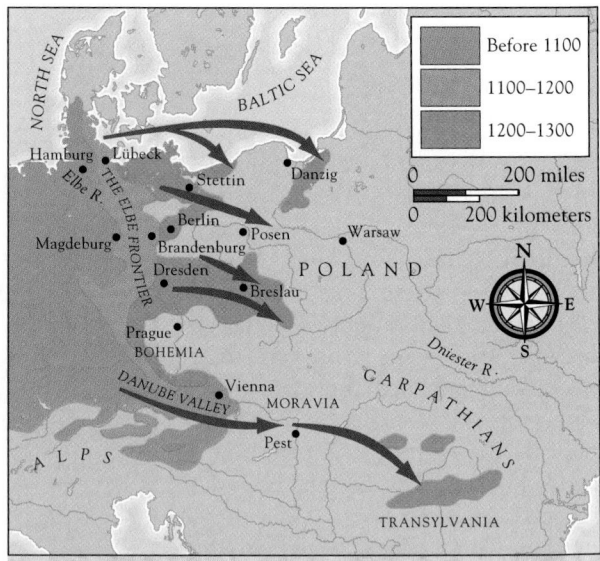

THINKING ABOUT GEOGRAPHY

MAP 8.1   *German Migration Eastward*

This map shows the new eastern settlements from about 1000 to 1300. ◾ **Notice** the steady progress eastward to promising agricultural lands. **Consider** the long expanse of time this migration encompassed. ◾ **Notice** the locations of the many cities that grew up in the north near the Baltic Sea. **What** do you think will be the impact of these new northern cities on trade routes around the Baltic?

rivers. In the cities, coal burning poured clouds of dangerous pollutants into the air. Still, the population kept expanding, and more and more people appreciated being freed from the land to populate the burgeoning cities and towns.

Those Outside the Order: Town Life

As we saw in the quotation that began this chapter, when medieval writers identified an ordered world of "those who work," they imagined agricultural laborers providing for the lords who ruled and the clergy who prayed. Yet, there were others who labored outside this well-defined hierarchy who did not fit medieval understandings based on a rural society. Yet, it was in these towns that people forged the real future of modern urban western European culture.

The few towns of the early Middle Ages were primarily administrative centers, serving as the residences of bishops or occasionally of a count. These towns were walled for protection from the surrounding violence of the feudal world. After 1000, more cities grew up and began to take on more commercial roles. In the process, they grew not only larger, but wealthier, and they developed new ways to govern their increasingly prosperous lives.

COMMUNES AND GUILDS: LIFE IN A MEDIEVAL TOWN

People moved to towns that offered work in a thriving trade and a lively demand for goods. By present-day standards, most medieval towns were small. For example, of the 3,000 identified "towns" in late medieval Germany, 2,800 had populations of only about 1,000. Europe did have a few great cities, however. Cologne was home to some 40,000 people, and London's population approached that figure by the fourteenth century. The Italian cities of Florence and Venice boasted almost 100,000 residents each.

Men and women living in these small towns had little in common with the feudal society that surrounded them. To escape the many requirements imposed on village serfs, towns negotiated charters with the lords on whose lands the town stood. These charters granted townspeople freedom from labor obligations and freedom to travel at will. They also protected the growing town profits from unreasonable taxation and seizure, and some charters allowed the towns to run their own law courts. All these rights made towns islands of freedom in a tightly ordered world, and in return, the lords received money from the prosperous burgs. Towns also served as magnets drawing those who wished to escape from the ordered constraints of the feudal world. In most towns, if a serf could live for "a year and a day" without being caught, he had earned his freedom to stay in the town.

Sometimes townspeople could not peacefully obtain the liberties they desired, and they joined together in sworn associations called "communes" and staged violent revolutions to take communal liberties that they believed came with urban life. The communes elected their own officials, regulated taxation within the

Communes and guilds

town, and generally conducted the business of running the urban centers. These communes were not democratic, for most people accepted it as natural that the rich citizens would govern the town. In Italy, the communes became so strong that the cities developed into independent city-states. In the French and English lands, by contrast, all the towns remained subject to the political authority of the king. In all cases, however, towns encouraged people to develop their skills, learn a trade, and make money.

Tradesmen within towns formed guilds, or organizations to protect their interests and control the trade and manufacturing within the towns. These guilds regulated the quality of such products as gold work, shoes, bread, and so forth; they managed their own membership and set prices. In part because urban women outnumbered men, they participated in the guilds, and families arranged marriages to cement bonds of loyalty and control of commerce. Widows in particular ran businesses and took their husbands' places in the trade organizations. Boys and girls served as apprentices in the shops until they learned their trade. Then they could work as "journeymen"—paid employees under the guidance of a master. Finally, journeymen would present a sample of their best work—whether a gold piece or a loaf of bread—to the guild masters to see if this "masterpiece" would qualify them to become full guild masters. In these ways, the guild could control both the quality of the products and the number of guild members involved in the trade.

For other groups, town life offered a more mixed set of opportunities and limits. Since the time of the Roman Empire, many medieval towns had a significant population of Jews. For centuries, Jews had played a vital role in town life as merchants, artisans, and members of many other professions. By the eleventh and twelfth centuries, however, Christian merchants and craftspeople began to view the Jewish community as competition. Slowly, they excluded Jews from guilds and, in some places, kept them from owning land. However, Jews still engaged in commerce and many Christians found them valuable—although separate—members of the town. For example, a late-eleventh-century charter was granted by a bishop (Rudgar) to Jews who were willing to settle in the German town of Speyer. He wrote that he thought "it would greatly add to its [Speyer's] honor if I should establish some Jews in it." He gave them a section of the city for their use (and walled

Urban Jews

OLC

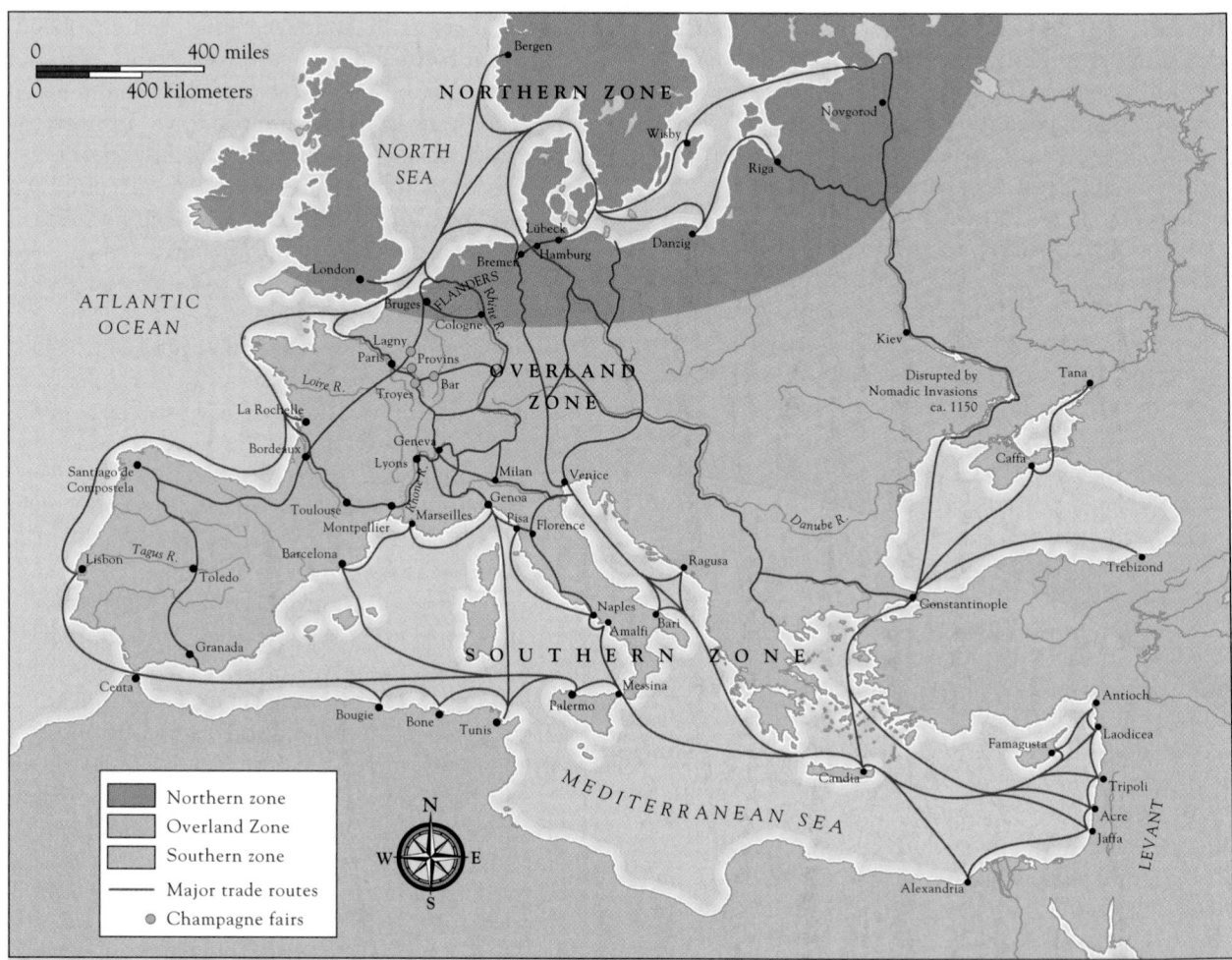

THINKING ABOUT GEOGRAPHY

MAP 8.2 *Trade Routes, Twelfth and Thirteenth Centuries*

This map shows the major trading areas of the High Middle Ages, including the three principal zones of trade. **Notice** the importance of sea and river routes. **Why** were the Italian cities particularly well suited to take advantage of the southern trade? **What** northern cities were well placed for sea and river trade? **Locate** the Champagne fairs. **Consider** why their location might be favorable in bringing together the northern and southern trade zones.

it off to provide protection from less-enlightened Christians) and offered them special concessions for trading.

The Bishop of Speyer also gave Jews the right to freely change coins, and slowly, urban Jews such as those in Speyer began to enter into moneylending, which is essential to commercial enterprises. The Christian religion forbade its followers to collect in-

terest on loans, for they believed that it was unseemly to make money from time, which belonged to God. One thirteenth-century church authority (Guillaume d'Auxerre) wrote of people who charged interest for loans: "The usurer acts in contravention to universal natural law, because he sells time. . . . " While many Christians continued to engage in the lucrative practice of moneylending, slowly through the late Middle

Ages, Jewish bankers increasingly began to take over the practice because Judaic practice contained no such strictures against lending money. The two urban groups thus depended on each other in an uneasy co-existence throughout most of the Middle Ages.

§§ THE WIDENING WEB OF TRADE

The impetus for the growth of towns and wealth in the Middle Ages came not from manufacturing, but from trade. Therefore, the most important towns were those that served as bustling centers for moving goods—throughout the Middle Ages most of the trade centered on luxury goods. Northern Italy, especially, became a significant nexus in southern Europe, and Venice, Pisa, and Genoa took the lead. As early as 998, Venetians had received charters from the Byzantine emperor that gave them complete freedom in Byzantine waters, and Pisa and Genoa had negotiated treaties with Muslim rulers that opened new markets. Thus, the way was paved for merchants to sail to the eastern Mediterranean and buy silks and spices passing through the great Muslim bazaars in Baghdad. They then brought the goods westward to Spain and southern France. Whereas the Mediterranean trade had been the commercial center during the Roman Empire, the medieval world opened a new trading hub in the north.

Cities in Flanders (particularly Bruges and Ghent) joined the Italian cities as commercial centers. They supplied fine wool cloth to all of northern Europe and acted as a supply center for Scandinavian products— particularly furs and hunting hawks— that were in demand all over Europe. The growth of the cloth industry, and the handsome profits to be made, led many northern men to replace at the looms the women who had dominated the industry. Map 8.2 shows the two major trade zones, northern and southern, that distributed goods. However, through the eleventh century, there was no easy mechanism for joining those two zones.

Early in the twelfth century, the French count of Champagne saw an opportunity to make a large profit by hosting fairs in his lands at which merchants could sell goods *Champagne fairs* from both the northern and southern trade routes. He granted the right to various towns in his county to organize such gatherings. (Map 8.2 shows the major towns of the Champagne fairs.) The counts of Champagne provided the space, set up booths, arranged for police to keep order, and invited money-lenders. Each day, the trade featured a different product, and the counts collected a sales tax from all the transactions made.

Figure 8.2 depicts one such medieval fair. At the booths, people gather to purchase animals, bolts of cloth, and fine artifacts. At the center of the illustration, the bishop of Paris opens the fair by bestowing God's blessing on the enterprise. The fairs featured products from all over Europe: leather from Spain,

FIGURE 8.2
A medieval fair in France.

iron from Germany, copper and tin from Bohemia, and smoked fish and furs from Scandinavia. They also offered an outlet for local products such as cheeses and wines. The fairs also drew people from the medieval underbelly of society; thieves, con-artists, actors and prostitutes plied their trade among the bustling crowds.

In the late thirteenth century, many cities in northern Germany created the Hanseatic League, an *Hanseatic League* association that united to capitalize on the prosperous northern trade. The cities formed a political as well as an economic power, and they were able to acquire a monopoly on the Baltic trade, replacing Flanders as the center of the northern trading zone. At its height, the Hanseatic League included 70 or 80 cities, led by Lubeck, Bremen, Cologne, and Hamburg. By the fourteenth century, they offered their own great fairs that replaced the French fairs. By looking at Maps 8.1 and 8.2, we can see that the eastward settlements around the Baltic Sea helped spawn prosperous trade regions that brought centers of wealth ever north-ward from the Mediterranean Sea.

THE GLORY OF GOD: CHURCH ARCHITECTURE

With the wealth that came pouring into the cities, townspeople built great churches to celebrate the glory of God and express their pride in their own towns. From about the tenth century until the twelfth, church architecture was dominated by the Romanesque style. Mostly monastic structures, these buildings were large and dark with long, central aisles made of barrel vaults and round arches. They seemed so solid and formidable, people often called them "fortresses of God."

Figure 8.3a shows the interior of the monastery church of La Madeleine at Vézeley in Burgundy. Built in the early twelfth century, this structure represents the highest achievement of Romanesque architec-ture. Because the barrel vault was high, it could not support the heavy stone roof by itself, so builders made the walls extra thick and the windows small. As a result, such churches were dark inside.

In about 1140, Abbot Suger of the Church of St. Denis near Paris decided to change all this. He envi-sioned a majestic church built in a new style—a church that reached up toward the heavens and that was filled with light. Architects and builders set

about making this vision a reality, and to do so, they adopted innovative techniques. Instead of round arches, they used pointed ones, as shown in Figure 8.3b. Some scholars *Gothic architecture* believe the use of the pointed arch originated in In-dia and found its way through the trade networks to France. Regardless of its origin, the new arch style di-rected the weight of the roof down the building's massive columns instead of its walls. But such tall walls were vulnerable to cracking under the pressure of high winds. To guard against this danger, architects developed "flying buttresses," large braces that sup-ported the outside of the building.

With these innovations, the walls no longer needed to be thick to provide the support for the church. Builders could therefore add large windows that let light fill the interior. *Stained glass* Glassmakers gathered in nearby forests to burn the hardwood needed to blow glass, and they added metallic oxides to make rich primary colors. Artists fitted the colored glass into intricate lead webs to form magnificent pictures showing everything from biblical stories to scenes of medieval life. Abbot Suger himself contracted the stained glass windows for his new church. Delighted with the result, he wrote, "The en-tire sanctuary is pervaded by a wonderful and contin-uous light." The thirteenth-century royal chapel in Paris shown in Figure 8.4 contains some of the most remarkable examples of stained glass, for the windows make up three-quarters of the wall surface.

Beginning in the mid-twelfth century, these im-mense Gothic cathedrals, with their pointed arches, stained-glass windows, and flying buttresses, began ap-pearing in all the great cities of Europe. Designed to accommodate the entire population of a city (some can hold as many as 10,000 people standing during mass), they were also designed to attract admiring pil-grims. The cathedrals vied to acquire and feature relics of famous saints (see Chapter 5) that drew the faithful seeking solace and miracles. These pilgrims brought money to both the church and the city and helped stimulate movement throughout medieval Eu-rope. The skylines of medieval Europe were reshaped by the towers of these striking new cathedrals.

THE RISE OF UNIVERSITIES

The cathedrals became more than just centers of wor-ship and pilgrimage; they began serving as places of learning. Scholars and students gathered at cathedrals

OLC

FIGURE 8.3
Romanesque and Gothic architecture. (a) Romanesque: La Madeleine at Vézeley, ca. 1104. (b) Gothic: Cologne cathedral (begun 1248).

to study, and these cathedral schools became vibrant centers. It soon became clear that the informal organization of these schools was inadequate. Document 8.1 on page D8.1 describes the drawbacks of some educators in the noble households. Townspeople frequently protested to the bishop against the students, who were often rowdy and sometimes violent. Students, on their part, resented the high prices that townspeople charged for rooms, food, and drink, and

they needed protection against incompetent teachers. By the twelfth century, new structures emerged to address some of these problems, establishing the beginnings of universities.

Just as townspeople founded guilds and used charters to protect their interests, students and scholars did the same. In some places (like Paris) masters grouped themselves into guilds, and in other cities (like Bologna), students organized themselves. These

Advanced students interested in focusing on a specialized course of study could continue their studies and receive a doctorate degree. Students might study medicine in Salerno, where masters taught Arabic medicine and | *Advanced degrees* sometimes dissected human cadavers. Others might go to Bologna to study law based on Justinian's *Corpus* (discussed in Chapter 6), or study theology—the "queen of all the sciences"—in Paris. The many medieval universities of Europe are shown in Map 8.3. This map gives some idea of the potential for students to move from school to school as they sought different masters and different curricula. It also suggests how these institutes of learning served to link the intellectual life of such a broad geographic area.

The universities gave rise to a new kind of life for the young men who attended them. Many students eagerly devoured the ideas and knowledge that percolated at these centers of learning. The classroom pictured in Figure 8.5 shows students with differing degrees of enthusiasm—those in the front listen attentively while some in the back talk during the lecture and another in the foreground sleeps. The less serious students deeply enjoyed the freedom of university life, drinking in the local bars and brawling in the streets, and raising the townspeople's ire. In Paris, a law was passed forbidding students to gamble with dice on the altar of the cathedral while mass was being said! All this freedom cost money; many letters in which students ask their parents to send more cash survive from this era. Yet, despite the occasional disruptions and distractions of life in the universities, students and teachers managed to engage in stimulating dialogues that led to exciting new ideas.

SCHOLASTICISM: THE HEIGHT OF MEDIEVAL PHILOSOPHY

The main goal of medieval philosophy was to reconcile faith with reason—that is, to understand with one's mind what one believed in one's heart. The medieval thinkers applied a particular form of logic, called dialectic, which involves using logic to explore various sides of an issue, and these writings often take the form of questioning. The greatest thinkers drawn to the new universities in the twelfth century wrestled constantly with this problem, and in doing so shaped both knowledge and faith.

The earliest medieval philosopher to explore the religious applications of dialectic was Anselm of Canterbury (1033–1109). Anselm's motto was "faith seeking

FIGURE 8.4
Stained glass windows in Saint Chapelle, Paris, ca. 1245.

organizations were called "universities"—from the Latin word *universitas*, which means "guild." These universities received charters that confirmed the guild's autonomy and authority to license teachers.

Young men (some only 14 years old) from all social classes attended universities; wealthy younger sons of the nobility and promising young village boys could eventually hope for lucrative jobs in the church or courts. (Women were not permitted to attend universities.) Students completed the traditional course of study that had been established centuries before at Charlemagne's (r. 768–814) court. First, they studied the trivium—grammar, rhetoric, and logic—and then the quadrivium—arithmetic, geometry, music, and astronomy. Upon completion, they would receive first a bachelor's degree and then a master's degree.

THINKING ABOUT GEOGRAPHY

MAP 8.3 *Medieval Universities*

This map shows the many universities that were founded throughout the Middle Ages and many of the dates of their foundations. ❧ **Notice** which universities were founded earliest, so you can identify the earliest centers of intellectual activity. ❧ **Notice** the great concentration of universities in Italy. **What** effect might this clustering have on the overall numbers of people educated in that region and on the local culture?

understanding" and his most famous effort involved showing a logical connection between the belief that God is a perfect being and a proof (by the rules of logic) that God exists. He argued that because God was perfect he *must* exist, or else he would not be perfect (for Anselm per-

Anselm and Abelard

fection demonstrated a real existence). Anselm wrote a number of works on logic, and his treatise *Why God Became Man* became the most important explanation of the central Christian mystery. Anselm established the exciting possibility that human reason could be brought to study the deep mysteries of Creation.

FIGURE 8.5
University classroom.

One of the most esteemed scholastic scholars was Peter Abelard (1079–1142), who taught at Paris. In his mid-thirties, Abelard was hired to tutor Heloise (1100?–1163), the talented 17-year-old niece of a local church official. Teacher and student were soon lovers, and Heloise became pregnant. The couple married secretly because Heloise feared that a traditional marriage would hurt Abelard's reputation as a teacher, but her infuriated uncle had Abelard castrated. Leaving their child to be raised by relatives, both Heloise and Abelard entered monasteries, where they each continued brilliant careers of learning and influence.

Abelard established a method of applying critical reason to even sacred texts. His most famous work, *Yes and No* (*Sic et Non*), assembled a variety of authoritative sources, from the Bible to church fathers, that seemed to contradict each other. From these, the scholar compiled 150 theological questions and the passages relevant to each question, which allowed scholars to consider the full range of the questions. Although his book has such provocative chapters as "Is God the Author of Evil, or No?" Abelard had no desire to undermine faith; on the contrary, he believed that this kind of inquiry would strengthen

Biography

📀 RAMÓN LULL (1232?–1316)

📷 **Notice** how Ramón was shaped by the main intellectual currents of the time, from poetry to chivalry to philosophy.

📷 **Consider** how he brought philosophy to bear on the overriding problem of the day—the proximity of the Muslims.

Ramón Lull was born in about 1232 on Majorca, one of the Balearic Islands off the east coast of Spain. As a young man, Ramón was deeply drawn to the love poetry of the troubadours. He composed songs and poems of love and the life of luxury. However, at about age 30, he had a transforming experience. One night, as he crafted a love song for his lady, he beheld a vision of Jesus hanging on the cross. After a few more such visions, Ramón decided to renounce his frivolous life and turn his efforts to religion. In his view, God had called him to convert the Muslims to Christianity.

Ramón began to train for his new vocation. To learn Arabic so he could preach to the Muslims, he bought a Muslim slave. He studied with the slave for nine years and became fluent in Arabic. Toward the end of his studies, the slave tried to murder Ramón, perhaps to keep him from preaching Christianity to Muslims. The scholar survived the attack and had the slave arrested, but he felt torn about what to do with him. He did not want to order him killed, because that seemed un-Christian. At the same time he felt unsafe freeing him. As he wrestled with this problem, the slave committed suicide in prison. Ramón interpreted the suicide as God's way of releasing him from his dilemma. He concluded that the death of his Muslim slave confirmed the correctness of his own desire to convert the followers of Islam.

Ramón then set out to build the skills he saw as essential for carrying the Christian message to the Muslim world. He attended the university at Paris to study theology and honed his skill in the formal logic practiced by the scholastics. All this preparation revealed Ramón's passion for education. He founded a school in Majorca and wrote many books intended to bring knowledge to the faithful. His influential work, *The Order of Chivalry*, set forth a call for an educated and virtuous knightly class. However, Ramón still believed that his real calling was to educate the Muslims. In 1292, when he was a ripe 60 years old, he traveled to North Africa to begin his missionary work.

In Tunis, a bustling Muslim city near Carthage, Ramón invited all the local Muslim scholars to debate with him the merits of the two religions. He stood by the scholastic idea that one could "prove" the truth of the Trinity over the truth of Muhammad through the power of Aristotelian logic. One Muslim scholar warned his fellows: "Beware ye! . . . He will bring such arguments against our law that it will be impossible to answer them."

Troubadour, Scholar, and Missionary to the Muslims

Ramón eventually realized that logic alone could not make people change their views on matters of faith, but he never abandoned his belief in dialectic as a missionary tool. At the time, the great scholastics from Anselm to Aquinas already knew this. They saw scholasticism primarily as a way for the faithful to understand with their minds what they already knew in their hearts. It is not surprising that Ramón made few converts.

The rest of Ramón's life proved just as dramatic as his early and middle years. Tired of his preaching, the Muslims imprisoned Ramón for a time and then placed him on a ship to Italy, but a great storm sank the ship. The robust 76-year-old lost all his books and clothes but managed to swim ashore and survive the adventure. He again resumed his efforts to convert the Muslims. In 1311, he even implored the pope to call another crusade, but his request was ignored. Ramón Lull returned to Tunis when he was 83 years old, where he roamed the streets striking up conversations with anyone who would listen to his advocacy of Christianity. Tunisian authorities finally lost patience with him in 1316 and executed him. Throughout his life, Ramón expressed the major medieval passions and accomplishments. From a love of poetry, chivalry, and philosophy to a single-minded desire to transform the Muslim world at his doorstep, Ramón's interests paralleled those of his greatest contemporaries. But few pursued so many of them as relentlessly as this vigorous, long-lived man.

faith through the discovery of truth. This was an academic exercise in which students were expected to reconcile apparent contradictions.

Throughout the Middle Ages, there had always been people who believed that it was not possible or even desirable to reach God through reason. Abelard's adversary, Bernard of Clairveaux (1090–1153), condemned many of Abelard's writings, primarily because he disapproved of the process of inquiry. Bernard wrote passionately: "I thought it unfitting that the grounds of the faith should be handed over to human reasonings for discussion." Although Bernard approved of rational inquiry in non-religious areas, he firmly believed the way to God lay in faith and love—in other words, in emotion, not intellect. He wrote beautiful tracts on the mystic approach to God through feeling and faith, and many men and women chose to seek God through this mystic path rather than through logic.

Through the twelfth century, Islamic scholars also continued the great intellectual strides that had been begun by scholars like Avicenna (980–1037) (in Biography, Chapter 6). Muslim scholars from centers as far apart as Baghdad in the east and Toledo in Spain studied the classical works of Aristotle and others with a sophistication lacking in the western kingdoms. The Muslim scholar Averroës (1126–1198) and the eminent Jewish scholar Maimonides (1135–1204) interpreted Aristotle's works and left extensive commentaries on the sophisticated ideas. These texts were discovered in Arabic libraries in Spain as Christians slowly reconquered Muslim territory, and the emergence of these commentaries along with the advanced logic of Aristotle generated much intellectual excitement in the university communities of western Europe.

Some of Aristotle's ideas as interpreted by these non-Christian commentators (such as his belief in the eternity of the world) seemed to contradict Christian faith. In spite of some controversy, many readers thrilled at the intellectual possibilities contained in such texts and felt confident that faith and reason could be reconciled. The Biography of Ramón Lull tells of one remarkable man's expression of this passion for reason.

The scholastic enterprise reached its height in the thirteenth century with the works of Thomas Aquinas (1225–1274), an Italian churchman whom many regard as the greatest scholar of the Middle Ages. Aquinas wrote many works, from commentaries on biblical books and Aristotelian texts to essays on philosophical problems and the *Summa Contra Gentiles*, a work

Thomas Aquinas

probably intended for missionary use in converting heretics, Muslims, and Jews. However, his most important work was the *Summa Theologiae* (*Summary of Theology*), which was intended to offer a comprehensive summary of all knowledge available at the time.

Aquinas taught that faith and reason were compatible paths to a single truth, but that the mind by itself could grasp only the truth of the physical world. Faith (given by God's grace), however, could help reason grasp spiritual truths such as the Trinity. This central understanding—that faith and nature cannot contradict each other and that each can inform the other—has remained one of Aquinas's most important contributions. The scholar wrote, "Our intellect is led by our senses to divine knowledge."

The most famous examples of his use of nature to yield divine truth were his "proofs" of God's existence in which, like Anselm, he wanted to use logic available in the physical world to "understand" the mysteries of God. For instance, he showed that we can observe motion on earth, and all earthly motion is caused by some other motion. When we trace back all the motion that is caused, our logical mind leads us to the first mover that originated all other motion—the "unmoved mover"—who is God. Thus, our understanding of the physical world of motion, combined with faith, leads us to an understanding of one of the elements of God.

Aquinas's *Summa* remains one of the masterpieces of philosophy, but all medieval thinkers did not find it satisfying. For some, it was too speculative and abstract. For all Aquinas's emphasis on using the natural world as a path to truth, he did not study the natural world very much. Instead, he read Aristotle's views on the natural world. Yet some of the great minds of the age turned directly to matters of the physical world. In this area, they would find plenty to think about.

DISCOVERING THE PHYSICAL WORLD

The passion with which university scholars read Aristotle and the other ancient writers led them to adhere to classical views of physics and medicine. The educated man or woman of the thirteenth century held the same view of the physical universe as had the ancient Greeks: a motionless world made of earth, water, air, and fire. In the east, Muslim astronomers made huge strides in building upon classical wisdom in studying the heavens. The Muslim astronomer/mathematician al-Tusi (born 1201) recalculated ancient Greek understandings of planetary orbits with a precision that would not be matched in western Europe until the sixteenth century.

In the West, scientific advances came (albeit slowly) in the fields of medicine as physicians built on the works of Galen and Avicenna. Physicians studying at the medical school in Salerno learned Galen's theory of the four "humors" (discussed in Chapter 5) and studied how to bring the body back in balance.

Since classical times, the study of women's health had been limited by the fact that midwives did not write medical texts. Yet, male physicians, who did write the texts, frequently misunderstood women's bodies. In the Middle Ages, a few women wrote books that in part corrected this problem and thus contributed much to the field of women's health. The most well known was Hildegard of Bingen (1098–1179), an abbess and mystic in Germany. She wrote compelling accounts of her visions, which showed the same blend of faith and scholarly knowledge that marked the university-trained scholastics. Perhaps most interesting, however, Hildegard authored a medical tract, *Of Causes and Cures*. In this important work, she took the classical view of human beings as consisting of either hot, cold, wet, or dry, and applied it to women's health. In addition, she included in her text the popular cures she practiced as she ministered to the sick in the community, and she gave German and Latin names for drugs—all things that were not part of traditional scholarly writings. Hildegard's work pointed to the possibility of combining women's practical wisdom about women's health with traditional medical knowledge.

Hildegard of Bingen

Despite such contributions, by the thirteenth century women began to be excluded from medicine, as universities gained exclusive right to train physicians. In doing so, they prevented many charlatans from practicing medicine, but they were also slowly moving women out of healing occupations that for centuries they had shared informally with men. This exclusion sometimes severely damaged the careers of women healers. By the early fourteenth century, for example, there was a famous case of a female Jewish physician (Jacoba Felicie) who had a thriving practice in Paris. She was prosecuted for practicing medicine without a university license, but so many of her patients testified to her skill that the action against her was withdrawn. Nevertheless, Jacoba was ordered to stop practicing medicine.

Some scholars noticed the loss in wisdom that accompanied the separation of practical experience from the universities. One Oxford master, Robert Grosseteste (1168–1253) challenged his students to develop an experimental method to question the ancients. His most famous student, Roger Bacon (1214?–1292), continued Grosseteste's work and is usually credited with popularizing his teacher's movement toward a scientific method. Bacon's greatest practical contribution came in the field of optics, when he discovered how to make glasses by grinding lenses. Perhaps more important than any specific invention, Grosseteste and Bacon demonstrated the value of experimentation over pure logic, thus challenging the ancient scholars who formed the core of the traditional courses of study at the universities. In the centuries to come, the major discoveries in the physical world would come from people like Bacon, who had the courage to think for themselves instead of simply looking to ancient experts.

Experimental science

This intellectual expansion was one of many measures of the vitality of medieval life. The cities and the universities were growing in ways the medieval world hardly understood, much less expected, but this was not the only expansion of the Middle Ages. The world of "those who fight" began to see a dramatic growth.

Those Who Fight: Nobles and Knights

As the population of Europe multiplied in the eleventh century, it prompted a surge of construction of homes for the nobility. The aristocracy required fortresses and towers to "keep the peace" (and to collect the taxes paid by the peasantry). The characteristic defensive structure of the nobility was the castle, which came to define the landscape of the medieval world.

CASTLES: MEDIEVAL HOMES AND HAVENS

In the tenth century, castles were actually private fortresses made of timber and earth that were built on *Living quarters* mounds. By the thirteenth century, they had become large, defensive structures of wood and stone and were virtually impregnable. Many castles consisted of a large exterior wall surrounded by a moat filled with water, and an interior fortified structure that served as the noble family's home and an extra line of defense should invaders breach the outer wall. The inner fortress contained a deep well, for the castle's ability to endure a long siege depended on the availability of food and water as well as a strong defense. The Welsh castle in Figure 8.6 shows the varied circles of defense that protected the interior. Instead of a moat, this castle was actually built on an island in a lake, and the exterior wall in the foreground stood on the outer shore of the lake. Invaders who made it through this formidable outer wall would find themselves confronted by a lake and further walls. Protected by such features, a few people could withstand the assault of many.

The main household of a castle consisted of a large public hall where the castle residents ate, played games, and entertained themselves while gathered around the open hearth in the center of the room. There were also smaller, private chambers where the lord and lady slept, the women of the household did the weaving and sewing, and children were born. In such a private chamber, the lord also stored a strongbox filled with coins and other valuables. In an age with no banking, most nobles guarded their wealth themselves.

By the thirteenth century, these living quarters were designed for comfort as well as safety. Noble families lived in high towers, where it was safe to have glass windows, and the open hearth was moved to the wall as a fireplace to reduce the smoke in the room. Latrines were built into the walls of adjacent rooms, and pipes brought water to the upper floors. The tower inhabitants decorated—and warmed—the stone walls by hanging intricate tapestries from ceiling to floor.

Thirteenth-century castles stood as marvels of engineering, and those who designed them were much in demand. One English architect designed and supervised the building of 10 castles over a 30-year period. However, these structures also took their toll on the environment. More great forests were cleared for timber to shore up the stones and build scaffolds as the workers rushed to complete the castles, and defenders wanted the surrounding area clear-cut so they could see approaching foes. The Castle of Windsor, for example, required the wood of more than 4,000 oak trees in its construction. As the castle rose, its stone towers replaced the forests as the prominent feature of the landscape.

THE IDEALS OF CHIVALRY

The contractual form of feudalism (see Chapter 7) persisted throughout the Middle Ages as a way to provide armies for lords and kings. By the twelfth century, the feudal tie became interwoven with an elaborate code of values and symbolic rituals that served somewhat to tame the violent world of warriors. This code and culture of the ruling class was called chivalry, and its values became evident in church writings, romantic literature, and treatises. Ramón Lull, whose life was described in the Biography on page 273, wrote *The Order of Chivalry*, one of the most famous of such treatises.

According to the texts, a knight should be strong and disciplined, yet use his power to defend the church, the poor, and women in need. Knights were expected to possess the virtue of military prowess, but they also had to be loyal, generous, courteous, and "of noble bearing." In reality, knights probably violated these ethics as often as they adhered to them; the

FIGURE 8.6
Caerphilly Castle, Wales, ca. thirteenth century.

FIGURE 8.7
Joust watched by noble women.

tried to ban tournaments, but the code of chivalry proved too powerful. Tournaments and jousts not only satisfied a profound social need, but they also provided a practical way for young men to win horses and armor—the victors in these contests took the equipment of the losers.

The very vehemence with which the aristocracy clung to demanding rituals of behavior points to a weakness in their rule. As the Middle Ages wore on, the public role of the nobility—defending and administering Europe—was weakening. Merchants had more wealth, so chivalry was in part a way to hold on to privileges that were eroding. Yet, the nobility convinced itself of its special place in the world through elaborate ceremonies, proper dress, staged battles, and a mania for genealogy. And in the evenings, members of the warrior class entertained one another with stories celebrating the chivalric ideals.

THE LITERATURE OF CHIVALRY

During many of the evening gatherings, people listened to *chansons de geste*, or "songs of deeds," which celebrated the ideals of Christian knighthood in the eleventh and twelfth centuries. The most famous of these literary works are the French *Song of Roland* and the Spanish *Poem of the Cid*. Both poems extol the virtues of feudal heroes—Roland, a perfect vassal of Charlemagne; and Rodrigo Díaz de Vivar, known as El Cid ("my lord"), the perfect vassal of King Alfonso VI (r. 1065–1109) of Aragon. In both accounts, the knights embody the values of prowess and loyalty to a fault. Roland was too brave to call for help in the face of overwhelming forces, and El Cid showed perfect fidelity to an unworthy lord. Both stories feature specific details of battle and bloody victories designed to delight an audience of warriors.

These poems also show another side of the chivalric ideal—men's strong emotional ties with one another. The loyalty and camaraderie formed on the battlefield pervaded many aspects of warriors' lives. Roland, for example, wept and swooned at the death of his friend Oliver. In these works, as in the many handbooks on chivalry, women played a peripheral role. They were expected only to incite men to greater deeds and existed mainly to be protected and to provide noble heirs. With the emergence of a new form of literature and a new social code, however, these attitudes shifted somewhat.

code of chivalry provided only a veneer of symbols and ceremonies that overlay the violence at the heart of "those who fight."

One activity required of chivalrous knights was participation in mock battles called jousts or tourna-

Jousts and tournaments ments. Figure 8.7 shows a joust, which involved single encounters between two knights. (Tournaments were mock battles between teams of knights.) In this painted illustration, the knights display heraldic figures on their horses and shields. These figures reveal their noble lineage and suggest the importance of noble blood to the ideals of chivalry. Women watch the contest and incite the men on to greater deeds of valor.

These were only mock battles, yet many combatants came away from them with debilitating—and sometimes fatal—injuries. The church repeatedly

IN PRAISE OF ROMANTIC LOVE

In the twelfth century, a new kind of poetry appeared in southern France that changed the social code between men and women—the poetry of the troubadours, or court poets. Historians are divided on why this new sensibility emerged at this time; some postulate an influence of Arabic love poetry from Spain, others emphasize the patronage of wealthy noble women. Whatever its origin, the new poetry was highly influential in shaping people's ideas of love. In these works, the poets praised love between men and women as an ennobling idea worthy of being cultivated. Troubadour poetry is diverse, but from it we can distill some basic characteristics of this new romantic love. The ideal love was one in which a man grew more noble by loving and serving a high-born woman (not necessarily his wife and often somebody else's). As they complimented high-born ladies, poets wrote lines promising complete obedience: "And there's no task that's burdensome to me / If it should please my lady master." Knights who pledged this kind of service hoped to be rewarded ultimately with sexual favors: "Surely there'll some day be a time, / My lady beautiful and good / When you can pass me secretly / The sweet reward of a little kiss." This kind of love was meant to be difficult to attain, secret, and highly exciting.

In the twelfth century, Andrew the Chaplain wrote a book titled *The Art of Courtly Love* that paralleled earlier treatises on knightly chivalry. In this work, Andrew described how lovers must always turn pale in the presence of the beloved and stressed that secrecy and jealousy were essential for intensifying feelings of love. The ideal of courtly love was as much the exclusive property of the nobility as the ideals of chivalry had been. For example, Andrew wrote that if a nobleman fell in love with a mere peasant woman, "do not hesitate to take what you seek and to embrace her by force." Andrew and his noble patrons believed that only the nobility could "love properly"—that is, possess the leisure and money to engage in this elaborate game. Andrew warned of the consequence of peasants who might enjoy romantic love: Their "farms may through lack of cultivation prove useless to us."

Historians have argued about whether the ideal of courtly love improved the actual treatment of women, given that men supposedly bettered themselves in order to win women's hearts. Certainly Andrew's advice about raping peasant women helps answer this question. The poetry written by women troubadours also reveals something about women's experience of this kind of love. Some of this poetry describes the tension between women and the men who claimed to love them, but then left to embark on great deeds. The women's poetry shows a desire to have men remain present and attentive. As one poet wrote: "Handsome friend, as a lover true / I loved you, for you pleased me / but now I see I was a fool / for I've barely seen you since."

At least in the literature of courtly love women occupied the center of the narrative. Figure 8.8 shows a lady and her knight out hawking together. In contrast to Figure 8.7, the woman is in the forefront of the image. She holds the hawk and is courted by the attentive lover. The nobility of each is shown by the

FIGURE 8.8
Noble couple hunting.

coats of arms above them. The artist also enhanced the woman's prestige by showing her on a dappled horse, the most expensive breed.

Troubadour poetry spread beyond France to other areas of Europe. Poets also wrote long romances describing the courtly love tradition. The earliest of these writers, Chretien de Troyes, penned a number of romances set in the court of the imagined hero King Arthur. (The historical Arthur was the Celtic Roman general described in Chapter 6.) These works told of love, loyalty, and great deeds, and served to entertain a nobility that was as enthralled with courtly love as it was with chivalry. These stories and the ideal of romantic love profoundly influenced modern notions of the nature of love between men and women.

The Rise of Centralized Monarchies

While noble men and women cultivated ideals of war and love, real warfare struck with relentless regularity. Kings were constantly trying to reestablish control over provinces that had drifted away during the turbulent tenth century. At the same time, nobles struggled to keep and even increase their own power. The repeated conflicts between monarch and aristocrat transformed the political map of Europe.

ENGLAND: FROM CONQUEST TO PARLIAMENT

In the early eleventh century, England had been ruled by the able Danish king Canute (r. 1016–1035) (see Chapter 7), but after his death his Scandinavian empire did not hold together. Canute, before his death, and the English nobility turned to a surviving member of the family of the Anglo-Saxon king Alfred. Thus, Edward the Confessor (r. 1042–1066) reestablished the Anglo-Saxon monarchy. However, a dynasty requires heirs to be stable, and Edward did not have any children. A new succession crisis would lead to the conquest of England.

In 1066, when Edward the Confessor died without an heir, the Anglo-Saxon Witan crowned one of their own—Harold Godwinson—as king, and the Anglo-Saxon kingdom was poised to continue as it had before. However, two men believed they had better claims on the English crown. First, Harold Hardradi of Norway landed in the north of England. Harold Godwinson defeated him at the Battle of Stamford Bridge, but that was to be the last battle won by an Anglo-Saxon king.

Conquest of England

As Halley's comet streaked across the skies that year, seeming to predict disaster, the other claimant, Duke William of Normandy prepared to sail. William was Edward the Confessor's cousin, and he also claimed that the Anglo-Saxon king had promised him the throne; he aimed to take what he believed was his right. William sailed a fleet across the English Channel and engineered the last successful large-scale invasion of England. The Anglo-Saxon king was killed at the Battle of Hastings and henceforth Duke William reigned as William the Conqueror (r. 1066–1087).

William brought a highly controlled feudal system to the island as he redistributed the Anglo-Saxon nobles' lands to his Norman followers. Although he allowed them to have subvassals, he required everyone to take an oath to him as liege lord (see Chapter 7), so the future Anglo-Norman kings could avoid some of the decentralization implicit in feudalism. William wanted to know exactly what lands he ruled, so he sent out royal officials to make a record of his holdings. The resulting text—the Domesday Book—is an invaluable historical record of the times. While William kept the local officials (like sheriffs) that had been so effective in Anglo-Saxon times, he replaced the Anglo-Saxon Witan with his own assembly of vassals—the *curia regis*. In this assembly, or Great Council, vassals satisfied their feudal obligations to give the king advice and help him pass judgment. This advisory council would become one of the precedents for the growth of parliament.

William's court spoke only ancient French, and the long coexistence of the two languages led to the incorporation of many French words into what became the modern English language. For example, the Anglo-Saxon words "pig" and "cow" turned into the French-derived "pork" and "beef" as they came to the table of the conquerors. Over the next centuries, however, the hybrid language that emerged was closer to Old English than to French.

The Norman conquest of England had implications for the French monarchy as well, for now the king of England held lands in France—Normandy—as vassal to the king of France. However, this vassal was stronger than the French kings, and this ambiguous situation would lead to repeated tensions between the English and French royalty over these possessions in France (see Chapter 9).

William's son Henry I (r. 1100–1135) was as able an administrator as his father. To make the *curia regis*

Henry I and II more efficient, Henry created separate departments. The financial department—known as the exchequer—with a "chancellor" at its head, became extremely important in making sure the crown remained fiscally solvent. Wealth remained the mainstay of power for the medieval monarchies; the other source was the law. Henry I used the law courts to maintain royal control over his vassals. However, a civil war over succession erupted after Henry's death, and during this time of troubles, the monarchy was weakened at the expense of strong nobles. It would take another strong monarch to restore the power of the kings. England found this monarch in Henry II (r. 1154–1189).

Henry II (who introduced the Angevin dynasty of English kings) left a permanent impact on the government and law of England. He continued Henry I's fiscal policies and expanded royal control of justice in the land. He sent traveling justices (called Justices in Eyre) empowered with royal authority around the countryside. They traveled regularly to the courts of the shire investigating and punishing crimes. Henry's legal reforms led to controversies with church courts (described later in this chapter), but they strengthened the power of the king.

Primarily through his marriage, Henry II greatly increased the English holdings in France. In 1152, Henry married Eleanor of Aquitaine, a great heiress (whose first marriage to the king of France had been annulled). She brought to the marriage her extensive family estates in France, and Map 8.4 shows how

Legend:
French Royal Domain
- 987
- 987-1180
- 1180-1328
- English holdings in France 1180
- English holdings in France 1328
- Holy Roman Empire ca. 1200
- Battle site

0   400 miles
0   400 kilometers

THINKING ABOUT GEOGRAPHY

MAP 8.4 *Medieval France, England, and Germany, Tenth Through Fourteenth Centuries*

This map shows England, with the major cities and battles of the eleventh century, and the patchwork of lands that made up medieval France and Germany. It also shows the slow centralization of royal control in France. ◾ **Notice** how small the French royal domain was in 987. **Notice** the fragmented way in which lands were added to royal control. **Consider** what this pattern of expansion indicates about how the lands were acquired, and how kings might want to connect their scattered holdings. ◾ **Locate** Flanders. **Consider** why it was a profitable outlet for English wool. ◾ **Notice** the many small principalities within the Holy Roman Empire. **Consider** how difficult it would be to centralize the region.

much of France was under English control. This great English empire was increasingly threatening to the French kings, and it would have been even more so, but Henry and Eleanor's sons dissipated much of the royal wealth and power.

Henry's eldest son, Richard I (r. 1189–1199)—known as "the Lion-Hearted"—much preferred fighting to administering the land, and he spent all but 10 months of his reign on campaign outside England. He died from a neglected wound received when he was besieging a castle, and the crown went to his younger brother, John.

The reign of John (r. 1199–1216) was marked by a series of humiliations. He fought costly wars in Normandy to try to defend his possessions against the French king's intrusions. To raise money, John departed from feudal custom in many regards; for example, he married heiresses to the highest bidders and even extorted money from his subjects.

Finally, in the spring of 1215, the barons, disgusted by John's high-handed behavior, staged a rebellion.

Magna Carta They even took over London, forcing the king to retreat to a broad field south of the city. There, under duress, John signed the Magna Carta (the "Great Charter"), which asserted that kings were not above the law. Beyond establishing this general principle, the charter was a feudal document that promised the king would not impinge on noblemen's traditional rights. However, the charter also included two principles that shaped the future of English (and North American) law: The king would impose no new taxes without the consent of the governed and would not violate the due process of law. This document is treasured as one of the precedents of constitutional law.

Another central institution that arose in the Middle Ages with special implications for England was

Parliament parliament. As part of their feudal obligations, nobles were to give advice to their lords, and kings all over Europe gathered their vassals and wealthy townspeople in councils—called parliaments—to discuss matters of the realm, which included everything from justice to collecting new taxes. In England in the thirteenth century, this council took a significant turn and became an institution that was able to restrict the power of the king.

The English king Edward I (r. 1272–1307) desperately needed new taxes to finance his wars. Ordinarily English kings asked their nobles in parliament to give additional aid, and then sent their agents to cities throughout the land asking for additional

money from wealthy merchants. Edward simplified this process by calling for two knights from every county and two burgesses, or townsmen, from every city "to be elected without delay, and to . . . come to us at the aforesaid time and place."

This body with its expanded representation was called the "Model Parliament," and it became precedent setting. As they gathered, the knights and the lower nobility sat with the burgesses and began to act together for their mutual benefit, while the clergy sat with the upper nobility. Figure 8.9 shows one of these meetings of Parliament as called by Edward I. The bishops sit to the right and the barons to the left. The judges in the center sit on wool sacks to indicate the importance of the wool trade to England—the source of much of the burgesses' wealth. Edward presides with the king of Scotland and the Prince of Wales, while two archbishops sit on the extreme right and left. In time, the nobles—shown sitting with Edward—would become the House of Lords, and

FIGURE 8.9
The English Parliament under Edward I.

the burgesses with the lower nobility the House of Commons. At first, the House of Commons did little more than approve the rulings of the Lords, but in time this institution came to rule England.

THE SPANISH RECONQUER THEIR LANDS

On the Iberian Peninsula, kings and nobles still fought over the issue of centralization, but a larger political problem—the reconquest of Muslim lands—overshadowed this concern. Land that in other countries might have been held by the nobility emerged as small individual kingdoms—Aragon, Castille-Leon, and Navarre (see Map 8.5). These kingdoms sometimes presented a united front to the Muslims and other times fought each other to increase their power. With the threat of the Muslims constantly lurking on their borders, they simply could not afford to focus on unifying the Iberian kingdoms. In the twelfth century, Portugal continued the forces of decentralization when it emerged as a separate kingdom. Portugal had once been part of Leon, but King Alfonso VI (r. 1065–1109) gave it as an independent country to his illegitimate daughter and her crusader husband.

Map 8.5 shows the Iberians' slow reconquest of the peninsula from the Muslims. As the map indicates, each Iberian kingdom pursued its expansion southward at the expense of the Muslims. Kings then consolidated their hold on the new lands by establishing Christian settlers and building castles on the border lands. To encourage town settlements, which brought in profitable taxation, kings often gave privileges to Muslim and Jewish artisans and merchants. With this policy, the Iberian Peninsula became a hub for the fertile exchange of ideas among the three religious cultures.

The Reconquest

The miraculous tenth-century discovery of the bones of Saint James

the Elder stepped up the crusading zeal of the Iberian Christians. A peasant discovered the relics after a vision of brilliant stars shining over a field revealed their location to him. A great shrine—Santiago de Compostela (St. James of the Starry Field)—was built to house the bones. This shrine became a renowned pilgrimage site, attracting the faithful from as far as Scandinavia. Such pilgrims brought both money and arms, which supported the Iberians' battle against the Muslims. Visitors to the shrine also brought artistic

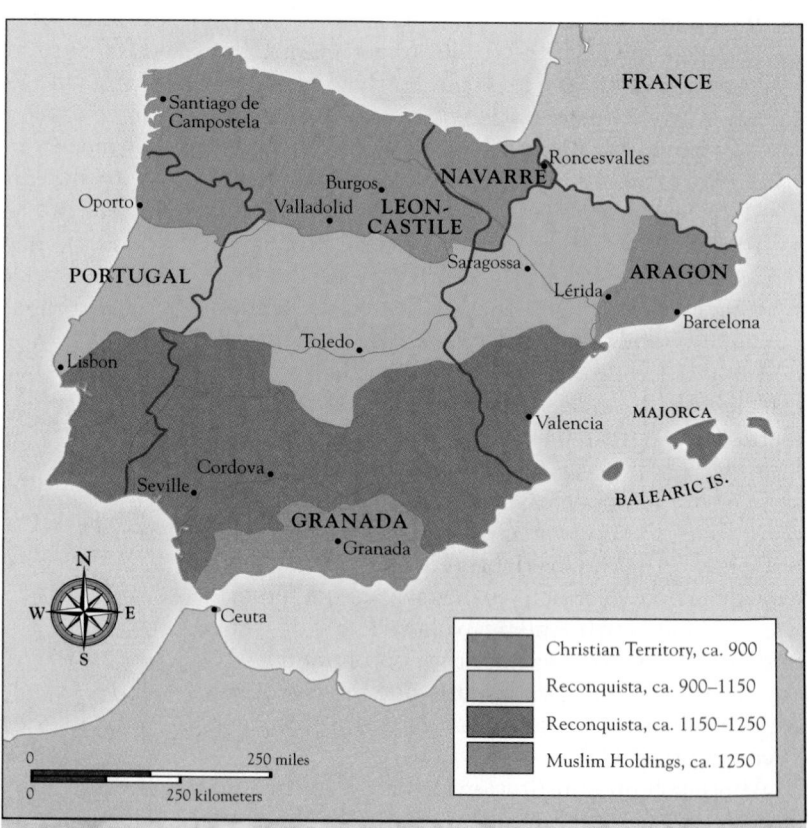

THINKING ABOUT GEOGRAPHY

MAP 8.5 *Christian Expansion in Iberia*

This map shows the location of the Christian kingdoms on the Iberian Peninsula, and the location and dates of their expansion southward into the Muslim territories. ◼ **Why** was Toledo so important strategically to the Iberians? ◼ **Locate** Majorca in the Balearic Islands, birthplace of Ramón Lull, who was profiled in this chapter's biography. **Does** this location help explain why he was drawn to North Africa? ◼ **Locate** Santiago de Compostela, which will become an important pilgrimage site. **How** would its location stimulate the reconquest?

talent, and traveling builders designed and built great Gothic churches along the pilgrimage route. Christian warriors believed that Saint James appeared on a white horse at the front of Christian armies. Their faith seems to have spurred on their efforts.

The Iberian armies fighting in the culturally diverse land made a significant contribution to the intellectual life of western Europe, for in 1085, King Alfonso VI retook the important city of Toledo, which dominated the peninsula's central plateau. There churchmen following Alfonso's army recovered the precious manuscripts of Aristotle and the Muslim and Jewish scholars (discussed earlier) that made such an impact on the universities of Europe. As Map 8.5 shows, by the late thirteenth century, the Muslim lands had dwindled to the city of Granada in the south and the surrounding countryside.

FRANCE AND ITS PATIENT KINGS

By late in the tenth century, the Carolingian family finally lost the royal title west of the Rhine. The descendants of Charlemagne had not exercised effective control of the great feudal princes for a hundred years, yet the title of king still brought some measure of prestige. In 987, Hugh Capet, the lord of the Île-de-France (the region surrounding Paris), was elected by the nobles to the French throne. The church legitimized his rule and a new dynasty was in place in France (see Map 8.4 on page 280). The rule of the Capetians involved a long history of slowly reasserting control over the great nobles of their lands. As Map 8.4 also shows, the kings had to wrestle with the problem of the extensive English holdings in France.

Capetian dynasty

The history of France from the tenth through the fourteenth centuries suggests the patience of the French kings. Map 8.4 shows how they gained control over one province after another. These monarchs seldom resorted to war and conquest, but used the means provided under feudal contract law to bring regions back under their control. They also made prudent marriages with wealthy heiresses who brought their inheritances back into royal control. Perhaps most important, the Capetians were fortunate enough to produce sons to inherit their throne.

Philip II Augustus (r. 1180–1223) made great strides in centralizing his lands by directly addressing the English holdings. In wars against the English, Philip finally defeated King John and took over the English lands of Normandy, Maine, and Anjou (see Map 8.4). Through these conquests, Philip quadrupled the income of the French monarchy. This talented king recognized the need to develop new ways to maintain his control over the widely disbursed patchwork that was France. Instead of relying on the feudal hierarchy to govern locally, he appointed salaried officials—bailiffs—to collect taxes and represent his interests. These ambitious men, most well-educated at the University of Paris, did much to strengthen royal power at the expense of the feudal nobility.

The fortunes of the Capetians were dramatically forwarded by Louis IX (r. 1226–1270), whom many consider the greatest of the medieval kings. He was a pious man who went to church at least twice a day and cared for the poor and sick, and he achieved a distinction highly unusual for a king: he was proclaimed a saint by the church.

Louis IX

For all his piety, Louis did not neglect matters of the realm. Although he did not try to extend the royal domain, he nevertheless expected his nobles to be good vassals. He also took an interest in law and justice and wanted royal justice to be available to all his subjects. The king himself liked to sit in the open under a great oak to receive petitions. Figure 8.10 shows Louis listening to the pleas of his humble subjects—a monk and women. On the left, hanged criminals dangle from trees, demonstrating that the saintly king kept good order in his land. However, Louis did more than dispense personal justice; his advisors began to codify the laws of France, and he was the first king to legislate for all of France. Finally, Louis confirmed the Parlement of Paris—a court, not a representative assembly—as the highest court in France. (It held this position until 1789.) Saint Louis died while on crusade, and his successors continued to ride the Capetian momentum, slowly centralizing their authority.

King Philip IV "the Fair" (r. 1285–1314) believed that the greatest obstacle to his power was Edward I of England and his extensive French fief of Gascony (see Map 8.4). Philip engaged in intermittent wars against Edward from 1294 to 1302. Philip even tried to attack the important English wool industry by blocking importation of English wool into Flanders, but the Flemish towns revolted against him. All these wars were expensive and drove Philip to look for additional funds. The king tried to collect money from the church, which led to a protracted struggle with Pope Boniface VIII (described fully in Chapter 9).

Philip IV

FIGURE 8.10
King Louis hears the petitions of his subjects.

In 1302, Philip needed the support of the realm in his struggles against the pope and to raise money. In response, he summoned representatives from church, nobility, and towns to the first meeting of the Estates General. As these men gathered to advise their king, they sat according to the medieval order—those who prayed, fought, and worked (including townsmen) deliberated separately. This triple arrangement, so different from the two houses of Parliament that grew up in England, helped diffuse each group's power, allowing kings to maintain tight control. This had dramatic consequences for the future of France.

By the end of the thirteenth century, the French monarchy was the best-governed and wealthiest in Europe. It was a power to be reckoned with, but there were clouds on the horizon. The Flemish towns remained defiant, England continued to hold and contest lands in France, and the religious struggles had just begun. Philip's successors would face great difficulties.

THE MYTH OF UNIVERSAL RULE: THE HOLY ROMAN EMPIRE

Map 8.4 depicts a large, seemingly powerful neighbor—the Holy Roman Empire—looming to the east of France. But that empire was not as potent as its size might suggest. Early in the tenth century, the last direct descendant of Charlemagne died. The German dukes recognized the need for a leader, and in 919 elected one of their number (Henry of Saxony) to be king. His descendants held the German monarchy until 1024.

The most powerful of this line of kings was Otto I (r. 936–973), who restored the title of emperor. Otto in *Saxon dynasty* many ways resembled Charlemagne. He was a warrior king who stopped the advance of the Magyars in 955 and won further conquests in northern Italy. Also like Charlemagne, Otto fostered a revival of learning in Germany in which literature and art flourished. (Otto had married a Byzantine princess, and she brought artists from Byzantium to enhance the German court.) Finally, the German king marched into Rome to receive the crown of the Roman emperor from Pope John XII, much as Charlemagne had done a century and a half earlier. For hundreds of years after this ceremony, an emperor would be proclaimed in German lands—later to be called the Holy Roman Empire. However, it is one thing to claim a far-flung empire and quite another to exert consistent control over it. Like other rulers in the west, Otto and his successors faced repeated challenges from the strength of the independent nobles within their lands. (Map 8.4 shows many of the principalities within the empire.)

The Ottonian dynasty ended in 1024, and the German nobles selected Henry III (r. 1039–1056) from another branch of the Saxon family. Henry began the Salian dynasty of *Salian dynasty* Germany. He was an able king who looked for ways to exert more control in his lands, and he increasingly used bishops and abbots that he appointed as his administrators. When his son Henry IV (r. 1056–1106) tried to continue that policy, he ignited a firestorm of debate called the "investiture controversy" (see page 286).

The Emperor Frederick I (r. 1152–1190), known as Barbarossa, or "red-beard," elected from the house of Hohenstaufen, came close to establishing a consolidated German empire. He planned to exert tight control over three contiguous regions that could form the core of royal lands. He had inherited Burgundy and Swabia (see Map 8.4), and **Hohenstaufen dynasty** invaded Italy to subdue Lombardy in the north. However, while this policy was theoretically sound, it proved ill conceived, and the German emperors were weakened by their continued involvement in Italian politics. Italy's city-states and a strong papacy refused to submit to German rule. The resulting, almost incessant, wars in Italy drained rather than strengthened the emperors' resources.

The rule of Emperor Frederick II Hohenstaufen (r. 1215–1250) effectively ended any chance of a unified German monarchy. Frederick was a brilliant ruler and patron of the arts, who had been raised in Sicily and had come to love the diverse Muslim and Christian cultures that coexisted in that sunny land. His policy was to confer upon the German princes and nobility virtual sovereignty within their own territories—he retained only the right to set the foreign policy of the empire. His goal was to take as much profit as possible from the German lands, but focus his rule in Italy—particularly the Kingdom of the Two Sicilies in the south.

In southern Italy, he rigorously centralized his administration and imposed a monetary tax on all his subjects. He used Muslims as soldiers and was reputed to have a harem of Muslim women. He turned Sicily into a highly organized and culturally exciting monarchy, guided by his firm rule. Although many historians praise Frederick as the first modern ruler—highly organized and practically calculating—the pope and the northern Italian towns feared his expanding policies in Italy. Their fears were well-founded, for Frederick led a campaign against the cities of northern Italy (the Lombard League) and scored some victories in 1237. The popes and the towns feared Frederick's encirclement. The pope excommunicated Frederick, and both sides conducted public relations campaigns to discredit the other. Frederick's attempts to unify Italy ended with his death in 1250.

The German princes wanted to preserve the freedoms they had acquired under Frederick II, so they **Habsburg dynasty** elected a man they considered a weak prince—Rudolph of Habsburg—as emperor. Eventually, the Habsburgs acquired the duchies of Austria, which became the chief foundation for the powerful Habsburg dynasty, (see Chapter 11). Burdened by independent nobles and worn down by political trouble in Italy, medieval German emperors had little hope of holding their so-called empire together.

Those Who Pray: Imperial Popes and Expanding Christendom

Like the monarchies which had seen their political power fragment during the tumultuous tenth century, the church, too, had decentralized. Local lords saw the churches on their manors as their own property and priests as their own vassals. Nobles sometimes treated bishoprics as rewards for loyal subjects rather than as religious positions. Critics of these practices began to voice demands for reform as Documents 8.3 on page D8.2 show. In addition, the reformers sought an authentic leader who could preside over a universal Christendom.

A CALL FOR CHURCH REFORM

One obvious candidate to reform the church was the Holy Roman Emperor. In 1046, when the German Henry III (r. 1039–1056) traveled to Rome to receive the imperial crown, he found the papacy dominated by Roman aristocrats and interfamilial disputes. When he arrived, three rival popes were vying for power. He deposed them all and established a pope (Clement II) loyal to Henry and a strengthened papal court. In the search for order in the Christian world, it seemed that the German emperors might preside over a unified Christendom.

But the eleventh-century popes also began to step forward as a force for reform. Pope Nicholas II (r. 1058–1061) began to free the papacy from military dependence on the German emperor by allying himself with the Normans in southern Italy. However, he also recognized that the church as a whole needed to be free from lay intervention. He was the first pope who expressly condemned the practice of "lay investiture": Popes disapproved of a lay person (a secular ruler) giving a churchmen the symbols of spiritual office (the ring and staff) because it appeared that the ruler was the source of spiritual authority. Nicholas was not be able to stop that long-standing practice, but his voice would not be the last on this subject.

However, he was able to move the selection of popes from lay interference, for he called a Roman council in 1059, which defined the principles by which popes were chosen by a college of cardinals, a practice that continues today. It seemed as if the popes might be able to preside over a unified Christendom.

Calls for church reform also came from another source: the ecclesiastical network of Cluniac monasteries that had been established in the early tenth century (see Chapter 7) began to raise its voice. From their foundation, Cluniacs had supported a strong papacy, and their influence increased even further when a cardinal highly sympathetic to the Cluniac order became Pope Gregory VII (r. 1073–1085). Gregory decided that popes, not kings or emperors, should guide Christendom. This outlook led him directly into conflict with the Holy Roman Emperor Henry IV (r. 1056–1106).

THE INVESTITURE CONTROVERSY

The controversy between Gregory and Henry was triggered by the question of who should appoint or invest bishops in Germany, a matter that was as much political as religious. As we have seen, the emperors had used their right to choose bishops to appoint men to act as royal representatives throughout the lands of their independence-hungry nobles. The pope also understood the importance of having allies in distant lands, and he wanted his loyal men in the German churches. This controversy arose out of the dual allegiances bishops faced—to whom did they owe their principal loyalty, pope or king? Through the struggle, the two sides liberally wielded their weapons: Henry sent his armies marching into Italy; Gregory threatened to excommunicate the emperor (and indeed later did so), claiming that this action could free the ever-rebellious vassals from their feudal obligations. Gregory also had the support of a powerful patron, Matilda, Countess of Tuscany. This skilled tactician promptly challenged Henry's military strength, leading her own armies into battle against him.

Figure 8.11 shows a crucial incident in the investiture controversy. Henry IV kneels at Matilda's feet, while she is shown framed by her strong castle of Canossa. He begs her and Abbot Hugh of Cluny to intercede for him, so that he may receive forgiveness from the pope, which Henry desperately needed to control his princes who saw this dispute as a way to gain more independence. This illustration also re-

R exrogat Abbatem. Mathildim Supplicat Atq.

FIGURE 8.11

Henry IV pleading with Matilda of Tuscany, twelfth century.

veals the important roles both Matilda and the monks of Cluny played in the controversy, but the question of the independence of the church would not be easily solved. In a dramatic incident at Canossa, Henry waited three days in the snow dressed in the sackcloth of a penitent begging the pope's forgiveness. Gregory as a priest was obliged to forgive a sinner professing sorrow, so the two temporarily made peace.

Within three years, pope and king were again locked in combat. This time, however, when Henry invaded Italy, Gregory's Norman mercenaries caused so much damage in Rome that the outraged citizens forced the pope to abandon the city. He died in exile in 1085, bitterly convinced he had failed in forwarding papal authority. But Henry was unable to secure a decisive victory either, and spent the remainder of his life trying to recover his authority in Germany. The issue of investiture was left for a later king and pope to resolve.

In 1122 the new emperor, Henry V, negotiated a compromise in the investiture controversy, the Concordat of Worms. Pope and emperor decided the pope could invest new bishops with their symbols of office, indicating the priority of the church over its churchmen. However, the emperor could be present at and influence the elections of bishops. This compromise actually represented a victory for the popes, who now had an opening for exerting authority within the rising national monarchies all over Europe. But the papal victory would not come easily nor unopposed.

Concordat of Worms

Such tensions persisted between clergy and lay rulers who wanted to strengthen their own rule in their home territories. In England, the struggle took the form of a deadly clash between King Henry II (r. 1154–1189) and his archbishop and once-best-friend, Thomas Becket. Becket wanted to preserve the church's right to be exempt from the legal authority Henry was using to consolidate his power over his land. One day, a small group of knights seeking to please their king surprised Becket in his church at Canterbury and split his head with their swords. Becket died on the altar he had served so well. Their plan to eliminate the influence of the archbishop backfired, however: Becket quickly became a martyr in the battle for church autonomy. In the face of popular revulsion for the crime, Henry was forced to compromise with the pope to gain forgiveness for his archbishop's murder. Henry had to allow the papacy to be the court of appeal from English ecclesiastical courts, and this concession brought the English church more closely into the sphere of Rome.

Thomas Becket

The power of the popes grew; the example of Becket showed that their weapons of excommunication and spiritual leadership were impossible to fight with swords. As church power grew, the papacy developed structures that increasingly resembled the powerful medieval monarchies. Just as monarchs began to rely on bureaucracy, court systems, and money to consolidate their power, the pope created a papal curia—an administrative unit—to handle financial matters. He also created a branch to handle legal appeals with the growing body of canon law, which were the compilations of religious laws that slowly came to govern much of medieval life.

By the beginning of the thirteenth century, popes could with some accuracy claim that they presided over a universal Christendom, and one of the most powerful was Innocent III (r. 1198–1216). Innocent was able to exert leadership over princes of Europe: He reprimanded the kings of England, Aragon, Portugal, France, Poland, and Norway, and insisted that they obey him. He vigorously fought heretics and wanted to clarify Christian belief. To accomplish the latter, he called the Fourth Lateran Council, which met in 1215. Among other things, this council identified exactly seven sacraments and reaffirmed their essential role in reaching salvation. The council also pronounced on many other matters, from qualifications for the priesthood to monastic life and veneration of relics. With the clarity expressed by the council, the medieval church was firmly defined. In effect, the church had become an empire that superseded all other empires. Like any empire, it even became involved in warfare. As early as 1095, the popes called for legions of armed Christians to embark on a march to retake the Holy Land from the Muslims.

Innocent III

CHRISTIANS ON THE MARCH: THE CRUSADES, 1096–1291

From as early as the fourth century, Christians began to visit holy places, and with the prosperity of the eleventh century, these pilgrimages had become even more popular. One of the favorite pilgrimage destinations (along with Santiago de Compostela described earlier) was Palestine, where Jesus had lived. Sometimes bands of thousands would travel, and when they journeyed to the Holy Land, they passed through Byzantine lands to reach the Muslim territories that included the holy places. For centuries, these trips—albeit hazardous—were possible.

However, in the eleventh century, the balance of power between the Byzantine Empire and its Muslim neighbors had shifted. Islam had gained strength from the movement of the Seljuk Turks, a fierce central Asian tribe who had converted to Islam and reinforced the Muslim armies threatening Byzantium. The Turks did not consciously stop the pilgrim traffic, but they did impose taxes on travelers, and to many Christians it seemed that the Holy Land should not be controlled by these Turks. Furthermore, internal struggles had weakened the empire, and in 1071 the Byzantine forces suffered a crushing defeat by the Turks at the Battle of Manzikert. The victorious Turks then drove deeper into the empire, capturing all of Asia Minor and taking control of some of the Byzantines' richest land. Now the Turks seemed to threaten Europe itself.

Islam strengthened

A new emperor, Alexius I Comnenus (r. 1081–1118), desperately cast about for ways to check the Turkish advance. He sent an appeal to Pope Urban II (r. 1088–1099) pleading for help to supplement his forces. In 1096 Urban responded vigorously, calling for Christians to begin a holy war against the newly strengthened Muslims.

The text of Urban's speech was preserved by several (sometimes conflicting) chroniclers, yet all agree **Pope Urban's call** that it shows a clear perception of the needs of the West and the motives of crusaders. He reminds his audience that western Europe was becoming too confining: "For this land which you inhabit, . . . is too narrow for your large population; nor does it abound in wealth; and it furnishes scarcely food enough for its cultivators." He further promised crusaders remission of sins if they undertook this journey. Urban's call was spectacularly successful, and members of the aristocracy began to plan the journey to the Holy Land.

Urban told departing soldiers to wear the sign of the cross on their breasts and encouraged them to earn the right to wear the symbol on their back when they returned, a symbol proving they had successfully fulfilled their vow to fight in this holy cause. The series of military engagements against the Muslims that continued for 200 years are called "the Crusades," named for the cross under which the Christians fought. People went on crusade for a number of reasons. Many were driven by sincere religious motivation, although their lofty purposes frequently deteriorated in the heat of battle. Some propertyless nobles hoped to find some land of their own, and other people sought wealth to bring home.

People responded to Urban's call with a fervor that surprised even the planners of the crusade. The first to respond included large numbers of peasants who followed two self-appointed leaders—Peter the Hermit and Walter the Penniless—to the east to free the Holy Land. Long before they reached the Holy Land, their zeal led them to violence in the west. They terrorized local people, looting for food and supplies to take on their way. Figure 8.12 shows a group of Hungarians attacking the peasants on crusade to reclaim their stolen goods. A contemporary chronicler also told how their religious fervor led to other violence: "Led by their zeal for Christianity, they persecuted the hated race of the Jews wherever they were found and strove either to destroy them completely or to compel them to become Christians." These early excesses would mark many of the subsequent Crusades. When these peasants arrived in Constantinople, the emperor quickly shipped them over to Asia Minor, where they were massacred by the Turks.

The earliest crusaders were vividly described by the Byzantine emperor's daughter Anna Comnena in *The Alexiad*, a history of her father's reign. According to this historian, even the crusaders who arrived after the peasants were little more than untrustworthy soldiers of fortune. She described the crusaders' "uncontrollable passion,

FIGURE 8.12
Peasants' Crusade.

their erratic character and their irresolution, not to mention their . . . greed for money, for example, which always led them to break their own agreements without scruple." Western sources, however, describe the flower of chivalry off to fulfill a high purpose: "The Franks straightway began to sew the cross on the right shoulders of their garments, saying that they would all with one accord follow in the footsteps of Christ." These contrasting accounts underscored the widening split between East and West, which was fueled by a fundamental misunderstanding: The crusaders wanted land in exchange for their military service (Western-style feudalism), but Alexius just wanted to pay them and have them turn over the land to him. The Muslims wanted them all to stay away from their lands.

Anna Comnena's "soldiers of fortune" were highly skilled and successful warriors, and they relentlessly swept the Muslim forces out of the Holy Land. In 1099, when they took Jerusalem after a five-week siege, the carnage was brutal. The eyewitness Fulcher of Chartres tells of the bloodshed: "Within Solomon's Temple, about ten thousand were beheaded. If you had been there, your feet would have been stained up to the ankles with the blood of the slain." When the violence died down, the crusaders took the Holy Land and established kingdoms there. Map 8.6 shows the routes of the Crusades and the locations of the crusader states.

The crusader principalities served as outposts of western European culture in the East. They entertained pilgrims, fought skirmishes on their borders, and learned about life in the eastern Mediterranean. *Crusader states* Generations of western Europeans living in proximity with Muslims were changed somewhat by the interactions. They learned to eat different foods, began to value bathing, and acquired a taste for urban life, unlike their rural cousins at home. Even a Muslim chronicler noticed the transformation: "Everyone who is a fresh emigrant from the Frankish lands is ruder in character than those who have become acclimatized and have held long association with Muslims."

However, the official relationship between crusader and Muslim was not friendly. Document 8.2 on page D8.1 shows the tension that undergirded the relationship between Christian and Muslim. Map 8.6 shows the precarious location of these states, surrounded by the Muslim world. As early as the 1120s, the Muslims had begun to strike back, and Edessa fell in 1144.

Christians in the west mounted further Crusades to support their fellows in the Holy Land, but the subsequent crusades were not as successful as the first, even though some illustrious western kings participated.

Map 8.6 shows the routes and dates of the two subsequent Crusades. The Second Crusade was urged on by Bernard of Clairveaux (Peter *Subsequent Crusades* Abelard's foe described earlier), but the two leaders—King Louis VII of France and Emperor Conrad III of Germany—could not coordinate their efforts enough to make any difference.

Things became worse for the crusader states: The Muslims of Syria produced a vigorous leader named Saladin, who controlled Syria and Egypt. He conducted a coordinated force that retook Jerusalem in 1187. Saladin did not permit a massacre of civilians, and he even tolerated a continuation of Christian services, but the West was ablaze with calls for a new Crusade. Three major monarchs responded: Emperor Frederick Barbarossa, Richard the Lion-Hearted of England, and Philip II of France. Everyone thought these pillars of chivalry could retake the Holy City, but they, too, had problems coordinating their efforts. After some stunning successes, Frederick Barbarossa drowned while swimming and his army went home. The French king also retreated after some losses, leaving Richard and Saladin to negotiate a settlement whereby Christian pilgrims could have free access to Jerusalem. However, these concessions seemed humiliating to Christians in the West who unrealistically hoped for a decisive victory.

The crusades spurred the emergence of new religious orders who followed a monastic rule and who served as a crucial part of the permanent garrison guarding the Holy *Knights Templars* Land. Their principal function was to serve God by fighting Muslims, and Muslims and Christians alike respected their military accomplishments. The Knights Templars, the most famous of these orders, protected pilgrims and served as bankers for those traveling to the Holy Land, but they grew so powerful that many began to resent their strength and organization. Saladin hated the Templars, saying, "Let us rid the earth of the air they breathe," but they remained a central force in the Holy Land. Again, the medieval social "order" blurred, as one group of those who prayed also began to specialize in warfare.

The noble ideal of crusading deteriorated over time as Christians began to focus less on the Holy Land itself and more on Christendom's perceived

CRITICISM OF THE CHURCH

In the West under the guidance of many skilled popes, the church had established a strong organization and wielded much authority. Yet some Christians, called heretics by the orthodox, disagreed with established doctrine and criticized the direction the church had taken. Some of these people believed that the church had erred in becoming rich as early as the reign of the Roman emperor Constantine (r. 306–337) (discussed in Chapter 5). These critics wanted to follow the example of the apostles described in the Bible and live a more simple life by being poor, preaching, and reading the sacred text. This criticism also reflected a new reality in the West—there now existed a richer and increasingly urban world with the kind of visible inequities that seemed worth rejecting.

The best-known proponent of this life was Valdes of Lyons. (Later he became incorrectly called Peter Waldo, and he is often remembered by *Waldensians* that name.) A rich merchant in his younger years, Valdes gave up all his material possessions in order to wander, beg, and preach. Many ordinary Christians were drawn to the holy simplicity of his life, but churchmen were threatened by his implicit criticism of churches decorated with gold. The pope condemned Valdes and his followers as heretics in 1181, but many of his supporters, called Waldensians, stayed loyal to their beliefs, and in fact, Waldensian churches exist today.

Several similar sects arose that advocated the apostolic life (called *vita apostolica*). Indeed, numerous men and women throughout the Middle Ages continued to consider wealth and Christianity incompatible. Taken together, such movements represented a growing discomfort with a church that seemed too powerful and too embroiled in the gritty details of the physical world to fulfill the spiritual needs of men and women. The thirteenth-century church met these criticisms with both accommodation and repression.

THE CHURCH ACCOMMODATES:
FRANCISCANS AND DOMINICANS

New monastic movements had always been a source of reform for the church and an outlet for men and women who sought different ways of expressing their religious impulses. In the thirteenth century, popes approved two such movements, the Franciscans and the Dominicans, that promised to address the criticism that had arisen so strongly against the church. In previous monastic movements, men and women isolated themselves behind great walls to devote themselves to God. By contrast, the new religious impulses called for holy men and women to mingle among the people in the growing towns of Europe and help alleviate the new problems of urban poverty and suffering. Therefore, Franciscans and Dominicans did not retire from society as monks, but were called "mendicant orders" (literally "begging orders," which alludes to their poverty) and served God by helping the needy within their villages and towns.

The Franciscan movement was founded by Francis of Assisi (1182–1226), the son of a wealthy Italian merchant. Like Valdes of Lyon, Francis *Francis of Assisi* had a conversion experience that inspired him to give up all his earthly goods to live in poverty. He survived by begging, and he helped care for the poor people of Assisi and other nearby towns. His gentle demeanor and charismatic preaching had broad appeal. Francis attracted a number of followers among the young in Assisi. One young woman, Clare, heard him speak, and in 1212 she followed him into a religious life. She established a mendicant order for women and presided over a group of women dedicated to the same ideals she had embraced. These "Poor Ladies" of Assisi, sometimes called "Poor Clares," became the female counterparts of the Franciscans, but soon their lives were structured differently from that of their male counterparts: Instead of wandering and preaching, they lived in silence in enclosed convents. In spite of this change, this spiritual life still attracted many followers.

Although Franciscans in some ways resembled the Waldensians, who had been condemned as heretics, they differed in one significant respect: They believed in obedience to the pope. Because of this humility, Francis received papal dispensation to establish a new order of "friars," who would live in poverty and preach.

The Franciscans appealed to those who believed in a poor and humble church, but their work did not satisfy all the critics. Many people *Dominican order* thought that the church had fallen into error because of ignorance. Another new mendicant order, the Dominicans, arose to address this problem. The Dominicans were led by the Spanish priest Dominic de Guzmán (1170–1221), an intellectual who believed that heresy could be fought through preaching. In 1217, Pope Honorius approved the "Order of Preachers," or the Dominicans, who like the Franciscans, took an oath of poverty and lived among the townspeople instead of in monasteries. However, they emphasized preaching rather than poverty and stressed study at universities to ensure that their preaching was strictly orthodox. The Dominicans thus appealed to people's minds, whereas the Franciscans spoke to their hearts. Through permitting both of these orders, the church had responded to the spiritual needs of its followers by authorizing dedicated men and women to teach and practice among the people. Christians hungering for a more profound sense of spiritual connectedness welcomed the lessons they received from these pious teachers.

The Church Suppresses: The Albigensian Crusade and the Inquisition

The church did not always prove so accommodating in the face of criticism. In the late twelfth century, a heretical movement became very popular, particularly in southern France. This movement, called Catharism (from the Greek word for "pure") was similar to Zoroastrianism (described in Chapter 1) in that it professed a dualist system of two principles (or two deities)—light and darkness—fighting for supremacy. They identified the god of darkness with the Old Testament deity who created the world and the god of light with the New Testament and spiritual salvation. They believed that people had to struggle to help the good principle trapped in everyone escape the evil world of the flesh. Because a center of this group was in Albi in southern France, they are also commonly known as "Albigensians."

Albigensians were particularly threatening to the church because their ideas struck at the very heart of Christian belief that considered the material world as good. Pope Innocent III first sent preachers to Albi to show people the error of their ways. However, in 1209, after some violence against papal representatives, the pope lost patience and called a crusade against the heretics. Northern French nobles, eager to break the power of

Albigensian Crusade

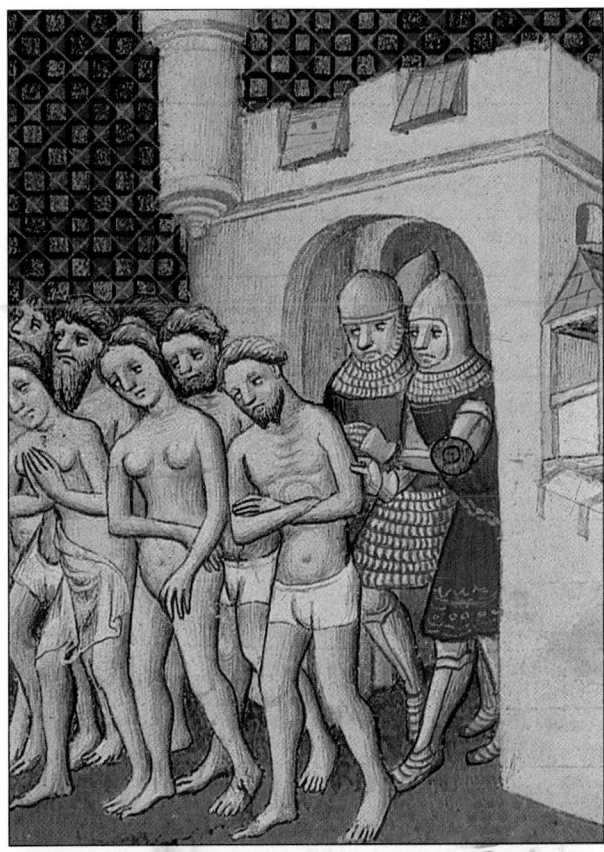

FIGURE 8.13
Expulsion of Albigensians from the town of Carcassone in 1209.

the strong southern lords, participated avidly in the savage campaign. Figure 8.13 shows Albigensians being expelled from one of the major heretical strongholds of Carcassone. This illustration contrasts the simplicity of the men and women heretics with the fierce crusaders, perhaps revealing some compassion for the heretics, because during the crusade's 20 years, thousands of people were massacred. In one especially tragic example, 7,000 men, women, and children of the town of Béziers took refuge from the crusaders in the local cathedral. When soldiers asked the papal representative how they could distinguish between heretics and the faithful, he reportedly replied, "Kill them all; God will know his own." All 7,000 of the townspeople—heretic and orthodox alike—died that day in the church's attempt to stamp out heresy.

Even after such brutal displays of power, church leaders still felt endangered by diversity of beliefs. In the mid-thirteenth century, the church established a new court—the inquisition—designed to ferret out and eradicate threatening ideas. Unlike secular courts, which determined the guilt or innocence of actions, the inquisition aimed to detect wrong beliefs. *The inquisition* The court recognized the difficulty in examining people's ideas and developed special means by which to determine what people were thinking. Often it relied on the Dominicans, with their training in understanding heresy, to serve as the inquisitor generals. These generals used questioning, starvation, and other forms of torture to force people to reveal their beliefs. Many unfortunate victims "confessed" to escape further torture or execution, and although they were released, many faced extreme "penances," such as renunciation of property or imprisonment. All self-confessed heretics faced severe social repercussions from their neighbors who no longer wanted to associate with the "guilty." Those who were deemed guilty and unrepentant were turned over to the secular authority to be executed, usually by burning.

The inquisition swept through much of Europe, inflicting more damage in some communities than in others. It is truly a dark chapter in the history of the church. Perhaps the only way to understand this phenomenon is to remember that people in the Middle Ages were deeply concerned about the state of their souls and their own salvation. They believed that exposure to incorrect religious ideas could jeopardize that salvation, and this was a risk they simply could not take. In their emphasis on community over the individual, they did not share modern beliefs that efforts to save one another from "wrong" ideas potentially put all ideas in peril.

By 1300, many in medieval Europe were convinced that order was established in the world. Bishop Gerard of Cambrai, whose quotation opened this chapter, elaborated on the three-part structure of this perfectly ordered society: Those who pray are able to enjoy this "holy leisure" because of the efforts of those who fight, who guarantee their security. Both of these groups are able to fill their functions because those who work see to the needs of their bodies. The world seemed perfectly appointed.

Summary

At the turn of the first millennium A.D., agricultural innovations sparked a dramatic surge in the European population. This growth fueled an expansion of western European civilization that represented the high point of the Middle Ages. During this time of expansion, western Europeans made great intellectual innovations—philosophical systems, engineering wonders, and creative literature. Kings slowly changed their feudal lands into national monarchies—sometimes by exerting their legal rights and sometimes by violent confrontations with their nobles. The church, too, increased its central power, ultimately claiming to rule over a Europe united in faith, although it had to resort to extreme measures to preserve this fiction.

Finally, the West was strong enough to expand its horizons and again confront the great cultures on its borders and beyond. With the violent crusades in the eastern Mediterranean, Christians challenged the power of Islam and lost; with the reconquest of Spain, however, Christians prevailed over the Muslims. More significantly, Christians learned much about science, technology, and life from the Muslims. However, this ordered, prosperous age would confront dramatic challenges in the fourteenth century, when disasters would strike. Would medieval structures prove resilient enough to withstand the pressure?

REVIEW, ANALYZE, AND ANTICIPATE

REVIEW THE PREVIOUS CHAPTER

Chapter 7—"The Struggle to Restore Order"—described manorialism and the feudal contract as the organizing structures of medieval life. It also described the invasions of the ninth and tenth centuries that undermined the developing order in the West.

1. Review the obligations of peasants and the nature of village life described in Chapter 7 and consider the strengths of these structures that allowed for the agricultural boom in the eleventh century.

2. Review the invasions by Vikings and others that caused a decentralization of power and the weakening of kings. How did this decentralization influence the growth of England and France from the eleventh through the thirteenth centuries?

ANALYZE THIS CHAPTER

Chapter 8—"Order Perfected"—traces the High Middle Ages and follows the fortunes of the social groups and political entities that made up the West.

1. Consider the growth of towns and the related developments of trade. How did towns govern themselves? How was the prevalence of Gothic cathedrals and pilgrimages related to the growing prosperity of towns?

2. One of the themes of this chapter is the struggle between popes and emperors or kings to decide who should lead a Christian Europe. Review these struggles and consider the advantages and disadvantages of each party's position.

3. Review the Crusades. Why did the crusaders go to the Holy Land, and what did they accomplish?

ANTICIPATE THE NEXT CHAPTER

Chapter 9—"Despair in the West, Empires in the East"—shows how the disasters of the fourteenth century undermined the structures that had ordered western Europe for centuries, and also shows the growth of empires in eastern Europe.

1. What structures—manorialism, feudal contracts, centralized monarchies, or a central church organization—do you think would be most vulnerable to social, economic, and military disasters? Why?

BEYOND THE CLASSROOM

THOSE WHO WORK: AGRICULTURAL LABOR

Hanawalt, B. *The Ties That Bind: Peasant Families in Medieval England.* New York: Oxford University Press, 1986. An eminent historian provides a vivid and engaging picture of peasant life.

Sweeny, Del, ed. *Agriculture in the Middle Ages: Technology, Practice and Representation.* Philadelphia, PA: University of Pennsylvania Press, 1995. Presents a collection of essays on various aspects of medieval agriculture that also shows the sources for such information.

THOSE OUTSIDE THE ORDER: TOWN LIFE

Bennet, Judith M. *Ale, Beer, and Brewsters in England: Women's Work in a Changing World.* Oxford: Oxford University Press, 1999. An excellent discussion of the changing economic roles of women as the medieval economy grew.

Evans, G.R. *Philosophy and Theology in the Middle Ages.* New York: Routledge, 1993. A sound, comprehensive survey of intellectual thought, showing the ties between philosophy and theology.

Gies, Frances, and Joseph Gies. *Cathedral, Forge, and Waterwheel: Technology and Invention in the Middle Ages.* New York: HarperCollins, 1994. An engaging discussion of the many inventions of the Middle Ages that shows the influence of the East in spreading innovations.

Herlihy, David. *Opera Muliebria: Women and Work in Medieval Europe.* New York: McGraw-Hill, 1990. A short, yet scholarly, summary of the varied jobs of women in the Middle Ages that considers the way their work changed over time.

Timeline: A Closer Look

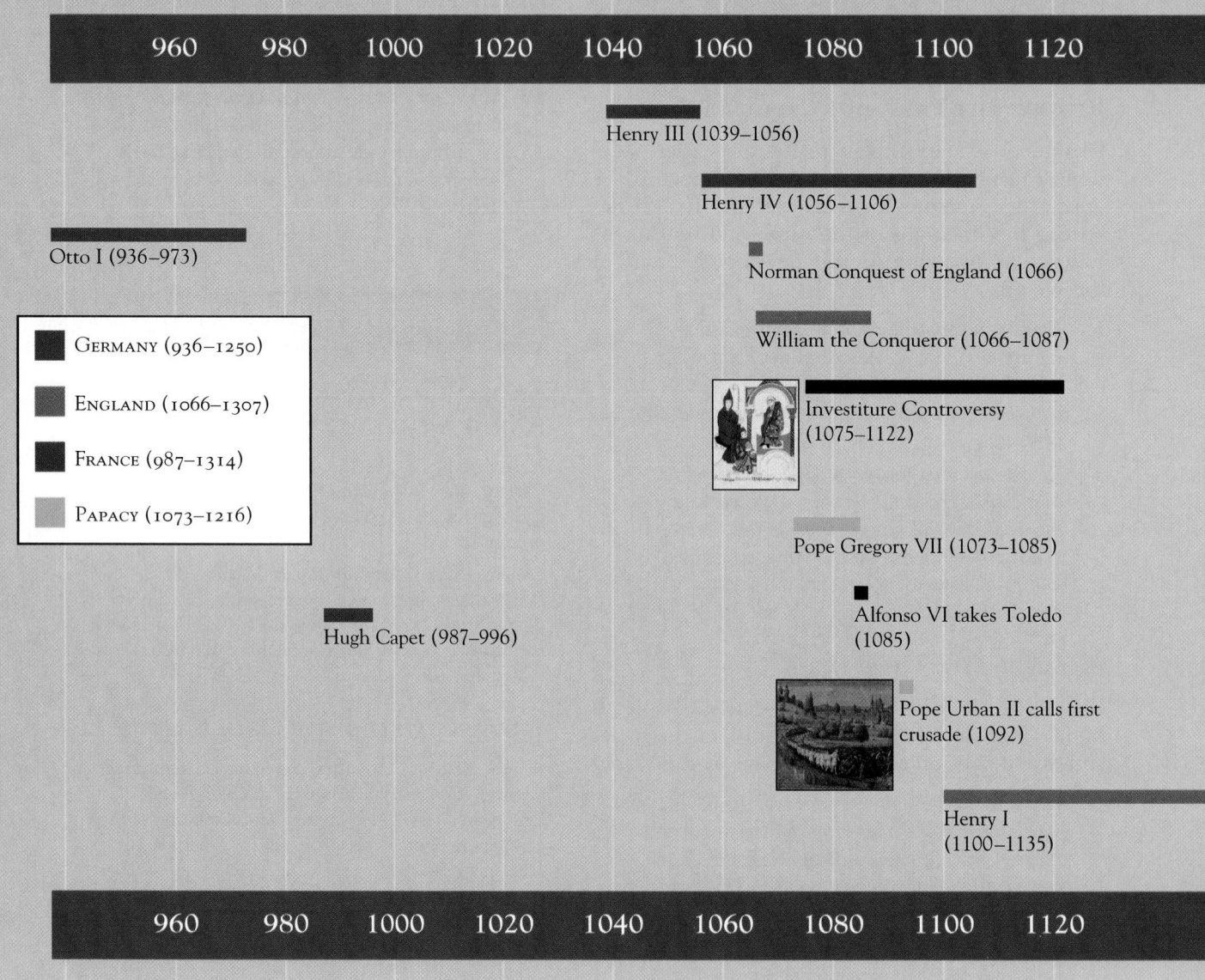

| 960 | 980 | 1000 | 1020 | 1040 | 1060 | 1080 | 1100 | 1120 |

Henry III (1039–1056)

Henry IV (1056–1106)

Otto I (936–973)

Norman Conquest of England (1066)

William the Conqueror (1066–1087)

Investiture Controversy
(1075–1122)

GERMANY (936–1250)

ENGLAND (1066–1307)

FRANCE (987–1314)

PAPACY (1073–1216)

Pope Gregory VII (1073–1085)

Alfonso VI takes Toledo
(1085)

Hugh Capet (987–996)

Pope Urban II calls first
crusade (1092)

Henry I
(1100–1135)

| 960 | 980 | 1000 | 1020 | 1040 | 1060 | 1080 | 1100 | 1120 |

Lopez, Robert S. *The Commercial Revolution of the Middle Ages, 950–1350.* New York: Cambridge University Press, 1976. Shows that there was a substantial growth in commerce in the Middle Ages and traces its effects.

Ridder-Symoens, Hilde de. *A History of the University in Europe: Universities in the Middle Ages.* New York: Cambridge University Press, 1991. A current summary of the subject that incorporates the latest scholarship.

THOSE WHO FIGHT: NOBLES AND KNIGHTS

Duby, George. *Love and Marriage in the Middle Ages.* Chicago: University of Chicago Press, 1996. An engaging study by an eminent historian.

Gies, J. and F. Gies. *Life in a Medieval Castle.* New York: Harper & Row, 1974. A popular, illustrated work that offers a summary of noble life. Although not scholarly, it is nevertheless accurate and engaging.

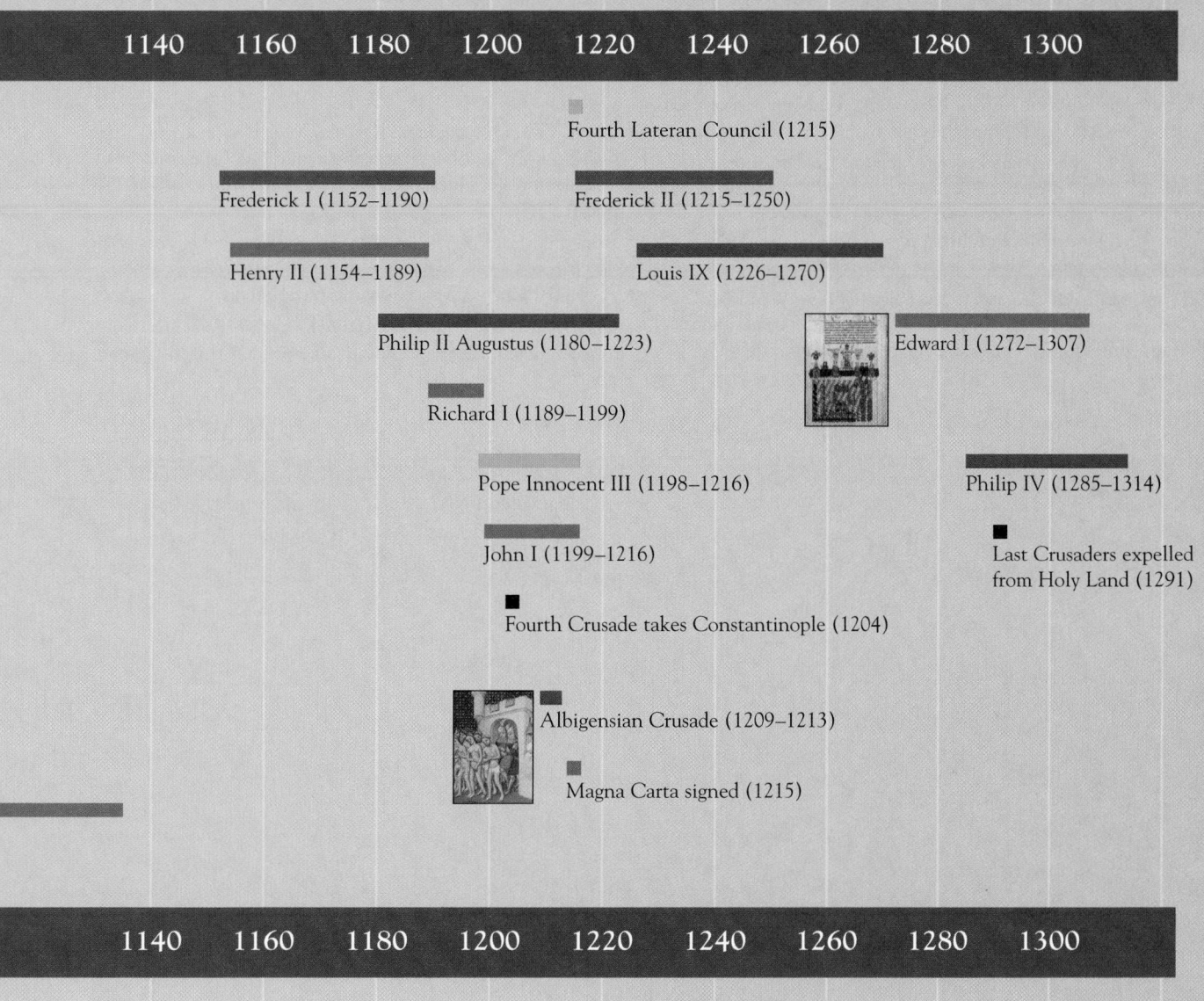

1140	1160	1180	1200	1220	1240	1260	1280	1300

Fourth Lateran Council (1215)

Frederick I (1152–1190)

Frederick II (1215–1250)

Henry II (1154–1189)

Louis IX (1226–1270)

Philip II Augustus (1180–1223)

Edward I (1272–1307)

Richard I (1189–1199)

Pope Innocent III (1198–1216)

Philip IV (1285–1314)

John I (1199–1216)

Last Crusaders expelled from Holy Land (1291)

Fourth Crusade takes Constantinople (1204)

Albigensian Crusade (1209–1213)

Magna Carta signed (1215)

1140	1160	1180	1200	1220	1240	1260	1280	1300

Keen, Maurice. *Chivalry*. New Haven, CT: Yale University Press, 1984. A comprehensive, well-illustrated work that will remain a classic on this subject.

The Rise of Centralized Monarchies

Fletcher, Richard. *Moorish Spain*. New York: H. Holt, 1992. A concise survey of the Iberian Peninsula from the Muslim invasion to the fall of Granada shows the significant impact of the reconquest.

Furman, Horst. *Germany in the High Middle Ages, c. 1050–1200*. trans. T. Reuter. New York: Cambridge University Press, 1986. Offers a clear and engaging survey of a complex time.

Hallam, Elizabeth M. *Capetian France, 987–1328*. New York: Longman, 1980. Chronicles the slow consolidation of these French kings as they expanded their power.

Painter, Sidney. *The Rise of the Feudal Monarchies*. Westport, CT: Greenwood Publishing Company, 1951, reprint, 1982. A readable survey of the major events leading to the growth of France, England, and Germany in the Middle Ages.

THOSE WHO PRAY: IMPERIAL POPES AND EXPANDING CHRISTENDOM

Evans, Austin P. *Heresies of the High Middle Ages*. New York: Columbia University Press, 1991. A good explanation of the many heresies that plagued the church and appealed to many.

Ladurie, LeRoy. *Montaillou: The Promised Land of Error*, trans. Barbara Brey. NY: Vintage Books, 1979. A classic study of the Inquisition records of Albigensian villagers in Southern France. It reads like a novel with the insights of a master historian.

Lyons, Malcolm C. *Saladin: The Politics of Holy War*. New York: Cambridge University Press, 1985. A fine study of one of the most remarkable figures involved in the Crusades.

Morris, Colin. *The Papal Monarchy: The Western Church from 1050–1250*. New York: Oxford University Press, 1991. Offers a balanced interpretation of the whole structure of the church in the formative central Middle Ages as the popes rose in power.

Peters, Edward. *Inquisition*. Berkeley, CA: University of California Press, 1989. Traces the evolution of the concept of "Inquisition" as represented in modern literature, art, and political theory.

Riley-Smith, Jonathan, ed. *The Oxford Illustrated History of the Crusades*. New York: Cambridge University Press, 1995. A comprehensive, beautifully illustrated study.

Sayers, Jane. *Innocent III: Leader of Europe, 1198–1216*. New York: Longman, 1994. Examines all aspects of this influential pontiff.

> For quiz questions that tie the book to the videos and additional primary sources, please go to the *Primary Source Investigator* CD.

Documents

DOCUMENT 8.1
Guibert of Nogent Describes His Education

In the early twelfth century, Guibert, the abbot of Nogent in France, wrote a remarkable autobiography that offers an intimate glimpse into twelfth-century life. Guibert's parents had promised him to the church at his birth and raised him to become a monk. In this account, he gives a rare description of child-rearing practices. Clearly, even privileged medieval children did not have it easy!

■ **Investigate the Document**

Why did Guibert's mother have to settle for a mediocre tutor? What methods of instruction did the tutor use? What did Guibert think of his tutor? How did medieval ideas of education differ from modern notions?

There was a little before that time, and in a measure there is still in my time, such a scarcity of grammarians that in the towns hardly anyone, and in the cities very few, could be found, and those who by good hap could be discovered, had but slight knowledge and could not be compared with the itinerant clerks of these days. And so the man in whose charge my mother decided to put me, had begun to learn grammar late in life and was the more unskilled in the art through having imbibed little of it when young. Yet of such sobriety was he, that what he wanted in letters, he made up for in honesty.

Placed under him I was taught with such purity and checked with such honesty in the excesses which are wont to spring up in my youth, that I was kept well-guarded from the common wolves and never allowed to leave his company, or to eat anywhere than at home, or to accept gifts from anyone without his leave; in everything I had to show self-control in word, look or act, so that he seemed to require of me the conduct of a monk rather than a clerk. For whereas others of my age wandered everywhere at will and were unchecked in the indulgence of such incli-

nations to their age, I, hedged in with constant restraints, would sit and look on in my clerical chasuble at the troops of players like a beast awaiting sacrifice.

Although, therefore, he crushed me by such severity, yet in other ways he made it quite plain that he loved me as well as he did himself. With such watchful care did he devote himself to me, with such foresight did he secure my welfare against the spite of others and teach me on what authority I should beware of the dissolute manners of some who paid court to me, and so long did he argue with my mother about the elaborate richness of my dress, that he was regarded as exercising the guardianship not of a master, but of a parent, and not over my body only, but my soul, too. As for me, considering the dull sensibility of my age and my littleness, great was the love I conceived for him in response, in spite of the many weals with which he marked my tender skin so that not through fear, as is common in those of my age, but through a sort of love deeply implanted in my heart, I obeyed him in utter forgetfulness of his severity.

DOCUMENT 8.2
Pope Innocent III Prohibits Trade with Muslims

While Western Crusaders sent waves of armed knights to try to hold the Crusader states in the Holy Land, Venetians grew rich trading with Muslims. Pope Innocent III tried to forbid trade that would help Muslims in their war against the Crusaders. But as you can see from this source, even the pope could not fully regulate the growing commercial ties between Christians and Muslims.

■ **Investigate the Document**

What kinds of goods did Innocent permit Venetians to trade? What kinds did he forbid? How successful do you think such prohibitions were?

In support of the eastern province [that is, the crusading states], in addition to the forgiveness of sins which we promise those who, at their own expense,

Source: Guibert de Nogent. *The Autobiography of Guibert, Abbot of Nogent-Sous-Coucy.* Translated by C.C. Swinton Bland (London: George Routledge & Sons, Ltd. and E.P. Dutton & Co., New York, 1926), p. 32.

Source: Oliver J. Thatcher and Edgar H. McNeal. *A Source Book for Mediaeval History*, (New York: Charles Scribner's Sons, 1905), pp. 536–537.

set out thither, and besides the papal protection which we give those who aid that land, we have renewed that decree of the Lateran council [held under Alexander III, 1179], which excommunicated those Christians who shall furnish the Saracens with weapons, iron, or timbers for their galleys, and those who serve the Saracens as helmsmen or in any other way on their galleys and other piratical craft, and which furthermore ordered that their property be confiscated by the secular princes and the consuls of the cities, and that, if any such persons should be taken prisoner, they should be the slaves of those who captured them. We furthermore excommunicated all those Christians who shall hereafter have anything to do with the Saracens either directly or indirectly, or shall attempt to give them aid in any way so long as the war between them and us shall last. But recently our beloved sons, Andreas Donatus and Benedict Grilion, your messengers, came and explained to us that your city was suffering great loss by this our decree, because Venice does not engage in agriculture, but in shipping and commerce. Nevertheless, we are led by the paternal love which we have for you to forbid you to aid the Saracens by selling them, giving them, or exchanging with them, iron, flax (oakum), pitch, sharp instruments, rope, weapons, galleys, ships, and timbers, whether hewn or in the rough. But for the present and until we order to the contrary, we permit those who are going to Egypt to carry other kinds of merchandise whenever it shall be necessary. In return for this favor you should be willing to go to the aid of the province of Jerusalem and you should not attempt to evade our apostolic command. For there is no doubt that he who, against his own conscience, shall fraudulently try to evade this prohibition, shall be under divine condemnation.

DOCUMENT 8.3

Papal Reformers Impose Clerical Celibacy

In the eleventh century, the Investiture Controversy represented a power struggle between popes and emperors over which of them should rule the Christian world. As part of this jockeying for control, papal reformers began imposing clerical celibacy on clergy members. As the sources below suggest, the motivations behind this policy centered as much on breaking up family ties as on ad- *dressing issues of sexual purity. All these excerpts link prohibitions of simony (the sale of church offices) with celibacy, showing the degree to which the reformers connected these notions in their minds.*

■ **Investigate the Document**

> **Which** sin—simony or clerical marriage—most disturbed the authors of these sources? **What** was the argument against clerical celibacy? **Why** do you think the party advocating clerical celibacy prevailed?

Sigebert of Gembloux, 1074

Pope Gregory [VII] held a synod in which he anathematized all who were guilty of simony. He also forbade all clergy who were married to say mass, and all laymen were forbidden to be present when such a married priest should officiate. In this he seemed to many to act contrary to the decisions of the holy fathers who have declared that the sacraments of the church are neither made more effective by the good qualities, nor less effective by the sins, of the officiating priest, because it is the Holy Spirit who makes them effective.

The Roman Council, 1074

Those who have been advanced to any grade of holy orders, or to any office, through simony, that is, by the payment of money, shall hereafter have no right to officiate in the holy church. Those also who have secured churches by giving money shall certainly be deprived of them. And in the future, it shall be illegal for anyone to buy or sell [any ecclesiastical office, etc.].

Nor shall clergymen who are married say mass or serve the altar in any way. We decree also that if they refuse to obey our orders, or rather those of the holy fathers, the people shall refuse to receive their ministrations, in order that those who disregard the love of God and the dignity of their office may be brought to their senses through feeling the shame of the world and the reproof of the people.

Ninth Lateran Council, 1123

We forbid priests, deacons, and subdeacons to live with wives or concubines, and no woman shall live with a clergyman except those who are permitted by

Source: Oliver J. Thatcher and Edgar N. McNeal, *A Source Book for Mediaeval History*, (New York: Charles Scribner's Sons, 1905), pp. 134–135.

the council of Nicaea, that is: mother, sister, aunt, or others of such sort that no suspicion may justly arise concerning them.

DOCUMENT 8.4
Walter of Henley Writes an Agricultural Instruction Manual

The prosperity of the High Middle Ages stemmed from agricultural innovations. New techniques, including the use of horses to increase plowing capacity, drove these innovations. However, the historical sources show that farming remained a difficult, skill-intensive task. This reading comes from an instruction manual revealing some of the difficulties facing those who wanted to make a profit from the land. Written in the thirteenth century, the manual offers a valuable glimpse into medieval farm life.

■ **Investigate the Document**

What major difficulties did farm overseers face? **What** challenges did the use of horses instead of oxen present? **Why** did many farmers delay adding horses to their plow teams?

At the beginning of fallowing and second fallowing and of sowing let the bailiff, and the messer, or the provost, be all the time with the ploughmen, to

Source: *Walter of Henley's Husbandry,* trans. Elizabeth Lamond, (London: Longmans, Green and Co., 1890), pp. 11–13

see that they do their work well and thoroughly, and at the end of the day see how much they have done, and for so much shall they answer each day after unless they can show a sure hindrance. And because customary servants neglect their work it is necessary to guard against their fraud; further, it is necessary that they are overseen often; and besides the bailiff must oversee all, that they all work well, and if they do not well let them be reproved.

With a team of oxen with two horses you draw quicker than with a team all horses, if the ground is not so stony that oxen cannot help themselves with their feet. Why? I will tell you: the horse costs more than the ox. Besides a plough of oxen will go as far in the year as a plough of horses, because the malice of ploughmen will not allow the plough [of horses] to go beyond their pace, no more than the plough of oxen. Further, in very hard ground, where the plough of horses will stop, the plough of oxen will pass. And will you see how the horse costs more than the ox? I will tell you. It is usual and right that plough beasts should be in the stall between the feast of St. Luke and the feast of the Holy Cross in May, five-and-twenty weeks, and if the horse is to be in a condition to do his daily work, it is necessary that he should have every night at the least the sixth part of a bushel of oats, price one halfpenny, and at the least twelve pennyworth of grass in summer. And each week more or less a penny in shoeing, if he must be shod on all four feet. The sum is twelve shillings and fivepence in the year, without fodder and chaff.

St. Sebastian Interceding for the Plague-Stricken, by Josse Lieferinxe

The dominating event of the fourteenth century was the plague that swept through Europe killing more than one-third of the population. This painting shows the horror of the plague as people bury the dead in their burial shrouds. Saint Sebastian—shown in the sky pierced with arrows—prays for the ill. Priests, too, pray for the dead and the living, but death still reigned.

CHAPTER 9

Despair in the West, Empires in the East

The Late Middle Ages, ca. 1300–1500

STUDY • Famine, Plague, and Revolts • Avignon Papacy and Great Schism • Hundred Years' War • Intellectual Responses • Rise of Eastern Empires

🌍NOTICE how the empires in the east grew more powerful as the western kingdoms were swept by disasters.

"In the year of the Lord 1315, shall begin a great famine on earth. . . . Also the Church shall totter and the line of Saint Peter shall be execrated. Also the blood of many shall be poured out on the ground." A fourteenth-century priest, Jean de Venette, told of this prophecy that appeared in a dream, and it came all too true as the century brought a series of disasters that would break down the medieval order that had seemed so secure a century before.

At the beginning of the century, bad weather ruined harvests and introduced years of famine, which drove many people from their lands to search for food. This misery was compounded when a terrible plague swept from east Asia and raged through western Europe, killing over a third of the population and bringing fear and despair to many survivors. Peasants in the countryside and urban workers responded by staging revolts that further seemed to attack the social order itself. In the High Middle Ages, people looked to the church and the pope to bring comfort and order, but in the fourteenth century the church too was split by controversy as disputed papal elections brought several popes to power at once. As these disasters swept over Europe, England and France engaged in a violent war—the Hundred Years' War—that brought destruction to civilians and mounted knights alike. In eastern Europe and Islam, new empires threatened western Europe from the outside.

At the end of the century and a half of devastation, the feudal, manorial, and many of the intellectual structures of the medieval world had been undermined. Many believed these disasters heralded the end of the world; instead, western Europe was transformed by the horrors that swept over it, and moved in exciting new directions.

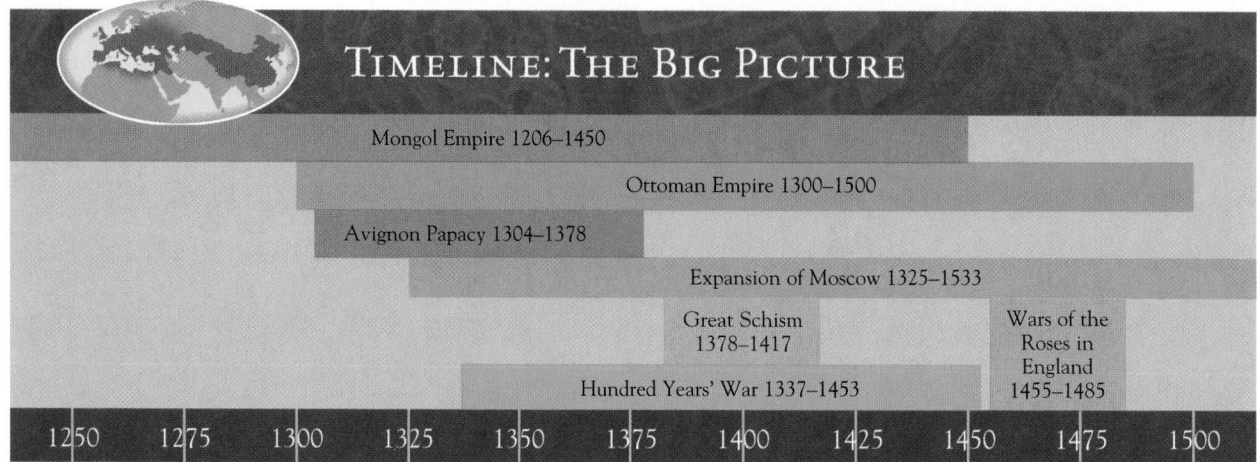

TIMELINE: THE BIG PICTURE

Mongol Empire 1206–1450

Ottoman Empire 1300–1500

Avignon Papacy 1304–1378

Expansion of Moscow 1325–1533

Great Schism 1378–1417

Wars of the Roses in England 1455–1485

Hundred Years' War 1337–1453

1250   1275   1300   1325   1350   1375   1400   1425   1450   1475   1500

Economic and Social Misery

The town of Douai in medieval Flanders (now in France) was a prosperous place, where men and women produced woolen cloth in a booming cottage industry that made many merchants rich. Some people spun the wool, others wove it, and still others dyed the cloth. Then they turned it over to the merchants with whom they held their labor contracts. In prosperous times, there were good wages to be had, but early in the fourteenth century, hard times suddenly came. Years of bad harvests began in 1315, and the shops in Douai no longer had enough food to satisfy the town's needs. Tensions erupted in 1322, when rumors spread that the rich merchants were hoarding grain. Many of the cloth workers took to the streets, and in the legal records of the town, we learn that 18 workers—including two women—were arrested in the turmoil. The workers "in the full marketplace" had urged an assault on grain merchants to take the needed food from their warehouses. The two women were charged with being especially vocal, and in punishment they had their tongues cut off before being banished from the city for life. This was only one small incident in a century that brought suffering and despair to many in Europe.

FAMINE

The growth of European society stemmed mostly from agricultural innovations that had generated the boom of the eleventh century. By 1300, however, the burgeoning population began to put a strain on medieval technology. People were cultivating poorer lands, and crop yields were dwindling; on some marginal lands, farmers might harvest only three bushels for every one planted. After setting aside one bushel to plant the following year, the remainder was hardly enough to maintain a fixed population.

As the population grew, people tried to bring more and more lands into cultivation to make up for the scarcities, and this often resulted in plowing the common fields on which villagers grazed their animals. Unable to feed their livestock, people were forced to kill many of their animals—from ¼ to ⅓ of their animals were slaughtered. This significant reduction of livestock, also reduced the amount of manure for fertilizer, and yields fell again. By the beginning of the fourteenth century, farmers faced increasing difficulties accumulating a surplus of food—and then the weather worsened.

A series of years with too much rain began in 1310; lands were drenched. Chroniclers all over Europe wrote that the rains—with unusually deafening thunder and terrible lightning— *Bad weather* were steady from April throughout the summer. The winds and overcast skies made the whole growing season abnormally cool. The rains came when the seed had just been scattered—washing much of it away—and continued to fall through the summer, flooding the lower croplands. When farmers tried to harvest the meager crop, the rains came again. Rivers flooded, bridges were swept away, and the crops, with previously low yields, failed.

Famine began in 1315, and in some parts of Europe lasted until 1322. During these years, cold winters followed by cool and extraordinarily wet summers brought disastrous harvests. Aching hunger drove peasants from their lands in search of food, and according to some reports, starving farmers at times even resorted to cannibalism. Still, the disasters of this century were only beginning. Many who did not starve suffered from malnutrition and were susceptible

OLC

to infection. Respiratory illnesses and intestinal ailments reached epidemic proportions in this century, but an even greater threat appeared.

THE BLACK DEATH: BUBONIC PLAGUE

As we saw in Chapter 1, some of the most devastating diseases have been those that move from animals to humans, and in the fourteenth century beginning in Asia, a virulent bacillus (*Yersinia pestis*) infected rodents in Manchuria and then spread to black rats. This disease was passed from rodent to rodent through the bites of infected fleas, and humans could also be bitten. This "Black Death," or bubonic plague, caused worldwide devastation. The disease spread over vast areas, helped by increased trade from ships moving through the Mediterranean and by the expansion of the Mongol Empire. (See "Global Connections" page 321.) There is general agreement that the plague arrived in Europe in about 1348 on ships of Genoese merchants who traveled between Sicily and the Middle East. They brought ships laden with goods—and with infected stowaway rats. As the sailors disembarked, so did the rats, carrying the fleas and the bacilli into western Europe.

Bubonic plague brought a high fever, aching joints and a swelling of the lymph nodes. Sometimes this disease reached a person's lungs, becoming "pneumonic" plague, which spread even more rapidly through sneezing and coughing. In its various forms, the plague raced through Europe, killing a shocking one-third to one-half of the population. The plague spread quickly in the summer and declined in the winter months—the cold, wet summers helped the plague spread. Map 9.1 shows the progress of the plague and the dates that the disease slowly moved north from Italy to Scandinavia.

The psychological impact of so great a plague was perhaps even more important than the actual loss of life. Law and tradition broke down, and many survivors saw no point in trying to preserve medieval customs. Boccaccio, a fourteenth-century observer, wrote: "In this sore affliction and misery of our city, the authority of the laws, both human and divine, was all dissolved and fell into decay," and he described how many sick died untended in the streets. The painting on page 300 shows people desperately trying to give their loved ones a decent burial, but the sheer volume of death interfered with people's good intentions.

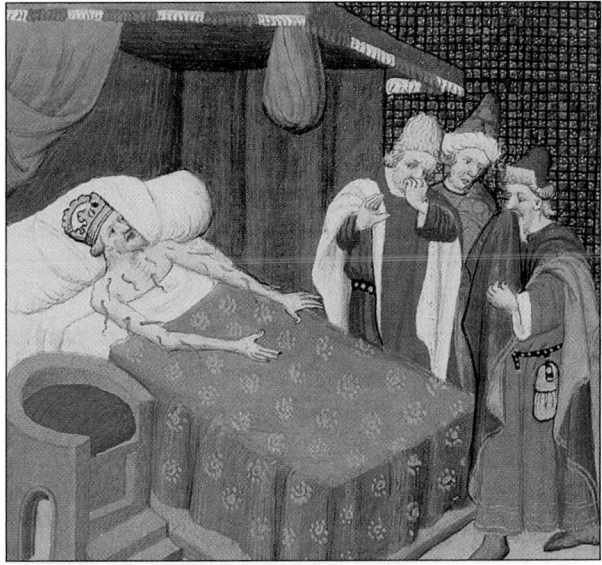

FIGURE 9.1
Physicians applying leeches to an ill king.

At the time, people did not realize that the disease was caused by bacteria and transmitted by fleas. Theories of the Black Death's etiology ranged from punishment by God to "bad air." Victims could expect only traditional treatments from physicians. In Figure 9.1 an ill king is attended by his doctors. One holds his nose to indicate the belief that the disease left an offensive smell owing to the buildup of bad "humors." The physicians have applied leeches, used on previous patients, to the king to remove excessive blood—a lethal practice that is equivalent to sharing needles between patients who have a blood-borne disease.

As medicine failed to offer solace for this horrifying disease, some people resorted to extreme measures to try to eliminate the plague. One group—the flagellants—thought that by *Flagellants* inflicting pain on themselves, they could ask God to relieve the suffering of others. Figure 9.2 shows a group of flagellants banded together in a procession. In this image, the procession is led by men carrying a cross and a dragon as a mark of their brotherhood. Flagellants beat themselves three times a day with leather thongs tipped in lead. They marched from town to town "splashing the church walls with their blood," according to contemporary witnesses. This movement reflected the desperation of people searching for ways to appease a seemingly angry God.

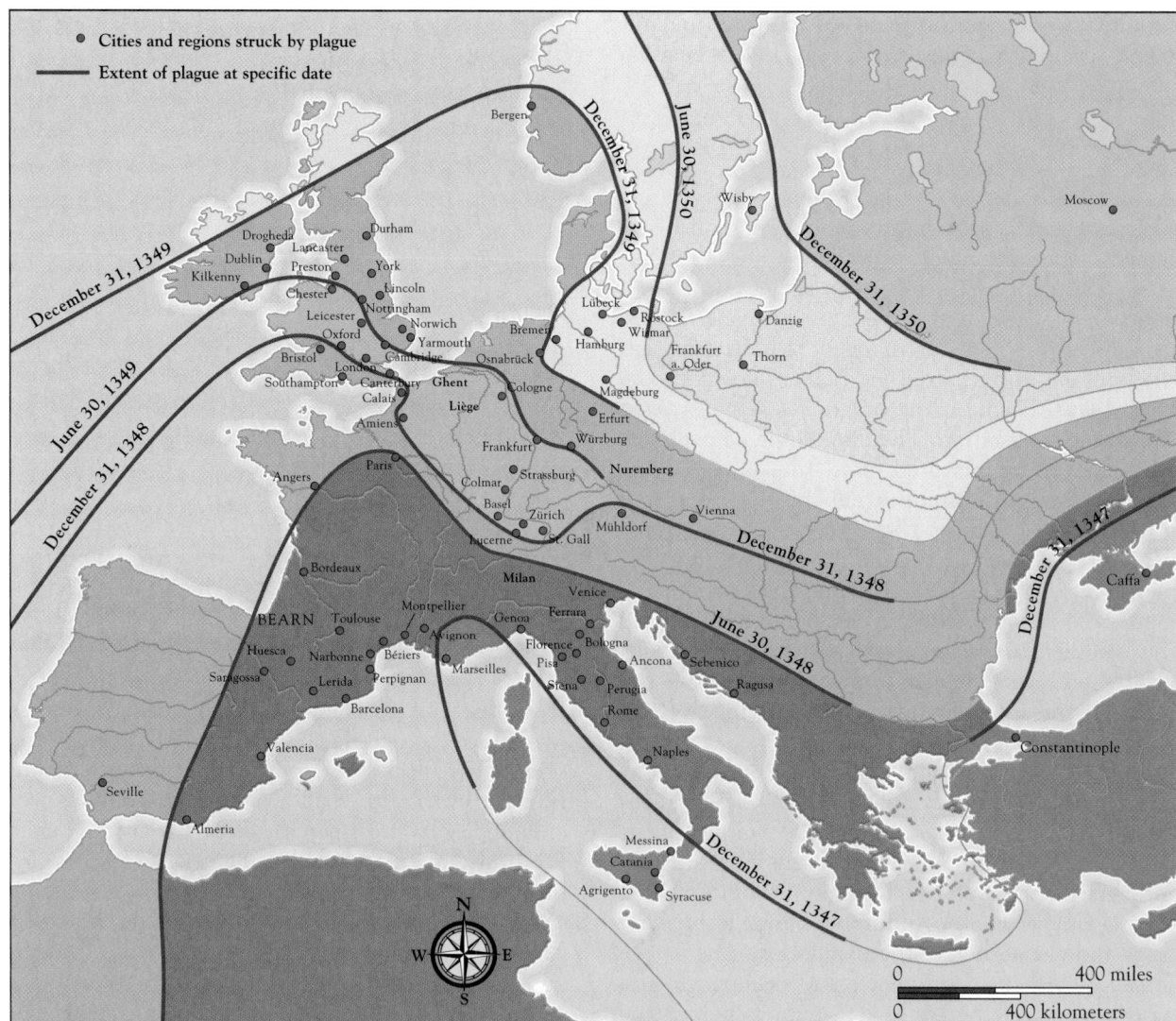

Legend:
- Cities and regions struck by plague
- Extent of plague at specific date

THINKING ABOUT GEOGRAPHY

MAP 9.1 *The Spread of the Black Death*

This map shows the slow progress of the plague as it spread gradually northward. ❧ **Notice** how long it took the plague to travel northward. **Consider** how winter and slow travel conditions might have delayed the progress. ❧ **Notice** the regions and cities largely spared. **What** might the cities have done to keep the plague from entering?

In their fear, some people turned against their neighbors, and in many cities, Jews were accused of bringing the plague by poisoning wells. The persecutions fell particularly heavily on Jewish communities in Germany because periodically throughout the thirteenth century, the English and French kings had forced Jews out of their lands and many had moved eastward. Because there was a larger presence of Jews in Germany, their Christian neighbors used them as a focus of their fears. A contemporary chronicler

(Jacob von Konigshofen) described a pogrom in Strasbourg that killed thousands of Jews accused of causing the plague: "On Saturday . . . they burnt the Jews on a wooden platform in their cemetery. There were about two thousand people of them. Many small children were taken out of the fire and baptized against the will of their fathers and mothers." In a practical aside, Jacob noted that the persecutors also had money on their minds, because they confiscated the property of the Jews: "The money was indeed the thing that killed the Jews. If they had been poor and if the feudal lords had not been in debt to them, they would not have been burnt. . . . "

Anti-Semitism

In spite of the foolishness of blaming people who were also dying from the plague, anti-Semitic persecutions spread. Over 60 major Jewish communities in Germany had been exterminated by 1351. Many Jews fled to eastern Europe—to Russia and Poland—where they received protection, and slowly many Jewish communities moved their homes even further east.

The plague continued to ravage Europe in waves into the seventeenth and even early eighteenth centuries. These subsequent visitations of the disease also took a large toll on the population. The plague finally abated when the larger, meaner Norwegian brown rat (today's urban rat) displaced the European black rats. The brown rats had thicker fur, which resisted the flea bites of the black rat fleas, so the disease bacillus slowly lost its host pool. Even though the disease eventually disappeared, it left a legacy of fear and despair that haunted Europe for centuries.

PEASANTS AND TOWNSPEOPLE REVOLT

As an immediate result of the plague, the European countryside suffered a disabling shortage of labor. Desperate lords tried to increase their customary—and already excessive—labor requirements in an effort to farm their lands. Free laborers, detecting an opportunity, began to demand higher wages, prompting some countries to pass laws freezing earnings. For example, a statute of laborers passed in England in 1351 said, "No one shall pay or promise to pay to anyone more wages . . . or salary than was accustomed." This policy enraged peasants across Europe. Determined to resist, they roamed the countryside, burning manor houses and slaughtering the occupants.

FIGURE 9.2
Flagellants, fifteenth century.

In some of these uprisings, popular preachers arose as leaders who combined social reform with religious hopes. Living in an age crippled by plague and famine, many believed that these "times of troubles" presaged a better world in which Christ would return. The most famous of these preachers was John Ball of England, who rallied listeners by calling for the overthrow of the social order: "Oh good people, things . . . will not go well until everything is held in common and there are no more serfs or lords." His most famous couplet attacked the very hierarchical privilege that had marked the three orders of medieval society. He said simply: "When Adam delved and Eve span, where then were all the gentlemen?" When Adam and Eve lived in the Garden of Eden, both worked the soil and no one was a noble "gentleman."

John Ball

The illustration in Figure 9.3 shows a confrontation between English peasants and the king's forces in 1381. John Ball rides the horse, and another popular preacher—Wat Tyler—stands in the foreground, holding a banner with the English coat of arms. This illustration shows two main things: First, the peasants had the support of well-armed and disciplined soldiers who had been trained to defend the English coast. Second, both sides hold the same royal banners, indicating that the peasants did not blame the king for their misery, but remained loyal to the teenaged Richard II (r. 1377–1399) (son of the Black Prince described in the Biography on page 313). They blamed his advisors and the local nobility for their misery. Their loyalty made no difference in the outcome—the king joined in repressing the revolt.

French peasants, too, rose up against their lords in a revolt called the "Jacquerie." French chroniclers told in horror of peasants storming manor houses and brutally killing noblemen and their families. English peasants burned houses of aristocrats, lawyers, and government officials, at times burning the records that they believed contributed to their oppression. However, the peasants in all regions could not hold out for long against the aristocracy and its superior arms. Eventually, all the revolts were suppressed with many peasants and their leaders massacred. Yet the violence, the labor shortages, and the prevailing belief that things were changing had begun to erode the old medieval manorial system. Over time, peasants who owed only rent gradually replaced serfs who had owed labor as well as rents. For these new peasants, their labor was now their own, giving them more freedom and opportunities to work for their own profit. Although the condition of many peasants improved, the trend was not uniform throughout Europe. The situation of peasants in western Europe improved more quickly than of those in eastern Europe.

As the anecdote about the town of Douai that opened this chapter indicates, the unrest was not limited to the countryside. As population dropped, the *Urban revolts* declining demand for goods led to falling prices, and some industries suffered. Merchants and manufacturers responded by trying to limit competition and reduce the freedoms of the lower classes in the towns. Revolts broke out in many towns throughout Europe. In addition to Douai, vio-

FIGURE 9.3
John Ball leading the English peasants' revolt of 1381.

lence erupted in Ghent, Rouen, and Florence. (This last was the famous *Ciompi* revolt in 1378—named for the wooden shoes worn by wool workers who rioted.) While some of these revolts led to short-term gains, most were crushed. Improvements for urban workers would eventually come with the labor shortages caused by the high death rates. But the rural and urban revolts of the fourteenth century set off social conflicts that periodically resurfaced throughout Western history.

Imperial Papacy Besieged

Throughout these troubled times, many medieval men and women looked to the church, especially the papacy, to guide them. Yet the popes were grappling with their own problems, and these very troubles undermined people's confidence in the church. Early in the fourteenth century, the issue of the relative sovereignty of kings and popes resurfaced once more over the taxation of church lands and the clergy's claim to immunity from royal courts. Document 9.2 on page D9.1 illustrates this struggle. This time, the French king proved stronger than the popes. In the course of this dispute, the French king, Philip IV (r. 1285–1314), ordered his troops to arrest Pope Boniface VIII (r. 1294–1303). Although the pope was quickly freed by his supporters, the elderly pope died soon afterward as a result of the rough treatment. Unlike Henry II of England after the death of Becket (described in Chapter 8), Philip IV was able to capitalize on the violence against the church. He brought pressure on the college of cardinals—which had elected popes since 1059—and they elected his favored French cardinal as pope.

Popes Move to Avignon

Philip expected this pope to support French interests, and to forward this aim, the king persuaded the pope to rule from Avignon, on the east bank of the Rhône River. Although the city was in the Holy Roman Empire, the French influence there was strong. The new pope, Clement V (r. 1304–1314) complied, and set up his court in Avignon. The popes never again tried to exert authority of taxation and legal immunity over the French kings. However, the pope's absence from Rome raised serious issues. After all, the pope was the bishop of Rome and was obligated to be there and guide the faithful in his charge.

For 72 years after the election of Clement V, the popes ruled from Avignon—in the shadow of the French king. Many Christians objected to this "Babylonian Captivity," as the Italian Petrarch (1304–1374) called it. Some people believed this shocking breach of tradition contributed to the subsequent plague, famine, and violence that accompanied the pope's residence in Avignon, and they urged the popes to resume ruling from Rome. The Avignon popes also expanded their administration, and they streamlined and made more efficient their collection of ecclesiastical taxes because they could not depend on the income from their lands in Rome. To many, it seemed that the church had become all too secular when the world was in desperate need of spiritual leadership.

An influential mystic, Catherine of Siena (1347–1380), felt called by God to intervene in this situation. Catherine had experienced a number of visions and was highly respected in her home *Return to Rome* city in the mountains south of Florence in Italy. Catherine wrote a series of letters to Pope Gregory XI (r. 1370–1378) in which she urged him to return to Rome, and in 1376 she traveled to Avignon to urge him in person. The painting in Figure 9.4 shows this emotion-charged meeting. Catherine kneels before the pope, pleading with him to once more take up his duties in Rome. He was persuaded, and in that year he tried to correct the decline in the papal prestige by returning to Rome. But the church's problems only increased.

Things Get Worse: The Great Schism

Gregory XI died in Rome in 1378, and the situation was volatile. The citizens of Rome feared that the college of cardinals would choose another French pope who would return to Avignon. Indeed, the guard of the cardinals warned them that they "ran the risk of being torn in pieces" if they did not elect an Italian. The fearful cardinals elected an Italian, Pope Urban VI (r. 1378–1389). Urban almost immediately indicated his plans to reduce the French influence in the college of cardinals, and not surprisingly, the French cardinals—claiming that the election of Urban VI was invalid because they had been coerced by the Roman mob—left Rome. The dissenting cardinals elected a Frenchman—Pope Clement VII (r. 1378–1394)—who took up residence in the papal palace in Avignon. Now there were two popes, initiating what has been called the Great Schism of the church. (This is not to be confused with the schism of 1054, which divided the church into the Latin west and the Greek Orthodox east. See Chapter 6.)

Many people chose to follow one pope over the other based on political rather than religious motivations, and Map 9.2 shows the respective alliances. Each pope denounced the other as the anti-Christ, and each tried to increase the revenues that now were split in half as Christians were divided in their loyalties. Many people began to criticize the church for its seeming concern for money over spiritual matters, and they advocated restoring a unified leadership to the divided Christendom. As the Black Death plundered Europe, the papacy lost its moral authority as the ruler of a united Christendom. Who could restore unity?

The Conciliar Movement

Church theorists had long speculated on who might rule the church if the pope should become incompetent. Some suggested the college of cardinals would be the logical body, but the college was split in two, so some theologians suggested that a general council of bishops might be able to restore the order and reform the abuses of the church. There was ample precedent for church councils to meet to resolve controversies, for as early as the fourth century, Emperor Constantine had called the bishops together at Nicaea (see Chapter 5). However, these new "conciliarists" wanted to convert the church to a kind of constitutional monarchy in which the power of the popes would be limited. This would be a dramatic step, but the times seemed to call for radical measures.

The first test of the Conciliar movement came at the Council of Pisa, convened in 1409 by cardinals of both Rome and Avignon. This council asserted its supremacy by deposing the two reigning popes and electing a new pope. Although this should have solved the problem, it only exacerbated it—the two previous popes would not step down, so now *three* popes reigned.

Finally, a second council was called. Some 400 churchmen assembled at the Council of Constance (1414–1418), which was the greatest international gathering in the Middle Ages. This august body deposed all three of the popes and elected a Roman cardinal—Martin V (r. 1417–1431). The Great Schism was finally over and the Western church was once more united under a single head. However, never again did the popes have the power that the medieval popes had, and church councils gathered periodically to address changes in the church.

NEW CRITICS OF THE CHURCH

Not surprisingly, as men and women became disenchanted with the established church, they sought new ways to approach God so as to address the pressing challenges of the age. Criticisms of the church that had been expressed periodically throughout the Middle Ages appeared with more urgency in this age

FIGURE 9.4
Paolo di Giovanni Fei, Saint Catherine of Siena persuades Pope Gregory XI to leave his exile in Avignon and return to Rome, ca. 1447.

of crisis. The preacher John Ball was simply one of many who offered a different view of religion, and even the dreaded inquisition could not silence the new critics.

The Englishman and Oxford theologian John Wycliffe (1320?–1384) offered a serious critique that struck at the heart of the organized church. Wycliffe argued that there was no scriptural basis for papal claims of earthly power and that the Bible should be a Christian's sole authority. In the course of his writings, he attacked many of the practices of the medieval church (such as pilgrimages, the veneration of saints, and many of the rituals that had grown up over the centuries). Furthermore, Wycliffe argued that the church (and the popes in particular) should renounce earthly

John Wycliffe

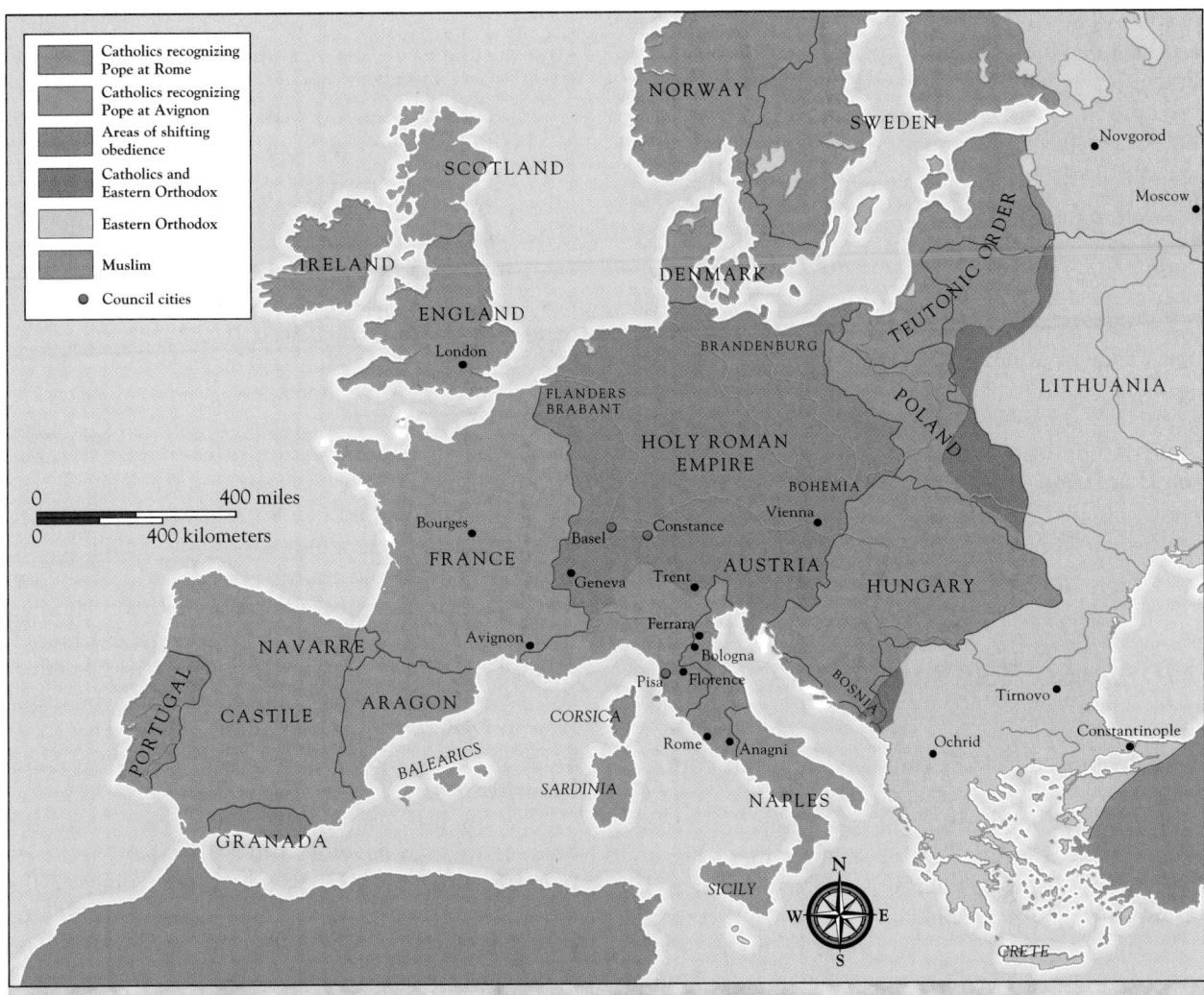

THINKING ABOUT GEOGRAPHY

MAP 9.2 *The Great Schism, 1378–1417*

This map shows the split loyalties of countries divided between the competing popes in Rome and Avignon. ◆ **Notice** the areas of specific loyalty. **Consider** what political advantage each country would gain by its allegiance. ◆ **Consider** what contributed to the Holy Roman Empire's shifting allegiances.

power, leaving it to kings. As he put it, "the pope [should] leave his worldly lordship to worldly lords." Wycliffe wanted a more simple church, led by a clergy that rejected all wealth. This would have been a major renunciation because the church was by far the greatest landlord in Europe. There was a great deal at stake.

Though Wycliffe's ideas were profoundly threatening to the established church, he had powerful protectors in the English court, who kept him **Jan Hus** unharmed until he died. Many of his followers (called Lollards) were condemned, but not until the early 1400s when his ideas seemed to stimulate treasonous acts. One of the most famous proponents of some of Wycliffe's ideas was Jan Hus (1373–1415), a popular preacher and rector of the university in Prague. Hus and his followers demanded a reform of the church, and his ideas were joined to a desire for Bohemian freedom from German dominance. Hus was certain that his beliefs were correct and defended them before the influential Council of Constance. However, the Czech scholar was found guilty of heresy and was burned. An eyewitness to the execution wrote that Hus died bravely with the words of the Lord's Prayer on his lips. Many Czechs remembered Hus as a martyr both to conscience and to a growing desire for Czech independence. While the council could silence Hus, it could not silence the growing numbers of voices calling for a significant transformation of the medieval church. As we will see in Chapter 11, these calls for reform would eventually be heard.

More Destruction: The Hundred Years' War, 1337–1453

As if famine, plague, revolts, and religious controversy weren't enough, England and France entered into the Hundred Years' War—a century-long conflict that became the closing chapter in an age in which long-standing traditions and social contracts crumbled. The issue that triggered the conflict was the succession to the throne of France—the Capetians' good luck in producing male heirs finally ran out in 1328, when the last Capetian died. The nearest male relative was King Edward III of England, son of a Capetian king's (Philip IV's) daughter (Isabel). The Parlement of Paris (the supreme court of France) claimed that a woman could not transmit a claim to the crown, so Philip VI of Valois, a first cousin of the previous ruler, became king. Edward at first did not dispute this decision, but he soon found cause to do so. Document 9.1 on page D9.1 reveals the early motivations of this complex war.

ENGLAND VS. FRANCE

There were two other reasons for the two kings to clash: one was economic—urban revolts in Flanders gave Philip VI an excuse to interfere in the lucrative wool trade between England and Flanders. The Flemish asked Edward to assert his claim to the French crown so the rich trade could continue unim-

peded. The second cause was feudal—the French king wanted to claim the status of liege lord over the lands in southern France held by Edward III. (See Chapter 8 to review how the English kings came to hold land in France as vassals to the king of France). Edward, as a king himself, did not believe he should accept Philip as his liege lord. In response, Philip declared Edward's lands forfeit and Edward decided to exert his dynastic claim to be king of both England and France.

The long struggle began with some stunning English victories. The English first secured their communications across the Channel with a naval victory at Sluys in 1340 (see Map 9.3); they then could turn to a land invasion of France. *New weapons* Although the French outnumbered the English, the English skillfully used new tactics and new weapons to supplement their mounted knights. In their wars against the Scots in the thirteenth century, the English learned of the effectiveness of the Scottish longbow and brought archers to fight against the French cavalry. The longbow was a simple yet highly effective device that had a greater range than the crossbow and could be fired with unprecedented speed. A longbowman could loose up to 10 arrows a minute, compared with the crossbowman's 2.

The English armies also took advantage of the pike—a weapon developed in Switzerland and used to good effect against the mounted armies of the Holy Roman Emperor. Footsoldiers wielded the long spears and braced them on the ground to fend off the charge of mounted knights. Some English footsoldiers brought pikes to France to support England's horsemen, who were outnumbered by the French cavalry.

While longbows and pikes challenged the ascendancy of mounted knights, their obsolescence was sealed with the spread of gunpowder from China. Iron shot appeared in England as early as 1346 and Italy in 1341, but the powder was unstable and did not explode immediately. In the 1420s, a new kind of gunpowder was developed that was not only stable, but exploded virtually instantly. Then guns and cannons became relatively efficient weapons. Throughout the war, desperate soldiers used new (and frequently unreliable) guns to bring down knights, and equally desperate armorers tried to make plate armor stronger and curved so it could deflect bullets. However, the mounted knights simply grew too expensive and ineffective for the new warfare; the future lay with the infantry.

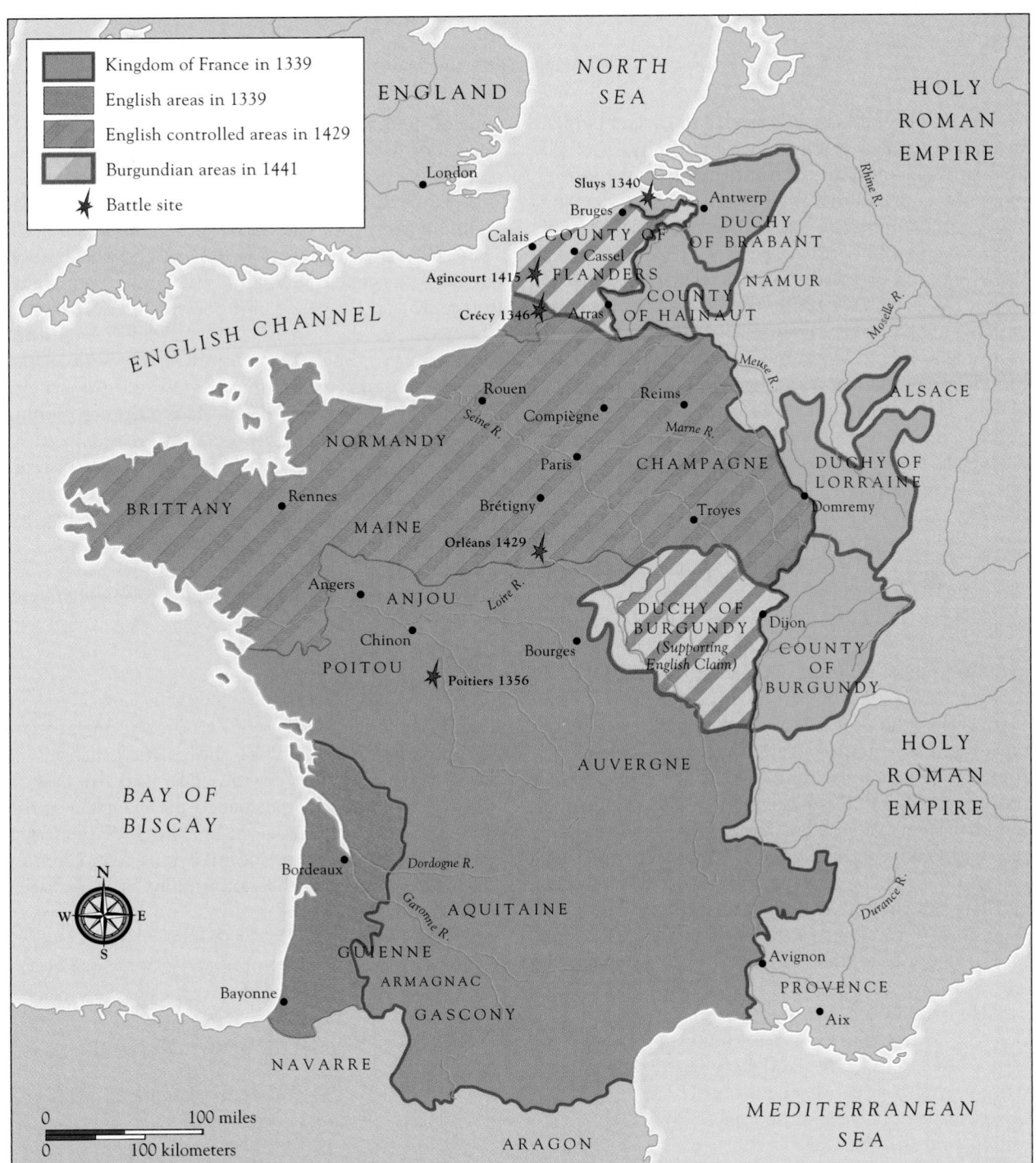

Legend:
- Kingdom of France in 1339
- English areas in 1339
- English controlled areas in 1429
- Burgundian areas in 1441
- ★ Battle site

ENGLAND

NORTH SEA

HOLY ROMAN EMPIRE

London

Rhine R.

Sluys 1340

Bruges

Antwerp

DUCHY OF BRABANT

Calais

COUNTY OF FLANDERS

Cassel

NAMUR

Agincourt 1415

Crécy 1346

Arras

COUNTY OF HAINAUT

ENGLISH CHANNEL

Meuse R.

ALSACE

Rouen

Reims

Seine R.

Compiègne

Marne R.

Moselle R.

NORMANDY

Paris

CHAMPAGNE

DUCHY OF LORRAINE

BRITTANY

Rennes

Brétigny

Troyes

Domremy

MAINE

Orléans 1429

Angers

Loire R.

ANJOU

DUCHY OF BURGUNDY

Dijon

Chinon

Bourges

(Supporting English Claim)

COUNTY OF BURGUNDY

POITOU

Poitiers 1356

BAY OF BISCAY

AUVERGNE

HOLY ROMAN EMPIRE

Bordeaux

Dordogne R.

Garonne R.

AQUITAINE

Durance R.

GUIENNE

Avignon

Bayonne

ARMAGNAC

PROVENCE

GASCONY

Aix

NAVARRE

MEDITERRANEAN SEA

0   100 miles

0   100 kilometers

ARAGON

N W E S

THINKING ABOUT GEOGRAPHY

MAP 9.3 *The Hundred Years' War, 1337–1453*

This map shows the Hundred Years' War between England and France. ✒ **Notice** that the major battle sites and areas of war were in the north, even though the English claims in France lay in the south. **What** does this pattern of warfare suggest about the significance of the various causes of the war? ✒ **Locate** the battle at Orléans, where Joan of Arc made her decisive victory. **Consider** why its location along the Loire River might prove strategically significant.

The English—led by Edward III and accompanied by his son the Black Prince (see Biography)—forged across the Channel to confront the superior force of French mounted knights. Edward brought a strong

English victories infantry, and eyewitness accounts of the Battle of Crécy in 1346 described a sky blackened by English arrows. By the end of the battle, the flower of French knighthood lay crushed, which struck a blow against feudalism itself when "those who fought" lost. In this victory, the English had secured Flanders and the important port of Calais. The strategy was repeated at Poitiers in 1356, and the exhausted French were forced to sue for peace (the Peace of Bretigny) in 1360. By the terms of this peace, King Edward renounced his claim to the French throne in exchange for Calais and enlarged holdings in Aquitaine.

The French were not willing to allow so much of their land to remain in English hands, so the war was reopened in 1369 under the French king Charles V (r. 1364–1380). He introduced a wise strategy of avoiding major military confrontation and instead wearing down the English forces on the Continent. During this phase of the war, soldiers on both sides devastated the countryside, plundering villages and ruining crops and vineyards. The illustration in Figure 9.5 shows soldiers pillaging a house during the Hundred Years' War. They carry out chests and barrels, and some search for valuables hidden in pots and jars while others break open wine casks. This sort of civilian destruction contributed to the misery of the fourteenth century.

The cautious tactics of Charles V led to French victories. By 1380, the English had almost been pushed out

A seesaw battle of France—they held only Calais and a small strip of land between Bordeaux and Bayonne. But once again the English rallied, and the last stage of the war (from 1415–1453) was marked by rapidly changing fortunes between the two sides. Early in the fifteenth century, France itself seemed to be disintegrating, for the powerful duke of Burgundy used the turmoil to increase his own land at the expense of the French kings. (Map 9.3 shows the location of Burgundy.) The Burgundians leapt into the fray on the

side of the English, and the alliance was at first devastating to the French crown. With this new ally, the English king Henry V (r. 1413–1422) reasserted his claims to the French throne, invaded, and had a brilliant victory at the Battle of Agincourt in 1415. This battle was a replay of Crécy, and the French cavalry was defeated again. The French king was forced to sue for peace and declare his heir (called the Dauphin) illegitimate. England got direct control of northern France as far south as the Loire River and the promise that Henry's son would inherit the throne of France. For all practical purposes, France was defeated. The Dauphin could not accept these terms, but he seemed unable to rally any systematic resistance. In 1428, the English laid siege to Orléans, and its fall would have assured the English control of all the lands north of the Loire River. It seemed it would take a miracle to restore the French monarchy, and remarkably, many people believed they got one.

JOAN OF ARC

During these darkest days of France, a young peasant girl—Joan of Arc (1412–1431) believed she saw visions in which angels urged her to lead the French troops to victory. She persuaded the Dauphin of the authenticity of her mission, and he gave her command of an army. Joan donned armor and almost miraculously stirred the determination of France's

FIGURE 9.5
Soldiers pillaging a farm.

Biography

EDWARD: THE BLACK PRINCE, 1330–1376

❧ **Notice** the clash in values between the perfect chivalrous knight and the new circumstances of the fourteenth century that made his skills less effective.

❧ **Notice also** how the use of mercenary troops led to more misery for the civilian population.

When King Edward III was only 17 years old, he fathered his eldest son, named him Edward, and prepared him to be his heir. The young Edward was tutored in reading, writing, Latin, and arithmetic, but his real education took place outdoors in the training for war. By the time he was eight years old, he had a complete suit of armor (with a spare helmet for jousting). The boy was also prepared to receive stately visitors: When he was seven he received a delegation of important cardinals, and the documents say he was dressed in a new robe of purple velvet and a special hat with a scarlet border sewn with pearls. (He would maintain his love of elaborate dress and jewels throughout his life.)

The young man learned the art of war well, and at 16 he accompanied his father to France to participate in the opening volleys of the Hundred Years' War. The young Prince of Wales (a title given to the heir to the English throne) proved brilliant in battle, and he is remembered as the "Black Prince," probably because of the color of his armor. Froissart, a chronicler of the war, describes (probably with more romance than accuracy) that at the Battle of Crécy the young prince was surrounded, but his father did not send help, allowing him to earn his "spurs"—that is, to become knighted. In 1356, he commanded his own troops and won his most famous victory over the French at Poitiers, where he took the French king John II captive. The Black Prince treated the captive king with all the courtesy that a code of chivalry required and collected a huge ransom of 3,000,000 gold coins for his prisoner. In addition, the French negotiated a treaty that gave the French lands of Aquitaine to the English. The prince seemed at the height of his glory, and he was also given the title Prince of Aquitaine to mark his victories.

Much to his father's dismay, Prince Edward married his cousin Joan (one year older than he), who seemed unsuitable for many reasons: She was so closely related to him that they needed a papal dispensation to marry, and she was already divorced once and a widow. Nevertheless, the Black Prince insisted on having his way, and he married the woman the chroniclers described as "pleasing and wise." The prince seemed to embody the highest medieval values: he was romantic and a great warrior. His eulogy boasted "he never attacked a people whom he did not conquer; he never besieged a city which he did not take." He loved jousting, falconry, hunting, and gambling, and he spent money lavishly (way beyond his means). But the medieval world was rapidly changing, and the Black Prince was not prepared for this new world.

In the course of the warfare in France, the prince had to rely more and more on mercenary troops, and they were expensive. He tried to raise money in Aquitaine and so alienated his people that he was confronted with urban and rural revolts in his lands. He became involved in warfare in Spain—to help the besieged ruler, Pedro the Cruel—in return for a promise of wealth, which he never collected. His hired troops plundered the lands of France in recompense for their back pay. The days when being the perfect chivalrous knight was enough seemed to be over—money and land armies were the new essentials.

Chivalric Warrior and Spendthrift

The Black Prince was ultimately defeated by disease—another mark of the fourteenth century. He survived the bubonic plague that had taken his younger sister in 1348, but while fighting in Spain, he caught some other debilitating illness. He seems to have suffered from dysentery or malaria, and his limbs became so swollen that he could hardly get up from his bed. By the age of 38, the great warrior had reached the end of his active career. By 1371, the Black Prince gave up his lands in Aquitaine—telling his father they did not offer enough monetary resources to support him. He lingered on until 1376, when he succumbed to the illnesses that had plagued him.

The English remembered him as the "unconquerable prince," the greatest warrior in an age that loved knights in shining black armor. The young son of the Black Prince would rule in his stead as Richard II, and he would have to confront the peasant revolts that further disrupted England in the fourteenth century.

FIGURE 9.6
Joan of Arc announces the liberation of Orléans, fifteenth century.

armies and lifted the siege at Orléans. Figure 9.6 shows Joan dressed in armor announcing the liberation of Orléans to the prince who emerged from the castle to welcome her. After this victory, she escorted the Dauphin to Reims—the city where French kings were traditionally crowned—where he received the crown of France, thus renouncing the previous treaty. The French embraced the cause of their new king and the new national spirit seemed to revitalize the French armies. The illustrator of Figure 9.6 shows this spirit by portraying the many knights following Joan

as she leads on her stunning white horse. They rallied, and by 1453 only Calais was left in English hands.

However, Joan did not live to see the victory. She was captured in 1431 by the Burgundians, who turned her over to their English allies who put her on trial for witchcraft and heresy. The record of her trial provides a fascinating *Joan executed* glimpse into the experience of this extraordinary woman. She repeatedly restated her conviction that her voices were from God and that she was following a just cause. Ultimately, she refused to abandon her men's clothing and acknowledge that she had been wrong, so she was condemned to be burned at the stake. Document 9.3 on page D9.2 reveals this deeply poignant episode in her trial. The French honored Joan of Arc as a savior of France, and in 1920 she was declared a saint of the Catholic Church.

RESULTS OF THE WAR

The new weaponry that was used during the Hundred Years' War set European armies on a new course. The feudal system that demanded knights' military service began to break down, and lords increasingly accepted money (called "scutage") instead of military service. Now lords could hire professional armies—called "free companies" because they had no feudal ties and sold their services to the highest bidder—which were becoming more effective than traditional knights. (The knights continued to fight in their beloved tournaments long after they were less welcome on the battlefields.) Like many other kings, the Black Prince featured in the Biography had repeated difficulties paying his free companies, and they ravaged the countryside in lieu of their pay. Under these pressures, the deterioration of the feudal system accelerated into what is sometimes called "bastard feudalism," in which the old ties of loyalty were replaced with cash payments. Nobles, like kings, simply hired soldiers, dressed them in elaborate uniforms sporting the special colors of the noble families, and created their own private armies.

As a result of the Hundred Years' War, the English were expelled from French soil; the French king emerged more powerful than all his vassals, and the slow consolidation of royal rule was effectively complete. The monarchy had a permanent army, a strong tax base, and a great deal of prestige among people who were coming to see themselves as "French."

England had a longer struggle after its loss in the war. England's monarchy was seriously weakened as Parliament took more control of the purse strings after the wartime excesses. During the turmoil, the Lan-

Wars of the Roses

caster and York families unleashed a civil war as they competed for the throne. Each family had a different color rose as its emblem, so this sporadic conflict was called the "Wars of the Roses" (1455–1485). The fighting perpetuated the worst aspects of feudal life as it degenerated into local skirmishes orchestrated by the nobility, and many old noble families were decimated in the course

of this war. In 1485, Henry Tudor, a Lancastrian, finally vanquished Richard III of the house of York at the Battle of Bosworth Field and was crowned Henry VII (r. 1485–1509). Henry proved to be a very competent king. To heal the breach between the noble factions, he married Elizabeth of York; at last, the civil war ended. England was now freed from its entanglements on the Continent and was poised to expand beyond the seas (see Chapter 12).

Responses to Disaster and Despair

As war and revolt have shown, one of the ways people responded to the fourteenth-century disasters was to consider new approaches to old problems. Wycliffe and Hus questioned church practices; Edward III of England thought of new battle strategies to confront French knights. These are only two of many famous and anonymous people who changed their world with creative new ideas. Philosophers, writers, and artists, too, produced works that dramatically changed the direction of Western thought.

WILLIAM OF OCKHAM RECONSIDERS SCHOLASTICISM

Within a century after Thomas Aquinas's brilliant synthesis (described in Chapter 8), a new breed of thinkers challenged the premises of scholasticism and questioned the ties between faith and reason. William of Ockham (1285?–1349) was the most prominent of these thinkers. Scholasticism was based on the idea that thinkers could extract general truths (or "universals") from individual cases. Ockham was a brilliant English philosopher who argued that universals had no connection with reality, and this philosophy was called "New Nominalism." (Ockham used "nominalism," derived from the Latin word for "name," because he said that universals were only convenient names for things.) For Ockham, philosophy was an interesting logical, linguistic exercise, not a path to certain truth. New Nominalists believed that it was impossible to know God or prove his existence through reason—because God was all-powerful, he did not have to act logically. Therefore, according to Ockham, scholasticism was a misguided waste of time.

So what should philosophers do? Ockham's studies spawned a decline in abstract logic, but a rise in interest in scientific observation that would bear much fruit in later generations. Ockham also founded a fundamental principle that remained the basis of much scientific analysis. Called "Ockham's razor," this principle says that between alternative explanations for the same phenomenon, the simpler is always to be preferred. People who have studied the material world ever since would look to simple, elegant explanations to satisfy Ockham's razor. New Nominalism became popular in universities, and Ockhamite philosophy became known as the *via moderna* ("modern way"). Indeed, intellectuals were beginning to reject the old and look at the world in a new way.

New Literary Giants

In the fourteenth century, more authors began to write in the vernacular, their national languages, instead of Latin, which had been the language of great literature throughout the Middle Ages. (Latin still remained the language of the church and of official government documents.) In the Middle Ages, romances and other poetry had been written in the vernacular (see Chapter 8), but in fourteenth-century Italy in particular, a new kind of literature emerged that explored people's place in the world. Italian poets from Tuscany made Italian a literary language and composed some of the greatest literature of all time.

The first of these writers was Dante Alighieri (1265–1321), who was born in Florence. In 1302, he

Dante became embroiled in the turbulent political situation of his city and was exiled. He always hoped to return to his beloved city, but never succeeded, and he grew to be a bitter, disillusioned man wandering from city to city until he died in 1321. While in exile, he composed his masterpiece, now called the *Divine Comedy*. The work became so popular that a century after his death, Florence recognized his genius and commissioned the painting shown in Figure 9.7 to honor the man they had exiled. He stands in the center holding the book that brought such posthumous fame to the man and the city that spawned him.

The *Divine Comedy* is a magnificent allegory of a soul's journey through despair to salvation. The lengthy work is divided into three sections—Hell, Purgatory, and Paradise—and the poet journeys through them all. He is first led through Hell by Virgil, the Roman poet whose works still formed the

basis of a good education. Dante described the punishments of the damned in gruesome detail: In one location he saw "long lines of people in a river of excrement that seemed the overflow of the world's latrines," and in these pits Dante placed his contemporaries (as well as historical figures) who deserved punishment. The damned are shown in Figure 9.7 on the lower left descending into Hell. Dante then leaves Hell and climbs the mountain of Purgatory (shown in the background of Figure 9.7), where sinners who would ultimately be saved were doing penance for their sins. Finally, Dante was led into Paradise by a mysterious woman—Beatrice—who was reputed to be the love of the poet's life.

Some scholars consider the *Divine Comedy* a perfect medieval work: It incorporates Aquinas's theology and Aristotle's science, and the whole work has the complexity of a Gothic cathedral or a *Summa Theologiae* (the philosophic summaries described in Chapter 8). Other scholars see in the work something new—a departure from the medieval world that shaped the poet. Dante, after all, was a layman who presumed to express theology of salvation. Furthermore, he articulated the growing criticism of the medieval church by placing many popes in Hell. Finally, his beloved guide through Hell and Purgatory was a classic poet—Virgil, who represented reason. His final tour through heaven was conducted by Beatrice, who was an allegory of faith. As we will see in Chapter 10, many thinkers who like Dante struggled with the despair of the age would find solace in pagan classics and faith in God's grace.

Another Florentine who had a profound impact on literature was Giovanni Boccaccio (1313–1375), who witnessed the devastating plague as it swept through his city. In his most famous *Boccaccio* work, *The Decameron*, Boccaccio offers a poignant eyewitness description of the plague, with insights into how various people responded to catastrophe, for he said some shut themselves off from everyone else, others prayed diligently in hopes of avoiding early death, and still others denied themselves nothing, "drinking and reveling incessantly from tavern to tavern." This description set the stage for the heart of the book, in which 10 young people escape to a villa outside Florence and decide to amuse themselves by telling stories. *The Decameron* is the collection of the stories they tell, and most are highly entertaining.

The stories reflect a new, permissive attitude that arose in the wake of the plague, for the stories talk frankly of sex, lies, and ordinary people. The heroes

FIGURE 9.7
Domenico di Michelino, *Dante Standing Before the City of Florence*, 1465.

are not knights or philosophers, but clever men and women who live by their wits, and their stories were intended more to amuse than to teach moral lessons. In his later years, Boccaccio became uneasy with his lighthearted works, and in a letter written in 1373 he urged someone to not let women read his stories, warning, "You know how much in them is less than decent and opposed to modesty." However, there was no return to a more modest, conservative age—the fourteenth century had disrupted much that was traditional, and many people welcomed a new way to look at life. In these dark times, many found a lighthearted tribute to pleasure particularly satisfying.

One of the world's most gifted poets—the Englishman Geoffrey Chaucer (1340?–1400)—also drew from tales like Boccaccio's to offer a different view of the turbulent fourteenth century. Chaucer's most famous work, *The Canterbury Tales*, was written in English and tells of a group of 29 pilgrims who journey from Southwark (outside London) to Canterbury to the shrine of Thomas Becket. Like Boccaccio's youths, Chaucer's pilgrims tell tales to pass the time on their journey, but unlike Boccaccio, Chaucer draws each pilgrim vividly, with a clear personality so each stands out as an individual. The stories are varied, from knightly romances to bawdy tales, and they still delight readers today.

Chaucer

Chaucer's descriptions of the pilgrims offer a subtle, yet revealing, look at fourteenth-century society. He criticized corruption in the church by commenting on monks who would rather hunt than pray, or Friars who were not interested in the poor: "He knew the taverns well in every town. / The barmaids and innkeepers pleased his mind / Better than beggars and lepers and their kind." However, Chaucer was also a medieval man who looked back to what he imagined was a golden age when knights were virtuous crusaders, priests cared nothing for money, and scholars loved only knowledge. If that golden age ever existed, it was gone by the fourteenth century—money was rapidly becoming the measure of success, and the future belonged to bright individuals with as much character as Chaucer's pilgrims.

A NEW VIEW: JAN VAN EYCK

Just as Chaucer carefully and precisely created his pilgrims with words on a page, painters in Flanders began to re-create their world in paint with a precision that continues to astonish the viewer. One of the most famous of the Flemish artists is Jan van Eyck (1370?–1440?), who was among the first to use oil paint—a medium that allowed the artist to capture realistic details. In the painting of a husband and his bride shown in Figure 9.8, van Eyck portrays the scene with amazing realism, down to the witnesses to the marriage who are reflected in the mirror on the wall in the background. Both the new medium and the technical skill of the artist point to the new directions that European culture took in this period.

Like Chaucer and Dante, van Eyck was breaking new ground in the arts, but he also looked back to the Middle Ages and preserved much of their ideals. In the medieval world, people looked to intense and detailed symbolism to both *Realism and symbolism* reveal and explain their world, and van Eyck filled the painting shown in Figure 9.8 with symbolism. The dog is a symbol of fidelity, and the carving on the bedpost is of Saint Margaret, the patron saint of childbirth. The single lighted candle indicates God's presence and blessing of the couple's wedding night. The combination of realism infused with symbolic meaning is characteristic of the late Middle Ages, and the Flemish painter captured this spirit perfectly.

The disasters of the long fourteenth century had caused many to question their traditional views and values. As the ordered world they had known was crumbling, however, room was being made for new ideas and new approaches. As we will see in the next chapter, the West would take a fresh and exciting path, but in the East, dramatic changes were also taking place. There, new empires were forming that dominated the political landscapes of these regions for centuries.

FIGURE 9.8

Jan van Eyck, *Giovanni Arnolfini and His Bride*, 1434.

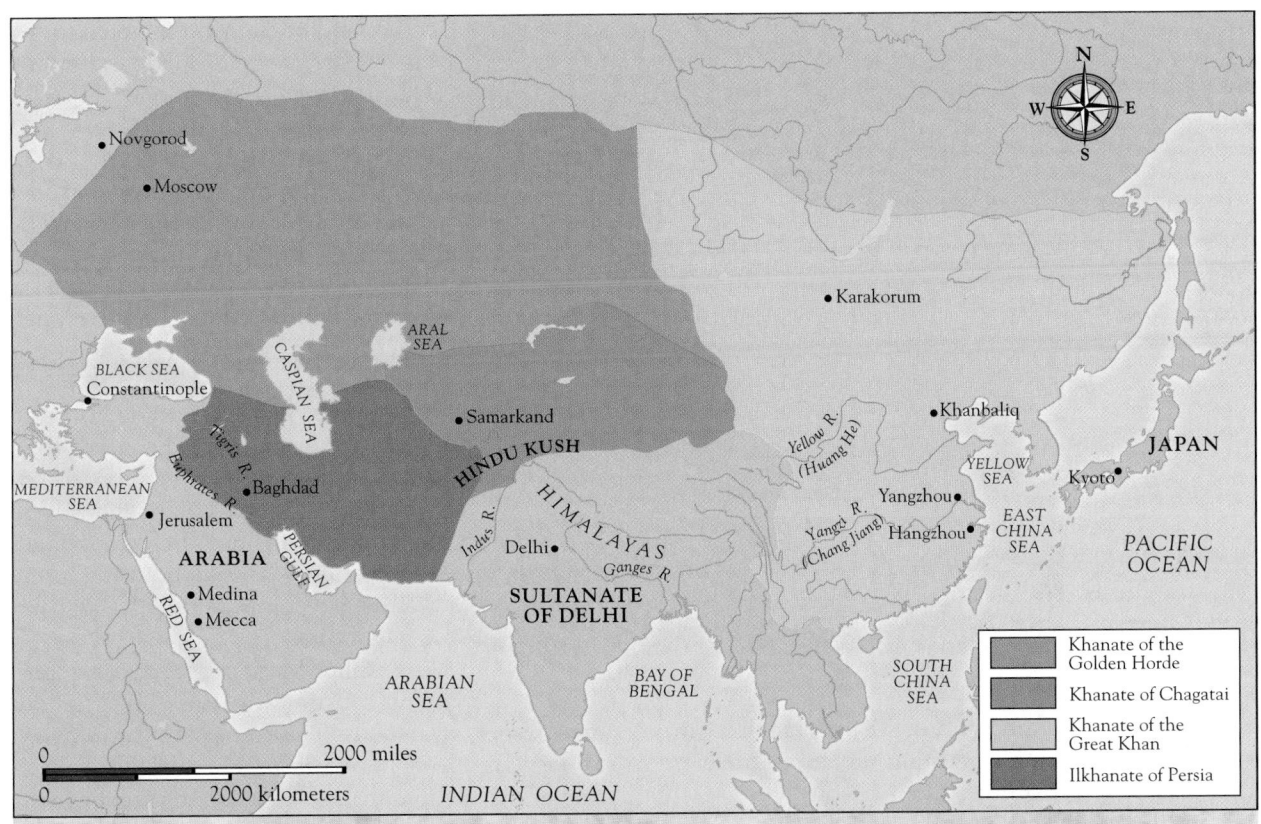

THINKING ABOUT GEOGRAPHY

MAP 9.4 *The Mongol Empire, ca. 1300*

This map shows the greatest expanse of the Mongol Empire as it extended from the Pacific Ocean to the Black Sea. ❧ **Notice** the extent of the empire and the scale of the map. **Consider** how many different cultures were ruled by the Mongols, and the problems the Mongols might face governing such a large empire. ❧ **How** might the Mongolian conquests have stimulated cross-cultural contacts between the West and non-West? ❧ **Locate** Constantinople and Novgorod. **Consider** why the Byzantine Empire and the Russian state would be threatened by the proximity of the Mongol Empire.

Empires in the East

EASTERN UNIVERSALISM: THE MONGOLS

As early as the thirteenth century, while the West struggled between localism and centralization, dynamic conquerors swept out of Mongolia and established a new, unified empire extending from eastern Europe across Asia to the Pacific Ocean. In 1206, Genghis Khan (r. 1206–1227) united diverse nomadic groups and forged a formidable army that he led with consummate skill. Genghis Khan was an extraordinary figure who is remembered for his appalling cruelty as well as for his wisdom and talent as a leader, for after the violence of his initial conquest, Genghis established a peaceful, tolerant rule. He implemented the first Mongol written language and promulgated the first law code for his nomadic people. His grandson, Kublai Khan (r. 1260–1294), was

FIGURE 9.9
Venetian merchants trading cloth for spices, mid-fourteenth century.

an equally powerful ruler, whose wealthy empire, centered in China, offered a tantalizing lure to travelers from the west. (See Global Connections.)

Map 9.4 shows the remarkable extent of the Mongol Empire in about 1300—from China and Korea in the east to Moscow and Ukraine in the west. The rulers of the Scandinavian/Slavic state *Mongol Empire* centered in Kiev had already moved their capital to the far north in Novgorod, and this Russian state had to pay tribute to the Mongol Empire to its south. This empire encompassed an extraordinary diversity of peoples and religions—from Muslims to Christians to Buddhists—and it accommodated them seemingly without conflict. This unified empire also created a huge trade area through which goods and ideas traveled easily.

As we saw in Chapter 8, the Venetians in particular were well placed to take advantage of this trade. By the fourteenth century, the Venetians had established many trading posts where they could engage in a lucrative commerce. Figure 9.9 shows Venetian merchants trading cloth for oriental products—possibly spices—with traders who had landed in a Mediterranean port.

Certainly the most famous western Europeans who took advantage of the Venetian experience in trade were the Venetians Marco Polo (1254–1324) and his father and uncle, who traveled to the far reaches of the Mongolian Empire. During several trading journeys, the Polos traveled all *Marco Polo* the way to the court of the great Kublai Khan in Khanbalik, as described in Global Connections. The journey took them three and a half years by horseback. The Polos stayed at the khan's court for seventeen years, and Marco apparently served as an emissary of the khan himself. When the Polos returned home to Venice, they brought back a wealth of spices, silks, and other luxurious curiosities. The extravagant items were so impressive that other anonymous merchants followed; by 1300 there was even a community of Italians living in China.

Perhaps Marco Polo's most important contribution was a book about his voyages, which has been translated into English as *The Travels of Marco Polo*. His writings told of things that people in the West found unbelievable. For example, the merchants found it extraordinary that the Chinese used paper money; as Marco wrote: "The coinage of this paper money is authenticated with as much form and ceremony as if it were actually of pure gold and silver." Even more astonishing, Marco described "a sort of black stone, which they dig out of the mountains. When lighted it burns like charcoal." The Chinese had been burning coal since about 100 B.C., but in the West such a feat seemed implausible. Few believed the exotic tales of the traveler, but the book did excite the imaginations of adventurers. It fueled the great age of exploration that followed—Christopher Columbus carried a well-marked copy of the book through his voyages.

THE OTTOMAN EMPIRE, CA. 1300–1566

Change continued to come to eastern Europe as more peoples emigrated from further east. In the thirteenth century, a group of Asiatic nomads (later called Ottoman Turks) migrated westward from the expansive Asian steppes. Along the way, they converted to Islam and brought new vigor to Muslim expansion. The Turks were ruled by sultans, who were supposedly the

Global Connections

The Mongols Establish the Yuan Dynasty in China

▪ **Consider** how the Mongols' desire to preserve their identity benefited Western travelers. **NOTICE** how the Mongols were able to rule the majority Chinese.

In the mid-1220s, eastern Europeans had briefly fought the Mongols—fierce warriors who swept in from the steppes of Asia. The Mongols' brilliant leader, Genghis Khan (Chingiskhan), had conquered lands from the Pacific Ocean to the Volga River. Turning back to address problems in his heartland, he died in 1227. On his deathbed, he reportedly predicted that his stunning success on the battlefield would lead to the loss of the nomadic life he so loved. He said: "My descendants will go clothed in gold-embroidered stuffs; they will feed on the choicest meats, they will bestride superb steeds and press in their arms the most beautiful of young women. And they will have forgotten to whom they owe all that." He was wrong about history forgetting his accomplishments, but he was right about the changing lifestyle of his descendants. His grandson Kublai Khan, robed in golden cloth, became the Emperor of China—the first leader in the Yuan Dynasty—as well as the Great Khan of the Mongols.

When Genghis's great empire split apart into four empires (see Map 9.4), the western empire—the Khanate of the Golden Horde—threatened to extend its conquests into eastern Europe. However, the wealthiest portion—the Khanate of the Great Khan—lay in China. The ruling Mongols faced the problem of how to control this vast populous land while maintaining their Mongol identity. In the Ilkhanate of Persia, Mongols eventually were assimilated into Persian/Muslim culture, and the danger of assimilation was even stronger in the huge ancient land of China. Kublai took two steps to solidify the Mongols as the rulers of China. First, he moved his capital from Karakorum in Mongolia (shown on Map 9.4) to a newly built city near modern Beijing. He named the city Ta-Tu (Great Capital), but everyone knew this was a Mongol creation and called it "Khanbaliq" (City of the Khan). Second, in 1272, Kublai issued an edict claiming that the new dynasty would henceforth take the name of Yuan, which means "the origin." He had now firmly established his empire in China and assumed the trappings of Chinese emperors.

Now that he was established as the Chinese emperor, Kublai had to use subtle means to preserve his Mongolian heritage. Kublai reputedly planted steppe grass near his palace to always remind himself of his roots, and he kept 10,000 white mares to provide milk for his family to drink during ceremonies. More significant, he created a separation between the Mongol overlords and the more numerous Chinese. He forbade intermarriage between the two and made it a crime for Chinese even to learn Mongolian, the language of government. To satisfy his administrative needs, Kublai relied on non-Chinese people—Arabs, Persians, and even westerners—from throughout his empire. In light of this tolerance—indeed acceptance—of strangers (as long as they weren't Chinese) it's perhaps not surprising that the Mongols also sponsored trade among the vast regions of all the Khans. Indeed, when the Venetian merchants, the Polos, arrived at Khanbaliq in about 1262, they found a welcoming environment. Marco Polo wrote that Kublai himself "entered graciously into conversation with them and made earnest inquiries on the subject of the western parts of the world."

Thanks to Kublai's policies, commerce and travel quickened during the Yuan Dynasty. But the movement of peoples brought unforeseen results. In the 1330s, plague erupted in southwestern China and spread throughout the Mongol empires, finally reaching the west as the Black Death in the 1340s. This catastrophe put overwhelming pressure on the empire, and in 1368 rebel Chinese forces—disdainful of their Mongol overlords—captured Khanbaliq. The Mongols fled China and returned to their homeland in the steppes of central Asia.

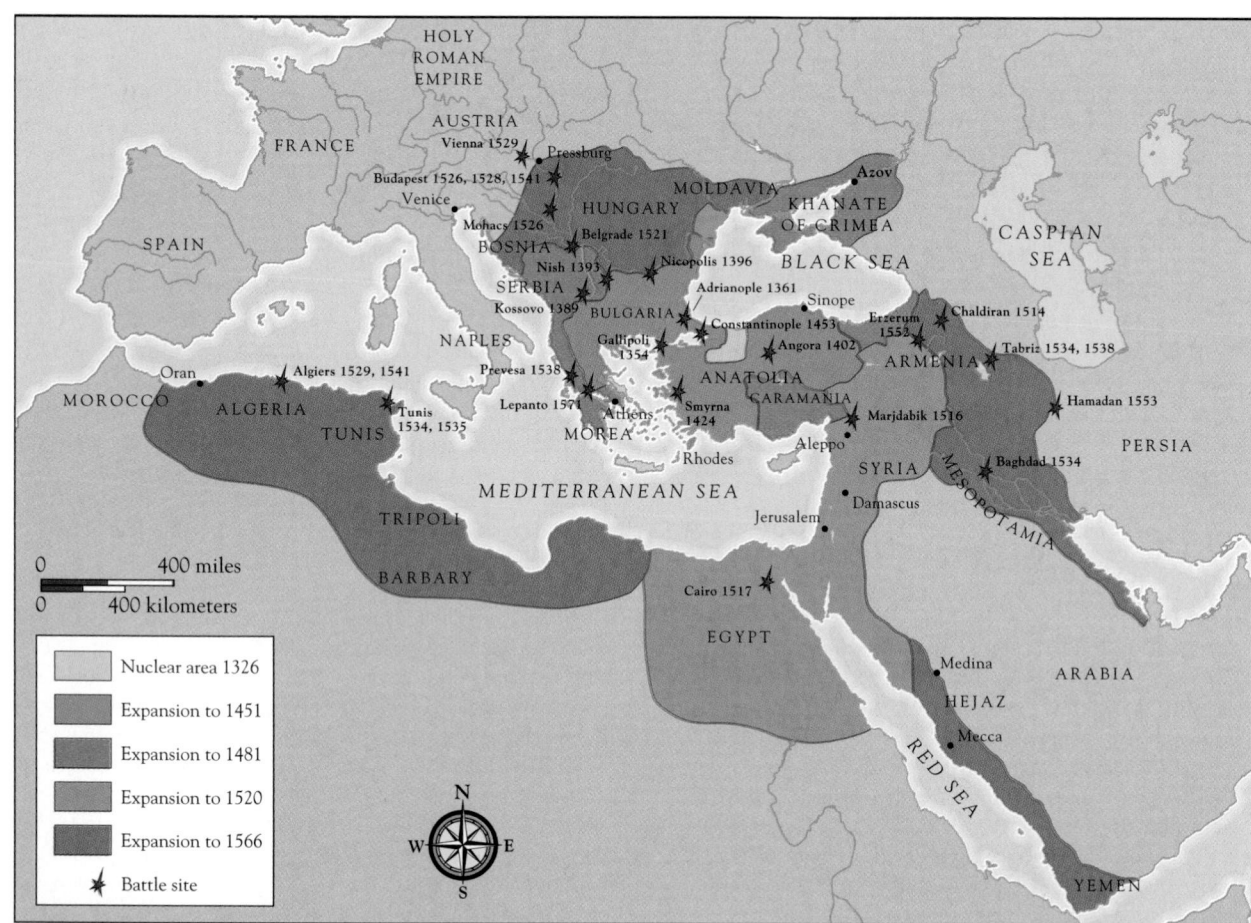

THINKING ABOUT GEOGRAPHY

MAP 9.5 *The Ottoman Empire, 1300–1566*

This map shows the spread of the Ottoman Empire, and the major battles that marked its expansion. ❖ **Notice** the nuclear area of the Turks in 1326. **Consider** how that placed them well to expand into the Byzantine Empire. ❖ **Locate** Constantinople. **Notice** the date of its fall and how it had been surrounded by 1451. **Was** there any chance it would have avoided capture with external help? ❖ **Notice** how far the Turks expanded into the Balkans and threatened Vienna, at the doorway to western Europe. **Consider** how western Europeans would have felt threatened by the invigorated empire as of 1566.

successors of Muhammad and therefore empowered to interpret Muslim law. In this way, the sultans drew on 700 years of history to legitimize their authority.

As Map 9.5 shows, by 1355 the Ottomans had effectively surrounded the Byzantine Empire that had stood for so long as a powerful state and a buffer for the West. Finally a powerful sultan—Mehmed II (r. 1451–1481)—committed his government to a pol-

icy of conquest. This sultan brought his cannons to the walls of Constantinople and attacked the ancient city by land and sea. After a heroic struggle, Constantinople fell in 1453, and the last emperor of the East— Constantine XI Palaeologus—died in the battle. The Byzantine Empire—heir to the Roman Empire—had fallen. Mehmed, now known as the "conqueror,"

Conquest of Constantinople

made Constantinople his capital under the name of Istanbul, by which it is known today. (The name was not formally changed until 1930.) Mehmed extended his power into the Balkans and around the Black Sea.

Almost a century later, the sultan Suleiman I the Magnificent (r. 1520–1566) brought the Ottoman Empire to the height of its power. As Map 9.5 shows, the Ottoman Empire extended throughout the Middle East and into North Africa. In order to secure his holdings in the eastern Mediterranean, Suleiman made the Ottomans into a major naval power. Suleiman's newly expanded navy had to confront the last Christian outpost in an otherwise Ottoman sea—the island of Rhodes (shown on Map 9.5), a highly fortified location held by the crusading order, Knights of Saint John. The sultan lost many men in repeated assaults on the fortified island, but eventually the knights surrendered. They were allowed to leave the island with their weapons and they moved to the island of Malta in the central Mediterranean, where they continued to fight against Muslim expansion. However, Suleiman's victory consolidated his hold in the east, and Christian merchants seeking to capitalize on the rich trade with the east found themselves confronted by the sultan's ships and tax collectors. As we will see in Chapter 12, westerners became highly motivated to find new routes to the rich lands of east Asia.

Suleiman I

With the sea secure, Suleiman turned his attention northward, and in 1529 he even threatened Vienna in the heartland of Europe. From now on, the new monarchies of western Europe would have to conduct their diplomatic and military escapades with the Turks in mind, and as we will see in the next chapters, the Turkish presence posed a significant threat to the West.

RUSSIA: THE THIRD ROME

Map 9.6 traces the rise of another great power in the east—the principality of Moscow. As the map shows, the princes of Moscow slowly expanded their territory. Ivan I (r. 1328–1341) extended his possessions and even recognized the need to curry favor with the powerful Mongol Khanate of the Golden Horde. Ivan received the right to collect the Mongol tribute within Russia, and he grew so rich in the process (probably by withholding most of the money due the Mongols) that he earned the nickname "moneybags." This money fostered the growth of the Russian

Empire in the fifteenth century, when the Mongols' fortunes declined. The khanate's hold on the territories of Russia and Ukraine loosened, and the Duchy of Moscow took the lead in overthrowing the last of Mongol rule.

Ivan III ("the Great") (r. 1462–1505), shown in Figure 9.10, pushed back the final Mongol advance on Moscow in 1480 and established himself as the first ruler of the new Russian state. Ivan had married a niece of the last Byzantine emperor, so the Russian declared himself the heir to the Byzantine Empire—he proclaimed Moscow the "Third Rome" and took the title caesar, or "tsar." His image shown in Figure 9.10 is portrayed in the traditional Byzantine manner and is designed to associate the ruler with the weight of a long tradition. His fur cape proclaimed his wealth and he holds a sword, the emblem of his victory in war. The tsar strove to reestablish the greatness of the Byzantine Empire, and like the Byzantines, he closely allied with the Orthodox Church in his land. The Orthodox Church had flourished in Russia with the support of the Mongols, who gave the church immunity from taxation. The Metropolitan Bishop of Moscow had become

Ivan III

FIGURE 9.10
Ivan III.

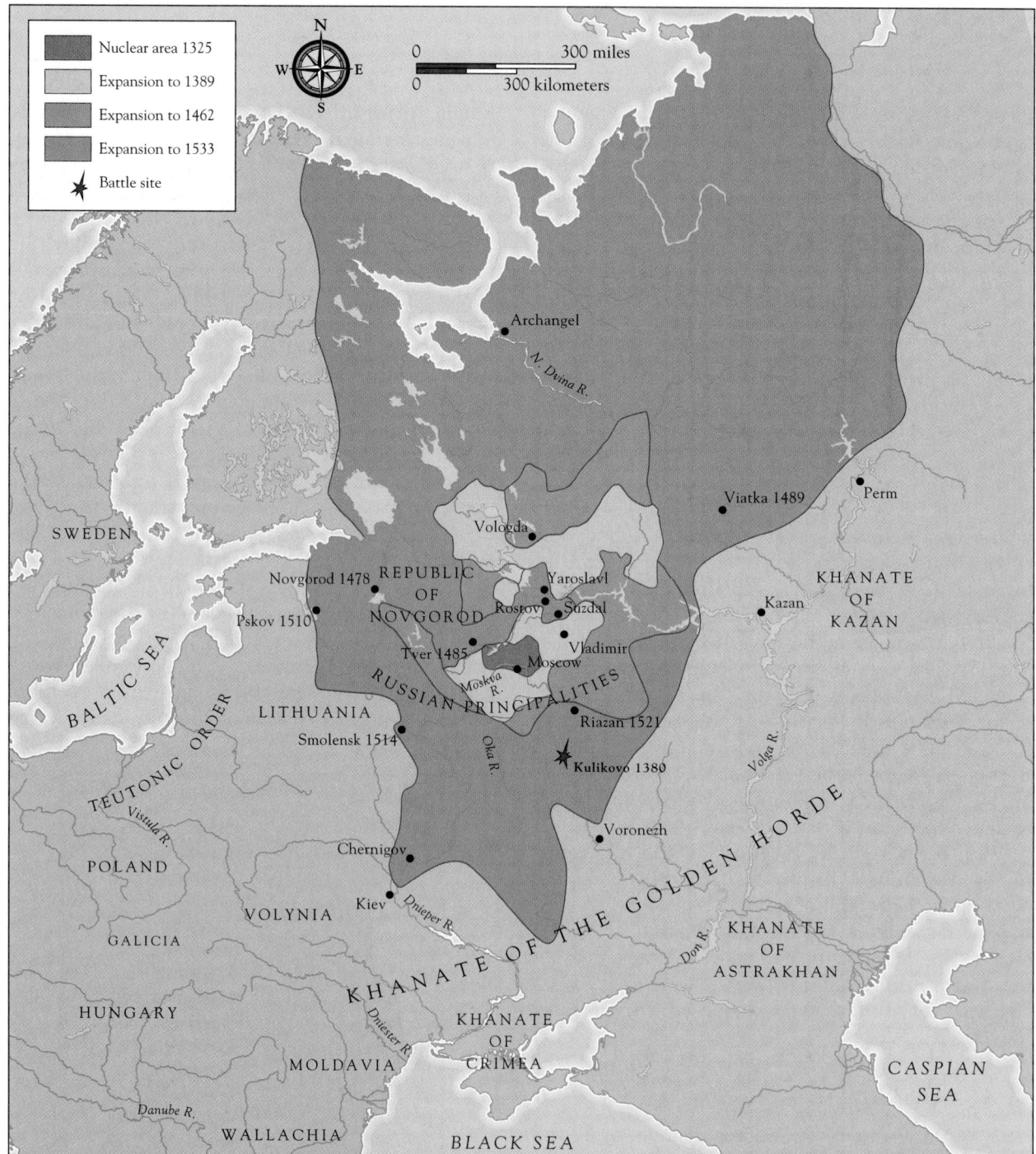

Legend:
- Nuclear area 1325
- Expansion to 1389
- Expansion to 1462
- Expansion to 1533
- ★ Battle site

N · S · E · W (compass)

0 — 300 miles
0 — 300 kilometers

Archangel

N. Dvina R.

Viatka 1489 · Perm

Vologda

SWEDEN

REPUBLIC OF NOVGOROD

KHANATE OF KAZAN

Novgorod 1478 · Yaroslavl

Pskov 1510 · Rostov · Suzdal

Kazan

Tver 1485 · Vladimir

Moskva R. · Moscow

RUSSIAN PRINCIPALITIES

BALTIC SEA

LITHUANIA

Riazan 1521

Smolensk 1514

Oka R.

★ **Kulikovo 1380**

Volga R.

TEUTONIC ORDER

Vistula R.

Voronezh

KHANATE OF THE GOLDEN HORDE

POLAND

Chernigov

Don R. · KHANATE OF ASTRAKHAN

VOLYNIA

Kiev · *Dnieper R.*

GALICIA

HUNGARY

Dniester R.

KHANATE OF CRIMEA

CASPIAN SEA

MOLDAVIA

Danube R.

WALLACHIA

BLACK SEA

THINKING ABOUT GEOGRAPHY

MAP 9.6   *The Rise of Moscow, 1325–1533*

This map shows the expansion of the principality of Moscow as it moved from a small state in 1325 to a large empire in 1533. ▧ **Notice** the location of the Khanate of the Golden Horde. ▧ **Compare** this map with Map 9.4. **How** was Russia well placed to take advantage of the Mongols' retreat from their westernmost province? ▧ **Compare** this map with Map 9.5. **Why** would Russia consider itself the logical heir to the Byzantine Empire in being the guardian of Christianity in the face of a growing Muslim threat?

independent from the patriarch of Constantinople as early as 1448, and in 1589, the bishop was proclaimed a Patriarch—one of the five who presided over the eastern Orthodox Church. (See Chapter 6 for the origins of this church.) The Orthodox church supported the tsar's claim that Moscow was the spiritual heir to Constantinople. Thus, religion and tradition supported the tsar's claim for absolute and universal authority. A new conservative empire had arisen in the east.

The fourteenth century dawned bringing with it a series of disasters in the West that broke down the medieval order that had prevailed before. Famine and plague killed tens of thousands, depopulating villages and towns. Revolts broke out in towns and across the countryside, not only bringing more violence but also raising the shocking specter of people attacking the very order of society. The manorial system in which serfs labored for their lords slowly broke down under the pressure, leaving a monetary system of rents and labor for hire. If one survived the disasters, life (at least in western Europe) might be better—higher wages and more opportunities awaited.

The papacy, too, fell prey to disasters. After new struggles with the kings of France, the popes lost prestige as they left Rome to live in Avignon and, subsequently, precipitated the Great Schism when disputed elections left two, then three, popes ruling at the same time. The medieval imperial papacy could not recover from such blows. Feudalism with its knights in shining armor also proved to be inadequate in the new age. During the devastating Hundred Years' War, infantry armed with bows and arrows, pikes, and later guns, proved more effective than knights, and kings slowly began to prefer money to military service from their vassals.

In eastern Europe, new empires arose with strong, autocratic rulers, and with the strengthening of these empires East and West grew further apart. The tensions that emerged between the two profoundly influenced European life in the future. However, these eastern empires would soon face a western Europe with ideas and values dramatically different from those of the medieval West. What form would this new sensibility take?

REVIEW, ANALYZE, AND ANTICIPATE

REVIEW THE PREVIOUS CHAPTER

Chapter 8—"Order Perfected"—described the three orders of the High Middle Ages and traced the fortunes of the social groups and the kings who ruled them. It also looked at the intellectual and religious accomplishments of that vigorous age.

1. *Review the agricultural innovations that allowed for expansion during the High Middle Ages and consider why these no longer proved adequate in the fourteenth century.*

2. *Review the development of England and France in the High Middle Ages to see how they came to the violent confrontation of the Hundred Years' War in the fourteenth century.*

ANALYZE THIS CHAPTER

Chapter 9—"Despair in the West, Empires in the East"—traces the disasters of the fourteenth century that undermined the medieval structures, and it also shows the growth of empires in eastern Europe.

1. *In the struggle between popes and kings over who should lead a Christian Europe, popes had dominated in the thirteenth century. When the struggle reopened in the fourteenth century, the kings prevailed. Review the events that led to the Great Schism and its resolution.*

2. *How did the disasters of the fourteenth century undermine the feudal and manorial systems?*

3. *What were the eastern empires that came to power by the end of the fifteenth century, and what were their relative strengths?*

TIMELINE: A CLOSER LOOK

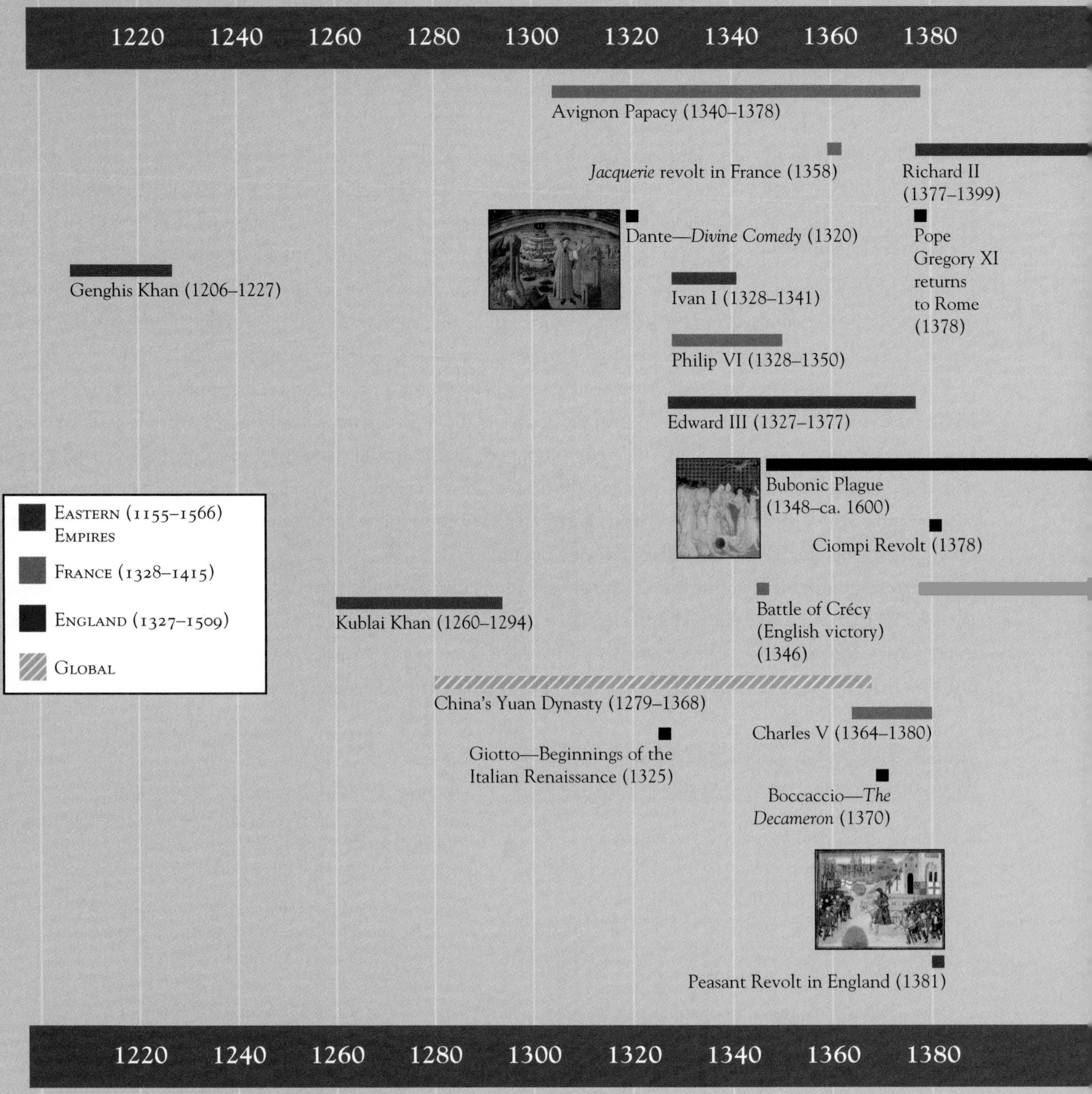

1220	1240	1260	1280	1300	1320	1340	1360	1380

Avignon Papacy (1340–1378)

Jacquerie revolt in France (1358)

Richard II (1377–1399)

Dante—*Divine Comedy* (1320)

Pope Gregory XI returns to Rome (1378)

Ivan I (1328–1341)

Genghis Khan (1206–1227)

Philip VI (1328–1350)

Edward III (1327–1377)

Bubonic Plague (1348–ca. 1600)

Ciompi Revolt (1378)

Legend:

- ■ EASTERN (1155–1566) EMPIRES
- ■ FRANCE (1328–1415)
- ■ ENGLAND (1327–1509)
- ▨ GLOBAL

Kublai Khan (1260–1294)

Battle of Crécy (English victory) (1346)

China's Yuan Dynasty (1279–1368)

Charles V (1364–1380)

Giotto—Beginnings of the Italian Renaissance (1325)

Boccaccio—*The Decameron* (1370)

Peasant Revolt in England (1381)

1220	1240	1260	1280	1300	1320	1340	1360	1380

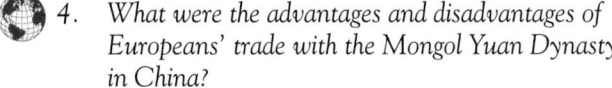

4. *What were the advantages and disadvantages of Europeans' trade with the Mongol Yuan Dynasty in China?*

ANTICIPATE THE NEXT CHAPTER

Chapter 10—"A New Spirit in the West"—will survey the Renaissance ideas of individualism, realism, and activism that began in Italy and spread north to the rest of Europe.

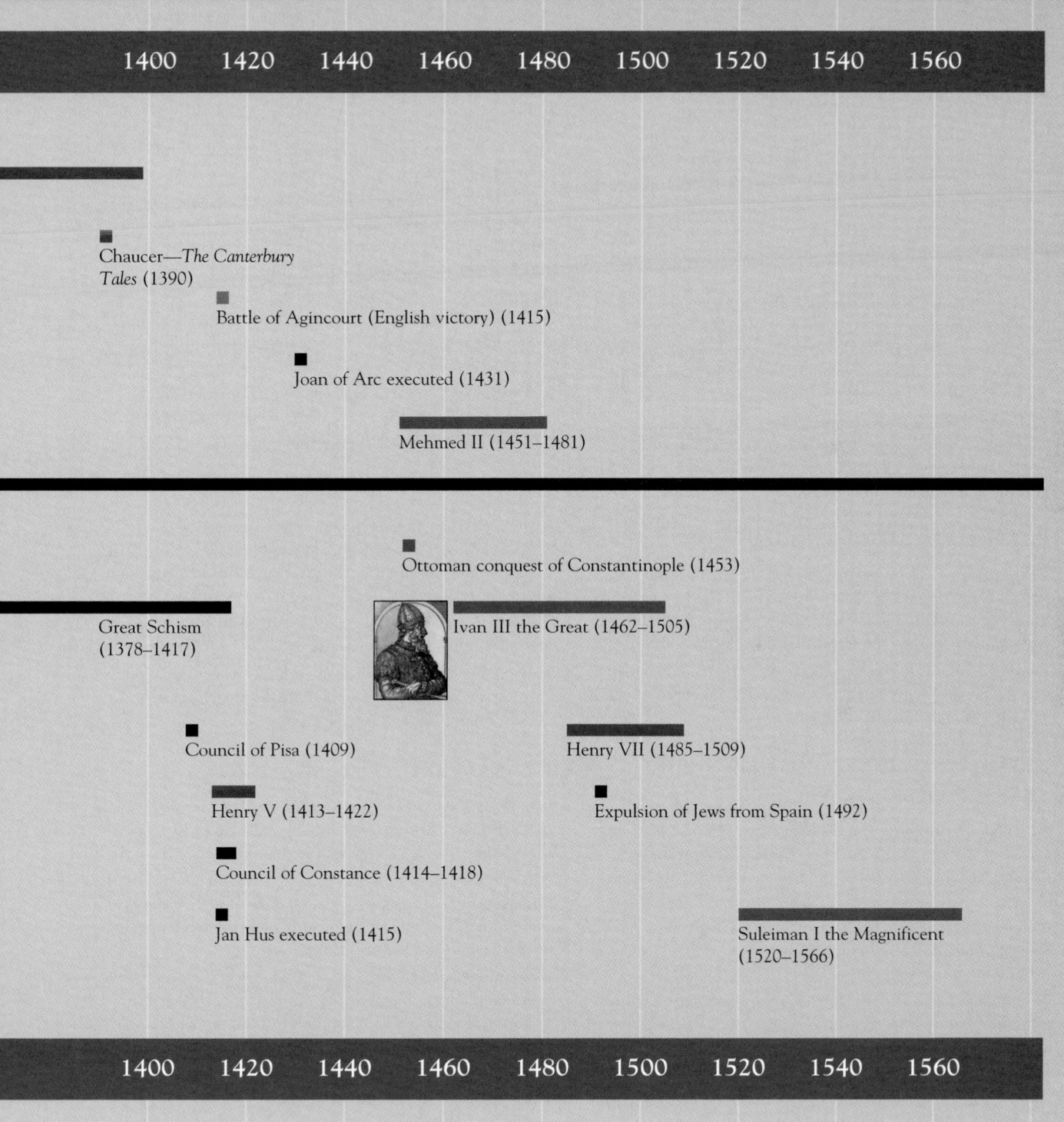

| 1400 | 1420 | 1440 | 1460 | 1480 | 1500 | 1520 | 1540 | 1560 |

Chaucer—*The Canterbury Tales* (1390)

Battle of Agincourt (English victory) (1415)

Joan of Arc executed (1431)

Mehmed II (1451–1481)

Ottoman conquest of Constantinople (1453)

Great Schism (1378–1417)

Ivan III the Great (1462–1505)

Council of Pisa (1409)

Henry VII (1485–1509)

Henry V (1413–1422)

Expulsion of Jews from Spain (1492)

Council of Constance (1414–1418)

Jan Hus executed (1415)

Suleiman I the Magnificent (1520–1566)

| 1400 | 1420 | 1440 | 1460 | 1480 | 1500 | 1520 | 1540 | 1560 |

1. *Review the struggle between popes and emperors discussed in Chapter 8 that prevented the Italian city-states from being unified under a strong monarchy; consider how this very independence might foster a new spirit of individual achievement.*

2. *Review the ideas of Dante, Boccaccio, and Chaucer, and consider how the Italian writers might foreshadow a new spirit more so than the English writer did.*

BEYOND THE CLASSROOM

ECONOMIC AND SOCIAL MISERY

Herlihy, D. *The Black Death and the Transformation of the West*. Cambridge, MA: Harvard University Press, 1997. A revisionist look at this devastating disease that reconsiders how many diseases were involved.

Hilton, Rodney. *Bond Men Made Free*. New York: Methuen, 1973. The classic, highly sympathetic study of peasant unrest in the Late Middle Ages.

Jordan, William Chester. *The Great Famine*. Princeton, NJ: Princeton University Press, 1996. A comprehensive study of this devastating event that looks at the causes, impact, and responses to the famine—certain to remain the classic work on the subject.

Tuchman, Barbara W. *A Distant Mirror: The Calamitous Fourteenth Century*. New York: Ballantine Books, Inc., 1987. Although this book has not found favor with some historians, it remains a popular account of the period.

IMPERIAL PAPACY BESIEGED

Oakley, Francis. *The Western Church in the Later Middle Ages*. Ithaca, NY: Cornell University Press, 1979. The best general history of the church in the late Middle Ages that is particularly strong on the Great Schism and conciliarism.

Renouard, Yves. *The Avignon Papacy (1305–1403)*. Hamden, CT: Archon, 1970. A balanced view of the accomplishments and failures of the Avignon Papacy.

MORE DESTRUCTION: THE HUNDRED YEARS' WAR

Allmand, Christopher. *The Hundred Years' War: England and France at War, ca. 1300–ca. 1450*. Cambridge, England: Cambridge University Press, 1988. The classic survey of the war.

Curry, Anne. *The Hundred Years' War*. New York: St. Martin's Press, 1993. A brief diplomatic study of the international relations during the period of the war.

Gillingham, John. *The Wars of the Roses: Peace and Conflict in Fifteenth-Century England*. Baton Rouge, LA: Louisiana State University Press, 1981. A political and military history of this influential conflict.

Warner, Marina. *Joan of Arc: The Image of Female Heroism*. New York: Knopf, 1981. Examines Joan's life and legend.

RESPONSES TO DISASTER AND DESPAIR

Bergin, Thomas Goddard. *Boccaccio*. New York: Viking Press, 1981. A scholarly study of the life and thought of this influential writer.

Hicks, Michael. *Bastard Feudalism*. NY: Longmans, 1995. This careful work revisits the development of Bastard Feudalism in England, particularly in the fifteenth century, and shows that it is an acceleration of previous trends.

Huizinga, Johan. *The Waning of the Middle Ages*. New York: St. Martin's Press, 1967. A brilliant study of the mentality of the people in the late Middle Ages, including art, literature, and general outlook.

Leff, Gordon. *William of Ockham*. Manchester, England: Manchester University Press, 1975. The authoritative study that makes the ideas of this difficult philosopher accessible.

EMPIRES IN THE EAST

Inalcik, H. *The Ottoman Empire: The Classical Age, 1300–1600*. London: Weidenfeld and Nicolson, 1973. An excellent general survey of the growth of the Ottoman state.

Martin, Janet. *Medieval Russia, 980–1584*. New York: Cambridge University Press, 1995. A well-written, accessible account of the growth of Russia.

Morgan, David. *The Mongols*. New York: Blackwell, 1986. This survey stresses the impact of the Mongol Empire on eastern Europe.

GLOBAL CONNECTIONS

Chambers, James. *The Devil's Horsemen: The Mongol Invasion of Europe*. NY: Atheneum, 1985. A well-written history of the Khanate of the Golden Horde that threatened Russia and Europe.

Grousset, René. *Conqueror of the World*. NY: The Orion Press, 1966. Extremely engaging life of Genghis Khan based on the detailed legends of his life.

Morgan, David. *The Mongols*. Oxford: Basil Blackwell, 1986. A readable yet thorough survey of the Mongols from their origin on the steppes through their fortunes under the communist regime in China. This work contains an excellent explanation of the sources.

For quiz questions that tie the book to the videos and additional primary sources, please go to the Primary Source Investigator CD.

Documents

DOCUMENT 9.1
Edward III of England Seeks Allies

By the end of the Hundred Years War, people living in England and France began to feel a strong identification with their homelands. At the beginning of the conflict, however, people had viewed themselves as fighting just one more feudal war within a larger Christian Europe. This source describes that earlier time. In it, Edward III seeks the support of the Holy Roman Emperor as he launches a campaign against the French king.

■ **Investigate the Document**

> **What** *aspects of the agreement between Edward and the emperor reveal a feudal relationship between them?* **How** *long did the nobles think the war would last?* **Why** *do you think they miscalculated the time frame so badly?*

When the emperor learned of the approach of king Edward, he set out from his place to meet him, and after travelling four days he met him near Coblenz, receiving him there with great honor. Two richly decorated thrones were set up in the market-place, and on these the emperor and the king sat. There were present in attendance four dukes, three archbishops, six bishops, and thirty-seven counts, besides a great number, estimated by the heralds at 17,000, of barons, baronets, knights, and others. The emperor held in his right hand the imperial sceptre, and in his left the golden globe as a symbol of world-wide authority. A certain knight held a drawn sword above his head. And the emperor in the presence of the people gathered here proclaimed to all the crimes, disobedience, and wickedness of the king of France. And after he had declared that the king of France had broken his faith to the emperor, he published a decree of forfeiture against him and his followers. Then the emperor made king Edward his vicar and gave him authority over the land from Cologne to the sea, presenting him with a charter of this in the sight of all the people.

Source: Oliver J. Thatcher and Edgar H. McNeal, *A Source Book for Mediaeval History*, (New York: Charles Scribner's Sons, 1905), pp. 282–283.

On the next day the emperor and the king of England and their nobles assembled in the cathedral, and the archbishop of Cologne said mass. And after mass the emperor and all his nobles swore to aid the king of England and to maintain his quarrel against the king of France with their lives for seven years, if the war between the said kings should last so long. They also swore that all the nobles in the territory from Cologne to the sea would come at the summons of the king of England to join him in an attack upon the king of France at any place and at any time set by him. If any one of them should fail to obey the king of England in these matters, all the other nobles of northern Germany would attack and destroy him. These affairs having been arranged and settled, the king of England received the grant of authority and returned to Brabant.

DOCUMENT 9.2
Pope Boniface VIII Wrests Control of the Church from Kings

In the fourteenth century, a unified Christian Europe led by a respected pope broke apart as pontiffs and kings jockeyed for power. The first salvo in this confrontation for leadership came over the issue of taxation of clergy. The French and English kings had begun to levy heavy assessments against their clergy. Boniface VIII issued this bull (papal edict) to reassert the liberty of the church from encroaching royal power.

■ **Investigate the Document**

> **Why** *did some clergy pay the taxes imposed by kings?* **What** *sanctions did the pope impose to stop this taxation?* **How** *do you think the kings responded to this bull?*

It is said that in times past laymen practiced great violence against the clergy, and our experience clearly shows that they are doing so at present, since they are not content to keep within the limits pre-

Source: Oliver J. Thatcher and Edgar H. McNeal, *A Source Book for Mediaeval History*, (New York: Charles Scribner's Sons, 1905), pp. 311–313.

scribed for them, but strive to do that which is prohibited and illegal. And they pay no attention to the fact that they are forbidden to exercise authority over the clergy and ecclesiastical persons and their possessions. But they are laying heavy burdens on bishops, churches, and clergy, both regular and secular, by taxing them, levying contributions on them, and extorting the half, or the tenth, or the twentieth, or some other part of their income and possessions. They are striving in many ways to reduce the clergy to servitude and to subject them to their own sway. And we grieve to say it, but some bishops and clergy, fearing where they should not, and seeking a temporary peace, and fearing more to offend man than God, submit, improvidently rather than rashly, to these abuses [and pay the sums demanded], without receiving the papal permission. Wishing to prevent these evils, with the counsel of our brethren, and by our apostolic authority, we decree that if any bishops or clergy, regular or secular, of any grade, condition, or rank, shall pay, or promise, or consent to pay to laymen any contributions, or taxes, or the tenth, or the twentieth, or the hundredth, or any other part of their income or of their possessions, or of their value, real or estimated, under the name of aid, or loan, or subvention, or subsidy, or gift, or under any other name or pretext, without the permission of the pope, they shall, by the very act, incur the sentence of excommunication. And we also decree that emperors, kings, princes, dukes, counts, barons, *podestà, capitanei,* and governors of cities, fortresses, and of all other places everywhere, by whatever names such governors may be called, and all other persons of whatever power, condition, or rank, who shall impose, demand, or receive such taxes, or shall seize, or cause to be seized, the property of churches or of the clergy, which has been deposited in sacred buildings, or shall receive such property after it has been seized, or shall give aid, counsel, or support in such things either openly or secretly, shall by that very act incur the sentence of excommunication. We also put under the interdict all communities which shall be culpable in such matters. And under the threat of deposition we strictly command all bishops and clergy, in accordance with their oath of obedience, not to submit to such taxes without the express permission of the pope. They shall not pay anything under the pretext that they had already promised or agreed to do so before the prohibition came to their knowledge. They

shall not pay, nor shall the above-named laymen receive anything in any way. And if the ones shall pay, or the others receive anything, they shall by that very act fall under the sentence of excommunication. From this sentence of excommunication and interdict no one can be absolved except in the moment of death, without the authority and special permission of the pope. . . .

DOCUMENT **9.3**
Joan of Arc Is Defiant

The trial records of Joan of Arc offer a fascinating glimpse into both the inquisitorial proceedings of the late Middle Ages and the psychology of the accused. Earlier in her trial, Joan claimed to renounce the voices that had guided her and meekly agreed to adopt women's clothing again. However, when the judges visited her in prison the following day, she had donned men's clothing again and renounced her previous recanation.

■ **Investigate the Document**

> **Why** was clothing style so important in this event? **Notice** how clothing symbolizes gender roles and obedience. **Why** did Joan take back her confession? **What** was the church's sentence?

Wednesday, May 9th, We, the Judges, . . . did cause Jeanne to be brought before us. We did require and warn her: To speak the truth to Us on divers and numerous points on which she had hitherto refused to reply or had replied untruthfully, the which are established in the highest degree by informations, proofs, and grave presumptions. A great number of these points was read and shown to her. Then she was told that, if she would not tell the truth, she would immediately be put to the torture, the instruments of which were here, in this same tower, under her eyes. There also were present the executioners, who by Our order had made all the necessary preparations for torturing her, in order to bring her back by this means into the way and knowledge of the truth, and thus to procure for her salvation both of body and soul, which she did expose to such grave peril by her lying inventions.

Source: Saint Joan of Arc Center, Albuquerque, NM, "The Relapse, the final adjudication and the sentence of death," www.stjoan-center.com.

To which Jeanne replied in this manner: "Truly if you were to tear me limb from limb, and separate soul from body, I will tell you nothing more; and, if I were to say anything else, I should always afterwards declare that you made me say it by force.

"Last Thursday (1) . . . . **(The Day of the Holy Cross, May 3rd.)** I received comfort from Saint Gabriel; I believe it was Saint Gabriel : I knew by my Voices it was he. I asked counsel of my Voices if I ought to submit to the Church, because the Clergy were pressing me hard to submit, and they said to me: 'If you want God to come to your help, wait on Him for all your doings.' I know that Our Lord had always been the Master of all my doings, and that the Devil had never had power over them. I asked of my Voices if I should be burned, and my Voices answered me: 'Wait on Our Lord, He will help thee.' "

[Joan is found guilty and agrees to recant:]

Then, in the presence of all the aforenamed, in presence of an immense number of people and Clergy, she did make and utter her recantation and abjuration, following a formula written in French, which was read to her; a formula which she did pronounce herself, and the schedule of which she did sign with her own hand, and of which the tenor follows:

". . . I, Jeanne, commonly called the Maid, a miserable sinner, after that I had recognized the snares of error in the which I was held, and [after] that, by the grace of God, I had returned to our Holy Mother Church, in order that it may be seen that, not pretending but with a good heart and good will, I have returned thereto; I confess that I have most grievously sinned, in pretending untruthfully to have had revelations and apparitions from God, from the Angels, and Saint Catherine and Saint Margaret; in seducing others; in believing foolishly and lightly; in making superstitious divinations; in blaspheming God and His Saints; in breaking the Divine Law, Holy Scripture, and the lawful Canons; in wearing a dissolute habit, misshapen and immodest and against the propriety of nature, and hair clipped 'en ronde' in the style of a man, against all the modesty of the feminine sex; . . .

And the same day, **Thursday, May 24th, in the afternoon,** We [the judges] did repair to the place in the prison where Jeanne was to be found.

We, and the persons assisting us, did set forth before her how God had on this day had mercy on her, and how the Clergy had shown themselves merciful in receiving her to the Grace and pardon of Holy Mother Church. In return, it was right that she, Jeanne, should obey with humility the sentence and orders of the Judges and the Ecclesiastics; that she should wholly give up her errors and all her inventions, never to return to them. . . . We told her to leave off her man's dress and to take a woman's garments, as the Church had ordered her. In all our observations Jeanne did reply that she would willingly take woman's garments, and that in all things she would obey the Church. Woman's garments having been offered to her, she at once dressed herself in them, after having taken off the man's dress she was wearing; and her hair, which up to this time had been cut "en ronde" above her ears, she desired and permitted them to shave and take away.

Monday, May 28th, the day following Trinity Sunday.

We, the aforesaid Judges, repaired to the place of Jeanne's prison, to learn the state and disposition of her soul. . . .

And because Jeanne was dressed in the dress of a man—that is to say, a short mantle, a hood, a doublet and other effects used by men—although, by our orders, she had, several days before, consented to give up these garments, we asked her when and for what reason she had resumed this dress.

She answered us:

"I have but now resumed the dress of a man and put off the woman's dress."

"Why did you take it, and who made you take it?"

"I took it of my own free will, and with no constraint: I prefer a man's dress to a woman's dress."

"You promised and swore not to resume a man's dress."

"I never meant to swear that I would not resume it."

"Why have you resumed it?"

"Because it is more lawful and suitable for me to resume it and to wear man's dress, being with men, than to have a woman's dress. I have resumed it because the promise made to me has not been kept; that is to say, that I should go to Mass and should receive my Savior and that I should be taken out of irons."

"Did you not abjure and promise not to resume this dress?"

"I would rather die than be in irons! but if I am allowed to go to Mass, and am taken out of irons and put into a gracious prison, and [may have a woman for companion] . . . I will be good, and do as the Church wills."

And as We, the Judges, heard from several persons that she had returned to her old illusions on the subject of her pretended revelations. We put to her this question:

"Since last Thursday [the day of her abjuration] have you heard your Voices at all?"

"Yes, I have heard them."

"What did they say to you?"

"They said to me: . . . 'God had sent me word by St. Catherine and St. Margaret of the great pity it is, this treason to which I have consented, to abjure and recant in order to save my life! I have damned myself to save my life!' Before last Thursday, my Voices did indeed tell me what I should do and what I did on that day. When I was on the scaffold on Thursday, my Voices said to me, while the preacher was speaking: 'Answer him boldly, this preacher!' And in truth he is a false preacher; he reproached me with many things I never did. If I said that God had not sent me, I should damn myself, for it is true that God has sent me; my Voices have said to me since Thursday: 'You have done a great evil in declaring that what you have done was wrong.' All I said and revoked, I said for fear of the fire."

"Do you believe that your Voices are Saint Catherine and Saint Margaret?"

"Yes, I believe it, and that they come from God."

"Tell us the truth on the subject of this crown which is mentioned in your Trial."

"In everything, I told you the truth about it in my Trial, as well as I know."

"On the scaffold, at the moment of your abjuration, you did admit before us, your Judges, and before many others, in presence of all the people, that you had untruthfully boasted your Voices to be Saint Catherine and Saint Margaret."

"I did not intend so to do or say. I did not intend to deny my apparitions that is to say, that they were Saint Catherine and Saint Margaret; what I said was from fear of the fire: I revoked nothing that was not against the truth. I would rather do penance once for all—that is die—than endure any longer the suffering of a prison. I have done nothing against God or the Faith, in spite of all they have made me revoke. What was in the schedule of abjuration I did not understand. I did not intend to revoke anything except according to God's good pleasure. If the Judges wish, I will resume a woman's dress: for the rest, I can do no more." After hearing this. We retired from her, to act and proceed later according to law and reason.

Wednesday, May 30th, towards 9 o'clock in the morning, . . .

We, the Bishop and Vicar aforesaid, having regard to all that has gone before, in which it is shown that this woman had never truly abandoned her errors, her obstinate temerity, nor her unheard-of crimes; that she had even shown the malice of her diabolical obstinacy in this deceitful semblance of contrition, penitence, and amendment; malice rendered still more damnable by perjury of the Holy Name of God and blasphemy of His ineffable Majesty; considering her on all these grounds obstinate, incorrigible, heretic, relapsed into heresy, and altogether unworthy of the grace and of the Communion which, by our former sentence. We did mercifully accord to her; all of which being seen and considered, after mature deliberation and counsel of a great number of Doctors. We have at last proceeded to the Final Sentence on these terms:

For the causes, declaring thee fallen again into your old errors, and under the sentence of excommunication which you have formerly incurred. WE DECREE THAT YOU ART A RELAPSED HERETIC, by our present sentence which, seated in tribunal, we utter and pronounce in this writing; we denounce thee as a rotten member, and that you may not vitiate others, as cast out from the unity of the Church, separate from her Body, abandoned to the secular power as, indeed, by these presents, we do cast thee off, separate and abandon thee:—praying this same secular power, so far as concerns death and the mutilation of the limbs, to moderate its judgment towards thee, and, if true signs of penitence should appear in thee, [to permit] that the Sacrament of Penance be administered to thee.

Domenico Ghirlandaio, *Old Man with a Child*, ca. 1480

This portrait captures many characteristics of Renaissance art: realistic portrayal of individuals (even the subject's misshapen nose), perspective of the landscape in the background to show three-dimensional space, and the importance of family life. A dramatic new spirit was appearing in the West.

CHAPTER 10

A New Spirit in the West

The Renaissance, ca. 1300–1640

STUDY • Characteristics of the Renaissance • Politics of the Italian city-states • Urban Life • Artistic and Scientific developments • Renaissance ideas in France and England. NOTICE how ideas of individualism and Greco-Roman values permeated all facets of this movement.

"This age is dominated by great men [who] labored much to aggrandize themselves and to acquire glory. And yet, would it not have been better if they had undertaken fewer enterprises and been more afraid of offending God and of persecuting their subjects and neighbors?" With these words, a contemporary biographer of Louis the Spider, king of France during the Renaissance, pinpointed both the strengths and weaknesses of this new age: Talented individuals accomplished much, yet often to the neglect of those in their care.

The Renaissance (which means "rebirth") was mainly a cultural movement that emphasized the study of Greek and Roman classics and praised individual achievement. It first emerged in Italy in the fourteenth century and then spread throughout Europe as the disasters of the fourteenth century broke down the old medieval structures. Renaissance ideas fostered especially striking accomplishments in literature, architecture, and the visual arts. Politics, as well, came under the influence of the age: Princes and monarchs governed their states in new ways, developing innovative military strategies and novel ways of conducting diplomacy. At the same time, public policies in these centuries often worsened the lot of the poor and the powerless. Nevertheless, this era was an exciting, vibrant time that ushered Europe from the medieval world toward the modern one.

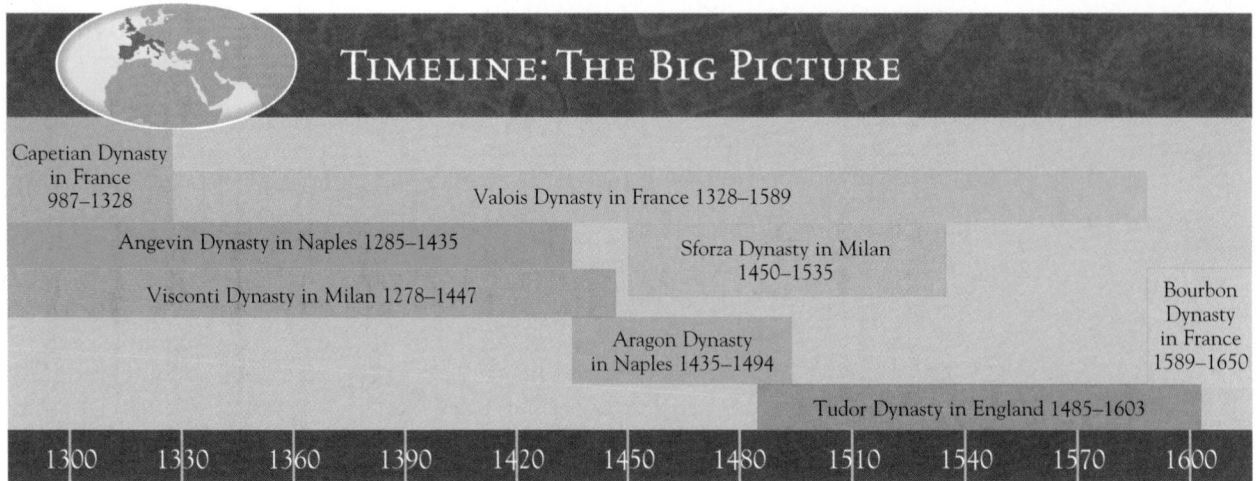

TIMELINE: THE BIG PICTURE

Capetian Dynasty
in France
987–1328

Valois Dynasty in France 1328–1589

Angevin Dynasty in Naples 1285–1435

Sforza Dynasty in Milan
1450–1535

Visconti Dynasty in Milan 1278–1447

Bourbon
Dynasty
in France
1589–1650

Aragon Dynasty
in Naples 1435–1494

Tudor Dynasty in England 1485–1603

1300   1330   1360   1390   1420   1450   1480   1510   1540   1570   1600

A New Spirit Emerges: Individualism, Realism, and Activism

In the late thirteenth century, Cimabue, an important painter from the Italian city-state of Florence, was walking in the countryside and saw a young shepherd boy drawing sheep on a rock. The painter recognized the boy's talent and took him on as an apprentice. The young shepherd, Giotto (1267?–1337), flourished under his master's tutelage, and stories arose about the youth's talent for realistic painting—and his independent spirit. He was said to have once painted a fly on the nose of a face that Cimabue was painting, and the fly was so lifelike that the master tried to brush it off several times before he grasped his student's joke. Giotto grew up to vastly surpass his master and create paintings of such realism and emotional honesty that they helped change the direction of painting. As the new century dawned, there would be others like Giotto who creatively broke new ground.

THE RENAISSANCE: A CONTROVERSIAL IDEA

For centuries historians have struggled with the very idea of whether this age beginning in the fourteenth century in Italy constituted a turning point—the Renaissance. People living in fourteenth-century Italy themselves identified this era as characterized by a return to the sources of knowledge and standards of beauty that had created the great civilizations of classical Greece and Rome. ("Classical literature," as they defined it, covered a period from about 800 B.C. to about A.D. 400.) Francesco Petrarch (1304–1374), an Italian writer who studied the classics and wrote poetry, was an early proponent of Renaissance ideas. Petrarch lamented because he felt that he could find no one in his own times who could serve as a model of virtuous behavior—he mirrored the example of many in the fourteenth century who despaired of their times (see Chapter 9). However, through his studies, he came to revere figures from antiquity who seemed to understand proper values and follow them regardless of worldly distractions. Petrarch even wrote letters to ancient figures, and in one such letter to the Roman historian Livy (discussed in Chapter 5), he wrote: "I only wish, that I had been born in your time or you in ours. . . . I have to thank you . . . because you have so often helped me forget the evils of today." Later Renaissance thinkers would follow Petrarch's example and see in ancient Greece and Rome the models to shape a new world.

Yet, they overstated their case—medieval scholars had never lost touch with the Latin texts, and no one gazing at the Gothic cathedrals and the magnificent illuminated manuscripts of the Middle Ages can doubt that medieval people had an exquisite sense of beauty. Indeed, most of the qualities that we identify with the Renaissance had existed in some form throughout the Middle Ages. For this reason, some modern scholars have suggested that the Renaissance should not be considered a separate historical era. Others argue that a different spirit clearly emerged during the period that we have come to call the Renaissance.

Medieval antecedents

In its simplest sense, the Renaissance was an age of accelerated change that began in Italy and that spread new ideas more rapidly than ever. Many people, especially urban dwellers, questioned medieval values of hierarchy, community, and reliance on authority, and replaced them with a focus on ambitious individualism and realism (both of which had to some extent existed in the Middle Ages, but received new emphasis). Some no longer used the classic texts to reinforce the status quo as had become common in the medieval universities; instead, they studied to transform themselves. Petrarch eagerly noted that the texts "sow into our hearts love of the best and eager desire for it." As they strove for excellence, the men and women of the Renaissance ushered in a new age.

Thus, many historians identify the Renaissance as a unique state of mind or set of ideas about everything from art to politics. Having first sprouted in Italy in the fourteenth century, these ideas slowly spread north as the prevailing medieval culture was rocked by the disasters of the fourteenth century. Just as historians disagree about the nature of the Renaissance, they also differ on exactly why these new ideas took root in Italy. What was it about the Italian situation in the early fourteenth century that made that land ripe for fresh ideas about individualism and realism and that fostered the rise of enterprising people?

WHY ITALY?

Because the people of the Renaissance themselves believed the heart of their rebirth was a recovery of the spirit of classical Greece and Rome, the ancient ruins provided a continuing stimulus for such reflections. As Petrarch mapped the ruins, he said the pastime was wonderfully pleasant "not so much because of what I actually saw, as from the recollection of our ancestors, who left such illustrious memorials of Roman virtue . . ." For Petrarch and others, these ruins were an ever-present reminder of an age that they believed was dramatically different from their own—an age they sought to recapture.

A fresh reading of the classics certainly stimulated in some literate Italians a desire to recover a spirit of classical greatness, but were readings alone enough to change a culture's sensibilities so dramatically? Some historians argue instead that the tumultuous politics of the Italian city-states particularly favored the growth of new ideas. Incessant warfare among the states opened the door for skilled, innovative leaders to come forward. These leaders in turn surrounded themselves with talented courtiers who willingly broke from tradition to forward their own careers as they pleased their princes. A new spirit found fertile ground in these ambitious, upwardly mobile men.

Others point to the Black Death that entered Italy in 1348 as the catalyst that transformed the old order (see Chapter 9). The plague's drastic *Plague disruptions* reduction of the population engendered huge economic changes. Prices plummeted, and trade in luxuries such as silk, jewelry, spices, and glass quickened. Italy was ideally placed to profit from this commerce, for throughout the Middle Ages, the Italian city-states had dominated trade in the eastern Mediterranean. During the fourteenth century, individuals, families, and institutions accumulated a good deal of capital, and men and women used some of this money to support the arts. Some have vividly suggested that the Renaissance became one long shopping spree that supported the talented artists whose vision helped define this controversial era—the bridge that began to move Western history from the Middle Ages to modernity.

A MULTIFACETED MOVEMENT

At its core, the Renaissance emphasized and celebrated humans and their achievements. It thus revived an advocacy of individualism that the West had not seen since the time of ancients. As the Italian writer Giovanni Pico della Mirandola (1463–1494) optimistically wrote in his *Oration on the Dignity of Man*, "Man is rightly . . . considered a great miracle and a truly marvelous creature," and in addition to this, Pico said that people *Individualism* could determine their own destiny. This optimistic faith in the human potential was an exciting new idea. Renaissance thinkers asserted a powerful belief in the human ability to choose right and wrong and to act on these choices.

During the Renaissance, Europeans favored a biblical verse from Genesis that described humans as being created in God's "image and likeness." Figure 10.1 shows one portion of the Italian artist Michelangelo's (1475–1564) revered painting on the ceiling of the Sistine Chapel. In this image, the realistic and beautifully proportioned figure of Adam mirrors the physical beauty of the Creator. Michelangelo also portrayed Adam as more than a piece of inert clay waiting for the divine spark to bring him life. Instead, Adam reaches up to God, meeting him halfway in the act of Creation. For Michelangelo and many other artists of the time, man was indeed created in God's image—not merely spiritually and morally, but also as a creator himself, shaping his own destiny. Here Michelangelo echoes Pico in expressing this idea that was the essence of Renaissance thought.

Renaissance men and women also prided themselves on their accurate view of the world. This form *Realism* of realism appears vividly in the art of the period—consider, for example, how the illustration that opens this chapter unflinchingly portrays the grandfather's bulbous nose. Throughout the rest of this chapter, the various examples of artwork from these centuries show a similarly realistic portrayal of the world.

Another prevailing theme in the Renaissance came with the emergence of activism. Petrarch himself succinctly expressed the energetic spirit of the age, writing, "It is better to will the good than to

know the truth." In other words, being wise was not enough; one had to exert one's will actively in the world to make a difference. Leon Battista Alberti (1404–1472) expressed the same senti- *Activism* ment: "Men can do all things if they will." As we saw, Michelangelo's Adam in Figure 10.1 participates in his own creation by reaching up to receive the spark of life, and people were encouraged to imitate this active involvement.

A final characteristic of this new spirit was that it was secular—that is, it did not take place in the churches, monasteries, or universi- *A secular spirit* ties that were dominated by religious thought. That is not to say Renaissance thinkers were antireligious, for they were not—Petrarch explained quite clearly: "Christ is my God; Cicero is the prince of the language I use." While most believed deeply in God and many worked in the church, their vocation was to apply the new spirit to this world, not the next.

Renaissance thinkers felt that the spirit of the classical worlds of Greece and Rome had been reborn before their very eyes. In part, they were right. This vital new age witnessed a renewed belief in human beings' capacity to perfect themselves, to assess the

FIGURE 10.1
Michelangelo, *Creation of Adam*, from the Sistine Chapel, 1508–1512.

world realistically, and to act vigorously to make an impact on their society. The key to this transformation was education.

Humanism: The Path to Self-Improvement

The urban dwellers of the Italian cities knew that education was the key to success. Men entering business had to be trained at least in reading, writing, and mathematics. In Florence at the beginning of the fourteenth century, the number of students enrolled in private schools testifies to the value practical Florentines placed on education: Out of a total population of about 100,000, some 10,000 youths attended private schools to obtain a basic education. Of those, about 1,000 went to special schools to learn advanced business mathematics. However, another 500 pursued a more general liberal education. From these latter emerged an educational movement that defined and perpetuated the Renaissance spirit and changed the course of Western thought.

Petrarch departed from the traditional medieval course of study and from his father's desire that he prepare for a career in law. In-

Humanist curriculum

stead, he pursued a general study of classical literature. The cities of Italy spawned many young men like Petrarch, who wanted an education separated from the church-dominated universities that had monopolized learning for centuries. Such students sought to understand the causes of human actions through the writings of the ancients, and in turn improve themselves. The humanities—literature, history, and philosophy—thus formed the core of the ideal Renaissance education, which aimed to shape students so that they could excel in anything. Proponents of this teaching method were called humanists.

Humanists stressed grammar (particularly Latin and Greek so students could read the classics), poetry, history, and ethics. Following the ancient Roman model, humanists capped off their education with rhetoric, the art of persuasive speaking, which prepared men to serve in a public capacity. Although this course of study may not appear revolutionary, it proved to be.

The early humanists' passion for classical texts led them to search out manuscripts that might yield even greater wisdom from the ancients. As they read and compared manuscripts, they discovered that mistakes had crept into texts that had been painstakingly copied over and over in the medieval monasteries. So the early humanists carefully pored over the many copies of texts to compile accurate versions. These techniques established standards for historical and literary criticism that continue today. Our debt to these literary scholars is incalculable as we enjoy accurate editions of works written thousands of years ago.

The Renaissance emphasis on study and self-improvement inspired some writers to comment on educational theory. Christine of Pizan (1365–1430?) was a pro-

Self-improvement books

fessional writer who worked in the French court. She supported herself and her children through her works of poetry and prose. Reflecting the interests of the times, she also wrote several pedagogical treatises: one instructing women on their roles in society (*The Book of Three Virtues*), a manual of good government for the French Dauphin (*The Book of Deeds of King Charles V*), and even a military handbook (*The Book of Feats of Arms and of Chivalry*).

In the same vein, many others authored self-improvement books. The best known of these is *The Book of the Courtier*, by the Italian author Baldassare Castiglione (1478–1529). In this popular work, the author summarizes the expected behavior of men of the court. For Castiglione, native endowments were only the beginning—a courtier had to cultivate military skills, a classical education, and an appreciation of art through music, drawing, and painting. Castiglione turned the Renaissance ideal of an active, well-developed individual into a social ideal of the aristocracy.

Other humanists proposed more formal educational settings. One educator (Guarino da Verona) established a model secondary school at Mantua, in Italy, called the "Happy House," which taught humanities, religion, mathematics, and physical education. The school even included lessons on diet and dress; no facet of the whole human was neglected in the effort at improvement.

Urban families who prized education for their sons also expected their daughters to be educated, but not to the same degree. The eminent Italian humanist Leonardo Bruni

Women humanists

(1374–1444) wrote an oft-quoted letter praising a humanist—but not a full—education for women. For example, he argued that rhetoric in particular

Biography

ISABELLA D'ESTE (1474–1539)

🔳 **Consider** how Isabella's life sheds light on the importance of patronage during the Renaissance, the position of women, and the significance of family ties.

Isabella d'Este was born the daughter of a duke in 1474 in the small Duchy of Ferrara, just south of Venice. She grew up in a court that both appreciated Renaissance education and art and succumbed to the violence that marked fifteenth-century Italy.

When Isabella was only two, her father's nephew attacked the palace in an effort to seize power from the duke. Before Isabella was eight years old, Venetian armies had invaded Ferrara to try to dominate the small duchy. Yet Isabella's father was a skillful diplomat and withstood these and many other challenges. In the process, his daughter began learning about Renaissance diplomacy.

The young girl was educated in the best humanist tradition. Her tutors taught her to read the great classics of the Roman world in the original Latin. She learned quickly and spoke Latin fluently at an early age. She also was an accomplished musician and excelled at singing and playing the lute.

When she was six years old, Isabella's parents began searching for a suitable future husband for her. They approached the family of the nearby Duke of Mantua to discuss a betrothal between Isabella and their eldest son, Francesco. When representatives of Francesco's family interviewed the young child, they wrote back to the prospective in-laws that they were astonished at her precocious intelligence. They sent Francesco's parents a portrait of the lovely black-eyed, blond child, but assured that "her marvelous knowledge and intelligence are far more worthy of admiration [than her beauty]." A betrothal was arranged that would unite the two houses trying to maintain independence from their powerful neighbors, Milan and Venice.

Isabella and Francesco were married in 1490, when she was 15. An elaborate ceremony joined the two families, and in her old age, Isabella proudly wrote of her memories of the gifts, decorations, and lavish banquet that marked this turning point of her life.

Duchess of Mantua, Diplomat, and Patron of the Arts

Under the skillful rule of Francesco and Isabella, Mantua rose to the foremost rank of the smaller Italian city-states. Isabella involved herself in the art of diplomacy throughout the couple's reign. She wrote more than 2,000 letters—many

was inappropriate for women: "For why exhaust a woman with the concerns of . . . [rhetoric] when she will never be seen in the forum?" His comments reveal the crux of the matter: Women could be educated, but they were not to use their education in a public way, and since rhetoric was central to the humanists, educated Renaissance women were caught in a paradox.

As one example, Isotta Nogarola (1418–1466) earned much recognition from her family and some family friends for her learning. However, as soon as she tried to engage in a public dialogue (through letters), male humanists reprimanded her and deemed her "immoral" for her public display. She retired into the seclusion of her study, just as other women took refuge in convents to pursue their research.

wrong, and all that is possible will be done for the good of your subjects." This talented woman was as good as her word, for when Francesco was captured in 1509 and imprisoned, Isabella ruled in his stead and valiantly saved the city from invasion.

Like other Italians influenced by Renaissance pseudo-science, Isabella avidly believed in astrology. She embarked on no important venture without consulting her astrologers. But she also took an interest in the real-world findings of the time. She received correspondence about Columbus's discovery of America and the "intelligent and gentle" natives he found there.

Yet the educated duchess is most remembered as a patron of the arts. She wrote explicit instructions for the works she commissioned: One painting prompted her to pen as many as 40 letters. Recognizing excellence, she wanted to commission a work from Leonardo da Vinci, but the artist never found the time to oblige her. (See Document 10.2 page D10.1.)

With a love of literature nurtured since her youth, Isabella accumulated a library that became one of the best in Italy. She took advantage of the new printing industry to acquire the first editions of the great classics as well as the contemporary works of Petrarch and Dante. Her requests for these editions show her appreciation of beauty even in her search for literature: She asked for books printed on parchment (instead of paper) and bound in leather.

When Isabella was 64 years old, Francesco died. The aging duchess turned to her many children and grandchildren for comfort and companionship. She took particular delight in one grandchild who could recite Virgil at the age of only five. Isabella died in 1539, a year after losing her husband. In the last months of her life, a great scholar of the age called her "the wisest and most fortunate of women"—an apt epitaph for someone who so personified the Renaissance spirit.

FIGURE 10.2

Isabella d'Este.

of them to popes, kings, and other Italian rulers. In one letter to her husband, Isabella assured him that he could concentrate completely on military matters, for "I intend to govern the State . . . in such a manner that you will suffer no

Rulers, of course, were exempt from such prohibitions of public use of education, and royal women made good use of the latest Renaissance notions of study. Queens such as Elizabeth I of England (r. 1558–1603) and Isabella of Castille (r. 1474–1504) employed their education to rule effectively, support the arts, and encourage the new educational methods. The Biography of Isabella d'Este describes the life of one Italian woman who possessed so much political authority that she became a renowned patron of the arts and of education.

Humanist scholarship was crucial in shaping the new spirit of the Renaissance, but it was not sufficient in itself. Scholars and artists and talented young men would have made little impact without the generosity of patrons such as Isabella, who supported the new talent and assiduously purchased their productions. The spirit of the Renaissance thrived on the money that flowed abundantly (albeit unevenly, as we will see) in the Italian cities.

THE GENEROSITY OF PATRONS: SUPPORTING NEW IDEAS

The talented writers and artists of the Renaissance depended on generous patrons to support them. During the early Renaissance, cities themselves served as artistic patrons, stimulating the creation of art by offering prizes and subsidies for their talented citizens. Guilds, too, served as artistic patrons, commissioning great public monuments to enhance the spaces of their cities. The public art that graced the streets and squares enhanced the reputation of the city itself and in turn forwarded the new ideas of the gifted artists.

In time, warfare and internal strife caused cities to have less money to use in support of art, and patronage was taken over by wealthy individuals. In addition to Isabella d'Este, many other rulers, such as the Medici in Florence and the Sforza in Milan, used their wealth to stimulate the creation of spectacular

works of art. In return, patrons gained social and political status by surrounding themselves with objects of beauty or intellect. Not only rulers, but rising bourgeoisie could enhance their social status by owning works of art, and this activity served to spur the production of art. Document 10.2 on page D10.1 describes Isabella d'Este trying to contract a painting.

The church also supported the arts. Religious fraternities commissioned many paintings, and popes financially backed numerous artists. Like cities and individuals, churches gained status through their patronage, but churches also recognized a religious purpose of art. *Religious patronage* Many people attributed miraculous power to visual portrayals of religious themes and churchmen supported this belief. For example, the Florentines customarily brought an image of the Virgin Mary (called the *Madonna of Impruneta*) down from the hills to Florence in times of crisis, and in 1483, a procession of the Madonna was credited with stopping a destructive, month-long rainfall.

Such ceremonies also served the civic purpose of bringing the faithful together in a public way. The painting in Figure 10.3 shows a religious procession

FIGURE 10.3
Gentile Bellini, *Procession of Eucharist*.

FIGURE 10.4
A printing shop.

the West by the late fourteenth century. By the early fifteenth century, Asian printers replaced wooden type with bronze type, which was much more durable and offered a more consistent print. This method, too, rapidly spread to the West.

In the 1440s, these early printing techniques reached their culmination with the development of moveable type and the adaptation of an oil press to print pages more rapidly. A German silversmith named Johannes Gutenberg (1400?–1470) is credited with bringing all these innovations together to produce the first printed Bible in 1455. Suddenly, literature became more available and thereby ultimately affecting all of Western civilization. Figure 10.4 depicts a printing shop in the late fifteenth century. At the right of the image, a worker sets the type in a tray so as to match the lettering in the manuscript in front of him. The printer at the left presses a plate of type on the paper, producing copies that are admired (and perhaps proofread) by the worker in the foreground. The worker standing at the left mixes the ink that will be applied to the letters to produce the image on the paper.

The development and proliferation of the printing press was a testimony to the growing confidence that there was a market for books. In addition to a demand for their product, print shops also needed something to print on. Paper technology gave them the necessary cheap medium to replace the expensive parchment used during the Middle Ages. The technique of papermaking came to Europe from China through the Muslim world. By the fourteenth century, Italian paper mills were using old rags to make inexpensive, yet high-quality, paper. Although some wealthy patrons, such as Isabella d'Este, often preferred the more traditional parchment, the future lay with the new paper.

Printing presses spread rapidly through Europe—by the 1480s many Italian cities had established their own presses, and by 1500 there were about a thousand presses all over the Continent. Map 10.1 shows the rapid spread of this popular new technology. Previously, valuable books, painstakingly copied by hand, belonged to the patron who paid for the copy. Now the literary world looked to a broader reading public for support, consequently igniting a rapid spread of ideas that carried the new spirit throughout Europe. Subsequent notions—from the excitement of international discoveries to intellectual challenges to religious ideology—also spread rapidly.

in Venice, in which the sacred Eucharist was paraded through the square encased in a magnificently ornate carrier. The painting reinforces the way these religious festivities united the residents and indeed celebrated the beautiful public spaces of the city itself.

Thus, dynamic city life and a new emphasis on education stimulated new ideas, and generous patronage helped them grow. However, the new spirit spread rapidly by the late Renaissance owing to a revolutionary advance in technology.

THE INVENTION OF THE PRINTING PRESS: SPREADING NEW IDEAS

Throughout the Middle Ages, precious texts had to be laboriously copied by hand, making books relatively scarce and expensive. As we saw in Chapter 1, one of the significant advantages to the growth of civilization is the ability for more people to read and have access to the written word. In Asia (China and Korea) inventors had developed a way to reproduce texts and pictures more quickly—wood-block printing. With this technique, images and some text were carved into wooden blocks and then could be mass produced by printing. This technique had spread to

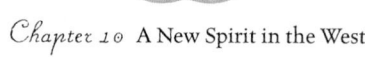

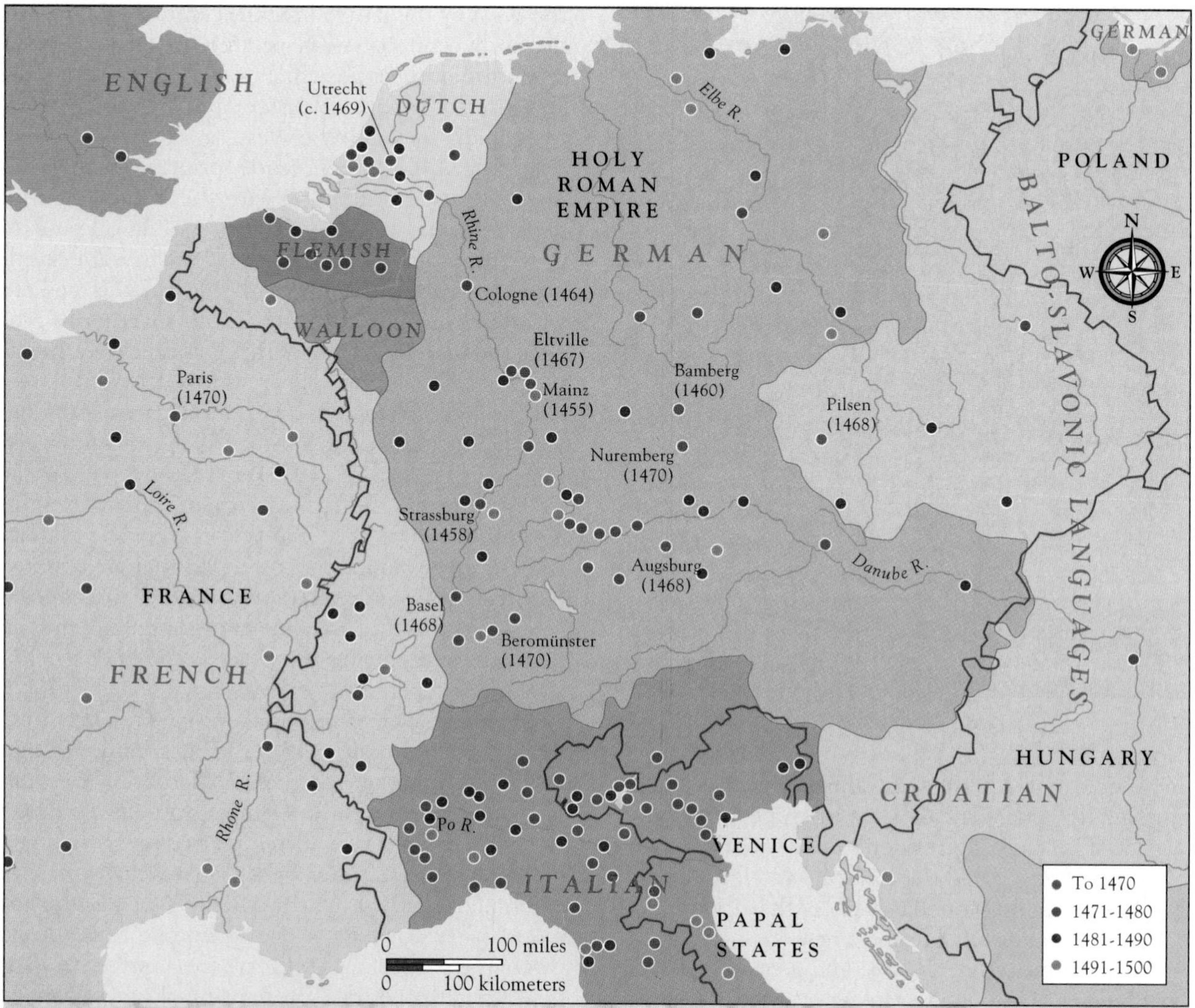

THINKING ABOUT GEOGRAPHY

MAP 10.1 *The Spread of Printing Before 1500*

This map shows how rapidly printing spread in the short time from 1470 to 1500. ◙ **Locate** Mainz along the Rhine River, the location from where printing spread. ◙ **Notice** how most of the centers of printing were located along the major rivers. **Consider** what that pattern suggests about the significance of waterways as means of communication. ◙ **Consider** why printing spread with such astonishing speed.

The pace of change in Western civilization quickened as the European presses circulated ideas with unprecedented speed.

All the elements were in place for the transformation of thought that we have come to know as the Renaissance. The study of classical texts had helped change people's views of themselves and their approach to the world. Money flowed in support of talented and enterprising individuals, and technology helped spread the ideas rapidly. Finally, men actively implemented these ideas in many fields, from art to business to politics.

The Politics of Individual Effort

The medieval power struggle between emperors and popes left an enormous power vacuum in northern Italy. This vacuum allowed small city-states, or cities that controlled the surrounding countryside, to become used to independence. As the fourteenth century opened, most of the northern cities were free communes (see Chapter 8) with republican forms of government, but as the fourteenth century progressed, changes occurred.

THE ITALIAN CITY-STATES

These city-states engaged in almost constant warfare over their borders and commercial interests, and within the cities, classes and political factions fought for control of the government. In such unstable times, most of the republican governments were under pressure, and strong men with dictatorial power took over. As we saw in Chapter 9, mercenary armies had become a significant feature of warfare, and they also became a force in Italian politics as city-states hired army captains (called *condottieri*) with their armies to come fight their wars. These mercenaries frequently ravaged the countryside, bringing more misery than protection to the population. Through the fourteenth and fifteenth centuries, city-states would see repeated internal and external strife as they wrestled with their neighbors and with internal governing. These turbulent times brought misery to many but opportunity to others. Sometimes strong, talented individuals rose to positions of authority without constitutional or hereditary legitimacy. Such rulers introduced a new kind of politics and perhaps inadvertently stimulated the new spirit of the Renaissance.

Map 10.2 shows Italy in 1454. Notice that the northern areas consisted of a patchwork quilt of city-states. Among these, Venice, Milan, and Florence were the largest and most powerful. Popes controlled the large, central strip of the peninsula, and the Kingdom of Naples dominated the south. It was the competition among the northern states that fueled the politics of individual effort that so influenced Renaissance ideas such as individualism and activism.

The Italian city-states fell into two general categories: republics and principalities. Republics featured the institutions of the medieval city communes, in which an urban elite governed. For the most part, Venice and Florence preserved the republican form of government during most of the Renaissance. Principalities, on the other hand, were ruled by one dynasty. Milan and Naples were the most notable examples of this form of government.

FLORENCE: BIRTHPLACE OF THE RENAISSANCE

Florence at the beginning of the fourteenth century was a vibrant republic where Renaissance ideas seem to have been first fostered. Florence prided itself on its republican form of government in which eligible men held office by random selection. But the city was an uneasy republic indeed, fragmented by local rivalries that always threatened to break out into violence within the urban spaces themselves. Only guild members could participate in the government, and an oligarchy of the leading families was frequently able to control the government. Florence was badly hit by the plague—in 1348 alone, almost 40 percent of its population was killed, and its economy, too, was badly damaged as cloth production declined. Warfare with Milan in the early fifteenth century bankrupted many of the city's leading commercial families and created a massive public debt. In their troubles, the Florentines turned to the wealthiest banking family in Europe—the Medici. The republic got more than it bargained for.

In 1434, Cosimo de Medici (1388–1464) took control of the Florentine oligarchy and exiled his rivals. In the tradition of Caesar Augustus, whom he admired, Cosimo concentrated power in his *The Medici* household while ostensibly keeping a republican form of government. Under this shrewd family, Florence and the arts flourished. Cosimo's grandson, Lorenzo the Magnificent (r. 1478–1492), epitomized the ideal Renaissance ruler. A great statesman, he was also a patron of the arts, a poet, and an athlete.

Yet even Lorenzo could not bring peace to the contentious Florentine people. During his life he faced intrigue and assassination attempts and had to use all his diplomatic skills to preserve Florence from foreign foes. Late in his tenure, voices began to be raised against the Renaissance ideals that he so actively supported. Shortly after Lorenzo's death, the rule of the Medici could not withstand the growing pressures from outside and within the city.

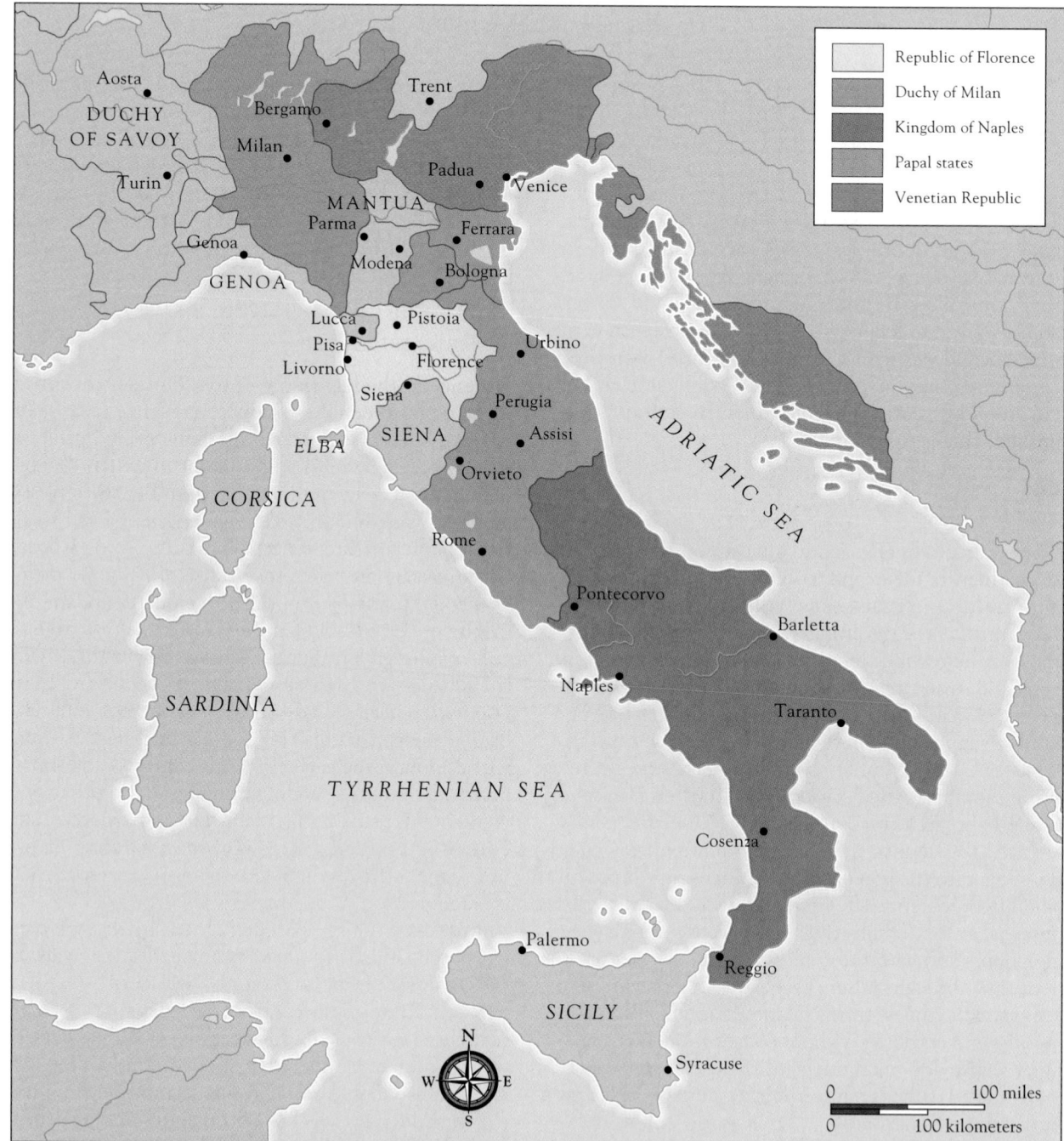

THINKING ABOUT GEOGRAPHY

MAP 10.2 *Italy in 1454*

This map shows the political divisions of Italy in the fifteenth century. ■ **Notice** the location of the major city-states of the north. **Which** were likely to be most immediately threatened by the expansion of the Papal states? ■ **Locate** Venice. **Consider** why it was so well placed to dominate trade in the eastern Mediterranean. **Which** states were threatened by Venice's expansion into the peninsula? ■ **Locate** the Kingdom of Naples. **What** contributed to Naples' relative isolation from the politics of the northern states?

In 1494, French armies invaded the countryside around Florence, and the city-state was again buffeted with financial and material woes. *Savonarola* The French armies found an ally within the city in the person of a fiery preacher who had objected to the rule of the Medici and to the passionate acquisition of money and art that had dominated the early Renaissance.

Girolamo Savonarola (1452–1498) was a courageous, yet uncompromising, man who had resented the rule of the Medici and accused the clergy of corruption from the papacy on down. He argued vigorously against the lust for money that motivated citizens in the high-tempo Florentine economy. Perhaps most of all, he despised humanism, which he believed poisoned everything from art to religion by placing humans in the spotlight. The passionate preacher clearly recognized the changing times, but he advocated a different response to these changes.

Helped by the disruptions caused by the French invasions, Savonarola was able to arrange for the Medici to be expelled from the city and for a republic to be reintroduced. But Savonarola also wanted to return people's sensibilities to what he perceived to be a more pious age. He preached against nude paintings and sculptures, and in 1497 presided over a public "burning of the vanities"—a huge bonfire into which people tossed ornaments, pictures, cards, and other "frivolous" items. This event is described by an eyewitness in Document 10.1 on page D10.1.

Eventually, the monk's zeal sparked opposition. The pope chafed at Savonarola's attacks and finally excommunicated him and forbade him to preach. Savonarola himself came to an ironic, fiery end: He was condemned and burned in the public square of Florence—exactly where the "vanities" had been burned.

Like the other great figures of the age, Savonarola was a product of the Renaissance—he felt the same civic pride and shared the same love of education. But, instead of responding to these forces with a sense of humanism and realism, he looked for a spiritual reaction, a religious renewal that he believed should shape the future. In time, northern Europeans picked up Savonarola's call for religious renewal, but not yet. In Florence the Medici were restored by the sixteenth century, and the republic was formally dissolved in 1530.

At first glance, it may seem incongruous that the stormy political history of Florence spawned the creative ideas that we have come to identify with the Renaissance. However, the very environment that made people feel they had to be actively involved in their city and fight for their own interests stimulated the driving individualism that characterized this age. Politicians vied to prove themselves superior to their rivals, often by supporting artists whose products contributed to their own status. In the republican turmoil, the Renaissance was born.

VENICE: THE SERENE REPUBLIC?

Venice preserved its republic with much less turmoil than Florence, although there, too, an oligarchy ruled. Venice's constitution called for only its aristocratic merchant families—numbering about 2,000—to serve in its Great Council. From among this number, they chose one man to serve as the council leader, or "doge," for life, but most men were in their 70s before being elected to this office. This rule by the elders made political life in Venice remarkably stable—indeed, the city called itself the "Most Serene Republic." This title underplayed the ever-present factional strife that plagued the Italian cities, but Venetians were always able to suppress the strife, and many believed their self-proclaimed myth of serenity.

This peace also stemmed from the prosperity generated by overseas trade, which Venice dominated owing to its advantageous location on the Adriatic Sea. Map 10.3 shows how Venice's location perfectly situated it to take advantage of the lucrative trade in the eastern Mediter- *Overseas trade* ranean. From Venice's earliest history, it enjoyed a privileged position in the trade with Byzantium, and as we saw in Chapter 8, during the Fourth Crusade in 1204, the Venetians led in the conquest of Constantinople itself. The painting of St. Mark's Square in Figure 10.3 shows not only the wealth of Venice, but the domed church in the background reveals the continuing influence of Byzantium on the aesthetics of the city that was formed by the interactions with east. The end of the crusader kingdoms did not end the Venetian dominance of trade, and at the beginning of the Renaissance, wealth continued to pour into the Serene Republic. To consolidate its hold on the eastern Mediterranean, Venice built an empire of coastal cities and islands—as shown on Map 10.3.

Venice was built on a collection of islands in a lagoon, and the Grand Canal that continues to mark its main thoroughfare is a perfect representation of the city's maritime orientation. Of the city-state's

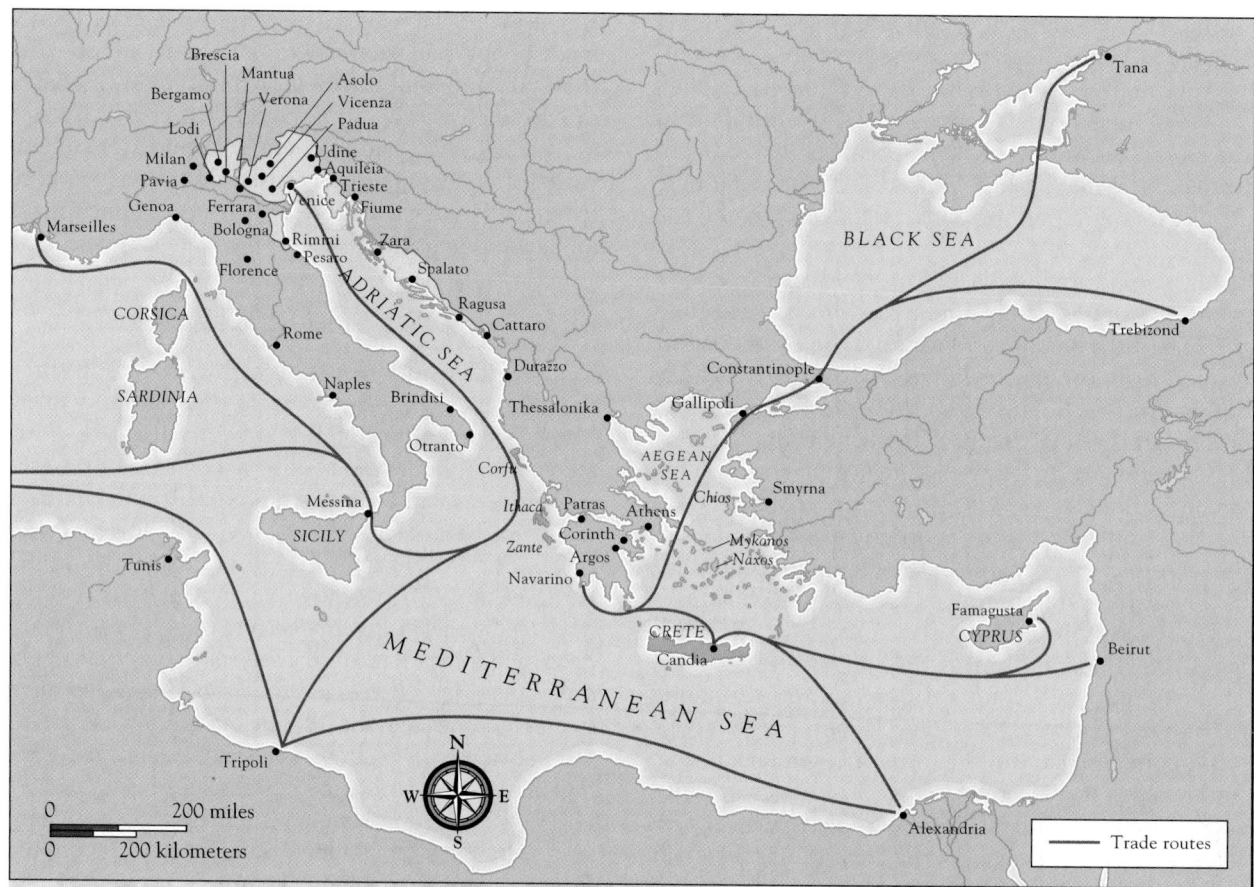

THINKING ABOUT GEOGRAPHY

MAP 10.3 *The Venetian Empire in the Fifteenth Century*

This map shows the Venetian empire, with the red lines indicting the main trade routes of Venice's prosperous commercial ventures. ❧ **Notice** Venice's dominance of the Adriatic Sea. **Locate** Crete. **Consider** how control of these two areas would facilitate Venice's ascendancy of the trade in the eastern Mediterranean. ❧ **Locate** the Muslim cities of Tripoli, Tunis, Alexandria, and Beirut. **Consider** how trade with these centers might facilitate cross-cultural interactions.

total population of about 150,000 people, more than 30,000 were sailors. Venice's navy boasted 45 galleys—large warships with sails and oars—and 300 hefty sailing ships.

In the beginning of the fifteenth century, Venice began to engage in a policy of expanding into the Italian mainland—the city-state wanted to secure its food supply as well as its overland trade routes. Map 10.3 shows the cities that became Venetian dependencies. Although this expansionist policy made sense to the Venetians, it understandably upset the neighboring states of Milan and Florence.

The Venetians perhaps should have looked more carefully at their maritime holdings, for as we saw in Chapter 9, Turkish expansion in the eastern Mediterranean (with the capture of Rhodes) seriously challenged Venetian supremacy in the seas. (See Chapter 11 for the subsequent confrontation.)

Through the Renaissance, however, this calm republic helped forward the progress of the new spirit. Its leaders wanted to grace their city with the magnificent new art, so their patronage brought talent to the fore, and their ships helped disseminate the new ideas along with the Italian trade goods.

MILAN AND NAPLES: TWO PRINCIPALITIES

Milan's violent history mirrored that of Florence, but this city-state more quickly moved from a republican form of government to an hereditary principality. During the thirteenth century, rival political factions in the city had constantly vied for power. In desperation, the commune invited a soldier from a family named Visconti to come in and keep the peace; he stayed on to rule as prince and established a dynasty that reigned in Milan from 1278 to 1447. The Visconti family recognized the volatility of Italian politics and focused on the military strength that had brought them to power in the first place. After fending off attempts to establish a republic, the Visconti established a principality that coveted the lands of the rest of northern Italy. Only the diplomatic and military talents of Florence, Venice, and its other neighbors kept this aggressive principality in check. Finally, in 1447, the Visconti dynasty ended when the prince died without an heir—the door was open for a new power struggle in Milan.

In 1450 another strong dynasty took power. The Sforza family kept the city-state's proud military tradition, yet also served as patrons of the arts to enhance their own political reputations. The Sforza continued to rule until the early sixteenth century, though always under the pressure of growing republican aspirations.

The Kingdom of Naples in the south was the only region of Italy that preserved a feudal form of government ruled by an hereditary monarchy. In the *Naples* early fourteenth century, Naples was ruled by Angevin kings who were descendants of the king of France. Under these kings the ideas of the Renaissance came to the feudal and rural south. Giotto (the shepherd-painter whose story opened this chapter) and Boccaccio (see Chapter 9) spent time in Naples under the patronage of King Robert (r. 1309–1343), and even Petrarch called Robert "the only king of our times who has been a friend of learning and of virtue."

However, after Robert's rule, Naples became a battleground with claimants from the Angevins and the Spanish Aragonese competing for the throne.

In 1435, the king of Aragon, Alfonso the Magnanimous (r. 1435–1458), was able to reunite the crowns of Naples and Sicily. He worked to centralize his administration but was unable fully to subdue his barons, and Naples remained a feudal kingdom. Alfonso was a passionate devotee of Italian culture and served as a patron of the Renaissance. However, the dynastic claims on this throne by other kings in Europe would disrupt Italian politics in years to come.

THE PAPAL STATES

As Map 10.2 shows, the papacy was not just a spiritual presence. When the popes returned to Rome after their sojourn in Avignon (see Chapter 9), they found their traditional lands reduced and many under the control of their neighbors. They faced the question of whether they were to be more secular or more spiritual leaders. One supporter of papal rule said that "virtue without power would be ridiculous." Therefore, like the Italian princes, the Renaissance popes strove to resume control of central Italy and succeeded.

As rulers of central Italy, the popes had a particular advantage in that their rule was a theocracy that derived its legitimacy from God (and election by the college of cardinals), so that issues of republicanism and tyranny did not apply. However, their religious role also brought complications. For example, as worldly rulers in the Italian tradition, they were expected to improve the fortunes of their families, so they frequently (and accurately) fell prey to the charge of nepotism as they created positions for their relatives. The popes also looked backward to their medieval struggles with the Holy Roman Emperors to control Italy (see Chapter 8), so many felt they had a right—indeed an obligation—to expand papal lands on the peninsula. All these factors helped propel the popes into the frequently violent sphere of Italian politics. But they also leaped into the exciting, brilliant world of Renaissance creativity.

Just as other Italian princes discovered that art could enhance their prestige, the popes, too, became avid patrons of the arts. In doing so, *Papal patronage* they transformed Rome into one of Europe's major cultural centers. Figure 10.5 shows Pope Sixtus IV (r. 1471–1484) seated in as much grandeur

FIGURE 10.5

Melozzo da Forlí, *Sixtus IV Receives Platina, Keeper of the Vatican Library.*

and surrounded by as much wealth as any king. His courtiers talk among themselves while the pope receives the humanist Platina (kneeling in the center). This painting commemorated the founding of the Vatican library, to be run by Platina. Even today, the library remains a major learning center. The cardinal standing in the center of the painting later became Pope Julius II. The courtiers on the left are Sixtus's nephews, who later participated in a plot to murder one of the Medicis. This painting depicts the Renaissance love of learning—as well as its penchant for nepotism and intrigue.

To increase (or even maintain) their secular power, the popes waded into the quagmire of Italian

The Borgia Family politics, and by the end of the Renaissance, a pope was elected from an influential family—the Borgia. Like many other Renaissance princes, the Borgia Pope Alexander VI (r. 1492–1503) tried to reclaim his lands from his acquisitive neighbors. Alexander also proved worldly in his personal life; gossips gleefully circulated accounts

of his sexual escapades. He still upheld the tradition of Renaissance family life, however, favoring his illegitimate children by placing them in advantageous positions. The pope's warrior son, Cesare Borgia (1475?–1507), seemed a candidate for uniting Italy under Alexander's authority. For his daughter Lucrezia, Alexander arranged three marriages designed to advance the family's dynastic aims. Isabella d'Este (featured in the Biography on page 336) arranged one of these marriages to protect the Este family's interests. All these manipulations came to nothing, however: Alexander died suddenly, and the family's ambitions failed. The reputation of the papacy as a spiritual authority also declined.

One of the most memorable of the Renaissance popes, Julius II (r. 1503–1513) embodied the ambitious values of the times, but without the scandals that had plagued Alexander. Julius was as perfect a Renaissance ruler as Florence's *Julius II* Lorenzo de Medici. A patron of the arts, he made Rome a cultural hub on par with the greatness of Florence. He was also an experienced warrior, personally leading his armies into battle as he carried on Alexander's expansionist policies. Julius II summoned Michelangelo to Rome and commissioned him to decorate the ceiling of the Sistine Chapel (see Figure 10.1). Michelangelo also worked on the new St. Peter's Church in Rome that was being built at the time. Although Julius and Michelangelo had a stormy relationship, the patron helped his artist produce some of the most beautiful work of the Renaissance. But such creations cost money, and, as we will see in Chapter 11, many people, especially in northern Europe, began to criticize these popes for what some called worldly extravagance.

THE ART OF DIPLOMACY

The wars, shifting alliances, and courtly intrigue of Italian politics sparked a new interest (and expertise) in the art of diplomacy. Not since the early Byzantine state had courtiers devoted such attention to the details of successful diplomacy. States exchanged ambassadors to facilitate official communication and sent spies to maintain advantages.

The most noted writer on political skill and diplomacy was Niccolò Machiavelli (1469–1527), whose book *The Prince* still influences many modern-day political thinkers. Machiavelli recognized the danger confronting Florence in the fifteenth century as

OLC

French armies threatened the independence of the city-states, and he wrote to offer advice about how to survive—indeed prevail—in these turbulent times. His was an eminently practical guide that looked at politics with a cold-blooded realism that had not been seen before. For Machiavelli, the most important element for a successful ruler (the prince) was his strength of will. He insisted that while princes might appear to have such traditional virtues as charity and generosity, they could not rely on these traits to hold power. They must actually be ruthless, expedient, strong, and clever if they were to maintain their rule. As he said, "It is better for a ruler to be feared than loved."

Machiavelli

Machiavelli's blunt description of political power articulated a striking departure from medieval political ideals. During the Middle Ages, the perfect ruler was Louis IX of France (r. 1226–1270) (described in Chapter 8), who proved so virtuous that he was made a saint. With the Renaissance, men like Cosimo de Medici and Cesare Borgia—self-made rulers who methodically cultivated their talents and grasped power boldly—took power. Machiavelli's book captured the new statecraft and showed realistic politics often meant a brutal disregard for ethics. Indeed, many Europeans living during the Renaissance showed a social indifference and personal immorality that we might find dismaying today.

Individualism as Self-Interest: Life During the Renaissance

In spite of efforts to hone their diplomatic skills to a fine art, many Italians still resorted to brute force to get what they wanted. In all the city-states, some individuals came to power by stimulating social strife among competing factions or even using violence to vanquish their rivals. Taking part in politics could also get one in deep trouble. Petrarch's father, for example, like many other men of his time, made the mistake of supporting a losing political struggle in Florence, and the victors punished him by amputating his hand. Individuals struggling to better themselves politically and economically often did so at the expense of their neighbors.

Aside from the occasional opportunity to improve one's social position, Renaissance cities still had a clearly defined social hierarchy. The Florentines referred to these divisions as the "little people" and the "fat people." The "little people" consisted of merchants, artisans, and workers, and made up about 60 percent of the population. Slaves and servants assumed even lower status, beneath the "little people." The "fat people" included well-to-do merchants and professionals, and made up about 30 percent of the population. The wealthiest elite—bankers and merchants owning more than one-quarter of the city's wealth—made up only 1 percent of the population.

Whenever there is a great disparity between rich and poor in a situation of some social mobility, crime tends to run high. This was true throughout Renaissance Europe. One Florentine merchant, Luca Landucci, who kept a detailed diary of the events of his age, regularly wrote of crime and punishment as he heard his neighbors gossip about the shocking misdeeds of the day. In one diary entry, he repeats news of a young woman who killed a child for the pearl necklace the girl was wearing. In another, he tells of the townspeople watching as a man was beheaded for "coining false money." Luca's dreary lists of crimes seem endless.

Rising crime

Many people blamed wanderers for the alarming rise in crime. According to such observers, soldiers discharged from mercenary armies, the poor fleeing poverty in cities and countryside, and other displaced persons made the highways more dangerous than ever. Italy and other states tried to control crime, but their methods were usually ineffective as well as misplaced. As in other times of rapid social change, rulers increased the regulation of social behavior. For example, in England in 1547 a new law stipulated that vagabonds be branded and enslaved for two years. The law tells us a great deal about Renaissance society's intense fear of crime and strangers.

GROWING INTOLERANCE

Renaissance governments enacted harsh legislation on people they found threatening, from prostitutes to paupers. This same impulse contributed to an increasing intolerance of other religions and cultures, as evidenced by an intensifying anti-Semitism. In Italy, Christians passed laws against sexual relations between Christians and Jews, and authorities in Rome reputedly burned 50 Jewish prostitutes to death for having intercourse with Christian men. Laws also restricted Jews to certain parts of cities and required them to wear identifiable clothing. In some instances the clothing included colors that had been set aside for prostitutes. This cruel association left Jewish women open to ridicule, criticism, and sometimes abuse from non-Jewish neighbors.

Anti-Semitism existed during the Middle Ages—thirteenth-century kings of England and France had expelled Jews from their lands, and communities of Jews had experienced periodic violence. (As we saw in Chapter 9, Jews were subjected to particular violence in the wake of the bubonic plague.) However, increasing anti-Semitism in the fifteenth century led to large-scale expulsions of Jewish communities from many cities and countries. Vienna began expelling Jews in 1421, and many other German cities followed. Figure 10.6 is taken from a fifteenth-century Hebrew manuscript, and it shows Jews driven from a German town. The group was allowed to take their animals and a wagon for the women, children, and elderly as they headed down the hills seeking a new home. Most German Jews moved eastward into Poland and Russia, and the center of Judaism shifted from western Europe to the East.

Ferdinand and Isabella forced all of Spain's Jews to leave in 1492, causing one of the largest movements of peoples in the era. Portugal did the same in 1497. Many Iberian Jews fled to the Muslim lands in North Africa, and some people today still trace their ancestry back to this exodus. As a result of this intolerance, western Europe lost the talents of the many Jews who had inhabited these lands for centuries.

FIGURE 10.6

Jews driven from a German city, Hebrew manuscript, ca. 1427.

ECONOMIC BOOM TIMES

The new ideas of the Renaissance (both good and bad) developed against the backdrop of the fourteenth-century crises but were fostered in the fifteenth century by a vigorous economic life. Individualism was stimulated by the economic potential, and excess money made the all-important patronage possible. Growing commerce and industries brought money into Italy, stimulating the local economy and allowing wealthy people to indulge their desire for beauty and comfort.

Venice shone as the greatest merchant city in the world, importing tons of cotton, silk, and spices every year and exporting woolen cloth and mounds of silver coins to pay for their imports. As the sixteenth century opened, 1.5 million pounds of spices came through Venice alone every year. Venetians did not simply rest on their commercial wealth; some enterprising citizens developed and manufactured new products—most prominently, forks and windowpane glass—that would in time sweep through the world.

By contrast, Milan and Florence were craft-industrial cities. Florence, with its 270 workshops, led the way in wool cloth making. Renaissance Italy also profited from another new industry: silk. *Wool and silk* As early as the twelfth century, travelers had smuggled silkworms into Italy from China so that Italians could begin to produce the precious fabric locally. But the industry really blossomed after the thirteenth century, when the Chinese silk loom appeared in Italy. Italians powered the looms with waterwheels and produced large amounts of silk cloth. In the fourteenth century, one city had a silk mill employing 480 spindles rapidly spinning the precious silk. By the fifteenth century, Florence boasted 83 workshops devoted to silk production. The wealth let Florence take part in the thriving economy generated by the cloth trade network that connected countries like Italy and the Netherlands all the way to the New

World. In the wake of this prosperous trade, even a shopkeeper in Florence wrote excitedly about his first taste of sugar brought in from overseas.

But the most profitable industry was banking. Throughout the Middle Ages, the development of *Banking* banking and commerce had been impeded by the Christian belief in the immorality of usury, or charging interest, but enterprising merchants found ways around the prohibition. Some people offered gifts in gratitude for a loan of money, thus effectively paying back more than they borrowed. However, the easiest way to collect interest was by changing money and making a profit on the exchange rate. By the thirteenth century, Christians all over Europe began to engage in the lucrative trade of money lending, but it was the Italian bankers of the Renaissance who really first perfected the art of using money to make money. In the process, many raked in fortunes—for example, the rich families in Florence purchased state-guaranteed government bonds that paid over 15 percent interest. It is not surprising that the "fat people" got even "fatter" as the Renaissance rolled on.

SLAVERY REVIVED

The booming economy of the Renaissance led to new institutional oppression—the revival of slavery in Europe. Why was slavery reintroduced precisely when even serfs were being freed from their bondage? Some historians suggest that the labor shortage of the late fourteenth century caused by the bubonic plague drove people to look for fresh hands. However, this explanation is not satisfactory, because the new slaves were by and large not used in agriculture or industry. Instead, it seems that newly wealthy people trying to make their lives more comfortable looked to new sources for scarce domestic help.

Slavery had some complex facets. Renaissance families, for example, often considered slaves part of the household. One Florentine woman in 1469 wrote a letter to her husband asking him to acquire a slave-girl to care for their young child or a "black boy" to become the child's playmate. Occasionally slaves bore children fathered by their owners, who sometimes raised them as legitimate heirs. Figure 10.7 is a portrait of a slave named Katharina drawn by Albrecht Dürer (1471–1528), a popular engraver commissioned to render portraits of many famous people. Katharina was in the service of a Portuguese com-

mercial agent living in Antwerp who became friends with Dürer in 1520. This portrait shows the high regard in which this owner held Katharina.

She is well dressed, and the fact that she sat for a portrait shows that she was a valued member of the household. Nevertheless, Dürer captured a sadness in her eyes that must have marked even the best-placed slaves.

The Venetians, positioned near the eastern Mediterranean, capitalized on this trade first, dealing mostly in Muslim and Greek Orthodox slaves *Sources of slaves* obtained through warfare or simply taken captive. Between 1414 and 1423, Venetian traders sold about 10,000 slaves in their markets. Most of these slaves were young girls sold into service as domestic servants. The fall of Constantinople to the Turks in 1453 (see Chapter 9) led to a decline in

FIGURE 10.7
Albrecht Dürer, *Portrait of Katharina*, 1520.

FIGURE 10.8
Botticelli, *Wedding Feast of Nastagio degli Onesti,* 1483.

slaves from eastern lands, and Europeans began to look for new sources of captives. In the early fifteenth century, the Portuguese conquered the Canary Islands off the western coast of Africa, and what had been a trickle of African slaves into Europe swelled. In the following decades, Portuguese traders eager to compete with the wealthy Venetians brought some 140,000 sub-Saharan African slaves into Europe.

Many people questioned the reestablishment of slavery in Europe. The church disapproved of it, and numerous slaveowners considered it too expensive in the long run. Slavery gradually disappeared in Europe by the end of the Renaissance. However, the precedent had been reestablished, and traders would later find a flourishing slave market in the New World (see Chapters 12 and 15).

FINDING COMFORT IN FAMILY

In the rugged world that emphasized individual achievement, the family assumed central importance as the one constant, dependable structure in Renais-

sance society. Men and women believed they could count on their kin when all else failed and highlighted these connections in art, literature, and the decisions they made in their daily lives. The emphasis on family loyalty was not limited to the upper classes. Artisan workshops, for example, were family affairs in which fathers trained sons and sons-in-law to carry on the family business.

Family ties also defined ethics in a world in which morality seemed relative. In a book about family written by Leon Battista Alberti (1404–1472), a Florentine architect, the author argued that whatever increased a man's power to help his family was good. Riches, however gained, fell into this category. Still, as Isabella d'Este proved, nothing beat a good marriage alliance for improving a family's standing.

Figure 10.8, a painting by Sandro Botticelli (1447–1510), depicts a wedding banquet marking the alliance between two wealthy Florentine families. The families and *Marriage alliances* their supporters sit facing each other at the tables. The image suggests that these families, though once separate, will be joined after the wedding. The lines of servants extending beyond the margins of the image imply the unlimited bounty that the two families bring to the festivities.

Plans for such beneficial alliances began as early as the birth of a girl, when wealthy Florentine fathers would open an account with the public dowry fund, which paid as much as 21 percent interest. Family alliances depended on both parties bringing resources to the match. Wealthy families with sons wanted to be certain that their resources would not be diminished by marriage. Thus, parents of girls had to ensure that their daughters could bring enough money to an alliance to ensure a match with well-placed families. The dowry fund was implemented to guarantee that a girl had a sizeable dowry when she reached marriageable age. Some Renaissance families could not afford dowries for all their daughters and encouraged some to enter convents (which required smaller dowries). Indeed, the number of convents in Florence increased from only 5 in 1350 to 47 in 1550.

Of course, all these efforts to secure important family alliances had an equal impact on men and women. In the literature and art of the period, too, both men and women appear, but here women played a strikingly different role than they did in real life. Frequently following the medieval traditions of courtly love, women were given a prominent place as idealized beings who inspired men. Dante Alighieri (1265–1321) (discussed in Chapter 9), whose *Divine Comedy* stands at the cusp between the Middle Ages and the Renaissance, featured a young woman, Beatrice, as his guide into heaven. Petrarch devoted many sonnets to Laura, a young woman who served as his inspiration. Painters, too, portrayed numerous women, many of them nudes who represented idealized beauty and longing for perfection. Artists may have played with the notion of idealized women, but Renaissance men depended on real women to preside over the haven that was their family and their security for the future.

CHILDREN'S LIVES

Though idealized visions of women signaled the importance of the continuity that families provided, and Renaissance families wanted and loved their children, child-rearing practices undermined the hopes of many a proud parent. Middle-class and wealthy families of the Renaissance believed that it was unhealthy (and

FIGURE 10.9
Andrea Mantegna, *The Cardinal Francesco Gonzaga Returning from Rome.*

perhaps even unsavory) for women to breast-feed their infants. Therefore, they customarily sent their newborns to live with peasant women, who were paid to serve as wet nurses until the children were weaned. Some nurses took meticulous care of these infants; others were less attentive. Peasant mothers suffered from poor diets themselves and had insufficient milk to nurse a fosterling along with her own infants. Foster babies faced other dangers in the villages as well: Criminal records tell horrifying stories of death in the countryside, such as that of a peasant man who murdered four children under the age of eight. Florentine city-dwellers hearing such tales sometimes worried about their children's safety in the countryside, but the force of custom sent infants away to depend on the kindness of strangers.

Most urban parents reclaimed their children when they were weaned, at about two years old. These young strangers then had to fit into large households teeming

Childhood hardships

with older children, stepchildren, and a host of other relatives. With busy parents and stepparents, children often formed their principal attachment with an older sibling or aunt or uncle. The artist Andrea Mantegna was commissioned to paint a cycle of frescoes for the Gonzaga family, who ruled the Duchy of Mantua, and Figure 10.9 shows one portion of this magnificent work. Against the stunning background of the city, the painter shows a man with presumably three of his sons. The youngest in the foreground holds tightly to the eldest's hand, perhaps reflecting the situation in many crowded settings as older children cared for younger.

Child-rearing experts warned parents against pampering their offspring, and in general the parents obeyed. Ironically, in this culture of wealth and luxury, people raised their children with a degree of strictness that may seem extreme to us today. One writer (the Dominican Giovanni Dominici), for example, urged mothers to prepare children for hardship by making them sleep in the cold on a hard chest instead of a bed. To toughen them, parents fed children bitter-tasting objects such as peachstones and sometimes gave them "harmless" nausea-inducing herbs so as to accustom them to illness. A humanist (Filarete) writing about an ideal school recommended that children be fed only tough meat so they would learn to eat slowly. This same writer recommended that children eat standing up until they were twenty years old. Many parents let their children sleep only six to eight hours a night to keep them from getting lazy.

Within these strict guidelines, boys and girls were treated quite differently. One humanist (Paola da Certaldo) advised feeding and clothing boys well. For girls, he recommended: "Dress the girl well but as for eating, it doesn't matter as long as it keeps her alive; don't let her get fat."

At about seven years old, middle-class boys were sent to school to learn reading and mathematics and to ready themselves for the complex world of Renaissance economics. As the boys prepared for careers, fathers arranged marriages for their young daughters.

Girls were married relatively young—between 17 and 20 years old (although sometimes younger)—to bridegrooms in their 30s who had established their careers. (See Isabella d'Este's biography.) Many brides, still children themselves when they began having babies, did not survive the experience of giving birth. One Florentine man recorded in his memoirs that, between 1390 and 1431, he had four wives who gave him a total of 24 children. The first three wives died in childbirth.

The harshness of childhood took its toll on many boys and girls; mortality among children reached astonishing rates. In fifteenth-century Florence, 45 percent of children died before the age of 20, most of them girls. The 1427 census in Florence showed a surprising gender ratio: 100 women to every 110 men. This statistic reversed the situation that had prevailed through the High Middle Ages, when women outnumbered men, and testifies to the hardships that even wealthy Renaissance girls and women faced. Families eager to preserve their dynasties nevertheless neglected the very children on whom their futures depended.

An Age of Talent and Beauty: Renaissance Culture and Science

Renaissance life had its unsavory side—as rich men struggled to get richer, powerful men worked for more power, and small children sometimes suffered. But at the same time, Renaissance society produced some astonishingly talented people whose works have transformed not only our ideas about beauty but also the very appearance of the world we live in today. During the Renaissance—as in classical Athens—people expected art to be a public thing, to be available to and appreciated by people as they strolled through the cities. Public art nurtured civic pride.

ARTISTS AND ARTISANS

During the Renaissance, many upper-class boys pursued humanistic literary studies to prepare for the day they would play a public role in city life, but their families generally discouraged them from following careers in the visual arts. Filippo Brunelleschi (1377–1446), for example, greatly displeased his

OLC

father when he declared his interest in sculpting and architecture; his family had fully expected Filippo to become a physician or a notary. Michelangelo's father dismissed his son's interest in art as "shameful." Peasant boys, too, had little chance at a career in the arts, for without family connections, there was little chance of entry into the art world. If a country boy was a talented artist, he would probably not have the good fortune to be discovered like the shepherd Giotto whose story opened this chapter.

The majority of Renaissance artists came from artisan families. As boys worked as apprentices in artisan workshops, masters recognized and supported genius. Botticelli, the great Florentine painter, was apprenticed at age 13, as was Michelangelo. These examples were typical—a boy entering adulthood had to learn to take his place in the world, and that place often began in the artisan workshops. As a young man developed his skill, people began to recognize that he was no longer a simple craftsman, an artisan, making goods, but instead an artist, a creator of beauty.

Women ordinarily were excluded from taking this path. Yet, in spite of this lack of official acceptance, a number of female artists won renown during the Renaissance. Two, in particular, were highly respected by their contemporaries. Sofonisba Anguissola (1532?–1625) achieved fame as an artist through her skill and the support of her wealthy, aristocratic father. More typical was the case of Lavinia Fontana (1552–1614), the daughter of an artist who trained in her father's workshop. Despite these successes, the public role of artists precluded many women from active careers in art. For example, Anguissola delayed marriage until she was in her late 40s so she could paint—a privilege that most Renaissance fathers did not grant.

Late in the Renaissance, artists overall gained new respect—wealthy patrons stopped viewing them as simply manual laborers and began to recognize them as artists. Michelangelo even earned the title "*Il Divino*," the Divine One. Europeans during the Renaissance valued genius, and these artistic geniuses obliged by creating magnificent works.

ARCHITECTURE: ECHOING THE HUMAN FORM

The most expensive investment a patron of the arts could make was in architecture, and artists competed for these lucrative contracts. In the process, they designed innovative churches and other buildings that contributed to the prestige of their cities. Where did architects learn these new ideas? Part of the answer comes from the training of architects. Artisans did not consider architecture a separate craft, so there was no direct apprenticeship for this profession that rigidly inculcated old design ideas. Indeed, the greatest architects had all trained for other fields: Brunelleschi, for example, was a goldsmith, and Alberti a university-trained humanist. The Renaissance passion for the glory of classical Greece and Rome led would-be architects to look carefully at the old ruins that had stood for so long; their love of the individual caused them to put humans at the center of their enterprise. The resulting architecture, while looking back to classical models, was strikingly and beautifully new.

Instead of soaring Gothic cathedrals dominated by vertical heights, architects followed classical models of balance and simplicity and combined circular forms with linear supports to break up the monotony of vertical lines. Instead of creating structures that made humans seem small *Human architecture* and insignificant before God, they built to glorify the human form and proportions. The fifteenth-century architectural drawings pictured in Figure 10.10 show the ideal of buildings designed along human proportions. The drawing on the left shows a front view of a building with a man standing to indicate the proper proportions, while the one on the right shows a floor plan with the man lying down in the building.

The most influential architectural treatise, *On Building* by Alberti, dominated the field for centuries and expressed an architectural aesthetic that echoed that of the ancient Greeks. Alberti argued that buildings should mirror the human body in their supports and openings, and this sentiment is shown in Figure 10.10. Repeating the same principle, Michelangelo claimed that anyone who had not mastered anatomy and painting of the human form could not understand architecture. "The different parts of a building," he explained, "derive from human members." Thus, much of the architecture of the Renaissance was created in the image and likeness of the human form.

It is easy to miss the subtleties of human proportion within architecture as we look at the graceful buildings, but there is no overlooking one of the architects' debts to Rome—domes instead of *Domes* Gothic spires now began to rise with more frequency over the skylines of Renaissance cities. Figure 10.11 shows the cathedral of Florence, with its dome designed by Brunelleschi. The architect had admired the Pantheon dome in Rome (see Chapter 4), and he

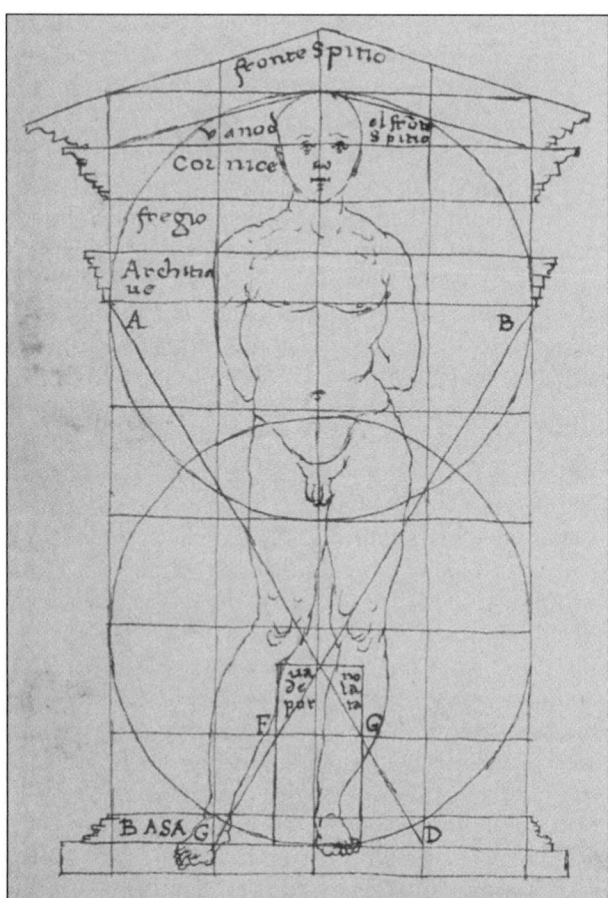
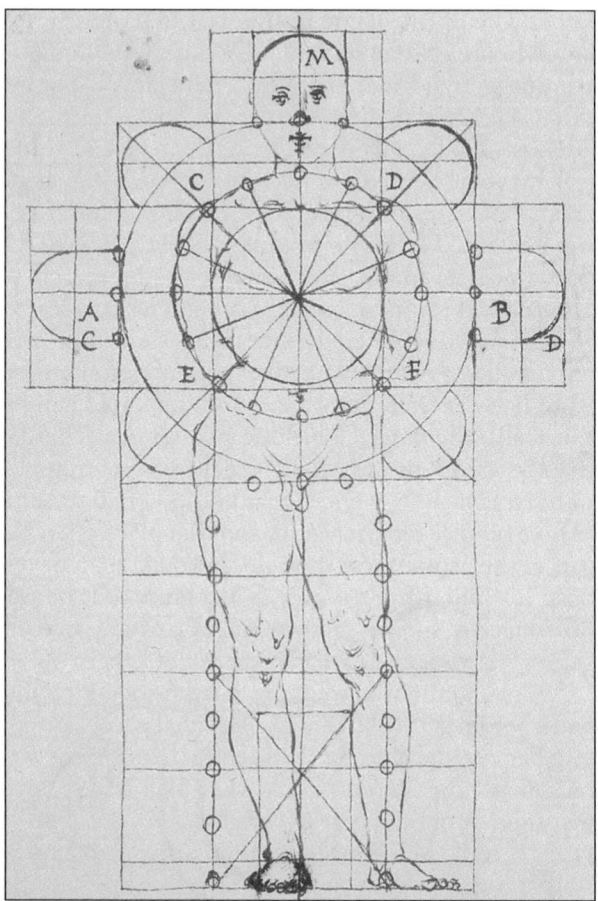

FIGURE 10.10
Francesco di Giorgio Martini, human-proportion architecture.

wanted to erect a massive dome to span the huge base of the new cathedral in Florence. However, Brunelleschi realized that the Roman dome was not suitable to the large space, so the architect creatively took the Gothic technique of using architectural ribs to create a magnificent new structure for the city. Brunelleschi designed the dome of the Florence cathedral with an inner and outer shell, both attached to the eight ribs of the octagonal structure. The inset in Figure 10.11 shows a drawing of the structural design. Between the two shells the architect placed 16 ribs to strengthen the dome. The two shells thus supported each other and shared the weight of the whole. Many Florentines predicted that the dome would collapse, yet Brunelleschi's handiwork continues to dominate the skyline of Florence.

The Renaissance study of architecture also extended beyond individual buildings to town planning in general. In the fifteenth century, planners began to dream of laying out towns in the simple and logical grid pattern that characterizes our modern cities. Indeed, older European cities still feature a medieval center with curved and random streets surrounded by tidy, post-Renaissance grids. In Latin America, by contrast, towns founded by fifteenth-century Europeans were created in a grid pattern centered on the town square. On the peripheries of such towns, however, streets wove randomly in the tradition of the villages that predated the Renaissance town centers. All these new ideas about buildings and street planning reshaped the cities of the West.

Town planning

SCULPTURE COMES INTO ITS OWN

Just as Brunelleschi's admiration of the ancients led him to re-create domed architecture, sculptors also drew from classical models. Italians, who had admired free-standing images from the ancient world, began to demand similar beauty for their cities. City communes and individuals commissioned life-sized figures to stand free in the public spaces of cities.

Figure 10.12 shows Michelangelo's widely admired statue of David, the biblical figure who killed the giant Goliath. The statue stands more *Michelangelo's David* than 18 feet high and took the master three years to carve from a block of supposedly flawed marble. The work exhibits all the innovations of Renaissance sculpture: It is a huge, free-standing nude that depicts the classical ideal of repose, in which the subject rests his weight on one leg in a pose called *contra posto*. The figure exemplifies the confidence and the glorification of the human body that marked Renaissance pride.

Michelangelo's statue shows another hallmark of Renaissance spirit—an exuberant praise of realism; the sculptor knew anatomy and realistically portrayed the human body. Renaissance sculptors had to look at life carefully in order to reproduce it with such accuracy, and the audience, too, was led to an appreciation of realism through admiring the great sculptures that graced the public areas.

The statue also carried a political message, a common characteristic of the civic humanism of the day. In 1494, when the French invasion of Florence caused a temporary fall of the Medici rule, the newly restored Republic of Florence had commissioned Michelangelo to create a work with a patriotic theme—something that would celebrate the overthrow of the family that had dominated the city for so long. The sculptor chose David the "giant killer" to symbolize the republic's ousting of the goliath Medici. Michelangelo portrayed David before his fight with Goliath—the youth is confident and defiant, just as Florence saw itself confronting the rest of the world. In this masterpiece, art joined with politics in the best Renaissance tradition.

PAINTING FROM A NEW PERSPECTIVE

The shepherd Giotto di Bondone (1267?–1337), whose artistic talents were recognized by a Florentine master, was to revolutionize painting for Florence and

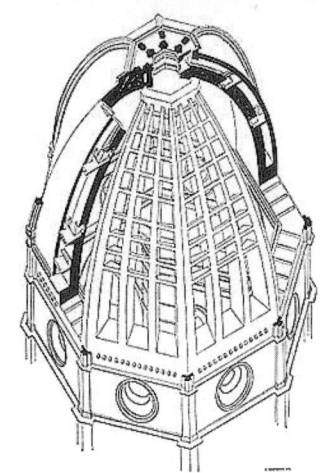

FIGURE 10.11 Brunelleschi's dome of the Florence Cathedral, 1420–1436.

the West. The young apprentice who fooled his master with a painting of a fly turned his talents to magnificent religious paintings, and he created realistic figures that showed a full range of human expression. For example, his virgins were not portrayed as remote queens of heaven, but instead painted as realistic young girls struggling to be caring mothers.

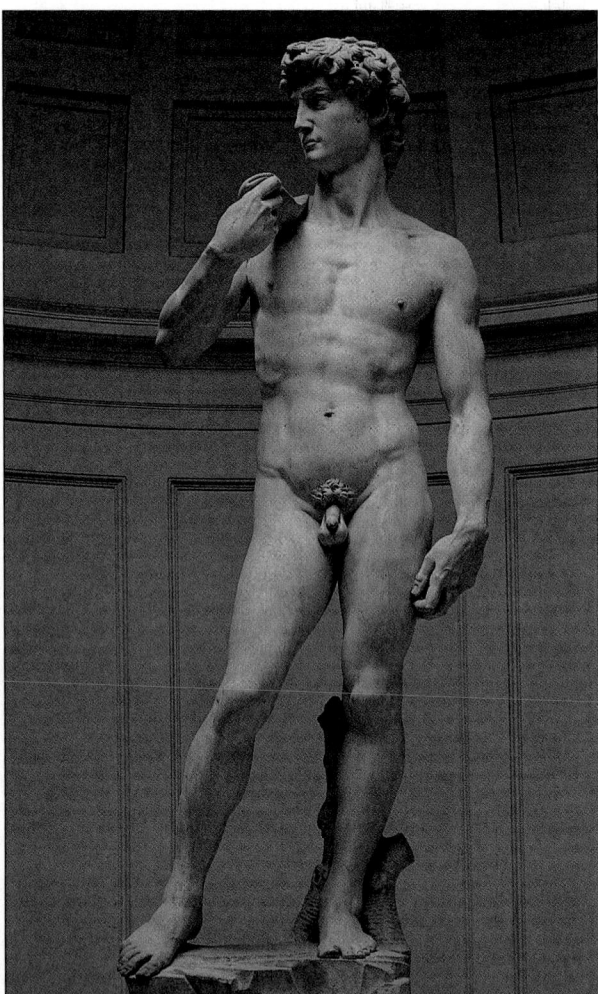

FIGURE 10.12
Michelangelo, *David*, 1504.

FIGURE 10.13
Giotto, *Lamentation over Christ*, ca. 1305.

Figure 10.13 shows Giotto's fresco of the *Lamentation over Christ*, in which the faithful mourn the death of Christ. The painting looks back to medieval tradition with gold leaf on the halos and the theme of the painting. However, the painter points to the future with his three-dimensional figures and a new realistic portrayal of emotion. Giotto's talent was recognized during his lifetime, and his paintings were in great demand. Toward the end of his life, his city of Florence issued a proclamation that in part captures the painter's influence: "Many will profit from his knowledge and learning and the city's beauty

will be enhanced." Painters following Giotto built on his techniques and further revolutionized this visual art.

Like architects and sculptors, Renaissance painters developed striking new techniques, including oil painting on canvas and the perfection of portraiture. However, perhaps their *Linear perspective* best-known innovation was linear perspective, which allowed painters to enhance the realism of paintings by creating the illusion of three-dimensional space on a two-dimensional surface. (Recall the perspective created by the landscape in the background of the painting on page 330.) The Florentines—and Brunelleschi in particular—proudly claimed to have invented this technique of painting. Whether they did or not is probably irrelevant; regardless of who invented linear perspective, the Florentines perfected it.

Before beginning to paint, Brunelleschi organized the painting around a central point and then drew a grid to place objects precisely in relation to each other. His real innovation, however, came when he calculated the mathematic ratios by which objects seem to get smaller as they recede from view. In this way, he knew exactly how big to paint each object in his grid to achieve a realistic illusion of receding space. In commenting on Brunelleschi's creations, Alberti asserted that a painting should be pleasing to the eye, but also should appeal to the mind with optical and mathematical accuracy. And here is the essence of these complex works: They used all the intellectual skill of the artists to create images profoundly appealing to the senses.

Perspective also grew from and appealed to the Renaissance emphasis on the individual, for it assumed that a painting would be viewed from one single spot in front of the work. As one art critic wrote, "Every painting that used perspective proposed to the spectator that he was the unique center of the world." In other words, the painter designed the painting with the eye of the beholder in mind. For the next 400 years, Renaissance ideas of perspective and space set the standard for Western painting.

The painter Raphael (1483–1520) was widely regarded as one of Italy's best painters of the High

Raphael Renaissance (the late fifteenth and early sixteenth centuries). His painting *The Marriage of the Virgin* is shown in Figure 10.14. Modern art critics agree with the accolades that Raphael's contemporaries gave him and claim that he embodied all the qualities to which Renaissance artists aspired. As Figure 10.14 reveals, Raphael's paintings are both realistic and transcendent. To give the scene a realistic quality, he used the technique of perspective in the grid of the courtyard as it recedes to the building in the background. Although the painting contains a religious theme, Raphael drew the figures from contemporary Italian life, thus celebrating Italian urban life and its emphasis on kinship joined through marriage. At the same time, however, the religious theme and the ethereal portrayal of the Virgin Mary encourage the viewer to transcend the realism of the scene and contemplate the divine.

SCIENCE OR PSEUDOSCIENCE?

The Renaissance passion for direct observation and realistic assessment that led to such magnificent achievements in the visual and literary arts catalyzed a process that ultimately led to the scientific accomplishments of the seventeenth century. During the fourteenth and fifteenth centuries, however, much scientific inquiry was shaped by a desire to control as well as understand the world. This combination led to the pursuit of what we consider pseudoscientific studies.

FIGURE 10.14
Raphael, *The Marriage of the Virgin*, 1504.

As the biography of Isabella d'Este indicated, astrology was extremely popular during these centuries. Even some popes hired their own astrologers. The bright appearance of Halley's comet in 1456 provoked a flurry of both dire and inspiring prophecies. For example, one humanist physician explained the outbreak of syphilis in Europe in terms of a conjunction of the planets Saturn, Jupiter, and Mars in the sign of Cancer. Alchemy was the early practice of chemistry, but the alchemists' interests were dramatically different from those of modern scientists. Their main goal was to find a "philosopher stone" that would turn base metals into gold. This science was perhaps even more popular than astrology.

Astrology and alchemy

Such pseudoscience aside, the Renaissance did succeed in combining visual arts with scientific observation. The study of linear perspective, for example, depended on an understanding of mathematics, and scholars spread the use of Arabic numerals to replace the Roman numerals that had previously dominated the West. The use of these numbers facilitated higher orders of calculations, like algebra, which was also learned from the Muslims. Realistic sculpture and painting required a study of anatomy, and this science also progressed. Amidst these advancements, the Renaissance saw the birth of a man who came to represent the entire range and combination of talents that so defined this age.

Mathematics and anatomy

FIGURE 10.15
Leonardo da Vinci, *Mona Lisa*, ca. 1504.

LEONARDO DA VINCI: THE "RENAISSANCE MAN"

Leonardo da Vinci (1453–1519) personifies the idea of the "Renaissance man"—the person who can supposedly do anything well. As a young man, he had contributed to the architecture of Florence by helping to make the golden ball that topped Brunelleschi's dome (see Figure 10.11), but he excelled in much more than architecture and sculpture.

This multitalented Italian served in the courts of a number of patrons, from the Medici to the Sforza of Milan—even Isabella d'Este had tried to woo him. At these courts, Leonardo painted magnificent portraits and beautiful religious works. Figure 10.15 shows Leonardo's celebrated *Mona Lisa*, probably the most famous portrait from the Renaissance. Her famous hint of a smile and calm pose were strikingly original at the time and inspired many later portraits.

Painting

Although Leonardo's skill as a painter would have satisfied most men longing for greatness, he saw this medium only as a beginning, a means to a larger end. "Painting should increase the artist's knowledge of the physical world," he explained.

Leonardo left a collection of notebooks that showed his intense interest in the world. His drawings of plants revealed a skill and meticulousness that any botanist would envy, and his sketches of water in motion would have impressed the most accomplished of engineers. Leonardo's imagination seemed boundless—his sketches included tanks and other war machines, a submarine, textile machines, paddle boats, a "horseless carriage," and many other inventions that lay in the future. Document 10.3 on page D10.2 shows Leonardo's confidence in the marketability of his inventions.

Scientific notebooks

Leonardo also took an interest in the inner workings of the human body. Although some medieval physicians conducted dissections, the practice was not common. During the Renaissance, however, physicians and scholars began to approach the study of the human body empirically by regularly dissecting cadavers. At the time, both artists and physicians saw dissection as a way to improve their portrayal of the human form. Like many other artists, Leonardo dissected cadavers to understand anatomy and thereby make his paintings as realistic as possible (as well as to satisfy his insatiable curiosity). Figure 10.16 shows Leonardo's sketches and descriptions of human

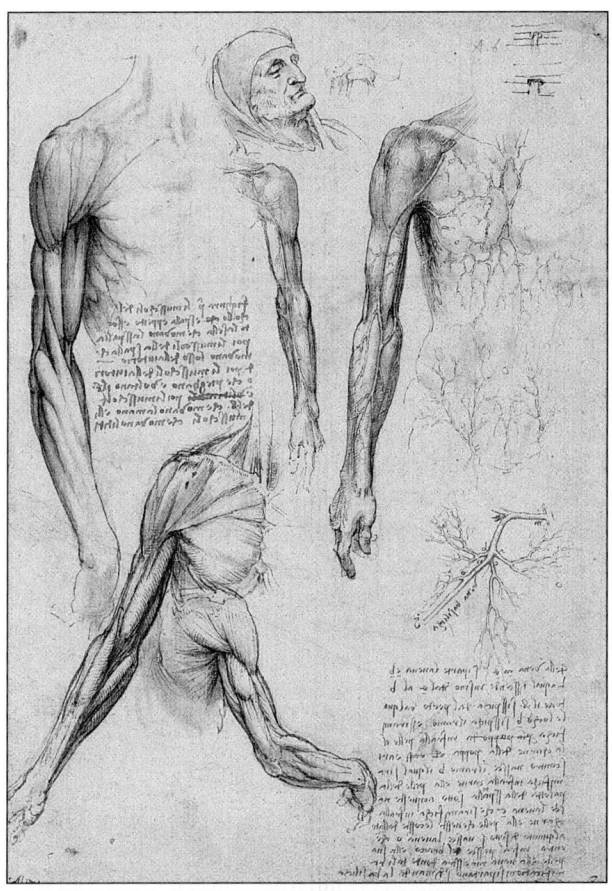

FIGURE 10.16
Leonardo da Vinci, study of a shoulder and arm.

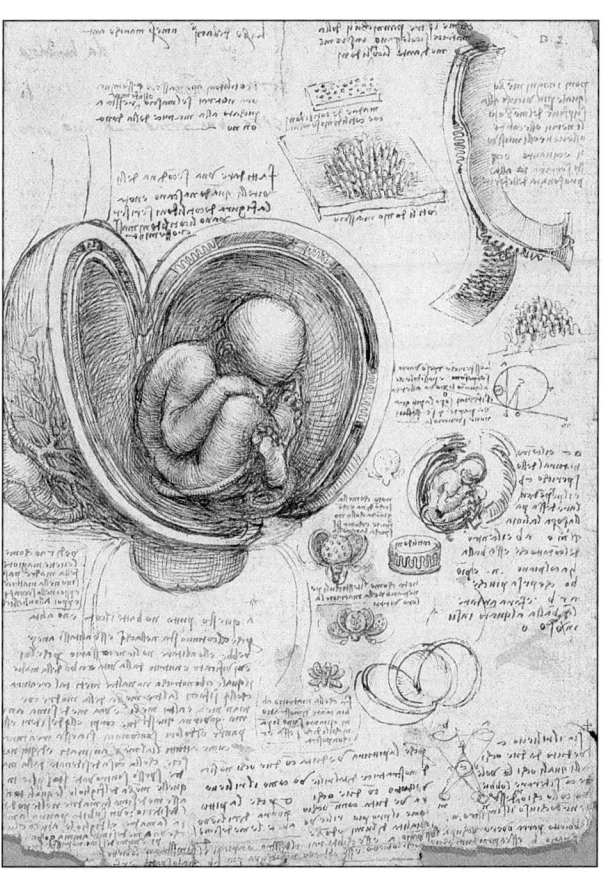

FIGURE 10.17
Leonardo da Vinci, child in womb.

shoulders and arms, including their intricate network of veins and capillaries. The drawing of the head of an old man whose body Leonardo had dissected suggests the artist's awareness of humanity even in his mechanical analysis of the body.

Figure 10.17, a depiction of a child in the womb, reveals the wide range of Leonardo's interests as well as his scientific curiosity. It is the oldest surviving illustration in the West of the actual position of an unborn child. To make this drawing, Leonardo secured a dispensation to dissect a deceased pregnant woman. In addition to capturing the correct positioning, the drawing also explains the function of the placenta.

King Francis I of France (r. 1515–1547) once said of Leonardo, "No other man had been born who knew so much." Unfortunately for the future of science and engineering, Leonardo's voluminous

notebooks were lost for centuries after his death. In retrospect, perhaps Leonardo's greatest achievement was that he showed how multitalented human beings could be. He proved the humanists' belief that an educated man could accomplish anything in all fields. Leonardo died at the court of Francis I, who had proudly served as his patron.

Renaissance of the "New Monarchies" of the North: 1453–1640

As we saw in Chapter 9, the medieval political structures of Europe began to fall apart under the pressures of the many disasters of the fourteenth century. The monarchies of the fifteenth century could no longer rely on feudal contracts and armies of mounted knights and began to search for new ways to rule their countries. To bypass their sometimes unreliable nobility, monarchs concentrated their royal authority by appointing bureaucrats who owed their status only to the will of the king or queen. As they looked for new sources of income to pay growing mercenary armies, kings and queens kept imposing new taxes and, in general, were receptive to new ideas to help them consolidate their power. Many hired Italians trained in the humanist tradition to work in their courts, and slowly and fitfully from the late thirteenth through the sixteenth centuries, the ideas of the Renaissance spread to northern European countries. As Renaissance notions traveled north and bore fruit in the courts of powerful rulers, the ideas were further transformed. This migration of ideas also accelerated the changes triggered by the disasters of the fourteenth century.

FRANCE: UNDER THE ITALIAN INFLUENCE

France offers a case study in how slowly and sporadically Renaissance ideas moved and how much this new spirit depended on the patronage of monarchs. The French king Charles V (r. 1364–1380), known as "the Wise," encouraged Renaissance learning among his subjects, gathering a circle of intellectuals around him. However, this early flowering of learning withered when his mentally unstable son, Charles VI (r. 1380–1422), took power. Integration of Renaissance ideals in this northern court would have to wait until the end of the Hundred Years' War in 1453 (discussed in Chapter 9).

France eventually triumphed in the Hundred Years' War, but a new threat from the neighboring state of Burgundy immediately arose.

Louis the Spider

As we saw in Chapter 9, Burgundy had allied with England to weaken France, and England's defeat did not weaken Burgundy's land hunger. As Map 10.4 shows, the rulers of Burgundy were trying to forge a state between France and the Holy Roman Empire, and their hundred-year expansion represented a real threat to France. Instead of leading armies in the old chivalric manner, however, the French king, Louis XI (r. 1461–1483) skillfully brought a new kind of diplomacy to bear in confronting

this next challenge. His contemporaries called him "Louis the Spider" because he spun a complex web of intrigue and diplomatic machinations worthy of Machiavelli—bribing his allies and murdering his enemies. Louis subsidized Swiss mercenaries who eventually defeated the Burgundian ruler. France then seized the Duchy of Burgundy and added the sizeable new territory to its lands. (As Map 10.4 shows, the Low Countries remained in the hands of Mary, the Duke of Burgundy's daughter, and this later formed part of the inheritance of her grandson, Charles V, whose fortunes we will follow in Chapter 11). Louis left France strong and prosperous and well placed to play a powerful political role in the coming centuries.

As Map 10.4 shows, the French kings succeeded in slowly taking the lands from the nobles who had retained their holdings since the Middle Ages. With its increasing strength, France next began expanding across the Alps into Italy to assert dynastic claims in Naples, because, as we saw previously, the French royal family was related to the rulers in Naples. However, the French came back with much more than wealth. Nobles leading mercenary armies in the Italian campaigns of 1494 came in search of land and left feeling dazzled by the cultural accomplishments of the Italian Renaissance. In a letter to his courtiers back home, the French king Charles VIII (r. 1483–1498) gushed about discovering the "best artists" in Italy. He returned home with some 20 Italian workmen whom he instructed to build "in the Italian style." The aesthetic ideals of Italy thus moved north with the retreating French armies, and the early Renaissance spirit in France was reawakened.

Italian influence increased further with the substantial growth of the French court, which opened positions to Italian humanists and diplomats. France's kings employed more officials than any other state in Europe—one esti-

Italians in France

mate places the number of bureaucrats at more than 4,000 during the reign of Francis I (r. 1515–1547). (Leonardo da Vinci was among those brought to France by this powerful and sophisticated patron.) Under Francis's rule, humanist literature flourished, and the new learning influenced university curricula from languages to mathematics to law. The king even ordered Castiglione's *The Book of the Courtier* to be translated into French and read to him nightly.

NORTH
SEA

ENGLAND

HOLY
ROMAN
EMPIRE

London

Bruges Antwerp

Calais

Brussels

Scheldt R.

Meuse R.

Rhine R.

Moselle R.

Etaples

FLANDERS

PICARDY

Amiens

ALSACE

Rouen

Reims

Verdun Metz

NORMANDY

Marne R.

CHAMPAGNE

Paris

Toul

Brest

Orléans

LORRAINE

BRITTANY

ORLEANS

Blois

MAINE

Tours

Dijon

FRANCHE-
COMTE

Loire R.

Amboise

DUCHY OF
BURGUNDY

Nantes

ANJOU

Bourges

POITOU

AUVERGNE

SAVOY

ANGOULEME

Lyons

Grenoble

Dordogne R.

DAUPHINE

Bordeaux

GUIENNE

Avignon

Toulouse

PROVENCE

LANGUEDOC

Marseilles

Perpignan

CERDAGNE

ROUSSILLON

MEDITERRANEAN
SEA

Legend:

— Holy Roman Empire boundary

- - - Ile de France boundary

Royal domain in 1461

Areas added to 1483

Areas added to 1498

Areas added to 1515

Areas added to 1547

Areas added to 1559

Burgundian areas in 1477:
those in the Holy Roman
Empire to be inherited
by the Habsburgs; those
to the West by France.

Semi-independent areas

Scale: 0 — 100 miles / 0 — 100 kilometers

THINKING ABOUT GEOGRAPHY

Map 10.4   *France in the Fifteenth and Sixteenth Centuries*

This map shows the growth of the royal domain of the French kings from 1461 through 1559. **Locate** the Duchy of Burgundy that extends from Flanders down to Savoy. **Consider** why this state posed such a threat to the French kings. **Locate** Avignon, where the popes had lived for so long. **Consider** why many in Europe accused those popes of being pro-French.

The French Renaissance did not merely copy the Italian movement. Indeed, many works by French artists and writers during this period show a unique blend of humorous skepticism and creative power. The imaginative humanist François Rabelais embodies this unmistakable French version of Renaissance ideals. His books *Pantagruel* and *Gargantua*—bawdy tales about giants with enormous appetites—are masterpieces of satire. Both stories continue to captivate modern readers. France had left its own mark on the Renaissance spirit.

English Humanism

When Henry VII (r. 1485–1509) became king in England after the Wars of the Roses (see Chapter 9), he succeeded in taming the rowdy and independent nobility and established a strong, centralized monarchy. Under the dynasty that he initiated, England again prospered. The English monarchs now turned their attention to the new spirit emanating from the south as they began to surround themselves with courtiers and art that served as the hallmarks of the courts of new monarchs. Delayed because of internal strife, the English Renaissance (1500–1640) gained momentum just as the Italian movement waned.

During the reign of Henry VII, English scholars intrigued by Renaissance thought traveled to Italy and studied under noted humanists. They frequented the newly established Vatican library and consulted with Platina, the papal librarian shown in Figure 10.5, and then returned home brimming with new ideas. By 1500, these scholars had so transformed the curriculum at Oxford that England could offer as fine a classical education as Italy.

Henry VIII (r. 1509–1547) proved an even more vigorous patron of Renaissance learning than his father. As we will see in Chapter 11, Henry met the French king Francis I and tried to outdo that Renaissance prince in splendor and patronage. The English king cultivated interest in astronomy, literature, and music—all the fields advocated by the humanists. Still, the talented monarch was outdone by his Lord Chancellor, Sir Thomas More (1478–1535).

More published a biography of the humanist Pico della Mirandola that revealed the author's debt to the Italian movement. The English scholar mastered classical learning and the humanist curriculum and applied his skills in public life in the best tradition of civic humanism. More's masterpiece, however, was *Utopia,* a work that commented on contemporary evils while offering a vision of a society free of poverty, crime, and corruption. More's work, with its visions of exploration and decidedly political orientation, points to distinct characteristics of the English Renaissance. More's studies gave him strong views on religion, which, as we will see in Chapter 11, led to a fatal conflict with his king.

Thomas More

Many Englishwomen also wrote during this Renaissance. The first wife of Henry VIII, Catherine of Aragon (1485–1536) had grown up with a love of the new learning encouraged by her mother, Isabella of Castille. When Catherine came to England, she stimulated interest among courtiers and scholars in the proper education of women. Consequently, Englishwomen wrote more publicly than their Italian counterparts. In fact, Italian travelers to England wrote disparagingly of the "brazen and violently assertive" Englishwomen. This tradition of education strongly influenced Queen Elizabeth I (r. 1558–1603), under whose rule England prospered and the Renaissance flowered.

Renaissance queens

Renaissance London: A Booming City

Sixteenth-century London—a vibrant city—scintillated during the English Renaissance, expanding physically and intellectually. Between 1560 and 1603, the population almost doubled, from 120,000 to more than 200,000, and travelers flocked there to see its wonders. Figure 10.18 shows a 1616 painting of London by Claes von Visscher. In this cityscape, the great sailing ships that made London a bustling commercial hub waft by, along with small vessels that supplied the city's growing population. Rows of houses stand in front of St. Paul's cathedral, which dominates the skyline.

In the foreground of the painting is the south bank of the Thames, which had been a center of prostitution from the time of the Roman settlement of London. The south bank remained the unseemly quarter of the city, inhabited by criminals and prostitutes, and notorious for its violent forms of entertainment such as bear baiting and dog fights. The south bank also housed private prisons, including the infamous "clink" that housed some

The South Bank

of the fiercest criminals. Yet, the south bank was also home to the theaters where crowds gathered to watch the plays of the great Renaissance dramatists. The two tall, round structures in the foreground are examples of these theaters. The one on the right is inaccurately labeled "The Globe." Known as Shakespeare's theater, the building had burned down in 1613, before Visscher painted his London scene. During the late-sixteenth century, however, the Globe served as a backdrop for the work of the greatest writer England has ever produced, and crowds today gather to see plays performed in a newly rebuilt Globe Theater on the south bank of the Thames.

ENGLAND'S PRIDE: WILLIAM SHAKESPEARE

The new social mobility of the Renaissance permitted William Shakespeare (1564–1616) to rise to prominence. William's father, a modest glove maker, married a woman above his station, the daughter of a wealthy landowner. Shakespeare probably attended the local school in Stratford-upon-Avon and received a humanist education. At the age of 18, the young scholar married Anne Hathaway, about eight years his elder, who was pregnant with their first child. In 1592, William journeyed to London, where he worked as an actor and wrote comedies, histories, and tragedies.

This master of the English language articulated all the Renaissance ideals: Shakespeare's love of the classics showed in his use of Roman histories in his plays (*Julius Caesar*) and in his study of Roman playwrights that offered him models of theater. Furthermore, Hamlet's words, "What a piece of work is man," expressed Renaissance optimism in human accomplishment; *Romeo and Juliet* re-created the story of "star-crossed lovers" (a reference to the Renaissance love of astrology) in the streets of Italy. *The Tempest* featured Renaissance

magicians, and Shakespeare's histories described the fortunes of princes as surely as Machiavelli's analysis of history and politics had. In Shakespeare's hands, the ideals of the Renaissance were given a new enduring form—popular theater that reached the masses. However, some modern literary critics believe the great playwright accomplished much more than perfecting Renaissance ideas. Some claim that by expressing complex human emotions in magnificent language, Shakespeare created an understanding of humanity for the West. In this, perhaps, we can see the ideals of the Renaissance come full circle—the early humanists in Italy transformed themselves by the texts they read, and Shakespeare used the written word to shape our understanding of who we are. Western civilization was dramatically transformed.

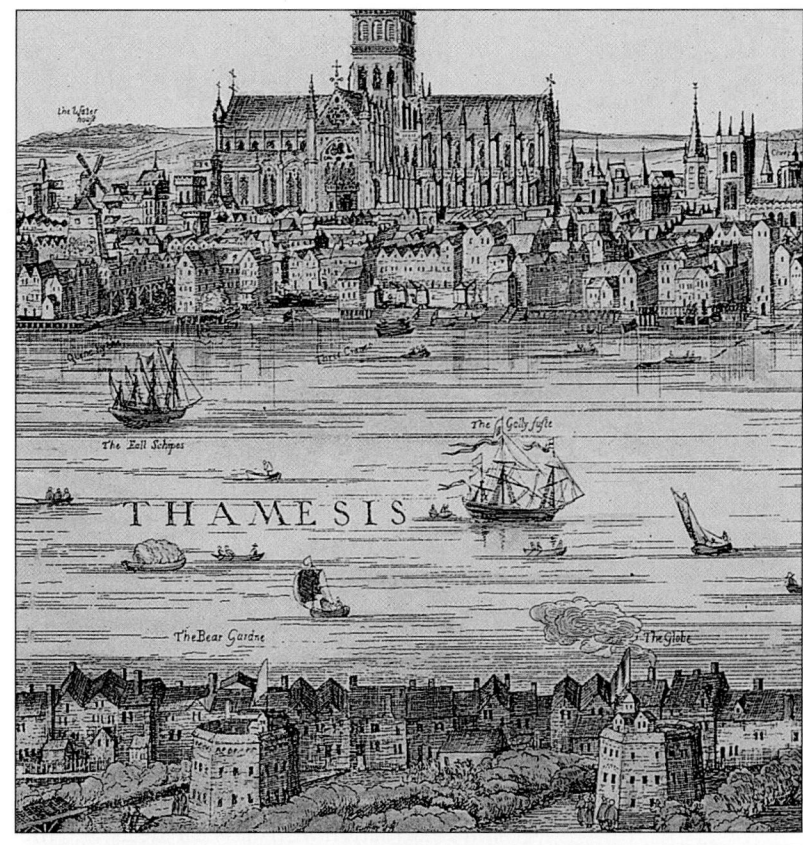

FIGURE 10.18
Claes von Visscher, *Map of London*, detail, 1616.

Timeline: A Closer Look

1320	1340	1360	1380	1400	1420	1440	1460	1480

Brunelleschi's Dome (1420)

Dante—*Divine Comedy* (1320)

Cosimo de Medici (1434–1464)

Giotto (1325)

Alfonso the Magnanimous
(1435–1458)

Beginning of Bubonic Plague (1348)

Gutenberg prints Bible
(1455)

Louis XI
the Spider
(1461–1483)

- ■ ITALY (1320–1513)
- ■ ENGLAND (1485–1610)
- ■ FRANCE (1364–1547)

Charles V the Wise (1364–1380)

Pope
Sixtus IV
(1471–1484)

Boccaccio—*The Decameron* (1370)

Lorenzo the Magnificent
(1478–1492)

1320	1340	1360	1380	1400	1420	1440	1460	1480

Summary

In the crucible of the fourteenth century—in which plague, famine, warfare, and religious instability swirled—new ideas percolated in the turbulent Italian city-states. Scholars and statesmen alike resuscitated a pride in human dignity, a confidence in human activism, and a fascination with classical ideals, and they expressed these ideas primarily in the secular arena. Writers, painters, and politicians looked with new realism at the world around them and strove to exert an impact on it. Although all these ideas had a precedent in the Middle Ages, nevertheless, their prevalence and novel applications created a new spirit that historians call the Renaissance.

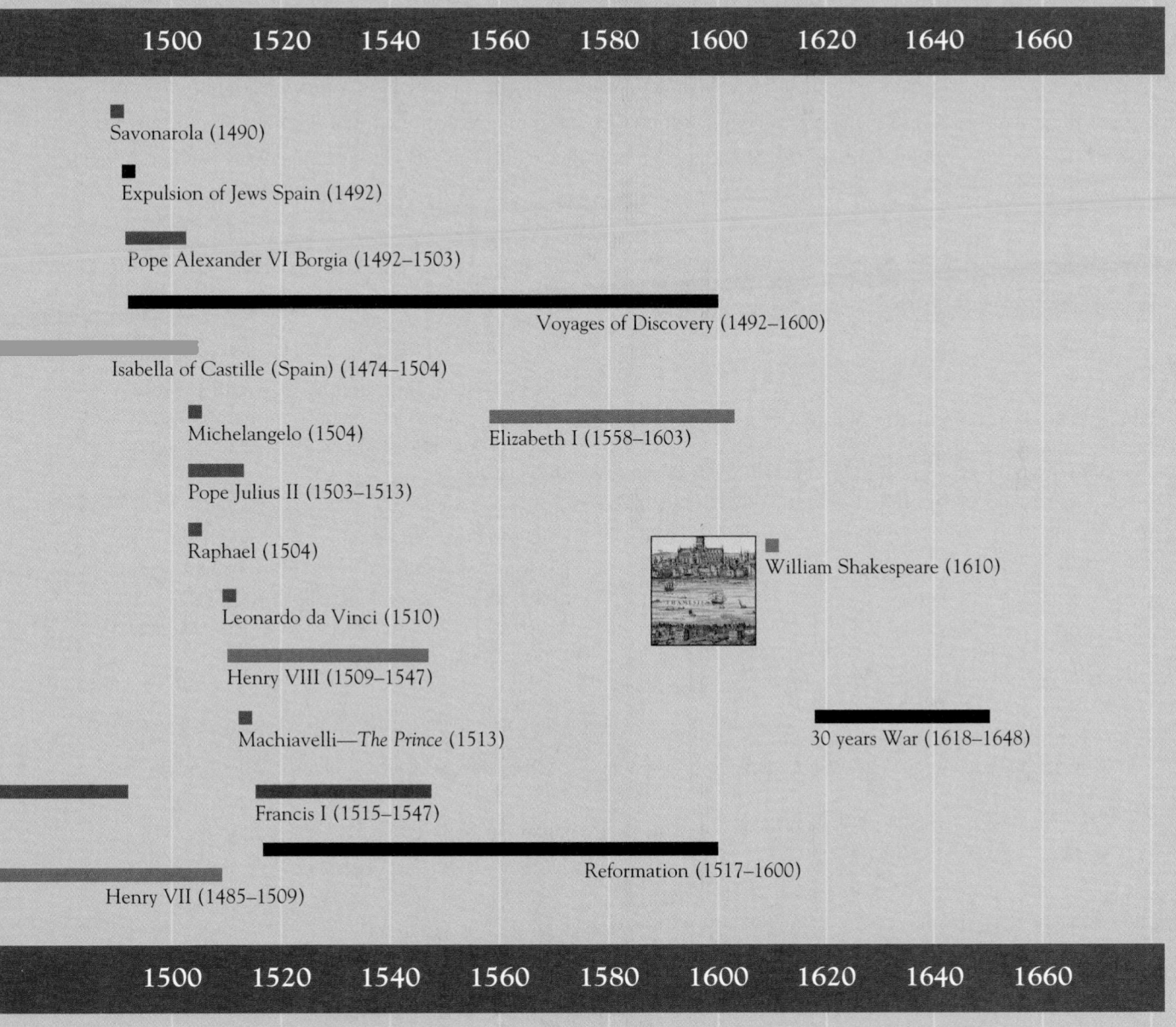

| 1500 | 1520 | 1540 | 1560 | 1580 | 1600 | 1620 | 1640 | 1660 |

Savonarola (1490)

Expulsion of Jews Spain (1492)

Pope Alexander VI Borgia (1492–1503)

Voyages of Discovery (1492–1600)

Isabella of Castille (Spain) (1474–1504)

Michelangelo (1504)

Elizabeth I (1558–1603)

Pope Julius II (1503–1513)

Raphael (1504)

William Shakespeare (1610)

Leonardo da Vinci (1510)

Henry VIII (1509–1547)

Machiavelli—*The Prince* (1513)

30 years War (1618–1648)

Francis I (1515–1547)

Reformation (1517–1600)

Henry VII (1485–1509)

| 1500 | 1520 | 1540 | 1560 | 1580 | 1600 | 1620 | 1640 | 1660 |

This age of the Renaissance ushered in a period that had both great and shameful aspects. In booming economies, Italian city-states were able to support architects and artists who created masterpieces that have set Western standards of beauty for centuries. At the same time, many of these enterprising individualists turned a blind eye to social problems—increased crime, new slavery, and growing anti-Semitism.

The new ideas of the Renaissance flowed northward with humanist courtiers and talented artists and artisans. In the process, they helped transform the old feudal monarchies. At the same time, scholars in each country put their own stamp on the Renaissance spirit. For example, France gloried in court architecture and brilliant satire, and England most notably brought these ideas to the popular theater.

As we will see in Chapter 11, Spain and Germany, too, would mold the praise of individualism and literary criticism to their own interests. Like Savonarola in Florence, German humanists applied Renaissance ideas to spiritual matters. Their efforts would eventually bring about an upheaval in religion as great as the Renaissance revolution in art and ideas.

REVIEW, ANALYZE, AND ANTICIPATE

REVIEW THE PREVIOUS CHAPTER

Chapter 9—"Despair in the West, Empires in the East"—told of the disasters of the fourteenth century that contributed to the breakdown of medieval structures. It also told of the rise of empires in the East that would soon cast a long shadow on politics in the West.

1. *Review the political order of northern Europe in the Middle Ages and contrast it with the political life of fourteenth-century Italy. How did the turbulent politics of Italy contribute to the growth of Renaissance thought?*

2. *Contrast medieval art, architecture, and literature with that of the Renaissance artists and humanists.*

ANALYZE THIS CHAPTER

Chapter 10—"A New Spirit in the West"—considers the characteristics we have come to associate with the term "Renaissance." It looks at the politics and social life of the Italian city-states that fostered these ideas and the magnificent accomplishments in the arts and science that accompanied them. It also follows the fortunes of the "new monarchies" of the north as Renaissance ideas spread.

1. *Review the characteristics of the Renaissance and consider what contributed to the development.*

2. *One theme this chapter traces is the relationship between ideas—like individualism and realism—and actual events and accomplishments. Analyze some aspects of life and accomplishments of Renaissance Italy in light of these values and consider how they were related.*

3. *How did Renaissance ideas spread northward, and how were they transformed in France and England?*

ANTICIPATE THE NEXT CHAPTER

Chapter 11—"Alone Before God"—will explore political developments as northern monarchs jockey for increased power. It will also explore major changes in religious beliefs.

1. *How do you think Renaissance ideas like individualism and scholarly criticism of texts might influence traditional religious convictions?*

2. *What states do you think will emerge as the strongest in the sixteenth century, and what areas do you think they might threaten the most?*

BEYOND THE CLASSROOM

A NEW SPIRIT EMERGES: INDIVIDUALISM, REALISM, AND ACTIVISM

Dean, T., and C. Wickham. *City and Countryside in Late Medieval and Renaissance Italy.* London: Hambledon Press, 1990. Collection of essays that offer a different look at the Renaissance by focusing on Siena rather than Florence.

Eisenstein, Elizabeth. *The Printing Revolution in Early Modern Europe.* New York: Cambridge University Press, 1983. Studies the shift from script to print and looks at the relationship between changes in communication and other developments.

Goldthwaite, Richard A. *Wealth and the Demand for Art in Italy, 1300–1600.* Baltimore, MD: Johns Hopkins University Press, 1993. An original and important look at art in relationship to the society and economy that produced it.

King, Margaret L., and Albert Rabil. *Her Immaculate Hand: Selected Works by and About the Women Humanists of Quattrocento Italy.* Asheville, NC: Pegasus Press, 1998. Presents writings of women humanists to illuminate an often-neglected side of the Renaissance.

Marek, G. *The Bed and the Throne: Isabelle d'Este*. New York: Harper & Row, 1976. A dazzling story of culture, art, and politics through the life of this talented ruler.

THE POLITICS OF INDIVIDUAL EFFORT

Burckhardt, Jacob. *The Civilization of the Renaissance*. NY: Modern Library, 2002. This is a reissued edition of the 19th century classic that began serious historical analysis of the Renaissance.

Jones, P.J. *The Italian City-State: From Commune to Signoria*. Oxford: Clarendon Press, 1997. An impressive, scholarly study of the political history of the Italian city-states.

Rosenberg, Charles M. *Art and Politics in Late Medieval and Early Renaissance Italy, 1250–1500*. South Bend, IN: University of Notre Dame Press, 1991. Considers the interaction of art and politics from various points of view.

Strauss, Leo. *Thoughts on Machiavelli*. Chicago: University of Chicago Press, 1995. A critical study of the ideas of Machiavelli.

INDIVIDUALISM AS SELF-INTEREST: LIFE DURING THE RENAISSANCE

Haas, Louis. *The Renaissance Man and His Children*. New York: St. Martin's Press, 1991. Sheds light on how Florentine parents (primarily fathers) viewed, reared, and cared for their children.

Herlihy, David, and C. Klapisch-Zuher. *Tuscans and Their Families*. New Haven, CT: Yale University Press, 1985. A well-written, fascinating study of families—the classic in the field.

King, Margaret L. *Women of the Renaissance*. Chicago: University of Chicago Press, 1991. A short, accessible summary of women in the family, the church, and participating in high culture.

McIntosh, Marjorie. *Controlling Misbehavior in England, 1370–1600*. Cambridge: Cambridge University Press, 2002. An in-depth study of the growing efforts of states to regulate behavior they deemed threatened public order.

Miskimin, H.A. *The Economy of Later Renaissance Europe, 1460–1600*. Cambridge: Cambridge University Press, 1978. A classic study of the changing economy.

Trexler, Richard. *Public Life in Renaissance Florence*. Ithaca, NY.: Cornell University Press, 1991. Describes the way Florentines from Dante to Michelangelo interacted with one another, with foreigners, and with their God.

AN AGE OF TALENT AND BEAUTY: RENAISSANCE CULTURE AND SCIENCE

James, Frank A. *Renaissance and Revolution: Humanists, Scholars, Craftsmen and Natural Philosophers in Early Modern Europe*. New York: Cambridge University Press, 1994. A clear and engaging survey of the history of science and technology between 1400 and 1750.

Kaufmann, Thomas D. *The Mastery of Nature: Aspects of Art, Science and Humanism in the Renaissance*. Princeton, NJ.: Princeton University Press, 1993. A rich collection of essays that contribute to the study of art history and the history of science.

Paletti, John T., and Gary M. Radke. *Art in Renaissance Italy*. New York: Harry N. Abrams, Inc., 1997. A good survey.

RENAISSANCE OF THE "NEW MONARCHIES" OF THE NORTH: 1453–1640

Bloom, Harold. Shakespeare: *The Invention of the Human*. New York: Riverhead Books, 1998. A controversial but influential study of all Shakespeare's plays that argues that Shakespeare shaped the way we define ourselves.

Kendall, P.M. *Louis XI, The Universal Spider*. New York: W.W. Norton, 1971. A remarkable presentation of the French king Louis XI as one of the formidable personalities of Europe and one of the shapers of the modern world.

Shennan, J.H. *The Origins of the Modern European State, 1450–1725*. London: Hutchinson, 1974. Looks at the theory as well as the practice of the modern state.

Unfamiliar words? See our Glossary at the back for pronunciation and definitions.

See our Web Page at www.mhhe.com/sherman2updated for additional readings, map exercises, practice quizzes, and more activities.

For quiz questions that tie the book to the videos and additional primary sources, please go to the Primary Source Investigator CD.

Documents

DOCUMENT 10.1
The Friar Savonarola Ignites a "Bonfire of the Vanities"

Born in 1436, Luca Landucci ran a small apothecary shop in Florence and kept a diary chronicling these turbulent times. This excerpt tells of the notorious incident in which the reforming friar Savonarola (whom Landucci calls Fra Girolamo) ordered his followers—young boys—to collect Florentine art works and other "frivolities" and burn them in the square.

■ Investigate the Document

What kinds of objects did the friar's followers collect? Who supported the friar? Was Landucci sympathetic to Savonarola? Why was Florence a particularly appropriate place for this act?

27th February (the Carnival). There was made on the *Piazza de' Signori* a pile of vain things, nude statues and playing-boards, heretic books, Morganti [poems], mirrors, and many other vain things, of great value, estimated at thousands of florins. Although some lukewarm people gave trouble, throwing dead cats and other dirt upon it, the boys nevertheless set it on fire and burnt everything, for there was plenty of small brushwood. And it is to be observed that the pile was not made by children; there was a rectangular woodwork measuring more than *12 braccia* [about 23 feet] each way, which had taken the carpenters several days to make, with many workmen, so that it was necessary for many armed men to keep guard the night before, as certain lukewarm persons, specially certain young men called *Compagnacci* wanted to destroy it. The *Frate* was held in such veneration by those who had faith in him, that this morning, although it was Carnival, Fra Girolamo said mass in *San Marco*, and gave the Sacrament with his hands to all his friars, and afterwards to several thousand men and women; and then he came on to a pulpit outside the door of the church with the Host, and showing it to the people, blessed them, with many prayers: *Fac salvum populum*

tuum Domine, etc. There was a great crowd, who had come in the expectation of seeing signs; the lukewarm laughed and mocked, saying: "He is excommunicated, and he gives the Communion to others." And certainly it seemed a mistake to me, although I had faith in him; but I never wished to endanger myself by going to hear him, since he was excommunicated.

Source: Luca Landucci, *A Florentine Diary From 1450 to 1516*, Trans, Alice de Rosen Jervice (London: Dent. 1927), pp. 130–131.

DOCUMENT 10.2
Isabella d'Este Implores Leonardo da Vinci to Paint for Her

The flowering of the arts during the Renaissance depended largely on patronage—whereby wealthy buyers contracted works of art. However, tensions often arose between the purchaser's desires and the artist's aesthetic inclinations. The letters of Isabella d'Este of Mantua (see Biography, Chapter 10) to Leonardo da Vinci suggest these tensions. Isabella never got the painting she wanted.

■ Investigate the Document

What specific painting does Isabella want? What are your thoughts about how specific her request is? Notice how Leonardo's uncle gets involved (see Letter 2). What does the uncle's participation suggest about the relationship between family connections and patronage?

Letter 1.   "To Master Leonardo Vinci, the painter. M. Leonardo,—Hearing that you are settled at Florence, we have begun to hope that our cherished desire to obtain a work by your hand may be at length realised. When you were in this city, and drew our portrait in carbon, you promised us that you would some day paint it in colours. But because this would be almost impossible, since you are unable to come here, we beg you to keep your promise by converting our portrait into another figure, which would be still more acceptable to us; that is to say, a youthful Christ of about twelve years, which would be the age He

Source: Julia Cartwright, *Isabella d'Este, Marchioness of Mantua, 1474–1539*, (NY: E. P. Dutton & Co., 1903), Vol. 1, pp. 324–327.

had attained when He disputed with the doctors in the temple, executed with all that sweetness and charm of atmosphere which is the peculiar excellence of your art. If you will consent to gratify this our great desire, remember that apart from the payment, which you shall fix yourself, we shall remain so deeply obliged to you that our sole desire will be to do what you wish, and from this time forth we are ready to do your service and pleasure, hoping to receive an answer in the affirmative." Mantua, May 14, 1504.

Letter 2.   On the 27th of May, Angelo del Tovaglia replied:—

"I received the letter of Your Highness, together with the one for Leonardo da Vinci, to whom I presented it, and at the same time tried to persuade and induce him, with powerful reasons, to oblige Your Excellency by painting the little figure of Christ, according to your request. He has promised me without fail to paint it in such times and hours as he can snatch from the work on which he is engaged for this Signory. I will not fail to entreat Leonardo, and also Perugino, as to the other subject. Both make liberal promises, and seem to have the greatest wish to serve Your Highness. Nevertheless, I think it will be a race between them which is the slower! I hardly know which of the two is likely to win, but expect Leonardo will be the conqueror. All the same, I will do my utmost."

DOCUMENT 10.3
Leonardo Seeks a Patron

While Leonardo high-handedly ignored Isabella d'Este's pleas for a painting, in this letter, he actively seeks a patron who would employ him to produce materials of war. To sweeten the deal, Leonardo casually offers to produce a sculpture praising the house of Sforza—his desired patron.

■ **Investigate the Document**

What kinds of weapons does Leonardo promise to develop? What does this list tell you about Renaissance warfare? Why does Leonardo offer to create a sculpture for Sforza?

If a place cannot be reduced by the method of bombardment, either through the height of its glacis or the strength of its position, I have plans for destroying every fortress or other stronghold unless it has been founded upon rock.

I have also plans for making cannon, very convenient and easy of transport, with which to hurl small stones in the manner almost of hail, causing great terror to the enemy from their smoke, and great loss and confusion. . . .

Also I can make armored cars, safe and unassailable, which will enter the serried ranks of the enemy with their artillery, and there is no company of men at arms so great that they will not break it. . . .

And if it should happen that the engagement is at sea, I have plans for constructing many engines most suitable either for attack or defense, and ships which can resist the fire of all the heaviest cannon, and powder and smoke.

Moreover, I would undertake the work of the bronze horse, which shall perpetuate with immortal glory and eternal honor the auspicious memory of the Prince your father and of the illustrious house of Sforza.

Source: Jean Paul Richter, *The Literary Works of Leonardo da Vinci*, (Oxford: Phaidon Press Ltd., 1939), pp. 92–93.

Pieter Brueghel (Elder), *The Massacre of the Innocents*, 1565

This painting depicts the biblical incident when King Herod of Jerusalem ordered all infant boys killed in an attempt to kill the newborn Jesus—who was prophesied to become a king. While referring to an ancient time, the image gives visual impact to an especially violent era in European history—a time when people were preoccupied with new religious direction while warfare and bloodshed ripped at the social fabric. Many an innocent was massacred during this period of religious upheaval.

CHAPTER 11

"Alone Before God"
Religious Reform and Warfare, 1500–1648

STUDY • Dynastic warfare •
Protestant Religious Reform •
Catholic Reformation • Religious
wars • Changes in society.
NOTICE how new religious ideas
significantly and sometimes
violently changed European
politics and society.

"They used thumbscrews, which they cleverly made out of their pistols, to torture the peasants, as if they wanted to burn witches. . . . They put one of the captured peasants in the bake-oven and lighted a fire in it." This horrifying description of war in Germany (by a soldier, Jakob von Grimmelshausen) characterizes a period in European history when many innocents suffered horrible deaths. Rulers launched their armies at each other in an attempt to win new territory and enhance their power, and these armies fighting with new weapons unleashed untold misery.

At the same time, new ideas about how to worship God began to spread throughout Europe—religious reformers introduced an intellectual revolution that would not only alter how people viewed their relationship with God, but would also redefine their ideas about society, politics, and the very nature of human beings. However, as monarchs confronted the religious diversity boiling within their countries, they increased the violence: Civil wars over religion erupted and brought this period to a bloody close.

Out of this turmoil came a reform in religion that split the Christian body into many Christian churches. In the course of this reform, many men and women who were spared the bloodshed of warfare were killed for their beliefs. This religious reform also generated more subtle changes in society—ideas of love, marriage, education, and charity were transformed as some people rethought their relationship to God. The West was irrevocably changed.

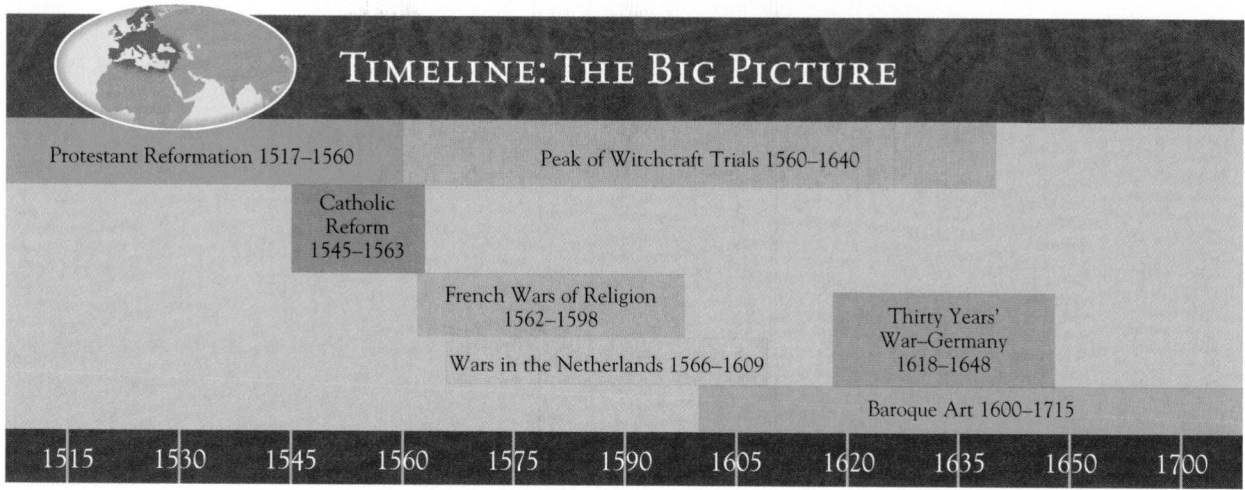

TIMELINE: THE BIG PICTURE

Protestant Reformation 1517–1560

Peak of Witchcraft Trials 1560–1640

Catholic Reform 1545–1563

French Wars of Religion 1562–1598

Wars in the Netherlands 1566–1609

Thirty Years' War–Germany 1618–1648

Baroque Art 1600–1715

| 1515 | 1530 | 1545 | 1560 | 1575 | 1590 | 1605 | 1620 | 1635 | 1650 | 1700 |

The Clash of Dynasties, 1515–1555

In 1520 two of the most powerful kings in Europe met in France to hold a tournament and discuss matters of state. Francis I (r. 1515–1547) of France had invited Henry VIII (r. 1509–1547) of England to his court to seek an alliance against his powerful enemy, the Holy Roman Emperor Charles V (r. 1519–1556). Francis hoped to impress Henry with his extravagant wealth, but the ostentatious display generated only more rivalry. Each king approached the meeting with as much state as he could muster. The kings, their followers, and even their horses wore clothing made of silver and gold thread. Silk and gold decorated the walls of the French palace and even the tents on the palace grounds that offered shade from the noonday sun. The meeting was dubbed the "Field of the Cloth of Gold." All this opulence underscored the character of the sixteenth century—there was money to spend and kings thought excess bought power. However, Francis had offended Henry by outspending him, and he did not get the alliance he sought. Instead, much to Francis's dismay, Henry met with Charles V, who approached the king in a frugal and reserved manner—and received his alliance. The struggle for land and power between Francis I and the Holy Roman Emperor would not take place on a golden tournament field; instead,

these kings opened a violent century by warfare, while Henry waited to see who would be left standing. The Italian city—states—too small to compete on fields of golden cloth—became the battleground in this bitter contest.

The kings of France and England ruled strong, unified states, but at the beginning of the sixteenth century, nation-states were not necessarily the ideal political form. Indeed, kings sought to extend their reach even further and acquire multinational empires like that held by the Holy Roman Emperor, Charles V. Ignoring considerations of common culture or the difficulties of holding large empires, each king believed simply that bigger was better.

LAND-HUNGRY MONARCHS

Charles V was the grandson of Ferdinand and Isabella of Spain. Thanks to the prudent dynastic marriages of his ancestors, he had inherited a sprawling, multinational empire. Map 11.1 shows the Habsburg lands of Charles V, which included the Netherlands, Spain, and lands in Austria, and highlights all the battles to indicate how warfare dominated Charles's reign. The map also shows the extensive empire of the Ottoman Turks that threatened Charles in the East.

As we saw in Chapter 9, events in the eastern Mediterranean had complicated western European rivalry, for the empire of the Ottoman Turks had gained strength. After the Turks conquered Constantinople in 1453, they consolidated their rule and

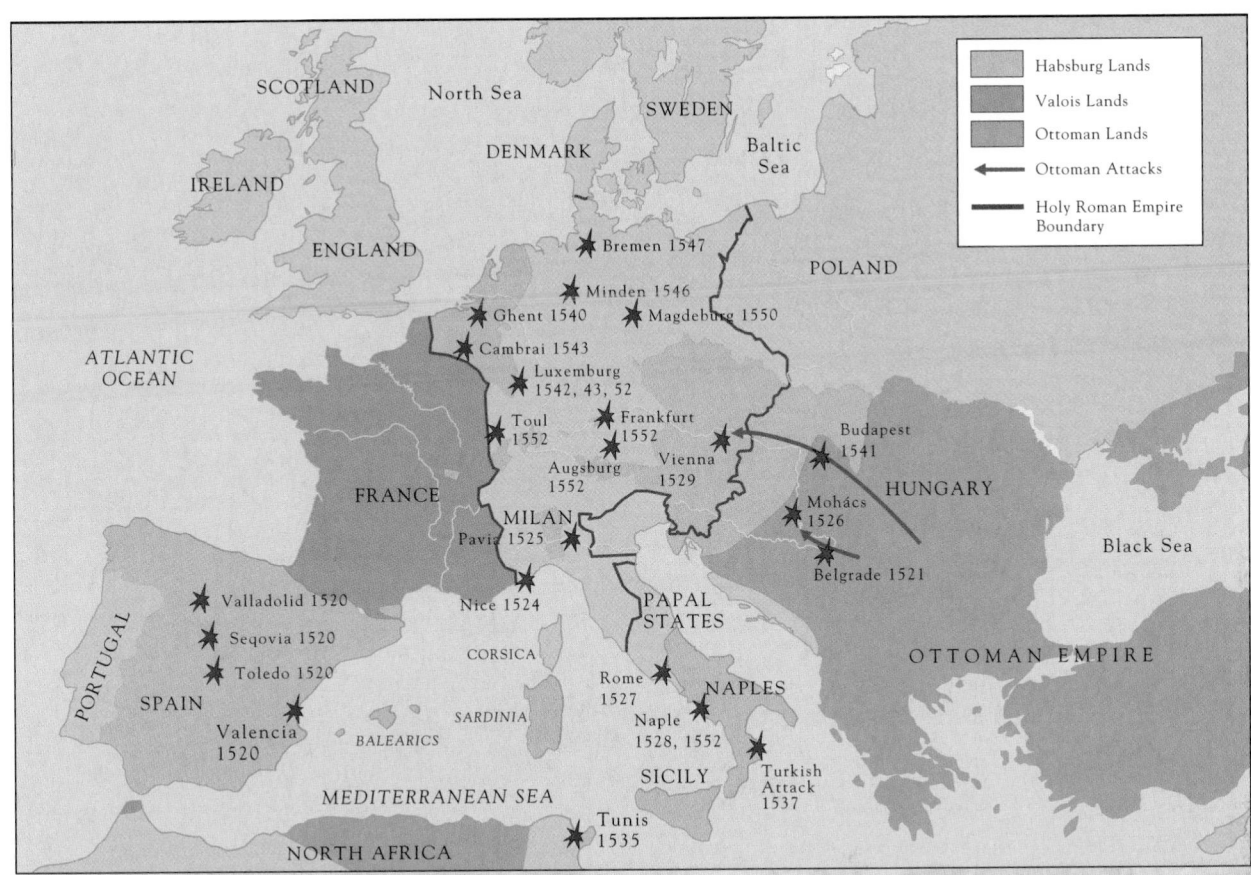

THINKING ABOUT GEOGRAPHY

MAP 11.1 *Europe in 1526—Habsburg-Valois Wars*

This map shows the political division of Europe in 1526, highlighting the lands inherited by Charles V and the Ottoman Empire on his borders. ❧ **Notice** Charles V's extensive holdings. **Why** would the French king have felt threatened by his powerful neighbor? ❧ **Locate** the Ottoman Empire and notice its proximity to Charles' territory. ❧ **Notice** all the battles Charles fought. **Consider** the impact of all this warfare both on the people and on the ability of the emperor to rule.

developed a sophisticated administration and a well-trained military. Under Suleiman I the Magnificent (r. 1520–1566), the Turks began to advance again, this time toward the very heart of Europe. Map 11.2 shows the sixteenth-century advance of the Ottoman Empire and indicates why western Europeans felt threatened by the growing power of the Muslims.

Turkish expansion

In 1521 the Turks marched up the Danube valley and seized Belgrade and Hungary, creating a panic throughout central Europe. By 1529, they were outside the walls of Vienna, the core of the Austrian Habsburg lands. At the same time, Turkish ships proved so effective in the eastern Mediterranean that all the western rulers wondered how long they could hold onto their share of the lucrative sea trade in that

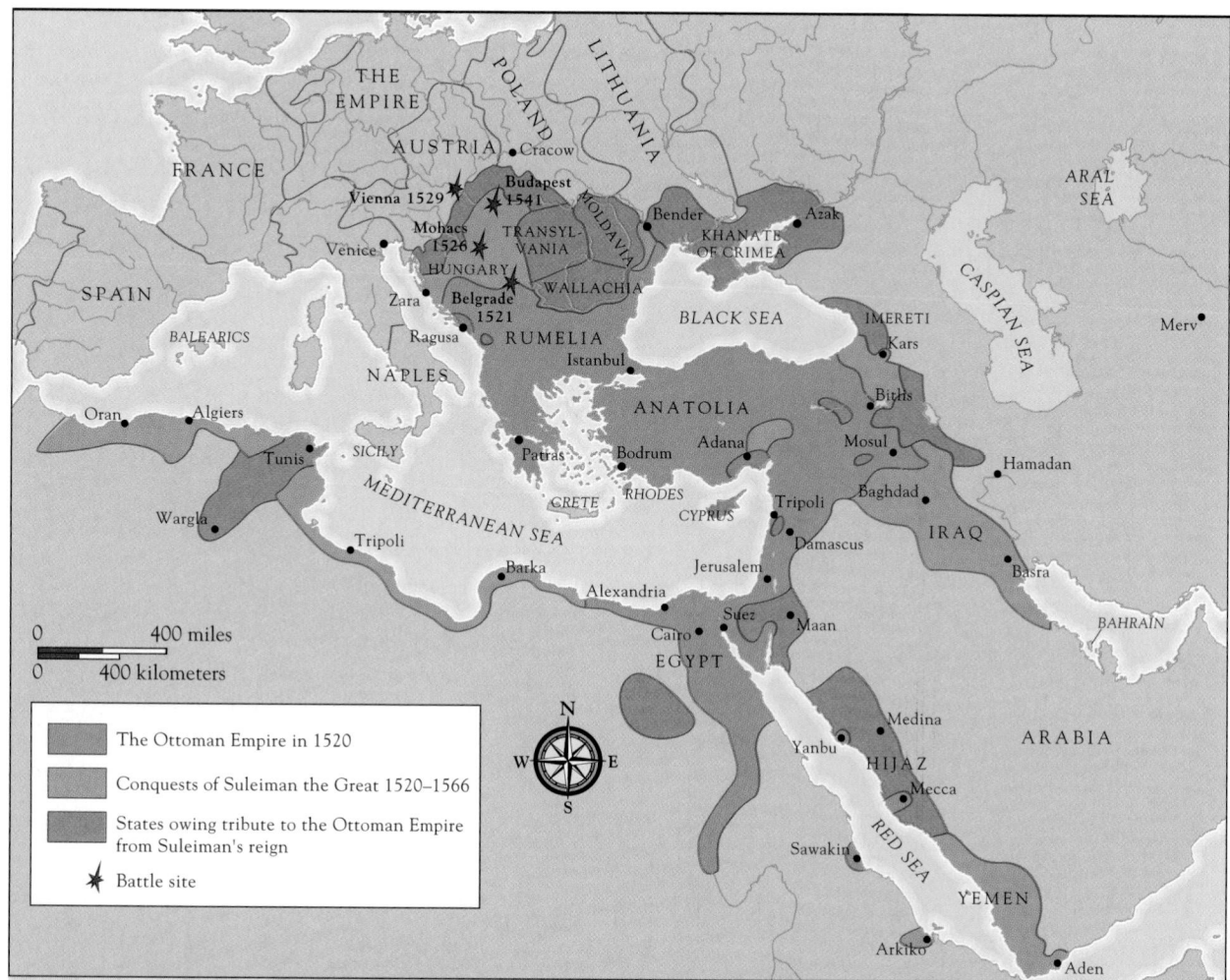

THINKING ABOUT GEOGRAPHY

MAP 11.2   *The Ottoman Empire, 1520–1566*

This map shows the remarkable growth of the Ottoman Empire under Suleiman the Great. ❂ **Notice** the spread of the Muslims into the Balkan area. **Consider** the long-term effects of this expansion and the resulting blending of peoples in this region. ❂ **Locate** Vienna. **Consider** its strategic location as a gateway into Europe from the east. **Consider** the impact on western Europe if Vienna should fall.

area. For Charles V in particular, however, the Ottoman Empire had become a major, distracting presence in the east as he struggled to extend his empire in the west. All these monarchs had to grapple with new complexities in their seemingly endless struggles with each other, for the scale of warfare was increasing, and the old rules no longer applied.

THE CHANGING RULES OF WARFARE

As we saw in Chapter 9, the mounted knights of the Middle Ages were being replaced by infantry, and by the sixteenth century, that trend was complete. The primary reason for this change was military technology. By 1500, Europeans had improved on the unreliable early guns of the Hundred Years' War. Now guns with 50-inch-long barrels gave marksmen a good deal of power and accuracy, and soon the Spanish developed the musket, a six-foot-long gun that could shoot lead bullets up to 200 yards. Now, soldiers could do a great deal more damage. As one observer noted: "Often and frequently ... a virile brave hero is killed by some forsaken knave with a gun." Indeed, warfare was now dramatically changed, and kings had to pay the price in men and materials for new armies.

The new weapons dictated different military strategies. Now, captains arrayed their troops in a series of long, narrow lines. The infantrymen carried muskets, and were backed by tight formations of pike-wielding foot soldiers. In this new kind of warfare, sheer numbers often determined a king's success, so monarchs strove to bolster the size of their armies. At the beginning of the century, most armies had fewer than 50,000 men; Charles V's forces boasted a whopping 148,000 (although they were widely dispersed through Charles's extensive lands).

Growing armies

To enlarge their armies, rulers had to resort to creative new ways to fill their ranks. In part, kings relied on mercenaries, hiring soldiers of fortune who offered their services to the highest bidder, but these were never sufficient. Traditionally, kings claimed the right to draft an army from among the able-bodied men of the land. Originally, these draftees were required only to fight on their home soil, but in 1544 Henry VIII sent his conscripts overseas. No one objected, and a useful precedent was set that helped kings boost their foreign armies. Sometimes men did not wait to be drafted into the growing armies, but instead volunteered. These soldiers joined up for various reasons—some wanted to escape poverty or the hardships of village life; others sought adventure. Martin Guerre, described in the Biography, was one such villager; he volunteered for the wars probably to escape the responsibilities of family life.

Not surprisingly, armies made up of poorly paid mercenaries, conscripts, and volunteers brought new problems to the art of making war. Officers repeatedly complained of soldiers' lack of discipline, and they imposed drilling and strict penalties for disobedience. Military leaders developed other strategies as well to manage their expanding forces. The Spanish evolved a complex military administration, which included the first battlefield hospitals. The Dutch introduced standardized caliber weapons to help solve the problem of supplying larger numbers of infantrymen. Feeding and outfitting armies was still no easy matter, however. Wives, children, prostitutes, and servants trailed behind the lines to take advantage of the regular pay that the armies offered their men. These followers also needed to eat, of course, and at times they plundered the countryside through which the army moved.

Modernized warfare carried a high price. Heavy artillery was especially costly for both offensive and defensive forces. Not only did armies have to spend valuable currency to equip their armies with cannons, but rulers had to rebuild cities into massive fortresses with forts and gun emplacements to guard against opposing artillery. The new warfare also required larger navies, and ships, too, were expensive. Between 1542 and 1550, England spent more than twice its royal revenue on military campaigns. Other European powers also bankrupted themselves on these incessant wars. For example, between 1520 and 1532, Charles V borrowed an astounding 5.4 million gold coins from rich merchants to pay his troops—still, he could not compensate them completely. At his death, Francis I owed bankers one full year's income of all the crown lands.

WINNERS AND LOSERS

Kings were seldom able to deliver a decisive victory in this seemingly endless warfare, and small victories were soon avenged. Therefore, very few combatants "won" these military contests or profited at all. However, some individuals were able to gain a huge profit. Bankers who lent money to kings recklessly supplying ever larger armies struck it rich. Guns and ammunition manufacturers, especially in the Netherlands, also profited hugely.

Overall, however, losers vastly outnumbered winners in these wars. As armies ballooned, so did casualties. With the increasing use of bullets and gunpowder, the nature of combat injuries also changed. In the Middle Ages, battlefield surgeons had been skilled at treating sword injuries; in the sixteenth century, surgeons more often had to amputate limbs crushed by artillery shells (as happened to Martin Guerre, in the Biography). As one soldier wrote of the new guns: "Would to God that this unhappy weapon had never been

Casualties of war

Biography

MARTIN GUERRE (1524–1594)

Notice what this case reveals about the tumultuous sixteenth century, when people resorted to magic to solve problems, foreign wars disrupted families, and changing religious ideas split communities.

In 1527, a peasant family moved from their village in the Basque country, on the border between France and Spain, to a village in southern France. The Guerre family prospered in their new home and by the time their young son, Martin, was fourteen, his parents had contracted a promising marriage for him with the daughter of a relatively well-to-do peasant family nearby.

Martin and his new bride, Bertrande, spent their wedding night in the Guerre household, where neighbor women gave them a heavily seasoned drink designed to stimulate their ardor and fertility. The potion failed. Martin remained impotent for eight years, while the village discussed whether he was "under a spell" and teased him mercilessly for not fulfilling his duty. Finally, an old woman told the young couple how to lift the spell through special prayers and cakes. The marriage was consummated, and Bertrande became pregnant immediately and bore a son. Martin, however, was not a happy young man. After quarreling with his father one day in 1548, the 24-year-old fled the village and was not heard from for years.

Martin traveled to Spain, where he served in the Spanish army in Flanders and France. During the fighting, he was shot in the leg; the limb then had to be amputated. Still, he sent no word to his village. In his absence, his parents died. Bertrande remained under the care of Martin's uncle Pierre as she raised their son and awaited the return of her husband.

Then, in 1556, a man strolled into the village and claimed to be Martin Guerre. He was actually an imposter, Arnaud du Tilh, who had left his own French village after a dissolute youth and joined the Spanish army fighting in Flanders. He had met Martin and learned about his life and marriage. Now, when Arnaud was ready to settle down into a new life, Martin's village seemed to offer that opportunity.

The village welcomed Arnaud as the lost Martin, and Bertrande took him in as her husband. If she had doubts about the newly passionate "Martin," she apparently set them aside. The couple harmoniously lived together for three years, during which Bertrande gave birth to two daughters.

Soon dissension arose in the village as Protestant ideas began to spread through the region. Bertrande's parents became Protestant, and Arnaud may have been drawn to Protestant ideas as well. As in so many villages throughout Europe, a split in religion caused tensions in previously unified villages, and these religious ideas may have exacerbated the suspicions that were growing in Bertrande's family. Arnaud and Martin's uncle increasingly began to quarrel over land and ideas, which caused Pierre to question Arnaud's very identity. Finally, Pierre had Arnaud arrested, and charged him with impersonating his nephew. At Arnaud's trial, hundreds of villagers testified for both sides. Some were certain that Arnaud was the real Martin; others felt equally convinced that he was not. Most of them simply could not decide. The case went to appellate court, where the legal tide

Peasant, Soldier, and Reluctant Family Man

seemed about to turn in Arnaud's favor. However, one day during the appeal proceedings, the real Martin Guerre, outfitted with crutches and a peg leg, suddenly limped into the courtroom to reclaim his identity and his family.

The imposter was condemned to death, and Bertrande was judged an innocent victim of Arnaud's duplicity and returned to her husband. Over the coming years, Martin and Bertrande had two more sons. The historical records reveal nothing about Bertrande's response to Martin's return. In 1594, Martin died.

This extraordinary case was recorded by a contemporary witness, Jean de Coras, who was fascinated by the motivations of the various parties. Coras's account was widely circulated throughout France, although the author did not live long enough to enjoy the fame. The Protestant Coras was killed in the French wars of religion—a few months after the Saint Bartholomew's Day Massacre in 1572. Villagers related the tale of the impersonation of Martin Guerre for centuries.

invented." In Figure 11.1, a painting by the Dutch artist, Pieter Brueghel (1525?–1569), the wounded men's artificial limbs are depicted as particularly short. In this way, Brueghel emphasized the loss and disability that came with amputation. To survive, many legless or armless veterans resorted to begging in the towns and villages of Europe.

The wars of this period also contributed to inflation and ruined harvests, both of which tormented even noncombatants. Horrified contemporary witnesses repeatedly described the legions of poor, starving civilians who wandered the landscape in search of food and died along the way. One French writer told of "some thousands of poor people, . . . subdued like skeletons, the majority leaning on crutches and dragging themselves along as best they could to ask for a piece of bread." People weakened by hunger and traveling through the countryside also fell prey to all manner of diseases. In the sixteenth century, outbreaks of plague, typhoid fever, typhus, smallpox, and influenza took a terrible toll.

THE HABSBURG-VALOIS WARS, 1521–1544

All these costs of making war still did not deter kings from their drive for land and power, and the city-states of Italy—where both Francis I and Charles V had dynastic claims— became the battlefield. Thus began the Habsburg-Valois Wars, named after the ruling houses of Austria and France. These wars were fought sporadically for about 25 years.

The wars devastated the Italian city-states, demonstrating that only large states could successfully field large *Weary imperialists* enough armies for the new warfare. Charles also learned a hazard in using mercenary troops, for in 1527 the emperor was unable to pay them, and his enraged armies stormed Rome in search of booty to cover their pay.

Neither Charles nor Francis could win a decisive victory, so the two men finally negotiated a peace in 1544, and by its terms, Francis agreed to renounce his claim on Italy. Charles,

too, wearied by all his problems, and in ill health, troubled by gout, decided to give up his imperial ambitions. He abdicated his various thrones between 1555 and 1556 and split his extensive holdings. He bestowed his Austrian and German lands to his brother Ferdinand I (r. 1558–1564) and the Low Countries, Spain, and Naples to his son Philip II (r. 1556–1598). Weary and disheartened, the ailing Charles V retired to a palace in Spain, where he died two years later. From this point on, these two branches of the Habsburg family went their separate ways.

During the wars, the kings had been willing to ally with unlikely partners. Sometimes Francis sought help from the Turks against Charles, and at times both Catholic kings courted critics of the church— "Lutherans"—to help against the other's Catholic forces. However, the treaty that ended the war attempted to present the Catholic kings as a united front against religious diversity that had flourished in their lands. Charles and Francis agreed to focus their energies on defeating "Muslims and Lutherans" who were threatening the Christian world. The Muslims had been a traditional enemy, but who were

FIGURE 11.1
Pieter Brueghel the Elder, *The Cripples*, 1568.

these Lutherans who appeared in the sixteenth century and who by 1544 seemed such a threat to the Christian kings?

A Tide of Religious Reform

The powerful medieval Christian church had called itself "Catholic," which meant "universal." In the hands of reformers, however, "Catholic" began to mean the traditional church, which even in the Middle Ages had come under criticism. Medieval critics had questioned some of the beliefs and practices of the church—its power, its wealth, and its insistence on obedience to the pope as necessary for spiritual salvation. The last point was central, because from the beginning, Christians had focused on salvation—everything from the best way to worship God to getting into heaven after death. As the sixteenth century opened, criticism began to intensify and many people wondered if their salvation was in good hands.

The Best Path to Salvation?

The church had promised Christians that the path to salvation lay in the hierarchy of the church and its sacramental system that offered grace to the faithful through the seven sacraments. To further confirm this, the Fourth Lateran Council in 1215 (described in Chapter 8) had declared that there was no salvation outside the church. Churchmen also promised that the faithful would be supported by the community of Christians, including the Virgin Mary, all the saints, and the congregations on earth. No Catholic believer, the church claimed, would have to face God alone in the afterlife.

A new popular piety and personal mysticism, along with the spread of Renaissance ideas of individualism, began to raise questions about this path to salvation. Many men and women who called themselves the Brethren of the Common Life tried to create a devout personal relationship between themselves and Christ, to supplement the complex Catholic theology. This style of popular religion was called the *devotio moderna* ("modern devotion"), and it influenced many subsequent believers.

One pious follower of the *devotio moderna*, Thomas à Kempis (1380–1471), is reputed to be the author of the best articulation of their ideas in *The Imitation of Christ* (1425). In this profoundly influential text, Thomas argued that personal piety and ethics were as important as religious dogma. In Thomas's view, individuals could work toward salvation by focusing on their own spiritual growth, and many agreed passionately with Thomas's assertion: "Blessed is the soul which hears the Lord speak within it and receives consolation from his mouth." Many longed for this kind of personal contact with God that, as Thomas pointed out, would make society as a whole more spiritual. As devoted Christians began to experiment with new forms of a Christian life, intellectuals began to contemplate some of the more complicated aspects of Christian thought.

Desiderius Erasmus: "Prince of Humanists"

As humanism spread to northern Europe, scholars applied the techniques of humanist education to Christian thought. The greatest Christian humanist was Desiderius Erasmus (1466–1536), who became known as the "Prince of the Humanists." Erasmus knew firsthand that some elements of the church needed reform, because he was born in Holland as the illegitimate son of a supposedly celibate priest. He studied at a school that was the center of the Brethren of the Common Life and grew up imbued in the new devotion that called for people to approach God directly in their hearts. Erasmus became a priest and went to study in a traditional university in Paris, which he hated. He dropped out of school, complaining that the university offered "theology as stale as their eggs."

The young priest then went to England, where his intellect was awakened by the humanists in Henry VIII's London. Erasmus became great friends with Thomas More and began a course of study based on a humanist curriculum. His interests remained religious, however, and he turned the humanist emphasis on original texts to biblical studies. He learned Greek so he could immerse himself in the mental world of the New Testament, and like the Italian humanists, he insisted that language study had to be the starting point for any education: "Our first care must be to learn the three languages, Latin, Greek, and Hebrew, for it is plain that the mystery of all Scripture is revealed in them." In this statement, we can see the literary work of the humanists applied to the highest Christian purpose.

Erasmus's greatest contribution to the intellectual life of the West was his critical edition of the New Testament. To approach this, Erasmus rejected the officially accepted version of the Bible—Jerome's (340?–420) Latin translation, called the Vulgate—and returned to the Greek and Hebrew texts to create a new rendition. Erasmus even corrected portions of the Vulgate, and his edition became the basis for later translations of the Bible.

The humanist also criticized corruption in the church in many writings. For example, he wrote a satire, *Julius Excluded from Heaven* (1517), in which he showed the famous Renaissance warrior-pope *Religious satires* Julius II (see Chapter 10) unable to enter heaven, even though popes had always claimed to hold its keys. His most famous satire, however, was *The Praise of Folly* (1511), in which he used his sharp wit to promote a greater spirituality in religion. In this book, his character, Folly, catalogs vices, and in the process makes fun of the author himself, his friends, and the follies of everyday life. His attacks also probed deeply into many of the religious practices of the day, and as readers laughed at his attacks on people who "worshiped" the Virgin Mary over her son and popes who did not live like Jesus, their ideas on worship itself began to change.

Perhaps even more than his disappointment at church corruption, it was his humanist love of education that led him to propose a radically different approach to Christian life. Erasmus argued that Christians should read the Bible directly, rather than relying on priests to interpret it for them: "I would that even the lowliest women read the Gospels and the Pauline Epistles. And I would that they were translated into all languages." A scholar to the core, Erasmus did not advocate separation from the church, but a contemporary of his recognized the long-term impact of the humanist's thought, saying that "Erasmus laid the egg Luther hatched." Revolution in religious thinking had been planted, and Document 11.1 on page D11.1 reveal the anger that served as fertile ground.

LUTHER'S REVOLUTION

Martin Luther (1483–1546), the intelligent son of an upwardly mobile family in Germany, was an improbable revolutionary. His father, a successful mine owner, expected him to further the family fortune by becoming a lawyer, but young Luther's life took a dramatically different turn. During a fierce thunderstorm, Luther was struck to the ground by a bolt of lightning. Frightened, Luther cried out to Saint Anne (the Virgin Mary's mother): "Help me and I will become a monk." He survived the storm and fulfilled his vow (much to his father's initial disapproval). Luther threw himself into his new calling—becoming a monk, priest, and doctor of theology—but he remained plagued with a deep sense of sin and a deep fear of damnation. He even believed he actually saw the devil during the torments of his conscience.

For all Luther's study, prayer, and attempts to live a Christian life, he still did not believe he could ever be worthy of salvation. Even the church's promise of grace in the sacraments and "good works" of the church brought him no comfort. Finally, he found peace in the Bible, especially its statement that the "just shall live by his faith" (Rom. 1:17). Luther interpreted this statement as meaning that people were saved only through God's mercy, not through their own efforts to live as good Christians. Faith alone—not ritual—would save their souls. For Luther, Christ's sacrifice had been complete and for all time, so humans did not have to do anything else for their own salvation. This central point of Luther's belief is called "justification by faith."

Inflamed by his newfound belief, Luther challenged church doctrine over the issue of indulgences. Through the Middle Ages, the Catholic Church had developed a complex understand- *Attack on indulgences* ing of how people are forgiven for their sins, including confession, penance, and absolution. As part of this process, churchmen claimed that people had to perform certain "works"—like prayers, fastings, pilgrimages, or similar activities—to receive forgiveness for their sins. If people died before completing full repentance for their transgressions, they could expect to suffer for them in purgatory before they could enter heaven, and late medieval people had come to believe it would be virtually impossible for anyone to do full penance for their sins before death.

In the Middle Ages, the pope had begun to alleviate some people's fears by offering an "indulgence," a remission of the need to do penance for sins. The pope claimed to control a "treasury of merit"—an infinite supply of good works that had been done by the saints and the Virgin Mary from which he could draw to remit sins. These remissions came in the form of "indulgences," documents that popes gave people in return for certain pious acts. Dating from the fourteenth century, a pious act might be a contribution of money to the church.

In 1517, Pope Leo X had issued a special indulgence to finance the construction of a new St. Peter's Church in Rome that would replace an old, smaller one. Johann Tetzel, a well-known Dominican friar, appeared to sell these indulgences to rich and poor alike in Germany and sent the money to Leo. Tetzel was reputed to have used the crude words: "As soon as the coin in the coffer rings, the soul from purgatory springs." Luther, horrified by this apparent trafficking in God's grace, wrote a series of statements decrying the selling of these indulgences and protesting the flow of money from Germany to Rome. Figure 11.2 shows an engraving that depicts the apparent sale of indulgences. The church-

FIGURE 11.2
Jörg Breu, *The Sale of Indulgences*, ca. 1530.

men (called pardoners) on the right ride carrying crosses, one with elaborate seals and ribbons that authenticate their privilege. The faithful put money in the barrel in the middle or hand it to the man on the left who is issuing the certificates of indulgence. The locked chest at the lower left held the money as they traveled throughout the German lands.

Tradition says that Luther tacked his list of arguments—the Ninety-Five Theses—to the door of the
Ninety-Five Theses church in Wittenberg, but he may well have simply sent it to his bishop. It seems that Luther merely wanted to engage a scholarly debate on the subject, but too many people were profoundly interested in this topic. The inflammatory theses were soon translated into German and circulated even more widely than if they had been publicly posted on the church doors—they spread rapidly throughout Germany and beyond by way of the printing press. Their clearly drawn arguments and the passion that lay beneath them appealed to many intellectuals who criticized the church and to Germans who had begun to resent German money going to Italy. With Luther's strong words, "It is foolish to think that papal indulgences . . . can absolve a man," the battle lines were drawn.

Luther's commitment to individual conscience over institutional obedience catalyzed major changes in his life that in turn shaped the emergence of the reformed church. It is somewhat ironic that within a generation, reformers would be enforcing institutional obedience with as much enthusiasm as the Catholics ever had. However, Luther himself pursued the logical consequences of his ideas. In Luther's new understanding, the monastic life made no religious sense; in the presence of God's grace, there was no need for heroic renunciations. Therefore, he left the monastery and married Katherina von Bora, a former nun, and wrote influential works on Christian marriage. He also composed moving hymns that transformed religious services. Furthermore, because he came to his understanding of religion through reading the Bible, he believed that it should be accessible to everyone, so he translated it into German. Indeed, this translation became his most influential legacy. Not only did it make the Bible available to an even wider group of readers, it also, through its popularity, helped shape the form of the developing German language.

PROTESTANT RELIGIOUS IDEAS

Luther articulated a core of beliefs that subsequent religious groups would share, even as they departed from "Lutheranism." Christian churches (except the Roman Catholic and Eastern Orthodox) that share

OLC

these beliefs today are called "Protestant." The word derives from the "protest" of some German princes at the Diet (assembly) of Speier in 1529. Over the objection of the Lutheran princes, that body decided to protect the Catholic Church's right to offer services in Lutheran lands while denying the same privilege to Lutherans. The name "Protestant" remained long after the issue had been resolved.

For Luther and subsequent Protestant reformers, at the heart of religious belief lay a faith in God's mercy that transcended the need for any "good works." The **Priesthood of all believers** Protestants thus conceived of a "priesthood of all believers," in which women and men were responsible for their own salvation. There was no need for an ordained priesthood to convey grace to believers by performing the sacraments. Church leaders (whom Protestants called ministers, pastors, or preachers) could teach, preach, and guide Christian followers, but they could not help them achieve salvation. Each person stood alone before God throughout his or her life, and on judgment day prayers to saints and to the Virgin Mary were no more helpful than prayers offered by any other Christian. When people's spiritual quests combined with the Renaissance sense of individualism, it changed even the path to God.

With their emphasis on the individual's relationship to God, Protestants rejected many of the elements that had characterized the medieval church. No longer were the faithful to venerate saints or the Virgin Mary, so many claimed the relics of saints and martyrs that filled the churches of Europe were worthless. Protestant faithful would not become pilgrims traveling to the great cathedrals and saints' shrines in search of blessings or miracles. Indeed, the statues of the saints and other icons seemed to many Protestants to promote idolatry, and there was periodic Protestant iconoclasm, or destroying of the sacred images in the churches.

Just as Protestants downplayed the importance of the priesthood and the intercession of saints, they restricted the significance and number of the sacra- **Sacraments** ments. In the Middle Ages, Catholics had identified seven sacraments important for salvation (including marriage and the last rites at death). Most (but not all) Protestant reformers accepted only two sacraments—baptism and the Eucharist (the celebration of Christ's Last Supper before his Crucifixion). Furthermore, they rejected "transubstantiation," which said that the bread and wine

offered up at mass were turned into the actual body and blood of Christ—a transformation that only an ordained priest could perform. Although Protestants may have rejected transubstantiation, they held various views on how Christ was present in the Eucharist, but because the bread and wine were not transformed, any believer could celebrate the Last Supper. As other Protestant groups branched off from Luther's initial thinking, they would emphasize some points of this theology over others. However, all of them shared the same basic principles: salvation by faith, not works; the Bible as the sole authority; and a "priesthood" made up of all believers.

These ideas spread rapidly in large part because they offered a simple and elegant answer to the question that had plagued so many: "How do I know I am saved?" Printing presses produced pamphlets and flyers offering these notions to the literate of towns and manors, and popular preachers told peasants in villages about Luther's challenge. Luther's seeds of revolution disseminated widely and found fertile soil.

THE REFORMED CHURCH TAKES ROOT IN GERMANY

Luther's attack on tradition and hierarchy could not go unnoticed. In July 1519, at the Leipzig Debate, the Catholic theologian Johann Eck forced Luther to look at the logical consequences of his stand on indulgences and actually to deny the authority of popes and councils. After this turning point, Luther was more and more ready to make a full break with Rome. Finally, in 1521, Luther was called to appear before Charles V at the Diet of Worms to defend his views. Though confronted with over a thousand years of tradition, Luther nevertheless adhered to his understanding of scripture, and he reputedly made the famous reply: "To go against conscience is neither right nor safe. Here I stand, I cannot do otherwise." During the Middle Ages, many men and women who had similarly stood by their beliefs had been executed for their stance. The political situation in Germany in the sixteenth century saved Luther from this fate—and turned his personal stance into a religious revolution.

Under pressure from Charles V to recant, Luther sought and received the protection of his prince, the powerful Frederick the Wise of Saxony. Figure 11.3 shows Frederick surrounded by Protestant reformers under his protection. Frederick, at the center of the image, has an imposing presence, with his gold

FIGURE 11.3

Lucas Cranach the Younger, *Martin Luther and the Wittenberg Reformers*, sixteenth century

chains and richly embroidered clothing. The reformers gather behind him, Martin Luther at the prince's right arm. This painting suggests the degree to which the Reformation drew strength from the support of powerful local leaders.

In addition to reasons of conscience, German princes had other motives for supporting Luther's ideas. The reformer's call to stop sending German money to Rome suited princes who felt the sharp sting of inflation. Princes could also benefit from confiscating wealthy Catholic properties (like churches and monasteries) in the name of religion. Luther's call for a break with Rome also appealed to a growing sense of German nationalism as distinct from the international Christendom represented by the Catholic Church. Some princes may have hoped that any weakening of the pope's authority would also diminish the power of the Holy Roman Emperor Charles V, whose authority derived in part from papal support. A weakened emperor meant more opportunities for the princes to bolster their own power.

Many poor, too, rallied to Luther's banner of religious reform, and this support took a particularly violent form in Germany. Spurred on by fiery preachers, peasants who suffered from *Peasants' war* hunger, inflation, and skyrocketing manorial dues made Luther's attack on religious abuses part of their revolutionary program. In 1524, German peasants circulated the "Twelve Articles," in which they demanded such things as a reduction of manorial dues and services and preservation of their rights to use meadows and woods. These wants dealt directly with the peasants' concerns, but they couched their demands in references to Scripture—a direct consequence of Luther's call for people to conduct their lives in accordance with their biblical readings. The "Twelve Articles" claimed to "give a Christian reason for the disobedience or even the revolt of the entire peasantry," and further promised "[if any of] the articles here set forth should not be in agreement with the word of God . . . we will willingly recede from [it]." This widely circulated pamphlet linked Protestant theology directly with revolution, and Germany erupted.

In 1524, a violent peasant war broke out. As the peasants took up arms and stormed manor houses, they called for support from Luther's religious reformers. However, Luther was no John Ball (the religious leader who had led the peasant revolt in England in 1381). He advocated religious reform, not social revolution, for he believed the Bible called for people to obey secular rulers. Appalled by the violence in the countryside, Luther wrote a treatise called "Against the Robbing and Murdering Hordes of Peasants," in which he reprimanded peasants for defying legitimate government. He also urged those in power to "smite, slay and stab" rebellious peasants, but the nobility needed no urging from Luther to protect their privileges. The rebellion was brutally suppressed—more than 100,000 peasants were killed. The princes appreciated Luther's support of their repression and judged the movement perfectly consistent with their political needs. The Protestant Reformation thus found a warm welcome in the courts of many German princes.

By the time Charles V could turn his attention from the wars in Italy in the west and the Turkish threat in the east back to his German lands, the reformed church had taken firm root. At this point, Charles was in no position to uproot Lutheranism, which was supported by many of the great princes of the land. Furthermore, Charles's armies contained many Lutherans—as early as 1527, men among the rioting troops in Rome purportedly were calling for a silk rope to hang the pope. The emperor could not govern any longer without some accommodation.

In 1555, Charles's successor, Ferdinand, met with the German princes to negotiate a compromise to settle the religious turmoil. The resulting Peace of Augsburg established the Lutheran Church as a legitimate alternative to Catholicism in Germany. By this treaty, each prince defined his principality as either Catholic or Lutheran. Residents of any principality who did not agree with their prince's religious decision were free to move to a more congenial location. The Catholic emperor Ferdinand, the pope, and many churchmen did not like this concession to Lutheranism, which split the unity of the Christian church. However, they had no choice but to accept the compromise forced by the strong German princes.

Peace of Augsburg

The Augsburg treaty opened the door for the Reformation to fragment Christian Europe into a complex mix of different Christian sects. In addition, other monarchs and princes besides those in Germany saw the advantage in separating from Rome. Scandinavian kings, for instance, followed the example of German princes in supporting Lutheranism. These conversions left many problems unsolved—what about groups other than Lutherans? What about dissenting voices within either Catholic or Protestant principalities? What was the relationship between the state and religion? While these questions smoldered, the fire of religious reform continued to spread through Europe.

BRINGING REFORM TO THE STATES IN SWITZERLAND

While Luther's call for reform was the first to gain a large audience, his was not a solitary voice. Shortly after Luther's challenge, reformers in Switzerland successfully challenged old religious ideas. Switzerland consisted of a loose confederation of states (called *cantons*) in which many residents were ready for change, and the very independence of the cantons facilitated acceptance of new religious ideas. In addition, many of the young men from the Swiss cantons served as mercenaries in the seemingly insatiable armies of Europe, and service generated a growing disdain for the established order. Just as in Germany, dissatisfaction and growing national spirit combined with a desire for religious reform.

The first leader of the Reformation in Switzerland was Ulrich Zwingli (1484–1531), who lived in the northern canton of Zurich. Zwingli had been strongly influenced by Erasmus's writings, and when he served as a chaplain with Swiss mercenaries, his longing for religious reform became joined with a desire to remove the Swiss confederation from the horrible wars.

Zwingli

In 1519 (a mere two years after Luther's challenge with his Ninety-Five Theses), Zwingli became the priest of the main church in Zurich, and from there he began his own attack on traditional church practices. He believed Christians should practice only those things found in Scripture, so his church in Zurich rejected such things as the veneration of saints, pilgrimages, purgatory, clerical celibacy, and most of the sacraments. In 1523, the city government in Zurich approved Zwingli's reforms, and Zurich became a Protestant city.

Zwingli and Luther shared many ideas, but would Protestants join together and form one church to oppose Catholicism? One German prince—Philip of Hesse—saw the advantages of consolidation and brought Luther and Zwingli together in 1529 at a meeting in Marburg to try to bring about an alliance. Although the two reformers agreed on virtually all points of doctrine, the meeting fell apart over their respective understanding of the nature of Christ's presence in the celebration of the Eucharist. Zwingli insisted the remembrance was symbolic, whereas Luther insisted that Christ's body was present as well as his spirit. As neither man could compromise with his conscience, there would be no united Protestant church or state. The new reformed churches would go their separate ways.

Just as in Germany, Protestantism came to the Swiss cantons with violence. In 1529, civil wars broke out between Protestant and Catholic cantons, and Zwingli himself died on the battlefield in 1531. The cantons reached a resolution similar to that of the later Peace of Augsburg in Germany—each canton would determine its own religion. However, the fires of reform stirred in more consciences and continued to spread, bringing both more hope and more violence.

ANABAPTISTS: THE RADICAL REFORMERS

The reforms of Luther and Zwingli appealed to many people, but were implemented by princes or urban governments. However, many people saw power and religion as incompatible. New groups took a more radical turn in their efforts to reform the church and to keep it untainted by politics, and these reformers seemed threatening even to Protestants like Lutherans and Swiss reformers. Most members of these sects were referred to by their opponents as "Anabaptists," meaning "rebaptizers," (although many of them preferred to be called simply "Baptists") because they believed baptism should be reserved for adults, who could make a conscious choice to receive the grace of the sacrament. The radical sects drew heavily from peasants and artisans, especially those suffering from poverty and the relentless warfare of the period.

Confrontation between Anabaptists and the rest of society stemmed mainly from the Anabaptists' views *Church vs. state* on the relationship between church and state. Many radical reformers advocated a complete separation of these two institutions. They even argued that the "saved" (or the "elect") should not participate in government (including serving in the armies that were vigorously recruiting in the villages). One especially pacifist form of Anabaptism emerged in the Netherlands, developed by Menno Simons (1496–1561). Simons led his followers, the Mennonites, into Germany and Poland; eventually members of this sect emigrated to the United States, where they settled as early as the seventeenth century. Document 11.3 on page D11.2 describes the persecution some Anabaptist women experienced.

While most Anabaptist groups were pacifists, others became revolutionaries fighting for what they *Radical reformers* believed was a religious cause—the ushering in of a biblically promised age of peace and prosperity during which the "meek shall inherit the earth." Some saw the horrors of war and famine in the sixteenth century as the expected biblical disasters and chose to take up arms to help fight against those who had previously oppressed the poor. In Germany in 1534, a fiery preacher named Melchior established a sect (called the Melchiorites) that gained political control of their city of Munster.

They burned all books but the Bible, abolished private property, and introduced polygamy as they settled down to await the expected second coming of Christ. Lutherans and Catholics alike believed this was a threat to society, so they captured the city and massacred the Melchiorites. Thereafter, the radicals were persecuted by Catholics and other Protestants alike.

CALVINISM AND THE GROWING MIDDLE CLASS

As we have seen, the Swiss cantons with their prosperous middle class had voiced religious longings and aspirations under the guidance of Zwingli. In the mid-sixteenth century, another voice also appealed to many of these well-to-do people in cities throughout Europe. Many people found intellectual and spiritual satisfaction in the teachings of the brilliant French scholar John Calvin (1509–1564), shown in Figure 11.4 surrounded by books to remind everyone of his erudition. While preparing for a career in law, Calvin had studied many humanist writings, and in about 1533, Calvin read some of Martin Luther's works. He experienced a profound calling to Protestant theology, as he said: "God by a sudden conversion subdued and brought my mind to a teachable frame." The new reformer soon experienced pressure from royal authorities who in the reign of Francis I began a periodic suppression of reformers. Calvin had to flee France to avoid persecution and found a safe haven in the Swiss city of Geneva, where he published the first edition of his master work, *The Institutes of the Christian Religion* (1536).

What was the nature of Calvin's vision that appealed particularly to the hardworking and often prosperous middle classes? Calvin accepted the basic elements of Protestant belief that Luther had articulated, but he added his own emphasis. Whereas Luther had focused on salvation as the goal of human struggle, Calvin urged people to recognize the majesty, power, and justice of God. Perhaps Calvin's greatest contribution to Reformation thought was to redirect theological speculation from individual salvation to a larger question of humans' place in the universe.

When he turned to the question of salvation, Calvin again emphasized the power of God, shown in predestination, the belief that God *Predestination* preordained who would be saved or damned, even before a person was born. Calvin explained that if God were *only* just, everyone would be damned, for all people were sinful. However, God

FIGURE 11.4
John Calvin.

Huguenots. German cities, too, began attracting Calvinist minorities—a problem because the Peace of Augsburg recognized only Lutheranism and Catholicism as acceptable religions. The Scot John Knox (1514–1572) was dazzled by Calvin in Geneva and returned to Scotland, where he established Calvinism as the predominant form of Protestantism. Like Knox, others from the British Isles were drawn to the exciting ideas of the reformers.

HENRY VIII AND THE ENGLISH CHURCH

In England in the 1520s, men with Protestant sympathies gathered to discuss some of Luther's writings that had been smuggled in. Perhaps even more exciting to the reformers was William Tyndale's English translation of the New Testament, which began to circulate in England in 1526. Protestant sympathies were growing on the island, but they would bear fruit from the actions of an unlikely ally—the king himself.

Henry VIII (r. 1509–1547), the proud king who appeared in state at the "Field of the Cloth of Gold," was not initially a reformer. In fact, he had written an attack against Martin Luther in 1521 called the *Defense of the Seven Sacraments,* and Pope Leo X awarded him the title "Defender of the Faith" for his support. (Ironically, Protestant English monarchs still retain this title.) Although many English people wanted religious reform and some felt a strong antipathy toward the pope, it did not seem as if their king would lead them in a break with Rome. But Henry's desperate need for a male heir changed all this.

Remembering the devastating Wars of the Roses (Chapter 10) that had brought his Tudor dynasty to power, Henry believed he needed a male heir to secure the succession. His wife of 18 years, Catherine of Aragon, had *Seeking a male heir* failed to produce one. Henry began to believe that God disapproved of this marriage, for he had married the widow of his brother (a practice normally forbidden) and had received special permission from the pope to do so. Henry also had fallen in love with a beautiful and bright young woman, Anne Boleyn. Anne did not want to become another of the king's mistresses, so she held off his amorous advances, insisting on a promise of marriage; first, Henry needed an annulment from the pope to end his first marriage.

Ordinarily, such royal annulments were easy to obtain because the popes had traditionally acquiesced to royal wishes. However, just as Charles V's absence

tempered his justice with mercy, reaching down into the flames of damnation and plucking some souls out to share salvation. Calvin called these souls that were predestined to be saved the "elect"; the rest would experience eternal damnation. Many believers who, like Luther, felt that humans could do nothing to earn their salvation, found comfort in the concept of predestination. Although predestination was at the core of Calvin's beliefs, he never stressed it as much as his followers in subsequent generations did.

As Calvinism took hold, Geneva became a vibrant center for Calvinist missionary work. Between 1555 and 1562, Calvin dispersed 100 preachers to the *Spread of Calvinism* far-flung corners of Europe. Calvin had impressive organizational abilities, and he laid out directions for organizing congregations that explained how believers could establish underground groups to adopt Calvinism even where civil authorities were hostile. These techniques worked. The Netherlands were particularly receptive to Calvinist thought. In addition, many French cities soon amassed substantial Calvinist minorities, called from Germany in the Italian Habsburg-Valois Wars allowed Lutheranism to take hold, it also facilitated religious reform in England. Henry wanted his divorce in 1527, just as Charles V's troops were sacking Rome and virtually holding Pope Clement VII prisoner. The pope needed the goodwill of Charles to restore order and Henry's queen, Catherine, was Charles V's aunt. The pope dragged his feet in granting Henry his annulment.

In 1533, Anne Boleyn, persuaded that the king would marry her, became pregnant. Now Henry was running out of time for his annul-

Henry's annulment

ment, for he wanted Anne's child to be born legitimate. Henry's two principal advisors—Thomas Cranmer, archbishop of Canterbury, and Thomas Cromwell—devised a way for Henry to get his annulment. Parliament passed an act making the archbishop of Canterbury the highest ecclesiastical official in England (cutting off the pope's authority). Then Thomas Cranmer ruled that Henry's marriage to Catherine was "null and void," so Henry was free to marry Anne. He did so, and three months later, much to the king's dismay, she gave birth to a girl, the future Queen Elizabeth. (Henry finally had a male heir by his third wife, after Anne was beheaded for adultery, but the king would eventually marry six women in his quest for heirs and personal happiness.) Document 11.2 on page D11.1 gives a politically inspired account of Anne's execution.

Henry had gotten his annulment, but the force of religious reform he had unleashed continued its momentum. Parliament passed a num-

Church of England

ber of measures designed to control the Catholic clergy and finally passed an "Act of Supremacy" (1534) that declared the king the "supreme head of the Church of England." This break with the papacy established the Church of England as a separate church (that later was also called Protestant), but not everyone in England welcomed this major reform. The most notable dissenter was the humanist Thomas More (1478–1535) (see Chapter 10), whose conscience would not allow him to obey a secular ruler in matters of faith, and he refused to swear an oath acknowledging the king's ecclesiastical supremacy. More was beheaded for his dissent, and this man of high integrity died blessing the king who had been his great friend, saying: "I die the king's good servant, but God's first."

Henry's position toward the reformers vacillated throughout his life. He did not support all the Protestant religious ideas—for example, he reaffirmed tran-

substantiation, which all the Protestants rejected. In fact, he considered himself a Catholic, although not a "Roman" Catholic. However, the powerful king readily implemented Reformation ideas that enriched his coffers and weakened the power of the Catholic Church. He shared the reformers' rejection of the monastic life and dissolved all the monasteries in England, confiscating their extensive lands and wealth. The king's treasury bulged from the confiscations, and many English religious reformers were satisfied with his new policies. However, the Church of England (also called the Anglican Church) really became Protestant under the reign of Henry's son.

Henry's third wife, Jane Seymour, finally bore him a son, Edward, in 1537. However, the boy was sickly when he took the throne upon Henry's death in 1547. Edward VI (r. 1547–1553)

Edward VI

was a bright youth who was fond of Protestant theology, but he was young. Because of Edward's age, England was in fact ruled by a council of regents who wanted to solidify Protestantism in England. The painting in Figure 11.5 shows the young king at the center of the portrait, receiving his father's (dying on the left) blessing to rule. Beneath the young king, the pope and monks are crushed by the Scriptures, while outside the window, iconoclastic Protestants destroy churches and images. Archbishop Thomas Cranmer issued a Protestant manual of worship, *The Book of Common Prayer,* and Parliament issued an "Act of Uniformity" in 1549, making the prayer book's use mandatory for religious service throughout the kingdom. It seemed as if the Church of England was securely established, but the English would suffer more upheavals before religious peace reigned.

The 16-year-old Edward died without an heir, and the kingdom next went to his elder sister, Mary (r. 1553–1558), daughter of Catherine of Aragon, Henry's first wife. A staunch

"Bloody Mary"

Catholic, Mary promptly set about undoing the Protestant reforms and returning England to the protective bosom of Rome. Although many prominent Protestants had fled to the continent upon Mary's accession, the queen attempted to force remaining Protestants to renounce their beliefs. "Bloody Mary" ordered some 280 Protestants burned for "religious treason," including Archbishop Cranmer, who had originally granted Henry VIII his divorce. The English public was even more upset by her marriage to Charles V's son Philip II, the Catholic king of Spain. However, the marriage did not produce an heir who could continue her Catholic policies.

FIGURE 11.5
Edward VI and the pope (attrib.).

Upon Mary's death, the throne went to her half-sister, Anne Boleyn's daughter, Elizabeth I (r. 1558–1603), whose rule would earn her the affectionate nickname "Good Queen Bess." Elizabeth (shown in Figure 11.6) proved a brilliant politician who skillfully positioned herself at the center of a contentious court. As the portrait in Figure 11.6 shows, she portrayed herself as a haughty, yet gracious queen who cared deeply for her subjects. She also remained unmarried (the ermine on her left arm in the painting is the symbol of virginity) and used that condition for her own diplomatic advantage by holding out the possibility of marrying into other European royal houses. Though arrogant and vain, Elizabeth was also a shrewd and frugal ruler who well deserved her people's grateful affection.

In matters of religion, Elizabeth did not worry about the fine points of theology. The young queen was appalled at the violence and destruction caused by the religious controversies, and she felt deeply responsible for maintaining peace in her realm while allowing people to follow their consciences. However, she was insistent on loyalty above all else, and she persecuted Catholics, who she felt had divided loyalties. She wanted to unify England around a Protestant core but also allow her loyal subjects latitude in religious practice and belief. For example, the prayer book that she instituted let people of differing convictions pray together in a national church. This moderate approach was effective: For a while, England basked in a time of peace that fostered an intellectual flowering (see Chapter 10) and an era of international expansion (see Chapter 12).

By the end of the seventeenth century, the old medieval notion of a Europe united under the protection of a uniform Christianity had evaporated. Map 11.3

Elizabeth I

shows the religious diversity that characterized Christian Europe at the end of the sixteenth century.

Europe divided Lutheran and Anglican churches were accepted by princes and rulers. Calvinists formed a solid minority in many areas. Many rulers struggled to grapple with even this degree of diversity. Yet Protestantism, by its very nature, had the potential to yield even more divisions. Once the door had opened for individuals to define their own way to God, there was no limit to the paths that people might create. However, the Catholic Church could not ignore these theological controversies and cries for reform, and in the sixteenth century, Catholicism, searched its own conscience.

The Catholic Reformation

Even before Luther circulated his devastating criticism, many leaders in the Catholic Church were working to reform abuses and bring to Catholic worship new insights about textual criticism of Christian humanism. Girolamo Savonarola (1452–1498) in Florence, for example, had urged reform of the Renaissance papacy (see Chapter 10). His was not an isolated voice, though, for even popes in the early sixteenth century called councils and promulgated decrees aimed at reform. However, the popes faced a tough challenge in implementing reforms at that time, because the Habsburg-Valois Wars occupied the attention of the Catholic kings Charles V and Francis I, who, in normal times, would have backed the papacy. These wars also carried a high financial price for the popes—during the sack of Rome in 1527, for example, imperial troops made off with mounds of gold coins from the papal treasury. To recover their losses, the popes stepped up the sort of fund-raising that had so incited Luther. Practical reform had to wait for peace.

THE STIRRING OF REFORM IN SPAIN

Like the Protestants, many Catholic reformers were strongly influenced by Christian humanism. When Charles V became ruler of Spain and the Netherlands in 1516, the writings of the great Dutch humanists—especially Erasmus—filtered into Spain. Cardinal Ximénez de Cisneros (1436–1517) led the Spanish humanist movement. Ximénez was particularly impressed with Erasmus's emphasis on scholarly study of Scripture and the works of the church fathers, and he wanted to strengthen this kind of education in Spain. In 1498, Ximénez received permission from the Borgia pope Alexander VI to found a new university at Alcalá de

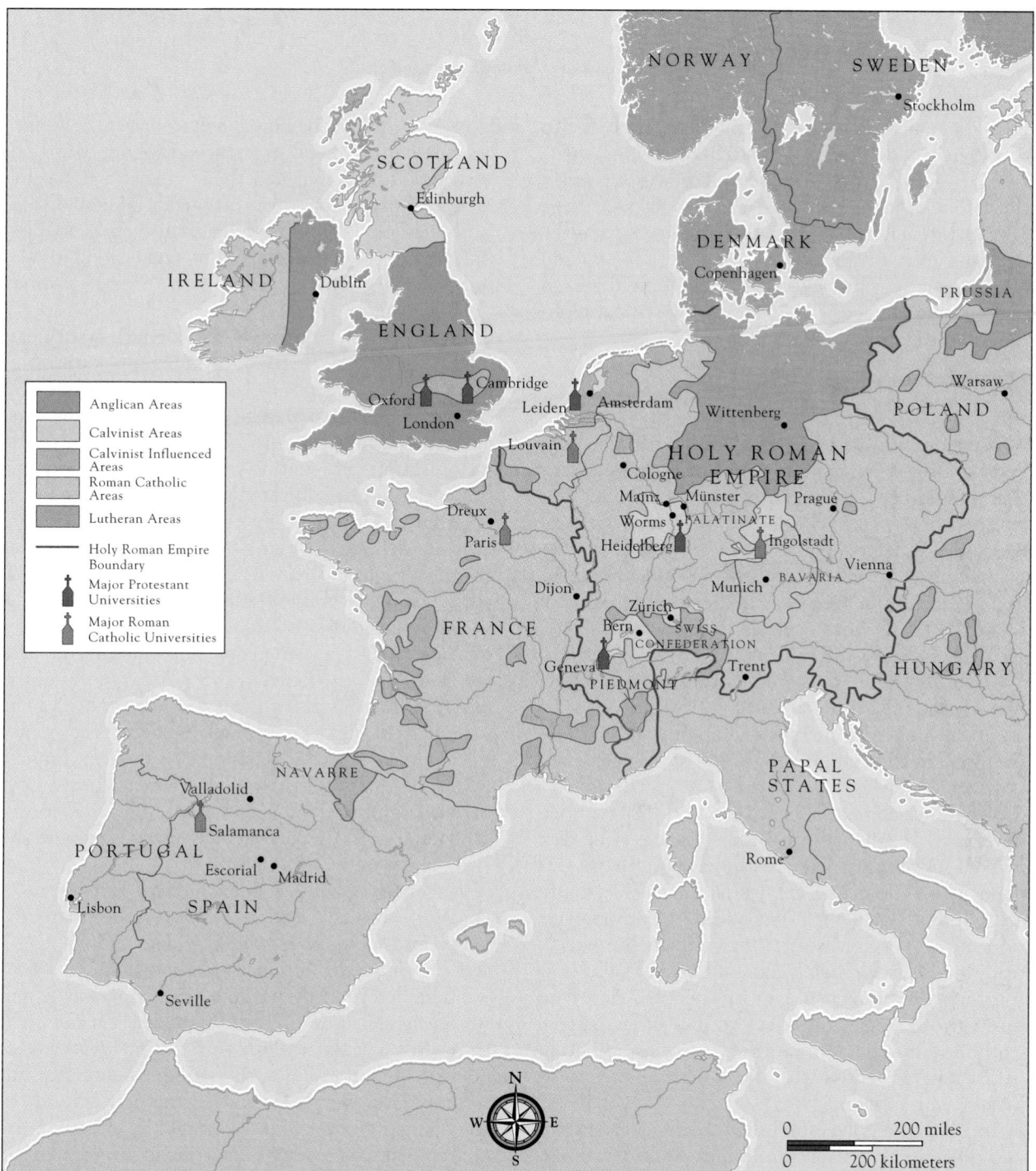

Map legend:

- Anglican Areas
- Calvinist Areas
- Calvinist Influenced Areas
- Roman Catholic Areas
- Lutheran Areas
- Holy Roman Empire Boundary
- Major Protestant Universities
- Major Roman Catholic Universities

NORWAY

SWEDEN

Stockholm

SCOTLAND

Edinburgh

DENMARK

Copenhagen

PRUSSIA

IRELAND

Dublin

ENGLAND

Oxford   Cambridge

London

Leiden   Amsterdam

Wittenberg

POLAND

Warsaw

Louvain

HOLY ROMAN EMPIRE

Cologne

Dreux

Mainz   Münster

Prague

Paris

Worms   PALATINATE

Heidelberg   Ingolstadt

Vienna

Dijon

BAVARIA

FRANCE

Munich

Zürich

Bern   SWISS CONFEDERATION

Geneva

Trent

HUNGARY

PIEDMONT

NAVARRE

PAPAL STATES

Valladolid

Salamanca

PORTUGAL

Escorial   Madrid

Rome

Lisbon   SPAIN

Seville

N   W   E   S

0   200 miles

0   200 kilometers

THINKING ABOUT GEOGRAPHY

MAP 11.3   *Religions in Europe, ca. 1600*

This map shows the distribution of the major centers of Catholics and Protestants in Europe at the end of the sixteenth century. ▶ **Notice** the contrast between those countries that had established Protestant churches and those in which the Protestants (especially the Calvinists) constituted a significant minority. **Where** might the Protestant minorities be most likely to confront religious turmoil?

Henares that would feature humanist approaches to theological and ecclesiastical studies. The high quality of the scholarship at the school drew notice with the publication of the *Complutensian Polyglot Bible* (1520), an edition of the Bible written in three columns that compared the Hebrew, Greek, and Latin versions. This scholarship represented a high point in humanistic learning and new critical techniques in the study of the Bible.

THE SOCIETY OF JESUS

Throughout its history, the Catholic Church had been reformed by monastic and mendicant orders that infused new life and ideas into the church. This pattern continued in the sixteenth century. Several new orders emerged, but the most influential was the Society of Jesus, whose members were called Jesuits.

The Society of Jesus was founded by Ignatius of Loyola (1491–1556), a soldier in the service of the Spanish monarch. In battle a cannon-ball shattered Loyola's legs, and he had a long and painful recovery—his legs had to be set and rebroken twice (without anesthesia) because they were healing crookedly. During his recuperation, Loyola read stories of Christian saints and decided to dedicate himself as a soldier of Christ. Loyola trained himself for a spiritual life with the same rigor that marked his military practice. In his quest, he was influenced by Thomas à Kempis's *The Imitation of Christ* and wrote his own book that offered a Catholic version of the personal search for God. In the widely read work, *The Spiritual Exercises,* Loyola taught how spiritual discipline could satisfy people's desire to reach up to God while obeying the orders of the Catholic Church. Here was the perfect combination of Catholic orthodoxy with the longings expressed by Protestant reformers.

Jesuits established

In 1540, the pope established the Society of Jesus as a religious order, and the Jesuits, who vowed perfect obedience to the papacy, became the vanguard of reformed Catholicism. These men devoted themselves to education, sharing Cardinal Ximénez's belief that a Christian humanist education would combat the threat of Protestantism. Their schools became among the best in Europe, drawing even some Protestants who were willing to risk their children's conversion to Catholicism in exchange for the fine education. Jesuits also served as missionaries to bring Catholicism to the New World (see Chapter 12).

However, in time the new shock troops of the papacy became controversial in their own right—the vigor with which they pursued their aims and the vehemence of their support of the papacy alienated some Catholics and Protestants alike. But, there is no question that in the sixteenth century and beyond, the Jesuits would be a powerful force in the reformed Catholicism.

Figure 11.7, a painting by the Flemish artist Peter Paul Rubens (1577–1640), captures the spirit of reformed Catholicism. *The Miracles of St. Ignatius* was commissioned in 1620 to be placed in the Jesuits' first church in Antwerp in 1622 on the occasion of the canonization of Ignatius of Loyola. The painting shows the saint performing miracles: easing the pain of childbirth (on the right), reviving a suicide victim long enough for the dying man to take the last rites (in the foreground), and casting out demons (on the left). The image praises traditional Catholic doctrine, showing the efficacy of saints by representing them as intermediaries between people and God. In the same way Loyola is positioned in the vertical center of the painting. Rubens also affirms the importance of the sacrament of "last rites" (attacked by the Protestants) by depicting it as the occasion of a miracle. Finally, this work points out that, in less than a century, Loyola's accomplishments had earned him the status of sainthood and his Society of Jesus had become the army of the new Catholicism.

Rubens's painting is an example of a new style of painting (and the arts in general) called baroque, which also served to forward the ideas and spirit of reformed Catholicism. Baroque art was characterized by passion, drama, and awe, and was designed to involve the audience. Catholic patrons, in particular, spurred this art that spoke as eloquently of Catholic doctrine and passion as a Jesuit sermon. However, before either the new art style or the energetic order of Jesuits could be effective, the church had to agree on its doctrine in response to the Protestant critique.

Baroque art

THE COUNCIL OF TRENT, 1545–1563

With the conclusion of the Habsburg-Valois Wars, the Catholic monarchs could focus on the divisive religious questions of the day. After the treaty of 1544 that ended the wars, church leaders from all over Europe gathered in northern Italy at Trent, and the council met

Reforming corruption

intermittently from 1545 to 1563. Charles wanted the council to concentrate on reforming abuses, and they confronted this thorny issue honestly, establishing stern measures to clean up clerical corruption, ignorance, and apathy. They even banned the selling of indulgences and the office of indulgence-seller (like the pardoners shown in Figure 11.2). But the real work of the council took place when they confronted the theological debate that had driven the Protestants from the church. As these leaders clarified their beliefs, it became obvious that there would be no compromise with Protestant Christianity.

The Council of Trent determined that Catholics did *not* stand alone before God. Rather, they claimed, the community of the faithful, both living *Affirming doctrine* and dead, could help a Catholic to salvation. Thus prayers to the saints and to the Virgin Mary *did* matter. The church also affirmed the existence of purgatory and the power of prayer and even indulgences to free souls from their punishment.

These churchmen further departed from the Protestants by declaring that Christians needed both faith and good works to go to heaven. For Catholics, the sacraments by their very nature conveyed grace, so the council reaffirmed the existence of all seven rites. In further rejection of Protestant criticism, Catholics supported the idea of transubstantiation, by which priests presided over the transformation of the wine and host into the blood and body of Christ.

Like Rubens, the Spanish painter El Greco ("the Greek") (1547–1614) was a baroque painter who reaffirmed Catholic theology. El Greco's painting *El Greco* *Burial of the Count of Orgaz* (Figure 11.8) is less about the burial of one man than about the theological stance of the Council of Trent. The dead count does not face his maker alone. Instead, he is buried with the full ceremony of the church presided over by the bishop. El Greco also shows

FIGURE 11.7
Peter Paul Rubens, *The Miracles of St. Ignatius*, 1620.

saints Augustine and Stephen miraculously appearing and helping with the burial. The count's way to heaven is paved by the prayers of the living who surround the scene and the Virgin Mary, who sits between the dead man and Jesus as an intermediary for the count's soul. The painting depicts heaven as filled with saints and the souls of other saved individuals, who also pray for the count and help him enter their community. By all these means, the picture visually reaffirms the theology established at the Council of Trent.

While debating and refining their beliefs, the churchmen attending the council looked to two authorities—Scripture and tradition. Armed with these pillars of Christian thought, they prepared to answer Luther and the other Protestants, who recognized only their own consciences and the complete authority of the Holy Book. Catholics, the Trent council argued, could draw strength from the body of practices that the faithful had accumulated over the course of a millennium. With its doctrine thus established, the Catholic Church showed a new strength and confidence. Dissenters had gone to other sects, leaving a vigorous corps of dedicated believers to challenge the Protestants head-on.

Scripture and tradition

CATHOLICS ON THE OFFENSE

Throughout this period, as we have seen with baroque art, many Catholics expressed their faith with more passion and mystical emotion than they had shown in centuries. Teresa of Avila, Spain (1515–1582), a sixteenth-century mystic who quickly became a saint, exemplified this newfound energy. The daughter of a converted Jew, Teresa entered a convent and experienced a series of visions. Not only a mystic, Teresa was an active reformer, establishing new convents for women as part of her dedication to a reinvigorated Catholicism. Her mystical writing, *Way of Perfection*, ensured her influence, for it inspired the pope to declare her a "Doctor of the Church" (which means that her writings were worthy of study). Soon she became the patron saint of Spain, replacing Saint James (Santiago), who had held that honor throughout the Middle Ages. The example of Teresa and other mystics offered the church a strong weapon to show skeptics the deep and passionate faith that came with Catholic worship. However, they also used stronger measures than the writings of gentle mystics.

Reinvigorated, and considering themselves at war with Protestants, the Catholics moved to repress opposition to their views. The Spanish Inquisition, which Charles V's grandparents Ferdinand and Isabella introduced in 1478, took a forceful role in this battle over religious diversity. (This court was separate from the Papal inquisition that, as we saw in Chapter 8, had been introduced into Europe in the thirteenth century.) Inquisitors now added Lutherans and Calvinists to converted Jews and Muslims in their definition of suspect populations and launched a new round of

Spanish Inquisition

FIGURE 11.8
El Greco, *Burial of the Count of Orgaz*, ca. 1586.

public trials and executions. In 1542, the Inquisition was reestablished in Rome, as the popes also felt compelled to take extreme measures to protect Catholics themselves from incorrect ideas. In addition, the papacy began to publish an "Index of Prohibited Books" in 1557, which it updated and reissued regularly. (The index was finally abolished in 1966.)

Philip II

While such measures aimed to control people's beliefs, the church looked to the Spanish king to champion the Catholic cause in the political and military arena. Philip II (r. 1556–1588), Charles V's heir to the kingdoms of Spain and the Netherlands, had an unparalleled zeal for both the Catholic religion and empire. Philip moved his capital from Toledo, the cramped medieval city, to the newly built city of Madrid, chosen because it was the geographic center of the Iberian Peninsula.

Philip faced two dire threats to the Catholic faith: the Turks in the eastern Mediterranean and the Protestants in the north. In 1571, he assembled a league that included a number of Italian city-states and set out to challenge the Turks' supremacy in the Mediterranean. The Venetians, with their large fleet and who were highly motivated by their trading interests in the eastern Mediterranean, were particularly eager to join Philip's navy. Outfitted with 208 galleys—sleek warships rowed by slaves and armed with cannons—Philip's navy confronted the Turks' 230 warships at the Battle of Lepanto, off the coast of Greece. Figure 11.9 depicts what the scene may have looked like. In this graphic image, cannons blaze and battering rams thrust forward as the galleys draw together.

When the smoke cleared after this spectacular battle, Philip's coalition had scored a decisive victory. The Turks lost 200 warships, the Europeans only 10. Tens of thousands of men on both sides died in the fighting, and contemporary witnesses described the sea as running red with blood. Nevertheless, the success at Lepanto raised Catholics' spirits throughout the West. The navy had proved that Turkish power in the Mediterranean was not invincible after all. Indeed, some Western Catholics began toying with the idea of invading the Ottoman Empire itself. But the Catholic monarchs had other adversaries in mind. Again, the kings of Europe went to war. This time, though, they marched against the Protestants in a series of battles that would drag on for a century and tear apart the soul of Europe.

Europe Erupts Again: A Century of Religious Warfare, 1559–1648

The Reformation had done far more than just establish alternative Christian sects—it raised the possibility that individuals might follow their own consciences in matters of religion. In a society in which the church served as the central institution in people's lives, this radical new idea struck at the very foundation of European politics and social realities. From the time the Roman emperor Constantine supported the Catholic Church (see Chapter 5), people always assumed that there was an identity of belief between rulers and subjects. Political loyalty was considered a religious phenomenon; the Protestant Reformation questioned this assumed fact.

In fact, the wars of religion that scourged Europe from 1559 to 1648 involved much more than the proper way to worship God. They also centered on the question of what constituted a state—specifically, whether one state could encompass various religious expressions. Like the peasant wars in Germany in 1524, these new hostilities involved religion, but they had significant economic, political, and social dimensions as well.

FRENCH WARS OF RELIGION, 1562–1598

By the 1550s, Calvinism had gained a good deal of strength in France among the peasants and in the towns of the south and southwest (including villages like that of Martin Guerre in the Biography). Although the French Calvinists (Huguenots) remained a minority—only about 7 percent of the population—they were well organized. Local congregations governed by ministers sent representatives to district assemblies that in turn coordinated their efforts with a national assembly and even mustered troops from local churches. This impressive minority even began to recruit members from the nobility—possibly 40 percent of French nobles had become Huguenots. Great noble families took the lead in forwarding their religious (and in turn political) interests—the Guises led the Catholics, and the Bourbons championed the

FIGURE 11.9
The Battle of Lepanto.

Huguenots. By the mid-sixteenth century, French Protestantism was a force to be reckoned with and the French kings took notice.

Francis I (r. 1515–1547) and his heir, Henry II (r. 1547–1559), were both powerful kings who based their authority in part on a strong Catholic stance. However, this royal power was broken by a freak accident. King Henry was celebrating the wedding of his daughter by fighting in a joust (the war game still much beloved by the nobility), but during the last joust of the day, his opponent's lance shattered, gouging Henry's eye. Henry died of complications of this wound, leaving his widow, the Italian Catherine de' Medici, to rule as regent for her young sons from 1559 to 1589.

Catherine tried to preserve royal control, but her efforts were impeded by the struggle for power between the Guises and the Bour- *Catholics vs. Huguenots* bons, both of whom had family ties to the monarchy and hoped to inherit the throne. Politics here intertwined with religion and the time was ripe for civil war. Fighting broke out in 1562, when the Duke of Guise massacred a Huguenot congregation, and it continued for about 36 years (with brief respites). The Huguenot forces, though outnumbered, were too well organized to be defeated. The most infamous point of these wars was the Saint Bartholomew's Day Massacre, which took place on August 23, 1572, just when peace seemed imminent.

A religious compromise seemed to be on the horizon with a marriage between Catherine's daughter and the Bourbon leader of the Huguenots, Henry of Navarre. However, the *Saint Bartholomew's Day Massacre* mutual suspicions and desire for revenge had not subsided—the Guise family persuaded the young king Charles IX (r. 1560–1574) that the Huguenot gathering for the wedding was a plot against the crown. The king then ordered his guard to kill all the Protestant leadership. On the morning of St. Bartholomew's Day, the soldiers unleashed a massacre against Protestants.

Although the young bridegroom escaped assassination, many others did not. Thousands were murdered, and the painting shown in Figure 11.10 depicts a

FIGURE 11.10
Françoise Dubois, *St. Bartholomew's Day Massacre.*

contemporary witness's memory of the slaughter. The massacre raged for six days, and as the image shows, it was particularly brutal. Women and infants were not spared, and the painting shows that even corpses were mutilated as religious fervor introduced a bloodbath. This violence did not end the wars, however. Civil war continued in France until King Henry III (r. 1574–1589) was assassinated, leaving no heir.

The next in line for the throne was Henry of Navarre—the Protestant bridegroom who survived the massacre. Recognizing that the overwhelmingly *Peace in France* Catholic population would not accept a reformist king, he converted to Catholicism, reputedly saying, "Paris is worth a mass." Sympathetic to both religions, the new king Henry IV (r. 1589–1610) issued the Edict of Nantes (1598), which ended the religious wars and introduced religious toleration in France. However, a subsequent king (Louis XIV, discussed in Chapter 13)

who believed that a nation was defined by loyalty to one religion would overturn Henry's policy. But for the time being at least, France gained a small respite from the violence of intolerance. The rest of Europe was not so lucky.

A "COUNCIL OF BLOOD" IN THE NETHERLANDS, 1566–1609

In addition to Spain, the Catholic king Philip II ruled over the Netherlands, which consisted of 17 provinces. (Today these provinces are Netherlands, Belgium, and Luxembourg.) Trouble began when Philip began to exert more control over the provinces—he restructured the Catholic Church to weaken the local aristocracy, and he insisted on billeting troops locally, which offended the Dutch.

In response, riots broke out in 1566 and Dutch Protestants, though still a tiny minority, rebelled against their Spanish, Catholic overlords. In a spasm of violence, they destroyed Catholic Church property, smashing images of saints and desecrating the host. Philip was enraged. Vowing to silence the rebels, he sent the largest land army ever assembled into the Netherlands to crush the Protestants and bring the province back under his Catholic rule. In 1572, organized revolt broke out and war officially began.

Revolt breaks out

Philip's crackdown ignited a savage 40-year contest in which the Spanish general, the "iron duke of Alba" presided over a slaughter of thousands of Protestants in what he called a "Council of Troubles," but what the Protestants called the "Council of Blood." Calvinist preachers retaliated by giving their congregations complete license to kill the invaders. To protect themselves, the towns of the Netherlands even opened their dikes to flood their country rather than give in to Philip's armies. The Dutch found an able leader in William of Orange, a nobleman known for his wise counsel, who took charge in 1580. William was assassinated four years later, and the murderer was publicly tortured to death as blood continued to flow in the Netherlands.

The defiance of the Dutch cost Philip more than the loss of soldiers and huge amounts of gold to finance the wars. It also diverted his attention northward, away from his victory over the Turks at Lepanto in 1571. Preoccupied by events in the Netherlands, he failed to ride the wave of widespread Christian antipathy toward the Turks and launch a decisive campaign against the enemy in the eastern Mediterranean.

Philip also tried to "save" England from the Protestantism that Henry VIII had introduced. Philip had married Henry's Catholic daughter Mary (r. 1553–1558), and when she died without an heir, the Spanish king proposed matrimony to her sister, Elizabeth I.

Armada against England

But the Protestant Elizabeth refused his attentions and even dared support the Netherlands against him. Philip struck back by hurling the full force of his navy against England, sending a huge fleet across the English Channel in 1588. What happened next stood in stark contrast to Philip's triumph at Lepanto. Instead of scoring an easy victory, the Spanish Armada was wiped out by the well-armed English ships and the sudden onslaught of violent storms in the North Sea (what the English would later call a "Protestant wind").

Philip never succeeded in subduing the Protestants in the Netherlands; the conflict dragged on until the deaths of both Philip and Elizabeth. In 1609, the two sides finally drew up an agreement that gave the northern provinces virtual independence. The final recognition of an independent Netherlands would have to wait until the Peace of Westphalia in 1648. After the final settlement, Protestants in the southern provinces moved north to escape continuing Spanish rule in the south, so the two provinces became divided along religious lines. The northern provinces became the Protestant Dutch Republic, and the southern (and French-speaking) Spanish Netherlands (which later became Belgium) remained Catholic. But this solution still could not quell the religious tensions tearing at Europe. Instead, the wars shifted east, where they culminated in the bloodiest engagement of them all.

Netherlands split

THE THIRTY YEARS' WAR, 1618–1648

The Peace of Augsburg had only temporarily answered the question of religious diversity in the Holy Roman Empire. For 50 years after Augsburg, pressure mounted as more and more people followed their consciences and as diverse spiritual beliefs proliferated in the principalities. These tensions reached the boiling point in 1618, when a Catholic prince took over Bohemia (in the modern Czech Republic) and set out to vanquish the substantial Protestant minority in his state. Protestant Bohemian nobles responded by throwing the prince's representatives out the castle window in Prague. The hapless officials landed unhurt in a pile of manure, but the Catholic explanation was that their fall had been broken by angels. The two sides seemed to have irreconcilable points of view.

But the Holy Roman Empire's political structure contained a unique feature that made religious tensions much harder to resolve than by merely pushing bureaucrats out of windows. The essential problem was that Protestant and Catholic electors (princes who elected the Holy Roman Emperor) were roughly equal in number. If Bohemia went to a Protestant prince, the balance of power would shift away from the ruling Catholic Habsburgs. Fearing this possibility, the Holy Roman Emperor Ferdinand II (r. 1619–1637) went to war to reclaim Bohemia for Catholicism. His action provoked a civil war that began over the key issue of the authority of the emperor over the princes in

War breaks out

Germany, but that quickly turned international as Protestants and Catholics across the Holy Roman Empire faced each other in battle.

The first 12 years of the war were marked by the success of Emperor Ferdinand's forces, and it seemed as if the Catholic Habsburgs would be able to roll back the Protestant gains in the German lands. The powerful Catholic Maximilian of Bavaria put an army at Ferdinand's disposal that won a stunning victory over the Bohemians at the Battle of White Mountain in 1620 (shown on Map 11.4). The Bohemian rebels were killed or exiled, and it seemed as if the war was over. However, the Protestants continued their struggle, but with few gains.

In 1624, the emperor received considerable help when a soldier of fortune came to offer his services to the Catholic cause. Albrecht von Wallen- **Wallenstein** stein, a minor Bohemian nobleman, recognized that the emperor needed a new army if he was to succeed, and Wallenstein offered to raise the force if he could billet it and raise its supplies wherever it happened to be stationed. Ferdinand agreed, and by 1627 Wallenstein's army had begun to conquer the northern region of the empire—the center of Protestant strength. Ferdinand grew so confident that he issued the Edict of Restitution in 1629, ordering all territories lost to Protestants since 1552 to be restored to Catholics. Wallenstein—brilliant general and opportunist—became one of the richest men in the empire.

By 1630, the tide and nature of the war began to change. With help from abroad, Protestants made gains, but the war began to shift from a religious strug- **From religion to politics** gle to a purely political quest—to weaken the power of the Habsburgs; for example, the Catholic French king was willing to join Protestants in support of this cause. Protestant forces found a worthy champion in the Swedish king Gustavus Adolphus (r. 1611–1632), who was appalled by Ferdinand's treatment of Protestants, and at the same time, he feared a Habsburg threat to Swedish lands around the Baltic Sea (see Map 11.4). A decisive battle was fought at Lutzen in 1632, where Gustavus's armies beat Wallenstein's forces. Unfortunately, Gustavus was killed in that battle, so the Swedish forces did not follow up on the victory. (The German princes eventually forced Ferdinand to turn against Wallenstein, and the emperor had his general assassinated a few months later.)

Gustavus's successes opened the final phase of the war (from 1632–1648) during which the emperor lost all his previous gains. The Protestant princes raised new armies, and by 1635, Ferdinand had to agree to suspend the Edict of Restitution and to grant amnesty to most of the Protestant princes. In return, the Protestants joined the imperial troops in driving the Swedes out of German lands. However, the Catholic French declared open war on Ferdinand in 1635, and for the next 13 years, French and Swedish troops rampaged through the lands, causing destruction and devastation.

By the 1640s, the war had reached a stalemate. The kings and princes who had started the hostilities had all died, and their successors (as well as civilians) were exhausted. Both sides laid down their arms and took stock of their losses. This war had **Devastation** raged with a violence that astonished even contemporary witnesses used to sixteenth-century battle methods, for armies on both sides had swept through villages and towns and laid to waste everything in their paths. The war had exacted a staggering price: Germany's population had plummeted (although historians do not agree on the figures, some suggest a population loss as high as 30 percent). The economy, too, was damaged. Spain had gone bankrupt and would never recover its standing as a leader on the European stage. France and Sweden emerged somewhat victoriously, gaining some land at the expense of the exhausted German states.

PEACE AT WESTPHALIA

The series of agreements that ended the Thirty Years' War are collectively known as the Peace of Westphalia, named for the region of Germany where the agreements were drafted. German princes now had the freedom to choose their own religion, but the religious desires of individuals within the states were still not accepted. However, for the first time, Calvinism was included among the tolerated faiths. The religious landmark of Europe was roughly established along north-south lines. The northwest—England, Holland, Scandinavia, and the northern German states—was Protestant, whereas the south remained Catholic.

The war had marked political overtones at the end, and the treaty accordingly addressed issues of power beyond religious choice. The **Political results** peace set the political geography of Europe for the next century and established a precedent for diplomacy that would shape the way nations

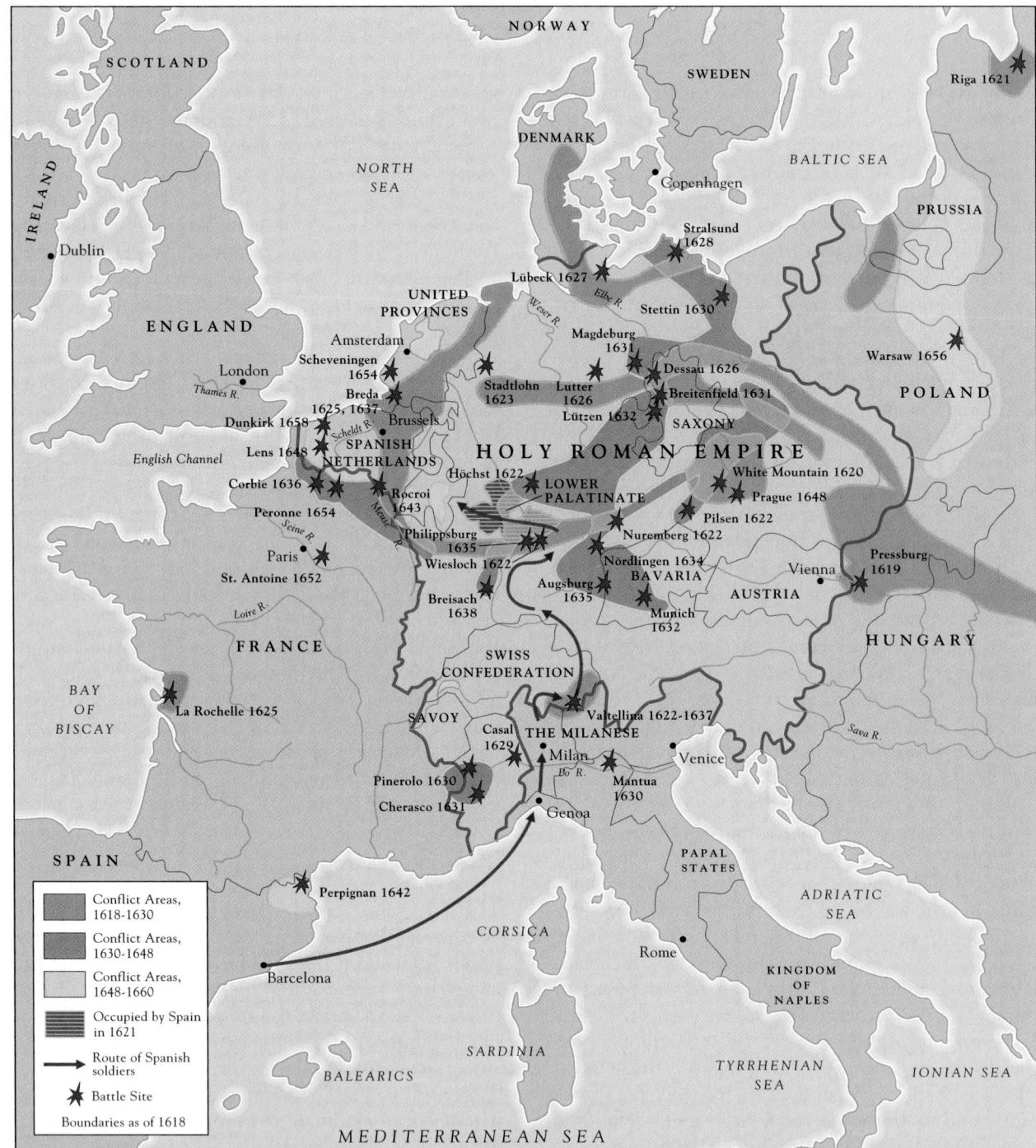

THINKING ABOUT GEOGRAPHY

MAP 11.4   *The Thirty Years' War, 1618–1648*

This map shows the major participants and the main battles of the long war that took place on German territory. ◾ **Notice** the location of Swedish lands. **Consider** why the king of Sweden became involved in this war. ◾ **Compare** this map with Map 11.3. **Consider** which regions were Protestant and which were Catholic. **Which** regions departed from their religious interests to fight primarily for political reasons?

THINKING ABOUT GEOGRAPHY

MAP 11.5   *Europe in 1648*

This map shows the political configuration of Europe after the Peace of Westphalia that ended the Thirty Years' War. ◼ **Notice** which countries appear large and cohesive after the settlement of Westphalia, and see the description in the text of the countries that gained the most. ◼ **Notice also** the countries that control territories distant from their main nations. **Which** of these more remote areas might become centers of conflict in the future?

resolved political problems in the coming centuries. Map 11.5 outlines the aftermath of the Peace of Westphalia. The representatives at Westphalia conducted all these negotiations with an eye toward "balance of power," a relatively new principle that

emerged in fifteenth-century Italy and now applied to European politics. They believed that they could ensure peace by making all the European powers roughly as strong as their neighbors. This strategy would dominate European diplomacy for centuries.

Life After the Reformation

The early modern wars of religion were finally over. Christians with different beliefs would now have to learn to coexist. As the storms of religious rage subsided, Europeans began noticing the dramatic changes in other aspects of everyday life and thought that the Protestant Reformation had provoked.

NEW DEFINITIONS OF COURTSHIP AND MARRIAGE

When the Protestants excluded marriage as a sacrament, the institution changed in ways they could not have foreseen. After Martin Luther left the monastery and married Katherina, the couple formed a loving partnership and raised five children (along with caring for orphans). Luther explored this relationship in his writings and saw in marriage part of God's plan for humanity. Calvin, too, rejected the church fathers' "too superstitious admiration of celibacy" and extolled the benefits of conjugal partnerships. Although divorce was not easy in any of the Protestant groups, it was possible. With all these changes, the ideal of marriage shifted. Couples began to expect "mutual love between man and wife," instead of simply duty that bound extended families together. The Catholic Church also was influenced by the new marital values, and in the late sixteenth century, church manuals began to use the word "love" to refer to conjugal relations.

People still did not marry just for love, however; instead, families continued to arrange suitable matches between young people. Arranged marriages were an essential and logical part of a view that valued family prosperity and continuity more than an individual's happiness. Individuals were seen as mere moments in the larger life of the family. Nevertheless, something new was

Courtship

going on in family relations. Although parents still negotiated a suitable match, prospective couples were allowed to consider their compatibility before marriage, and daughters had some say in vetoing disagreeable matches. Courtship customs grew more complex, as men and women evaluated whether they would have a "harmonious" union. In Figure 11.11, a painting titled *The Suitor's Visit*, a young man calls on a woman in one of many visits intended for the couple to get to know each other. Presumably, the suitor greets the young woman's mother, who will chaperone the courtship and approve the joining of the families that marriage still represented. The prospective bride is in the background playing her lute; young women in these years cultivated their skills at making music and clever conversation so as to beguile potential mates and convince them of their qualities as life partners.

FIGURE 11.11
Gerard Ter Borch, *The Suitor's Visit*, 1658.

FORGING A LINK BETWEEN EDUCATION AND WORK

The Christian humanists from Erasmus on urged everyone to learn to read. Reformed Catholicism under the Jesuits also stressed education as central to a

Valuing literacy Christian life, and parochial schools and armies of nuns gave young children the rudiments of education. Protestants, too, urged study. As Luther and others emphasized Bible study as part of essential Christian behavior and translated the Book into vernacular languages, the next logical step was to broaden literacy. Luther encouraged the cities and villages in Saxony to establish publicly funded schools, and many Protestants followed his call. A Bohemian reformer, Jan Amos Comenius (1592–1670) wrote: "All alike, boys and girls, both noble and ignoble, rich and poor, in all cities and towns, villages and hamlets, should be sent to school." This egalitarian notion would take centuries to implement, but it established a new educational goal in the West.

The painter Jan Steen's depiction of an early-seventeenth-century classroom (shown in Figure 11.12) embodies the Protestant ideals of education. This is a village school where both boys and girls study. The strict schoolmaster slaps a boy's hand in reprimand for the poorly done assignment on the floor, while the boy cries. The girl on the boy's right smiles rather too gleefully at his distress. This scene must have played out repeatedly in the many small village schools that began to spring up as more children began to receive formal education.

Although education was intended primarily to help people study the Bible and learn to serve as their

Valuing work own spiritual guides, it also had profound implications for the way people viewed work. In response to critics who complained about educating "rustics," the Bohemian educational reformer Comenius answered that universal education would help everyone avoid "that idleness which is so dangerous to flesh and blood." His words hinted at a new philosophy that stressed the value of work.

In the Middle Ages, "those who work" were relegated to the bottom of the social scale. The upper crust consisted of only those who could live off the income of their land and did not need to work to survive. The bourgeoisie—the middle class—that was becoming more and more prosperous since the

FIGURE 11.12
Jan Steen, *The Village School*, ca. 1655.

Renaissance began to change that view and brought a new valuing of work into the consciousness of Western society. The Protestant reformers that appealed to many of the residents of these growing urban areas lent religious support to new ideas about work. In Luther's writings, even women were defined by the work they did. He described the ideal wife as follows: "She likes working.... She girds her loins and stretches her arms, works with energy in the house."

Calvin, too, believed that men and women were "called" to work and that work itself was a virtuous activity. Centuries later, the German sociologist Max Weber, in *The Protestant Ethic and the Spirit of Capitalism* (1904), would argue that Calvinists' emphasis on work legitimized and therefore boosted the growth of capitalism in the West. Many Calvinists believed that hard work, efficiency, and frugality all indicated a person predestined to salvation. Not surprisingly, then, Protestants embraced what has come to be called the "work ethic" with fervor. Historians dispute the details of Weber's thesis, but his argument still offers us an insight into the way religious ideas shaped modern-day views of work in the West. In the Catholic Middle Ages, people had seen work as the curse of Adam laid on the damned; in the Protestant early modern period, work became God's gift to a saved humanity.

ANXIETY AND SPIRITUAL INSECURITY

The striking revolution in thought that the Protestant reformers introduced also prompted some spiritual anxiety and insecurity among Christians. In part, this unease stemmed from the hardship spawned by the relentless warfare of the period. The "community of the faithful" that Catholicism once represented had fragmented, and for Protestants encouraged to "stand alone before God," the new religious individualism often felt frightening.

The new mind-set began to raise questions about charitable institutions and their relationship with religious bodies. Where once the universal church

Charitable institutions looked after the poor and widows and orphans, now separate congregations had to care for their own. The question of who was responsible for whom sometimes became quite murky, and a sense of individual responsibility for one's own plight slowly replaced a collective sense of charity. For example, civic authorities began to consider ways to help the needy, building workhouses for the poor and passing laws prohibiting begging. Such laws could never completely succeed, given the scale of need that we saw in the painting of the "Cripples" in Figure 11.1. Yet, more and more societies tried designing institutional solutions to the problems of poverty.

Figure 11.13 depicts a girls' dining hall in a Protestant orphanage in Amsterdam. The painting emphasizes the institutional quality of charity in the early seventeenth century. The orphans are dressed alike, for exam-

ple, and the girls in the foreground serve watery soup for dinner while the matrons watch. The scene utterly lacks a sense of compassion.

As communities redivided themselves along religious loyalties, many people's sense of personal anxiety increased. The Catholic Church had *Decline of "magic"* also provided community support and at least the hope of miraculous cures for the sick and troubled. Men and women could themselves pray to saints or the Virgin Mary for help, and priests could say prayers for members of their congregation in need. The Catholic Church even turned a blind eye to "white" magic (like that described in the village of Martin Guerre in the Biography), but Protestants rejected saints and any forms of "magic." As village rituals split apart, it became harder to define "community." As changing times and beliefs generated anxieties, some people began looking for scapegoats.

SEARCHING FOR SCAPEGOATS: THE HUNT FOR WITCHES

Catholics and Protestants alike believed that there were people who had special powers to cause people good or harm. In England, belief in witchcraft was grounded in the popular beliefs of the time, which

FIGURE 11.13

Jan Victors, *The Girls' Dining Hall in the Reformed Parish Orphanage*, ca. 1651.

argued that witches harmed humans or animals, brought on bad weather, or destroyed fertility. Protestant preachers argued regularly against "superstitious magical practices," but people remained attached to charms and spells.

On the Continent, fear of witches became more firmly linked to the Devil—a force that Protestants and Catholics alike deeply feared. Martin

Devil worship Luther himself claimed to have confronted the Devil several times and constantly remained alert to the presence of this evil being. Church authorities began to stress that witches were in league with the Devil and performed mysterious ceremonies in his service. To stamp out the Devil's assistants, many accused supposed witches, putting them on trial and executing them.

Indeed, people in the sixteenth century were fascinated by the possibility of witchcraft. The best-known work on the subject was the *Malleus Maleficarum* (the "Hammer of Witches"), which had been written in the late fifteenth century (before the start of the Reformation) for inquisitors to try witches. However, by 1669 it had been reissued in 40 editions and had become extraordinarily popular, appealing to Protestants and Catholics alike. In France alone, 345 books about witchcraft were published between 1550 and 1650.

Figure 11.14, a painting from the seventeenth century, reveals the characteristics of witches as imagined by Europeans of this period. Those accused of witchcraft were predominantly female (90 percent of those executed for witchcraft were women), many of whom were old. In this picture, the witches prepare magic potions drawn from body parts taken from the corpse hanging on the left and the heart impaled on the sword in the center. At the right, a witch carries an infant who will be killed and whose body will be used for magical purposes. In the center is a broomstick. People believed that witches rode these and used them to apply hallucinogenic potions to their vaginas.

FIGURE 11.14
Salvator Rosa, *Witches at Their Incantations* (detail), late seventeenth century.

Catholics and Protestants alike persecuted witches, and the trials in Europe peaked between 1560 and 1640. Although precise numbers elude us, *Persecutions* more than 100,000 people were executed for witchcraft, and 200,000 may have endured trials. These trials are probably the most disturbing indicator of the rampant anxiety stirred by the intellectual and social changes of the sixteenth century.

By the eighteenth century, the witchcraft panic ebbed and the trials gradually ceased, as men and women adjusted to the religious diversity that had split their countries and their communities. However, the ideals of the Protestant Reformation—individualism, a desire for marital harmony, an emphasis on hard work, and a staunch reliance on conscience—left a permanent mark on European society. As they recovered from the horrible wars that had plagued the Continent, Europeans were poised to spread their culture outside the boundaries of Europe and throughout the world.

TIMELINE: A CLOSER LOOK

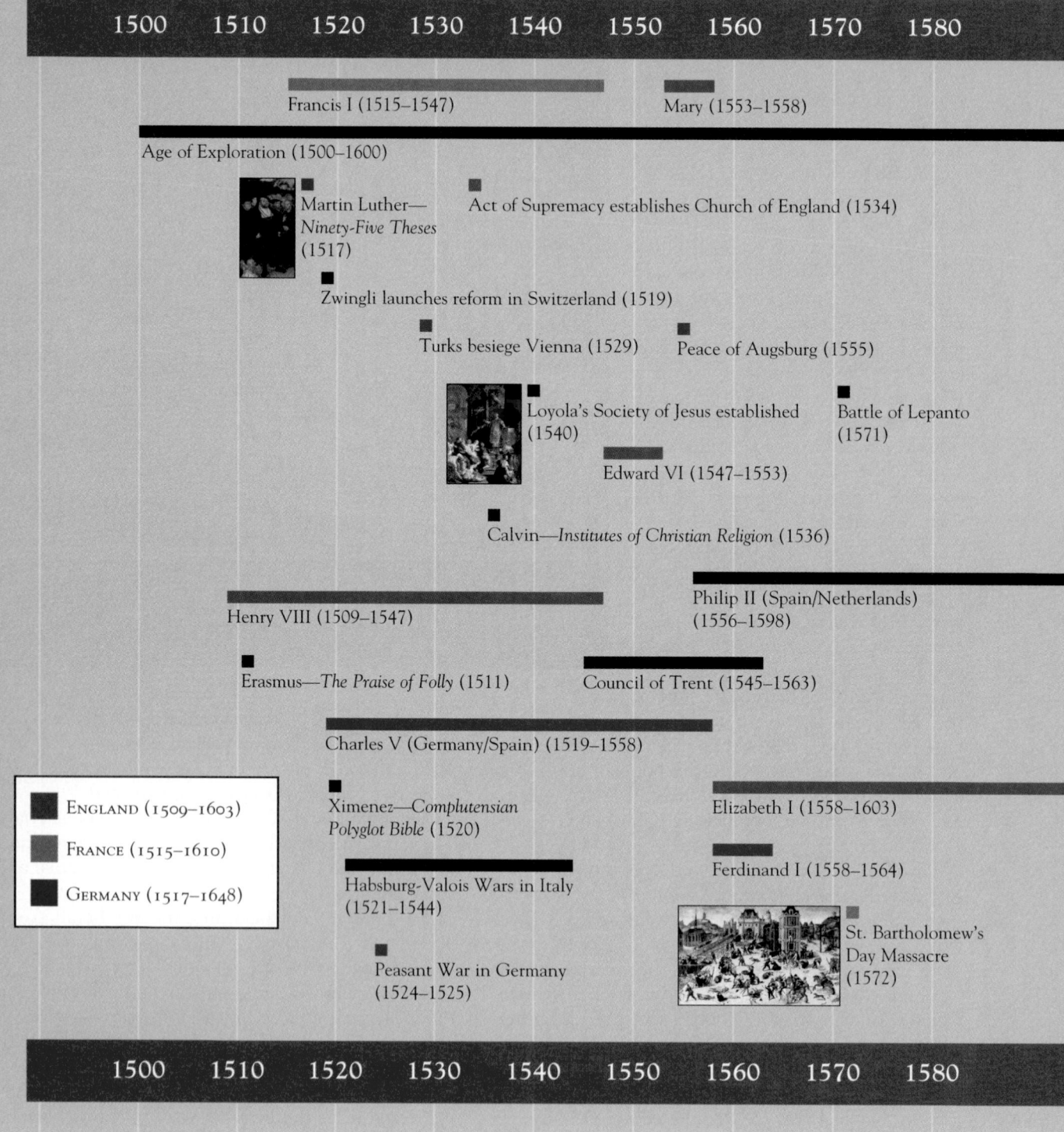

| | 1500 | 1510 | 1520 | 1530 | 1540 | 1550 | 1560 | 1570 | 1580 |

Francis I (1515–1547)

Mary (1553–1558)

Age of Exploration (1500–1600)

Martin Luther—*Ninety-Five Theses* (1517)

Act of Supremacy establishes Church of England (1534)

Zwingli launches reform in Switzerland (1519)

Turks besiege Vienna (1529)

Peace of Augsburg (1555)

Loyola's Society of Jesus established (1540)

Battle of Lepanto (1571)

Edward VI (1547–1553)

Calvin—*Institutes of Christian Religion* (1536)

Philip II (Spain/Netherlands) (1556–1598)

Henry VIII (1509–1547)

Erasmus—*The Praise of Folly* (1511)

Council of Trent (1545–1563)

Charles V (Germany/Spain) (1519–1558)

ENGLAND (1509–1603)

FRANCE (1515–1610)

GERMANY (1517–1648)

Ximenez—*Complutensian Polyglot Bible* (1520)

Elizabeth I (1558–1603)

Ferdinand I (1558–1564)

Habsburg-Valois Wars in Italy (1521–1544)

St. Bartholomew's Day Massacre (1572)

Peasant War in Germany (1524–1525)

| | 1500 | 1510 | 1520 | 1530 | 1540 | 1550 | 1560 | 1570 | 1580 |

Spanish Armada attacks England (1588)

Henry IV (1598–1610)

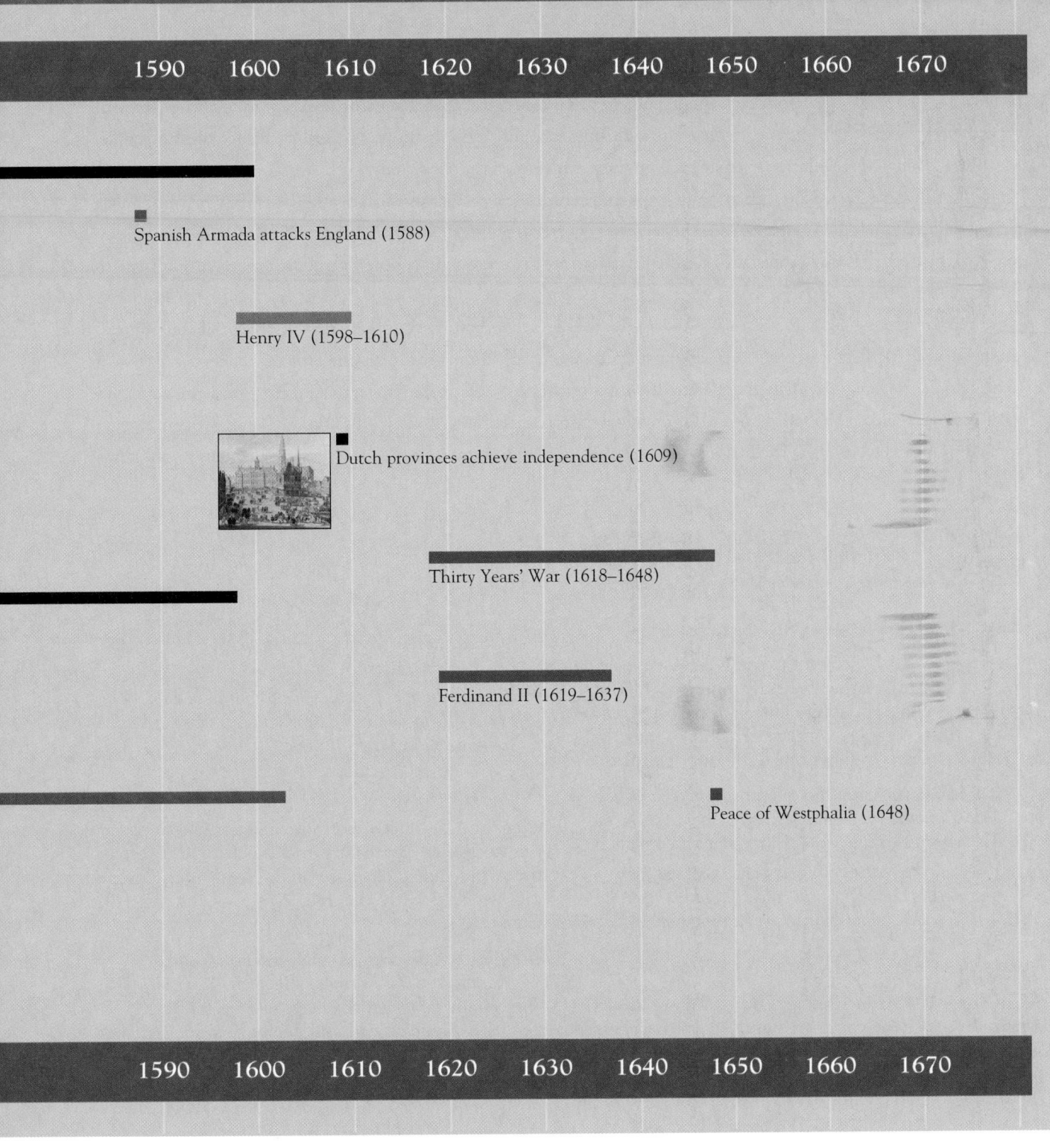

Dutch provinces achieve independence (1609)

Thirty Years' War (1618–1648)

Ferdinand II (1619–1637)

Peace of Westphalia (1648)

Summary

Through the sixteenth century, the monarchs of the unified states of Europe—England, France, Spain, and the Holy Roman Empire—struggled to snatch power, wealth, and land from each other. The wars that resulted accomplished little except to bankrupt some of the kings, leave the European countryside in ruins, and inflict misery on the people. Meanwhile, religious revolutionaries stepped up their criticism of the thousand-year history of Christian tradition. These Protestants effected a reformation that spurred century-long religious warfare and that split Christendom as people followed their own paths to God. The religious quest had political ramifications as well—kings involved themselves in the Catholics' and Protestants' conflict in part to try to exert religious hegemony over their own lands and to gain land from their neighbors.

When the century of religious wars in Europe ended, it left a legacy of economic devastation, social and political change, and an intellectual revolution that transformed Western culture. More boys and girls in village schools began to read and write, men and women hoped to find love in marriage, and people began to take more pride in work over leisure. Nevertheless, the Protestant revolution failed to stop the competition for Christian souls. In the centuries to come, Europeans would take the battle between Protestants and Catholics across the seas, as they discovered lands that were new to them.

REVIEW, ANALYZE, AND ANTICIPATE

REVIEW THE PREVIOUS CHAPTER

Chapter 10—"A New Spirit in the West"—described the characteristics that we have come to identify with the Renaissance. In addition, Chapter 10 also discussed the complex political structure of Italy that engaged popes as well as princes in power politics.

1. Which Renaissance characteristics also describe the ideas of the Protestant reformers? Consider how the Renaissance influenced the Protestant Reformation.

2. Review the policies of Renaissance popes as they strove to become political powers in Italy. How did those policies contribute to the Reformation?

ANALYZE THIS CHAPTER

Chapter 11—"Alone Before God"—follows the expansion of warfare until it engulfed all of Europe in the sixteenth century. It also looks at the new religious ideas that split the Catholic Church and brought about a change in life in the West.

1. Review the various religious beliefs of the different Protestant sects and consider the relationship of these ideas to the different social and economic groups who were attracted to them.

2. How did the differing appeal help lead to the century of religious warfare? What were the results of this warfare?

3. Review the reform movements of the Catholic Church. How did the church respond to the critique of the Protestants?

4. How did the Reformation help contribute to changing social and cultural patterns that marked seventeenth-century Europe?

ANTICIPATE THE NEXT CHAPTER

Chapter 12—"Faith, Fortune, and Fame"—looks at the European expansion into much of the rest of the world that took place at the same time Europe was wracked with the religious wars discussed in Chapter 11.

1. Based on the strengths and weaknesses of the various states discussed in Chapter 11, which countries do you think might take the lead in the explorations and which might be left behind? Why?

2. Which Christian churches do you think might be most vigorous in missionary activities? Review Chapter 11's discussion of the characteristics of each sect's relative theology as you decide.

BEYOND THE CLASSROOM

THE CLASH OF DYNASTIES

Bonney, Richard. *The European Dynastic States, 1494–1660*. Oxford: Oxford University Press, 1991. A rich survey that includes eastern as well as western Europe and provides an excellent overview (although it does exclude England).

Braudel, Fernand. *The Mediterranean and the Mediterranean World in the Age of Philip II*. New York: Harper and Row, 1972. An extraordinary analysis of the Mediterranean world that, in its consideration of geography, ecology, social history, economic history, and politics, offers a broad background for the period.

Davis, Natalie Zemon. *The Return of Martin Guerre*. Cambridge, MA: Harvard University Press, 1983. The classic study of Martin Guerre (the subject of the Chapter 11 Biography).

Parker, Geoffrey. *European Soldiers, 1550–1650*. New York: Cambridge University Press, 1997. A short, beautifully illustrated look into the lives of European soldiers.

A TIDE OF RELIGIOUS REFORM

Bainton, Roland H. *Here I Stand: A Life of Martin Luther*. New York: Meridian, 1995. First published in 1950, but it remains the best and most sensitive study of the man and his impact.

Baylor, Michael G. *The Radical Reformation*. New York: Cambridge University Press, 1991. Collects letters and other documents to illustrate the rich diversity and the fragile unity that existed in the political thinking of some of the major radical reformers in Germany.

Edwards, Mark Jr. *Printing, Propaganda and Martin Luther*. Berkeley, CA: University of California Press, 1994. A study of the literature that tried to redefine the church and its beliefs.

Haigh, Christopher. *English Reformations: Religion, Politics, and Society Under the Tudors*. Oxford: Clarendon Press, 1993. A scholarly work that draws on a wealth of primary materials from catechisms to churchwardens' accounts to offer a full picture of the English Reformation.

Ozment, Steven. *The Age of Reform, 1250–1550*. New Haven, CT: Yale University Press, 1980. A clear study that explains how the reformers transformed medieval theological debates.

Steinmetz, David. *Calvin in Context*. New York: Oxford University Press, 1995. A general and well-balanced introduction to Calvin's thought.

THE CATHOLIC REFORMATION

Ahlgren, Gillian. *Teresa of Avila and the Politics of Sanctity*. Ithaca, NY: Cornell University Press, 1996. Considers Teresa's struggle in the context of a world that did not always look kindly on an outspoken woman.

Jones, Martin D. *The Counter Reformation: Religion and Society in Early Modern Europe*. New York: Cambridge University Press, 1995. A good, up-to-date survey.

EUROPE ERUPTS AGAIN: A CENTURY OF RELIGIOUS WARFARE, 1559–1648

Knecht, R.J. *The French Wars of Religion: 1554–1598*. New York: Longman, 1989. A good survey.

MacCaffrey, Wallace. *Elizabeth I: War and Politics, 1588–1603*. Princeton, NJ: Princeton University Press, 1992. Recounts the conduct of the war with Spain and describes the diplomacy of alliances of the period.

Parker, Geoffrey. *The Thirty Years' War*. New York: Routledge, 1997. A readable general history by one of the foremost military historians.

LIFE AFTER THE REFORMATION

Harrington, Joel. *Reordering Marriage and Society in Reformation Germany*. Cambridge, England: Cambridge University Press, 1994. A provocative and sound interpretation.

Thomas, Keith. *Religion and the Decline of Magic*. 1971. An important book that investigates many sources to study the changing character of religious beliefs and the replacement of "superstition" with science.

Weber, Max. *The Protestant Ethic and the Spirit of Capitalism*. Los Angeles: Roxbury Publishing Co., 1998. Originally published in 1904, this study of how the Reformation helped create the modern world has generated much controversy, but has also shaped much of the historical thinking about the Reformation.

For quiz questions that tie the book to the videos and additional primary sources, please go to the Primary Source Investigator CD.

QUIZ

Documents

DOCUMENT 11.1

Germans Rage against Papal Exploitation

Well before Luther complained about the Catholic Church, others in Germany raged against what they saw as exploitation of Germans by a distant pope. The first was written in 1480 by an unknown author. The second was written in 1503 by a Franciscan monk, Myconius, who was appalled at Tetzel's sale of indulgences. These documents show that Luther's critique launched in 1517 would find fertile soil.

■ **Investigate the Document**

> **What** *were the main criticisms of the church?* **Notice** *the angry rhetoric of these texts.* **How** *will that contribute to the coming of the Reformation?*

1. Critique of Church Wealth, ca. 1480. Author anonymous.

It is as clear as day that by means of smooth and crafty words the clergy have deprived us of our rightful possessions. For they blinded the eyes of our forefathers, and persuaded them to buy the kingdom of heaven with their lands and possessions. If you priests give the poor and the chosen children of God their paternal inheritance, which before God you owe them, God will perhaps grant you such grace that you will know yourselves. But so long as you spend your money on your dear harlots and profligates, instead of upon the children of God, you may be sure that God will reward you according to your merits. For you have angered and overburdened all the people of the empire. The time is coming when your possessions will be seized and divided as if they were the possessions of an enemy. As you have oppressed the people, they will rise up against you so that you will not know where to find a place to stay.

2. Against Abuses in Indulgences, Myconius, 1512

Anno 1512. Tetzel gained by his preaching in Germany an immense sum of money which he sent to Rome. A very large sum was collected at the new

Source: Oliver J. Thatcher and Edgar H. McNeal, *A Source Book for Mediaeval History*, (New York: Charles Scribner's Sons, 1905), pp. 336–340.

mining works at St. Annaberg, where I heard him for two years. It is incredible what this ignorant and impudent monk used to say. . . . He declared that if they contributed readily and bought grace and indulgence, all the hills of St. Annaberg would become pure massive silver. Also, that, as soon as the coin clinked in the chest, the soul for whom the money was paid would go straight to heaven. . . . The indulgence was so highly prized that when the agent came to a city the bull was carried on a satin or gold cloth, and all the priests and monks, the town council, schoolmaster, scholars, men, women, girls, and children went out in procession to meet it with banners, candles, and songs. All the bells were rung and organs played. He was conducted into the church, a red cross was erected in the center of the church, and the pope's banner displayed. . . .

DOCUMENT 11.2

An English Historian Chronicles the Execution of Anne Boleyn

Holinshed's Chronicles, *as Raphaell Holinshed's best-known work is called, was the most influential narrative history in late-fifteenth-century England. This passage records the semi-public execution of Henry's queen, Anne Boleyn, on the green of the Tower of London. Holinshed wrote this account in a way he thought would please the reigning monarch, Queen Elizabeth I.*

■ **Investigate the Document**

> **Which** *parts of Anne's speech might have been propaganda designed to flatter her mother, Queen Elizabeth, and support Elizabeth's Protestant agenda?*

From the year 1536.

About five of the clock in the afternoon, queen Anne of Boleyn was brought to the tower of London... and when she came to the tower gate, entering in she fell on her knees before the said lords, beseeching God to help her, as she was not guilty of that whereof she was accused, and then desired the said lords to beseech the king's grace to be good unto her, and so they left her there prisoner. On the fifteenth of May queen Anne was arraigned in the tower of London on a scaffold for that purpose, made in the king's hall, before the duke of Norfolk, who sat under the cloth of estate as high steward of England. . . . The king's commission being read, the constable of the tower, and the lieutenant brought the queen to the bar, where was made a chair for her to sit down in, and there her indictment was read, whereunto she made so wise and discreet answers, that she seemed fully to clear herself of all matters laid to her charge; but being tried by her peers, whereof the duke of Sufolk was chief, she was by them found guilty, and had judgement pronounced by the duke of Norfolk.

The words of queen Anne at her death:

Good Christian people, I am come hither to die, for according to the law, and by the law as I am judged to die, and therefore I will speak nothing against it. I am come hither to accuse no man, nor to speak any thing of that whereof I am accused and condemned to die, but I pray God save the king and send him long to reign over you, for a gentler, nor a more merciful prince was there never, and to me he was ever a good, a gentle, and a sovereign lord. And if any person will meddle of my cause, I require them to judge the best. And thus I take my leave of the world, and of you all, and I heartily desire you all to pray for me. Oh Lord have mercy on, to God I commend my soul. Jesus receive my soul; diverse times repeating those words, till that her head was striken off with the sword.

DOCUMENT 11.3
A Ducal Order Mandates Persecution of Anabaptist Women

The Reformation encouraged Christians to follow their consciences in matters of faith. But this principle often tore families apart. In 1584, a Duke issued an order addressing the problem of women who converted to Anabaptism recommending punishing women for their beliefs.

Source: Raphaell Holinshed, *Holinshed's Chronicles of England, Scotland, and Ireland*, 6 vol. (London: Johnson, Rivington, et al., 1808), pp. 796–97. [I have modernized the spelling.]

■ **Investigate the Document**

Why does the author oppose banishment as a punishment for these women? What retribution does he recommend instead? How did some husbands respond to the ducal order?

For a few years it has often occurred and come to pass that women whose husbands are not Anabaptists but of the correct religion are misled and drawn into error by others. They do not let themselves be led back to proper, circumspect behavior and well-directed energy by the commissioners and magistrates or by the chancellery, and they are unaffected by the reminders and fervent petitions of their husbands. Instead they persist in their error, and for this reason they have previously been dealt with by banishment from the land, as is the case with men by virtue of ordinance. But this has caused many great burdens to small untrained, even nursing children. For this reason, and also because of the earnest, plaintive requests of the husbands, such cases have been dealt with leniently, and such wives have been handed over to their husbands to be chained in the house. Officials have earnestly been instructed to permit no access to them and to take care that such erring women not presume to lead their families or others astray. . . .

Previously, however, we have learned that when it was thought that the women were chained and secured, they had been freed secretly with the help of their husbands or their servants. . . . Now since they have used deception, the command must be all the most serious from now on, and a considerable punishment of fine or imprisonment must be enjoined and inflicted upon the men given such a serious, high trust.

Source: "How to Proceed Against Anabaptist Women" in *Lives and Voices: Sources in European Women's History*, ed. Lisa DiCaprio and Merry E. Wiesner, (NY: Houghton Mifflin Co., 2001), pp. 216–217.

Sailing ship detail from Fall of the Icarus, by Pieter Brueghel the Elder

In the sixteenth century, Europeans struck out over uncharted seas, traveling to new lands and discovering new peoples. These explorations were made possible by small but sturdy ships rigged for capturing the winds that would allow the ships to sail in whatever direction the breezes blew. This detail of a sixteenth-century ship shows the kind of magnificent vessel that would take Europeans around the world. The voyages of discovery and the resulting blending of cultures utterly changed the world.

CHAPTER 12

Faith, Fortune, and Fame

European Expansion, 1450–1700

STUDY • The world imagined • Discovery of new lands and sea routes • Confrontation of cultures • The growth of a world market and commercial revolution ⊕NOTICE how the mingling of various cultures transformed all of them to some degree.

"To serve God and the King, to give light to those who are in darkness, and to grow rich, as all men desire to do."

With these words, the Portuguese explorer Bartholomeu Dias (1450–1500) explained purposes that drove men to sail their ships across uncharted oceans during the sixteenth and seventeenth centuries. At the same time that Italian Renaissance ideas spread and the Reformation created new martyrs, daring Europeans ventured where they had never gone before. Kings and queens sponsored these explorers in the hopes that the new territories and riches they promised would give monarchs an advantage over their dynastic rivals.

The adventurers traveled by ship east to China, Japan, and other places in the Pacific, and west to strange new islands and continents. As they journeyed, they met peoples living in great empires in the East and in the mountains and jungles of South and Central America. They traded with many others from tribes and kingdoms in sub-Saharan Africa, the Caribbean, and North America. The interactions among the many cultures prompted the emergence of new markets and the discovery of unusual products that whetted Europeans' appetites for yet more novelties. Sadly, the commingling also led to the transmission of deadly new diseases and other hardships. Europeans were irrevocably altered by these cultural contacts, and so were the cultures they encountered.

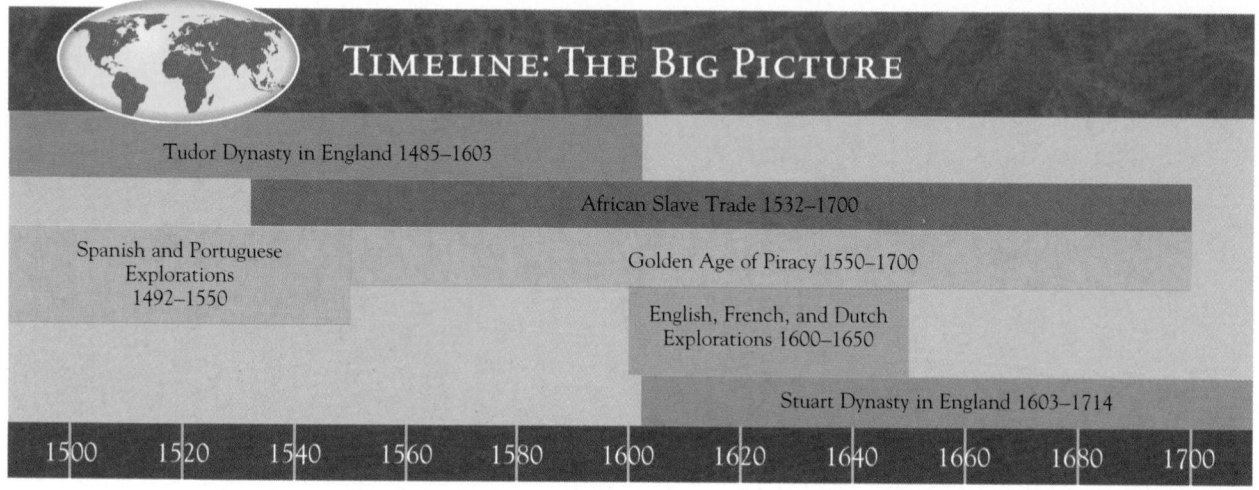

TIMELINE: THE BIG PICTURE

Tudor Dynasty in England 1485–1603

African Slave Trade 1532–1700

Spanish and Portuguese
Explorations
1492–1550

Golden Age of Piracy 1550–1700

English, French, and Dutch
Explorations 1600–1650

Stuart Dynasty in England 1603–1714

1500 1520 1540 1560 1580 1600 1620 1640 1660 1680 1700

The World Imagined

In 1498, four Portuguese ships led by Vasco da Gama sailed south from Europe and rounded the southern tip of Africa to reach India in the east. Gaspar Correa accompanied this journey, keeping a careful chronicle that told of the exciting, frightening voyage. In order to sail south with prevailing northwesterly winds, the navigators could not hug the shore, but instead had to direct the ships southwest, tacking into the wind and going far away from the sight of land into the unknown sea. For two months, Vasco da Gama tacked out to sea to make sure when they turned to shore, the ships would "double the cape," skirting the African continent. Correa wrote of the hardships of this venture into the Atlantic: "The fury of the sea [made] the ships seem every moment to be going to pieces. The crews grew sick with fear and hardship, . . . and all clamored for putting back to Portugal. . . . At times they met with such cold rains that the men could not prepare their food. All cried out to God for mercy upon their souls." Vasco da Gama finally ordered the ships about and they sailed southeast again. They circled the southern tip of Africa and with much celebration they headed northeast toward India.

The ships were to face much more hardship. They pulled into great rivers in Africa looking for food and for people to tell them where they were. They ate unknown fruits—one so toxic it made their gums swell and their teeth loosen. The captain ordered his ill men to rinse their mouths with urine to ease their gums, and the cure worked. Somehow, through all the adversity the crews carried on, and finally docked in India at a city where citizens flocked to the shore, amazed at the Western ships. Correa succinctly and accurately described the confrontation between East and West: "All were much amazed at seeing what they had never before seen." Vasco da Gama's crew was not unique in the fifteenth century; brave sailors sailed east and west from Europe, and the world was transformed as Europeans and indigenous peoples almost everywhere were "amazed" at their new confrontation.

THE LURE OF THE "EAST"

Western Europeans had long coveted goods from the "East," which they generally considered China and India. When they used the name "China," they also meant Japan and the other lands of eastern Asia. When they referred to "India," they included southeast Asia and the many islands dotting the Pacific, and although Vasco da Gama *Eastern trade* reached the mainland of India, he would have been content to land on any of the Pacific islands. More than just a geographic entity, though, the East, in many Europeans' minds, was the source of valuable luxury goods.

Since the Middle Ages, Europe had lusted after the silks, fine carpets, pottery, and precious jewels produced in the East. Europeans were so impressed by these exotic goods that they praised the Chinese as the "finest craftsmen in the world." Yet it was the spices from the Orient that riveted westerners' attention. European diets were bland, and those who depended only on local seasonings—garlic, saffron, and the ever-present salt—found the food tiresome. Recipes of the time and records showing commercial demand reveal that people clamored for cloves, cinnamon, coriander, and pepper in particular—all available only in the East. Throughout the Middle Ages, these products came overland through the Byzantine Empire into western Europe.

But after 1400, intensifying warfare in eastern Europe and Asia made overland travel difficult. (See Chapter 9 for the increased threat posed by the Turks.) Europeans began looking for new trade routes through the eastern Mediterranean to satisfy their appetite for spice. They revived centuries-old memories of journeys to the East by reading accounts like that of the Venetian explorer Marco Polo (1254–1324), who wrote detailed descriptions of his visits to China (see Chapter 9). These works were incorrect in much of their geography, however; for example, Marco Polo believed that Japan was 1,500 miles east of China. Furthermore, most of these older accounts contained exaggerated descriptions of botanical and biological features of eastern lands. Nevertheless, no tale of the exotic "East" seemed too far-fetched to fifteenth-century European imaginations.

FIGURE 12.1

"Monstrous races" pictured in manuscript of Marco Polo's travels, fifteenth century.

IMAGINED PEOPLES

Since the time of the Roman scholar Pliny the Elder (23–79), people had heard of unusual races of people who inhabited parts of the world outside the Mediterranean. Pliny's works had been read, copied, and embellished over the centuries, and by the fifteenth century, explorers expected to find beings as bizarre as dog-headed humans, headless people, one-legged "sciopods," and—south of the equator— "antipods," whose feet reportedly faced backward.

Figure 12.1 shows an illustration from a fifteenth-century manuscript about the travels of Marco Polo. Although Marco Polo never claimed to have seen such creatures, later Europeans imagined that he did. On the left of the illustration is a blemmyae, a headless man whose face is located on his chest. In the center is a sciopod, a one-legged creature believed to use his large foot as a parasol against the sun. These two beings are greeted by a cyclops approaching from the right.

A more plausible person the explorers expected to meet was "Prester John," supposedly a rich and powerful Christian king reigning in the heart of Africa. By the Renaissance, Europeans hoped to enlist this king as an ally against the Muslims. Document 12.1 on page D12.1 gives a famous medieval example of a description of the imagined Prester John's court. However, the search for both Prester John and the fascinating creatures in Marco Polo's tales was stymied by an inaccurate geographic sense of the world that, like the descriptions of the "monstrous races," the explorers had inherited from the ancients.

PTOLEMY'S MAP

During the fifteenth century, western Europeans acquired the *Geography* of Ptolemy (100?–178?). This guide had been translated from Greek, reproduced by the new printing presses, and widely distributed. Now Renaissance explorers had a picture of the world that they could use to venture into the Atlantic, or the "green sea of darkness," as the Arabic commentators called it.

Ptolemy's world view

Ptolemy portrayed the world as a globe, divided into the familiar 360 degrees of longitude. Figure 12.2, from a 1482 edition of the *Geography*, shows Ptolemy's map of the world. This ancient geographer believed that the world consisted of three continents—Asia, Africa, and Europe—and two oceans—the Indian Ocean and the Western Ocean. The map is surrounded by figures representing the many winds so crucial to a sailing society. In addition to mistaking the number of continents, Ptolemy made two major errors.

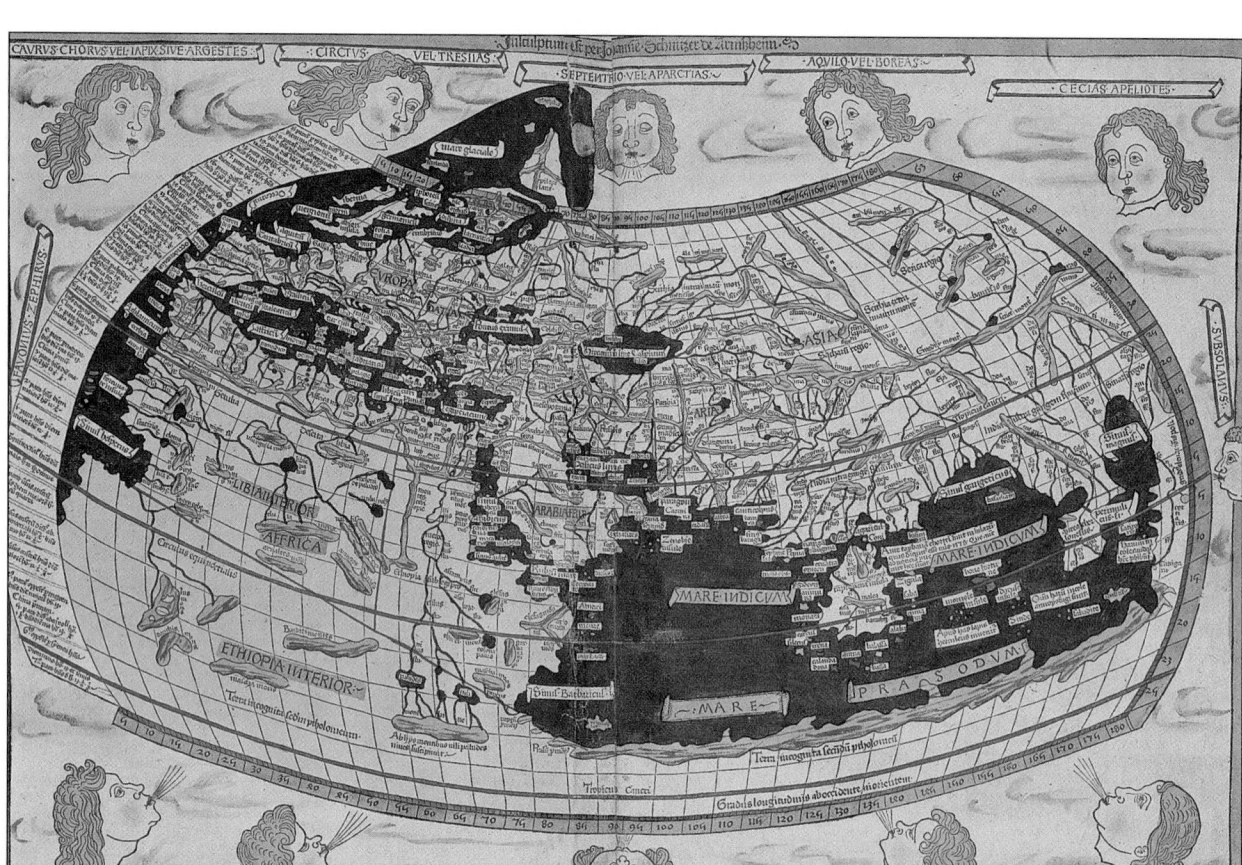

FIGURE 12.2
Ptolemy's image of the world.

He underestimated the extent of the oceans, suggesting that land covered three-fourths of the earth's surface, and he miscalculated the earth as being one-sixth smaller than its true size. With only Ptolemy's map to guide them, later explorers understandably expected the journey east to be shorter than it really was. During this age of discovery, however, the theories of Ptolemy dissolved in the face of experience.

The World Discovered

The explorers expected to capitalize on Europe's desire for Eastern goods and bring back wealth for themselves and their sovereigns. Sixteenth-century rulers were desperate for money to field their expensive armies, and the conquest of Constantinople by the Turks in 1453 increased the price of the valuable spices as they imposed steep taxes on the goods. This costly trade siphoned precious metals away from an already coin-poor western Europe, and monarchs were willing to reward anyone who hunted for new wealth. Brave, enterprising men eager for fame and fortune took up the challenge.

FAME, FORTUNE, AND FAITH: THE DRIVE TO EXPLORE

Though the lure of wealth motivated explorers and the sovereigns who funded them, some adventurers had other incentives for embarking on these risky travels. As Bartholomeu Dias implied in the quotation that introduced this chapter, religion also served as a major impulse for Europeans to seek new worlds. Christians during the fifteenth and sixteenth centuries felt besieged by the Islamic empire of the Ottoman Turks that loomed on Europe's eastern border (see Chapter 11). Some voyages aimed to find allies against the Turks. For example, the Portuguese Prince Henry the Navigator (1394–1460) sponsored voyages down the coast of Africa to search for "Prester John." The Reformation within Europe also stimulated explorations and migrations, as Catholics sought converts to Catholicism overseas and Protestants looked for new lands where they could practice their faith. Faith joined with fame and fortune to drive Europeans across the seas.

New Technologies and Travel

Europeans had a passion for adventure, but they also needed strong navigational tools and skills if they were to survive these hazardous journeys. Fortunately for them, *Navigation instruments* sailors in the Middle Ages had perfected instruments to help them sail out of sight of land. One device, the quadrant, aligned with the fixed North Star at night to let navigators determine their latitude. However, this was not useful in the Southern Hemisphere, where the North Star was not visible. Sailors going south had to confront uncharted heavens as well as unmapped lands. During the day, sailors in both Northern and Southern hemispheres could check their calculations with the astrolabe, which measured the height of the sun during the day or the altitude of a known star at night.

Finally, mapmakers had gained experience in charting the seas and lands and could graphically document their travels with some accuracy. Earlier skilled seafarers like the Vikings who first discovered North America lacked the cartography skills to allow them to reproduce their long sea voyages with as much certainty as the sixteenth-century explorers. Navigators felt confident in their charts, and the newly discovered map of Ptolemy, though inaccurate, at least gave them a basic sense of direction.

Sailors lacked only the ships to carry them safely on long ventures. The galleys that had ruled the Mediterranean in the fourteenth century had large, square sails, but their locomotion came primarily from the many slaves who rowed the big ships. These ships were unsuitable for long distances and had little extra space left in their holds to store the provisions necessary for a lengthy sea voyage.

All this changed in the late fifteenth century, when the Portuguese built ships that marked the highest development of a long evolution of Mediterranean sailing ships. In the Middle Ages, shipbuilders had developed a new kind of sail rigging that *Improved ships* allowed ships to maneuver near shore in uncertain winds. By the sixteenth century, shipbuilders had improved the mobility of the sails and the rigging of the ropes so that the sails could be moved readily. Figure 12.3 shows a sixteenth-century watercolor of Portuguese caravels—the small (70 to 80 feet long) ships that conquered the great seas. The large square sails allowed the ships to move in the direction of the

Figure 12.3
Sixteenth-century watercolor of Portuguese ships.

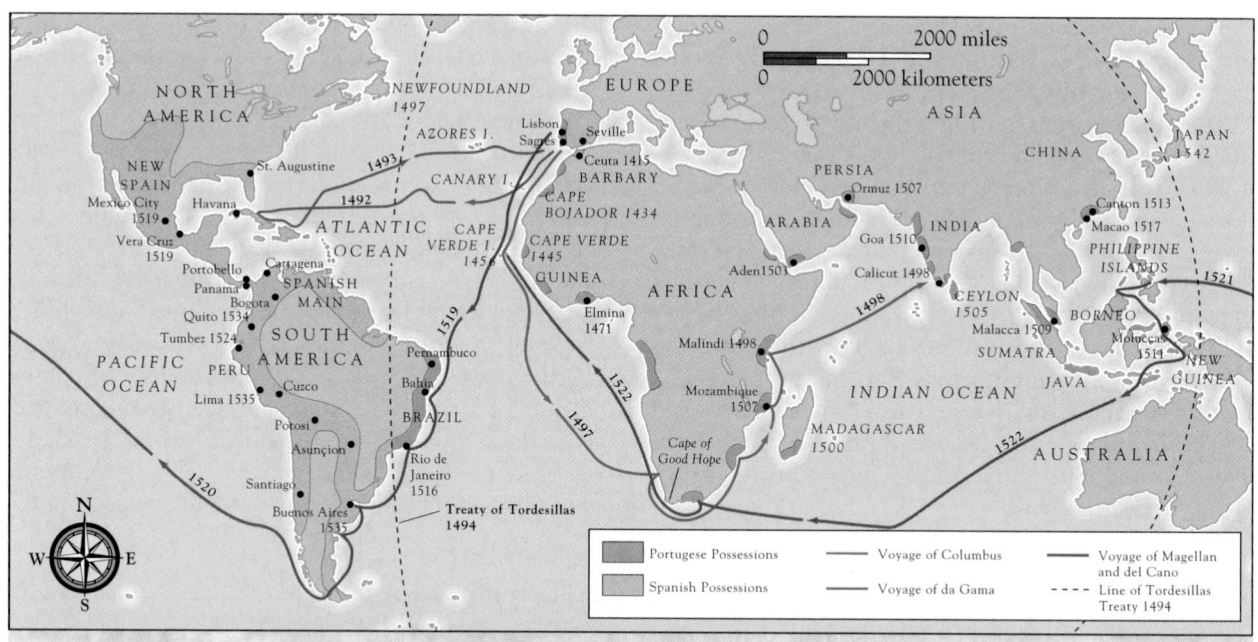

THINKING ABOUT GEOGRAPHY

MAP 12.1 *Exploration and Conquest: Fifteenth and Sixteenth Centuries*

This map shows the routes and dates of the explorations of the fifteenth and sixteenth centuries, as well as the possessions claimed by the Spanish and Portuguese. ❂ **Notice** the differences in the patterns of settlement in the Americas, Africa, and Asia. **What** do you think accounted for those differences? ❂ **Notice** the location of the Treaty of Tordesillas line that divided up the world between Portugal and Spain. **Notice** how the wealthiest and most populated regions went to Portugal. **How** did this treaty influence the differing settlement patterns of the Spanish and the Portuguese?

wind, or downwind. The real secret to long-distance sailing, however, was the lateen, a triangular, mobile sail at the rear (furled in Figure 12.3, but the ship pictured on page 406 is sailing with its lateen). This device not only let the ship sail faster, it also allowed it to sail at an angle to the wind and thus progress upwind—a crucial advantage for traveling into the prevailing westerly winds of the Atlantic. This ship, with its absence of oar banks, stands in striking contrast to the Mediterranean galleys shown in Figure 11.9. The ships had to be heavy to withstand the storms of the Atlantic, and this weight gave the West an unforeseen advantage: They could support heavy cannons, giving them a military advantage over the lighter ships of the east that sailed the calmer Indian ocean. On these innovative vessels, the Portuguese set out on voyages of discovery that changed the world.

THE PORTUGUESE RACE FOR THE EAST, 1450–1600

As the chronicler of Vasco da Gama's voyage described in the account at the beginning of this chapter, the Portuguese explorers had an immediate goal in mind: to venture south around Africa to the Indian Ocean and trade directly with natives in India for spices and other luxury items. This route would eliminate the troublesome role of the Ottoman Turks as key players in the eastern Mediterranean trade network. Beginning in 1418, Prince Henry the Navigator (1394–1460) of Portugal sponsored annual expeditions down the west coast of Africa. Bartholomeu Dias continued Henry's work with great success, rounding the southern tip of Africa in 1488.

King John II of Portugal (r. 1481–1495), expecting this route to yield the riches of the East, named the tip the "Cape of Good Hope." But Dias never reached India. His frightened crew had experienced the storms and hardships that Correa described, but Dias did not maintain the iron control that Vasco da Gama would, and his crew mutinied as he sailed north along the eastern coast of Africa. He was forced to return home. In 1498, his countryman Vasco da Gama (1460?–1524) set out with four ships to complete Dias's ill-fated voyage to India. He succeeded and returned to Portugal with ships laden with spices worth 60 times the cost of the journey.

Portuguese explorers scored spectacular successes in opening up the trade to the east. As one pleasant *Trading outposts* surprise, they discovered that "India" was not simply one location—it included the Moluccas, "spice islands," from which wafted the delightful aroma of cloves as the Portuguese ships approached. As Map 12.1 shows, the Portuguese established a string of trading outposts throughout the East. In these small settlements, Europeans lived peacefully near native settlements in a mutually profitable relationship. Portugal's successful entry into the Indian Ocean trade struck a dramatic blow to the economy of the Muslims, who had previously held a monopoly on that trade. At the same time, their neighbors, the Spanish, took a quite different approach. Spain's explorers sailed westward in hopes of reaching the fabulous Orient, believing Ptolemy's claim that the land of plenty lay just over the horizon.

SPAIN'S WESTWARD DISCOVERIES, 1492–1522

Christopher Columbus (1446–1506) perhaps best exemplifies Spain's travel ambitions. The son of an Italian (Genoese) weaver, Columbus traveled to Portugal in 1476 to learn about Portuguese shipbuilding and sailing. During his visit, he became captivated by the accounts of Marco Polo and the *Geography* of Ptolemy. Inflamed by images of glory and wealth, he asked the Portuguese king to sponsor him on a trip west to Asia. The king rejected him; like many others, he dismissed Columbus as a vague dreamer. Columbus then presented his idea to the Spanish monarchs Ferdinand and Isabella. The queen, impressed with Columbus's proposal, made him an admiral in 1492 and financed his expedition.

Figure 12.4
Woodcut of Columbus landing.

Columbus embarked on his journey with three ships, the *Niña,* the *Pinta,* and the *Santa María.* In October, the small fleet landed on an island in the Caribbean Sea. *Columbus's discoveries* According to the admiral's account, as he stepped ashore, Columbus "claimed all the lands for their Highnesses, by proclamation and with the royal standard displayed." According to Columbus, the many islanders who watched him did not object to his claims, so he accepted this as their tacit agreement—ignoring the language barrier that separated them. Subsequent explorers followed his lead, claiming ownership of already inhabited lands.

Figure 12.4 is a contemporary woodcut that was intended to capture this incident, and it shows all the essential elements: The King of Spain, on the left, gives Columbus the authority for his voyage. The three ships are featured in the center, and Columbus is shown landing on an island to claim it for the king. The island is depicted as a place as fanciful as any in the literature of imaginative travel, with exotic trees and beautiful, naked natives. The reality of the landing proved much less idyllic.

Columbus made four voyages between 1492 and 1502, during which he established settlements on several more Caribbean islands and visited the northern coast of South America and Central America. On his third voyage, he brought women from Spain to ensure the permanence of the settlements. The explorer was not a good administrator, and when Spain sent a judge to look into a revolt in the new lands, Columbus was brought back to Spain in chains. Though he was later released and made a final fourth voyage to the New World, Columbus never received the riches and acclaim he sought. Throughout these years, the Italian adventurer apparently felt sure that he had found Asian islands. He even referred to the natives as "Indians" because he was certain he was in the general region of "India." Columbus never realized that he had discovered a world unknown by virtually all Europeans. Instead, he clung to the image of the world he had imagined. His continued misconceptions encouraged other voyagers, who would soon prove him wrong.

As the Spanish and Portuguese both raced to claim lands on their way east, they inevitably came into conflict. The Catholic sovereigns of Spain and Portugal appealed to the pope to divide the world into two spheres of influence. In the 1494 Treaty of Tordesillas (shown on Map 12.1), the Spanish received exclusive rights to the lands west of a line drawn 370 leagues (about 1,200 miles) west of the Cape Verde Islands off the west coast of Africa, and the Portuguese received rights to the lands east of the line. This agreement (which was virtually ignored by the other European monarchs) was one of many attempts to apportion the world without regard for the opinions of indigenous residents.

Treaty of Tordesillas

Soon, subsequent travelers convinced Europeans that Columbus was wrong and that a great new land mass had been found. The most influential of these explorers was Amerigo Vespucci (1451–1512), an educated "Renaissance man" who worked for the Medici family of Florence (discussed in Chapter 10). In 1499, Vespucci set off on a voyage of discovery that took him westward from Spain and across the vast ocean to South America. During his voyage, he took careful navigational measurements and wrote colorful letters to his Medici patron, which were widely circulated. In the introduction to these works, Amerigo's publisher even suggested that Vespucci's name be given to the *Mundus Novus* (the "New World") he had popularized with his maps and vivid tales of a continent across the ocean. The suggestion caught on, and the name "America" became attached to the western land mass

that newly captured the European imagination. (Document 12.2 on page D12.2 has an example of one of Vespucci's vivid descriptions.)

After Vespucci's voyages, people set out purposefully to visit the new continent. For example, the Spanish adventurer Vasco Núñez de Balboa (1475–1517) trekked across the Isthmus of Panama, eventually reaching the Pacific Ocean on the other side. Besides adding to the evidence that a new continent existed, Balboa's discovery intensified the race to the riches of the East. New men with even bigger dreams of wealth joined the rush.

Circumnavigating the globe

Ferdinand Magellan (1480?–1521) was one of these men. A Portuguese explorer in the service of Spain, Magellan began the first expedition that succeeded in encircling the world. He sailed west from Spain in 1519 with three ships and discovered (and named) the Straits of Magellan at the southern tip of South America. The straits gave him access to the Pacific Ocean (which he also named). He and his crew braved the huge expanses of ocean and withstood mutinies. In 1521, Magellan was killed while interfering in a local war in the Philippines. His navigator, Sebastian Elcano (1476?–1526), finished the journey to Asia and through the Indian Ocean back to Spain. Elcano's voyage took three years and he returned home with only one ship. But that ship was packed with enough spices not only to pay for the cost of the expedition, but also to make the crew very rich.

Magellan's and Elcano's successful circumnavigation of the globe revealed not that the world was round (they knew that), but its true size. It also demonstrated the impracticality of sailing to the Orient by way of the Pacific. The Spanish would have to search for new sources of wealth—this time in the New World.

THE NORTHERN EUROPEANS JOIN THE RACE, 1600–1650

England, France, and the Netherlands came late to the race for the riches of the New World. Understandably, they were unwilling to accept the terms of the Treaty of Tordesillas. Instead, they began their own explorations. They started by looking for a "northwest passage" to the East that would parallel the southern route around South America. In about 1497, the Genoese captain John Cabot (1450–1498) and his son Sebastian (1476–1557), who both had

OLC

settled in England, received a letter from the English king Henry VII (r. 1485–1509) authorizing them to take possession for England any new lands unclaimed by any Christian nation. So empowered, father and son sailed across the North Atlantic to Newfoundland and Maine. They found codfish so plentiful that their ships could not pass through the thick schools of fish. However, the voyage was immediately disappointing because they neither reached Asia nor returned laden with spices.

The French also hunted for a northwest passage to the East. In 1534, Jacques Cartier led three voyages *Settlements in Canada* that explored the St. Lawrence River in what is today Canada. He and his crew got as far as Montreal, but the great waterway led only inland, not out to the Pacific Northwest. An early settlement effort in the region of Quebec in 1541 failed, owing to the harsh winter and indigenes' hostility. In about 1600, Samuel de Champlain (1567?–1635) made another try at establishing a settlement in North America. He founded Quebec, signing treaties with the natives to secure the settlement. Canadian settlements remained small in both size and number through the seventeenth century, but their existence ensured the continuous presence of European traders and missionaries in this northern land.

When the much sought after northwest passage proved elusive, northern Europeans shifted their journeys of discovery farther south and began to confront the Iberians directly. In 1602, the *Dutch colonies* Dutch chartered the East India Company and established trading posts in the Spice Islands. The Dutch warships proved their superiority and expelled the Portuguese from the islands that we now know as Indonesia. The Dutch also redesigned their ships to haul more cargo (like the ship pictured on page 406) than the small Portuguese caravels that had first mastered the oceans. They then dominated the lucrative spice trade, founding colonies in strategic locations to protect their growing trade empire. As one example, they colonized the tip of South Africa to facilitate their eastern trade and planted colonies in North America (most famously on Manhattan Island) and in the Caribbean.

The English, for their part, began to install settlements along the North American Atlantic seaboard *English colonies* in the seventeenth century: By 1700, about 250,000 colonists lived along the coast. Many of these people moved there to escape the religious persecution that swept Europe in the sev-

enteenth century. For this reason, they traveled west with their entire families, with the intent to stay. Their presence irrevocably altered the face of North America. Map 12.2 shows the status of the European colonization in about 1700, and it illustrates how the northern European countries had joined the Spanish and Portuguese in their race around the world.

Confrontation of Cultures

When the Europeans arrived in the New World, it was already abundantly populated by peoples who had lived there in resilient societies for millennia. From as early as 35,000 B.C., small groups of people walked from Asia northward across a land bridge from Siberia to Alaska. Slowly, over tens of thousands of years, families, clans, and tribes moved southward and settled throughout North, Central, and South America. At first all these tribes pursued a highly effective hunting-and-gathering existence, with devastating consequences for their future development. As the hunters came through North America, they confronted great herds of large mammals—horses, elephants, camels, and giant ground sloths. Within a few centuries of human arrival, all those large mammals were extinct, probably because of effective hunting. However, this meant that there were no more large animals in North America for domestication—this would represent a fatal disadvantage when the Amerindians confronted Europeans millennia later.

THE ORIGINAL AMERICANS

In about 5500 B.C., tribes in central Mexico first developed agriculture, which, as we saw in Chapter 1, allowed large settled populations to become established. These civilizations would become tempting, wealthy targets for European explorers. *Agriculture* Agriculture spread north and south from there, but very slowly. The differing latitudes and varied growing seasons of the large American continents caused agriculture to diffuse more slowly in the Americas than it had in Europe and Asia, where crops spread primarily within similar latitudes. In the Americas, for example, it took about 3,500 years for maize (what we usually call corn) and beans to spread 700 miles from Mexico to the southern farmlands of the modern United States.

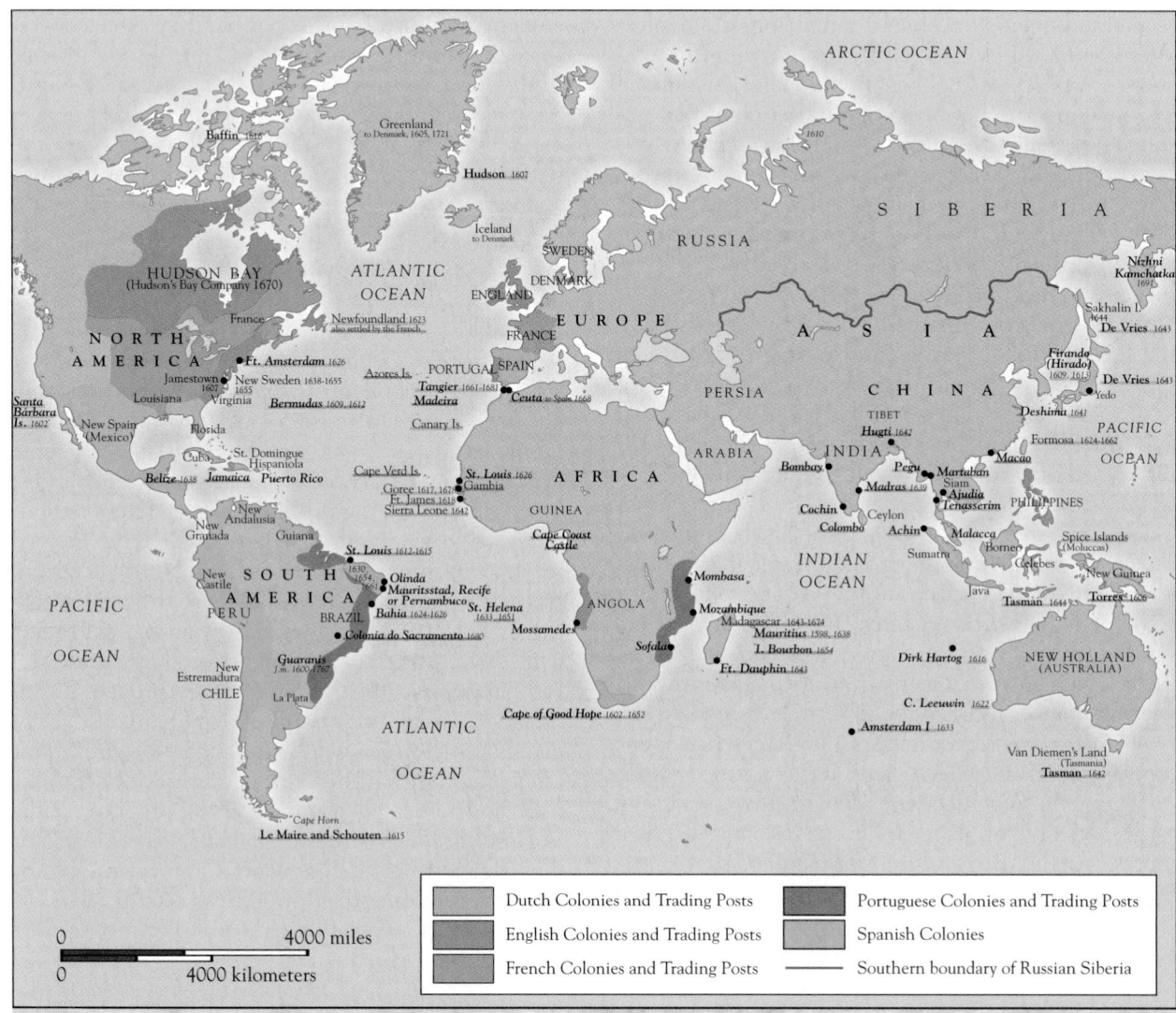

THINKING ABOUT GEOGRAPHY

MAP 12.2 *European Expansion, ca. 1700*

This map shows the world around 1700, when Europeans had farther expanded throughout the globe. **Notice** where the people from the various countries settled. **Compare** the different settlement patterns of the Americas and Africa and Asia. **What** accounts for this difference? **Compare** this map with Map 12.1. **Consider** what caused the major differences.

Some North American tribes—in Canada and the great central plains of the modern United States—maintained their hunting and gathering culture; others—mostly in the southwest and east—developed agricultural societies that permitted fairly large concentrations of population. With the early use of agriculture in Central America and the western mountains of South America, populations grew large and elaborate empires—the Maya, Aztec, Inca, and others—developed. These civilizations thrived mainly through the cultivation of maize. This highly nutritious, versatile crop originally grew wild in the New World, but had been cultivated for so long that it no longer grew without human help. Maize offered high yields with very little effort. Cultivators worked only about 50 days a year to produce an abundant crop that could be eaten even before it was ripe.

In these maize-growing societies, men cut and burned brush to clear the land to plant the grain, and women ground the hard kernels into flour to make tortillas, or flat bread. Girolamo Benzoni, a traveler in Central and South America in 1541, drew women in the process of making the essential cornbread (Figure 12.5). The woman on the right boils the husked corn with lime, and then the woman on the left grinds it to make flour for the woman at the center cooking the dough on the griddle.

The Incas, a people living in the Andes Mountains of South America, also cultivated a crop indigenous to that region—potatoes. An excellent alternative to maize, which did not grow in the high country, this hardy vegetable grew easily in the adverse conditions and high altitudes of mountain ranges and provided a hearty food supply. Once planted, potatoes required little work to harvest and prepare. Incas living in the mountains dried potatoes for long-term storage.

The small amount of time required to cultivate and harvest maize and potatoes left many days free *Empire building* for other work, and the great Central and South American empires developed a religious and aristocratic culture that demanded human labor for immense building projects. The Maya, Aztecs, and Incas built magnificent cities and roads and imposing pyramids. These constructions seem even more remarkable when we realize that they were built with Stone Age technology and without use of the wheel and (in most places) without the help of powerful, domesticated animals. Among these civilizations, only the Incas had domesticated the llama and alpaca as beasts of burden; throughout the rest of North and South America, people raised only dogs and fowl.

Map 12.3 shows the locations of the large South American empires as they existed when the Europeans arrived in the fifteenth century. The illustration shows the narrow Isthmus of Panama, which formed an effective geographic barrier between the two major empires, and which also served to dis-

Figure 12.5
Women preparing corn for tortillas, ca. 1541.

advantage the Amerindians in developing increasingly complex societies. For example, the Aztecs in Mexico invented a wheel, but because they lacked draft animals, the wheel remained a children's toy. The Incas had domesticated the llama, but had no wheel to convert this animal into an effective beast of burden.

In Mexico, the Aztecs had located their capital at the great city of Tenochtitlán, built on a lake and accessible only by boat or causeway. (Tenochtitlán is the site of present-day Mexico City.) The *Aztec Empire* Aztecs called themselves Meshica, where we get the word "Mexico." The Aztecs had conquered all the surrounding local tribes and claimed tribute from the vanquished, including humans sacrificed to the demanding Aztec gods who people believed claimed human blood to delay an inevitable destruction of Aztec society. Much of the visual information we have on the South American tribes comes from manuscripts written in the sixteenth century after the Spanish conquests. Authors included drawings within these books—many created by the Amerindians themselves. From these drawings, we can gain information about life before and after the Spanish invasions. Figure 12.6 is one such drawing, which shows the ritual human sacrifice. In the sacrificial ceremony, victims were forced to the top of a pyramid and stretched over a stone. A priest then used a sharp, stone knife to cut out the victim's heart and offer it—still beating—to the god. The voracious demand for such tribute from the subject peoples catalyzed resentment among them—a force that the new conquerors from Europe would find useful in overpowering the Aztecs.

EARLY CONTACTS

Christopher Columbus set the tone for the relationship between the original Americans and Europeans when he claimed land in the New World for the Spanish monarchs and when he treated the people as sources of revenue for the Spanish crown. With few exceptions, subsequent European explorers viewed the native peoples in the same way. Sometimes they traded with them; other times they used them as labor. Still other times, they killed or enslaved the men and women they found living in the new lands.

Explorers of the New World believed they encountered a major problem: these lands lacked the spices and luxury goods of the East that had brought so much immediate wealth to merchants. These new explorers had to find other forms of riches to bring home. Sometimes they enslaved natives, but this was not particularly lucrative. Instead, they searched for silver and gold to take back to Europe. According to one contemporary observer, when an Amerindian asked a Spaniard what Europeans ate, the Spaniard responded, "Gold and silver." (We do not know whether this exchange actually took place, but the anecdote testifies to the insatiable European appetite for precious metals.)

European contacts with the North American tribes took place about 25 to 100 years later than the early South and Central American contacts, and some of

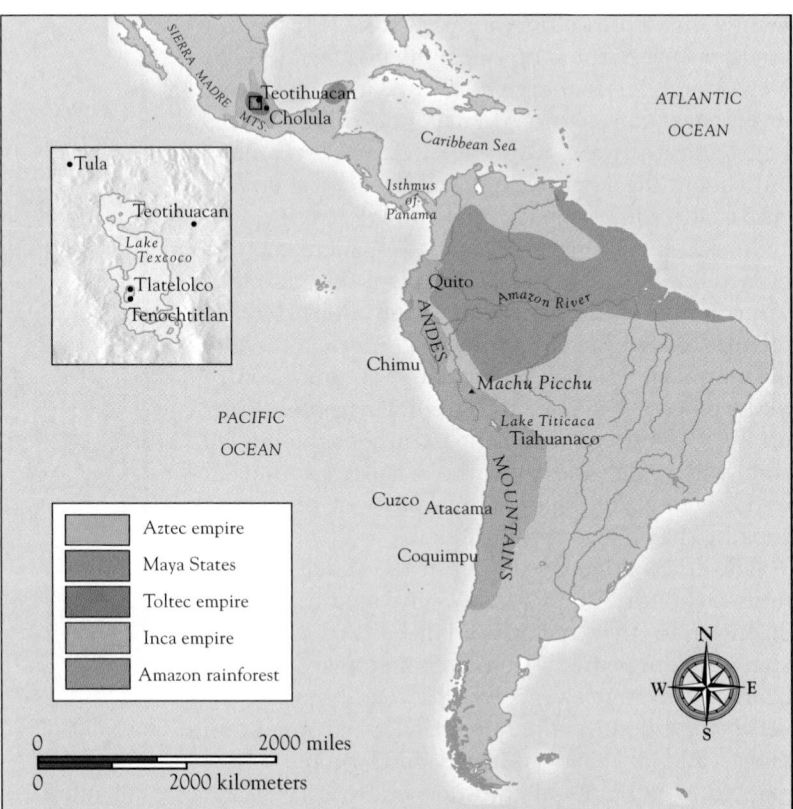

THINKING ABOUT GEOGRAPHY

MAP 12.3 *Indigenous Empires in the Americas, ca. 1500*

This map shows the locations of the Inca and Aztec Empires in North and South America. ◙ **Notice** how distant the Inca Empire is from the Aztec and Maya in Mesoamerica. **How** might these distances and geographic barriers have contributed to the striking differences among these populations?

the early European chroniclers of these engagements offer interesting details about the local customs. For example, a shipwreck stranded a Spaniard, Cabeza de Vaca (1409?–1560?) with his three companions (including an African slave) in southwest North America. For eight years, they wandered among the southern nomadic tribes until they encountered a Spanish colony in 1536. Cabeza de Vaca wrote of his experiences shortly after his return to Spain, and his narrative stimulated interest in the New World.

North American contacts

Cabeza de Vaca told most profoundly about the scarcity of food among these tribes of the Southwest, who lived on cactus fruit and game. The Spaniards were welcomed, and they worked side by side with the tribes they visited. The author wrote how he was pleased to be given an animal hide to scrape and tan for leather, for he "scraped it very deep in order to eat the parings, which would last me two or three days." His account of hunger, hospitality, and warfare among the Amerindians shaped many Europeans' views of the original Americans.

An English chronicler observed more prosperous, but equally generous, tribes in what would become the colony of North Carolina. In 1584, Arthur Barlow accompanied an expedition that established excellent relations with the tribes—trading goods and hospitality with these "very handsome and goodly people, in their behavior as mannerly and civil as any of Europe."

We are also fortunate to have a visual record of this tribe of agriculturists, for an artist, John White, accompanied three voyages to this colony of Roanoke. White's detailed watercolors were copied by an engraver in the Netherlands and published in 1590; they remain an excellent source of information about life in some North American tribes before the impact of Europeans. The village White portrays in Figure 12.7 is prosperous and orderly and shows the abundant food available. In the upper left of the etching, Amerindians hunt deer. In the hut at the upper right, a watchman makes "continual cries and noise" to frighten animals and birds from the fields, which grow maize and pumpkins on the right and tobacco in the circular field on the left. Villagers celebrate the abundance by dancing (lower right) and feasting (center).

However, within a few years, relations between Europeans and Amerindians had soured, and the at- *Deteriorating relations* tractive village White painted was destroyed. As a subsequent chronicler of the new colony wrote, "Their amicable relations with the natives were now to receive a rude

Figure 12.6
Aztec human sacrifice, ca. 1570, in the *Codex Magliabecchiano.*

shock, from which they never recovered." An Amerindian stole a silver cup, and although he returned it, the colonists wanted to teach a lesson about property. "For this enormous offence the English burned the town and barbarously destroyed the growing corn." Strife like this was repeated many times, and the two cultures that newly confronted each other beginning in the sixteenth century would engage in increasing conflict.

CONQUEST OF THE GREAT EMPIRES, 1520–1550

While in the Caribbean, the Spanish explorer Hernando Cortés (1485–1547) heard of a fabulously rich society to the west. Their curiosity *Cortés's explorations* aroused, he and 600 men sailed across the Gulf of Mexico in search of gold and glory. When Cortés landed on the Yucatan peninsula in southeast Mexico, the people he met there told him of a wealthy civilization in the interior (the Aztecs). As Cortés moved inland, he acquired a gift that proved more valuable to his quest than anything else—the slave woman Malinche.

Figure 12.7
Amerindian village in North America. Theodore DeBry, *Grands et Petits Voyages*, 1590.

Figure 12.8
Cortés and Malinche meet Montezuma. *Lecuzo de Tlaxcala*, sixteenth century, copied in eighteenth century.

According to later Spanish sources, Malinche was a princess whose father had died when she was young. The girl's mother gave her to local slave traders when the mother remarried, and the traders included the young woman in their gifts to Cortés. Malinche spoke four Amerindian languages, including the Nahuatl of the Aztecs, and she easily learned Spanish. She converted to Christianity and took the baptismal name of Marina. Malinche was constantly at Cortés's side, interpreting and advising him on matters of policy and customs as he made his way west. The various peoples they encountered on their journey recognized her importance, calling Cortés "Malinche's Captain."

Eventually Cortés's group marched 250 miles into the interior of Mexico and reached the Aztec capital of Tenochtitlán. There, Cortés and Malinche met with Montezuma II (1502–1520), the Aztec emperor. Figure 12.8 depicts this meeting. This drawing was taken from a valuable cloth that was painted in the mid-sixteenth century by a Mexican tribe that helped Cortés conquer the Aztecs. (Unfortunately, the original cloth has disappeared, but a copy was made in Mexico in the eighteenth century.)

Confronting the Aztecs

By skilled use of images, the painter emphasized the role of Malinche in the conquest. In the illustration, Cortés and Malinche use the same gesture, showing that they speak with one voice. Montezuma sits in state, his nobles standing behind him. The Aztecs have gathered gifts for Cortés, drawn at the bottom of the page. The illustration foreshadows the coming European conquest: In the center of the picture the Aztec royal headdress moves toward Cortés; in the upper-right corner, the hand of God reaches down to bless the proceedings.

Global Connections

The Inca Empire Falls

⬛ **Consider** how technological differences between the Incas and the Spanish contributed to the brutality of the Spanish rule. **NOTICE** how internal problems and Spanish military technology led to the Incas' defeat.

Ten years after Hernando Cortes had sailed from Spain and conquered the Aztec Empire in Mexico in 1521, another conquistador, Francisco Pizarro, set off to seek his own fortune in the New World. He landed on the west coast of South America—which included the 2,500-mile border of the mountainous Inca Empire. (See Map 12.3.) The Inca ruler used a hierarchic bureaucracy to govern a population of about 11.5 million peasants.

Before Pizarro even landed in South America, the great Inca Empire had endured deep troubles. Powerful earthquakes accompanied by giant waves had pounded the coast. Lightning had struck the palace of Huayna Capac. Messengers had also told Huayna that strange beings with beards had landed on the coast. In the midst of these disasters, the ruler remembered a prophecy claiming that during the reign of the twelfth ruler, strange men would invade and destroy the empire. Huayna was the eleventh. On his deathbed, he purportedly advised his subjects to submit to the newcomers, who would surely arrive soon in fulfillment of the prophecy.

But the empire's ruling house had suffered other problems as well. Civil war between two half brothers over the succession erupted after the death of Huayna Capac. Atahualpa, Huayna's illegitimate son, challenged Huascar, the legitimate heir. In 1533, Atahualpa captured Huascar, but resistance to Atahualpa's rule continued in the region of Cuzco. (See Map 12.3.) At this volatile moment, Pizarro arrived. Some of Huascar's supporters claimed that their god, Viracochas, had sent the armed men to place Huascar on the throne. This account of Inca beliefs on the eve of Pizarro's conquest was recorded in the early sixteenth century by the conquerors themselves. Historians have used it in part to explain how Pizarro—with a force of only 62 mounted men and 106 foot soldiers—could overwhelm between 100,000 and 400,000 armed Incas. Yet, it was neither their fatalism nor Pizarro's temporary alliance with Huascar that gave the Spanish the advantage; it was their technological superiority.

In the sixteenth century, warfare had honed both the weapons and the tactical skills of the Spanish. Their horses made a huge difference, adding power and reach to the mounted soldier. Pizarro wrote that the horsemen "did all the fighting, because the. . . Indians hold the footsoldiers in slight account." Furthermore, the Spanish fighters' steel swords, spears, and pikes so outmatched the Incas' most effective weapon, the sling, that the armored invaders could engage many Indians without much fear of injury themselves. Yet, even with these advantages, the Spanish took seven years to fully conquer the extensive empire. Despite the Incas' lack of advanced weaponry, they quickly assessed the Spanish tactics and bravely exploited what weaknesses they could find.

Due to the cultural and technological chasm between the Spanish and the Incas, the conquest took on unprecedented brutality. One conquistador wrote, "I can bear witness that this is the most dreadful and cruel war in the world. For between Christians and Muslims there is some well-feeling. . . But in this Indian war there is no such feeling on either side. They give each other the cruelest deaths they can imagine." After finally crushing the Incas, the Spanish had little inclination to treat their captives with any humanity. The early Spanish rule—with its forced labor programs—proved as brutal as the conquest itself.

OLC

Cortés knew that to transport the riches of the Aztecs back to Spain, he first had to vanquish this mighty civilization. With the help of Malinche, he garnered the support of nearly 100,000 people from neighboring tribes who were eager to throw off the Aztec yoke. Even with the advantage of gunpowder, armor, horses, and fierce dogs, it took him nearly a year to subdue the empire, and contemporary witnesses captured the violence of the struggle. Bernal Díaz del Castillo described the capture of the last stronghold: "I have read of the destruction of Jerusalem, but I know not if that slaughter was more fearful than this—the earth, the lagoons, and the buttresses were full of corpses and the stench was more than any man could bear." In 1522, Cortés proclaimed the Aztec Empire "New Spain," and he prepared to rule. Although he had fathered a son with Malinche, he gave her as a bride to one of his soldiers and presented her with expensive estates to thank her for her help.

Aztecs conquered

The Inca Empire fell to another conquistador, Francisco Pizarro (1475?–1541). In 1532, Pizarro landed on the west coast of South America and began to march to Cuzco, the Incan capital. (See Global Connections box.) The Inca rulers had just endured a five-year civil war over a disputed succession, and the newly victorious ruler, Atahualpa, apparently underestimated the Spanish. Atahualpa came unguarded to meet with Pizarro, and he was promptly captured. He offered a roomful of gold as his ransom, which the Spanish accepted. After collecting the ransom, they killed their hostage. The Incas fought fiercely for a few years after the fall of their leader, but they were unable to overcome the Spanish technical advantages. A new order arose in South America.

Incas conquered

How did these small numbers of Europeans manage to conquer the impressive Amerindian empires? They gained a clear advantage from their steel weapons, horses, and high organization (including writing, which allowed them to communicate effectively). However, in the long run, their greatest weapon was biological—germs they brought from Europe. When previously isolated populations mingle, it is common for epidemics to break out, but the confrontation between Europeans and Amerindians was particularly devastating because the New World had no history of interaction with domesticated animals. The most devastating acute diseases

Germs

that Eurasians faced came initially from their animals: measles, tuberculosis, flu, whooping cough, and perhaps most deadly, smallpox. With thousands of years of exposure to these diseases, Europeans had developed immunities. Amerindians had not. In what turned out to be a biological tragedy that clinched the European conquest, disease and death followed the colonists everywhere they ventured. As one Huron woman said of the Jesuit missionaries, "They set themselves up in a village where everyone is feeling fine; no sooner are they there but everyone dies except for three or four people. They move to another place, and the same thing happens."

LIFE AND DEATH UNDER EUROPEAN RULE, 1550–1700

The goal of the newly established European colonial empires was to enrich the home countries. To meet this aim, the colonists exploited natural resources and Amerindian peoples to their fullest. The Spanish crown divided up the lands, placing "viceroys" in charge of each section. These royal representatives were responsible for delivering to the crown the profits taken from the new lands. The crown claimed one-fifth of all gold and silver mined in the New World, and the treasure ships departed the coasts of the Americas heavily laden.

To get the human labor he needed to search and mine for precious metals, Christopher Columbus proposed enslaving the native peoples. Queen Isabella rejected the plan, for she considered the New World peoples her subjects. Instead, the Spanish forced labor contracts on subject peoples. Sometimes these contracts stipulated a lifetime of labor (though the subject peoples remained personally free); other times, the Amerindians had to work for the Spanish for a fixed number of years. Life under these contracts proved extremely harsh—hard labor and shortage of food—and many laborers died while working for their new overseers.

Enforced labor

For the Spanish, the arrangement yielded untold wealth, exemplified by the silver mine in Bolivia—the Potosí—shown in the painting in Figure 12.9. In the background of this picture, workers and pack-trains climb steep peaks that lead to the veins of ore. The workers' homes are shown in the middle of the painting. In the foreground, other local Amerindians process the ore. First they watch a hydraulic wheel crush the raw ore; then they pound the ore with large hammers until it is reduced to powder. The waterwheel is fed by long canals that convey melting snow and rainwater from the mountain. The last step in the process was to mix the ore with mercury and convert it into a paste. This technique, brought from Europe in 1557, increased silver production tenfold. From 1580 to 1620, the great age of Spanish imperialism was financed by the silver extracted primarily from the Potosí mine.

Figure 12.9 also hints at the amount of work necessary to run sixteenth-century mines and the reason that the mine owners saw the enforced labor of the locals as essential. The Spanish crown gave the mine owners of the Potosí the conscripted labor of 13,300 Amerindians. These workers had to report to the mine on Monday morning and toil underground until Saturday evening. The mine owners did not provide meals; throughout the work week, the men's wives had to bring them food. Many workers perished under the inhumane conditions.

Not everyone accepted this colonial brutality as a natural consequence of the need for silver. The most severe critic among these was the Dominican friar Bartolomé de Las Casas (1474–1566). In his book *The Tears of the Indians,* Las Casas wrote: "There is nothing more detestable or more cruel, than the tyranny which the Spaniards use toward the Indian." Historians have disagreed about the exact number of lives lost in the Spanish domination of Central and South America, but all the estimates are shocking. Diseases, overwork, and warfare took a terrible toll on indigenous people everywhere in the New World. When Columbus landed in 1492, for example, the population of the Caribbean Islands was about 6,000,000 people, and 50 years later, it numbered only a few thousand. The native population of Peru fell from about 1,250,000 in 1570 to just 500,000 in 1620. Mexico fared worse: About 24 million native individuals died between 1519 and 1605. Many fell victim to diseases, over-

Amerindian mortality

Figure 12.9
The Potosí silver mine in Bolivia, ca. 1584.

work, and the abuse that Las Casas had described. Some Europeans abhorred this destruction, but many saw it as merely a source of worry about where to get enough labor to work their mines and the plantations.

In another tragic turn of events, Las Casas proposed a solution that he thought might free the native workers from their burden of labor. He suggested that the king of Spain offer Spanish men and women a license to settle in the New World. In addition to land, each license would give permission for the holder to import a dozen African slaves to the Americas. In his old age, Las Casas recognized the problems with this policy. To his regret, the plan brought a shameful new injustice to the New World: the African slave trade.

THE AFRICAN SLAVE TRADE

By the beginning of the seventeenth century, the new rulers in the Americas were facing alarming labor shortages. The original Americans had died in huge numbers just as colonists stepped up the need for labor in their profitable enterprises. As we saw earlier, mining required countless workers. The sprawling plantations built to exploit demand for new crops also desperately depended on large numbers of ill-paid workers.

Sugar is the overriding example. Although sugarcane grew in Egypt and North Africa, it remained *Sugar plantations* scarce and expensive. Europeans discovered that the cane flourished in the New World and began to cultivate it avidly in hopes of satisfying the intense European craving for its sweet flavor. Sugar also fueled a new vice—the alcoholic beverages (like rum) that it helped make. Throughout the Caribbean and in Brazil, colonists established grand sugar plantations and began using African slaves to work them. On the plantations, like the one in Barbados shown in Figure 12.10, workers tended the sugarcane and harvested it with large, sharp knives—a practice that often led to serious injuries. Then the cane had to be crushed to extract its juice. In this illustration, the cane is crushed in the background with grindstones. In the center, the crushed cane is cooked in vats to produce molasses,

and then the product is distilled into rum (in the lower left). The whole process was guided by overseers like the one in the foreground holding his stick to beat any recalcitrant slaves.

Sugar and other plantations (for example, cotton in North America) were designed to produce enough of their specified crop to satisfy a world market. Plantation owners took a consuming interest in the success of these endeavors. Indeed, the German naturalist Maria Merian (see the Biography on page 434) wrote that she was ridiculed in the colony of Surinam, in South America, because she was interested in things other than sugar. This monoculture, or focus on a single crop, forced the plantations to trade with the rest of the world for all their remaining necessities, including labor.

As we saw in Chapter 10, slavery on a small scale began to be reintroduced into Europe during the Renaissance, and the sixteenth-century warfare escalating between Christians and Muslims stimulated even more enslavements in North Africa. For example, in

Figure 12.10
Sugar plantation engraving, 1667.

1627 Muslim pirates from the Mediterranean raided distant Iceland and enslaved nearly 400 descendants of the Vikings. Current studies suggest that between 1580 and 1680, some 850,000 Christian captives were enslaved in Muslim North Africa. Some of these captives who escaped or were ransomed engaged in their own slaving raids against Muslims as a form of revenge.

This growth of slavery between Christians and Muslims likely suggested to Europeans a solution for *African slaves* the labor shortages in the New World. In 1532, the first slave shipments departed from Africa to transport slaves directly across the Atlantic to the plantations of the West Indies and Brazil. Before 1650, only about 7,000 slaves annually crossed the Atlantic, but the figure doubled to about 14,000 between 1650 and 1675. Before the 1680s, the Atlantic slave trade almost exclusively provided slaves for these sugar plantations. During the seventeenth century, blacks brought to North America came from the Caribbean, not directly from Africa—many had European surnames and knew a European language. A significant fraction of these early "servants for life" in North America became free, and some appear in the early records of the colonies (even in the South) as freeholders and voters. By the eighteenth century, the rise in plantations in North America caused slaves to be imported directly from Africa in large numbers (see Chapter 15).

The slave trade generated huge profits, not only for the Europeans, but also for African chiefs who *Impact in Africa* supplied slaves to the traders. Because of long, but periodic, contact with Europe for millennia, Africans had substantial resistance to European disease, so they survived in larger numbers than the Amerindians had. Slavery had always been part of African warfare, and as early as the seventh century, Muslims profited from slaves brought across the Sahara Desert. However, in the sixteenth century the huge profits created a new scale of trade—chiefs traded slaves to the Europeans in exchange for guns to gain advantage over their traditional rivals. Some tribes (such as the Congo in central Africa) were initially opposed to the trade, but became heavily involved to stay competitive with their neighbors.

The political consequences of the trade in Africa varied. In the kingdom of the Congo, the Portuguese quest for slaves weakened the monarchy and led to local warfare and a decentralization of power. In the military kingdom of Dahomey on the west coast of Africa, kings made the slave trade a royal monopoly and profited enormously. When the trade ended, however, the resulting economic depression in Dahomey led to severe political disturbance. Although this discussion shows it is possible to treat the slave trade as one more manifestation of the growing world economy, one cannot ignore the fact that the trade of human beings rendered incalculable costs in human misery.

By 1700, traders delivered about 30,000 slaves each year, and that number continued to escalate into the late eighteenth century. Packed tightly into the holds of ships and subjected to lack of food, water, and sanitary facilities, as many as 25 percent of these human beings died in transit. Anyone who survived the trip then faced new horrors: starvation and overwork and sometimes harsh physical discipline by their owners.

Some slaves ran away. In Brazil, in particular, many escapees fled into the forest and founded their own communities. The largest of the settlements was Palmares, which the Portuguese at- *Slave rebellions* tacked in 1692 and destroyed three years later. Although it is impossible to get exact figures, it seems the community consisted of perhaps 10,000 fugitives who had formed a kingdom and designated a king and a council of elders. Other slaves devised more subtle forms of rebellion, including slow labor. In one interesting instance, an African woman in Surinam told the naturalist Maria Merian (see the Biography on page 434) that the slaves practiced birth control to avoid bringing children into slavery. Although we know that Africans practiced some birth control in Africa, we cannot know for sure that it took a new purpose under slavery, but it may have.

GATHERING SOULS IN THE NEW LANDS

Early explorers were partially motivated to travel by their desire to spread the Christian faith, and this desire only increased as Europeans found so many "heathens" around the world. Cultures all over the world became exposed to the Christian message. Many missionaries worked to alleviate the misery caused by the conquests, but others traveled from Europe with the zeal of crusaders and with the dogged insensitivity of the *conquistadors*. Some of them baptized natives in large groups, with no concern for their spiritual inclinations. Columbus and other early explorers, ignorant

tablecloth of tapestry from India. The woman's clothing is made of oriental silk—an unusual luxury for everyday dress. Even the woman's movement to open a window suggests wealth, for expensive, leaded glass windows originally had been used only in churches. Vermeer completes this picture of prosperity with a leather map of the world hanging on the wall—a fitting symbol of the new global commerce.

What exactly stepped up the global demand for luxury goods? In *Inflation* part, the demand was fueled by population growth in the sixteenth and seventeenth centuries. During the sixteenth century, the number of Europeans expanded from about 80 million to 105 million as Europe recovered from the devastation of the Black Death. These increases continued. As the population steadily rose, goods became scarce. Demand intensified and drove prices up. In the sixteenth century, cereal prices escalated about fivefold, and the price of manufactured goods tripled. Contemporary witnesses repeatedly expressed shock at the inflation. As one sixteenth-century Spaniard lamented, "Today a pound of mutton costs as much as a whole sheep used to." People complained, but no one had concrete solutions to the problem.

At mid-century, some Europeans began blaming the influx of precious metals from the New World for their inflation woes. Their frustration was understandable. The Potosí mine alone yielded millions of Spanish coins a year, which poured unchecked into the European economy, moving rapidly from one country to the next. As just one example of the interconnected economy, the massive Spanish ships that transported silver across the Atlantic depended on French canvas for their sails. Silver coins from the New World paid for those sails. As one French author wrote, "They may have the ships, but we have their wings." Economists can trace Spanish silver from Europe to as far as China, where European merchants snapped up the silks and spices that initially inspired

Figure 12.12
Jan Vermeer, *Young Woman with a Water Pitcher*, ca. 1664.

the explorations. Yet the flood of coins into Europe was only part of the picture. In truth, the "price revolution" stemmed from a combination of the new money, a surge in population growth, and unprecedented appetites for new goods.

THE RISE OF COMMERCIAL CAPITALISM

Inflation always hurts those with fixed incomes, but high prices also provide incentives for enterprising people to make a profit. The energetic sixteenth-century pursuit of trade stimulated new forms of production and economic concepts that together have been called the "commercial revolution," but might more accurately be termed a "commercial acceleration," during which trading practices developed in the Middle Ages spread and flourished. During this vital era, a set of business practices (and perceptions) arose that we know as capitalism. The word *capitalism* was actually not used until the nineteenth century. By the mid-seventeenth century, however, some individuals were called *capitalists*, a word indicating how they handled money. Capitalists were people who chose to invest their funds in business activities in order to make more money (capital). For these entrepreneurs, the most lucrative business opportunity was the growing world trade. Document 12.3 on page D12.3 presents a seventeenth century testimonial on the benefits of this long-distance trade.

Dutch entrepreneurs led the way in implementing capitalist ideas as they engaged in worldwide trade. *Capitalist ideas* For example, merchants in Amsterdam built huge warehouses to store goods so that they could control supplies and keep prices high. Through new strategies like this and through individual initiative (rather than through government policy), the Netherlands became the leading commercial center in Europe in the sixteenth century. Indeed, it was this very success that generated the wealth depicted in the households painted by Vermeer.

Capitalist initiative gave rise to fluctuations in demand for goods. We can follow an early example of this economic cycle in the tulip industry. Tulips originally were imported into the Netherlands from Turkey, in the sixteenth century. A Dutch botanist discovered how to grow the many varied colors of this versatile flower. By 1634, buyers not only in the Netherlands but also all over Europe were so enthralled by the exotic and beautiful plants that one rare tulip bulb sold for 1,000 pounds of cheese, four oxen, eight pigs, 12 sheep, a bed, and a suit of clothes. Investors rushed to take advantage of the lucrative tulip market and the supply of the bulbs ballooned. Three years later, however, the increased supply drove down the price, ruining many who had gambled on the rare flower. Novice capitalists learned the hard way about the cruel whims of the market economy.

People with moderate means also yearned to participate in promising financial ventures. To accommodate them, businesses built *Joint-stock companies* upon medieval concepts of trading partnerships and stock exchanges and developed an innovative entity called the joint-stock company. This new economic structure allowed ordinary investors to buy shares in commercial ventures that were run by boards of directors. With successes in such investments, modest capitalists might generate enough money to set out on their own and gamble on higher-risk opportunities. These joint-stock companies made it easier to raise enough capital for trading ventures around the world—enterprising people in the colony of New York began trading shares at a tree at the end of Wall Street.

MERCANTILISM: CONTROLLING THE BALANCE OF TRADE

Whereas the Dutch fostered individualistic business practices, other western European governments attempted centralized regulation of their economies—mercantilism—to profit from the expanded global trade. Mercantilism was based on the assumption that the amount of worldwide wealth was fixed, so countries competed to get a larger piece of the pie. This was essentially economic nationalism, in which governments controlled their economies to increase their acquisition of hard currency. The simple principle "buy low, sell high" led these governments to discourage imports, particularly expensive ones, and encourage exports. In 1586, one Spanish bureaucrat asked King Philip II to forbid the import of candles, glass trinkets, jewelry, cutlery, and other such items, because these sorts of "useless" luxuries drained away precious Spanish gold. Such policies aimed to create a favorable balance of trade and fill bank vaults with gold. *Economic nationalism*

Mercantilist governments passed laws to ensure a favorable trade balance. They imposed tariffs on imports and discouraged manufacturing in their colonies to force them to buy exports from the home country. Thus, hard currency would flow from the colonies to enrich royal treasuries in Europe. In fact, mercantilist policy encouraged the founding of new colonies to create new markets to purchase European exports. When other things failed, governments debased their coins to try to maintain a favorable balance. *Economic regulations*

Some governments even tried to keep wages low so that citizens would have little discretionary income with which to buy expensive imports. All these efforts were meant to enrich the states, not the fortunes of wealthy citizens. Mercantilist policies placed the state before the individual. They achieved their goal, vastly enriching the powerful monarchies of western Europe. Sadly, they also financed the destructive wars that swept over Europe through the mid-seventeenth century (discussed in Chapter 11). Mercantilist economic policy would continue to shape government policy into the eighteenth century (as we will see in Chapter 15).

THE GROWTH OF BANKING

Neither private capitalism nor mercantilism could have succeeded without innovations in banking practices. Medieval ideas that forbade charging interest and that kept royal treasuries locked in chests in royal bedrooms had become obsolete. In this new age, people needed easier access to a lot of money, and they refined banking techniques that had been developed in the late Middle Ages in the Italian cities of the Renaissance. Medieval bankers had developed bills of exchange and complex account books to facilitate commerce, but in the late fifteenth century, bankers added checks, bank drafts, and sophisticated double-entry bookkeeping to their skills, all of which made commercial ventures easier than ever.

Through the sixteenth century, private bankers handled most financial transactions. The Fuggers of Germany were the most successful at this profession, taking over a role that the Medicis in Florence had dominated in the fifteenth century. The Fugger family became so wealthy that they even lent money to Emperor Charles V. With the emergence of mercantilist ideas about economics serving the state, this kind of practice waned. Instead, government banks developed that controlled profits going to individuals. The Bank of Amsterdam was founded in 1609, followed by the Bank of Sweden in 1657, and the Bank of England in 1694. However, new banking policies could not ensure that even mercantilist governments would grow rich.

State banks

THE DANGER OF OVERSPENDING: SPAIN LEARNS A LESSON

At first, Europeans believed that the wealth flowing into Europe from the New World was the primary payoff from their explorations. Entire countries became rich, and imperial powers grew in previously unheard-of ways. Spain immediately capitalized on the new wealth, its treasure ships offering unlimited prosperity and power to the monarchs. Yet, the vast influx of silver was deceiving, and the Spanish king spent it wastefully on the incessant wars that dominated the sixteenth and early seventeenth centuries.

Consequently, the Spanish crown had to declare bankruptcy several times in the course of the sixteenth and seventeenth centuries. Spain's financial troubles hurt merchants in Germany and Italy, but the real burden fell on the Spanish taxpayers, who were soon saddled with debt. Instead of relieving their debt burdens, the politics of empire only added to them. Spanish domination of the New World passed to the governments of other countries (notably Holland and England) that proved more efficient in fiscal matters.

Ultimately, much of the gold and silver that motivated the expansionist countries did not even end up in Europe. A large percentage of this currency eventually flowed to the East for the purchase of luxury items. As Spain discovered, these precious metals were not enough to keep profligate governments in power.

REDEFINING WORK ROLES

The commercial revolution both enlarged the scale of business and redefined the way people viewed their work. While most people still worked the land, in the cities, which served as the nerve centers of the new economies, people experienced the most remarkable shifts in how they made their living. As the middle class rose to economic power on the dual waves of trade and hard work, the lives of urban women in particular diverged dramatically from earlier times. In the early Middle Ages, women had labored in the stores and workshops of Europe's cities. They dominated trades that they had controlled in the home—textile making and brewing, for example. Women had such a presence in these fields that feminine forms of certain words (ending in "ster") derived from these jobs—for instance, "webster" (from "weaver") and "brewster" (from "brewer")—arose and even became common surnames. Women also owned taverns in such numbers that an instruction manual written for merchants in 1515 assumed that the innkeeper would be a woman and gave instructions on "how to ask the *hostess* how much one has spent."

Women's work

Still, women's access to the workforce came primarily through their families. Daughters, like most sons, mastered trades in the family workshops, just as Maria Merian (in the Biography on page 434–435) learned printing from her stepfather. Wives worked with their husbands, and widows frequently ran businesses and took their husbands' place in the guilds. During the late Middle Ages, men slowly began to replace women in some of the most lucrative jobs, like cloth making, and just as in banking and commercial enterprises, this late-medieval trend accelerated in the early modern period.

Into the sixteenth century, as work generated more capital and power, it began losing its association with the family and became more linked to the public political arena. Many people *Leaving the workforce* (women and men alike) believed that public work and control of money were more appropriately managed by men than women. Late in the sixteenth century, cities accordingly began to issue ordinances restricting women's entry into guilds, which had taken on markedly political overtones. For example, a ruling in France in 1583 limited silk-making apprentices (who had previously been predominantly female) to only two males per master. In another example, a 1508 ordinance in the Netherlands referred to a "brotherhood and sisterhood" of a guild, but the reissued ordinance in 1552 mentioned only a "brotherhood of trimmers." By 1563, when the ordinances were again revised, even widows' rights had been omitted.

Similar examples emerged at local levels throughout Europe. As the commercial revolution spread and urban merchants grew powerful, the old divisions of those who worked and those who did not began to blur. Instead, the growing middle class began to divide the world between those who worked outside the home in the public, political arena, and those who worked inside the home. Urban women, relegated increasingly to the domestic sphere, lost much of their visibility in the public arena.

PIRACY: BANDITRY ON A WORLD SCALE, 1550–1700

The expansion of trade into the Atlantic and Pacific brought with it another nettlesome problem: a rise in piracy. Piracy was as old as Mediterranean shipping, when seagoing robbers had preyed mercilessly on the ponderous merchant roundships that moved goods through the inland sea. As the pace of the world economy quickened, pirates moved to take advantage. From about 1550 to about 1700, a "pirate belt" developed that stretched from the West Indies to East Asia. The new entrepreneurial raiding coincided with the weakening of the great Turkish, Spanish, and Chinese empires that we saw in Chapter 11, because these navies could no longer effectively patrol their territorial waters.

Piracy as a way of life actually had a somewhat benign origin—monarchs had often issued licenses for people to steal from other countries in unofficial warfare. Before the seventeenth century, the word *pirate* rarely appeared. Instead, seagoing raiders were called *privateers* or *corsairs*, terms meaning that *Early privateers* they had the authorization of formal commissions from their rulers. Even as late as the eighteenth century, the United States Constitution gave Congress the right to issue letters of "marque and reprisal," essentially to hire pirate ships. Privateers earned their profits from captured booty, and in the freewheeling raids that took place on the open seas, it was impossible to distinguish them from pirates acting on their own. The ships that were robbed probably did not draw any distinction between the two.

The difficulties of discerning pirate from privateer may be seen in the famous early English privateers, particularly Francis Drake (1540?–1596). By 1571, Drake had become a major force in the Caribbean, and this champion of the British was considered a ruthless pirate by the Spanish. Drake had numerous bases on land and gained the admiration and support of unconquered Amerindians and Spanish-hating escaped slaves. With the backing and affection of Queen Elizabeth I (r. 1558–1603), Drake and his fellow privateers relentlessly harassed the Spanish ships they found sailing in the Caribbean.

The fortunes of Drake's compatriot, Walter Raleigh (1554?–1618), showed how fragile royal support of these independent captains could be. Elizabeth backed Raleigh in his flamboyant enterprises, even knighting her champion. However, her successor, James I (r. 1603–1625) found the privateer less useful. As James began to have political difficulties with English Protestants, he sought an alliance with Spain (as we will see in Chapter 13). As a token of good will to Spain, James imprisoned Raleigh in the Tower of London and executed him in 1618.

Pirates included many Africans who had been captured as slaves, because after seizing wealthy slave-trading ships, pirates frequently gave the slaves the choice to continue on their way or join the pirate band. The eighteenth-century trial records of a pirate on the ship *Whydah* indicates that about 30 to 50 of the men on his ship were African and one *Pirate life* was an Amerindian. The freedom of the pirate life drew many who had few choices elsewhere.

With all its hazards—from fickle royal supporters to war on the high seas—the pirate life could bring amazing riches even for those without a royal patron.

Pirate cities sprang up based solely on the illicit trade. For example, Algiers in North Africa became a prosperous Muslim pirate city, and Malta in the Mediterranean was its Christian counterpart. Other pirate cities dotted the Caribbean from the coast of the Yucatán to the islands of the West Indies. These cities served as havens for the violent, reckless sea raiders and their families. They also were places where talented outsiders could rise to positions of considerable power. For example, a poor North African shepherd boy rose through the pirate ranks to become "king" of Algiers in 1569. During the eighteenth century, several women even took command of pirate ships.

By the eighteenth century, however, governments began expanding their navies and set out to suppress the buccaneers. The British admiralty discouraged privateering because it lured sailors away from serving in the navy. The age of informal warfare came to a close and accounts of the bandits' careers retreated to literary works that romanticized their lives. For example, literary pirates made their victims walk the plank; real pirates would not have wasted time on such rituals. If they wanted to kill their captives, they unceremoniously threw them overboard.

The World Transformed

The booming world market that stimulated the movement of goods and the enterprise of pirates also served to spread other aspects of European culture around the world. During the sixteenth century, more than 200,000 Spanish people, 10 percent of them women, migrated to Latin America. In the next century, comparable numbers of English, French, and Dutch settled in North America. These immigrants became a new ruling class that transfused much of European culture into the New World. They built cities featuring the grid pattern that marked Renaissance urban planning and placed their churches in the city centers.

EUROPEAN CULTURE SPREADS

The new immigrants brought their languages and religions, but also unique livestock, tools, plants, and other goods that transformed the lives of native peoples. When European horses escaped (or were stolen), for example, some indigenous peoples took them into their midst. The Plains Indians in the southwest of North America soon made horses cen-

tral to their way of life. In time, guns, liquor, and many other goods also found their way into the many native cultures.

Plants from Europe, some of them intentionally cultivated, made their mark on the New World as well. For example, Europeans brought wheat to make the bread that had long served as their dietary staple. Along with their domesticated plants, they also transported their traditional farming methods. Figure 12.13 shows Amerindians cultivating wheat on a Spanish plantation. The laborers use the same kinds of tools, including the overburdened donkey in the lower-left corner, that their European peasant counterparts had employed.

Plants

Europeans unwittingly altered the ecology of the New World in many other ways. As we have seen, they brought diseases that ravaged native populations. Less destructive but equally ubiquitous, plants transported to the New World spread with vigor. A sixteenth-century Inca observer (Garcilaso de la Vega) described how quickly the ecology of Peru had been transformed by invasive plants: "Some of them

Figure 12.13
Amerindians planting wheat in America.

are becoming mischievous, such as the mustard, mint, and camomile, which have spread. . . [and] the first endives and spinach multiplied in such a way that a horse could not force its way through them." Inadvertent transportation of weed seeds also displaced native species. Dandelions are a particularly apt example of a European weed that spread accidentally as people, plants, and animals moved across the sea.

Europeans traveling and trading in Africa and Asia took New World plants to other regions of the world, transforming local consumption habits and economies. Africa, for example, received sweet potatoes and maize in the sixteenth century. In the Congo, the Portuguese introduced maize, although at first the tribes dismissed the vegetable as more suitable for pigs than human beings. In time, these plants became so central to the local culture that people no longer remembered that they were once strange imports. Because the societies of east Asia kept most Europeans at arm's length, they were less influenced by European culture than were the peoples of North and South America, and it would take several more centuries for European trade to exert its full impact in that region.

Finally, the populations themselves mixed as immigrants settled among native societies. Because European men greatly outnumbered women from their home continent, many of them married native and slave women or kept them as concubines. Generations of children born of mixed background, called *mestizos,* preserved aspects of both their parents' cultures. These generations ultimately made the Americas vastly different from Europe in spite of common languages, religions, and political structures.

Population mixing

EUROPEAN CULTURE TRANSFORMED

Europeans were as much transformed by contact with the New World as the original Americans were by their European conquerors. In one of the less-savory examples of this exchange, the earliest explorers to the New World probably brought back a virulent form of syphilis. New archaeological excavations have revealed that some form of syphilis existed in Europe from classical times, but this new strain of the sexually transmitted disease ravaged Europe until the twentieth century, when the advent of penicillin offered a cure. The disease never took the kind of toll on Europeans that plagues such as smallpox and measles imposed on native populations. Nevethe-

less, its presence caused much misery and made some people more cautious about sexual activity.

New foods changed Europeans' diets and even the landscape. It is difficult to imagine Ireland without the hardy, nutritious potatoes that flourish today in that rocky land, but until the conquest of the Incas, the population of Ireland had to struggle to sustain itself. The tomato—a New World fruit that people first rejected as poisonous—was eventually embraced as an aphrodisiac and became an often-used ingredient in European cuisine. Maize spread more slowly, for Europeans, like the Africans, did not initially view it as a food fit for humans. However, as early as 1500, it began thriving in Spain, from where it soon spread to Italy (near Venice) and eventually to the rest of Europe. Maize had immediate use as animal feed and peasant fare and allowed farming families to sell their more expensive wheat.

New foods

In addition to new staples, certain food stimulants from the Americas proved enormously popular in Europe. Chocolate, for example, came to Spain from Aztec Mexico in about 1520 in the form of loaves and tablets that were boiled into a drink. A luxury at first, chocolate became a common beverage by the eighteenth century. Tea, too, had been a rare treat in the Middle Ages, when some traders brought small amounts from China. Over time, more and more Europeans developed an unquenchable thirst for tea, making the East India Company rich in the process.

New stimulants

Coffee appeared in Europe for the first time in the early seventeenth century and replaced tea and chocolate as the most popular stimulant drink. Coffee seems to have first come from Africa and then spread to the Muslim lands—it was in Mecca by 1511, and Istanbul in 1517. By 1615, coffee reached Venice, and merchants spread the product rapidly through Europe from there. Physicians praised the drink as medicinal for many ailments, from heart disease to "short breath, colds which attack the lungs, and worms." By the eighteenth century, coffee was so central to European society that even the social life of the West began to be centered at coffee shops.

But it was tobacco that made the biggest impression on European culture. Columbus saw Amerindians smoking it and brought the plant back home as an object of curiosity. Europeans cultivated tobacco at first for medicinal purposes—one sixteenth-century Parisian claimed that it cured all ills—and

Biography

MARIA SIBYLLA MERIAN (1647–1717)

Notice how Merian's life exemplifies this exciting age that combined deep religious faith, world exploration, scientific curiosity, and astonishing opportunities for enterprising women and men.

Maria Sibylla was born in Frankfurt, Germany, the daughter of a well-known engraver and publisher and his second wife, Johanna. Maria's father also had a keen interest in the explorations of the age. He published editions of *Grands Voyages*, which contained accounts of journeys to the New World (including the illustration shown in Figure 12.7). Although he died in 1650 when Maria was only three years old, she grew up to excel in the same fields that had so captivated her father. Maria's mother married a painter and art dealer, and the young girl cultivated her artistic interests and skills in her stepfather's workshop.

In her later years, Maria remembered acquiring an additional passion: "I have been concerned with the study of insects. This led me to collect all the caterpillars I could find in order to study their metamorphoses . . . and to work at my painter's art so that I could sketch them from life and represent them in lifelike colors."

Maria married Johann Andreas Graff, an artist and publisher, in 1665, and the couple had two daughters. Ten years later, she published her first book of copperplate engravings. This work consisted solely of illustrations of flowers and some insects. It contained no text but was used to provide patterns for artists and embroiderers, who preferred to work from an illustration rather than from life. This work established Merian's reputation as an artist and naturalist, and she was included in a contemporary book on German art.

Naturalist, Artist, and Traveler

A few years later, she published *Wonderful Transformation and Singular Flower-Food of Caterpillars*. This work contained her detailed observations and commentaries on the habits of caterpillars and was hailed as "amazing."

Yet Merian's scientific work was soon interrupted by dramatic changes in her personal life. In 1685, she was consumed with a fervor for religious renewal. With her elderly mother and two daughters, she joined a radical Protestant sect, the Labadists, in the Netherlands. The group established a community of the "elect," who held their property in common and

the plant then spread rapidly all over the world. By the mid-seventeenth century, it had reached as far as China, where virtually the entire population took up the smoking habit. The difficulties of planting tobacco also stimulated settlement expansion. Because the crop rapidly depletes the soil, in an age without chemical fertilizers colonists seeking to profit from the lucrative crop constantly had to annex and cultivate new lands.

Tobacco

The New World's reshaping of European culture unfolded slowly. New products became available gradually, whetting appetites for yet more novelties. The commercial revolution stimulated the movement of goods all over the world, creating more and more demand that fueled further explorations and commerce. Ironically, the demand for spices, and particularly pepper, that had originally served as the main force behind the voyages of exploration waned

FIGURE 12.14

Maria Sibylla Merian. Frontispiece to Merian *Der Rupsen*, 1717.

lived in isolation from what they saw as a sinful world. When Merian's husband pleaded with her to return to him and bring home their daughters, she refused. He acquired a divorce and remarried.

After some years, the closed Labadist community must have felt too confining to the talented, curious Merian. She and her daughters left the group and settled in Amsterdam, the thriving port city that bustled with exotic goods and hummed with exciting tales of travel. Recognized for her previous work, Merian was welcomed into the circle of naturalists in Amsterdam.

Despite the attractions of her new life, Merian continued to find fascination in insects. In 1699, she and her daughter Dorothea sailed from Amsterdam to Surinam, the Dutch colony on the northern shore of South America. The Labadists had established a community there, but it had failed due to the hardships of the tropics. Merian might well have heard about Surinam during her earlier stay with the Labadists and decided to go there to study tropical insects, butterflies, and plants.

The devoted naturalist lived in Surinam for two years. With the help of Amerindians and African slaves, she collected thousands of specimens and made hundreds of drawings of plant and insect species unknown in Europe. In 1701 she returned to Amsterdam and several years later published *Metamorphosis of the Insects of Surinam* in both Dutch and Latin. Her drawings were praised as "the most beautiful work ever painted in America" (see Figure 12.15). Merian lived the rest of her days in Amsterdam, consulted by other naturalists and continuing to seek out interesting new caterpillar specimens. Her book remained widely read by naturalists well into the next century.

by the eighteenth century. Europeans had found other, more intriguing products to satisfy their restless desire for culinary novelties.

 A NEW WORLDVIEW

When Europeans first set off across the seas, they had a false, though highly imaginative, view of what they would find. The world proved larger and far more diverse than they had ever imagined, and travelers began to study and write about the new reality. Amerigo Vespucci, the Italian mapmaker and chronicler we met *Scientific observations* earlier, wrote with awe in 1499 about New World flora: "The trees were so beautiful and so fragrant that we thought we were in a terrestrial paradise. Not one of those trees or its fruit was like those in our part of the globe." Such early descriptions were followed by

Figure 12.15 shows an illustration from *Metamorphosis of the Insects of Surinam* by Maria Sibylla Merian (1647–1717) (see Biography). In this painstakingly rendered illustration, one can see both the detail that marked these kinds of studies and the artist's fascination with the exotic. Merian drew a guava tree (one of the fruits that Vespucci had found so strange) populated with spiders and ants. In the drawing, most of the spiders are eating ants. One of them, however, is shown attacking a nest of hummingbird eggs. Here Merian was illustrating a story told to her by the Surinam locals. (In fact, spider attacks on birds' nests are extremely rare.) This illustration, with its blend of careful attention to detail and elements of fantasy, typifies the European fascination with the newly discovered world.

The new maps created as explorers traveled the global coastlines and great rivers were almost as precise as the naturalists' drawings. These representations offered a much more realistic picture of the world than Ptolemy's map that guided Columbus. The map in Figure 12.16 shows the globe flattened out. This projection method, which let sailors plot straight-line courses, was developed by the Flemish cartographer Gerhard Mercator (1512–1594), who first published in 1569. Many modern European maps are still based on this technique.

Mercator maps

The mercator projection was a huge step forward in mapmaking, but it still allowed for some measure of geographic illusion. By flattening out the map and placing Europe in the center, mapmakers could not help distorting their graphic representation of the world. Greenland, for example, appears much larger than it is, India becomes smaller, and Asia is divided, thus seeming to have less mass than it really does. Not surprisingly, the Mercator map encouraged the illusion that Europeans occupied the center of the world. This idea shaped Europeans' future mapmaking techniques and their attitudes and actions toward the rest of the globe.

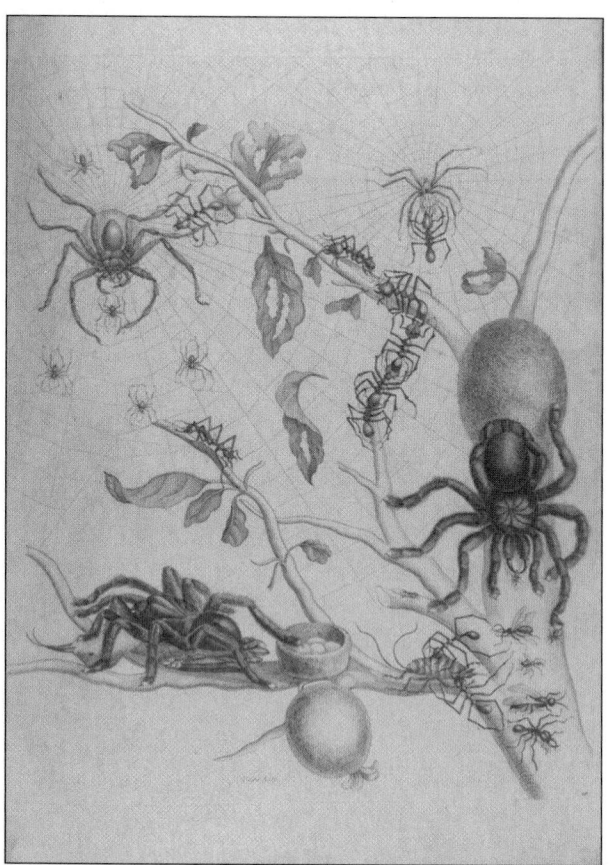

Figure 12.15
Spiders and Ants on a Guava Tree. Maria Sibylla Merian, *Metamorphosis*, plate 18, ca. 1705.

more systematic studies in the seventeenth century. For example, in 1648 a Dutch prince sponsored an expedition that published the *Natural History of Brazil*, followed by many other books by naturalists cataloging the wonders of the Americas.

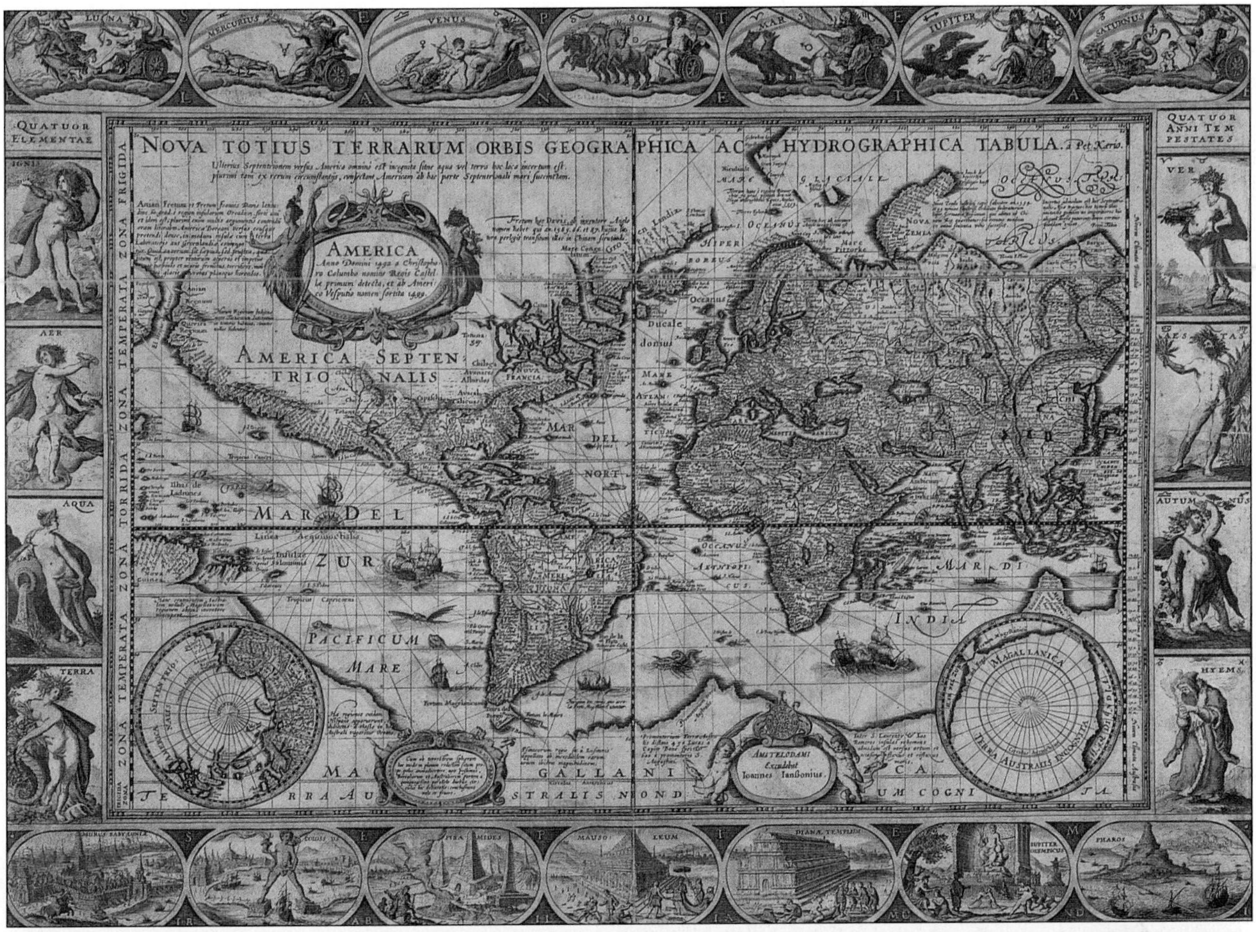

Figure 12.16
Mercator projection of the world in 1608.

Summary

By the early sixteenth century, Western culture was no longer contained within Europe. Lured by faith, fame, and fortune, Europeans sailed all over the world. They also settled in the newfound lands, conquering and colonizing the Americas and establishing trading posts in the East. Merchants and entrepreneurs followed the explorers and established a world market that stimulated the growth of commercial capitalism, new banking techniques, and widespread popular interest in economic opportunity. Some governments began to set economic policy and tried to control the flow of money to and from their countries.

In this great movement of peoples and confrontation of cultures, Europeans generated enormous wealth—and equally unprecedented misery. Native populations were virtually eliminated by warfare, disease, and abuse, and hundreds of thousands of Africans were enslaved and taken by force from their homelands. The resultant blending of peoples, ideas, and goods profoundly affected the entire world and whetted European appetites for yet more exploration and conquest.

TIMELINE: A CLOSER LOOK

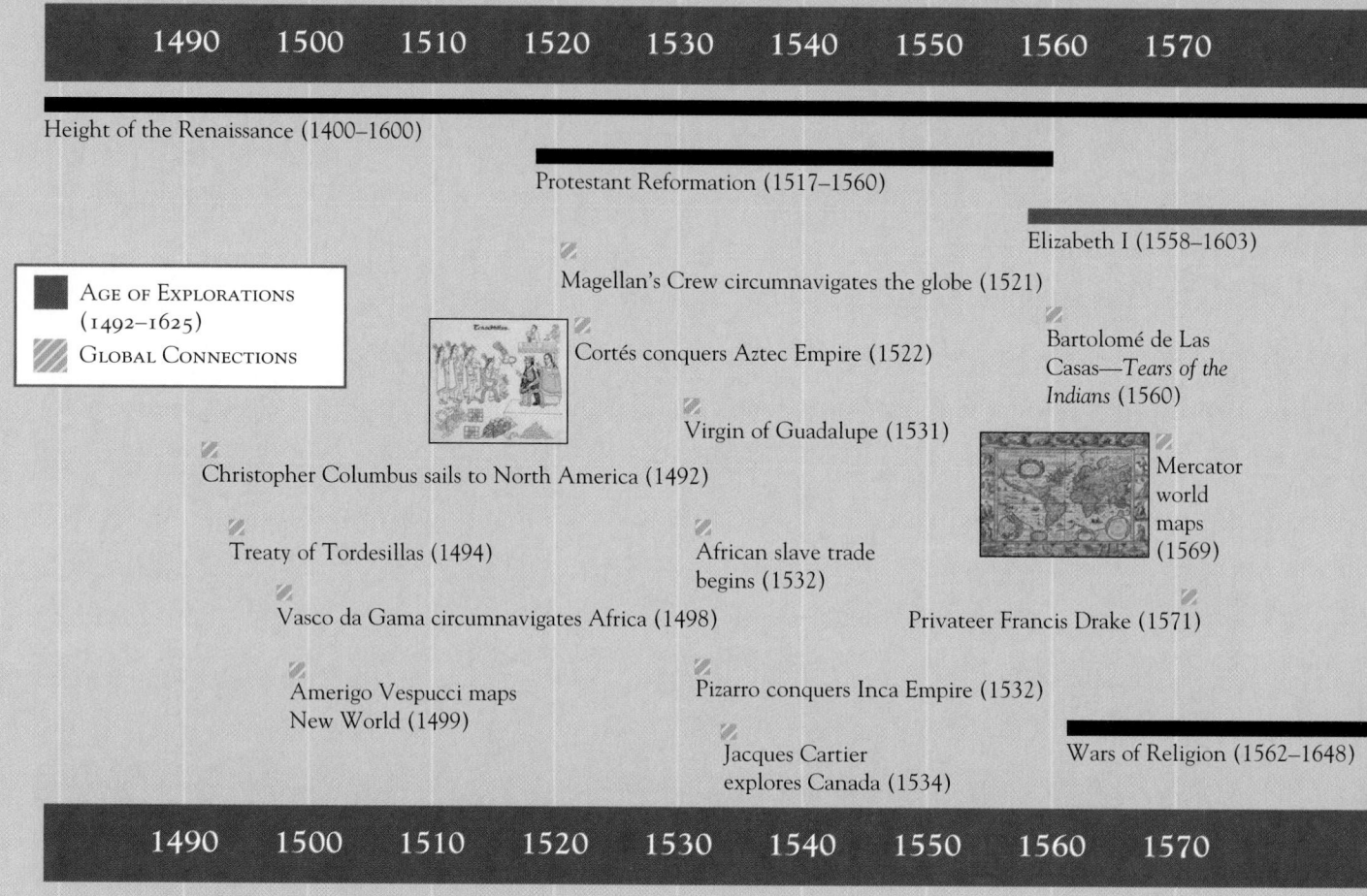

| 1490 | 1500 | 1510 | 1520 | 1530 | 1540 | 1550 | 1560 | 1570 |

Height of the Renaissance (1400–1600)

Protestant Reformation (1517–1560)

Elizabeth I (1558–1603)

AGE OF EXPLORATIONS (1492–1625)
GLOBAL CONNECTIONS

Magellan's Crew circumnavigates the globe (1521)

Cortés conquers Aztec Empire (1522)

Bartolomé de Las Casas—*Tears of the Indians* (1560)

Virgin of Guadalupe (1531)

Christopher Columbus sails to North America (1492)

Mercator world maps (1569)

Treaty of Tordesillas (1494)

African slave trade begins (1532)

Vasco da Gama circumnavigates Africa (1498)

Privateer Francis Drake (1571)

Amerigo Vespucci maps New World (1499)

Pizarro conquers Inca Empire (1532)

Jacques Cartier explores Canada (1534)

Wars of Religion (1562–1648)

| 1490 | 1500 | 1510 | 1520 | 1530 | 1540 | 1550 | 1560 | 1570 |

REVIEW, ANALYZE, AND ANTICIPATE

REVIEW THE PREVIOUS CHAPTER

Chapter 10—"A New Spirit in the West"—analyzed the revolution in thought that we have come to call the Renaissance, and in Chapter 11—"Alone Before God"—we saw how the new ideas were put into practice in religion. Chapter 11 also told the story of the struggles of European states as they competed with each other to claim superiority.

1. Review the characteristics of Renaissance thought and consider how they contributed to the sixteenth-century interest in discovering previously unknown areas of the world.

2. Review the Chapter 11 discussion of sixteenth-century European warfare and religious reforms.

How did these wars and reforms affect the global exploration that was occurring at the same time?

ANALYZE THIS CHAPTER

Chapter 12—"Faith, Fortune, and Fame"—describes and analyzes the European explorations and conquests that spread Western culture around the world and, in turn, transformed Europe.

1. Review the areas of Spanish and Portuguese exploration and consider where these early efforts forced England, France, and the Netherlands to focus their attention. Which areas turned out to be most profitable in the long run? Why?

2. Consider the complex relationship between technology, commercial exchange, and the lure of exploration and conquest and review how this relationship was expressed in this chapter.

1580	1590	1600	1610	1620	1630	1640	1650	1660

Privateer Walter Raleigh (1600)

James I (1603–1625)

Jamestown colony founded (1607)

Dutch provinces achieve independence (1609)

1580	1590	1600	1610	1620	1630	1640	1650	1660

3. *What advantages did the Spanish have in their conquests in the New World? How did the Spanish perceptions of the natives shape their treatment of them?*

ANTICIPATE THE NEXT CHAPTER

Chapter 13—"The Struggle for Survival and Sovereignty"—returns to the events occurring on the European subcontinent and explores political and religious tensions as nobles struggled for power with kings claiming ever more privileges.

1. *As kings in the seventeenth century strive to exert control over their nobles, who might they ally with given the new wealth generated in the years of commercial revolution and discovery?*

2. *What social group do you think might develop an economic theory to challenge mercantilism? Why?*

BEYOND THE CLASSROOM

THE WORLD IMAGINED

Friedman, John Block. *The Monstrous Races in Medieval Art and Thought.* Cambridge, MA: Harvard University Press, 1981. The best study on this subject—scholarly, fascinating, and well illustrated.

Russell, Jeffrey B. *Inventing the Flat Earth: Columbus and Modern Historians.* Westport, CT: Greenwood, 1991. Studies the origin of the myth that only Columbus believed the earth was round.

THE WORLD DISCOVERED

Greenhill, Basil. *The Evolution of the Sailing Ship, 1250–1589.* Annapolis, MD: Naval Institute Press, 1996. A clear explanation of the technology of sailing ships that does not get bogged down in unduly technical language.

McNeill, William. *History of the Human Community*, 5th edition. Englewood Cliffs, NJ: Prentice Hall, 1996. A look at world history showing the complex interactions that have always marked our global society.

Subrahmanyam, Sanjay. *The Portuguese Empire in Asia, 1500–1700: A Political and Economic History.* New York: Longman, 1993. A comprehensive look at the economic and diplomatic history of the whole Portuguese Asian empire.

CONFRONTATION OF CULTURES

Berlin, Ira. *Many Thousands Gone.* Cambridge, MA: Harvard University Press, 1998. A sensitive study of the changing nature of the history of African-American slavery in mainland North America.

Diamond, Jared. *Guns, Germs, and Steel.* New York: W.W. Norton & Co., 1997. A Pulitzer Prize-winning analysis of the interactions of cultures around the world that is utterly riveting.

Fagan, Brian M. *Clash of Cultures.* New York: W.H. Freeman and Company, 1984. Concentrates on the first period of European exploration and settlement beginning in 1488.

Karlen, Arno. *Men and Microbes: Diseases and Plagues in History and Modern Times.* NY: Touchstone, 1996. This detailed look at the history of diseases demonstrates how infections are always part of the changing natural and social human environment. Particularly strong on modern times.

Pagden, Anthony. *European Encounters with the New World: From Renaissance to Romanticism.* New Haven, CT: Yale University Press, 1993. A fascinating study of the ways in which European ideas were changed by encounters with the peoples of the New World.

Palmer, Colin. *The First Passage: Blacks in the Americas (1501–1617).* New York: Oxford University Publishing Press, 1995. A comprehensive study that includes differences among African cultures and the changes that went on in Africa as a result of the African diaspora.

Standard, David E. *American Holocaust: Columbus and the Conquest of the New World.* New York: Oxford University Press, 1993. Describes in horrible detail the mass destruction of the New World societies in the wake of European contact.

Thornton, John. *Africa and Africans in the Making of the Atlantic World, 1400–1680.* Cambridge: Cambridge University Press, 1992. Offers the controversial perspective that Africans were voluntary and active participants in the Atlantic world.

THE WORLD MARKET AND COMMERCIAL REVOLUTION

Braudel, Fernand. *Civilization and Capitalism, 15th to 18th Centuries,* 3 volumes. Translated by S. Reynolds. New York:

Harper & Row, 1981. A celebrated author's detailed economic history that analyzes patterns in European and world economy—particularly rich in details.

Magnusson, Lars. *Mercantilism: The Shaping of an Economic Language.* New York: Routledge, 1994. Directly deals with how nations could increase their wealth specifically through international trade.

Smith, Alan K. *Creating a World Economy: Merchant Capital, Colonialism and World Trade, 1400–1825.* Boulder, CO: Westview Press, 1991. Deals with the first world economy, an entity that was shaped by the emergence of merchant capital in early modern Europe.

THE WORLD TRANSFORMED

Crosby, A.W. *Columbian Exchange: Biological and Cultural Consequences of 1492.* Westport, CT: Greenwood, 1972. Unravels the impact of Columbus's voyages on the global ecosystem.

Crosby, A.W. *Ecological Imperialism: The Biological Expansion of Europe, 900–1900.* Cambridge: Cambridge University Press, 1986. Discusses the expansion of Europeans and the animals, weeds, and pathogens that accompanied them.

Davis, Natalie Zemon. *Women on the Margins: Three Seventeenth-Century Lives.* Cambridge, MA: Harvard University Press, 1997. Explores seventeenth-century culture through the lives of three women—a Catholic missionary, a Jewish storyteller, and the Protestant Merian (described in the chapter's Biography box).

Fuentes, Carlos. *The Buried Mirror: Reflections on Spain and the New World.* Boston: Houghton Mifflin, 1992. A fascinating essay by one of Mexico's greatest writers on the blending of cultures of Spain and the New World.

GLOBAL CONNECTIONS

Andrien, Kenneth J., and Rolena Adorno. *Translatlantic Encounters: Europeans and Andeans in the Sixteenth Century.* Berkeley: University of California Press, 1991. Particularly good analysis of the warfare of the period as well as economic conditions after the conquest.

Rostoworowski de Diez Canseco, Maria. *History of the Inca Realm.* Cambridge: Cambridge University Press, 1999. Thorough and readable account drawing from the latest scholarship.

Wachtgel, Nathan. *The Vision of the Vanquished: The Spanish Conquest of Peru Through Indian Eyes, 1530–1570.* New York: Barnes and Noble, 1971. A comprehensive, readable account sensitively drawn from the few sources giving the Indian point of view.

Documents

DOCUMENT 12.1

Explorers Describe Prester John, a Mythical Christian King in Africa

When European explorers headed for Africa, they were partly motivated by accounts of a powerful Christian king names Prester John who reputedly lived there. As this excerpt shows, the explorers imagined Prester John's court in fanciful yet compelling ways.

■ **Investigate the Document**

What *would explorers find so attractive about Prester John's court?* **How** *did the organization of this imagined court mirror that of medieval Europe?* **How** *might Muslim ideals of holy war and paradise have influenced this account?*

This emperor, Prester John, holds full great land, and hath many full noble cities and good towns in his realm and many great diverse isles and large. For all the country of Ind is devised in isles for the great floods that come from Paradise, that depart all the land in many parts. And also in the sea he hath full many isles. And the best city in the Isle of Pentexoire is Nyse, that is a full royal city and a noble, and full rich.

In the land of Prester John be many diverse things and many precious stones, so great and so large, that men make of them vessels, as platters, dishes, and cups. And many other marvels be there, that it were too cumbrous and too long to put it in scripture of books; but of the principal isles and of his estate and of his law, I shall tell you some part.

This Emperor Prester John is Christian, and a great part of his country also. But yet, they have not all the articles of our faith as we have. They believe well in the Father, in the Son, and in the Holy Ghost. And they be full devout and right true one to another. And they set not by no barrets, nor by cautels, nor of no deceits.

Source: Medieval Sourcebook: Mandeville on Prester John, http://www.fordham.edu/halsall/source/mandeville.html.

And he hath under him seventy-two provinces, and in every province is a king. And these kings have kings under them, and all be tributaries to Prester John. And he hath in his lordships many great marvels.

This Emperor Prester John hath evermore seven kings with him to serve him, and they depart their service by certain months. And with these kings serve always seventy-two dukes and three hundred and sixty earls. And all the days of the year, there eat in his household and in his court, twelve anchbishops and twenty bishops. And the patriarch of Saint Thomas is there as is the pope here. And the archbishops and the bishops and the abbots in that country be all kings. And he had also, in that place, the fairest damsels that might be found, under the age of fifteen years, and the fairest young striplings that men might get, of that same age. And all they were clothed in cloths of gold, full richly. And he said that those were angels.

And when that any good knight, that was hardy and noble, came to see this royalty, he would lead him into his paradise, and show him these wonderful things to his disport, and the marvellous and delicious song of diverse birds, and the fair damsels, and the fair wells of milk, of wine, and of honey, plenteously running. And he would let make divers instruments of music to sound in an high tower, so merrily, that it was joy for to hear; and no man should see the craft thereof. And those, he said, were angels of God, and that place was paradise, that God had behight to his friends, saying, *Dabo vobic terram fluentem lacte et melle*. And then would he make them to drink of certain drink, whereof anon they should be drunk. And then would them think greater delight than they had before. And then would he say to them that if they would die for him and for his love, that after their death they should come to his paradise; and they should be of the age of those damosels, and they should play with them, and yet be maidens. And after that yet should he put them in a fairer paradise, where that they should see God of nature visibly, in his majesty and in his bliss. And then would he shew them his intent, and say them; that if they would go slay such a lord, or such a man that was his enemy or contrarious to his list, that they should not dread to do it and for to be slain therefore themselves. For

FIGURE 13.2
The Rich Noble, the Poor Peasant.

the women, children, and elderly who had to shoulder the men's share of the labor. Soldiers embroiled in nearby battles plundered what they could from the villages they passed.

Officials also came with new tax assessments, even though peasants already owed much to those above them. Traditional taxes to the government, tithes to the church, and rents to large landowners used up more than half of the already scant wealth peasants produced. Figure 13.2, a mid-seventeenth-century print, caustically depicts some of the peasants' grievances. On the left, the well-dressed noble sits authoritatively on his padded chair to receive the peasant ("thin as the noble's terrier"), who is bringing money in his right hand, fruits and vegetables in his left hand, and a sack of wheat at his feet. Above the noble is a spider and a fly caught in its web. As the caption on the lower left states, "The noble is the spider and the peasant the fly." The noble says, "You must pay or serve." The peasant can only reply, "To all masters, all honors."

Peasants avoided collectors and hid what assets they could. In countless incidents, peasants and city-

dwellers across Europe rose against increasing taxes and attacked the hated collectors. In the 1630s, for example, French peasants rose against tax increases and forced temporary concessions from local officials, only to have those victories reversed by the state. Farther south, in 1647, women demanding more bread led riots that swept through the city of Palermo in Spanish-occupied Italy. Rebels in the city chanted, "down with taxes!" As in France, government forces eventually reversed early victories and crushed the revolt.

Tax revolts

Other intrusions further eroded the traditional isolation that characterized rural life. Officials and merchants ventured more and more often to the countryside to buy grain for cities, creating food shortages in rural villages. Moreover, as members of the local nobility departed for capital cities and the king's court, new officials appeared and began administering affairs and rendering judgments in courts. For good or ill, villagers found themselves increasingly drawn into the web of national affairs.

PRESSURES ON THE UPPER ORDERS

Monarchs faced pressures of their own, especially the demands of war. In the competition for territory and status, kings won by fielding ever larger armies and mustering the resources needed to support them. During the seventeenth century, armies doubled and redoubled in size, as did the central governments that supported them (see Chapter 11). The costs of making war and supporting government increased accordingly. Governments devoted half or more of their income to the military, and monarchs desperate for money levied more and more taxes just to stay even. The ability to collect taxes could make or break a ruler. More than anything else, a king's unrelenting demands for more taxes sparked widespread resistance to his rule.

Competing centers of power added to the kings' problems. Independent town officials, church leaders, and provincial officials tried to hold on to their authority over local matters. Religious dissidents, for their part, guarded what independence they could. Finally, those who resented the royal tax collectors resisted the crown's reach. But the greatest threat to monarchical power came from aristocrats, who tried to retain as much of their social and economic dominance as possible. These nobles often challenged royal policies and

Competing centers of power

decried royal "tyranny" as a violation of divine law. They guarded their traditional rights and local authority, and many of them refused to give up their tax exemptions. Should the crown falter, they stood ready to take back any powers they might have lost.

Monarchs argued with, fought, and schemed against these forms of opposition. They justified their power as a divine right, because they represented God on Earth, and surrounded themselves with compliant advisors and admirers. As Document 13.1 reveals (see page D13.1), their favored supporters, such as France's court preacher and royal tutor, Bishop Jacques Bossuet (1627–1704), backed them. Bossuet declared, "The whole state is included in him [the monarch], the will of all the people is enclosed within his own."

Yet the kings used more than words and "yes-men" in this power struggle. Bypassing representative institutions, they sent their royal law courts into the provinces as a way to extend their authority. Sometimes they appointed new local leaders to gain allies. Other times, they attracted aristocrats from the provinces to the royal court, thereby creating a power vacuum that they then filled with their own men. When great nobles resisted being turned into obedient officials, rulers often turned to the lesser nobility or members of the wealthy middle class—men such as Chancellor Seguier, whom we met in the photo on p. 442. Such royal servants received titles or land and were elevated to high office as compensation for their loyalty.

Women also became entwined in these struggles between monarchs and aristocrats. With the royal courts growing in size, many women became important friends and unofficial advisors to kings and influential aristocrats. They used their intelligence, wit, services, and advice to gain privileged positions in royal courts. There they won titles, offices, lands, money, and advantageous marriages for themselves and their families. Mothers encouraged their daughters not to let good marriage opportunities pass by. "It is true that [the proposed groom] is some fifteen years older than you," wrote one aristocratic mother in 1622. "[B]ut . . . you are going to marry a man . . . who has spent his life honorably at court and at the wars and has been granted considerable payments by the king." Royal mistresses also achieved important positions in the king's household. Françoise d'Aubigné (Marquise de Maintenon), mistress (and, secretly, wife) of France's king Louis XIV, influenced court appointments and founded a royal school for

the daughters of impoverished nobles in 1686. Some mistresses even persuaded kings to acknowledge their children as "royal bastards" and grant them titles and privileges.

This system of elevated royal authority has been called "royal absolutism" because the kings of the day commanded more loyalty, control, and resources than their predecessors *Royal absolutism* had, and because they justified their right to rule as an absolute. However, no monarch gained true absolute power. Most people understood that even the strongest ruler, divinely ordained, was vaguely subject to tradition and law. As one seventeenth-century French jurist explained, the king's power "seems to place him above the law, . . . [but] his rank obliges him to subordinate his personal interests to the general good of the state." Further, with so many local centers of power, with scores of nobles who persisted in their independent ways, and with too much information to control, no king in this era could hope to dominate everything. Some monarchs even found themselves on losing ends of internal battles for power.

Royal Absolutism in France

In western Europe, the efforts of French kings to maximize their power exemplified the development of royal absolutism. Building upon the work of predecessors who had enhanced the power of the monarchy, Louis XIV (r. 1643–1715) took personal control of the French monarchy in 1661. By then, France had supplanted Spain as the most powerful nation in Europe. Under Louis's long rule, royal absolutism reached its peak and inspired other monarchs to emulate his style.

HENRY IV SECURES THE MONARCHY

French absolutism had its immediate roots in the reign of Henry IV (r. 1589–1610). When Henry IV ascended the French throne in 1589, his country had endured several decades of wars between Protestants and Catholics, combined with conflicts between different political factions. Law and order had broken down, and powerful nobles had reasserted their authority. The finances of the central government lay in disarray, and French prestige abroad had sunk to a low level.

The talented, witty Henry, in his prime at 36, set out to change all this. He defused the religious turmoil by issuing the Edict of Nantes (see Chapter 11), which granted to Huguenots (French Protestants) religious toleration and control of some 200 fortified cities and towns as a guarantee against future oppression. He appealed to the traditional nobility by developing an image as a cultured warrior-king who could be trusted to enforce the law. He catered to rich lawyers, merchants, and landowners by selling new governmental offices, which often came with ennoblement as well as prestige. This growing elite became known as the nobility of the robe because their robes of office, rather than the arms borne by the traditional nobility of the sword, represented their power (see p. 442). Many of these nobles gladly paid annual fees for the right to pass their offices on to heirs. For the peasantry, Henry suggested that prosperity should bring "a chicken in the pot of every peasant for Sunday dinner." Not surprisingly, Henry's authority and popularity soared.

With the help of his able, methodical administrator, the duke of Sully (1560–1641), Henry also launched a comprehensive program of economic reconstruction. Agriculture and commerce benefited from the increased security of life and property brought by better law enforcement; from improved transportation facilitated by the repair of roads, bridges, and harbors; and from the freeing of trade, thanks to lower internal tariff barriers. The monarchy even subsidized and protected new industries that produced luxuries such as glass, porcelain, lace, silk, tapestries, fine leather, and textiles. Sully's efficient collection of taxes and administration of expenditures produced a rare budget surplus.

Henry also dreamed of making France secure from ambitious foreign states and of ensuring his country a supreme position in all of Europe. However, the powerful Spanish and Austrian Habsburgs on France's borders stood in his way. In 1610, he prepared to join his armies for a campaign against his rivals. Yet before he could set out, he was assassinated by a fanatic, and his plans died with him.

RICHELIEU ELEVATES ROYAL AUTHORITY

For several years after Henry's death, his Italian wife, Marie de Médicis (1573–1642), ruled as regent for their son, the young Louis XIII (r. 1610–1643). Marie kept opponents at arm's length, but made little head-way in strengthening the position of the monarchy. Then in 1624, one of her favorite advisors, Cardinal Richelieu (1585–1642), became chief minister and began exercising power from behind the throne. Having come from a minor noble family and possessing a keen intellect, the arrogant and calculating Richelieu handled the young king deftly and controlled others through a skillful blend of patronage and punishment. His twofold policy was to make royal power supreme in France and to maneuver France into a position of dominance in Europe. To Louis XIII, Richelieu promised "to ruin the Huguenot party, to abase the pride of the nobles, to bring back all your subjects to their duty, and to elevate your name among foreign nations to the point where it belongs."

With the royal army at his disposal, Richelieu boldly destroyed the castles of nobles who opposed the king; he disbanded their private armies and executed a number of the most recalcitrant among them. When Huguenot nobles in the southwest rebelled, Richelieu sent in the army and stripped the Huguenots of the special military and political privileges that Henry IV had granted them. Only their religious liberties remained intact. To dilute local centers of political power, the dynamic minister divided France into some 30 administrative districts, placing each under the control of a powerful *intendant*, who was an agent of the crown. He chose these intendants from the ranks of the middle class and recently ennobled people and shifted them around frequently, lest they become too sympathetic with their localities. Finally, Richelieu plunged France into the Thirty Years' War in Germany (see Chapter 11). His purpose was to weaken the Habsburgs, chief rivals of the French monarchs for European supremacy.

By the time of his death in 1642, Richelieu had firmly secured royal power in France and elevated France's position in Europe. Nevertheless, the imperious cardinal, having more than doubled taxes to promote his policies, had gained few friends. Far more French subjects rejoiced in his death than mourned his passing.

MAZARIN OVERCOMES THE OPPOSITION

Richelieu was succeeded by his protégé, Cardinal Jules Mazarin (1602–1661). Louis XIII's death in 1643, a few months after that of his great minister, left the throne to Louis XIV, a child of five. Mazarin, who began his career as a gambler and diplomat, played the same role in the early reign of Louis XIV and his regent, Anne of Austria (1601–1666), that Richelieu had played during the reign of Louis XIII.

Early on, Mazarin, Anne, and the child-king faced a series of wide-ranging, uncoordinated revolts that *The Fronde* forced them to flee Paris. Known collectively as the Fronde (the name of a child's slingshot game, which implied that the participants were childish), these revolts stemmed primarily from French subjects' objections to high taxes and increasing royal power. Between 1648 and 1653, ambitious nobles, footloose soldiers returning from war, urban artisans, and even some peasants fought the monarchy and its supporters in what amounted to a civil war at times. Bad harvests added to the chaos and suffering: "People massacre each other daily with every sort of cruelty," wrote an observer in 1652. "The soldiers steal from one another when they have denuded everyone else . . . all the armies are equally undisciplined and vie with one another in lawlessness." Nobles conspired and shifted alliances for their own gains, resulting in growing disillusionment with their cause. Gaining support from city-dwellers and peasants longing for peace, and shrewdly buying off one noble after another, Mazarin quashed the revolts by 1653. The crown gradually reasserted itself as the basis for order in France.

The Fronde was paralleled by other revolts during the 1640s in Spain, the Italian states, and much more seriously, in England. In each case, the catalysts included new taxes, the demand for more men and supplies for the military, and monarchies' efforts to acquire more power. In the Spanish provinces of Catalonia and Portugal, as well as in the Italian states of Naples and Sicily, rebels murdered tax officials, peasants took up arms, and local nobles joined the fray. Localities demanded and sometimes got concessions, but many of these victories proved short lived when the crown reasserted its authority. As we will see, matters grew much worse in England. Taken together, these mid-century rebellions served as a warning to monarchs not to push unpopular policies too far—and to the aristocracy not to underestimate the power of the crown.

The Sun King Rises

Upon Mazarin's death in 1661, the 23-year-old Louis XIV finally stepped forward to rule in his own right. "Up to this moment I have been pleased to entrust the government of my affairs to the late Cardinal," he announced. "It is now time that I govern them myself." With his regal bearing and stolid build, young Louis fit the part well. His lack of intellectual brilliance was offset by a sharp memory, a sense of responsibility, and a capacity for tedious work. "One reigns only by dint of hard work," he warned his own son. Haunted by childhood memories of fleeing in terror across the tiled rooftops of Paris during the Fronde revolts, he remained determined to prevent further challenges from rebellious aristocrats. By his mother, Mazarin, and a succession of tutors, Louis had been convinced that he was God's appointed deputy for France. Supporting him was the most famous exponent of royal absolutism, Bishop Bossuet, who argued that the monarchy "is sacred, it is paternal, it is absolute, and it is subject to reason . . . the royal throne is not that of a man but the throne of God Himself." As Document 13.2 indicates (see page D13.2), Louis XIV learned these lessons well. In words commonly attributed to Louis, "*L'état, c'est moi*" ("I am the state").

However, Louis could not possibly perform all the functions of government personally. The great bulk of the details were handled by a series of councils and bureaus and administered locally by the intendants. Distrusting the traditional nobility, Louis instead usually appointed members of modest noble backgrounds to the important offices of his government. Well supervised by the industrious king, the administrative machinery hummed along.

To raise his stature, Louis XIV initiated massive public-works projects that glorified him, his government, and his reign. His greatest architectural project was a new palace. Hating the *Versailles* tumult of Paris, with its streets teeming with commoners, he selected Versailles, 11 miles southwest of the city, as the new seat of government. There, as many as 35,000 workmen toiled for more than 40 years to turn marshes and sand into Europe's most splendid palace and grounds.

Figure 13.3 shows Versailles in 1668. Over the next 43 years, successive teams of workers added rear gardens and more than doubled the size of the buildings. This painting, which shows the roads, paths, and gardens of Versailles geometrically laid out, gives a sense of the scale of the project. In the foreground to the right, the royal coach, with its train of followers, arrives at the front gates. The exterior of Versailles was designed in long, horizontal, classic lines.

FIGURE 13.3
Pierre Patel the Elder, *Versailles*, 1668.

The interior boasted a lavish baroque style with richly colored marbles, mosaics, inlaid woods, gilt, silver, silk, velvet, and brocade. Ceiling-to-floor windows and mirrors and crystal chandeliers holding thousands of candles illuminated the salons and halls. In terms of sheer capacity, the palace could house 5,000 people and serve thousands more visitors each day. It faced hundreds of acres of groves, walks, canals, pools, terraces, fountains, statues, flower beds, and clipped shrubs—all laid out in formal geometric patterns symbolizing the triumph of engineering over nature. So dazzling was this hallmark of royal absolutism that other European monarchs soon attempted to copy it.

Louis used Versailles, images of himself, and symbols to enhance his authority among the nobility and everyone else. "The peoples over whom we reign, be-ing unable to apprehend the basic reality of things, usually derive their opinions from what they can see with their eyes," he explained. Figure 13.4, a painting by an anonymous seventeenth-century artist, shows Louis—in the center astride a white horse—as he rides into the gardens at Versailles. His favored courtiers throng around him, hoping to be seen by him and others more than to see him. Servants mingle in the crowd as well. Above is the king's chosen symbol, the sun, with its light radiating out. As Louis put it, "The symbol that I have adopted and that you see all around you represents the duties of a Prince . . . endlessly promoting life, joy and growth." It is "the most dazzling and most beautiful image of the monarch."

The "Sun King" finally moved to Versailles in 1682. Once established there, he lured the men and women of the nobility away from their local centers of power where they might make trouble and turned them into domesticated court "butterflies." He subjected them to a complex system of etiquette and favoritism that made every aspect of Louis' daily life the center of their concern. Court became a theater where those already in favor, as well as aspiring favorites, had to scheme for gifts, patronage, and position. Winners might secure lucrative rewards, and losers might spend themselves broke trying to stay in the race.

Despite the grandeur of Versailles, this glittering monument to royal absolutism had its critics. In her novel *The Princess of Clèves* (1678), the Countess de Lafayette com-

Versailles critics plained that at Versailles "everybody was busily trying to better their position by pleasing, by helping, or by hindering somebody else." The court reportedly seethed with gossip, scandal, and intrigue. Critics such as Pierre Jurieu, a French Calvinist pastor who fled to Holland, lamented that the king "is the idol to which are sacrificed princes, great men and small, families, provinces, cities, finances and generally everything." Resentful nobles once proudly drawing high status from their lands and lineage came to depend on the approval of and service to the king as the primary route to power. Many hard-toiling, heavily taxed French commoners also grumbled about living in the reflected glory of a pretentious monarch.

To enhance the glory of his court, Louis XIV subsidized and attracted to Versailles leading French artists and literary figures. The elegance, the sense of order,

"Classical" literature and the formalism of royalty all found expression in much of the literature of this "classical" period in French culture. Pierre Corneille (1606–1684), for example, wrote elegant plays modeled on the ancient Greek tragedies. Human beings' conflicts with their own nature and with the workings of fate and the universe furnished the plots. Even more exquisite were the perfectly rhymed and metered couplets of Jean Racine's (1639–1699) dramas. Finally, in his profound come-

FIGURE 13.4
Louis XIV on horseback at Versailles.

dies, Jean-Baptiste Molière (1622–1673) satirized pompous scholars, social climbers, false priests, and quack physicians. Louis and his court had little to fear from this literature. On the contrary, they appreciated its formal order and laughed along with other audiences at its satire, which was aimed at humankind in general rather than at specific ruling regimes.

At court and elsewhere, many members of the elite also read historical romances. Perhaps the most popular of these was *Grand Cyrus* by Madeleine de Scudéry (1608–1701), a writer who rose from an impoverished background. The fact that this book was published under the name of the author's brother, Georges, hints at the difficulties women faced in expressing their cultural talents. Other forms of literature included letters and memoirs. The courtier Madame de Sévigné (1626–1696), for example, wrote almost 2,000 letters to her daughter that reported what the king said and did as well as news of marriages, deaths, gossip, fads, and conspiracies that

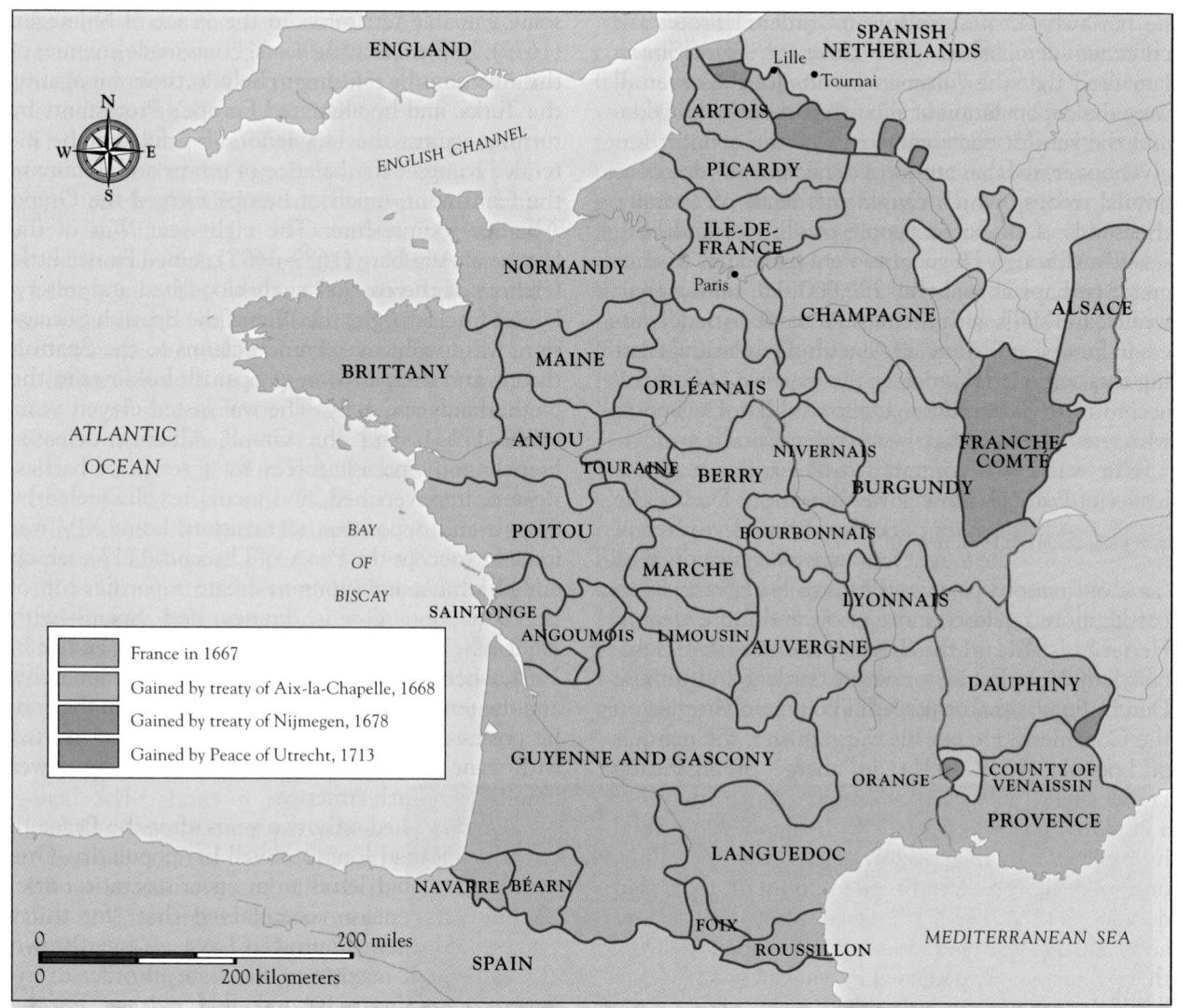

THINKING ABOUT GEOGRAPHY

MAP 13.1 *France under Louis XIV, 1661–1715*

This map shows France's provinces and the territorial gains it made during the reign of Louis XIV. ❧
Notice that most of Louis' gains came from Spanish lands and German states on France's eastern border.
What might this imply about vulnerable areas of Europe and changing power relationships? ❧ **Consider**
how little France's gains were despite almost endless, costly wars. **What** were the likely consequences for
France's finances and the popularity of its monarch?

Louis XIV became the model of absolutism. However his expenditures and wars created unprecedented misery for most commoners saddled with relentlessly rising taxes, more military service, and famines.

Recognizing that the continued power of the state required some support of the people, Louis's successors would try to avoid his mistakes and ameliorate the worst threats to the lives of French people.

The Struggle for Sovereignty in Eastern Europe

In eastern Europe, people struggled just as fiercely to survive and to define sovereignty as they did in the west. However, the two regions differed sharply, and those differences affected the outcomes of battles over these issues. States east of the Elbe River (see Map 13.2) were less commercially developed than those in western Europe. Instead of farms worked by legally free and mobile peasants, estate agriculture (large landed estates owned by lords and worked by their serfs) dominated those economies. By the sixteenth century, the nobles who owned these estates had reversed the medieval trends toward greater freedom for the peasantry and the growth of towns. Most people who worked the fields sank into serfdom, bound to the land and owing ever-increasing services to their lords. The middle classes in the towns also declined, failing to gain in numbers and wealth like their counterparts in western Europe. Finally, most central governments at the beginning of the seventeenth century proved weaker than those in western European states, as powerful nobles retained much independence. Despite all this, several monarchs decided to change things in their own favor.

CENTRALIZING THE STATE IN BRANDENBURG-PRUSSIA

In Brandenburg-Prussia, the "Great Elector" Frederick William (r. 1640–1688) inherited a scattered patchwork of poorly managed lands weakened by years of war and population decline. He faced a number of other problems as well. His army was tiny—too weak to keep foreign forces out of his lands or to discipline internal opponents. His nobles, or *Junkers*, had an independent streak and had found ways to avoid most taxes. Finally, his cities remained uncooperative, asserting their long-established political and economic independence.

Frederick William set out to correct the situation. He believed that the key was to strengthen his standing army. Only then could he gain control of his lands and make Brandenburg-Prussia a desired ally in international affairs. During the 1640s he more than tripled the size of his army. This new strength and effective diplomacy won him several new territories at the end of the Thirty Years' War (see Map 13.2). With energy and skill, he next centralized and administered the governments of his fragmented holdings—while continuing to boost the size of his army. He prevailed over the Estates—the representative assemblies of the realm—and acquired the crucial authority to collect taxes. He then used his newly powerful army to enforce tax payments and organize state resources. In a pivotal compromise with landed aristocrats, he allowed them complete control over their serfs in return for support and service in his bureaucracy and army. Through mercantilistic policies, he protected industries, improved communications, and promoted agriculture. Though he could not afford a lavish court like that of Louis XIV, Frederick William's policies ratcheted up his power. "Hold fast to the eminence of your superior position . . . [and] rely on your own strength," he advised his son. At the Great Elector's death in 1688, Brandenburg-Prussia was well on the road to becoming a major player in European politics. He also left a legacy of military values and reliance on armed might that would influence much of Prussia's subsequent history.

In 1701, his son, Frederick I (r. 1688–1713), increased the dynasty's status by acquiring the title of King of Prussia in return for helping the Holy Roman Emperor in a war against France. He used state revenues to turn his Berlin court into a great social and cultural center. By his death in 1713, Brandenburg-Prussia had become a respected force in eastern Europe.

AUSTRIA CONFRONTS THE OTTOMANS AND EXPANDS ITS CONTROL

Austria's Leopold I (r. 1657–1705), facing extreme local, language, and ethnic differences within his diverse lands, could not hope to acquire the same power as that enjoyed by Louis XIV in France or even Frederick William in Prussia. Localities retained considerable autonomy, especially in matters of taxation. The practical Leopold focused on securing his own Habsburg lands, rather than cementing the minimal control he had over the Holy Roman Empire, and allied himself closely with the Catholic Church. He gained the allegiance of the nobles by making them his chief advisors and granting them rights to exploit lands and the peasants on them. Some peasants revolted, but as elsewhere in Europe, they did not pose a serious challenge to authorities.

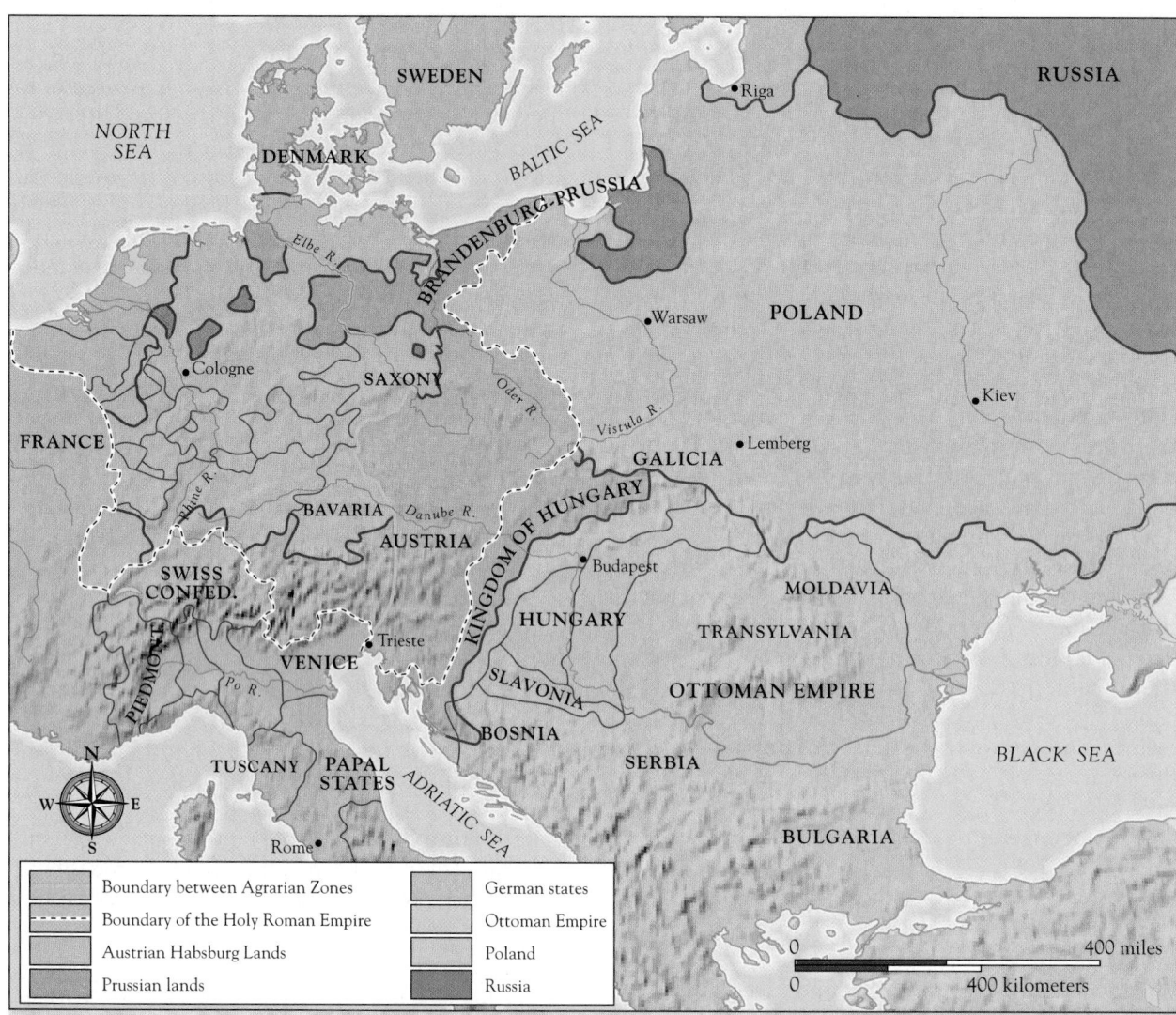

THINKING ABOUT GEOGRAPHY

MAP 13.2 *Central and Eastern Europe, 1648*

This map shows the border between the western and eastern agrarian zones, running from the mouth of the Elbe River south to Trieste on the Adriatic Sea. ◙ **Notice** which states are to the east of this line. **What** might this imply about social differences between eastern and western European states? **What** problems might these differences pose for eastern European states such as Austria and Brandenburg-Prussia, which controlled provinces to the west of this line?

With the help of Poland's king, Jan Sobieski (r. 1674–1696), Leopold also fought the Ottoman Turks, who controlled most of Hungary as part of their large and still-powerful empire. The Ottoman rulers had their own problems maintaining authority in the face of competition from bandit armies, mutinous army officers, and squabbling elites. However, in times of crisis, the sultans usually managed to bring these forces under control. In 1683, Ottoman forces pushed into Austrian lands and laid siege to the capital,

Vienna. Leopold and Sobieski's forces saved the city and then brought most of Hungary under Austrian control (see Map 13.3 on page 461). During the following decades, Ottoman power and imperial leadership would deteriorate as weakened rulers struggled against political corruption, provincial revolts, and military insubordination.

After his victory in Vienna, the Austria king tried to install his own nobility in Hungarian lands and ally himself with powerful Hungarian nobles at the expense of the peasantry. He succeeded only partially, and the still-independent Hungarian nobles remained a thorn in the side of the Austrian monarchy. Facing west, Leopold helped build a coalition that stood against Louis XIV. By the Austrian king's death in 1705, the Habsburg state had become one of the most powerful in Europe.

RUSSIA AND ITS TSARS GAIN PROMINENCE

Even farther east, the Russian monarchy slowly rose to prominence. Already in the sixteenth century, Ivan IV ("the Terrible") (r. 1533–1584) had added both to the authority of the Russian *tsars* (*caesars*, or emperors) and to the span of territories over which they ruled. He destroyed the remaining power of the Mongols in southeastern Russia and annexed most of their territory. Next, he began Russia's conquest of Siberia. Within his expanding state, Ivan ruled as a ruthless autocrat, creating his own service gentry to bypass powerful nobles and using torture and terror to silence all he saw as his opponents.

A difficult period known as the "Time of Troubles" (1584–1613) followed Ivan IV's death. Ivan's feeble-minded son Fydor ruled ineffectively *The Romanovs* and left no successor upon his death in 1598. Great nobles vied for power among themselves and against weak tsars. To end the political chaos, a group of leading nobles in 1613 chose the 17-year-old Michael Romanov (r. 1613–1645) to rule as tsar. He began a dynasty that ruled Russia for over 300 years.

Despite the political stability Michael and his immediate successors brought, discontent among those below the tsar and the nobility mounted during the century as the authorities increasingly restricted the freedom of the masses. The notorious Law Code of 1649, for example, merged peasants and slaves into a class of serfs and gave the landowning nobility the power to treat them as property. In a spate of uprisings between the late 1640s and early 1670s, the lower classes rebelled against landowners and officials by killing them and looting or burning their estates. The discontent reached a climax in the late 1660s and early 1670s with the revolts of Cossacks ("free warriors") in south Russia led by Stenka Razin. A shrewd, seasoned warrior, Razin claimed to "fight only the boyars and the wealthy lords. As for the poor and the plain folk, I shall treat them as brothers." His rebel army marched north, and many towns opened their gates to welcome Razin's forces, now swelling with the addition of discontented peasants and the urban poor. Russian soldiers finally caught, tortured, and executed Razin, and the uprisings tapered off.

By the final decades of the seventeenth century, the Romanov tsars had shored up the government's central administration and extended their authority throughout the country. Lured by visions of wealth from access to Siber- *Russian expansion* ian furs, Russians had driven eastward into Asia, establishing fortified settlements, bringing indigenous peoples under their control (in the process decimating them with raids and diseases such as smallpox), and planting their flag on the shores of the Pacific. Moreover, through increased trade and travel, Russia's commercial and cultural contacts with the West expanded, bringing new European goods and ideas into the country. The stage was set for a dynamic tsar to propel Russia more fully into European affairs.

This new, energetic emperor came in the person of Peter I ("the Great") (r. 1689–1725). Standing nearly seven feet tall, Peter seemed born to rule. At the age of 17, he seized the *Peter the Great* reins of government from his elder sister. He soon concluded that the best way to bolster his own political and military power was to copy Western practices. To this end, he traveled to western Europe and learned as much as he could about Western politics, customs, and technology.

Back home, he took decisive steps to solidify his authority. In 1698 he crushed a revolt of his bodyguards and silenced critics with a ruthlessness that cowed all potential troublemakers. "Every day was deemed fit and lawful for torturing," wrote an observer. He also made five years of education away from home and state service requirements for the nobility and allowed movement within the ranks only through merit. Peter applied the bureaucratic system of western European monarchs to both central and local government to secure his rule. He also brought

Western technicians to Russia in large numbers and protected new industries with mercantilistic policies. Western social customs were introduced to the upper and middle classes of Russian society, such as bringing Russian women out of seclusion to appear in Western dresses at official dinners and social gatherings. In addition, Peter banned the long beards and flowing Oriental robes that Russian men traditionally wore. When the patriarch of the Russian Orthodox Church opposed the tsar's authority and some of his westernizing policies, Peter took control of the church and confiscated much of its wealth. Henceforth, the Orthodox Church served as a powerful instrument of the Russian government.

FIGURE 13.6
Louis Karavack, *Peter the Great*.

All these reforms left the peasantry in even worse straits than before. Peasants made up 97 percent of Russia's population during Peter's reign, and they became tied down in a system of serfdom bordering on slavery. The taxes they were forced to pay ballooned by a whopping 500 percent, and their feudal obligations and military service increased. Nowhere was peasant life harsher than in Russia, and Peter's efforts to westernize the nobility only widened the gap between the educated elites and the enserfed peasantry. *Russia's military establishment*

To keep Russia in step with the West and support his ambitions for territorial expansion, Peter devoted particular attention to his military establishment. He built a navy and patterned his expanded and modernized conscript army on the model of Prussia. Recruits were drafted for life and even branded with a cross on their left hand to deter desertion. Officials arbitrarily assigned serfs to work in mines and manufacturing establishments to supply the military with equipment and arms.

Peter meant to use his new military might. Figure 13.6 depicts the clean-shaven tsar Peter the Great in heroic military pose. Clad in armor and carrying a sword, Peter asserts his authority over all potential rivals, who offer him their swords. Beneath the feet of his horse lays a defeated dragon. Above, an angel crowns Peter with divine authority. The tsar waged numerous military campaigns over his long reign, and he designed many of his great reforms to strengthen and modernize his armed forces. In the background of the painting, his troops surge to victory in a mighty battle.

Lacking warm-water access to the west, Peter tried to seize lands bordering the Black Sea that the Ottoman Turks held. Though they had weakened during the seventeenth century, the Ottoman Turks remained a formidable obstacle, and Peter's armies could not dislodge *Conflict with Sweden*

Global Connections

The Rise and Fall of the Mughal Empire In India

▣ **Consider** the similarities between European and Mughal monarchs, particularly Louis XIV of France and Aurangzeb of India. **NOTICE** the policies that weakened their respective states.

While monarchs in Europe struggled to consolidate their authority during the seventeenth century, powerful rulers rose in the Asian states. These emperors would become strong enough to rival the Western powers and control relations with European traders. The Asian leaders had a proud history. During the sixteenth century, the Mughals [Moguls], a fierce Islamic Turkish tribe, had swept into the Indian subcontinent and established a flourishing realm ruled by able emperors such as Babur (1483–1530) and Akbar (1542–1605).

In 1605, the 38-year-old Jahangir succeeded the great Mughal leader Akbar and assumed the title of "the world-subduing emperor." In his memoir, he described the lavish ceremonies accompanying his crowning. During the festivities, the high officials of the empire, "covered from head to foot in gold and jewels, and shoulder to shoulder, stood round in brilliant array, also waiting for the commands of their sovereign."

By that time, the Portuguese had already established a flourishing trading base on the west Indian coast. As the seventeenth century unfolded, the Mughals also allowed the English, French, and Dutch to establish trading bases in India, but without power to be of any concern. The Mughals themselves paid little attention to foreign trade, but welcomed the revenues from the commerce into their treasuries.

Though Jahangir wielded power arbitrarily, he also felt compelled to follow certain traditions and laws. In his view, to bring "prompt punishment to the man who violates the laws of his country is an alternative with which no person entrusted with the reins of power is authorized to dispense." Jahangir also struggled to bring unruly sections of his empire more firmly under his control, at one time ordering a bloody campaign against rebellious Afghans. The Mughal emperor

recorded how prisoners from one battle were paraded before him "yoked together, with the heads of the seventeen thousand slain in the battle suspended from their necks." Reflecting on the burdens of office, Jahangir lamented, "There is no pain or anxiety equal to that which attends the possession of sovereign power, for to the possessor there is not in this world a moment's rest." Nevertheless, the emperor gave his wife, Nur Jahan, a major role in running the government. He also managed to find time to support and enjoy sports, literature, and art as well as to smoke opium regularly. He completed his *Memoirs* before his death in 1627.

An eventual successor, Aurangzeb, became Mughal emperor in 1658 and held power for almost 50 years. One of his chroniclers, Bakhta'war Khan, claimed it was "a great object with this Emperor that all Muslims should follow the principles of the religion." The biographer also boasted that his emperor "has learned the Qur'an by heart." But Aurangzeb's reign marked both the apex of Mughal power and the beginning of its end. By the time of his death in 1707, reckless spending, endless military campaigns, and persecution of Hindus and Sikhs had weakened the regime. Widespread rebellions broke out, which Aurangzeb's weaker successors failed to overcome. In the 1720s, one observer, Khafi Khan, reported that many townships "have been so far ruined and devastated that they have become forests infested by tigers and lions, and the villages are so utterly ruined and desolate that there is no sign of habitation on the routes."

As the Mughal empire disintegrated, rivals quickly took power. Europeans traders also gained influence—especially the British and French, who were competing for the Indian trade in textiles, spices, and sugar. By the mid-eighteenth century, the land controlled by Aurangzeb's successors had dwindled to Delhi. Meanwhile, the British and French forged strategic political alliances with Indian states and jockeyed for a dominant position on the subcontinent.

between classes and lost their solitary struggle against absolutism. In England, however, there had been a tradition of joint parliamentary action by nobles and commoners who owned land, and this helped contribute to a different outcome in the struggle for sovereignty. Instead of government residing in the person of an absolute monarch, it rested in written law—constitutions, not kings, would come to rule.

THE NOBILITY LOSES RESPECT

For over 1,000 years, the English had taken for granted the idea of separate social classes. Peasants and members of the middle classes showed the high nobility an unmistakable deference, turning out to greet them when they emerged, gazing downward and holding their hats respectfully in their hands. Even upwardly mobile landowners with some wealth (the "gentry") knew that they ranked well below the "peers" (the old nobility). In England, there were only about 400 noble families and they jealously guarded their exclusive position. Commentators wrote that "nobility is a precious gift" and accepted this privilege as the natural order of things: "Men naturally favor nobility."

By the beginning of the seventeenth century, several disturbing incidents pointed to ominous cracks in the wall of privilege. One member of the gentry actually jostled and swore at an earl as the two passed in a narrow passageway, and some tenant farmers neglected to turn out, hats in hand, to welcome passing noblemen. Later, a Protestant sect, the Quakers, enacted a religious policy that forbade members to take off their hats to men in authority. Something had changed and nobles no longer seemed so essential nor so noble.

What explained this apparent loss of respect for the English upper crust? We can find a partial answer *New wealth* in the shifting role of money. In the early modern world, the old wealth of the nobility had declined relative to the "new money" of merchants and other enterprising individuals. Furthermore, the medieval base of noble power, the military, had also declined. No longer were nobles in charge of defending the realm; mercenary armies made up of commoners now took care of these matters. England had a relatively large sector of independent craftsmen compared to other countries, and noblemen depended more on "free labor"—that is, on wage laborers who could enter into contracts for

their labor. These differences led commoners increasingly to feel they could control their own lives rather than defer to their "betters." In addition, education had become the key to upward mobility. More and more, knowledge and service, rather than birth, seemed the measure of a man.

The members of the nobility did not relinquish their traditional place easily. Indeed, critics complained that noblemen were becoming more arrogant than ever in exerting their privileges. Sometimes, nobles even exceeded the bounds of propriety. In 1635 the earl of Arundel lost his temper when the mayor of a city did not turn out to greet him in the traditional way. The earl sought out the mayor, grabbed his staff of office, and proceeded to beat him with it, shouting, "I will teach you to . . . attend Peers of the Realm!"

As early as the sixteenth century, laws throughout Europe had begun to supplement tradition in keeping the social classes separate, and England was no different. Governments issued sumptuary laws to regulate what kinds of clothing were appropriate for members of each social class. For example, an individual could not wear velvet unless he had an independent income of over 100 pounds a year, and laborers could not wear cloth costing more than two shillings a yard. These laws were supposed to preserve social distinction, but the newly rich recognized that the path to gaining social respect lay in part in *looking* noble. Thus, men and women insisted on purchasing luxurious clothing to rival that of the highest classes. In 1714, a Sicilian traveler observed: "Nothing makes noble persons despise the gilded costume so much as to see it on the bodies of the lowest men in the world." Now, it seemed, there was no visual marker of a person's noble status.

The nobles had more success in guarding their property rights than their fashion privileges. In 1671, Parliament passed game laws giving the nobility the exclusive prerogative to hunt on their own lands. The new mandates even allowed them to set lethal trapguns to kill poachers. Not surprisingly, these laws only exacerbated the common people's anger, as the poor continued to poach simply to survive in times of hunger. Still, many members of the nobility tried to hang on to their privilege while others pressed to undo them.

The portrait of James Stuart, a member of the royal family, shown in Figure 13.7, captures the arrogance and complacency of the typical English nobleman of 1630, who was oblivious to the gathering with the kind of deference that James had come to expect. Sadly for members of the nobility, they would receive fewer and fewer admiring glances from their fellow humans.

PROTESTANTISM REVITALIZED

A good deal of social criticism also came from Protestants, many of whom believed that the implementation of Reformation ideas in England had not gone far enough. Because many Protestants were involved in the increasingly lucrative commerce, their wealth helped make their concerns more visible. For many, the compromise of Elizabeth I (discussed in Chapter 11) that allowed worshipers of many beliefs to share one Church of England was unacceptable. These critics believed that the Church of England (the Anglican Church) should be "purified"—that is, trimmed of any practice that lacked biblical precedent or smacked of Catholicism. They especially objected to priestly garments and the elaborate rituals of the Anglican Church. Some wanted to eliminate bishops altogether, preferring rule by church elders instead. (This was the practice common in Scotland, where Protestant churches became called "Presbyterian"— "ruled by elders").

In their zeal, many Protestants became increasingly anti-Catholic, and their political actions were shaped by this prejudice. Other Protestants even wanted to purify daily life, objecting to theater, cockfights, and other seemingly frivolous activities. Although individuals disagreed among themselves on exactly how they wanted the Church of England purified, they all concurred that change was essential. Many members of this loose group of critics, called Puritans, became influential members of Parliament.

Puritans in England reconsidered the political relationship between monarchs and their subjects, wondering about competing loyalties between law and conscience, for example. These questions formed the backdrop of a struggle for sovereignty that dominated the seventeenth century. As early as 1561, the Scottish reformer John Knox warned Queen Mary of Scotland that monarchs were responsible to their subjects: "If their princes exceed their bounds, Madam, no doubt they may be resisted, even by power." This was tantamount to a call to revolution. As Puritans gathered to discuss the purification of the church, they could not help but consider the possibility of political action.

FIGURE 13.7

Anthony Van Dyck, *James Stuart, Duke of Richmond and Lennox*, ca. 1630.

social storm that would soon disrupt his idyllic world. James stands proudly dressed in the opulent clothing of the nobility that the sumptuary laws carefully tried to preserve. His stockings are made of the finest silk, and the lace at his throat is expensive and handcrafted. Adorning his jacket sleeve is a sun image embroidered in silver thread—an early forerunner of Louis XIV's trademark symbol. The painting portrays James with his huge hunting dog, again proclaiming his privileged position through his hunting rights. The dog gazes up adoringly at his master

JAMES I INVOKES THE DIVINE RIGHT OF KINGS

Because Queen Elizabeth I had died childless, the throne went to her cousin, the king of Scotland, who became King James I of England (r. 1603–1625). As soon as James heard of Elizabeth's death, he rushed to England brimming with great plans. He made promises to many who greeted him on his way south to London, rapidly knighted thousands of gentry, and even ordered an accused thief hanged without a trial—assuming incorrectly that as king he had the right to do so. Many of his subjects turned out to see their affable new monarch, but, unfortunately for him, he would not prove as popular, nor as politically shrewd as "Good Queen Bess."

The honeymoon of the new monarch and his people faded rather quickly, for unlike his predecessor, he

Religious problems was unable to mollify the varying religious beliefs of his people. He was a Calvinist, yet he favored Anglicanism, and his most enduring heritage was the translation of the Bible he commissioned, the King James Bible, which remains widely admired as both religion and beautiful literature. However, the king managed to offend his subjects who hoped for his support for religious change. At the beginning of his reign, Calvinists approached the king, hoping to eliminate the Anglican episcopal system and bring it in line with the Presbyterian Scottish practice with which the king was familiar. They were sadly disappointed, for James threatened to "harry them out of the land" if they did not conform to Anglicanism.

James also offended his Catholic subjects, banning Jesuits and seminary priests. In 1605, a conspiracy of Catholics planned to blow up Parliament while it was in session. The plot failed and the conspirators were executed. Yet, the "gunpowder plot," as it came to be known, increased the anti-Catholic feelings in the country, which were exacerbated when James planned a political marriage between his son and a Catholic Spanish princess. Although the marriage negotiations fell through, the attempt alienated Calvinists and Anglicans alike.

Thus by 1610, there was much animosity between the king and many of his subjects. James thought the English ungrateful and they found him arbitrary and arrogant. Unlike Elizabeth before him, James was dis-

inclined to compromise his theoretical notions of divine right monarchy. Even before he ascended the throne, James had written two treatises in *Divine right* which he asserted the divine right of kings, and in 1610 he presented this position to a skeptical Parliament. As he put it, "Kings have power of . . . life and death; [they are] judges over all their subjects and in all causes, and yet accountable to none but God." This position was consistent with his hasty execution of the accused thief, but it offended many Puritans in the House of Commons, as well as many Lords who viewed the king as subject to the law of the land.

During James's rule, the English colonies in North America grew. In part, the attention to the New World stemmed from James's financial diffi- *Colonies* culties: The first permanent English colony, named Jamestown after the monarch, was founded in Virginia in 1607. James hoped to generate new income from the Virginia colonies, which in 1619 had imported slaves from Africa to grow tobacco, an increasingly popular crop. Colonial settlement was also forwarded by James's high-handed attitude toward religious dissidents. When the king threatened to harry nonconformists out of the land, some took him literally and emigrated to North America to establish colonies. They avoided Jamestown, which was sympathetic to the Church of England, and instead landed farther north, founding their first colony in Plymouth, Massachusetts, in 1620. The New World was not to be the solution to either James's religious or fiscal problems. He died leaving a shortage of money and an oversupply of ill will among both Parliament and Protestants.

CHARLES I ALIENATES PARLIAMENT

James's son, Charles I (r. 1625–1649), inherited both his father's rule and his policies. This sober monarch, continuing to invoke the divine right of kings, considered himself answerable only to God, not Parliament. His relationship with his subjects deteriorated rapidly. He approached Parliament in the same way his father had—calling it when he needed money and disbanding it when the members demanded concessions.

Showing a remarkable insensitivity to his Protestant subjects, Charles married a sister of the Catholic king Louis XIII of France. Soon after his wedding, Charles granted concessions to English Catholics,

OLC

even allowing the queen and her entourage to practice Catholic rituals in the court itself. English

Concessions to Catholics

Protestants were horrified at what they saw as outrageous behavior by the family of the titular head of the Church of England. Charles responded to critics by persecuting Puritans, whom he viewed as disloyal. More Puritans fled to North America, settling so many colonies in the northeast that the region came to be called New England. Meanwhile, the situation in old England grew more desperate.

As we saw in Chapter 11, warfare had become extremely expensive, and Charles's

Parliament gains power

costly and fruitless wars with Spain and France had so strained his finances that he even tried to pawn the crown jewels. The king called Parliament several times in the 1620s, only to disband them repeatedly. Things came to a head in 1640, when the Scots, who also objected to the king's high-handed religious policies, invaded the north of England. To raise the army and funds he needed to fight the Scots, Charles called Parliament again. This time, Parliament forced him to agree that he could not disband them without their consent. The first crack in Charles's armor of divine right had appeared. The "Long Parliament," as it came to be called, continued to meet from 1640 to 1653. Over time, it acquired a measure of power and established protections for the religious freedom of Anglicans and Puritans alike.

However, the temporary compromise between the king and Parliament came to an end when troubles in Ireland caused both to agree to send troops. However, their alliance ended there. The question of who would command the army remained. Parliament did not trust the king to suppress his religious sympathies to fight the Catholic Irish, and the king did not trust Parliament to share control of any army it raised. In the end, Parliament appointed officers to raise an army, and Charles withdrew from London to raise an army of his own. The Irish no longer seemed the immediate enemy for either side.

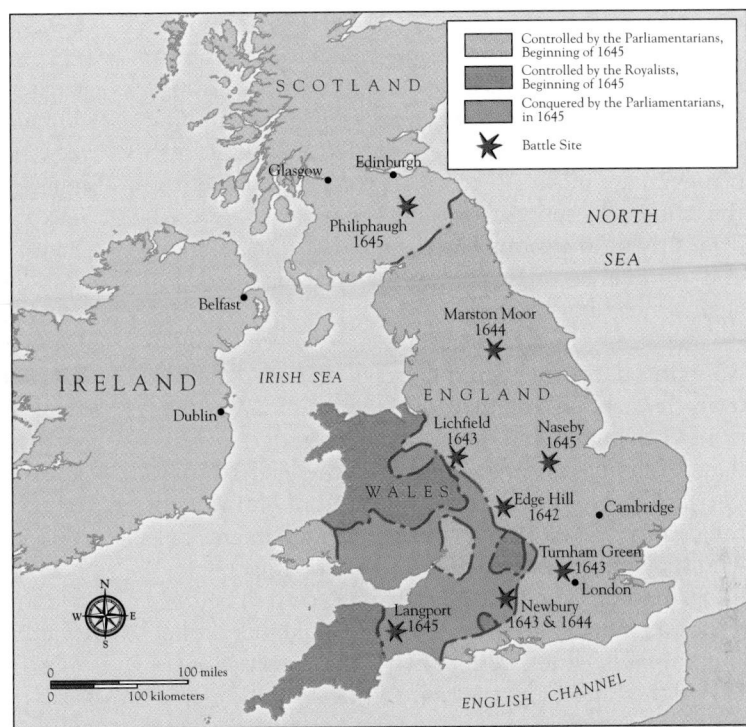

THINKING ABOUT GEOGRAPHY

MAP 13.4 *The English Civil War, 1642–1649*

This map shows England during the civil war years, the locations of the parliament and royalist supporters, and the major battles. ◼ **Notice** the scale of the map and **consider** how this might have affected the progress of the war. ◼ **Notice** the regions that initially supported the king and **consider** why the royalists drew from rural rather than the urban centers. ◼ **Notice** the locations of Ireland, Scotland, and Wales, which would be incorporated into what would become Great Britain.

"GOD MADE MEN AND THE DEVIL MADE KINGS": CIVIL WAR, 1642–1649

As Map 13.4 shows, the alignments in the English civil war show some divisions in English life. The rural areas were more likely to support the king, and the Puritan strongholds in the cities followed the forces of Parliament. In response to Charles's call for support, noblemen, cavalry officers, and Irish Catholics rallied to his banner. His royalist supporters were called Cavaliers, or horsemen, as a reference to medieval knights who fought for their kings. Back in London, Parliament recruited an army 13,000 strong, drawn from the commoners, merchants, a few noblemen, Scots, and Puritans. All these generalizations, however, are drawn in broad strokes, and frequently the choice to support one side or another derived from private decisions based sometimes on religion and sometimes on long-standing personal grudges against neighbors.

The strength of the parliamentary forces, called Roundheads for their short haircuts, stemmed mainly from their skilled infantry, the support of major sections of the navy, and their religious conviction. Parliament's forces also benefited from the leadership of Oliver Cromwell, a Puritan who not only forwarded the cause of revolutionary change in Parliament, but who took charge of the army and forged it into a formidable force called the New Model Army. The royalists had more experience in battles and more skilled generals. The lines were drawn—the royalist forces led by the king fought a civil war against the forces led by Cromwell.

By 1646, Parliament forces had won a series of victories, and Charles surrendered to the Scots, who

Charles captured later turned him over to Parliament in exchange for their back military pay. While the king was moved from prison to prison as royalists conspired to free him, leaders of Parliament confronted new challenges: a series of social upheavals as more and more people were drawn into the turbulent events of the 1640s.

Women from all social groups participated in unprecedented numbers in the English civil war. In their husbands' absence, a number of noble women defended their fortified castles against parliamentary

Women in war forces, inspiring many accounts of "great heroics" considered surprising in the "weaker sex." Working women disguised as men also passed themselves off as Roundhead soldiers. In 1643, Charles issued a proclamation intending to prevent women from joining the army: "Let no woman presume to counterfeit her sex by wearing man's apparel under pain of the severest punishment which law shall inflict." However, the king was in no position to enforce this edict, and women continued to serve as soldiers. It is impossible to know exactly how many women fought for their cause, but the fact that Charles tried to legislate their exclusion suggests that at least he and his advisors thought the numbers significant.

Women were well suited as spies, because people expected them to be noncombatants. One such woman, Jane Whorwood, dedicated herself fiercely to the king's cause. The tall redhead repeatedly tried to free Charles during his imprisonment after 1646. She smuggled money to him and once brought in acid to weaken the metal bars so that he could break free. One of Charles's aides described Whorwood as "the most loyal person to King Charles I in his miseries."

Other previously uninvolved members of society also jumped into the fray. After 1646, radicals, both men and women, raised new demands for social justice. Their complaints stemmed **Levellers** mostly from the severe economic problems that had hamstrung England in the 1640s. A series of bad harvests caused food shortages and rising prices, and disabled soldiers returning home discovered they could no longer earn a living. Crime increased as people stole to feed their families, and the social order deteriorated. One contemporary observed: "Necessity dissolves all laws and government, and hunger will break through stone walls." From these difficult circumstances, groups of radical Protestants arose. Known as Levellers, they insisted that social justice become part of Parliament's agenda. A pamphlet sympathetic to their cause claimed that "God made men and the Devil made kings."

Levellers were as varied a group as the Puritans, encompassing people with a broad array of agendas. In general, however, they harked back to a tradition of English religious radicals like John Ball (see Chapter 9), and espoused as their goal to "level" social differences. To that end, they advocated some reforms of Parliament. For example, they believed Parliament should be chosen by the vote of all male heads of households, which would represent a dramatic broadening of the vote. Furthermore, they wanted members of Parliament to be paid, so that even those with no independent income could serve. Although these ideas may seem natural to us, they posed a major threat to those who believed that only property brought privilege.

THE KING LAID LOW

In the midst of these controversies, the civil war broke out again in 1648 as Charles encouraged his supporters to rise up to free him. Cromwell's forces promptly crushed the uprisings, and some army leaders concluded that they would never come to peaceful terms

OLC

FIGURE 13.8
Weesop, *Execution of Charles I, 1649.*

with the king. With Cromwell's support, they demanded that Charles be tried for treason. The majority of Parliament members refused to take this extreme step, but in December 1648 invading soldiers purged Parliament of the cautious. The remaining members, scornfully called the Rump Parliament by opponents and historians, brought the king to trial.

The Rump Parliament tried Charles as a king, rather than deposing him first and then trying him as a private citizen. In other words, they wanted to find the *king* guilty, not just the man. This bold act represented a direct clash between two theories of government—one claiming that the king stood above Parliament, the other declaring that he must answer to it. This unprecedented, highly public trial became the first in history to receive full press coverage. Newspapers had initially emerged in England in 1641, on the eve of the civil war; by 1649, six licensed newspapers recorded the testimony in the trial and provided differing opinions on the proceedings.

Charles was accused of claiming to rule by divine right: He who had been "trusted with a limited power to govern . . . had conceived a wicked design to . . . uphold in himself an unlimited and tyrannical power

to rule according to his will. . . ." Though he genuinely believed in divine right, Charles refused to answer this or any other charge. Instead he claimed that Parliament had no right to bring charges against him at all. He gained much popular support over the few days of the trial as he consistently reiterated his position, rising above a stutter that had plagued him all his life in order to express his views firmly and with dignity. He challenged Parliament to justify "by what power I am called hither." Both sides clearly understood the magnitude of the trial's central question: Who had sovereignty? Charles claimed that God had sovereignty and had delegated it to the king; the Puritans in Parliament claimed that they had sovereignty. There was no room for compromise, and neither side gave way. Charles was found guilty and sentenced to die.

On January 30, 1649, the condemned king was led to a scaffold erected in front of Whitehall Palace. His public execution inspired a rash of etchings and paintings. Figure 13.8 depicts the crowds who gathered to watch, including women, whose interest in the execution seemed remarkable to contemporary commentators. Many in

Charles executed

the crowd were sympathetic to their king. Jane Whorwood, for example, who had worked tirelessly to free Charles, ran forward to greet the king as he walked to the scaffold. Figure 13.8 shows some of these sympathizers; note the old man in the foreground, leaning on his cane and crying, and the woman fainting in the center.

Charles bravely addressed the few people near him on the scaffold and repeated his views on sovereignty: "I must tell you that the liberty and freedom [of the people] consists in having a government. . . . It is not for having a share in government. Sir, that is nothing pertaining to them. A subject and a sovereign are clear different things." Charles then laid his head on the block, and the executioner severed it cleanly with one blow. The man on the side of the platform in Figure 13.8 holds the king's head up to show the crowd. The monarchy had ended, and a new form of government arose to take its place: a republic in which sovereignty rested with representatives of those who owned property. England called its new republic the Commonwealth.

A PURITAN REPUBLIC IS BORN: THE COMMONWEALTH, 1649–1660

As the Rump Parliament began to rule the republic, chaos erupted throughout the realm. The new commonwealth faced warfare outside its borders and dissension within. Fortunately, Parliament had an able champion in Oliver Cromwell (1599–1658). While Parliament ruled, Cromwell with his army controlled the policies.

Rebellions broke out in Catholic Ireland and Protestant Scotland, and Cromwell led his army to those lands, putting down the revolts so brutally that the Irish still remember his invasion with anger. However, Cromwell was effective and brought Scotland and Ireland tightly under English rule. Yet Parliament had more to worry about than just these expensive wars.

Within England, Levellers continued to agitate for social reform, and many of their leaders were imprisoned. Then, in 1649, a gathering of women entered the House of Commons bringing a petition asking for "those rights and freedoms of the nation that you promised us." One member of Parliament taunted the women, saying their public stance was "strange," to which a petitioner responded, "It was strange that you cut off the king's head." These were odd times indeed, and many wondered whether Parliament's victory in the civil war had created more disorder than it had resolved.

Domestic distress

The 1649 cartoon in Figure 13.9 expresses the fears of royalists and moderates alike during this difficult era and serves to illustrate the tumultuous times of the Commonwealth. In this complex image, ax-wielding men (representing the Roundheads) chop down "the Royal Oak of Britain," England's longtime symbol of authority and tradition. The oak teeters, threatening to fall and take with it the Bible, the Magna Carta, and the traditional rule of law. Soldiers assist the woodsmen in destroying the tree and the order it represents. The pigs in the center symbolize the common people, being "fattened for the slaughter." Oliver Cromwell stands at the left, supervising the destruction. Below his feet is hell, although he is oblivious to how close he is to damnation. While this cartoon clearly vilifies Cromwell and all he embodied, it also reveals the disorder that had torn at England since the civil war began. Could the parliamentary forces under Oliver Cromwell resolve these fears and tensions?

Parliament seemed incapable of uniting the various constituents that demanded action after Charles's death. In 1653, when the House of Commons considered a proposal to dismantle Cromwell's large army, the general lost patience. He disbanded Parliament altogether, named himself "Lord Protector" of the Commonwealth of England, Scotland, and Ireland, and established a military dictatorship—the republic remained only as an ideal. Cromwell faced the same problems that had confronted Parliament and the king—foreign wars and religious struggles. A pious Puritan, Cromwell set out to make England the model of a Protestant land, banning horse races, cockfights, and even theater. He ultimately proved as intolerant of Anglicans as they had been of Puritans, and he alienated most of the population with his intrusive policies. The brief experiment with a rule purely by Parliament had failed, and a military dictatorship could not be popular in a land with such a tradition of participatory government.

Lord Protector

WHO HAS THE POWER TO RULE?

Charles's trial and execution, and the disorder that followed, did not resolve the issue of who had the ultimate power in England. In 1651, the English philosopher Thomas Hobbes (1588–1679) wrote a

FIGURE 13.9
The Royal Oak of Britain, 1649.

political treatise, *The Leviathan*, that offered an answer to this question in the form of a new theory of government. Perhaps shaken by the chaos of the civil war, Hobbes harbored a pessimistic view of human nature. He claimed that everyone was driven by a quest for power and that given the chance, people would try to exercise their power at the expense of their neighbors—even if it meant taking their property and their lives. In this "state of nature" where there was no controlling authority, Hobbes described human life as "solitary, poor, nasty, brutish and short." However, he held out a ray of hope. Humans, he explained, recognized their inability to live peacefully, so they created a "social contract" by which they erected a ruler above them. By this contract, subjects willingly surrendered their sovereignty to a ruler who, in turn, agreed to rule over them absolutely.

Thomas Hobbes

With this explanation, Hobbes reconciled the Protestant views of sovereignty—in which the people held the right to rule—with absolute monarchy, where the ruler (the king or "Lord Protector") possessed sole sovereignty. In the famous frontispiece of *The Leviathan*, shown in Figure 13.10, Hobbes visually portrayed the benefits of his system. The ruler is shown at the top wielding the sword and scepter of absolute power. Even more significant, he comprises all the people of the land—he is the "body politic." The king derives his power from his subjects, without whom he would not exist. However, with this delegated power, he presides over an orderly and peaceful countryside and village. Church, state, the army, and Parliament are all neatly ordered along the sides of the page. This tidy, comforting vision stands in stark contrast to the chaos shown in Figure 13.9 and reveals Hobbes's hope that absolute monarchy would guarantee peace in the land.

Hobbes omitted a key point in his thesis: Absolute rule is only as effective as the ruler. Although Cromwell preserved order (albeit while offending many), he failed to develop an institution that could maintain the Puritan republic. When he died in 1658, he named his son Richard his successor. However, the young man could not lead with the same energy and fervor that his father had shown. Under pressure from members of Parliament, Richard resigned, and the right to govern again returned to the people's representatives.

THE MONARCHY RESTORED, 1660–1688

Sobered by the chaos that had followed Charles's execution, Parliament decided to reinstate the monarchy. It invited Charles II (r. 1660–1685), son of the executed king, to resume the throne. Ships sailed from England to Holland to escort the king home from his place of exile. Among those in attendance when the king returned was Samuel Pepys (see Biography), an English diarist who became noted for the detailed accounts he kept of events from 1660 to 1669. According to Pepys, the people of England greeted their new king with much fanfare and excitement. Charles II came home to a restored monarchy that had all the luxury that his father had enjoyed—and all the problems that had plagued this troubled institution. (See Document 13.3 on page D13.2)

Samuel Pepys devoted several pages of his diary to Charles's coronation in 1661. "So glorious was the show with gold and silver," he wrote, "that we were

FIGURE 13.10
Frontispiece of *The Leviathan* by Thomas Hobbes, 1651.

not able to look at it, our eyes at last being so much overcome with it." Like most of his countrymen, Pepys drank ale with wild abandon during the celebration—the years of Puritan temperance seemed to melt away in a haze of drunkenness.

Yet, not everyone got caught up in the celebration. Former Cromwell supporters saw the Restoration in a very different light. John *John Bunyan* Bunyan (1628–1688), for example, who had fought with Cromwell, was imprisoned in 1660 for preaching against the Restoration. His original sentence of three months was extended to 12 years because he refused to stop preaching. After his release in 1672, he continued to preach and wrote his

masterpiece, *Pilgrim's Progress*, in 1678. Probably the most widely read book by an English author, *Pilgrim's Progress* tells of a hero named Christian and his search for salvation through an allegorical world. This tale of hope and confidence in the human power to prevail through times of tribulation was balanced by Bunyan's lesser-known work, *The Life and Death of Mr. Badman* (1680). In this allegory, Bunyan criticized the loose life of Restoration England by describing the journey of a man who goes straight to hell. Bunyan's works strongly suggested that the Restoration had definitely not solved the political struggles of England.

Charles II grappled with the same fiscal problems that had plagued James I and Charles I, but he had to face a Parliament that had proven its *Fiscal problems* strength during the civil wars. The king was bound by law to call Parliament at least every three years, and the members of Parliament had severely curtailed royal power over taxation. Like his predecessors, Charles needed money, and to buttress his revenues without the restrictions Parliament imposed, the new king tried to exert more control over the colonies in North America. He increased the customs duties permitted by the Navigation Acts (imposed in 1651) and fought a war with the Dutch in 1665. This conflict ended in a treaty that gave the English New York in exchange for Dutch control of Surinam in South America.

Charles's international dealings were hampered by disasters at home. In 1665, England experienced a plague of frightening intensity—70,000 *Plague and fire* people died in London alone. The following year, a devastating fire broke out in London, engulfing the city and destroying 13,000 dwellings and 87 churches, including the venerable St. Paul's Cathedral. After the fire had died out, Charles ordered the city rebuilt and hired the skilled architect Sir Christopher Wren to redesign the main buildings. Wren's masterpiece, the new St. Paul's Cathedral, still marks the London skyline.

In addition to these disasters, the issue of religion again came to the fore. Charles had Catholic sympathies, and to circumvent Parliament, he had several times turned to the Catholic king Louis XIV of France for help and money. The Protestant Parliament, wary of Charles's granting concessions to Catholics, passed the "Test Act" in 1673. The law required an oath of Protestant loyalties to prevent Catholics from holding public offices, but legislation could not affect the king's conscience, nor alleviate Parliament's fears of Catholicism. In 1685, Charles died after converting to Roman Catholicism on his deathbed.

Charles's successor, his brother James II (r. 1685–1688), was not able to avoid direct confrontation with the Protestant Parliament. A Catholic, James demanded in vain that Parliament repeal the Test Act, and he proceeded to place Catholics in high office in violation of Parliament's law. Many English feared that James would adopt Louis XIV's policies against Protestants and even try to institute absolute rule. They may well have been right, but the members of Parliament were not going to wait and see. In 1688, when James's Catholic wife produced a Catholic heir to the throne of England, leading members of Parliament took action.

THE GLORIOUS REVOLUTION

To preempt James, Parliamentary leaders turned to the king's eldest daughter, Mary, a Protestant and the wife of William of Orange of the Netherlands. William staunchly opposed the policies of the *William and Mary* Catholic Louis XIV, so both his politics and his religion suited the English Protestants. William gathered a fleet and an army of 14,000 men and landed in England in November 1688. He marched slowly and peacefully toward London, while most of the English population rallied to his side. Recalling Charles I's fate, James decided to flee to France "for the security of my person." Louis XIV received his Catholic counterpart with kindness.

The Irish Catholics did not welcome the new Protestant king. Indeed, they thought of James II as a Catholic hero, and Irish leaders conspired with James to help him retake his throne while the French king helped fund this enterprise. Early in his reign William led an army into Ireland and ruthlessly suppressed what he saw as Catholic treason. Abandoning both Ireland and his claim to the throne, James lived out his life in lavish exile in France, leaving the Irish to bear the brunt of William's wrath. The new king reduced Ireland to colonial status and offered new opportunity for English landlords to take possession of Irish Catholic lands. Irish anger toward the English festered and would grow, but William's victory was cheered in England.

William and Parliament turned to the immediate task of establishing the legitimacy of his kingship. Parliament decided that James's flight from England constituted an abdication of the throne. The sovereignty that, according to Hobbes, the people had surrendered to their king had been returned to *England's Bill of Rights* parliament, who now had the right to install a new monarch. Parliament determined to clarify its relationship with the king. As revealed in Document 13.4 (see page D13.4), in 1689 it passed a Bill of Rights firmly stating that kings were subject to the laws of the land, thus creating a constitutional monarchy—the triumph of constitutionalism. Within the Bill of Rights, William agreed to "deliver this kingdom from popery [Catholicism] and arbitrary power" and to preserve freedom of speech, election, and the rule of law. The bill secured the position of Protestantism in England by ruling that "no person embracing Catholicism or married to a Catholic is eligible to succeed to the throne." Through this bloodless "Glorious Revolution," Parliament had finally demonstrated that the power to rule rested with the people through their representatives, rather than absolutely with the king. After this, Parliament began to meet annually, which was a practical way to secure its authority.

ROYALISM RECONSIDERED: JOHN LOCKE

Many English men and women were proud of their bloodless "revolution" that so peacefully changed their monarch, but others were uncertain about the legality of this step. The English philosopher John Locke (1623–1704) wrote an influential political tract—*The Second Treatise of Government* (1690)—to justify "to the world [and] the people of England" the Revolution of 1688, and proclaim the legitimacy of William. Locke did much more—he articulated a new relationship between king and subjects that provided a theoretical framework for constitutional forms of government. Like Hobbes, Locke believed that power originally rested with the people and that citizens themselves established a monarchy to keep order. However, whereas Hobbes had said that the people turned over their sovereignty completely to the monarch, Locke claimed that they retained it but created a contract of mutual obligations with their ruler. Locke argued that if the king broke the contract, the people had the right to depose him and install a new monarch, just as Parliament had done during the Glorious Revolution.

Locke's political theories were not intended to support full democracies—in his time, the "people" meant only those who owned property. He did not

Biography

SAMUEL PEPYS (1633–1703)

▪ **Notice** that Pepys' diary shows how the political events of the day—the Glorious Revolution and the growing importance of Parliament—affected his life.

▪ **Consider** the effects of educational opportunities on the lives of seventeenth-century people.

Samuel Pepys was born in London on February 23, 1633, the fifth of 11 children. Only he and two of his siblings survived childhood. Samuel's father was a relatively modest tailor and his mother was the sister of a butcher. Nevertheless, the family had relatives who included landed gentry, lawyers, and a physician. The Pepyses were Puritans, and although Samuel uncharitably recalled his mother as "quarrelsome and feeble-minded" and his father as "always needing some kind of aid," the family did provide him with the educational opportunities he needed to succeed.

As a young boy, Pepys was sent to live with an uncle and attend the same grammar school where the young Oliver Cromwell had been educated. Samuel must have seemed a promising student, for when he was about 13 he returned to London to attend St. Paul's School, a stronghold of Puritanism and classical learning. He won scholarships to attend Cambridge University and received his bachelor's degree in 1654. After graduating, he found a job as secretary to a distant relative who had taken an important position in Cromwell's new Commonwealth.

A year later, Pepys married Elizabeth, the 15-year-old daughter of a French Protestant refugee. She brought no dowry to the marriage, though Samuel was probably drawn to her beauty—throughout his diary, he repeatedly made notes about attractive women. His domestic life proved stormy, but he wrote often about being pleased with his marriage during the more harmonious times in his household. Pepys complained that Elizabeth was untidy and that she mismanaged the household. For his part, Samuel was no model husband; he always kept his wife short of money and was relentlessly unfaithful to her. He recorded the details of his infidelities and of Elizabeth's pained reactions to them. Elizabeth died young and childless in 1669, and Samuel never remarried.

Enterprising Clerk, Member of Parliament, and Diarist

Through the late seventeenth century, Pepys was an active participant and a careful chronicler of the major events of the era. While still at Cambridge, he witnessed the execution of Charles I and supported the Commonwealth as a clerk.

---

intend for individuals, such as the landless Levellers, to threaten property owners. Nor did he view women as sharing in the popular sovereignty of the privileged social order. Locke's highly influential rhetoric, in which he claimed natural rights of "life, liberty, and property" actually applied to relatively few people in 1690. However, in time, his theory would broaden to form the basis for democracy as well as constitutional monarchy.

Parliament soon had the opportunity to exert its king-making authority once again. William and Mary died without an heir, so the crown went to James II's Protestant daughter, Anne. Queen Anne (r. 1701–1714) also died without an heir, whereby the Protestant Stuart dynasty evaporated. Parliament then passed the crown to George I (r. 1714–1727), a great-grandson of James I, who ruled the German principality of Hanover, introducing the

Hanover Dynasty

Pepys began his diary in 1660 and for nine years detailed the events of his times, both great and small. In this extraordinary text, we have an eyewitness account of the devastating plague that scourged London in 1665, followed by the great fire the year after. Pepys juxtaposed historical events with the most intimate details of his daily life, from the food he ate to the arguments he had with his wife. He stopped keeping his diary in 1669 because his eyesight was failing him.

Pepys took an active role in political life by working in the naval office. In 1685 he was even elected to the House of Commons. He continued to receive the benefits of royal patronage under the reigns of Charles II and James II, but the Glorious Revolution of 1688 caused his fortunes to change. He lost the parliamentary election in 1689, and in the following year he was arrested on suspicion that he supported the deposed James II. Pepys had always been more interested in observing political events rather than engaging passionately in them, and when he was released from prison he removed himself from political life. He spent the rest of his years reading, playing music, and exchanging letters with friends, including such eminent scholars as Isaac Newton. His last years were devoted to building a substantial library that he bequeathed at his death to his alma mater, where it still remains intact and unaltered. He died peacefully in 1703.

Pepys wrote his diary in a shorthand that was used by clerks in the seventeenth century; Newton used the same shorthand for taking his notes. The four-volume, handwritten, leatherbound diary written in a forgotten code lay ignored on the library shelves until the nineteenth century. Then, an undergraduate of the college took on the gigantic task of transcribing the diary (omitting the erotic passages) and it became an instant success. Modern editions of the complete diary continue to engage readers with its direct picture of seventeenth-century England. It has ensured that Samuel Pepys will not be forgotten. See Document 13.4 on page D13.4 for an excerpt of Pepys' diary.

FIGURE 13.11
J. Hayls, *Samuel Pepys*, 1666.

However, he must have harbored royalist sympathies, for his political career blossomed in 1660 with the Restoration. Pepys accompanied the fleet that escorted the new monarch back to England, and his contacts on that journey ensured him a position suited to his many talents.

Hanoverian dynasty to England. This peaceful transition demonstrated once and for all that the struggle for sovereignty in England was over—Parliament ruled.

THE NETHERLANDS: THE SOVEREIGNTY OF LOCAL AUTHORITY

The English nobles asserted their rights over the king by exercising their authority through a parliament that ruled over a highly centralized government. This struggle created a strong constitutional monarchy that preserved popular sovereignty while creating a state that would prove highly stable. Another way for people to preserve their sovereignty was to resist a strong central government in order to strengthen local institutions. In the seventeenth century, the Netherlands developed this political structure that also gave power to the people instead of to absolute rulers. They instituted another form of constitutionalism that structured the government around consent of the propertied.

When the Low Countries split in 1609, the southern Catholic regions remained subject to the absolutist monarch, Philip III of Spain. Map 13.5 shows the division of the Low Countries in 1609. The Spanish Netherlands of the south (now Belgium) formed a buffer between the United Provinces of the north and the divine right monarchy of France. In the United Provinces,

The United Provinces

which became largely Calvinist after the wars with Catholic Spain, a Protestant state developed that successfully resisted any attempts at royal absolutism. The United Provinces—also known as the Dutch Republic—became a republic in which sovereignty remained with the people and power stayed at the local level. Figure 13.12 shows how little central authority there was and how this authority was effectively controlled by the provincial assemblies. Document 13.5 on page D13.5 provides a description of the governmental structure of the Dutch Republic. The 1648 Treaty of Westphalia that ended the Thirty Years' War (see Chapter 11) formally recognized the Republic of the United Provinces.

What were the special circumstances that led the Netherlands to develop and maintain this strong sense of local sovereignty when other areas of Europe were moving to centralized governments? In large part, such political independence was facilitated by prosperity. The seventeenth century has been called the "golden age" of the United Provinces, for this small region was a tremendous European and colonial power. Amsterdam became the commercial and financial center of Europe as ships brought huge quantities of herring from the North Sea, as well as sugar, tobacco, glass, and many other items from around the world, through the bustling port. Figure 13.13, a contemporary painting of busy merchants and shoppers in the central square of seventeenth-century Amsterdam, reveals the prosperity of this wealthy city.

Dutch prosperity

The Dutch also grew rich from their activities as major slave traders in the New World. The population of Amsterdam grew from about 30,000 people in 1570 to 200,000 by 1660, and the growth was testimony to the wealth and opportunities people saw there. Its financial importance was secured in 1609 by the foundation of the Exchange Bank of Amsterdam, the greatest public bank in northern Europe. Europeans were astonished by the prosperity and enterprise of the Dutch, and they recognized that there was an intimate link between prosperity and freedom.

The Dutch had other elements that contributed to their resistance of absolutism. The Dutch aristocracy was not as wealthy as that of England or France, for example. Their wealth lay more in commerce than in land, so the aristocracy had more in common with the merchants of their land than they did with the

THINKING ABOUT GEOGRAPHY

MAP 13.5 *The United Provinces and the Spanish Netherlands, 1609*

This map shows the location of the Netherlands in Europe and its division into two separate states. ◼ **Notice** the scale of this map. **Consider** how small the United Provinces were. **What** about their location contributed to their wealth and importance in the seventeenth century? ◼ **Notice** the proximity of the Catholic Spanish Netherlands to France. **Consider** how this region might have served as a buffer for the Protestant United Provinces.

landed gentry in England or with the nobility at the court of Versailles. Furthermore, in the United Provinces, the Protestant faith cultivated an ideology of moderation—rather than the aristocratic excess that marked the nobility of other states. That is not to say that the seventeenth-century United Provinces espoused notions of egalitarian democracy—the nobility were as interested in trying to increase their power as those of other countries. They were just not able to exert much centralized control over the prosperous, Protestant residents that were the wonder of Europe.

Overall, the Dutch exhibited an unusual degree of religious toleration for their time. They even allowed *Religious toleration* Catholics and Jews to practice their religions, a policy that encouraged religious refugees to flock to the Netherlands from all over Europe. These refugees greatly enriched the cultural and economic life of the republic. Not only did the United Provinces attract intellectuals, such as René Descartes from France and John Locke from England, but the open-minded assemblies stimulated the spread of ideas through the press. The United Provinces became a leading center for book publishing and transmitted ideas, even revolutionary ones, all over Europe. In 1649, for example, an anonymous pamphlet published in the Netherlands attacked Cromwell's government for not supporting the ideas of the Levellers. The pamphlet called for an "equality of goods and lands" and condemned the government that "hangs a poor man if he do steal, when they have wrongfully taken from him all his maintenance."

The refugees streaming into the Netherlands included some destitute travelers and in some ways burdened the small country. The Dutch, however, generously assisted the needy, who never sank to the same depths of hardship that faced the poor in many other European cities. In his brief stay in the Netherlands, Samuel Pepys recorded in his diary the provisions the Dutch made for the poor. He observed a guesthouse, "where it was very pleasant to see what neat preparation there is for the poor." He further noted that there were special entertainment taxes to raise money for the needy.

The wealthy middle classes treated themselves well also. For example, they commissioned paintings that depicted their unique way of life. The Dutch artist Jan

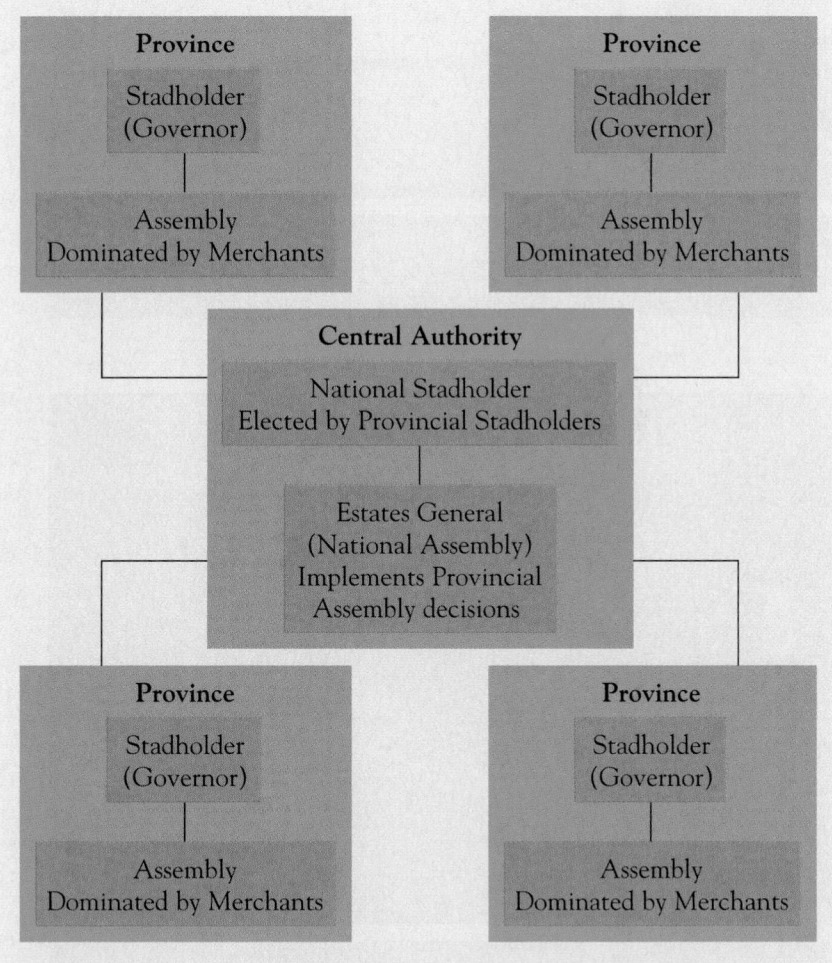

FIGURE 13.12

Governmental structure of the Dutch United Provinces.

FIGURE 13.13
Jacob van der Ulft, Dam Square in Amsterdam, 1659.

FIGURE 13.14
Rembrandt van Rijn, *Syndics of the Cloth Guild.*

Vermeer (see Chapter 12) was one of several whose talents flourished in the free Dutch environment. Even more celebrated was the Dutch artist Rembrandt van Rijn (1606–1669), whose brilliant use of light and forceful expressiveness made him among the greatest of western European painters.

In the painting *Syndics of the Cloth Guild* (Figure 13.14) Rembrandt portrays the serious, successful merchants who had been chosen to manage the wealthy guild. The artist captures the proud intensity with which they work over a book on the table. In the uniformity in their clothing, they stand in striking contrast to the man in Figure 13.7 on page 463, who boasts luxurious designs and fabrics that set him apart from people precisely like these successful syndics. Rembrandt offered this painting to the cloth guild in thanks for their charity—the painter, who had fallen on hard times, needed coal to heat his house for the winter, and the cloth guild had provided it.

The preeminence of the Dutch in the seventeenth century began to wane by the beginning of the next century. The economies of England and France had gathered strength both in Europe and abroad and encroached on the commercial empire forged by the Dutch. Yet the two geographically small countries of England and the Netherlands had contributed much to the political development of the West. Both established the sovereignty of the people through constitutionalism—England through Parliament, and the Netherlands through local autonomy. For all their tremendous impact for the future, at the opening of the eighteenth century both nations seemed hardly whispers in a Europe dominated by strong monarchs proclaiming a divine right to rule.

For upper-crust members of Western societies, the seventeenth century was a period of both comfort and struggle. The comfort came from these elites' continued dominance. From the beginning to the end of the century, they held most of the riches, status, and power. Those below them sometimes revolted, but the real threats came from competing colleagues and the monarch above. The efforts by monarchs to increase their power, to become "absolute" in both theory and practice, sparked intense struggles within states. In some places, such as France, Prussia, and Russia, strong monarchs offering order and stability won. In other places, such as Poland, England, and the Netherlands, powerful nobles—sometimes allied with commoners—overcame kings.

For the vast majority who toiled the fields, the period offered struggle without much comfort. In western Europe, demands from expanding central governments for taxes and conscripts only aggravated the hardships wrought by unusually bad harvests and disease. In eastern Europe, landowning nobles added to these problems by burdening peasants under an increasingly heavy yoke of serfdom.

Thus the structure of this hierarchical society may have loosened enough for some people in western Europe to improve their lot. However, that structure only tightened in eastern Europe. For all of Europe, war, revolt, and even revolution shook societies without breaking the traditional hierarchies. Nevertheless, some traditions started to crumble. Important changes in science and thought were already afoot that would soon transform the intellectual foundations of Western society.

REVIEW, ANALYZE, AND ANTICIPATE

REVIEW THE PREVIOUS CHAPTER

Chapter 11—"Alone Before God"—examines the Reformation, which shattered the unity of Western Christendom, and the entwined religious and dynastic wars that followed. Chapter 12—"Faith, Fortune, and Fame"—told how several European powers expanded overseas during this same period and grew rich from the commerce developed in their colonies.

1. *Analyze how the religious divisions and wars of the sixteenth and seventeenth centuries lay the groundwork for both the growth of absolutism in France and central Europe as well as the struggle against it in England and the Netherlands.*

2. *In what ways might the competition for overseas empires and the commerce that resulted have affected the power of central governments and their responsibilities? How might the Netherlands' political structure have contributed to its commercial expansion?*

ANALYZE THIS CHAPTER

Chapter 13—"The Struggle for Survival and Sovereignty"—describes how kings and nobles battled for power, the resolutions of those struggles, and their impact on the millions of people outside the elites.

1. *Analyze the ways monarchs tried to increase their power.*

2. *What groups opposed the increase in monarchical power, and what political theories were developed to support their positions?*

3. *In what ways might the term "absolutism" also apply to the Mughal emperors?*

4. *How do you explain why in some areas monarchs won the battle for sovereignty, whereas in others they lost?*

5. *Describe the struggles peasants throughout Europe faced during the seventeenth century. How did their conditions differ in western and eastern Europe?*

ANTICIPATE THE NEXT CHAPTER

Chapter 14—"A New World of Reason and Reform" —examines the changing intellectual foundations of the West.

TIMELINE: A CLOSER LOOK

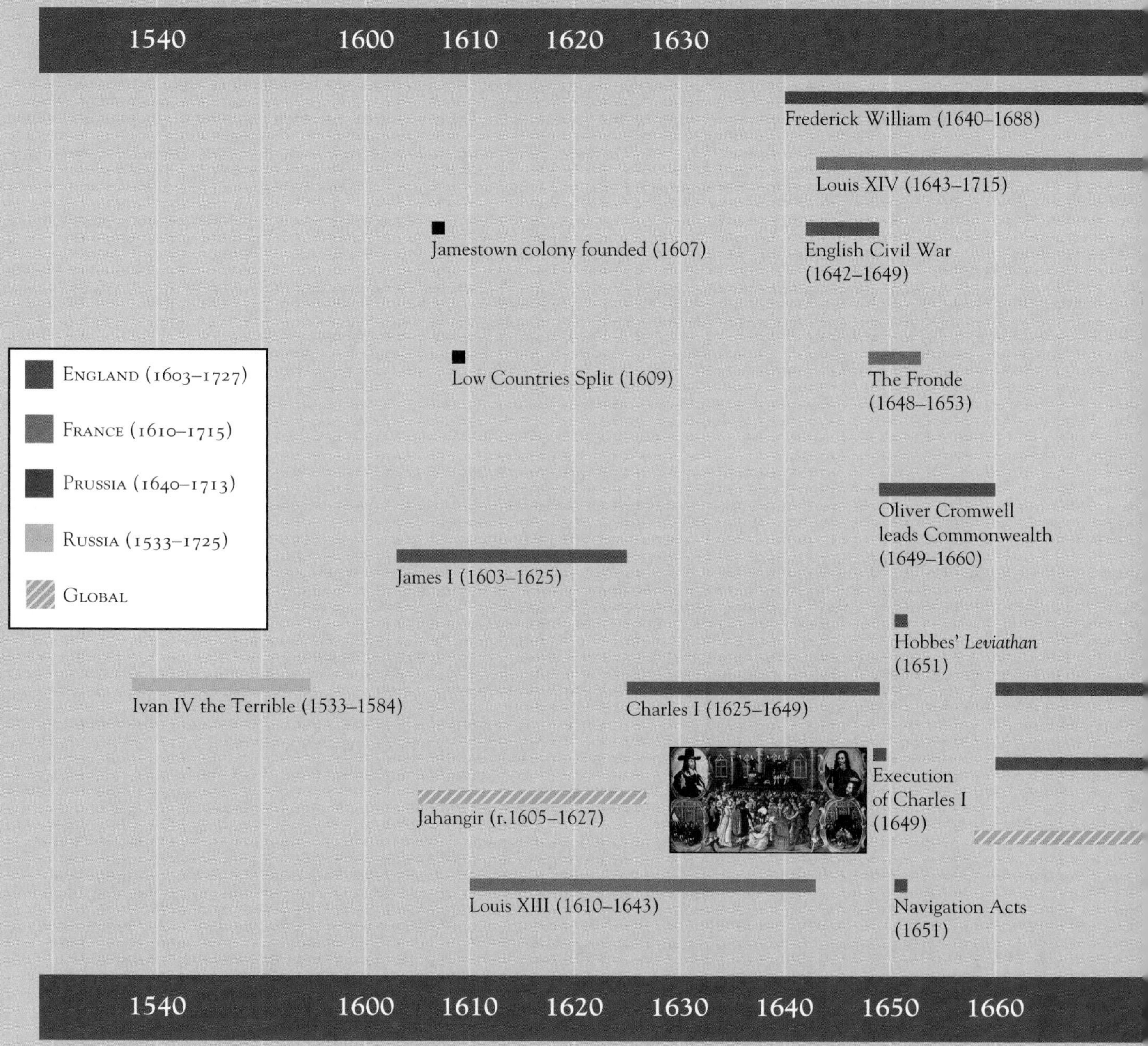

1540	1600	1610	1620	1630

Frederick William (1640–1688)

Louis XIV (1643–1715)

■ Jamestown colony founded (1607)

English Civil War
(1642–1649)

ENGLAND (1603–1727)

FRANCE (1610–1715)

PRUSSIA (1640–1713)

RUSSIA (1533–1725)

GLOBAL

■ Low Countries Split (1609)

The Fronde
(1648–1653)

Oliver Cromwell
leads Commonwealth
(1649–1660)

James I (1603–1625)

Hobbes' *Leviathan*
(1651)

Ivan IV the Terrible (1533–1584)

Charles I (1625–1649)

Execution
of Charles I
(1649)

Jahangir (r.1605–1627)

Louis XIII (1610–1643)

Navigation Acts
(1651)

1540	1600	1610	1620	1630	1640	1650	1660

1. What kinds of intellectual changes do you think might undermine the traditional social and political order during the seventeenth and eighteenth centuries? Why?

2. What groups and institutions are most likely to be threatened by or resist intellectual changes? Why?

BEYOND THE CLASSROOM

STRESSES IN TRADITIONAL SOCIETY

Braudel, Fernand. *Civilization and Capitalism: The Structures of Everyday Life*. New York: Harper & Row, 1981. An

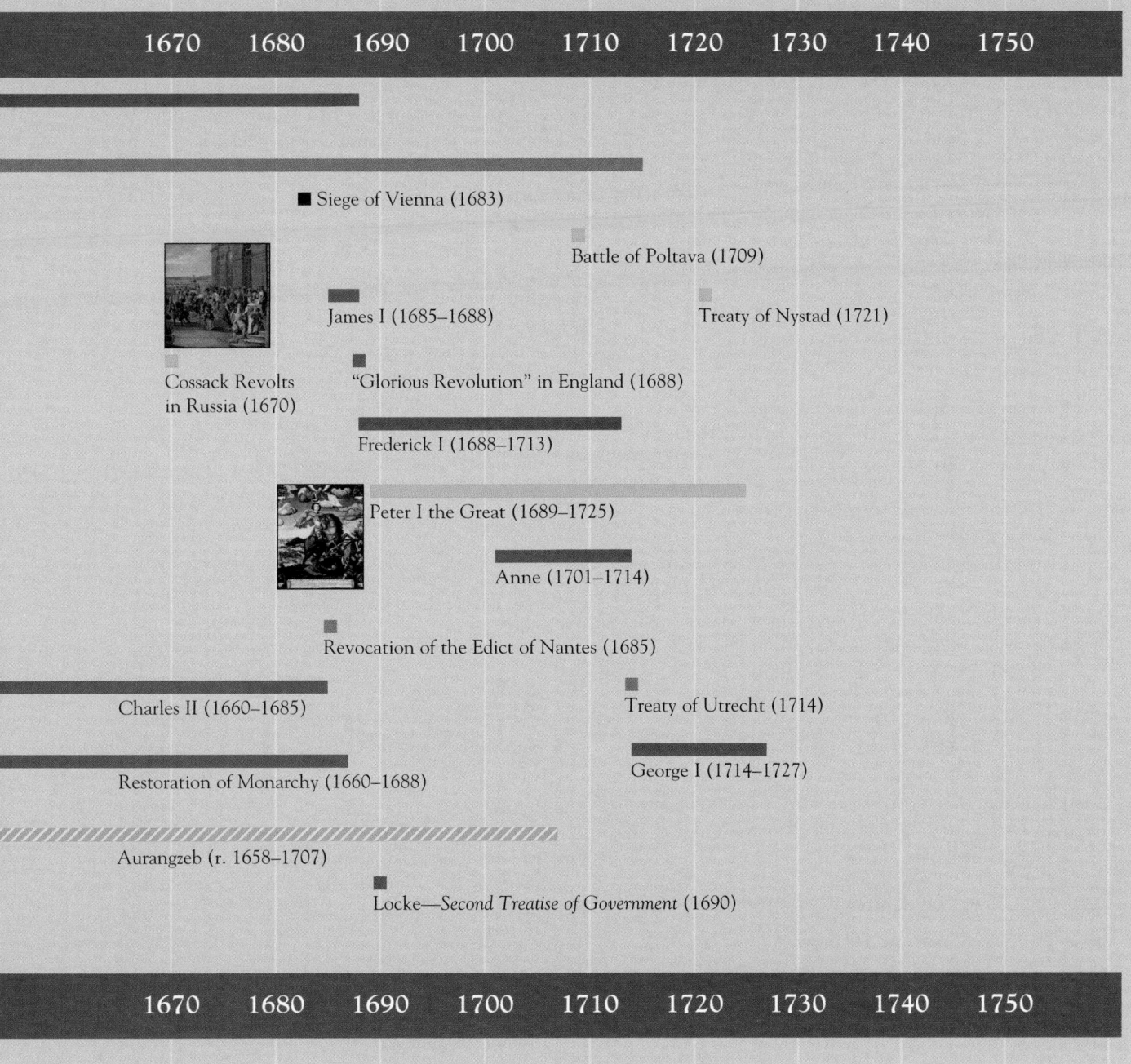

| 1670 | 1680 | 1690 | 1700 | 1710 | 1720 | 1730 | 1740 | 1750 |

■ Siege of Vienna (1683)

Battle of Poltava (1709)

James I (1685–1688)

Treaty of Nystad (1721)

Cossack Revolts
in Russia (1670)

"Glorious Revolution" in England (1688)

Frederick I (1688–1713)

Peter I the Great (1689–1725)

Anne (1701–1714)

Revocation of the Edict of Nantes (1685)

Charles II (1660–1685)

Treaty of Utrecht (1714)

Restoration of Monarchy (1660–1688)

George I (1714–1727)

Aurangzeb (r. 1658–1707)

Locke—*Second Treatise of Government* (1690)

| 1670 | 1680 | 1690 | 1700 | 1710 | 1720 | 1730 | 1740 | 1750 |

excellent survey by an important historian that details the transformations in economic and social history.

Bush, Michael. *Noble Privilege*. New York: Holmes & Meier, 1983. Analyzes the role of the nobility in the seventeenth century.

Chartier, Roger, ed. *A History of Private Life, Vol. III: Passions of the Renaissance*. Cambridge, MA: Harvard University Press, 1989. Part of a fine series that describes the creation of the sphere of private life.

Gottlieb, Beatrice. *The Family in the Western World from the Black Death to the Industrial Age*. Oxford: Oxford University Press, 1994. A thorough survey of the transformations in family life.

ROYAL ABSOLUTISM IN FRANCE

Bercé, Yves-Marie. *The Birth of Absolutism*. London: Macmillan, 1996. A solid examination of French absolutism from the reign of Louis XIV to 1789.

Campbell, Peter R. *Louis XIV, 1661–1715*. London: Longman, 1993. A brief examination of the subject with supporting documents and a good bibliography.

Muchembled, Robert. *Popular Culture and Elite Culture in France, 1400–1750*. Baton Rouge, LA: Louisiana State University Press, 1985. Examines popular culture and the means by which higher authorities attempted to destroy it.

THE STRUGGLE FOR SOVEREIGNTY IN EASTERN EUROPE

Bérenger, Jean. *A History of the Habsburg Empire, 1273–1700*. London: Longman, 1990. A useful survey, particularly for this period.

Hughes, Lindsey. *Russia in the Age of Peter the Great*. New Haven, CT: Yale University Press, 1998. The most recent study of this important figure.

Kirby, David G. *Northern Europe in the Early Modern Period: The Baltic World, 1492–1772*. London: Longman, 1990. A good survey of the region during this period.

Vierhaus, Rudolf. *Germany in the Age of Absolutism*. New York: Cambridge University Press, 1988. An informative discussion of the German states during the seventeenth century.

GLOBAL CONNECTIONS

 Richards, John F. *The Mughal Empire*. Cambridge: Cambridge University Press, 1993. A solid, useful survey of Mughal history.

THE TRIUMPH OF CONSTITUTIONALISM

Coward, Barry. *The Stuart Age: A History of England, 1603–1714*. White Plains, NY: Longman Publishing Group, 1995. A readable and balanced narrative of the whole course of the history of England.

van Deursen, Arie Theodorus. *Plain Lives in a Golden Age: Popular Culture, Religion, and Society in Seventeenth-Century Holland*. Trans. M. Ultree. New York: Cambridge University Press, 1991. A fascinating analysis of how laborers, peasants, and sailors made their living.

Durston, Christopher, ed. *Culture of English Puritanism, 1560–1700*. New York: Saint Martin's Press, 1996. A look into the lives and times of the English Puritans.

Fraser, Antonia. *The Weaker Vessel*. New York: Alfred A. Knopf, 1984. A detailed, illustrated, and comprehensive study of women in seventeenth-century England.

Gaunt, Peter. *Oliver Cromwell*. Cambridge, MA: Blackwell Publishers, 1995. A good study on the life and career of the Lord Protector.

Geyl, Pieter. *History of the Low Countries: Episodes and Problems*. New York: St. Martin's Press, 1964. A collection of essays by a preeminent scholar that illuminates this important period in the Low Countries.

Hill, Christopher. *A Nation of Change and Novelty: Radical Politics, Religion, and Literature in Seventeenth-Century England*. London: Routledge, 1990. The standard history of the revolution by an eminent historian.

Miller, John. *Restoration and the England of Charles II*, 2nd ed. White Plains, NY: Longman Publishing Group, 1997. Clarifies the complex issues of the major political and religious themes surrounding the Restoration.

Sharpe, Kevin. *Culture and Politics in Early Stuart England*. Stanford, CA: Stanford University Press, 1994. A revisionist look at the culture and politics in England at this time.

Unfamiliar words? See our Glossary at the back for pronunciation and definitions.

See our Web Page at www.mhhe.com/sherman2updated for additional readings, map exercises, practice quizzes, and more activities.

For quiz questions that tie the book to the videos and additional primary sources, please go to the Primary Source Investigator CD.

Documents

DOCUMENT 13.1

Bishop Bossuet Justifies Monarchical Absolutism

In their efforts to acquire as much power as possible, European monarchs and their supporters sought justifications for monarchical rights. One of the most explicit and influential justifications was written and preached by Jacques Bénigne Bossuet (1627–1704), a French bishop and tutor to the son of Louis XIV. In the following excerpt from his Politics Drawn from the Very Words of Holy Scripture, *Bossuet argues for the divine right of kings.*

■ **Investigate the Document**

What, *according to Bossuet, are the nature and properties of royal authority?* **How** *does Bossuet justify the various qualities of royal authority?* **How** *absolute is the power of kings?*

Article I

There are four characters or qualities essential to royal authority: First, royal authority is sacred; second, it is paternal; third, it is absolute; fourth, it is ruled by reason. . . .

Article II

Royal authority is sacred.

Proposition 1

God established kings as his ministers and rules peoples by them.

We have already seen that all power comes from God. "The prince," St. Paul adds, "is the minister of God to thee for good. But if thou do that which is evil, be afraid; for he beareth not the sword in vain; for he is the minister of God, a revenger to execute wrath upon him that doeth evil."

Thus princes act as ministers of God, and as his lieutenants on earth. It is by them that he exercises his rule. . . .

Proposition 2

The person of kings is sacred.

It thus appears that the person of kings is sacred and that to make an attempt on their lives is a sacrilege. . . .

The title of Christ is given to kings; and they are everywhere called christs, or the anointed of the lord. . . .

Proposition 3

The prince must provide for the needs of the people.

It is a royal right to provide for the needs of the people. He who undertakes it at the expense of the prince undertakes royalty: this is why it has been established. The obligation to care for the people is the foundation of all the rights that sovereigns have over their subjects. . . .

Article I

The royal authority is absolute.

. . . The prince is by his office the father of his people; he is placed by his grandeur above all petty interests; even more: all his grandeur and his natural interests are that the people shall be conserved, for once the people fail him he is no longer prince. There is thus nothing better than to give all the power of the state to him who has the greatest interest in the conservation and greatness of the state itself. . . .

Proposition 4

Kings are not by this above the laws. . . .

Kings therefore are subject like any others to the equity of the laws both because they must be just and because they owe to the people the example of protecting justice; but they are not subject to the penalties of the laws; or, as theology puts it, they are subject to the laws, not in terms of its coactive power but in terms of its directive power.

Source: J. B. Bossuet, *Politics Drawn from the Very Words of Holy Scripture* (1709), in Brian Tierney and Joan Scott, *Western Societies, A Documentary History,* Volume II (New York: McGraw-Hill, 1984), pp. 11–13.

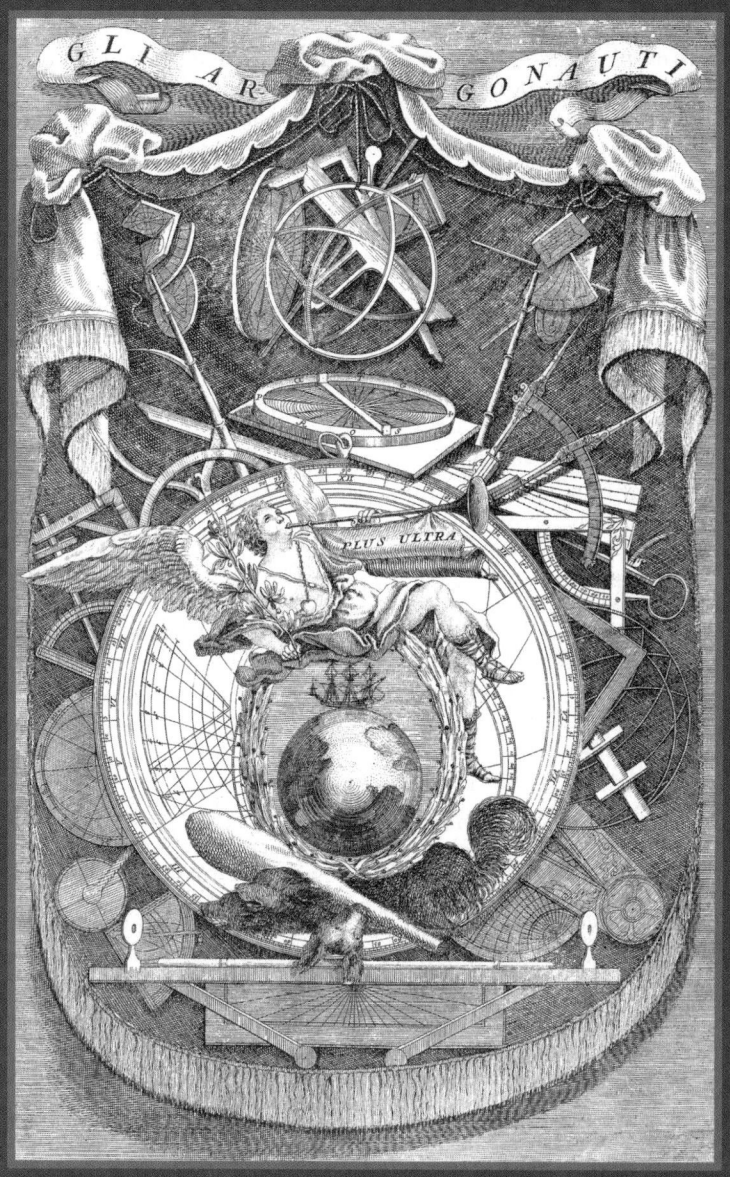

Frontispiece to Marco Vincenzo Coronelli's Atlas, 1691

In this frontispiece from an atlas, a globe and ship occupy center stage and represent the West's exploration of the world. Just above, the banner of a trumpeting angel reads, "Yet farther"—words that contrast sharply with the traditional medieval expression "No farther." Drawings of the numerous instruments that characterized the new age of exploration and science occupy the periphery of the image.

CHAPTER 14

A New World of Reason and Reform

The Scientific Revolution and the Enlightenment, 1600–1800

STUDY • The traditional worldview • The modern scientific worldview • Spreading science • The Enlightenment. 🌐 NOTICE the connections between the scientific revolution and the Enlightenment.

In 1655, French scientist Blaise Pascal (1623–1662) retired from his studies and began recording his thoughts in writing. "Man is but a reed, the most feeble thing in nature; but he is a thinking reed," he wrote. "All our dignity consists, then, in thought . . . by thought I comprehend the world." Pascal's words hint at the changes emerging in scholars' thinking about ideas, the world, and the place of humans in it.

We can detect more clues about these changes in the artwork on page 482. The 1691 world atlas itself, published by the accomplished Venetian mapmaker and mathematician Marco Coronelli (1650–1718), echoes the overseas expansion of Europe, already two centuries old. It also reveals the underlying culture of the Renaissance, which stressed learning and exploration through reading and art. Coronelli chose this illustration to open his new atlas. With the images of a ship, the earth, scientific instruments, and the provocative phrasing "Yet farther," he declared the end of limits to the search for knowledge. The entire illustration suggests a people proudly using science to fuel their growing power—over other peoples as well as nature itself.

Buoyed by the accumulation of scientific discoveries, this optimism about the power of thought and the search for knowledge grew and spread throughout the West during the eighteenth century. Widening circles of intellectuals and the reading public learned about the new ways of thinking being applied to all fields, from politics and religion to economics and criminology. Despite resistance from church and state, this dawning of what became known as the Age of Reason would gather strength, filter down through the ranks of society, and form the intellectual foundation for life in the modern West. Certainly the West was not unique in reasoning about the world. In the centuries preceding Europe's Renaissance, the Chinese had made many scholarly and scientific advances. The Arabs had not only prized learning and science, but also had provided Europeans with tools such as translations of Greek science and Arabic numerals that were essential for Europe's scientists. On the other hand, by the sixteenth century most European scientists had university educations, whereas non-Western civilizations lacked institutions comparable to the medieval universities in places such as Bologna, Paris, and Oxford. Moreover, during the seventeenth and eighteenth centuries, the Islamic, Chinese, Japanese, and other civilizations of the world declined to question their traditional ways. Only westerners challenged the standard assumptions of their civilization. The power and attitudes that the West gained from this intellectual exploration helped redefine Western civilization and distinguish it from the non-Western world.

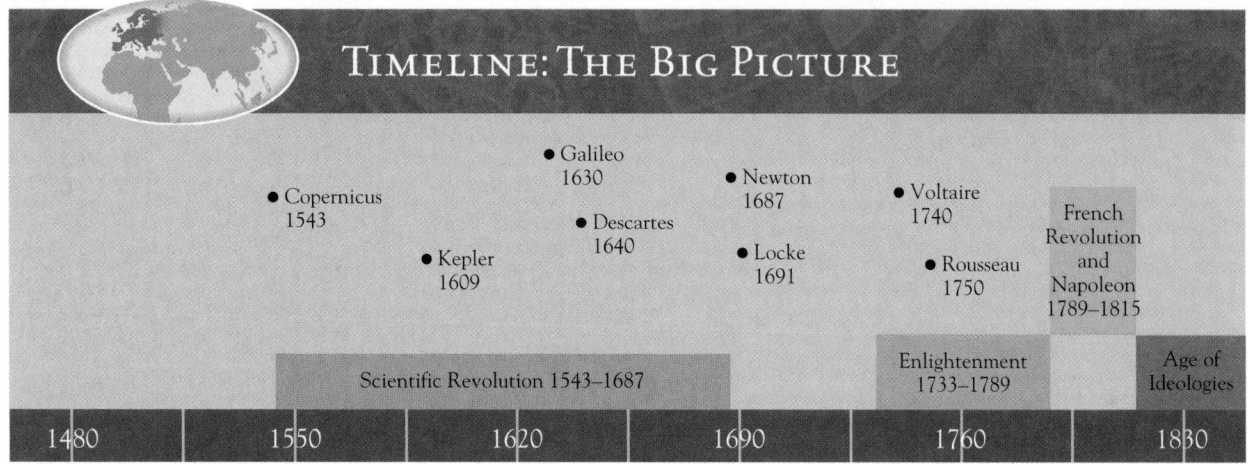

TIMELINE: THE BIG PICTURE

● Galileo
1630

● Newton
1687

● Copernicus
1543

● Voltaire
1740

● Descartes
1640

French
Revolution
and
Napoleon
1789–1815

● Kepler
1609

● Locke
1691

● Rousseau
1750

Scientific Revolution 1543–1687

Enlightenment
1733–1789

Age of
Ideologies

1480   1550   1620   1690   1760   1830

Questioning Truth and Authority

On June 22, 1633, the well-known Italian scientist Galileo Galilei (1564–1642) knelt in a Roman convent before the cardinals who served as judges of the Inquisition. The cardinals informed Galileo that he was "vehemently suspected of heresy." They also showed him the customary instruments of torture, though they did not use them. Next, they ordered him to deny "the false opinion that the sun is the center of the universe and immovable, and that the earth is not the center of the same"—views that Galileo had supported in a book he published the previous year. Threatened with being tried and burned as a heretic, Galileo had to denounce his views as heresy. The court and papacy sentenced Galileo to house arrest in Florence for the rest of his life and forbade him to publish on the topic again. Nevertheless, Galileo would not change his mind. The sequence of events leading to Galileo's trial and conviction is a story of its own, but the conflict lay at the core of a major development of the age: the scientific revolution.

THE OLD VIEW

Until the sixteenth century, most European scholars shared the standard medieval understanding of the physical nature of the earth and the universe. This understanding was based on a long legacy stretching back to the views of the fourth-century B.C. Greek philosopher Aristotle. His ideas had been modified in the second century A.D. by Ptolemy of Alexandria

and then passed on through Byzantine and Arab scholars to medieval European thinkers. After the thirteenth century, Europeans translated Aristotle's works into Latin and merged his thinking with Christian ideas about the universe.

According to this Christian medieval understanding, illustrated in the woodcut in Figure 14.1, the earth rested at the center of an unchanging universe. *The Earth-centered universe* Around it in ascending order rose the perfect spheres of air, fire, the sun, the planets, and the stars (the "firmament"), with God (the "prime mover") just beyond. The signs of the zodiac are recorded on one band in the illustration, revealing the importance of astrology. Westerners accounted for the succession of day and night by explaining that this finite universe rotated in precise circles around the earth once every 24 hours. The heavenly abode of angels consisted of pure matter, and the earthly home of humans was made of changeable, corrupt matter. This universe was clear, finite, and satisfyingly focused on the earthly center of God's concern.

Common sense supported this worldview. A glance at the sky confirmed that the sun and stars indeed circled around the earth each day. Under foot, the earth felt motionless. To careful observers, the motion of planets, whose position often changed, was more perplexing. To explain this mystery, Ptolemy and others had modified their theories, concluding that planets moved in small, individual orbits as they traveled predictably around the earth. People had lived by the wisdom of the ancients and authoritative interpretations of the Bible for centuries. Accordingly, investigation of the physical universe generally consisted of making deductions from these long-accepted guides.

UNDERMINING THE OLD VIEW

During the fifteenth and sixteenth centuries, new problems began undermining this traditional view. Authorities of all kinds—including Aristotle—came into question during the Renaissance. Some of this questioning stemmed from the Renaissance search for classical writings, which led scholars to discover and read the works of Greek authorities who contradicted Aristotle. Neoplatonism, based on the ideas of Plato, stressed the belief that one should search beyond appearances for true knowledge; truth about both nature and God could be found in abstract reasoning and be best expressed by mathematics. Neoplatonic Hermetic doctrine provided especially powerful alternatives to Aristotelian thought.

According to Hermetic doctrine, based on writings mistakenly attributed to Hermes Trismegistus (supposedly an ancient Egyptian priest), all matter *Hermetic doctrine* contained the divine spirit, which humans ought to seek to understand. Among many scholars, this doctrine stimulated intense interest in botany, chemistry, metallurgy, and other studies that promised to help people unlock the secrets of nature. The Hermetic approach also held that mathematical harmonies helped explain the divine spirit and represented a crucial pathway to understanding God's physical world. This approach encouraged scholars to use mathematics and to measure, map, and quantify nature. Moreover, Hermetic doctrine also held that the sun was the most important agency for transmission of the divine spirit, and thus rightly occupied the center of the universe. Finally, these beliefs fostered the idea of the natural magician who could unleash the powers of nature through alchemy (the study of how to purify and transform metals, such as turning common minerals into gold), astrology (the study of how stars affect people), and magic. Scholars often saw no distinction between seeking to understand the harmony, oneness, and spiritual aspects of the natural world and what we would call scientific observation and experimentation. Although Hermetic doctrine often proved not useful, all these ideas encouraged investigators to question traditionally accepted knowledge.

Figure 14.2, an illustration from a book on alchemy by the German Heinrich Khunrath shows these close connections between spiritual beliefs and the "science" or "Hermetic art" of alchemy. At the

FIGURE 14.1
The medieval view of the universe, 1559.

left, the author prays in a small chapel. Lettering on the drapery of the chapel states, "When we attend strictly to our work, God himself will help us." At the center, musical instruments and a pair of scales rest on a table, representing the links among music, harmony, and number so characteristic in alchemy. The inscription on the table reads, "Sacred music disperses sadness in evil spirits." On the floor lie containers and other apparatus used to mix materials, and at the upper right are flasks and other storage containers.

In addition to new ideas and beliefs, geographic exploration during the Renaissance also upset traditional assumptions. The discovery of the *Exploration* New World, for example, disproved Ptolemaic geography. Furthermore, overseas voyages stimulated demand for new instruments and precise

certainties, sixteenth- and seventeenth-century scholars hoped to establish new, even sounder certainties and thereby regain a sense of mastery over nature.

Developing a Modern Scientific View

Even with these rumblings of change, no sudden breakthrough cleared away the centuries-old understanding of nature. Most scientific work still proceeded slowly, as did scholarly and public acceptance of its findings. Investigators had to demonstrate the effectiveness of their new methods again and again to convince even their colleagues. Indeed, few scholars suggested a wholesale rejection of traditional authorities; most simply chipped away at old notions. By the end of the seventeenth century, however, an entirely new scientific view of reality, initiated by just a handful of scholars, had replaced the traditional view. To understand this startling shift, we need to trace developments in astronomy, physics, and scientific methodology.

ASTRONOMY AND PHYSICS: FROM COPERNICUS TO NEWTON

During the sixteenth and seventeenth centuries, astronomy and physics attracted the most systematic attention from scholars. Researchers in these fields became particularly dissatisfied with the inability of Aristotelian theory to explain, simply and efficiently, careful observations and mathematical calculations of the stars. The Ptolemaic system for predicting planetary movements seemed overly complex and cumbersome to these scholars. Their findings would dramatically alter westerners' perceptions of nature and of the earth's place in the universe. As the English poet John Donne complained in 1611, "New philosophy calls all in doubt."

Nicolaus Copernicus (1473–1543), a Polish clergyman with an interest in astronomy, astrology, mathematics, and church law, took the first steps in this intellectual adventure. Like so many other

measurements for navigation. This demand, in turn, encouraged research, especially in astronomy and mathematics.

Finally, the recently invented printing press enabled even out-of-favor scholars to publish their find-*The printing press* ings, which spread new ideas and discoveries even further. Renaissance rulers supported all these efforts in hopes of gaining prestige as well as practical tools for war, construction, and mining. Church authorities did the same at times, especially backing research in astronomy in the hopes of improving the calendar to date Easter more accurately.

Like the Renaissance, the Reformation also unleashed forces that provoked the questioning of long-held views. Most researchers had religious motives for their work, though those motives were not necessarily grounded in tradition. In particular, they yearned for insights into the perfection of God's universe. As we read in Chapter 11, the Reformation shattered confidence in religious authorities. By upsetting hallowed northern European scholars, he crossed the Alps to study in an Italian university. There he became influenced by the rediscovery of Greek scholarship, Neoplatonism, and the Hermetic doctrine. Copernicus sought a simpler mathematical formulation to explain how the universe operated. His search convinced him that the earth was *not* at the center of the universe. Instead, he believed that the sun "sits upon a royal throne" in that location, "ruling his children, the planets which circle around him." Moreover, Copernicus concluded that the earth was not stationary: "What appears to be a motion of the sun is in truth a motion of the earth." According to Copernicus, the earth moved in perfect, "divine" circles around the sun, as did other bodies in the universe. Day passed into night because the earth turned on its axis. Figure 14.3 shows this view of the universe. At the center is the sun, circled by the earth ("this globe of mortality") and other planets, all bounded by an infinity of stars ("fixed" and "immovable") and the heavens ("the palace of happiness . . . the habitat for the elect"). This change from an Earth-centered (geocentric) to a sun-centered (heliocentric) universe would become known as the Copernican revolution.

Nicolaus Copernicus

Copernicus worked on his heliocentric model of the universe for almost 25 years. However, fearing ridicule and disapproval from the clergy, he waited until 1543—what became the year of his death—to publish it. Few people outside a limited circle of scholars knew of his views, and even fewer accepted them. Nevertheless, Catholic and Protestant authorities who were wedded to the Earth-centered system soon recognized the threat to the Christian conception of the universe that these ideas represented. They denounced the Copernican system as illogical, unbiblical, and unsettling to the Christian faith. One Protestant associate of Martin Luther complained that "certain men . . . have concluded that the earth moves. . . . It is want of honesty and decency to assert such notions publicly. . . . It is part of a good mind to accept the truth as revealed by God and to acquiesce in it."

Still, Copernicus's thinking had some supporters. An Italian monk, Giordano Bruno (1548–1600), tested Catholic authorities by openly teaching and extending Copernican thought, arguing that "the universe is entirely infinite because it has neither edge, limit, nor surfaces." Bruno also professed a series of unusual religious notions. Outraged, the Catholic Inquisition burned Bruno at the stake.

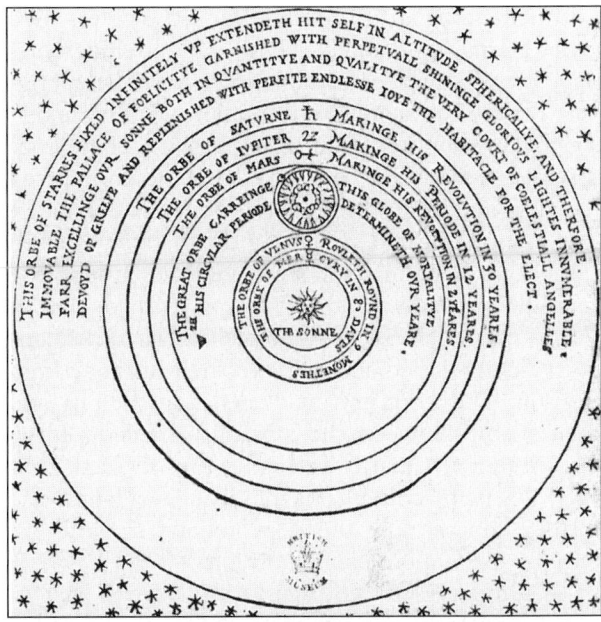

FIGURE 14.3

The Copernican view of the universe, 1576. *Tycho Brahe*

Nevertheless, Copernicus's views began to influence other scholars who were investigating the physical nature of the universe.

The Danish aristocrat Tycho Brahe (1546–1601) did not share Copernicus's belief in a heliocentric universe, nor did he grasp the sophisticated mathematics of the day. Still, he became *Tycho Brahe* the next most important astronomer of the sixteenth century. He persuaded the king of Denmark to build for him the most advanced astronomy laboratory in Europe. There he recorded thousands of unusually accurate, detailed observations about the planets and stars over a period of 20 years—all without a telescope. His discoveries of a new star in 1572 and a comet in 1577 undermined the Aristotelian belief in a sky of fixed, unalterable stars moving in crystalline spheres. Although Brahe mistakenly concluded that some planets revolved around the sun, which itself moved around the earth, other astronomers with better understandings of mathematics would use his observations to draw very different conclusions.

Tycho Brahe's assistant, Johannes Kepler (1571–1630), built on Brahe's observations to support the Copernican heliocentric theory. A German

Lutheran from an aristocratic family, Kepler—like other Hermetic scholars—believed in an underlying mathematical harmony of mystical significance to the physical universe. He sought one harmony that would fit with Brahe's observations. Between 1609 and 1619, he announced his most important findings: the three laws of planetary motion. After determining the first law—which stated that the planets moved in ellipses around the sun—he excitedly wrote, "It was as if I had awaken from a sleep." The second law declared that the planets' velocity varied according to their distance from the sun. The third law concluded that the physical relationship between the moving planets could be expressed mathematically. Kepler thus showed "that the celestial machine . . . is the likeness of [a] clock," further undermining the Aristotelian view and extending the Copernican revolution.

Johannes Kepler

Document 14.1 (see page D14.1) reveals that in 1597, Kepler responded to a letter from Galileo Galilei, the Italian astronomer, physicist, and mathematician discussed at the beginning of this chapter. Although Galileo expressed a reluctance to publicize his beliefs in Copernican ideas, Kepler encouraged him to take the risk. "Be of good cheer, Galileo, and appear in public. If I am not mistaken there are only a few among the distinguished mathematicians of Europe who would dissociate themselves from us. So great is the power of truth."

Galileo Galilei

Galileo already believed that the world could be described in purely mathematical terms. "Philosophy," he wrote, "is written in this grand book, the universe, which stands continually open to our gaze. . . . It is written in the language of mathematics, and its characters are triangles, circles, and other geometric figures without which it is humanly impossible to understand a single word of it. . . . " Galileo also felt that harmonies could be discovered through experimentation and mathematics. By conducting controlled experiments such as rolling balls down inclines, he demonstrated how motion could be described mathematically. He rejected the old view that objects in their natural state were at rest and that all motion needed a purpose. Instead, he formulated the principle of inertia, showing that bodies, once set into motion, will tend to stay in motion. He thus overturned Aristotelian ideas and established rules for experimental physics.

Galileo, hearing about the recent invention of the telescope, then studied the skies through a telescope that he built in 1609 out of a long tube and magnifying lenses. Figure 14.4 shows what he saw. He sketched this illustration of the moon for his book *Starry Messenger*. Instead of being a perfect, smooth heavenly body, the moon's surface was rugged (like the earth's), with craters and mountains indicated by lines and shading. The telescope also revealed that Jupiter had moons and that the sun had spots. These observations confirmed the view that other heavenly bodies besides the earth were imperfect and further convinced him of the validity of Copernicus's hypothesis. For years, Galileo had feared the disapproval of the Catholic Church. Now, however, he was ready to publicly argue that "in discussions of physical problems we ought to begin not from the authority of scriptural passages, but from sense-experiences and necessary demonstrations." Galileo published his findings in 1610.

Six years later, the church attacked his proposition that "the earth is not the center of the world nor immovable, but moves as a whole, and also with a daily motion." This statement, the church said, was "foolish and absurd philosophically, and formally heretical." To back up its claim, the church cited the authority of both the Bible and itself. For the next several years, Galileo kept his thoughts to himself. In

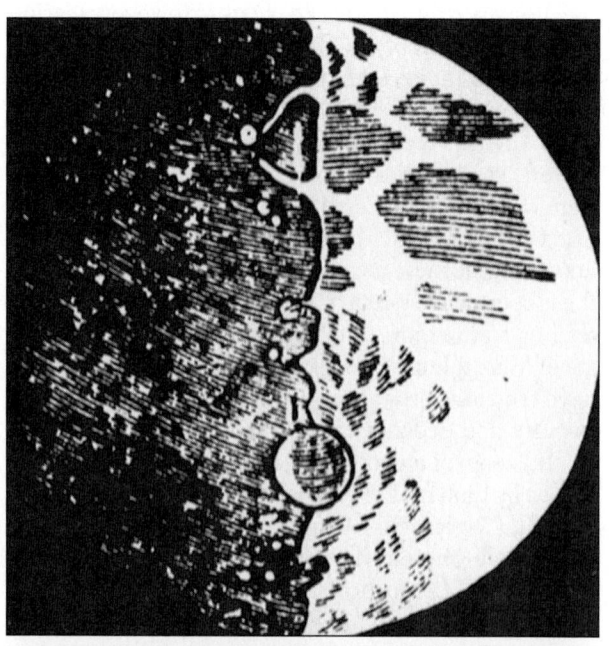

FIGURE 14.4
Galileo Galilei, *The Moon*, 1610.

1632, believing that the church might be more open, he decided again to present his views. To avoid challenging the church, he submitted his book to the official church censors and agreed to some changes they demanded. Finally he published his *Dialogue on the Two Chief Systems of the World*—in Italian rather than the less-accessible Latin. This text advocated Copernicanism, portrayed opponents of the Copernican system (such as the Jesuits) as simpletons, and brought Galileo directly into public conflict with conservative forces in the Catholic Church. Because Galileo could show that his book had already been approved by church officials, prosecutors had to use questionable evidence against him. As we saw at the beginning of the chapter, the Roman Inquisition ultimately forced him to renounce his views.

News of Galileo's sensational trial spread throughout Europe, as did fear of publishing other radical views. Soon, however, his book was translated and published elsewhere in Europe, and his views began to win acceptance by other scientists. Even though Galileo admitted that the new science was beyond the grasp of "the shallow minds of the common people," he effectively communicated its ideas to his peers. By the time of his death in 1642, Europe's intellectual elite had begun to embrace the Copernican outlook.

In England, Isaac Newton (1642–1727) picked up the trail blazed by Copernicus, Brahe, Kepler, and Galileo. Late in life, Newton described *Isaac Newton* his career modestly: "I do not know what I may appear to the world; but to myself I seem to have been only like a boy playing on the sea-shore, and diverting myself in now and then finding a smoother pebble or a prettier shell than ordinary, while the great ocean of truth lay all undiscovered before me." Newton may have held himself in humble regard, but his accomplishments were astonishing.

In 1661, Newton entered Cambridge University, where he studied the ideas of Copernicus and Galileo as well as the advantages of scientific investigation. He distinguished himself enough in mathematics to be chosen to stay on as a professor after his graduation. Like most other figures of the scientific revolution, Newton was also profoundly religious and, as indicated by Document 14.2 (see page D14.1), hoped to harmonize his Christian beliefs with the principles of science. He also believed in alchemy and elements of Hermeticism.

Starting in his early 20s, Newton made some of the most important discoveries in the history of science.

He developed calculus and investigated the nature of light; he also formulated and mathematically described three laws of motion: inertia, acceleration, and action/reaction. *Newton's Principia* Yet he is best known for discovering the law of universal attraction, or gravitation. After working on the concept for years, he finally published it in 1687 in his great work *Principia (The Mathematical Principles of Natural Knowledge)*. In the book, he stated the law with simplicity and precision: "Every particle of matter in the universe attracts every other particle with a force varying inversely as the square of the distance between them and directly proportional to the product of their masses." In his view, this law applied equally to all objects, from the most massive planet to a small apple falling from a tree.

Newton had managed to synthesize the new findings in astronomy and physics into a systematic explanation of physical laws that applied to the earth as well as the heavens. This Newtonian universe was infinite and had no center. Uniform and mathematically describable, it was held together by explainable forces and was atomic in nature. Essentially, everything in the universe consisted of only one thing: matter in motion.

THE REVOLUTION SPREADS: MEDICINE, ANATOMY, AND CHEMISTRY

Although astronomy and physics led the way in dramatic scientific findings, researchers in other fields made important discoveries as well. Many of these advances also had roots in the sixteenth century. For example, several scholars developed new ideas in the related fields of medicine, anatomy, and chemistry.

In medicine, a flamboyant Swiss alchemist-physician known as Paracelsus (1493–1541) strongly influenced the healing arts. A believer in *Paracelsus* Hermetic doctrine, Paracelsus openly opposed medical orthodoxy and taught that healers should not look for truth in libraries ("the more learned, the more perverted," he warned) but in the Book of Nature. "I have not been ashamed to learn from tramps, butchers, and barbers," he boasted. As a teacher and wandering practitioner, he treated patients, experimented with chemicals, recorded his observations, and developed new theories. Paracelsus concluded that all matter was composed of salt, sulfur, and mercury—not the traditional earth, water, fire, and air. Rejecting the standard view that an

shows the 28-year-old Vesalius displaying one of his studies on human anatomy from his 1543 treatise, *On the Fabric of the Human Body.* This figure is one of more than 200 woodcut illustrations showing the composition of the body, stage by stage. Vesalius himself dissected cadavers, as suggested by the scalpel resting on the table. A notable aspect of this illustration is that Vesalius boldly looks the viewer in the eye, perhaps to challenge directly the old, authoritative assumptions about human anatomy. Nevertheless, his dissections of human bodies brought him into conflict with traditional physicians and scholars. Disgusted, he finally gave up his scientific studies and became the personal physician to Emperor Charles V.

Andreas Vesalius

Despite relentless criticism, other scholars continued anatomical research. A line from a poem written for the opening of the Amsterdam Anatomical Theatre in the early seventeenth century reflects the sense that this research needed special justification: "Evil doers who while living have done damage are of benefit after their death." In other words, the body parts of criminals "afford a lesson to you, the Living." The most important of these researchers was William Harvey (1578–1657), an Englishman who, like Vesalius, studied at the University of Padua in Italy. Harvey dissected hundreds of animals, including dogs, pigs, lobsters, shrimp, and snakes. He discovered that the human heart worked like a pump, with valves that allowed blood to circulate through the body: "The movement of the blood occurs constantly in a circular manner and is the result of the beating of the heart." Yet, despite this mechanistic view, he also considered the heart the physical and spiritual center of life—in his words, "the sovereign of everything."

William Harvey

By the seventeenth century, anatomists and others benefited from several newly invented scientific instruments, such as the microscope. Anton van Leeuwenhoek (1632–1723), a Dutchman, became the chief pioneer in the use of this instrument. In observations during the 1670s, he described seeing "little animals or animalcules" in water from a lake. "It was wonderful to see: and I judge that some of these little creatures were above a thousand times smaller than the smallest ones I have ever yet seen, upon the rind of cheese, in wheaten flour, mould and the like." Leeuwenhoek discovered what would later be identified as bacteria in his own saliva: "little eels or worms,

Anton van Leeuwenhoek

imbalance in the humors of the body caused disease, he instead looked to specific chemical imbalances to explain what caused each illness. He also encouraged research and experimentation to find natural remedies for bodily disorders, such as administering mercury or arsenic at astrologically correct moments. Though rejected by most established physicians, Paracelsus's ideas became particularly popular among common practitioners and would later influence the study of chemistry.

Other researchers founded the modern science of anatomy. In the sixteenth century, Andreas Vesalius (1514–1564), a Fleming living in Italy, wrote the first comprehensive textbook on the structure of the human body based on careful observation. Figure 14.5

Developing a Modern Scientific View

lying all huddled up together and wriggling . . . This was for me, among all the marvels that I have discovered in nature, the most marvellous of all."

Around this same time, Robert Boyle (1627–1691), an Irish nobleman particularly interested in medical chemistry, helped lay the foundations for modern chemistry. Drawing inspiration from Paracelsus, Boyle attacked many assumptions inherited from the ancients and began a systematic search for the basic elements of matter. Relying on the experimental method and using new instruments, he argued that all matter was composed of indestructible atoms that behaved in predictable ways. Boyle also discovered a law—which still bears his name—that governs the pressure of gases. His exacting procedures set a standard for the scientific practice of chemistry.

Robert Boyle

THE METHODOLOGY OF SCIENCE EMERGES

The scientists who challenged traditional views in their fields also used new methods of discovery—of uncovering how things worked and of determining "truth." Indeed, this innovative methodology lay at the heart of the scientific revolution. Earlier techniques for ascertaining the truth—by referring to long-trusted authorities and making deductions from their propositions—became unacceptable to the new scientists. They instead emphasized systematic skepticism, experimentation, and reasoning based solely on observed facts and mathematical laws. The two most important philosophers of this methodology were Francis Bacon and René Descartes.

Francis Bacon (1561–1626), an English politician who was once lord chancellor of England under James I, took a passionate interest in the new science. He rejected reliance on ancient authorities and advocated the collection of data without preconceived notions. From such data, he explained, scientific conclusions could be reached through inductive reasoning—drawing general conclusions from particular concrete observations. "Deriv[ing] axioms from . . . particulars, rising by gradual and unbroken ascent, so that it arrives at the most general axioms of all. This is the true way," he proclaimed. In addition, Bacon argued that scientific knowledge would be useful knowledge: "I am laboring to lay the foundation not of any sect or doctrine, but of human utility and power." He believed that sci-

Francis Bacon

OLC

ence would benefit commerce and industry and improve the human condition by giving people unprecedented power over their environment.

Figure 14.6, the title page from Bacon's 1620 book *New Instrument*, graphically depicts these views. The illustration shows a ship of discovery sailing out from the western end of the Mediterranean Sea into the unknown. Below is the quotation, "Many shall venture forth and science shall be increased." Here is an optimistic assertion that knowledge is limitless and that science constitutes a voyage of discovery—a view that would be echoed again and again, as we saw in

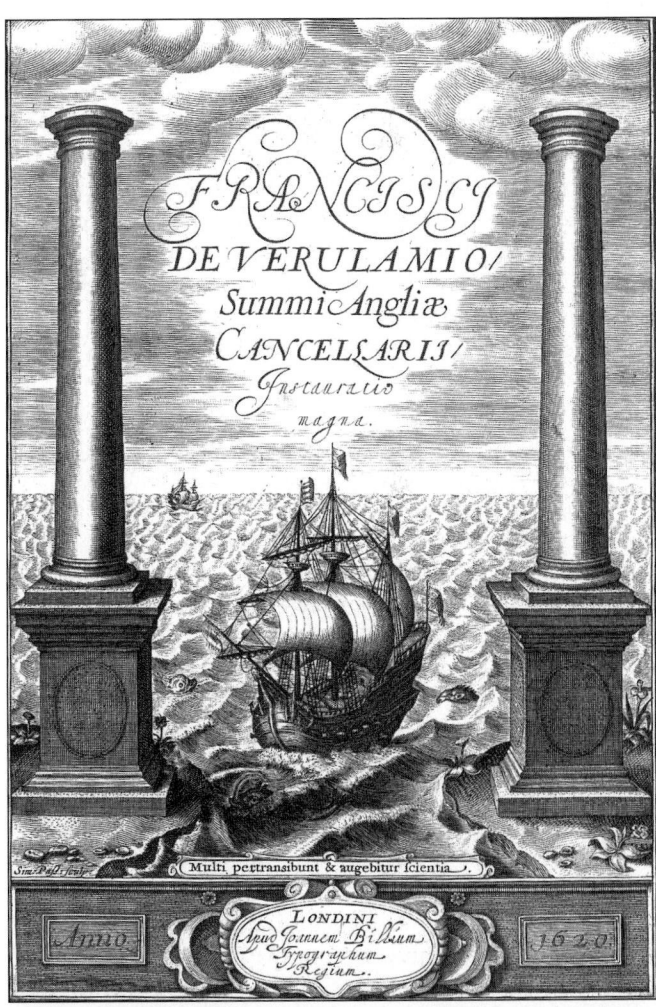

FIGURE 14.6
Title page of Francis Bacon's *New Instrument*, 1620.

the picture at the beginning of this chapter. As Document 14.3 (see p. D14.2) suggests, Bacon thus became a noted propagandist for the new science as well as a proponent of the empirical method.

Despite his brilliance, Bacon did not have a thorough understanding of mathematics and the role it could play in the new science. His contemporary, René Descartes (1596–1650), would be the one to excel in this arena. Born in France, René Descartes received training in scholastic philosophy and mathematics at one of France's best Jesuit schools and took a degree in law. He entered military service and served during the Thirty Years' War. During his travels, he met a Dutch mathematician and became interested in the new science. An ecstatic experience in 1619 convinced him to commit to a life of the mind. He spent his most productive years as a mathematician, physicist, and metaphysical philosopher in Holland. In 1637, he published his philosophy and scientific methodology in the *Discourse on Method*—in French, not Latin. The book presented an eloquent defense of skepticism and of abstract deductive reasoning—deriving conclusions that logically flowed from a premise. "Inquiries should be directed, not to what others have thought, nor to what we ourselves conjecture, but to what we can clearly and perspicuously behold and with certainty deduce; for knowledge is not won in any other way."

Descartes questioned all forms of authority, no matter how venerable—be it Aristotle or even the Bible. He tried to remove systematically all assumptions about knowledge and advocated doubting the senses, which he claimed could be deceptive. Taken to its logical conclusion, his argument left him with one God-given experiential fact—that he was thinking. "I think, therefore I am" became his starting point. From there he followed a rigorous process of deductive reasoning to draw a variety of conclusions, including the existence of God and the physical world. He argued that there were two kinds of reality: mind, or subjective thinking and experiencing; and body, or objective physical matter. According to this philosophy, known as Cartesian dualism, the objective physical universe could be understood in terms of extension (matter occupying space) and motion (matter in motion). "Give me extension and motion," vowed Descartes, "and I will create the universe." He considered the body nothing more than "an earthen machine." In his opinion, only the mind was exempt from mechanical laws.

Descartes emphasized the power of the detached, reasoning individual mind to discover truths about nature. Unlike Bacon, he put his faith in mathematical reasoning, not in empirical investigation. By challenging all established authority, by accepting as truth only what could be known by reason, and by assuming a purely mechanical physical universe, Descartes established a philosophy and methodology that became the core of the new science.

Supporting and Spreading Science

Only a small group of people actually participated in the scientific revolution. Of these, a handful of women managed to overcome barriers to take part as patrons for scientists or as scientists themselves. Men ignored or discounted their work, and scientific societies usually excluded them. The few women engaged in science such as the naturalist Maria Sibilla Merian (see Biography, pages 434–435) and the German astronomer Maria Winkelmann (1647–1717) had to rely on their own resources or work in collaboration with their husbands.

Few scientific scholars—whether male or female—got far without calling on a network of peers and soliciting the support of wealthy patrons. To spread their ideas, these scientists needed to publish their works, interact with like-minded colleagues, and gain the backing of prestigious elites. Fortunately for them, these elites were eager to comply.

COURTS AND SALONS

Governments and wealthy aristocrats served as benefactors and employers of scientists. Kepler, for example, received help from the imperial court, serving in Bohemia as Rudolf II's official mathematician. Galileo became court mathematician to Cosimo de' Medici in Tuscany. Vesalius served as physician to Holy Roman Emperor Charles V, and Harvey as royal physician in England.

Queen Christina of Sweden, like several other monarchs, invited scholars and artists to her court. Figure 14.7 shows her in 1649 with the French philosopher and mathematician René Descartes (on the right pointing to papers). Books, papers, and instruments attest to the importance of the new science at this meeting. In this Protestant country, the religious figure on the far right seems to indicate that there is little conflict between science and religion. The artist portrays Christina, a deeply religious person (who would later become a Catholic), as an interested and gracious benefactor helping to bring to light scientific findings.

Rulers had their own motives—namely practicality and prestige—for assisting scholars and scientists. Royals especially hoped that scholarship and scientific inquiry would yield discoveries that would enhance the strength and prosperity of the state. For example, they sought experts in building projects, armaments, map-making, navigation, and mining. They also tried to burnish their own reputations as powerful, educated people by patronizing scholarship, science, and the arts. In this way, support of science became a supposed hallmark of good government. Enticed by this assistance, learned people gathered at royal courts, which gradually filled rooms with new tools, machines, exotic plants and animals, and books.

Beyond the court, people formed private salons and local academies where those interested in science could meet. In the 1540s, the first academy for scientific study was established in Naples. Women ran several important salons where scientists discussed their findings along with literature, art, and politics. Some scientists even found benefactors at these meetings.

FIGURE 14.7
Queen Christina and Descartes, 1649.

THE RISE OF ROYAL SOCIETIES

During the second half of the seventeenth century, central governments stepped up their support of scientific experimentation, publications, and academies. In 1662, for example, Charles II chartered the Royal Society in England; four years later, Louis XIV's finance minister, Jean Baptiste Colbert, founded the Académie des Sciences in France. Figure

14.8 illustrates royal interest in these academies. In this 1666 painting, members of the French Royal Academy of Science gather for their first meeting. In the center sits Louis XIV, boasting a plumed hat, and standing to his right is Colbert, who hands a scroll to a bowing leader of the Academy. On the far right is a plan for improved military fortifications. Throughout the room are instruments and specimens for studies in cartography, geography, astronomy, physics, chemistry, and natural history—all supported by the Académie. Through the window on the right we can see a new Royal Observatory being built. These organizations, and others patterned after them, furnished laboratories, granted subsidies, brought scientists together to exchange ideas, published their findings, and honored scientific achievements. This governmental support of science added to the growing prestige of science and the scientific community.

RELIGION AND THE NEW SCIENCE

Religious organizations played a mixed role in the spread of the new science. Traditionally, the Catholic Church supported scholarship and learning in general, including natural science. Moreover, religious orders staffed most universities, and many key figures of the scientific revolution held university positions. Numerous leading scholars also felt a profound sense of spirituality. Copernicus, for example, who dedicated his work to the pope, was a cleric, as were many other natural scientists. Although we may be tempted to assume that the skepticism inherent in the scientific method would lead to atheism, the great scientists attacked neither faith nor established religion. Nor were they dispassionate investigators holding themselves apart from the spiritual nature of their age. They often believed in magic, ghosts, and witchcraft, and typically considered alchemy, astrology, and numerology (predicting events from numbers) valuable components of natural science. Galileo, though he later decried his trial as the triumph of "ignorance, impiety, fraud and deceit," remained a believing Catholic. Even Robert Boyle, who like others came to think of the universe as a machine, attributed its origin to God: "God, indeed, gave motion to matter . . . and established those rules of motion, and that order amongst things . . . which we call the laws of nature." Newton agreed: "This most beautiful system of the sun, planets, and comets, could only proceed from the counsel and dominion of an intelligent and powerful Being. . . . He endures forever, and is everywhere present. . . ."

Nevertheless, the new science did challenge certain tenets of faith and the traditional Christian conception of God's place in the ordering of the world. Neither Protestant nor Catholic leaders welcomed Copernican ideas and the implications of the new science. The Catholic Church, itself ordered in a hierar-

FIGURE 14.8
Henri Testelin, *The Inaugural Meeting of the French Royal Academy of Sciences, 1666.*

chy that paralleled the old view of the universe, stayed particularly committed to established authorities. Moreover the church's condemnation of Galileo in 1633 discouraged scientific investigations throughout much of Catholic Europe. Descartes was not alone in deciding not to publish ideas incorporating Copernican assumptions. As he explained in 1634, "It is not my temperament to set sail against the wind . . . I want to be able to live in peace . . . out of sight." Although the French government would actively promote science, after the mid-seventeenth century most scientific work and publishing took place in Protestant areas—particularly in England and the Netherlands.

THE NEW WORLDVIEW

By the end of the seventeenth century, the accumulation of convincing scientific findings and the support for those findings among the educated elites had broken the Aristotelian-medieval worldview and replaced it with the Copernican-Newtonian paradigm. According to the new view, the earth, *The Copernican-Newtonian paradigm* along with the planets, moved around the sun in an infinite universe of other similar bodies. The natural order consisted of matter in motion, acting according to mathematically expressible laws. Scientific truths came from observing, measuring, experimenting, and making reasoned conclusions through the use of sophisticated mathematics. Religious truths still had their place, and the orderliness of nature reflected God's design (see Document 14.2 on page D14.1). However, science now claimed precedence in explaining the material world.

In the sixteenth and early-seventeenth centuries, great thinkers such as Copernicus and Galileo had been ridiculed and persecuted for their ideas. By the late-seventeenth and early-eighteenth centuries, Isaac Newton's fate revealed the acceptance of the new paradigm among educated elites. Famous and popular, Newton became a member of Parliament, served for many years as director of the Royal Mint, and was knighted by Queen Anne.

Laying the Foundations for the Enlightenment

In the course of the eighteenth century, the ideas of the scientific revolution spread widely and were applied in stunning new ways. With this broadening, the eighteenth century witnessed the birth of a major cultural movement known as the Enlightenment. At the heart of this movement lay the firm conviction—especially among intellectuals—that human reason should determine understanding of the world and the rules of social life. "[H]ave the courage to use your own intelligence," and leave your "self-caused immaturity," exhorted the German philosopher Immanuel Kant (1724–1804). "All that is required for this enlightenment is freedom, and particularly . . . the freedom for man to make public use of his reason in all matters."

The Enlightenment hit its full stride in the middle decades of the eighteenth century, when it particularly influenced literate elites of Europe and North America. Yet, its roots stretched back to the end of the seventeenth century. At that time, the thinking that would characterize the Enlightenment emerged in the writings of people who popularized science, applied a skeptical attitude toward religious standards of truth, and criticized accepted traditions and authorities.

SCIENCE POPULARIZED

Unevenly educated and facing challenging findings, members of scientific societies often struggled to understand one another's work. For the nonscientific public, the problem of communicating new, complex ideas was even worse. Late in the seventeenth century, several talented writers, nonscientists themselves but believing that science had established a new standard of truth, began explaining in clear language the meaning of science to the literate public. For example, the French writer Bernard de Fontenelle (1657–1757) enjoyed a long, brilliant career as a popularizer of science. In *Conversations on the Plurality of Worlds* (1686), he presented the Copernican view of the universe in a series of conversations between an aristocratic woman and her lover under starry skies. The English essayist and publisher, Joseph Addison (1672–1719), in March 12, 1711 issue of his newspaper, *The Spectator*, said that he hoped to bring "philosophy out of closets and libraries, schools and colleges, to dwell in clubs and assemblies, at tea-tables and in coffee-houses." He aimed his daily paper not only at men, but at women "of a more elevated life and conversation, that move in an exalted sphere of knowledge and virtue, that join all the beauties of the mind to the ornaments of dress, and inspire a kind of awe and respect, as well as love, in their male beholders." Other writers also targeted women. In 1737, for example, *Newtonianism for Women* was published in Naples and was soon translated into English. Writings such as these helped make science fashionable in elite circles.

By the mid-eighteenth century, this popularization of science merged with another foundation of Enlightenment thinking: the belief that every educated man and woman should be familiar with the nature and methods of science. Figure 14.9, an illustration from a British book on the arts and sciences, depicts this connection between science and education. Here a teacher instructs three young men in the principles of astronomy by demonstrating the planetary movements on a new machine—the orrery. The stuffed animals hanging from the ceiling underscore the importance of natural history. Atop the bookcase and on the floor are seminal instruments of science—an air pump, a microscope, a telescope, and a globe. A human skeleton hangs in the closet.

Teaching science

Soon scientific ideas were being taught to children of the middle and upper classes. For example, the year 1761 saw the publication of *The Newtonian System of Philosophy, Adapted to the Capacities of Young Gentlemen and Ladies*, a book engagingly advertised as the "Philosophy of Tops and Balls." In it, a fictional boy named Tom Telescope gave lectures on science topics to children while also teaching the virtues of good manners and citizenship. The book proved immensely popular, going through many editions in Britain and in other countries.

Many of these books emphasized Newton—and for understandable reasons. Enlightenment thinkers saw this brilliant Englishman as the great synthesizer of the scientific revolution, an astute observer who rightly described the universe as ordered, mechanical, material, and set into motion by God. From Newton, they concluded that reason and nature were compatible: Nature functioned logically

Glorifying Newton: Reason and nature

and discernibly; therefore, what was natural was also reasonable. Many writers of the day agreed with the spirit of a poem written for Newton by the English author Alexander Pope upon the scientist's death in 1727:

Nature and Nature's Laws lay hid in Night.
God said, "Let Newton be," and all was Light.

In simple terms, Newton had become a European cultural hero, as Figure 14.10 suggests. At the left-center of this allegorical painting, a great urn "wherein is supposed to be deposited the Remains of the deceased Hero" is displayed. Above the urn shines a beam of light, broken into the colors of the spectrum by a prism—a bow to Newton's famous prism experiments. At the right are pages filled with mathematical calculations; below them, a globe and measuring instruments. Various figures in classical dress admire these objects and perhaps discuss Newton's ideas. The entire painting glorifies not only Newton, but all of science.

Enlightenment thinkers also admired the ideas of Newton's compatriot John Locke (1632–1704), who applied scientific thinking to human psychology. This English

The psychology of John Locke

philosopher did not hold the mind exempt from the mechanical laws of the material universe. In his *Essay Concerning Human Understanding* (1690), Locke pictured the human brain at birth as a blank sheet of paper that sensory perception and reason filled as a person aged. "Our observation, employed either about external sensible objects or about the internal operations of our minds perceived and reflected on by ourselves, is that which supplies our understanding with all the materials of thinking." Locke's empirical psychology rejected the notion that human beings were born with innate ideas or that revelation was a reliable source of truth. What we become, he argued, depends solely on our experiences—on the information received

FIGURE 14.9
Science, education, and enlightenment, 1759.

through the senses. Schools and social institutions should therefore play a major role in molding the individual from childhood to adulthood. These ideas, like those of Newton and the scientific revolution, also set the stage for the skeptical questioning of received wisdom.

SKEPTICISM AND RELIGION

Locke's ideas, along with those of Newton and the scientific revolution, *Pierre Bayle* set the stage for the questioning of established wisdom that came to define the Enlightenment. Among several writers, skepticism—or doubts about religious dogmas—mounted. Pierre Bayle (1647–1706), a French Huguenot forced to flee to the Dutch Republic because of Louis XIV's religious persecutions, became the leading proponent of skepticism in the late seventeenth century. In his *News from the Republic of Letters* (1684), Bayle bitterly attacked the intolerance of the French monarchy and the Catholic Church. In most of Europe, where religious principles shared by ruler and ruled underlay all political systems, nonconformity was a major challenge. Therefore, the book earned him condemnation in Paris and Rome. Eventually, however, Bayle would have the last word. In 1697 he published the *Historical and Critical Dictionary*, which contained a list of religious views and beliefs that Bayle maintained did not stand up to criticism. Bayle cited human reason and common sense as his standard of criticism: "Any particular dogma, whatever it may be, whether it is advanced on the authority of the Scriptures, or whatever else may be its origins, is to be regarded as false if it clashes with the clear and definite conclusions of the natural understanding." Bayle also argued that "morals and religion, far from being

FIGURE 14.10
Giovanni Battista Pittori, *Allegorical Monument to Isaac Newton*, 1727–1730.

inseparable, are completely independent of each other." For Bayle, a person's moral behavior had little to do with any particular religious doctrine or creed. With these stands, Bayle pushed much harder than

Galileo in challenging the Catholic Church and other religious beliefs. He became recognized as an international authority on religious toleration and skeptical criticism of the Bible.

New information and arguments added weight to Bayle's criticism of biblical authority. For example, *David Hume* geological discoveries suggested that life on Earth had actually begun earlier than biblical accounts claimed. Investigators also began casting doubt on reports of miracles and prophecies. David Hume (1711–1776), a first-rate Scottish philosopher and historian, carried the skeptical argument even further. In *An Essay Concerning Human Understanding* (1748), he insisted that nothing—not even the existence of God or our own existence—could be known for sure. Reality consisted only of human perceptions. To Hume, established religions were based on nothing but "hope and fear." Reason demanded that people live with skeptical uncertainty rather than dogmatic faith.

BROADENING CRITICISM OF AUTHORITY AND TRADITION

Travel writing had a long history, and by the eighteenth century many Enlightenment thinkers had read explanations of China's lucid Confucian traditions as well as *Travel writings of Montesquieu and Voltaire* accounts of customs and beliefs in Islamic, Buddhist, and Hindu lands. Several writers—among them Baron de Montesquieu (1689–1755), a wealthy judge in a provincial French court, and the French author Voltaire (1694–1778)—used comparisons of place and time to criticize authority and tradition during the early decades of the eighteenth century. Journeying abroad and writing about their experiences gave such people a new perspective on their home societies. Montesquieu and Voltaire, for their part, chastised European customs in general and French institutions in particular for being contrary to reason and good ethics.

Both presented the traveler as an objective observer. In his best-selling book *Persian Letters* (1721), Montesquieu bitingly satirized the customs, morals, and practices of Europeans from the point of view of two Persian travelers. Through this comparative perspective, Montesquieu painted the French as lacking in both good morals and effective government. Voltaire, in his widely read *Letters Concerning the English Nation* (1733), similarly criticized French politics

and Catholic intolerance. In the island nation, "one thinks freely and nobly without being held back by any servile fear." Like many people, Voltaire idealized England because it allowed greater individual freedom, religious differences, and political reform than most other countries, especially France. England was also enviably prosperous and was the home of Newton and Locke, so admired in France. Many French intellectuals wanted for their own country what the English already seemed to have.

Other writers took a new historical perspective to criticize tradition and trumpet rapid change. For them, the tools of science and reason enabled people to surpass their historical predecessors, even the admired Greeks and Romans of antiquity. History became a story of *History and progress* relentless human progress, and people living in the eighteenth century stood on the brink of unprecedented historical achievements. Some people, such as the American scientist and philosopher Benjamin Franklin (1706–1790), embraced the idea of progress with an almost religious fervor: "The rapid Progress of *true* Science now occasions my regretting sometimes that I was born so soon. It is impossible to imagine the Height to which may be carried . . . the Power of Man over Matter, . . . all diseases may by sure means be prevented, . . . and our lives lengthened at pleasure."

The Enlightenment in Full Stride

Building on the foundations of science, skepticism, and criticism, Western intellectuals systematically investigated the ethical, political, social, and economic implications of science after the 1730s. For them, nature—with its laws, order, simplicity, and rationality—served as a guide for human thought and society. "The source of man's unhappiness is his ignorance of Nature," claimed France's influential Baron d'Holbach (1723–1789). The Marquis de Condorcet argued, "The Time will therefore come when the sun will shine only on free men who know no other master but their reason (see Document 14.4 on p. D14.2). These optimistic intellectuals pushed for reform and change, using critical and empirical reasoning to back up their arguments. Specifically, they urged people to shrug off the shackles of tradition and custom and to participate in the accelerating progress of civilization. The spark of reason would soon dispel ignorance and enlighten all human understanding. Indeed, it was this image that lent the Enlightenment its name.

THE PHILOSOPHES

Although Enlightenment ideas bubbled up throughout Europe and North America, France was the true heart of the movement. There Enlightenment thinkers came to be called *philosophes*, the French term for "philosophers." In a sense, the questions these thinkers grappled with were philosophical: How do we discover truth? How should we live our lives? Yet the *philosophes* were not traditional philosophers. Coming from both noble and middle-class origins, they were intellectuals—though often not formally trained by or associated with a university. They tended to extend, apply, or propagandize others' ideas rather than initiate new concepts themselves. They also wrote more plays, satires, histories, novels, encyclopedia entries, and short pamphlets than formal philosophical treatises. Finally, they considered themselves part of a common intellectual culture, an international "republic of letters" held together by literature, correspondence, and private gatherings. In the eyes of leading *philosophes* such as Jean Le Rond d'Alembert (1717–1783), this republic of letters should "establish the laws of philosophy and taste for the rest of the nation."

The witty, versatile François Arouet, who took the pen name Voltaire (1694–1778), best represented the *philosophes*. The son of a Parisian lawyer, Voltaire received a fine classical education from the Jesuits and soon denounced their religious doctrine. He became the idol of French intellectuals while only in his 20s, and the enemy of many others. He soon ran afoul of state authorities, who imprisoned him in the Bastille for writing verses that criticized the crown. Released, he became embroiled in a dangerous conflict with a prominent nobleman and again landed in the Bastille. By promising to leave the country, he gained his freedom. In England, he encountered the ideas of Newton and Locke and came to admire English parliamentary government and the nation's religious tolerance. As we saw, he popularized Newton's and Locke's ideas and extolled the virtues of English society in his writings.

Slipping back into France, Voltaire hid for a time under the protection of Émilie du Châtelet (1706–

Voltaire

1749), a wealthy woman who became his lover and match. Châtelet had already shown brilliance as a child. By the age of 12, she could speak four languages and had already translated Greek and Latin texts. Her mother worried that she would not find a mate because she "flaunts her mind, and frightens away the suitors her other excesses have not driven off." In 1733, she insisted on joining a group of male intellectuals who met regularly at a Parisian coffeehouse, donning men's clothes after the management refused to admit her because of her gender. Voltaire lived openly with Châtelet and her husband. In the great hall of their country chateau, she hung rods, pipes, and balls from the ceiling for her experiments in physics. She made her reputation by publishing a three-volume work on the German mathematician and philosopher Leibnitz and translating Newton's *Principles of Mathematics*. A *philosophe*, accomplished scientist, and leading proponent of Newtonian thought in her own right, Châtelet helped Voltaire gain a better understanding of the sciences and their significance. When she died in childbirth in 1749, the despondent Voltaire accepted an invitation from King Frederick II of Prussia to join his court.

Émilie du Châtelet

Figure 14.11 shows the two men at an opulent luncheon in Prussia. At the left, Voltaire leans forward in conversation with Frederick, seated directly across the table and also leaning forward to catch every word from his learned guest. Around the table other men engage in conversation, but most have their eyes on the celebrity, Voltaire. This painting reveals the image of the great Enlightenment thinker in conversation and with the international stature sufficient to gain the ear of "enlightened" monarchs such as Frederick. However, they soon argued, and Voltaire returned to France.

Having made both a fortune in financial speculations and a rich network of friends and acquaintances, Voltaire was not without resources. He wrote poetry, drama, history, essays, letters, and scientific treatises—90 volumes in all. The novel *Candide* (1759) became his best-known work. In this dark satire, Voltaire created the epitome of the "ivory-tower" intellectual, ridiculed the pretensions of the nobility and clergy, and skewered the naiveté of optimists who believed that "this is the best of all possible worlds and all things turn out for the best." He aimed his cynical wit especially at the Catholic church and Christian institutions. His *Philosophical Dictionary*

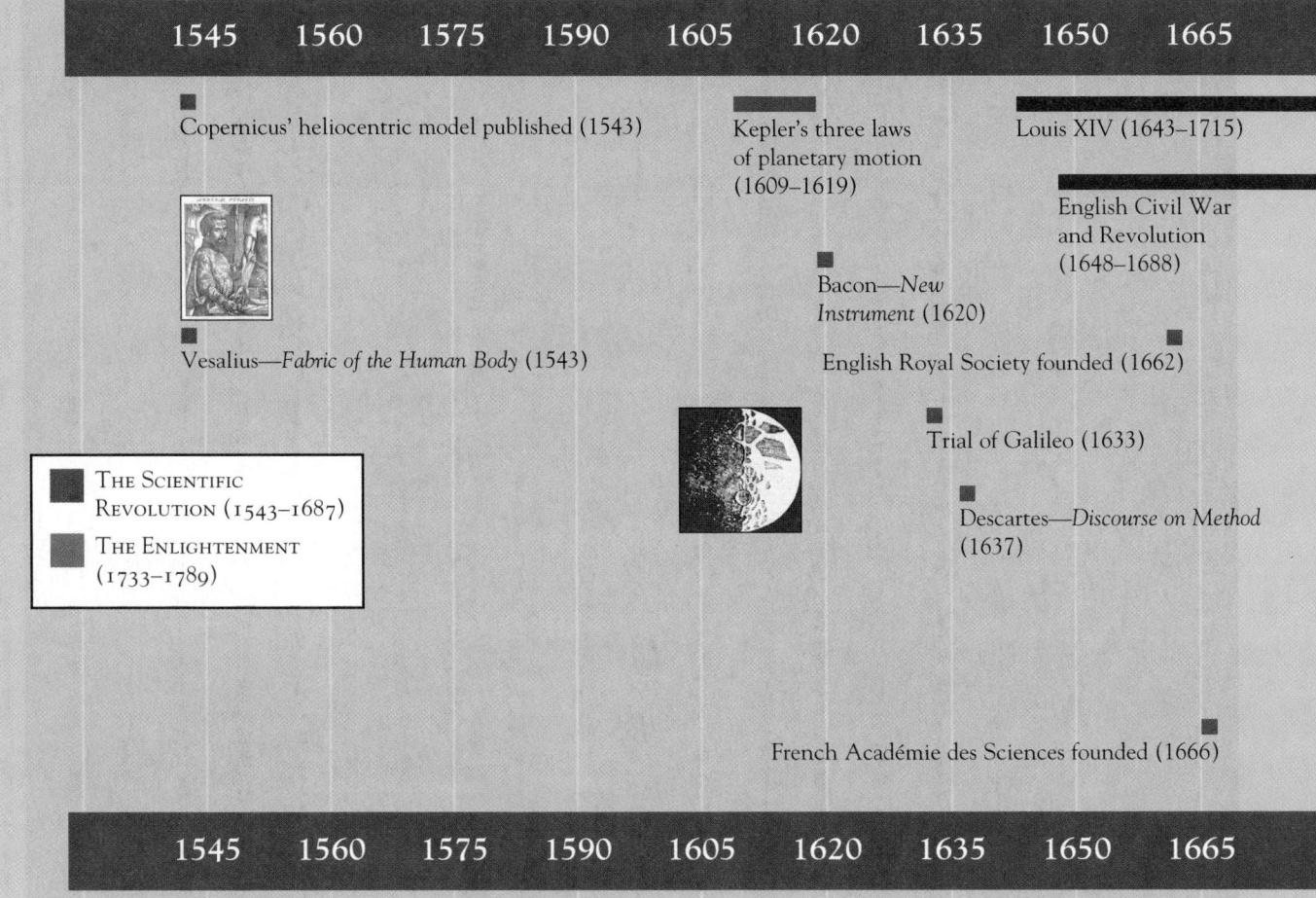

| 1545 | 1560 | 1575 | 1590 | 1605 | 1620 | 1635 | 1650 | 1665 |

Copernicus' heliocentric model published (1543)

Kepler's three laws of planetary motion (1609–1619)

Louis XIV (1643–1715)

English Civil War and Revolution (1648–1688)

Bacon—*New Instrument* (1620)

Vesalius—*Fabric of the Human Body* (1543)

English Royal Society founded (1662)

Trial of Galileo (1633)

■ THE SCIENTIFIC REVOLUTION (1543–1687)
■ THE ENLIGHTENMENT (1733–1789)

Descartes—*Discourse on Method* (1637)

French Académie des Sciences founded (1666)

| 1545 | 1560 | 1575 | 1590 | 1605 | 1620 | 1635 | 1650 | 1665 |

societies, libraries, and coffeehouses. In addition, most municipalities had clubs where the social and intellectual elites could mingle.

Even bookstores, where people could purchase books or pay small fees to read recent works, became *Bookstores* hotbeds of Enlightenment ideas. Figure 14.15 shows an eighteenth-century bookstore. In the doorway stand two women, reading books. Just outside are packages of books being delivered from or to Spain, Portugal, Rome, and Naples. In the street, apparently drawn to the bookstore, are people of all classes, from a peasant with his scythe at the left to a cleric in his white robes at the center. The name of the bookstore, "The Shield of Minerva," refers to the Roman goddess of wisdom. In a growing number of bookstores such as this, all sorts of works became increasingly available, from religious tracts and chivalric tales to new novels and Enlightenment literature.

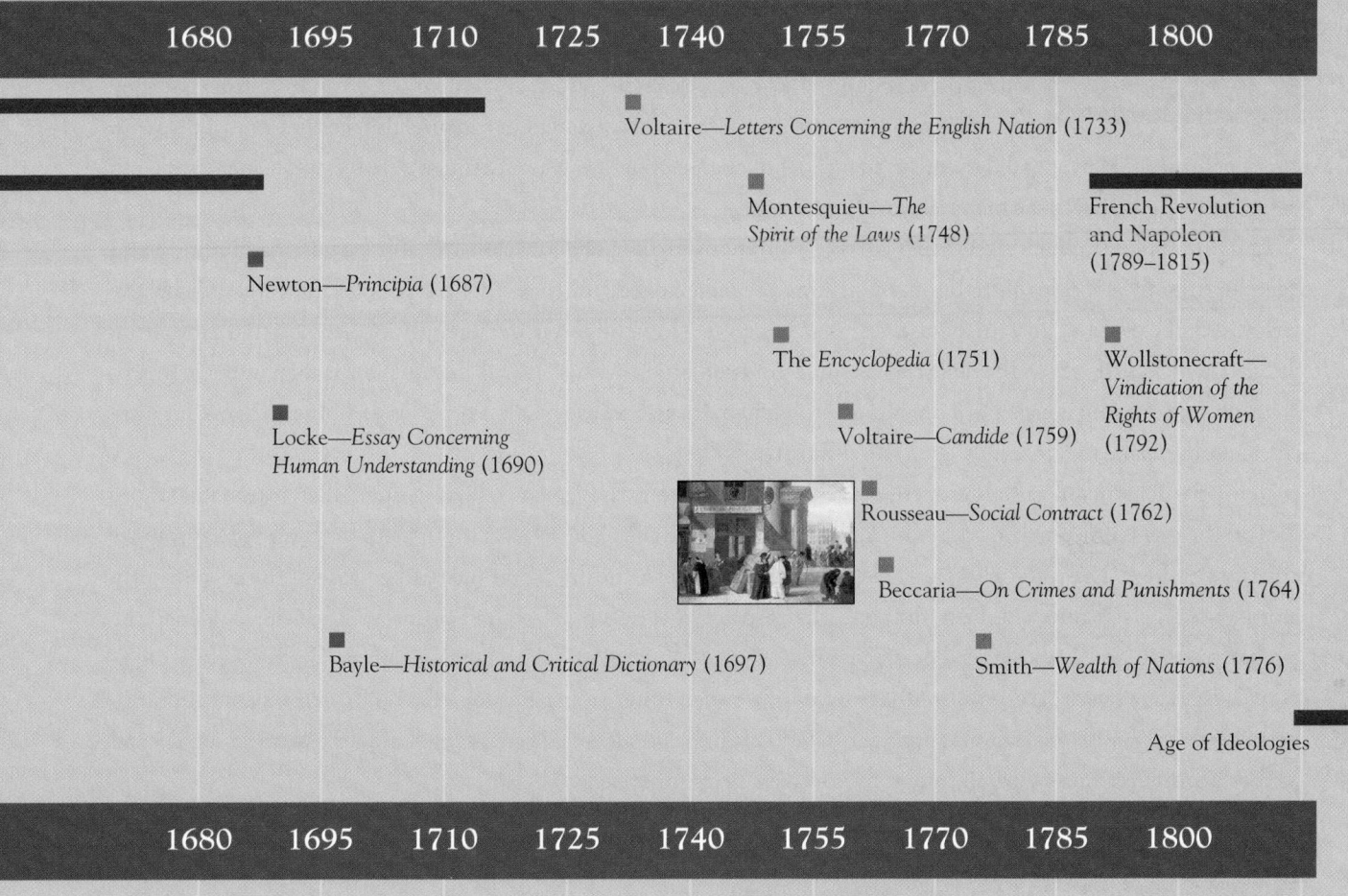

1680　1695　1710　1725　1740　1755　1770　1785　1800

Voltaire—*Letters Concerning the English Nation* (1733)

Montesquieu—*The Spirit of the Laws* (1748)

French Revolution and Napoleon (1789–1815)

Newton—*Principia* (1687)

The *Encyclopedia* (1751)

Wollstonecraft—*Vindication of the Rights of Women* (1792)

Locke—*Essay Concerning Human Understanding* (1690)

Voltaire—*Candide* (1759)

Rousseau—*Social Contract* (1762)

Beccaria—*On Crimes and Punishments* (1764)

Bayle—*Historical and Critical Dictionary* (1697)

Smith—*Wealth of Nations* (1776)

Age of Ideologies

1680　1695　1710　1725　1740　1755　1770　1785　1800

These gatherings and interchanges spread the ideas of the Enlightenment throughout society and enhanced the social respectability of intellectuals. They also helped create a common intellectual culture that crossed class lines and political borders and that contributed to an informed body of public opinion. People who participated in these interchanges came to sense that they could freely express ideas as well as debate political and social issues. By the last quarter of the eighteenth century, Enlightenment ideas could be heard even in the camps of the *philosophes'* traditional opponents—the clergy, governmental officials, and monarchs. As we will see, these ideas pushed some monarchs to enact "enlightened" reforms and encouraged many other people to demand revolutionary change.

Summary

The great intellectual revolution of the seventeenth and eighteenth centuries was fueled by advances in science. Brimming with new scientific ideas and discoveries, Western civilization relinquished its medieval assumptions and embarked on an innovative journey unique among the cultures of the world. This change in direction became one of the main forces behind the power and dynamism that came to characterize the West. Through science, westerners hoped to gain greater control over the material world and nature.

Enlightenment thinkers carried these daring aspirations further, self-consciously leading a mission of reform and freedom from the shackles of tradition. By striking the match of reason, they believed, people could at last dispel the darkness of the past and liberate themselves as never before. Thus enlightened, humanity as a whole could move from childhood to adulthood. As the *philosophe* Baron d'Holbach proclaimed, "The *enlightened man*, is man in his maturity, in his perfection; who is capable of pursuing his own happiness; because he has learned to examine, to think for himself, and not to take that for truth upon the authority of others."

Many participants in Enlightenment circles have since been criticized as self-concerned dilettantes reluctant to take on the risks of real reform. Most historians, however, see the *philosophes* as thoughtful, sincere, and sometimes brilliant thinkers. The *philosophes* clearly left a mark on Western culture. Their ideas, like those of the seventeenth-century scientists, threatened the traditional order, especially the church. As their primary legacy, they widened the gap between religiously influenced doctrines and accepted scholarly thought. Equally significant, they set the intellectual stage for a series of revolutions that would soon sweep America and Europe. Above all, their way of thinking—stressing reason, individualism, and progress—would form the intellectual foundation of modern Western society and further distinguish this civilization from its non-Western counterparts.

REVIEW, ANALYZE, AND ANTICIPATE

REVIEW THE PREVIOUS CHAPTER

Chapter 12—"Faith, Fortune, and Fame"—told how several European powers expanded overseas during the fifteenth, sixteenth, and seventeenth centuries and grew rich from the commerce. Chapter 13—"The Struggle for Survival and Sovereignty"—focused on how kings and nobles battled for power, the resolutions of those struggles, and their impact on the millions of people outside the elite.

1. *Analyze how the expansion of Europe might have stimulated scientific research.*

2. *In what ways did the effort of monarchs to increase their power and create stability relate to the promotion of science and the desire for greater intellectual certainty?*

ANALYZE THIS CHAPTER

Chapter 14—"A New World of Reason and Reform"—examines the changing intellectual foundations of the West.

1. *List and analyze the differences between the new scientific views of the world and traditional medieval views. How did standards for ascertaining the "truth" differ between these two perspectives?*

2. *Analyze the beliefs and motives of three central figures in the scientific revolution. What barriers did they have to overcome to present their views?*

3. *Do you think the Enlightenment merely popularized the scientific revolution, or did it accomplish something more?*

4. *In what ways did the Enlightenment threaten traditional views and authorities?*

ANTICIPATE THE NEXT CHAPTER

In Chapter 15—"Competing for Power and Wealth"—the struggles of Western powers over land, position, and commerce, as well as the economic and social changes affecting life in several Western societies during the eighteenth century, will be examined.

1. *What kinds of reforms—actual changes in governments and institutions—would most likely flow from Enlightenment ideas?*

2. *What social groups might try to adopt the ideas of the Enlightenment as a basis for demanding political and social reforms? Why might some monarchs consider enacting Enlightenment ideas?*

BEYOND THE CLASSROOM

QUESTIONING TRUTH AND AUTHORITY

Debus, Allen. *Man and Nature in the Renaissance*. Cambridge: Cambridge University Press, 1978. A solid, thoughtful analysis of the intellectual roots of scientific thought.

Kuhn, Thomas S. *The Structure of Scientific Revolutions*, 2nd ed. Chicago: University of Chicago Press, 1970. A landmark analysis of the nature, causes, and consequences of transformations in scientific concepts.

Mandrou, Robert. *From Humanism to Science*. Atlantic Highlands, NJ: Humanities Press, 1979. Describes how the role of intellectuals changed between 1480 and 1700.

Teresi, Dick. *Lost Discoveries: The Ancient Roots of Modern Science—From the Babylonians to the Maya*. New York: Simon & Schuster, 2003. A recent book that focuses on discoveries from non-Western societies that pre-dated Europe's Scientific Revolution.

DEVELOPING A MODERN SCIENTIFIC VIEW

Cohen, H.F. *The Scientific Revolution*. Chicago: University of Chicago Press, 1994. An analysis of when and where modern science began.

Hall, Rupert A. *The Revolution in Science, 1500–1750*. London: Longman, 1983. A useful introduction to the developments in science during this period.

Schiebinger, Londa. *The Mind Has No Sex? Women in the Origins of Modern Science*. Cambridge, MA: Harvard University Press, 1990. Examines the participation of women in science and stresses how science reflected male biases.

Shapin, Steven, *The Scientific Revolution*. Chicago: University of Chicago Press, 1996. A concise, new interpretation questioning whether there was a "scientific revolution."

Webster, Charles. *The Great Instauration: Science, Medicine, and Reform*. New York: Holmes & Meier Publishers, 1976. An excellent study that connects the development of scientific attitudes to England's Puritan revolution.

Westfall, Richard. *The Construction of Modern Science: Mechanisms and Mechanics*. New York: Cambridge University Press, 1977. A good survey of scientific developments during the seventeenth century that emphasizes the importance of mathematics and mechanics.

Westfall, Richard. *The Life of Isaac Newton*. Cambridge: Cambridge University Press, 1993. A full-scale biography of Isaac Newton.

SUPPORTING AND SPREADING SCIENCE

Jacob, Margaret C. *The Cultural Meaning of the Scientific Revolution*. New York: Alfred A. Knopf, 1988. Examines the evolution of science within its political, social, and cultural context.

Moran, Bruce T., ed. *Patronage and Institutions: Science, Technology and Medicine at the European Court, 1500–1750*. Rochester, NY: Boydell Press, 1991. Examines the role of royal courts in supporting and shaping science during this period.

LAYING THE FOUNDATIONS FOR THE ENLIGHTENMENT

Hampson, Norman. *The Enlightenment*. London: Penguin Books, 1982. A thorough survey that relates the Enlightenment to contemporary events.

Imhof, Ulrich. *The Enlightenment*. Oxford: Blackwell, 1994. A recent examination and evaluation of the Enlightenment.

Sklar, Judith. *Montesquieu*. Oxford: Oxford University Press, 1987. A concise, well-written study of Montesquieu and his ideas.

THE ENLIGHTENMENT IN FULL STRIDE

Besterman, Theodore. *Voltaire*, 3rd ed. Chicago: University of Chicago Press, 1976. A useful biography of this major Enlightenment figure.

Chartier, Roger. *The Cultural Uses of Print in Early Modern France*. Princeton, NJ: Princeton University Press, 1987. Examines changing reading habits and the connections between culture and society in eighteenth-century France.

Darton, Robert. *The Business of Enlightenment: A Publishing History of the Encyclopedia, 1775–1800*. Cambridge, Mass.: Belknap Press, 1979. A well-written social history and analysis of the publication of the Encyclopedia.

Gay, Peter. *The Enlightenment: An Interpretation*, 2 volumes. New York: Alfred A. Knopf, 1966–1969. A classic study, exhaustive, but with a strong point of view.

Goodman, Dena. *The Republic of Letters: A Cultural History of the French Enlightenment*. Ithaca, NY: Cornell University Press, 1994. A study of the cultural and intellectual life of eighteenth-century France that concentrates on the role played by the salons.

Lougee, Carolyn. *Le Paradis des Femmes. Women, Salons, and Social Stratification in Seventeenth-Century France*. Princeton, N.J.: Princeton University Press, 1976. Analyzes the foundations and importance of the French salons, emphasizing the role played by women in them.

For quiz questions that tie the book to the videos and additional primary sources, please go to the Primary Source Investigator CD.

QUIZ

Documents

DOCUMENT 14.1
Kepler and Galileo Exchange Letters about Science

Many leading European scholars of the Scientific Revolution feared publishing their views, which were often unpopular with religious authorities. Such scholars sometimes turned to each other for support, as the following late-sixteenth-century letters between Kepler and Galileo suggest. Here the two men discuss their beliefs in Copernican theory.

■ **Investigate the Document**

Why *is Galileo reluctant to publish his views on the Copernican position?* **How** *does Kepler respond to Galileo's concerns?*

Galileo to Kepler: "Like you, I accepted the Copernican position several years ago. I have written up many reasons on the subject, but have not dared until now to bring them into the open. I would dare publish my thoughts if there were many like you; but, since there are not, I shall forbear."

Kepler's Reply: "I could only have wished that you, who have so profound an insight, would choose another way. You advise us to retreat before the general ignorance and not to expose ourselves to the violent attacks of the mob of scholars. But after a tremendous task has been begun in our time, first by Copernicus and then by many very learned mathematicians, and when the assertion that the Earth moves can no longer be considered something new, would it not be much better to pull the wagon to its goal by our joint efforts, now that we have got it under way, and gradually, with powerful voices, to shout down the common herd? Be of good cheer, Galileo, and come out publicly! If I judge correctly, there are only a few of the distinguished mathematicians of Europe who would part company with us, so great is the power of truth. If Italy seems a less favorable place for your publication, perhaps Germany will allow us this freedom."

Source: Giorgio de Santillana, *The Crime of Galileo* (Chicago: University of Chicago Press, 1955), pp. 11 and 14–15.

DOCUMENT 14.2
Isaac Newton: God in a Scientific Universe

Like Galileo and Descartes, Newton was well aware that his ideas had profound implications for theology. His views, he realized, might even be considered contrary to religious doctrine. Yet Newton was a deeply spiritual man and took pains to distinguish the appropriate realms of science and religion. In the following selection from Opticks (1704), his analysis of light, Newton emphasizes that his ideas and systems still allow room for God in the universe.

■ **Investigate the Document**

What *is Newton's view of the role played by God in the universe?* **Might** *scientists today have any objections to these ideas? If so,* **what** *might they be?*

All these things being consider'd, it seems probable to me, that God in the Beginning form'd Matter in solid, massy, hard, impenetrable moveable Particles, of such Sizes and Figures, and with such other Properties, and in such Proportion to Space, as most conduced to the End for which he form'd them; and that these primitive Particles being Solids, are incomparably harder than any porous Bodies compounded of them; even so very hard, as never to wear or break in pieces; no ordinary Power being able to divide what God himself made one in the first Creation. . . .

It seems to me farther, that these Particles have not only a *Vis inertiae*, accompanied with such passive Laws of Motion as naturally result from that Force, but also that they are moved by certain active Principles, such as is that of Gravity, and that which causes Fermentation, and the Cohesion of Bodies. These Principles I consider, not as occult Qualities, supposed to result from the specifick Forms of Things, but as general Laws of Nature, by which the Things themselves are form'd; their Truth appearing to us by Phaenomena, though their Causes be not yet discover'd. . . .

Source: Sir Isaac Newton, *Opticks*, 4th ed. (London: 1730), pp. 400–402.

Now by the help of these Principles, all material Things seem to have been composed of the hard and solid Particles above-mention'd, variously associated in the first Creation by the Counsel of an intelligent Agent. For it became him who created them to set them in order. And if he did no, it's unphilosophical to seek for any other Origin of the World, or to pretend that it might arise out of a Chaos by the mere Laws of Nature; though being once form'd, it may continue by those Laws for many Ages.

DOCUMENT 14.3

Francis Bacon Promotes a New Method of Inquiry

In the early seventeenth century, English lawyer and scholar Francis Bacon (1561-1626) attacked what he considered the "in fashion" path to truths and proposed, in its place, a new "scientific" method of inquiry. The following is an excerpt from his New Organon, *first published in 1620. His work and his optimistic spirit influenced many other scholars, leading some to call him a prophet of the Scientific Revolution.*

■ **Investigate the Document**

*According to Bacon, **what** is the "true way" of "searching into and discovering truth?" **Why** is Bacon so optimistic about the potential of his method?*

I. Man, being the servant and interpreter of Nature, can do and understand so much and so much only as he has observed in fact or in thought of the course of nature: beyond this he neither knows anything nor can do anything.

II. Neither the naked hand nor the understanding left to itself can effect much. It is by instruments and helps that the work is done, which are as much wanted for the understanding as for the hand. And as the instruments of the hand either give motion or guide it, so the instruments of the mind supply either suggestions for the understanding or cautions.

Source: James Spedding, R. L. Ellis, and Doublas Heath, eds., The Works of Francis Bacon (New York: Hurd and Houghton, 1864), Vol 10, pp. 67, 74, 132.

III. Human knowledge and human power meet in one; for where the cause is not known the effect cannot be produced. Nature to be commanded must be obeyed; and that which in contemplation is as the cause is in operation as the rule. . . .

XIX. There are and can be only two ways of searching into and discovering truth. The one files from the senses and particulars to the most general axioms, and from these principles, the truth of which it takes for settled and immovable, proceeds to judgment and to the discovery of middle axioms. And this way is now in fashion. The other derives axioms from the senses and particulars, rising by a gradual and unbroken ascent, so that it arrives at the most general axioms last of all. This is the truth way, but as yet untried. . . .

XXII. Both ways set out from the senses and particulars, and rest in the highest generalizes, but the difference between them is infinite. For the one just glances at experiment and particulars in passing, the other swells duly and orderly among them. The one, again, begins at once by establishing certain abstract and useless generalities, the other rises by gradual steps to that which is prior and better known in the order of nature. . . .

There is therefore much ground for hoping that there are still laid up in the womb of nature many secrets of excellent use, having no affinity or parallelism with any thing that is now known, but lying entirely out of the beat of the imagination, which have not yet been found out. They too no doubt will some time or other, in the course and revolution of many ages, come to light of themselves, just as the others did; only by the method of which we are now treating they can be speedily and suddenly and simultaneously presented and anticipated.

DOCUMENT 14.4

Condorcet Lauds the Power of Reason

No one lauded the power of reason and the Enlightenment, or had more hope for the future—thanks to the Enlightenment—that the French mathematician and philosophe, the Marquis de Condorcet (1743–1794). The following is an excerpt from his Sketch of the Progress of the Human Mind, *a book tracing human "progress" over time, that he completed in 1794.*

■ **Investigate the Document**

What "hopes" does Condorcet have for the future of humanity? According to Condorcet, what will open the door to such great progress?

Our hopes for the future condition of the human race can be subsumed under three important heads: the abolition of inequality between nations, the progress of equality within each nation, and the true perfection of mankind. Will all nations one day attain that state of civilization which the most enlightened, the freest and the least burdened by prejudices, such as the French and the Anglo-Americans, have attained already? Will the vast gulf that separates these peoples from the slavery of nations under the rule of monarchs, from the barbarism of African tribes, from the ignorance of savages, little by little disappear? . . .

In answering these three questions we shall find in the experience of the past, in the observation of the progress that the sciences and civilization have already made, in the analysis of the progress of the human mind and of the development of its faculties, the strongest reasons for believing that nature has set no limit to the realization of our hopes.

If we glance at the state of the world today we see first of all that in Europe the principles of the French constitution are already those of all enlightened men. We see them too widely propagated, too seriously professed, for priests and despots to prevent their gradual penetration even into the hovels of their slaves; there they will soon awaken in these slaves the remnants of their common sense and inspire them with that smoldering indignation which not even constant humiliation and fear can smother in the soul of the oppressed. . . .

The time will therefore come when the sun will shine only on free men who know no other master but their reason; when tyrants and slaves, priests and their stupid or hypocritical instruments will exist only in works of history and on the stage; and when we shall think of them only to pity their victims and their dupes; to maintain ourselves in a state of vigilance by thinking on their excesses; and to learn how

to recognize and so to destroy, by force of reason, the first seeds of tyranny and superstition, should they ever dare to reappear amongst us.

DOCUMENT 14.5
Cesare Beccaria on Crimes and Punishments

Many eighteenth-century analyses of social and political institutions reflected the philosophy of the Enlightenment. Cesare Beccaria (1735–1794), an Italian aristocrat and government official, made one of the most influential calls for enlightened reform. In On Crimes and Punishments *(1764), he severely criticized the criminology and penology of the* ancien régime *and suggested reforms.*

■ **Investigate the Document**

What principles underlie Beccaria's ideas about crime and punishment? How do his ideas relate to the spirit of the Enlightenment?

We have seen what the true measure of crimes is—namely, the *harm done to society*. This is one of those palpable truths which, though requiring neither quadrants nor telescopes for their discovery, and lying well within the capacity of any ordinary intellect, are, nevertheless, because of a marvelous combination of circumstances, known with clarity and precision only by some few thinking men in every nation and in every age. . . .

They were in error who believed that the true measure of crimes is to be found in the intention of the person who commits them. Intention depends on the impression objects actually make and on the precedent disposition of the mind; these vary in all men and in each man, according to the swift succession of ideas, of passions, and of circumstances. . . .

Others measure crimes rather by the dignity of the injured person than by the importance [of the offense] with respect to the public good. If this were the true measure of crimes, an irreverence toward the Being of beings ought to be more severely punished than the assassination of a monarch, the superiority of nature constituting infinite compensation for the difference in the injury.

Source: Jean Antoine Nicholas Caritat Marquis de Condorcet, *Sketch for a Historical Picture on the Progress of the Human Mind*, tr. June Barraclough. London: Weidenfeld and Nicolson (Orion Books), 1955, pp 236–237, 244.

Source: Cesare Beccaria, *On Crimes and Punishments*, Henry Paolucci, Trans, (New York: Bobbs-Merrill Co., Inc, 1963), pp. 64–65, 93–99.

Finally, some have thought that the gravity of sinfulness ought to enter into the measure of crimes. The fallacy of this opinion will at once appear to the eye of an impartial examiner of the true relations between men and men, and between men and God. . . .

It is better to prevent crimes than to punish them. This is the ultimate end of every good legislation, which, to use the general terms for assessing the good and evils of life, is the art of leading men to the greatest possible happiness or to the least possible unhappiness. . . .

Do you want to prevent crimes? See to it that the laws are clear and simple and that the entire force of a nation is united in their defense, and that no part of it is employed to destroy them. See to it that the laws favor not so much classes of men as men themselves. See to it that men fear the laws and fear nothing else. . . .

Another way of preventing crimes is to reward virtue. Upon this subject I notice a general silence in the laws of all the nations of our day. If the prizes offered by the academies to discoverers of useful truths have increased our knowledge and have multiplied good books, why should not prizes distributed by the beneficent hand of the sovereign serve in a similar way to multiply virtuous actions? The coin of honor is always inexhaustible and fruitful in the hands of the wise distributor.

Finally, the surest but most difficult way to prevent crimes is by perfecting education. . . .

From what has thus far been demonstrated, one may deduce a general theorem of considerable utility, though hardly conformable with custom, the usual legislator of nations; it is this: *In order for punishment not to be, in every instance, an act of violence of one or of many against a private citizen, it must be essentially public, prompt, necessary, the least possible in the given circumstances, proportionate to the crimes, dictated by the laws.*

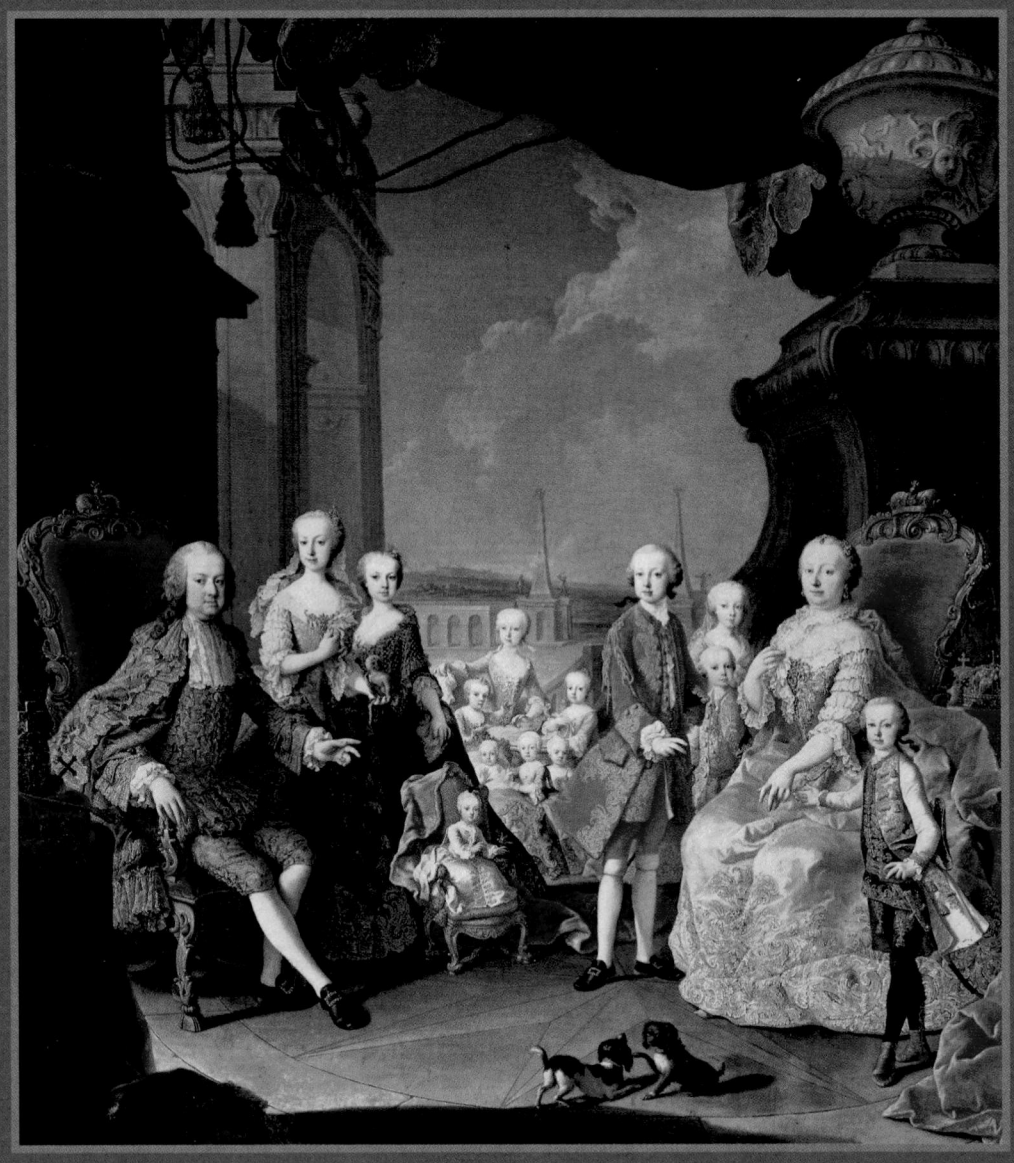

Martin Meytens, Maria Theresa and Her Family, 1750

In 1750, Habsburg court artist Martin Meytens (1695–1770) painted Austria's powerful monarch, Maria Theresa (1717–1780), with her husband (seated on the left) and thirteen of her sixteen children. Her son, Joseph, heir to the throne, stands in a favored place at the center of the star floor. As this painting suggests, even though she led Austria through two major wars, Maria Theresa often chose to present herself as a good mother to both her family and her nation.

CHAPTER 15

Competing for Power and Wealth

The Old Regime, 1715–1789

STUDY • Statebuilding and warfare • Enlightened Absolutism • Country and city life • Culture of the elite • Culture for the lower classes • The American Revolution. 🌐NOTICE the connections between politics, war, and society during the eighteenth century.

"A reasonable man is always happy if he has what is necessary for him according to his condition [social rank], that is to say, if he has the protection of the laws, and can live as his father lived before him," wrote a French observer in 1747. The political lesson behind these words was clear: "Essential . . . to the good of a nation is being governed in one constant and uniform manner." Most people living in the eighteenth century would have nodded their heads in agreement. Indeed, they actively upheld the social order—ranked, governed, and sanctioned as it was by tradition and Christian teachings.

Despite this affirmation of stability, change was afoot in these years, even among monarchs such as Austria's Maria Theresa (r. 1740–1780) (p. 514). During the seventeenth century, kings and queens had struggled with nobles in their own countries for control and with other monarchs to increase their nations' sway. In their continuing competition for power and wealth, eighteenth-century kings and queens tried to strengthen their states while gaining status—often through war—in the international arena. Below them, ambitious aristocrats flexed their muscles, sometimes challenging their monarchs, sometimes forging alliances with them, and often reveling in the new wealth and culture that now lay within their reach. They, along with the growing number of commoners, began to see much promise in the new ways to produce food and organize manufacturing, all fueled by accelerating commerce—especially with overseas colonies. Moreover, many elites—including some monarchs themselves—also recognized the strength of Enlightenment ideas and began to think of ways to institute "enlightened" reforms. At the base of Western society, the mass of peasants and workers toiled, as they always had. However, their numbers were increasing, and their ways of life were slowly adjusting to the pressures of change. This society and its politics would later be known as the Old Regime, but many living at the time detected the quickening pulse of a new era.

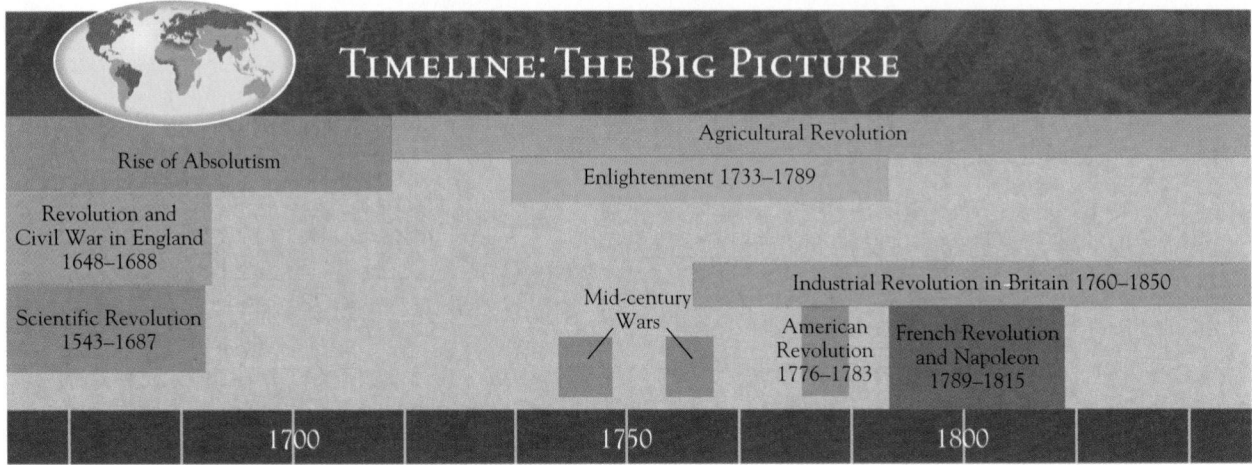

TIMELINE: THE BIG PICTURE

Rise of Absolutism

Agricultural Revolution

Enlightenment 1733–1789

Revolution and
Civil War in England
1648–1688

Industrial Revolution in Britain 1760–1850

Mid-century
Wars

Scientific Revolution
1543–1687

American
Revolution
1776–1783

French Revolution
and Napoleon
1789–1815

1700   1750   1800

Statebuilding and War

In August 1715, the old and sad Louis XIV fell ill. His legs swelled and turned black as gangrene set in. Remarkably, he had outlived both his son and grandson. On his deathbed, Louis warned his five-year-old great-grandson, who would succeed him as Louis XV (r. 1715–1774), not to "imitate my love of building nor my liking of war." Neither Louis XV nor many other rulers of the time managed to follow this advice for long. War and building might cost lives and drain royal treasuries, but they made a spectacular show of power in a competitive world. The rulers of Europe clung to their statebuilding ways, straining to secure their central governments and ensure their own position at the top.

During the seventeenth century, this competitiveness had plunged Europe into a series of bloody conflicts—the very battles Louis XIV regretted on his deathbed (see Chapter 13). In western Europe, the violence stopped with the Peace of Utrecht in 1713–1714. Seven years later, the Treaty of Nystad (1721) ended the conflicts in eastern Europe (see Map 15.1). For a while, the two treaties held. Monarchs throughout Europe tried to adhere to the principle of a balance of power to prevent any one state or alliance from dominating the others. Nevertheless, anyone hoping for an extended period free of war would be sorely disappointed. Up-and-coming states such as Prussia and Britain bristled with ambition and vied with their established competitors for power, prestige, and wealth. Their struggles spread beyond the borders of Europe to overseas colonies on continents from North America to Asia, in this sense turning European wars into global conflicts. As we will see, this competition subjected millions of people to a fresh round of hardship and irrevocably altered the fate and fortunes of nations throughout the West.

RISING AMBITIONS IN EASTERN EUROPE

Within Europe, the fiercest competition took place in eastern Europe. There, Russia and Brandenburg-Prussia were on the rise. Under Peter the Great, Russia had already defeated Sweden, grabbing much of the northeastern Baltic coast in the process. Russia next hoped to take advantage of the sprawling but weak Polish state farther west (see Chapter 13) and to benefit from the decline of the Ottoman Empire, which controlled the Black Sea to Russia's south. Brandenburg-Prussia also saw opportunities in Poland, which divided and bordered its lands. This militaristic state also coveted some of the holdings of the bloated Austro-Hungarian Empire to the south, which in turn intended to hold its own in the power struggle. Someone would have to pay the price for all these ambitions.

Peter the Great had done much to turn Russia toward the west and make it a great power. By the time of his death in 1725, he had modernized Russia's government and military, established Russia as the dominant power in northeastern Europe, and pressured the Russian nobility into the state bureaucracy and army officer corps. In the process, he made many enemies, from the peasants who paid dearly for Peter's accomplishments to all those who had a stake in the very social, cultural, and religious traditions that Peter attacked. His successors would have to face these enemies and shoulder the task of sustaining Russia's expansion to the south and west.

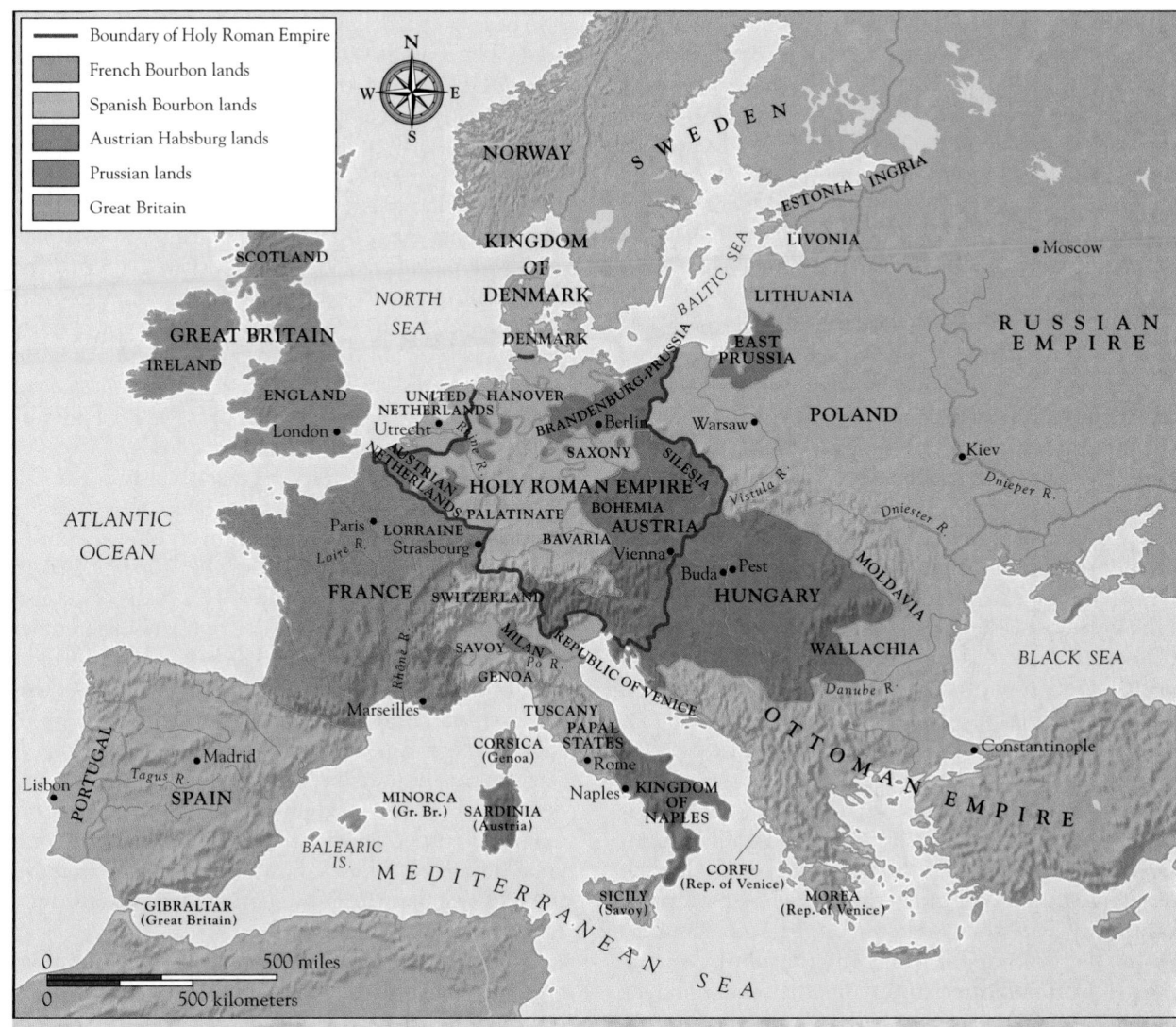

THINKING ABOUT GEOGRAPHY

MAP 15.1 *Europe, 1721*

This map shows Europe after the Treaties of Utrecht (1714) and Nystad (1721). ◼ **Notice** that although France and Spain are ruled by Bourbon monarchs, the two nations remain separate. **How** might their union have altered the balance of power in Europe? ◼ **Locate** the large states in eastern Europe. **Which** of these states, despite their size, are declining powers? ◼ **Notice** the lands controlled by Austria. **Why might** this power's holdings be vulnerable?

Six mediocre rulers followed Peter—including an infant, a boy of twelve, and a mentally unstable tsar. Despite this shaky leadership, Russia held its ground. From 1725 to 1762, its population increased, and the landowning elite grew wealthier than ever. The nobility took back some of the authority it had lost to Peter, diminishing the service it owed to the state; in 1762, nobles freed themselves of all such obligations.

Nevertheless, they still staffed the bureaucracy and military officer corps. Moreover, nobles cracked down

New leadership in expanding Russia

even more on their serfs, reducing their status to that of mere property. The 1767 Decree on Serfs made the situation crystal clear: "Serfs and peasants . . . owe their landlords proper submission and absolute obedience in all matters."

The decades of weak leadership ended when a dynamic new leader ascended the Russian throne.

Catherine the Great

Catherine the Great (r. 1762–1796) grew up an obscure princess from one of the little German states. For political reasons, her family married her to young Peter III (r. 1762), the tyrannical and intellectually limited grandson of Peter the Great and heir to the Russian crown. He soon rejected her in all ways, and after he became tsar, he quickly lost most of his supporters as well. Catherine had no intention of languishing in obscurity. "I did not care about Peter," she later wrote, "but I did care about the crown." Less than a year after he took the throne, Catherine conspired with a group of aristocratic army officers, who assassinated him and declared Catherine tsarina of Russia.

The new empress used her striking intelligence, charm, and political talent to assert her own power and expand Russian territory and might. Well educated, she thought of herself as attuned to Enlightenment ideas. She often corresponded with French *philosophes* such as Denis Diderot, who spent some time at St. Petersburg as her guest. In 1766, she congratulated Voltaire for triumphing "against the enemies of mankind: superstition, fanaticism, ignorance, quibbling, evil judges, and the power that rests in their hands." Voltaire returned the favor with constant praise for Catherine. She relaxed the traditionally tight constraints on the press in Russia and she confiscated church lands—policies that seemed in line with Enlightenment thinking. Her educational reforms, by which she established new local schools, teachers' colleges, and schools for girls, also suggested a forward-thinking monarch. Most stunningly, Catherine convened a legislative commission, half of whose members were commoners (some even peasants), to reform Russia's legal code. She wrote the *Instruction* (1767) to that commission herself, relying on the works of key Enlightenment figures such as Montesquieu and Beccaria. Her *Instruction* called for equality before the law, the abolition of torture, and other liberal reforms.

These programs promised more than they delivered. The commission members squabbled among themselves, and in the end, the effort yielded only minor reforms before it was finally abandoned. Catherine's early talk of easing the burdens on the peasantry also came to little; in return for the support of noble landowners, she allowed them to subjugate the peasants even further. As Document 15.1 suggests (see page D15.1), some observers criticized the treatment of Russia's serfs. For example, Alexander Radischev argued, "What good does it do the country that every year a few thousand more bushels of grain are grown, if those who produce it are valued on a par with the ox whose job it is to break the heavy furrow?" Catherine imprisoned him.

In 1768, Catherine provoked a war against the Ottoman Empire. The event seems to have signaled her turn away from enlightened reform and toward power politics. A massive insurrection by Russian serfs in 1773 under the leadership of a Don Cossack, Yemelyan Pugachev (1726–1775), further soured her on reform. Pugachev claimed to be Catherine's murdered husband, a "redeemer tsar," and promised his followers land and freedom. Thousands of serfs in southwestern Russia turned against their masters—slaughtering hundreds of landlords and officials—and demanded an end to their plight. Catherine's army managed to put down the rebellion, but only with great difficulty. When some disgruntled followers betrayed Pugachev, the army captured him and tortured him to death.

Catherine proved more successful in her ambitious foreign policy. She defeated the Turks in 1774, extending Russia to the Black Sea and the Balkan Peninsula. Map 15.2 shows Russia's expansion to the south and west during the eighteenth century. For the Ottoman Empire, this defeat marked another step in an unstoppable decline.

Catherine then turned on Poland. At the beginning of the eighteenth century, Poland was the third-largest country in Europe. Yet, as

The Partition of Poland

we saw in Chapter 13, it lacked natural boundaries and a strong central government. Weak and without allies, it became a power vacuum that proved all too tempting to its ambitious neighbors. In 1772, Russia, Prussia, and Austria—having plotted Poland's demise among themselves—annexed slices of Polish territory. This aggression at long last stirred the Polish government to action. The Diet passed sweeping reforms, improved the lot

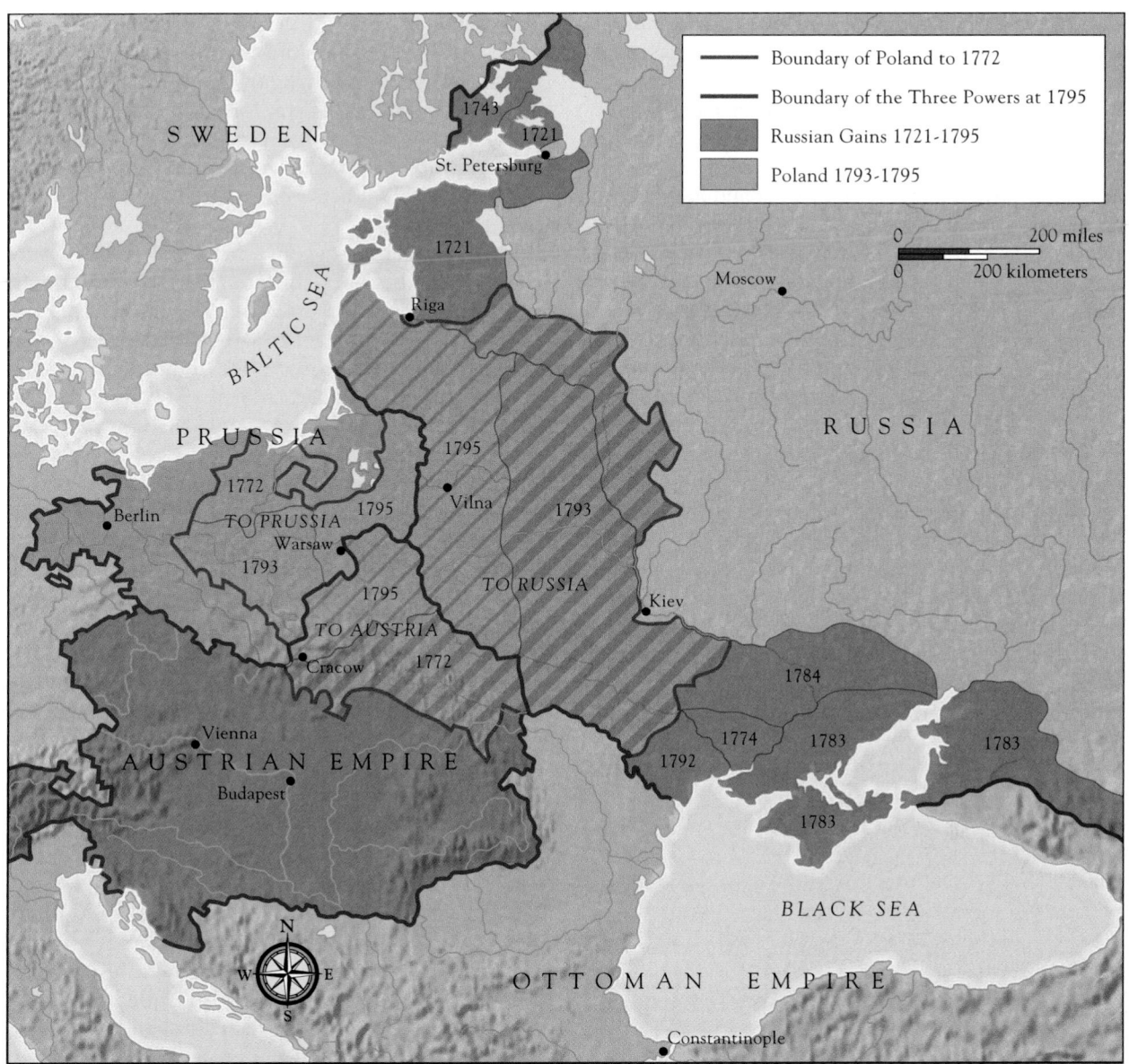

Legend:
— Boundary of Poland to 1772
— Boundary of the Three Powers at 1795
Russian Gains 1721-1795
Poland 1793-1795

THINKING ABOUT GEOGRAPHY

MAP 15.2 *The Expansion of Russia and the Partition of Poland, 1721–1795*

This map shows eastern Europe during the eighteenth century. **Notice** the division of Poland. **In what ways** did the partition of Poland benefit Russia, Prussia, and Austria? **How** might Poland's decline change the balance of power? **Notice** the expansion of Russia and Prussia. **Where** might these rising powers look for further expansion?

of commoners, and gave the central government power to act effectively. These changes came too late. Poland still could not match the combined armies of its enemies, and in 1795, the three aggressors divided the remainder of the hapless nation among themselves. Map 15.2 shows the eventual dismemberment of Poland, which left Russia, Prussia, and Austria the dominant powers in eastern Europe. When Catherine died in 1796 after 35 years of rule, Russia had grown to an ominous size and had taken its place as a major power in world affairs.

In east-central Europe, the small but rising Brandenburg-Prussia set its sights on the Austrian Empire, *Forging a military state in Prussia* a large power struggling to maintain control over its far-flung lands. From 1713 to 1740, the vigorous Frederick William I ruled Prussia. The king was obsessed with unquestioned absolutism, centralized bureaucratic administration, and above all, the military. His martial uniforms and preoccupation with Prussian soldiery earned him the label the "Sergeant King."

Frederick William's mental image of the perfect military dominated his policies and Prussian society. While he employed his army for road and canal building as well as traditional military service, some 70 percent of the state's budget went to the armed forces, whose size he more than doubled during his reign. Rather than relying on mercenaries, the king required all men to register for military service in local units commanded by German noble officers. The localities, in turn, had to recruit and support these regiments, and soldiers were billeted among the civilian population.

As Figure 15.1 suggests, drills and parades were common sights. The tight formation shown in the illustration resembles the fighting formations the Prussians strove to achieve in actual battle. Here is an image of near-perfect discipline and order, mastered through endless drill and professional command. The wooden horse at the left was used to punish undisciplined soldiers. The presence of the townspeople in the background on the right suggests that exercises such as these typically took place within towns rather than at separate military centers. No other state in Europe could boast such a high proportion of men, from peasant to noble, in the military. Nor could any other state point to such a regimented society. In Prussia, the higher ranks of the military and state bureaucracy were reserved for the nobility; the middle classes were clearly prevented from rising to noble status; and the peasantry was a subordinate, overburdened people, often still serfs living in almost slavelike relationships to their landowning masters.

Despite the martial tenor of life in Prussia, the king left a surprisingly progressive legacy. Frederick William I avoided wars, promoted a strong economy, welcomed Protestant and Jewish refugees, and filled the treasury. In 1740 he passed all that he had built, intact, on to his talented son Frederick II (r. 1740–1786), later known as Frederick the Great. The new king soon used this army—the fourth largest in Europe—and the money his father had accumulated to make a bold bid for Austrian lands.

In the same year that Frederick II ascended the throne in Prussia, Maria Theresa (r. 1740–1780) be- *Austria tries to hold on* came empress of the Austrian Habsburg dominions. Austria was not a tightly controlled, militaristic state like Prussia. Rather, it had already lost

FIGURE 15.1
Prussian troops at drill.

most of the indirect control it once held over the central German states as head of the Holy Roman Empire. Austria's own lands contained a complex array of language groups and consisted of some semiautonomous territories. Austria could barely control Hungary, and its nobility fully dominated its serfs, who paid most taxes directly to their lords rather than to the crown. As a result, Maria Theresa could afford only a relatively small army.

The empress's father had feared that these weaknesses might prove Austria's undoing when he died. Moreover, there was only weak precedent for a female ruler of Habsburg lands. Therefore, he spent the final 20 years of his life securing agreement among all the European powers (embodied in a document called the Pragmatic Sanction) that his daughter would succeed him without question. In spite of his diligence, when he died in 1740, competitors arose to challenge her authority. As for the principle of balance of power among states implying a desire for peace, Frederick II of Prussia dismissed the idea bluntly: "The fundamental rule of governments is the principle of extending their territories."

As soon as Maria Theresa took the crown, Frederick challenged her authority, a common occurrence

The mid-century land wars when a succession was questionable in any way. Acting on his maxim that "the safety and greater good for the state demands that treaties should be broken under certain circumstances," the Prussian king marched his troops into Silesia (see Map 15.3), the richest of the Habsburg provinces. He also shrewdly forged alliances with other German states against Austria. His aggressive scheming plunged most of the major European states into a series of wars for the mastery of central Europe.

The War of the Austrian Succession dragged on for eight years (1740–1748). Maria Theresa rallied Hungarian arms to her defense and repelled Prussia's allies—Bavarians, Saxons, French, and Spanish. The conflict eventually turned into a military stalemate, which led to a 1748 peace treaty that ended the hostilities. Maria Theresa had managed to preserve the Habsburg state as a major power, but she had been unable to dislodge Frederick from Silesia.

Neither she nor her advisors intended to tolerate this robbery of their fair province by the upstart Prussians—even if it meant starting negotiations for an alliance with their traditional rival, France. Frederick grew fearful of being isolated by his enemies and left vulnerable to invasions. In 1756, when he signed an alliance with Great Britain—Prussia's opponent only a few years earlier—Maria Theresa solidified a new alliance with France. Docu-

ment 15.2 (see page D15.1) *The Diplomatic Revolution* reveals how difficult the change of allies was for Maria Theresa. This astounding shift of alliances—the so-called Diplomatic Revolution—suddenly transformed former enemies into friends. Meanwhile, Maria Theresa shored up Austria's internal resources by honing her government's control over taxation, diminishing burdens on the peasantry, and reorganizing the bureaucracy. All this strengthened her position as a ruler who could command strong forces and who enjoyed backing from a powerful ally.

Not one to wait for his enemies to strike first, Frederick reopened hostilities by overrunning Saxony in 1756, initiating the Seven Years' War (1756–1763). However, Frederick soon found himself at bay as France and Austria—now joined by Russia and Sweden, both of which hoped to gain lands at Prussia's expense—closed in on him from all directions. His only backing came from Britain, which saw an opportunity to weaken its longtime opponent, France. After holding off his enemies for six years, the exhausted Prussian king finally seemed near defeat. "I believe all is lost," he confessed in private. Then in 1762 his luck revived. The Russian tsarina Elizabeth, one of his most reviled enemies, died. Her successor, the weak Peter III, happened to admire Frederick and suddenly pulled Russia out of the war. The remaining allies soon lost stomach for the fight. The peace in 1763 left matters much as they had been before the war began, but as we will see (p. 527–531), the fighting in Europe spread to India, the Caribbean, and North America.

Having narrowly escaped destruction, Frederick spent the remaining 23 years of his life reconstructing his war-ravaged territories. He encouraged agriculture, subsidized and protected industry, and invited immigrants into his well-governed territories. At no time, though, did he neglect his army or lose his sense of practicality. Indeed, in 1772 he joined Austria and Russia in the first partition of Poland. Map 15.3 shows Prussia's expansion under Frederick, first at the expense of the Austrian Empire when he took Silesia, and then at the expense of Poland as he used the territory to unify the main portions of his country. The map also shows Prussia's chief competitor, Austria, with its more far-flung territories. By the time of his death in 1786, Frederick had raised Prussia to the status of a great power and shared the leadership of central Europe with Austria.

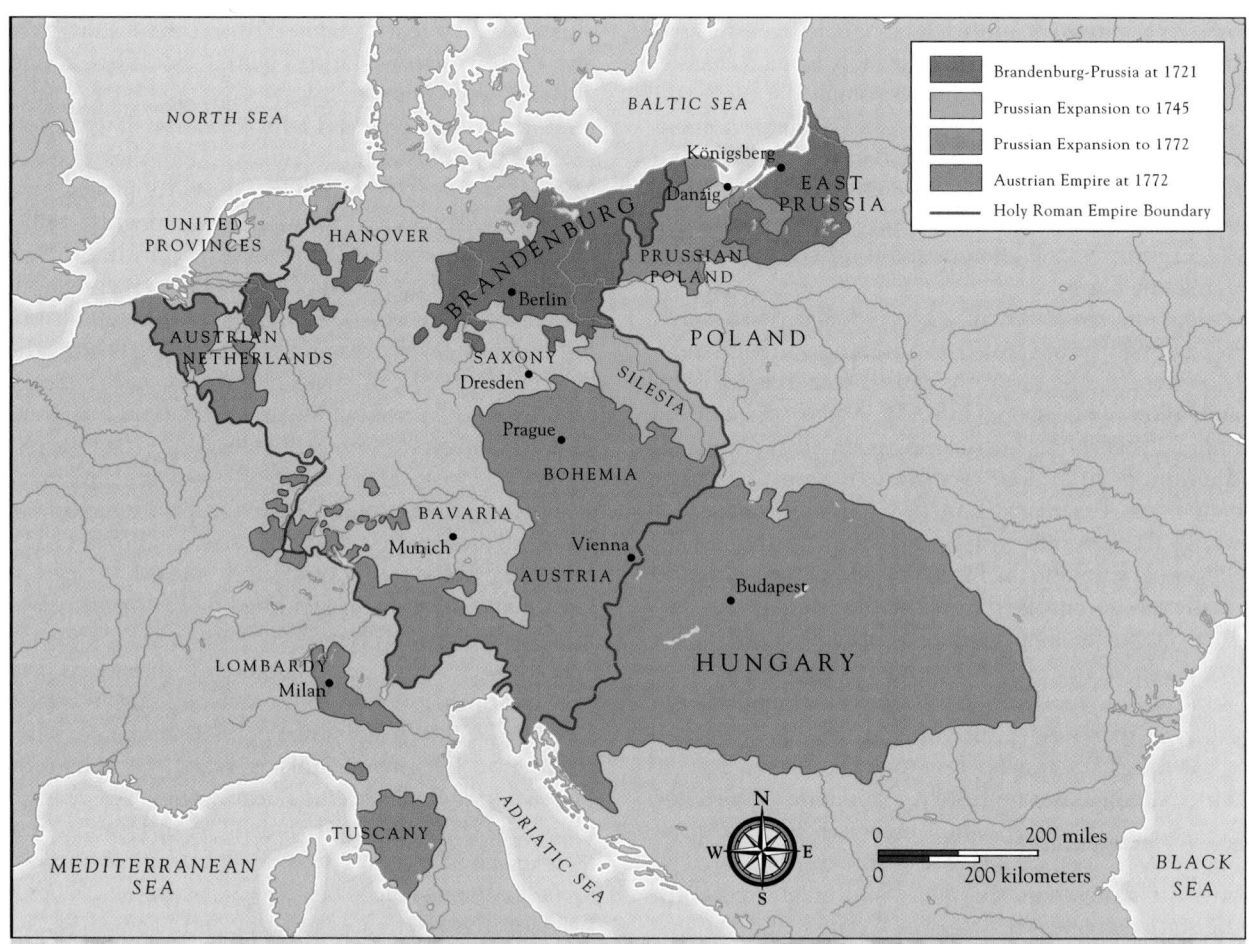

THINKING ABOUT GEOGRAPHY

MAP 15.3 *Prussia and the Austrian Empire, 1721–1772*

This map shows two growing eighteenth-century powers, Prussia and Austria. ❧ **Compare** the holdings of these two states. **Which** do you think might be considered the stronger? **What** problems face both in creating a strong, unified state? ❧ **Notice** France to the west and Russia to the east—both large and unified states. **Where** are Austria and Prussia most likely to compete with each other or expand?

WARFARE IN THE EIGHTEENTH CENTURY

The nature of wars fought by these eighteenth-century nations had evolved and changed from earlier times. Now armies consisted primarily of professional forces whose size and elaborate organization mirrored the centralized, bureaucratic governments they served. Officers were paid as full-time servants of the state in both peace and war. However, the troops they commanded were not all so "professional." Conscripts, volunteers, mercenaries, and even criminals made up their rank and file. In this sense, armies served as a depository for men without means and for those seen as threats to the social order. Officers tried to tame these motley groups by stressing harsh discipline and incessant drilling (see Figure 15.1).

Weapons and tactics were also changing. Reliable muskets; bayonets that no longer hindered fire; mobile cannons; and skilled coordination of troops, artillery, and cavalry all made warfare potentially more destructive than ever. Still, generals typically avoided all-out battles, preferring to expend their resources judiciously. "I do not favor pitched battles, especially at the beginning of a war," said Marshall Saxe, a leading French officer and writer on war tactics, in 1732. "I am convinced that a skillful general could make war all his life without being forced into one." Even Frederick the Great—not one to shy away from warfare—expressed this preference in his *Instructions for His Generals* (1747): "The greatest secret of war and the masterpiece of a skillful general is to starve his enemy." Instead of embarking on grand, decisive battles, then, eighteenth-century generals focused on building fortifications, initiating and maintaining sieges, securing supply lines, gaining superior positions, and piling up small advantages. Moreover, most military campaigns lasted only four or five months a year. Meanwhile, life outside the military—commerce, farming, culture, travel, and politics—went on as usual.

Yet, as Frederick the Great recognized, "war is [ultimately] decided only by battles and is not finished except by them." Outright fighting, when it finally occurred, took a heavy toll in human lives. Typically, soldiers arranged themselves in dense rows at least three men deep and fired their muskets, row by row, on command. Each side hurled artillery fire into the opposing troops and sent the cavalry charging in. Casualties mounted, but at the end of the day generals usually pulled their forces back from the battle with enough survivors to fight again.

Maritime battles cost fewer lives than land wars but could be crucial in the overall outcome of war. The largest ships of war in the eighteenth century carried up to 100 cannons. Figure 15.2, a cutaway view of a French warship, shows cannons poking out of the top three decks. Sailors are depicted at drill and at rest. At the upper right are officers' quarters, and the bottom decks house supplies, including livestock. Often firing at each other at point-blank range, many warships were destroyed or suffered grievous damage in these brutal clashes, and thousands of sailors perished.

A single battle, whether on land or sea, rarely led to a definitive outcome. More likely, the relentless draining away of money and men prompted diplomats to come to the bargaining table and end the war. This hemorrhaging of money and men was not missed by critics of the military, especially Enlightenment thinkers, who denigrated the old warrior

FIGURE 15.2
An eighteenth-century French warship. *Iconographic Encyclopaedia*, 1851.

FIGURE 15.3
William Hogarth, *Canvassing for Votes—The Election,* 1754.

staunchly opposed to any return of the Catholic Stuarts to the crown. Whigs also championed popular rights more than the conservative Tories did. Tories usually favored large landowners and a strong monarchy and had stood less firmly against the Stuarts than the Whigs had.

Differences between the two groups came to a head in 1714. That year, the Tories considered supporting James, a Catholic Stuart raised in France, against George I. An unsuccessful rebellion in favor of James discredited the Tories in the eyes of the monarchy. In 1746, the English army put down another rebellion in Scotland that had attempted to support a Catholic Stuart. This latest fiasco further alienated the Tory leadership from the British crown.

For these reasons, George I and his son George II (r. 1727–1760) selected their ministers from the Whigs rather than the Tories. The two kings' lack of talent and public support made them all the more dependent on Whig leadership for governance. That leadership came in the person of Robert Walpole (1676–1745). Already recognized as a superb speaker and leading Whig in the House of Commons, Walpole became First Lord of the Treasury and the most important minister in George I's Privy Council in 1721. Much of Walpole's prominence derived from his successful handling of a financial crisis after an overseas trading company collapsed in 1720 (the South Sea Bubble). After that coup, he brought in other Whigs who could control votes in Parliament. He flattered and "managed" the monarch to remain in favor. Through patronage—control over money, contracts, offices, and honors—and the manipulation of elections, he ensured the dominance of the Whigs and his own leadership for 20 years.

Many complained about this pattern of political corruption, which both Whigs and Tories used. One critic—the British artist William Hogarth (1697–1764)—produced many prints lambasting British political and social life. In Figure 15.3, one of a series of works on British elections, Hogarth shows a corrupt political campaign in progress. At the center, a voter emerges drunk from a riotous tavern. He

had died. The crown passed to George I (r. 1714–1727), the first of the German Hanoverian line. The

Making the British system work

British monarchy had already sustained damage from the civil war and revolution of the seventeenth century (see Chapter 13). Though the king remained the chief executive of the state, ordained by God and tradition, Parliament now had the upper hand. Divided into the House of Lords (for nobles only) and House of Commons (elected representatives of commoners), Parliament controlled critical functions such as taxation, lawmaking, and the process for bringing grievances to the monarchy. Clearly, king and Parliament had to find a way to work together rather than in opposition.

The answer came in the form of a new institution: the cabinet system. Under this structure, the king chose members of Parliament, usually from the House of Commons, to serve as his ministers. If he hoped to enact policies, he had to select ministers who could command plenty of votes. These men tended to be the leaders of the major groups, or parties, in the House of Commons. By the eighteenth century, two groups dominated the House. Whigs, favoring commercial interests and a strong Parliament, remained has been bribed and is being instructed how to vote, which at the time was done publicly. At the left, the Tory candidate is purchasing cheap jewelry for a woman on the balcony. He makes his purchase from a Jewish merchant, despite his own anti-Jewish record in Parliament.

Walpole's successors continued his strategy of patronage to ensure parliamentary support, and the Whigs held office for another 20 years. By the middle of the eighteenth century, a pattern had emerged. A group of ministers—themselves led by a prime minister, chosen from Parliament, who could command enough votes in the House of Commons to pass legislation—served the monarch and remained responsible to Parliament. Unlike in France, where most political debate took place outside the government, in Britain, debate occurred within Parliament between the party in power and the "loyal opposition." People thus perceived the nation as being governed by the rule of law rather than the whim of a monarch. This system often moved slowly, but it worked.

Although Britain's government may have been more representative than France's, it was far from democratic. Only some 200,000—most of them the wealthiest males—could vote. Rich landowners and powerful local elites staffed the government. Not surprisingly, Parliament listened most carefully to representatives of the 400 families whose massive estates included one-fourth of Britain's arable land. British officials did not seek to exempt themselves from taxation, as did most of their counterparts in France, but instead ruled along with the crown by controlling Parliament.

Prosperity formed the foundation of Britain's strong position in these years. The middle class in particular agreed with the popular British author and observer Daniel Defoe that "the greatness of the British nation is not owing to war and conquests . . . it is all owing to trade, to the increase of our commerce at home, and the extending it abroad." Goods poured into Britain from India and North America. The nation transformed itself into an agricultural exporter and a flourishing manufacturing center. By the middle of the eighteenth century, Great Britain had become Europe's leading economic power. It pursued its interest in European affairs through diplomacy, alliances, and the subsidizing of its allies' arms. Its naval dominance alone made it a formidable opponent. After 1740, Britain used both its economic strength and its military might in the great midcentury wars with France that stretched across three con-

tinents. To understand this story, we must shift our attention to the West's overseas colonies and the nature of trade among them.

More than anything else, France and Britain fought over colonies. For both countries, foreign trade quadrupled in the eighteenth century, and a large part of that increase de- *Colonies, trade, and war*
rived from transactions with colonies. The two nations also made their greatest profits from trade across the Atlantic. However, their overseas presence differed crucially. The French had only 56,000 colonists living in North America in 1740—a fraction of the British colonial population. Yet French colonists carried out an extensive, highly profitable fur trade. Further, because of their small numbers and trade arrangements, they experienced limited conflict with Amerindians.

British colonists, clustered along the eastern seaboard, had a different experience. First, they grew rapidly—from 250,000 in 1700 to 1.7 million in 1760. As they occupied and exploited more and more land, they pushed the Amerindians out. Their expansion, combined with resistance from local tribes, led to savage battles. The fighting, in turn, convinced the colonists that removing or even exterminating the Amerindians was justified. As they became more firmly established, the British colonists bought manufactured goods from Britain in return for tobacco, rice, cotton, and indigo dye, much of which Britain re-exported to the European continent.

These North American colonists participated in the even more lucrative triangle of trade that connected Europe, Africa, and the *The triangle of trade*
Americas and that centered on the Caribbean (see Map 15.4). The British and French, along with the Dutch and Spanish, held islands there that supported sugar, rum, coffee, and dyestuffs trade produced by slave labor. In particular, the demand for sugar and coffee seemed endless. European craving for these items grew so much that, for many, they became necessities rather than occasional luxuries.

At the heart of this thriving colonial commerce was the slave trade (see Chapter 11). Slavery was long common throughout Africa and in other *The slave trade*
societies. For centuries, Islamic merchants had purchased slaves through well-established African networks and transported them by caravan across the Sahara Desert to the Mediterranean basin or by ship from east African ports across the Indian Ocean to Asia.

By the eighteenth century, the dramatic demand for slaves in the Americas shifted Africa's slave trade westward to the Atlantic coast. Ships from Europe carried manufactured goods (most notably, guns) and gin to western Africa and traded them for slaves—two-thirds of them males, because they best provided heavy labor. Usually captured by African middlemen, slaves languished in pens in towns or forts on the African coast. European trading ships then carried them across the Atlantic in a perilous two-month sea voyage known as the Middle Passage.

Figure 15.4, an 1846 watercolor, suggests what conditions were like below decks on a slave ship. Typically, slaves were packed like cargo into the holds of ships "where the light of day does not penetrate." As many as 700 slaves—naked, branded, and shackled—might be crammed into one ship. A French writer describing these voyages told of a "continuous state of alarm on the part of the white men, who fear a revolt, and . . . a cruel state of uncertainty on the part of the Negroes, who do not know the fate awaiting them." In Document 15.3 (see page D15.2), Olaudah Equiano, a captured African, describes how this middle-passage experience soon made him "so sick and low" that he "wished for the last friend, death."

Traders took most of their slaves to the West Indies and Brazil; less than 10 percent went to North American destinations. After unloading their human cargo, the ships filled up with sugar, rum, and other goods—sometimes stopping farther north in the American colonies to take on additional products such as cotton, tobacco, timber, and furs. From there, the ships returned to Europe. Merchants then re-exported many of these products to other European nations.

Disease, abuse, and suicide took the lives of many slaves. In addition, African women often suffered the horror of rape by their captors. Those who survived the "Middle Passage" were then sold for profit and put to work on a plantation or in the mines or households of colonists. Figure 15.5 depicts slaves harvesting sugar cane on a West Indies plantation. Men, women, and children share the difficult work. In the foreground, a manager on horseback gives orders to a

FIGURE 15.4
A transatlantic slave ship.

slave, who looks up deferentially to his master. On the right, sugar cane is being loaded into a cart, to be carried to the mill in the distant background. Slaves suffered from poor diets, inadequate housing, broken families, and stiff corporal punishment. The uprooting, the trauma of transportation, and the harsh conditions in the colonies stripped much away from these people. Still, slaves often resisted their masters by working slowly, sabotaging equipment, running away, and revolting. Despite their lack of freedom, slaves built hybrid cultural traditions from African, American, and European sources.

Within the slave societies of Brazil, the West Indies, and North America, the notion of race was becoming tied to slavery, adding to earlier notions of racial prejudice. The unprecedented dependence on slavery and the associated development of racism would stain these societies in ways that would persist to this day.

The consequences of the slave trade also rippled through sub-Saharan Africa. Traditional trade routes north to the Mediterranean and east to the Indian Ocean disintegrated as more lucrative commerce shifted west to the Atlantic coast of Africa. To supply more human cargo to the Europeans, West African kingdoms raided inland tribes. Bloody internal wars erupted—more deadly than ever thanks to the guns supplied by Europeans to the Africans.

Because many slaves perished in the Americas, and the plantations that depended on them kept expanding, the demand for fresh supplies of slaves increased relentlessly. This rising need perpetuated the triangular commerce among Europe, Africa, and the Americas. European traders took 50,000 to 100,000 slaves across the Atlantic each year during most of the eighteenth century. By the time slave trafficking abated in the mid-nineteenth century, more than 11 million Africans had been ripped from their homes, transported across the Atlantic, and sold into slavery. Another 4 million died resisting seizure or while in transport.

Planters and merchants on both sides of the Atlantic profited from this trade, and European cities serving as slave-trade ports flourished, particularly in England. The coastal town of Liverpool, for example, grew from a small town to a major city in the eighteenth century. In 1750, its slave merchants and fleet of almost 200 ships carried almost half of Europe's slave trade. Thousands of men from Liverpool worked on both merchant and naval ships, and more than a dozen banks and several insurance companies served slave-trade merchants. The wealth spread outward from Liverpool, helping to finance Britain's burgeoning industry as well as its rising position on the world stage. "Our West-Indies and African Trades are the most nationally beneficial of any we carry on. . . . The Trade to Africa is the branch which renders our American Colonies and Plantations so advantageous to Great Britain," argued one British defender of the slave system in 1746. "The daily bread of the most considerable part of our British Manufacturers are owing primarily to the labor of Negroes." Although the statement may be an exaggeration, slavery generated much commerce and wealth in this eighteenth-century Atlantic economy, whether by direct or indirect means.

As Europeans' commercial activities, profits, and presence increased in the Americas, so did competition and friction, especially between the French and the British. In North America, British colonists along the eastern seaboard pushed inland, beyond the Appalachian Mountains into the Ohio Valley. The French strengthened their holdings by building forts along the Great Lakes and the large rivers of the St. Lawrence and Mississippi valleys. *Fighting on three continents* When the War of the Austrian Succession broke out in Europe in 1740, Britain and France soon locked horns on the Continent as well as overseas. Most of the fighting took place in the Americas, however. Wins and losses on each side balanced out, and by the time the conflict ended in 1748, each side had settled for what it had held in the beginning.

The peace would not last long. In 1755, war—sometimes known as the French and Indian War—erupted again, this time initiated by a British offensive against a French stronghold near Pittsburgh in North America. At the same time, the two powers were also competing in India, each trying to take advantage of the declining power of the Mughals (India's Muslim rulers—see Global Connections). After 1715, the subcontinent had split apart into bickering, independent kingdoms. India became a fertile ground for the British and French, working through their chartered trading companies and backed by their superior weapons of war, to make deals, gain influence, and line up allies among India's opposing princes and political factions. This competition between the British and French for trade and imperial power

FIGURE 15.5
A West Indies sugar plantation, 1823.

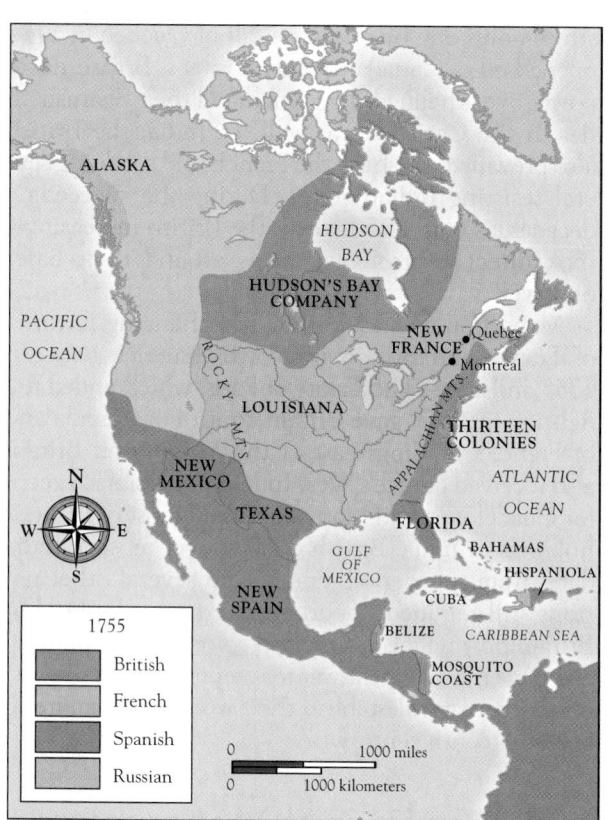

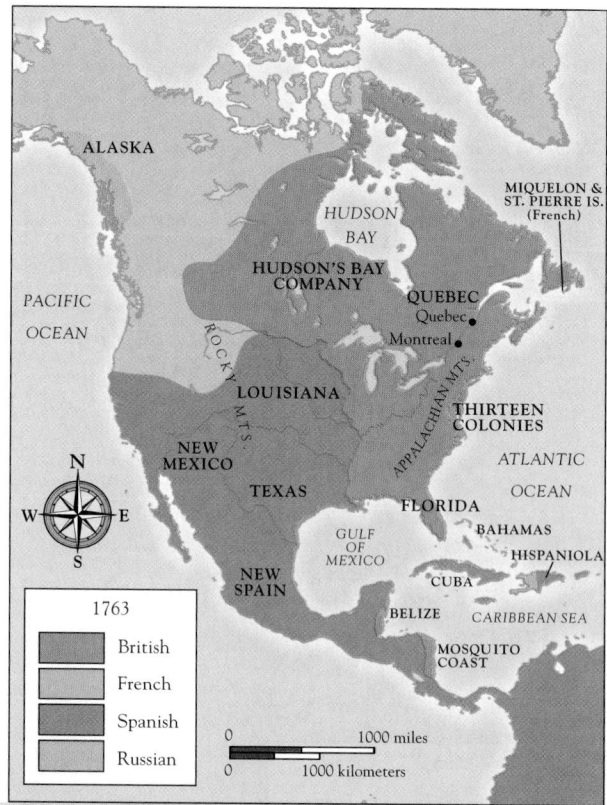

THINKING ABOUT GEOGRAPHY

MAPS 15.6 AND 15.7 *North America, 1755 and 1763*

These maps show North America before and after the Seven Years' War. ▣ **Notice** France's large holdings in 1755. **What** advantages helped the British defeat France in this part of the world? **What** new problems faced Britain as a result of this victory? ▣ **Notice** what other competitors to the British remained in North America after 1763. **Assess** their relative strength.

these rulers from their predecessors, calling them "enlightened absolutists" or simply "enlightened." Yet, how valid is this characterization? Several historians claim that these monarchs primarily followed the long tradition of trying to buttress the central government's power and efficiency. Other historians argue that they genuinely initiated reforms in line with Enlightenment thinking.

The most sensational of the self-described enlightened monarchs was Frederick the Great (Frederick II) of Prussia. Even as a boy, Frederick loved music, poetry, and philosophy. After ascending to the throne, he still found time to perform in concerts as an accomplished flutist

Frederick the Great

in his Palace of San Souci. There he also hobnobbed with towering cultural figures such as Voltaire, savored books in his library, and carried on a lively correspondence with leading French intellectuals. He knew and spoke the phrases of the Enlightenment. Like several other monarchs, he also wanted to display his awareness of culture and intellectual life to help justify his position as monarch. He described "the good monarch" as one who behaved "as if he were each moment liable to render an account of his administration to his fellow citizens." He claimed to act only in the common interest of the people, declaring himself to be "the first servant of the state" rather than a divinely appointed ruler.

At the end of the Seven Years' War (1756–1763), the second of his two wars of aggression, Frederick made some attempts at "enlightened" reforms. For example, he initiated codification of the laws, abolished torture, and ended most capital punishment. Believing that "all religions, if one examines them, are founded on superstitious systems, more or less absurd," he proclaimed religious toleration. Nevertheless, he considered Jews "useless to the state" and taxed them heavily. He advocated public education, but spent very little on it compared with what he spent on his army. In his economic policy, Frederick did share the Physiocrats' appreciation of the importance of agriculture and tried to introduce new methods of cultivation (see p. 504). Yet he did nothing to free the serfs or lessen their burdens. Neither his wars nor his involvement in the partition of Poland revealed any hint of "enlightened" principles different from the monarchs who preceded him.

No one tried more sincerely to be "enlightened" than Joseph II of Austria (r. 1780–1790). "Since I have ascended the throne," he said in 1781, "I have made *philosophy* the legislator of my empire." Viewing his rule as a moral and holy calling, Joseph issued thousands of decrees. Unfortunately, he lacked the practical sense of Frederick the Great. He did change laws that had previously limited freedom of the press and religion (including Judaism). He also restricted the death penalty, promoted education, and enacted and tried to enforce equality before the law.

Joseph II

Nevertheless, Joseph still ruled as an autocrat, antagonizing most of the powerful groups in his lands. Even peasants, unable to understand exactly what all the decrees meant, failed to support him. His well-meaning but ill-conceived efforts—to centralize the administration of the widely dispersed Habsburg territories, to replace the numerous languages of his subjects with German, to subordinate the strongly entrenched Roman Catholic Church, and to free the serfs in a society still based on feudalism—all backfired. Opposition and even open revolt swelled in his lands. In 1787, Joseph lamented, "[I] hope that when I am no more, posterity will examine, and judge more equitably . . . all that I have done for my people." His vision would not come to pass. Within a few years of his death in 1790, most of his reforms were abolished and the Habsburg lands reacquired their old, conservative ways.

Other monarchs, such as those of Sweden, Sardinia, Spain, and Portugal, attempted or enacted reforms that could be seen as enlightened. In Russia, Catherine the Great certainly prided herself on being "enlightened" (see pp. 518). She once described the true aim of monarchy as "not to deprive People of their natural Liberty; but to correct their Actions, in order to attain the supreme good." Ultimately, however, Catherine failed to put most of her reforms into practice. Instead, she resorted to the tried-and-true tactic of appeasing elites at a price paid by the peasantry.

Certainly these monarchs found it easier to manifest their "enlightenment" in style rather than substance. Moreover, they rarely lost sight of traditional goals: to increase their own military and economic power. Few attempted to enact fundamental social, political, or economic reforms dictated by Enlightenment thought. Even those who tried, such as Joseph II in Austria, generally failed to overcome opposition to those reforms from tradition-minded people.

Style, substance, or survival?

Nevertheless, thoughtful observers of the eighteenth century—looking for tendencies and possibilities for reform rather than revolutionary change—believed that several rulers displayed the enlightened spirit of the times. Despite great obstacles to reform within the traditional order, some of these rulers made progress toward fulfilling the *philosophes'* agenda of promoting more religious tolerance, humane social institutions, and rational administration. In the eyes of contemporaries, they earned the label "enlightened."

Finally, from another perspective, "enlightened absolutism" also may have reflected a growing sense that, in the long run, monarchs could no longer *claim* to embody the state. The need for governmental efficiency had grown too much to be entrusted to a poorly qualified individual who happened to be a king or queen. If the institution of monarchy were to survive, kings and queens had to justify their position in these new, ostensibly "enlightened" ways.

Changes in Country and City Life

Eighteenth-century European monarchs and officials faced not only the risky politics and wars of their times, but also the changes unfolding in their very societies. Especially in western Europe, new economic and social forces began to upset old traditions (see

Chapter 13). For some, these changes created a sense that life was improving and would continue to do so. For others, the changes only deepened their misery. The greatest shifts emerged in the countryside, where the vast majority of the population (some 80 percent) lived and depended on agriculture for their livelihood and very survival.

Historically, toiling in the fields within Europe's traditional subsistence economies produced little more than enough food to survive. During the late seventeenth and eighteenth centuries, new methods of agricultural production that had originated in Holland spread to England and then to other areas of western Europe. These innovative methods allowed fewer people to work the fields and still produce far more food than they needed. The new techniques and the changes flowing from them became so important that they are known as the agricultural revolution.

THE AGRICULTURAL REVOLUTION

Most early-eighteenth-century farmers used methods that differed only marginally from those employed in previous centuries. They grew the same crops year after year, left one-third to one-half of the land fallow (unplanted) to allow the soil to replenish itself with nutrients for the next planting, and saved only enough fodder to feed small numbers of domestic animals during the winters. Individual families worked small strips of land, and large, uncultivated fields, brushlands, and forests (the "commons") were reserved for general use by the community. Traditional community practices usually determined decisions about crops, animals, and land use. Overall, only a small minority of people made their living outside of agriculture, and an even smaller percentage had the good fortune to afford luxuries.

This traditional, agricultural economy had the potential to support a limited measure of population growth. In the eighteenth century, population increases stepped up the demand for food, and hence for hands to clear fields, drain swamps, terrace hillsides, carry water, and till the soil. Most of these efforts were simply an intensification of old methods for increasing agricultural yields, and the growing population consumed most of the extra food they produced. Something had to change if large numbers of Europeans hoped to increase their standard of living and provide enough food for people living in the cities as well as the countryside.

At the heart of the agricultural revolution lay two developments: first, the introduction of new crops and the use of new farming techniques that dramatically boosted agricultural yields; and second, the transformation of rural lands farmed for subsistence into large, controlled properties that produced crops for commerce. The primary agricultural advances came first in Holland and Britain, where farmers began experimenting with new crops such as clover, turnips, and legumes, as well as the potato from America. These crops replenished the soil rather than depleted it, and therefore could be grown on lands that farmers periodically had to leave fallow. Farmers now used the new crops to feed livestock during the hard winters. More cattle meant more protein-rich dairy products; more horses and oxen eased the workload for humans and provided transportation; and more sheep produced more wool. All this livestock, improving with new crossbreeding practices, yielded more meat, leather, and soap as well as manure with which to fertilize fields. Other new foods, such as nutrient-rich potatoes, also made the land more productive than ever before. Some landowners became renowned for their farming innovations. In England, for example, Charles "Turnip" Townshend (1674–1738) experimented with crop rotation and growing turnips. His compatriot, Jethro Tull (1674–1741), advocated the use of a seed drill and manure, which made planting more efficient and productive.

New crops and techniques

Not all farmers adopted the new agricultural methods. For many, traditional ways were comfortably familiar. Even those who realized how much profit they might make by selling their surpluses in the cities and other distant markets needed money to fund the new farming methods. They also required control over larger tracts of land to introduce the new crops, apply the innovative methods, and specialize in certain products—whether sheep for wool, grain for flour, or cattle for meat and dairy.

By all means, fair and foul, these market-oriented landowners dispossessed individuals of their small plots and communities of their commons to enclose land with fences, hedges, and walls as their own. Figure 15.6, a mid-eighteenth century English painting, shows a large, rich estate in Gloucestershire, England. The fields are consolidated and enclosed. In the center, organized groups of men and women workers toil on the harvest while wagons haul away the produce, destined for commerce rather

Enclosures

FIGURE 15.6
The Fields of Gloucestershire, England.

than local consumption. Other fields are carefully planned and managed for the marketplace. Gone are the small farms, subsistance crops, and open fields that used to dominate the English countryside. After 1750, Britain's Parliament furthered this trend by authorizing a wave of these enclosures. Over the decades, wealthy landowners created large, controlled tracts that yielded products for the market. They reserved only a small part of their land for their own needs or bought their food elsewhere. Through this process, thousands of small, independent landowners, sharecroppers, and tenant farmers lost their land—and the status and security that had come with it. Rural communities disintegrated, eroding the support and human interactions that had so characterized life in the country.

MANUFACTURING SPREADS IN THE COUNTRYSIDE: COTTAGE INDUSTRY

The spreading agricultural revolution became one force pushing, forcing, or freeing people to work more in nonagricultural jobs. When families lost their self-sufficient farms, they had to find new sources of income to supplement the meager day-labor wages their landowning employers paid them. Manufacturing seemed to offer a solution. Growing commerce, particularly overseas trade, had heightened demand for manufactured goods—and thus workers to pro-

duce them. Traditionally, well-paid urban artisans had done this sort of work. Now, with demand high and rural workers available by the thousands, merchants turned to the countryside to increase production and take advantage of the cheap labor. Moreover, by shifting more production itself to the countryside, merchants avoided urban guild regulations that historically had controlled wages and the quantity and quality of goods.

All these changes stimulated the growth of "cottage industry," also known as the "putting-out system." This system, which had already existed in the sixteenth and seventeenth centuries but to a much smaller degree, worked in a specific way. An entrepreneur provided raw materials (usually for production of textiles such as wool or linen) and sometimes equipment (such as a handloom or a spinning wheel) to peasants. The entrepreneur might be anyone—from a city merchant to a rural landowner—who managed to amass enough money to make an initial investment in raw materials and perhaps equipment. Peasants, who sought employment during times of the year when there was less need for agricultural labor, worked in their homes (hence the term "cottage industry") to turn these raw materials into finished products. Mainly, they spun wool into yarn and wove the yarn into cloth. Sometimes enterprising peasants contracted out raw material to other spinners to keep weavers busy, since weavers depended on

fell into poverty. A governmental commission in Austria reported to Empress Maria Theresa that "the peasants live in a condition of real slavery. . . . In their ruinous huts, the parents sleep on straw, the children naked on the wide shelves of earthenware stoves . . . all the charges of the Kingdom are born by the peasants, who are the sole taxpayers." Despite a widespread sense that people were better off than ever and that things would improve, in truth more people meant more misery.

In a desperate attempt to survive, poor people fled to the cities, hoping to find work in trade and manufacturing or as day-laborers and domestics. Only some of them managed to find jobs; the rest were left to fend for themselves. A large percentage of urban dwellers missed out on the new wealth and opportunities of the cities. They eked out a living at little more than a subsistence level, and their lot worsened as more and more of them crowded in from the countryside.

Indeed, the surplus of workers; inflation; and disasters such as war, disease, and failed harvests hit the poor in cities and countryside alike. In France, economist Jacques Turgot (1727–1781) described the disastrous harvest of 1769: "The people could exist only by exhausting their resources, by selling at a miserable price their articles of furniture and even their clothes. Many of the inhabitants have been obliged to disperse themselves through other provinces to seek work or to beg, leaving their wives and children to the charity of the parishes. . . ." One Spanish official described how "wives and children are without work, and all, piled together in cities or large towns, live at the expense of charity . . . " Even for those who found steady employment, wages simply did not keep pace with escalating prices.

In bad times, food riots and tax revolts broke out in cities and rural areas across Europe. A rise in the price of grain often sparked attacks on merchants, granaries, and convoys of grain slated for armies. People turned on officials as well, blaming them for not keeping grain prices affordable or for allowing food to be shipped out to higher bidders elsewhere. Crime increased and more people slept along the sides of rural roads and city streets. Crowds of mothers pushed into foundling hospitals, desperate to leave children they could not care for. Some foundling hospitals established lotteries to determine which children they could afford to take in. Others found ways to make it easier for women to give up their children. Figure 15.10 depicts a woman abandoning her baby at an

Italian foundling home. Desperate mothers could give up a baby at any time of day without embarrassing questions by placing the child on a revolving table. The nun or nurse on duty would then rotate the table and take in the child. Here the worried mother looks back to see if anyone is looking. Scenes such as this took place in many countries during the eighteenth century.

This deepening of poverty put a huge strain on traditional systems for aiding the poor, such as through the church or private charity. Some people were reduced to begging and to teaching their children this dubious art. Some authorities sympathized; others turned a blind eye. As one French official put it, "Beggary is the apprenticeship of crime; it begins by creating a love of idleness . . . in this state the beggar does not long resist the temptation to steal." A few countries devised legislation, such as the English Poor Laws, that required the impoverished to work on public projects or in workhouses. Officials used these sorts of laws more to control and discipline the poor than to help them. Often the same institution served as a workshop for the unfortunate, a hospital, and a prison. True, the poor had always suffered. Now, however, the population boom pushed their numbers to overwhelming new heights.

FIGURE 15.10 Abandoning children.

Prosperity and the Bourgeoisie

Like the agricultural revolution, urban growth made life worse for some and better for others. Those who gained most during this era were the middle and aristocratic classes, particularly those who seized opportunities in commerce and industry and in the expanding governmental bureaucracies. The urban middle class—in French, the *bourgeoisie*—expanded and found itself in a particularly odd situation. Wealthier than most, the bourgeoisie lived off their investments in trade, manufacturing, or land rather than working with their hands like their fellow commoners. They also found ways to avoid the restrictions of the guild system of production. While those laboring "below" them envied and resented their success, the bourgeoisie tried to distance themselves from "less respectable" commoners.

Middle-class people also had difficult relationships with those above them—the aristocracy. Successful members of the bourgeoisie resented the privileges enjoyed by the aristocracy, but—even more strongly—they wanted those privileges for themselves. They longed to join the aristocracy, and they were willing to spend money to do it. Money got them titles and offices, large estates, and judicious marriages—the trappings of success that they hoped would earn them acceptance into the ranks of the aristocracy. The aristocrats, for their part, viewed this method of "social climbing"—and the people who attempted it—with disdain. As they saw it, true nobility derived from birth, not wealth.

Nevertheless, the bourgeoisie persisted and thrived. These merchants, manufacturers, and professionals made money, expanded their businesses, invested in government bonds, and took chances on shaky financial schemes. They valued hard work and the accumulation of money. Moreover, they had the means to purchase a vast variety of luxuries, from coffee and chocolate to wallpaper, cotton clothing, and watch chains—goods produced outside the home, often even outside the country. For them, the market—rather than the household—supplied staples as well as conveniences and luxuries.

Over time, the richest among the bourgeoisie might manage to gain entrance into the aristocracy. Yet even if they could not get into the courts, estates, and homes of the aristocracy, the bourgeoisie developed a public culture of their own. They educated their children at universities, and attended public theaters, music halls, and galleries. They filled tearooms, coffeehouses, literary societies, and clubs, and devoured newspapers, journals, and books written especially for them. Over time, they acquired their own sense of identity, as well as an impatience when further opportunities to rise in society were denied them.

The Culture of the Elite: Combining the Old and the New

The culture of the bourgeoisie and the aristocracy reflected the continuance of old trends along with the new developments that characterized the eighteenth century. For example, the courts of Europe still sponsored painters, composers, and musicians. In their private halls, aristocrats savored these artists' paintings, concerts, and operas. The prevailing spirit remained classical, inspired by the Greek and Roman appreciation for formal symmetry, proportion, and reason. On the other hand, artistic styles were changing. Several artists and authors put a new emphasis on emotion and nature in their works, an artistic trend sometimes referred to as the "cult of sensibility." Audiences for these new cultural forms expanded, and the stream of literature being published for the growing numbers of literate westerners swelled.

The Advent of the Modern Novel

Much of the reading public consisted of members of the middle class, and not surprisingly, the modern novel reflected middle-class tastes. A compelling story, complex and varied characters, and realistic social situations formed the core of this new literary form. Novels also conveyed current ideas, manners, news, and information in witty and dramatic ways. In several popular novels, the English writer Daniel Defoe (1660–1731) wrote about individuals who planned ahead and used their entrepreneurial skills to meet challenges. The adventures of a character in a Defoe novel might take place at home in England or on exotic islands, as in *Robinson Crusoe* (1719). Similarly, Defoe's book *Moll Flanders* (1722) tells of a woman of lower-class origins who manages to navigate through all sorts of difficult situations, from prisons to a position in high society, in England and America.

Samuel Richardson (1689–1761) and Henry Fielding (1707–1754), also British, used the novel to analyze human personality, emotions, and psychology. In *Pamela, or Virtue Rewarded* (1740), Richardson recounts the story of a servant girl who tries to retain her "virtue" in the face of her wealthy employer's sexual advances. The book's characters and circumstances powerfully reflected contemporary realities, and the novel inspired a wave of similar works. Henry Fielding, for one, expanded on Richardson's effort, weaving a rich tapestry of English society in his novel *Tom Jones* (1749).

Many novels appealed particularly to women readers. British writer Fanny Burney (1752–1840) gained fame with the publication of her novel *Evelina or A Young Lady's Entrance into the World* (1778). The book portrays a provincial girl who makes a life for herself in London. Although the story ends with a marriage, it also reveals the social restrictions and dangers facing eighteenth-century women who tried to live an independent life. Burney would go on to publish several other popular novels.

During the second half of the century, novels and works of poetry by authors such as Jean-Jacques Rousseau in France and Johann Wolfgang von Goethe (1749–1832) in the German states emphasized emotion, relationships, and social problems. These authors presented the emotions as natural virtues, rejecting the artificiality of formal manners.

Their style, which would become known as romanticism, grew in popularity during the last quarter of the century.

PRIDE AND SENTIMENT IN ART AND ARCHITECTURE

Unlike literature, the fine arts still typically reflected the tastes of the dominant aristocracy. Artists vied with one another for commissions to paint the portraits of royals and aristocrats, depicting their proud subjects adorned with plumes, buckles, silks, brocades, and laces. The scenes might include children and dogs and, in the background, lavish estate grounds. The distinctive clothing, haughty poses, and elaborate settings marked subjects as members of the landowning elite.

Many paintings showed intimate scenes of aristocratic private life—meetings, picnics, flirtations, and conversations among the upper classes. In Antoine Watteau's (1684–1721) popular paintings, for example, the context might be classical mythology, but the figures were eighteenth-century aristocrats. In *A Pilgrimage to Cythera* (a mythical island of love), shown in Figure 15.11, aristocrats wander leisurely through an idyllic garden of nature. Cupids at the left and Venus at the right bless the scene. The line between life, mythology, and the social roles played by the subjects blurs in this lush scene. The painting also has an underlying seriousness, as the lovers, reluctantly preparing to depart to the everyday world, enjoy a moment of life that will pass too quickly.

Whereas the aristocracy tended to populate Watteau's works, other artists painted well-received, sentimental scenes of ordinary people experiencing dramatic moments. Figure 15.12, a painting by the French artist Jean-Baptiste Greuze (1725–1805), shows one of these works. Here, the father at the left curses his departing son, who is determined to find his own way through life by joining the army. The young man's mother and other members of the family try in vain to reconcile the two men and to prevent the breakup of the family on such a painful note. In an accompanying painting, the grief-stricken son returns to find his father on his death

FIGURE 15.11
Antoine Watteau, *A Pilgrimage to Cythera*, 1717.

bed. William Hogarth's engravings (see Figures 15.3 and 15.14) also explored everyday experiences in the lives of ordinary people, but usually from a satirical or moralistic perspective.

Eighteenth-century architecture could not portray sentiments in the same detail as paintings, but buildings in the baroque style still expressed well the gaudy splendor of the eighteenth-century monarchs and their courts. At the same time, architects began de-emphasizing size and instead relied on multiple curves and lacy, shell-like ornamentation to convey a sense of pleasing luxury. This style is usually referred to as rococo. Some new government buildings and urban residences followed a more neoclassical style, which stressed clarity of line and form modeled on Greek and Roman ideals.

Gardens complemented the buildings they accompanied, extending them and reflecting the mix of old and new tastes. As we saw in Louis XIV's Versailles palace (see Chapter 13), the French garden in particular emphasized rational, geometric forms marked off by hedges. Here, nature was shown completely tamed by human power and reason. By contrast, the eighteenth-century English garden looked freer and more natural. In fact, these gardens were not natural at all. Landscape architects designed them to imitate a vision of nature or to turn the grounds of an estate into an idealized version of nature. This managing of nature in English gardens was a compromise between old and new ideas about human beings' place in the natural world.

REACHING NEW HEIGHTS IN MUSIC

Of all the eighteenth-century arts, music left the most profound legacy. Much of it reflected the tastes of its royal, aristocratic, and ecclesiastical patrons. Composers and musicians, therefore, usually stuck to established forms, and music was typically heard as a pleasing background to conversations, balls, and other social occasions in the bastions of the aristocracy. Increasingly, however, music was played in public concert halls to a larger audience. Opera houses opened everywhere, and com-

posers could now hope to make money from paying audiences as well as from court and aristocratic patronage. Several cities became well-known musical centers, but Vienna topped them all. This Austrian city became the musical heart of Europe, drawing hundreds of musicians who competed for favor there.

The first half of the eighteenth century saw the high point of baroque music, a style that had originated in the seventeenth century and that was still favored in royal courts and aristocratic homes. The greatest practitioners of the baroque style were Johann Sebastian Bach (1685–1750) and George Frideric Handel (1685–1759). Bach was a member of a German family long distinguished by its musical talent. Noted in his own lifetime chiefly as an organist rather than a composer, he created a vast array of great music for organ, harpsichord, clavichord (forerunner of the piano), orchestra, and chorus. Sadly, much of Bach's work has been lost. Much of his music was religiously inspired, but he also wrote a large amount of secular music. Handel was born in central Germany in the same year and same region as Bach. He studied Italian opera in Germany and Italy and wrote 46 operas himself. He also became court musician in Hanover. Later, he made

Baroque music

FIGURE 15.12
Jean-Baptiste Greuze, *The Father's Curse.*

Biography

WOLFGANG AMADEUS MOZART (1756–1791)

• **Consider** how Mozart's career reflected eighteenth-century society—still dominated by the aristocracy but with a growing middle class interested in the culture of the day.

Musicians quickly recognized the young Wolfgang Amadeus Mozart as a unique genius. His father, Leopold, a well-known Austrian composer and violinist, called him the "miracle which God let be born in Salzburg." Born in 1756, Wolfgang wrote his first compositions when he was just five years old. He embarked on the first of many tours throughout Europe as a six-year-old child prodigy, playing the clavier with his elder sister, Nannerl, also a child prodigy, and his father (see Figure 15.13). They played at several royal courts for monarchs such as Louis XV of France, Maria Theresa of Austria, and George III of Britain. They also performed at the homes of leading nobles as well as in public theaters. Wolfgang's father, always eager to promote his young son, wrote that "our great and mighty Wolfgang seems to know everything at the age of seven that a man acquires at the age of forty."

By the time he had reached 14, Mozart had composed several concertos, sonatas, and an opera. Announcements for his performances stressed his virtuosity. For example, for a concert in Italy, the 14 year old would play "A Symphony of his own composition; a harpsichord concerto which will be handed to him, and which he will play on first sight; a sonata handed him in like manner, which he will provide with variations, and afterwards repeat in another key. . . ." The boy could play the organ and violin almost as well. After hearing Mozart in 1771, one well-known composer said, "This boy will cause us all to be forgotten." The prestigious Haydn, who strongly influenced Wolfgang's music, would later tell Wolfgang's father that "your son is the greatest composer known to me. . . ."

Child-Prodigy, Musical Genius

In 1781 Mozart settled in Vienna as a teacher and composer. Short, slim, with engaging blue eyes and a full head of fine hair, the young man enjoyed an active social life,

his home in England, as did the elector, who became King George I of England. Handel wrote an enormous quantity of music—both instrumental and vocal—all of it marked by dignity, formal elegance, and harmony.

During the last decades of the century, the restrained baroque style gave way to the more melodic "classical" style, with its striking depth, structure, and emotion. Franz Joseph Haydn (1732–1809) and Wolfgang Amadeus Mozart (1756–1791) led the way. Their most stunning work was the symphony; by the end of their careers, they had created symphonies of rich harmonic complexity and emotional depth within the restrained classical

The classical style

form. During his long career in Vienna, Haydn wrote more than a hundred symphonies in addition to scores of compositions for other forms, particularly chamber music. Toward the end of his career, he became so popular that he left noble patrons and signed a lucrative contract with his music publisher.

Haydn became a friend and a source of inspiration for the young Mozart (see Biography). Figure 15.13 shows the seven-year-old Wolfgang playing the piano. Accompanying him are his father on the violin and his sister, who is singing. Here the performers are exquisitely dressed for their aristocratic audience. Ultimately, Mozart composed more than 600 works and excelled in all forms, but he became including billiards and dancing. Yet music preoccupied him. He wrote, "You know that I am, so to speak, swallowed up in music, that I am busy with it all day—speculating, studying, considering." Keenly aware of his own talents, he at times arrogantly criticized other musicians' limitations. He felt certain that he could outshine any rival.

In 1782, despite the doubts of his father and sister, Mozart married Constanze Weber, a singer. Mozart wrote that "as soon as we were married, my wife and I both began to weep" for joy. Their marriage seems to have been happy. They would have six children, of whom only two survived. Neither parent managed the family finances well. Even though Mozart became brilliantly successful as a composer, a virtuoso pianist, and a teacher; received numerous commissions and fees; and attained appointment as royal chamber composer to Emperor Joseph II of Austria, he continually borrowed money to support his growing family.

Wolfgang could never quite satisfy his demanding and increasingly distant father. Hearing that Leopold had fallen seriously ill in 1787, Mozart wrote a letter of consolation that included his own views on death: "As death . . . is the true goal of our existence, I have formed during the last few years such close relations with this best and truest friend of mankind that his image is no longer terrifying to me but rather very soothing and consoling." Leopold died a month later. In July 1791, a stranger appeared at Wolfgang's door with a commission to write a Requiem in secrecy. Mozart was still working on the project in December when he died in relative poverty. He was just 35. Although he probably had succumbed to an infection and fever, unsubstantiated rumors circulated for years that a competitor had poisoned him.

FIGURE 15.13

The Mozarts.

most appreciated for his symphonies, piano concertos, and operas. His music was stunningly clear, melodic, elegant, and graceful. In his hands, the classical style reached its peak.

THE GRAND TOUR

The music, art, and literature of the elites was part of a broader, cosmopolitan culture that spilled across national boundaries. This culture manifested itself in elaborate styles of dress, polished manners, and highly structured conversation. French was its international language. The growing popularity of travel and travel literature added to the sense of a common European cultural identity, at least among elites. Indeed, the wealthy often considered the "grand tour" a necessary part of education. Travelers on the tour stopped in main cities to indulge in coffeehouses, storefront window displays, public gardens, theaters, opera houses, and galleries. They might also visit art dealers or public auctions to purchase quality paintings. Family connections offered them accommodations and introduced them to local society, Enlightenment salons, or potential candidates for marriage. The tour usually continued to historical ruins, which featured revered models of Greek and Roman antiquity that further strengthened the viewers' sense of a common cultural identity.

Culture for the Lower Classes

The lower classes were not without cultural outlets that fit their lives and provided a sense of common identity. For peasants, artisans, and the urban poor, culture typically came in the form of shared recreation, songs, tales, and the passing down of wisdom at gatherings and celebrations. Many of these activities also coincided with religious gatherings and celebrations.

FESTIVALS AND POPULAR LITERATURE

Villagers worked together and celebrated together—at fairs, harvests, plowings, weddings, and religious holidays. Numerous festivals and public ceremonies had seasonal themes that were of particular importance and interest to people so dependent on agriculture. Other celebratory events related to the Christian calendar and centered on holidays, such as Christmas and Easter. Traditional weddings involved a community procession and festivities as well as a religious ceremony, and they featured music, dancing, feasts, games, and play. In the cities, artisans participated in their own organizations that combined recreational activities with mutual aid and religious celebrations.

Certain forms of literature also became popular among ordinary people. Literacy was growing, thanks to the printing press, the demands of business, and an increase in the number of primary schools. By the end of the eighteenth century, some 40 to 60 percent of the population in England and France could read (more men than women). With the rise in literacy, popular literature also expanded. Stirring religious tracts, almanacs, and tales of chivalric valor—typically, small, cheap booklets—circulated widely. More often, however, the "literature" of ordinary people was passed on orally. At night, people might gather to share folktales and songs that told of traditional wisdom, the hardships of everyday life, the hopes of common people, the dangers of life in the forests or of strangers who could be monsters or princes, and the ways to get along in life.

In the past, elites had fully participated in this popular culture, but during the eighteenth century they increasingly abandoned it to the lower classes. The "respectable" classes now often considered the leisure activities of ordinary people too disorderly and crude. Nevertheless, the middle and upper classes read some of the same popular literature enjoyed by the lower classes. Moreover, everyone—aristocrats and peasants alike—might be found at village festivals, fairs, and sporting events or enjoying jugglers, acrobats, magic lantern shows, and touring troops of actors. Men of all classes watched and wagered on cockfights and dogfights. Other sports, such as soccer and cricket, gained popularity and drew large, animated crowds.

GIN AND BEER

All the social classes also engaged in drinking—whether wine or brandy in the privacy of a wealthy home, or gin and beer in popular taverns. Especially in England, the ravages of drinking gin seemed to grow to alarming proportions. Figure 15.14, another moralistic work by William Hogarth, graphically

FIGURE 15.14
William Hogarth, *Gin Lane*, 1750.

depicts the evils of gin drinking in England. At the center a pox-ridden, impoverished, and drunken woman lets her baby fall over a wooden rail. Near her, a man slowly starves to death. In the background, workers haul bodies away, a man hangs himself in an upstairs tenement, children drink glasses of gin, and buildings collapse for want of repair. The scene is one of physical, social, and moral decay from excessive alcohol consumption. Though this image is an exaggeration, the actual problems caused by drinking were so extensive that in 1751 the British government passed a heavy tax on cheap gin to curtail its consumption.

Religious Revivals

Popular culture also merged with deeply felt spiritual beliefs and religious activities. Despite the many secular trends of the period, Christianity still stood at the center of Western culture and life. Churches rather than the state ran the schools and hospitals. The poor, aged, and crippled relied on churches for social services. Church bells announced the time of day everywhere, and religious holidays marked the year.

Within this Western religious culture, popular piety persisted. Indeed, especially among Protestants, a sense grew among ordinary churchgoers that official *Pietism* churches were becoming bureaucratized, complacent, and unresponsive to peoples' spiritual needs. In response, religious revivals spread from community to community and across national borders. In the German and Scandinavian states, pietism—which minimized dogma and formal ritual in favor of inner piety, holy living, and the private emotional experience of worshiping—gained strength. Revival movements in Britain and its North American colonies attracted thousands to huge gatherings.

The greatest of these revival movements was Methodism, founded in England by John Wesley (1703–1791). While studying for the Anglican ministry at Oxford, Wesley and a band of fellow students became disillusioned with the spiritual emptiness that had fallen upon the Anglican Church as well as its subservience to the government and the aristocracy. The group's lives became such examples of piety and moderate regularity that their fellow students branded them "Methodists" in derision. Methodism stressed humble faith, abstinence, and hard work. Barred from preaching in the Anglican churches, Wesley rode horseback from one end of England to the other until well into his 80s, preaching the "glad tidings" of salvation in thousands of sermons in streets, fields, and anywhere else he could find even a small audience. He claimed "to lower religion to the level of the lowest people's capacities."

Among Catholics, similar movements—such as Jansenism in France and Italy and Quietism in Spain—spread among elites and others. East European Jews had their own revivalist movement with the founding of the Hasidic sect in the 1740s. Hasidim (meaning "most pious") spread throughout Poland, rejecting formalism, stressing simplicity, and engaging in loud, joyful singing prayers. These religious movements revealed the power with which spiritual matters still influenced people in the West. Nevertheless, like the broader cultural forms of the time, religious revivals left the overall social order intact.

Foreshadowing Upheaval: The American Revolution

For most of the eighteenth century, neither wars, colonial rivalries, nor changes in country and city life upset the fundamental social and political stability of Western societies. In the last quarter of the eighteenth century, however, new forces erupted that would ultimately transform the West. The first of these disturbances occurred in Britain's 13 North American colonies. This upheaval shifted the tide of events in North America and foreshadowed a far deeper and broader revolution that would strike at the heart of Europe itself.

Insults, Interests, and Principles: The Seeds of Revolt

By the mid-eighteenth century, over 2 million people lived in the colonies. The seaboard cities in particular flourished, benefiting from a thriving commerce with Europe, Africa, and the West Indies. The colonists thought of themselves as British. Furthermore, the 13 colonies in theory were part of Great Britain, governed in the same way and therefore subject to British trade regulations. In practice, however, the colonists often acted as they pleased, even if that meant quietly ignoring those regulations. They developed their own patterns of local government, manipulated British governors, and worked around British mercantilist policies.

FIGURE 15.15
John Singleton Copley, *Paul Revere*, 1768–1770.

Tensions between the island nation and these prospering colonies arose just after the Seven Years' War ended in 1763. Feeling that they had helped defend the American colonists against the hostile French and Indians, the British expected the colonists *New commercial regulations and taxes* to help pay off the huge debt incurred in the fighting. To tighten their control over the colonial empire for which Britain had just fought so long and hard, British officials enacted new commercial regulations and taxes. Perhaps the most irritating of these was the Stamp Act of 1765, which taxed printed documents such as newspapers, pamphlets, and wills.

The colonists reacted to the new policies with complaints, boycotts, protest meetings, outrage, and sometimes riots. Because colonists were not represented in Britain's Parliament, headlines in newspapers and pamphlets screamed, "No taxation without representation!" In their Stamp Act Congress of 1765, colonists announced that they were "entitled to all the inherent rights and liberties of his [the king's] natural born subjects within the kingdom of Great Britain." Local circumstances and the distance from Britain meant that "the only representatives of these colonies are persons chosen therein by themselves, and that no taxes ever have been, or can be constitutionally imposed on them, but by their respective legislatures." The British compromised, repealing most of the taxes, but many colonists were still not satisfied.

Figure 15.15 is a portrait of one of these dissatisfied colonists, Paul Revere (1735–1818), before he became a hero of the American Revolution. This neoclassical painting by John Singleton Copley (1738–1815), one of America's outstanding artists, shows the 33-year-old Revere as a well-known, confident silversmith. Here he proudly holds one of his silver teapots; his engraving tools lie nearby on the table. This ambitious, up-and-coming merchant-craftsman created products that competed directly with similar items from England, and he rebelled against British efforts to tax and control American commerce.

Both sides translated their disagreements into ideological terms. American newspapers, propagandists, and political groups, echoing Enlightenment ideas, argued that violation of their fundamental rights justified a fight for independence. Most people in Britain stood against rebellion and for parliamentary sovereignty as a matter of principle. They argued that they were making only reasonable and minimal demands on the colonies.

In the end, each side felt backed into a corner. The notion of full independence gained appeal among the colonists. American political leaders who were critical of British policies organized the First Continental Congress in 1774, hoping to persuade Parliament to abandon its efforts to directly control colonial affairs. In response, King George III increased British armed forces in America, convinced that "blows must decide whether they are to be subject to the Country or Independent."

A WAR FOR INDEPENDENCE

The first "blows" were exchanged in 1775 between British troops and American militiamen in New England. The Second Continental Congress appointed George Washington (1732–1799) its military commander, setting the course for armed rebellion and independence. On July 4, 1776, that Congress issued

the Declaration of Independence, written primarily by Thomas Jefferson (1743–1826) and based on the ideas of John Locke and other Enlightenment thinkers. Citing "self-evident" truths; "inalienable" natural rights such as "Life, Liberty, and the pursuit of Happiness"; and "a long train of abuses" to reduce the people under "absolute Despotism," the Declaration passionately justified rebellion.

Odds favored the stronger British forces, and at first they had the upper hand. Indeed, many British leaders viewed the rebel troops with disdain, one official calling the rebels a "rude rabble without a plan." Nevertheless, despite much internal division, an American victory at Saratoga in 1777 persuaded the French to help the Americans with money, ships, and troops against France's longtime enemy. The Dutch and Spanish eventually declared war on Britain, increasing the stakes for the British. Now British possessions in the West Indies, the Mediterranean, and perhaps even India hung in the balance. In 1781 the victory of the French fleet off Virginia forced a large British army to surrender at Yorktown. This indignity convinced the British that the effort to keep the American colonies was not worth the costs. After two years of negotiations, the combatants drew up the Treaty of Paris in 1783. Britain agreed to recognize American independence and ceded to the United States the lands between the Mississippi River to the west, Canada to the north, and Spanish Florida to the south.

CREATING THE NEW NATION

By 1787, a new American constitution established a central government balanced by a separation of powers and strong states' rights. A Bill of Rights was soon enacted, protecting individual liberties and separating church and state. These principles, though lofty, did not apply to everyone. Although the Declaration of Independence had proclaimed that "all men are created equal" as a "self-evident" truth, one-fifth of the people remained slaves, and only property owners and men could vote. Nevertheless, the new nation had instituted—to an unprecedented degree—popular control, personal freedom, and formal toleration.

Some historians deem the American rebellion a war for independence, and others call it a revolution. At the time, people throughout the West—not just in America and Great Britain—viewed the *War for independence or revolution?* events as dramatic and significant. A growing body of European readers avidly followed the action in newspaper accounts. Many of these readers saw the American Revolution as a victory for Enlightenment ideas. The French in particular celebrated the Revolution as a triumph in their own competition with their British rivals. They did not realize at the time that the debts incurred by France and the ideas promoted by the American Revolution would soon come back to haunt the French monarchy.

Summary

On the surface, life between 1715 and 1789 seemed to change only incrementally for most westerners. The vast majority still lived in the countryside and worked the fields. Moreover, society and politics in the so-called Old Regime remained dominated by the aristocracy and, in most places, the monarchy. As in the seventeenth century, cultural forms still reflected elite tastes and the traditional values of commoners below them.

Below the surface, however, the West changed in crucial ways during this period. The political balance of power shifted as Russia and Prussia rose in the east while Britain gained prominence in the west. Success in the international arena often reflected how well central governments conducted their internal affairs. Some monarchs managed to dominate or work with the nobility, enact reforms, and even take on the trappings of "enlightened" rulers, whereas others—such as the French kings—failed in these ways. More important, mushrooming commerce, the agricultural revolution, and the spreading of cottage industry altered the ways by which millions of people earned a living, and these changes generated enormous new wealth. Finally, across the Atlantic in Britain's North American colonies, the

Timeline: A Closer Look

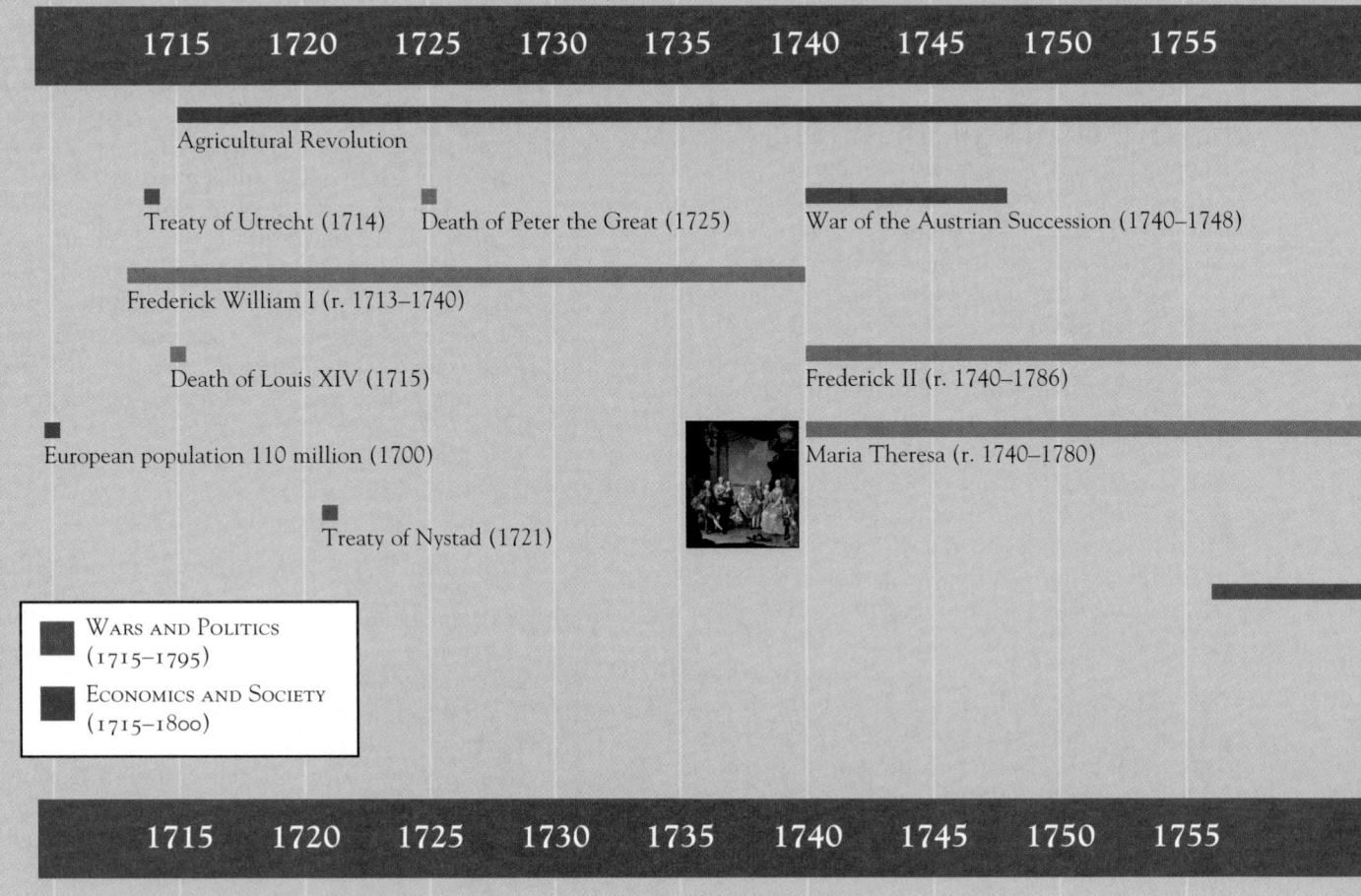

| | 1715 | 1720 | 1725 | 1730 | 1735 | 1740 | 1745 | 1750 | 1755 |

Agricultural Revolution

Treaty of Utrecht (1714)   Death of Peter the Great (1725)   War of the Austrian Succession (1740–1748)

Frederick William I (r. 1713–1740)

Death of Louis XIV (1715)   Frederick II (r. 1740–1786)

European population 110 million (1700)   Maria Theresa (r. 1740–1780)

Treaty of Nystad (1721)

WARS AND POLITICS
(1715–1795)
ECONOMICS AND SOCIETY
(1715–1800)

| | 1715 | 1720 | 1725 | 1730 | 1735 | 1740 | 1745 | 1750 | 1755 |

American Revolution posed a challenge to the status quo that the French would soon take up in a much more fundamental way. These developments, combined with the spread of Enlightenment ideas, mark the eighteenth century as a period in which westerners—knowingly or not—laid foundations for the great transformations to come.

REVIEW, ANALYZE, AND ANTICIPATE

REVIEW THE PREVIOUS CHAPTER

Chapter 13—"The Struggle for Survival and Sovereignty"—told the story of kings and nobles battling for power, the results of those struggles, and their impact on millions of people throughout the West. Chapter 14—"A New World of Reason and Re-

form"—shifted focus to the changing intellectual foundations of the West.

1. *In what ways was the eighteenth century a continuation of the struggle between monarchs and elites that had marked the seventeenth century?*

2. *Analyze how Enlightenment ideas—themselves stemming from the scientific revolution—affected Western society and especially politics during the eighteenth century.*

Catherine the Great (r. 1762–1796)

European population 190 million (1800)

Partitions of Poland (1792 and 1795)

Serfs revolt in Russia (1773–1775)

American Revolution (1776–1783)

Seven Years' War (1756–1763)

Decree on Serfs (1767)

ANALYZE THIS CHAPTER

Chapter 15—"Competing for Power and Wealth"—examines the battles of Western powers over land, position, and commerce, as well as the economic and social changes affecting eighteenth-century life in the West.

1. Which nations do you think were the biggest winners and which the biggest losers in this period? How do you explain their varying fortunes?

2. How did eighteenth-century rulers try to shore up and justify their own powers and those of their central governments?

3. Analyze the impact of slavery on Africa, the Americas, and Europe.

4. Analyze the benefits and costs of the growing commerce, the agricultural revolution, and cottage industry.

5. Why might this period be considered one of both growing prosperity and deepening social misery?

6. Delineate the differences between elite and popular culture during this period. How do you explain those differences?

ANTICIPATE THE NEXT CHAPTER

Chapter 16—"Overturning the Political and Social Order"—will examine the great upheaval in France that shook and transformed the West.

1. Why might the French monarchy have been particularly vulnerable to a revolution?

2. *In what ways might the American Revolution—as a revolution and in its principles—have foreshadowed the political upheaval that would break out in France?*

BEYOND THE CLASSROOM

STATEBUILDING AND WAR

Anderson, M.S. *Europe in the Eighteenth Century, 1713–1783*, 3rd ed. London: Longman, 1987. A thorough survey of the period.

Clark, J.C.D. *English Society, 1688–1832*. Cambridge: Cambridge University Press, 1985. A major reinterpretation of political thought and behavior that emphasizes the role of religion in English political life.

Davis, Ralph. *The Rise of the Atlantic Economies*. Ithaca, NY: Cornell University Press, 1973. A survey of the early modern economic history of the countries on the Western fringe of Europe and their colonies in North and South America.

de Madariaga, Isabel. *Catherine the Great: A Short History*. New Haven, CT: Yale University Press, 1990. A solid, useful study.

Manning, Patrick. *Slavery and African Life: Occidental, Oriental and African Slave Trades*. Cambridge: Cambridge University Press, 1990. A wide-ranging study that demonstrates how the external slave trade affected African societies.

Ritter, Gerhard. *Frederick the Great*. Berkeley, CA: University of California Press, 1968. More of an extended essay than a standard biography, but useful.

Weigley, R.F. *The Age of Battles: The Quest for Decisive Warfare from Breitenfeld to Waterloo*. Bloomington: Indiana University Press. 1991. A study of the period between 1631 and 1815 when economic, social, and technological circumstances enabled governments to concentrate large forces in the field.

 ### GLOBAL CONNECTIONS

Conniff, Michael, and Davis, Thomas. *Africans in the Americas: A History of the Black Diaspora*. New York: St. Martin's Press, 1998. Excellent coverage of the slave trade and the African diaspora.

THE TWILIGHT OF MONARCHIES? THE QUESTION OF ENLIGHTENED ABSOLUTISM

Gagliardo, John G. *Enlightened Despotism*. Arlington Heights, IL: AHM Publishing Co., 1967. A respected examination of the topic in its European context.

Scott, H.M., ed. *Enlightened Despotism*. Ann Arbor, MI: University of Michigan Press, 1990. Essays by leading historians analyzing Europe's rulers and nobility.

CHANGES IN COUNTRY AND CITY LIFE

Blum, Jerome. *The End of the Old Order in Rural Europe*. Princeton, NJ: Princeton University Press, 1978. A comprehensive study of life in rural Europe from the early eighteenth to the mid-nineteenth centuries; especially good on the abolition of serfdom.

Chambers, J.D., and G.E. Mingay. *The Agricultural Revolution*. London: Batsord, 1966. Covers various aspects of the agricultural revolution, such as enclosures and technological improvements, and relates agriculture to the socioeconomic life of the period.

Clarkson, Leslie A. *Proto-Industrialization: The First Phase of Industrialization?* London: Macmillan, 1985. Stresses the importance of cottage industry for the beginning of industrialization.

THE CULTURE OF THE ELITE: COMBINING THE OLD AND THE NEW

Black, Jeremy. *Eighteenth-Century Europe*. London: Macmillan, 1990. A thorough survey of the period.

Watt, Ian. *The Rise of the Novel*. Berkeley, CA: University of California Press, 1957. A study of the intellectual and social conditions that produced the novel in eighteenth-century England.

CULTURE FOR THE LOWER CLASSES

Burke, Peter. *Popular Culture in Early Modern Europe*. New York: Harper & Row, 1978. Surveys popular culture from the Renaissance to the French Revolution.

Muchembled, Robert. *Popular Culture and Elite Culture in France, 1400–1750*. Baton Rouge, LA:

Louisiana State University Press, 1985. Examines popular culture and the means higher authorities used to destroy it.

FORESHADOWING UPHEAVAL: THE AMERICAN REVOLUTION

Countryman, Edward. *The American Revolution*. New York: Hill and Wang, 1985. A social history of the American Revolution.

Middlekauff, Robert. *The Glorious Cause: The American Revolution, 1763–1789*. New York: Oxford University Press, 1981. A narrative account of the Anglo-American conflict.

For quiz questions that tie the book to the videos and additional primary sources, please go to the Primary Source Investigator CD.

Documents

DOCUMENT 15.1

Landlords and Serfs in Russia

During the eighteenth century, Russian serfs probably fared worse than peasants elsewhere in Europe. Toward the end of the century, Alexander Radischev published a description of Russian serfs and their treatment by noble landowners. For this daring act, the author was imprisoned by Catherine II.

■ **Investigate the Document**

In what ways does the landowner described in this excerpt treat his serfs? How does the author criticize this treatment of serfs?

"A certain man left the capital, acquired a small village of one or two hundred souls [i.e., serfs], and determined to make his living by agriculture. . . .To this end he thought it the surest method to make his peasants resemble tools that have neither will nor impulse; and to a certain extent he actually made them like the soldiers of the present time who are commanded in a mass, who move to battle in a mass, and who count for nothing when acting singly. To attain this end he took away from his peasants the small allotment of plough land and the hay meadows which noblemen usually give them for their bare maintenance, as a recompense for all the forced labor which they demand from them. In a word, this nobleman forced all his peasants and their wives and children to work every day of the year for him. Lest they should starve, he doled out to them a definite quantity of bread. . . .If there was any real meat, it was only in Easter Week.

"These serfs also receive clothing befitting their condition. . . .Naturally these serfs had no cows, horses, ewes, or rams. Their master did not withhold from these serfs the permission, but rather the means to have them. Whoever was a little better off and ate sparingly, kept a few chickens, which the master sometimes took for himself, paying for them as he pleased.

"In a short time he added to his two hundred souls another two hundred as victims of his greed, and proceeding with them just as with the first, he increased his holdings year after year, thus multiplying the number of those groaning in his fields. Now he counts them by the thousands and is praised as a famous agriculturalist.

"Barbarian! What good does it do the country that every year a few thousand more bushels of grain are grown, if those who produce it are valued on a par with the ox whose job it is to break the heavy furrow? Or do we think our citizens happy because our granaries are full and their stomachs empty?"

DOCUMENT 15.2

Austria's Empress Explains the Diplomatic Revolution

During the eighteenth century, alliances among European states often shifted. They changed most dramatically in the 1756 "Diplomatic Revolution" preceding the Seven Years' War (1756–1763). In the following excerpt, Empress Maria Theresa of Austria explains why she turned toward her traditional adversary, France, to form a coalition against the newly allied Prussia and Great Britain.

■ **Investigate the Document**

Why does Maria Theresa forge an alliance with France? What problems does she anticipate in allying Austria with France?

"I have not abandoned the old system, but Great Britain has abandoned me and the system, by concluding the Prussian treaty, the first intelligence of which struck me like a fit of apoplexy. I and the king of Prussia are incompatible; and no consideration on earth will ever induce me to enter into any engagement to which he is a party. Why should you be surprised if, following your example in concluding a treaty with Prussia, I should now enter into an engagement with France?

"I am far from being French in my disposition, and do not deny that the court of Versailles has been my bitterest enemy, but I have little to fear from France, and I have no other recourse than to form such arrangements as will secure what remains to me. My

Source: Alexander Radischev, *A Journey from St. Petersburg to Moscow* (1790).

Source: William Coxe, *History of the House of Austria,* vol. 3 (London: Bohn, 1847), pp. 363–364.

principal aim is to secure my hereditary possessions. I have truly but two enemies whom I really dread, the king of Prussia and the Turks; and while I and Russia continue on the same good terms as now exist between us; we shall, I trust, be able to convince Europe, that we are in a condition to defend ourselves against those adversaries, however formidable."

DOCUMENT 15.3

Olaudah Equiano Describes the Middle Passage

The slave trade between Africa and the Americas involved the horrors of capture and the "Middle Passage," a harrowing two-month voyage across the Atlantic. In the account below, Olaudah Equiano (1745–1797)—a west African who was captured by slave raiders when he was 10 years old—describes the ocean journey. He survived the voyage and 21 years of slavery before purchasing his freedom.

■ **Investigate the Document**

How were captured Africans treated on the slave ship? **In what ways** *did they try to resist?*

The first object which saluted my eyes when I arrived on the coast was the sea, and a slave ship which was then riding at anchor and waiting for its cargo. These filled me with astonishment, which was soon converted into terror when I was carried on board. I was immediately handled and tossed up to see if I were sound by some of the crew, and I was now persuaded that I had gotten into a world of bad spirits and that they were going to kill me. . . .

I was not long suffered to indulge my grief; I was soon put down under the decks, and there I received such a salutation in my nostrils as I had never experienced in my life; so that with the loathsomeness of the stench and crying together, I became so sick and low that I was not able to eat, nor had I the least desire to taste anything. I now wished for the last friend, death, to relieve me; but soon, to my grief, two of the white men offered me eatables, and on my refusing to eat, one of them held me fast by the hands and laid me across I think the windlass and tied my feet while the other flogged me severely. I had never experienced anything of this kind before, and although not being used to the water I naturally feared that element the first time I saw it, yet nevertheless if I could have gotten over the nettings I would have jumped over the side, but I could not; and besides, the crew used to watch very closely over those of us who were not chained down to the decks, lest we should leap into the water, and I have seen some of these poor African prisoners most severely cut for attempting to do so, and hourly whipped for not eating. This indeed was often the case with myself. . . .

One day when we had a smooth sea and moderate wind, two of my wearied countrymen who were chained together (I was near them at the time), preferring death to such a life of misery, somehow made through the nettings and jumped into the sea; immediately another quite dejected fellow, who on account of his illness was suffered to be out of irons, also followed their example; and I believe many more would very soon have done the same if they had not been prevented by the ship's crew, who were instantly alarmed. Those of us that were the most active were in a moment put down under the deck, and there was such a noise and confusion amongst the people of the ship as I never heard before, to stop her and get the boat to go after the slaves. However, two of the wretches were drowned, but they got the other and afterwards flogged him unmercifully for thus attempting to prefer death to slavery. In this manner we continued to undergo more hardships than I can now relate, hardships which are inseparable from this accursed trade.

Source: Olaudah Equiano, *The Interesting Narrative of the Life of Olaudah Equiano, or Gustavus Vassa, the African, Written by Himself,* 2 vols (London, 1789).

Storming the Bastille

On July 14, 1789, a crowd of Parisians stormed the Bastille, a castle-prison that stood as a symbol of all that was oppressive under the Old Regime. For most people, this event marked the beginning of the French Revolution.

CHAPTER 16

Overturning the Political and Social Order

The French Revolution and Napoleon, 1789–1815

STUDY • Causes of the French Revolution • Creating a new order in France • The Radical Republic • The rise and fall of Napoleon Bonaparte. NOTICE how the French Revolution and Napoleon transformed politics and society.

France was beginning to stir. On October 17, 1787, Arthur Young, a British farmer and diarist traveling through France, described "a great ferment amongst all ranks of men, who are eager for some change, without knowing what to look to, or to hope for." People whom Young talked with in Paris concluded that "they are on the eve of some great revolution in the government."

Two years later, the French Revolution brought the French monarchy to its knees. During the following 10 years, revolutionaries eliminated the monarchy, overturned the social system of France's Old Regime, and transformed France's institutions. Moreover, the Revolution, with its compelling banner of "Liberty, Equality, Fraternity," proved so potent that its impact spread far beyond the borders of France. It soon spawned wars that engulfed most of Europe for more than two decades. Riding the twin forces of revolutionary turmoil and war, one individual—Napoleon Bonaparte—would rise to a legendary pinnacle of power. He would rule over a new French Empire and a nearly conquered continent. In the process, Napoleon spread the ideals of the French Revolution well beyond France. This tide of change, turmoil, and war mounted by the French Revolution and Napoleon would eventually subside, but for France—and for much of Western civilization—the course of history had shifted permanently.

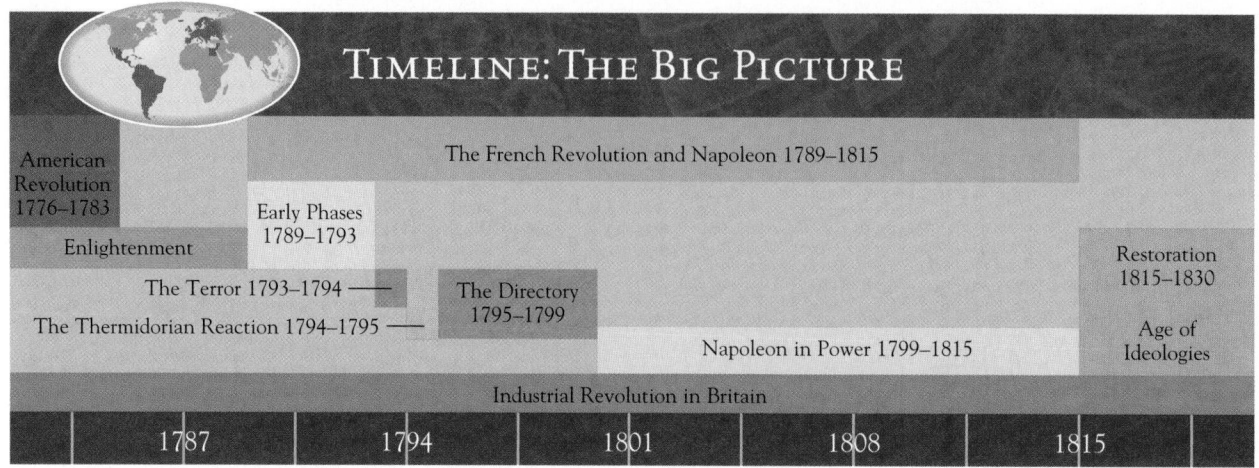

American Revolution 1776–1783

The French Revolution and Napoleon 1789–1815

Enlightenment

Early Phases 1789–1793

The Terror 1793–1794 ———

The Thermidorian Reaction 1794–1795 ———

The Directory 1795–1799

Restoration 1815–1830

Napoleon in Power 1799–1815

Age of Ideologies

Industrial Revolution in Britain

1787   1794   1801   1808   1815

"A Great Ferment": Trouble Brewing in France

Arthur Young recognized discontent percolating among the French population, but there was good reason for people everywhere to assume that any crises would pass without a fundamental change in the monarchy or social order. The French monarchy had remained intact for centuries. Both Louis XVI and his predecessor, Louis XV, ruled over the leading nation on the Continent—a country more populous, wealthy, and educated than ever. Although neither king could claim much popularity, Louis XVI could at least bask in the glory of supporting the American revolutionaries in their victory over the British, France's chief competitor.

Then what caused the "great ferment" in France described by our British traveler? Below the surface bubbled growing complaints within France's social orders. Members of the aristocracy and middle classes, many influenced by the ideas of the Enlightenment, wanted more rights and power from the monarchy. Peasants suffered hardships that could, as in the past, create disorder and uprisings. However, the immediate, visible problem came from a conflict over France's finances.

THE FINANCIAL CRISIS WEAKENS THE MONARCHY

When Louis XVI ascended the throne in 1774, he inherited a large—and constantly growing—national debt. Much of that debt had been incurred financing wars and maintaining the military (see Chapter 15). Yet this debt should not have broken a nation as rich as France. Great Britain and the Netherlands had higher per-capita debts than France, but these countries also boasted taxation systems and banks to support their debts. *The taxation system* France lacked an adequate banking system, and most of the national debt was short term and privately held. Moreover, France's taxation system offered little help. The French nobility, clergy, and much of the bourgeoisie controlled the bulk of France's wealth and had long been exempt from most taxes. Nearly all direct taxes fell on the struggling peasantry. There was no consistent set of rules or method for collecting taxes throughout the country, and private tax collectors diverted much revenue from the treasury into their own pockets. Unless something was done, royal bankruptcy loomed ahead.

To stave off financial ruin, Louis XVI appointed the Physiocrat Jacques Turgot (1727–1781), a friend of Voltaire, as his minister of finance in 1774. Turgot proposed to abolish guilds, *Reform efforts* eliminate restriction on the commerce in grain, institute a small new tax on landowners, and cut down on expenses at court. However, people who benefited from the old system soon engineered his dismissal, and his modest reform measures were rescinded. A succession of ministers tried all kinds of temporary solutions, but to no avail. Costs incurred to support the Americans in their war of independence against England made matters worse. Now interest payments on the debt ate up half of all government expenditures. Bankers began refusing to lend the government money.

Desperate, Louis called an Assembly of Notables in 1787 and pleaded with these selected nobles, clergy, and officials to consent to new taxes and financial reforms. Still they refused, as did the judges (all members of the nobility) in the *parlement,* or law court, of

554

Paris when Louis turned to them. Instead, leading nobles and officials demanded a meeting of an old representative institution, the Estates General. They fully expected to control these proceedings and thereby assert their own interests. With bankruptcy imminent and nowhere else to turn for help, the king gave in. No one knew it at the time, but Louis's decision set the stage for turning France's financial crisis into a political and social movement of epic proportions.

THE UNDERLYING CAUSES OF THE REVOLUTION

Louis's financial woes were just the most visible part of France's problems. When these tensions combined

Revolt of the nobility

with the conflicts tugging at the fabric of French society, a dangerous blend resulted. One of the most troubling conflicts stemmed from the relationship between the monarchy and the nobility. For centuries, the French nobility, less than 2 percent of the population, had been the foundation on which the monarchy established its rule. However, the nobility was also the monarchy's chief rival for power, and it had grown increasingly assertive during the eighteenth century (see Chapter 15). Through institutions such as the *parlements* that they controlled, nobles resisted ministerial efforts to tax them. More and more, nobles claimed to be protecting their rights as well as France itself from "ministerial despotism." So when the monarchy turned to this group for financial help, the nobles refused for two reasons. First, they wanted to protect their own financial interests. Second, they used the crisis to assert their independence. Indeed, they argued that they represented the nation. They established a price for their cooperation: a greater share of power. Understandably, France's kings refused to pay that price. Thus, when the Assembly of Notables turned a deaf ear to Louis's pleas in 1787 and instead demanded a meeting of the Estates General, the king faced a financial crisis that was linked to a virtual revolt of his own nobility.

Louis might have thought he could find allies within the middle class in his standoff with the nobility. After all, French and other European kings had

Middle-class demands

occasionally turned to wealthy members of this class for support in the past. Nevertheless, as events would prove in the tumultuous months of 1789, the middle class had changed—it now nursed its own set of grievances.

This growing social sector—having almost tripled during the century to some 9 percent of the population—had benefited greatly from France's general prosperity and population boom after 1715. Many talented, wealthy, and ambitious members of the middle class managed to gain the high offices, titles, and privileges enjoyed by the nobility. Others rubbed shoulders and shared ideas with the nobility in salons and did their best to copy the nobles' style of life. Moreover, most had found ways to avoid paying heavy taxes.

However, numerous members of the bourgeoisie—particularly younger administrators, lawyers, journalists, and intellectuals—had encountered frustrating barriers to the offices and prestige enjoyed by the nobility. They also had grown impatient with the monarchy's failure to enact reforms that would benefit them specifically. By 1789, many applauded broad attacks on the privileged orders and the status quo. An example of such an attack was Abbé Emmanuel-Joseph Sieyès' widely circulated pamphlet *What Is the Third Estate?* According to Sieyès, "If the privileged order should be abolished, the nation would be nothing less, but something more." The sorts of reforms that these middle-class critics had in mind were no more palatable to the monarchy than those of the nobility.

People from both the middle class and the nobility had begun expressing ideas and using highly charged political terms that profoundly threatened the monarchy. In the decades before 1789, salon meetings and new publica-

Enlightenment ideas and language

tions had spread key ideas of the Enlightenment to an increasingly literate public, particularly the aristocratic and middle-class elite in Paris and other French cities (see Chapter 14). These ideas emphasized the validity of reason and natural rights and questioned long-established institutions. They also undermined notions of the divine rights of kings and traditional ways of life—all while intensifying expectations of rapid reforms. In addition, terms such as "nation," "citizen," and "general will" had increasingly cropped up in the political discourse and reflected a growing sense that politics should include more than the concerns of the monarch and a tiny elite. So, when nobles asserted their own interests against the king, they often used language and ideas that attacked monarchical absolutists as unjustified tyrants and that accused the king's minister of "despotism." Middle-class men and women shared these sentiments and later extended them to demands for legal equality.

Thus, given all the resentments brewing among the nobility and the middle class, Louis and his often unpopular ministers risked much after they exposed themselves to discussions of reform within the Estates General. Three other developments—all beyond the powers of the king, nobility, and middle class—added an underlying sense of disappointment, desperation, and disorder among the French people in these decades.

First, a gap opened between rosy expectations and frightening realities. Before 1770, France had enjoyed a long period of prosperity. This growing wealth engendered a sense of rising expectations—that economically, things would keep getting better and better. After 1770, a series of *Disappointed expectations* economic depressions struck, turning these high expectations into bitter disappointment and frustration. Worse, in 1788 the countryside suffered unusually bad harvests. In May and July of that year, hailstorms wiped out crops throughout France. Drought and then the most severe winter in decades followed. The price of bread soared, and with it came hunger, desperation, and even starvation. Droves of peasants crowded into the cities in search of jobs and help, but the agricultural depression had already spread there and had thrown thousands of artisans and laborers out of work. In the spring of 1789, peasants and urban poor looking for food turned to violence in France's cities and villages. Women led groups demanding grain and lower prices for flour. Desperate people attacked bakeries and stores of grain wherever they could find them. Arthur Young wrote, "the want of bread is terrible: accounts arrive every moment from the provinces of riots and disturbances, and calling in the military, to preserve the peace of the markets." The populace angrily blamed governmental figures and "parasitical agents" of the Old Regime for their plight.

By 1789, many pamphlets and cartoons portraying the connection between suffering and France's privileged orders circulated throughout France. Figure 16.1 is an apt example of these publications. This illustration shows the thin "common man," who represents the vast majority of the people, carrying three heavy figures from the privileged classes on his back. In front, wielding a whip and claiming feudal rights, is an aristocrat or perhaps the king himself. Just above him is a clergyman in robes, brandishing papers representing the threat of an inquisition and clerical privileges. In back rides a judge with a list of

the jealously guarded rights of the noble-controlled *parlements*. The illustration depicts the common man as a naked beast kept under control by reins, chains, and a blindfold. He crawls pitifully across barren fields, bleeding from the hands, knees, and loins, while his tormentors spur him on.

The second unsettling development came with the increasing demands for political participation and governmental reform *Demands for political participation* throughout the West in the years before 1789. These movements, arising in various countries, were led by ambitious elites. In Poland, agitation for independence from Russian influence surfaced between 1772 and 1792. Across the Atlantic, what started as a tax revolt in Britain's North American colonies turned into the American Revolution and war for independence that directly involved French aristocrats and common soldiers alike, and led to government without a king (see Chapter 15). In the Dutch Republic, demands for reform in the 1780s erupted into open revolt in 1787. In the Austrian Netherlands (Belgium and Luxembourg),

FIGURE 16.1
France's privileged orders.

elites rose against the reforms initiated by Emperor Joseph II in 1787. Well-informed French elites, keeping abreast of these disturbances, began to surmise that they, too, might successfully challenge the political status quo.

The economic hardship and political uprisings across Europe were damaging enough. A third problem—the French people's disrespect for

Unpopular kings

their own king—made matters worse. For much of the eighteenth century, France had been ruled by the unremarkable, unpopular, and long-lived King Louis XV. Unlike some of his European counterparts, neither he nor his successor, Louis XVI, managed to forge an effective alliance with the nobility or consistently assert their authority over it. Nor did they succeed in enacting reforms or even give the impression of being "enlightened" monarchs. Louis XVI had little particular taste or talent for rule, and his unpopular Austrian wife, Queen Marie Antoinette, increasingly drew fire for her supposed extravagance and indifference to those below her. According to a widely circulated story, she dismissed reports that the poor could not buy bread with the phrase, "Let them eat cake!" Though the story was untrue, it reflected the growing anger against the king and queen.

Desperate to stave off the immediate threat of bankruptcy, the relatively weak Louis XVI looked for support. Instead of able allies, he found a jealous nobility, a disgruntled middle class, a bitter and frustrated peasantry, and an urban poor made desperate by hunger.

THE "TENNIS COURT OATH"

In this ominous atmosphere, Louis XVI summoned the Estates General in 1788. This representative body, which had not met since 1614, was divided

The Estates General

into France's three traditional orders, or estates: the first estate, the clergy, owned over 10 percent of France's best land; the second estate, the nobility, owned more than 20 percent of the land; and the third estate, the so-called commoners, included the bourgeoisie, the peasantry, and the urban populace. During the early months of 1789, elections of representatives to the Estates General were held. All men who had reached the age of 25 and who paid taxes could vote. In thousands of meetings to draw up lists of grievances to present to the king, people found their political voices and connected their dissatisfactions with inflating expecta-

tions of reform. Hundreds of pamphlets appeared and public debate spread widely. Each of the three estates elected its own representatives. Because the third estate made up more than nine-tenths of the total population, Louis XVI agreed to grant it as many seats as the other two estates combined. However, by tradition, the three estates sat separately, and each group had one vote.

In April 1789, delegates began streaming into Versailles armed only with *cahiers*, or the lists of grievances from all classes of people, that had been called for by the king. Of the 600 representatives of the third estate, not one came from the peasantry. Except for a handful of liberal clergy and nobles elected to the third estate, these delegates—mostly ambitious lawyers, petty officials, administrators, and other professionals—were all members of the bourgeoisie. They fully expected to solve the financial crisis quickly and then move on to addressing the long lists of complaints that they had been accumulating for years. Most bourgeois representatives, like many liberal nobles, wanted to create a constitutional government with a national assembly that would meet regularly to pass taxes and laws.

After religious services and a solemn procession in Paris, the delegates met in Versailles on May 5. Immediately they debated the voting system. The two privileged estates demanded that, according to custom, the three estates meet separately and vote by order—that is, each estate cast one vote. This procedure would place power squarely in the hands of the nobility, which controlled most of the first estate as well as its own order. The third estate demanded that all the orders meet jointly and that delegates vote by head. This method would favor the third estate, for not only did this order boast as many members as the other two combined, but a number of liberal clergy and nobles in the first and second estates sympathized with the reforms called for by the third estate. All sides realized that the outcome of this voting issue would be decisive.

The delegates haggled for six weeks. Louis waffled from one side to the other. Finally, the third estate, backed by some clergy from the

The National Assembly

first estate, took action and declared itself the National Assembly of France on June 17 and invited the other two estates to join it in enacting legislation. Three days later, when the third estate deputies arrived at their meeting hall, they found it locked. Adjourning to a nearby building that

FIGURE 16.2
School of Jacques-Louis David, *The Tennis Court Oath.*

served as an indoor tennis court, they took the "Tennis Court Oath," vowing not to disband until France had a constitution.

Figure 16.2 dramatizes and glorifies this act of defiance. The painting is based on a pen and ink drawing by Jacques-Louis David (1748–1825), a talented contemporary painter and active supporter of the Revolution. In the center of the picture, the presiding officer, Jean-Sylvain Bailly (1736–1793) (soon to become mayor of Paris), raises his arm in a pledge and reads the oath aloud. Below him, from left to right, a white-robed Carthusian monk represents the second estate, a black-robed Catholic curate the first estate, and the brown-clad Protestant minister the third estate. These same three figures also stand for France's main religious groups: the secular clergy, the regular clergy, and Protestantism. All three figures join, symbolizing the transformation of the meeting into the newly formed National Assembly. Around these fig-

ures, representatives also take the oath. From above, light streams through billowing curtains as if blessing the heroic activities below, and members of the populace approvingly watch the scene.

On June 23, the king met with the three estates in a royal session. He offered many reforms but also commanded the estates to meet separately and vote by order. Then the king, his ministers, and members of the first two estates regally filed out. The third-estate representatives, however, defiantly remained seated. When the royal master of ceremonies returned to remind them of the king's orders, Count Mirabeau (1749–1791), a liberal nobleman elected by the third estate, jumped to his feet. "Go and tell those who sent you," he shouted, "that we are here by the will of the people and will not leave this place except at the point of the bayonet!" When the startled courtier dutifully repeated these words to his master, Louis XVI, with characteristic weakness, replied,

"They mean to stay. Well, damn it, let them stay." A few days later, the king reversed himself and ordered the three estates to meet jointly and vote by head. The third estate had won the first round.

STORMING THE BASTILLE

The monarchy might have been able to reassert control had not the new National Assembly received unexpected support from two sources: the Parisian populace and the French peasantry. Both groups had been suffering from the unusually poor economic conditions initiated by bad harvests. Revolutionary events raised expectations in hard times, making these people in the city and countryside particularly volatile. The first important disturbances broke out in Paris, whose population of 600,000 made it one of the largest cities in Europe. In early July, rumors that the king was calling the professional troops of the frontier garrison to Versailles raced through the streets of Paris. Alarmed, residents concluded that the king meant to use force against them. Then Louis dismissed his popular finance minister, Jacques Necker (1732–1804). This move seemed to confirm the fears of the third estate, who saw Necker as an ally.

At this critical juncture, the common people of Paris acted on their own. On July 14, riotous crowds of men and women searching for arms marched on the Bastille, a gloomy old fortress-prison in a working-class quarter. Few people were actually in the weakly guarded Bastille, but it symbolized the old order. Many died in the confused battle. With the help of mutinous troops, however, the crowd eventually took the Bastille, hacked its governor to death, and paraded around Paris with his head on a pike. "This glorious day must amaze our enemies, and finally usher in for us the triumph of justice and liberty," proclaimed a Paris newspaper.

The scene on page 552, one of many paintings and drawings made to celebrate this event, reveals the importance of this famous battle. The Bastille is portrayed as a massive castle that, against all odds, has come under attack by commoners and troops who have rallied to the side of the people. Only a few cannons seem necessary, for the people supposedly have heroic revolutionary spirit and numbers enough to surge forward and somehow storm across the bridge toward the Bastille entrance. The picture poignantly captures the symbolism of the act—the Bastille, representing the old feudal regime of the past, falls because of corruption within and the heroic power of an outraged people fighting under the revolutionary banner of Liberty, Equality, and Fraternity. In fact, this show of force by the artisans, shop owners, and laborers of Paris stayed the king's hand and sparked uprisings in other cities across France. Under pressure, royal authority began to crumble.

Uprisings in the countryside echoed events in Paris. That July and August, peasants throughout France revolted against their lords. *Peasant revolts* Burning tax rolls, the peasantry attacked manors, reoccupied enclosed lands, and rejected the traditional rights of noble landowners—dues on land, flour mills, wine presses, and law courts, and the tithes (taxes) landlords charged their tenants. These revolts intensified with the spreading of unfounded rumors that bands of brigands, perhaps assembled by nobles, were on the loose in the countryside. *The "Great Fear"* Panicked by this "Great Fear," many nobles—including one of the king's brothers—fled France and became known as the *émigrés* (exiles).

THE END OF THE OLD ORDER

Now the nobility as well as the monarchy was in retreat. The National Assembly—dominated by the middle-class deputies from the third estate but now including many deputies from the clergy and nobility—tried to pacify the aroused peasantry. On August 4, during a night session of the National Assembly, one nobleman after another stood up and renounced his traditional rights and privileges in an effort to make the best of a bad situation. A leader of the Assembly hailed the "end of feudalism." As Document 16.1 (see page D16.1) shows, the National Assembly quickly decreed the end of serfdom, traditional dues owed to landlords, special taxation rights, and privileged access to official posts. The peasantry seemed pacified for the time being.

Success spurred the National Assembly to take further steps. The most important of these actions occurred on August 26, when the Assembly proclaimed the Declaration of *Declaration of Rights of Man and Citizen* Rights of Man and Citizen. Enlightenment ideas and phrases similar to those in the American Declaration of Independence filled this document. "Men are born and remain free and equal in rights," it stated. The natural rights included "liberty, property, security, and resistance to oppression." Sovereignty—supreme authority—rested

OLC

FIGURE 16.3
Parisian women march to Versailles.

crowd of Parisian women, already infuriated by high bread prices and food shortages, marched 11 miles through the rain to Versailles. The contemporary print shown in Figure 16.3 depicts *March to Versailles* the marchers, armed with pikes, axes, swords, and cannon. With the exception of the well-dressed, reluctant figure at the left, their faces express a striking determination and authority. (Notice the woman riding in the cart with the cannon and the woman at the front to the far right).

At Versailles, the marchers surrounded the palace. With the help of members of the recently formed National Guard—units of armed civilians under Lafayette—they forced the king and his family to accompany them back to Paris, bringing him closer to the people and away from the protected isolation of Versailles and the king's aristocratic advisors. As the carriage bearing the royal family rolled toward the capital, where the royal family would be virtually imprisoned in the Tuileries Palace, the surrounding crowd of women and men shouted jubilantly, "We have the baker [the king], the baker's wife, and the little cook boy! Now we shall have bread!" Although this image of women taking political action into their own hands made them heroines of the Revolution in some eyes, others would nervously look back on the women's behavior as something inappropriate and even frightening. Most men were not ready to accept such a change in women's traditional roles.

A few days later, the National Assembly moved its sessions to Paris. The third estate, building on the anger and hunger of the peasantry and the urban poor, had triumphed. The old order had disintegrated.

with the nation as a whole, not the monarchy. Enacted laws should express the "general will"—a term and idea made popular by Jean-Jacques Rousseau (see Chapter 14). The document proclaimed freedom of opinion "even in religion," freedom of the press, and freedom from arbitrary arrest. In 1791, this spirit would lead to the liberation of France's Jews from old legal disabilities.

Some of these rights, such as freedom of the press, applied to women as well as men, but only men gained the full measure of new social and political rights. In the months and years that followed, many women objected to this limitation. Organizing groups and writing petitions and pamphlets, these women demanded to be included. In 1791, Olympe de Gouges (1748–1793), a writer and strong supporter of the Revolution, wrote one of the best-known and more challenging pamphlets, the *Declaration of the Rights of Women.* She argued that women should have the same political and social rights as men: "The only limits on the exercise of the natural rights of woman are perpetual male tyranny; these limits are to be reformed by the laws of nature and reason." Some members of the government, such as the marquis de Condorcet (1743–1794) voiced similar demands. However, their arguments fell on deaf ears.

Despite this rising tide of defiance, Louis refused to sign the August decrees. Instead, he once more assembled troops around Versailles and Paris. In answer to this new threat of force, on October 5 and 6 a huge

The Constitutional Monarchy: Establishing a New Order

Flushed with success, the National Assembly now turned to the task of transforming French institutions. Guiding principles were represented by the revolutionary banner "Liberty, Equality, and Fraternity." At that time, the idea of liberty meant freedom from arbitrary authority and freedom of speech, press, conscience, assembly, and profession. Equality meant

Liberty, Equality, Fraternity equal treatment under the law and equality of economic opportunity—at least for men. Fraternity meant comradeship as citizens of the nation. During the next two years, the Assembly passed a series of sweeping reforms that altered almost all aspects of life in France.

The central government, now based on national sovereignty, was transformed into what amounted to a constitutional monarchy. The National Assembly served as its legislature, and the king (still an impor-

Constitutional monarchy tant symbol of authority for many) remained its chief executive officer. Because only tax-paying males could vote and win election to office, the bourgeoisie firmly held the reins of power. For the time being, the governance of France was decentralized. To undermine

old loyalties and the power of the provincial nobility, the National Assembly created 83 newly named departments, each almost equal in size and administered by locally elected assemblies and officials (Maps 16.1 and 16.2). Similarly, the National Assembly took France's judicial system out of the hands of the nobility and clergy. It created new civil and criminal courts, with elected judges. France's complex, unequal system of taxation was also swept away, replaced by uniform taxes on land and the profits of trade and industry.

The new government linked reform of the Catholic Church with the financial problems it faced. Repudiating France's debt was out of the question because part of it was owed to members of the bourgeoisie. To pay for its expenditures, the National Assembly issued what amounted to paper money called *assignats*. To back up the *assignats*, pay off the

THINKING ABOUT GEOGRAPHY

MAPS 16.1 AND 16.2 *Reorganizing France in 1789*

These maps show France's historic provinces, each with its own political identity, and the nation's revolutionary departments after 1789. ◙ **Notice** the different sizes of the old provinces and the almost equal size of the new departments. ◙ **Notice** that the historic names of the provinces have been eliminated, and most of the new departments are named for geographical features (mountains, such as the Alps; rivers, such as the Seine). **Consider** why France's Assembly reorganized the nation in this way.

On August 10, local leaders in Paris organized a huge Parisian crowd of men and women who attacked the king's palace. The royal family fled for their lives to the Legislative Assembly. The invading crowd wrecked the interior of the palace and slaughtered hundreds of the king's guards. The Legislative Assembly suspended and imprisoned the hapless Louis XVI. Under pressure from the people of Paris, it called elections—this time with almost all men enjoying the right to vote—for a National Convention to draw up a new, more radical constitution.

Meanwhile, one of the Jacobin leaders, Georges-Jacques Danton (1759–1794), used his great skills as *Panic and massacres* an orator and organizer to gather recruits for the army and rush them to the front. As the recruits prepared to leave Paris to meet the invading Prussians, rumors—spurred by the propaganda of radical journalists like Jean-Paul Marat (1743–1793)—spread that reactionary clergy and nobles planned to murder their wives and children. Frightened and enraged people began murdering members of the nonjuring clergy (who would not swear allegiance to the new order) and nobles being held in the prisons of Paris. During the first three weeks of September 1792, more than a thousand fell victim to these massacres.

In the elections for the National Convention, held amid this hysteria, republicans—favoring elimination of the monarchy altogether *National Convention* and the creation of a French republic—won a sweeping victory. Document 16.2 (see page D16.1) reveals how the Jacobin club of Paris, branding the king "Louis the Last," pushed for a republic and legislators who favored Jacobin views. Most of the conservative elements fearfully stayed away from the polls. This Convention ruled France for the next three years, taking the Revolution down a new, more radical road.

RADICAL REPUBLICANS STRUGGLE FOR POWER

The struggle for political dominance among the different Jacobin factions intensified after the election. *Girondins and Jacobins* The Girondins, so called because many of their leaders came from the vicinity of Bordeaux in the department of the Gironde, had once been the most powerful and radical faction of the Legislative Assembly. Because they had sat on the speaker's left, they had come to be

known as "the Left." In the new National Convention, the Girondins found themselves on the Right as the more conservative faction. Now the Left consisted mostly of members of the Jacobin political club from Paris. These Jacobins came to be called "the Mountain" because they occupied the highest seats in the convention hall.

On September 22, 1792, the National Convention declared France a republic. The government then disposed of the king, who had *The Republic* squandered most of his support since his flight to Varennes in 1791. The Convention tried Louis and found him guilty of treasonable communication with the enemy. An extended debate ensued over whether to execute the king, with most of the Girondins opposed and the Mountain in favor. On January 21, 1793, the Convention voted by a narrow margin to execute Louis.

Figure 16.4 depicts the scene of Louis's execution. On the platform, Louis addressed the crowd for the last time: "I die innocent." An eyewitness described how the execu- *Execution of the king* tioners "dragged him under the axe of the guillotine, which with one stroke severed his head from his body." The revolutionary government adopted the newly invented guillotine as its instrument of choice because it considered the device more efficient and therefore humane than other methods of execution, such as hanging and the axe. Here an executioner holds up the head of the king for the troops and crowd to view. An observer reported that a few seconds later, "cries of 'Vive la Républic' [long live the Republic] were heard . . . and in less than ten minutes this cry, a thousand times repeated, became the universal shout of the multitude, and every hat was in the air." The troops, with their backs to the crowd, are there to witness what is presented as a patriotic event. Although other executions would not have the same significance or draw the same crowds, this scene would be repeated thousands of times over the next two years. Beheadings not only served as affirmations of revolutionary justice, they also provided entertainment—people often rented chairs and purchased food, drinks, and souvenirs, including miniature guillotines. Those who could not attend might purchase widely sold prints such as the one pictured.

Ten months later the queen, Marie Antoinette, followed Louis XVI to the guillotine. These executions sent a shudder of horror through the royal courts of Europe, as did the new French army recruits'

FIGURE 16.4
Execution of Louis XVI.

surprising success against the Austrian and Prussian coalition. The hastily assembled revolutionary armies, swelling with numbers and enthusiasm, had checked the advancing Austrian and Prussian armies at Valmy in September 1792. France now went on the offensive. Alarmed, Britain, the Dutch Netherlands, Spain, Portugal, Sardinia, and Naples joined Austria and Prussia in a great coalition against France. This new external threat was compounded by internal threats to the revolutionary government. The peasants of the Vendée region in western France, stirred up by the nonjuring clergy and others, rebelled against the republican government. "We want our king, our priests and the Old Regime," cried the rebels. The uprising spread until some 60 of the 83 departments suffered revolts. Lyons, France's second largest city, rose against the government in May. Toulon, the chief French naval base on the Mediter-

Internal and external enemies

ranean, invited in the British fleet to help in the fight against France's radical government. All-too-real enemies outside and within France's borders surged forward to fight against the Revolution.

THE TERROR

Faced with a seemingly inevitable demise of their cause and threatened by radical demands from the *sans-culottes*, the leaders of the Mountain decided to take drastic action. For support they turned to the Paris Commune, as the city government was called, which radicals and the *sans-culottes* controlled. The *sans-culottes* wanted to carry the Revolution even further, toward more direct democracy and governmental controls over the price of bread. Although the Mountain's leaders did not fully agree with the *sans-culottes*, they were willing to work with them to gain supremacy.

Biography

MANON ROLAND (1754–1793)

✎ Consider what Manon Roland's life reveals about the attitudes underlying the Revolution and the rapidly changing events that disrupted people's lives.

Manon Roland, describing herself as a "friend of humanity" and "lover of liberty," welcomed the French Revolution "with rapture." Born in 1754 into the family of a Parisian engraver, she learned to read by the age of four. By her early 20s, she was fluent in two foreign languages, had mastered the Greek and Roman classics, and embraced the ideas of Rousseau. She also rejected her Catholic faith and formed a lasting hatred for the pretensions of the aristocracy—and of the royal family in particular. She married a lawyer 20 years her senior who gained a position as inspector of manufacturers in Lyons. At the outbreak of the Revolution in 1789, she was at the center of a group of idealistic intellectuals and admirers who met regularly in Lyons. She argued for a republic rather than a constitutional monarchy and demanded that the royal family be put on trial.

The turmoil of revolutionary events created opportunities for the couple. In 1791, the city government of Lyons sent Manon's husband to Paris as a negotiator. Manon accompanied him, thrilled to be at the political center of France. They attended meetings of the Jacobin Club, and Manon quickly gathered around her a social circle of men, including Robespierre, whom she would later describe as "ardent, jealous, avid for popularity." The Rolands also associated with Girondins.

Manon's husband often attended gatherings of this circle, and Manon let him do all the public speaking for both of them. Upholding the traditional, formal role of a proper wife, mother, and homemaker, she mostly listened. "I knew the role that suited my sex, and I never abandoned it," she noted. Similarly, she did not argue for the rights of women or even invite other women to these gatherings, but she often resented men's attitudes toward women: it takes "a great deal of patience or vanity to hear with cool head, from men's own mouths, the value they attach to their superiority over us." Yet she was more politically and intellectually ambitious than her husband. Often, she was the force behind her husband's words and the author of writings that came out under his name. Figure 16.5 shows this strong woman looking directly at the viewer, pen in hand.

In 1792, with the rise to power of the Girondins, Manon's husband was offered the high post of minister of the interior. She talked him into accepting it and, from behind the scenes, shared his new position of power and prominence. It was she

---

The National Convention, now dominated by the Mountain and surrounded by a threatening Parisian crowd of women and men urged on by *sans-culotte* leaders, voted the expulsion and arrest of their chief competitors, the Girondin leaders, on June 2, 1793. To pacify the *sans-culottes*, the National Convention also agreed to enact the Law of the Maximum to control the price of bread, flour, and other essentials. Finally, the Convention drafted a democratic constitution based on universal male suffrage that promised rights to education and even subsistence (a job or poor relief). However, the Convention soon suspended the constitution and formed the 12-member Committee of Public Safety to guide the country. The committee had two main tasks: to secure the Republic against its enemies—both internal and external—and to carry out a radical republican program. With the vast authority granted by the Convention, it enjoyed dictatorial powers. The committee came

Committee of Public Safety

FIGURE 16.5

Manon Roland.

who did most of the necessary writing—the instructions, circulars, and public announcements—and who accepted visitors eager to get an audience with the busy minister.

Events, however, moved too rapidly for Manon Roland as her life and the Revolution took more radical turns. She fell

in love with Buzot, a young Girondin in her circle. She told her husband of her feelings, and although the two honored the form of their marriage out of a sense of propriety and discipline, they were miserable together. Manon made new political enemies, particularly Danton and the more radical Jacobins. The radical press called her a whore and her salon a hotbed of intrigue. Then the Girondins began to lose power, and Manon's husband's career stumbled as well. He resigned from office two days after the execution of the king in early 1793. The Revolution had gone too far even for Manon Roland, who wrote that she was "ashamed of it. It has been dishonored by scoundrels." Over the next few months both Rolands drew criticism from the press and their political enemies. Threatening groups of *sans-culottes* lurked in front of their apartment.

Too late, the Rolands tried to flee Paris. On May 31, 1793, Manon's husband, like many other Girondins, was arrested. He soon escaped, but then Manon suffered the same fate. After languishing in jail for months and writing her memoirs (modeled on Rousseau's *Memoirs*), she was tried on November 8, 1793, and found guilty of crimes against the Republic. That same day, she was escorted to the very guillotine where her longtime enemies Louis XVI and Marie Antoinette had perished. On the platform, she raised her eyes to David's statue representing liberty and lamented, "O Liberty, what crimes are committed in thy name." Upon hearing of her death, her husband committed suicide. Just weeks later, her love, Buzot, facing arrest himself, also committed suicide.

Revolutionary events that had drawn Manon to Paris and initially fulfilled her hopes quickly spun out of control. At the forefront of change in 1789, she found herself left behind and labeled an enemy of the Revolution just four years later. For Manon Roland and so many like her who rose with the Revolution, the wry statement of a moderate observer held true: "The Revolution . . . devours its children."

under the ideological leadership of the gifted and feared Maximilien Robespierre (1758–1794). A lawyer from the provinces when elected to the Estates General in 1789, he quickly rose to head the Jacobin Club in Paris. This stern, determined idealist was influenced by Rousseau and was bent upon the creation of a virtuous republic. In pursuit of this dream, Robespierre and his fellow committee members struggled both to appease and control the unpredictable, threatening *sans-culottes*.

To protect the Republic from its internal enemies and to satisfy demands from the *sans-culottes* for immediate action, the Committee of Public Safety instituted a Reign of Terror. | **Reign of Terror** |

"We must annihilate the enemies of the Republic at home and abroad, or else we shall perish," Robespierre warned. He justified the Terror by arguing that in this time of revolution, "the first maxim of our politics ought to be to lead the people by means of reason and the enemies of the people by terror."

Accordingly, agents of the committee searched out and summarily tried anyone suspected of being counterrevolutionaries. Even those who had once supported the Revolution—such as the Girondins, whose views had fallen out of favor—were arrested and executed. Jean-Sylvain Bailly, shown leading the 1789 Tennis Court Oath in Figure 16.2; Manon Roland (see Biography); and Olympe de Gouges, the woman who argued so strongly for revolutionary principles in the beginning, fell to the guillotine. Though many people became victims of arbitrary justice, officials used the Terror most often where real threats arose—regions in revolt and vulnerable areas near France's borders. During this violent phase of the Revolution, probably between 200,000 and 400,000 victims of the Terror went to prison. Some 25,000 to 50,000 died in jail or at the hands of executioners.

To secure the Republic against external enemies, the government ordered a *levée en masse,* or general **Levée en masse** call-up of all men, women, and children to serve the nation. As able-bodied young men were rapidly trained and rushed to the front, the army swelled to 850,000 men—a number that far exceeded the forces of France's opponents. Everyone else was supposed to contribute to the war effort by collecting or manufacturing supplies for the troops and by bolstering spirit. Women stitched clothing and served as nurses, children made bandages, and old men delivered stirring, patriotic speeches. This united activity for defense of the country produced an intense national patriotism. One soldier wrote home from the front to explain his feelings: "When *la patrie* calls us to her defense, we ought to fly there. . . . Our life, our wealth, and our talents do not belong to us. It is to the nation, *la patrie,* that all that belongs." With the officer corps now open to talent and the massive mobilization of men, materials, and spirit, the citizen armies turned back coalition forces by the end of 1793. By the summer of the following year, they carried the war beyond France's borders.

THE REPUBLIC OF VIRTUE

While fighting this war, Robespierre and the Committee of Public Safety carried out their radical republican program. They attempted to reform institutions and infuse all aspects of French life with revolutionary politics. They intended to create a Republic of Virtue based on Rousseauian ideas of reason and natural law.

First, they targeted those institutions that, in their view, represented the worst of the Old Regime. Many officials saw the Catholic **Attacking the Catholic Church** Church in this negative light and sold church buildings, turned them into warehouses, or rededicated them as "temples of reason." Angry radicals disfigured religious statues, even sending some wooden figures of saints to the guillotine and melting down church treasures. The most enthusiastic radicals searched out nonjuring clergy for prosecution and pressured even the clergy that had sworn to uphold the Revolution to leave their vocations. Some radical leaders hoped that the new festivals established to celebrate the Revolution would provide a sufficient substitute for Christian rituals. Other revolutionaries tried to create new beliefs, such as the Cult of Reason, to replace Christianity. Robespierre tried in vain to institute his own deistic Cult of the Supreme Being.

The National Convention also enacted legislation that took the rules governing family life and education away from the church and **Family life and education** placed them in state hands. Marriage became a civil rather than a religiously ordained act. New rules for divorce allowed thousands of couples to end marriages they would have been bound to under church rules. Births were registered at city halls rather than local churches. Women could sue for equal inheritance for the first time. Education became a responsibility of the state. New legislation mandated free primary schooling for all girls and boys and state-run secondary schooling, though in fact the government had neither the funds nor enough trained teachers to support such a system.

Women—especially those living in the cities—welcomed the new marriage, divorce, inheritance, and education laws, for they increased women's rights. However, the Jacobins had no desire to free women from their traditional role in the private sphere. Rather, they rejected women's participation in politics and outlawed female associations such as the Society of Revolutionary Republican Women. Jacobins declared that women's primary duties lay in nurturing children. They concluded that women had no proper role as active citizens and that women's political groups only disrupted the republican order. As one member of the government explained, "It is horrible, it is contrary to all laws of nature for a woman to want to make herself a man."

Revolutionary symbols The new government went far beyond simply rooting out opponents of the Revolution and attacking institutions tied to the Old Regime. It also tried to create support for the Republic by infusing the objects and activities of everyday life with revolutionary symbols. The figure of Liberty replaced royal symbols on everything from coins and statues to plates and posters. Patriotic groups planted liberty trees throughout France. Women adopted the flowing robes and hairstyles of ancient Greece that reflected rejection of the traditional social order. People sported revolutionary ribbons on their hats. Songs such as the Marseillaise, rallying the "children of the nation . . . against . . . the bloody standard of tyranny!" rang out among crowds and troops. Plays and paintings that supported the Revolution were encouraged. Officials promoted festivals that featured revolutionary symbols, mass loyalty oaths, and patriotic celebrations. Titles of all kinds were discarded and replaced with the terms "citizen" and "citizeness."

Pamphlets and posters spread throughout France, proclaiming what the Republic stood for. The 1792 poster shown in Figure 16.6, printed just after France became a republic, is a typical example. The poster announces principles at the core of the Republic:

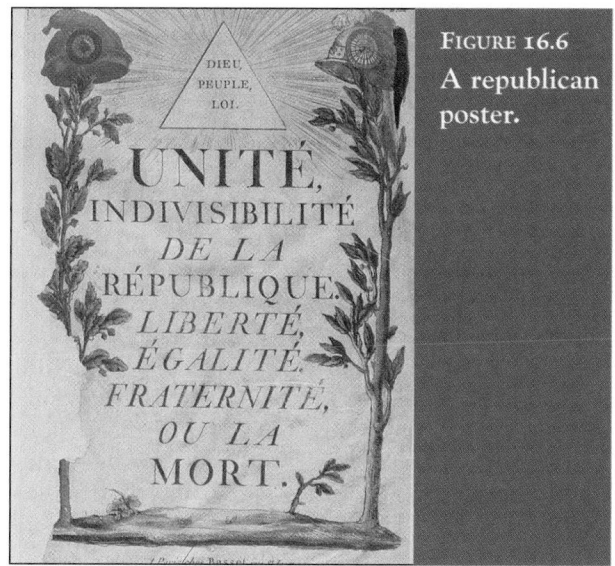

FIGURE 16.6
A republican poster.

"Unity, indivisibility of the Republic. Liberty, equality, fraternity, or death." A triangle of authorities—"God, People, Law"—shines its blessings on these principles. Also blessed are the liberty trees that symbolize the Revolution, the one at the left topped by a "liberty cap"; the one at the right, by a helmet from France's citizen army.

In the name of reason and revolutionary principles, the government revamped the calendar, making the months equal in length and naming them after the seasons. Weeks were made 10 days long, with one day of rest. (This change eliminated Sunday, a day of traditional Christian importance.) September 22, 1792—the date of the declaration of the Republic—became the first day of Year I. The new metric system of weights and measures based on units of 10 was introduced and eventually would spread beyond France's borders to countries throughout the world.

THE REVOLUTION SPREADS OUTSIDE OF FRANCE

Since 1792, France had fended off various coalitions of European powers. After initial defeats, France's citizen armies had gone on the offensive. *Sister republics* During the struggles that ensued, France incorporated lands on its northern and eastern borders, claiming that these additions conformed to France's "natural boundaries" of the Rhine and the Alps. By 1799, more victories on the battlefield enabled France to set up "sister" republics in Holland, Switzerland, and Italy. To these areas, the French brought their own Enlightenment-inspired revolutionary principles and legislation. However, the gains carried a tremendous price tag. Hundreds of thousands died in the fighting, and the constant warfare disrupted trade and created shortages of essential goods.

The Revolution also powerfully influenced opinion outside France. Initially many groups in nearby countries supported the Revolution *Outside opinion* and its principles. However, part of that support rested on seeing France, a powerful rival, weakened. As people began to understand the seriousness of the attacks on monarchy and aristocracy and the threat to their own political independence, support waned. Still, many intellectuals and liberal political groups continued to uphold the ideals of the Revolution, at least until 1793 when the Revolution took a more radical turn.

FIGURE 16.7
Slave rebellion in St. Domingue (Haiti), 1791.

The Revolution helped promote other developments farther away. In Poland, patriots tried to use inspiration from France to assert independence from Russia. Despite some initial successes, however, their efforts failed. In Ireland, the revolutionary doctrines of liberty, equality, and natural rights touched many, encouraging them to rise against their British lords and make Ireland a republic. Irish patriots even anticipated a French invasion to help their own rebellion, although the invasion never took place.

In the Caribbean, slaves in France's lucrative colony of St. Domingue (Haiti) took heart from revolutionary principles and revolted. As Figure 16.7, a French print, reveals, the 1791 slave uprising struck fear in the hearts of white settlers. Slaves, outnumbering white settlers, attack a plantation. Women and men fall under the knives, swords, and cannon of the slaves, while plantation buildings go up in flames. Reports from French settlers, such as the wealthy Madame de Rouvray, described how the slaves "slaughtered and torched much of the countryside hereabouts," and warned, "how can we stay in a

country where slaves have raised their hands against their masters?"

After much maneuvering and the abolishing of slavery by the National Convention in February 1794, the rebel leader Toussaint L'Ouverture and his black generals gained control of St. Domingue. The determined group would go on to successfully oppose English, Spanish, and French armies, turning the island into the independent republic of Haiti in 1804.

RESISTANCE TO THE REPUBLIC RISES

Despite the Reign of Terror and efforts to establish a Republic of Virtue, violent resistance to the Republic persisted and, in some cases, grew. Its leadership consisted primarily of local aristocrats and notables, officials who had fallen out of favor with the Jacobins, Girondin sympathizers, and members of the nonjuring clergy who had gone underground. They gathered additional support from remaining royalists, conservative peasants who had already gained most of what they wanted, opponents of military conscription, and the many citizens who remained loyal to Catholicism and their nonjuring priests. Of the many armed revolts that broke out across France, the most important occurred in the Vendée, a region in western France. In what amounted to a regional civil war that raged for most of 1793 and dragged on for years thereafter, both sides committed atrocities and thousands lost their lives before republican soldiers gained the upper hand.

Figure 16.8 reveals another form of resistance and the symbols of conflict during the radical phase of the Revolution. The painting, by the politically active artist Jacques-Louis David, depicts the death of Jean-Paul Marat, a journalist and leading radical deputy, in July 1793. Marat, ironically already suffering from a terminal skin condition, was working in his bathtub when Charlotte Corday, a supporter of the Girondins, assassinated him. Corday felt that it was her duty to kill Marat because of his persistent demands for more executions. This painting shows the mortally wounded Marat with pen and paper still in his hands and Corday's knife on the floor. David and others eulogized Marat as a martyr for the Revolution. On the side of his writing stand are the words, "Not having been able to corrupt me, they assassinated me." Corday, widely denounced but convinced that she had "avenged many innocent victims," was soon guillotined.

Uprisings

Meanwhile, discontent with Robespierre and his policies increased. With the defeat of the invading coalition armies and the suppression of internal rebellion, most people no longer saw *Thermidorian reaction* any need for the Terror—yet the Terror only intensified. When the influential Danton counseled moderation, Robespierre sent him and his most prominent followers to the guillotine. No one, not even the members of the National Convention, felt safe. Finally, on July 27, 1794 (9 Thermidor on the Revolutionary calendar, and thus referred to as the "Thermidorian reaction"), the Convention overthrew Robespierre. In an ironic ending, the Jacobin leader died by the guillotine: the same device to which he had sent so many others to their deaths.

REACTION: THE "WHITE" TERROR AND THE DIRECTORY

With the leader of the Terror now dead, the propertied bourgeoisie quickly gained control of the government. Eliminating the "Red" Terror of the Committee of Public Safety, they replaced it with the "White" Terror of reaction. They executed the former terrorists and imprisoned many supporters of Robespierre, including the painter, Jacques-Louis David. Armed bands of bourgeois hirelings roved around beating and killing Jacobins. Restrictive measures of Robespierre's regime were repealed, and many individuals, weary of the Republic's code of discipline and restraint, reveled in an outburst of licentious living. Middle- and upper-class women wore more revealing clothing; mistresses appeared more publicly, even in the political arena. On the other hand, women of the poor in the small towns and countryside often turned back to the Catholic Church. They hoped that a return to God would end the turmoil of the revolutionary years.

A new constitution in 1795 reflected conservative reaction. The right to vote for members of the legislative bodies was limited to the wealthier property owners. Executive functions were placed in the hands of five directors—the Directory.

Men of reasonable competence staffed the Directory (1795–1799), but they failed to restore tranquility. War dragged on, governmental finances unraveled further, and brigands terrorized the countryside and the cities. The five directors tried to balance threats from the royalists on the Right and the Jacobins on the Left. They turned against the *sans-culottes* by re-

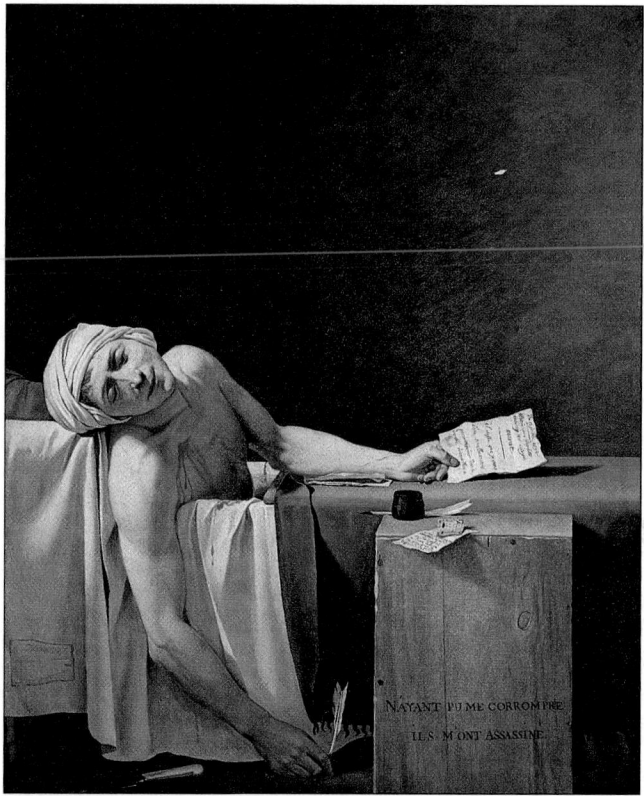

FIGURE 16.8
Jacques-Louis David, *The Death of Marat,* 1793.

moving price controls and had to be saved by governmental forces when the *sans-culottes* stormed the Convention in May 1795. Five months later, the government barely put down a royalist uprising, thanks to a quick-acting artillery officer named Napoleon Bonaparte. The directors finally resorted to purges to control the legislature and increasingly relied on the army for support. All in all, the situation was ripe for the arrival of a strongman who could bring both order at home and peace abroad.

Napoleon Bonaparte

Within France, the Revolution provided unprecedented opportunities for ambitious soldiers of talent. Most prerevolutionary army officers had come from the nobility, and had fled the country or lost their commands as the Revolution gathered momentum. This leadership drain, as well as the need to expand the army, created a huge demand for skilled officers. Napoleon Bonaparte, a talented artillery officer, stepped in to take full advantage of these opportunities.

NAPOLEON'S RISE TO POWER

Born into a poor but well-known family on Corsica in 1769, just a few months after the Mediterranean island was transferred from the Republic of Genoa to France, Napoleon was hardworking, assertive, independent, and even arrogant as a youth. These qualities would stay with him for the rest of his life. The young Napoleon attended French military school (where he proved particularly strong in mathematics) and received his commission as second lieutenant when he was just 16. When the Revolution broke out in 1789, Napoleon was already familiar with Enlightenment ideas and resented the aristocratic pretensions of those around him. He quickly sided with the revolutionaries. In 1793, he attracted attention during the recapture of Toulon. Two years later, when he happened to be in Paris, the National Convention called on him to quell a threatening Parisian crowd. Using artillery—his legendary "whiff of grape-shot"—Napoleon quickly dispersed the crowd and became the hero of the Convention. He fell in love with and married the politically well-connected Josephine de Beauharnais (1763–1814), a 32-year-old widow eager to provide security for her children.

Napoleon then used his growing prominence to secure command of the French army still fighting in *Italian campaign* northern Italy. Calling his forces "soldiers of liberty" and announcing to the people of Italy that "the French army comes to break your chains," he skillfully galvanized the lethargic French forces into defeating the Austrians and Sardinians. Along with loads of Italian art, Napoleon sent home glowing reports of his exploits. In 1797, he personally negotiated a favorable Treaty of Campo Formio with Austria, which recognized French expansion and the creation of the Cisalpine Republic in northern Italy (Map 16.3). Over the next two years, French armies moved south, helping to set up more French-controlled republics throughout the Italian peninsula. Napoleon's successes in Italy established his reputation as a brilliant military leader and able statesman.

Turning toward the British, Napoleon and the Directory concluded that an expedition to Egypt would deal a telling blow to British commerce with its colonies in Asia. Egypt could also serve as the foundation for a new French colony. Moreover, a conquest there might enhance Napoleon's image as a daring, heroic conqueror. Yet, despite some spectacular battlefield *Expedition to Egypt* successes, the expedition failed; Admiral Nelson (1758–1805), who became one of Britain's most admired naval commanders, destroyed the French fleet at the Battle of the Nile on August 1, 1798. The French land campaign in Egypt and Syria persisted for a while, but it was doomed by a lack of supplies and reinforcements. Napoleon avoided personal disaster by slipping back to France with a few chosen followers, cleverly controlling the reports from Egypt and emphasizing the expedition's scientific explorations and exotic discoveries (he sent 165 scholars to Egypt in hopes that they might help him control the country) as well as its few victories. For example, in April 1799, General Junot and 500 French troops fought one of the rare successful battles of this failed campaign. Just three weeks later, with an eye toward creating an image of success, Napoleon ordered a commemorating painting of the difficult but stunning victory over 6,000 Turkish and Arab troops in the Holy Land. The artist of Figure 16.9, Antoine-Jean Gros (1771–1835), shows the hero of this battle, General Junot, at the left on a white horse, raising his saber against a mounted Mameluke attacker. Around him and in the background, the life-and-death struggle rages on this desert battlefield. In the end, the French took no Turkish prisoners; they had all been killed.

Meanwhile, matters took a bad turn for France's government, the Directory. The expedition to Egypt prompted Great Britain, Austria, and Russia to join in a new coalition. These allies inflicted *Coup d'état* defeats on French armies and threatened to invade France itself. Eyeing this foreign threat, as well as bankruptcy, insubordinate army commanders, and disruptions in the countryside, rival factions within France vied for power. One conservative faction, led by a member of the Directory, Abbé Sieyès, concluded that a coup d'état would gain them needed control over the government. This situation provided Napoleon with another opportunity to advance his career. Sieyès and others conspired with him to overthrow the Directory on November 9, 1799 (18 Brumaire). The conspirators expected that the 30-year-old military hero would make a popular figurehead representing authority, and they would actually govern the country. As events would prove, they were very mistaken.

NORTH SEA

ENGLAND

PRUSSIA

BATAVIAN
REPUBLIC 1798
Amsterdam

AUSTRIAN
NETHERLANDS
(BELGIUM)
AND RHINELAND
PROVINCES
1795

Paris

ATLANTIC
OCEAN

BAVARIA

FRANCE

AUSTRIAN
EMPIRE

Geneva

HELVETIC
REPUBLIC 1798

Bordeaux

SAVOY
1792

Lyons

Turin

Milan

VENICE

Campoformio

PIEDMONT

Venice

CISALPINE
REPUBLIC 1797

Marseilles

Genoa

OTTOMA
EMPIRE

NICE
1792

TUSCANY

ADRIATIC SEA

ROMAN
REPUBLIC
1798

SPAIN

CORSICA

Rome

NAPOLEON'S INVASION OF EGYPT 1798

PARTHENOPIAN
REPUBLIC 1799

SARDINIA

Naples

French Republic
at 1792

Annexed to France
1792-1795

Sister Republics

N
W   E
S

0   200 miles
0   200 kilometers

MEDITERRANEAN SEA

SICILY

THINKING ABOUT GEOGRAPHY

MAP 16.3   *France and Its Sister Republics*

This map shows the expansion of France and the creation of its sister republics between 1792 and 1798.
❧ **Notice** the dates of annexation and creation of sister republics. **Consider** who was most threatened by
these developments. ❧ **Notice** the arrow indicating Napoleon's invasion of Egypt in 1798. **Why** might
Napoleon have moved against British interests in Egypt rather than Great Britain itself?

FIGURE 16.9
Antoine-Jean Gros, *Battle of Nazareth*, 1801. Musée des Beaux-Arts, Nantes.

NAPOLEON CONSOLIDATES CONTROL

Napoleon quickly outmaneuvered his partners. He had a new "short and obscure" constitution drawn up and accepted by members of the old legislature. In a national plebiscite where people could vote to accept or reject the new constitution, the French overwhelmingly approved it (though the government falsified the results to give it a more lopsided victory). As one observer explained, people "believed quite sincerely that Bonaparte . . . would save us from the perils of anarchy." Napoleon named himself "first consul" and assumed the powers necessary to rule—all with the ready support of the Senate. The remaining two consuls, as well as voters and the handpicked legislative bodies they thought they were electing, had only minimal powers. Next, Napoleon placed each of France's 83 departments under the control of a powerful agent of the central government—the *prefect*. Thus at both the local and the national levels, Napoleon ended meaningful democracy in France.

First consul

With the touch of a skilled authoritarian politician, Napoleon proceeded to gather support. He welcomed former Old Regime officials as well as moderate Jacobins into his service. By approving the end of serfdom and feudal privileges as well as all transfers of property that had occurred during the Revolution, he won favor with the peasantry. He gained the backing of the middle class by affirming the property rights and formal equality before the law that adult males had secured during the Revolution. He welcomed back to France all but the most reactionary émigrés, most of whom had come from France's old aristocracy. The educated elite admired Napoleon for patronizing science and inviting leading scientists to join him in his government. To deter opposition, he created a secret police force, suppressed independent political organizations, and censored newspapers and artistic works. Finally, for those who displayed the highest loyalty and the most spectacular achievements (particularly in the military), he created the prestigious Legion of Honor.

The Concordat

Keenly aware of the political and social importance of religion—once calling religion "excellent stuff for keeping the common people quiet"—Napoleon made peace with the pope and ended the 10-year struggle between the French revolutionary governments and the Roman Catholic church. Their Concordat (formal agreement) of 1801 declared the Catholic religion the religion of the majority of the French people, but ensured freedom for Protestants. Later, Napoleon granted new rights to Jews, as well. Under his rule, the clergy was paid by the state and required to take an oath of allegiance to the state. Confiscated Catholic Church property was not returned.

REFORMING FRANCE

Napoleonic Code

Napoleon followed up this pattern of blending compromise and authoritarian control with a remaking of France's legal, financial, and educational systems. The Civil Code of 1804 (the Napoleonic Code), for example, generally affirmed the Enlightenment-inspired legal reforms that the early French revolutionaries had sought. Progressives throughout Europe and even overseas would embrace this law code. For men, the code guaranteed legal equality, careers open to talent, and paternal authority over women, children, and property. In particular, it catered to middle-class employers by forbidding strikes and trade unions. At the same time, the code rejected many of the rights and liberties gained in 1789 as well as the more radical measures enacted after 1792. For women, the code represented a clear defeat. Rather than granting them legal or political equality, it gave power over property and the family to men and left married women legally and economically dependent on their husbands. The code also severely restricted the right to divorce, particularly for women. These measures reflected Napoleon's belief that women belonged in the home and that their concerns should center on domestic life.

To stabilize France financially, Napoleon established the Bank of France to handle governmental *Finance and education* funds and issue money. To promote economic health, he involved the state in a huge program of public works, supported certain industries, and established price controls. To restructure educational institutions, he created a long-lasting system of secondary schools tied to the University of France and infused it with patriotic trappings. Napoleon also actively supported scientific research and rewarded surgeons, chemists, mathematicians, and other scientists with governmental posts and honors.

CREATING THE EMPIRE

Napoleon's rise to power hinged on his ability to remove external military threats as well as internal disruptions. This he managed by crossing the Alps in 1800 with a French army to crush the Austrian forces in Northern Italy and knock Austria out of the coalition of powers opposing France. Next, he made peace with Russia and persuaded Great Britain to sign the Peace of Amiens in 1802.

In the first five years of his rule, Napoleon scored spectacular successes. Law and order reigned at home, and he secured peace abroad. Public morale was high. Napoleon's vision of a centralized, paternalistic state that would make France the model of a modern nation through reason, authority, and science seemed almost real.

However, two problems lurked beneath this promising exterior. First, Napoleon had an insatiable craving for public recognition and legitimacy. He satisfied

FIGURE 16.10
Jacques-Louis David, *Napoleon's Coronation.*

this need at least partially with a bold move in 1804. That year, with the approval of the Senate and the French people in a lopsided plebiscite, Napoleon formally estab- *Emperor Napoleon* lished France as an empire—and then crowned himself emperor.

As Jacques-Louis David's painting in Figure 16.10 reveals, Napoleon controlled all aspects of the coronation. Although he invited Pope Pius VII (seated behind him) to preside over the ceremony, it is Napoleon—ever the self-made man—who takes matters into his own hands. As splendidly dressed spectators look on, Napoleon raises a crown, preparing to place it on the kneeling Josephine's head to make her his empress. He has already boldly crowned himself emperor with a laurel wreath that alludes back to Roman emperors and Charlemagne, crowned emperor by the pope in the year 800. Aware of the importance of details, Napoleon had shrewdly instructed his ardent supporter David to paint the reluctant pope raising his hand in blessing.

The new emperor then elevated members of his family to princely status and granted new titles and honors to his wealthy supporters who had proved themselves, usually as officers on the battlefield. Later, he divorced empress Josephine, whose relationship with Napoleon became more formal than intimate, and who failed to produce a male heir. He married Princess Marie-Louise of Austria, giving him a stronger image as legitimate royalty.

In addition to his hunger for formal recognition, Napoleon had a second problem. He had risen to prominence and power through his military conquests. *Need for conquests* "I am an upstart soldier," he admitted. "My domination will not survive the day when I cease to be strong, and therefore feared." These martial ties would push Napoleon to seek still greater conquests on the battlefield. "Conquest has made me what I am; only conquest can maintain me." Yet even when battle after battle brought him victory, war also came at great cost and risk.

WAR AND CONQUEST

The interests of Great Britain and Napoleon clashed too often for their peace to last long. By the end of *Battle of Trafalgar* 1803, the two countries were again at war, and by 1805, the ambitious Napoleon had to battle a new coalition of European powers. That year, he marched to the English Channel with a huge army and seemed poised to invade England. Before him stretched 24 miles of water and British sea power. To overcome those barriers, Napoleon amassed a combined French and Spanish fleet and plotted his next move. Alert for any opportunity, he suddenly turned his army eastward, surrounded an exposed Austrian army, and on October 20, forced it to surrender. The next day, however, England's Admiral Nelson sighted the combined French and Spanish fleets off Cape Trafalgar on the southwest point of Spain and annihilated them. Although Nelson perished early in the battle, his navy's victory saved Great Britain from the menace of an invasion and limited Napoleon's conquests to the European continent.

On land, Napoleon fared much better—in fact, he seemed invincible. His success stemmed in part from his independent units that could move quickly and then join in a mass attack. Equally important, he possessed an unusually talented officer *Military strengths* corps and enjoyed the loyalty of a large number of nationalistic citizen-soldiers. The strategy of sending a mass of spirited soldiers in a column of attack aimed at dividing opposing forces served Napoleon well. Fighting alongside his troops, he cleverly used these military strengths to crush the combined forces of Austria and Russia at Austerlitz in December 1805. Prussia made the mistake of declaring war on France after it was too late to join the Austrians and Russians. As the French troops moved east through villages and cities, people reported how "the dreadful cry was heard in the streets, 'the French are coming!'" Napoleon virtually obliterated the Prussian forces. When the Russian troops began massing again, Napoleon moved eastward and decisively defeated them in the great Battle of Friedland (1807). Although the resulting Treaties of Tilsit (July 1807) were technically between equals, they actually left Russia only a junior partner to France. France commanded the greater resources, and Napoleon expected to have his way on the European continent.

Despite all these triumphs, Napoleon still could not find a way to get his troops across the Channel to attack England directly. He finally hit on an alternative *The Continental System* plan—the "Continental System"—that he hoped would destroy his rival's commercial economy by preventing the importation of British goods into continental Europe. To implement the plan, he ordered a continent wide blockade against British ships, confiscated all British goods, and set French privateers upon British merchant ships. Britain responded with new regulations that amounted to its own blockade on shipping to continental ports. Now the naval war between France and Britain affected even neutral states, including the United States.

By 1810, Napoleon had redrawn the map of Europe (Map 16.4) and the political balance of power. He had dismembered Prussia *The new European order* and abolished the Holy Roman Empire. Now most German states were unified into the Confederation of the Rhine. Holland and the Italian peninsula had come under French control. Spain was a dependent state, and Austria, Russia, and a diminished Prussia had become reluctant allies of France. Only Great Britain and still-defiant parts of Spain and Portugal remained active opponents.

In those areas annexed to France, Napoleon ruled directly and imposed all of France's laws and

Map legend:
- French Empire
- Satellite Kingdoms
- Allies of Napoleon
- Hostile to Napoleon
- Confederation of the Rhine Boundary
- ✹ Major battles

THINKING ABOUT GEOGRAPHY

MAP 16.4 *Europe, 1810*

This map shows Europe at the height of Napoleon's empire. ▣ **Notice** the extent of area Napoleon controlled—directly and indirectly. **Where** would you expect Napoleon's rule to exert the greatest impact? **What** geographical problems did Napoleon face trying to control his empire? ▣ **Locate** those areas that remained hostile to Napoleon. **How** might geography help explain why those areas retained their independence?

institutions. In dependent states, he installed French-controlled governments to rule with the help of local elites. He usually made members of his family monarchs in these areas—his brother Louis, king of Holland, his brother Jérôme, king of Westphalia, and his brother Joseph, king of Spain. As Document 16.3 suggests (see page D16.2), some of France's "enlightened" institutions and policies were introduced.

These usually included constitutional government, equality before the law, careers open to talent, the Napoleonic Civil Code, civil rights to Jews and other religious minorities, and the creation of similar public works improvements—schools, roads, bridges—that Napoleon supported in France. Wherever Napoleon conquered, except Russia, he abolished serfdom. At the same time, the reforms included tax increases and conscription quotas to help finance and provide soldiers for Napoleon's armies.

THE IMPACT OVERSEAS

Naturally, Napoleon's policies exerted their greatest impact in Europe, but other areas—particularly in the Western Hemisphere and the British Empire—also felt the effects of his rule and expansion. In the Caribbean, Napoleon failed to put down the black population's struggle for independence and freedom in Saint Domingue (Haiti) (see p. 570). He also cut

FIGURE 16.11
Simón Bolívar.

his losses in North America and sold Louisiana to the United States.

The Napoleonic Wars had dramatic consequences in the colonies of Spain and Portugal in the Americas. Discontent with colonial rule had been mounting during the eighteenth century. In particular, the colonists resented the economic and political restrictions imposed by the "mother" country. As the native-born "Creoles" began to outnumber the Spanish- and Portuguese-born settlers, the ties of loyalty to home countries weakened. The successful revolt of the English colonies to the north and the birth of the United States also impressed colonial liberals and intellectuals. Spanish colonists' attachment to Spain faltered further when Napoleon overthrew the Spanish king and placed his own brother, Joseph Bonaparte, on the throne. By 1810, many colonists were in open revolt.

Revolt in Latin America

Over the next 10 years, Spain struggled to regain its colonies. In 1814, Argentina drove off a Spanish army and won its independence. Elsewhere, Simón Bolívar (1783–1830), known as "The Liberator," led the fight for independence against Spanish forces. Figure 16.11 shows him in heroic pose, probably to symbolize his military campaigns in Venezuela, Colombia, Ecuador, and Peru. The painting is modeled on a well-known work by David that portrays Napoleon leading his troops across the Alps. Bolívar points upward while a wind blows at his back—a traditional posture of victory.

As Map 16.5 shows, by 1822 almost all of Spain's colonies, as well as Portugal's huge colony of Brazil, had gained their independence. Nevertheless, Bolívar's and other's hopes for unity within Spain's old colonies soon faded as various South American regions began dividing into separate states. Most of these new states would adopt the Napoleonic Code as their basis of civil law, and oppressive white minorities would rule them for many years.

Napoleon's dominance over the European continent inspired England to step up its overseas expansion and tighten control over its own colonies and areas of influence. Sea power enabled it to capture and take over French and Dutch colonies in Africa, Asia, and America. In addition, England began trading more briskly with South America. However, one of England's strategies—its counterblockade of Napoleonic Europe—had a major, unintended drawback. By enforcing the blockade, England ended up embroiled

England's overseas expansion

in the War of 1812 with the United States. That war, in turn, spread further north when the United States attempted to invade Britain's loyal colonies in Canada.

In the decades that followed, states from Asia to the Americas that reformed their own governments and laws would look to the Napoleonic Code and adopt parts of it. In this way, some of the *Adopting the Napoleonic Code* ideals of the Enlightenment and the French Revolution would be translated through the Napoleonic Code to many areas around the globe.

DECLINE AND FALL

Napoleon had an even more ambitious vision—to rule Europe as the head of a single imperial administration. Before he could make his vision real, new problems plagued him. Even at the height of his power, Napoleon and his empire suffered from dangerous weaknesses. Between 1808 and 1812, three crucial vulnerabilities—flawed policies, resistance to his rule, and overextension of his military reach—would intensify and erode Napoleon's power.

The Continental System that Napoleon devised to cripple England economically was not working well enough. With control of the sea, Great Britain applied an effective counterblockade against the Napoleon-dominated Continent. Port cities and industries relying on external commerce suffered. Smuggling further weakened the system. In *Flawed policies* some areas, such as Holland and Russia, the restrictions of the system became a constant source of irritation and resentment against the French. In the long run, the Continental System stiffened opposition to

Napoleon on the Continent and failed to weaken England. Again and again, that island nation would finance Napoleon's enemies.

People across Europe had other reasons besides the Continental System to resist Napoleon's rule. In the wake of France's conquering armies, a new national

THINKING ABOUT GEOGRAPHY

MAP 16.5 *Latin America After Independence*

This map shows that within a twelve-year period Spain and Portugal lost most of their possessions in the Americas. **❧ Notice** that in several areas there are differences between the date of independence from the colonial power and the date of separation from other states. **What** might these differences mean? **❧ Locate** those territories still held by European nations. **What** might differ these territories from those that gained their independence?

FIGURE 16.12
Francicso de Goya, *The Third of May, 1808.*

spirit developed among many subject peoples. In Spain, for example, Napoleon had no sooner placed *Growing resistance* his brother Joseph on the Spanish throne when his unwilling subjects rose up against him. The painting in Figure 16.12 by the influential Spanish artist Francisco de Goya depicts the popular resistance in Spain to the Napoleonic occupation and the reprisals that resulted. Here, in a night scene on May 3, 1808, a firing squad of anonymous French soldiers brutally executes citizens in retaliation for riots against French troops in Madrid. The magnitude of the French atrocity is emphasized by the central figure, who resembles a crucified Christ about to be shot. Monks and commoners,

selected at random for execution, surround the man at the center, and the bodies of those already executed lie scattered on the bloody earth around him. Goya, who painted this scene six years after the actual event, intended the work as a statement against the evils of war.

The Madrid rebellion and reprisals by Napoleon's soldiers inspired other Spanish uprisings and organized resistance against French troops in the years to come. Larger French armies, even when led by Napoleon himself, managed only limited success against the hit-and-run guerrilla tactics used by the Spanish. England took advantage of the situation by sending supplies and troops to Spain under the duke of Wellington (1769–1852), the British commander who would plague Napoleon's forces to the end. Spain became a running abscess that drained Napoleon's military strength.

In Prussia, similar national sentiments encouraged the government—partly in secret—to modernize its army and civil institutions in preparation for liberation from France. In Austria, the government again declared war on Napoleon in a premature effort to free itself from subservience to the French emperor. In Holland, opposition to Napoleon's policies ran so strong that in 1810 he had to annex the country to France to bring it under control. All this resistance drained French forces and raised the specter of open revolt at the least opportunity.

Napoleon himself created that opportunity by overextending his imperial reach. Successes on the

Overextension battlefield added to his growing dreams of creating an empire ruled from Paris that would encompass all of Europe. Russia, already chafing against the commercial restrictions of the Continental System and harboring its own ambitions for expansion in eastern Europe, stood as the main barrier to Napoleon's dreams. In 1812, these conflict-

Invasion of Russia ing ambitions soured the alliance between Russia and France. Against the advice of his closest associates, Napoleon decided to invade Russia. Amassing an immense army of more than 600,000, he plunged into the vastness of Russia. Half of his troops, however, were unenthusiastic conscripts from dependent states. The Russian army retreated into the interior of their huge country, following a scorched-earth policy and luring Napoleon ever farther from his base of supplies. "We believed that once in Russia, we need do nothing but forage—which, however, proved to be an illusion. . . . All the villages were already stripped before we could enter," wrote Jakob Walter, a German conscript in Napoleon's army. One of Napoleon's aides explained the deepening problem: "We were in the heart of inhabited Russia and yet we were like a vessel without a compass in the midst of a vast ocean, knowing nothing of what was happening around us." At Borodino, the Russians turned and made a stand. In one of the bloodiest battles of the nineteenth century—taking a toll of more than 80,000 casualties—the two armies fought until the Russians withdrew.

The French army may have won the battle, but it failed to destroy Russia's forces. In September, Napoleon's Grand Army, weakened by battlefield losses and even more so by hunger, fatigue, and disease, finally entered Moscow. Tsar Alexander I, however, refused to capitulate. The future looked even worse for the French when a fire destroyed much of Moscow, leaving the invaders without enough shelter or supplies to ride out the notorious Russian winter. "Here in the white country we'll all have to die of hunger," wrote Hohann Wärncke, a German soldier in Napoleon's army. Napoleon began his retreat, but too late. The winter caught his forces overburdened with loot. Tens of thousands of them froze, starved, or succumbed to disease. Russian Cossacks, riding out of the blizzards, cut down or captured thousands more. Many of Napoleon's men surrendered to Russian forces. Of the original 600,000 who marched into Russia, fewer than 100,000 struggled home.

Napoleon himself was able to dash back to France. Behind him, one nation after another, aided by British money, joined the Russians in a war of liberation. Back home, Napoleon raised new conscripts for his army and again rushed them east-

Defeat at Leipzig ward. At Leipzig in central Germany, in October 1813, allied armies at last decisively defeated Napoleon. The next year, the allies entered Paris and exiled Napoleon to the island of Elba, off the coast of Italy.

Napoleon still had some fight left in him. While the allies squabbled over the peace settlement and discontent weakened France's new government under Louis XVIII, Napoleon escaped back to France. "Soldiers! In exile I heard your voice," he announced. "Now I have landed [in France]." He quickly raised yet another army from the remains of his old, still loyal supporters. However he was

Waterloo finally defeated in June 1815 by British and Prussian forces at Waterloo in Belgium. This time his captors imprisoned him on the bleak island of St. Helena in the South Atlantic. "Posterity will do me justice," he wrote while in exile. "The truth will be known; and the good I have done will be compared with the faults I have committed." Six years later, Napoleon died, probably of stomach cancer.

Timeline: A Closer Look

| 1789 | 1790 | 1791 | 1792 | 1793 | 1794 | 1795 |

Meeting of the Estates General (May 5, 1789)

War breaks out (April 1792)

Tennis Court Oath (June 20, 1789)

France declared a Republic (September 1792)

Fall of the Bastille (July 14, 1789)

Flight to Varennes (June 20, 1791)

Renunciation of noble privileges (August 4, 1789)

Louis XVI executed (January 1793)

Assembly of Notables (1787)

■ **French Revolutionary Developments** (1789–1799)
■ **Age of Napoleon** (1799–1815)
▨ **Global**

Declaration of Rights of Man and Citizen (August 26, 1789)

Slave Revolt in St. Domingue (Haiti) (August 1791)

Thermidorian Reaction (1794–1795)

Legislative Assembly (October 1791)

March to Versailles (October 5–6, 1789)

The Terror (1793–1794)

| 1789 | 1790 | 1791 | 1792 | 1793 | 1794 | 1795 |

Summary

In 1815, a king from the old house of Bourbon again ruled France. Many aristocrats and royalists hoped to turn back the clock to the days before 1789, when they enjoyed unchallenged power and prestige. However, too much had changed. The Revolution had destroyed a French monarchy based on the divine right of kings. French aristocrats might still boast impressive titles, but the revolutionaries and Napoleon had secured legal equality for French men, if not women. Members of the middle class, though no longer enjoying the control they had exercised during the revolutionary years, would not relinquish the opportunities for position and prestige that they had gained. The peasantry, which had played such an important role during the early months of the Revolution, would never again be burdened by the traditional dues and services they once owed to lords. Finally, the Catholic Church had forever lost the lands and position it had once possessed before the Revolution.

Napoleon's connection to the Revolution was contradictory. He subverted key elements of the Revolution by removing the substance from representative institutions and eliminating freedom of speech and press. On the other hand, he preserved other elements of the Revolution by affirming the end of feudalism, protecting the rights of

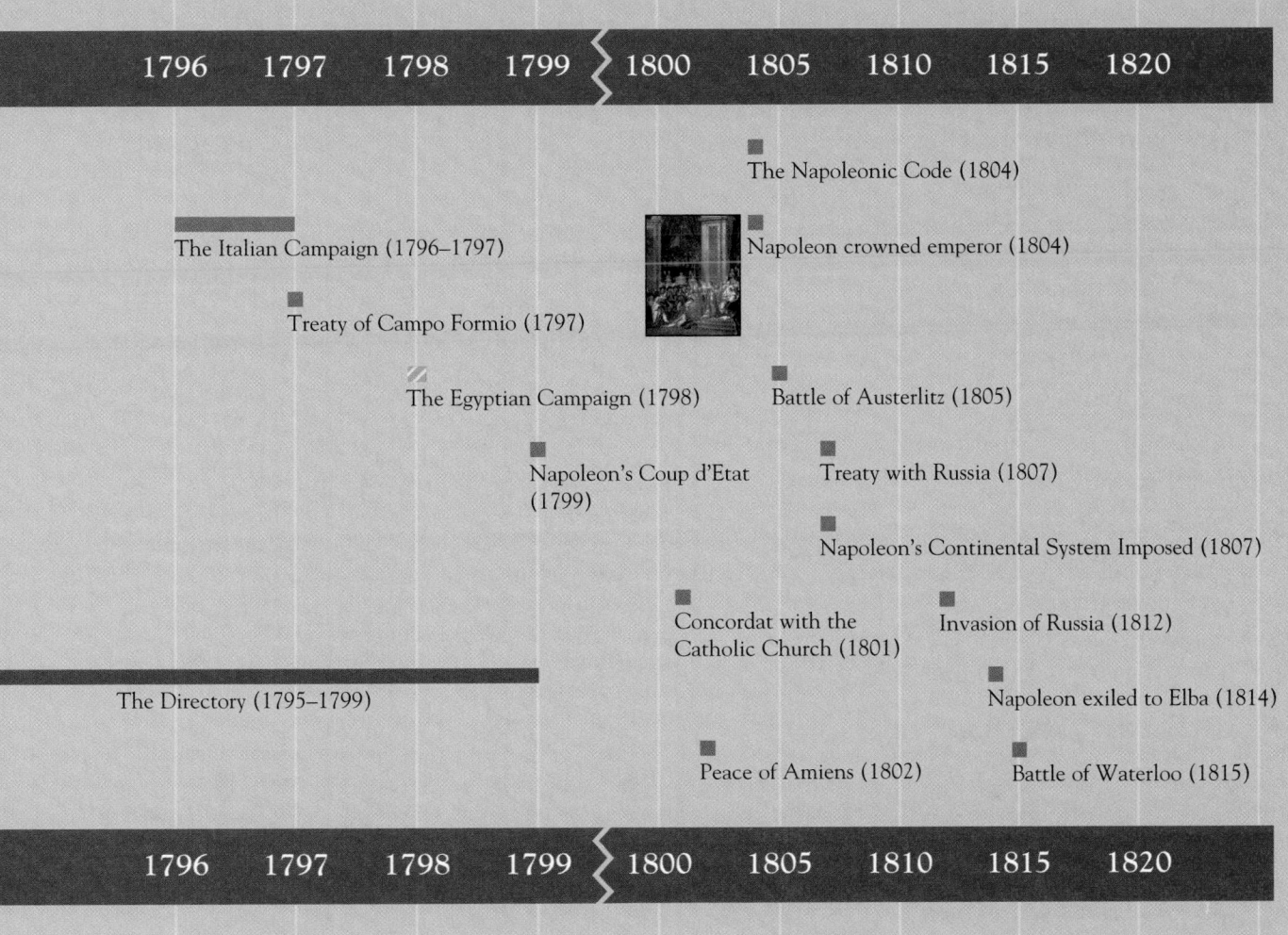

1796   1797   1798   1799   1800   1805   1810   1815   1820

The Napoleonic Code (1804)

The Italian Campaign (1796–1797)

Napoleon crowned emperor (1804)

Treaty of Campo Formio (1797)

The Egyptian Campaign (1798)

Battle of Austerlitz (1805)

Napoleon's Coup d'Etat (1799)

Treaty with Russia (1807)

Napoleon's Continental System Imposed (1807)

Concordat with the Catholic Church (1801)

Invasion of Russia (1812)

The Directory (1795–1799)

Napoleon exiled to Elba (1814)

Peace of Amiens (1802)

Battle of Waterloo (1815)

1796   1797   1798   1799   1800   1805   1810   1815   1820

property, and ensuring equality before the law for men; through his conquests, he spread the ideas and institutions of the Revolution beyond France's borders. When he maximized the political and military power of the state by rationalizing the government, he acted like an eighteenth-century enlightened despot.

Finally, the French Revolution and Napoleon created two potent, long-lasting images. First, people had learned that a popular revolution could topple the government and social order of even the most powerful country. This image would inspire revolutionaries and unnerve those representing the status quo for decades to come. Second, westerners also saw in Napoleon a nationalistic, charismatic leader who could suddenly seize power and exert his will with ease. This compelling image would inspire other individuals who envisioned themselves as potential Napoleons. Perhaps even more important, it would seduce people who yearned for easy, decisive solutions to complex problems.

After 1815, the old forces of order tried desperately to reassert their control. Although they scored some temporary successes, the ideas and institutions of the Revolution, spread by the armies of the French Republic and Napoleon, had taken root permanently in France and beyond its borders. The French Revolution had become a watershed event, and those who ignored it did so at peril.

REVIEW, ANALYZE, AND ANTICIPATE

REVIEW THE PREVIOUS CHAPTERS

Chapter 14—"A New World of Reason and Reform"—revealed how Enlightenment ideas challenged traditional values and institutions in the West. Chapter 15—"Competing for Power and Wealth"—followed the battles of Western powers over land, position, and commerce as well as the economic and social changes affecting eighteenth-century life in the West.

1. *In what ways were Enlightenment ideas reflected in the values and reforms of the French Revolution?*

2. *Do you think the French Revolution conformed to or contradicted the main political trends of the eighteenth century?*

3. *In what ways did Napoleon embody the eighteenth-century trend toward "Enlightened Absolutism?"*

ANALYZE THIS CHAPTER

Chapter 16—"Overturning the Political and Social Order"—examines the great upheaval in France that shocked and transformed the West.

1. *Analyze the roles of France's aristocracy, bourgeoisie, peasantry, and urban workers in causing the French Revolution.*

2. *What might Louis XVI have done to keep his throne?*

3. *Why do you think the Revolution turned more radical, resulting in the establishment of a republic and leading to the Reign of Terror?*

4. *How do you explain Napoleon's rise? Was his rise a logical consequence of revolutionary events?*

5. *Analyze Napoleon's accomplishments. Do you think they were worth the costs?*

ANTICIPATE THE NEXT CHAPTER

In Chapter 17—"Factories, Cities, and Families in the Industrial Age"—the industrial revolution and its accompanying social changes will be examined.

1. *With the industrial revolution beginning in Britain at about the same period as the French Revolution on the Continent, in what ways should this period be considered a watershed ushering in the modern era?*

BEYOND THE CLASSROOM

"A GREAT FERMENT": TROUBLE BREWING IN FRANCE

Chartier, Roger. *The Cultural Origins of the French Revolution.* Trans. Lydia G. Cochrane. Durham, NC: Duke University Press, 1991. Examines the developments that contributed to the cultural destabilization of the Old Regime.

Furet, François. *Interpreting the French Revolution.* Cambridge: Cambridge University Press, 1981. An important book that refutes the traditional theory of the French Revolution as a bourgeois revolution.

Landes, Joan. *Women and the Public Sphere in the Age of the French Revolution.* Ithaca, NY: Cornell University Press, 1988. Explores the historical evolution of the male-oriented public sphere and the consignment of women to the private realm of domesticity.

Lefebvre, Georges. *The Coming of the French Revolution.* Translated by R.R. Palmer. Princeton, NJ: Princeton University Press, 1947. A landmark analysis of the social structure of prerevolutionary France and the opening phase of the Revolution.

Lucas, Colin, ed. *Rewriting the French Revolution.* Oxford: Clarendon Press, 1991. Essays on social development, politics, religion, and ideas during the French Revolution by eight scholars.

Schama, Simon. *Citizens: A Chronicle of the French Revolution.* New York: Random House, 1990. A popular, well-written narrative of events.

Sutherland, Donald M.G. *France, 1789–1815: Revolution and Counter-Revolution.* New York: Oxford University Press, 1986. A departure from the traditional theory of the French Revolution as an attempt by the bourgeoisie to overthrow the aristocracy and install a capitalist order.

THE CONSTITUTIONAL MONARCHY: ESTABLISHING A NEW ORDER

Hunt, Lynn. Politics, *Culture and Class in the French Revolution.* Berkeley, CA: University of California Press, 1984. Focuses on the political culture of language, dress, and festivals created by the revolutionaries.

Jones, P. *The Peasantry in the French Revolution.* New York: Cambridge University Press, 1988. Examines the role of the peasantry in the revolutionary events from 1789–1799.

Rudé, George. *The Crowd in the French Revolution.* Oxford: Clarendon Press, 1959. A study of the composition of the crowds that participated in revolutionary events such as the storming of the Bastille.

To the Radical Republic and Back

Bertaud, Jean-Paul. *The Army of the French Revolution*. Princeton, NJ: Princeton University Press, 1988. Analyzes the role of the army in overthrowing the Old Regime and how the army changed during the revolutionary years.

Hufton, Olwen. *Women and the Limits of Citizenship in the French Revolution*. Toronto: University of Toronto Press, 1992. Analyzes attitudes toward women during the French Revolution that led to female exclusion from the rights of citizenship.

Kennedy, Emmet. *A Cultural History of the French Revolution*. New Haven, CT: Yale University Press, 1989. Examines the role of the arts, clubs, and intellectual institutions during the Revolution.

Lyons, Martyn. *France Under the Directory*. New York: Cambridge University Press, 1975. A brief yet wide-ranging survey of the Directory period.

Palmer, Robert R. *Twelve Who Ruled: The Committee of Public Safety During the Terror*. Princeton, NJ: Princeton University Press, 1970. A well-written account of the Terror and its leaders.

Napoleon Bonaparte

Connelly, Owen. *Blundering to Glory: Napoleon's Military Campaigns*. Wilmington, DE: Scholarly Resources, 1987. An assessment of Napoleon's military strategy and achievements.

Kafker, Frank A., and James M. Laux, eds. *Napoleon and His Times: Selected Interpretations*. Malabar, FL: Krieger Publishing Co., 1989. A fine collection of articles on many aspects of Napoleon's regime.

Lyons, Martyn. *Napoleon Bonaparte and the Legacy of the French Revolution*. New York: St. Martin's Press, 1994. A solid reevaluation of Napoleon and his legacy.

Schom, Alan. *Napoleon Bonaparte: A Life*. New York: HarperCollins, 1998. An up-to-date, critical biography of Napoleon.

For quiz questions that tie the book to the videos and additional primary sources, please go to the Primary Source Investigator CD.

Documents

DOCUMENT 16.1
New Laws End the Feudal System in France

During the summer of 1789, revolutionary activities swept France. On July 14, a mob stormed the Bastille, symbolizing a violent tearing down of the ancien régime. In the countryside, the peasantry rose against the nobility. Cracking under these pressures, nobles in the National Assembly moved on August 4 and 5 to abolish their own feudal rights and privileges. The following excerpts describe some of the laws passed to end the feudal system and other ancien régime institutions.

■ Investigate the Document

In what ways did these laws transform the ancient régime? How did these laws change the relationship between commoners and nobility, as well as between citizens and the king?

ARTICLE I. The National Assembly hereby completely abolishes the feudal system. It decrees that, among the existing rights and dues, . . . all those originating in or representing real or personal serfdom or personal servitude, shall be abolished without indemnification.

IV. All manorial courts are hereby suppressed without indemnification. . . .

V. Tithes of every description, as well as the dues which have been substituted for them . . . are abolished, on condition, however, that some other method be devised to provide for the expenses of divine worship, the support of the officiating clergy, for the assistance of the poor, for repairs and rebuilding of churches and parsonages, and for the maintenance of all institutions, seminaries, schools, academies, asylums, and organizations to which the present funds are devoted.

VII. The sale of judicial and municipal offices shall be suppressed forthwith. Justice shall be dispensed *gratis.*

IX. Pecuniary privileges, personal or real, in the payment of taxes are abolished forever. Taxes shall be collected from all the citizens, and from all property, in the same manner and in the same form. . . .

X. . . . All the peculiar privileges, pecuniary or otherwise, of the provinces, principalities, districts, cantons, cities and communes, are once for all abolished and are absorbed into the law common to all Frenchmen.

XI. All citizens, without distinction of birth, are eligible to any office or dignity, whether ecclesiastical, civil or military; and no profession shall imply any derogation.

DOCUMENT 16.2
The Jacobins' Revolutionary Politics

In the years following 1789, the Jacobin club of Paris became the most influential political club in the city and, with many affiliated clubs outside of Paris, the most important in France. The Jacobins pushed politics in an increasingly more radical direction. The following document, which they circulated on September 12, 1792, reveals some of the club's evolving goals and tactics.

■ Investigate the Document

What is the club's vision of the monarchy and its supporters? What does the club stand for? What tensions within France does this document expose?

Since the 10th of August conspirators have expiated their offences; the public spirit has risen again; the sovereign, recovered possession of its rights, triumphs at length over the scoundrels leagued against its liberty and its welfare. Nevertheless, the people of Paris have felt the necessity of preserving an imposing attitude and of exercising a strict surveillance over the Minions and agents of the traitor, Louis the

Source: James Harvey Robinson, ed., *Translations and Reprints from the Original Sources of European History,* vol. I, no. 5 (Philadelphia: University of Pennsylvania Press, 1898), pp. 2–5.

Source: F. M. Anderson, ed., *The Constitution and Other Select Documents Illustrative of the History of France 1789–1901,* (Minneapolis: H. W. Wilson Co., 1904), pp. 127–128.

Last. Be apprehensive, brothers and friends, lest new intrigues shall follow the baffled intrigues. The head, the cause and the pretext of the machinations still lives! Despotism moves in the darkness; let us be ready to engage in a combat to the death with it, under whatever form it presents itself. . . .

Let us impress our minds then with the spirit of the orders of the electoral body of Paris; they along can save us from all sorts of despotism and the dangers of convulsions too long a time prolonged, etc.

These orders are in substance:

The purgatorial examination of the National Convention, in order to reject from its midst the suspected members who may have escaped the sagacity of the primary assemblies;

The revocability of the deputies to the National Convention who have attacked or who attack by any motions the rights of the sovereign;

The sanction, or the popular revision of all the constitutional decrees of the National Convention;

The entire abolition of royalty and the penalty of death against those who may propose to reestablish it;

The form of a republican government.

These, friends and brothers, are the important matters which the electors, the Commune, and the Primary Assemblies of Paris, invite us to discuss earnestly in order to fortify and encompass the National Convention with your opinion upon these matters.

DOCUMENT 16.3
Napoleon Issues an Imperial Decree at Madrid

When Napoleon scored military successes outside of France, he demanded more from the conquered peoples than subservience to French rule. Typically he applied some of the same reforms and institutions of the French Revolution to the conquered lands. This policy is shown in the following decree, issued from Napoleon's imperial camp at Madrid on December 4, 1808.

■ **Investigate the Document**

What benefits might Napoleon have been hoping for by issuing this decree? In what ways are these measures consistent with the spirit of the French Revolution?

To date from the publication of the present decree, feudal rights are abolished in Spain.

All personal obligations, all exclusive fishing rights and other rights of similar nature on the coast or on rivers and streams, all feudal monopolies (*banalités*) of ovens, mills, and inns are suppressed. It shall be free to every one who shall conform to the laws to develop his industry without restraint.

The tribunal of the Inquisition is abolished, as inconsistent with the civil sovereignty and authority.

The property of the Inquisition shall be sequestered and fall to the Spanish state, to serve as security for the bonded debt.

Considering that the members of the various monastic orders have increased to an undue degree and that, although a certain number of them are useful in assisting the ministers of the altar in the administration of the sacraments, the existence of too great a number interferes with the prosperity of the state, we have decreed and do decree as follows:

The number of convents now in existence in Spain shall be reduced to a third of their present number. This reduction shall be accomplished by uniting the members of several convents of the same order into one.

All regular ecclesiastics who desire to renounce the monastic life and live as secular ecclesiastics are at liberty to leave their monasteries . . .

In view of the fact that the institution which stands most in the way of the internal prosperity of Spain is that of the customs lines separating the provinces, we have decreed and do decree what follows:

To date from January 1 next, the barriers existing between the provinces shall be suppressed. The custom houses shall be removed to the frontiers and there established.

Source: James Harvey Robinson, ed., *Readings in European History*, vol. II (Boston: Gin, 1904), p. 512.

Industrial Manchester, 1851

By 1851, Manchester in northern England had grown into an industrial city of some 400,000 inhabitants. The city "chiefly consists of dense masses of houses, inhabited by the population engaged in the great manufactories of the cotton trade," explained James Kay, a contemporary observer, "but the opulent merchants chiefly reside in the country." This painting captures the common vision of industrial cities standing in stark contrast to the surrounding countryside.

CHAPTER 17

Factories, Cities, and Families in the Industrial Age

The Industrial Revolution, 1780–1850

STUDY • Causes of the industrial revolution • New markets, machines, and power • The spread of industrialization • The benefits and burdens of industrialization • Life in the growing cities • Public health and medicine • Family ideals and realities.

NOTICE the social consequences of industrialization.

In 1828, a German visitor described Britain as a land where the "new creations springing into life every year bordered on the fabulous." These creations were the machines and factories of the industrial revolution that were replacing agriculture and handicrafts as the basis of the traditional economy. They turned industrial cities like Manchester into what the French writer Alexis de Tocqueville called "the greatest stream of human industry" that "flows out to fertilize the whole world."

However, this wave of industrial developments, which made Britain wealthy and envied, brought disturbing consequences in its wake: great swings of economic prosperity and depression and a new working class harnessed to the rhythm of machines. A British journal in 1826 spoke of a growing "accumulation of misery endured by thousands" in industrial areas. A few years later, the French consul in Edinburgh argued, "Who would want the prosperity of Liverpool and Manchester in France...beside these base miseries offered by manufacturing establishments?"

These "miseries" haunted not only the new factories and mines. Workers hoping for jobs crowded into unprepared cities. There, life for them as well as for middle-class employers, professionals, and shopkeepers was rapidly changing. In bad times, unemployment and business failures made urban life particularly harsh. In prosperous times, filth and disease still marked these cities. Here even the family, which for so long labored together as a cooperating unit of economic life, was shifting under the weight of new ideas and pressures. Western societies were entering the industrial age.

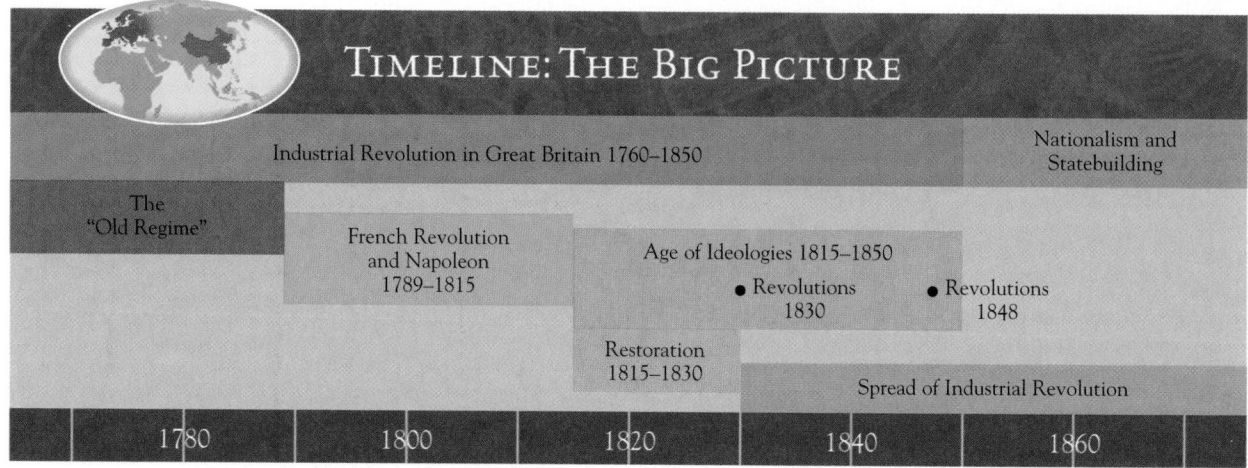

TIMELINE: THE BIG PICTURE

Industrial Revolution in Great Britain 1760–1850

Nationalism and Statebuilding

The "Old Regime"

French Revolution and Napoleon 1789–1815

Age of Ideologies 1815–1850
● Revolutions 1830
● Revolutions 1848

Restoration 1815–1830

Spread of Industrial Revolution

1780 1800 1820 1840 1860

The Industrial Revolution Begins

In this new era, Britain led the way. There a middle-class couple such as Richard and Elizabeth Cadbury (see the Biography on pages 612–613) might expect to work hard and see the cloth and dry goods store they opened in 1794 support them and their several children. Thirty-five years later their sons, Benjamin and John, had become wealthy retailers and manufacturers.

Others did not consider the industrial age such a boon. One railroad worker told of a day when 2,000 of his coworkers lost their jobs: "They were all starving, the heap of them, or next door to it." This worker had recently injured his leg at work and was laid up for one month, living "all that time on charity; on what the chaps would come and give me. When I could get about again, the work was all stopped, and I couldn't get none to do. . . . I went to a lodginghouse in the Borough, and I sold all my things—shovel and grafting-tool and all, to have a meal of food. When all my things was gone, I didn't know where to go. . . . Now I'm dead beat, though I'm only twenty-eight next August."

Stories about successful merchants like the Cadburys and less fortunate laborers like this railroad worker give us a glimpse at the two faces of Britain's industrial revolution. Year by year, the work and home lives of these people and others changed only gradually. However, between the 1780s and 1850s—little more than a single lifetime—astonishing developments transformed economic and social life in Britain.

The scene pictured on page 586 captures some of what that transformation meant to people. In the foreground of this 1851 painting is a romanticized vision of nature and the countryside, featuring trees, bushes, rock formations, hills, and a road winding around a lake. On the left, a couple, perhaps enjoying a picnic, relax with their dog—all apparently at one with nature. In the distance looms Manchester, which between 1780 and 1851 grew from a small country town to a large, industrialized city. Manchester's numerous factory chimneys belch clouds of smoke into the air. The sense of contrast is striking: In the city, people grind out the new wealth of this civilization, all while enduring crowds and filth away from the imagined delights of nature and the rural life they once knew.

In the mid-eighteenth century, most British people had lived in the countryside. Women and men who laboriously spun fibers into thread and yarn and then wove it into cloth with the aid of only simple tools and handlooms barely noticed the few new machines that could quickly spin American cotton into thread and weave it into cloth by the thousands of yards. At the edges of forests where wood was available for smelting iron, most iron masters still forged metal using slow methods inherited from their ancestors. To transport their goods to markets, these people, like their predecessors from centuries back, relied on coaches drawn by horses over rutted dirt roads, and on wooden ships pushed by currents and winds across the seas. Steam engines, already present for several decades, were inefficient and rare outside of coal mines.

By 1850, things had changed dramatically. Over half of Britain's population, which had more than doubled during the period, now lived in cities. Cotton factories churned out hundreds of millions of yards of cloth that were sold throughout the world every year and were driving those who still made cloth the old way out of business. New mines, machines, and production techniques made vast quantities of iron cheap to produce, easy to work, and available everywhere. Railroads carried people and merchandise to their destinations quickly, inexpensively, and reliably. Recent generations of efficient coal-burning steam engines powered these factories, foundries, and railroads. Waves of inventions and innovations built on earlier breakthroughs cheapened production while improving quality. Entrepreneurs and business organizations applied these machines and production methods to other industries in Britain and elsewhere in the West. Although marked by periodic crises and downturns, a self-sustaining process of economic growth and technological change had been achieved and would continue through the decades after 1850.

Figure 17.1, an 1830 British print, reveals the impact on people's imaginations of the new industrial age. In this fanciful view, all sorts of vehicles powered by smoke-belching steam engines race down one of London's main streets—White Chapel Road. The old mixes oddly with the new: The street remains unpaved, some of the vehicles are little different than the horse-drawn carts and coaches of the period, and despite the jam of traffic there is still room for dogs to roam down the road at a leisurely pace. Yet the image is one of life in the process of being transformed by the new technology.

What created this phenomenon—which French observers in the 1820s termed an "industrial revolution"—and why did it happen first in the West and particularly in Britain?

A BOOMING COMMERCIAL ECONOMY IN THE WEST

Why the industrial revolution emerged first in the West rather than in other civilizations such as China or India is difficult to say. Before 1500, Europeans enjoyed no fundamental advantages in how they produced goods over their Asian counterparts; in some areas, such as iron and steel production, they even lagged behind. Many qualities, such as intellectual traditions and politics, differed Eastern civilizations from the West and may help explain the early appearance of the industrial revolution in the West. However, the rise of commerce during the sixteenth, seventeenth, and eighteenth centuries distinguished the West economically. Civilizations elsewhere usually participated in this growing commerce only reluctantly. China, for example, may have produced luxury goods dearly desired by westerners, but, except for gold and silver, the Chinese wanted little in trade from the West (see Global Connections). Moreover, the occupation of merchant had a low social status in China, further discouraging any potential bloom of commerce in that part of the world. In the West, however, the growth of commerce encouraged people to produce more agricultural and manufactured goods and sell them for a profit in the marketplace. Merchants and entrepreneurs became devoted to "buying low" and "selling high," thereby amassing more and more wealth. The growth of commerce helped create the potential markets, producers, entrepreneurs, and capitalists that would fuel the industrial revolution in the West.

The Western and non-Western worlds

FIGURE 7.1
Technology transforming life.

Global Connections

CROSS-CULTURAL MISUNDERSTANDINGS: CHINA AND GREAT BRITAIN

Consider the contrasting views about China held by the British and Chinese. **NOTICE** the British response to China's isolation.

As industrialization spread in England during the last decades of the eighteenth century, British merchants sought new markets across the globe for their manufactured goods. China constituted a huge potential market for trade. In 1776, the British economist Adam Smith concluded that China's home market was "perhaps in extent not much inferior to the market of all the different countries of Europe put together." Indeed, during the eighteenth century, China under the Qing (Ch'ing) dynasty enjoyed considerable peace, prosperity, and population growth. But the emperors had always limited European merchants' access to China. Moreover, the Qing, determined to minimize foreign influences on their society, imposed strict restrictions on Western commerce within China.

Eager to widen the opening to China, the East India Company persuaded the British government to send an experienced diplomat, Lord George Macartney, to China in 1792. There, Macartney presented a formal request from King George III for a lessening of trade restrictions. But Emperor Qianlong (Ch'ien Lung) (r. 1736–1796), a capable and humane ruler, rejected the request. In a letter to King George III, he stressed that China "possesses all things in prolific abundance and lacks no product within its own borders." Therefore, China had "no need to import manufactures of outside barbarians [Europeans] in exchange for our own produce." Clearly, in the emperor's mind, it was the British who "yearned after the blessings of our civilization" and not the reverse. Indeed, Qianlong expressed sympathy for the British, condemned as they were to "the lonely remoteness of your island, cut off from the world by intervening wastes of sea." He

went on to lament the persistent desire of Christian missionaries for greater access to China. The Chinese had no need for these missionaries, he argued. "Ever since the beginning of history, sage Emperors and wise rulers have bestowed on China a moral system [Confucianism] and inculcated a code, which from time immemorial has been religiously observed by the myriads of my subjects." The emperor ended his letter by denying all British requests for greater access to China. He also threatened to treat any future violations of his rules harshly: "Do not say that you were not warned in due time!"

Lord Macartney, in turn, criticized the Chinese. "Morality is a mere pretense in their practice, though a common topic of their discourse." As for science, the Chinese, he claimed, considered it a mere "intruder." However, Macartney admitted that China was "an old first-rate man of war, which a succession of vigilant officers has continued to keep afloat." And in the government as well as the family, he observed, authority was "usually exercised with kindness and indulgence."

In 1816, the British tried again, sending Lord Amherst on a similar mission to China. This effort, too, met with failure. However, British observers had even more positive things to say about China than Lord Macartney had. One official under Lord Amherst noted that the "lower orders of Chinese seem to me more neat and clean than any Europeans of the same class." Many other Western observers who traveled in China during the first half of the nineteenth century agreed with Robert Fortune's conclusion: "In no country in the world is there less real misery and want than in China."

By this time, however, China's population growth was outstripping its economic growth. The government struggled to cope with its people's needs, but poverty worsened. Local banditry rose and rebellions broke out with alarming frequency. The weakening Qing empire was losing its ability to meet the growing challenges from the British and the West.

BRITAIN'S UNIQUE SET OF ADVANTAGES

Commerce also helps explain why Britain industrialized first. During the sixteenth and seventeenth centuries, commercial activity in England intensified along with English *Commercial vigor* sea power and overseas holdings. In the eighteenth century, Britain became Europe's leading commercial and colonial power (see Chapter 15). Britain's economy efficiently turned out goods for export, and the island nation enjoyed considerable access to expanding markets—both internal, from its rapidly growing and relatively wealthy population, and external, from its colonies and established commercial connections.

Commercial vigor, however, is not enough to answer the question of why Britain led the industrial revolution. Other areas of Europe enjoyed advantages that would be important for industrialization. For example, during the first half of the eighteenth century, Holland's agriculture and financial institutions were second to none. France was the wealthiest nation in the West. Britain, however, boasted a unique combination of advantages that, when added to its commercial leadership, laid a solid foundation for the birth of the industrial revolution.

Water transportation—far cheaper and quicker than overland shipping—played a crucial role in moving the *Transportation* coal, iron, cloth, and machines pumped out by Britain's new factories and mines. Already crisscrossed with countless navigable rivers (see Map 17.1), Britain enhanced its natural internal transportation system even more by building an extensive network of canals after 1760.

Certain raw materials—especially coal, iron, and cotton—also had an essential part in the island's in-

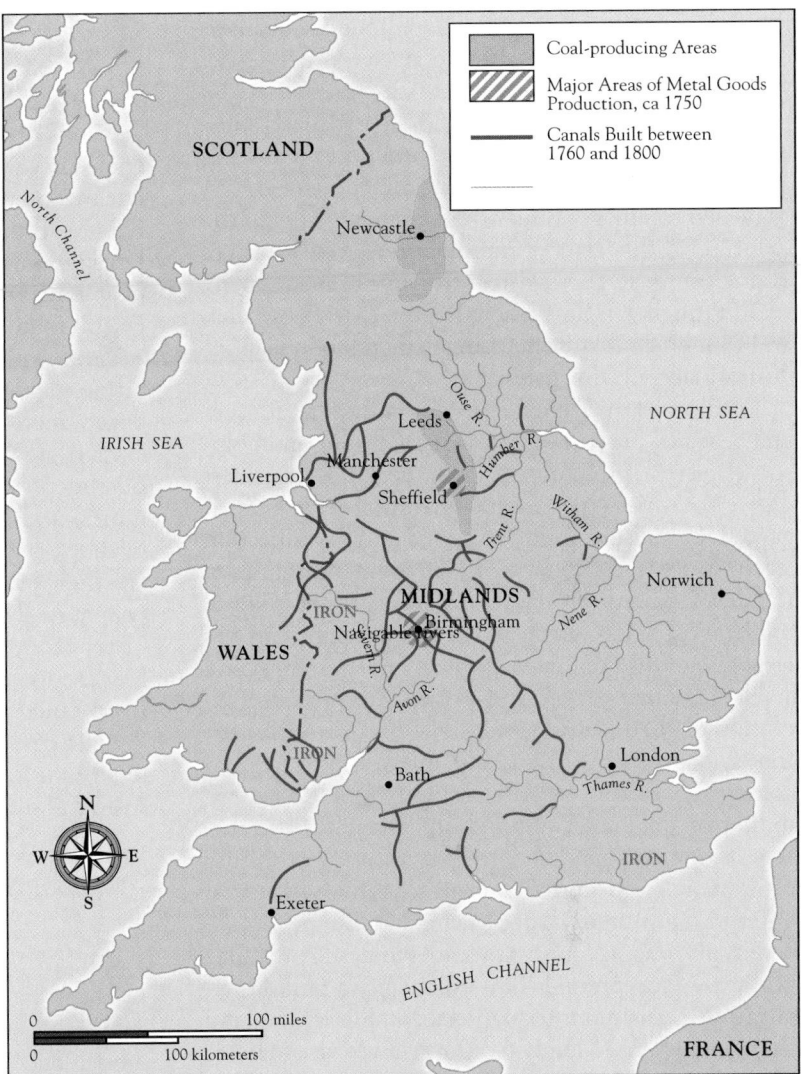

THINKING ABOUT GEOGRAPHY

MAP 17.1 *Eighteenth-Century England*

This map shows England's system of navigable waterways and areas of coal and iron production in the eighteenth century.
Consider the advantages of England's natural resources for industrialization. **How** did the English add to those advantages during the second half of the eighteenth century?

dustrialization. Britain's American colonies harvested large quantities of cotton. The British *Raw materials* countryside not only contained plentiful deposits of coal, but they were often conveniently located near iron deposits where foundry workers used the two materials in the newer processes of smelting to make iron products.

An expanding population and a particularly large and mobile force of both skilled and unskilled work-ers gave Britain another advantage. Already less tied to villages than others in many parts of the Continent, this class of rural laborers grew as waves of enclosures in the eighteenth century made many small farmers landless (see Chapter 15). These men and women could fill the rising demand for cheap in-dustrial labor in the cities.

Labor

Britain had the capital to invest in industry for sev-eral reasons. First, its growing agricultural and com-mercial prosperity made it one of the wealthiest countries—per capita—in Europe. Second, it gained an unusual ability to amass and mobilize that wealth into capital for potential investment, thanks to the development of a national banking system. Third, unlike most of its continental competitors, Britain was long free of internal tariff barriers, had a uniform and stable monetary system, and—since the Glorious Rev-olution of 1688 (see Chapter 13)—had a government that sympathized with business interests. All this en-couraged wealthy individuals and families to risk money on commerce and industry. Therefore, inven-tors, innovators, and those who saw an opportunity could more easily find the means to start an industrial enterprise in Britain than elsewhere in Europe.

Capital

Finally, and according to some analysts, most im-portantly, entrepreneurship—at the heart of industri-alization—was more socially acceptable in England than elsewhere. Members of England's aristocratic families—especially younger sons left without inher-ited lands—often sought careers in commerce and manufacturing. Social barriers between them and the business-minded mid-dle class were lower than elsewhere. More than in most European nations, British merchants and entre-preneurs occupied a strong, respected place in society. On the other hand, in France, for example, most elites looked on commerce and industry as a means—often regrettable—to gain money to purchase office, estates, and aristocratic status; as soon as possible, French aristocrats usually left commerce or distanced themselves from their businesses.

Entrepreneurship

In short, Britain had the most potential both to nurture and to take advantage of Europe's first indus-trial stirrings. Yet, what was it that finally trans-formed this potential into reality? Oddly, the crucial development came with advances in agriculture.

A REVOLUTION IN AGRICULTURE

The agricultural revolution, with its new crops, methods of rotating crops, breeding of animals, and enclosures of open fields, spread in Britain during the late seventeenth and eighteenth centuries (see Chap-ter 15). Production increased, as did profits for the large landowners who shipped their crops to markets near and far. Declining food prices enabled more British families to purchase manufactured goods such as shoes, knives, and cloth. As the agricultural revo-lution picked up speed, fewer and fewer people pro-duced more and more food. The new, large-scale farmers grew crops and livestock to feed the growing number of people working in factories, digging in the mines, and building their lives in the cities. More-over, these well-to-do, enterprising landowners could use their profits to invest in the many business and commercial opportunities becoming available.

By 1850, the majority of Britain's population no longer raised food or lived in the countryside. Most lived and worked in cities and factory towns. Whether people were better off in these urban cen-ters is a question we will turn to later. For now, the stage was set for Britain's industrial revolution.

New Markets, Machines, and Power

As wealth increased and people moved away from subsistence farming toward the burgeoning urban centers, the demand for manufactured goods reached unheard-of levels. Inventors and entrepreneurs rushed to fill this demand, dreaming up new ma-chines and designing novel manufacturing methods. The machines, gaining complexity almost every year, seemed like mechanical wonders. The methods of production transformed the workplace. Coal and steam provided all the power necessary to make these machines and production methods work. Manufac-tured goods poured forth, available to all with the money to purchase them.

THE RISING DEMAND FOR GOODS

The old methods of production—slow, unreliable, and costly—could not satisfy the rising clamor for manu-factured goods (see pages 535–536). In fact, the popu-lation growth in Britain and Europe alone created an

OLC

ever-expanding pool of potential customers for low-cost clothing, nails, pottery, knives, and so forth. Eager overseas buyers, particularly in the colonies, offered raw materials in return for Britain's manufactured goods. At home, Britain's own successful farmers and merchants added to the demand.

Between the middle decades of the eighteenth century and 1850, inventors and entrepreneurs introduced new machines and methods that began to satisfy these hungry markets. Most inventors were practical men who embodied the widespread British interest in devices, gadgets, and machines of all kinds and had more talent as curious tinkerers than as scientific thinkers. Industrial entrepreneurs were also practical. Sometimes inventors themselves, they more often used the new devices and processes invented by others. Entrepreneurs purchased machines, employed workers, ran factories and mines, and found the necessary capital and markets.

Inventors and entrepreneurs

Some entrepreneurs were landowning aristocrats; others rose from rags to riches. Many were Protestant dissenters, such as Calvinists and Quakers, who had been discriminated against by the dominant Anglican Church. Denied careers in government, they jumped at the opportunities presented by commerce and industry. Most, however, came from the middle classes. They took advantage of journals that promoted new techniques and ideas, divided and redivided the processes of production, and trained a work force unaccustomed to working with machines in factory conditions. Buying raw materials from both local and distant suppliers, they promoted their products to the public. Through their resourcefulness and sometimes outright greed, they pursued profits. Navigating a risky competitive environment, they often reinvested their profits in their shops and factories, buying new machines and boosting production. The story of how they took advantage of new markets in the early decades of the industrial revolution is a narrative of new developments in cotton, iron, and steam.

COTTON LEADS THE WAY

Changes in cotton production came first and with dramatic results. Before 1750, most thread and yarn was spun by women and woven into cloth by men who worked in rural cottages or small urban shops. Using only simple spinning wheels and handlooms, these laborers produced thread, yarn, and cloth of uneven quality. How much they produced was limited by many things—the supply of fiber, farmwork that took them away from their spinning and weaving, the wages paid by the entrepreneurs who organized much of this work, and, above all, the tools and methods they used.

In 1733, John Kay (1704–1764) invented a device called the flying shuttle, which doubled the speed at which cloth could be woven on a loom. The shuttle, in turn, intensified the demand for thread. In the 1760s, James Hargreaves (d. 1778) invented the spinning jenny, which revolutionized thread production. By 1812, one spinner could produce as much cotton thread as 200 spinners had in 1760. Other inventions, such as Richard Arkwright's (1732–1792) water frame and Edmund Cartwright's (1743–1823) power loom, allowed weavers to turn cotton into cloth in tremendous quantities. Two American developments added to the acceleration in textile production: Eli Whitney's (1765–1825) cotton gin (1793), which efficiently removed seeds from raw cotton; and the expanding slave plantation system in the South. Indeed, British manufacturers' growing demand for cotton became an important force perpetuating slavery in the cotton-growing areas of the United States.

Weaving and spinning

By 1850, British cotton manufacturers had boosted cloth production from less than 40 million yards per year during the 1780s to more than 2,000 million yards per year. Cotton had become hugely popular and, alone, accounted for some 40 percent of British exports.

IRON: NEW PROCESSES TRANSFORM PRODUCTION

Machines for the new cotton industry were just one source of a growing demand for iron. Armies needed guns and cannons; civilians needed nails and pans. Until the eighteenth century, British iron makers were limited by the island nation's dwindling forests, for they knew how to smelt iron ore only with charcoal, which came from wood. Even during the days of plentiful charcoal, ironworkers had only their own and their animals' muscle power with which to work the iron into usable forms. Figure 17.2, a painting by the British artist Joseph Wright of Derby (1734–1797), shows a typical eighteenth-century iron forge. As this picture suggests, most production came out of small family firms or homes of artisans. The men—posing proudly—use only hand-powered tools to

FIGURE 17.2
Joseph Wright of Derby, *The Iron Forge*, 1772.

transform the iron, while women and children stand by, averting their eyes or turning away from the white-hot metal.

Abraham Darby's (1678?–1717) discovery in 1708 of an efficient way to smelt iron with coal in a blast
Smelting with coal furnace started the iron industry down a new path. By the end of the century, other novel processes enabled iron makers to double production again and again in the years that followed. Foundry workers began using the steam engine to operate smelting furnaces, drive forge hammers to shape the iron, and roll the iron into sheets. By 1850, ironworks, with their tall, smoke-belching furnaces, had joined cotton factories as a pillar of the industrial revolution.

THE STEAM ENGINE AND THE FACTORY SYSTEM

Both the cotton and the iron industries created ever higher demand for power. At the beginning of the eighteenth century, people had to rely on muscle, wind, and water to supply the energy to do their work. Early mills used water power, which meant that their owners had to build them near waterfalls. A drought in the summer or a cold snap in the

winter could threaten to dry up or freeze this essential power source.

The steam engine, first used in the early eighteenth century to pump water out of deepening coal mines, provided a solution and would become the industrial revolution's most important technological advance. Portable and easily controlled, the earliest models were nevertheless not yet efficient enough for widespread application. Over the course of the eighteenth century, inventors such as Thomas Newcomen (1663–1729) and James Watt (1736–1819) improved the power and efficiency of these engines. Watt, a skilled craftsman backed by the daring entrepreneur Matthew Boulton (1728–1809), worked for years on the engine, making several design changes and eventually converting the reciprocal motion of the piston into a rotary motion. Now steam engines could be used not only to pump coal mines but also to drive the other new machines of the day, such as powering bellows for iron forges, mills for grains, and looms for textiles. Figure 17.1 indicates that the steam engine came to symbolize the new industrial age.

Reliable power from steam engines also made it possible for entrepreneurs to locate factories away from water power sites and build even larger cotton, iron, and other factories. In huge buildings, entrepreneurs hoped to guard their industrial secrets and mold a new labor force. Hundreds of workers, who produced goods in a repetitive series of steps and specialized tasks, tended rows of machines. The factory system had emerged. "The principle of the factory system . . . is to substitute mechanical science for hand skill, and the partition of a process into its essential constituents, for the division or graduation of labor," explained Andrew Ure, a professor of applied science, in 1835 (see Document 17.1 on page D17.1). As we will see, factories generated unprecedented wealth for their owners and investors, but brought new hardships for the people who toiled in them.

Figure 17.3 reveals the nature of the factory system. This realistic 1859 painting of a factory interior in France shows the mixture of raw materials (zinc ore), machines, and division of labor that epitomized factories in the industrial age. In the upper left and center, workers bring ore from the mines and dump it into machines for initial washing and processing. After the ore is split and sorted, workers shovel it into large ovens to be melted down. Men, women, and children work together in this hot, noisy building; the men have the more authoritative and skilled jobs (a foreman sits in the rear to the left), while the women and children are assigned to sorting and splitting chunks of ore.

COAL: FUELING THE REVOLUTION

As the industrial revolution hit its stride, the demand for coal also intensified. Steam engines devoured coal as fuel. Iron makers required more and more coal to run their furnaces. Britain's doubling population needed coal to heat their homes.

People poured huge amounts of money and labor into digging mines, extracting the coal, and developing the roads, canals, and rails necessary to transport the mineral to waiting customers. Coal not only fueled the industrial revolution; mining and manufacturing became so entwined that it was hard for people to think of one without the other.

RAILROADS: CARRYING INDUSTRIALIZATION ACROSS THE LAND

The advent of the railroad age brought everything together. In the eighteenth century, horses had pulled carts along rails radiating out from mines, hauled barges along the growing network of canals, and pulled carriages along roads. Only wind in the sails of ships could move heavy cargoes and passengers across the seas.

During the 1820s, as steam engines began to power ships, the British inventor George Stephenson (1781–1848) developed the practical modern railroad. In 1830 his new train, "the Rocket," initiated the Liverpool-to-Manchester railway line. The Rocket's speed (16 miles per hour) and reliability

FIGURE 17.3
Francois Bonhomme, *Workshop with Mechanical Sieves,* 1859.

excited the imaginations of everyone. People eagerly invested in railway companies, rode the new lines out of curiosity, and traveled by rail to vacation spots.

The railway carried heavy freight with unprecedented ease and speed. By 1850, trains were chugging over 2,000 miles of track in Britain, reaching astonishing speeds of up to 50 miles an hour. Steaming across bridges and through tunnels to the railway stations dotting the land, the new locomotives embodied the power and the promise that seemed to characterize the industrial age.

Figure 17.4, a lithograph by the British industrial artist John Cooke Bourne, portrays the drama of the railroad age. The piece shows a locomotive on the Great Western Railway, with its shining copper

FIGURE 17.4
John Cooke Bourne, *Tunnel and the Great Western Railway.*

haystack boiler, bursting out of a newly built tunnel into daylight near Bristol in 1846. The image captures the combination of power, practicality, science, and art that characterized the early years of the railroads. Painted at the height of a speculative boom in railway stocks, it reflects the visions of optimistic observers such as the British politician Edward Stanley, who argued that "of all the promoters of civilization, the Railway System of communication will be amongst the foremost in its effects, for it cannot fail to produce many and mighty changes in manufactures, in commerce, in trade, and in science."

The railroad seemed to pull together all the trends that emerged during the industrial revolution. It ignited demand for an array of related products—coal-thirsty steam *Effects of the railroad* engines to power the trains, iron to build the rails and cars, cloth and leather to make furnishings, and bricks and glass to erect the new stations. Like the cotton factories, iron foundries, and coal mines, the railroad industry created new jobs while destroying old ones. In addition, it left its own permanent mark on the land and neighborhoods it affected. As Charles Dickens (1812–1870) described in *Dombey and Son* (1846), a new rail line meant that "houses were knocked down; streets broken through and stopped; deep pits and trenches dug in the ground; enormous heaps of earth and clay thrown up . . . everywhere carcasses of ragged tenements, and fragments of unfinished walls and arches, and piles of scaffolding, and wilderness of bricks, . . . mounds of ashes blocked up rights of way." All this "wholly changed the law and custom of the neighborhood," before the railroad "trailed smoothly away, upon its mighty course of civilization and improvement."

Finally, like the other new industries, the railroads could be a risky investment opportunity. Some owners and investors grew fabulously wealthy; others suffered devastating financial losses. Just as the cotton and iron industries continued to face competition from older methods such as the putting-out system (cottage industry), handicrafts, small family firms, and agriculture, the railroads had to fight to steal business from the roads and canal systems that were expanding across Britain at the same time. Those who had thrown their lot in with the railroads need not have worried too long about the wisdom of their investment, however. Like the cotton and iron factories, the railways were the wave of the future, and they rolled inexorably across the British landscape.

FIGURE 17.5
The Crystal Palace Exhibition.

BRITAIN'S TRIUMPH: THE CRYSTAL PALACE EXHIBITION

In 1851, that shining future was put on display for all the world to admire. That year, London hosted the first international industrial fair at the glass-and-iron Crystal Palace. At this dazzling exhibit, millions of visitors came to gaze reverently at the British miracle.

Figure 17.5 shows the interior of the Crystal Palace—its arching glass roof like a cathedral, its steel framing a testament to modern engineering. Matthew Wyatt, one of the directors of the exhibition, proudly described the construction of the palace as an industrial triumph: "But for the perfect system of discipline, which frequent practice in directing the labour of masses of workmen has now made general throughout England, it would have been impossible to have fashioned, in so short a time, so novel and so vast a structure . . . the gates of which may . . . be thrown open to the world at large, for many years to come." To Wyatt and many others in 1851, the Crystal Palace was at once an architectural masterpiece and a jewel of mass production that could not help but appeal to popular taste. In addition to admiring the building itself, visitors could view displays from various nations. No exhibit was more impressive, however, than the British-manufactured products and machines. Figure 17.6 shows one of these British triumphs, a lathe for forming railway wheels.

FIGURE 17.6
British machinery displayed at the Crystal Palace Exhibition.

The awe-inspiring palace confirmed economic realities. Britain produced more than half the world's cotton cloth and iron, and, despite periodic downturns, the nation enjoyed sustained economic growth. Britain had become the world's first industrialized nation.

Industrialization Spreads to the Continent

It was not until after 1830 that industrialization spread with much force outside Britain (see Figure 17.7). Before then, people from France, the German states, and elsewhere were interested in Britain's economic wonders. Some traveled to Britain to copy machines, and others enticed British technicians and capital to their own countries. A few modern industrial shops and machines sprang up on the Continent, but overall, agriculture and tradition still dominated economic life there.

After 1830, industrialization spread to certain regions, especially Belgium, northeastern France, the

Governmental aid

northern German states, and northwestern Italy (see Figure 17.7). These areas had plenty of urban laborers, deposits of iron and coal, and developed transportation facilities. Envious of British wealth, pressured by British competition, and recognizing the military potential of cheap iron and rail transportation, continental governments took a more active role in supporting

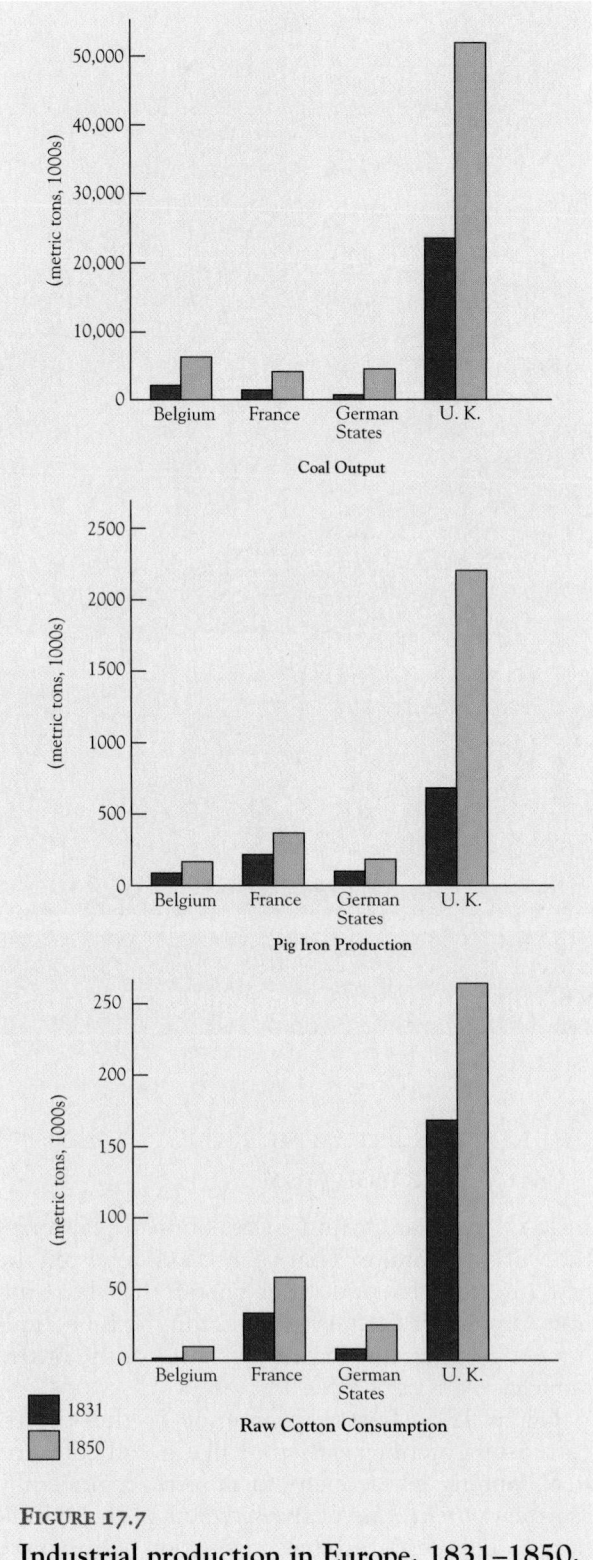

FIGURE 17.7

Industrial production in Europe, 1831–1850.

industrialization than British rulers had. They enacted tariffs to protect their manufacturers from British goods and they subsidized new industries. Railroads, partially financed by governments and foreign capital, led rather than followed the advent of other industries, widening markets and creating demand for coal and iron. These countries could not yet hope to catch up to Britain. At mid-century, a German official complained that Germany would never "be able to reach the level of production of coal and iron currently attained in England." But soon Germany and other nations would manage to industrialize more selectively and quickly, thanks to the groundwork that Britain had laid.

As Map 17.2 indicates, by 1850 large industrial centers had arisen in Belgium, France, and those areas of northern Germany bounded by the 1834 *Zollverein* (a customs union that eliminated tariffs between independent German states). Other regions, particularly around Milan in northern Italy and in the northeastern United States, had also begun to industrialize.

Most of southern, central, and eastern Europe, however, remained virtually untouched by industrial development. Lacking *Remaining traditional economies* well-placed resources, efficient transportation, mobile work forces, commercialized agriculture, and capital for investment, these regions retained their traditional and rural character. The vast majority of people in these areas remained in the countryside tied to subsistence farms or, especially in the east, large agricultural estates. Small villages rather than booming cities were the rule. Wealthy urban elites might purchase manufactured goods from industrial regions to the west, but their own countries could not produce them in the same way. Governments and perhaps a few ambitious and wealthy individuals sometimes imported the latest machines and built a few railroad lines, but these signs of industrialization primarily had symbolic or military value. Relying on old methods of production, merchants in these lands had trouble selling their manufactured goods in international markets. Nations, such as Spain and Russia, that once exported cloth saw their sales dry up in the face of British textiles.

There were a few exceptions in these traditional economies. For example, Austria's Bohemian lands developed a spinning industry, and a few factories sprang up around St. Petersburg and Moscow in Russia. Even so, British technicians and industrialists were often needed to support these limited efforts. On the whole, all these countries would have to wait before experiencing both the benefits and the burdens of the industrial revolution.

Balancing Benefits and Burdens of Industrialization

How did industrialization affect everyday life for Europeans? To answer this complex question, we might first explore the impact of the new machines, factories, and railroads on people's work conditions, home lives, and social relationships. It is also important to ask who received the lion's share of the new wealth.

Foreign observers marveled at Britain's wealth; indeed, to this day many of us associate machines, factories, and railroads with prosperity. *New wealth* Statistics seem to confirm this impression: Britain's national product increased more than threefold between 1780 and 1850. The population in Europe also surged during the same period and absorbed some of the new wealth. Probably thanks to better food supplies (especially cultivation of the potato), earlier marriages, and declining mortality rates, Europe's population bal- *Population growth* looned from fewer than 175 million in 1780 to 266 million in 1850. During this same period, Britain's population more than doubled.

These startling numbers suggest a sense of economic well-being on the part of Europeans, but they also frightened some contemporaries. In his influential *Essay on the Principle of Population* (1798), British economist Thomas Malthus (1766–1834) warned that population growth would inevitably outstrip food supplies. A few years later, another well-known economist, David Ricardo (1772–1823), argued that overpopulation would restrict wages to no more than subsistence levels.

Nevertheless, industrialization generated new wealth so rapidly that personal income rose faster than population growth in these years. Between 1800 and 1850, per-capita income skyrocketed by a whopping 75 percent in Britain. As other countries—such as Belgium, Germany, and France—industrialized, they too enjoyed similar gains. But who exactly was receiving these new riches?

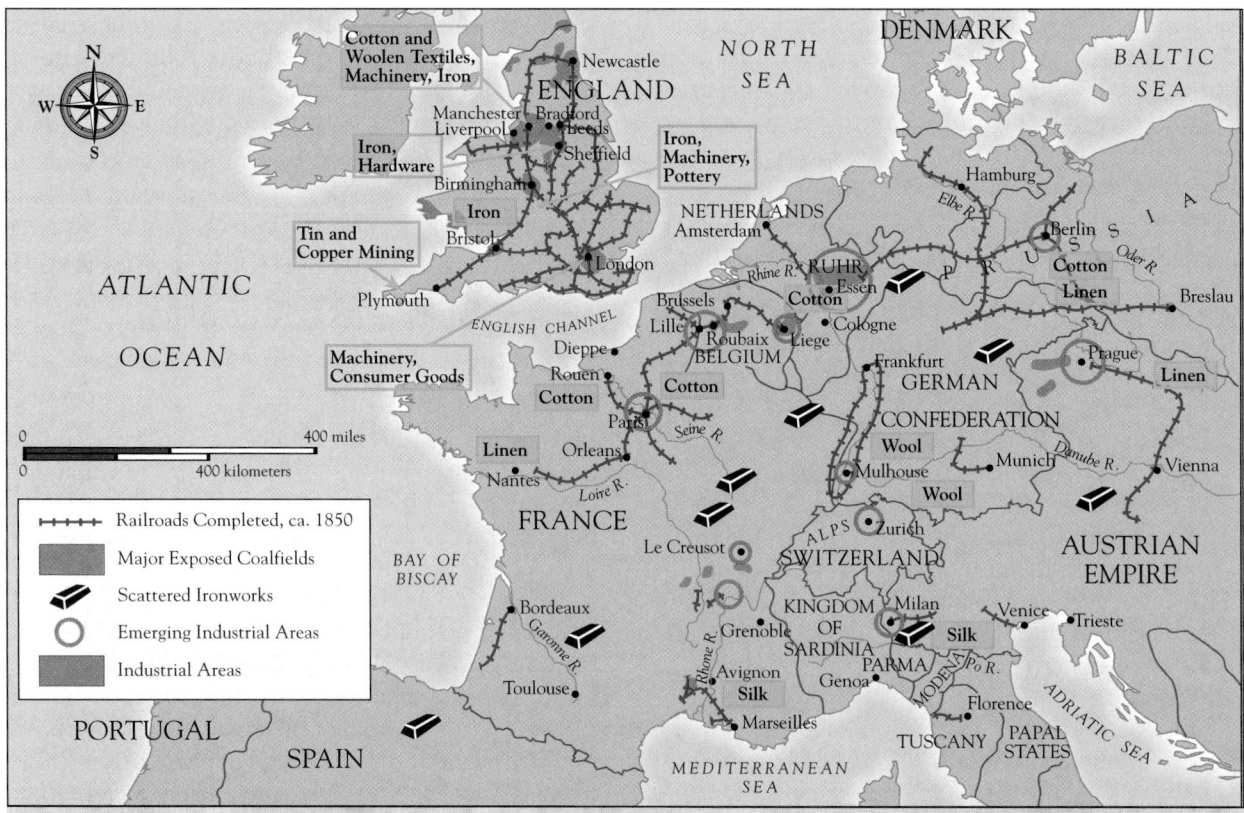

THINKING ABOUT GEOGRAPHY

MAP 17.2 *The Industrial Revolution in Europe, 1850*

This map reveals the spread of industrialization in Europe by 1850. ◼ **Locate** industrial areas. **What** connections are there between these areas, resources—such as coalfields—and access to transportation by water or rail? **Compare** the extent of British industrialization to that in continental nations. ◼ **Notice** the location of railways. **What** does this suggest about the kinds of areas that early railways were intended to serve?

THE MIDDLE CLASS

The middle classes (bourgeoisie), still a minority of the population even in Britain, prospered. The newest, most dynamic group within the middle classes were the industrial entrepreneurs—the factory and mine owners. They gained the most, some amassing enormous fortunes. Many bankers, smaller factory owners, professionals, merchants, and shopkeepers enjoyed more modest gains, as did those who earned interest and profits from investing their savings in industrial and commercial ventures. All investments, however, did not pay off. Some loans were not repaid. People took financial risks, and some lost their bets. Firms failed all the time, and periodic economic downturns spawned a string of losses and bankruptcies.

Still, over the long haul, the middle class as a whole benefited the most from industrialization. As their wealth and numbers grew, so did their prestige, political power, and cultural influence. The middle class, marked by their modest, sober clothing, gradually displaced the once glittering aristocracy who were still tied by tradition to the land. This process unfolded slowly, and some aristocrats and landowners managed to adjust quite well to the change.

❧ THE WORKING CLASSES

The picture is far less clear for the working classes—those who labored in the factories, tended the machines, and toiled in the mines. For people who shifted from the agricultural life or jobs as artisans to work as factory laborers, industrialization may have hurt more than it helped, especially in its earlier decades. These people worked six days a week, 12 to 16 hours a day, earning only subsistence-level wages. William Harter, a British silk manufacturer, justified the long hours to a parliamentary commission: Reducing the hours of labor "would instantly much reduce the value of my mill and machines . . . every machine is valuable in proportion to the quantity of work which it will turn off in a given time." In textile factories, whole families typically labored together. Women's earnings were between one-third and two-thirds of men's, and children's wages were a mere fraction of that. As a result, factory owners employed women and children whenever possible to save money, and they even contracted with orphanages to provide cheap child laborers.

Figure 17.8, an 1853 woodcut, shows the interior of a cotton factory. Here the supervisor of an English cotton factory whips a boy as a woman in tattered clothing looks on. Whipping was one way in which supervisors disciplined child workers to the rhythms of the machinery. In the scene's background, women and men tend the spinning machines while three other men talk, apparently unconcerned by the violence. Middle-class reformers such as Frances Trollope (1780–1863) used pictures like these to decry the harsh treatment of children in the cotton mills. One governmental investigation of child labor described how children "were rendered pale, weak and unhealthy" from "labouring for hours like little slaves." Employers, anxious to keep their machines running and wages low, replied that "it was absolutely necessary that the children should be employed within the mills from six o'clock in the morning till seven in the evening, summer and winter." Document 17.2 (see page D17.1) reveals some of the typical factory rules that employers insisted were necessary to keep their machines running smoothly and profitably.

After the 1820s, factory workers' wages started to climb. By the 1840s or 1850s, they were earning more than their agricultural counterparts. This change did not make them rich, however, for most of them had to spend some two-thirds of their income on food

Factory labor

THE
WHITE SLAVES
OF
ENGLAND.

FIGURE 17.8
Factory labor, 1853.

alone. In 1842, Flora Tristan reported that most workers in English factories "lack clothing, bed, furniture, fuel, wholesome food—even potatoes!" and that their bodies were "thin and frail, their limbs feeble, their complexions pale, their eyes dead."

Money was only one variable in the quality-of-life equation. Industrial workers faced job insecurity, physical dangers, and painful changes unique to their way of life. The worst insecurity centered on employment itself. Even in good times, some firms failed. During economic downturns and crises, such as the "Great Hunger" of the 1840s, wages plummeted below subsistence levels, and many workers lost their jobs. For these industrial laborers there was no unemployment insurance to turn to, and no

Insecurity

foraging, cottage industry, or gardening that people living in the countryside could resort to in hard times.

The work itself carried a high risk of severe physical injury. Factory owners made no provisions for safety. In cotton factories, children regularly climbed under and on top of the equipment to free jammed machines, collect cotton, and tie broken threads; many young workers suffered terrible injuries to their hands and even lost fingers. Long hours and exposure to chemicals, dust, smoke, and industrial residue all led to ill health. Indeed, industrial populations had a far shorter life expectancy and higher incidence of disease and deformity than rural populations. In the 1840s, the military turned down 90 percent of volunteers from some urban areas for health reasons—double the rate of rejection for rural volunteers.

Risks of injury

Besides job insecurity, injury, and ill health, the new industrial age brought other lifestyle changes that are harder to evaluate. Industrial workers experienced a new rhythm of labor that no longer bore any resemblance to the natural rhythms of daylight and seasonal changes. Now, workers toiled unrelentingly to keep pace with the machines and schedules of the factory owner. Employers and their stewards maintained workplace discipline with fines, curses, and whippings. Children who could not keep up were beaten at times (see Figure 17.8); some were even chained to their machines. There were no slack days, like the traditional Monday of preindustrial times. Wages took the form of cash, which workers had to save and apportion carefully over the week for food and housing despite the temptations of alcohol and other leisure activities. At the end of the long workday, laborers trudged home to poor housing clustered around noisy mills or mine entrances or to cheap, overcrowded rooms and cellars of industrial cities.

Lifestyle changes

The question remains: Did the overall quality of life improve for the working classes in the early decades of the industrial revolution? One way to judge is to ask what would have happened to these people without industrialization. Communal villages and agricultural labor had their advantages. In a widely popular poem, "The Deserted Village," (1770) Oliver Goldsmith lamented the loss of rural life:

Ill fares the land, to hastening ills a prey
Where wealth accumulated . . .
But a bold peasantry, their country's pride
When once destroyed, can never be supplied.

People growing up on farms and in small villages at least had traditions they could rely on. But this traditional life also had its own harsh side. Poverty was no stranger to the countryside, nor was child labor, cold, uncertainty, and squalor in windowless hovels. One contemporary, Frederick Eden, argued that the difficulties experienced by small farmers and villagers were only "temporary" and a small price to pay for "the greater good which may be expected from the improvement." However we evaluate all this, life in the city did give the working class something no one could have foreseen: a new sense of class consciousness, an awareness of their own unique burdens and hardships that emboldened them into action and alarmed the onlooking middle classes.

DEVELOPING WORKING-CLASS CONSCIOUSNESS

Because industrial workers lived in the same areas, labored in the same oppressive buildings, grappled with similar problems, socialized and commiserated together, and joined the same trade or civic organizations, they began to see themselves as a separate class. This sense of solidarity came partly from a tradition among artisans and craftsmen of membership in guilds. Although guilds were made illegal after 1791 and were opposed by middle-class people committed to gaining control over the workplace, other workers' organizations such as fraternal societies, trade organizations, and mutual aid societies persisted. These groups laid the foundation for the emergence of trade unions, made legal (though severely restricted) in England in 1824 and elsewhere after 1850.

Workers' organizations

Figure 17.9, a nineteenth-century trade union membership certificate, reveals the pride and values in union labor during this industrial age. Like most unions of the period, the Associated Shipwright's Society—a British shipbuilders' union—was made up of skilled workers. Toward the top of this membership certificate is a blue shield; above it are two hands clasped in brotherhood, below it are the words, "WE ARE AS ONE." In the center is a construction site where ships are being built. Just above are pictures of ships, particularly the steamships that carried people and commerce throughout the world. On the bottom of the certificate are pictures of some of the typical benefits of union membership, including accident insurance, retirement income, and death payments. By mid-century, labor leaders had formed the beginnings

FIGURE 17.9
Trade Union membership certificate.

where as the industrial revolution spread. In the 1830s, silk workers in Lyons, France, rose up against attempts to lower their pay. In 1836, Spanish workers burned a textile factory in Barcelona. During the 1840s, several governments had to call out troops against strikers.

Most of these efforts brought few concrete results in the period before 1850. In addition to the power wielded by wealthier classes and governments, many internally divisive forces chipped away at the fledgling working-class solidarity. Labor leaders, for example, who usually came from the more skilled trades—the cabinetmakers, printers, tailors, masons, and blacksmiths—tended to look down on unskilled industrial workers. Most women were not invited to join worker organizations, though they forged some of their own trade associations. Other loyalties based on religion, region, trade, or even neighborhood undermined worker unity. Sometimes the only connection holding laborers together was a sense of shared problems, the belief that workers had a right to a "just wage," and the impression that their employers were exploiters rather than economic partners.

Despite the forces dividing them, workers' sense of themselves as a separate, unique class strengthened over time. Increasingly, members of the middle class began to see them as dangerous and even savage. As we will see in following chapters, with the sharpening of working-class consciousness, the power of the traditional artisan groups and the peasantry would decline—quickly in the decades after 1850, especially in highly industrialized places such as Britain, Belgium, and parts of Germany. The process would unfold more gradually in moderately industrialized places, such as France, and slowly in most of southern and eastern Europe.

For good or ill, industrialization was transforming everyday life across Europe. The economic and human balance shifted from the countryside to the city. Now the dramatic social transformations took place in the growing urban centers where, as one young worker described London in the 1820s, "a wilderness of human beings" lived.

Life in the Growing Cities

The unprecedented growth of cities from 1780 to 1850 stemmed from a combination of forces. Population was increasing in both urban and rural areas. Enclosures of

of national unions, such as the Grand National Consolidated Trades Union in Britain in 1834, the National Trades Union in the United States in 1834, and the General Workers' Brotherhood in Germany in 1848.

Sometimes workers turned to violence against what they saw as threats from industrialization by destroying the new machines. After 1811, English hand weavers, losing their work to the new power looms, went on rampages, smashing the machines to pieces or campaigning to get rid of them. Glove makers, too, destroyed the new stocking frames that threatened their jobs. These forms of protest came to be known as Luddism in honor of a legendary (and perhaps fictitious) leader, Ned Ludd. The British Parliament quickly named industrial sabotage a capital offense and heavily suppressed the violence. Nevertheless, sporadic episodes of violence continued to erupt for several years, not only in Britain but else-

Luddism

land by market-oriented landowners that dispossessed individuals of their small farms and communities of their commons further uprooted rural families. These pressures pushed people from the land. At the same time, the cities, with their promise of jobs and the lure of beer halls and theaters, attracted people in droves. Industrial towns sprang up where none had existed before. Towns ballooned into cities, and already large cities grew even more imposing. Some of the most spectacular urban growth happened in industrial cities, such as Manchester, which expanded from 25,000 in 1772 to 367,000 in 1850; and Birmingham, Leeds, and St. Etienne in France, which more than tripled in size. Other already substantial cities, such as London and Paris, became increasingly crowded and sprouted new suburbs.

Urban growth

Most cities flourished through industrial activity, such as mining and manufacturing. Other areas scarcely touched by industrialization, such as Naples, St. Petersburg, and Vienna, also grew dramatically through the expansion of governmental bureaucracies and traditional commerce.

The Promise and Pitfalls of Work in the Cities

Industry, however, had the strongest pull. It inevitably attracted new commerce and gave rise to a broad range of consumer and service needs. Women flocked to the textile factories, but even more women living in the cities worked as domestics. Many young women came for what jobs they could find, perhaps hoping to send home part of their pay and still save enough to start a new life. The building trades drew growing numbers of men, who sometimes left their wives and children in the countryside to survive on a patch of land and dwindling cottage industry employment. Many men periodically returned to the countryside, particularly in winter when construction slowed, or during planting and harvest times.

Living with Urban Growth

Industrialization and urbanization also altered the landscape that people traveled through to reach the cities. Forests shrank as people cut down more and more trees for construction of cities, mines, factories, and railroads. The same mines and railroads cut scars into the land, and the cities and factories ate up rural landscapes. Rivers once fit for fish or drinking became polluted with industrial and human wastes.

Approaching the cities, travelers saw smoke in the air from the dirty coal fires used to heat buildings and from the engines of industry. In the city, and particularly in the poor working-class areas, the air smelled foul, for there were no modern sewers, sorely inadequate toilet facilities, and not enough clean water. Garbage and animal waste collected in the streets until heavy rains washed them away. In Manchester, only two-thirds of the houses had toilets, and many of those flushed into inadequate cesspools. Human and animal waste mixed in rivers that people used for drinking water. Charles Dickens' description of the fictionalized Coketown in his novel *Hard Times* (1854) would have struck a familiar chord for nineteenth-century travelers to Britain's industrial cities: "It was a town of machinery and tall chimneys, out of which interminable serpents of smoke trailed themselves for ever and ever. . . . It had a black canal in it, and a river that ran purple with ill-smelling dye, and vast piles of buildings full of windows where there was a rattling and a trembling all day long, and where the piston of the steam-engine worked monotonously up and down."

Environmental changes

Overwhelmed by these surroundings, newcomers to the cities tended to settle in areas where they knew someone else. Whole neighborhoods grew up populated by people who had come from the same rural region. This tendency led to a sense of segregation and separate identities within the cities, as people familiar with one another clustered together.

Few neighborhoods were planned. Indeed, the expansion of most cities became increasingly uncontrolled. The rampant growth created far more problems for the working class than for anyone else. The middle classes, for example, most likely lived in lower-floor apartments in the more desirable sections of town and had the benefit of some running water. They also could afford to employ servants. It was in the working-class sections and poverty-stricken areas that the social ills and squalor of the age reached their worst levels. As the manufacturer and socialist Frederich Engels (1820–1895) described, "The houses are packed from cellar to attic and they are as dirty inside as outside." In the Irish quarter of London, as many as 38 people crowded into small buildings down narrow alleys where the walls were crumbling, and "piles of refuse and ashes lie all over the place and the slops thrown out into the street collect in pools which emit a foul stench." In the bad

Different neighborhoods

quarters lived "the poorest of the poor. Here the worst-paid workers rub shoulders with thieves, rogues and prostitutes."

Document 17.3 (see page D17.2) describes conditions where poor workers lived. Figure 17.10, a mid-nineteenth-century woodcut by the French artist Gustave Doré (1832–1883), also portrays the squalor and crowding of a London slum. In the center, a young child carries a baby, perhaps because her mother is working. Around her in the alley, dejected men, women, and children stand listlessly. Dark tenements tower over them, and laundry sags from clotheslines. Though criticized for overdramatizing the plight of the poor, Doré effectively conveys the anguish of unemployment, poverty, and crowding marring this rich city. As this and other works by novelists such as Charles Dickens, Elizabeth Gaskell, Frances Trollope, and Honoré de Balzac showed, the burgeoning cities were fostering a whole set of social concerns.

Worrying about Urban Society: Rising Crime

One of those social concerns centered on patterns of criminal behavior. People in the upper classes complained about crime and the social disorder it implied. Had cities become hotbeds of crime, as some middle-class observers claimed, or were these critics simply overly worried about their own safety and well-being?

Crime certainly plagued people in the West long before the industrial revolution. In rural areas, along highways, and in the preindustrial cities of Europe, crimes ranging from pickpocketing to murder occurred all too frequently. Professional thieves reportedly ran rampant in Germany, England, and France in past centuries.

In the early stages of industrialization, theft and robbery in particular did rise in the cities. Crowds provided prime opportunities for pickpockets. In urban taverns and dance halls, men sometimes fell into violent brawling, sometimes over women. In these establishments, alcohol flowed freely and almost certainly played a role in outbreaks of fighting. The widening gaps between rich and poor and the desperation of living in hard times also made tempers short. Finally, the anonymity of life in the city and the tempting array of luxury items to steal made crime harder to resist.

Whether justified by the realities of more crime or not, the specter of urban crime and fear of disorder prompted new efforts to improve law enforcement. In

FIGURE 17.10
Gustave Doré, *A London Slum.*

1828, under the leadership of Robert Peel, Parliament passed a law establishing the first modern police force in London. Peel's
Crime and law enforcement
new police, called "Bobbies" in his honor, emphasized regular patrols by uniformed officers as a way to deter crime and present a visual image of security. Both the middle and the working classes accepted the Bobbies, in part because the police were not allowed to be engaged for political purposes such as domestic espionage, and in part because people saw them as the first line of defense against all disorder. By the early 1830s, there were some 3,000 uniformed officers in the force.

The frightening consequences of rapid urbanization were becoming all too apparent. Year by year, the cities grew more densely packed and seemingly more dangerous. In bad times, they teemed with desperate people hoping to find jobs; in good times, they drew even more people eager to take advantage of the available work and other opportunities. Contemporaries associated the cities with overcrowding, filth, crime, moral degeneracy, and an unruly working class. "They [the working class] live precisely like brutes . . . they eat, drink, breed, work and die," complained a middle-class British observer in 1850. "The richer and more intelligent classes are obliged to guard them with police." Perhaps most disturbing, however, was the disease and death that haunted urban centers.

Public Health and Medicine in the Industrial Age

People had good reason to fear for their health and safety in the growing cities, especially in the poorer sections of town. On average, city-dwellers fell ill more often and died at a far earlier age than their rural counterparts. Within the cities, the poor lived half as long as the rich.

Industrialization itself was dangerous. The new machines maimed factory workers, and cave-ins, floods, and explosions killed miners. Various diseases stemmed directly from mining and manufacturing. Coal miners became ill and died from black-lung disease. Cotton workers developed brown-lung disease. In textile factories, women suffered particularly high mortality rates. Metalworkers, especially grinders, developed lung diseases from inhaling shavings. Poisonings from mercury, lead, and phosphorus used in industrial processes also increased.

THE DANGER OF DISEASE

The greatest danger came from infectious diseases. They were the great causes of sickness and death before the nineteenth century, and the rapid growth of crowded cities that lacked sanitation facilities made matters worse. People living in working-class quarters and urban slums were most vulnerable. Tuberculosis and diphtheria thrived in the most heavily populated areas and killed millions during the nineteenth century.

Worse, plagues periodically swept through cities. Cholera epidemics struck Europe several times, causing great panic as people in city after city awaited the arrival of the illness (see Map 17.3). Suggested remedies included taking several measures to restore warmth to the body, giving laudanum (opium dissolved in alcohol), and seeking medical aid. In 1831 alone, cholera killed some 100,000 in France and 50,000 in England.

People disagreed about the causes of diseases. Some observers blamed illnesses on physical weakness and immorality of individuals. In
Causes of disease
these critics' view, disease was rooted in inferior genetic background, overindulgence, degenerate lifestyle, poor hygiene, and irresponsibility. Only self-help could solve the problem, they argued.

Other commentators and some doctors theorized that disease spread through contagion—that people caught diseases from one another. This theory had more to do with magic, belief in the devil, or a desire to keep the ill out of sight than any notion of modern germ theory. It seemed to explain sexually transmitted diseases like syphilis, but could not answer the question of why some people contracted various diseases while others did not. In these commentators' minds, quarantine offered the best solution to fighting contagious diseases.

Most doctors eventually concluded that disease stemmed less from personal contact than from environmental forces. They believed in "miasma," the centuries-old notion that people caught diseases by breathing fumes given off by human waste, rotting vegetables, decaying flesh, marshes, or stagnant ponds. They also blamed poor diets for weakening resistance to these sources of disease. In a widely respected 1840 study, the French physician Louis Villermé attributed the prevalence of disease in the working-class slums of Lille to the cellars and crowded rooms where "the air is never renewed," where "everywhere are piles of garbage, of ashes, of debris from vegetables picked up from the streets, of rotten straw," where "one is exhausted in these hovels by a stale, nauseating, . . . odor of filth, odor of garbage." This helped him and others explain why people living in barracks, workhouses, and the worst parts of cities more often fell ill and died.

SEEKING MEDICAL CARE

None of these theories about disease aided individuals seeking medical care. Doctors may have been

Doctors well-meaning, but in 1850, anyone visiting a doctor was more likely to be hurt than helped. Most people consulted physicians reluctantly and had little trust in the power of treatments or medicine. To our twentieth-century sensibilities, medicine in the

early 1800s can indeed seem quite alarming. To alleviate a fever, for example, doctors often turned to traditional cures such as initiating bloodletting by opening a vein or applying leeches to the skin, or they recommended laxatives to purge the "bad humors" and fluids from the body. Physicians routinely prescribed pills that at best did nothing and more likely contained toxic substances such as mercury. Frequently, the addictive drug laudanum was suggested for the treatment of pain, sleeping problems, difficulties with children, and a variety of other complaints. Such treatments more often led to fluid depletion, poisoning, and addiction than any improvement of the patient's condition.

More benignly, doctors might recommend fresh-air cures or "taking the waters" at health spas. Many of the wealthy traveled to coastal resorts and centers in Caldas da Rainha in Portugal, Bath in England, and Baden Baden in Germany for these health cures. They may have gained some temporary relief from conditions such as arthritis, but they more likely enjoyed the lively social events and casinos that also attracted them to these spas.

Figure 17.11, an 1820 print by the French artist Caroline Naudet (1775–1839), reveals popular attitudes toward physicians. Titled *Journey of a Dying Man to the Other World,* the print depicts a wealthy doctor in black robes leading a procession that includes a dying man, a clergyman pointing up, a surgeon with a fluttering bat over his head, a sinister-looking apothecary carrying an enema device, and an undertaker. The solemn physician carries a banner that describes the traditional treatment for diseases: "To give a clyster [enema], after that to bleed, finally to purge."

Many sufferers looked for treatments opposed by ordinary doctors to cure their ailments. Homeopathy, which emphasized *Alternative medicine* the use of herbal drugs and natural remedies, gained in popularity during the period. Other options—from vegetable laxatives, claimed to be effective for all

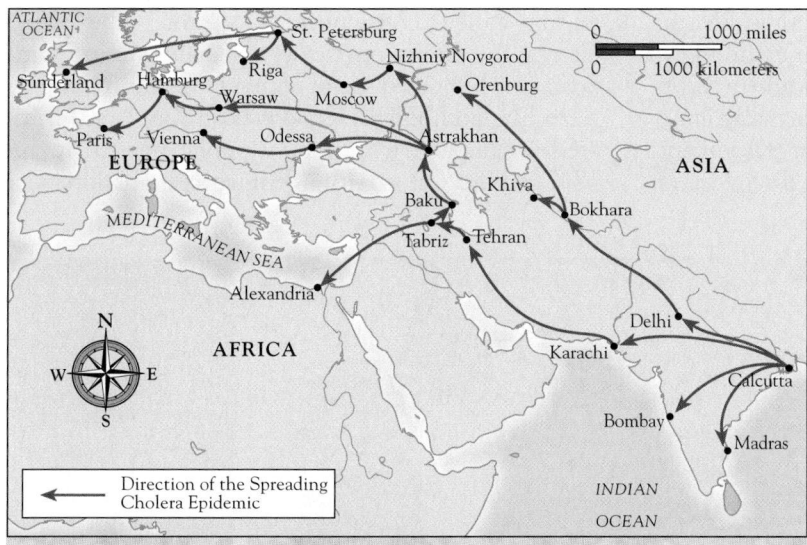

THINKING ABOUT GEOGRAPHY

MAP 17.3 *The Spread of a Cholera Epidemic*

This map shows the spread of a cholera epidemic, which originally broke out in eastern India in 1817 and struck France and England so hard in the 1830s. ✒ **Notice** how, over time, the epidemic spread north and west. **Consider** what this reveals about the growing connections between the Western and non-Western worlds.

ills, to faith healers—saw wide use. These alternatives at least gave sufferers a sense of controlling their own health.

As for surgery, people turned to this option only as a last resort. Surgical methods became safer in the *Surgery* first half of the nineteenth century, but anesthesia and antiseptics still lay in the future. Those who managed to survive the pain of an operation faced a likelihood of dying from an infection afterward.

PROMISING DEVELOPMENTS FOR PUBLIC HEALTH

Despite all the dangers, the period had a few bright spots for the future of public health. Improvements in diet probably held the most promise. Many nutritious foods had become more available than ever, especially potatoes, which were an affordable, rich source of vitamin C and minerals; dairy products, which helped newborns survive infancy and childhood; and meat, which contained high-grade proteins. Inexpensive cotton underwear, thanks to the new cotton mills, kept people warmer and cleaner than before. The smallpox vaccine, developed during the eighteenth century and made into a safe form in 1796 by Edward Jenner in England, would virtually erase a disease that had once afflicted almost 80 percent of Europeans and killed millions. The discovery of

anesthetics—nitrous oxide and, after 1846, ether and chloroform—began to make surgical trauma bearable.

Other developments showed some potential as well. Following the lead of a small group of influential French physicians, European doctors applied scientific methods to medicine and made great strides in pathology and physiology. *New developments in medicine* Hospitals proliferated and increasingly became places to observe the sick and gather information. New laboratories allowed doctors to conduct more experiments. Professional organizations and educational institutions for doctors and nurses formed, and governments, particularly in France, began taking some responsibility for medical education and licensing.

Many doctors no longer relied solely on a patient's description of the problem. Physical examinations became common—feeling the pulse, sounding the chest, taking the blood pressure, looking down the throat. Some doctors used the new stethoscope, which became a crucial tool for diagnosing bronchitis, pneumonia, and pulmonary tuberculosis (commonly called consumption). Among the upper classes, the family physician was even gaining some favor as a respected social contact and confidant.

In England, Edwin Chadwick (1800–1890) initiated a campaign to improve public health. In his 1842 report for a parliamentary commission, *The*

OLC

FIGURE 17.11
Caroline Naudet, *Journey of a Dying Man to the Other World,* 1820.

Sanitary Condition of the Laboring Population of Britain, he emphasized that the accumulation of human and animal waste near people's dwellings was a crucial cause of disease. He proposed a system of underground tunnels that would allow constantly running water to carry waste out of the city.

Nevertheless, the gains from these promising new developments would not come until the second half of the nineteenth century. In Britain, one of every three people still died of contagious diseases in the decades surrounding 1850. Health, therefore, remained a great public and private concern. It was not the only concern that crossed the lines between public and private life, however. The day-to-day events in everybody's lives, whether in illness or health, unfolded within a crucial setting: the family. In this period of industrialization and urbanization, the family as an institution and the roles within it began to shift in the face of enormous economic and social pressures.

Family Ideals and Realities

The ways that people come together into families and the roles they play in their families usually evolve slowly, if at all. During this period, however, the middle class redefined accepted notions of the family, and working-class families struggled under the new pressures beleaguering them. In subtle but important ways, family ideals and realities were changing.

MIDDLE-CLASS IDEALS: AFFECTION, CHILDREN, AND PRIVACY

With their numbers, wealth, and status in urban societies rising, the middle class not only developed its own ideas about what the proper family should be; it propagated those ideas as the norm for everyone else. The result was an evolution of, rather than a break from, old notions about the family. Compared with families of earlier times, the ideal middle-class family emphasized emotional bonds, attention to children, and privacy.

People were supposed to marry because of affection, love, and emotional compatibility. Social rank and wealth remained important, but these values exerted less influence than they had in the past. Love could bridge social and economic gaps. Indeed, one of the great themes in the flood of new novels that appeared during the nineteenth century centered on this very conflict: the tension between love and money in marriage. In stories that ended happily, love won out—though most characters in these plots never were relegated to a life of poverty as a consequence of their choice.

Marriage

The new middle-class family was smaller and more child-centered than before. Europeans were choosing to limit the size of their families, and by mid-century this preference led to declining rates of population growth. Women gave birth to fewer children—two or three rather than the five or six of an earlier era—and more infants than ever survived the first, riskiest years of life. Unlike workers and peasants, middle-class parents did not have to view their children as economic assets—as hands to work the fields, help with the crafts, or labor in the factories. Wealthier urban parents could afford to raise perhaps just two or three children as fulfilling products of a good home. More than ever, children came to be seen as innocent, impressionable, vulnerable persons who should be separated from the corrupting influences of adult society. Mothers and fathers began investing more time, effort, and other resources in child rearing. Boys, especially, needed training and education designed to ensure their success as adults in the changing urban world. To arm them with these essentials, parents extended the time period of childhood and economic dependence. All this required planning and intensified emotional ties between parents and children. Parents increasingly centered their attention and family activities on children.

Family size

Children

More than ever, mothers and fathers idealized their home as a private "haven in a heartless world," separate from and above the world of paid work. The home represented the reward for competing on the job—a protected, glorified place for a satisfying personal life. There husband and wife could enjoy the delights of material possessions and, hopefully, the rewarding intimacy of family life. As indicated by the growing number of popular books by authors such as Jane Austen (1775–1817), Mary Ann Evans (1819–1880) (writing under the pen name George Eliot), and Charlotte Brontë (1816–1855), home was a setting of many appealing, moralizing dramas where the virtues of prudence, love, sacrifice, self-reliance, and persistence could usually overcome all obstacles.

The home

SEPARATE SPHERES: CHANGING ROLES FOR MIDDLE-CLASS WOMEN AND MEN

With the rise of industrialization and urban life, the roles of middle-class husbands and wives grew more and more separate. In the seventeenth and eighteenth centuries, most middle-class families had worked together as one economic unit—sharing the responsibilities of running a shop or business and living near their place of work in back rooms, upstairs, or next door. During the nineteenth century, the tasks assigned to men and women, and the private world of home and the public place of paid work, became increasingly distinct. As the locus of work shifted from the home to the factory, store, or office, women lost their traditional employments that contributed to the family economy. Paid employees working outside the home now occupied the role previously played by women who had run thriving family businesses. The new economic growth also allowed middle-class families to afford the homes, servants, and leisure previously reserved for the elite. Eventually, the ability of middle-class women to devote more time to their homes and families without having to do paid work, and to hire servants to lighten domestic burdens, became symbols of social success. The home became women's sphere, and within the home, child rearing began requiring far more maternal attention than ever. As the task of raising children and socializing them with the values and training needed for success expanded, so did the responsibilities of motherhood. Becoming "rational mothers," fully able to meet the new demands of child rearing, turned into a revered duty.

The man was supposed to be the respected economic provider who operated primarily in his sphere: *The man's sphere* the competitive world of work outside the home. He was expected to behave in an authoritative, competent, and controlled manner. These qualities reflected the legal and economic realities of the time. Under British common law and the Napoleonic Code on the Continent, for example, a man had legal authority over his wife and children. He also had control over his wife's personal property as well as over any money earned by her. Furthermore, only men could vote. Most positions in the middle-class world of work were reserved for men. Those jobs usually required specialized skills in plan-

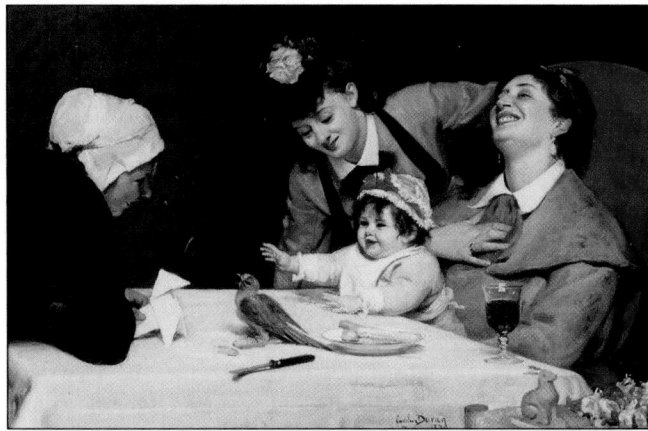

FIGURE 17.12
Carolus Duran, *The Merrymakers.*

ning and information managing—abilities that came primarily from formal schooling. Young men were more likely than women to receive a formal education in areas of study such as accounting or law. Through apprenticeships and clerkships in commerce, industry, or finance, men also found many opportunities to equip themselves for success in the growing industrial-urban economy.

Women faced a very different set of cultural expectations. A host of marriage manuals, medical tracts, advice books, and religious dictates reminded women that their place was *The woman's domestic sphere* within the domestic sphere. A woman should provide emotional support for her husband and cultivate a virtuous home environment to counteract the amoral, competitive marketplace. She should care for the children, make sure the house was clean and the meals served, supervise domestic servants (a requirement for any middle-class home), and manage other domestic tasks from sewing to administering household accounts.

In the mid-nineteenth-century painting shown in Figure 17.12, Carolus Duran depicts two middle-class women at home. The center of the women's attention, and the painting, is a playful child sitting on her mother's lap and reaching for a pet bird or figurine. Across the table from the two well-dressed women, a maid or house servant leans toward the child with a folded paper figurine, perhaps in mock play with the bird. On the lower right are more petlike figurines.

Indeed, middle-class families often considered pets as much a part of domestic life as the food and drink on the table.

In some ways, a middle-class woman's domestic sphere extended outside the home. She might manage the family's social life, for example, or lead in religious matters. If she had the time and means, she might also participate in philanthropic activities, social movements such as temperance or the abolition of slavery, and certain cultural events—but only as long as these activities added to her image as virtuous, dutiful, maternal, supportive, and sensitive. These activities put women in a position of power as representatives of the family in religious, social, and cultural matters and often gave them the last word on such matters within the family.

Involvement in politics was out of the question for most women. A few middle-class women joined movements to gain political and legal rights, but their efforts did not lead to real reforms during this period. Nor did paid work fit the domestic image. Although a woman might serve without wages as a clerk or secretary in her husband's store or office, paid work outside the home was considered inappropriate and generally not available to married women. Even for unmarried women, only occupations directly connected to the domestic role, such as governess, elementary schoolteacher, lady's companion, or seller of women's clothing were deemed acceptable. There were exceptions, especially in cultural fields such as painting and writing, but most people raised a skeptical, disapproving eyebrow at women who had such careers.

At home, a wife was expected to be the counterpart to her controlled, strong husband. "In every thing . . . that women attempt, they should show their consciousness of dependence" on men, explained Elizabeth Poole Sandford in her widely read book, *Woman in her Social and Domestic Character* (1842). Law hindered most married women from acquiring economic independence and generally placed them, as well as children, under the formal power and protection of men. Women were to be emotional and even frail, and therefore capable of only domestic tasks. The training of young women reinforced these qualities. Instead of a secondary schooling or professional education, women's formal training focused on religion, music, and perhaps languages. Any other skills a young woman might need, she picked up at home.

Educators and scientists generally agreed that women were ill suited for occupations outside the home and that they lacked the emotional control, mental acuity, and assertiveness of men. Doctors usually held the same views, and even believed that menstruation incapacitated women and that women had no interest in sex. Clothing, too, emphasized this vision of women's proper role. Middle-class husbands wore prudent and practical clothing for the world of work—trousers and jackets in modest black or gray. Their wives endured tight corsets and full decorative skirts more suited for display than action.

In short, the middle-class ideal was a small, private family bonded by love and authority. In such a family, the wife and husband willingly fulfilled the expected roles of their separate spheres. Families measured their success in achieving this ideal by the luxury items they bought, collected, and self-consciously displayed; by the accomplishments of their children; by how well their lives matched the uplifting dramas that the novels and paintings of the day depicted; and by their participation in appropriate social, religious, and philanthropic activities.

Middle-class success is well illustrated by the economic and social rise of wealthy commercial and industrial families such as the Cadburys (see Biography). The 1824 drawing by E. Wall Cousins in Figure 17.13 shows the *Middle-class success* still-modest Cadbury shops on Bull Street in Birmingham. To the right is Richard's original dry-goods (linens) store; to the left, his son John's tea and coffee shop. The plate-glass windows and the dress of people on the street indicate the store's intention to appeal to middle-class and wealthy clients. Above are the family's apartments, which include plants and pets. When the business expanded, the Cadburys moved away from this store to a suburban house, with separate nursery and schoolrooms for the children. The idea of separate rooms for children, and for eating, cooking, reading, and socializing was new and reflected the growing wealth of the middle class and how the idea of differentiation—separate areas for different tasks and the division of labor—already spreading in the industrial world affected the domestic sphere as well.

WORKING-CLASS REALITIES

The middle class assumed that its vision of the proper family served as the standard for all. However, this vision did not fit the urban and industrial realities facing the far more numerous working classes.

Biography

THE CADBURYS

Consider why the Cadburys benefited so greatly from the industrial revolution and how members of the family exhibited typical nineteenth-century middle-class values.

By the late eighteenth century, the Cadburys were a well-established Quaker family of shopkeepers in western England. Young Richard Tapper Cadbury used his father's connections to find positions as an apprentice and journeyman to drapers (selling retail cloth and dry goods) in Gloucester and London. In 1794, his father helped him again, giving him money to start his own cloth and dry goods store on a main street in Birmingham, one of Britain's leading industrial cities.

In 1800, Richard, his wife, Elizabeth, and their growing family moved into an apartment above their shop on Bull Street. Middle-class families such as the Cadburys typically lived in the same building as their business until they could afford to buy a separate home.

Elizabeth Cadbury, like most middle-class women of moderate means, worked in the family enterprise but had received no professional training. She picked up skills on the job, helping rather than leading, and taking over for her husband when he was away. As a married woman, Elizabeth had no independent legal identity and could not have owned a business on her own. Formally, their family business belonged to Richard, but like many businesses during the period, it also functioned as an informal partnership between the couple. In addition to working in the business, Elizabeth was also responsible for running the household, which included eight children and young apprentices.

Draper retailers such as the Cadbury family played a major role in the revolution of Britain's textile industries. Like producers, retailers benefited from the new sources of supply and expanding demand for cloth. The Cadbury shop expanded and brought in enough income for Richard and Elizabeth to rent a house and land for a garden on the outskirts of Birmingham in 1812. The younger children, their nurse, and their pets moved there. Elizabeth and her older daughters traveled back and forth, managing the two households.

A Rising Middle-Class Family

Richard and Elizabeth's sons eventually apprenticed in retail businesses in different cities—Benjamin as a draper, John as a tea and coffee dealer. The daughters had no such training. Instead they learned what they could from their mother as they helped in the shop, house, and garden.

John (1801–1889) opened a tea and coffee store next door to his parents' shop (see Figure 17.13). He and his first wife, who died in 1828, lived over the shop. When John accumulated enough money, he also opened a plant to manufacture

---

Industrialization pulled many working-class women away from their homes and into factory jobs. *Women workers* Employers preferred to hire women because they worked for lower salaries and seemed more pliable than men. In the early decades, young children often accompanied their mothers, providing even cheaper labor and falling victim to the harsh, disciplined factory environment.

During the 1830s and 1840s, public outcry against child labor (led by middle-class reformers, not the working class) prompted women to leave their younger children at home in care of an older child or neglectful "babyfarmers," women who took in far too many children. Many mothers resorted to drugging their children with laudanum to keep them out of harm's way while the adults were at work.

E. Wall Cousins, *The Cadbury Shops*, 1824.

the cocoa and chocolate for which the family name would become so famous. In 1834, John and his second wife, Candia, moved their home away from the city, with its filth and crowds, to a new, planned middle-class suburb just outside of Birmingham. Candia generally stayed at home, busy with her domestic tasks and gardening, while John rode to town every day to take care of business and political affairs. Candia could not look after the family business as her mother-in-law Elizabeth had, for the demands of child rearing had grown and the training necessary for John's more complex business had increased. John and Candia's spheres were much more distinct that the elder Cadburys' had been.

In 1861, John's sons, Richard and George, took over their father's failing business. They visited a chocolate factory in Holland that was using a new process to transform cocoa beans into cocoa and chocolate. In 1866, they successfully introduced that process into their own factory. This new technique helped them to break the near monopoly that French chocolate products had previously enjoyed in the British market. In the decades that followed, the brothers built Cadbury into a prosperous cocoa and chocolate manufacturing firm. Richard painted the designs for fancy Cadbury chocolate boxes that idealized children and their innocence, using his own children as models.

In 1879, the brothers moved their firm from industrialized Birmingham to a rural site they called Bournville. There they introduced improved conditions for their workers and a private social security program, reforms well ahead of their time. George, holding firmly to the Quaker views of his parents and grandparents, had long taught in a Birmingham "adult school" for workingmen. Concluding that poor housing lay at the root of many social evils, he began building high-quality working-class housing that featured gardens. By 1900, that community included 313 houses and served as a model for British "garden cities" and "garden suburbs."

In 1901, George and members of his family acquired the *London Daily News* and other newspapers, which they used to express their Liberal Party views. By this time, Cadbury, which had grown unevenly from the seeds planted by Richard and Elizabeth in 1794, had become a vast, worldwide company.

Middle-class critics demanded reforms that would limit women's ability to work away from home, although working-class women objected that they had no better alternatives. As one group of women factory workers from Manchester pointed out, "Hand loom has been almost totally superseded by power loom weaving, and no inconsiderable number of females, who must depend on their own exertions, . . . have been forced . . . into the manufactories, from their total inability to earn a livelihood at home." During recessions, women's plight worsened. Employers laid off the more highly paid men first, leaving women with the overwhelming burden of managing both a paid job and all the domestic tasks at home.

Timeline: A Closer Look

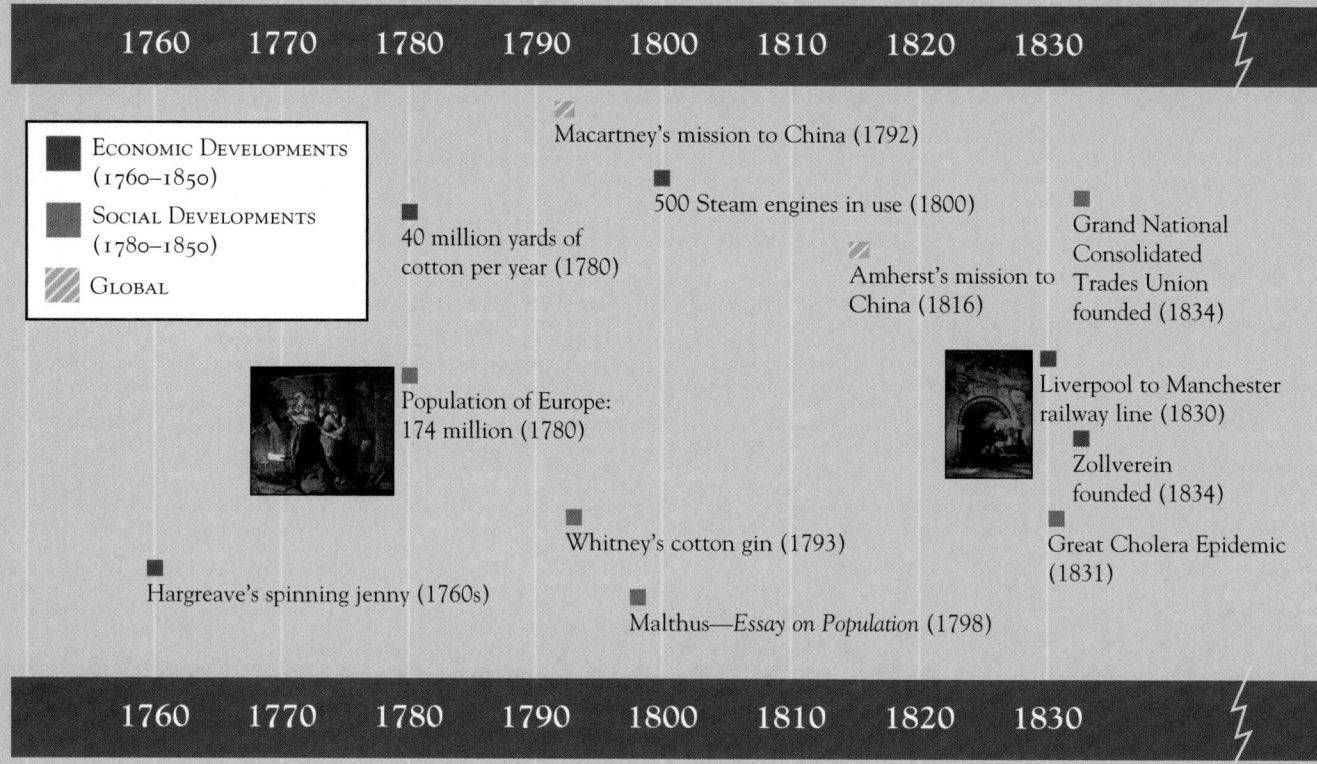

1760　1770　1780　1790　1800　1810　1820　1830

ECONOMIC DEVELOPMENTS (1760–1850)

SOCIAL DEVELOPMENTS (1780–1850)

GLOBAL

Macartney's mission to China (1792)

500 Steam engines in use (1800)

40 million yards of cotton per year (1780)

Amherst's mission to China (1816)

Grand National Consolidated Trades Union founded (1834)

Population of Europe: 174 million (1780)

Liverpool to Manchester railway line (1830)

Zollverein founded (1834)

Whitney's cotton gin (1793)

Great Cholera Epidemic (1831)

Hargreave's spinning jenny (1760s)

Malthus—*Essay on Population* (1798)

1760　1770　1780　1790　1800　1810　1820　1830

Working-class and peasant families were being pulled apart in other ways as well. Adolescent boys left home to seek work in the mines or cities. Daughters, too, sought jobs as factory laborers or as domestics in middle- or upper-class homes. In the cities, women were all the more vulnerable during economic downturns when low-paying jobs disappeared.

PROSTITUTION

Hard times left unmarried and married women alike in particularly desperate straits. To survive, some women turned to prostitution, which grew along with Europe's mushrooming cities. In 1850, there were probably some 30,000 prostitutes in Paris and 50,000 in London. Unemployment and the dangers of solitude were probably the main forces driving women to prostitution. Many prostitutes had come from outside the cities and had no family to help them. Others were out-of-work domestics, seamstresses in need of income during a slow season, daughters of unemployed workers, or women abandoned after being impregnated by masters or lovers. Low wages also led to prostitution; a woman earned as much money in one

night prostituting herself as she could acquire after an entire week of work at the factory.

Many of these women worked as prostitutes for relatively short periods, and only part time. While the work helped them financially, it also exposed them to venereal disease, which ran rampant during this period. Finally, in some people's minds, prostitution linked working-class women to images of urban crime and immorality. To middle-class moralists, prostitutes embodied unrestrained sexuality and therefore were the ultimate outcasts. However, despite its dangers, prostitution would persist as a sign of the difficulties that many working families faced in Europe's growing cities.

STRESS AND SURVIVAL IN THE WORKING CLASSES

The new tensions swirling through working-class family life had severe consequences for some. Peasant, artisan, and working-class families had worked together as economic units for longer than the middle class had, and industrialization and urbanization corroded this unity. The stresses proved so great

1840 1842 1844 1846 1848 1850 1852 1854 1856

Anesthetics become available (Late 1840s)

European Population: 266 million (1850)

Opium War (1839–1841)

Majority in Britain living in cities (1850)

Chadwick Report (1842)

2,000 million yards of cotton per year in Britain (1850)

Over 2,000 miles of railway track in Britain (1850)

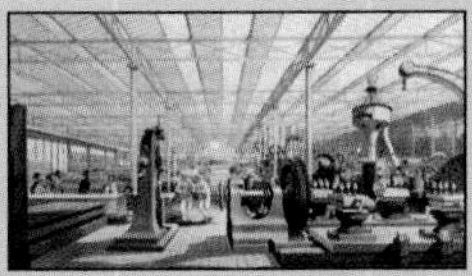

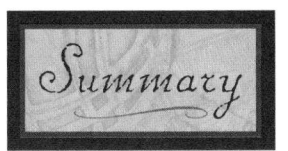

Crystal Palace Exhibition (1851)

1840 1842 1844 1846 1848 1850 1852 1854 1856

that some families broke apart, leaving a growing number of women to work and manage households on their own.

However, the picture was not all bleak. As a rule, the family survived, providing a haven for workers and a home for children. Like peasants' and artisans' families, many working-class families clung to the old putting-out system or the newer piece-work system, in which entrepreneurs distributed jobs, such as tailoring or decorating, to workers at their homes. Unions, better wages, and new social policies would ease the burdens on workers in the decades after 1850. In the end, most families adjusted and found ways to meet the many challenges of the industrial age.

Summary

Industrialization meant unprecedented, sustained economic growth, and it soon became a measure of whether people considered a society "modern" or "traditional." Carrying in its wake fundamental changes in literally all aspects of life, industrialization altered the ways people worked, what they could buy, how they lived their lives, and where they stood on the social ladder. Its railroads, dams, bridges, factories, and mines transformed the land, the rivers, and the air. Nations that industrialized left others behind in the competition for wealth. That wealth was all too easily translated into power, leaving traditional agrarian societies in the West vulnerable to their industrialized neighbors.

The new riches pumped out by the machines of industry also propelled the West into an even stronger position to dominate over unindustrialized, non-Western societies throughout the world. Decade after decade, a widening gap of wealth and power opened up between the industrializing regions of the West and nonindustrializing regions of Asia, Africa, and Latin America.

At the same time, the cities grew. There, old ties to traditional communities and beliefs loosened; long-established religions even lost some of their influence. Despite a host of social problems, the cities had a vibrancy and an image of opportunity that continued to attract people. While some people lost when they migrated to the cities, others gained, whether by hard work, luck, or the advantages of birth. Perhaps life in the countryside, with its slower pace and simpler pleasures, simply could not compete with what the city promised.

Through these decades, most families found ways to adapt to new circumstances. Middle-class families responded to their improving positions by developing a compelling new set of ideals about how men and women should behave. Working-class families did their best to hold themselves together in the face of divisive forces; looking to the future, workers began seeing themselves as a new class of people who just might have the power to determine their own fate.

This growing awareness by both classes added to the fundamental changes being wrought by industrialism. Conflict—whether in an intellectual realm, at the work site, in the courts, or on the barricades—would often be the result. These conflicts, along with those stemming from the French Revolution, would profoundly shape social and political life in the West in the decades to come.

REVIEW, ANALYZE, AND ANTICIPATE

REVIEW THE PREVIOUS CHAPTER

Chapter 16—"Overturning the Political and Social Order"—examined the revolution that transformed France and whose consequences were felt throughout the West. The chapter also focused on the role Napoleon played during that period and the battles he waged throughout Europe until his final defeat in 1815.

1. *Who do you think were the main beneficiaries of the French Revolution and the industrial revolution? Were they the same groups?*

2. *In what ways might the French Revolution and the industrial revolution be related?*

ANALYZE THIS CHAPTER

Chapter 17—"Factories, Cities, and Families in the Industrial Age"—analyzes the industrial revolution and urbanization.

1. *How do you explain why Britain industrialized before other European nations and non-Western societies such as China?*

2. *Compare the consequences of industrialization for the middle class and the working class.*

3. *In what ways did moving from the countryside to the city change people's lives during this period?*

4. *Analyze how the family and ideas about women's and men's roles altered within the middle class. In what ways were circumstances different for working-class families?*

ANTICIPATE THE NEXT CHAPTER

In Chapter 18—"Coping with Change"—we will examine the political developments, theories of change, and revolutionary movements of the period between 1815 and 1850.

1. *What sorts of problems do you think the industrial revolution will pose for governments? What policies might they adopt to solve those problems?*

2. *Consider which ideas about the industrial revolution might be favored by people sympathetic to the workers. What about people sympathetic to middle-class employers?*

BEYOND THE CLASSROOM

THE INDUSTRIAL REVOLUTION BEGINS

Brown, Richard. *Society and Economy in Modern Britain, 1700–1850.* New York: Routledge, 1991. Argues that Britain's industrial development was gradual and quite regionally varied.

Landes, David. *The Wealth and Poverty of Nations.* New York: W. W. Norton, 1999. Connects cultures to economic development in a broad international context.

Mathias, Peter. *The First Industrial Nation*, 2nd ed. London: Methuen, 1983. Attempts to account for the origins of industrialization in eighteenth-century Britain and traces its development during the nineteenth century.

O'Brien, Patrick K., and Roland Quinault, eds. *The Industrial Revolution and British Society*. Cambridge: Cambridge University Press, 1993. Essays by noted scholars that stress the origins and consequences of the industrial revolution in Britain.

GLOBAL CONNECTIONS

Pomeranz, Kenneth. *The Great Divergence: China, Europe, and the Making of the Modern World Economy*. Princeton: Princeton University Press, 2000. A bold comparison of economic development in Europe and Asia.

NEW MARKETS, MACHINES, AND POWER

Deane, Phyllis. *The First Industrial Revolution*, 2nd ed. Cambridge: Cambridge University Press, 1979. A respected account of British industrialization and its consequences.

Goodman, Jordan, and Katrina Honeyman. *Gainful Pursuits: The Making of Industrial Europe, 1600–1914*. London: Edward Arnold, 1988. A wide-ranging examination.

Landes, David S. *The Unbound Prometheus: Technological Change and Industrial Development in Western Europe from 1750 to the Present*. London: Cambridge University Press, 1969. A classic treatment of technological development in a broad social and economic context.

Mokyr, Joel. *The Lever of Riches: Technological Creativity and Economic Progress*. New York: Oxford University Press, 1992. Attempts to explain why technological creativity occurred in some places and not in others.

INDUSTRIALIZATION SPREADS TO THE CONTINENT

Pollard, Sidney. *Peaceful Conquest: The Industrialization of Europe, 1760–1970*. Oxford: Oxford University Press, 1981. Charts the process of industrialization as it spread from Britain to the European continent.

Sylla, Richard, and Gianni Toniolo, eds. *Patterns of European Industrialization*. London: Routledge, 1993. A comparative analysis of industrialization in Europe.

BALANCING THE BENEFITS AND BURDENS OF INDUSTRIALIZATION

Chinn, Carl. *Poverty Amidst Prosperity: The Urban Poor in England, 1834–1914*. Manchester: Manchester University Press, 1995. Focuses on the poverty created by the industrial revolution.

Nardinelli, Clark. *Child Labor and the Industrial Revolution*. Bloomington, IN: Indiana University Press, 1990. A sympathetic portrait of the topic.

Thompson, E.P. *The Making of the English Working Class*. New York: Random House, 1966. A remarkable book of sympathy and insight that has been hugely controversial and influential.

LIFE IN THE GROWING CITIES

Lawton, Richard, and Robert Lee, eds. *Urban Population Development in Western Europe from the Late Eighteenth to the Early Twentieth Century*. Liverpool: Liverpool University Press, 1989. Examines urban growth throughout western Europe.

Traugott, Mark, ed. *The French Worker: Autobiographies from the Early Industrial Era*. Berkeley, CA: University of California Press, 1993. Presents a working-class perspective on the effects of industrialization.

PUBLIC HEALTH AND MEDICINE IN THE INDUSTRIAL AGE

Porter, Roy. *A Medical History of Humanity*. New York: W.W. Norton & Co., 1998. A wide-ranging and interesting survey that covers the period well.

FAMILY IDEALS AND REALITIES

Davidoff, Leonore, and Catherine Hall. *Family Fortunes: Men and Women of the English Middle Class, 1750–1850*. Chicago: University of Chicago Press, 1987. An interesting analysis of the interaction between gender and class that reconstructs every dimension of middle-class life.

Maynes, Mary Jo. *Taking the Hard Road*. Chapel Hill, NC: University of North Carolina Press, 1995. Examines German and French workers' lives during the industrial revolution.

Tilly, Louise, and Joan Scott. *Women, Work and Family*. New York: Holt, Rinehart and Winston, 1978. A classic study of the family as an economic unit, especially during the first half of the nineteenth century.

For quiz questions that tie the book to the videos and additional primary sources, please go to the Primary Source Investigator CD.

QUIZ

Anton Ziegler, The Barricade in Michaeler Square on the Night of May 26th

This painting by the Austrian artist Anton Ziegler depicts the "glory days" of the 1848 revolutions. In the image, men and women of various classes in Vienna guard a revolutionary barricade made of paving stones, timbers, and carts. Behind the barricade, a community of people stand ready to help one another politely in the common effort (notice the man aiding a woman across a wooden footbridge). The atmosphere has an almost festive quality, and nothing in the picture hints at the violence and loss of life that came with this turbulent year.

CHAPTER 18

Coping With Change

Ideology, Politics, and Revolution, 1815–1850

STUDY • The Congress of Vienna • Ideologies • The Restoration • Revolution and reform • 1848.
NOTICE the sets of beliefs about the world that shaped politics and social action.

Prince Clemens von Metternich (1773–1859), Austria's conservative and powerful minister of foreign affairs, discussed ideas in candlelit salons as easily as he wielded power in somber cabinet meetings. Like other cosmopolitan aristocrats born into traditional eighteenth-century societies, he spoke French as well as the German of his birthplace. In 1820, five years after the fall of Napoleon, he wrote to his ally, Tsar Alexander I (r. 1801–1825) of Russia. "Kings have to calculate the chances of their very existence in the immediate future," he complained. "Passions are let loose and league together to overthrow everything which society respects as the basis of its existence; religion, public morality, laws, customs, rights, and duties, all are attacked, confounded, overthrown, or called to question."

Metternich, Alexander I, and people everywhere were struggling to adjust to the political and social forces unleashed by the French Revolution and Napoleon's domination of Europe. The industrial revolution, wherever it set its roots, spawned another set of problems along with the wealth it created. Together, these waves of change were undermining traditional political, social, and economic orders.

Some, such as Metternich, fought to maintain the old order; others, displaying the "passions" Metternich complained about, fought for all-encompassing reforms. People on all sides turned to ideologies—sets of ideas, attitudes, and beliefs about how the world is and should be—to try to cope with the new realities of Western life in the nineteenth century. One of those realities was the possibility of revolution again raising its unpredictable head. The outcomes of these struggles of ideologies and politics would profoundly shape much of nineteenth-century history.

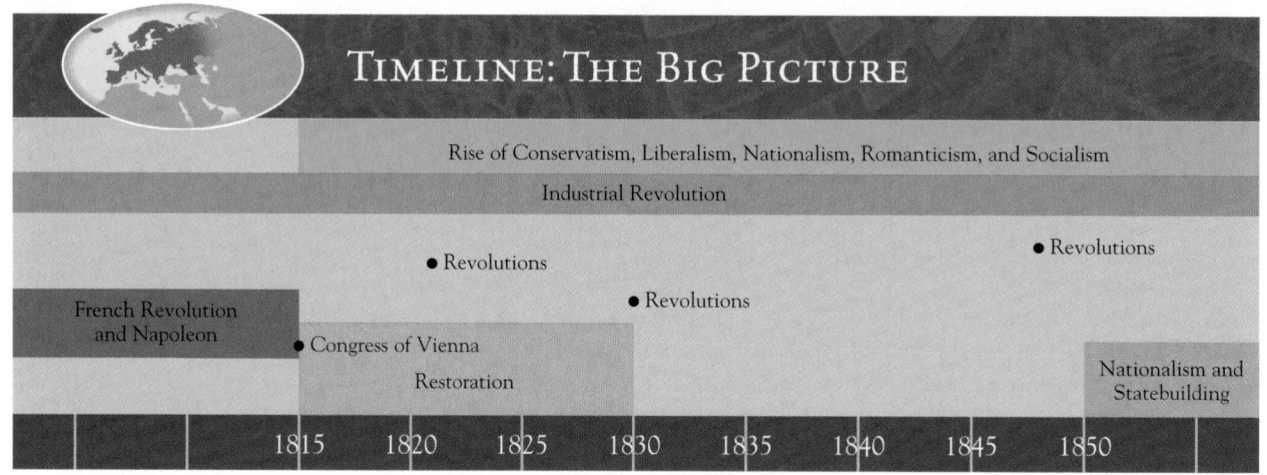

TIMELINE: THE BIG PICTURE

Rise of Conservatism, Liberalism, Nationalism, Romanticism, and Socialism

Industrial Revolution

• Revolutions

• Revolutions

• Revolutions

French Revolution
and Napoleon

• Congress of Vienna

Restoration

Nationalism and
Statebuilding

1815   1820   1825   1830   1835   1840   1845   1850

The Congress of Vienna: A Gathering of Victors

In the autumn of 1814, the leaders of the powers who had finally vanquished Napoleon gathered to redraw territorial boundaries and fashion a lasting peace. The conference also attracted representatives of every state in Europe, hundreds of dispossessed princes, agents of every interest, and adventurers. Nearly everyone who thought he or she was somebody of importance in "high circles" attended. The representatives reveled in the glittering gatherings and entertainments. In addition to the public conferences, many private meetings took place—though just how private remains uncertain, for Austrian spies regularly opened letters and searched wastebaskets. Elsewhere, in newspapers from St. Petersburg, Rome, and Paris to London and even Boston, people closely followed the daily events in the beautiful Austrian capital. Something immensely important and exciting seemed to be unfolding there.

The victors The four major victors over Napoleon—Great Britain, Prussia, Russia, and Austria—set peace terms with France around the time of Napoleon's overthrow in April, and these four dominated the congress. The able Lord Castlereagh (1769–1822) represented Great Britain and the experienced Baron Hardenberg (1750–1822) represented Prussia. Russia's tsar, the unsteady Alexander I, headed his own delegation. The elegant, arrogant Metternich led the Austrian delegation and became the most influential figure of the congress.

Jean-Baptiste Isabey's formal portrait of the principal figures at the Congress of Vienna (Figure 18.1) gives a sense of the seriousness of this event and the ideals that the victors represented. From left to right, Austria's polished Metternich stands before a chair, Great Britain's Castlereagh sits with crossed legs, and the elderly Talleyrand (1754–1838) of France rests with his right arm on the table. In a fine but businesslike eighteenth-century salon, these powerful men are gathered around a table to participate in the reading and signing of crucial documents. Their clothing marks them as members of the aristocracy: almost all the men sport gold trim and knee breeches with high stockings, some wear military coats and carry swords reflecting victory in the field over Napoleon. Most display medals symbolizing their achievements and position. Yet these clothes also hint at change: most of the figures in the painting lack the more elegant clothing and wigs of the eighteenth century. Above the men, as if approving of what they are doing, hangs a symbol of the restoration of the old regime: a portrait of a king draped in regal robes.

Legitimacy and stability As guiding principles in the negotiations, the conferees decided on "legitimacy" and "stability." By *legitimacy* they meant that territories should once more be placed under the control of the old ruling houses of the traditional order. By *stability* they meant establishing and maintaining a balance of power within Europe, with particular focus on restraining France. The main powers agreed that the settlement should apply to all of Europe.

Yet the conferees proved lenient in their settlement toward France. Thanks to the victors' desire to turn France into an ally rather than a resentful enemy and to Talleyrand's diplomatic skills, France, the original force behind all the turmoil, escaped the proceedings with only light penalties. Having already restored the French throne to the Bourbons, the powers merely reduced France roughly to its 1789

FIGURE 18.1

Jean-Baptiste Isabey, *The Congress of Vienna.*

boundaries. Because of Napoleon's 100-day return (see p. 581), they also required France to pay an indemnity of 700 million francs, return stolen art treasures, and submit to occupation by allied forces until the indemnity was paid.

To confine France within its frontiers and discourage future French aggression, the powers established strong buffer states along France's borders. As Map 18.1 shows, Prussia received a *Territorial arrangements* sizable block of territory along the Rhine; the Austrian Netherlands (Belgium) and the Dutch Netherlands were unified; Piedmont-Sardinia in northern Italy was enlarged; and the old monarchy was restored in Spain.

Trading among themselves, the four main powers took new territories. Great Britain gained several strategic islands and colonies, all of which boosted its sea power and overseas dominance. Prussia added some areas in central Europe. Russia acquired control over a reduced, nominally independent Poland, thereby edging farther into the heart of central Europe. Russia also took Finland from Sweden, which in turn got Norway at the expense of Napoleon's ally, Denmark. Austria gained Lombardy and Venetia in northern Italy as well as the permanent presidency over the weak German Confederation—the 39 German states that remained after Napoleon's destruction of the Holy Roman Empire.

Although they displayed little concern for the wishes of the peoples being placed under the control of one power or the other, the conferees did produce a settlement that contributed to a century of freedom

THINKING ABOUT GEOGRAPHY

MAP 18.1 *Europe, 1815*

This map shows Europe after the Congress of Vienna in 1815. ✪ **Compare** this map with that of Napoleon's empire in Chapter 16 (Map 16.4). **What** are the main changes? ✪ **Locate** the enlarged states—the Netherlands, Prussia, and Piedmont-Sardinia. **Why** did the Congress of Vienna strengthen these states? ✪ **Consider** the effect of the settlement on the major European powers. **Did** the settlement severely punish France?

from Europe-wide war. Moreover, thanks to the persistent efforts of the British, the powers agreed in principle to abolish the slave trade. They also achieved—at least temporarily—their conservative goals of promoting legitimacy and stability that meant so much to them.

THE CONCERT OF EUROPE: SECURING THE VIENNA SETTLEMENT

Metternich and his colleagues, pleased with their handiwork, set up the political machinery for perpetuating the Vienna settlement. Con-

The Holy Alliance

veniently at hand was the Holy Alliance, conceived by Alexander I to establish and safeguard the principles of Christianity. Russia, Austria, and Prussia—the three bastions of conservatism—formed the nucleus of this alliance. Though Metternich and professional diplomats put little faith in it, the Holy Alliance did symbolize a commitment to preserving the Vienna settlement. Perhaps more important, it suggested a possible willingness to intervene in other countries in support of its conservative principles.

The Quadruple Alliance, also known as the Concert of Europe, proved a much more earthly agency

The Concert of Europe

for perpetuating the Vienna settlement. Austria, Russia, Prussia, and Great Britain created this military alliance in November 1815 to guarantee the Vienna settlement. The powers agreed to hold periodic meetings to discuss common problems. In 1818, France completed its payment of indemnities and joined the Alliance.

Soon this conservative partnership showed its strength. In 1821 it authorized an Austrian army to put down an insurrection in Naples against King Ferdinand I. The Neapolitan liberal rebels, no match for the Austrian troops, were soon defeated and their leaders executed, imprisoned, or exiled. In 1822 the Alliance, despite Britain's withdrawal, authorized France to intervene against a liberal revolt in Spain. A French army streamed across the Pyrenees and easily crushed the rebellion. That same year, the conservative powers supported Alexander's proposal to send a Russian fleet to help put down the revolt of Spain's Latin American colonies (see Chapter 16).

The great strength of the Alliance, however, remained bound within the European continent. Across the Atlantic Ocean, President Monroe of the United States announced what would come to be called the Monroe Doctrine: The United States would regard any interference on the part of European powers in the affairs of the Western Hemisphere as an "unfriendly act." British support of the doctrine—stemming from Britain's own economic interests in Latin America—killed any further thought of Holy Alliance intervention in the Western Hemisphere, for Great Britain enjoyed unchallenged dominance of the seas.

Ideologies: How the World Should Be

The principles underlying the settlement at Vienna and the international cooperation to enforce it reflected the deep conservatism of Metternich and many others during these years. Their conservatism was more than just a whim or political mood. Under the impact of the French Revolution and the industrial revolution, the centuries-old aristocratic order and agriculturally based society had started to crumble. Intellectuals in particular tried to grasp these changes by exploring ideologies, or sets of beliefs about the world and how it should be. These ideologies exerted immense power. People wrote, marched, fought, and died for them. Indeed, they fueled many of the struggles that would erupt in the years to come and ultimately would shape our very definition of the modern world.

CONSERVATISM: RESTORING THE TRADITIONAL ORDER

The changes initiated during the French Revolution and supported by Enlightenment ideas threatened and even terrified conservatives. They wanted desperately to preserve the traditional way of life. Conservatism provided the ideas to refute Enlightenment and revolutionary principles and all those who stood behind them. At the heart of conservatism lay a belief in order and hierarchy. The social and political order, conservatives believed, should be based on a hierarchy of authoritative institutions whose legitimacy rested on God and tradition. As conservatives saw it, the revolutionary notion of equality was wrong. The elite was equipped to rule; the rest were not. The most formidable enemy was the bourgeoisie, "this intermediary class" ready to "abandon itself with a blind fury and animosity . . . to all the means which seem proper to assuage its thirst for power," according to Metternich. Conservatives also warned that the idea of individualism promoted by the Enlightenment and favored by the rising middle class would fragment society and lead to anarchy. In the mind of a conservative, all change was suspect. If change did come, it should take the form of slow evolution of social and political institutions.

In 1790, the influential Anglo-Irish writer and statesman Edmund Burke (1729–1797), horrified *Burke* with the outbreak of the French Revolution, outlined some of the principles of conservatism (see p. 562). He argued that the revolutionaries' radical reforms based on abstract reason and notions of equality unraveled hard-won victories against savagery: "[I]t is with infinite caution that any man ought to venture upon pulling down an edifice which has answered . . . for ages the common purposes of society." The monarchy and nobility should be preserved because they, like the church, were established links to an organic past and the best hopes for preserving the order necessary for societies to thrive.

The French writers Joseph de Maistre (1753–1821) and Louis de Bonald (1754–1840) represented a later generation of conservative thinkers who proved more rigid and ultraroyalist than Burke. As Document 18.1 *de Maistre and de Bonald* suggests (see page D18.1), they attacked everything about the French Revolution and Enlightenment as contrary to religion, order, and civilization. De Maistre called the French Revolution an "insurrection against God." Both writers argued that authority rightly rests in the monarchy and the church, both of which derive that authority from God. "When monarchy and Christianity are both attacked, society returns to savagery," declared de Bonald. These conservatives felt that deep down, humans were more wicked than good, more irrational than rational. Only the time-tested traditions and institutions could hold the bad impulses of humans in check. All means, including fear and violence, should be used to roll back the changes from the French revolutionary and Napoleonic periods and return to societies dominated by monarchs, aristocrats, and clergy.

Not surprisingly, people from these same three groups found conservatism most appealing. Conservatism also attracted many who believed in a Christian view of society, particularly members of the established churches rather than religious minorities.

Some even saw the revolutionary and Napoleonic periods as divine retribution for the presumption and evil that had long marred human beings. In the international field, *Appeal of conservatism* conservatism was epitomized by Metternich's policies, the Holy Alliance, and the Concert of Europe. In domestic policies, this conservatism was characterized by the restoration of power to the traditional monarchs and aristocrats, the renewed influence of Christianity, and the suppression of liberal and nationalistic movements.

However, conservatives faced formidable opponents, even during the early years after the fall of Napoleon. The French Revolution had turned the ideas of liberalism into a powerful, persistent force. The clash between conservatism and liberalism had just begun and would endure into the twentieth century.

LIBERALISM: INDIVIDUAL FREEDOM AND POLITICAL REFORM

In contrast to conservatism, liberalism drew on the promises of the French Revolution and the Enlightenment. Conservatives sought to maintain traditional society; liberals fought to change it. Liberals wanted a society that promoted individual freedom, or liberty. However, many laws, customs, and conditions of the traditional order stood in their way. Liberals therefore opposed the dominance of politics and society by monarchs, aristocrats, and clergy, and governments' arbitrary interference with individual liberty. To the extent that these elements of the traditional order remained in place, liberals demanded reform and fought resisting conservatives.

From the Enlightenment and the theories of John Locke, liberals adopted ideas about natural laws, natural rights, toleration, and the application of reason to human affairs *Sources of liberalism* (see Chapter 14). From political thinkers such as Montesquieu, they took the idea that governmental powers should be separated and restricted by checks and balances. From the French and American Revolutions, they drew on the principles of freedom, equality before the law, popular sovereignty, and sanctity of property.

Liberalism reflected the aspirations of the middle class, which was gaining wealth but lacked political and social power in the traditional order. Not surprisingly, then, liberals advocated government limited by written constitutions, the elimination of political and social privileges, and extension of voting rights to men of some property and education (most liberals stopped short of suggesting universal male suffrage or extension of the vote to women.) In addition, liberals desired representative institutions where none existed and an extension of the right to participate in representative institutions that remained the preserve of the aristocratic and wealthy elite. They demanded that governments guarantee the sanctity of property and individual rights, such as freedom of the press, speech, assembly, and religion.

Certain economic policies also had great importance to liberals and reflected the stake that the middle class had in commerce and industry. The *Smith* Scottish economist Adam Smith (1723–1790) formulated the ideas that guided economic liberalism (see p. 504). In *The Wealth of Nations* (1776), Smith argued that economics, like the physical world, had its own natural laws. The most basic economic law was of supply and demand, he explained. When left to operate alone, economic laws, like an "invisible hand," would keep the economy in balance and, in the long run, create the most wealth. According to Smith, self-interest—even greed—was the engine that motivated people to work hard and produce wealth. Governments should therefore follow a policy of laissez-faire (hands-off), limiting their involvement in the economy to little more than maintaining law and order so that an unfettered marketplace could flourish.

Other liberal economic thinkers extended Smith's ideas. The British economist Thomas Malthus (1766–1834) cast gloom on hopes for progress among *Malthus and Ricardo* workers. He argued that population would always increase more than food supplies, resulting in poverty and death by "the whole train of common disease, and epidemics, wars, plague and famine." Malthus concluded that workers themselves are "the cause of their own poverty," because they lacked the moral discipline to avoid sexual activity. The politically influential Englishman David Ricardo (1772–1823) refined Malthus' arguments into the "iron law of wages," explaining that wages would always sink to subsistence levels or below because higher salaries just caused workers to multiply, thereby glutting the labor market and lowering wages. He emphasized that the economy was controlled by objective laws. The lessons for these "classical" liberals (to distinguish them from modern American liberals, who usually favor government programs to regulate certain economic

and social affairs) were clear: No intervention in economic matters by government, no tariffs or unions that artificially raise prices or wages, and no restrictions on individual enterprise.

Over time, liberalism evolved and developed several variations. The English philosopher Jeremy Bentham (1748–1832) and his followers advocated a kind of liberalism that became particularly *Bentham* influential in Britain. Known as utilitarianism, it held that all activities and policies should be judged by the standard of usefulness. "Nature has placed mankind under the governance of two sovereign masters, *pain* and *pleasure*," explained Bentham. What was useful, the utilitarians decreed, was what created more pleasure than pain; the best laws and policies were therefore those that promoted "the greatest good for the greatest number" of people. Bentham's utilitarians fought for more governmental intervention in economic and social affairs than other liberals. For example, they supported reforms to protect women and children workers in factories and to improve urban sanitation. Democracy was implicit in utilitarianism, for the best way for the greatest number to maximize their own happiness was for each person to vote. Nevertheless, most liberals during this period actually opposed democracy. They feared the supposedly unruly "masses" and hoped to keep government in the hands of the propertied and well *Mill* educated. They would not start to embrace democratic reforms until the middle of the nineteenth century. At that time, some of them, such as John Stuart Mill (1806–1873) (see Biography), would also begin arguing for major social programs to protect workers and even the right to vote for women.

As we saw earlier, liberalism appealed especially to the rising middle classes, who were prospering from commerce and industry and wanted political power along with their growing wealth and confidence. Liberals had faith that history was on their side, that liberalism, like progress, was inevitable and that the forces they opposed were of the past. That optimism gave them strength to fight against the conservative forces of tradition and rally to protect their gains.

NATIONALISM: A COMMON IDENTITY AND NATIONAL LIBERATION

Like the liberals, nationalists harbored a spirit of optimism. They, too, were aroused by the French Revolution, for it promoted the idea that sovereignty

Biography

JOHN STUART MILL (1806–1873) AND HARRIET TAYLOR (1807–1858)

▪ **Consider** why Mill is labeled a leading proponent of liberalism.

▪ **Compare** the Mill family and the Cadbury family discussed in Chapter 17.

John Stuart Mill and Harriet Taylor were one of the most famous and extraordinary couples of the nineteenth century. Born in 1806, John described his own childhood as "remarkable." His father, the well-known liberal philosopher James Mill (1773–1836), raised John according to the cut-and-dried principles of Jeremy Bentham's utilitarianism. John learned Greek at the age of three, Latin when he was seven, logic at twelve, and economics at thirteen. On their daily walks, James encouraged little John to summarize assigned readings for him. He wanted to turn John's mind into a logical machine for radical thought and utilitarian reform.

In 1822, John and several other young men founded the liberal Utilitarian Society. John, like other liberals, had great faith in the power of knowledge and reason to right human errors: "Knowledge has triumphed. It has worked the downfall of much that is mischievous." For the young Mill, utilitarianism was virtually "a religion." In 1823, John took his first job with the East India Company, the vehicle of British rule in India. He would remain with that company for thirty-five years, reading dispatches from the company's agents in India and drafting replies.

In 1826 he suffered a "crisis." Recoiling from his sterile, intellectualized upbringing, John came to doubt the value of his education and ambition, concluding that neither of these qualities led to happiness. He turned to romanticism—a movement that featured the lush music and especially the writings of Wordsworth, Goethe, and other cultural icons of the day. In time, he came to believe that "poetry is higher than logic, and . . . the union of the two is philosophy."

During these same years, nineteen-year-old Harriet Hardy had married John Taylor, a wealthy partner in a wholesale drug firm. Taylor adored his intellectual wife, who was bolder and more brilliant than he. However, after giving birth to two children, Harriet began to lose interest in John. She increasingly found sex with him an unpleasant imposition and criticized marriage as a sexual contract that was unfair to women.

Extraordinary Victorians

In 1830 Harriet Taylor and John Stuart Mill met. They became "intimate and confidential friends." Mill was a constant visitor to the Taylor household and a frequent companion to Harriet in London. Although their relationship created a scandal in London society, John Taylor, unwilling to see his wife unhappy, acquiesced in it.

rested not in a monarch or a church, but in the people, and that they, banded together, constituted the nation. Nationalism promised to unify nations, liberate subject peoples from foreign rule, create a sense of fraternity among members of a national community, and lead that community to a common destiny. At its core was a feeling of cultural identity among distinct groups of people who shared a common language and traditions and who belonged in a nation-state of their own.

France became an early source of nationalist sentiments. There a sense of membership in the state became especially important when the Revolution transformed the kingdom into a nation. Popular

In 1843, Mill published *A System of Logic*, the first of several major works that marked him as one of the leading thinkers of the nineteenth century. In 1851 Harriet published anonymously *The Enfranchisement of Women*, which argued for universal suffrage and more equal companionship between men and women. Mill would go on to publish *On Liberty* (1859), his most famous political work, in which he argued for freedom of thought and warned against the tyranny of the majority. In 1869 he published *The Subjection of Women*, which made him one of the leading feminists of the century. It is fundamentally wrong, he said, for society to "ordain that to be born a girl instead of a boy, any more than to be born black instead of white, or a commoner instead of a nobleman, shall decide the person's position through all life."

Mill was happy to describe most of his works as jointly produced by himself and Harriet. But Mill may have been too generous in his praise of her role. Just how much she contributed has long been a matter of heated debate. In 1849, two discreet years after John Taylor's death, Mill and Harriet Taylor married. They were proud that their relationship was based on rationality, intellectual companionship, affection, and intimacy, but not sex. They imagined their marriage as a utopian union of equals. It lasted until 1858, when Harriet died.

In the years before his death in 1873, Mill was elected to the House of Commons, where he argued for liberal reforms such as the abolition of capital punishment, feminist reforms such as the extension of suffrage to women and socialist reforms such as poor relief. Figure 18.2 shows a caricature drawing of Mill that was published in the widely read journal Punch in 1867. Readers could easily recognize the famous liberal intellectual (depicted with an unusually large head). The illustration shows him leading women, who are demanding the right to vote, by pushing aside resisting men with his arm and his logical arguments. He concluded that "the social problem of the future" would center on "how to unite the greatest individual liberty of action with a common ownership in the raw material of the globe."

Thus Harriet and John embodied many nineteenth-century trends. Liberalism, romanticism, and socialism all played a role in their lives. In addition, what brought them together was the middle-class ideal—affection, companionship, the shared life at home. In other ways, however, they did not reflect the times at all. Their views on marriage and relations between men and women, for example, the long triangular relationship with John Taylor, and the intensity of their intellectual collaboration all alarmed many of their contemporaries. Only in the decades to come would these unusual views gain more favor.

FIGURE 18.2

John Stuart Mill.

sovereignty, wider political participation, and abolition of old provincial boundary lines gave the French a feeling of solidarity among themselves and with the national government. Universal conscription into the revolutionary armies added to feelings of fraternity in a righteous cause and helped make those armies strong. Powerful new symbols, such as the tricolor flag, stood for national unity and willingness to sacrifice for the sake of the nation.

Nationalism also moved people who did not yet share a state. In the German-speaking areas, for example, scholars and intellectuals developed a cultural basis for nationalism. Writers such as Johann Gottfried

The French Revolution

von Herder (1744–1803) fostered a sense of common national identity arising from German folk culture and oral traditions. Georg Wilhelm Friedrich Hegel (1770–1831) provided philosophi-

Cultural nationalism

cal and historical bases for German nationalism and the importance of the national state. Romantics such as Ernst Moritz Arndt (1769–1860) urged Prussians, Austrians, Bavarians, and others with common roots to "be Germans, be one, will to be one by love and loyalty, and no devil will vanquish you." Groups and secret societies such as Young Germany—usually composed of students, intellectuals, and members of the middle class—promoted a sense of national identity and unity.

In Italy, Poland, and elsewhere, nationalists formed similar organizations and intellectuals created interest in national languages and folk culture. Scholars resurrected and developed languages from previous eras and elevated myths to national histories. Schoolteachers taught these languages and histories to their students and thereby spread a sense of ethnic unity. Nationalists used this growing interest in language and history to proclaim their nation's special mission—for example, of the Czechs to become leaders of the Slavs, or the Italians to lead Europe again as it had during Roman times.

Nationalism promised a new sense of community as the old order with its traditional allegiances declined. It offered a sense of strength

Sense of community

and unity that appealed to many peoples: to those threatened with foreign domination, such as the Spaniards and Italians under the French during the Napoleonic era; to those dissatisfied with the dominance of one ethnic group, such as Czechs, Magyars, or Serbs under the Germans within the Habsburg Empire; and to those feeling suppressed by what they considered foreign domination, such as the Greeks under the Ottomans, the Poles under the Russians, and the Italians under the Austrians.

From such sources, it was a short step to calls for national liberation and political unification. Nationalism

National liberation and unification

soon acquired attributes of a religion and became a powerful political force. For example, the Italian nationalist Giuseppe Mazzini (1805–1872), who founded the revolutionary Young Italy movement in 1831, called Italy "the purpose, the soul, the consolation of our thoughts, the country chosen of God and oppressed by men." Some nationalist leaders such as Mazzini began demanding loyalty and solidarity from members of their organizations.

Before 1848, most nationalists supported liberal causes, for liberals also struggled for national rights. Both liberals and nationalists typically believed that sovereignty should rest with the people, united by common loyalties and language. They also had faith that change would bring political, social, and economic progress. Campaigns by liberals to promote agricultural improvement and industrial development often merged into German, Italian, and Hungarian calls for national unity.

Later, nationalists would ally themselves with conservatives, for both believed in the value of historical traditions and in an organic society over the rights of the individual. Nationalism would also become more entwined with notions of national superiority and special national missions that so often appealed to conservatives. All nationalists, however, insisted that each nation of people, unified into a self-governing state, should be the primary focus of political loyalty and that the political boundaries of the state should be the same as ethnic boundaries of the people. The widespread political and emotional appeal of nationalism made it an increasingly powerful ideology over the course of the century.

ROMANTICISM: FREEDOM, INSTINCT, AND SPONTANEITY

The origins of nationalism in literature and history also made it attractive to believers in romanticism. This ideology became the dominant spirit in literature and art during the first half of the nineteenth century. Its significance stretched beyond culture, however. Romanticism reflected a new recognition that human beings were complex, emotional, and only sometimes rational creatures. In a civilization that was growing ever more scientific, materialistic, industrial, and urban, romanticism became a counterweight for the human experience. It stood against eighteenth-century classicism and the Enlightenment, and the ideals of reason and order that so characterized those eras. Instead, romanticism emphasized individual freedom and spontaneity.

Origins of romanticism can be traced back to Jean-Jacques Rousseau, the acclaimed writer and philosopher we met in Chapter 14. Though

Rousseau

a central figure of the Enlightenment, Rousseau had stressed feeling, instinct, emotions, and love of nature. He described walking away from the city into the fields and woods, stretching himself out on the ground, digging his fingers and toes into the dirt, kissing the earth, and weeping for joy. In several of his most widely read writings, he seemed to idealize love, childhood, and "the noble savage."

Other strands of romanticism came from the German "Storm and Stress" (Sturm und Drang) literature of the late eighteenth century. German writers gave **"Storm and Stress" literature** much weight to inner feelings fully experienced and expressed by sensitive individuals. Johann Wolfgang von Goethe provided a model of the emotional individual searching for love and self-understanding in his novel *The Sorrows of the Young Werther* (1774). Like Rousseau, Goethe had many interests. He delved into philosophy, science, and public affairs as well as literature. His masterpiece, the philosophical drama *Faust,* featured a medieval scholar who, dissatisfied with the fruits of knowledge, sells his soul to the devil in return for earthly pleasure and wisdom. In Goethe's medieval interests, his emotional spontaneity, and his love of nature and of individual personality, this renowned writer exemplified the heart of romanticism.

All these qualities explored by Rousseau and Goethe came to characterize the work of succeeding romantic writers and artists. Many romantics ex-**Reviving the Middle Ages** pressed a new interest in the Middle Ages. They revived the popularity of medieval tales, Gothic architecture, the Knights of the Round Table, and heroic figures, thereby turning the medieval era from the "Dark Ages" into the "Age of Faith."

This fascination with the Middle Ages reflected romanticism's passionate concern with the drama of history. Written by scholars such as Thomas Babing-**History** ton Macaulay (1800–1859) in Great Britain, history was literary and exciting, featuring heroic individuals, great accomplishments, and national struggles. These same themes were explored by the Prussian philosopher Hegel. In Hegel's view, history was a great spiritual drama of heroic individuals that would lead to a new sense of national identity and freedom.

Romanticism also stressed the emotion of Christianity and the mystical presence of God in nature. According to romantic theologians, the important **Christianity** part of religion was the feeling of dependence on an infinite God rather than religious dogma or institutions. In his widely read book, *The Genius of Christianity,* the French writer François Auguste-René de Chateaubriand (1768–1848) described in lush words how "every thing in a Gothic church reminds you of the labyrinths of a forest; every thing excites a feeling of religious awe, of mystery, and of the Divinity." In part, religious revivals during the late eighteenth and early nineteenth centuries, with their stress on piety and emotional outpourings, reflected these spiritual qualities of romanticism.

The connections among the love of nature, the spiritual presence of God, and the power of emotions were most striking in the romantic literature, art, and music of the period. In the literary realm, the English poets William Wordsworth (1770–1850) **Literature** and Samuel Taylor Coleridge (1772–1834) became closely associated with the beautiful lake country of northwest England—Wordsworth by birth and Coleridge by adoption. Together the two men traveled to Germany, where they fell under the influence of German romanticists. They collaborated on *Lyrical Ballads* (1798), which included Wordsworth's "Lines Composed a Few Miles Above Tintern Abbey" and Coleridge's "Rime of the Ancient Mariner." Both writers glorified nature and sensed a brooding, mystical presence of the divine. Wordsworth saw in nature a higher wisdom than what scholars might offer:

> One impulse from a vernal wood
> May teach you more of man,
> Of moral evil and of good
> Than all the sages can.

Wordsworth's and Coleridge's ardent appreciation of nature, their introspective concern for the individual, and their preoccupation with the spiritual rather than the material made them leaders among Britain's many romantic poets.

In France, Germaine de Staël (1766–1817) led the romantic movement in literature. Although she admired the passionate Rousseau, she attacked most Enlightenment thinkers for not being free enough. She turned to writing in order to grapple with her own emotional experiences with several lovers and to argue for living the passionate life. Often writing about female heroes and genius in works such as *Corinne,* de Staël also looked to history for a vision of another, better world. She and other romantics created an image of the ideal romantic heroine who followed her emotions rather than tradition or reason—a model that some tried to follow in life. Also in France, George Sand (Amandine Dupin Dudevant) (1804–1876) became an extraordinarily creative writer and an unconventional, even threatening woman. Abandoning her tyrannical husband for an independent life in Paris, Sand became an intellectual leader whose private life included several love affairs with well-known people. At her own convenience, she dressed as a man or a woman (see Figure 18.5). Like several other women writers, she also took a male pseudonym to add legitimacy to her writings. Several of her novels explored romantic love and featured strong, intensely emotional heroines.

Leading romantic painters also stressed emotional images. Figure 18.3, an oil painting by the German **Art** artist Karl Friedrich Schinkel, shows an idealized image of a medieval town at twilight. In the center stands a magnificent Gothic cathedral, its spires stretching toward the heavens above. The parting clouds and setting sun seem to bless this church and

town. Below, humble workers bring abundant supplies from the river. They are dwarfed by the cathedral, the central stairs leading up to the cathedral, the high-arching bridge that echoes the arches of the cathedral, their finely built town on the right, and nature above. The painting contains the key elements of romanticism: glorification of nature, religious mysticism, adoration of an idealized medieval era, and expression of emotion.

The romantic love of magnificent landscapes can be found in Figure 18.4. This 1817 painting emphasizes the theme of the poet both immersed in nature and conjuring up a majestic natural setting like a god. Here the robed poet with his harp stands on a cliff, his arm

FIGURE 18.3
Karl Friedrich Schinkel, *Medieval Town on a River*, 1815.

FIGURE 18.4
John Martin, *The Bard*, 1817.

stretched out to the swirling heavens above. Below him, waters rage and a knight on a white horse (lower left) gallops off into the distance. In the background stands a medieval castle built into the mountains.

In music, a number of romantic composers followed in the footsteps of Ludwig van Beethoven *Music* (1770–1827). The music of this famed German composer overflowed the bounds of classic forms, becoming freer, more individualistic, and emotional than anything that had come before. Beethoven composed his *Pastoral Symphony* as a musical link to nature. "How happy I am," he wrote in 1810, "to be able to stroll in the woods, among the trees, bushes, wild flowers and rocks. No one can love the country as much as I do." The lyrics to one of his choral works explain his feelings about music:

When the magic of sound holds sway
and works bring inspiration,
glorious things must appear,
darkness and turmoil become light.

One critic explained that romantic music should "paint to the eyes of the soul the splendors of nature, the delights of contemplation, the character of nations, the tumult of their passions, and the languor of their sufferings. . . ."

The painting by the Austrian artist Josef Danhauser shown in Figure 18.5 brings together leading figures of romantic art and literature. At the center, the Hungarian virtuoso and composer Franz Liszt plays the piano for his friends. Standing, from left to right, are the French writer Victor Hugo, the Italian violinist Niccolò Paganini, and the composer Antonio Rossini. Sitting are the French writers Alexandre Dumas, George Sand (characteristically in men's clothing), and Daniel Stern (Marie d'Agoult, who had a long-term liaison with Liszt). Above the group hangs a portrait of Lord Byron and a bust of Beethoven, the deceased "saints" of romantic poetry and music.

Through much of romanticism, strands from all the ideologies combined and recombined in a variety of ways. Nationalism, for ex- *Connections to nationalism* ample, played a prominent role in some romantics' lives. In the 1820s, England's romantic poet Lord Byron (1788–1824) fought for Greek national independence against the Turks (see Figure 18.8). Some of Frederic Chopin's (1810–1849) dramatic music self-consciously evoked nationalistic sentiments for his native Poland, which was still under Russian rule. The Italian Giuseppe Verdi (1813–1901) and the German Richard Wagner (1813–1883), who developed the opera into a fully integrated artform of music, theater, ballet, and special effects, were among many other composers whose works brought together romantic and openly nationalistic themes.

Liberals, too, found comfort in various aspects of romanticism, which helps explain the movement's wide appeal. By breaking sharply with past forms, romanticism attracted liberal and *Connections to liberalism* revolutionary spirits. Indeed, many romantic writers and artists sided with liberal causes. Germaine de Staël, for example, in her own life as well as in her novels, histories, and political tracts, fostered romanticism and liberalism in France. Few liberal romantics, however, were more popular than the French writer Victor Hugo (1802–1885), who idealized the masses of underprivileged humanity and preached redemption and purification through suffering.

At the same time, certain dimensions of romanticism appealed to conservatives as well—especially the return to the past, the emphasis on Christianity, and the stand against *Connections to conservatism* the rationalism of the Enlightenment. Sir Walter Scott (1771–1832), who in novel and verse glorified the Middle Ages and his native Scotland, was a conservative. So was the French writer François Auguste-René de Chateaubriand, who advocated a return to mystic Catholicism and dreamed of noble Indians in tropical America.

Romanticism found expression in many cultural forms—in the new English gardens that imitated nature rather than confining it to geometric forms, in the image of the artist as a nonconforming genius, in the glorification of walks down wooded lanes, in the popularity of the Grimm fairy tales that evoked images of medieval life, and in the sentimentalization of love in life and literature. In its qualities, its popularity, and its persistence, romanticism proved to be more than a casual change of taste or a mood. It reflected the revolutionary social, political, and intellectual developments of the era.

FIGURE 18.5
Josef Danhauser, *Liszt at the Piano*, 1840.

EARLY SOCIALISM: ENDING COMPETITION AND INEQUITIES

Romantics questioned the existing system from cultural and emotional perspectives. Socialists questioned it from social and economic perspectives. As socialists saw it, the common people—the workers—were missing out on the astounding power and wealth generated by the industrial revolution. Socialists called for a reordering of society so as to end the competition and class divisions that caused inequalities and suffering. Such calls made the socialists enemies of both the conservative and liberal camps.

During the early decades of the nineteenth century, a few intellectuals—some of whom came to be called Utopian Socialists—contended that society should be based on cooperation rather than competitive individualism and that property should be owned communally. One of the first of these early socialists was the French nobleman Henri de Saint-Simon (1760–1825). During the French *Utopian Socialists* Revolution, Saint-Simon abandoned his noble title. Turning to land speculation, he made and lost a fortune. He and his followers believed that society should be reorganized on the basis of a "religion of humanity," that all people should work, and that the inheritance of private property should be abolished. In Saint-Simon's ideal world, women would be elevated from their inferior social positions. Superior artists, scientists, engineers, and business people would be rewarded according to the *Saint-Simon* formula: "from each according to his capacity, to each according to his desserts." Saint-Simon's influential followers became convinced that the best scientists and managers could use their expertise to plan and run prosperous societies for the benefit of everyone.

Charles Fourier (1772–1837) was also an early Utopian Socialist who, like Saint-Simon, gathered a following. A Frenchman who had been a traveling salesman, he advocated doing away with *Fourier* economic competition, which he saw as the very source of evil. In his utopian society, agriculture and industry would be carried on by voluntary cooperatives whose members would pool their resources and live in communal apartment houses (*phalansteries*). Housework and child care would be a shared responsibility of the community. Women, like men, would have the right to work and to control their own money. Fourier also considered traditional marriage too restrictive sexually. Work and pleasure would merge as people did as they pleased while still carrying out the tasks their society required to survive. People would be paid according to the labor, capital, and talent that each contributed.

Figure 18.6 reveals the dream of Fourier and his followers. In the background, an imagined phalanstery—geometrically ordered and laid out in a style reminiscent of the palace at Versailles—rests in an idyllic setting away from large cities. A classical temple on the shoreline offers tranquillity to people arriving in boats. On a hill in the foreground, Fourier—depicted as a saintly father figure with his arm lovingly around a child—instructs his followers. In fact, the communities that Fourier's followers established in the United States and Europe rarely lasted for long. Fourier's ideas, however, inspired many people looking for a more joyful, communal alternative to the competitive industrial societies spreading in the West.

Robert Owen (1771–1858) had different ideas. Born in Wales, Owen quickly made an industrial fortune in Manchester and bought large cotton mills in New Lanark, Scotland. Early in the nineteenth century, he set out to make New Lanark a model community. He raised wages, shortened work hours, improved working conditions, abolished child labor, provided educational and recreational facilities for employees, and established sickness and old-age insurance. Productivity in his mills soared, and profits rose. Owen spent years drawing up plans for model socialist communities, which he envisioned as being located in rural settings and as mostly self-sufficient. The plans called for community members to raise children together and for women to share in governing. Like Fourier, Owen advocated loosening the bounds of marriage to create greater sexual freedom for women and men. Several such communities were established in America, most notably New Harmony, Indiana. However, all soon succumbed to internal disagreements and economic difficulties. The efforts cost Owen most of his fortune. He retained his fame, especially within the labor movement and among

Owen

FIGURE 18.6
Fourier and his phalanstery.

those establishing modest workers' cooperatives. However, he died in 1858 without having created a lasting alternative to the harsh industrial capitalism he deplored.

In the 1830s, several Frenchwomen began linking socialist demands with calls for the emancipation of women. The most famous of these women was Flora Tristan (1801–1844), a Frenchwoman influenced by Fourier's ideas. French law discriminated against women in many ways, including automatically awarding custody of children to fathers after a marital separation. When Tristan's abusive husband was awarded their children, she fought back. Eventually she turned this dispute into a campaign to end discrimination against women within marriage, in the law, and on the job. She traveled throughout Europe and Latin America, speaking passionately for unions and the creation of centers for the care and education of workers. In her *Worker's Union* (1843), she argued that equality between women and men could free the whole working class and transform civilization.

Tristan

These and other early socialists recognized both the significance of the industrial revolution and its possibilities. They attacked the unbridled pursuit of profits in an unregulated, industrial economy. Only a well-organized society, they explained, could eliminate the misery of industrial capitalism and promote happiness. Most also attacked middle-class restrictions on women, emphasized the importance of sensual pleasure, and questioned traditional Christianity.

The wave of socialist thought that these leaders unleashed became profoundly influential by the middle decades of the nineteenth century. As it evolved, it took on a more revolutionary quality, and it bore the distinctive stamp of one of the most authoritative thinkers of the nineteenth century: Karl Marx.

"SCIENTIFIC SOCIALISM": KARL MARX AND THE COMMUNIST MANIFESTO

"A specter is haunting Europe—the specter of Communism," announced Karl Marx (1818–1883) in 1848. "Let the ruling classes tremble at a Communist revolution." Born into a German middle-class family, his father was a Jewish lawyer who had converted to Christianity. A brilliant student, Marx attained his doctorate in philosophy and history, but he was denied an academic position because of his radical views. After embarking on a career in journalism, he was exiled from Germany for his attacks on censorship and his economic views; later France exiled him because of his revolutionary socialist ideas. He spent the last 34 years of his life in London researching, writing, and trying to build organizations to put his ideas into action. Marx collaborated with his friend Friedrich Engels (1820–1895), son of a wealthy German manufacturer, in writing the seminal work, *The Communist Manifesto* (1848). This treatise, along with the later *Das Kapital,* contained the fundamentals of what Marx called "scientific socialism."

Marx argued that economic interest, more than anything else, drove human behavior. He also thought that the dominant characteristic of each historical epoch was its prevailing system of economic production—how people made a living. In his view, politics, religion, and culture were all shaped mainly by economic and social realities.

Economic interest

Marx also described how human societies in each historical era became divided into the "haves" and the "have-nots." The haves owned the means of economic production—in nineteenth century Britain, for example, the industrial capitalists who owned the machines and factories. They also controlled the state and the ideas that dominated their societies. The have-nots were the exploited laborers—for example, Britain's industrial working class. Each side consisted of classes of people with opposing interests. As Marx wrote, "[T]he history of all hitherto existing society is the history of class struggle." At a certain point, economic and so-

Class struggle

cial change would bring these class struggles to a revolutionary crisis. The French Revolution, he explained, was an example of one of those conflicts coming to a violent head, as the bourgeoisie (the middle-class capitalists) overcame the aristocracy (the feudal landlords.)

Marx focused much of his analysis on his own industrial society of the nineteenth century. In this society, he explained, the bourgeoisie (capitalists) exploited workers by paying them only subsistence wages rather than compensating them for the true value created by their work. "These labourers, who must sell themselves piecemeal, are a commodity, like every other article of commerce," Marx lamented. At the same time, Marx saw capitalists as locked in a competitive struggle with one another. This contest forced them continually to introduce new, costly machines and build larger factories: "Constant revolutionizing of production, uninterrupted disturbance of all social conditions, ever-lasting uncertainty and agitation distinguish the bourgeois epoch from all earlier ones." Soon, Marx warned, greater and greater quantities of goods would be produced by a system running out of control. Eventually, the relentless competition and the periodic economic crises that plague industrial societies would thin the ranks of the bourgeoisie. At the same time, the working class would grow stronger as its numbers and consciousness increased. Inevitably, the workers—with "nothing to lose but their chains" and with "a world to win"—would revolt, seize the factories, destroy the capitalist system, abolish private property, and establish a classless socialist society.

Industrial capitalism

Marx only hinted at the general nature of this new socialist society. His writings suggest that the elimination of capitalism would end the division of society into classes of haves (capitalists) and have-nots (workers). The state itself would eventually wither away, for its only purpose was to protect the interests of the haves against the have-nots. Freed from exploitation and the pressures of capitalist competition, all people would lead more varied, cooperative, creative lives—in this sense, free and truly human.

Socialist society

Marx's socialism gained immense appeal. Because he based much of his analysis on evidence and logic, it attracted intellectuals and students. Because his socialism reflected the social and emotional turmoil being produced by the industrial revolution, especially the suffering of the working poor, it spoke convincingly

Appeal of socialism

to workers and their leaders. During the second half of the nineteenth century, Marx's socialism would become a major force in the West.

Restoration and Repression

Socialism as well as the other ideologies reflected the political and social realities of their era, particularly the efforts of people to understand and cope with changes that either threatened them or offered promise. In the three decades following 1815, however, socialism played only a limited part in the great struggles for policies and power. During these years, it was the forces representing conservatism, liberalism, and nationalism that instead took center stage.

The struggles for influence and power among believers of these ideologies took place in pamphlets and newspapers, in courts and parliaments, in universities and police barracks, and in streets and fields throughout Europe. In the first years after the defeat of Napoleon, conservatism held sway in international and diplomatic affairs. The Vienna agreements and the cooperative arrangements to repress the threat of revolution in Europe epitomized this ideology. Conservatism also prevailed in domestic politics across most of Europe.

THE RETURN OF THE BOURBONS IN FRANCE

When the victorious armies of the coalition powers entered France and deposed Napoleon in the spring of 1814, they brought "in their baggage" the members of the Bourbon royal family who had fled the Revolution. In their wake trooped the émigré nobility. The brother of the guillotined Louis XVI was placed on the throne as Louis XVIII (r. 1814–1824). (The son of Louis XVI, who had died in prison without having ruled, was considered Louis XVII.)

Louis XVIII

The "restored" king ruled with an odd mixture of conservatism and moderation. He issued a charter that retained Napoleon's administrative and legal system as well as civil and religious liberties. He also placed lawmaking in the hands of a two-chamber legislature. However, only a small, wealthy elite could vote, and the king kept most of the power.

Nevertheless, Louis XVIII used his authority with moderation, thinking that a mild leadership style would help ensure his hold on the crown and tranquillity in France. Most of the returned émigrés, however, had little appreciation for his relaxed rule—they were more conservative and angry than he was and wanted action. Led by the king's younger brother, Comte d'Artois, these ultraroyalists controlled the legislature. Through the rest of Louis XVIII's reign, they agitated for a return of their privileges and indemnification for their lost lands.

After Louis XVIII's death in 1824, d'Artois was crowned King Charles X (r. 1824–1830); he followed more conservative policies that favored the old aristocracy and the Catholic Church. He offered money to indemnify those who had lost land in the Revolution and gave the church greater control over education. Those policies provoked growing opposition to his rule. When elections increased the size of the opposition, he dissolved the Chamber of Deputies. In the face of still-increasing opposition, he abolished freedom of the press and drastically restricted the right to vote.

Charles X

REACTION AND REPRESSION IN THE GERMAN STATES

The Germanies in 1815 consisted of 37 little states and 2 large ones—Prussia and Austria. All belonged to the German Confederation, which lacked an army, a treasury, and even a flag. Austria and Prussia politically dominated the German lands. Both states were firmly conservative, if not reactionary.

In multilingual Austria, the Habsburg emperor and Metternich, the conservative diplomat we met at the beginning of the chapter, held sway. The Austrian leaders had good reason to fear liberalism and nationalism like the plague, for the empire included many ethnic groups—including Hungarians, Czechs, Serbs, and Italians—with their own languages and customs. In the wake of the French Revolution, they began to stir with national consciousness. Metternich used all means—police, spies, censorship, and travel restrictions—to ensure the status quo. The only possible threats to conservative control came from within some of the small states in the weak German Confederation, and Austria enjoyed permanent presidency over that organization.

Metternich

When students and professors formed organizations and staged festivals that supported liberal and nationalistic principles, conservative officials became alarmed. "We want a constitution for the people that fits in with the spirit of the times and with people's own level of enlightenment," explained one student. "[A]bove all, we want Germany to be considered *one* land and the people *one* people."

OLC

The murder of a conservative dramatist by a member of a student organization, Karl Sand, gave Metternich his opportunity to strike. After Sand's trial and public execution, Metternich called the princes of the leading German states to Carlsbad and had them draw up a set of harsh decrees outlawing the organizations. He also issued an ominous warning: "The duty of especial watchfulness in this matter should be impressed upon the special agents of the government." The Carlsbad Decrees established strict censorship and supervision of classrooms and libraries. Spies and police terrorized liberal students and professors. Although Sand became a political martyr in the eyes of many young nationalists, the crackdown worked: the small liberal and nationalistic movements evaporated.

Carlsbad Decrees

In Prussia, the conservative, militaristic Hohenzollern kings reigned. Behind them stood the equally conservative landed aristocracy, the *Junkers*. The Junkers served as officers in the Prussian army and filled the key posts in the civil service and administration. They had no sympathy for any reforms that seemed even faintly liberal or nationalistic, and they reversed many of the changes of the Napoleonic era. However, to better connect its separated territories, Prussia began making commercial treaties with its smaller German neighbors, providing for the free flow of trade among them. By 1834, nearly all the states of the German Confederation except Austria had joined the Prussian-sponsored *Zollverein* (customs union), which would prove of great importance in the march toward national unity.

Prussia

RESTORATION IN ITALY

Austria dominated Italy even more completely than Germany. Metternich described Italy as only a "geographical expression." Austria annexed the northern states of Lombardy and Venetia outright. Most other states were ruled by Austrian princes or under Austria's protection and guidance. Piedmont-Sardinia in the northwest was free from Austrian control, but its ruling House of Savoy was no less conservative than Metternich.

In 1815 the deposed aristocracy and clericals trooped back to the Italian states intent on regaining their old positions. They and their Austrian masters soon sent nearly all the Italian intelligentsia to prison or exile. When revolts in Naples, Sicily, and Piedmont flared up in 1820, the forces of order quickly used overwhelming force to put them down.

The Papal States in central Italy were no exception in this period of restoration. Pope Pius VII revived the Inquisition, reconstituted the *Index* of prohibited books, annulled Napoleonic laws of religious toleration, and even did away with French innovations such as street lighting. His successor, Pius VIII, followed equally conservative ideas. In 1829, he condemned almost everything even faintly liberal, including secular education and civil marriage.

CONSERVATISM IN RUSSIA

Russia remained a vast agricultural nation with a feudal social structure and a tiny urban bourgeoisie. The Orthodox Christian Church, dominated by an upper clergy drawn from the aristocracy, served as an arm of the government. After fighting against the French, suffering a ravaging invasion in 1812, and playing a major role in Napoleon's defeat, Russia commanded considerable respect and power in Europe. Russia's tsar was the unstable Alexander I—at first a man open to reform, such as granting the Poles a constitution and proclaiming religious toleration, and later more of a reactionary mystic who resumed religious repression. He fell under the influence of Metternich in international affairs and his own aristocratic magnates at home. At his death in 1825, Russia remained a champion of autocracy and conservatism.

His successor, Nicholas I (r. 1825–1855), was an austere autocrat whose military career wedded him to the concepts of discipline and authority. When he assumed the throne in December, 1825, a group of his young liberal military officers—hoping to write a constitution and free the serfs—revolted. Nicholas immediately crushed these "Decembrists" and bitterly turned against any hints of liberalism. He followed a policy of demanding submission of everyone to the autocracy and to the Orthodox Church. Although the Decembrists would later gain a reputation as liberal political martyrs, Russia's government now stood as a bastion of conservatism and would remain so for many decades.

HOLDING THE LINE IN GREAT BRITAIN

Although Great Britain had for years been a home of representative government, conservatives dominated its government in 1815. Property qualifications so

FIGURE 18.7
George Cruikshank, *The Peterloo Massacre, 1819*

severely restricted the suffrage that only about 5 percent of adult males could vote. The distribution of seats in Parliament was so distorted that a relatively small number of families dominated the House of Commons. Furthermore, the emerging industrial cities of the north were scarcely represented at all. The conservative landed aristocracy and the Tory Party, which had seen the country through the Napoleonic Wars, had a firm grip on power.

Things became even more restricted when an economic depression left thousands of returning veterans *Peterloo Massacre* jobless. Luddite riots (see p. 603) and the specter of revolutionary activity prompted the government to take strong measures against the restless workers. The climax came in 1819 when troops charged on a crowd that had assembled in St. Peter's Fields, outside Manchester, to listen to reform speeches. A number were killed and hundreds injured in this "Peterloo Massacre."

Figure 18.7, a print by George Cruikshank, shows the troops of the conservative British government breaking up this rally for liberal and radical political reform. On the platform, women and men wave banners demanding universal suffrage, religious freedom, and liberty; their banners are topped with liberty caps, a radical symbol from the French Revolution. This depiction of the violence that erupted at St. Peter's Fields near Manchester seeks to evoke sympa-

thy for the reformers. It portrays merciless troops on horseback striking down and trampling nonresisting women, men, and children. An army officer on horseback repeats orders from a higher authority, "Cut them down." A participant confirmed this depiction: "Women, white-vested maids, and tender youths, were indiscriminately sabred or trampled. . . . In ten minutes from the commencement of the havoc the field was an open and almost deserted space." Parliament would not back down. It soon passed the Six Acts of 1819, which further restricted public meetings and facilitated prosecution of radicals.

The government treated the Irish no less harshly. The Irish had long been ruled and exploited as a conquered people. In the 1801 Act of Union, Britain formally absorbed Ireland into the United Kingdom. In this predominantly Catholic land, the Protestant minority con- *Ireland* trolled most of the land and political power. The Catholic peasantry suffered from such acute poverty that the threat of famine was not uncommon. Irish nationalists organized to agitate for the right to send elected Catholic representatives to Parliament. In 1829, fearing a civil war in Ireland, the conservative British government reluctantly passed the Catholic Emancipation Act, which allowed Roman Catholics to become members of Parliament.

A Wave of Revolution and Reform

Despite conservative efforts to maintain order and halt change during the years after 1815, liberal and nationalistic causes simmered just under the surface. The demands for greater political participation and recognition of national identity strengthened and spread. Moreover, Europeans could no longer ignore the changes stemming from early industrialization and urbanization. In some cases, revolts and revolutions broke out. In other cases, people clamored for and gained major reforms.

THE GREEK WAR FOR INDEPENDENCE

A hint of the problems to come occurred during the 1820s, when Greeks mounted a national liberation movement against their Ottoman Turk overlords. The Ottoman Empire still sprawled over vast territories, from the north African coast and southwest Asia to southeastern Europe, but it had been weakened by internal dissention and external threats. By 1815, revolts had enabled Serbia to gain virtual independence, and in Egypt, Mehemet Ali ruled with only nominal subordination to the Ottomans. The Greek revolt began in 1821, which resulted in the death of many defenseless Turks. After the Turks met Greek insurrections with force and atrocities, romantic and liberal idealists formed an international movement to support Greek independence. Britain's well-known romantic poet Lord Byron was one of several who traveled to Greece to contribute to the cause. He brought money and enlisted in a regiment, but lost his life to malaria at Missolonghi.

Figure 18.8, by the romantic French artist Eugène Delacroix (1798–1863), captures Greece's struggle for independence. The year is 1826, during the months when the Turks laid siege to the Greek stronghold of Missolonghi and the garrison of 4,000 finally succumbed to 35,000 attackers and the Ottoman fleet. The remaining defenders blew up the city and themselves rather than surrender to the Turks. Greece is represented as a beautiful, defenseless peasant woman and a classical symbol of liberty. Under a dark, foreboding sky, she kneels on what are both the ruins of Missolonghi's city walls and the stone remains of Greek culture in a desperate, mute appeal for aid. But it is already too late for the martyred freedom fighter (perhaps evoking the memory of the fallen Byron), whose arm is thrust forward toward the viewer. Behind the woman, a Turkish soldier strikes a victorious pose. The painting, like the Greek cause in Europe, blends the themes of romanticism, liberalism, and nationalism that so characterized the era.

In the end, intervention by Great Britain, France, and Russia finally secured Greek independence. Although Europeans thought of Greece sympathetically as Christian and as the birthplace of European civilization, these countries' motives had more to do with their own greedy hopes of gains at the expense of the Turks than genuinely supporting the Greek revolutionaries. They achieved their objective, but this dramatic chapter in Greek history still revealed the strength of nationalistic movements and the power of liberal and romantic ideals to fuel these movements.

LIBERAL TRIUMPHS IN WESTERN EUROPE

In 1830, a new series of revolutions tested and sometimes overwhelmed established governments. In France, a struggle arose for liberal reforms against the reactionary King Charles X. Since ascending the throne in 1824, Charles had tried to reverse the

FIGURE 18.8
Eugène Delacroix, *Greece on the Ruins of Missolonghi*, 1827.

moderate policies of his predecessor, Louis XVIII, and return France to the days before the French Revolution. He aligned himself with the most extreme ultraroyalists and the Catholic Church, angering the wealthy bourgeoisie and even the peasantry with his reactionary policies. Support for his regime weakened and he lost control over the Chamber of Deputies, the most representative of France's two-chamber legislature. His efforts to dissolve the Chamber, censor the press, and narrow the electoral laws only stiffened liberal opposition. In July 1830, things came to a head. Liberals in Paris joined with workers outraged by rising food prices. Workers took to the streets of Paris and set up barriers against the king's unenthusiastic troops. Uprisings—fueled by hunger, suspicions of hoarding, and resentment against taxes—spread throughout France. After three days of haphazard fighting, the insurgents gained the upper hand. Charles X, the last Bourbon king of France, fled to Great Britain.

The July Revolution in France

Figure 18.9, a painting by Horace Vernet, reveals how the victors in France's revolution of 1830 interpreted the dramatic events of that year. In the center of the painting, the new constitutional monarch, Louis-Philippe, rides victoriously to the Hôtel de Ville (city hall), the seat of power in Paris. Before him a man carries the French revolutionary tricolor flag, replacing the old Bourbon flag of Charles X. Louis-Philippe's horse picks his way through the paving stones, which the people of Paris had used to construct barricades and hurl at the royal troops. In the foreground, rich and poor walk arm-in-arm with regular and irregular soldiers in victory; a wealthy man stops to drop alms into a basket for the poor or fallen. Women and men of all classes hail the new king and the revolutionary cause.

While many in France had hoped for a republic to replace the Bourbon monarchy, more conservative liberals took control and created a constitutional "Bourgeois monarchy" under Charles X's cousin, Louis-Philippe

(r. 1830–1848). Recognizing that a new, more liberal era had dawned in France, Louis-Philippe assumed the role of "citizen king," casting aside the clothes and ornaments of royalty and dressing in the style of his Parisian upper-middle-class supporters. He reduced property qualifications for voting, thereby doubling the electorate (though still only the property-owning elite could vote).

The year 1830 also brought revolutionary trouble in the Belgian provinces of the kingdom of the Netherlands. The union forced on Belgium (predominantly Catholic) and the Netherlands (mainly Calvinist) at Vienna had never been a happy one. Although numerically a minority, the Dutch staffed most of the country's political institutions. As one Belgian nationalist put it in 1830, "By what right do two million Dutchmen command four million Belgians?" Desires

Revolution in Belgium

FIGURE 18.9
Horace Vernet, *The Duc d'Orléans Proceeds to the Hotel-de-Ville, July 31, 1830,* 1833.

for national liberation combined with tensions over high food prices to fuel a revolt in August 1830. When the half-hearted efforts of the Dutch government failed to suppress the revolt, Austria and Russia threatened to intervene. Britain and France resisted the intervention and secured Belgian independence. Belgium soon adopted a liberal constitution.

By that time, liberal reformers had also scored successes in Switzerland, making that country the first to

Switzerland and Spain grant universal male suffrage. In 1834, a new constitution introduced at least the form of liberal institutions to Spain as well.

TESTING AUTHORITY IN EASTERN AND SOUTHERN EUROPE

As Map 18.2 shows, revolutionaries also tested regimes in eastern and southern Europe. In November 1830, a Polish nationalistic movement led by stu-

Poland dents and army cadets tried to end Russian rule. They managed to establish a provisional government in Warsaw, but conflict within different social groups and among reformers weakened that government. Russian troops soon defeated the revolutionaries. Nicholas sent thousands of Poles to Siberia in chains and began a harsh program of Russification to crush any hint of Polish independence.

In Italy, nationalists began gathering in secret societies called *Carbonari*. (The word means "charcoal

Italy burners," suggesting an image of common people meeting around charcoal fires.) The Carbonari had long plotted for political freedom and national unification. In 1831, liberal and nationalist revolutions broke out in central Italy, but Austrian forces promptly suppressed them. The movement again went underground, but was kept alive under the leadership of the romantic nationalist Giuseppe Mazzini (1805–1872).

LIBERAL DEMANDS IN GREAT BRITAIN

In Britain, conservatives had to contend not only with demands for liberal reforms but also with pressures rising from early industrialization and urbanization. Despite the Peterloo Massacre and the restrictive Six Acts, Britain had already shown signs of political flexibility in response to public opinion in the 1820s. By 1822, it had deserted the conservative Concert of Europe. The government repealed laws preventing labor-

ers from organizing unions and removed civil restrictions against nonconforming Protestants and Catholics. Yet these measures, however encouraging to liberals, did not get at the fundamental issue that had raised reform demands for decades: broadening popular participation in the government.

Now the industrial middle class, gaining in wealth and number, added weight to radicals' demands to extend the right to vote and relocate political strength from the countryside to the underrepresented industrial cities. However, the conservative Tories, who controlled Parliament, remained un-

willing or unable to effect electoral *Reform Bill of 1832* reform. In 1830, elections brought the more liberal Whigs to power. These Whigs believed that moderate reform rather than reactionary intransigence was the best way to preserve elite institutions from revolutionary change. Worried that the July Revolution in France might spread to Britain, and facing increasing public demonstrations for reform as well as violent acts of protest, the Whigs decided to bend rather than break. They introduced the Reform Bill of 1832, which answered some of the demands. Speaking in favor of the bill, the English historian and politician Thomas Babington Macaulay warned that "now, while the crash of the proudest throne of the Continent [France] is still resounding in our ears . . . now, while the heart of England is still sound," the Reform Bill must be passed. After considerable effort, the Whigs finally enacted the new law.

The Reform Bill did not grant the universal manhood suffrage called for by radicals, but it lowered property qualifications so that most upper-middle-class men (still a small minority) could vote. More important, the bill redistributed electoral districts, taking power away from the "rotten boroughs" (no-longer-important towns and rural areas) and giving it to the underrepresented cities where commercial and industrial elites dominated. The political struggle to pass the bill enabled the House of Commons to gain power over the House of Lords, which had opposed the law. The long era of dominance by the conservative landed aristocracy was ending. More liberal property owners, including the commercial and industrial bourgeoisie, rose to power. From that point on, Britain's leading political groups realigned themselves into the modern Conservative and Liberal parties.

Britain's government soon turned to other reforms. Britain had for several decades led in the antislavery movement, abolishing its own slave trade in

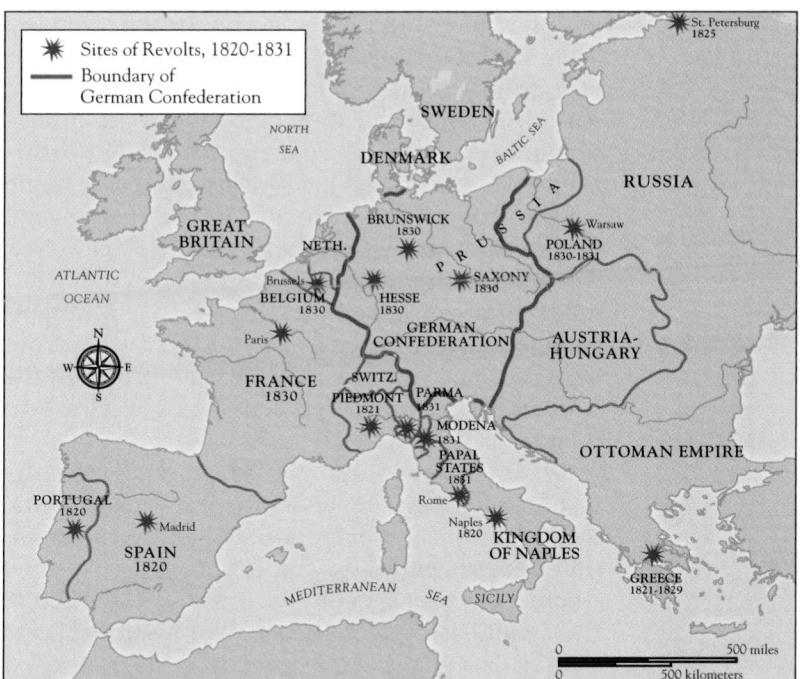

Sites of Revolts, 1820-1831

Boundary of German Confederation

THINKING ABOUT GEOGRAPHY

MAP 18.2 *European Revolts, 1820–1831*

This map shows the locations of revolts in Europe between 1820 and 1831. ◙ **Notice** the geographic extent of these revolts. **What** problems might this have posed for the efforts of the Concert of Europe to maintain the status quo through international cooperation? ◙ **Consider** which of these revolts had the most lasting consequences.

1807 and pushing the Congress of Vienna to declare against the trade in 1815. Europeans, however, often *Antislavery* violated principled declarations against slavery and shipped hundreds of thousands more African slaves to the Americas—especially to the Caribbean and Brazil. In 1833, Parliament bowed to humanitarian radicals and Protestant reformers and abolished slavery in Britain's colonies. Fifteen years later, France would follow suit by abolishing slavery in its colonies, and in 1888, Brazil joined the list, ending slavery in the Americas.

Britain's Parliament and reformers also tried to cope with growing pressures exerted by the industrial revolution. Several new laws aimed to ease some of the disturbing harshness of industrial employment. Between 1833 and 1847, Parliament forbade the em-

ployment of women and children in underground mines, prohibited the employment of children under nine in textile mills, and limited children nine or older *Economic and social reforms* and women to 10 hours a day in those factories. Other legislation also reflected the British economy's shift from agriculture to industry. In the name of free trade and lower bread prices, liberals mounted a major attack on the Corn Laws, which imposed tariffs on grain imports. An anti-Corn Law movement spread throughout the country, accusing the aristocratic landowners who benefited from the Corn Laws of being enemies of the middle *Corn Laws* and working classes. Victory for the movement came in 1846 with the repeal of the Corn Laws. The repeal reduced the price of bread, but it also opened up the possibility that employers—knowing that workers could afford the cheaper bread—would slash wages.

These liberal principles and reforms, however, only added to the suffering of millions facing the horrible potato famine in Ireland. This mostly rural and impoverished population relied on the potato for food. In 1845, a new, unknown fungus attacked potato plants, ruin- *Irish famine* ing the crop. Famine spread as the crops failed year after year. Despite some charitable assistance, Britain's liberal government concluded that the state should not meddle in the economy. Figure 18.10, a painting by British artist George Frederick Watts (1817–1904), depicts the Irish famine. A family sits in a barren landscape under a bleak sky. The pale mother, holding her baby in her arms, looks to her husband for help, but he, dismayed, can only look off in the distance. At the right the grandmother bends down in exhaustion and misery. No help is in the offing for this displaced, starving Irish family. More than a million died in Ireland and another million fled overseas while Britain's liberals—often sympathetic and believing that the free market would alleviate the distress—held fast to their principles and did little.

FIGURE 18.10
George Frederick Watts, *The Irish Famine,*
1849–1850.

Nor were liberal reforms enough for the hard-pressed urban workers. They were bitterly aware that they had been bypassed by the Reform Bill of 1832: "The Reform Act has effected a transfer of power | *Chartism* | from one domineering faction to another, and left the people as helpless as before," explained one of their leaders. They also complained that Britain's unprecedented national prosperity had not benefitted workers: "With all these elements of national prosperity, and with every disposition and capacity to take advantage of them, we find ourselves overwhelmed with public and private suffering." In 1838, working-class leaders took action and drew up The People's Charter. The document called for several democratic reforms, including universal male suffrage, election by secret ballot, and the removal of property qualifications for office. "We perform the duties of freemen; we must have the privileges of freemen," announced the charter.

The so-called Chartists presented their demands twice to Parliament, which summarily rejected them. Nevertheless, the movement persisted within the working class for years. Women aided the cause by raising money and passing petitions for signatures. They also, unsuccessfully, demanded that the charter include provisions for female suffrage. Finally, in April 1848, the Chartists planned a huge demonstration in London to back up their petition. The frightened government and middle classes prepared to use force to control the gathering, as they had several times against strikes and workers' protests. However, when the reforms were refused once more, only a few mild protests arose, and the Chartist movement sputtered out. Nevertheless, Britain's political parties were becoming aware of the growing influence of the working classes and began considering ways to win their favor.

In Britain, then, reforms designed to meet demands for broader representation and manage the social consequences of industrialization and urbanization were under way by the 1840s. Under pressure, Britain's government bent enough to satisfy much of the middle class. The discontented working classes were not yet powerful enough to force their views on the resisting government. Liberalism, the strongest ideology challenging Britain's traditional order, remained a force for reform rather than revolution.

On the Continent, however, nations followed a different path. Throughout western Europe, liberal and nationalistic movements gained stunning successes in these same years. In eastern and southern Europe, these two ideologies also rose and served notice, but, with the exception of Greece, the conservative forces of order beat them down. In 1848, however, the complicated interplay among all these movements finally reached a volatile turning point.

The Dam Bursts: 1848

On New Year's Day, 1848, one could look back to 1830 and conclude that the forces that had opened the gates to a wave of revolutions and reforms had since been held under control. In February 1848, everything would change.

Trouble had already been brewing across Europe. In 1846 and 1847, poor harvests had driven up food prices and even brought famine. These disasters, along with financial crises, undermined markets for manufactured goods, created business failures, and left thousands of workers jobless. Governments tried to maintain order, but the growing resentments of liberals, nationalists, and now socialists, who blamed governments for failing to enact overdue reforms, made things even more difficult.

Antigovernment groups had also begun taking on a disturbing complexity and variety. Some protesters wanted only to widen political participation and institute accepted liberal reforms; others demanded full democracy. Several ethnic groups desired national autonomy; workers wanted jobs and rights. Together, the potential opposition to established governments not only loomed large but also cut across class and ideological lines. Intense, shared opposition to the status quo masked any differences these groups might have had. As the pressure of their frustration mounted, the economic crisis threatened to unlock the floodgates.

The "Glory Days"

The dam broke first in France. Louis-Philippe's constitutional monarchy had allied moderate conservatives and moderate liberals into a regime of wealthy property owners. Presenting itself as the bearer of national patriotism and political caution, the government managed to quiet both conservative and radical opponents during the 1830s. However, beneath the surface of this apparently stable regime, discontent grew. The king and his chief minister during the 1840s—the moderately liberal historian Francois Guizot—opposed any further extension of the suffrage. Workers, who had not shared in the relative prosperity of the period, clamored for the right to vote and the right to organize unions, but got neither. The poor harvests and financial crises in 1846 and 1847 heightened frustration with the regime. In Paris, more than 40 percent of the workforce were without a job. One Parisian radical complained, "While half of the population of Paris dies of starvation, the other half eats for two."

The parliamentary opposition and bourgeois reformers began holding banquets to rally support for widening the right to vote. When a banquet to be held in Paris on February 22 in honor of George Washington's birthday (the United States served as a symbol of democracy in this period) promised to attract thousands of sympathetic workers, the government tried to prohibit the event. Opposition erupted in the Parisian streets. King Louis-Philippe tried to quiet people by dismissing his unpopular prime minister, Francois Guizot (1787–1874). Long in office,

Guizot's response to those not rich enough to have the right to vote was, "Get rich, then you can vote." The king's effort at appeasement failed. A shot fired during a brawl between a crowd and troops guarding government houses unnerved the troops, who fired a murderous volley into the mob and set off a full-scale insurrection. Barricades against governmental troops flew up all over Paris, and when the king's citizen militia, the National Guard, began taking the rebels' side, Louis-Philippe followed Guizot into exile.

Figure 18.11 depicts the triumph of the revolutionaries and the already simmering political battles to come. In the center, the well-dressed liberal and romantic poet Alphonse de Lamartine (1790–1869) stands with his arm raised in front of the Paris city hall. He persuades the crowd to keep the tricolor flag to represent the new republic rather than the more radical red flag, carried by a woman in plain dress riding a white horse on the left. On the right, troops and ordinary citizens march under the flag in unity. On the left, citizens bring objects of wealth gathered to support the new republic. At the bottom are the paving stones used in the battle and a fallen victim of the struggle.

Lamartine and a group of bourgeois liberals proclaimed the Second Republic and hastily set up a provisional government. The new ruling body was republican in sentiment, but tellingly, it had only one prominent radical member: the socialist writer Louis Blanc (1811–1882). The provisional government immediately called for the election by universal male suffrage of an assembly to draw up a new constitution. Yet that government turned down demands for political and economic rights by the new woman's newspaper, *The Voice of Women*, and by women's political clubs. Under the pressure of the Paris populace, the provisional government did admit workers to the National Guard, and therefore access to arms.

Document 18.2 (see page D18.1) reveals that the government, in response to popular demand for the "right to work," also set up national workshops. The workshops—an idea once proposed by Louis Blanc—however, were a parody of Blanc's socialist vision. Blanc lamented that they were deliberately planned so as to ensure failure. In this ill-designed undertaking, laborers were assigned to hastily arranged projects. When more laborers enrolled than could be used, the surplus workers were paid almost as much as the employed ones to remain idle. To make matters worse, tens of thousands

FIGURE 18.11

Henri-Félix Emmanuel Philippoteaux, Revolutionary triumph in Paris, 1848.

of job-hungry laborers rushed to Paris to join the workshops. The resulting demoralization of labor and the cost to the taxpayers frightened peasant and bourgeois property owners alike. Elections held in April 1848 swept conservative republicans and monarchists back into office.

As Map 18.3 reveals, the February explosion in Paris set central Europe aflame with revolt. One core *Austria* of the revolutions settled in Vienna, the seat of the Habsburg government. After news of the Paris events arrived in Vienna, Austrian students, middle-class reformers, and workers charged into the streets, clamoring for an end to Metternich's system. There, as elsewhere in the streets of Europe's cities, women joined men in the effort, building the barricades, taking care of the wounded, supplying the fighters with meals, and sometimes taking part in battles against armed forces. The painting on page 618 captures the flavor of this revolutionary activity. As the uprising gained momentum, Metternich fled for his life. The Habsburg emperor, Ferdinand I, hastily abolished the country's most repressive laws, ended serfdom, and promised constitutional reform.

In Hungary, the Magyars, under the leadership of the eloquent Louis Kossuth (1802–1894), rose and demanded national autonomy from Austria. The Czechs followed suit in Bohemia and called for a Pan-Slavic congress to meet at Prague. In Austria's Italian provinces of Lombardy and *Hungary* Venetia, the rebellious populace drove the Austrian forces into defensive fortresses and declared their independence. By June 1848, it appeared that the Habsburg Empire was splintering along ethnic lines and that its German core would commit to liberal reforms.

When the Hohenzollern ruler of Prussia, Frederick William IV (r. 1840–1861), heard of events in Austria, he granted some reforms and promised a *Prussia* liberal constitution. Nevertheless, as Document 18.3 suggests (see page D18.2), the news from Paris and Vienna sent middle-class liberals and artisans demonstrating in the streets of Berlin, the capital of Prussia. Frederick William sent in the troops, but their brutality stiffened support for the revolutionary cause. A few days later, he withdrew his troops and promised more reforms and support for German national unity. Hohenzollern Prussia, like Habsburg Austria, appeared on the road to liberal government.

In several other German states, rulers quickly gave in to revolutionary demands. Then a self-appointed group of liberal leaders made a bold move: they called for a popularly elected assembly representing all German states to meet at Frankfurt to construct a liberal German nation. "[A]t last the great opportunity had arrived for giving to the German people the liberty which was their birthright and to the German fatherland its unity and greatness," explained a participant. Three crucial questions confronted the Frankfurt Assembly: (1) whether German-speaking portions of the multilingual Habsburg Empire and other states should be included in the projected German nation, (2) what should be done with non-German ethnic groups living within German states, and (3) who should head the new nation. After almost a year of debate, the assembly decided on a smaller Germany and offered the crown to the king of Prussia.

Frankfurt Assembly

Meanwhile, in Italy several states established new constitutions. The movement for national unification kept alive by the idealist Giuseppi Mazzini found additional strength. He backed up his ideas with action: "Insurrection—by means of guerrilla bands—is the true method of warfare for all nations desirous of emancipating themselves from a foreign yoke," he explained. Just one year after the first revolt broke out in France, popular demonstrations brought down the papal government and forced Pius IX to flee Rome. Mazzini soon gained a foothold as head of the newly formed Republic of Rome.

Italy

THE RETURN TO ORDER

For the revolutionaries of 1848, a new, victorious age seemed to have dawned. Within a few months, the old governments almost everywhere had been swept from power or seriously weakened. The upheavals were so widespread that at one point Tsar Nicholas I of Russia exclaimed to Britain's Queen Victoria, "What remains standing in Europe? Great Britain and Russia." Unfortunately for the revolutionaries, however, the forces of order showed resiliency and even new strength when events took more radical turns.

In France, divisions rose among those once unified against the monarchy. The more conservative peasantry and landowners in the countryside stepped back from the radical reforms demanded by Parisian artisans, shopowners, and intellectuals. The gap also widened between the middle class, which felt that reforms had gone far enough or even too far, and workers, who agitated for more social programs. These divisions reached a boiling point when the Constitutional Assembly, which had been elected in the late spring of 1848, abolished the national workshops. Officials told the workers to join the army or go look for work in the provinces. The desperate men and women of the Paris working class resorted to arms and barricades. For four days, war raged in the streets of Paris between the working

June Days in France

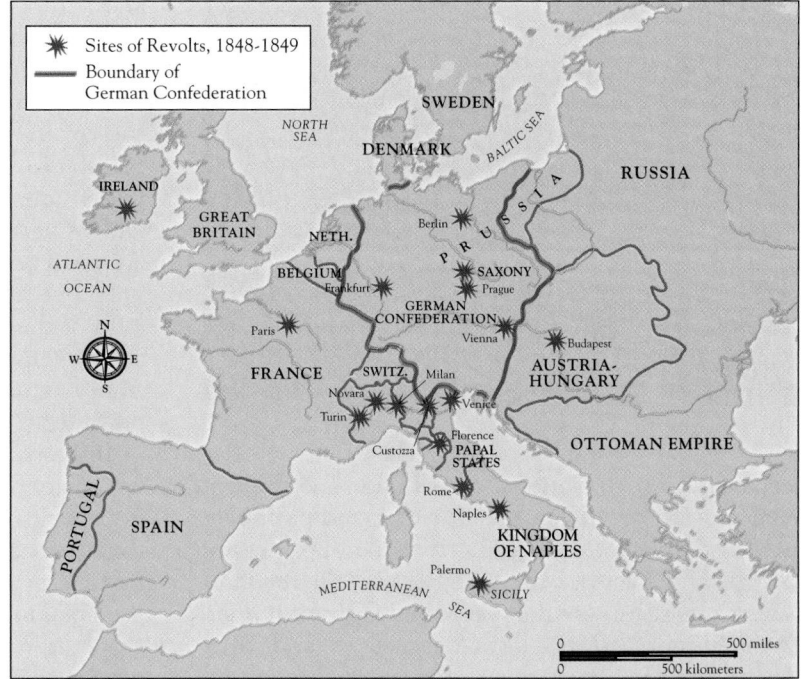

Sites of Revolts, 1848-1849
Boundary of German Confederation

THINKING ABOUT GEOGRAPHY

MAP 18.3 *European Revolts, 1848–1849*

This map shows the location of the 1848 revolutions. ⬛ **Consider** the possible reasons for the eruption of so many revolutions over this wide geographic area. ⬛ **Compare** this map with Map 18.2. **What** do the two maps reveal about the breath of revolutionary activity between 1820 and 1848 and the challenges faced by the conservative forces of order?

FIGURE 18.12
Jean-Louis-Ernest Meissonier, *Memory of Civil War (The Barricade)*, 1849.

fired on the people. The artist, Meissonier (1815–1891), witnessed these defenders "slain, shot down, thrown from the windows, covering the ground with their corpses, the earth not yet having drunk up all the blood." Meissonier intended his painting to serve as "a sober warning to the rebels of the future." When the last barricade had fallen during the bloody June Days, some 1,500, mostly workingmen, had perished. Several hundred were sent overseas to French colonial prisons. Louis Blanc fled to Great Britain. The events widened the cleavage between radical urban Paris and conservative rural France—a cleavage that would long complicate France's public life. As a final insult to the revolutionaries, the December presidential elections swept Louis-Napoleon Bonaparte (1808–1873), nephew of Napoleon Bonaparte, to victory. Promising something for everyone and projecting an image of order and authority, Louis-Napoleon held office for three years and then destroyed the republic in 1851 by taking power for himself in a coup d'état.

In Austria, the revolutionaries' inexperience and the rivalries among various ethnic groups gave the Habsburgs the upper hand. Playing off one group against another *Austria and Hungary* and using their still-formidable military force, the Austrian rulers beat down the liberal and national revolts one after the other. In Hungary, they had the help of the reactionary Nicholas I of Russia, whose army overwhelmed the Magyar rebels. In Italy, Austrian might (and in Rome, French arms) eventually prevailed.

In Prussia, Frederick William IV fell under the influence of his militaristic and reactionary Junker advisors. Heartened by the news from Vienna *Prussia* that the Habsburgs had regained their position, he spurned the German crown offered him by the Frankfurt Assembly, contemptuously calling it "a crown from the gutter." His rejection of the crown blasted the Frankfurt Assembly's hopes for a united, liberal Germany. He accused liberals in the Frankfurt Assembly of "fighting the battle of godlessness, perjury, and robbery, and kindling a war against monarchy," and his Prussian troops drove the point home by ousting the few remaining liberals determined to keep the assembly alive. Figure 18.13 depicts the street fighting in Frankfurt in September 1848. The king's well-ordered professional troops move up the street against a barricade thrown up by revolutionaries. The

class, armed with National Guard rifles, and the regular army. The French liberal writer and politician Alexis de Tocqueville (1805–1859), an observer of the events, described the June Days as "the revolt of one whole section of the population against another. Women took part in it as well as men . . . and when at last the time had come to surrender, the women were the last to yield."

Figure 18.12 depicts the fate of the revolutionary workers of Paris during the "June Days" of 1848. Here the paving stones used so successfully for the barricades in February 1848, are scattered in the rout of the revolutionaries. The revolutionaries and the radical demands they represented—symbolized by the red, white, and blue of a fallen fighter's clothing—lie crushed by army troops, who this time have willingly untrained revolutionaries and their supporters fire from windows and hurl stones, chairs, and bottles at the uniformed troops. This time, the revolutionaries proved no match for the king's forces.

WHAT HAPPENED?

By 1850, the conservative forces of order had regained control. What happened? How could so many victories by liberals, nationalists, workers, and students be turned into defeats so quickly?

There are several explanations. First, the alliances among middle-class liberals, radicals, socialists, artisans, and workers was one of convenience (their shared opposition to the status quo) rather than genuine fellowship. After revolutionary forces gained power, the interests of the various groups proved too divergent for the alliances to endure. These divisions emerged most clearly in France, where the frightened middle class and conservative peasantry broke with the Parisian working classes. Lamartine, a poet and leading politician at the time, explained how the revolutionaries were divided into two groups: the republicans "were inspired by the hatred of royalty," while the socialists "were inspired . . . by the progress of humanity. The republic and equality was the aim of the one; social renovation and fraternity the aim of the other. They had nothing in common but impatience . . . and hope. . . ."

Internal divisions

Second, liberal and nationalistic forces worked best together when out of power; in power, they often stood at cross-purposes. This lack of harmony between liberals and nationalists was particularly pronounced in central Europe, where the nationalist aspirations of German, Polish, Magyar, Croatian, Serbian, and other groups conflicted with efforts to form new governments with liberal institutions. For example, liberals in the Frankfurt Assembly who sought to unify Germany turned against other nationalities who rose up against German rule in Austria and Prussia.

Holding power: Liberalism vs. nationalism

Third, the strength of conservatism should not be underestimated. With industrialization just beginning to emerge in central Europe, the middle and working classes—both discontented with the conser-

FIGURE 18.13
The forces of order in Frankfurt, September, 1848.

vative status quo—were still weak. Revolutionary leaders were inexperienced as well. In Germany, for example, the journalist Carl Schurz explained the failure of the Frankfurt parliament: "That parliament was laboring under an overabundance of learning and virtue and under a want of . . . political experience."

Conservatism

Finally, once the shock of initial defeat at the hands of revolutionaries had faded, the seasoned leaders of the forces of order marshaled their resources, drew on their own armies and those of allies, and overcame the divided revolutionary forces. After they reestablished control, conservative leaders tore up most of the reforms and imprisoned, executed, or exiled revolutionaries. In December 1848, Pope Pius IX summarized the views of angry conservatives: "We . . . declare null and of no effect, and altogether illegal, every act" of reform during 1848. In fact, a few liberal reforms, such as the abolition of serfdom in Austria and Hungary and the limited constitutions in Piedmont and Prussia, would survive, but the great changes and power that for a few months seemed within the grasp of revolutionaries were gone.

Force

TIMELINE: A CLOSER LOOK

1816	1818	1820	1822	1824	1826	1828	1830	1832

■ POLITICS

■ REVOLUTIONS

■ REFORMS AND REFORM MOVEMENTS

Greek Independence (1829)

British Reform Bill (1832)

Congress of Vienna (1814–1815)

Decemberists Revolt in Russia (1825)

The Quadruple Alliance (1815)

Revolutions in France, Belgium, Poland, and Italy (1830–1831)

Carlsbad Decrees (1819)

Peterloo Massacre (1819)

Revolt in Naples, Sicily, and Piedmont (1821)

Young Italy founded (1831)

Metternich (1773–1859)

Revolt in Spain (1822)

1816	1818	1820	1822	1824	1826	1828	1830	1832

Summary

In 1815, the conservative forces of order tried to secure their own survival by repressing all those heartened by the principles and reforms of the French Revolution and the Enlightenment. Change became the enemy of conservatives, but the industrial revolution and the growing strength of ideologies such as liberalism, nationalism, and socialism strengthened demands for change.

In the early 1820s, a cycle of revolution and reform timidly emerged. In 1830, revolutionary forces posed a broader challenge, gaining some important victories in western Europe. The cycle returned in full force in 1848, as revolutions broke out through Europe and scored victory after victory. Those victories proved short-lived. By 1850, conservatives were back in power. This quick reversal of fortunes has led many historians to call the revolutions of 1848 "the turning point at which modern history failed to turn."

Yet the revolutions of 1848 left several important legacies. In a few cases, some liberal reforms were retained; in other cases, reforms in modified forms would be passed in succeeding years. Moreover, the overall failure of 1848 did not necessarily ensure a permanent victory for conservatism. As industrialization and urbanization spread year by

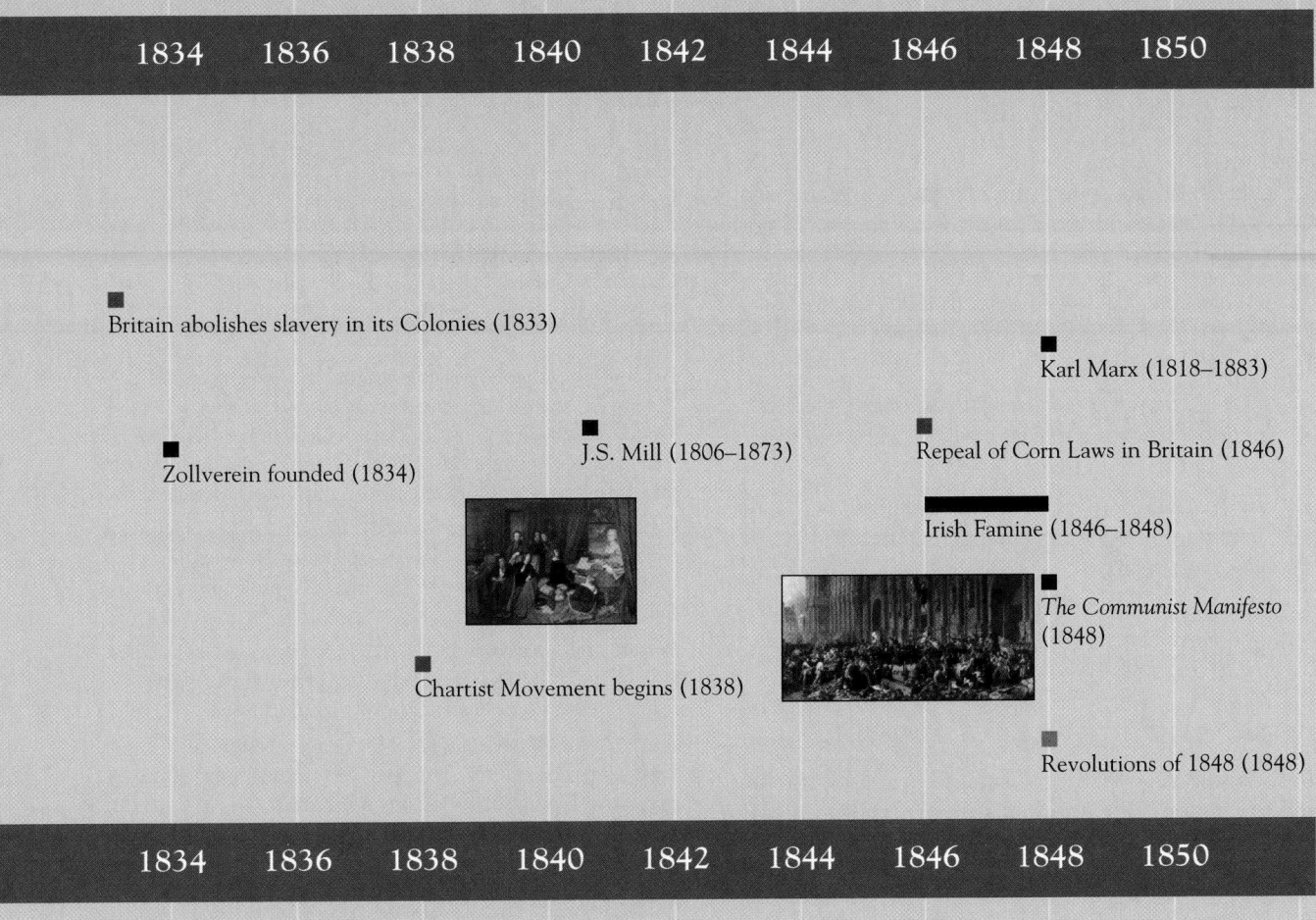

Britain abolishes slavery in its Colonies (1833)

Karl Marx (1818–1883)

Zollverein founded (1834)

J.S. Mill (1806–1873)

Repeal of Corn Laws in Britain (1846)

Irish Famine (1846–1848)

The Communist Manifesto (1848)

Chartist Movement begins (1838)

Revolutions of 1848 (1848)

1834   1836   1838   1840   1842   1844   1846   1848   1850

year, traditional life and the old order it represented kept crumbling. Perhaps most significant, participants and observers had witnessed the power of ideologies, as well as economic and social realities, to galvanize people into political action.

However, the reestablished governments had learned important lessons from 1848, too, and would try to secure their positions with new vigor. They repaired the dam that broke in February 1848. For the time being, at least, everything seemed under control.

REVIEW, ANALYZE, AND ANTICIPATE

REVIEW THE PREVIOUS CHAPTER

Chapter 17—"Factories, Cities, and Families in the Industrial Age"—analyzed the industrial revolution and urbanization. Chapter 16—"Overturning the Political and Social Order"—examined the revolution whose consequences were felt throughout the West.

1. *In what ways might the developments described in Chapter 18 be considered a reaction to the French Revolution and industrial revolution discussed in the previous two chapters?*

2. *What forces stemming from the French Revolution and industrial revolution did conservatives try to*

repress or contain? To what extent do you think conservatives succeeded?

ANALYZE THIS CHAPTER

Chapter 18—"Coping with Change"—analyzes the struggles between competing ideologies and political forces during the period between Napoleon's fall and the revolutions of 1848.

1. *Analyze the ideas of conservatism and policies of the forces of order in the years between 1815 and 1830.*

2. *In what ways did the ideas and actions of liberals, nationalists, and socialists challenge conservatives between 1815 and 1850?*

3. *In what ways did romanticism become a new cultural movement and an important ideology?*

4. *Analyze the commonalties in the several revolutions and movements for reform that developed between 1820 and 1848.*

ANTICIPATE THE NEXT CHAPTER

In Chapter 19—"Nationalism and Statebuilding"— the movements for national strength and unity will be examined.

1. *What "lessons" do you think governments and different social groups will have learned from the decades just preceding 1850 and, in particular, the revolutions of 1848?*

2. *Why might the ideologies of liberalism, nationalism, and socialism—which apparently suffered a stunning defeat between 1848 and 1850— persist and even grow in strength in the following decades?*

BEYOND THE CLASSROOM

THE CONGRESS OF VIENNA: A GATHERING OF VICTORS

Bridge, F. R. *The Great Powers and the European States System, 1815–1914.* London: Longman, 1980. A thorough diplomatic history of the period.

Nicolson, Harold. *The Congress of Vienna: A Study in Allied Unity, 1812–1822.* New York: Viking Press, 1961. A classic study of the Congress of Vienna and its accomplishments.

IDEOLOGIES: HOW THE WORLD SHOULD BE

Arblaster, Anthony. *The Rise and Decline of Western Liberalism.* Oxford, England: B. Blackwell, 1984. An analysis of the evolution and key components of liberalism.

Beecher, Jonathan. *Charles Fourier: The Visionary and His World.* Berkeley, CA: University of California Press, 1986. Traces the development of Fourier's ideas through his early years to his emergence as a political prophet and founder of one of the most significant early socialist movements.

Carlisle, Robert B. *The Proferred Crown: Saint-Simonianism and the Doctrine of Hope.* Baltimore: Johns Hopkins University Press, 1987. Studies the social philosophy of Saint-Simonianism.

Porter, Roy, and Mikulas Teich, eds. *Romanticism in National Context.* Cambridge: Cambridge University Press, 1988. A series of essays on romanticism by noted historians.

Smith, Denis Mack. *Mazzini.* New Haven, CT: Yale University Press, 1999. The most recent biography of this important figure by a well-known historian.

RESTORATION AND REPRESSION

Gildea, Robert. *Barricades and Borders: Europe 1800–1914.* New York: Oxford University Press, 1987. A broad survey stressing social and political developments during the period.

Jardin, André, and André-Jean Tudesq. *Restoration and Reaction, 1815–1848.* Cambridge: Cambridge University Press, 1988. A solid survey of France during this period.

Sheehan, James J. *German History, 1770–1866.* New York: Oxford University Press, 1989. A comprehensive, exhaustive examination of the changes in German social, political, and economic history.

Sked, Alan. *The Decline and Fall of the Habsburg Empire, 1815–1918.* London: Longman, 1989. Studies the growing problems facing the Habsburg Empire during the nineteenth century.

A WAVE OF REVOLUTION AND REFORM

Church, Clive. *Europe in 1830: Revolution and Political Change.* London: Allen & Unwin, 1983. Examines the revolutions that swept across Europe in a comparative context.

Thompson, Dorothy. *The Chartists: Popular Politics in the Industrial Revolution*. New York: Pantheon Books, 1984. An important and extensive treatment of the Chartist movement in Britain.

THE DAM BURSTS: 1848

Price, Roger. *The Revolutions of 1848*. Atlantic Highlands, NJ: Humanities Press International, 1989. A useful, wide-ranging survey.

Sperber, Jonathan. *The European Revolutions, 1848–1851*. Cambridge: Cambridge University Press, 1994. A brief yet thorough account that covers the tumultuous events throughout Europe.

For quiz questions that tie the book to the videos and additional primary sources, please go to the Primary Source Investigator CD.

QUIZ

Documents

DOCUMENT 18.1
A Conservative Theorist Attacks Political Reform

Many conservatives resented the reforms sparked by the French Revolution. The extremely conservative theorist Joseph de Maistre was no exception. In the following excerpt from his Essay on the Generative Principle of Political Constitutions, *published in Russia in 1810 and then Paris in 1814, Maistre attacks written constitutions and the reform of political institutions.*

■ **Investigate the Document**

On what basis does Maistre object to written constitutions? Would any political reforms have merit according to Maistre?

"Every thing brings us back to the general rule—*man cannot create a constitution; and no legitimate constitution can be written.* The collection of fundamental laws, which must essentially constitute a civil or religious society, never has been written, and never will be, *a priori.* It is only when society finds itself already constituted, without being able to say how, that it is possible to make known, or explain, in writing, certain special articles; but in almost every case these declarations or explanations are the effect of very great evils, and always cost the people more than they are worth.

" . . . Not only does it not belong to man to create institutions, but it does not appear that his power, *unassisted,* extends even to change for the better institutions already established. . . . *Nothing* [says the philosopher, Origen] . . . *can be changed for the better among men, without God.* All men have a consciousness of this truth, without being in a state to explain it to themselves. Hence that instinctive aversion, in every good mind, to innovations. The word *reform,* in itself, and previous to all examinations, will be always suspected by wisdom, and the experience of every age justifies this sort of instinct.

" . . . To apply these maxims to a particular case . . . the great question of parliamentary reform, which has agitated minds in England so powerfully, and for so long a time, I still find myself constrained to believe, that this idea is pernicious, and that if the English yield themselves too readily to it, they will have occasion to repent."

DOCUMENT 18.2
France's Provisional Government Issues Decrees

Shortly after the 1848 revolution that ended the July Monarchy in France, the victors established a new provisional government. They issued the following decrees relating to workers on February 25, 1848—the day after creating the provisional government.

■ **Investigate the Document**

What do these decrees suggest about possible causes of the revolution? What might be the advantages and disadvantages of issuing these decrees?

The provisional government of the French republic decrees that the Tuileries shall serve hereafter as a home for the veterans of labor.

The provisional government of the French republic pledges itself to guarantee the means of subsistence of the workingman by labor.

It pledges itself to guarantee labor to all citizens.

It recognizes that workingmen ought to enter into associations among themselves in order to enjoy the advantage of their labor. . . .

The provisional government of the French republic decrees that all articles pledged at the pawn shops since the first of February, consisting of linen, garments, or clothes, etc., upon which the loan does not exceed ten francs, shall be given back to those who pledged them.

The provisional government of the republic decrees the immediate establishment of national work-

Source: Scholars' Facsimiles & Reprints (New York: Delmar, 1977), reprinting of the edition of Joseph de Maistre, *Essay on the Generative Principle of Political Constitutions,* (Boston: Little and Brown, 1847).

Source: James Harvey Robinson, ed., *Readings in European History,* vol. II (Boston: Ginn, 1904), pp. 560–561.

shops. The minister of public works is charged with the execution of the present decree.

DOCUMENT 18.3
German Liberals and Nationalists Rally for Reform

The February 1848 revolution ending Louis Philippe's regime and establishing a republic in France inspired many others throughout Europe who thirsted for reform. In Germany, liberals and nationalists rallied in hopes of uniting the German states and initiating liberal reforms. In the following selection, Carl Schurz (1829–1906) describes his participation in those events and the feelings he shared with others.

■ **Investigate the Document**

> **Why** *did the fall of Louis Philippe in France have such a strong effect on Schurz?* **What** *reforms did Schurz long for?*

One morning, toward the end of February, 1848, I sat quietly in my attic-chamber, working hard at my tragedy of "Ulrich von Hutten," [a sixteenth-century German knight] when suddenly a friend rushed breathlessly into the room, exclaiming, "What, you sitting here! Do you not know what has happened?"

"No; what?"

"The French have driven away Louis Philippe and proclaimed the republic."

I threw down my pen—and that was the end of "Ulrich von Hutten." I never touched the manuscript again. We tore down the stairs, into the street, to the market-square, the accustomed meeting-place for all the student societies after their midday dinner. Although it was still forenoon, the market was already crowded with young men talking excitedly. There was no shouting, no noise, only agitated conversation. What did we want there? This probably no one knew. But since the French had driven away Louis

Source: Carl Schurz, *The Reminiscences of Carl Schurz,* (New York: The McClure Co., 1907), vol. 1, pp. 112–113.

Philippe and proclaimed the republic, something of course must happen here, too. . . . We were dominated by a vague feeling as if a great outbreak of elemental forces had begun, as if an earthquake was impending of which we had felt the first shock, and we instinctively crowded together. . . .

The next morning there were the usual lectures to be attended. But how profitless! At last we closed with a sigh the notebook and went away, impelled by a feeling that now we had something more important to do—to devote ourselves to the affairs of the fatherland. And this we did by seeking as quickly as possible again the company of our friends, in order to discuss what had happened and what was to come. In these conversations, excited as they were, certain ideas and catchwords worked themselves to the surface, which expressed more or less the feelings of the people. Now had arrived in Germany the day for the establishment of "German Unity," and the founding of a great, powerful national German Empire. In the first line the convocation of a national parliament. Then the demands for civil rights and liberties, free speech, free press, the right of free assembly, equality before the law, a freely elected representation of the people with legislative power, responsibility of ministers, self-government of the communes, the right of the people to carry arms, the formation of a civic guard with elective officers, and so on—in short, that which was called a "constitutional form of government on a broad democratic basis." Republican ideas were at first only sparingly expressed. But the word democracy was soon on all tongues, and many, too, thought it a matter of course that if the princes should try to withhold from the people the rights and liberties demanded, force would take the place of mere petition. Of course, the regeneration of the fatherland must, if possible, be accomplished by peaceable means. . . . Like many of my friends, I was dominated by the feeling that at last the great opportunity had arrived for giving to the German people the liberty which was their birthright and to the German fatherland its unity and greatness, and that it was now the first duty of every German to do and to sacrifice everything for this sacred object.

Garibaldi Landing in Sicily

In this painting, the lifelong nationalist Giuseppe Garibaldi (1807–1882) heroically lands at the island of Sicily to fight for Italian unification. In the background, his band of volunteer soldiers (the "Red Shirts") pour from three ships and march in rough formation. Carrying a sword and a flag representing Italian unity, Garibaldi is welcomed by admiring children, women, men, and a priest. The image, though stirring, still cannot convey the effort and anguish required to turn nationalistic sentiment into political reality.

CHAPTER 19

Nationalism and Statebuilding

Unifying Nations, 1850–1870

STUDY • Italian unification • German unification • National unity in North America • Nationalism in France and Russia NOTICE the conflict of forces for and against national unification.

On May 31, 1860, just three weeks after landing in Sicily, the Italian nationalist leader Giuseppe Garibaldi toured Palermo, Sicily's main city. He entered the city at the head of a band of 1,000 volunteer soldiers to begin the liberation of southern Italy from the old, Austrian-supported Bourbon king. He called for "Italians" to "put an end, once and for all, to the miseries of so many centuries," and "prove to the world that it is no lie that Roman generations inhabited this land." An eyewitness described how "the popular idol, Garibaldi, in his red flannel shirt, with a loose colored handkerchief round his neck . . . was walking on foot among those cheering, laughing, crying, mad thousands." As he moved through the streets, "the people threw themselves forward to kiss his hands, or, at least, to touch the hem of his garment, as if it contained the panacea for all their past and perhaps coming suffering."

In the decades between 1850 and 1870, millions of others in the Italian states—and in regions ranging from the Americas in the west to the Ottoman Empire in the east—would rally, fight, and die in the name of national unity. In Europe, maps had to be redrawn as new nation-states emerged. In the United States, a wrenching battle was entered in the name of preserving the Union. Political leaders would use nationalistic appeals to build stronger states as well as to tear apart multinational empires. Nationalism was evolving from the ideals of earlier decades to the realities of power politics.

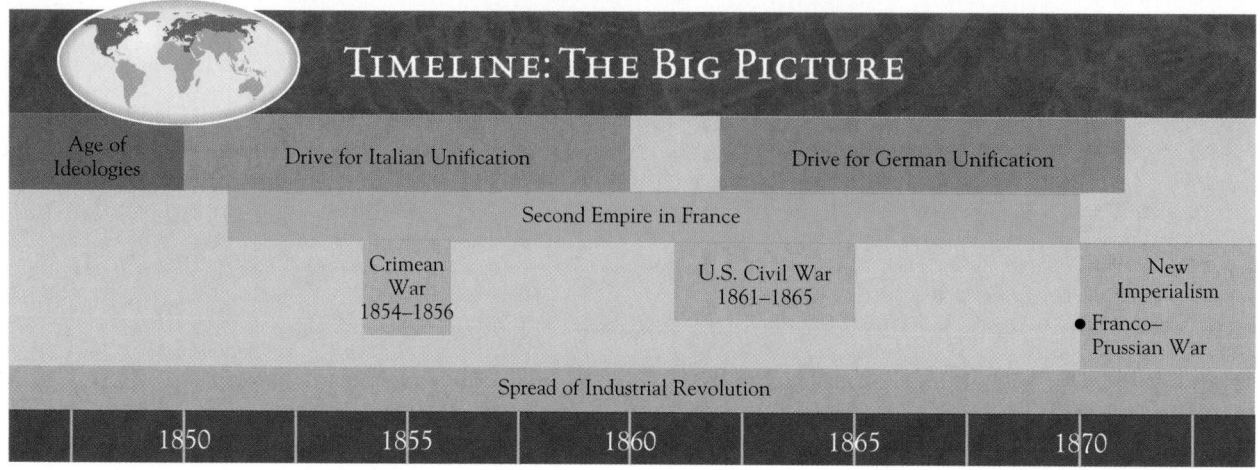

TIMELINE: THE BIG PICTURE

Age of Ideologies	Drive for Italian Unification		Drive for German Unification
	Second Empire in France		
	Crimean War 1854–1856	U.S. Civil War 1861–1865	New Imperialism ● Franco–Prussian War
	Spread of Industrial Revolution		
1850	1855	1860	1865	1870

Building Unified Nation-States

"Every German heart hoped for it," wrote the baroness Spitzemberg in Berlin in 1871. "United into one Reich, the greatest, the most powerful, the most feared in Europe; great by reason of its physical power, greater still by reason of its education and the intelligence which permeates it!" So the baroness expressed her longing for national unification, a passion felt by many others in the West.

In the two decades after 1850, no political force was stronger than nationalism. It pushed people toward national unity in Italy and Germany and threatened to tear the Habsburg and Ottoman Empires apart. In the United States, the principle of national unity helped spark a brutal civil war. In France and elsewhere, rulers enacted major reforms designed to bolster national unity and their authority as leaders of a nation of citizens. All these efforts were intended to build strong, unified nation-states led by central governments that could enjoy the support of their citizens.

Nationalism

Unlike in 1848, however, the nationalist political figures were neither revolutionaries nor idealists. As one advocate of Italian unification observed, "To defeat cannons and soldiers, cannons and soldiers are needed." From positions of established power, this new generation of leaders molded nationalism to fit harsh political realities. They focused their eyes on practical policies, not ideals. They gambled, compromised, manipulated, and fought to achieve their goals. Few struggled more persistently and cleverly than Count Camillo di Cavour (1810–1861).

Political realism

The Drive for Italian Unification

Cavour was born into a well-to-do, noble family living in Piedmont-Sardinia, a small, but relatively powerful independent state in northern Italy that also included the island of Sardinia. As a young man, he gambled, played the stock market, experimented with agricultural techniques, and succeeded in business—a pattern of taking calculated risks he would later try to follow in politics. By the 1840s, he had become committed to Italian unification. Shortly before the revolution of 1848, he founded the newspaper *Il Risorgimento* (*The Resurgence*), which passionately argued for a unified Italy. In 1850, Piedmont-Sardinia's king Victor Emmanuel II (r. 1849–1878) made Cavour his minister of commerce and agriculture and, two years later, prime minister.

Cavour

Cavour's goals were clear. First, he wanted to modernize Piedmont economically and thereby win strength and respect for his homeland. Second, he sought to make Piedmont the central engine of the drive for national unification. Third, he advocated forming a new Italian state as a constitutional monarchy under Piedmont's king rather than a democratic republic or a confederation under the pope. To achieve all these ends, Cavour lowered tariffs, built railroads, and balanced Piedmont's budget. He supported the nationalistic Italian National Society and its Feminine Committee, which worked toward national unification with Piedmont at the helm. Finally, he employed

Cavour's leadership

OLC